HU320-World Religions and Cultures

Denise L. Carmody /McGuire/Gary E. Kessler

D1517690

CENGAGE
Learning™

Australia • Brazil • Japan • Korea • Mexico • Singapore • Spain • United Kingdom • United States

CENGAGE
Learning™

HU320-World Religions and Cultures

Denise L. Carmody /McGuire/Gary E. Kessler

Executive Editor:
Michele Baird

Maureen Staudt

Michael Stranz

Project Development Editor:
Linda de Stefano

Senior Marketing Coordinators:
Sara Mercurio

Lindsay Shapiro

Production/Manufacturing Manager:
Donna M. Brown

PreMedia Services Supervisor:
Rebecca A. Walker

Rights & Permissions Specialist:
Kalina Hintz

Cover Image:
Getty Images*

For product information and technology assistance, contact us at
Cengage Learning Customer & Sales Support, 1-800-354-9706

For permission to use material from this text or product,
submit all requests online at **cengage.com/permissions**
Further permissions questions can be emailed to
permissionrequest@cengage.com

Library of Congress Control Number: 0000000000

ISBN-13: 978-0-495-41967-9

ISBN-10: 0-495-41967-2

Cengage Learning
5191 Natorp Boulevard
Mason, Ohio 45040
USA

Cengage Learning is a leading provider of customized learning solutions with office locations around the globe, including Singapore, the United Kingdom, Australia, Mexico, Brazil, and Japan. Locate your local office at:
international.cengage.com/region

Cengage Learning products are represented in Canada by Nelson Education, Ltd.

For your lifelong learning solutions, visit **custom.cengage.com**

Visit our corporate website at **cengage.com**

Printed in the United States of America
1 2 3 4 5 6 7 12 11 10 09 08

World Religion and Cultures

Table of Contents

WHAT IS RELIGION?

DEFINITION OF RELIGION

We define **religion** as

a system of symbols, myths, doctrines, ethics, and rituals for the expression of ultimate relevance.

Memorize that definition now. We will give you a more precise understanding of each of its component terms later, but your success in this course depends upon your ability to comprehend what religion is (and is not) and apply that definition to specific phenomena in order to figure out what is religious and what is something else.

Now let's see if you can apply that definition to a specific case. Picture yourself in New Delhi. You are outside Rajghat, the memorial to Mahatma Gandhi, the politician and holy man who led India to freedom from British colonial rule. Before you, squatting on the broken sidewalk, are three small boys with wooden flutes. They are piping tunes toward round wicker baskets. When they lift the baskets' covers, three silver cobras slowly weave their way out. You watch for several minutes, fearful but entranced. Then the boys shove the cobras back into their baskets and

RELIGIOUS WISDOM: TWENTY-FIVE KEY DATES		
when?	**where?**	**what?**
ca. 1500 B.C.E.	India	*Vedas*
ca. 1360 B.C.E.	Egypt	*Hymns* of Akhenaton
1000–500 B.C.E.	Palestine	*Redactions* of Pentateuch
800–400 B.C.E.	India	*Upanishads*
750–550 B.C.E.	Palestine	Hebrew *Prophets*
ca. 550 B.C.E.	Persia	oldest parts of Zoroastrian *Avesta*
ca. 500 B.C.E.	China	oldest parts of Confucian *Analects*
400–250 B.C.E.	Palestine, India	*Job; Ecclesiastes, Bhagavad Gita*
ca. 350 B.C.E.	Greece, China	Plato's *Laws; Tao De Jing*
ca. 330 B.C.E.	Greece	Aristotle's *Metaphysics*
160–80 B.C.E.	India	earliest Buddhist scriptures
50–90 C.E.	Roman Empire	New Testament writings
413–426 C.E.	Rome	Augustine's *City of God*
ca. 500 C.E.	Babylon	Talmud
ca. 650 C.E.	Arabia	canonization of the *Qur'an*
712–720 C.E.	Japan	Shinto *Chronicles*
ca. 1100 C.E.	Baghdad	Al-Ghazzali's *Revivification of the Sciences*
1175 C.E.	China	Ju Xi's Neo-Confucian Synthesis
1190 C.E.	Cordoba	Maimonides' *Guide for the Perplexed*
1270 C.E.	Paris	Aquinas' *Summa Theologica*
1536 C.E.	Geneva	Calvin's *Institutes*
1581 C.E.	India	compilation of Sikh Scripture, *Adi Granth*

Come up with your own definition of religion. Is it too broad or too narrow? (or both, or neither)? Let's try these examples.

DEFINITION 1: Religion is the acceptance of the existence of God.

PROBLEM: This is too narrow, because some religions do not have one supreme Deity but may recognize many lesser gods.

DEFINITION 2: Religion is a Sunday "get-together" to celebrate common values.

PROBLEM: This definition is too narrow because some religious denominations meet on Saturday or Friday for their religious services.

PROBLEM: This definition is too broad because it would also include some nonreligious get-togethers, such as a Super Bowl party.

Contribute to this discussion at
http://www.delphi.com/rel101

approach you for their fee. A few rupees seem fair enough—you don't want to upset those cobras.

Come back to the classroom and visualize your professor putting forth this question:

"Did you just witness (and maybe even participate in) something religious?"

The right answer is not a docile "yes" or a defiant "no" (and it is certainly not a dubious "maybe"). The right answer in this sort of course is analogous to the right answer in the field of jurisprudence; the product of the deliberation is less important than the process. Here is the way to proceed: Identify the pertinent issues to be resolved in determining the appropriate answer to the question by raising some other questions.

Are the youthful snake charmers just merchants trying to put on a show for the tourists, or are they recognized religious functionaries in some religious denomination?

Are the snakes just performing animals (akin to circus seals or an organ grinder's monkey), or are they seen as symbols of something religious (or even incarnations of gods)?

Is the music just a catchy tune to put the tourist in a generous mood, or does it have an established tradition in Indian religious rituals?

Is there something about the location (so close to the statue of Gandhi) that creates a religious context?

Of course, another issue is whether you can really *know* what is going on in other people's hearts and minds. All you can really do is observe what they do, listen to what they say, read what they have written. Anything beyond that is a matter of *inference* (reasoning from something directly observed to something else not directly observed).

These are the types of questions that would help you apply the definition of religion to the case at hand, but in order to answer those questions you would have to know a lot more about the culture and history of India. That is one of our central points: any religion can only be understood within the context of the people who live it. A study of religion must become a study of society, culture, and history.

Can we ever really *know* what another person is thinking? Or how committed he or she is to God? We observe what people say and do, and then *infer* something about their religious ideas and practices. Give an example of a time when you (or someone else) made an inference about religion based upon some observation that was made:

WHAT WAS OBSERVED? (describe a scene, event, or a person's behavior, speech or attire)

WHO MADE THE INFERENCE? (was it you or someone else who saw something and then came to a conclusion)

WHAT INFERENCE WAS MADE? (what conclusion was reached as to motive, cause, affiliation, etc.)

HOW APPROPRIATE WAS THE INFERENCE? IF IT WAS APPROPRIATE, WHAT FACTORS FACILITATED IT? IF IT WAS NOT APPROPRIATE, WHAT MISLED THE CONCLUSION?

Contribute to this discussion at
http://www.delphi.com/rel101

RELIGION VERSUS SCIENCE?

If you have already had a course in the physical sciences (e.g., physics), the life sciences (e.g., biology), or the social sciences (e.g., sociology), then you know something about how scientists go about trying to study and prove something. They use a method based upon objective and precise observation known as the **empirical method.** We are to believe a fact if it can be confirmed by a laboratory experiment or statistically analyzed survey. Truth is equated with **verifiable** factual data.

Although the sciences can often present useful perspectives on religious phenomena, we prefer to anchor our approach within the humanities—disciplines such as philosophy, art, and literature. Such an approach demands more self-awareness and personal engagement with materials than the scientific disciplines do. Pure science does not make great demands on a student's inner experiences of suffering or love. The humanities are disciplines that study our efforts at self-expression and self-understanding. The humanities involve more of such inner experiences because suffering and love shape so much of history and literature, yet even the humanities seldom deal with direct claims about ultimate relevance.

Only in the disciplines of philosophy and religion do we directly encounter systems about God, evil, and humanity's origin and end. Philosophy deals with such concepts principally in their rational forms, while religious studies meet them more directly in the myths, rituals, doctrines, behavior patterns, and institutions through which most human beings have been both drawn to the ultimate and yet terrified of it. More than in any other discipline, the student in a religious studies course is confronted with imperative claims. The religions are not normally warehouses where you pay your money and take your choice. Rather, they are impassioned heralds of ways of life. More than most people initially like, the religions speak of death, ignorance, and human viciousness. However, they also speak of peace and joy, forgiveness and harmony.

In order to understand the key differences between the scientific and the religious perspectives, let's set up an appropriate terminology to be used with each. Only in that way can we overcome the inherent

> ### WHAT'S WRONG WITH THIS DISCUSSION?
>
> ERIC: I can't understand why you belong to the XXX church. Their **beliefs** are just so ignorant.
>
> ASHLEY: But we base everything on the Bible.
>
> ERIC: That's just a book of **myths** and fairy tales.
>
> ASHLEY: But the Bible is **truth.**
>
> ERIC: That's just your **faith.** You can't **prove** that the Bible is **true.**
>
> ASHLEY: You can't **prove** that the Bible isn't **true,** and until you do I am going to **believe** it.
>
> Eric and Ashley will get nowhere until they start using a little more care with terms like *truth, proof, faith, belief,* and *myths.*

vagueness in the use of terms such as *truth, proof,* and *faith.* If we do not make these clarifications, some people will end up dismissing religion by saying, "Science deals with things you can prove, the truth, but religion is just faith." Both science and religion seek the truth, both have techniques for proof, and both involve faith. The difference between science and religion lies in the kind of truth, proof, and faith.

Suppose I make the statement: "I believe that it is about 70 degrees in this room." Is that statement true? Scientific truth must be descriptive (i.e., describe something in the physical world). Scientific truth must be *objective* (i.e., true whether I say it or someone else in the room says it, because it is the same temperature for both of us). The type of meaning involved is *cognitive* (i.e., it must involve precisely defined concepts). In other words, I am obligated to define what I mean by "70 degrees" (Fahrenheit? Celsius?). I would also have to describe those empirical procedures that would verify (prove) my claim: perhaps the use of a mercury thermometer. After making this measurement, I could discover if my initial statement was valid. But this type of belief is not something for which I would fight a holy crusade. Indeed, if someone else came up with a more precise measure of temperature, perhaps a digital thermometer, I would be willing to change my belief if it were to show, say, 74 degrees. The faith we put in any given scientific finding is contingent, and we should be willing to change our beliefs according to the discovery of new data in the next laboratory report.

Suppose I were to say: "I have faith in God." Are we dealing with the same type of truth, proof, faith? Religion and the humanities in general are more subjective, not in the sense of being vague, or incapable of consensus agreement, or beyond proof, but in the sense of depending upon the unique perspective of each individual. I may have faith in God, and someone else may not. Here is a different type of meaning and a different type of truth. We prefer to use the term **value** to describe religious truth. Values are prescriptive, **validity** is descriptive. The type of meaning involved is not mere cognitive definition, but **relevance**. Values cannot be comprehended as cognitive concepts, but are based upon relevance to some person: there is no relevance without a promise of a value or a threat to a value. The kind of faith we have in God must not be some fragile belief that is contingent upon the next laboratory report. We cannot prove the existence of God empirically: no telescope or microscope can discover Him.

The kind of faith we have in God is one of **commitment**. Over 90 percent of Americans agree that God exists, but that does not end the religious debate. That only begins the greater discussion: How do we work out the details of living daily that commitment to God? This is not something that can be verified by the discovery of any fact; it can only be **vindicated**—that is, proved in the realm of relevance—by the creation of a life filled with values.

This book is based upon the assumption that there is a center, a common core of values to which all humans are inextricably drawn. The world's religions are the journeys that people (in different times and places) have made toward that center.

Throughout history, individuals, families, and societies have had to make decisions about the religious doctrines and rituals to which they should commit. These decisions cannot be referred to the outcome of a laboratory experiment (as would be the verification of science). Let's take a look at one historical incident and how a people changed its religious commitments.

SCIENCE VERSUS RELIGION		
DIMENSION	SCIENCE	RELIGION
Knowledge from	observation	revelation
Focus on	object	subject
Terms	descriptive	prescriptive
Form of meaning	cognition	relevance
Truth	validity	value
Proof	verification	vindication
Faith	belief	commitment
Realization	discovery	creation
Past	history	myth
Driving force	mechanism	dynamism

Practice using these terms correctly. Download the drill **truth.exe** from the rel1 folder in the public filing cabinet at **http://www.ureach.com/tlbrink**

Go back about 1300 years. The place was medieval England, the date was 627 C.E. (**common era,** what we used to call A.D.). The Christian monk Paulinus came to King Edwin in northern England and urged him to convert his people to Christianity. After some debate, one of Edwin's counselors stood up and said: "Your majesty, on a winter night like this, it sometimes happens that a little bird flies in that far window, to enjoy the warmth and light of our fire. After a short while it passes out again, returning to the dark and the cold. As I see it, our human life is much the same. We have but a brief time between two great darknesses. If this monk can show us warmth and light, we should follow him."

When we first hear the story of the little bird, it is not clear what the counselor is talking about. Is he saying that the monk is just a little bird who came in from the cold and if we just ignore him, he will fly out of the castle and return to a warmer climate? When the counselor then explains his symbolism, we see that the bird stands for a seeker of values. According to this homily, if Christ offers us warmth and light (symbols of spiritual values), then we must commit ourselves to His way.

So religion and science are different ways to approach human reality, with different forms of truth, proof, and faith. We do not suggest that each one of us must choose to be religious *or* scientific. The two operate in different spheres of human life. A religious person can respect the findings of science. A great scientist can be religious. All we are cautioning against is that we should not expect to use the methods and language of science to understand religion, nor should we attempt to use the language and methods of religion to answer questions best left to the laboratory.

RELIGION VERSUS OTHER VALUES

Religion deals with values, but not all values are religious. Religion deals with values that are relevant in the realm of the **ultimate.** Most of the things that we find relevant to us on a daily basis are less than ultimate, although they are important and sometimes essential and urgent. Eating a good breakfast is relevant because it assures my health, and may even be a pleasant experience. Brushing my teeth is not intrinsically pleasant, but it also assures my health and prevents some degree of social embarrassment. Investing my retirement fund wisely can increase my overall level of wealth, so that too is valuable. Anything that deals with health or wealth is useful, but it is not ultimately valuable. So let's use the term *utilitarian* to describe such values to distinguish them from religious values (those which are ultimately relevant). **Utilitarian** relevance involves instrumental values (those which can be rationally shown to lead to some other goal). The type of commitment appropriate to such utilitarian relevance should be only contingent. If other, more effective means can be found, we should adopt those other means.

The relevance of some values is not immediately apparent to the neutral observer. Why does the alcoholic live as if the most important thing in his life is his next drink? Why do some gamblers throw away the rent money on the unlikely chance of winning the lottery? Why does an obsessive-compulsive patient waste most of her day washing her hands to remove any possible trace of germs or filth? We would say that such values are **ulterior** and irrational. Indeed, they do not lead to other values but may even serve to inhibit other values such as health and wealth.

Let's go back to our initial example about seeing the snake charmers in India. Was it a religious ritual? Whether or not you perceived the snake charmers as involved in a religious ritual depends upon how they themselves perceived the relevance of their actions. Were they doing it out of some fear that the snakes would curse them if they did not? If so, then most Westerners might regard this as superstitious behavior in the pursuit of inhibitory values: ulterior relevance. Do the snake charmers see what they are doing merely as a way to earn a living and strike up pleasant contacts with foreigners? If so, then this is clearly utilitarian, an instrumental means for wealth and pleasure. If the snake charmers see what they are doing within some ultimate context (worshipping gods, preparing for the next life, expiating sin), then it has a religious aspect for them.

What type of relevance did you yourself find in that ritual? You participated by watching and throwing some coins. If you did this out of pure irrational fear, then the relevance was inhibitory. If you did it as payment for an entertaining show, then it was utilitarian, much as buying a ticket to a motion picture theater. Only if you see how your presence and actions tie into ultimate issues of your life can you say that the experience was religious for you.

The great challenge of life is to figure out how to balance all of our different commitments. Should I rush home from mass on Sunday so I don't miss the opening kickoff? Should I contribute more to the temple even if it means that my daughter cannot go to her first-choice college? Every time we make a decision about how we spend our time or money, we are making a commitment. Life is not as simple as swearing off lottery tickets and soap operas so that we have more time to pray and money to put in the collection plate.

FORMS OF RELEVANCE			
DIMENSION	ULTIMATE	UTILITARIAN	ULTERIOR
Terms (prescriptive)	spiritual	technical	psychopathological
Truth (value)	intrinsic	instrumental	inhibitory
Proof (vindication)	transrational	rational	irrational
Faith (commitment)	absolute	contingent	rigid/fluid
Activity (proaction)	ritual	means	compulsive

THE HERMENEUTICS OF "BELIEF" AND "FAITH"

We suggest that the use of the terms *faith* and *belief* leads to confusion in the study of religions. To improve your writing, and thinking, about topics in religious studies, catch yourself when you are tempted to use the term *faith* and try to replace it with one of these: **denomination** (when referring to a religious *organization*), **doctrine** (when referring to a body of official *statements* about God, sin, and/or salvation), or **commitment** (when referring to the *strength* of a person's intention to follow a religion).

FUZZY	CLEAR
Rachel is a member of the Jewish faith.	Rachel is a member of the Jewish *denomination*.
The Trinity is an important element of Christian faith.	The Trinity is an important element of Christian *doctrine*.
Ali is very strong in his faith.	Ali is very strong in his religious *commitment*.

"By faith Abraham obeyed when he was called to go out to a place which he was to receive as an inheritance; and he went out, not knowing where he was to go" (*Hebrews* 11:8, Revised Standard Version).

Abraham was righteous in the sight of God because of his faith. It is clear from the context of this passage that the type of faith which saved Abraham was neither that of belonging to a certain denomination, nor that of having the theologically correct doctrine, but that of having a strong *commitment* to obey God, and do whatever He said.

We also suggest that the term *belief* be confined to "acceptance of factual statements" and that the terms *doctrine* and *commitment* be used for religious contexts. We *believe that* the Declaration of Independence was signed in 1776 (a factual statement), but we *believe in* freedom (in that we are committed to defending it).

The gospel of *John* uses the term *believe* over sixty times. Notice that the Evangelist usually says "believe in" or "believe on" rather than "believe that": "For God so loved the world that he gave his only Son, that whosoever believes in him should not perish but have eternal life" (*John* 3:16, Revised Standard Version).

COMPONENTS OF RELIGION

We opened with our definition of religion as a system of symbols, doctrines, myths, ethics, and rituals for the expression of ultimate relevance. Now let's look at each of those terms and see how they fit together.

A **symbol** is something that is used to represent something else. So is a sign. Symbols and signs present something to the senses, such as a visual icon, and the individual must then interpret what has been seen. If you are driving down the street and see a stop sign, you interpret the specific meaning conveyed: I had better stop or risk a traffic ticket. The relevance of signs is utilitarian because they promote safety and efficiency. Most corporate logos are signs; the Nike swoosh or McDonald's golden arches merely identify the brand. A symbol also points to something beyond itself, but in a less direct, more evocative way. A cross is a Christian symbol intended to evoke a memory of Jesus and his atonement for the sins of mankind. Religious symbols are intended to lift us out of the mundane, utilitarian basis of our existence and point us to the realm of the ultimate. Symbols are the foundation of other dimensions of religion.

Sometimes it is not possible for an outsider to understand how other people regard a certain icon: Is it mere sign or evocative symbol? Take your school's mascot (bronco, tiger, bulldog, etc.). If it merely serves to identify one team versus another, then it is only a sign. However, to the extent that it inspires a commitment among the loyal students, faculty, and alumni, it may be a powerful symbol.

You are probably familiar with several definitions of the term *myth*. One definition which we do not want to use in this course is the idea that a myth is the opposite of verified fact. We define **myth** as a story about the past that is told and retold in order to express certain values. History is also a story about the past that is told and retold. The difference is that history, like science, claims to be verifiable fact. The kind of faith we should place in a historical account is the mere belief that we would place in any scientific claim: a tentative faith subject to revision when more evidence comes in. Myths should not pretend factual claims, but serve only to express certain values. The proof of a myth is not whether some archaeologist can unearth evidence verifying the claim, but whether the values it conveys can be vindicated.

Let's take the case of the story of Adam and Eve in the book of *Genesis*. We take the position that this is a myth repeated for thousands of years because it expresses a truth (that is, a value) about the relationship of God to humans and the nature of sin. It might be hard to verify the claim that the *Genesis* story represents history. Even if historians, archaeologists, and paleontologists were able to come up with indisputable evidence that Eden never existed, most of us would still read *Genesis* and find it a relevant account of the human condition.

Are we saying that a story about the past is either history or myth (but not both)? Not at all! The *Bible* contains many myths and much history. Theologians may disagree among themselves about which myths are relevant to a contemporary understanding of God and the church. Historians may disagree about which biblical accounts can be verified by external evidence. For example, that a man named Jesus, son of Joseph, came from Nazareth and preached around Galilee and was executed in Jerusalem during the first century C.E. is generally accepted as historical fact. Whether you see his death as representing a myth about salvation will determine if you commit yourself to follow one of the denominations collectively known as Christian.

Symbols are often incorporated into myths as a way to alert us that we should evaluate them according to their relevance, not as valid accounts of historical events. Myths may also serve to explain the importance of symbols. For example, the cross is an important symbol in Christianity because it was the instrument for the crucifixion of Jesus.

Rituals are prescribed, formalized actions that dramatize religious symbols. Brushing my teeth is a prescribed action, but it is not a ritual, because it promotes dental health and reduces social embarrassment. Brushing my teeth has instrumental value, utilitarian relevance. Rituals are repeated in order to attain, or sustain, the individual's contact with ultimate relevance and to consolidate the cohesion of the community. Such rituals are usually performed in a sacred space: in a church or temple, in front of an altar, or the like. Rituals often have prescribed times for their performance: the Jewish sabbath meal on Friday night, an Aborigine subincision at the time a young male makes the transition to manhood, a Roman Catholic penance when some sins have been committed. Rituals usually employ music, dance, and special costumes to make ritualistic occasions the more impressive. Rituals carry the danger of becoming overly aesthetic, ends in themselves, antagonistic to doctrinal clarity, and legislated in all their details.

Religious rituals are fundamentally different from magic. Here we are not talking about stage magicians who perform for our entertainment. Indeed, the performers David Copperfield, Lance Burton, and Siegfried and Roy describe themselves as illusionists rather than magicians. **Magic** is the attempt to manipulate spiritual forces. Religious rituals seek to worship spiritual forces. Magical rituals are undertaken in private and are usually secret, while religious rituals are celebrated in public. Religion tries to invite humans into the realm of the ultimate, while magic tries to keep people in the realm of the ulterior.

The origins of rituals are often explained in myths. Many rituals are reenactments of myths. The performance of rituals usually involves the use of symbols. For example, each Sunday (time) Roman Catholics attend mass (a ritual) in a church (a sacred place). Just before the priest distributes a small wafer (a symbol) to devout participants, he retells the story (myth) of Jesus' last supper with his disciples. This explains the origin of the ritual and the importance of the symbol: the bread represents the body of Christ.

The primary purpose of myths and rituals is akin to that of symbols: to connote some profound understanding or evoke some commitment within the person who hears the myth or participates in the ritual. Symbols, myths, and rituals lack the precision found in signs, history, or actions undertaken as means to promote specific ends.

There are more denotative, precise aspects to religion. An example would be **ethical** prescriptions. Since religions are concerned with values, and certain actions can have a direct impact on values, religions say what must be done and what must not be done. Do the duties of your caste, and do them gladly, says the Hindu book, the *Bhagavad Gita*. Honor your parents says Confucius. Don't lie, steal, kill, or have sex outside marriage, say the rules at a Buddhist monastery. Don't worship idols, said Muhammad. Most of these sound familiar to the Ten Commandments of the Old Testament.

Ethical behavior is more tied to reason, than would be the case with ritual behaviors. We may gladly perform a ritual simply because it is tradition, but most people want to know the reason behind a moral precept. Most ethical pronouncements based upon a religious foundation are **deontological**, emphasizing specific duties and/or rights. Duties may be seen as coming from God, and rights are often seen as coming from the natural order of things. On the abortion debate, for example, the pro-life side argues from the starting point that we as a society have a duty (coming from "Thou Shalt Not Kill") to protect the right to life of the unborn fetus. The pro-choice side argues from the starting point that we have a duty to protect the right of the woman to choose whether or not she will become a parent, based upon the natural principle that she should have autonomy over her own body.

Another rational basis for ethics is the **utilitarian** approach. To determine if a given action or policy should be regarded as good or bad, right or wrong, consider the outcomes on everyone concerned. Does an act (or rule) increase their welfare or reduce it? In practice, this approach to morality says that we have to think through the ramifications and balance the good against the evil. For example, should I drive my car to work or take public transportation? I have to balance the convenience of taking my own vehicle versus the adverse impact on others through increased congestion, pollution, and depletion of fossil fuels.

Ethics ties into both myths and rituals. Myths often justify certain ethical positions by telling powerful stories that demonstrate virtuous or evil behavior. People often turn to rituals when ethical rules have been violated. The Roman Catholic may go to confession and perform a penance. The ancient Hebrews dealt with collective sin by the sacrifice of an animal.

Yet another area in which religions strive for precision is the area of **doctrine**. Doctrinal positions involve statements about the nature of the Deity (God) or deities (gods), sin, salvation, and/or afterlife. We prefer to use the term *doctrine* instead of *beliefs* because these statements are not like historical events or laboratory results that we are called upon to believe. Doctrine is proven (vindicated) because it expresses a religion's value. The Christian doctrine of heaven or the Hindu doctrine of transmigration express the values that people who do their duty should be rewarded after this life. Doctrine can be vindicated through

COMPONENTS OF RELIGION		
DIMENSION	THOUGHTS	ACTIONS
Denotative (precise)	**Doctrines** Statements made about deities, salvation, afterlife EXAMPLE: Jesus is the Son of God	**Ethics** Actions deemed to be right or wrong, sinful, or moral EXAMPLE: Thou shalt not kill
Connotative (evocative)	**Myths** Stories about the past retold because of the values they portray EXAMPLE: Jesus had a last supper with his disciples	**Rituals** Actions prescribed as ceremonies EXAMPLE: Holy Communion

its ethical implications. Doctrine cannot be proven (verified) in the same way that empirical statements can be. You cannot verify the existence of God by a telescope or microscope. No historian has been able to verify (or disprove) the doctrine of reincarnation.

Many students new to the study of religion make two serious mistakes. One is to rely on the structure of their own religion to provide a template for understanding other religions. Since most students of the English-speaking world come from a Protestant Christian background (e.g., Baptist, Methodist, Presbyterian, Episcopalian, Lutheran), they tend to overemphasize the importance of one of these components (doctrine) and try to reduce world religions to mere doctrinal comparison. Most tribal and ancient religions (along with Judaism and Hinduism) deemphasize doctrine in favor of ritual and ethics. (A Jew does not define himself in terms of his religion as "believing" or "not believing" but as "practicing" or "not practicing.") The different religions can be compared, however. (This process is known as a **homology**). Usually, more similarities can be found than differences, and rarely are the differences in doctrine the

most important. Usually, the most striking distinctions among religions can be attributed to differences in geography, culture, or historical events.

Another blind spot for most students is the tendency to conceive of a religion as a static system of doctrines, rituals, and ethics. Indeed, many Christian denominations base their claims to legitimacy or superiority on their perception that they are closer to "pure" original Christianity. However, since specific religions arise and develop within the context of human culture and history, religions change: doctrines and ethics may evolve, adapting to the changing times. Two thousand years ago, a main Jewish ritual was animal sacrifice. Then, in 70 C.E., the Romans destroyed the Jerusalem temple and the sacred site for this ritual was lost.

Myths, symbols, and rituals are especially susceptible to change via **syncretism** (the blending that takes place when different religions come into contact). Think of the two most important Christian holidays celebrated in North America: Christmas and Easter. Think of the symbols associated with those rituals. First-century Christians did not have evergreen trees for Christmas or colored eggs for Easter. These symbols came from Teutonic and Celtic traditions Christianity assimilated as it moved north.

The study of the changing structure and form of religion is known as **morphology**. Remember a popular kids' TV show a few years back (somewhere between the Ninja Turtles and Pokemon) known as the *Mighty Morphin Power Rangers?* Remember how

Contribute to this discussion. Come up with an *analogy* for understanding religion. Tie in the terminology introduced in this text.

EXAMPLE: Religion is like an onion. A person's religion involves rituals, symbols, and myths that are at the very core of life. Each additional layer of life is influenced by the shape of that core. This understanding of religion is especially appropriate for comprehending the role of religion in the lives of fundamentalists, who take scripture literally and attempt to apply it to daily life.

Contribute to this discussion at http://www.delphi.com/rel101

the heroes could quickly change their form? Religions can morph, maybe not as quickly as the Power Rangers, but a particular doctrine, ethical rule, symbol, ritual, or even myth may evolve in its relevance over time. So when we study what Buddha said 2,500 years ago in India, don't assume that his doctrine and monastic ethics completely comprehend the rituals followed by a modern-day Japanese.

GOD OR GODS?

Many students assume that religion centers around a doctrine about God. This is another example of the North American and Christian tendency to reduce religion to doctrine. Because of the tendency to use the term *God* almost as a proper name for the Deity described in the Old and New Testaments, we suggest that in this course the term *Deity* might be used to describe the one God of the Judeo-Christian-Islamic tradition.

The position that only one Deity exists is known as monotheism. This is a key element of doctrine in those religions coming out of the Middle East: Atonism, Zoroastrianism, Judaism, Christianity, Islam, and Bahai. Some monotheists are **theistic** and regard the Deity as personal: loving and merciful and/or wrathful when our sins have offended Him. Theists usually emphasize the importance of prayer and see it as important to the ongoing intimate relationship between creature and Creator. Most evangelical Christians could be described as theistic.

Another understanding of monotheism is deistic. **Deism** is the view that a supreme god or **deity** set up the natural world but does not actively intervene on a regular basis. The deistic approach is that God is impersonal, worthy of worship, but not interested in the details of the individual lives of humans. Many of the founders of the American Republic (e.g., Benjamin Franklin and Thomas Jefferson) could be described as deists.

A further twist of monotheism is **pantheism**, the doctrine that everything is God (or that nothing exists apart from the Deity). This doctrine was suggested by the *Upanishads* in India about 2,500 years ago. Pantheistic approaches assume that the Deity is **immanent** (in everyone and everything) while the more traditional monotheistic religions coming out

of the Middle East view God as **transcendent** (apart from this world, a Creator who preexisted and stands outside His creation).

Polytheism is the doctrine that several deities exist. Most of the religions of the ancient world (e.g., Egyptians, Mesopotamians, Canaanites, Greeks, Mayans, Aztecs, Incas) recognized several deities worthy of worship. These deities can take human form (i.e., be **anthropomorphic**) in terms of their bodies or characteristics, or the form of animals (i.e., be **theriomorphic**). Some polytheistic religions view these deities as unequal in function or importance. Myths may explain that one deity conquered another or was selected to be the king of the gods. Among the Babylonians and the Aztecs, the deities of the conquering tribes and the defeated peoples alike were in the pantheon, but the deities of the victors had a more important place. A **pantheon** is a structured hierarchy of deities and can also be found among the Egyptians, Greeks, Teutons, and Vedic Aryans.

Many tribal religions have an animistic doctrine. **Animism** is the doctrine that there are spirits in everything—not just each person, but animals, plants, places, and even natural phenomena. One debate within the history of religion has been whether an inevitable progression of doctrine has taken place throughout the ages. Did we all start off living in hunting and gathering tribes, with an animistic doctrine? As humans developed the herding of domesticated animals, settled agriculture, and cities, did polytheism arise? Did polytheism tend to structure its doctrine as civilizations grew, so that pantheons arose? The big question would be: How did these polytheistic pantheons lead to monotheism? One possible answer is **henotheism**: that one deity then emerged as most worthy of worship. Another step could have been the development of **monolatry**: the worship of one god (although the existence of other deities might be acknowledged). Scholars who have studied ancient religions disagree on whether the Egyptian pharaoh Akhenaton or the Hebrew patriarch Abraham should be regarded as true monotheists or merely monolatrous, advocating the worship of only one Deity while not clearly denying the existence of others.

Atheism is the position that no deities exist. Most atheists are committed to the scientific point of view and attempt to apply scientific standards of proof to

POSITION	VIEW OF DEITIES	WHERE FOUND
Animism	spirits are in everything	tribal cultures
Polytheism	several gods exist	ancient civilizations, Hindus
Pantheon	several gods, arranged in a hierarchy	Mayans, Aztecs, Greeks, Teutons, Vedic Aryans, Mesopotamians
Henotheism	several gods, some more important than others	Hindus
Monolatry	worship one deity	Akhenaton? Abraham?
Monotheism	only one deity exists	Judaism, Islam, Christianity
Theism	personal deity (deities) who answer prayer	some Christians, some Hindus
Deism	impersonal deity who does not actively intervene in world	Jefferson, Franklin
Pantheism	everything is God	Upanishadic Hinduism
Atheism	no deities exist	about 5% of U.S. population
Agnosticism	God's existence cannot be proved, so we must doubt	adolescence

religious doctrines, finding religious proofs inadequate. Another possible motive for the atheist position is the view that humans should confine their activities within the sphere of utilitarian relevance and that when religions try to lead people into the realm of the ultimate, the result is simply that the mass of people are led into the superstitiousness of ulterior relevance. In other words, some people may not want to acknowledge the existence of God because He would get in the way of their (sinful?) pursuit of pleasure. Although most people acknowledge some type of Deity (or higher power), between 5 and 10 percent of North Americans would describe themselves as atheists.

Many atheists are humanists. **Humanism** is the position that people are basically good and can work out their own salvation. This position may involve such an appreciation of human virtues and needs that it leads to focus on human concerns, sometimes to the neglect of divinity or ultimate reality.

Atheistic humanists would say that religion is not necessary to make people good. Not all atheists are humanists. (As we shall see, psychoanalyst Sigmund Freud embraced atheism, yet contended that religion helped control the evil impulses in humans.) Not all humanists are atheists. Humanistic doctrine can be found among some deists and theists. However, religion lives from present attainment, reaching out to the infinite. Humanism can define itself so as to be compatible with such transcendence, but frequently it does not. Secular humanism expressly does not, taking its name from the this-worldly horizon that at best brackets divine transcendence.

A position slightly less extreme than that of the atheist is that of the agnostic. **Agnosticism** says that God's existence is not provable and therefore we should doubt, but we can never know with the certainty that the monotheist claims for the existence of God or that certainty which the atheist has in the nonexistence of God. Clearly the agnostic, like the atheist, attempts to apply the same standards of proof (empirical verification) to religious doctrine as are appropriately applied to the realm of science. Although the number of lifelong agnostics is probably small, many adolescents and young adults go through an agnostic phase as they begin to question their own religious traditions. Most of these individuals will not remain agnostics. Perhaps some will go on to become confirmed atheists as their doubts harden into rejection of religion. Others will find another, more relevant denomination to which they will convert. Most will probably reembrace the religion of their childhood as the life tasks of matrimony and parenthood approach along the road of adulthood.

The purpose of this course is not to turn you into an atheist or agnostic, or to make you a convert to Buddhism or Catholicism, or to get you to reembrace the religion of your upbringing as a "born-again" adherent. However, we must ask you to suspend the standards of judgment of your own doctrines in order to comprehend the complexities of other religions. In other words, if you are a committed evangelical Christian, you cannot simply dismiss other religions as wrong because they do not follow the Bible (or perhaps do not follow it in the way that you do). If you are an atheist or agnostic, you cannot simply dismiss all religions as unscientific superstition.

RELIGION VERSUS GOVERNMENT

Church and state are two of the strongest institutions in most societies. Sometimes they work together, supporting each other's efforts in controlling human behavior and promoting values that have been jointly agreed upon.

A **theocracy** is a government run by religion, or at least one in which the religious leaders have a great deal of influence over governmental policy. In most ancient civilizations, the king supported the religious institutions financially and enforced laws that were based upon ethics. In some societies, the performance of religious rituals was compelled by the government. A good example would be ancient Israel. Kings such as David and Solomon understood their duty as enforcers of God's laws of the Old Testament (Torah). One contemporary example of a theocracy would be the Vatican. This is an area of several square blocks in Rome, which by virtue of a treaty with Italy, is recognized as a separate and sovereign country, complete with powers to conduct diplomatic relations with other nations. The chief executive of that country is the Pope of the Roman Catholic Church. Other contemporary examples would be Iran and Afghan-

Theologians use reason to fully develop the implications of doctrine and ethics. Averroes used the philosophy of Aristotle in order to comprehend some of the implications of Islam.

istan, where revolutions have brought religious-led factions into positions of leadership. These leaders have used their political power, guided by their religious values, to demand that women dress and behave in ways deemed appropriate.

A pro-religious government may lack the unity between church and state seen in a theocracy, but such a nation is not neutral when it comes to different denominations (or sects). Such sectarian governments may "tolerate" the rights of other denominations to worship, but one denomination is clearly favored. If a sectarian government has a monarchy, a requirement of succession may be that a prince or princess belong to the state religion in order to assume the throne. The next king of England must be Anglican. The next king of Spain must be Catholic. Even a nonmonarchy democracy such as Israel is clearly pro-religious, insofar as that state was created to be a

Theocracies, such as Iran since 1979, give religious leaders major authority within the government. The U.S. model is secularism: a separation of Church and State.

homeland for the Jews. Prior to the American Revolution, most of the British colonies in North America were sectarian. In most colonies, the Anglican Church was established and supported by taxes. In some New England colonies, it was the Congregational Church. In Rhode Island, it was the Baptists. The Quakers predominated in Pennsylvania, the Catholics in Maryland, and the Dutch Reformed Church in New York.

The U.S. Constitution outlined a different approach based upon the principle of neutrality. This approach was prompted by the realization that the different denominations in the United States probably could not agree on anything except that they all wanted to preserve their rights to worship without government interference. The First Amendment to the Constitution affirms this and promises to keep out of purely religious affairs. This has been interpreted to mean that neither the federal, state, nor local governments could support denominations with tax monies. Throughout the 1790s, many of the new

states were required to "disestablish" churches. The movement to oppose this constitutional requirement (and keep tax money supporting the churches) was known as *antidisestablishmentarianism* and eventually gave way to the nonsectarian position.

Secular is another name for this neutral approach. This may seem confusing because the word *secular* looks like *sectarian,* but they have opposite meanings (secular = nonsectarian). Public institutions funded by the government are supposed to be secular. Crafton Hills College, for example, is one of California's 108 tax-supported community colleges. Many of the faculty, administrators, and students who attend Crafton are very religiously committed individuals, but the taxpayers and the government expect faculty and administrators to do their jobs without advancing a religious agenda of any kind. Santa Clara University is a private university founded and still led by the Jesuit order of Roman Catholic priests. Many students and faculty members are non-Catholics, but all know that the university will

GOVERNMENT POSITIONS ON RELIGION		
APPROACH	POLICY ON RELIGION	EXAMPLES
Theocracy	Religious leaders run or influence the government	Vatican, ancient Israel, Iran since 1979
Pro-religious	Government supports certain denominations	England, Spain since 1939, Israel since 1948, American colonies before 1787
Secular	Government supports no denominations but protects the rights of all denominations	U.S. since 1787
Anticlerical	Government opposes the power of religious leaders	Mexico 1917–2000, Spain 1931–1939
Antireligious	Government suppresses worship by individuals	USSR 1930s, China 1950s
Is the U.S. government too pro-religious or too anti-religious? Join the discussion at http://www.delphi.com/rel101		

expose them to certain Catholic doctrines, symbols, and rituals and that many decisions will be guided by Catholic ethics. Santa Clara is sectarian; Crafton is secular.

An **anticlerical** government is one which sees the power of the nation's largest religion as a threat. An anticlerical government may not try to prevent individuals from worshipping, but it may try to limit the church's wealth or the influence of church leaders. One example would be Mexico in the 1920s. As the agrarian revolution led by Pancho Villa and Emiliano Zapata hardened into the bureaucracy of the Institutional Revolutionary Party (PRI), there was an inevitable conflict with the Roman Catholic Church. The government confiscated church lands, limited its role in the educational system, and told priests not to wear clerical garb in public. The result was the armed Cristero rebellion in western Mexico, in which the church recruited devout peasants to oppose these government measures. The PRI won that civil war, and for over seventy years a nation that was 95 percent Catholic was governed by a string of non-Catholic presidents (until 2000, when opposition

leader Vicente Fox was elected from the National Action Party, PAN, and for the first time Mexicans saw their president on television attending mass).

Another example of an anticlerical government comes from Spain in the 1930s. In 1931 a republic was declared, and in 1935 a leftist coalition of socialists, communists, anarchists, and syndicalists won the elections. Their reforms angered not only the wealthy, but also the Roman Catholic Church. The following year, units of the Spanish Army (led by General Francisco Franco) rose up against the government under the banner of defending Catholicism. After three bloody years of civil war, Franco won, establishing a right-wing dictatorship and a pro-religious government.

Some revolutionary governments have gone even farther in their opposition to religion. Communist governments have usually been suspicious of any other center of power in the nation, including religion. During the 1930s, the Soviet Union under Stalin became anti-religious, promoting atheism as an ideal and discouraging citizens from religious affiliation or worship. (In the 1940s, Stalin reversed his position,

(c) Archivio Iconografico, S.A./ CORBIS

Karl Marx, father of Communism, "Religion is the opiate of the masses."

seeking to get the support of the Russian Orthodox Church in the war against Nazi Germany.) Similar anti-religious extremism was reached in the 1950s in Mao's China and the 1960s in Castro's Cuba. Today, both China and Cuba try to appear more tolerant of religion, but oppression may wax and wane with political needs.

SACRED WRITINGS

Tribal societies often preserve their myths by repeating the stories ritually in an oral tradition. After the invention of writing, many religions started to write down their myths and doctrines. (Examples would be the book of *Genesis* for the Hebrews and the *Rig Veda* for the Aryans in India.) Priests also wrote down guidelines for those performing rituals. (Examples would be the book of *Leviticus* for the He-

brews and the later *Vedas* for the Hindus). Then there were books that recorded laws (e.g., Hammurabi in Babylonia) and ethical behaviors (e.g., *Deuteronomy* for the Hebrews). **Scripture** is the name given to sacred writings. Each of the modern religions has a **canon** (an official list of the writings to be regarded as scripture). In Hinduism this would be the *Vedas*; in Judaism, the *Torah*; in Islam, the *Qur'an*; in Christianity, the books of the *Bible*. Writings that have not been admitted to the canon, but are nevertheless revered for their historical or inspirational value, are sometimes called **apocryphal**. In Hinduism, this would include the *Brahamanas, Aranyakas, Upanishads* and *Bhagavad Gita* (although some Hindus might base more of their own doctrines and rituals on these books than the *Vedas*). Islam regards the Christian *Bible* as apocryphal (having many useful myths, but not as scripturally authoritative as the *Qur'an*). The Jewish and Protestant *Apocrypha* includes fourteen books written by Jewish prophets after 400 B.C.E. but before the birth of Jesus. (After 1500 C.E., the Catholic Church decided to include these intertestamental writings into the Catholic Old Testament canon.)

Hermeneutics constitute the principles of the interpretation of documents. Physically, a text is simply some marks on a piece of paper or some impressions in clay. These marks have to "speak" from the mind of the person who set them down to the minds of people like you who are trying to pick them up. Thus, the languages and assumptions of both minds come

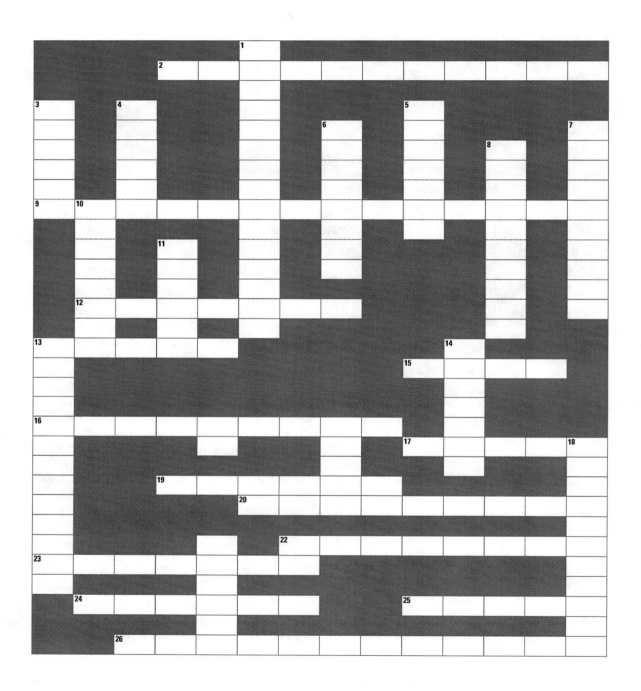

ACROSS

2   Doctrine that God's existence cannot be proven
9   Advocates literal interpretation of scripture
12 View that everything has a spirit
13 Another name for a "god"
15 A specific religious group
16 A government run by religious leaders
17 *Commitment* or *denomination* are terms for _____.
19 Something explained by a myth, used in a ritual
20 The doctrine that everything is God
22 Structured hierarchy of deities
23 The position that no deities exist
24 Religion does not deal with validity, but . . .
25 The view that God created the world, then left it alone
26 The view that there are many deities

DOWN

1   Deities with human form
3   *Doctrine* is a better term to use than religious _____
4   Era that began with the birth of Christ
5   Not sectarian
6   "People are basically good."
7   Doctrine that only one God exists
8   Scientific statements must be verified according to _____.
10 Religion is in the realm of _____ relevance.
11 View that God is personal
14 The U.S. Constitution makes our society _____.
18 Something useful in interpreting scripture
21 A ceremony using symbols

into play, your own as much as the author's. You can assume that you and the author share a great deal, since you are both human, but you must be careful about how you use this assumption. Boiled down, hermeneutics consist of walking the tightrope between the sameness we have as members of one species and the differences we have as individuals, people of different cultures, and people of different historical eras.

Hermeneutical techniques include the study of literary style as well as the historical context of those who wrote a document. We cannot simply rely upon translations of texts into modern English. To become expert in the interpretation of scripture, we would also have to have a knowledge of the ancient languages in which scripture was written, both the vocabulary and grammar. **Exegesis** is the attempt to arrive at the most relevant interpretation of a specific scriptural passage.

Fundamentalists are people who are strict about their religious doctrine and ethics. Fundamentalists usually emphasize literal interpretation of scripture and its strict application in daily life. Fundamentalists are often concerned about the growth of secular humanism in modern society, because it represents a trend away from the importance of religion in institutions and the daily lives of individuals.

RELIGIOUS ROLES

All social organizations, including religious denominations, have various roles which their members may assume.

Most adherents or followers of a given religious denomination are known as **lay** persons, or *laity,* in that they do not have leadership roles. Laypersons participate in rituals, but do not lead the rituals. Laypersons are supposed to accept the denomination's doctrine, but probably will not get a chance to vote on it. Those decisions will be made by the leadership.

In tribes that subsist largely by hunting and gathering, the major religious figure is the **shaman** (such as the medicine man in North American Indian tribes). Shamans are the intermediaries between the tribe and the world of the spirits and may have to arrange for a good hunt by negotiating with the keeper of the animals, by locating the herd, or by capturing the spirits of the game before the hunters capture their bodies. The shaman may have to guide the souls of the dead to an afterlife. Shamans have the primary duties of healing the sick through herbs or through exorcism (casting out evil spirits). Obviously, the specific duties of the shaman differ from tribe to tribe.

In societies that have developed a pastoral or agricultural economy, the main religious figure is usually a **priest,** who officiates at regularly scheduled rituals.

This shaman is from Tibet, but his role is similar to that of shamans in other tribal societies.

Most of these are sacrifices in which there is some offering made to the deities to propitiate human sin or the violation of a taboo or to encourage a rich harvest. In the early civilizations, calendars were developed, and rituals were scheduled for appropriate times.

Some contemporary Christian denominations use the term *priest* to describe their religious leaders: the Roman Catholics, Episcopalians, Mormons, and Eastern Orthodox. The sacrifice that is reenacted in the ritual of the mass is the Last Supper of Jesus (Eucharist). Brahmin priests are the highest caste of Hindu society. Priests were important in Jewish religion during the time of the Israelite kingdom, but for about two thousand years Jewish religious leaders have been known as **rabbis** ("teachers"), who are distinguished for their knowledge of the Jewish tradition. Most of the Protestant Christian denominations that arose during the period of the Reformation (sixteenth century, C.E.) refer to their officials as **ministers** or **parsons** or preachers. A **pastor** is a priest or minister who is in charge or a particular locality (e.g., a Roman Catholic parish).

The higher levels of leadership in the Christian church are also denoted by special roles. A **bishop** is in charge of several priests or ministers within a geographical area (e.g., a Roman Catholic diocese or Mormon ward). An archbishop (or metropolitan or patriarch in the Eastern Orthodox churches) is in charge over several bishops. In the Roman Catholic Church, the **Pope** is the Bishop of Rome, and is the head of the entire Church. He is not a prophet in terms of receiving specific revelations from God, but the Church accepts the Pope's ability to speak authoritatively, infallibly (Ex Cathedra) on doctrinal issues. The Pope selects certain archbishops to be **cardinals** who meet in large councils to proclaim church doctrine and to select a new pope upon the death of the old one.

A **psychic** (or **medium**) is a person who claims abilities such as foretelling the future (augury, soothsaying, omens, **divination**), perceiving objects despite

ROLE	FUNCTIONS	WHERE FOUND
Shaman, medicine man, witch doctor	exorcism, healing, finding game, making rain, guiding souls to afterlife	tribal cultures
Priest	rituals of calendar and propitiation, confession	ancient civilizations, Hebrews and Israelites, Hindus, Mormons, Roman Catholics, Episcopalians, Eastern Orthodox
Prophet	speaks for the one God	Hebrews and Israelites, Zoroastrianism, Islam, Mormonism, Japanese Buddhism
Diviner	predicts future	Africans, Celts, Mayans, Aztecs, Chinese, Greeks, Mesopotamians
Psychic, medium	predicts future, perceives distant events, reads minds, communicates with dead	worldwide: usually outside of religions
Mystic	seeks ecstatic union with God	Buddhists, Jainists, Neoplatonists, Gnostics, *Upanishads,* Taoists, Sufi Moslems, Hasidic and Cabbalist Jews, monastic Christians
Theologian	uses reason to defend doctrines and ethics	Paul, Augustine, Anselm, Aquinas, Averroes, Maimonides, Al-Ghazzali, Calvin, Arminius
Teacher	conveys doctrine and ethics	Jewish rabbis, Confucius
Layperson	no leadership role	most people in most denominations

distances or obstacles (**clairvoyance**), reading the mind of another person (**telepathy**), manipulating physical objects or energy fields without using one's muscles (**psychokinesis**, levitation), or contacting the spirits of the deceased (seances, channeling, necromancy). Although these psychic phenomena are more comparable to magic, some religious leaders may claim some psychic abilities. For example, shamans may conduct the spirits of the departed to the happy hunting ground, scare away troublesome ghosts, determine the location of game herds, and the like.

Do not confuse psychics with **prophets.** Some prophets do foretell the future, but what separates them from mere diviners is that the prophet claims to speak the will of God. Noah, Abraham, Moses, and most of the authors of the books of the Old Testament are regarded as prophets in Judaism because they received special revelations from God. One of the first prophets outside the Judaic tradition was the Persian Zoroaster (about 600 B.C.E.). Muhammad is regarded as the last and greatest prophet in Islam. Some recent religions have founders who have been regarded as prophets (e.g., Joseph Smith of the Mormons). Usually, prophets are found within the monotheistic religions coming out of the ancient Middle East. One exception would be the Buddhist

Nichiren (thirteenth century), who commanded that a temple be built.

Mystics seek to attain an altered state of consciousness that they understand as an intimate union with the Deity. The usual technique employed is the use of meditation. We could describe what they are doing as stripping away all pretense of cognitive meaning, utilitarian relevance, and ulterior relevance from their lives. The strategy is to reduce their lives to just one factor: ultimate relevance.

When mystics contemplate, they attempt to focus their minds on the whole of a scene or experience, or to commune with the ultimate directly. Perhaps contemplation may be distinguished from meditation as something more holistic, more affective, and less intellectual. It schools the human spirit in letting go of particulars and reaching out (or maybe pulling within) to receive the divine whole directly and lovingly.

Historically, mysticism began in the **Axial Age** (roughly 600 B.C.E–200 C.E.). Asian religions (Upanishadic Hinduism, Jainism, Buddhism, Taoism) urged a liberation from the material and social ties of this world. In Western monotheistic religions, mysticism has usually been seen as a potential source of heresy. Nevertheless, Judaism had Cabala in medieval times and Hasidism since the eighteenth century, Islam has had the Sufis, and the Christians have canonized mystics as saints in the Roman Catholic and Eastern Orthodox traditions. With the exception of Quakerism, Protestantism has rejected mysticism.

Many Christian and Buddhist mystics have been part of the tradition of **monasticism**: monks and nuns living in separate communities where they can be freed from the everyday concerns of utilitarian relevance such as earning a living. These monks and nuns are usually required to be **celibate**: they must avoid marriage and sex outside of marriage. The requirement of celibacy has also been made of Roman Catholic priests for the last thousand years. The only religion to require celibacy for all of its followers was the Shaker sect, which had dozens of utopian farm communities throughout the northeastern part of the United States in the nineteenth century (but has now nearly died out).

The mystic differs from other religious figures such as the psychic, shaman, prophet, priest, and theologian. The psychic also claims to enjoy altered

Give us an example. Take a scriptural passage and indicate how it portrays the role of Jesus. Is he portrayed as a . . .

PRIEST: absolving guilt, performing ritual?

MYSTIC: seeking an ecstatic union with God (similar to Lao Tzu, Buddha)?

TEACHER: trying to apply religious tradition to specific ethical questions (similar to Confucius)?

PROPHET: bringing new messages from God (similar to Zoroaster, Isaiah, Nichiren, Muhammed)?

SHAMAN: healing, exorcising?

Contribute to this discussion at http://www.delphi.com/rel101

states of consciousness, but these are associated with specific occult abilities. Prophets claim to have received a conceptual message from the Deity, while mystics have a nonconceptual message. Priests try to preserve the rituals, doctrines, and authority of established denominations, while mystics often transcend them for a direct union with what is ultimately relevant.

Mysticism has been criticized by established religions as "beginning in 'mist,' centering in 'I,' and ending in 'schism.'" The mystic usually tries to transcend established doctrine, rituals, and authority. The theologian champions the use of reason in the development of religious doctrine while the mystic seeks to transcend reason. (However, Augustine and Al-Ghazzali reconciled mysticism and theology.)

Theologians attempt to use philosophy and rational elaboration in order to explain or argue religious doctrine. In other words, theologians attempt to link religion back to the realm of cognitive meaning. One role of theology is to clarify a denomination's doctrine for priesthood and laity alike. Some theologians are engaged in trying to defend the doctrines of their denominations against atheists or the doctrines of other sects. This is known as *apologetics*. Some of the greatest theologians have been Paul, who distinguished Christian doctrine in the first century; Augustine, who blended Christianity with Plato; Aquinas, who blended Christianity with Aristotle; Maimonides, who blended Judaism with Plato; Aver-

ARGUMENTS ABOUT THE EXISTENCE OF GOD		
ARGUMENT	**PROPONENTS**	**SUBSTANCE**
Cosmological	Aristotle (384–322) B.C.E. and Aquinas (1224–1274)	Since every earthly event is the effect of some other event, which in turn must be caused by some other event, the beginning of this causal chain must be a *first cause* that lies outside of earthly events: God exists as the first cause.
Teleological	Paul (first century), Aquinas (1224–1274), and Paley (1743–1805)	All the wonders of nature, from the great planetary bodies to the intricate organs of the smallest forms of life, show evidence of complicated *design,* so there must exist a great designer whom we call God.
Ontological	Anselm (1033–1109) and Descartes (1596–1650)	God is defined as a perfect being and therefore possesses all the qualities of perfection: all knowing, all powerful, and good. Existence is also a quality of *perfection,* and therefore God also has that quality: God exists.
Moral	Kant (1724–1804)	We must *postulate* the existence of a good God who will compensate humans for the performance of their moral duties.
Wager	Pascal (1623–1662)	If God exists, and we do not accept Him, we will spend eternity in Hell, whereas if we accept God, and He does not exist, we have only missed out on some sins—so bet that God does exist.
Mystical	mystics	The universality of the mystical experience means that mystics are experiencing the same thing: God.
Theodicy	atheists	The existence of *evil* and suffering in the world means that there cannot exist a God who is good, all knowing, and all powerful.

roes, who blended Islam with Aristotle; and Al-Ghazzali, who resolved Islam, reason, and mysticism.

Theologians have offered various proofs for the existence of God. The **cosmological proof** says that everything is caused by something else that must have come before it, but how then could the first cause get started? God must be the uncaused first cause who stands outside the material world's causal chain. The teleological **proof** is also known as the **design argument:** since there is so much structure and purpose in the natural world, there must be a God who set the planets in their orbits and designed the intricacies of the organs of the body. The **ontological proof** is based upon a logical syllogism: God is defined as a perfect being, and since existence is one of the qualities of perfection, God must exist, by His very definition!

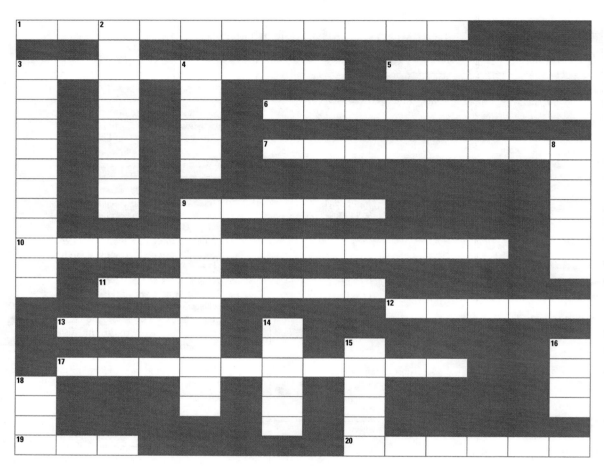

ACROSS

1 "God exists, because of the definition of perfection."
3 The problem of evil challenging God's existence
5 Member of contemporary Jewish clergy
6 Catholic priests, monks, and nuns take a vow to be _____.
7 Casting out demons
9 Period 600 B.C.E.–200 B.C.E.
10 "God exists as the first cause, prime mover."
11 Claims to receive revelations and speak for God
12 The attempt to manipulate spiritual forces
13 Head of the Roman Catholic Church
17 Predicting the future
19 A person who is not in a leadership role
20 Who officiates at sacrifices?

DOWN

2 Who uses reason to explain doctrine?
3 "God exists, because of the design in the universe."
4 The teleological argument is also known as the _____ argument
8 Seeking an immediate union with God
9 Branch of theology defending doctrine
14 Spiritual leader of tribal society
15 Supervises priests in a diocese
16 The bishop of Rome also has this higher role.
18 Theodicy deals with the problem of _____.

Theodicy (the problem of evil) is one of the best arguments for atheism. It runs like this . . .

"If God is to be defined as

OMNISCIENT (all knowing),

OMNIPOTENT (all powerful), and

BENEFICENT (good),

then God would not allow any evil or suffering in the world. Since evil does exist in the world, God cannot exist."

Can you support or counter this argument? *Do* define evil, using terms such as relevance, value, commitment, vindication, myth, symbol, ritual. *Don't* use terms such as truth, true, correct, false, wrong, right, accurate, proof, prove, faith, belief, believe, feel, felt. Be very cautious using the term *meaning*: use only when referring to a definition, not life's great purpose.

Contribute to this discussion at
http://www.delphi.com/rel101

Electronic flashcards and matching games
http://www.quia.com/jg/50265.html

hangman games
http://www.quia.com/hm/17774.html

word jumble games
http://www.quia.com/jw/8185.html

Download multiple choice, true-false, and fill-in drills from
http://www.ureach.com/tlbrink
Click on the public filing cabinet and folder rel2 and download m2.exe, t2.exe, and f2.exe.

The philosopher Immanuel Kant (1724–1804) presented a moral argument for God: since moral actions must be rewarded, we must postulate the existence of God.

There are also powerful rational arguments against the existence of a supreme Deity. One of the best is known as **theodicy**: the problem of evil. Let us assume three characteristics about the Deity (and most Christians would agree with these), that God is omnipotent (all powerful), omniscient (all knowing) and beneficent (good). The atheist now asks, "How would such a God, if He did exist, permit suffering or evil in the world?" Human disease, natural disasters, and the existence of any evil would be impossible if God really had all of those characteristics. While many atheists find this argument conclusive, many theists respond that the time when humans experience evil and suffering (such as the death of a loved one) is exactly when they are in the greatest need of divine consolation. In this way, the existence of God is vindicated.

SCHOLARLY APPROACHES

Throughout most of human history, the scholars who have written about religious topics have been theologians dedicated to the defense of the doctrines of a specific denomination. This was also true of those scholars who studied comparative religion. About 1700 C.E., Jesuit Catholic priests translated the works of Confucius and Taoism, but their main purpose was to facilitate their missionary efforts in China. Then Europe experienced a period known as the **Enlightenment.** This intellectual movement of the eighteenth century embraced humanism and secularism and attempted to extend the rational method of philosophy and the empirical method of science to the study of all human endeavors, including religion. By the nineteenth century, European scholars were writing objective accounts of the history and doctrine of non-Christian religions (e.g., Thomas Carlyle, 1795–1881, on Islam), but few scholars attempted to develop a comprehensive view of religion itself. The twentieth century saw the rise of a scholarly approach to the study of religion that emphasized the role of the social sciences: history, psychology, sociology, and anthropology.

A cognitive view of religion takes the perspective that it represents a merely rational attempt to explain the universe. This view was advanced by several nineteenth-century British scholars who were little more than "armchair anthropologists." E. B. **Tylor** (1832–1917) argued that religion at its core was animistic, and began in an attempt to explain ghosts. Sir James **Frazer** (1854–1941) thought that religion was merely the second stage in the development of human explanation—comprising magic (manipulation), religion (revelation), science (empiricism)—and would eventually disappear.

SCHOLARLY APPROACHES TO RELIGION				
THEORIST	DATES	FOCUS	EXAMPLES	MAIN POINTS
Müller	1823–1900	myth	Teutons, Greeks	confused speech: myth begins as a confusion with metaphor
Tylor	1832–1917	ghosts	Africans	animism: religion begins with speculation about ghosts
Robertson-Smith	1846–1894	totems	Semites	ethics and rituals show importance of tribe
Durkheim	1858–1917	rites	Australia	rituals celebrate and strengthen social cohesion
Mauss	1873–1950	gifts	Native Americans	gift exchange defines relationships
Frazer	1854–1941	myth	Greeks	first magic, then religion, then science
Marx	1818–1883	class	19th-century Europe	dialectical materialism: religion is the opiate of the masses
Fromm	1902–1980	class	20th-century Europe, Mexico	humanistic materialism: religion is a tool for exploitation or community
Otto	1869–1937	emotion		religion is an emotional encounter with the Holy: awe, fear
Freud	1856–1939	ritual, totem, taboo	patients	psychoanalysis: religion controls sex and aggression, but will die out
Jung	1875–1961	myth	patients	analytical psychology: religion fosters healthy contact with collective unconscious
James	1842–1910	mysticism	introspection, biographies	functionalism: judge religion by its fruits
Malinowski	1884–1942	magic	Pacific islands	functionalism: people use best available technology before turning to magic or religion
van Gennep	1873–1957	ritual	Africa	rites of passage: rituals transition people through life events
Erikson	1902–1994	ritual	biographies	psychoanalysis: religion transitions people through developmental tasks
Lévi-Strauss	1908-	totems	Australia	structuralism: cognitive thought is projected onto myths and social structures
Eliade	1907–1986	yoga, shamanism		phenomenology: consider each religion in its own context

This cognitive view was dealt a blow by the field work and functionalist theory of anthropologist Bronislaw **Malinowski** (1884–1942) who found that all peoples use the best technology available to them, but turn to magic and religion when the problems they confront exceed that technology.

The last remnant of a cognitive theory of religion can be found in the structuralism of linguists. Benjamin **Whorf** (1897–1941) argued that the structure of language determines the structure of our thoughts about things. Anthropologist Claude **Lévi-Strauss** (1908–) noted similar structures between the religions, languages, and clan organizations of primitive tribes.

The idea that religion is outside the sphere of the cognitive slowly gained favor among German scholars. Friedrich Max **Müller** (1823–1900) thought that religion has its origin in forms of confused speech in which metaphor was mistaken for objective description. Friedrich **Schleiermacher** (1768–1834) argued that religion transcends reason, and should be considered as an emotional response. Rudolf **Otto** (1869–1937) contended that the essence of religion was the human experience of the sacred, "the holy," and the profound emotions of awe and fear which accompanied this experience. Frenchman Lucien Lévy-Bruhl (1857–1939) argued that the emotional experience was different for primitives, who had a *participation mystique* in which there was no boundary between the individual and community or nature. A. **Ritschl** contended that facts and values were in completely different spheres and that no set of facts could prove or disprove a value claim. H. **Vaihinger** distinguished between facts and "guiding fictions," and he grouped religion under the latter. Fictions cannot be verified the way that facts are (empirically or logically) but they can be vindicated in the sense that they are relevant to the way people guide their lives. American philosopher and psychologist William **James** (1842–1910) contended that religious doctrines and practices should be judged by their fruits (i.e., their results) rather than their roots (i.e., their origins).

Twentieth-century psychological theory has also examined the role of religion as a human phenomenon. Sigmund **Freud** (1856–1939), the founder of psychoanalysis, contended that humans were driven by unconscious sexual and aggressive drives and that

Sigmund Freud, founder of psychoanalysis, "Religion is a childish, obsessional neurosis which mankind will outgrow."

religion was merely one of society's tools for controlling such drives. An atheist, Freud was not sympathetic to religion and noted parallels between religious ritual and obsessive-compulsive and other neurotic behaviors. Like Frazer, Freud predicted that religion would disappear, to be replaced by science (i.e., psychoanalysis). One of Freud's early colleagues was the Swiss psychiatrist Carl **Jung** (1875–1961), who held a more optimistic view of human nature, especially of the creative and nurturing capacities of the unconscious. For Jung, religion (along with art and literature) was one of the fundamental ways in which people used archetypal symbols to contact the potential of the collective unconscious. While Freud had contended that psychotherapy would replace religion in this century, Jung said that the only reason why modern people need psychotherapy was because they had turned away from their religious roots.

Favorable views of religion were offered by humanistic psychologists such as Gordon **Allport** ("ma-

Extrinsic motivation is what moves an individual to do something in order to get some external reward (e.g., a paycheck, praise from others) or avoid some external punishment (a prison sentence or monetary fine). *Intrinsic motivation* is what moves an individual to do something independent of any external consequences (e.g., working hard because you love your job, not breaking a commandment because you would experience guilt).

Social psychologist Gordon Allport noted that both of these motivations could be present in religious behavior, but he contended that "healthy" religion was more intrinsically oriented.

Is this a useful way of categorizing religious denominations or phenomena?

Contribute to this discussion at
http://www.delphi.com/rel101

Electronic flashcards and matching games
http://www.quia.com/jg/50562.html

hangman games
http://www.quia.com/hm/17945.html

word jumble games
http://www.quia.com/jw/8242.html

Download multiple choice, true-false, and fill-in drills from
http://www.ureach.com/tlbrink
Click on the public filing cabinet and folder rel3 and download m3.exe, t3.exe, and f3.exe.

ture religion leads to personal growth and not discrimination against other groups"), Erich **Fromm** ("religion can be used as a key to social progress and equality instead of oppression"), and Abraham **Maslow** ("the peak experience of mysticism represents the highest level of human functioning").

The founders of sociology and anthropology had much to say about religion. J. J. **Bachofen** viewed the transition from animism, to female fertility deities, to male tribal deities, as reflecting the development of society from promiscuity, to matriarchy, to patriarchy. Emile **Durkheim** (1858–1917) and Robertson-Smith (1846–1894) emphasized religion's role in promoting social cohesion, especially in tribal societies. Religious ritual is a celebration by the tribe of the tribe.

The role of socioeconomic aspects of religion was noted by Marx and Weber. Karl **Marx** (1818–1883), who is also known as the ideological father of communism, viewed religion as just another social institution which reflects and reinforces the prevailing social class structure. An atheist, Marx contended that religion merely served as a tool for oppressing the masses, a kind of "opiate" that distracted them from the misery of their exploitation by promising them a better life in the next world. Marx predicted that religion would die out in the perfect communist society because the masses would no longer need otherworldly promises to distract them. Max **Weber**

(1865–1920) argued the opposite relationship between religious ethics and economic systems: that doctrines and practices had nurtured the rise of economic systems. Specifically, Weber saw the rise of capitalism in northern Europe as reflecting the Protestant Ethic of hard work and saving. Marcel **Mauss** (1873–1950) focused on the exchange and transactions between members of the religious community (e.g., gifts) and between the worshippers and the deities (e.g., sacrifices and blessings).

The importance of religious ritual in the life cycle has been noted by anthropologists as well as psychologists. Anthropologists Arnold **van Gennep** (1873–1957) and Victor Turner looked at how religion helped individuals move through social roles and life events (e.g., childbirth, puberty, marriage, death) with rites of passage. Psychoanalyst Erik **Erikson** (1902–1994) agreed that such rituals were important in resolving life's developmental tasks and demonstrated this in case studies of sixteenth-century Protestant Reformer Martin Luther and India's twentieth-century leader Mahatma Gandhi.

An ongoing debate within these social science perspectives concerns **reductionism,** whether they fairly portray religion as a phenomenon in its own right or whether they reduce religion to physical, psychological or social phenomena. Freud, for example, would try to interpret any religious symbol as if it had arisen in the dream of one of his patients, as symbolic of something sexual that had been repressed. Marx would reduce any doctrine to a justification of the ruling powers, and any ethical constraints to an attempt to thwart revolutionary efforts. It is unclear how Marxists could explain away religious figures

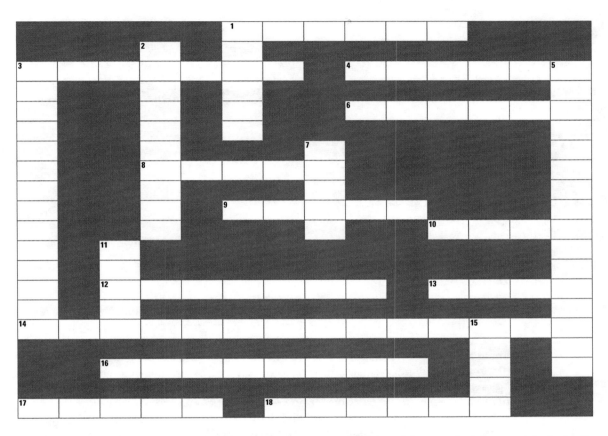

ACROSS

1. "Religion began as confused metaphorical speech."
3. "Religion has the same structure as the tribe." Lévi-_____
4. "Religion is based upon rites of passage." van _____
6. Phenomenological approach
8. "The Protestant ethic paved the way for capitalism."
9. "Judge religions by their fruits, not their roots."
10. "Religion is an emotional experience of the Holy."
12. "Religion helps with life role development."
13. "Religion presents symbols from the unconscious."
14. Approach that reduces religion to other factors

16. "Religion celebrates and reinforces social cohesion."
17. "Religion deals with mutual gift giving."
18. "Magic, then religion, then science."

DOWN

2. "People use the best available technology, then religion."
3. "Religion is an emotional experience of dependence."
5. Eliade's approach
7. "Religion can be a movement for social justice."
11. "Religion controls sex and aggression."
15. "Religion began as an attempt to deal with ghosts."

such as Gandhi or the movement for social justice in contemporary Catholicism, both of which are thorns in the side of the ruling political and economic hierarchies.

Opposed to the reductionistic approach has been the rise of the **phenomenological** approach of Geraldus van der Leeuw (1890–1950) and Mircea **Eliade** (1907–1986). While these scholars eagerly note homologies of ritual, symbol, and myth between diverse religious traditions, they also try to respect the unique perspective of each religion. The phenomenologists may find typical patterns (e.g., mysticism, sacrifice) but also unique configurations.

Diverse Views of Ultimate Reality

Introduction

MANY ARGUE THAT the idea of an ultimate reality is central to religion. This, however, need not be the case. For example, totemism (worship of a plant or animal thought to be an ancestor of the tribe), animism (worship of spirits thought to inhabit and animate aspects of nature), polytheism (worship of many gods) and henotheism (recognition that many gods exist, but worship of only one of them) characterize many religions. The totem, the spirit, and the god are real, but should we think of them as *ultimately* real or simply as *superior* powers? The whole notion of some ultimate, absolute, infinite, unconditioned, and highest reality probably would not make much sense from the totemic, animistic, polytheistic, and henotheistic viewpoints. From these viewpoints, any reality or power greater than humans and related to human beings and nature in important ways is worth worshipping.

However, many religions do claim that there is an ultimate reality (although they disagree about its nature). Some claim it is God in the sense of a personal being. This outlook is usually called theism. Others claim it is nonpersonal or transcends the categories of personal/nonpersonal. We could call this outlook nontheism. However, the use of the word *God* is tricky and often confusing. By "God" some mean simply that which is ultimate, in which case "God" designates whatever is understood by the term *ultimate reality.* Others restrict the use of the term to a personal being. I will use the term *ultimate reality* to designate whatever religions take to be ultimate insofar as they recognize that there *is* something ultimate. Hence, from my viewpoint, the idea of an ultimate reality can be understood both theistically and nontheistically.

What, if anything, is ultimate? In the history of religious thought, there have been many different answers to that question. Some hold that ultimate reality is the way nature operates. Thus Taoism holds that the Tao, or the Way of Nature, is ultimate. This view is sometimes called pantheism, but that word is misleading. Literally, *pantheism* means "everything is divine or God." Yet philosophical Taoism does not explicitly identify the Tao with the divine and holds that it is not only the Way of Nature but also the source or origin of nature. Is the source of something identical to it? Is such an ultimate personal? Certainly it includes persons, because persons are part of nature, but it includes much more as well.

Some argue that the term *panentheism* ("everything is *in* God") better characterizes the view that ultimate reality is the source of the universe (and hence not identical to the universe) and that the universe is also the self-expression of this source. However, according to Taoism, the Tao is subtle and elusive. It is the "Nameless" (see Reading 2.1).

Some Indian philosophers think of ultimate reality as *Satchitanada* (Being, Consciousness, Bliss). *Satchitanada* is the sole reality, and once humans realize this truth, they are released from suffering, thereby attaining bliss (see Reading 2.2). This reality may include a notion of a personal God as a lower manifestation, but ultimate reality is greater than a personal God or Lord. This is not unlike the distinction some Christian theologians have made between the Godhead (the essence of divinity or ultimate reality in itself) and God (the manifestation or expression of the Godhead apprehended by humans).

Monotheism usually insists that ultimate reality is personal (see Reading 2.3). There is only one personal God, and that God is either an absolute unity (unitarianism) or a tri-unity (trinitarianism). Typically Judaism and Islam emphasize the former, and Christianity (with some notable exceptions) the latter. In addition, God is said to possess all possible perfections (and hence to be ultimate). Thus God's knowledge, power, will, mercy, justice, and so on are of the greatest possible magnitude. Indeed God is infinite (unconditioned) in all respects, whereas the universe and humans are finite (conditioned).

If God is personal, does God have a gender? Certainly personal beings do. Is God a "he" or a "she"? Either answer appears both to reinforce sexism by elevating one sex over another and to limit God and thereby contradict the claim that God is an infinite, ultimate reality (see Reading 2.5).

The search for an ultimate reality takes human thought in a variety of different directions. Some Buddhist philosophers maintain that nothing less than "emptiness" will do as an adequate characterization of ultimacy. Ultimate reality is not a god, for *a* god is a limited being. True ultimacy cannot be a particular thing. If it were, it would be finite, or conditioned. Thus it must be a no-thing in the sense that it is not just another item in the universe. Then what are the items that make up the universe? Are they too empty? Ultimately they too are empty in the sense that they have no independent substantial existence (see Reading 2.4).

"Wait a minute," you might be saying, "this is going too fast. You have not even defined *ultimate reality* yet. What is it, anyway? Is it the most perfect actual being or the most perfect possible being? Is it even a being at all?"

These are very good questions, and they are not easy to answer. If reality is measured on a scale from 1 to 10, then the most perfect actual being might be an 8, because 8 is very high on the scale of perfection and is much greater than the second-most-perfect actual reality (say, a 4). But if a 10 is the top of the scale and there cannot ever be anything higher, then would not what is ultimate have to rank a 10? Yet could a mere being ever rank so high? Would not *being itself* or the ground or *source* of being rank higher? And if there is a source of both being and non-being, would not this be higher still? Is there a highest? If there is, can we even think it, let alone define it? Perhaps our language is just carrying us off into a never-never land of paradoxes (if not contradictions) when we try to talk about the nature of ultimate reality. Let's see.

2.1 The Tao

Scholars of Chinese religion use the term *Taoism* to refer to a complex interweaving of religious practices and philosophic thought. In 142 Chang Tao-ling had a vision of Lao-tzu, a legendary sage, as an Immortal being, who gave him the title of Heavenly Master. In this vision, Lao-tzu instructed Tao-ling to institute new forms of worship and to teach people to abandon the old gods. The group Tao-ling founded eventually combined with other reform movements that stressed meditation, breathing exercises, doing good deeds, diet, various healing practices, and alchemical searches for an elixir of immortality. The idea of a future heavenly state of peace and harmony that could be achieved on earth became part of the mix. Over time these elements coalesced into Taoism, one of the three major strands of Chinese religion (the other two are Confucianism and Buddhism)

But who was Lao-tzu? According to tradition, he was the author of a book called the *Tao Te Ching* (*The Book of the Way and Its Excellence*). There are stories about Lao-tzu and when he lived, but we have very little firm historical information. Some claim he was a contemporary of Confucius (551–479 B.C.E.), but others have placed his book later (403–221 B.C.E.).

The *Tao Te Ching* is a classic of world literature. However, its meaning is very obscure, and it has been interpreted in a wide variety of ways. Scholars have argued it is a treatise on how one should live, that it is a political manual offering advice to government officials on how best to govern, that it is a metaphysical discussion of the ultimate source of reality, that it is a collection of anti-Confucian sayings, and so on. I have selected those chapters of the *Tao Te Ching* that have to do with the Tao, which literally means "way or road," because our concerns here are with different views of ultimate reality. The word *Tao* is used by Taoists to refer to the Way of Nature. This Way is indescribable. It transcends human thought and vocabulary. The best humans can do is hint at its nature by the use of metaphors and analogies. Thus it is compared to a valley, the empty space between mountains that makes mountains possible. It is compared to water that is weak in its fluidity, yet strong in its ability to bring about change. It is like the empty space inside a bowel. Without that space, the bowel would be useless. It acts by "not acting," (*wu-wei* means "no action"); that is, its actions are spontaneous, free, and natural, unlike the formal, rigid, and artificial actions, manners, and customs that the Confucians (according to the Taoists) maintain are necessary for a peaceful society.

The Tao is the source of all things and pervades all things. It is the *Te* ("excellence, power, or virtue") of nature. If all things could realize their full potential, they would actualize their *te* and would thereby be living in harmony with the Way of nature (Tao).

The world generated by Tao is an ever-changing flow of oppositions. At times the *yin,* or the passive, dominates. At other times the *yang,* or the active, dominates.

Yin and yang stand for *complementary* opposites. You cannot have one without the other. The seasonal cycle is an example. Winter is the most *yin* season. Life processes are slow. It is cold and dark. However, winter contains an element of *yang* that develops until we reach spring, with its warmth, light, and flourishing life. *Yang* reaches its zenith in summer. Yet summer contains an element of *yin* that expands into fall and then winter again.

According to Lao-tzu, Tao is prior to the gods. It is the most basic and fundamental reality. It is that which is truly real. It is the organic harmony that is the foundation of all things.

Reading Questions

1. Why do you think the Tao is called the Nameless?
2. According to Chapter 2, what is the nature of opposites?
3. Why do you think the Tao is called the invisible, inaudible, and formless?
4. What do you think "reversion is the action of the Tao" means?
5. If to exist is to exist as a some-thing distinguishable from other things, can the Tao exist? Why or why not?

The Tao*

LAO-TZU

1

The Tao that can be told of is not the
   eternal Tao;
The name that can be named is not the
   eternal name.
The Nameless is the origin of Heaven and
   Earth;
The Named is the mother of all things.

Therefore let there always be non-being,
   so we may see their subtlety,
And let there always be being, so we may
   see their outcome.
The two are the same,
But after they are produced, they have
   different names.

They both may be called deep and
   profound.
Deeper and more profound,
The door of all subtleties!

2

When the people of the world all know
   beauty as beauty,
   There arises the recognition of ugliness.
When they all know the good as good,
   There arises the recognition of evil.
Therefore:
   Being and non-being produce each
     other;

* From *A Source Book of Chinese Philosophy,* translated by Wing-tsit Chan. Copyright © 1963 by Princeton University Press. Reprinted by permission of Princeton University Press, Princeton, NJ. Footnotes edited.

Difficult and easy complete each other;
Long and short contrast each other;
High and low distinguish each other;
Sound and voice harmonize each
    other;
Front and behind accompany each
    other.

Therefore the sage manages affairs
    without action
And spreads doctrines without words.
All things arise, and he does not turn
    away from them.
He produces them but does not take
    possession of them.
He acts but does not rely on his own
    ability.
He accomplishes his task but does not
    claim credit for it.
It is precisely because he does not claim
    credit that his accomplishment
    remains with him.

4

Tao is empty (like a bowl).
    It may be used but its capacity is never
        exhausted.
    It is bottomless, perhaps the ancestor
        of all things.
    It blunts its sharpness,
    It unties its tangles.
    It softens its light.
    It becomes one with the dusty world.
    Deep and still, it appears to exist
        forever.
    I do not know whose son it is.
    It seems to have existed before the
        Lord.

6

The spirit of the valley never dies.
    It is called the subtle and profound
        female.
The gate of the subtle and profound
    female
    Is the root of Heaven and Earth.

It is continuous, and seems to be always
    existing.
Use it and you will never wear it out.

8

The best (man)[1] is like water.
    Water is good; it benefits all things and
        does not compete with them.
It dwells in (lowly) places that all
    disdain.
This is why it is so near to Tao.

(The best man) in his dwelling loves the
    earth.
In his heart, he loves what is profound.
In his associations, he loves humanity.
In his words, he loves faithfulness.
In government, he loves order.
In handling affairs, he loves competence.
In his activities, he loves timeliness.
It is because he does not compete that he
    is without reproach.

11

Thirty spokes are united around the hub
    to make a wheel,
    But it is on its non-being that the
        utility of the carriage depends.
Clay is molded to form a utensil,
    But it is on its non-being that the
        utility of the utensil depends.
Doors and windows are cut out to make
    a room,
    But it is on its non-being that the
        utility of the room depends.
Therefore turn being into advantage, and
    turn non-being into utility.

14

We look at it and do not see it;
    Its name is The Invisible.
We listen to it and do not hear it;
    Its name is The Inaudible.
We touch it and do not find it;
    Its name is The Subtle (formless).

These three cannot be further inquired
  into,
And hence merge into one.
Going up high, it is not bright, and
  coming down low, it is not dark.
Infinite and boundless, it cannot be given
  any name;
It reverts to nothingness.
This is called shape without shape,
Form without objects.
It is The Vague and Elusive.
Meet it and you will not see its head.
Follow it and you will not see its back.
Hold on to the Tao of old in order to
  master the things of the present.
From this one may know the primeval
  beginning (of the universe).
This is called the bond[2] of Tao.

25

There was something undifferentiated
  and yet complete,
Which existed before heaven and earth.
Soundless and formless, it depends on
  nothing and does not change.
It operates everywhere and is free from
  danger.
It may be considered the mother of the
  universe.
I do not know its name; I call it Tao.
If forced to give it a name, I shall call it
  Great.
Now being great means functioning
  everywhere.
Functioning everywhere means
  far-reaching.
Being far-reaching means returning to the
  original point.

Therefore Tao is great.
Heaven is great.
Earth is great.
And the king[3] is also great.
There are four great things in the universe,
  and the king is one of them.
Man models himself after Earth.
Earth models itself after Heaven.

Heaven models itself after Tao.
And Tao models itself after Nature.

34

The Great Tao flows everywhere.
It may go left or right.
All things depend on it for life, and it does
  not turn away from them.
It accomplishes its task but does not claim
  credit for it.
It clothes and feeds all things but does not
  claim to be master over them.
Always without desires, it may be called
  The Small.
All things come to it and it does not master
  them; it may be called The Great.
Therefore (the sage) never strives himself
  for the great, and thereby the great is
  achieved.

37

Tao invariably takes no action, and yet
  there is nothing left undone.
If kings and barons can keep it, all things
  will transform spontaneously.
If, after transformation, they should desire
  to be active,
I would restrain them with simplicity,
  which has no name.
Simplicity, which has no name, is free of
  desires.
Being free of desires, it is tranquil.
And the world will be at peace of its own
  accord.

40

Reversion is the action of Tao.
Weakness is the function of Tao.
All things in the world come from being.
And being comes from non-being.[4]

42

Tao produced the One.
The One produced the two.
The two produced the three.

And the three produced the ten
    thousand things.
The ten thousand things carry the yin and
    embrace the yang, and through the
    blending of the material force they
    achieve harmony.

People hate to be children without
    parents, lonely people without spouses,
    or men without food to eat,
And yet kings and lords call themselves by
    these names.
Therefore it is often the case that things
    gain by losing and lose by gaining.

What others have taught, I teach also:
"Violent and fierce people do not die a
    natural death."
I shall make this the father of my teaching.

NOTES

1. Most commentators and translators have understood the Chinese phrase literally as "the highest good," but some commentators and translators, including Lin Yutang, Cheng Lin, and Bynner, have followed Wang Pi and taken the phrase to mean "the best man." Both interpretations are possible. The former interpretation has a parallel in chapter 38, which talks about the highest virtue, while the latter has a parallel in chapter 17, where both Wang Pi and Ho-shang Kung interpret *the best* to mean "the best ruler." I have followed Wang Pi, not only because his commentary on the text is the oldest and most reliable, but also because the *Lao Tzu* deals with man's way of life more than with abstract ideas.

2. *Chi*, literally "a thread," denotes tradition, discipline, principle, order, essence, etc. Generally it means the system, principle, or continuity that binds things together.

3. The Fu I and Fan Ying-yüan texts have *man* in place of *king*. This substitution has been accepted by Hsi T'ung, Ma Hsü-lun, Ch'en Chu, Jen Chi-yü, and Ch'u Ta-kao. They have been influenced, undoubtedly, by the concept of the trinity of Heaven, Earth, and man, without realizing that the king is considered here as representative of men. Moreover, in chapters 16 and 39, Heaven, Earth, and the king are spoken of together.

4. Cf. chapter 1. This seems to contradict the saying "Being and non-being produce each other" in chapter 2. But to produce means not to originate but to bring about.

2.2 Non-Dualism

Philosophical reflection on religion in India is ancient, rich, and diverse. The *Veda* is the name for the oldest scriptures of India, and the *Upanishads* form the last section. Hence they are called *Vedanta,* which means "the end of the *Veda.*" One of the many philosophical schools of India became known as *Vedanta* because its primary concern was to elaborate on the philosophical implications of the *Upanishads.* The most influential members of this school were Shankara, Ramanuja, and Madhva.

Shankara (c. 788–820) developed ideas that constitute *Advaita* (non-dualistic) *Vedanta.* Shankara was a philosopher, a religious reformer, a founder of an order of monks, a teacher, and an author. He presents his system as an explication of the meaning of the saying *tat tvam asi* ("Thou art That") found in the *Upanishads.*

According to Shankara, our task, when dealing with metaphysical questions related to the nature of reality, is to distinguish among reality, appearance, and unreality. To do this, we need a principle of discrimination called sublation.

Sublation is an act whereby a previous experience or judgment is corrected in light of a subsequent experience or judgment. For example, upon waking you reinterpret your previous experiences as dreaming. Your dream experiences are corrected, or sublated, by your waking experiences. Sublatability refers to the qualities something has that allow it to be sublated. These qualities are three. (1) It must be an object of the awareness of some subject. (2) It must be distinguishable from other objects, so the category of multiplicity is applicable to it. (3) It must be impermanent and hence subject to time and change.

If we define reality as what cannot be sublated, appearance as what can be sublated, and unreality as neither sublatable nor unsublatable (because nonexistent), then our philosophical task is to analyze our experiences in order to see into which of the three categories our experiences fall.

Shankara argues that everything experienced as internal—sensations, emotions, desires, thoughts, mind, intelligence, our ego or individual self—is sublatable. These are all objects of awareness, they are distinguishable from one another, and they change. But is consciousness itself sublatable? Shankara contends that consciousness in and of itself, pure consciousness, it not sublatable. He calls it the Atman (the true Self).

Let us now consider those objects of our experience that seem to be external. Are they appearance or reality? According to Shankara, they are sublatable by the divine because the divine is permanent, in contrast to the temporal and changing objects we experience as external. *Isvara* (Lord) is the name Shankara uses for the divine that has attributes (*saguna*) such as creator, good, merciful, and so on. *Isvara*, in turn, is sublatable by Brahman. Brahman is without attributes (*nirguna*). A reality without qualities is a non-dual reality beyond any multiplicity because nothing qualifies it.

Are there two ultimates, Atman and Brahman? There cannot be two ultimates. That is a contradiction in terms. Therefore Atman must be Brahman. This is the meaning of the saying in the *Upanishads tat tvam asi*. Atman and Brahman are non-dual.

Why, then, do we experience plurality—a world made up of many things? Plurality is an illusion or appearance (*maya*) that is due to our ignorance of the true nature of reality as non-dual. But whence comes such ignorance or nescience (*avidya*)?

It is due to superimposition. We superimpose on non-dual Brahman the images of many things. For example, we superimpose on a coiled rope the image of a snake. But do not our experiences show us that reality is plural, not non-dual?

Shankara distinguishes between lower knowledge—whose six sources are perception, inference, testimony, comparison, postulation, and noncognition (immediate cognition of the nonexistence of an object)—and higher knowledge—the immediate intuitive awareness of the identity of Atman with Brahman. Lower knowledge yields only knowledge of appearances: the way things seem to be to us. Higher knowledge gives us reality.

When we awake from our dreams, we think we know the way things really are rather than the way they appeared to be in our dreams. However, what we call being awake is just dreaming on another level. Beyond this is another awakening, and from the point of view of that higher knowledge, this will all appear to be a dream.

Shankara's views about what is ultimately real seemed so counterintuitive that they did not go unchallenged. Ramanuja (eleventh century) argued for a qualified non-dualism. He contended that the universe, the self, and God are all equally real, although the world and the self depend on God in an important way. Brahman or God has two forms: selves and matter. Yet these forms constitute irreducible realities. This viewpoint is a "qualified" non-dualism in the sense that both selves and matter are "forms" of Brahman although not reducible to Brahman.

Madhva (1197–1276) argued for dualism. There is God (Brahman) who is the eternally real and perfect. In addition, there are individual selves and matter. The distinctions among God and the individual self, God and matter, individual selves, selves and matter, and individual material substances are all fundamental and irreducible. The material universe and individual selves are not forms or aspects of Brahman, although they are dependent on Brahman for their existence.

Shankara, Ramanuja, and Madhva have differing notions of reality, but all three agree that true knowledge of reality can release or free (*mokhsa*) one from what appeared to many people in their society to be an endless round of painful reincarnations or transmigrations. Thus their philosophical reflections, however abstract, have a practical application.

The following selection represents Shankara's views. It is from his book *A Thousand Teachings*. The book consists of a metrical part in which he explains his key ideas and a prose part in which he engages in a dialogue with a pupil who wants to know how he can be released from "transmigratory existence." As Shankara answers, the pupil raises various objections, and Shankara (the teacher) provides a response. Do the responses convince you?

Reading Questions

1. Why will knowledge of Brahman, not action, destroy ignorance?
2. Why must we abandon the whole universe, our bodies, and even what we call our "I" in order to grasp Atman?
3. How is the highest Brahman characterized?
4. Who are we really, according to Shankara?
5. What is nescience (ignorance)?
6. How does the teacher (Shankara) respond to the objection by the pupil that "non-Atman cannot be superimposed upon Atman because Atman is not fully known"?
7. In paragraph 55 of the prose part, the pupil raises a crucial objection. What is the objection and how does the teacher answer? Do you find the teacher's answer adequate or not? Why?
8. Why is the pupil in doubt about being "transcendentally changeless," and how does the teacher respond?

Non-Dualism*

SHANKARA

A. *Metrical Part*

CHAPTER 1   PURE CONSCIOUSNESS

1. Salutation to the all-knowing Pure Consciousness which pervades all, is all, abides in the hearts of all beings, and is beyond all objects [of knowledge].

2. Having completed all the rituals, preceded by the marriage ceremony and the ceremony of installing the sacred fire, the *Veda* has now begun to utter knowledge of *Brahman*.

3. *Karmans* [as the results of actions, good or bad, in the past existence] produce association with a body. When there is association with a body, pleasant and unpleasant things are inevitable. From these result passion and aversion [and] from them actions.

4. [From actions] merit and demerit result [and] from merit and demerit there results an ignorant man's association with a body in the same manner again. Thus this transmigratory existence rolls onward powerfully forever like a wheel.

5. Since the root cause of this transmigratory existence is ignorance, its destruction is desired. Knowledge of *Brahman* therefore is entered on. Final beatitude results from this knowledge.

6. Only knowledge [of *Brahman*] can destroy ignorance; action cannot [destroy it] since [action] is not incompatible [with ignorance]. Unless ignorance is destroyed, passion and aversion will not be destroyed.

7. Unless passion and aversion are destroyed, action arises inevitably from [those] faults. Therefore, for the sake of final beatitude, only knowledge [of *Brahman*] is set forth here [in the Vedānta]. . . .

CHAPTER 6   HAVING CUT

1. *Ātman* Itself is not qualified by a hand which has been cut off and thrown away. Likewise, none of the rest [of the body] qualifies [*Ātman*].

2. Therefore, every qualification is the same as a hand which has been thrown away, since it is non-*Ātman*. Therefore, the Knower (= *Ātman*) is devoid of all qualifications.

3. This whole [universe] is qualification, like a beautiful ornament, which is superimposed [upon *Ātman*] through nescience. Therefore, when *Ātman* has been known, the whole [universe] becomes non-existent.

4. One should always grasp *Ātman* alone as the Knower, disconnected [from all qualifications], and abandon the object of knowledge. One should grasp that what is called "I" is also the same as a part which has been abandoned.

5. As long as the "this"-portion is a qualification [of *ātman*], that ["I"-portion] is different from [*Ātman*] Itself. When the qualification has been destroyed, the Knower is established [independently from it], as a man who owns a brindled cow [is established independently from it].

6. The learned should abandon the "this"-portion in what is called "I," understanding that it is not *Ātman*. ["I" in the sentence of the *Śruti*] "I am *Brahman*" (Brh. Up. I,4,10) is the portion which has been left unabandoned in accordance with the above teaching.

CHAPTER 8   THE NATURE OF PURE CONSCIOUSNESS

1. I Myself have the nature of Pure Consciousness, O Mind; [My apparent] connection with taste, etc., is caused by your delusion.

---

* From *A Thousand Teachings: The Upadesasahasri of Sankara.* Translated and edited by Sengaku Mayeda. Copyright © 1992 University of Tokyo Press. Reprinted by permission of State University of New York Press, Albany. Footnotes edited.

Therefore no result due to your activity would belong to Me, since I am free from all attributes.

2. Abandon here activity born of illusion and come ever to rest from search for the wrong, since I am forever the highest *Brahman,* released, as it were, unborn, one alone, and without duality.

3. And I am always the same to beings, one alone; [I am] the highest [*Brahman*] which, like the sky, is all-pervading, imperishable, auspicious, uninterrupted, undivided and devoid of action. Therefore no result from your efforts here pertains to Me.

4. I am one alone; No other than that [*Brahman*] is thought to be Mine. In like manner I do not belong to anything since I am free from attachment. I have by nature no attachment. Therefore I do not need you nor your work since I am non-dual.

5. Considering that people are attached to cause and effect, I have composed this dialogue, making [them] understand the meaning of the truth of their own nature, so that they may be released from [their] attachment to cause and effect.

6. If a man ponders on this dialogue, he will be released from ignorance, the origin of great fears. And such a man is always free from desire; being a knower of *Ātman,* he is ever free from sorrow, the same [to beings], and happy.

CHAPTER 10   SEEING

1. The highest [*Brahman*]—which is of the nature of Seeing, like the sky, ever-shining, unborn, one alone, imperishable, stainless, all-pervading, and non-dual—That am I and I am forever released. Om.[1]

2. I am Seeing, pure and by nature changeless. There is by nature no object for me. Being the Infinite, completely filled in front, across, up, down, and in every direction, I am unborn, abiding in Myself.

3. I am unborn, deathless, free from old age, immortal, self-effulgent, all-pervading, non-dual; I am neither cause nor effect, altogether stainless, always satisfied and therefore [constantly] released. Om.

4. Whether in the state of deep sleep or of waking or of dreaming, no delusive perception appears to pertain to Me in this world. As those [three states] have no existence, self-dependent or other-dependent, I am always the Fourth, the Seeing and the non-dual.

5. The continuous series of pains due to the body, the intellect and the senses is neither I nor of Me, for I am changeless. And this is because the continual series [of pain] is unreal; it is indeed unreal like an object seen by a dreaming man.

6. It is true that I have neither change nor any cause of change, since I am non-dual. I have neither good nor bad deeds, neither final release nor bondage, neither caste nor stages of life, since I am bodiless.

7. Since I am beginningless and attributeless, I have neither action nor result [of action]. Therefore I am the highest [*Ātman*], non-dual. Just as the ether, though all-pervading, is not stained, so am I not either, though abiding in the body, since I am subtle.

8. And I am always the same to [all] beings, the Lord, for I am superior to, and higher than, the perishable and the imperishable. Though I have the highest *Ātman* as my true nature and am non-dual, I am nevertheless covered with wrong knowledge which is nescience.

9. Being perfectly stainless, *Ātman* is distinguished from, and broken by, nescience, residual impression, and actions. Being filled with powers such as Seeing, I am non-dual, standing [perfect] in my own nature and motionless like the sky.

10. He who sees *Ātman* with the firm belief "I am the highest *Brahman*" "is born no more" (Kaṭh. Up. I,38), says the *Śruti.* When there is no seed, no fruit is produced. Therefore there is no birth, for there is no delusion.

11. "This is mine, being thus," "That is yours, being of such kind," "Likewise, I am so, not superior nor otherwise"—[such] assumptions of people concerning *Brahman,* which is the same [to all beings], non-dual and auspicious, are nothing but their stupidity.

12. When there is completely non-dual and stainless knowledge, then the great-souled experiences neither sorrow nor delusion. In the absence

of both there is neither action nor birth. This is the firm belief of those who know the *Veda*.

13. He who, in the waking state, like a man in the state of deep sleep, does not see duality, though [actually] seeing, because of his non-duality, and similarly he who, though [in fact] acting, is actionless—he [only] is the knower of *Ātman,* and nobody else. This is the firm conclusion here [in the Vedānta].

14. This view which has been declared by me from the standpoint of the highest truth is the supreme [view] as ascertained in the Vedānta. If a man has firm belief in it, he is released and not stained by actions, as others are.

CHAPTER 13   EYELESSNESS

1. As I am eyeless, I do not see. Likewise, as I am earless, how shall I hear? As I have no organ of speech, I do not speak. As I am mindless, how shall I think?

2. As I am devoid of the life principle,[2] I do not act. Being without intellect, I am not a knower. Therefore I have neither knowledge nor nescience, having the light of Pure Consciousness only.

3. Ever-free, pure, transcendentally changeless, invariable, immortal, imperishable, and thus always bodiless.

4. [All-] pervading like ether, I have neither hunger nor thirst, neither sorrow nor delusion, neither decay nor death, since I am bodiless.

5. As I have no sense of touch, I do not touch. As I have no tongue, I do not perceive taste. As I am of the nature of constant knowledge, I never have [either] knowledge or ignorance.

6. The modification of the mind, which is caused by the eye and takes on form-and-color [of its object], is certainly always seen by the constant Seeing of *Ātman.*

7. In like manner the modifications [of the mind] which are connected with the senses other [than the eye] and are colored by [external] objects; also [the modification of the mind] in the form of memory and in the forms of passion and the like; which is unconnected [from the senses], located in the mind;

8. and the modifications of the mind in the dreaming state are also seen to be an other's. The Seeing of the Seer is, therefore, constant, pure, infinite, and alone.

9. The Seeing is [wrongly] taken to be inconstant and impure because of the absence of discriminating knowledge with regard to It. Similarly, I experience pleasure and pain through [a seeing] which is the object and adjunct [of the Seeing].

10. Through deluded [seeing] all people think, "[I am] deluded," and again through a pure [seeing] they think, "[I am] pure"; for this reason they continue in transmigratory existence.

11. If one is a seeker after final release in this world, he should always remember *Ātman* which is ever-free, described in the scripture as eyeless, etc. [which] includes the exterior and the interior, and is unborn.

12. And as the scripture says that I am eyeless, etc., no senses at all belong to Me. And there are the words in the [Muṇḍ. Up. (II,1,2)] belonging to the *Atharvaveda,* "[He is . . .] breathless, mindless, pure."

13. As it is stated in the Kaṭh. Up. (I,3,15) that I do not have sound, etc., and [in the Muṇḍ. Up. (II,1,2) that I am] "without breath, without mind," I am indeed always changeless.

14. Therefore, mental restlessness does not belong to Me. Therefore, concentration does not belong to Me. Both mental restlessness and concentration belong [only] to the changeable mind.

15. As I am without mind and pure, how can those two (= restlessness and concentration) belong to Me? Freedom from mind and freedom from change belong to Me who am bodiless and [all-]pervading.

16. Thus, as long as I had this ignorance, I had duties to perform, though I am ever-free, pure, and always enlightened.

17. How can concentration, non-concentration, or anything else which is to be done belong to Me? For, having meditated on and known Me, they realize that they have completed [all] that had to be done.

18. "I am *Brahman*" (Bṛh. Up. I,4,10). I am all, always pure, enlightened and unfettered, unborn, all-pervading, undecaying, immortal, and imperishable.

19. In no being is there any Knower other than Myself; [I am] the Overseer of deeds, the Witness, the Observer, constant, attributeless, and non-dual.

20. I am neither existent nor non-existent nor both, being alone and auspicious. To Me, the Seeing, there is neither twilight nor night nor day at any time.

21. Just as ether is free from all forms, is subtle and non-dual, so am I devoid even of this [ether], I am *Brahman*, non-dual.

22. My separatedness, *i.e.,* in the form "my *ātman*," "his *ātman*," and "your *ātman*," is what is falsely constructed [on Me], just as the difference of one and the same ether arises from the difference of holes [in various objects].

23. Difference and non-difference, one and many, object of knowledge and knower, movement and mover—how can these [notions] be falsely constructed on Me who am one alone?

24. Nothing to be rejected or accepted belongs to Me, for I am changeless, always released and pure, always enlightened, attributeless, and non-dual.

25. Thus, with concentrated mind, one should always know everything as *Ātman*. Having known Me to be abiding in one's own body, one is a sage, released and immovable.

26. If a *Yogin* thus knows the meaning of the truth, he is one who has completed all that was to be done, a perfected one and knower of *Brahman.* [If he knows] otherwise, he is a slayer of *Ātman*.

27. The meaning of the *Veda* herein determined, which has been briefly related by me, should be imparted to serene wandering ascetics by one of disciplined intellect.

B. *Prose Part*

CHAPTER 2   AWARENESS

45. A certain student, who was tired of transmigratory existence characterized by birth and death and was seeking after final release, approached in the prescribed manner a knower of *Brahman* who was established in *Brahman* and sitting at his ease, and asked him, "Your Holiness, how can I be released from transmigratory existence? I am aware of the body, the senses and [their] objects; I experience pain in the waking state, and I experience it in the dreaming state after getting relief again and again by entering into the state of deep sleep again and again. Is it indeed my own nature or [is it] due to some cause, my own nature being different? If [this is] my own nature, there is no hope for me to attain final release, since one cannot avoid one's own nature. If [it is] due to some cause, final release is possible after the cause has been removed."

46. The teacher replied to him, "Listen, my child, this is not your own nature but is due to a cause."

47. When he was told this the pupil said, "What is the cause? And what will remove it? And what is my own nature? When the cause is removed, the effect due to the cause no [longer] exists; I will attain to my own nature like a sick person [who recovers his health] when the cause of his disease has been removed."

48. The teacher replied, "The cause is nescience; it is removed by knowledge. When nescience has been removed, you will be released from transmigratory existence which is characterized by birth and death, since its cause will be gone and you will no [longer] experience pain in the dreaming and waking states."

49. The pupil said, "What is that nescience? And what is its object? And what is knowledge, remover of nescience, by which I can realize my own nature?"

50. The teacher replied, "Though you are the highest *Ātman* and not a transmigrator, you hold the inverted view, 'I am a transmigrator.' Though you are neither an agent nor an experiencer, and exist [eternally], [you hold the inverted view, 'I am] an agent, an experiencer, and do not exist [eternally]'—this is nescience."

51. The pupil said, "Even though I exist [eternally], still I am not the highest *Ātman*. My nature is transmigratory existence which is characterized by agency and experiencership, since it is known by sense-perception and other means of

knowledge. [Transmigratory existence] has not nescience as its cause, since nescience cannot have one's own *Ātman* as its object.

Nescience is [defined as] the superimposition of the qualities of one [thing] upon another. For example, fully known silver is superimposed upon fully known mother-of-pearl, a fully known person upon a [fully known] tree trunk, or a fully known trunk upon a [fully known] person; but not an unknown [thing] upon [one that is] fully known nor a fully known [thing] upon one that is unknown. Nor is non-*Ātman* superimposed upon *Ātman* because *Ātman* is not fully known, nor *Ātman* [superimposed] upon non-*Ātman*, [again] because *Ātman* is not fully known."

52. The teacher said to him, "That is not right, since there is an exception. My child, it is not possible to make a general rule that a fully known [thing] is superimposed only upon a fully known [thing], since it is a matter of experience that [a fully known thing] is superimposed upon *Ātman*. [For example,] if one says, 'I am white,' 'I am dark,' this is [the superimposition] of qualities of the body upon *Ātman* which is the object of the 'I'-notion. And if one says, 'I am this,' this is [the superimposition of *Ātman*,] which is the object of the 'I'-notion, upon the body."

53. The pupil said, "In that case *Ātman* is indeed fully known as the object of the 'I'-notion; so is the body as 'this.' If so, [it is only a case of] the mutual superimposition of body and *Ātman*, both fully known, just like [the mutual superimposition] of tree-trunk and person, and of mother-of-pearl and silver. So, is there a particular reason why Your Holiness said that it is not possible to make a general rule that two fully known [things] are mutually superimposed?"

54. The teacher replied, "Listen. It is true that the body and *Ātman* are fully known; but they are not fully known to all people as the objects of distinct notions like a tree-trunk and a person."

"How [are they known] then?"

"[They are] always [known] as the objects of constantly non-distinct notions. Since nobody grasps the body and *Ātman* as two distinct no-

tions, saying, "This is the body, that is *Ātman*,' people are deluded with regard to *Ātman* and non-*Ātman*, thinking, '*Ātman* is thus' or '*Ātman* is not thus.' This is the particular reason why I said that it is impossible to make a general rule."

55. [The pupil raised another objection:] "Is it not experienced that the thing which is superimposed [upon something] else through nescience does not exist [in the latter]? For example, silver [does not exist] in a mother-of-pearl nor a person in a tree-trunk nor a snake in a rope; nor the dark color of the earth's surface in the sky. Likewise, if the body and *Ātman* are always mutually superimposed in the form of constantly non-distinct notions, then they cannot exist in each other at any time. Silver, etc., which are superimposed through nescience upon mother-of-pearl, etc., do not exist [in the latter] at any time in any way and *vice versa*; likewise the body and *Ātman* are mutually superimposed through nescience; this being the case, it would follow as the result that neither the body nor *Ātman* exists. And it is not acceptable, since it is the theory of the Nihilists.[3]

If, instead of mutual superimposition, [only] the body is superimposed upon *Ātman* through nescience, it would follow as the result that the body does not exist in *Ātman* while the latter exists. This is not acceptable either since it is contradictory to sense-perception and other [means of knowledge]. For this reason the body and *Ātman* are not superimposed upon each other through nescience."

"How then?"

"They are permanently connected with each other like bamboo and pillars [which are interlaced in the structure of a house]."

56. [The teacher said,] "No; because it would follow as the result that [*Ātman* is] non-eternal and exists for another's sake; since [in your opinion *Ātman*] is composite, [*Ātman* exists for another's sake and is non-eternal] just like bamboo, pillars, and so forth. Moreover, the *Ātman* which is assumed by some others to be connected with the body exists for another's sake since it is composite. [Therefore,] it has been

first established that the highest [*Ātman*] is not connected with the body, is different [from it], and is eternal.

57. [The pupil objected:] "Although [the *Ātman*] is not composite, It is [regarded] merely as the body and superimposed upon the body; from this follow the results that [the *Ātman*] does not exist and that [It] is non-eternal and so on. Then there would arise the fault that [you will] arrive at the Nihilists' position that the body has no *Ātman*."

58. [The teacher replied,] "Not so; because it is accepted that *Ātman*, like space, is by nature not composite. Although *Ātman* exists as connected with nothing, it does not follow that the body and other things are without *Ātman*, just as, although space is connected with nothing, it does not follow that nothing has space. Therefore, there would not arise the fault that [I shall] arrive at the Nihilists' position.

59. "Your further objection—namely that, if the body does not exist in *Ātman* [although *Ātman* exists], this would contradict sense-perception and the other [means of knowledge]: this is not right, because the existence of the body in *Ātman* is not cognized by sense-perception and the other [means of knowledge]; in *Ātman* — like a jujube-fruit in a pot, ghee in milk, oil in sesame and a picture on a wall—the body is not cognized by sense-perception and the other [means of knowledge]. Therefore there is no contradiction with sense-perception and the other [means of knowledge]."

60. [The pupil objected,] "How is the body then superimposed upon *Ātman* which is not established by sense-perception and the other [means of knowledge], and how is *Ātman* superimposed upon the body?"

61. [The teacher said,] "That is not a fault, because *Ātman* is established by Its own nature. A general rule cannot be made that superimposition is made only on that which is adventitiously established and not on that which is permanently established; for the dark color and other things on the surface of the earth are seen to be superimposed upon the sky [which is permanently established]."

62. [The pupil asked,] "Your Holiness, is the mutual superimposition of the body and *Ātman* made by the composite of the body and so on or by *Ātman*?"

63. The teacher said, "What would happen to you, if [the mutual superimposition] is made by the composite of the body and so on, or if [it] is made by *Ātman*?"

64. Then the pupil answered, "If I am merely the composite of the body and so on, then I am non-conscious, so I exist for another's sake; consequently, the mutual superimposition of body and *Ātman* is not effected by me. If I am the highest *Ātman* different from the composite [of the body and so on], then I am conscious, so I exist for my own sake; consequently, the superimposition [of body] which is the seed of every calamity is effected upon *Ātman* by me who am conscious."

65. To this the teacher responded, "If you know that the false superimposition is the seed of [every] calamity, then do not make it!"

66. "Your Holiness, I cannot help [it]. I am driven [to do it] by another; I am not independent."

67. [The teacher said,] "Then you are non-conscious, so you do not exist for your own sake. That by which you who are not self-dependent are driven to act is conscious and exists for its own sake; you are only a composite thing [of the body, etc.]."

68. [The pupil objected,] "If I am non-conscious, how do I perceive feelings of pleasure and pain, and [the words] you have spoken?"

69. The teacher said, "Are you different from feelings of pleasure and pain and from [the words] I have spoken, or are you identical [with them]?"

70. The pupil answered, "I am indeed not identical."

"Why?"

"Because I perceive both of them as objects just as [I perceive] a jar and other things [as objects]. If I were identical [with them] I could not perceive either of them; but I do perceive them, so I am different [from both of them]. If [I were] identical [with them] it would follow that the modifications of the feelings of pleasure and pain exist for their own sake and so do [the words] you have spoken; but it is not reasonable that any of them exists for their own sake, for the pleasure and pain produced by a sandal and a thorn are not for the sake of the sandal and the thorn, nor is use made of a jar for the sake of the jar. So, the sandal and other things serve my purpose, *i.e.*, the purpose of their perceiver, since I who am different from them perceive all the objects seated in the intellect."

71. The teacher said to him, "So, then, you exist for your own sake since you are conscious. You are not driven [to act] by another. A conscious being is neither dependent on another nor driven [to act] by another, for it is not reasonable that a conscious being should exist for the sake of another conscious being since they are equal like two lights. Nor does a conscious being exist for the sake of a non-conscious being since it is not reasonable that a nonconscious being should have any connection with its own object precisely because it is non-conscious. Nor does experience show that two non-conscious beings exist for each other, as for example a stick of wood and a wall do not fulfill each other's purposes."

72. [The pupil objected,] "Is it not experienced that a servant and his master, though they are equal in the sense of being conscious, exist for each other?"

73. [The teacher said,] "It is not so, for what [I] meant was that you have consciousness just as fire has heat and light. And [in this meaning I] cited the example, 'like two lights.' This being the case, you perceive everything seated in your intellect through your own nature, *i.e.*, the transcendentally changeless, eternal, pure consciousness which is equivalent to the heat and light of fire. And if you admit that *Ātman* is always without distinctions, why did you say, 'After getting relief again and again in the state of deep sleep, I perceive pain in the waking and dreaming states. Is this indeed my own nature or [is it] due to some cause?' Has this delusion left [you now] or not?"

74. To this the pupil replied, "Your Holiness, the delusion has gone thanks to your gracious assistance; but I am in doubt as to how I am transcendentally changeless."

"How?"

"Sound and other [external objects] are not self-established, since they are not conscious. But they [are established] through the rise of notions which take the forms of sound and other [external objects]. It is impossible for notions to be self-established, since they have mutually exclusive attributes and the forms [of external objects] such as blue and yellow. It is, therefore, understood that [notions] are caused by the forms of the external objects; so, [notions] are established as possessing the forms of external objects, *i.e.*, the forms of sound, etc. Likewise, notions, which are the modifications of a thing (= the intellect), the substratum of the 'I'-notion, are also composite, so it is reasonable that they are non-conscious; therefore, as it is impossible that they exist for their own sake, they, like sound and other [external objects], are established as objects to be perceived by a perceiver different in nature [from them]. If I am not composite, I have pure consciousness as my nature; so I exist for my own sake. Nevertheless, I am a perceiver of notions which have the forms [of the external objects] such as blue and yellow [and] so I am indeed subject to change. [For the above reason, I am] in doubt as to how [I am] transcendentally changeless."

75. The teacher said to him, "Your doubt is not reasonable. [Your] perception of those notions is necessary and entire; for this very reason [you] are not subject to transformation. It is, therefore, established that [you] are transcendentally changeless. But you have said that precisely the reason for the above positive conclusion—namely, that [you] perceive the entire movement of the mind—is the reason for [your] doubt [concerning your transcendental changelessness]. This is why [your doubt is not reasonable].

If indeed you were subject to transformation, you would not perceive the entire movement of the mind which is your object, just as the mind [does not perceive] its [entire] object and just as the senses [do not perceive] their [entire] objects, and similarly you as *Ātman* would not perceive even a part of your object. Therefore, you are transcendentally changeless."

76. Then [the pupil] said, "Perception is what is meant by the verbal root, that is, nothing but change; it is contradictory [to this fact] to say that [the nature of] the perceiver is transcendentally changeless."

77. [The teacher said,] "That is not right, for [the term] 'perception' is used figuratively in the sense of a change which is meant by the verbal root; whatever the notion of the intellect may be, that is what is meant by the verbal root; [the notion of the intellect] has change as its nature and end, with the result that the perception of Ātman falsely appears [as perceiver]; thus the notion of the intellect is figuratively indicated by the term, "perception." For example, the cutting action results [in the static state] that [the object to be cut] is separated in two parts; thus [the term, "cutting," in the sense of an object to be cut being separated in two parts,] is used figuratively as [the cutting action] which is meant by the verbal root."

78. To this the pupil objected, "Your Holiness, the example cannot explain my transcendental changelessness."

"Why not?"

"'Cutting' which results in a change in the object to be cut is used figuratively as [the cutting action] which is meant by the verbal root; in the same manner, if the notion of the intellect, which is figuratively indicated by the term 'perception' and is meant by the verbal root, results also in a change in the perception of Ātman, [the example] cannot explain Ātman's transcendental changelessness."

79. The teacher said, "It would be true, if there were a distinction between perception and perceiver. The perceiver is indeed nothing but eternal perception. And it is not [right] that perception and perceiver are different as in the doctrine of the logicians."

80. [The pupil said,] "How does that [action] which is meant by the verbal root result in perception?"

81. [The teacher] answered, "Listen, [I] said that [it] ends with the result that the perception

[of Ātman] falsely appears [as perceiver]. Did you not hear? I did not say that [it] results in the production of any change in Ātman."

82. The pupil said, "Why then did you say that if I am transcendentally changeless I am the perceiver of the entire movement of the mind which is my object?"

83. The teacher said to him, "I told [you] only the truth. Precisely because [you are the perceiver of the entire movement of the mind], I said, you are transcendentally changeless."

84. "If so, Your Holiness, I am of the nature of transcendentally changeless and eternal perception whereas the notions of the intellect, which have the forms of [external objects] such as sound, arise and end with the result that my own nature which is perception falsely appears [as perceiver]. Then what is my fault?"

85. [The teacher replied,] "You are right. [You] have no fault. The fault is only nescience as I have said before."

86. [The pupil said,] "If, Your Holiness, as in the state of deep sleep I undergo no change, how [do I experience] the dreaming and waking states?"

87. The teacher said to him, "But do you experience [these states] continuously?"

88. [The pupil answered,] "Certainly I do experience [them], but intermittently and not continuously."

89. The teacher said [to him,] "Both of them are adventitious [and] not your nature. If [they] were your nature [they] would be self-established and continuous like your nature, which is Pure Consciousness. Moreover, the dreaming and waking states are not your nature, for [they] depart [from you] like clothes and so on. It is certainly not experienced that the nature of anything, whatever it may be, departs from it. But the dreaming and waking states depart from the state of Pure Consciousness-only. If one's own nature were to depart [from oneself] in the state of deep sleep, it would be negated by saying, 'It has perished,' 'It does not exist,' since the adventitious attributes which are not one's own nature are seen to consist in both [perishableness and non-existence]; for example, wealth, clothes,

and the like are seen to perish and things which have been obtained in dream or delusion are seen to be non-existent."

90. [The pupil objected,] "[If] so, Your Holiness, it follows [either] that my own nature, *i.e.,* Pure Consciousness, is also adventitious, since [I] perceive in the dreaming and waking states but not in the state of deep sleep; or that I am not of the nature of Pure Consciousness."

91. [The teacher replied,] "No, Look. Because that is not reasonable. If you [insist on] looking your own nature, *i.e.* Pure Consciousness, as adventitious, do so! We cannot establish it logically even in a hundred years, nor can any other (*i.e.* non-conscious) being do so. As [that adventitious consciousness] is composite, nobody can logically deny that [it] exists for another's sake, is manifold and perishable; for what does not exist for its own sake is not self-established, as we have said before. Nobody can, however, deny that *Ātman,* which is of the nature of Pure Consciousness, is self-established; so It does not depend upon anything else, since It does not depart [from anybody]."

92. [The pupil objected,] "Did I not point out that [It] does depart [from me] when I said that in the state of deep sleep I do not see?"

93. [The teacher replied,] "That is not right, for it is contradictory."

"How is it a contradiction?"

"Although you are [in truth] seeing, you say, 'I do not see.' This is contradictory."

"But at no time in the state of deep sleep, Your Holiness, have I ever seen Pure Consciousness or anything else."

"Then you are seeing in the state of deep sleep; for you deny only the seen object, not the seeing. I said that your seeing is Pure Consciousness. That [eternally] existing one by which you deny [the existence of the seen object] when you say that nothing has been seen, [that precisely is the seeing] that is Pure Consciousness. Thus as [It] does not ever depart [from you] [Its] transcendental changelessness and eternity are established solely by Itself without depending upon any means of knowledge. The knower, though self-established, requires

means of knowledge for the discernment of an object to be known other [than itself]. And that eternal Discernment, which is required for discerning something else (= non-*Ātman*) which does not have Discernment as its nature—that is certainly eternal, transcendentally changeless, and of a self-effulgent nature. The eternal Discernment does not require any means of knowledge in order to be Itself the means of knowledge or the knower since the eternal Discernment is by nature the means of knowledge or the knower. [This is illustrated by the following] example: iron or water requires fire or sun [to obtain] light and heat since light and heat are not their nature; but fire and sun do not require [anything else] for light and heat since [these] are always their nature. . . .

109. [The pupil said,] "If so, Your Holiness, Apprehension is transcendentally changeless, eternal, indeed of the nature of the light of *Ātman,* and self-established, since It does not depend upon any means of knowledge with regard to Itself; everything other than This is non-conscious and exists for another's sake, since it acts together [with others].

And because of this nature of being apprehended as notion causing pleasure, pain, and delusion, [non-*Ātman*] exists for another's sake; on account of this very nature non-*Ātman* exists and not on account of any other nature. It is therefore merely non-existent from the standpoint of the highest truth. Just as it is experienced in this world that a snake [superimposed] upon a rope does not exist, nor water in a mirage, and the like, unless they are apprehended [as a notion], so it is reasonable that duality in the waking and dreaming states also does not exist unless it is apprehended [as a notion]. In this manner, Your Holiness, Apprehension, *i.e.,* the light of *Ātman,* is uninterrupted; so It is transcendentally changeless, eternal and non-dual, since It is never absent from any of the various notions. But various notions are absent from Apprehension. Just as in the dreaming state the notions in different forms such as blue and yellow, which are absent from that Apprehension, are said to be non-existent from the standpoint of the highest truth, so in the waking state also, the various notions such as blue and yellow, which are absent from this very Apprehension, must by nature be untrue. And there is no apprehender different from this Apprehension to apprehend It; therefore It can Itself neither be accepted nor rejected by Its own nature, since there is nothing else."

110. [The teacher said,] "Exactly so it is. It is nescience that is the cause of transmigratory existence which is characterized by the waking and dreaming states. The remover of this nescience is knowledge. And so you have reached fearlessness. From now on you will not perceive any pain in the waking and dreaming states. You are released from the sufferings of transmigratory existence."

111. [The pupil said,] "Om."

NOTES

1. *Om* is the sacred syllable called *praṇava* and sometimes compared with *Amen*. It is used at the opening of most Hindu works and as a sacred exclamation may be uttered at the beginning and end of Vedic recitation or before any prayer.

2. According to Śankara, the individual consists of the following six components: (1) the body, gross (*sthūla*) and subtle (*sūkṣma*), (2) the five senses (*buddhindriya*), (3) the five organs of action (*karmendriya*), (4) the internal organ (*antaḥkaraṇa*), (5) the principal vital air (*mukhya prāṇa*), and (6) *Ātman*. The term *prāṇa* in its wider sense comprises (2)–(5), and the term is probably used here in this wider sense. In the first stanza, (2) (eye and ear), (3) (organ of speech), and (4) (mind) are referred to.

3. "The Nihilists" (*Vaināśika*) indicates the Buddhists, especially the Śūnyavādins (or Mādhyamikas), who hold the view that everything is empty (*śūnya*) and who have Nāgārjuna (150–250) as their founder.

2.3 The Nature of God

Islam is the name of a religion that stems from a book of sacred scriptures called the *Qur'an*. Muslims (followers of Islam) believe that the *Qur'an* contains revelations from Allah (God) given to the prophet Muhammad (570–623). Muhammad, Muslims maintain, is the last in a long series of prophets stretching back to Abraham and including Jesus. Hence Jews and Christians are called "People of the Book."

Islam teaches a strict monotheism. There is one God (Allah), and Allah constitutes an absolute unity. Hence the tri-unity (Trinity) that Christians affirm is rejected. Allah is the absolute, ultimate, and unique divine reality:

Say: He is the One God;
God, the Eternal, the Uncaused Cause of all being.
He begets not, and neither is he begotten
and there is nothing that could be compared to him.
(*Qur'an* 112).

This monotheism is clearly stated in the first of the five pillars (the central practices) of Islam. A faithful Muslim must

1. Witness that there is no God but Allah and that Muhammad is his Prophet.
2. Perform mandatory prayers (*salat*).
3. Give mandatory alms (*zakat*).
4. Fast during the month of Ramadan.
5. At least once during life make a pilgrimage (*hajj*) to Mecca.

There is no doubt that Islam regards ultimate reality to be God or Allah. Exactly what this means, however, became a point of theological and philosophical debate as Islam developed. Some theologians (the *mujassima*) thought of God in anthropomorphic terms. They taught that God is very much like humans, who, after all, are created in God's image. Thus they attribute to God characteristics such as hearing, seeing, and speaking (all mentioned in the *Qur'an*). Of course God is vastly more powerful and more wise than humans. The difference, however, between God and humans is not one of kind, but one of degree.

These views of the *mujassima* were condemned by other Muslims as little more than idol worship. They (the *mu'attila*) argued that such attributes as hearing, seeing, and speaking apply only to physical things. God is not physical; hence they do not literally apply to God. When the *Qur'an* speaks in an anthropomorphic manner, it is doing so because that is the only kind of language humans are able to grasp.

In addition to the anthropomorphic view and that of the "negators" (*mu'attila*), there is also the affirmers' view. These theologians (the *muthbita*) argue that when the *Qur'an* speaks of God as though he had human-like qualities, it means it. God really does speak and has a real face and real hands. However, because there is "nothing like Him," these attributes are not like the attributes of humans or any other created thing. One wonders, of course, just exactly what a divine hand is if it is not like any other hand we know about. Such talk invites philosophical analysis.

Islamic philosophers entered this debate by using the resources of Greek philosophy to analyze the idea of ultimacy. There is no question that Allah is ultimate. But what does that mean? There appears to be a tension between an anthropomorphic and personal understanding of the divine and the philosophic view. As early as the sixth century B.C.E., Xenophanes claimed God is "in no way similar to mortals." Later Greek philosophers would describe God very impersonally and abstractly as an Unmoved Mover, as an eternal unchanging divine power, and as Pure Intelligence or Thought.

This tension between anthropomorphic and philosophical views is found in Judaism, Christianity, and Hinduism as well. Tertullian, a second-century Christian theologian, asked, "What has Athens to do with Jerusalem?" Much later, the French mathematician and philosopher Blaise Pascal (1623–1662) wondered what the God of the philosophers had to do with the God of Abraham, Isaac, and Jacob? Hinduism portrays God as male and female as well as beyond all personal and human-like traits. So how should we think of God? Is God at all like the sorts of beings we know?

Ibn Sina (known as Avicenna in the West), the author of the next selection, is a tenth-century Islamic philosopher who was very much concerned with the relationship between the God described in the *Qur'an* and the God described by the philosophers. He attempted to use philosophical reason to discover (as nearly as mortals can) the exact nature of God. He divided beings into two kinds: necessary and contingent. A necessary being is completely uncaused and unconditioned. All contingent beings, by contrast, are caused and conditioned. Hence God could not be reckoned among their numbers. God is a necessary being. All of God's other attributes—oneness, uncausedness, pure benevolence, true perfection, complete self-sufficiency, absolute knowledge, omnipotence and so on—can be logically deduced from the fact of God's necessity.

This philosophical analysis did not entirely relieve the tension between the anthropomorphic viewpoint and the philosophical. If God is unchanging, then how could God have created the universe, an act that seems to require a change from a state of not creating to a state of creating? If God is unchanging, how can God be compassionate and forgiving? If God has perfect foreknowledge, how can humans be free? If God is all-powerful, can God create a stone that even God cannot lift?

The idea of an ultimate reality combined with the idea of a loving, forgiving, creating God seems threatened with incoherence. It is not surprising to find al-Ghazali, a hundred years after Avicenna, writing a book called *The Incoherence of the Philosophers* and Averroes responding in the twelfth century with *The Incoherence of the Incoherence*. The debate goes on.

Reading Questions

1. What is the difference between a necessary being and a contingent being, and why would there be an infinite succession of beings if there were no necessary being?
2. Why is it, according to Avicenna, that it is impossible that "the Necessary Being should be two"?
3. What does it mean to say that a necessary being has no cause?
4. Why does the multiplicity of God's attributes *not* destroy God's unity?
5. How does Avicenna "prove" that God has one unchanging knowledge of all objects of knowledge? Do you find this "proof" convincing or not? Why?

The Nature of God*

AVICENNA

That there Is a Necessary Being

Whatever has being must either have a reason for its being, or have no reason for it. If it has a reason, then it is contingent, equally before it comes into being (if we make this mental hypothesis) and when it is in the state of being—for in the case of a thing whose being is contingent the mere fact of its entering upon being does not remove from it the contingent nature of its being. If on the other hand it has no reason for its being in any way whatsoever, then it is necessary in its being. This rule having been confirmed, I shall now proceed to prove that there is in being a being which has no reason for its being.

Such a being is either contingent or necessary. If it is necessary, then the point we sought to prove is established. If on the other hand it is contingent, that which is contingent cannot enter upon being except for some reason which sways the scales in favour of its being and against its not-being. If the reason is also contingent, there is then a chain of contingents linked one to the other, and there is no being at all; for this being which is the subject of our hypothesis cannot enter into being so long as it is not preceded by an infinite succession of beings, which is absurd. Therefore contingent beings end in a Necessary Being.

Of the Unicity of God

It is not possible in any way that the Necessary Being should be two. Demonstration: Let us suppose that there is another necessary being:

* From *Avicenna on Theology*. Translated by Arthur J. Arberry. Copyright © 1951 John Murray. Reprinted by permission of John Murray.

one must be distinguishable from the other, so that the terms "this" and "that" may be used with reference to them. This distinction must be either essential or accidental. If the distinction between them is accidental, this accidental element cannot but be present in each of them, or in one and not the other. If each of them has an accidental element by which it is distinguished from the other, both of them must be caused; for an accident is what is adjoined to a thing after its essence is realized. If the accidental element is regarded as adhering to its being, and is present in one of the two and not in the other, then the one which has no accidental element is a necessary being and the other is not a necessary being. If, however, the distinction is essential, the element of essentiality is that whereby the essence as such subsists; and if this element of essentiality is different in each and the two are distinguishable by virtue of it, then each of the two must be a compound; and compounds are caused; so that neither of them will be a necessary being. If the element of essentiality belongs to one only, and the other is one in every respect and there is no compounding of any kind in it, then the one which has no element of essentiality is a necessary being, and the other is not a necessary being. Since it is thus established that the Necessary Being cannot be two, but is All Truth, then by virtue of His Essential Reality, in respect of which He is a Truth, He is United and One, and no other shares with Him in that Unity: however the All-Truth attains existence, it is through Himself.

That God is Without Cause

A necessary being has no cause whatsoever. Causes are of four kinds: that from which a thing has being, or the active cause; that on account of which a thing has being, or the final and completive cause; that in which a thing has being, or the material cause; and that through which a thing has being, or the formal cause.

The justification for limiting causes to these four varieties is that the reason for a thing is either internal in its subsistence, or a part of its being, or external to it. If it is internal, then it is either that part in which the thing is, potentially and not actually, that is to say its matter; or it is that part in which the thing becomes actually, that is to say its form. If it is external, then it can only be either that from which the thing has being, that is to say the agent, or that on account of which the thing has being, that is to say its purpose and end.

Since it is established that these are the roots and principles of this matter, let us rest on them and clarify the problems which are constructed upon them.

Demonstration that He has no active cause: This is self-evident: for if He had any reason for being, this would be adventitious and that would be a necessary being. Since it is established that He has no active cause, it follows on this line of reasoning that His Quiddity is not other than His Identity, that is to say, other than His Being; neither will He be a subsistence or an accident. There cannot be two, each of which derives its being from the other; nor can He be a necessary being in one respect, and a contingent being in another respect.

Proof that His Quiddity is not other than His Identity, but rather that His Being is unified in His Reality: if His Being were not the same as His Reality, then His Being would be other than His Reality. Every accident is caused, and every thing caused requires a reason. Now this reason is either external to His Quiddity, or is itself His Quiddity: if it is external, then He is not a necessary being, and is not exempt from an active cause; while if the reason is itself the Quiddity, then the reason must necessarily be itself a complete being in order that the being of another may result from it. Quiddity before being has no being; and if it had being before this, it would not require a second being. The question therefore returns to the problem of being. If the Being of the Quiddity is accidental, whence did this Being supervene and adhere? It is therefore established that the Identity of the Necessary Being is His Quiddity, and that He has no active cause; the necessary nature of His Being is like the quiddity of all other things. From this it is evident that the Necessary Being does not resemble any other thing in any respect whatsoever; for with all other things their being is other than their quiddity.

Proof that He is not an accident: An accident is a being in a locus. The locus is precedent to it, and its being is not possible without the locus. But we have stated that a being which is necessary has no reason for its being.

Proof that there cannot be two necessary beings, each deriving its being from the other: Each of them, in as much as it derives its being from the other, would be subsequent to the other, while at the same time by virtue of supplying being to the other, each would be precedent to the other: but one and the same thing cannot be both precedent and subsequent in relation to its being. Moreover, if we assume for the sake of argument that the other is non-existent: would the first then be a necessary being, or not? If it were a necessary being, it would have no connexion with the other: if it were not a necessary being, it would be a contingent being and would require another necessary being. Since the Necessary Being is One, and does not derive Its being from any one, it follows that He is a Necessary Being in every respect; while anything else derives its being from another.

Proof that He cannot be a Necessary Being in one respect and a contingent being in another respect: Such a being, in as much as it is a contingent being, would be connected in being with something else, and so it has a reason; but in as much as it is a necessary being, it would have no connexions with anything else. In that case it would both have being and not have being; and that is absurd.

Demonstration that He has no material and receptive cause: The receptive cause is the cause for the provision of the place in which a thing is received; that is to say, the place prepared for the reception of being, or the perfection of being. Now the Necessary Being is a perfection in pure actuality, and is not impaired by any deficiency; every perfection belongs to Him, derives from Him, and is preceded by His Essence, while every deficiency, even if it be metaphorical, is negated to Him. All perfection and all beauty are of His Being; indeed, these are the vestiges of the perfection of His Being; how then should He derive perfection from any other? Since it is thus estab-

lished that He has no receptive cause, it follows that He does not possess anything potentially, and that He has no attribute yet to be awaited; on the contrary, His Perfection has been realized in actuality; and He has no material cause. We say "realized in actuality", using this as a common term of expression, meaning that every perfection belonging to any other is non-existent and yet to be awaited, whereas all perfection belonging to Him has being and is present. His Perfect Essence, preceding all relations, is One. From this it is manifest that His Attributes are not an augmentation of His Essence; for if they were an augmentation of His Essence, the Attributes would be potential with reference to the Essence and the Essence would be the reason for the Attributes. In that case the Attributes would be subsequent to a precedent, so that they would be in one respect active and in another receptive; their being active would be other than the aspect of their being receptive; and in consequence they would possess two mutually exclusive aspects. Now this is impossible in the case of anything whatsoever; when a body is in motion, the motivation is from one quarter and the movement from another.

If it were to be stated that His Attributes are not an augmentation of His Essence, but that they entered into the constitution of the Essence, and that the Essence cannot be conceived of as existing without these Attributes, then the Essence would be compound, and the Oneness would be destroyed. It is also evident, as a result of denying the existence of a receptive cause, that it is impossible for Him to change; for the meaning of change is the passing away of one attribute and the establishment of another; and if He were susceptible to change, He would possess potentially an element of passing-away and an element of establishment; and that is absurd. It is clear from this that He has no opposite and no contrary; for opposites are essences which succeed each other in the occupation of a single locus, there being between them the extreme of contrariety. But He is not receptive to accidents, much less to opposites. And if the term "opposite" is used to denote one who disputes with Him in His Rulership, it is clear too on this count that He has no opposite. It is further clear that it is impossible for Him not to be; for since it is established that His Being is necessary, it follows that it is impossible for Him not to be; because everything which exists potentially cannot exist actually, otherwise it would have two aspects. Anything which is receptive to a thing does not cease to be receptive when reception has actually taken place; if this were not so, it would result in the removal of both being and not-being, and that is untenable. This rule applies to every essence and every unified reality, such as angels and human spirits; they are not susceptible to not-being at all, since they are free from corporeal adjunctions.

Demonstration that He has no formal cause: A formal, corporeal cause only exists and is confirmed when a thing is possessed of matter: the matter has a share in the being of the form, in the same way that the form has a part in the disposition of the matter in being in actuality; such a thing is therefore caused. It is further evident as a result of denying this cause to Him, that He is also to be denied all corporeal attributes, such as time, space, direction, and being in one place to the exclusion of all other; in short, whatever is possible in relation to corporeal things is impossible in relation to Him.

Proof that He has no final cause: The final cause is that on account of which a thing has being; and the First Truth has not being for the sake of anything, rather does everything exist on account of the perfection of His Essence, being consequent to His Being and derived from His Being. Moreover the final cause, even if it be posterior in respect of being to all other causes, yet it is mentally prior to them all. It is the final cause which makes the active cause become a cause in actuality, that is to say in respect of its being a final cause.

Since it is established that He is exalted above this last kind of cause too, it is clear that there is no cause to His Attributes. It is also evident that He is Pure Benevolence and True Perfection; the meaning of His Self-Sufficiency likewise becomes manifest, namely that he approves of nothing and disapproves of nothing. For if He approved of anything, that thing would come into being and would continue to be; while if He disapproved of anything, that thing would be converted into not-being and would be annulled. The very divergency of these beings proves the nullity of such a proposition; for a thing which is one in every respect cannot approve of a thing and of its opposite. It is also not necessary for Him to observe the rule of greater expediency or of expediency, as certain Qualitarians have idly pretended; for if His acts of expediency were obligatory to Him, He would not merit gratitude and praise for such acts, since He would merely be fulfilling that which it is His obligation to perform, and He would be to all intents and purposes as one paying a debt; He would therefore deserve nothing at all for such benevolence. In fact His acts proceed on the contrary from Him and for Him, as we shall demonstrate later.

His Attributes as Interpreted According to the Foregoing Principles

Since it is established that God is a Necessary Being, that He is One in every respect, that He is exalted above all causes, and that He has no reason of any kind for His Being; since it is further established that His Attributes do not augment His Essence, and that He is qualified by the Attributes of Praise and Perfection; it follows necessarily that we must state that He is Knowing, Living, Willing, Omnipotent, Speaking, Seeing, Hearing, and Possessed of all the other Loveliest Attributes. It is also necessary to recognize that His Attributes are to be classified as negative, positive, and a compound of the two: since His Attributes are of this order, it follows that their multiplicity does not destroy His Unity or contradict the necessary nature of His Being. Pre-eternity for instance is essentially the negation of not-being in the first place, and the denial of causality and of primality in the second place; similarly the term One means that He is indivisible in every respect, both verbally and actually. When it is stated that He is a Necessary Being, this means that He is a Being without a cause, and that He is the Cause of other than Himself: this is a combination of the negative and the positive. Examples of the positive Attributes are His being Creator, Originator, Shaper, and the entire

Attributes of Action. As for the compound of both, this kind is illustrated by His being Willing and Omnipotent, for these Attributes are a compound of Knowledge with the addition of Creativeness.

God's Knowledge

God has knowledge of His Essence: His Knowledge, His Being Known and His Knowing are one and the same thing. He knows other than Himself, and all objects of knowledge. He knows all things by virtue of one knowledge, and in a single manner. His Knowledge does not change according to whether the thing known has being or not-being.

Proof that God has knowledge of His Essence: We have stated that God is One, and that He is exalted above all causes. The meaning of knowledge is the supervention of an idea divested of all corporeal coverings. Since it is established that He is One, and that He is divested of body, and His Attributes also; and as this idea as just described supervenes upon Him; and since whoever has an abstract idea supervening upon him is possessed of knowledge, and it is immaterial whether it is his essence or other than himself; and as further His Essence is not absent from Himself; it follows from all this that He knows Himself.

Proof that He is Knowledge, Knowing and Known: Knowledge is another term for an abstract idea. Since this idea is abstract, it follows that He is Knowledge; since this abstract idea belongs to Him, is present with Him, and is not veiled from Him, it follows that He is Knowing; and since this abstract idea does not supervene save through Him, it follows that He is Known. The terms employed in each case are different; otherwise it might be said that Knowledge, Knowing and Known are, in relation to His Essence, one. Take your own experience as a parallel. If you know yourself, the object of your knowledge is either yourself or something else; if the object of your knowledge is something other than yourself, then you do not know yourself. But if the object of your knowledge is yourself, then both the one knowing and the thing known are your self. If the image of your self is impressed

upon your self, then it is your self which is the knowledge. Now if you look back upon yourself reflectively, you will not find any impression of the idea and quiddity of your self in yourself a second time, so as to give rise within you to a sense that your self is more than one. Therefore since it is established that He has intelligence of His Essence, and since His Intelligence is His Essence and does not augment His Essence, it follows that He is Knowing, Knowledge and Known without any multiplicity attaching to Him through these Attributes; and there is no difference between "one who has knowledge" and "one who has intelligence", since both are terms for describing the negation of matter absolutely.

Proof that He has knowledge of other than Himself: Whoever knows himself, if thereafter he does not know other than himself this is due to some impediment. If the impediment is essential, this implies necessarily that he does not know himself either; while if the impediment is of an external nature, that which is external can be removed. Therefore it is possible—nay, necessary—that He should have knowledge of other than Himself, as you shall learn from this chapter.

Proof that He has knowledge of all objects of knowledge: Since it is established that He is a Necessary Being, that He is One, and that the universe is brought into being from Him and has resulted out of His Being; since it is established further that He has knowledge of His Own Essence, His Knowledge of His Essence being what it is, namely that He is the Origin of all realities and of all things that have being; it follows that nothing in heaven or earth is remote from His Knowledge—on the contrary, all that comes into being does so by reason of Him: He is the causer of all reasons, and He knows that of which He is the Reason, the Giver of being and the Originator.

Proof that He knows all things by virtue of one knowledge, in a manner which changes not according to the change in the thing known: It has been established that His Knowledge does not augment His Essence, and that He is the Origin of all things that have being, while being exalted above accident and changes; it therefore follows that He knows things in a manner unchanging. The objects of knowledge are a consequence of His Knowledge; His Knowledge is not a consequence of the things known, that it should change as they change; for His Knowledge of things is the reason for their having being. Hence it is manifest that Knowledge is itself Omnipotence. He knows all contingent things, even as He knows all things that have being, even though we know them not; for the contingent, in relation to us, is a thing whose being is possible and whose not-being is also possible; but in relation to Him one of the two alternatives is actually known. Therefore His Knowledge of genera, species, things with being, contingent things, manifest and secret things—this Knowledge is a single knowledge. . . .

2.4 Emptiness and God

If you were in search of two categories that you could use to characterize everything, the ideas of being and non-being might do nicely. Everything that exists, however diverse, has at least being or existence in common. Everything that does not exist has non-being in common. This, of course, is an odd way of talking, because presumably nothing exists in the category of non-being. In other words, non-being refers to nothing (although, somewhat paradoxically, we might characterize this nothing as everything that is not being). Some philosophers argue that because something (what has being) cannot come from nothing (non-being) and because non-being is the negation of being (and therefore grammatically and logically dependent on it), being has priority over non-being.

This line of reasoning has inspired much philosophical reflection on God among Jews, Christians, and Muslims. If the term *God* does refer to what is ultimate, then does it refer to being or to non-being? Surely, some argue, it must refer to being, because non-being is dependent on being and hence less than ultimate. Further, because all particular beings are dependent on being, being itself must be independent in the sense of not conditioned by anything else. Even further, being must be good and somehow concerned with the welfare of particular beings; otherwise, we would live in a totality nihilistic universe with no point or purpose.

It is something of a shock to those who think of God as ultimate reality and as being rather than non-being to encounter Buddhist philosophical reflection on ultimate reality. The religion known as Buddhism stems from the teachings and experiences of Siddhartha Gautama, a sixth- or possibly fifth-century B.C.E. Indian of the Sakya clan. He was called the Buddha, or Enlightened One, because he realized nirvana or release from suffering.

The core of the Buddha's teachings is the Four Noble Truths. First, life is suffering. All living creatures suffer to one degree or another during their lives. This suffering may be physical (disease, for example) or psychological (unhappiness, for example). Second, suffering is caused by desire. Attachment to pleasures and to life itself means that we live wanting more and more of what we do not have. It also means that we try to prevent things from changing. We cling to what we like and to what gives us pleasure and joy. Everything, however, eventually changes. Impermanence characterizes life. Ultimately we grow old and die, no matter how much we wish it were otherwise. Third, the release from suffering (nirvana) can be achieved by following the Eightfold Path or Middle Way. This Eightfold Path constitutes the fourth Noble Truth and it involves cultivating right views, right thought, right speech, right action, right livelihood, right effort, right mindfulness, and right concentration. Exactly what these phrases mean was worked out (and argued over) as the Buddhist tradition developed.

One of the right views that those who would overcome suffering needed to develop was an understanding of the Buddha's teaching known as "dependent co-origination." Everything that exists is dependent on something else that exists. Animals are dependent on food. Food is dependent on sunlight and water. Sunlight is dependent on the sun, and water on rain. Later Buddhist philosophers, reflecting on this teaching, came to a startling conclusion. If we mean by *being* that which can exist independently, then, if the doctrine of dependent co-origination is true, nothing can exist independently. Hence being is not ultimate. What is ultimate is empty of being. Further, if nirvana is the realization of release from all suffering, then it must be the realization of ultimate reality—that is, emptiness (*sunyata*).

What, however, is emptiness? Is it non-being? It would seem so, because being and non-being are ultimate categories. But perhaps not. Perhaps emptiness should be understood as no-thingness. If so, then it is very much like being, because being is also no-thingness in the sense that it is no particular being (it is not one of the beings) but is rather the source or ground of all beings. Emptiness is not a thing and neither is being, so it seems we have different words for the same reality. It is, however, not that simple, because Buddhist philosophers maintain that emptiness is beyond both being and non-being. It is, if you will, the source or ground of both. Thus those who might like to equate God and emptiness face a more difficult task than it first appears.

John B. Cobb, Jr. (1925–   ), Ingraham Professor of Theology at Claremont University and author of the following essay, is very much concerned with how the Buddhist conception of ultimate reality as emptiness is related to the Christian conception of God. He is a process theologian. Much Christian theology reflects a metaphysical viewpoint that assumes ultimate reality is static and substantive. The permanent is more real than process or change. Process theologians assume just the opposite and try to rethink the Christian theological tradition on a metaphysical basis that emphasizes process. Cobb finds this sort of metaphysics more like the metaphysical assumptions found in Buddhism. Hence he is particularly interested in that tradition and in the resources it may offer for understanding ultimacy.

Reading Questions

1. What is dualism?
2. What is being?
3. What does it mean to say that an event is empty?
4. What is dependent co-origination?
5. How does the "principle of rightness" differ from emptiness?
6. Why is that which is "ultimate" more easily conceived as a principle than as a personality?
7. Why, according to Cobb, must God be identified with the "principle of rightness rather than with the metaphysical ultimate"?
8. How might the duality between Emptiness and God be overcome, according to Cobb?
9. Cobb says that the affirmation of two different ultimates (Emptiness and God) is not contradictory. Do you agree or disagree? Why?

Emptiness and God*

JOHN B. COBB, JR.

MY TOPIC IS quite ambitious: it is the ultimate. In Buddhism the ultimate is often designated as Emptiness. In Christendom, at least traditionally, the ultimate has been declared to be God. One view of this situation is that Emptiness and God are but two names of the same reality, such that understanding between East and West is a matter of clarifying terminology. Another view is that these two names express opposing views of what the one ultimate reality is. In that case we can either engage in disputation or seek some sort of dialectical reconciliation. My own view is that Emptiness and God name two quite different ultimates to which we are related in two quite different ways. Indeed, there may be still other ultimates, such as the Whole or Cosmos, in relation to which segments of humanity have taken their bearings. If so, the question is whether human beings can develop their relations to this multiplicity of ultimates in ways that are not mutually exclusive. In this paper this question will be pressed only in terms of the Buddhist and Christian ultimate.

I propose to develop my position as follows. First, I will consider briefly the quest for the ultimate as it has led to Being in the West and to Brahman in the East. I will note how in Buddhism and in twentieth century philosophy Brahman or Being has been dissolved into Emptiness. Second, I will discuss the sense of rightness as pointing to another ultimate that has come most clearly to expression in Confucianism and Judaism. I will evaluate the efforts that have been made by the heirs of these traditions to assimilate the metaphysical ultimate to this ultimate principle of rightness. Third, I will consider the status of the idea of God in light of the dissolution of the ultimate into two ultimates, urging its renewal as a designation of the principle of rightness. Fourth, I will consider whether the realization of Emptiness and faith in God are mutually exclusive states, or whether they can be achieved in unity.

I. Being and Emptiness

Our efforts to understand reality in the West have led us again and again to dualism. This has grown out of our preoccupation with the subjective experience of the external object. The visual experience of a table, for example, has been a typical starting point of philosophical inquiry. This experience readily lends itself to analysis in terms of the one who sees and the entity that is seen. The one who sees is the subject; what is seen is the object. The subject is mental, the object, physical or material. The world, therefore, seems to be made up of mind and matter.

The philosophical problems generated by dualism are notorious. Hence Western philosophy is full of efforts to escape dualism. The easiest ways are by declaring the primacy either of the mental or of the material. Either mind can be viewed as the one source and locus of the data that are interpreted as matter, or mind can be viewed as an epiphenomenal by-product of changes in position of material particles. In these ways we can achieve idealist and materialist monisms, but since the ideal and the material are defined against each other, the taint of dualism is in fact not overcome.

There has been in the West a deeper response to the threat of dualism, a response which probes behind the differences between mind and matter to what they have in common. If both mental and material entities *are*, then what they have in common is existence or being. The tendency in

* From "Buddhist Emptiness and the Christian God" by John B. Cobb, Jr. *Journal of the American Academy of Religion* XLV (March 1977): 11–25. Reprinted by permission of the American Academy of Religion.

the West is often to suppose that this only means that existence or being names what is ultimate in the hierarchy of abstractions. That is, whereas only some entities are characterized by such particular qualities as squareness or redness, and whereas on the dualistic view thinking and extension are mutually exclusive characterizations of entities, existence or being characterizes all. But to view existence or being as simply the most abstract of characteristics, so abstract that it can be predicated of all things, is to misunderstand. Existence or being is not one more characteristic or essence that can be posited of things. It is that by virtue of which anything whatever can be posited. Hence it is related to things in a way totally different from the way in which abstractions or essences or forms are related to them. These differentiate types of things, but no combination of forms constitutes an existent thing: it constitutes only a more complex form. The existence of the existing thing is an entirely different matter. Hence existence as such, or being itself, is the ultimate reality by and through which every particular entity is or exists as qualified in its distinctive way.

The recognition of being itself as beyond and above all dualism and indeed all distinctions has played an important role in human thought. It is perceived as radically superior to all contingent things that have their being only through it. All things that are exist only by participation or derivation from being itself, whereas being itself is unaffected by them. As that by virtue of which all things are, as the ground of the being of all beings, it appears as infinitely more excellent than even the greatest being could be. It is absolute, immutable, omnipotent, and ineffable.

In the East the admiration for pure being went even further. As Brahman, its contrast with all contingent things led to viewing these things not merely as phenomenal but even as unreal or illusory. The goal for human life could be construed as release from involvement in this unreal and illusory world so as to be one with the real and changeless Brahman. This release could be affected by the realization of the identity of the being of the self and the being of all things.

Western mysticism at times came close to this position. Meister Eckhart identified being with the Godhead, and he was able to realize his own identity with this Godhead. But he did not draw conclusions about the unreality or illusoriness of the world comparable in their negations to those that can be found in the school of Sankara.

The point of these brief comments is to argue that the ultimate of metaphysical thought and of mysticism is one. In the Hindu tradition this is clear; for the greatest metaphysicians and the greatest mystics are often one. In the West it is less clear, but Rudolf Otto has pointed out how closely Meister Eckhart follows the metaphysics of Thomas Aquinas. This unity suggests that critics of metaphysics are wrong when they suppose that it deals only with abstractions remote from human experience. On the contrary, insofar as metaphysics penetrates to the ground of the being of beings it moves in tandem with the mystical penetration into ultimate reality. Metaphysics and mysticism inform one another. Mystical experience seems to confirm the metaphysical vision of Being Itself, the Ground of Being, or Brahman underlying and transcending the world of flux and expressing itself in that world.

The mystical literature both of the West and of Hinduism is full of negations as well as affirmations. Being or Brahman is utterly other than all things of which we can think, for all concepts are of forms rather than of being itself. Our habit of conceptual thinking can be broken only by repeated negations of all our efforts to conceive. The appeal can only be to intuition or experiential realization. Nevertheless, the mysticism of Being and of Brahman employs negations in support of affirmation. Being is not real as contingent things are real, but this is because it has an eminently superior reality of a wholly different order. Being is no-thing, because to be a thing is to be finite, and Being is without limitations of any kind. Being is empty in that it lacks all definition by forms; for such definition too is a mark of limitation and finitude.

Nevertheless, in Western and Hindu mysticism the negation served the cause of the affirmation of ultimate reality as Being or Brahman, the infinite source or ground of all things. Buddhism, on the other hand, from its origins insisted that the quest for the source or ground of things is idle, and this quickly came to be understood to imply that there is no such ground. Ultimate reality is not Being but Nothingness, Nirvana.

Even this was not radical enough to undergird the Buddhist requirement of total detachment. Nirvana could still be viewed as a blessed state or condition to be discovered or attained in contrast with the misery of Samsara, the phenomenal world. As long as this duality was allowed, one could be repelled by Samsara and crave Nirvana. Hence in the Madhyamika school, the distinction of Nirvana and Samsara was also negated, and in the Mahayana vision the identity of these opposites became fundamental. Nirvana is Samsara and Samsara is Nirvana; for both Nirvana and Samsara are "sunya" or empty. All that is, is Emptiness.

The dissolution of Being into Emptiness is also a dissolution of metaphysics into the language of things and of mysticism into the sheer immediacy of the world. We may, as a result, speak of the Buddhist denial or rejection of Being, of metaphysics, and of mysticism. But this would be misunderstood in the West where such denial usually arises by refusing the questions and the experiential probing that lead to Being, to metaphysics, and to mysticism. Buddhism overcomes Being by its analysis, metaphysics by metaphysical subtlety, and mysticism by mystical discipline. Hence it will be less confusing to continue to speak of Being, metaphysics, and mysticism, recognizing that in the Buddhist penetration they are dissolved and transformed.

The dissolution of Being into Emptiness is not designed to restore primacy to the finite things and events. Just as for Western and Hindu metaphysics and mysticism the finite things and events are nothing but expressions of Being; so for Buddhism they are nothing but expressions of Emptiness. Disengagement from attachment to things is as strong in Buddhism as in Hinduism. But this disengagement is not for the sake of a new engagement with ultimate reality. The ultimate that comes to expression in things, events, or experiences is Emptiness.

These Buddhist assertions are, and are intended to be, mind-boggling. As Buddhists insist, there is no simple way to explain them to those of us who have not experientially realized their truth. Still, much can be said, and I will try to indicate what I have understood or believe myself to have understood. What does it mean to say that an event, such as a moment of human experience, is empty?

First, it is empty of substance. There is no underlying self or "I" that unites separate moments of experience. Even in the single moment there is no subject to which the experience occurs. The happening of the experience brings into being the only subject that in any sense exists, and this subject is nothing other than the happening.

Second, the experience lacks all possession. That which makes up the experience does not belong to the experience. Its constituent elements are given to it. The experience is nothing but the coming together of that which is other than the experience.

Third, the experience is empty of form. It does not possess a form which it imposes on what constitutes it. The form is nothing but the result of the constitution, which is carried out by the constituting elements.

Fourth, it is empty of being. There is not, in addition to the coming together of the constituting elements something else which is the being of the new experience. Those constituting elements become the new experience, or rather, this becoming is the experience. Further, these elements, in their turn do not have being; for they in their turn are empty in the same way. There is no being—only Emptiness.

This explanation indicates that the Emptiness of an experience is the obverse side of the mode of its constitution. This mode is called *pratitya-samutpada* or dependent co-origination. That is, all the elements jointly constitute the new event which is then an element in the constitution of others. Both as event and as an element in other events it is empty.

The doctrine of Emptiness is not developed for the purpose of destroying all possible happiness and engendering bleak pessimism. On the contrary, it is developed to encourage the attainment of bliss through experiential realization of Emptiness. Indeed, there is no doubt that Buddhism succeeds in leading its adepts into a state of remarkable serenity and inner peace. Furthermore, just because all events are empty, they are also spontaneous and free.

The serenity and spontaneity attained by realization of Emptiness do not lead away from the awareness of what is occurring in one's world or reduce effectiveness of action. On the contrary, Buddhist meditation has been cultivated successfully for the sake of greater effectiveness in normal life. The Buddhist adept is able to be aware of every feature of her or his environment, responding to it freshly with enjoyment and appreciation without imposing upon it any meaning or emotional tone not immediately derived from it. Recent tests have vindicated this claim. In most meditative states persons are shown to respond differentially to stimuli. If a simple stimulus is frequently repeated, they respond with strong emotion initially, but eventually they become accustomed to it and do not respond at all. In a state of Zen meditation, however, persons respond to each repetition of the stimulus identically.

I mention this recent verification of Buddhist claims, not because Buddhist metaphysics is thereby proven, but to make it clear that we are not simply playing word-games. The experiential realization of being as Emptiness has definite effects, experienced as salvific by those who know them inwardly, and profoundly impressive to observers.

My knowledge of comparative religious practice and the results is not sufficient to allow me to judge between Western-Hindu mysticism and Buddhist meditation. But whereas until recently Western thought tended to support the view of being as Being Itself and the Ground of Being, in the twentieth century it has engaged in a dissolution of Being comparable to that of Buddhism. Hence there is special importance today in the encounter with Buddhism.

This reference to twentieth century development is especially focused on Martin Heidegger and Alfred North Whitehead. It is Heidegger who has done the major work in recovering for Western thought the question of being. It is he who has insisted upon the ontological difference between being and beings and worked through the history of Western philosophy in terms of his cognitive-experiential grasp of this difference. The results follow Buddhism in the insistence that there is no Being other than the being of the beings, and he goes far toward ridding this being of substantial character. Like Buddhism, he has dissolved metaphysics as onto-theo-logic.

Whitehead's work is remarkably compatible with that of Heidegger. He noted that every philosophy requires an ultimate that is actual only in its instantiations. In *Science and the Modern World* he called this ultimate "substantial activity," and he related it specifically to Spinoza's substance. But by the time he wrote *Process and Reality* the note of substantiality was gone. The ultimate is creativity, and creativity is nothing other than the many becoming one and being increased by one. Creativity is neither a being nor Being. It is remarkably like the ancient Buddhist dependent co-origination.

II. *The Principle of Rightness*

The dissolution of Being itself into Emptiness highlights the presence in the history of religions of another ultimate. Alongside the drive to go beyond the conditioned multiplicity of things to their common ground, which turns out to be groundlessness, there is another drive rightly to order action and experience. One finds this concern reflected in all the religious literatures of humankind, although in the religions of India it seems to be finally subordinated to the other concern for release through experiential realization of ultimate reality. In Judaism and in Confucianism it is paramount.

The rightness in question expresses itself in diverse ways. There is a rightness of style or form, propriety, appropriateness, good judgment, wisdom. Only in special circumstances is it expressed in clear-cut moral dualities of "ought" and "ought not." More often it functions as a discrimination of excellence from mediocrity. Still it is always bound up with norms of conduct that are broadly ethical.

It is particularly instructive to the Westerner to observe the struggle of the two ultimates in China. The first is represented by Taoism and is supported and strengthened subsequently by Buddhism. In Taoism efforts to improve society or to mold moral character are either ridiculed or viewed as clearly secondary to the fundamental goal of human beings, the realization of Tao. The embodiment of the second ultimate in Confucianism led to occasional attacks upon the escapism and amorality of Taoism. For the Confucian the goal must be rightly to order individual life and through it the corporate life. Moral considerations should never be subordinated to a mystical fulfillment of the private individual. They are as ultimate for the Confucian as is the unnamable Tao for the Taoist. But they are a radically different kind of ultimate.

Confucian thought was directed primarily to social theory and ethics. Hence it did not depend on agreed clarification of the metaphysical status of the ground or principle of rightness. Nevertheless, even a cursory reading of the texts allows one to say that in an important sense this principle is both immanent and transcendent for most Confucian thinkers. It is immanent in that it can be found by the sage through self-knowledge. The sense of rightness is a part of lived experience. We can grow in our ability to discern it well and to conform ourselves to it. But it is not imposed on us by alien authority. It is our own deepest nature.

At the same time, rightness is transcendent. It is not transcendent in the sense of having to be revealed or existing apart from human experience. But it is transcendent in that it is not created or chosen by human beings. It is given for us. It belongs to the nature of reality. It is prior to our acknowledgment of it or conformity to it. We individually derive it from beyond ourselves, and societies derive it from beyond themselves. The source or ground of its presence in our experience and nature is its prior characterization of heaven or of Tao. In its ultimacy it commands respect and even devotion, and that devotion is directed toward the cosmic ground of what is within.

All of this is familiar to the Westerner. Only in the last century have we come to see how even the most immanental interpretations of Western morality have in fact grounded themselves upon the transcendent. For only in the last century have we had radical critics of this transcendence who have argued that all appraisal of rightness is in fact a creation of norms rather than a recognition of a rightness already there. Kant's "moral law within" is as transcendent of human choice as is the prophet's "Thus says the Lord." The question is how to understand this transcendence. And to this question there has been far greater attention in the West than in China.

In Christianity there has been a transcending of morality. But this transcendence of morality should not be confused with the mystical transcending. In Paul morality is transcended because the effort to be righteous fails, not because being righteous is unimportant. What comes in the place of human fulfillment of the requirements of rightness is true righteousness as a gift. This involves conceiving of the principle of rightness as giving what it demands so that the believer can live out of this gift. It does not involve turning from the ultimate source of rightness to another ultimate that is beyond, or indifferent to, the distinctions of better and worse.

Just as it has proved possible to ignore and even to deny the metaphysical and mystical ultimate, so also it has proved possible to ignore and deny the ultimate of rightness. Cognitive confusion about both ultimates has contributed its share to the "positivistic" spirit. Nevertheless, these denials, however brilliant and important they have been, are best seen as phases in the process of cleansing our thought of these ultimates from conceptual accretions. Both remain present and functioning in human life when unrecognized, and in new forms they are recognized again and again. Our present experience as much as that of any previous epoch witnesses to the presence of a rightness in things more or less conformed to, just as the deepest intellectual and experiential penetration leads to the realization of a being that is Emptiness.

Clarification of each of the two ultimates and of what each means for human existence has taken place in separate traditions. I have suggested that the metaphysical-mystical ultimate is most fully clarified precisely in that tradition in which it is most fully freed of the last remnants of substantiality, namely Buddhism. But much can be learned of it in Hindu Brahmanism and Chinese Taoism as well. The ethical ultimate received its fullest development in the biblical and Confucian traditions.

In China the two ultimates were cultivated for centuries in partly separate traditions. Many Chinese embodied both in their lives, but an attempt at full synthesis in an inclusive philosophy awaited the advent of Neo-Confucianism. Chu Hsi is the greatest figure in this movement, and his synthesis can be treated in terms of the two concepts of T'ai-chi, the Great Ultimate, and Li, the principle of heaven and earth and the thousand things. Chu-Hsi declares that T'ai-chi is Li. This means that the metaphysical ultimate and the ultimate of rightness are one and the same. This identification does not, however, subordinate the directive character of Li to the transcendence of good and evil of the metaphysical ultimate. On the contrary, in Chu Hsi the metaphysical ultimate is viewed as characterized by the directivity derived from the ultimate principle of rightness.

In the West contact between Jewish and metaphysical thinking quickly drove Jewish thought to the claim that the ultimate principle of rightness to which it was directed must also be the metaphysical ultimate. Philo is the first great figure in this synthesis, and he has been followed by the major traditions of Christian theology. This synthesis could not be postponed or avoided as in China, because already in its dealings with the ultimate principle of rightness Israel had identified this as the creator of heaven and earth, and her praise of this creator heaped upon him every superlative attribute. It would be unthinkable to allow another ultimate beside this one. In later Christian theology, notably that of St. Thomas, the metaphysical ultimate was recognized as *esse,* the act of being, or Being Itself, but in Jewish and Christian thought, as in that of Neo-Confucian-

ism, the metaphysical ultimate is suffused with a directivity derived from the ultimate of rightness.

Hinduism and Buddhism have from the beginning dealt with the principle of rightness as well as with the metaphysical ultimate. In general, however, they have done so by distinguishing levels of human existence and attainment. The level at which considerations of rightness are relevant is finally transcended by the level at which the metaphysical ultimate is experientially realized. This final subordination of the ethical to the metaphysical is unacceptable to Confucianists and to heirs of the biblical tradition.

The question that confronts us now is whether the synthesis of the two ultimates effected in Neo-Confucianism and in most Western theology can be vindicated. Does the directivity in things, the orientation toward rightness, arise out of the relation to the metaphysical ultimate, or is the metaphysical ultimate finally neutral? If it is neutral, then is the ethical ultimate in fact not ultimate at all? Or is there an ultimate that is just as ultimate in its way as the metaphysical ultimate but that differs fundamentally from it?

The history of both Neo-Confucianism and of Western thought reveals a fundamental instability in the efforts to identify the two ultimates as one. To show that would be to retrace the history of these traditions in a way for which I have neither the knowledge nor the time. But the work of Heidegger and Whitehead indicates that the Buddhist analysis of the metaphysical-mystical ultimate as Emptiness carries us more fully into truth than any other. This emptiness cannot be identified with the ultimate of rightness. Hence either the ultimacy of this ultimate must be denied, or we are left with a duality of ultimates.

III. God

In the two preceding sections the word God has been avoided because it carries such heavy freight of meaning that it is difficult to discuss topics dispassionately once it is introduced. However, it is time now to ask to what this word has referred and what are its equivalents in other traditions and languages.

"God" is best used, first, to refer to whatever is worshipped. In this sense there are, superficially at least, many gods, and a god need have no ultimacy. But there is a drive in the act of worship itself to attribute ultimacy to what is worshipped, and this calls forth an effort to think through the specific object of worship to the ultimate that is worshipped in it. Hence "God," wherever the thought functions strongly, tends to name what is felt in some important way to be ultimate.

That "God" belongs with worship not only leads to association with ultimacy but also with actuality or concreteness. Within the context of worship there is a strong tendency to personalize the divine. But this tendency comes into tension with the other tendency toward ultimacy. What is actual, concrete, or personal seems always necessarily delimited and therefore limited. What is ultimate is more easily conceived as principle than as personality.

One solution to this problem is to hold that all worship is in fact directed to the metaphysical ultimate, but that it is psychologically necessary for all except the mystic to worship this ultimate through particular embodiments. The word God then can continue to attach to the supreme embodiment or embodiments of the ultimate, and some other word, such as "Godhead," can name the ultimate itself. This usage in Meister Eckhart was noted in Section I. It corresponds to the relation of Isvara and Brahman in Sankara, and to the relation of the Buddhas to the Buddhanature or Emptiness in much Buddhist thought.

In Confucian thought much less attention is given to the object of worship, but this could be identified as T'ai-yi, the Great One. In the Neo-Confucian philosophy of Chu Hsi, the Great One is explicitly identified with Li, the principle of rightness that functions as the directivity of all things. Li is also identified with the metaphysical ultimate, T'ai-chi, but in such a way that the metaphysical ultimate is assimilated to the ethical rather than the reverse. Hence, the God of Confucianism is the principle of rightness which may or may not also be viewed as metaphysically ultimate. The reality of God for Confucianism is bound up with the reality of a principle of right-

ness that is transcendent as well as immanent. But because worship is of minor importance to the Confucian, the identification of this principle as God is optional.

In the West God has meant the Ultimate, and the Ultimate has been both ethically and metaphysically ultimate. Hence belief in God faces a crisis when the one Ultimate is divided into two. The crisis has been precipitated especially by Heidegger, whose profound investigation of being led him to the conclusion that being is not God. If theologians are to continue to speak of God, they must identify God in another way. Heidegger lent his blessing to the proposal of Heinrich Ott that God is to faith as being is to thought, but this suggestive opening to a new mode of theology has thus far not been developed among Heideggerians.

On the contrary, the most influential philosophical theologian of our century, Paul Tillich, in spite of Heidegger's warning, identified God with Being. He recognized with Heidegger that this meant that God is not in any sense a being. Hence he was forced to remove from the idea of God much that had clung to the earlier understanding of Being when *esse* had been assimilated to an established understanding of deity. That is, in Tillich the classical identification of God and Being was continued, but whereas in Thomism the understanding of Being has been assimilated to the understanding of God, in Tillich the understanding of God was assimilated to the understanding of Being.

The contrast here should not be exaggerated. The understanding of God in philosophical theology had long been profoundly affected by its assimilation of Being. And in Tillich the understanding of Being as the Ground of Being and Depth of Being and much of his rhetoric and even doctrine shows the influence of an understanding of God shaped by the principle of rightness. Nevertheless, once the ontological difference between being and beings is unequivocally accepted, as it is by Tillich, the reversal is in principle effected.

The English theologian, John Macquarrie, made still more explicit and specific use of

Heidegger's renewal of the understanding of being. He freed being largely from the connotations of Ground of Being and Depth of Being that reflected Schelling and the Protestant mystics rather than Heidegger. Certainly much that he says about God as Being betrays the tension between the principle of rightness and the metaphysical ultimate. But he goes one step further in displaying the cost to Christianity of the identification of God with the metaphysical ultimate as this is progressively freed from the connotations of the principles of rightness. Although this kind of theological response to Heidegger continues, it appears to have decreasing power.

Whitehead agreed with Heidegger that the metaphysical ultimate is not God. This ultimate, creativity, was nevertheless appropriated by some of those influenced by him as God. Usually they coordinated his doctrine of creativity with that of Henry Nelson Wieman, thus restoring to it the association with the principle of rightness from which his own analysis freed it. Nevertheless, since Whitehead not only allowed and encouraged a different identification of God but himself developed it, Whitehead's primary theological influence has been the emergence of a school, process theology, that dissociates God from the metaphysical ultimate.

Even within the mainstream of process theology, however, the dissociation has been very incomplete. Charles Hartshorne has engaged more in a new interpretation of the metaphysical ultimate that introduces process into it than in a dissolution of the historic identification of the ultimate of metaphysics with the ultimate principle of rightness. For years I struggled to subordinate creativity to God, rather than to allow their radical difference to stand out clearly. It has required an encounter with Eastern thought to clarify the religious meaning of the work of both Heidegger and Whitehead and to force the issue of God. When that issue is forced, at least within process theology, but also wherever biblical faith is primary, God must be identified with the principle of rightness rather than with the metaphysical ultimate. The problem for Christian theology is then the right understanding of this principle in

its purity and distinctness instead of the effort to unite with it the metaphysical ultimate. To this task Whitehead has himself made a contribution whose full meaning has not yet been grasped or appropriated by his followers.

IV. The Realization of Emptiness and Faith in God

The analysis thus far has been primarily designed to show that an adequate account of the deepest level of human experience requires us to recognize that there are two ultimates, the metaphysical ultimate and the ultimate principle of rightness. I have also argued that the metaphysical ultimate is best understood precisely in its dissolution into dependent co-origination or Emptiness, and that the principle of rightness is properly designated as God.

The discussion has shown that the affirmation of these two ultimates is not contradictory. Indeed, the double affirmation is allowed and clarified in Heidegger and actually developed in Whitehead. Heidegger's being and Whitehead's creativity correspond remarkably with Buddhist Emptiness. And Whitehead has developed a cosmology in which God as the principle of rightness is clearly distinguished from and related to creativity as the metaphysical ultimate.

It is not so evident, however, that Buddhism can allow this dual ultimate. The question posed by Buddhism to this affirmation of God is whether it fully recognizes that God, too, insofar as God is, must be empty. That would mean recognizing that God does not possess a being different in kind from the being of other entities, which has been displayed as Emptiness. God, too, must be empty, just as the self, and all things are empty—empty of substantiality or own-being, and lacking in any given character of their own. God like all things must be an instance of dependent co-origination.

Whitehead's doctrine of God is open to this interpretation. God, like all things, is an instance of creativity, that is, of the many becoming one, which is his formulation of dependent co-origination. God is as much a creature of creativity as is any other entity, and God is not an exception to the categories. The principle of universal relativity includes God. Furthermore, God as understood by Whitehead supremely embodies the characteristics that follow from enlightenment. Accordingly God my be conceived as the totally enlightened one, the supreme and everlasting Buddha.

Whereas the unenlightened one discriminates, accentuating some stimuli and shutting out others, the enlightened one receives all for just what they are. Whereas the unenlightened one juxtaposes self-interest and the good of others, the enlightened one is equally benevolent toward all. Emptiness is freedom from all distorting perceptions and concerns and perfect openness to all that is, human and nonhuman alike.

Whitehead conceives God in much this way. God is constituted by the progressive unification of all actuality with all possibility. Each actuality and every possibility is allowed to be just what it is in the process of dependent co-origination or concrescence. God is undiscriminatingly benevolent towards all. There are no distortions in God's perceptions and concerns preventing God's perfect openness toward all that is, human and nonhuman alike. Thus "God" can be freed from the note of substantiality and dualism that makes this concept offensive to the Buddhist. Whether Buddhists can accept the remaining distinction between the one cosmic Buddha, the ultimate principle of rightness, and the many creaturely Buddhas is not yet clear.

Religiously some such acceptance seems to function in some Buddhist schools. The Christian conviction that personal trust in God, present in the world as Christ, is essential to salvation is paralleled in those Buddhist schools that teach salvation by the power of the Other, especially Amida Buddha, rather than by one's own efforts. Nevertheless, there is a profound difference.

For the Buddhists, even in those schools that emphasize total dependence on the power of the Other, the goal is that of enlightenment, or the realization of the ultimate reality of one's situation. This is the realization of the identity of one's true self as the Emptiness that is open to be filled by everything impartially. For Christians the goal is for the self to be progressively conformed to the gracious promptings or call of God, trusting the creative outcome of that surrender of the resistant selfhood to the divine wisdom and purpose.

We can now see that either goal is attainable, or rather that either may be approximated. For the Buddhist, even the Buddhist who stresses faith in the Other, the final goal is to attain freedom from the other power in becoming oneself a Buddha. For the Christian the final goal is to experience freedom as the perfect conformation to God, the principle of rightness.

When compared with ordinary states of self-centeredness, anxiety, isolation, and ambition, the Buddhist and Christian goals seem very much alike. But they overcome our ordinary pettiness and misery in fundamentally distinct ways. The differences can be stated as follows. Buddhists realize that they are at each and every moment, and hence without qualification, instances of dependent co-origination or, in Whitehead's language, concrescent processes. The actual standpoint of experience is never that of a completed entity, whereas all of our conceptuality, even about ourselves, turns us into such entities. This actual, existential realization frees the concrescent process of distortion and illusion, and it opens experience to what is as it is. Christians on the other hand, attend to God's aim for the concrescence, a directivity toward rightness that is the divine immanence in the concrescent process. This aim is both at an immediate achievement in that concrescence and at its appropriate effects beyond itself. These effects are upon other events and especially upon other human experiences.

I have tried to show in this presentation that the respective attainments of Buddhism and Christianity are not contradictory, but that they yet differ profoundly. Christians can agree that what is ultimate in the metaphysical sense is dependent co-origination, the many becoming one, creativity, or concrescence as such. They can understand, therefore, why metaphysicians and mystics have so often pushed through and past God to the metaphysical-mystical ultimate which can be called Being, Brahman, or Godhead. But they need not be intimidated. Buddhism teaches that this ultimate is indeed devoid of form and beyond good and evil, as mystics have often said. It is exemplified without discrimination in a cockroach, a human child, God, and an atomic explosion. It is not evident that this is the one ultimate that should guide all human attention, effort, and reflection. If there is importance in the shape that dependent co-origination or concrescence takes, if it matters whether the universe is full of life or allowed to die, then we should attend to God. God is not that ultimate that is actual only in its instantiations, but God is the ultimate instantiation of the ultimate. It is meaningless to speak of Emptiness as superior to God or of God as superior to Emptiness. They are incommensurable.

In this way the encounter with Buddhist Emptiness can free Christians to distinguish the Emptiness of God from the Emptiness which is the Godhead, without claiming for God the kind of ultimacy that belongs to Emptiness or to Godhead as such. But a still deeper question remain. How are Christians to relate themselves to that other form of human realization and perfection exemplified so purely in Buddhist enlightenment? Having recognized the possibility and reality of this fulfillment as well as its difference from Christian trust in God, are they to envy it in its superiority, condemn it as an inferior rival, recognize it as a legitimate option to be chosen by those so inclined, or attempt to appropriate it?

The argument of this paper counts against the first two of these options. That is, it finds no neutral grounds from which the respective worth of the two ultimates can be appraised. It opposes any claim to superiority between them. This implies that the orientation of human beings may be equally to Emptiness or to God. World history shows that the results of both orientations have been impressive, despite all their ambiguities, and that each exercises a certain attraction on the practitioners of the other. But the argument thus far has left fully open the question whether we are confronted here by existentially exclusive alternatives or whether this duality can in turn be transcended.

There are encouraging indications that the duality can be transcended. The hope that a synthesis of Buddhist and Christian achievements is possible is strengthened by the observation that the Buddhist saint appears to live and act as the Christian would expect one to live and act who is fully responsive to God. Although there is much talk of transcending the duality of good and evil, and although cheap imitations of Buddhism sometimes lead to amorality and immorality, authentic Buddhism does not have this character. The result of transcending the duality of good and evil is a pure and spontaneous goodness. It seems that when all discrimination and objectifying conceptualization are overcome, when one realizes what is as it is, the resultant concrescent process conforms effortlessly, without naming it, to the divine impulse.

Much Buddhist literature, indeed, witnesses to the conviction that Emptiness is not really neutral toward rightness. For example, in the treatment of the *Dharmakaya*, the Buddha-body or Buddha-nature, which is the truth and reality of all things, Buddhist writers employ notions of rightness, and especially of wisdom and compassion. Also, they attribute to the *Dharmakaya* the effecting of good works in those who realize it. Although the personalistic and value-laden language may be interpreted as a concession to popular understanding, it reflects a deep sense that what is realized in the realization of the metaphysical ultimate has its directivity toward wisdom and compassion.

This can be understood in terms of the double ultimate discussed above. Ultimate reality is the process of dependent co-origination in which the many that constitute the given world become a new, but ephemeral and insubstantial, one. Among these many, one is God, functioning in all things as a directivity toward rightness. The Buddhist who is completely empty is by that token completely open. To be completely open is to allow each element in the many to be what it is in the new one, that is, to function appropriately according to its own potentiality. To allow God so to function is to be spontaneously formed by the rightness appropriate in that moment. Thus to be truly open is to be spontaneously good. By being wholly indifferent to right and wrong the Buddhist achieves a perfect conformation to the immanent principle of right. It seems, therefore, that Buddhist enlightenment contains a synthesis of the two ultimates.

There is also a Christian approach to this synthesis. This is through attention to the principle of rightness. The Christian goal is to achieve sensitivity and responsiveness to the inner promptings of God. Spiritual discipline consists in discerning the spirits so as to discriminate the divine urge from the many other urges that affect us. Response to this directivity leads away from concern primarily with oneself to a broader concern and to sensitivity to the needs and feelings of others. In short, it leads toward openness to what occurs as it occurs and to self-constitution that is appropriate thereto. Perhaps when this is combined with the recognition that the reality of the self *is* this dependent co-origination, what is achieved through cultivated responsiveness to the directivity that is God's presence will converge with what is achieved through Buddhist enlightenment.

2.5 The Female Nature of God

Recently the press has reported controversy about using female terms for God. God is Mother or God is Goddess, or God is She. One might wonder what all the fuss is about. The sacred scriptures of Judaism, Christianity, and Islam, and many other religious traditions, affirm that God created human beings in the image of God. Women as well as men are human beings. Adam in Hebrew means "human being." So why do we not speak of God as mother as well as father, and why do we not use the pronoun *She* as well as *He* to refer to God?

The reason is that male and masculine metaphors have not only deeply infected our conception of God, but they have also infected our very thinking about ultimate reality. We live in a sexist society. Nearly everything we read or see on television or in the movies reinforces the notion that males are superior to females. We are comfortable with male metaphors for the divine but uncomfortable with female metaphors. Male images mask the sexuality of God. To say that God is "Father" has sexual connotations. Yet these connotations do not become obvious until we speak of God as "Mother."

Why do we not pray to "Mother–Father" God? "Well," you might say, "because we are taught by scripture and tradition to pray to a Father God." So? Does that which is ultimate, that which is the creator of the world—including both male and female—play favorites? If so, what we call "God" is not God.

One might argue that male metaphors for God are innocent. After all, in English, the pronoun *he* often is used to refer to any antecedent subject whose gender is not explicitly female. Is this really so innocent? Language and the symbols employed by language have profound and deep influences on how people think and act. How many of you think of God in primarily masculine terms?

Some scholars argue that we should substitute female and feminine terms for God. God is the Goddess, the Mother of all life. She is the eternal womb of all that is. Others argue that we must get beyond sexual metaphors entirely. God is the source of all that is. As such, God is neither male nor female but the ultimate reality that creates both.

Rosemary Radford Reuther, the author of the following essay, contends that we should conceive of God or ultimate reality as beyond the dualities of sex.

Dr. Reuther is Georgia Harkness Professor of Applied Theology at Garrett-Evangelical Theological Seminary and Northwestern University in Evanston, Illinois. She is the author or editor of over 17 books and has written extensively on topics relating to feminist theology.

Reading Questions

1. What is the problem with regarding God as male?
2. What is the point of Reuther's survey of "suppressed feminine images in patriarchal theology"?
3. According to Reuther, what is wrong with the "Goddess Movement"?
4. Why will bringing to the surface the suppressed "feminine" side of God not help the situation?
5. According to Reuther, how should we best envision God?
6. What do you think? Is Reuther right or not? Why?

The Female Nature of God*

ROSEMARY RADFORD REUTHER

THE EXCLUSIVELY MALE IMAGE of God in the Judaeo-Christian tradition has become a critical issue of contemporary religious life. This question does not originate first of all in theology or in hermeneutics. It originates in the experience of alienation from this male image of God experienced by feminist women. It is only when this alienation is taken seriously that the theological and exegetical questions begin to be raised.

1. What Is the Problem?

The problem of the male image of God cannot be treated as trivial or an accidental question of linguistics. It must be understood first of all as an ideological bias that reflects the sociology of patriarchal societies; that is, those societies dominated by male, property-holding heads of families. Although not all patriarchal societies have male monotheist religions, in those patriarchal societies which have this view of God, the God-image serves as the central reinforcement of the structure of patriarchal rule. The subordinate status of women in the social and legal order is reflected in the subordinate status of women in the cultus. The single male God is seen not only as creator and lawgiver of this secondary status of women. The very structure of spirituality in relation to this God enforces her secondary status.

What this means quite simply is the following. When God is projected in the image of one sex, rather than both sexes, and in the image of the ruling class of this sex, then this class of males is seen as consisting in the ones who possess the image of God primarily. Women are regarded as relating to God only secondarily and through inclusion in the male as their "head." This is stated very specifically by St. Augustine in his treatise *On the Trinity* (7, 7, 10).

* From "The Female Nature of God" by Rosemary Radford Reuther. *Concilium* 143: 1981. Reprinted by permission of Concilium.

The male monotheist image of God dictates a certain structure of divine-human relationship. God addresses directly only the patriarchal ruling class. All other groups—women, children, slaves—are addressed by God only indirectly and through the mediation of the patriarchal class. This hierarchal order of God/Man/Woman appears throughout Hebrew law. But it also reappears as a theological principle in the New Testament. Thus Paul (despite Gal. 3:28) in I Cor. 11:3 and 7 reaffirms this patriarchal order of relationships:

> But I want you to understand that the head of every man is Christ, the head of a woman is her husband, and the head of Christ is God. . . . For a man ought not to cover his head, since he is the image and glory of God; but the woman is the glory of man.

Thus the woman is seen as lacking the image of God or direct relation to God, in herself, but only secondarily, as mediated through the male.

2. The Suppressed "Feminine" in Patriarchal Theology

Recognising the fundamentally ideological, and even idolatrous, nature of this male-dominant image of God, some recent scholars have sought to show that this was never the whole story. God is not always described as a male. There is a small number of cases where God is described as a female. These texts occur in the Scriptures, particularly in the context of describing God's faithfulness to Israel and suffering on behalf of Israel. Here the labours of a woman in travail, giving birth to a child, and the fidelity of a mother who loves the child unconditionally, seemed to be more striking human analogies for these attributes of God than anything to be found in male activity. Thus in Isaiah we find:

> Yahweh goes forth, now I will cry out like a woman in travail, I will gasp and pant. (Isa. 42:13, 14).
> For Zion said, "Yahweh has forsaken me; my Lord has forgotten me. Can a woman forget her suckling child, that she should have no

compassion on the son of her womb? Even these may forget, yet I will not forget you." (Isa. 49:14, 15).

These analogies of God as female in Scripture have been collected in Leonard Swidler's *Biblical Affirmation of Woman* (Philadelphia: Westminster 1979).

There is a second use of the female image for God in Scripture. The female image also appears as a secondary *persona* of God in the work of mediation to creation. In biblical thought this is found primarily in the Wisdom tradition. Here Holy Wisdom is described as a daughter of God through whom God mediates the work of creation, providential guidance, revelation, and reconciliation to God. In relation to the Solomon, the paradigmatic royal person, Wisdom is described as a "bride of his soul." Of her Solomon says:

> I loved her and sought after her from my youth, and I desired to take her for my bride, and I became enamoured of her beauty. . . . Therefore I determined to take her to live with me, knowing that she would give me good counsel (Wisd. of Sol. 8:2, 9).

The same view of Wisdom as mediating creatrix is found in Proverbs (8:23–31). Here she is imaged as the mother who mediates wisdom to her sons.

Behind this powerful image of Divine Wisdom undoubtedly lies remnants of the ancient Near Eastern Goddess, Isis or Astarte. These Goddesses were imaged as creators and redeemers. They are linked particularly with Wisdom, defined as both social justice and harmony in nature, over against the threatening powers of Chaos. Raphael Patai, in his book, *The Hebrew Goddess* (Ktav 1967), has delineated the heritage of this ancient Near Eastern Goddess as she appeared in suppressed form in Hebrew theology.

Although the Sophia image disappears in rabbinic thought after the advent of the Christian era, possibly because of its use in gnosticism, a new image of God's mediating presence as female appears in the form of the *Shekinah*. The *Shekinah* is both the mediating presence of God in the midst of Israel, but also the reconciler of Israel with God. In rabbinic mystical speculation on the *galut* (exile), the *Shekinah* is seen as going into exile with Israel when God-as-father has turned away his face in anger. Each Shabbat celebration is seen as a mystical connubial embrace of God with his *Shekinah,* anticipating the final reuniting of God with creation in the messianic age. The exile of Israel from the land is seen ultimately as an exile within God, divorcing the masculine from the feminine "side" of God.

In Christianity this possibility of the immanence of God as feminine was eliminated. Christianity translated the Sophia concept into the Logos concept of Philo, defined as "son of God." It related this masculine mediating *persona* of God to the human person, Jesus. Thus the maleness of Jesus as a human person is correlated (or even fused into) the maleness of the Logos as "son of God." All possible speculation on a "female side" of God within trinitarian imagery was thus cut off from the beginning.

Some Sophia speculation does get revived in the Greek Orthodox tradition in relation to creation, the Church and Mariology. One somewhat maverick modern Orthodox thinker (Sergius Bulgakov *The Wisdom of God,* London 1937) even relates this sophiological aspect of God to the *ousia* or Being of God. Sophia is the matrix or ground of Being of the three (male) persons of God! But it is doubtful if most Orthodox thinkers would be comfortable with that idea.

In western thought speculation on feminine aspects of God were probably rejected early because of links with gnosticism. Some recent Catholic thinkers (i.e., Leonard Swidler) have tried to revive the Sophia/*Shekinah* idea and link it with the Holy Spirit. But this does not have roots in western trinitarian thought. Basically the Spirit is imaged as a "male" but nonanthropomorphic principle. As the power of God that "fecundates" the waters at creation and the womb of Mary, its human referent would seem to be closer to the male semen as medium of male power.

This means that in western Christian theology, the female image is expelled from any place within the doctrine of God. It appears instead on the creaturely side of the God/creation relation. The female is used as the image of that which is created by God, that which is the recipient of God's creation; namely, Nature, Church, the soul, and, finally, Mary as the paradigmatic image of the redeemed humanity.

One partial exception to this rule is found in the Jesus mysticism of the middle ages that finds its culmination in Juliana of Norwich. Here Jesus, as the one who feeds us with his body, is portrayed as both mother and father. Eucharistic spirituality particularly seems to foster this mothering, nurturing image of Jesus. However since both the divine and the human person of Jesus is firmly established in the orthodox theological tradition as male, this feminine reference to Jesus remains an attribute of a male person. Female-identified qualities, such as mothering and nurturing, are taken over by the male. But the female is not allowed "male" or "headship" capacities.

What I wish to argue then is that all of these suppressed feminine aspects of God in patriarchal theology still remain fundamentally within the context of the male-dominant structure of patriarchal relationships. The female can never appear as the icon of God in all divine fullness, parallel to the male image of God. It is allowed in certain limited references to God's faithfulness and suffering for Israel. Or it appears as a clearly subordinate principle that mediates the work and power of the Father, much as the mother in the family mediates to the children (sons) the dictates of the father. She can be daughter of the divine king; bride of the human king; mother of his sons; but never an autonomous person in her own right.

The "feminine" in patriarchal theology is basically allowed to act only within the same limited, subordinate or mediating roles that women are allowed to act in the patriarchal social order. The feminine is the recipient and mediator of male power to subordinate persons; i.e., sons, servants. In Christianity even these covert and marginal roles of the feminine as aspects of God disappear. Here the feminine is only allowed as image of the human recipient or mediator of divine grace, not as an aspect of the divine. In every relationship in which this "feminine" aspect appears in patriarchal theology, the dominant sovereign principle is always male; the female operating only as delegate of the male.

3. "Pagan Feminism": The Revolt Against the Biblical Patriarchal God

In the 1970s the feminist movement, particularly in the United States, began to develop an increasingly militant wing that identified patriarchal religion as the root of the problem of women's subordination. These women saw that efforts to create a more "androgynous" God within the biblical tradition would be insufficient. The female aspect of God would always be placed within this fundamentally male-centred perspective. They concluded that biblical religion must be rejected altogether.

In its place they would substitute a Goddess and nature religion that they believe to be the original human cult of matriarchal society before the rise of patriarchy. They believe that the witches of the European middle ages preserved this Goddess-centred nature religion. They were persecuted for this faith by the Christian Church who falsely accused them of malevolence and "devil worship." Feminist Wicca (or witchcraft) believes itself to be reviving this ancient Goddess religion. The book by Starhawk (Miriam Simos), *The Spiral Dance* (New York 1979), is a good expression of this feminist Goddess movement.

It is possible that we are witnessing in this movement the first strings of what may become a new stage of human religious consciousness. This possibility cannot be ruled out by the critical Christian. It may be that we have allowed divine revelation through the prophets and through Jesus to be so corrupted by an idolatrous androcentrism, that a fuller understanding of God that truly includes the female as person must come as superseding and judging patriarchal religion. However, Goddess religion in its present form manifests a number of immaturities that are open to criticism, even from the point of view of feminism.

Following outdated matriarchal anthropology from the nineteenth century, much of the pedigree claimed by this movement is of doubtful historicity. In fact, the patterns of Goddess religion reveal very clearly their roots in nineteenth-century European romanticism. The dualistic world view that sets the feminine, nature and immanence on one side, and the masculine, history and transcendence on the other, is fundamentally preserved in this movement. It simply exalts the feminine pole of the dualism and repudiates the masculine side. One must ask whether this does not entrap women in precisely the traditional stereotypes. The dualisms are not overcome, but merely given a reverse valuation. But, in practice, this still means that women, even in "rebellion," are confined to a powerless Utopianism in which males own and run "the world."

Moreover, within their own community, instead of transforming the male monotheist model, they have reversed it. Now the great Goddess is the predominant image of the Divine. Woman then becomes the one who fully images the Goddess and communicates directly with her. Males are either excluded or given a subordinate position that is analogous to the position traditionally accorded women in the patriarchal cult. This *coup d'etat* may feel satisfying in the short run, but in the long run would seem to reproduce the same fundamental pathology.

4. Does the Ancient Goddess Represent the Feminine?

Both biblical feminists, who search for the suppressed feminine in the Judaeo-Christian tradition, and Goddess worshipers, who wish to exalt the feminine at the expense of the masculine, share a common assumption. Both assume that the recovery of the female as icon of the divine means the vindication of the "feminine." Neither ask the more fundamental question of whether the concept of the feminine itself is not a patriarchal creation. Thus the vindication of the "feminine," as we have inherited that concept from patriarchy, will always be set within a dualistic scheme of complementary principles that segregate women on one side and men on the other. Even if this scheme is given a reversed valuation, the same dualism remains.

A recent study by Judith Ochshorn, *The Female Experience and the Nature of the Divine* (Indiana University Press 1980) raises some important questions about the appropriateness of identifying this patriarchally-defined feminine with the ancient goddesses of polytheistic cultures. What Ochshorn has discovered is that, in polytheistic cultures of the Ancient Near East, gods and goddesses do not fall into these stereotyped patterns of masculinity and femininity. A God or Goddess, when addressed in the context of their own cult, represents a fullness of divine attributes. The Goddess represents sovereignty, wisdom, justice, as well as aspects of sexual and natural fecundity. Likewise the God operates as a sexual and natural principle, as well as a principle for social relations. The Goddess displays all the fullness of divine power in a female image. She is not the expression of the "feminine." Ochshorn also believes that this more pluralistic schema allows women to play more equalitarian and even leading roles in the cultus.

The subordinate status of women, in which relation to God is mediated only through the patriarchal class, is absent from religions which have a plurality of divine foci in male and female forms. Although such a lost religious world is probably not revivable as an option today, such studies may help to point us to the relativity of our patriarchally-defined patterns of masculine or feminine. They alert us to the dangers of simply surfacing the suppressed "feminine side" of that dualism as part of the image of God, without further criticism.

5. Towards an Image of God Beyond Patriarchy

If we are to seek an image of God(ess) beyond patriarchy, certain basic principles must be acknowledged. First we must acknowledge that the male has no special priority in imaging God(ess). If male roles and functions; i.e., fathering, are only analogies for God, then those analogies are in no way superior to the parallel analogies drawn from female experience; i.e., mothering. God(ess) as Parent is as much Mother as Father.

But even the Parent image must be recognised as a limited analogy for God(ess), often reinforcing patterns of permanent spiritual infantilism and cutting off moral maturity and responsibility. God(ess) as creator must be seen as the Ground of the full personhood of men and women equally. A God(ess) who is a good parent, and not a neurotic parent, is one that promotes our growth towards responsible personhood, not one who sanctions dependency. The whole concept of our relation to God(ess) must be reimaged.

If God(ess) is not only creator, but also redeemer of the world from sin, then God(ess) cannot be seen as the sanctioner of the priority of male over female. To do so is to make God the creator and sanctioner of patriarchy. God becomes the architect of injustice. The image of God as predominantly male is fundamentally idolatrous. The same can be said of an image of God(ess) as predominantly female.

The God(ess) who can be imaged through the experience of men and women alike does not simply embrace these experiences and validate them in their traditional historical form. We cannot simply add the "mothering" to the "fathering" God, while preserving the same hierarchical patterns of male activity and female passivity. To vindicate the "feminine" in this form is merely to make God the sanctioner of patriarchy in new form.

God(ess) must be seen as beyond maleness and femaleness. Encompassing the full humanity of both men and women, God(ess) also speaks as judge and redeemer from the stereotyped roles in which men as "masculine" and women as "feminine" have been cast in patriarchal society. God(ess) restores both men and women to full humanity. This means not only a new humanity, but a new society, new personal and social patterns of human relationships. The God(ess) who is both male and female, and neither male or female, points us to an unrealised new humanity.

In this expanding image of God(ess) we glimpse our own expanding human potential, as selves and as social beings, that have remained truncated and confined in patriarchal, hierarchical relationships. We begin to give new content to the vision of the messianic humanity that is neither "Jew nor Greek, that is neither slave nor free, that is neither male nor female" (Gal. 3:28) in which God(ess) has "broken down the dividing wall of hostility" (Eph. 2:14).

2.6 Is the Concept of Ultimate Reality Coherent?

We have been looking at diverse views of ultimate reality (Tao, Brahman, God, Emptiness) in this chapter. As different as these views are and as incompatible as you may find them, they have in common the concern to describe or at least help us understand (however dimly) what is ultimate. It is time to take a step back from specific religious views and ask whether the notion of an ultimate reality makes any sense.

You might be inclined to argue that it does not. If that which is ultimate cannot be defined, if it transcends all names and forms, then we cannot form a clear conception of what it is. If we cannot form a clear conception, then why not conclude that the ultimate is incoherent or, at the very least, that we are not in a position to say one way or the other? As logicians have long pointed out, negative definitions do not help us very much. To say of the ultimate that it is "not this" and "not that," or to name it the Nameless, might seem like mere word play.

However, many find this strange way of talking very profound. How else could we talk (if we talk at all) about the ultimate? Yes, we should avoid negative definitions whenever possible. But perhaps there is just no other satisfactory way of proceeding when it comes to ultimacy. Still, questions remain.

What is it for something to be ultimate? Some support the "best widget" theory. What is ultimate is the best of all things that now exist. If we take this line of reasoning, then it would seem possible that at some future point, something better might come along. If so, *it* would then be ultimate. This raises the possibility that at some point in the past there was a better widget than there is now, even though the one we now have is the best of the present lot.

These sorts of speculations, others have argued, show that whatever is ultimate cannot be an *actual* being. They support the "best widget possible" theory. Ultimate reality is absolutely perfect. It is maximally perfect—the very best of all things that *might* exist. It is simply not possible for there to be a better widget.

If we follow this notion of ultimate reality as maximally perfect, then it seems that whatever is truly ultimate must have all possible perfections. Some perfections, however, are incompatible, such as being unchanging (a property frequently assigned to the ultimate) and being a perfect swimmer. Does it make sense to try to envision a reality that has all perfections? If some perfections are incompatible, then it would appear to be impossible for any being or reality to have all of them.

The next selection shows that other problems arise when we try to think through the concept of ultimate reality. William J. Wainwright (1935–   ) is a philosopher of religion teaching at the University of Wisconsin, Milwaukee. He supports the view that ultimate reality is best thought of as maximally perfect and defends its coherence in the face of critical objections.

Reading Questions

1. According to William James, what three beliefs characterize religious life?
2. What, according to Tillich, is the demand and the promise of an ultimate concern?
3. What reason does Wainwright give for concluding that "a *fully* appropriate object of ultimate concern must . . . be maximally perfect"?
4. How does Wainwright answer the objection that an appropriate object of ultimate concern need not be the most perfect *possible* reality, but only the most perfect *existing* (actual) reality?
5. What three reasons might lead us to think that the concept of a maximally perfect reality is incoherent, and what sort of response might be made to these objections?
6. What, according to Wainwright, conditions one's understanding of a maximally perfect reality as personal (theistic) or nonpersonal (nontheistic)?
7. What do you think? Does the concept of a maximally perfect reality make sense or not? Why?

Is the Concept of Ultimate Reality Coherent?*

WILLIAM J. WAINWRIGHT

ACCORDING TO WILLIAM JAMES (1842–1910), religious life includes three beliefs:

> "that the visible world is part of a more spiritual universe from which it draws its chief significance;
>
> that union or harmonious relation with that higher universe is our true end," and
>
> that life can be transformed for the better by making proper contact with it.

Religious people believe that "prayer or inner communion with the spirit thereof—be that spirit 'God' or 'law'—is a process wherein work is really done, and spiritual energy flows in and produces effects, psychological or material, within the phenomenal world."

James thinks that religion also involves "a new zest which adds itself to life, and takes the form either of lyrical enhancement or of appeal to earnestness and heroism." It provides, he says, "an assurance of safety and a temper of peace, and, in relation to others, a preponderance of loving affections."

Throughout history, men and women have turned to religion for comfort, strength, and assurance. Traditions like Buddhism, Christianity, and Islam give life depth and significance by explaining the nature of reality and our place in it, by assuring us of the possibility of victory over life's difficulties, and by providing means for achieving it.

Religion is rooted in human needs and yearnings—a conviction that ordinary life is flawed and that the powers of the "visible world" aren't sufficient to mend it. While suffering causes some to doubt the very existence of a "higher universe," it strengthens the convictions of many others. In Elizabeth Gaskell's novel *North and South,* a factory girl who is dying in miserable surroundings argues that this can't be all there is and that there must therefore be a "God to wipe away all tears from all eyes." The incompleteness and unsatis-

* From *Philosophy of Religion* by William J. Wainwright. Copywright © 1988 by Wadsworth, Inc. pp. 1–3, 6–12. Reprinted by permission of Wadsworth Publishing Company. Footnotes deleted.

factoriness of life—its inability to fully satisfy our yearnings or provide lasting happiness—leads many to hope or believe that the visible world isn't the whole of reality.

But religion isn't rooted only in needs and yearnings. The order and beauty of the world and even the fact that it exists at all seem to point to something beyond it. Furthermore, saints, mystics, prophets, and many ordinary men and women believe they have actually glimpsed a sovereign good that transcends life's contingencies and provides an answer to the quest for meaning and happiness.

Religion is thus rooted in human needs, yearnings, and experiences. The strength of conviction, hope, and commitment varies considerably from person to person. But, for the devout, the higher universe is a matter of what Paul Tillich (1886–1965) calls "ultimate concern."

Ultimate concern is "total." The self as a whole is caught up in it, and every other concern becomes secondary. The object of a person's ultimate concern is experienced as holy—distinct from all profane or ordinary realities. It is also experienced as a mystery. No matter how much one knows about it, it eludes one's grasp. One appears to be caught up in something so charged with power, so real and splendid that, in comparison, other things are empty and worthless. In short, the object of ultimate concern is experienced as overwhelming and supremely valuable. It thus demands total surrender and promises total fulfillment.

Whether ultimate concern is necessary for any kind of religious attitude is a matter of dispute. Nevertheless, it *is* characteristic of the religious attitudes idealized in Christianity, Buddhism, Islam, and other major religious traditions.

Ultimate concern can, however, take different forms. It often takes the form of worship and then involves praise, love, gratitude, supplication, confession, petition, and so on. It can also take the form of a quest for the ultimate good. The object of this quest is a knowledge of the ultimate good or a union with it that transfigures us and overcomes our wrongness. These forms of ultimate concern may be combined or they may exist separately. Christianity, for example, combines both. In Buddhism, however, ultimate concern usually takes the second form but not the first.

The fact that ultimate concern is an aspect of religious attitudes may have an important implication. Perhaps nothing can be a completely worthy object of these attitudes unless it is so great that we can conceive of nothing greater.

Why think this? It isn't sufficient for the object of these attitudes to be the greatest reality that actually exists, for the most perfect existing reality might be limited or defective. Suppose, for example, that the most perfect existing thing was wiser and better than other existing things but was ignorant of a number of matters and somewhat selfish. It would not be appropriate to surrender totally to a being of this sort. The defects or limitations of the most perfect existing thing might not be this striking. Nevertheless, if there is a possible reality that surpasses the most perfect existing thing, then the latter is limited or imperfect in comparison with the former. It thus seems that our admiration, concern, and commitment shouldn't be unconditional and without reservation. A *fully* appropriate object of ultimate concern must therefore be maximally perfect in the sense that it is the most perfect possible reality.

This conclusion isn't certain, and some philosophers doubt it. They grant that an appropriate object of ultimate concern must be greater than other *existing* beings. If it weren't, it wouldn't be ultimate. If another existing being was greater, our concern, loyalty, and commitment should be directed toward *it*. Suppose, though, that a being *is* greater than other existing beings, that it created heaven and earth, and is perfectly righteous. Suppose also that its power and knowledge are vastly greater than that of other existing beings although not as great as they could possibly be. While such a being would be the most perfect existing reality, it wouldn't be the most perfect possible reality. For we can conceive of something greater—a perfectly righteous creator of heaven and earth with *unlimited* power and knowledge. But isn't a most perfect existing reality of this kind an appropriate object of ultimate concern? It surely isn't *morally* wrong to worship it. Nor does it seem unfitting to totally commit ourselves to it, making it the object of our ultimate loyalty.

This is a plausible objection. Nevertheless, two things suggest that a *fully* appropriate object of ultimate concern must be the greatest possible reality.

Suppose a being has many perfections and is greater than other existing beings but that we can conceive of something greater. If the second being *had* existed, we ought to have given ourselves to *it* rather than the first. If we admit this, however, can we say that our commitment to the first is totally unreserved? Wouldn't this be like saying, "I love her unreservedly, but I might have met someone more beautiful and affectionate and, if I had, I would have loved her instead"? If one's love depends on not having met someone more loveable, is it truly unreserved? Similarly, is one's commitment to something unreserved if it depends on there not having been something more perfect?

The second point is this. Ultimate concern includes a number of attitudes—love, loyalty, and commitment but also reverence, awe, and admiration. Each is unreserved. Suppose something is greater than other existing beings but less great than some possible being. Even if unreserved love, loyalty, and commitment are appropriate, are unreserved reverence, awe, and admiration appropriate? Not clearly. I don't *unreservedly* admire a painting or a ball player if I think it would be possible for a painting or ball player to be better. Do I, then, unreservedly admire a being if I think a better being might have existed?

There are thus reasons for thinking that an appropriate object of ultimate concern must be *maximally* perfect. Classical Western theology has usually thought of God in this way. The issue is, however, controversial. . . .

Is the Concept of a Maximally Perfect Reality Coherent?

Critics sometimes argue that the concept of a maximally perfect reality is incoherent. If it is, then a maximally perfect reality isn't possible: either the object of the religious attitudes of Christians, Buddhists, and others doesn't exist, or it could be more perfect than it is.

There are three reasons for thinking that the concept is incoherent. Some critics argue that there are no standards in relation to which something could be said to be more perfect than everything else. Others contend that a maximally perfect reality would have logically incompatible properties. Still others maintain that some perfections have no maximum. According to them, the concept of a maximally perfect reality is ill-formed like the concept of the largest possible number or the longest possible line.

THE LACK OF STANDARDS

Charles Crittendon (1933–) puts the first objection in this way: "Normally when we say that something is 'greatest,' 'best,' 'most perfect,' etc., we mean greatest of *a given kind:* greatest symphony, best tennis player . . . most perfect likeness. The kind in question dictates which characteristics count for or against something's being greater, better, more perfect than something else. . . . [Thus] the best ball point pen would be one which smudges least, lasts longest, looks nicest, and so on; the best tennis player would be the one who wins the most important matches or something of the kind." But while one ball point pen or tennis player can be better than another, it makes no sense to say that my ball point pen is better than the winner of Wimbledon. There is no class that includes both within which meaningful comparisons could be made. If I were to say that my ball point pen is better than the winner of Wimbledon, I would invite the question "A better what?" There is no clear answer to this question. Comparisons presuppose standards, and standards are possible only when there is a common class within which things can be ranked as better or worse.

Just as there is no significant class of comparison that includes ball point pens and tennis players, there is no significant class of comparison that includes everything. To say that something is as good as, or better than, everything else is thus nonsense. The notion of a reality that nothing surpasses is therefore incoherent.

This objection rests on a mistake. That some reality, *x,* is at least as perfect as every other possible reality does not entail that there is a class of comparison within which everything can be ranked. What *is* entailed is that, for every other possible reality, *y,* there are classes of comparison that include both *x* and *y;* and in each of these *x* ranks at least as highly as *y.* This can be true even if there is no *single* class within which *x* can be compared with everything else. For example, God might be more perfect than other minds in virtue of His greater wisdom and righteousness and might be more perfect than material objects in virtue of features like greater power, permanence, and beauty. If God is maximally perfect, then (1) every possible reality can be compared with God in *some* respect and (2) no possible reality is better than God in *any* respect. This does not imply that God is better than everything else in the *same* respect and thus doesn't imply that God and everything else can be included in a common class of comparison.

THE INCOMPATIBILITY OF SOME PERFECTIONS

The second objection hinges on the fact that some perfections are logically incompatible. Immutability is the property something has if it cannot change in any respect. Incorporeality is the property of being bodiless. Both properties have been traditionally regarded as perfections, and both are incompatible with such perfections as being able to dance or play tennis well.

Why does this create a problem? A maximally perfect reality is sometimes described as a being that possesses all perfections. If some perfections are incompatible, then no possible being has all of them. Hence, no possible being is maximally perfect. There are two ways of responding to this objection.

First Response

One can distinguish between imperfections, "mixed" perfections, and "pure" perfections. Some imperfections are defects like blindness or unrighteousness. Others are limitations such as our inability to lift stones over a certain weight or the fact that our knowledge of the world can only be acquired piece by piece through time-consuming and difficult investigations. These properties are not defects since the fact that we are limited in these ways doesn't imply that we are imperfect specimens of humanity. Their possession does, however, imply that the human species is less perfect in these respects than are other species of being whose members could lift stones of any tonnage or whose knowledge of the world is intuitive and complete.

A mixed perfection is a property that makes something better but implies some defect or limitation. Repentance, for example, implies a defect (the moral failure that one repents). Being human or being corporeal implies limitations (susceptibility to physical damage, for example). A pure perfection, on the other hand, is a perfection that does not entail a defect or limitation. Being or actuality, goodness, love, power, knowledge, unity, and independence are sometimes mentioned as examples.

While theists have sometimes characterized a maximally perfect reality as a reality that possesses *every* perfection, they have implicitly meant "every *pure* perfection." Even if some perfections are mutually incompatible, pure perfections may be consistent with one another. If they are, the properties of a maximally perfect reality are mutually compatible.

Second Response

The concept of a maximally perfect reality is designed to pick out a *possible* reality that is at least as good as any other possible reality. If some perfections are incompatible, then a reality that possesses *all* perfections is not a *possible* reality and is thus not maximally perfect reality. A maximally perfect reality would possess a set of mutually consistent perfections that are as good as, or better than, any other set of mutually consistent perfections. However, it would not possess *all* perfections if there are some that are incompatible.

Both responses reject the assumption upon which the objection was based (that a maximally perfect reality must have all perfections). The first response insists that a maximally perfect reality need only have all *pure* perfections. The second insists that all that is needed is that it have an unsurpassable set of *mutually compatible* perfections.

THE LACK OF INTRINSIC MAXIMA

The third problem is created by the fact that certain perfections seem to lack "intrinsic maxima" (upper limits). Some properties admit of degrees and some do not. The sky can be more or less cloudy, but a tree can't be more or less of a maple. A day can be more or less hot, but it cannot be more or less in July. Some "degreed properties" have intrinsic maxima and others do not. Being cloudy, for example, has an upper limit (being completely cloudy). Being large, on the other hand, is a degreed property that does not have an upper limit. No matter how large an object is, it is logically possible that something can be larger.

Many of the perfections that have been ascribed to a maximally perfect reality are degreed properties—for example, knowledge, power, righteousness, love, and happiness. One being can know more than another, or be more powerful, and so on. Some of these appear to have intrinsic maxima. The knowledge of every true proposition or the power to bring about every contingent state of affairs may be the intrinsic maxima of knowledge and power respectively. Perhaps, too, nothing could be more righteous than a being whose dispositions and behavior never deviate from the appropriate moral standards—who is, for example, perfectly truthful, just, and faithful. Happiness, however, seems to lack an intrinsic maximum. No matter how happy a being is, it seems possible for it (or some other being) to be even happier.

The problem, then, is this. Most religions believe that a maximally perfect reality would be happy. But happiness doesn't seem to have an intrinsic maximum. Their notion of a maximally perfect reality is therefore incoherent. Why is this the case? To be maximally perfect, a thing must be happy. But happiness has no upper limit. Hence, it is possible that the maximally perfect reality, or some other thing, be even happier and thus more perfect in that respect. This statement is incoherent. It is impossible for something to be *more* perfect than a thing that is *maximally* perfect (as perfect as anything could possibly be). Two responses are again possible.

First Response

One might deny that happiness has no intrinsic maximum. Theists, for example, have traditionally believed that God's happiness consists in the possession and enjoyment of the highest good (namely, Himself). That is, God's happiness consists in His delight in His own nature, activity, and splendor. Perhaps a happiness of this kind could not be surpassed.

Second Response

One might also respond to the objection by adopting a suggestion made by Charles Hartshorne (1897–). Hartshorne argues that a maximally perfect reality should be understood as a reality that (1) cannot be surpassed with respect to properties which have maxima and (2) with respect to properties which do not have maxima, can only be surpassed by itself. Suppose, for example, that a maximally perfect reality would be powerful and joyous. Since power has a maximum, it would possess it. It would thus be impossible for anything to be more powerful. On the other hand, if there really is no upper limit to happiness, its happiness cannot be maximal. Nevertheless, because it is maximally perfect, its joy is so intense that even though *it* could be still happier, its joy could not be surpassed by the joy of any *other* possible being.

CONCLUSION

If our discussion has been sound, then the concept of a maximally perfect reality is probably coherent. It is not, however, sufficient to determine our understanding of divine reality, for the concept doesn't tell us precisely *what* properties a maximally perfect reality would have. It does provide some direction. If a property (1) is a perfection and (2) no equal or greater perfection is incompatible with it, then a maximally perfect reality would presumably have it. Nevertheless, it may be difficult to determine whether these conditions are met in particular cases. For example, whether immutability should be ascribed to a maximally perfect reality depends upon whether change is an imperfection. It also depends upon whether immutability is compatible with such perfections as creative activity.

The remainder of this chapter will examine problems that arise when one attempts to determine precisely what properties a maximally perfect reality would have.

Is a Perfect Reality Personal?

The difficulties in ascribing properties to a maximally perfect reality can be illustrated by considering the fundamental question of whether such a reality is personal or nonpersonal. Theists believe that, even though ultimate reality transcends all finite realities, it is more like a person than anything else. That is, they believe that ultimate reality should be understood as God—an infinitely wise, good, and powerful ruler of heaven and earth. Many important religious traditions, however, are nontheistic—for example, Advaita Vedānta and Buddhism. These traditions believe that ultimate reality is impersonal. They don't think of it as a god.

Advaita Vedānta's rejection of theism is a consequence of its emphasis upon ultimate reality's unity and incomprehensibility. Advaita believes that Brahman (the first principle) is an absolute unity. "Brahman is without parts or attributes . . . one without a second. In Brahman there is no diversity whatsoever." "All difference in Brahman is unreal."

The Brahman contains no plurality and transcends every distinction. It thus has no properties. Why is this the case? If the Brahman had properties, we could *distinguish* between the

Brahman and its properties. This would be incompatible with its absolute unity. But since Brahman has no properties and since we can only understand things by grasping their properties, it is incomprehensible. "It is the reality beyond all thought . . . outside the range of any mental conception."

If ultimate reality transcends *all* properties, it transcends the property of being a person. However, even if the Brahman is not *literally* a person, it might be more like a person than anything else. Why, then, does Advaita reject theism?

Persons are rational agents—beings who have beliefs about themselves and the world and act on the basis of their beliefs. Believing and willing are essential to personhood. The major theistic traditions, accordingly, describe ultimate reality as an omniscient mind and an omnipotent and active will. Advaita Vedānta is nontheistic because its emphasis upon the divine unity leads it to deny that Brahman is either a knower or a causal agent.

Knowledge presupposes a distinction between the knower and what it knows. Advaita concludes that the first principle is beyond thought and cognition. Even self-knowledge involves a distinction between the self as knower and the self as known and is therefore incompatible with the Brahman's unity. Hence, "all specific cognition such as seeing, and so on, is absent."

Why can't the Brahman be a causal agent? If the Brahman is maximally perfect, it must be unlimited. It is limited, however, if something exists outside it. The Brahman must therefore be identical with the whole of reality. But if the Brahman is identical with the whole of reality and if the Brahman contains no plurality, then reality as a whole must be an undifferentiated unity. The space-time world, with its distinctions between times, places, and events, is therefore unreal. Since a real causal relation is a relation between two real things, Brahman is not the cause of the space-time world or the events in it. The Brahman is thus neither the world's creator nor its ruler. "The Lord's being a Lord, his omniscience, his omnipotence, etc., all depend on . . . ignorance; while in reality none of these qualities belong to the Self [Brahman]. . . . In reality the relation of ruler and ruled [creator and created], does not exist." The Brahman is the "ground" of the world, but only in the sense that it is the real thing upon which people project the illusion of spatio-temporal reality. (This is compared with the way in which a person who mistakes a rope for a snake projects the illusory idea of the snake onto the rope.)

Advaita does, however, contain what one might call "theistic elements." It describes Brahman as infinite, joyous consciousness (although the consciousness has no objects or contents and is thus "empty"). Advaita also admits that the idea of an omniscient and omnipotent cause of the space-time world is superior to most conceptualizations of ultimate reality—though, like all conceptualizations, it too must be transcended.

Nevertheless, because Advaita refuses to ascribe either knowledge or activity to ultimate reality, it is essentially nontheistic. The maximally perfect reality is not the God of the theistic traditions—all powerful, all knowing, all loving, the ruler of heaven and earth. It is, rather, an "infinite ocean" of empty, joyous consciousness—impersonal, inactive, and anonymous. Brahman is "pure consciousness and infinite bliss"—"beyond all attributes, beyond action."

Some nontheistic traditions are devoid of theistic elements. According to Hīnayāna Buddhism, a person is simply a collection of interrelated experiences and body states called "dharmas." The dharmas are causally conditioned and transient. (They last for at most a few moments.) Consciousness is as conditioned and impermanent as the other dharmas. Furthermore, the realm of the transient and causally conditioned is the realm of suffering or unsatisfactoriness (duhka). One cannot therefore construe a maximally perfect reality as a person. To do so would imply that it was impermanent, causally conditioned, and unhappy. Ultimate reality (Nirvāna) is not a substance, it is not conscious, and it does not act. It is more like a transcendent place or state than a transcendent person.

Our discussion illustrates the way in which one's understanding of a maximally perfect real-

ity is determined by one's philosophical ideas, one's evaluations, and (as we shall see) one's interpretation of religious attitudes and experiences.

For example, we have seen how Advaita's emphasis upon the idea of absolute unity and Buddhism's analysis of personhood lead them to reject theism. One's evaluations are also important. Traditional thought places a high value on unity, permanence, and stability and a correspondingly low value on plurality, impermanence, and change. Persons appear to be complex, changing realities. An emphasis upon the values of unity, permanence, and stability may therefore lead one to deny that ultimate reality should be understood as a person.

These ideas and evaluations, however, are controversial. The Buddhist's analysis of personhood may be unable to account for the self's unity. Classical theists argue that God's unity, permanence, and stability do not entail impersonality. Some modern theists place a high value on change and complexity and ascribe them to the first principle. They believe, for example, that God's knowledge grows progressively richer and that He changes in response to His creatures.

One's understanding of the nature of a maximally perfect reality will also be influenced by one's attitude toward certain religious experiences. For example, Advaita Vedānta places a high value on "monistic mystical consciousness"—a joyous state of consciousness in which the mind is emptied of its contents and distinctions disappear. . . . Advaita privileges this experience and treats it as a model of the unifying and transfiguring knowledge (jnāna) that is the goal of the religious quest. It is thus not surprising that Advaita views the appropriate object of religious attitudes as "one without distinctions"—neither a knower nor a doer and hence not a god.

But other types of religious experience have different implications. . . . some of these experiences seem to have a person as their object. An emphasis upon them usually leads to theistic interpretations of maximal perfection.

Even the basic claim that a maximally perfect reality is a kind of person is thus subject to dispute. Let us assume, however, that the dispute has been resolved in favor of theism and turn to problems connected with three perfections traditionally ascribed to God—impassibility, omnipotence, and omniscience. Examining these problems will further illustrate the difficulties involved in working out the implications of the concept of a maximally perfect reality.

Suggestions for Further Reading

Afnan, Soheil Muhsin. *Avicenna, His Life and Works.* London: George Allen & Unwin, 1958.

Al-Ghazzali. *The Foundations of the Articles of Faith.* Translated by Nabih Amin Faris. Lahore, Pakistan: Sh. Muhammad Ashraf, 1969.

Armstrong, Karen, *A History of God: The 4000-Year Quest of Judaism, Christianity and Islam.* New York: Knopf, 1994.

Carter, Robert E. *The Nothingness Beyond God: An Introduction to the Philosophy of Mishida Kitaro.* New York: Paragon House, 1989.

Christ, Carol P. "Why Women Need the Goddess: Phenomenological, Psychological, and Political Reflections." In *Womanspirit Rising,* edited by Carol P. Christ and Judith Plaskow. New York: HarperCollins, 1979.

Cobb, Jr., John B. *Beyond Dialogue: Toward a Mutual Transformation of Christianity and Buddhism.* Philadelphia, PA: Fortress Press, 1982.

Creel, Harrlee G. *What Is Taoism?* Chicago: University of Chicago Press, 1970.

Daly, Mary. *Beyond God the Father.* Boston: Beacon Press, 1973.

Deutsch, Eliot. *Advaita Vedanta: A Philosophical Reconstruction.* Honolulu: East-West Center Press, 1969.

Deutsch, Eliot, and van Buitenen, J.A.B., eds. *A Source Book of Advaita Vedanta.* Honolulu: The University Press of Hawaii, 1971.

Eckel, Malcolm. *To See the Buddha: A Philosopher's Quest for the Meaning of Emptiness.* San Francisco: HarperCollins, 1992.

Fakhry, Majid. *A History of Islamic Philosophy.* New York: Columbia University Press, 1970.

Graham, A.C. *Disputers of the Tao: Philosophical Argument in Ancient China.* LaSalle, IL: Open Court, 1989.

Hartshorne, Charles. *The Divine Relativity.* New Haven, CT: Yale University Press, 1948.

Jayatilleke, K.N. *The Message of the Buddha.* New York: The Free Press, 1975.

Lafargue, Michael. *The Tao of the Tao Te Ching: A Translation and Commentary.* Albany: State University of New York Press, 1992.

McFague, Sallie. *Models of God: Theology for an Ecological, Nuclear Age.* Philadelphia, PA: Fortress Press, 1987.

Morewedge, Parviz, ed. *Islamic Philosophical Theology.* Albany, NY: State University of New York Press, 1979.

Nozick, Robert. "The Nature of God, The Nature of Faith." In *The Examined Life.* New York: Simon and Schuster, 1989.

Owen, H.P. *Concepts of Deity.* New York: Herder and Herder, 1971.

Sharma, Arvind. *The Philosophy of Religion and Advaita Vedanta: A Comparative Study in Religion and Reason.* University Park, PA: The Pennsylvania State University Press, 1995.

Sontag, Fredrick. *Divine Perfection: Possible Ideas of God.* New York: Harper and Brothers, 1962.

Sontag, Fredrick, and Bryant, M. Darrol, eds. *God: The Contemporary Discussion.* New York: The Rose of Sharon Press, 1982.

Welbon, Guy Richard. *The Buddhist Nirvana and Its Western Interpreters.* Chicago, IL: The University of Chicago Press, 1968.

The Provision of Meaning and Belonging

Religion represents an important tie between the individual and the larger social group, both as a **basis of association** and as an **expression of shared meanings.** In this chapter, we examine the provision of meaning for the individual and the larger social group. This provision of meaning is linked with the communal aspect of religion; a community of believers maintains a meaning system and mediates it to the individual. The religious processes described in this chapter are interesting in themselves, but we must ask the broader question: *What does our understanding of religion tell us about society itself?* Comprehending how the individual and the larger social group are linked in a community of shared meanings is important for the larger issue of how society is possible.

On a Monday morning in late March, 1997, my Sociology of Religion class wanted to understand "Why?": Why had a religious group of 39 people, ranging in age from 26 to 72, committed suicide together? Early news reports referred to the expectation of the End of Time, to hopes of escaping through a temporary "Heaven's Gate," to portents in the Hale-Bopp comet and UFOs, and to a group Web site with elaborate graphics of their imagined life "on the Next Level." Ever the sociologist, I reminded my class that, before we jumped to conclusions, we needed to wait for serious scholarly study of the group's consciously produced written and videotaped "record." Also, we should not be too quick to presume that all group suicides can be explained as simply a bunch of psychologically disturbed individuals who led each other down a twisted, crazy path. Indeed, news reports suggested that some of the young men and women in the "Heaven's Gate" group were not very different from ordinary university students. With as little as we knew about them, what could we understand about how their group's system of meaning and patterns of belonging contributed to the decision to commit suicide together?

We turned to this textbook (then in the fourth edition) and reviewed the parts of Chapters 2 and 3 that address these very issues:

- How do religious meanings help the individual and the group make "sense" of their lives?

- What happens to cause a "crisis of meaning"?

- What elements of this group's belief system—such as its fascination with UFOs, comets, and the millennium—are tied to the meaning-giving function of religion?[1]

- Are there other elements, such as a world image of warring forces of Good and Evil, that this group has in common with other millenarian social movements? And how do those beliefs give meaning and a sense of order to adherents' lives?

- How are these meanings linked with members' self-identities?

- What aspects of the group's way of life (such as their apparently monastic and celibate lifestyle, their relationship to their leader, and their intense involvement with the Internet) promoted a sense of belonging and commitment that could lead even to suicide?

- In what ways is this seemingly bizarre religious group not so different from other highly committed religious groups?[2]

RELIGION AND SYSTEMS OF MEANING

The capacity of religion to provide meaning for human experience has been a major theme in the sociology of religion since its early emphasis in the works of Weber (1958a). **Meaning** refers to the interpretation of situations and events in terms of some broader frame of reference. For example, the experience of losing one's job is given meaning when it is interpreted as "bad luck," "market forces," "the boss is trying to get rid of pro-union workers," "ethnic discrimination," or "God's will." As this example shows, meaning here refers to ordinary, everyday interpretations of experience. Sometimes meaning is expressed in grand, theoretical terms, such as elaborate theories of meaning formulated by philosophers and theologians. Most of what is meaningful to people in their everyday lives, however, is less complex.

---

1. Incidentally, early studies of the group, which only later referred to "Heaven's Gate," were specifically cited on pp. 45, 78, and 163 of the fourth edition, published only months before the group's suicide.

2 See Lingeman and Sorel, 1997, for clever humor on this point—a tongue-in-cheek guide to distinguishing a cult from a true religion.

Have you ever tried to write your autobiography? The ways in which you interpret your experiences and the events, persons, and experiences you choose to remember, as well as how you explain them, reflect the meanings you apply to events in your own life. This chapter discusses how that kind of meaning is attached to individual and social life.

People typically choose their personal meaning from a larger, socially available meaning system. Although the parts that constitute this personal meaning system are all interrelated, they are not necessarily coherent or internally consistent. People may believe in the idea of germs and in the seemingly contradictory idea of evil spirits as explanations for illness. They may simply use the concept of germs to interpret some illnesses and evil spirits to explain others.

Most historical religions are comprehensive meaning systems that locate all experiences of the individual and social group in a single general explanatory arrangement. A comprehensive meaning system such as these is called a **worldview** (Berger and Luckmann, 1966). We will use the concepts of "religious worldview" and "religious meaning system" more or less interchangeably because most historical religious meaning systems have been comprehensive. Nevertheless, in modern society, religious meaning systems compete with many other worldviews. Individuals are less likely to use any single comprehensive meaning system but may apply religious meanings to segments of their lives. For example, some meaning systems (e.g., astrology) explain only certain spheres of their adherents' lives, and believers find other meanings elsewhere.

According to some sociological definitions of religion (especially functional definitions, described in Chapter 1), *any* comprehensive meaning system is fundamentally religious, regardless of its content. For the purposes of this discussion, however, it is sufficient to say that comprehensive meaning systems that are not overtly religious (e.g., psychotherapeutic or political meaning systems) share most characteristics of specifically religious meaning systems. The process of conversion from one comprehensive meaning system to another is comparable, regardless of the belief content of either meaning system. We must also keep in mind that meaning systems are not abstract but are created and held by people.

According to Peter Berger (1967), the provision of meaning is particularly important for an understanding of religion because of the ways that meaning links the individual with the larger social group. *Meaning is not inherent in a situation, but is bestowed.* A person could interpret an event, such as losing one's job, by applying a wide variety of possible meanings. Although the individual may examine the event itself for clues about which meaning "fits" best, the final choice of meaning is *applied* to the event. The person fired might conclude that, although the boss cited uncooperative attitudes, the "real" meaning of the event points to a greater mission as an organizer of workers elsewhere. The experience is given meaning by this choice of interpretations. Attaching meaning to events is a human process (Berger, 1967:19).

Geertz (1966:40) suggests that religion serves as a template in establishing meaning. It not only interprets reality but also shapes it. The template of religion "fits" experiences of everyday life and "makes sense" of them; in turn, this meaning shapes the experiences themselves and orients the individual's actions.

A meaning system in which Satan is prominent can explain past events and experiences (e.g., temptation or illness) as evidence of Satan's effects and can shape future experiences (e.g., by warning believers to avoid certain places or activities where Satan is likely to ensnare them).

By examining how this meaning-giving process occurs, we can understand some of the ways religion links the individual with the larger social group.

Meaning for the Social Group

Meaning systems interpret an entire group's existence. Thus, the group's ways of doing things and its very existence are assigned meaning. The group, for example, may explain its moral norms as instituted by its god; its pattern of family life may be interpreted as copying the family of the gods; and its history may become meaningful as the story of the gods' relationship with their people. As Berger (1967:29–33) points out, the meaning system is both *explanatory* and *normative*; that is, it explains why things are the way they are and prescribes how things should be. The meaning system of the group "makes sense" of its **social order**—the present/existing and future/desired social arrangements of a group, such as its form of authority and power, its stratification system and allocation of roles, its distribution of resources and rewards, and so on. These qualities make the meaning system a strong legitimation for the social order of the group.

A **legitimation** is any form of socially established explanation that is given to justify a course of action. Legitimations include any explanation of social practices: Why do we do things this way? Why should we behave according to that norm? Why do we have this position in society? Particularly important are those legitimations that establish authority in the group (Berger, 1967:29ff.).

Legitimations are expressed in a wide variety of forms. Myths, legends, proverbs, folktales, and history are all invoked to justify certain social arrangements. Taken together, these legitimations may be viewed as the "story" out of which a group lives. These examples show that legitimations are seldom intellectual in form. Intellectual legitimations, such as those developed in philosophy, theology, and political and economic theory, are a highly specialized form of legitimation. Nonintellectual forms are far more common.

The Hindu creation myth in Box 2.1 used potent imagery of the functions and value of parts of the Creator's body to explain the human social structure, to justify the privileges of the higher classes, and to prescribe appropriate behavior of all social groups. The myth itself exemplifies a nonintellectual form of legitimation, but complex intellectual ideologies and legal codes were also eventually developed to justify the Hindu caste system.

Legitimations explain the ways in which the social group has behaved, but they also shape future action by justifying norms for appropriate or desirable action. Religious legitimations make especially strong claims for the bases of order and authority and for the specific arrangements of the social order by their references to a higher authority. Thus, *the social order is represented as more than human convention.* The European idea of the "divine right of kings," for example,

---

BOX 2.1   Cross-Cultural Comparison: Myth as Legitimation

In India, the ancient Hindu myth of four *varnas* legitimated the division of labor and subsequent rigid social class system developed by the thirteenth century (and continued well into the twentieth century). According to this myth, the highest social group, the Brahmins, issued from the mouth of the Creator. Duties assigned them by the Creator included various religious functions, study, teaching, sacrifice, almsgiving, and the perpetuation of the sacred literature. The next were Kshatryas, who were born from the arms of the Creator. Their special gift was power, and their duties included fighting and governing. From the thighs of the Creator came the Vaishyas, who were given the gift of strength; they were expected to cultivate the land and engage in other productive labor. The lowest social group, the Sudras, came from the Creator's feet. Theirs was the duty of serving the other three varnas (Lemercinier, 1981:164).

■ How does a creation myth legitimate moral norms and laws?
■ What are some myths in your own culture that have been used to legitimate social privileges?
■ How can religious traditions change, for example, toward an egalitarian society?

---

implied that the king ruled not merely as a political arrangement but as a permanent, God-given right. Contemporary examples of social arrangements that are religiously legitimated include the sanctity of marriage, the right to own and defend property, and the moral rightness of waging certain kinds of war.

The effectiveness of these legitimations often involves a certain amount of *mystification* (Berger, 1967:90). Anything suggesting that the social arrangements are purely human convention is allowed to be forgotten or is deliberately masked. The recent way of doing things is promoted as the "authentic tradition," and contrary evidence is not emphasized in the group's tale of its own history. For example, the Christian ideal of the institution of marriage is often represented as being exactly the ideal held during the whole history of Christianity. Actually, however, both the ideals and practices of marriage have changed considerably, and current religiously legitimated arrangements, such as the practice of church weddings, are relatively recent. The effectiveness of legitimations of present-day marriage practices depends on treating these practices as traditional and on forgetting or de-emphasizing those parts of history that are inconsistent with present norms and practices.

Although religious legitimations are generally used to justify existing social arrangements, they are also potent forms of criticism of the existing social order, as Chapter 7 shows in some detail. The Old Testament prophet Amos legitimated his denunciation of people's ways by reference to their God. Religious legitimations may be invoked to justify even revolutionary action. Thus, religious legitimations are not solely a tool of the dominant group but may justify actions of subordinate and dissenting groups as well.

> **BOX 2.2 Historical Perspective: The Invention of Church Weddings**
>
> The early Christian churches were ambivalent about marriage; some early church leaders thought that the ideal for committed Christians was celibacy or even castration, with a chaste marriage (i.e., without any sexual activity) as an accommodation for those who could not meet the difficult ideal (Bullough, 1982; Elliott, 1993). Until the sixteenth and seventeenth centuries, ordinary people typically wed by private self-marriage (later formalized as "common-law" marriage). Not until the sixteenth century was there a church prohibition of the practice of concubinage (Brundage, 1982). For most people, self-marriage was an acceptable pattern through the Middle Ages, though couples sometimes went to the church steps for a blessing. Only in the sixteenth century was church marriage declared a sacrament, but during the subsequent Reformation, many Protestant groups denied that marriage was a sacrament. Most Protestant groups did, however, keep the practice of church weddings, and they developed their own rituals for these ceremonies.
>
> - Why are some people disappointed to learn that Christians have not always had a tradition of church weddings?
> - Why are we surprised (or even shocked) that many early church leaders urged celibacy or even castration as a religious ideal?
> - Does knowing about how much a religious tradition has changed in history make you think differently about future changes?

The Individual's Meaning System

The individual does not construct a personal meaning system from nothing. An individual's meaning system is learned, for the most part, during the process of socialization. The interpretations that seem most plausible to a person are likely to be those that are familiar and held by others who are important to that individual. So although each individual operates with a highly personal meaning system, that set of meanings is greatly influenced by family, friends, institutions (e.g., education), and the larger society. Although the individual comes to accept some of the meanings communicated during socialization, the resulting meaning system is not an inevitable product of socialization. The individual can reject or modify meanings communicated by others. When several competing meaning systems are presented as alternatives (which happens especially in modern society), the individual can choose which meanings to accept. The individual may accept the meaning system presented by a subgroup in society, and not that of the larger society. Yet all personal meaning systems gain effectiveness by their link with some community in which they are shared.

Meaning and self-identity are intertwined. People locate themselves and their personal actions in a larger social order by means of their meaning systems. The individual selects subjectively meaningful interpretations of events and experiences from the larger interpretive scheme provided by the meaning system, and that personally held meaning system informs the individual's sense of self. The applied meaning system tells the individual what "kind" of person one is, the importance of the roles that one performs, the purpose of the events in which one participates, and the significance of being who one is. A meaning system, in other words, makes sense of one's identity and social being. Some societies emphasize subjective choice of meanings, while others take for granted group meanings, but all meaning systems are based on an intersection of self and social group.

People can bestow meaning on a situation in various ways. Beliefs are important in this process. Ideas can help locate an experience in a meaning system, but a meaning system cannot be reduced to its formal belief content. Miracles, magic, ritual, and symbols also contribute to a pervasive sense of meaning. The individual can apply meaning to a situation by performing an appropriate ritual for the event. Ritual practices and other religious actions, such as sharing a ritual meal, are ways by which the individual may subjectively—often bodily, as well as emotionally and mentally—experience social meanings. Similarly, by interpreting an event as miraculous or magical, the individual places special meaning on it. The application of meaning to human experience entails social processes. Through everyday conversation, the individual tries out interpretations of experiences. Interaction with others—especially with persons whose response "counts" to the individual—is a significant part of the process of bestowing meaning on a situation.

At the same time, the meaning system informs the individual of the values and norms of the larger group. The following interpretive statements illustrate the variety of ways in which norms and values can be embodied in a meaning system:

"Cleanliness is next to godliness."

"Masturbation is likely to lead to insanity."

"People who commit adultery will be punished by God."

"He brought his illness on himself by his bitter and hateful outlook on life."

"Hard work and patience are always rewarded."

Even though you may personally disagree with some or all of these statements, you can see how each statement can be used to *interpret* situations or experiences and to *evaluate* general kinds of behavior. Meaning systems embody *norms*—social evaluations of behavior. To the extent that one applies these normative interpretations to one's own behavior, the meaning system brings an evaluative element to one's identity. Thus, in terms of the interpretive framework, one may conclude: "I am a sinner," "I am a good mother," "I am a successful warrior," "I am ill-fated," or "I am a virtuous person."

The individual's meaning system makes possible the evaluation of past actions and the motivation of future actions. The ability to perceive events as ordered in some way enables one to plan and orient one's actions. If things are experienced as "just happening" in a chaotic, meaningless string of events, the person literally does not know what to do. If, however, these events are given meaning, their interpretation implies an appropriate course of action (even if that action consists in seemingly passive responses such as "suffering through it" or "praying over it"). By relating mundane social life to the realm of the transcendent, religion is particularly effective in motivating the individual's participation in the larger social group. The classic example of such motivation is the concept of *vocation,* the idea that one is "called" to an occupational or economic status by God. This idea gives special meaning to everyday work. By understanding such work in terms of vocation, individuals gain a sense of purpose and value to their labor, and society gains the willing contribution of its members (see Weber, 1958a:Chapter 3).

Both the individual and the social group draw on religion to give meaning to their existences. The meaning system provides interpretation for their experiences, locating human lives and events in terms of a larger framework. Religion also serves as an important form of legitimation, or justification, for both the individual and the social order. Religion interprets and evaluates the "way things are to be done" in the social group. These legitimations provide meaning for individual members of the group who accept these explanations and incorporate them into their ways of thinking about the world.

Nevertheless, we should not assume an overly intellectualized image of humans. Although a strong case can be made that meaning is a fundamental social requirement (Luckmann, 1967; see also Berger, 1967), we must keep in mind that all people do not necessarily equally desire to find meaning for *all* aspects of their lives. Some people are more tolerant than others of inconsistencies in their meaning systems. Some people desire intellectually elaborate systems of meaning; others are satisfied with quite simple views. Furthermore, meaning does not operate only at a cognitive level; for many people, ritual practice and religious experience effectively sustain the meaningfulness of their lives. Yet historical religions and quasi-religions address similar problems of meaning: discrepancies between the ideal and actual practices in the society; personal suffering and death; and group crises such as war, conquest, and natural disasters. By providing meaning in the face of meaning-threatening situations, religion enables the individual or group to cope with the situation. If the meaning-threatening situation can be successfully reintegrated into the group's sense of order, social life can continue.

CRISIS OF MEANING

The meaning system of the individual or group can integrate most routine events into an understandable pattern, a meaningful whole. Some events and experiences, however, are not so easily interpreted within the existing meaning system. The individual who experiences the death of a loved one, a painful illness, or serious economic misfortune may not be helped by the existing personal meaning system. An entire group can undergo similar meaning-threatening experiences: oppression by an enemy, famine, earthquake, or economic depression. Such events are particularly meaning-threatening if they appear to contradict important aspects of the existing meaning system. Groups who believe in a loving, personal god have more difficulty reconciling disastrous events with their meaning system than do groups whose god is remote and capricious.

Another situation that creates a problem of meaning is serious discrepancy between the ideal that a group promulgates and the actual practice. Inequality and injustice can be especially meaning-threatening when they are inconsistent with the group's ideals. Because the threat of the meaninglessness of such events is so great, individuals and groups try to build special legitimations into their meaning systems to justify these apparent contradictions or discrepancies. In other words, part of the meaning system itself interprets events and experiences that would seem to contradict the meaning system. These meanings are responses to the *problem of theodicy* (Weber, 1963:Chapter 9).

Theodicies

Theodicies are religious explanations that provide meaning for meaning-threatening experiences. Most religions, for example, offer theodicies of suffering and death. The content of these explanations differs among the various religions, but the desire to find meaning for such experiences appears virtually universal. Disaster and death create a problem of theodicy not because they are unpleasant, but because they threaten the fundamental assumptions of order underlying society itself (Berger, 1967:24). Theodicies tell the individual or group that the experience is not meaningless but is rather part of a larger system of order. Some successful theodicies are, in fact, nothing but assertions of order. A woman discussing her personal meaning crisis after her husband's premature death said: "I finally came to understand that it didn't matter whether I understood why he died when he did, but that God had a reason for it, and that was all that mattered." For this believer, knowing that an order exists behind events was more important than knowing *what* that order is.

Similarly, theodicies do not necessarily make the believer happy or even promise future happiness. A person suffering poverty and disease may be satisfied with the explanation that the situation has resulted from sins committed by the ancestors. Such an interpretation offers little hope for overcoming the poverty or disease, but it does offer meaning. It answers the question, "Why do I suffer?"

The capability of religion to provide meaning can be illustrated by how a society handles the especially meaning-threatening situation of dying and death. There is an inherent problem of meaning in the prospect of one's own or a loved one's death. Death seems to negate the individual's or group's sense of order. For this reason, the way in which a society handles the process of dying is revealing of its larger meaning system. Long before most individuals face death, their religion has been providing meaning for their various life stages (e.g., by rites of passage into adulthood or by legitimating the norms and prerogatives of old age). In many societies, the meaning system somewhat normalizes dying as a further stage of human development. Some meaning systems affirm an afterlife or a rebirth; others emphasize that people live on through their offspring or tribe.

In American society, dying and death have become particularly meaning-threatening. This problem of meaning partly results from the undermining of traditional theodicies; formerly used explanations have become less satisfying to many persons. The problem of the meaning of death is especially acute in this society because its value system assigns comparatively great worth to individual lives. Numerous social arrangements contribute to the problem. The dying person is typically segregated from one of the foremost meaning-providing social supports—the family. Furthermore, the specialized roles of those tending the dying seldom include the provision of meaning. Unlike their counterparts in traditional medical systems, modern doctors do not generally consider as part of their role helping the patient assign meaning to illness or death (Kleinman, 1988). Death and dying have become generally secularized processes, and the problem of their meaning has become acute.

Anomie

Sometimes a meaning system is completely unable to absorb a crisis experience. The theodicies applied may not be effective in reintegrating the experience into the meaning system, or the group supports of the entire meaning system may be so weakened by the crisis that people are unable to restore a sense of order and meaning. When an individual or group has lost its fundamental sense of meaning and order, ongoing social life becomes virtually impossible. Why should one want to do anything if everything seems senseless? When a meaning system is so weakened, the moral norms it supports are also undermined. And with no underlying order to existence, there is no apparent basis for distinguishing between "right" and "wrong" ways of behaving.

It becomes necessary, if social life is to continue, to establish a new basis of order and a new meaning system. If a group's way of life has been thoroughly disrupted by military conquest, for example, the group might reorganize itself around a social movement (e.g., followers of a new prophet) that offers a new basis of order and meaning for group members. The new meaning system sometimes consists of embracing new meanings (e.g., those of the conquerors) or **nativism**—a reaffirmation of old meanings and traditional ways of symbolizing the group's "native" identity. In the nineteenth century, many U.S. plains tribes adopted a nativistic religion, the Ghost Dance, a highly traditionalistic movement that foresaw the destruction of the white man. Although the movement itself was pacifist, its appeal and potential for uniting diverse tribes frightened the frontier army, culminating in the Battle of Wounded Knee, in which over two hundred men, women, and children were killed (see McNally, 1999; Mooney, 1965). Hopi tradition has a number of millenarian prophecies that are believed to predate the coming of Europeans. These indigenous narratives tell of the return of Maasaw, the spirit who guided the Hopis about how to live on the earth, granting them contingent temporary residence. The prophecies also speak to Maasaw's judgment of both the white and Hopi brothers, addressing culture contact and symbolic meaning for Hopi historical and political experience. These prophecies reaffirm tradition but proffer today's Hopi community in northern Arizona a sense of Hopi identity and destiny (Geertz, 1994).

Probably the most common new basis of meaning is **syncretism**—the interweaving of new meanings with the older meaning system. In colonial Brazil, for example, uprooted, enslaved Africans were allowed to celebrate the *congada*—a symbolic coronation of the King of the Congo, absorbed into the annual Catholic festival of Our Lady of the Rosary, who became patroness of blacks. Several symbolic homologies between Western African religion and Brazilian Catholicism made fertile ground for syncretism (Camara, 1988). Regardless of the source of elements for the new meaning system, its importance lies in its ability to reorganize the basis of order for the group. Social life is given new meaning.

The situation of crisis in the group's meaning and order is described in Durkheim's concept of **anomie** (or *anomy*). The word *anomie* means literally "without order." Durkheim applied this concept to social situations in which there was a deregulation of the public conscience. *Anomie* means a crisis in the moral order of a social group (Durkheim, 1951:246–257; see also Berger, 1967:22ff.). Although anomie has serious consequences for the individual (e.g., it might lead one to suicide), it is primarily a social situation referring to the inability of the social group to provide order and normative regulation for individual members. Religion's capability of providing meaning and order suggests that religion functions as a protection from anomie in two ways: A firm religious basis of order is a buffer against the occurrence of anomie in the first place; and if the group does experience an anomic situation, religion can potently respond to the crisis of moral meanings. Meaning is fundamental to a sense of order—without it, there is chaos. Indeed, Berger suggests that the opposite of "sacred" *is* "chaos." He states, "The sacred cosmos, which transcends and includes man in its ordering of reality, thus provides man's ultimate shield against the terror of anomy" (Berger, 1967:27; see also Geertz, 1966:14).

Although massive disruptions in a group's way of life (e.g., conquest and famine) are obvious starting points of such crises, less dramatic change is more common, and the sense of crisis is less profound. Members of the group may feel only a vague sense of malaise, a discomfort with the way things are going and a general ambiguity about what they as individuals should do. Rapid social change often leaves people unsure about where they "stand." Norms become open; although the old regulations no longer hold, new ones have not been crystallized. Examples of such ambiguities are found in the whole area of gender role expectations in contemporary societies.

Rapid social change is highly threatening to a group's meaning system, because the very *fact* of change undermines many legitimations of the existing social order. It temporarily humanizes the established rules and patterns of interaction by showing them to be changeable products of human convention. Before such change, the group's ways of doing things may have appeared immutable, but the very fact of change belies this perception. In this context, it is possible to understand, for example, the exasperation of a Roman Catholic who, during the period immediately after Vatican II, exclaimed, "How can it be that last year eating meat on Friday was a terrible and grave sin, and this year it is merely an optional and private sacrifice?" Even more threatening are the perceived changes in a social group's fundamental norms and values, such as patterns of family life. Periods of dramatic social change seriously challenge the existing meaning system of a group. Often these periods are marked by the rise of new religious movements that affirm an "improved" meaning system—new, traditional, or syncretic—that addresses the crisis in the moral order.

Some features of contemporary cultures may contribute to the continual sense of crisis of meaning. Some critics suggest that advanced capitalism's **commodification** of culture (i.e., the cultural product of transforming everything human into commodities to be bought and sold in a marketplace) has affected our ability to apply meaning to our experiences. They suggest that this commodification has changed our relationship to time and place and has undermined our sense of shared reality (see Jameson, 1991). How is our sense of meaning and order affected when our experienced "place" in our "world" includes, simultaneously, the "realities" of the mega-mall, the virtual space of computer game simulations, the televised images of the crew on the holodeck of a starship, juxtaposed with "infomercials" using the facade of information-giving to sell products, and the vacation stroll through Epcot center (where imitation villages of various foreign countries are constructed close enough that one can still be hearing the strains of the erstatz "German" oompah band as one arrives at the edge of the fake "medieval" English village)? One member of the Heaven's Gate group (discussed at the beginning of this chapter) described the group's communal sense of time and space before departing for "Beyond Human":

> We watch a lot of Star Trek, a lot of Star Wars; it's just . . . like going on a holodeck . . . now it's time to stop. The game's over. It's time to put into practice what we've learned. We take off the virtual reality helmet . . . go back out of the holodeck to be with . . . the other members of the craft in the heavens. (quoted in Urban, 2000:275)

How is religion's ability to provide meaning affected by commodification of time (e.g., "tradition") and place (e.g., sacred space)? For instance, the seventeenth-century Japanese poet, Basho, made a profoundly religious pilgrimage, on foot, in silence and austerity; contemporary Japanese tourists, however, celebrate Basho's fame by retracing his pilgrimage route traveling by bullet train (Frow, 1997). How is the meaning of their journey affected by the commodification of the travel itself and of the sites?

COMMUNITY AND RELIGIOUS BELONGING

A direct relationship exists between a community of believers and the strength of its shared meaning system. The unity of the group is expressed and enhanced by its shared meanings. The group's meaning system, in turn, depends on the group as its social base for its continued existence and importance. The idea of the "church" (i.e., community of believers) is not merely an organizational feature of religions but expresses a fundamental link between the meaning system and the community that holds it.

Religion as the Expression of Social Unity

Durkheim treated the essentially communal quality of religion as definitive. The collective nature of religion was central to Durkheim's analysis. He concluded that religious rituals and symbols are, at root, representations of the social group. These **collective representations** are the ways by which the group expresses something important about itself to its own members. Thus, by participating in group rituals, individual members renew their link with the group, and they learn and reaffirm shared meanings (Durkheim, 1965:257). We will explore Durkheim's theories of religious belonging further in Chapter 6.

For Durkheim, however, collective representations were not merely mental representations but were also collectively experienced. Thus, shared religious meanings expressed the group's unity, while shared experience produced that unity. Sociology has not developed an adequate understanding of religious experience, in part because the experiential aspect of religion has too often been treated as purely private (Spickard, 1993). An alternative approach, by contrast, suggests that some religious experience may reflect intense *intersubjectivity*. If people can share experiences intersubjectively, valued qualities, such as *communion* (literally, "union with") and *compassion* (literally, "co-feeling") can be experienced as actually—not just figuratively—real.

Plausibility Structures of Meaning

Berger emphasizes that meaning systems require social "bases" for their continued existence. These social bases are called *plausibility structures*—specific social processes or interactions within a network of persons sharing a meaning system. As the term implies, the meaning system continues to be plausible (i.e., believable) within these social structures. Berger asserts that all religious traditions require specific communities of believers for their continuing plausibility (1967:46). A sound plausibility structure allows the meaning system to be held as a common, taken-for-granted entity. Similarly, it strengthens the ability of individuals to believe, for the group gives them social support and reinforcement in their worldview.

Historically, most religious worldviews were coextensive with the societies that held them. Relatively simple societies exemplify especially well the link between the group's meaning system and networks of fellow believers. If one were born and socialized into a remote mountain tribe, for example, the religious meanings and rituals of the group would be taken for granted. Simply belonging to the tribe would make one a part of the religion, and the whole tribe would serve as social support for one's belief and practice. Indeed, it would be difficult for a member isolated in such a tribe to conceive of any other meaning system.

A societywide plausibility structure still exists in many relatively complex societies. In some parts of Latin America, religion is pervasive in all aspects of life, and a single, particular worldview dominates the society. Most people spend their daily lives solely in the company of people who share major elements of their worldview. Such massive social support for shared religious beliefs and practices makes it relatively easy for believers to take them for granted.

The significance of plausibility structures can also be seen in situations where believers of a worldview are separated from the social group that serves as its basis of plausibility. Missionaries typically went out in closely knit bands among the "unbelievers" (i.e., people with a different worldview from their own). This arrangement was not merely for mutual physical protection but, more importantly, for mutual protection of their view of reality (see Cohen, 1990, on how native worldviews influence missionaries). A meaning system shared even with only a few significant others is stronger than one held alone while surrounded by persons who do not share that meaning. In this context, we can appreciate how grave a punishment it was for some societies to exile a member. Exiles were cut off both from other members of the society and from the social support for their meaning system.

Pluralistic societies, by contrast, are characterized by the relatively unrestrained competition of several different meaning systems. Pluralism itself makes the maintenance of a meaning system problematic because it undermines the taken-for-granted quality of any single worldview. In pluralistic situations, each religious group must organize itself to serve as its own plausibility base because the society as a whole does not support its meaning system. Thus, in pluralistic societies such as the United States and Canada, religious groups often emphasize their communal ties, for example, by identifying strongly with an ethnic cultural heritage that sustains both the meaning and belonging aspects of the religious group. In the face of societal pluralism, many religious groups try to create a cultural enclave, characterized by frequent interaction with fellow believers and physical or symbolic withdrawal from the "world" of competing beliefs and values.

By contrast, religious groups that cannot sustain the experience of "belonging" in a pluralistic context may find their members less committed (see Chapter 3). One U.S. study found that "declining community attachment, more so than the erosion of traditional belief per se, is the critical factor in accounting for the declines in church support and participation" (Roof, 1978:136). The pervasiveness of community cultural reality is illustrated by the traditional rural Baptist church in the South, where kinship networks, shared sense of continuity of tradition, and everyday social practices and roles (such as gender roles) serve as plausibility structures for evangelical Christian beliefs and experience (Heriot, 1994). Persons with strong local community identification have a structure of social support to maintain the plausibility of their shared meaning system.

Modern societies, however, are characterized by weakened ties to a local community; urbanization and high levels of geographical mobility disperse families and communities. Increasingly, through mass media, education, and other wider social influences, even nonurban communities are exposed to competing worldviews. When a religious group holds a worldview not supported by the larger society, it must construct its own plausibility structures. Other processes that illustrate the way in which religious belonging supports a meaning system include socialization, conversion, and commitment, discussed further in Chapter 3.

EXTENDED APPLICATION: MILLENARIANISM AND DUALISM IN CONTEMPORARY SOCIAL MOVEMENTS

Many of the concepts presented in this chapter are particularly relevant to an understanding of contemporary meaning systems. The last part of this chapter is an extended example that applies some of these concepts to modern social movements. We begin by noticing certain themes common to many contemporary movements: millenarianism and dualism. What do these themes imply about the movements' responses to problems of meaning? More important, what does the attraction of such movements imply about recruits' relationship to the existing social order? This essay is one interpretation of the significance of millenarianism and dualism in contemporary social movements.[3]

These two themes appear regularly in the worldviews promulgated by many developing religious movements. A **dualistic worldview** holds that reality consists of two irreducible modes—Good versus Evil. **Millenarianism** is the expectation of an imminent collapse of the entire social order and its replacement with a perfect new order. The term is derived from occult Christian predictions that the world would end one thousand years after Jesus' birth. The occurrence and appeal of movements that emphasize these two elements reveal some of the problems of meaning in contemporary society.[4]

---

3. These themes are important indicators about the significance of contemporary social movements, but they are not sufficient explanations; important economic, political, and social structural factors are also involved.

4. Because this essay is presented as an example, it is necessarily somewhat oversimplified. See referenced sources for some of the complexities of interpreting social movements. The essay suggests only that dualistic and millenarian theodicies are effective responses to problems of meaning posed by anomie. That does not mean that these movements are "caused" by anomie. A full explanation of these phenomena would need to show that recruits had experienced anomie. It would also need to analyze the sources of problems of meaning in contemporary society.

These two elements of belief are not merely quaint characteristics of the movements but are central to their appeal. The appeal of the dualistic interpretation of reality and of millennial expectations results from a need for a new, firmer order in a time when the old basis of order appears to be collapsing. The elements of dualism and millenarianism represent the assertion of order in the face of felt disorder.

Two Opposing Principles: Good and Evil

A *dualistic worldview* depicts all reality as consisting of two fundamental modes or opposing principles—one Good and the other Evil. This dualistic perspective is especially important in the belief systems of groups growing from Western religious perspectives (e.g., Islam, Judaism, and especially Christianity). The idea of warring forces of Good and Evil has been recurrent in Christian ideologies, and contemporary expressions of this idea can be traced to enthusiastic religious movements of the sixteenth and seventeenth centuries. Some form of dualism is used by many Christian groups to explain the nature of humankind, the presence of evil, temptation, sin, suffering, and the need for God's help.

Many emerging religious movements particularly emphasize dualistic interpretations of the world (see, for example, Aho, 1990, 1994; Anthony and Robbins, 1997; Barker, 1984; Richardson et al., 1979; Wessinger, 2000a, 2000b; Westley, 1983). Through a new emphasis on mystery, magic, and miracle, believers perceive their world as full of evidence of the action of good and evil forces. Believers experience the world as remystified by the presence of God's spirit; it is also remystified by the presence of Satan in numerous forms. Just as God is influential in their world, so too is Satan immediate and active. Believers see the direct influence of God in the beneficial and pleasant events of their lives; at the same time, they see the Evil One as the source of doubts, temptations, dissension, sickness, and other troubles. This remystification of everyday life is in marked contrast to the usual, more secular interpretation of events.

Some dualistic belief systems identify and personify the forces of Evil in movements, issues, or people that threaten the values of the group. The Heaven's Gate group (described at the beginning of this chapter) explained on their Web site that 2,000 years ago, the Representative from the Kingdom Level Above Human was on earth to tell the civilization how to enter the true Kingdom of God. But he was killed by "humans under control of the adversarial space races" (quoted in Urban, 2000: 280). According to the Web site, in our time:

Where the space aliens have a major stronghold in playing "God" is through those humans with the most power. The power is the strongest among the very rich and the very righteous (their self-styled religion) who accept that it is their ("God-given") responsibility to maintain the world's stability. . . . These *powerful* individuals have a loose-knit worldwide "club" that for the most part dictates who their primary "monopoly" players are—those leaders in the strong societies. (Urban, 2000: 281)

Dualism in the ideology of some Black Muslims identifies the forces of Evil with the white oppressors (Lincoln, 1989). Similarly, various fundamentalist Christian groups identify communism with the forces of Evil (Ammerman, 1991), while neo-Nazi groups consider the "Jewish AntiChrist" to be the principal enemy (Aho, 1994; Lamy, 1997). Another dualistic religious group is the Unification Church of the Reverend Sun Myung Moon, whose belief system holds that the fundamental struggle is between communism and the "God-fearing world" of which the United States is the center (Anthony and Robbins, 1992).

Dualism is also a prominent feature of many religious nationalisms that interpret "our" people as God's people and "their" people as identified with the forces of Evil. In this way, dualism serves as a political ideology. In 1977 one militant Islamic fundamentalist wrote:

> Some people today divide the world into democratic or fascist [systems], labor or liberal parties. Islam does not recognize any parties except two: the Party of God and the Party of Satan. The Party of God are those who act as His agents on earth and govern by His laws. The others are the Party of Satan—whatever variation there may be in their system of government and regardless of the conflict among them. In the end, they are one coalition formed to oppose God the Mighty, the Omnipotent. (quoted in Arjomand, 1989:119–120)

A similar appeal to an apocalyptic dualism appears in the rhetoric of a U.S. neo-Nazi group that refuses to recognize the legitimacy of the U.S. government: "We are engaged in a struggle to the death between the people of the Kingdom of God, and the Kingdom of Satan" (quoted in Lamy, 1996:125).

The cosmic opposition implied in dualism provides a ready explanation for any felt opposition to one's own belief system. Numerous religious movements identify their own beliefs and practices as on the side of Good and decry competing religious movements as on the side of Evil. Often, however, Evil is identified with vague general forces that seem to work against the commitments of the religious group. Thus, one neo-Pentecostal member stated:

> I think Satan does his best. I think it's time we recognized that the power of evil lives in the world and that we as individuals have to cope with the evil that's in the world today. And again that's another thing, another advantage of having a prayer community. It's because we gather together for strength and you sort of get to be invincible in a group. If you try to hit it out on your own, I mean obviously, you just can't with those devils. You just don't stand a ghost of a chance. . . . I do believe that a lot of evil, a lot of sadness and sickness in this world is brought out by Satan. I think it's in his scheme of things to turn us against God. (quoted in McGuire, 1982:150)

The persistence and strength of dualistic beliefs suggest that dualism is not merely one characteristic of these movements but may indeed be central to their appeal.

Dualism as a Response to Anomie Dualistic interpretations are useful to both the group and the individual, especially as a response to anomie, which results in a sense of normlessness and powerlessness. Being out of touch with the source of moral power means being powerless in the face of the nameless terrors of the disordered universe. Only a firm reordering of the social order can provide an effective protection against such terror (Berger, 1967:27). A new order must be established and maintained continually against the occurrence of further order-threatening phenomena. Even a firmly established new order is threatened by occurrences such as suffering and death, which perpetually raise the problems of "meaning" and "order."

A dualistic worldview both provides a framework for the *construction* of a new order and legitimates its *maintenance*. Religious dualism is particularly effective in this reordering because it holds that both the sources of all problems and the "real" solutions to these problems derive from a transcendent realm (see Lofland, 1966:36). Dualism enables believers to name the sources of their anxieties, fears, and problems. This identification is in itself an important source of believers' sense of order and control. Identifying certain difficulties as caused by evil forces also implies a clear-cut course of action. Believers locate their personal courses of action within a cosmic struggle, a continual battle between the forces of Good and the forces of Evil. This identification provides explanations of all events—good and bad—that occur in their lives, and it gives meaning to everyday existence. Even trivial aspects of daily life become part of the order implied in the dualistic worldview.

This order-giving potential of dualism is partly responsible for believers' sense of spiritual opposition. The believer perceives frequent, regular evidence of the immediacy and influence of both good and evil spirits. This evidence, it should be emphasized, is usually in the form of actual events in everyday life. A dualistic worldview contains a built-in tendency to ascribe all good events to God and all bad ones to Satan. The tidiness and order of the dualistic interpretation of the world are part of the basic appeal of such movements. Dualistic figures of ultimate Good and Evil simplify the world to people who are overwhelmed by the ambiguity and complexity of modern life.

In facing the perceived opposition, the group gains cohesion and strength. This sense of opposition is also a useful legitimation for maintaining the new order because it enables believers to see significance in subsequent events, even those that would otherwise threaten their new beliefs. The dualistic worldview heightens the sense that the opposition is a conspiracy against believers and their group (cf. Barkun, 1974, 1994, 1998; Beckford, 1975b; Wessinger, 2000a).

There are two sides to the believer's sense of order. On the "negative" side is a sense of fearsome powers bent on a conspiratorial attack on believers and their values. On the "positive" side, the same sense of order provides the believer with a feeling of harmony and symmetry. Both positive and negative aspects involve the forming of patterns and imposing of a sense of order (Weil, 1973:178–179). The believer's worldview is founded on the expectation that everything is ordered; therefore, order and patterns in the world are subsequently perceived. The "positive" side of this spiritual order can be seen in the believer's constant discovery of "holy coincidence," "providence," and other evidences of the pattern of God's work in everyday life. The dualistic worldview gives form and a "cast of characters" to the patterns that believers perceive in the world around them.

Dualism as Theodicy Dualism also offers the believer an explanatory system for reinterpreting order-threatening events. As such, it functions as a theodicy. The theodicy provides meaning but not necessarily happiness, informing the believer, "You may be miserable, but be comforted that there is, at least, meaning to your suffering."

Dualism is a particularly effective form of theodicy because it is a closed system of legitimation; that is, built into the legitimating system itself is an "explanation" of every argument against the system. Thus, the same theodicy can explain both good and bad events, opposition and confirmation. It also provides a basis for self-justification and for the moral condemnation of others (cf. Rokeach, 1960:69).

Religious groups often use the dualistic theodicy to explain the doubts and uncertainties experienced by new believers: "Your doubts and anxieties are because the devil is trying to confuse and tempt you back to your old way of life." This theodicy gives meaning to the natural doubts and sense of uncertainty encountered by the new believer in the resocialization process. Armed with a concrete identification of the source of these difficulties, the new believer has a greater sense of power in facing such problems of belief. The theodicy that fears and doubts are planted by Satan is a welcome explanation.

The foremost function of dualism is the reshaping of believers' interpretations of everyday events. Believers reinterpret even their own roles. Dualism bestows significance on events that formerly seemed meaningless. Human failure, suffering, social problems, personal difficulties, and death are all given meaning. Events that formerly appeared to be random, haphazard, and disorderly come to be perceived as part of a clear pattern. One's sense of ambiguity and insecurity is resolved by perceiving one's personal role as part of "something big"—a great cosmic struggle in which one gains power and purpose by siding with the good forces.

Dualism enables the group to create order out of chaos. The source of threat is not only the external chaos of the anomic social world; intragroup problems constitute a threat, too. Internal conflict is especially disruptive because it undermines those interpersonal relationships that support the believers' worldview. Problems of "disorder" are inherent in the establishment of any new group, and much ambiguity arises during the developing stages of a movement. Also, if members perceive their new belief system to be a departure from their previous one, the fact of change may cause some uncertainty. Emphasizing the group's role in a cosmic dualistic confrontation enables the group to resolve its problems of uncertainty and ambiguity (Slater, 1966). Dualistic beliefs affirm the boundaries between the group and "the world," and they provide mechanisms (e.g., exorcism, confession, and healing) for dealing with internal conflict.

The group constructs and perceives its world in dualistic terms: Good versus Evil, truth versus deceptions, light versus darkness, purity versus pollution. For example, a recent dualistic religious movement in the United States symbolizes the forces of evil as all "impurity": germs, viruses, bacteria, dirt, sludge, filth, garbage, diseases (especially addictions, cancer, herpes, and AIDS), human "pests" and "rodents," and "unclean" persons (especially immigrants and "impure" racial groups) (Aho, 1990:85, 1997). Dualistic boundaries serve to enhance member commitment, even commitment to sacrifice for the group's goals (cf. Douglas, 1986).

The dualistic theodicy enhances the individual believer's sense of security. Recruits to these movements often express a strong desire to know for sure where they "stand" before God. This desire for certainty is fulfilled by a secure sense of order, which affirms a clear duality between the forces of Good and Evil and shows a distinct path for the believer who would side with Good. This simplified course of action informs the member that, having sided with the Good, one is safe and secure.

The Imminence of the Millennium

A dualistic theodicy is particularly forceful if combined with a millenarian theodicy. *Millenarianism,* the expectation of an imminent disintegration of the entire social order and its replacement with a perfect new order, is a recurring theme in religious movements. The millenarian theodicy informs the believer that the present chaotic social order, with its misery and deprivations, is transient and that in the coming new order the believer will have a better life and no longer experience the turmoil and malaise of the present. Millenarianism offers both an explanation of the wrongness of the present social order and a hope for future change; as such, it is a potent source of change-oriented behavior.

The millennial dream that the perfect new order is imminent is also a response to anomie. When the old order is seen as nearly defunct, the new order must be near (see Barkun, 1974). The perceived disorder of the United States is especially upsetting to some groups who believe that the nation has a special purpose in God's plan. One television preacher said:

> America's star is sinking fast. If Christians don't begin immediately to assert their influence, it may be too late to save America from the destruction toward which it is plunging. And, since America now stands as the key base camp for missions around the globe, to fail to save America now would almost certainly be to miss its last opportunity to save the world. (James Robison, from *Save America,* as quoted in Hadden and Swann, 1981:97)

Similarly, the Reverend Moon warned:

> But today America is retreating. It's not just an accident that great tragedy is constantly striking America and the world, such as the assassination of President Kennedy and the sudden death of Secretary-General Hammarskjöld of the United Nations, both in the same decade. The

spirit of America has declined since then. Unless this nation, unless the leadership of the nation lives up to the mission ordained by God, many troubles will plague you. God is beginning to leave America. This is God's warning. (quoted in Anthony and Robbins, 1978:84)

People who view this society as badly out of order and consider the established religions impotent to do anything about the "problems" are likely to hope for dramatic change. The ultimate religious "solution" is the end of the world. The coming of the millennium will not only destroy the old problematic order but will also vindicate the faith of the believers.

Religious Apocalypticism The idea of an apocalypse—a dramatic end of the world—is not a new religious theme. Many religious groups have anticipated the imminent end of the social order they define as ungodly. Some have expected a total physical cataclysm in which the world would end; others have awaited a God-sent revolutionary end in which the existing social order would cease and be replaced by a perfect new order. This latter hope has been frequently combined with the anticipation of a messiah who would bring about the new order. Such themes are particularly prominent in Western religions, especially Christianity (see Barkun, 1974; Cohn, 1970, 1993; Festinger et al., 1956; Moses, 1993). Several Shi'ite (Muslim) sects combine a messianic and millenarian expectation in their belief that the Twelfth (Hidden) Imam would reappear as the Mahdi (bringer of justice to the world) and the Riser of the Resurrection (who would preside over the end of the world and the last judgment). The religious leader, the Ayatollah Khomeini did not need to make explicit millenarian claims to tap the apocalyptic religious and political mood that prevailed in 1978 among many adherents of these Shi'ite sects in Iran in order to mobilize the revolutionary potential of the religion (Arjomand, 1993). His religious movement's overthrow of the U.S.-backed Shah of Iran surprised many international observers, who knew there was serious unrest in the region but gravely underestimated the potential for millenarian religious beliefs to become effectively revolutionary. While messianic hopes are linked with millenarianism in Christianity and Islam, other religious groups such as Sikh "fundamentalists" in India have used millenarian visions of alternative social systems in which their oppression by a more powerful religious group would end and utopias of harmony, purity, and justice would prevail (Oberoi, 1993).

Millenarian movements were widespread in the United States in the nineteenth century, sometimes combined with a messianic vision of a special destiny for the nation. The Mormons, Millerites, Christadelphians, and Jehovah's Witnesses are examples of groups in which the millenarian expectation was or is central (see Wilson, 1970). The early Seventh Day Adventists expected the end of the world imminently. The founders had been followers of William Miller who had prophesied the Second Coming of Christ on October 22, 1844. After his prophecy did not come to pass, the Adventist founders reinterpreted Miller's prophecy to signify the *beginning* of the end. Elaborating further "signs" of the end, one of the founders wrote:

> When Protestantism shall stretch her hand across the gulf to grasp the hand of the Roman power, when she shall reach over the abyss to clasp hands with spiritualism, when, under the influence of the threefold union, our country shall repudiate every principle of its Constitution as a Protestant and republican government . . . then we may know that the time has come for the marvelous working of Satan and that the end is near. (White, 1885, quoted in Lawson, 1997:211)

This expectation was problematic in the early years, because if the end was very near, there was no point in proselyting or even organizing the movement. Later, as the prophecy was downplayed and further reinterpreted, Adventism became one of the most active of proselytizing Christian groups worldwide. The movement has also softened its antigovernment and anti-Catholic stance, but fringe Adventists continue to appeal to the foundational position (Lawson, 1997). For example, the Branch Davidians (many of whom were killed in a standoff against federal agents in Waco, Texas) preached a radicalized version of Adventism (Anthony and Robbins, 1997).

Nativistic religious movements, which envisioned the millennium as the dramatic restoration of a traditional "native" way of life, arose in the nineteenth century among several Native American tribes, whose social and economic plight was desperate. The Ghost Dance,[5] Handsome Lake, Indian Shakers, and the peyote cult exemplify these movements by which Native Americans responded to the profound disruption of their traditional way of life wrought by white settlers, government policy, and the army (see Barnett, 1957; DeMallie, 1982; Mooney, 1965; Myerhoff, 1974). Among the Hopi people of the U.S. Southwest, a prophecy of Hopi rebirth developed, predicting their role as a cultural "chosen people" emerging from the degradation of both native and white colonial cultures (Geertz, 1994). A black syncretic movement, the Lost Found Nation of Islam (i.e., Black Muslims) appealed to both the millennial possibilities in Islam and U.S. blacks' familiarity with Christian millenarian themes. Its early teaching was that 1914 ended the 6,000 years of the "white devils'" rule, after which the lost Nation of Islam would finally realize its destiny (Lincoln, 1989). Later, however, the movement emphasized orthodox Sunni versions of Islam and abandoned this prophecy, while a splinter group headed by Louis Farrakhan reasserted it (Mamiya, 1982; Mamiya and Lincoln, 1988).

Belief in the imminence of the millennium is widespread among new religious movements as well as in Christian fundamentalist denominations and sects. Peculiarly modern forms of millenarianism include groups that base their millennial expectations on UFOs and extraterrestrial communications, eugenics, or cryonics (see Balch and Taylor, 1976, 1977; Bozeman, 1997; Davis, 2000; Festinger et al., 1956; Palmer, 1998; Urban, 2000; Wessinger, 2000a).

---

5. The Ghost Dance was a highly traditionalistic movement that foresaw the destruction of the white man. Although the movement itself was pacifist, its appeal and potential for uniting diverse tribes frightened the frontier army, culminating in the Battle of Wounded Knee, in which over two hundred men, women, and children were killed.

Members of Heaven's Gate committed mass suicide in San Diego, California, in 1997, to exit planet Earth and enter the realm of "Beyond Human" via a flying saucer that they believed was behind the Hale-Bopp comet (Davis, 2000; Urban, 2000; Wessinger, 2000a). The Order of the Solar Temple based its millenarian vision on the Western occult tradition—a combination of Gnostic Christianity, neo-Templar, Rosicrucianism, and hermetic Freemasonry. More than seventy members in Canada and Switzerland died violently, some by suicide and others by murder (in what group teachings called "transits"—departure to another planet) in 1994, 1995, and 1997 (Mayer, 1999; Wessinger, 2000).

Dispensational premillennialism among conservative Christians has been used for political ends. Building on the long history of millenarian thought, dispensational premillennialism proposes that the world's history is divided into periods of "dispensations," each ended by a wrathful judgment by God. Accordingly, the world is now in the final dispensation, which will end in a "great tribulation" marked by horrible wars and the destruction of much of the world's population; subsequently, Christ will return to reign. Many dispensationalists also believe that the "righteous" (i.e., true Christians like themselves) will be spared this tribulation by the "rapture" in which Christ will "catch" them up before the last seven years of the world. Unlike other millenarian movements that have held similar beliefs, this movement actively promotes certain political and military actions that are believed to hasten the end time (Harrell, 1984; Robertson, 1988). For example, despite their widespread anti-Semitism, dispensationalists have raised much money to help right-wing Jewish extremists reclaim the Temple Mount in Jerusalem from the Muslims who have one of their holiest, centuries-old shrines on the site. Unlike other millenarians who merely decry the crises and chaos as signs of impending doom, some Christian dispensationalists actively promote crises and strife.

Social and Political Millenarianism Not only specifically religious movements, but also many other social and political movements, have dominant millenarian themes. Several "isms" of the nineteenth and twentieth centuries projected a secular millennium. Thus, many forms of nationalism are based on a vision of a people realizing their destiny in the destruction of the old social order.

The Sendero Luminoso (Shining Path) movement, engaged in armed guerilla struggle in Peru, is a contemporary political expression that uses highly millenarian rhetoric (Gorriti, 1999). The articulator of its ideology, referred to by his nom de guerre as "President Gonzalo," said in an early speech:

> The trumpets start to sound, the rumor of the masses grows and it will grow more, it will deafen us, it will attract us to a powerful vortex . . . and in this way it will create the great rupture and we will be the makers of the definite dawn. We will transform the black fire into red and the red into light. That we are, this is the reconstitution. Comrades, we are reconstituted! (quoted in Díaz-Albertini, 1993:172)

The millenarian and messianic appeal of the Russian Revolution is another example. Indeed, a persuasive case can be made that the major revolutions of the twentieth century (Nazism, Soviet Communism, and Maoism[6]) were millenarian movements (see Ellwood, 1999; Sikkink and Regnerus, 1996). The potential for modern movements to create and sustain a sense of urgency and imminent disaster in a larger mass population can be partially attributed to the impact of mass media (see Barkun, 1974; Cohn, 1970). Even without reference to a supernatural realm, these belief systems are millenarian responses to problems of order and meaning.

Some social historians observe that there appears to be a cyclical pattern to the rise of millenarianism. In U.S. history, for example, the 1840s, 1890s, 1930s, and 1960s have been identified as periods of intense millenarianism in both religious and other social political forms. If there are recurring patterns, do these periods have certain factors (such as economic conditions, regional growth or decline, moral or political crises) in common (Barkun, 1985; Hammond, 1983; McLoughlin, 1983; Smith, 1983)?

Millenarian movements, even explicitly religious millenarianism, may have an inherent political quality to them, because members can draw the conclusion that the enormity of the end of "the World's" time invalidates previously binding rules and laws, including established governments' laws. Thus, millenarian movements have a built-in potential for **antinomian** behavior, because their key beliefs negate the temporal basis of the political order (Fields, 1993). Often government authorities correctly sense these movements' challenge to law and the existing order of the nation, but they fail to appreciate that the antinomian threat is deeply embedded in an apocalyptic vision that completely transforms the meanings of time, order, and behavior. Had U.S. authorities taken seriously the Branch Davidians' highly apocalyptic and millenarian beliefs as a basis for their behavior before and during the 1993 siege of their compound (resulting in the fiery deaths of eighty-six people), they would have realized that their approach to dealing with the group's antinomian conduct was counterproductive (O'Leary, 1994; Wessinger, 2000a; see also, Barkun, 1997; Foster et al., 1998; Robbins and Anthony, 1995).

Dualism and Millenarianism in Social Movements

Expectation of the millennium is not merely an incidental item of belief; rather, it is a significant part of the group's response to the problem of anomie. If people have experienced anomie, the solution par excellence is not only to

---

6. The messianic tone of Maoism had a precursor in the mid-nineteenth-century Chinese Taiping rebellion, a civil war in which some 20 million persons were killed in combat, massacres, and purges. The rebellion was based on a syncretic religious message that combined elements of Christianity—especially the idea of heavenly reign after the return of the Messiah—with popular Confucianism and Buddhism to justify both the authority of Hong Xiuquan and his platform calling for the destruction of old economic hierarchies to be replaced with egalitarian sharing of land and resources (Spence, 1996; see also Lowe, 2000).

affirm a new order for the present but also to believe in a future reordering that will reintegrate all problematic aspects of the present situation into an overall, meaningful perfect order.

The imminence of this dramatic reordering creates a sense of urgency and makes the mundane business of daily life "in the world" seem trivial. Millennial expectations therefore enhance members' commitment to the group through which they will help usher in the new order. The idea that the end of this world is near makes it much easier for members to give up possessions, jobs, education, and other things that have value only in the nearly defunct world. Like the dualistic theodicy, millenarianism encourages pattern-forming. Believers interpret seemingly random events as evidence for the imminence of the millennium. For example, in the 1990s some Christian, occult, and psychic groups saw signs of the impending end in current events: comets, earthquakes and volcanoes, ecodisasters, wars in the Mideast, economic crises, and so on. The approach of the year 2000 itself spurred some millennial expectations, such as one U.S.-based group whose members were deported from Israel where authorities feared they intended to provoke the apocalypse (Sontag, 1999). Meanwhile, other believers attempted elaborate calculations of the End based on symbolic numbers in the Bible, the occult prophecies of Nostradamus, or other prophecies.

The rhetoric of millenarianism combined with dualism provides a persuasive motivation for social movements, because it undermines the authority of the existing order, reorders the collective notion of time, and suggests a line of action in the face of that which the movement defines as evil (O'Leary, 1994).

The millenarian vision is likewise a theodicy for the discrepancies within the present order. Even after conversion, members are likely to have difficulties—friends and relatives "not understanding," prayers seemingly not answered, doubts and uncertainties, and the society still not on the "right track." The belief in the coming of the millennium relativizes the problems and opposition of the present by the knowledge that all of these will be overcome in a glorious future. Members can feel that although "things" are really bad now and will probably get worse, they are not personally threatened by the disorder and ambiguity because they know that they are allied in the present with the source of perfect order and will have a privileged position in the unknown glorious future.

Although infinite possible meanings can be attached to any given event, the themes of millenarianism and dualism illustrate how meaning systems interpret events and locate them in some larger framework. We have seen how individuals and groups use their belief systems to bestow meaning on the social world, and how elements of belief such as imminence of the millennium, messianic expectations, and dualism are responses to a social situation that appears chaotic, ambiguous, or hopeless. Individuals who hold dualistic or millenarian worldviews relate to their social world accordingly. Their worldview organizes their experiences and influences their associations and their very identities.

SUMMARY

This chapter has outlined some of the ways in which the meaning-providing and belonging components of religion are linked. Religion is both a basis of association and an expression of shared meanings, the importance of which depends largely on the social support of a community of believers.

Religious meaning systems are ways of interpreting events and experiences. They assign meaning to a group's existence and to an individual's identity. The meaning system of a group interprets its social order, serving as a legitimation of social arrangements. Meaning systems also locate human lives and events in terms of a larger framework, identifying the individual with an overarching order. The significance of meaning in individual and social life is illustrated by situations in which meaning is threatened. Theodicies are religious explanations that offer meaning for meaning-threatening experiences such as suffering and death. Some crises of meaning profoundly disrupt the social order. The concept of *anomie* describes the impact of such crises on the individual and group.

Analysis of the themes of millenarianism and dualism in contemporary social movements illustrates how groups bestow meaning on the social situation. These two themes can be interpreted as responses to problems of meaning and order. They represent an effort to posit a new order in response to the ambiguity and confusion of meanings produced by social change. Millenarianism and dualism are theodicies that locate believers' experiences in terms of a larger framework of order and meaning.

Religious belonging is a natural outcome of shared meaning systems. At the same time, a community of believers (however small) is important for maintaining the plausibility of a meaning system. Where a particular worldview has monolithic status in a society, these plausibility structures pervade the entire society. In pluralistic societies, by contrast, worldviews are in competition. The interrelationship of the meaning-providing and belonging aspects of religion is well illustrated in the social processes of religious socialization, conversion, and commitment, to be explored in Chapter 3.

JUDAISM

JUDAISM: TWENTY-FIVE KEY DATES	
Date	**Event**
ca. 1200 B.C.E.	Exodus: Moses leads Hebrews out of Egypt
1013–973 B.C.E.	David's rule
722 B.C.E.	fall of northern kingdom (Israel) to Assyria
586 B.C.E.	fall of southern kingdom (Judah) to Babylon; beginning of the Exile
331 B.C.E.	Alexander conquers Palestine
168 B.C.E.	Maccabean revolt against Hellenization
63 B.C.E.	Roman conquest of Jerusalem
70 C.E.	Romans destroy Temple; beginning of Diaspora
80–110 C.E.	assembly of Hebrew Scriptures (Old Testament)
ca. 200 C.E.	promulgation of the Mishnah
ca. 500 C.E.	Babylonian Talmud complete in rough form
640 C.E.	Muslim conquest of Middle East
1041 C.E.	birth of Rashi, Bible and Talmud commentator
1135 C.E.	birth of Maimonides in Cordoba, Spain
1187 C.E.	Muslims reconquer Jerusalem from Christian crusaders
1290–1309 C.E.	expulsion of Jews from England and France
1492–1496 C.E.	expulsion of Jews from Spain and Portugal
1516 C.E.	introduction of the ghetto in Venice
1521 C.E.	beginning of Jewish migrations to Palestine
1648 C.E.	massacre of Polish and Ukrainian Jews
1654–1658 C.E.	Jewish communities in New Amsterdam and Rhode Island
1760 C.E.	Death of Baal Shem-Tov
1897 C.E.	founding of Zionist movement
1938 C.E.	every synagogue in Germany burned
1948 C.E.	creation of modern state of Israel

The discussion of this tradition must begin with a clarification of confusing and overlapping terms. Terms like *Jew* and *Judaism* came into being in the sixth century B.C.E. Judaism is the name of the religious tradition. The term **Jew** refers to a follower of Judaism. Non-Jews are described as *goyim* (**Gentiles**). One can be considered a Jew if one is a convert to Judaism (which is rare, since this denomination is nonproselytizing) or if one is the son or daughter of a Jewish mother (the father's status does not count). One of the most listened-to voices on the radio, Dr. Laura Schlessinger, proudly acknowledges the Jewish foundation of the advice she dispenses. Her father was an American Jew, but her mother was a war bride from Italy (a Catholic). As an adult, Dr. Laura decided to embrace her Jewish roots. She found that she did not qualify as a Jew solely on the basis of matrilineal parentage, so she had to make a formal conversion.

The term *Jew* has also come to serve as an ethnic description, such as Irish, Polish, Latino, or African-American. Many atheists, agnostics, or converts to other denominations still regard themselves as Jewish, at least in terms of ethnic identification. Indeed, some of the persecution (**anti-Semitism**) that the Jews have received throughout history was based more on ethnic rather than religious prejudice. Jews could not escape the Nazi death camps by converting to another religion. Indeed, one Auschwitz victim was a nun recently sainted by the Catholic Church, Sister Edith Stein, who was killed because she was of Jewish parentage (although she converted to Catholicism and had become a nun as a young woman).

The book of *Genesis* figures of Abraham, Isaac, Jacob, and Joseph were known as the patriarchs of the tribe of Hebrews. Moses and the people who followed him out of Egypt used that name. The term may have come from a Mesopotamian term for "outside the city's walls" (implying "nomad" or even "outlaw"). We now use the term **Hebrew** to describe a language of the Semitic group (which also includes Arabic). The Old Testament was written in this language and Hebrew remains a language used in many Jewish rituals. (A different language was spoken in daily life by the Jews of eastern Europe: Yiddish, which has many similarities to German.)

The name **Israel** initially referred to a man, Jacob, a patriarch of the later Jews. About five hundred years later, when Joshua led the Hebrews across the Jordan River into the promised land of Palestine, the name *Israel* was given to the land. About three thousand years ago, Israel became a kingdom ruled by such monarchs as Saul, David, and Solomon. The subjects of this biblical kingdom were known as Israelites. The terms *Jew* and *Judaism* emerged in the seventh century B.C.E. and refer to the Kingdom of Judah (the "southern" kingdom), which had survived the Assyrian conquest of the northern kingdom of Israel.

In 1948, the United Nations created a modern homeland for the Jews and named this nation Israel. The citizens of this modern nation are known as Israelis (and the Arab peoples who lived in that land are now referred to as Palestinians).

HISTORY

THE BIBLICAL PERIOD

Even more than Hinduism, the development of Judaism is chronicled in its scripture. The **Torah** (also known as the *Pentateuch*) is found in the first five

books of the Christian Bible.) This Jewish scripture is sometimes simply referred to as "the Law" in order to distinguish it from the other, later parts of the Hebrew Scriptures (the **Old Testament**).

Tradition says that the Torah was written by Moses after the **Exodus** (the movement of the Hebrews out from Egypt). Through the use of hermeneutical tools, secular and liberal scholars (such as Graf and Wellhausen) over the past hundred years have wondered if the books might actually have been finally written down five hundred years later, a scissors-and-paste job from at least four different oral traditions. The more fundamentalist Jewish and Christian scholars have defended the plausibility of Moses' authorship. Rather than resolving the ongoing debate about the origin of the Old Testament, we point to a common agreement. Both sides agree that the Old Testament began as oral tradition (even those who take everything literally would say that Adam passed on what he knew to Seth, and then to his son, and so on until we get down to Moses). Both sides also agree that someone then put together oral tradition as a written document (if not Moses during the Exodus from Egypt, then the rabbis during the Babylonian Exile five hundred years later).

Materials such as these different strands of the Pentateuch were edited, probably several times, into the order of the biblical "books" that we find today. Each book of the *Bible* therefore is, to an extent, a composite work, and sometimes one finds apparent conflicts, within a given book or between one book and another. So, for example, *Exodus* gives us one perspective on Moses and *Deuteronomy* gives us another.

Although the first five books of the *Bible* have been accorded the most dignity and authority, the second section of the Old Testament has also been revered. Traditionally called *Prophets*, this section contains reinterpretations of events (especially the establishment of the covenant between Israel and God) suited to later crises, such as the removal of many leaders of the Israelite community to Babylon in the sixth century B.C.E. Still a third section of the Hebrew Scriptures, traditionally called *The Writings*, collects later and disparate materials, and while as a group it has had less status than either the first five books (collectively called the Pentateuch or Torah) or *Prophets*, its works have still been considered authoritative

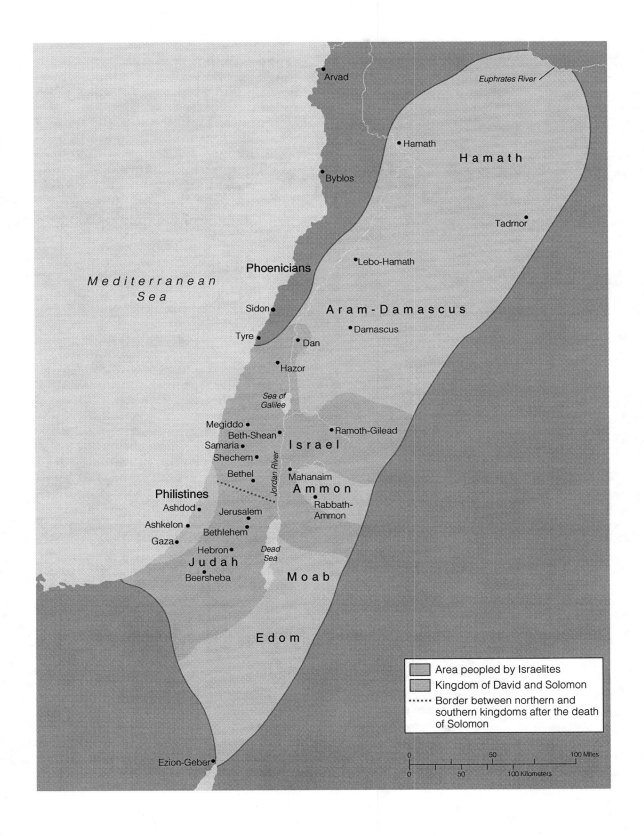

MAIN ELEMENTS OF JUDAISM	
Myths	Abraham was the patriarch of the Hebrews; Moses led the Exodus from Egypt and received the laws.
Doctrines	*Monotheism:* There is only one God. *Covenant:* The Jews were a people chosen by God to receive special revelations, a promised land, and responsibilities.
Ethics	Ten Commandments; pursue justice and mercy
Symbols	Star of David; Torah
Rituals	infant male circumcisions; *bar mitzvah* coming of age; weddings; funerals; annual holidays; weekly Sabbath
Leaders	Prophets in Old Testament times; priests conducting animal sacrifice (until 70 C.E.); rabbis (teachers of scripture)
Scripture	Torah (first five books of Bible); rest of Old Testament has lesser status
Commentary	Talmud (a later commentary)

interpretations of the relevance of Israelite existence. Together, these three sections of the *Bible* comprised the *Tanak,* an anagram comprised from the first letters for each section in Hebrew.

Whether or not events of the *Bible* are capable of independent verification by historians and archaeologists must be judged according to the standards of social science scholarship. Our concern in this book is less with these issues and more with viewing scripture as a record of myth. We use the term *myth* not to imply that the events described did not occur, but to view the Bible as a record of the values of the people who recited, wrote, compiled, and interpreted that record.

We see *Bible* events and figures as *paradigmatic* in that they can serve as three-dimensional lessons about the significance of Israel's experiences sojourning with its Lord though time. The biblical writers were more interested in the significance a given event had for the cultural challenges existing at the time of the writer or editor than in what may have happened (in a literal sense) originally (or how readers three thousand years later might interpret these writings). In other words, we are always involved in interpreting interpretations—dealing with the relevance of symbolism that people using the *Bible* paradigmatically found most absorbing.

To begin our historical survey, we take up an *integrationist* point of view, assuming a continuity between biblical Israel and later Judaism. In the beginning, the Jews were most likely a loose collection of seminomadic tribes that wandered in what is today Israel, Jordan, Lebanon, and Syria. They may have cultivated some crops, but their self-designation was "wandering Aramaeans" (*Deuteronomy:* 26:5). Thus, when scouts returned from Canaan (present-day western Israel) with grapes, pomegranates, and figs (products of settled cultivators), they caused quite a stir.

Members of an early Jewish extended family tended to worship their particular "god of the father," defining themselves largely in terms of their patriarch and his god. The cult therefore centered on clan remembrance of this god, who wandered with the tribe in its nomadic life. The common name for such a clan divinity was *el.* Before their settlement in Canaan, the people may have worshiped a variety of *els:* the god of the mountain, the god of seeing, the god of eternity, and so on. Usually they worshiped at altars constructed of unhewn stones, which they considered to be the god's house. In addition to the *els* were household deities and minor divinities and demons of the desert. In later orthodox Jewish interpretation, Abraham drew on whatever sense there was of a unity among these *els* or of a supreme *el* over the others to dedicate himself to a God who was beyond nature. That God, the creator of the world, Abraham called **Yahweh** (YHWH). (The connection between *Exodus* 3:14 and the *Genesis* story of Abraham is clear.)

For later orthodoxy, **Abraham** became the "Father" of the Hebrews (and therefore, the later Jews) and his God YHWH ("I am who I am") became their God. In that sense, Judaism as a religious tradition began with Abraham. Abraham probably lived around 1800 B.C.E. His descendants Isaac and Jacob, whose stories are recounted in the biblical book of *Genesis,* kept the Abrahamic covenant in the unique name of YHWH, "the Lord." From about 1650 to 1280 B.C.E., the people of Abraham, then known as Hebrews, were in Egypt, subjects of the Egyptian kingdom (or at least they were required to do forced labor there). According to the book of *Genesis* (chapters 39–50), the Hebrews' presence in Egypt was due to the success there of Jacob's son Joseph. Their leader at the end of their stay in Egypt was **Moses.**

In later Jewish theology, Moses functioned as the founder of the Jewish doctrine, ethics, and ritual because God revealed through Moses his will to make a covenant and fashion himself a people. In the incident at the burning bush (*Exodus,* chapter 3), Moses experienced God's self-revelation. God then commissioned Moses to lead the people out of Egypt, giving as his authoritative name only "I am who I am" (or "I am whatever I want to be"). Moses then led the Jewish people out of Egypt, an event that dominated the biblical authors' interpretation of everything that preceded and followed it. In the most significant episode in that exodus, Egyptian pursuers drowned in the sea. Free of them, the Israelites (the descendants of Jacob, Abraham's grandson) wandered in the desert until they entered the homeland that God had promised them. The deliverance from Egypt through the unexpected event at the Red Sea (probably not the present-day Red Sea) marked all subsequent Jewish doctrine. Looking back to this event, later generations clung to the hope that their God ruled history and would continue to liberate them from oppression.

In the desert, Moses and his people sought to understand the relevance of their exodus experience. They developed the doctrine that they were bound to God by a **covenant.** In this contract, similar to the relation between a Near Eastern overlord and vassal, God pledged care and the people pledged fidelity. The commandments accompanying this covenant gave the binding relationship (which some later commentators saw as prefigured in the figures of Adam, Noah, and Abraham) an ethical code: the basis of the Law (Torah) and the revelation that bound the people together. From laws about how to keep the Sabbath to traditions about how to sway while praying, Torah has encompassed all the traditions cherished as the basis of the people's identity and way to live worthy of their Lord.

When the Israelites finally settled in Canaan (Palestine) in the latter half of the thirteenth century B.C.E. under Moses' successor Joshua, they changed from a nomadic to an agricultural people. They were still a group of confederated tribes, but in settlement their bonds tended to loosen, as each group kept to its own area and developed its own ways. Only in times of common danger would the groups weld together, but war was so constant a feature of the period from the Exodus to the sixth century Exile in Babylon that the people had to cooperate. Settlement also meant religious changes, as local sanctuaries replaced the wandering ark of the covenant as the house of God. A somewhat professional priesthood (the tribe of *Levites*) apparently developed around these sanctuaries. Canaanite religion itself was a great influence on the Israelites. Before long, it produced a conflict between Israelites who favored the older God YHWH—the God of Abraham, Moses, and the covenant—and those who favored the agricultural gods (baals) of the Canaanites.

KINGS AND PROPHETS. From about 1200 to 1000 B.C.E., the Israelites had a government by *judges*—charismatic leaders, usually men but occasionally women, who took command in times of common danger. However, they eventually adopted monarchical rule, organizing a sturdy little kingdom under David at a new capital: Jerusalem. This kingdom unified the tribes of both north and south, and under Solomon, David's son, it had a brief but golden age of culture and empire. Some of the most striking narratives of the Hebrew Scriptures (Old Testament) derive from this period, including the brilliant memoir we find in 2 *Samuel,* chapters 13–20. In these narratives, David is portrayed as the ideal king and yet a man undeniably human—lustful for Bathsheba (willing to murder to get her), tragically at odds with his son Absalom. Much later, David's achievements in war and his fashioning a kingdom for peace made him the focus of messianic hopes—hopes for a king anointed by God who would usher in a new age of prosperity and peace. David, then, was the Jewish prototype for sacred kingship. Similarly, David's son

Solomon became the prototype for wisdom. Just as many pious Jews attributed the Psalms to David, so they attributed much of the Bible's wisdom literature (e.g., Proverbs) to Solomon.

Following Solomon's death, the northern and southern portions of the kingdom split apart. The north (Israel) lasted from 922 to 722 B.C.E., when it fell to Assyria. The south (Judah) lasted until 586 B.C.E., when it fell to Babylon. (Both Assyria and Babylon lay to the northeast.) These were centuries of great political strife and military conflict. They spawned a series of important religious **prophets**, who dominate the next phase of biblical history. Greatest of the early prophets was Elijah, who preached in the north against the corrupt kings Ahab and Ahaziah and the queen Jezebel. The legendary stories about Elijah portray him as a champion of YHWH and authentic prophecy against the false prophets of the Canaanite baals.

Around 750 B.C.E., the prophet Amos issued a clarion call for justice. Extending the notion that YHWH was simply Israel's protector, Amos made divine blessings dependent upon repentance from sin. His God was clearly in charge of nature, but the key access to divinity was social justice (human beings dealing with one another fairly). Hosea, another northern prophet, also spoke up for mercy and justice (and for a nonidolatrous cult), but he expressed God's role as symbolized by a spouse willing to suffer infidelity, unable to cast off his beloved (that is, the people covenanted to him).

In the south, the successors to these northern prophets were Isaiah, Jeremiah, and the prophet known as "Second Isaiah" (the source of *Isaiah,* chapters 40–55). They made the same demands, but with greater stress on punishment by foreign powers. Reading the signs of the times, they thought that God would subject his people to captivity because they had not relied on him in absolute commitment. However, both Jeremiah and Second Isaiah held out hope for a new beginning, assuring Judah that a remnant of the people would keep their commitment to the covenant. During the reign of the southern king Josiah (640–609 B.C.E.), there was a religious reform that many scripture scholars see as the source of the "Deuteronomic" recasting of the early Jewish tradition. It shaped not only the book of *Deuteronomy* but other historical writings as well. Among the

influential ideas were that YHWH had elected Israel to be his people; that observing the covenant laws was necessary for religious prosperity; that Jews ought to repudiate contacts with foreigners and foreign gods; that sacrificial rituals should be consolidated in Jerusalem; and that Israel ought to rely only on YHWH, since he controlled history and oversaw nature.

COVENANTAL THEOLOGY. From their Exile to Babylon, Jews thought they had learned an important lesson: commitment to the covenant is essential, infidelity to Torah leads to national disaster. God had chosen them by covenanting with them in a special way, and unless they responded with fidelity, they would reap not blessing but judgment. Consequently, the returnees stressed their isolation and uniqueness. Some prophets and religious thinkers suggested that God himself was universal, Lord of all peoples. His dominion included the foreign nations, for they had obviously served as his instruments for chastening Israel. He had punished through the Assyrians and Babylonians and freed through the Persians.

The stress on covenant by the Deuteronomic and postexilic leaders exalted Moses as the religious figure par excellence. However much David stood for kingly success, indeed for the very establishment of Jerusalem, Moses stood for the Torah—revelation, teaching, law. The Torah was a much more solid foundation than either kingship or Jerusalem. By the words of God's mouth, the heavens were made. By the words God spoke through Moses' mouth, the Jews were made a people. If the people kept to those words, they would choose life. If they forgot them or put them aside, they would choose death. Thus, Moses had said: "I call heaven and earth to witness against you this day, that I have set before you life and death, blessing and curse; therefore, choose life, that you and your descendants may live, loving the Lord your God, obeying his voice, and clinging to him" (*Deuteronomy* 30:19–20). In the sober climate that followed the return from Exile, the wise way for Jews seemed to be to keep to themselves and their own special laws.

WISDOM AND APOCALYPSE. Two other movements marked the later Jewish biblical period. The first is found in the wisdom literature of the Hebrew

CASE STUDY: JEREMIAH

It will be useful to consider the personality, career, and message of Jeremiah, for Jeremiah is a striking example of both the prophetic vocation and biblical spirituality. Born in the middle of the seventh century B.C.E. (in 645, according to some scholars), and coming from a priestly family, Jeremiah preached during the reigns of kings Josiah, Jehoiakim, and Zedekiah, until he was deported around 582 to Egypt, where he died. We know more about Jeremiah's personal life than that of the other prophets, and this shows a man completely dominated by God's call. He did not marry, because he wanted to draw attention to the risk that most children would not survive the troubles coming because of Israel's infidelities (*Jeremiah* 16:1–4). He would not take part in mourning ceremonies or festivals because soon there would be none left to mourn and nothing good to celebrate (16:5–8). As one might expect, these dire forecasts made Jeremiah very unpopular. Enemies conspired against his life (11:18–23), he was confined in the stocks (19:14–20:6), and for announcing the coming destruction of the Jerusalem Temple he was tried for blasphemy. King Jehoiakim considered Jeremiah his deadly enemy and had him flogged. Jeremiah reciprocated Jehoiakim's enmity, attacking him verbally. Indeed, his indictment of King Jehoiakim reveals so much about Jeremiah's character that the verses are worth reproducing:

> Woe to him who builds his house by unrighteousness, and his upper rooms by injustice; who makes his neighbor serve him for nothing, and does not give him his wages; Who says, "I will build myself a great house with spacious upper rooms," and cuts out windows for it, paneling it with cedar, and painting it with vermillion. Do you think you are a king because you compete in cedar? Did not your father eat and drink and do justice and righteousness? Then it was well with him. He judged the cause of the poor and needy; then it was well. "Is this not to know me?" says the Lord. "But you have eyes and heart only for your dishonest gain, for shedding innocent blood, and for practicing oppression and violence." Therefore thus says the Lord concerning Jehoi'akim the son of Josi'ah, king of Judah: "They shall not lament for him, saying, 'Ah my brother!' or 'Ah sister!' They shall not lament for him, saying 'Ah lord!' or 'Ah his majesty!' With the burial of an ass he shall be buried, dragged and cast forth beyond the gates of Jerusalem." (22:13–19 RSV)

Whence came this lashing tongue, this need to accuse the mighty to their faces? Jeremiah concluded that his painful vocation had been laid upon him by God, who had chosen him to be a prophet from the moment of his conception (1:5–10). His mission would extend beyond Israel, bringing the Lord's message to all the nations. Jeremiah apparently came to this understanding of his vocation while still a teenager, and the responsibility it imposed overwhelmed him. But the Lord would hear none of Jeremiah's protests, assuring him that if he spoke divine words he would receive divine support: "Behold I have put my words in your mouth" (1:9). "Be not afraid of them, for I am with you to deliver you" (1:8). So a prophet was formed, a man dominated by "the word of the Lord," the message his God impelled him to deliver.

Along with Jeremiah's calling came two visions (1:11–19). The first vision was of an almond tree. Punning on the similarity of the Hebrew words for "almond tree" and "to watch," God told Jeremiah that his vision of the almond tree was symbolically relevant: the Lord would watch over his word to perform it. The second vision was of a boiling pot, facing away from the north. Just as boiling water spilled out of the pot and swept away twigs and pebbles, so foes would sweep out of the north and inflict evil on Jeremiah's countrymen. Jeremiah himself would face strong opposition for delivering these oracles, but his enemies would not prevail. The Lord would be with him, to deliver him.

From the outset, therefore, Jeremiah was a troubled man. He felt a charge to bring before his people the unpleasant news that hard times were coming, as the just deserts of their irreligion. From the outset Jeremiah was also a poetic man, brimming with powerful imagery. In a few lines he could sketch the whole career of a dishonest king, withering him by contrast with his righteous father. In a few phrases he could etch the king's coming demise, depicting the funeral that none would mourn. The word of the Lord pouring from the mouth of this troubled man riveted his people's imagination and lashed their soul. Jeremiah's passion for justice, his almost obsessive sense that the people had abandoned the very basis of their existence by falling away from God, gave him the courage to flay kings and leaders publicly. Thus he asked the people, in the name of God, "What wrong did your fathers find in me, that they went far from me, and went after worthlessness, and became worthless?" (2:5).

As Jeremiah read the political situation, God would punish this worthless people, using Babylon as his instrument. King Zedekiah consulted with Jeremiah about the political situation, but the king's advisers were bitterly opposed to the prophet, fearing that his predictions of woe were destroying the people's will to resist the Babylonians. Babylon did lay siege to Jerusalem, and when in 588 or 587 Jeremiah used a brief break in the siege to leave Jerusalem, his enemies arrested him for desertion. Zedekiah soon released him from the dungeon but had him kept in confinement. Undeterred, Jeremiah continued to proclaim that the Babylonians would defeat the Jews, and for this stubbornness his enemies threw him into a cistern, with the intention that he should starve there. When Jerusalem finally fell in 586, the victorious Babylonians treated Jeremiah well, offering him the choice of living either in Babylon or Judah. Jeremiah chose Judah, and he urged his countrymen left in Judah to try to live in peace. Peace was not to be, however, for some discontented Jewish fugitives from the army killed Gedaliah, the governor appointed by the Babylonian ruler Nebuchadnezzar. Most of the Jewish community feared Baby-

lonian vengeance for this murder, but when the community appealed to Jeremiah for a divine oracle on whether they should flee to Egypt or stay where they were, Jeremiah told them to stay in their own country. The people would not accept this oracle, however, so they took Jeremiah and his scribe Baruch with them to Egypt. In Egypt Jeremiah continued his unpopular ways, predicting that the Babylonians would defeat the Egyptians and castigating Jews who fell to worshiping a heavenly queen. The Jews in Egypt rejected this rebuke, and, according to later legend, stoned Jeremiah to death. Overall, most of Jeremiah's warnings, visions, symbolic actions, and oracles were gloomy. Thinking that his people had enmeshed themselves in secular politics to the neglect of their religion, the prophet saw Judah becoming crushed by the much larger foreign powers surrounding it, and thought this fate a fitting punishment for Judah's defections. Still, not all Jeremiah's prophecies were gloomy. Like the other great prophets, his message balanced judgment with consolation. If God was judging the people harshly, because of their wanton irreligion, God was also assuring the people that the future would bring better times. Jeremiah's most consoling assurances occur in chapters 30–32, which are a high point of biblical poetry and theology.

Chapter 30 begins with the formulaic introductory phrase, "The word that came to Jeremiah from the Lord." This word was positive. The days were coming when God would restore his people's fortunes. He would bring them back to their land, lost when the northern kingdom fell in 722 to Assyria and threatened by Babylon. No matter how great the present pains grew, God would save the people from them. He would break the yoke of their foreign rulers, leading them back to serve him, the Lord their God, and a king like David.

With great poetic skill, the prophet plays variations on this theme. Behind the people's present sufferings is the hand of the Lord, punishing them for their transgressions. But that same hand will punish Israel's enemies: "Therefore all who devour you shall be devoured, and all your foes, every one of them, shall go into captivity, those who despoil you shall become a spoil, and all who prey on you I will make a prey" (30:16).

Similar poetry sings of what the restored people will enjoy: good fortune for the tents of Jacob, compassion on all Jacob's offspring's dwellings, songs of thanksgiving throughout the city and the palace, many voices making merry. "And you shall be my people, and I will be your God" (30:22). Harkening back to the exodus from Egypt, the prophet has God say that the people who survived the sword and found grace in the wilderness would come to know God most intimately. Why? Because "I have loved you with an everlasting love; therefore I have continued my faithfulness to you" (31:3).

Both the prophets and the Deuteronomic historian-theologians testified to the dangers to survival that Jews of their time experienced. Political subjugation by the much larger neighboring powers was ever a possibility, but it was less ominous than cultural assimilation. To preserve their identity, Jews would have to keep clear of their neighbors' fertility religion. Only an adherence to a quite different god—YHWH, the God of Moses and Abraham—could keep the people unique. Thus, the stress on a nonidolatrous cult and detailed religious law that we find after the period of captivity to Babylon was most likely a reaction to the threat of adopting non-Hebrew influences. For instance, both adopting kingship and holding agricultural celebrations could be false steps, be-

cause they could take the Israelites away from YHWH. When the Israelites were exiled to Babylon, Jews of the southern kingdom tested the prophets' theology. A few realized what they had lost by playing power politics and relying on new gods.

This Babylonian Captivity (or Babylonian Exile), when Judah fell to Babylon in 586 B.C.E., was a major divide in biblical history, everything before it qualifying as pre-exilic and everything after (or everything after within the pre–common era) qualifying as postexilic. The Exile highlighted the paradoxes of trying to give theological interpretations of history (say what God's purposes were in the Babylonian captivity as well as the significance of autonomous rule in one's own land for the full flowering of biblical tradition). Some of the most profound prophetic poetry of the Bible came from the cauldron of the Exile—parts of the present books of *Isaiah, Jeremiah,* and *Ezekiel.*

When the Persians gained control of the region from the Babylonians, Cyrus allowed Jews to return to Jerusalem. The relatively small number who did return lived a reformed life under Nehemiah and Ezra, choosing to rebuild the Temple the Babylonians had wrecked and to reestablish themselves on the basis of a strict adherence to the covenant law. Marriage to foreigners was prohibited, and priests strictly controlled the new Temple.

Scriptures. As many commentators point out, *Ecclesiastes* and *Proverbs* bear the marks of the prudential, reflective thought, expressed in maxims, that was available from Egypt. Somewhat incongruously, it grafted itself onto Jewish speculation about God's action, which suggests that postexilic Judaism found its times rather trying. At least, the wisdom literature is dour and sober compared with the historical and prophetic sections of the Bible. It retains a trust that God still has his hand on the tiller, but it finds the seas gray and choppy. Suffering had tempered the fire in the Jewish soul for poetry and prophecy.

The book of *Job,* however, is an exception. Job probes *theodicy* (the problem of evil and suffering), which surely is a wisdom concern, but it reaches poetic depths. Job reveals that the innocent do suffer mysteriously—that we cannot understand our fate, because all human life unfolds by the plan of a God whose mind we cannot know. This God set the boundaries of the seas, made the different species of all living things. He is not someone we can take to court, not someone who has to account to us. Rather, we can only cling to him in darkness and in trust. Because Job does not profess the older theology, in which punishment was in response to sin, instead proposing a mystery beyond legalistic logic, it brings the postexilic centuries some religious distinction.

By the end of the third century B.C.E., however, the constraints on Jewish national life brought about another reaction to the problems of suffering and providence. Job refers to **Satan**, an "adversary," and, perhaps because of Iranian influences, in the last years before the common era, a dualistic concern with good and evil came to the fore. God and his supporting angels fought against Satan and his minions. The world, in fact, was conceived of as a cosmic battlefield, with God and the forces of light against the forces of darkness. For the first time, Jewish religion started to focus on an afterlife. Pressed by the problem that the good do not necessarily meet with reward nor the evil with punishment, Jewish religion raised the notion that a divine judgment would mete out proper justice. Correspondingly, it started to imagine heavenly places for the good who pass judgment and infernal places for the wicked who fail.

The book of *Daniel* expresses these concerns through what scholars call *apocalyptic* imagination of the end of the current unjust world order. This imagination purports to be a revelation (**apocalypse**) from God about how the future will unfold. Psychologically, it is an effort to comfort people who are under stress with promises that they will find vindication. Theologically, it puts a sharp edge on the question of whether God controls history. The historical context of Daniel was the pressure of Antiochus Epiphanes to profane Jewish worship. The revolt of the Jews led by the Maccabees stemmed from this pressure.

Daniel joins apocalyptic concern with the older prophetic concern with a messiah, casting the future vindication of the Jews in terms of a heavenly being (the "Son of man") who will come on the clouds. His coming is the dramatic climax in the **eschatological** (end times) scenario that Jews developed in postexilic times. Thus, the Son of man came to figure in many apocalyptic writings (most of them not included in the Bible), and among those who were of a more apocalyptic orientation, he was the preferred version of the messianic king. (Christians seized on this figure as a principal explanation of Jesus.)

HELLENISM. From the end of the fourth century B.C.E., the political fate of the Jews lay in the hands first of the Greeks and then of the Romans. Thus, Greek and Roman influences mixed with Israel's wisdom and apocalyptic concerns. The ideals that some Jews accepted from Alexander the Great are commonly labeled **Hellenism**. Contact with Hellenism divided the Jewish community. Some priests and intellectuals took to Greek science, philosophy, and drama, but the majority of the people, sensing a threat to their identity, reacted adversely. By the time that Antiochus Epiphanes tried to enforce worship of Greek gods and destroy traditional Judaism, most Jews supported the (successful) revolt that the Maccabees led in 168 B.C.E. Herod the Great was appointed king of the Jews by the Roman Senate in 40 B.C.E. and helped to promote Hellenistic influences in Judea after the Roman conquest.

Overall, Hellenism influenced the Jewish conception of law, and it sparked the first strictly philosophical efforts to make the Torah appear reasonable to any clear-thinking person. Philo, a contemporary of Jesus, was a great expositor of this sort of philosophy. In the final decades of the biblical period, however, political and religious differences divided the Jewish communities. Some people, called the **Zealots**, urged political action, in the spirit of the Maccabean rebellion. These small guerrilla bands hid out in rugged terrain and ambushed columns of Roman soldiers. They also ambushed merchant caravans, giving the Zealots the status of mere robbers in the eyes of many middle-class Jews. (Note how the figure of Barabbas appears in the Christian gospels: robber or revolutionary depending upon the author.)

A different approach was advocated by another small group, the **Essenes**. Their solution was physical withdrawal from the influence of Roman law and Greek culture. The Essenes moved from the cities and relocated to the Qumran community around the Dead Sea. (The Dead Sea scrolls, found just sixty years ago, were probably deposited by this sect.) The Essenes devalued this earthly world and advocated aescetic purification for the coming Messiah, perhaps celibacy (approaches that did not resonate with either Judaism's past tradition or future focus).

A larger first-century movement was the **Pharisees**, laypeople who defended the tradition of the

COMPARISON OF FIRST-CENTURY JEWISH SECTS				
DIMENSION	PHARISEES	SADDUCEES	ESSENES	ZEALOTS
Greek culture	opposed	accepted	withdrew from	opposed
Roman rule	opposed	accepted	withdrew from	rebelled against
Laws of the Torah	strictly followed	loosely followed	other new doctrines	ignored
Appealed to	poor	wealthy	alienated	robbers
Apocalypse	coming soon	ignored	ignored	start it!
Role of the Messiah	great	ignored	ignored	ignored
Angels	accepted	rejected	ignored	ignored
Resurrection	accepted	rejected	transmigration	irrelevant
Heaven and hell	accepted	ignored	ignored	ignored

oral Torah and tried to update its relevance. The Pharisees were somewhat distant from the Temple that was the center of priestly, ritualistic Judaism. (The portrait of the Pharisees in the New Testament is colored by Jewish-Christian polemics and cannot be considered objective in its charges of hypocrisy.) Indeed, they were quite sincere in their efforts to follow strictly all of the more than six hundred rules of the Torah. Doctrinally, the Pharisees, like their contemporary Christian competitors, accepted the doctrines of angels, final judgment, a coming Messiah, and a resurrection of the dead. The Pharisees were probably most popular among the poor, who were attracted to the call to pride in Jewish traditions.

Another first-century movement was the **Sadducees.** They were composed of priests and upper-class members who were associated with the Jerusalem Temple and stressed the written Torah. They were willing to accommodate to Roman law and Greek culture. The Sadducees disappeared after the fall of the Jerusalem Temple in 70 C.E. They are presented in the New Testament as denying the notion of a resurrection and agreeing with the Roman establishment that Jesus was a threat to security in Judea.

RABBINIC JUDAISM

The forces who urged revolt against the Romans suffered a crushing defeat in 70 C.E., when the Romans destroyed the Temple in Jerusalem and cast most of the Jews out into the **Diaspora** (the forced resettlement of Jews outside Palestine). Despite the heroic resistance of many Zealots at Masada, a fortress of King Herod near the Dead Sea Valley, foreign rule stamped down all the harder.

The Pharisees and their successors picked up the pieces. The Pharisaic movement owed much of its concern for the punctilious observance of Torah to the lay scribes (lawyers) who arose in the postexilic Hellenistic period, but the Pharisees did not organize themselves as a distinct party until the second century B.C.E. Maccabean revolt. The Pharisees stood for a close observance of the covenant law, applying it in all aspects of daily life, trying to adapt it as new times required. This approach had come to dominate the scribes who preceded the Pharisees, and it dominated the rabbis (teachers) who came after them. The Pharisees sponsored vigorous debate about the application of Torah, which became a feature of subsequent rabbinic Judaism.

In the Diaspora these rabbis became the center of communal life. The Temple had fallen and with it the cultic priesthood. So the alternative to cultic sacrifice—an alternative that had begun in the Babylonian exile, when Jerusalem and the Temple were far away—filled the religious void. This alternative was the **synagogue**—the gathering place where the community could pray and hear expositions of the Torah. The synagogue became the central institution of Judaism after the destruction of the Temple of Solomon and the deportation of many Jews to Babylon in the sixth century B.C.E. In the absense of a place to perform priestly rituals, the custom of gathering for common study and prayer gained momentum. The synagogue rather naturally gave rise to the rabbinic movement, in that it emphasized study of the tradition focused in the Torah more than ritualistic sacrifice. Following the Diaspora of 70 C.E., the synagogue became the major Jewish institution, although archaeological remains suggest that synagogues varied considerably in their architecture and their degree of involvement in the rabbinic hegemony over Judaism.

As the teachers wanted to base their expositions on the teachings of their eminent predecessors, so they gathered a great collection of commentaries. Eventually, this collection became the Talmud ("the Learning"), a vast collection of the oral law that was composed of the *Mishnah* (itself a collection of interpretations of biblical legal materials) and the *Gemara* (commentaries on the *Mishnah*).

The *Mishnah* arose at the end of the first century B.C.E. from the new practice of settling legal disputes by a systematized appeal to recognized authorities. This practice prompted a conflict between the Sadducees and the Pharisees. The *Mishnah* represented a Pharisaic effort to outflank the Sadducees, who denied the binding character of the oral law and relied on the literal biblical text alone. After the Temple fell in 70 C.E. and times became tumultuous, a written record of all the great teachers' legal opinions became highly desirable. The recording took place in Jabneh, a town on the coast west of Jerusalem. Many teachers moved to Jabneh, among them the great Rabbi Akiba (50–135 C.E.), who later set up his own influential academy at Bene-Berak to the north. They began the real systematization of the *Mishnah* (the

word implies repetition). The *Mishnah* continued and even intensified the scrutiny of every scriptural jot and tittle, but it went hand in hand with more pastoral activities. The interest of the Mishnaic teachers was relatively practical, as they divided Jewish reality into different tractates and discoursed on how relationships ideally would be. For example, in the tractate on women they discussed especially the transitions that ought to occur when a woman passed from her father to her husband at marriage or when she passed from marriage to widowhood.

The *Gemara* was comment on and discussion of the *Mishnah*. The *Gemara* represents a second stage in the evolution of rabbinic Judaism, as the rabbis who gained more and more control during the Diaspora of the early centuries of the common era elaborated their views of the oral Law (which they thought had long accompanied the *Tanak*) and moved from collecting the teachings of the revered early sages (accomplished in the *Mishnah*) to collecting reflections, additions, and commentaries upon this first stratum of collected oral tradition. The *Gemara*, which collected commentaries on the *Mishnah*, plus the Mishnah itself, yielded the Talmud.

As this grand collection of commentary, the **Talmud** became the primary source of Jewish law and focus of rabbinic learning, composed of the *Mishnah* and the Gemara. The Talmud was probably virtually complete around 500 C.E. and existed in at least two important versions, that from Babylon and that from Palestine. It collected teachings, opinions, and decisions of rabbis concerned with continuing the tradition of the oral law—the ongoing interpretation of the Mosaic Torah. As Talmudic scholarship grew throughout the Middle Ages, the Talmudic texts became an encyclopedia of Jewish learning—science, linguistics, and theology, in addition to halakic theory. A traditional Jewish education was based on the Talmud, and it inculcated a good memory, a concern for legal precedent, a willingness to weigh authorities against one another, and a realization that interpretation was intrinsic to the Jewish experiences of both scripture and God.

Under the Roman emperor Hadrian, the Jews were so oppressed, especially by his decision to build a temple to Jupiter on the site of the great Jewish Temple in Jerusalem, that they mounted the shortlived revolt led by Bar Kokhba. The Romans crushed it in 135 C.E., and thenceforth Jews could enter Jerusalem only on the anniversary of the destruction of the Temple, when they might weep at the Western Wall.

In Babylon (present-day Iraq), to which many of the teachers fled, the Talmudic work went on. When Hadrian died in 138 C.E., Palestinian Jews' fortunes rose, and a new intellectual center soon was established in Galilee in northern Israel. There, under Rabbi Judah, the *Mishnah* was elaborated to the point where, when written down (around 200 C.E.), it could be both a practical code and a digest of the oral law. It consisted of six parts, whose subject matter reveals a great deal about the rabbis' conception of religious life. The first Order (part) deals with the biblical precepts concerning the rights of the poor, the rights of priests, the fruits of the harvest, and other agricultural matters. The second Order deals with the Sabbath, festivals, fasts, and the calendar. The third Order (entitled "Women") contains laws of marriage and divorce and other laws governing the relations between the sexes. The fourth Order, entitled "Damages," addresses civil and criminal law. The fifth Order deals with cultic matters and the slaughtering of animals, and the final Order concerns ritual cleanliness.

LAW AND LORE. Perhaps the best-known portion of the *Mishnah* is the *Pirke Avot* ("Sayings of the Fathers"), the last tractate of the fourth Order. It contains opinions of some of the oldest and most influential rabbis, but it is especially venerated for the spirit, the animating love, with which it infuses both the study of the Torah and the ethical life that the Torah should inspire. The *Pirke Avot* suggests the thought of sober, disciplined, studious minds—minds not unlike that of Ecclesiastes and the other wisdom writers. However, further study shows that the Fathers' sobriety encourages a study that reaches the heart and brings joy. This is explicit in Johanan ben Zacchai (2:13), but surely it is implicit in Hillel (1:12), Simeon the Just (1:2), and many others.

The rabbis called the legal portion of the Torah *halakah*. Through reason, analogies, and deep thought, *halakah* made the most minute applications of the Torah. For instance, it concerned itself with the

---

THE KOSHER DIETARY RULES

1. Certain land animals are prohibited:
   Cannot eat: pigs, hares, camels, badgers
   Permitted animals must have cloven hooves and chew cud
   Can eat: cows, goats, sheep, deer

2. Certain birds are prohibited, especially scavengers.
   Cannot eat: vultures, ravens
   Can eat: ducks, doves, turkeys, chickens, geese

3. Certain fish are prohibited.
   Cannot eat: crabs, shrimp, clams, oysters, lobsters
   Permitted fish have scales and fins
   Can eat: trout, bass, red snapper

4. All rodents, insects, amphibians, and reptiles are prohibited
   Cannot eat: frog legs

5. Butchering and preparation of meat must be done in a special fashion so as to be humane and to fully drain all blood.
   Cannot eat: blood sausage

6. Dairy foods and meat cannot be mixed.
   Cannot eat: cheeseburger, veal parmesan

---

dietary laws intended to keep the Jews' eating practices clean or fitting (kosher). It also went deeply into the laws for the observance of the Sabbath. For centuries such laws, in their biblical forms (for example, *Leviticus* and *Numbers*), had kept the Jews separate from their neighbors. As the scribes, Pharisees, and then the Diaspora rabbis concentrated their legal expertise, however, *halakah* became very complex. Certainly in the Roman empire, non-Jews strongly associated the Jews with their laws. Thus, *halakah* partly contributed to anti-Semitism (prejudice and discrimination against the Jews), insofar as it stressed the sense of "otherness" that often is used to justify bigotry.

Kosher meant habits that were considered consonant with the Torah. The dietary laws appear to have developed from a combination of ancient ideas about what was hygienic (apt to promote health and discourage disease) and what was fitting or normal in nature itself—for example, separating dairy and meat foods (that means no cheeseburgers, and for

---

119

some strict homes, separate dishes for meat and dairy products). Some rules governed the preparation of meats (e.g., draining all the blood), while the flesh of other animals were entirely prohibited (e.g., swine, camels, snakes, vultures, shellfish).

Kosher observance became a badge of Jewishness in many periods, serving to demarcate Jews from gentiles and helping to preserve the purity of the chosen people. Probably more Jews kept the laws for this reason than out of any strong sense that certain foods were intrinsically unclean or that God from all eternity had wanted housewives to need two sets of dishes.

Rabbis were most interested in **exegesis:** discerning the most relevant possible interpretation and elaboration of a given passage of scripture. Ancient techniques included the mystical and allegorical approaches. Modern approaches use *hermeneutics:* trying to determine the relevance intended by the original authors and latent in the text as a somewhat transhistorical entity. Exegetes usually stress knowing the original language in which the text was written, informing oneself about the original historical context, and studying the symbols through which the text seems to be trying to express its assumptions, messages, hopes, and the like.

Balancing the strictly legal teaching and lore, however, was the looser, more folkloric approach known as *aggadah.* This was a treasury of exegetical (interpretive) and homiletic (explanatory and preaching) stories that applied biblical passages to a congregation's present circumstances. Where *halakah* reasoned closely, *aggadah* was apt to employ symbols. *Aggadah* drew much of its authority from the fact that Jewish theology had always held (at least in the dominant Pharisaic opinion) that an oral Torah accompanied the written Law of Moses and the other books of the Hebrew Bible. *Aggadah* often presented pious reflection about traditional passages, especially those of scripture, that pictured God at work creating this world in which we live.

This approach probably began with Ezra in the postexilic period, and it flourished when the scribes came to dominate the reassembled community's spiritual life. *Aggadah* continued to develop side by side with *halakah* for at least a millennium, ministering to the needs that common folk had for a teaching that was vivid and exemplary.

In Babylon, under the rule of the Exilarch (as the head of the Diaspora community was known in the common era), scholars collected the fruits of discussions of Rabbi Judah's *Mishnah* conducted at various academies. In addition, they immersed themselves in the ideas and *responsa* (masters' answers to questions about the Law's application) that flowed back and forth between Babylon and Palestine. Both *halakah* and *aggadah* contributed to this broad collection of legal materials, and the final redaction of the Babylonian Talmud, probably accomplished early in the fifth century, amounted to an encyclopedia of scholarly opinion not only on the law but also on much of the other learning of the day, including biology, medicine, and astronomy, that formed the background for many of the discussions.

TALMUDIC RELIGION. In terms of theology proper, the Talmud (whether the Palestinian or the more influential Babylonian version) clung to scripture. Its central pillar was the Shema, the Jewish proclamation of God's unity based on *Deuteronomy* 6:4–9. The Shema has served to remind Jews that they are covenanted to the unique deity responsible for the creation of the world and the guidance of history. Their relation to this God ought to be one of wholehearted love, and they have the obligation to make this God the focus of the education they give their children, the culture they develop, and all the distinctive features of their community life. The call to "hear" implied listening, to the divine or prophetic or rabbinic word. It also implied obedience and loyalty, as well as a regular effort to remember the great things God had done for his chosen people, especially the victory of the Exodus and the gift of the promised land.

The Talmudic view of the Shema was practical rather than speculative. The oneness of God meant to them God's sole dominion over life. He was the Lord of all peoples. The most practical of God's attributes were his justice and his mercy, but how they correlated was not obvious. Clear enough, though, were the implications for ethics and piety: a person ought to reckon with God's justice by acting righteously and avoiding condemnation. A person also ought to rely on God's mercy, remembering that he is slow to anger and quick to forgive.

Through such righteous living, a person could look forward to God's kingdom, which would come

DOWN

1. Non-gentiles
2. Jewish house of worship
3. Orthodox Jews follow a kosher _____.
4. Jewish patriarch who started the covenant
5. David and Solomon were kings of _____.
6. Jewish dispersion after 70 C.E.
7. Jewish doctrine of one God

nature, but how one observed the Sabbath was clearly specified. A major effect of this ethical concern was the refinement of the already quite sensitive morality of the Hebrew Bible. For instance, the rabbis wanted to safeguard the body against even the threat of mortal injury, so they called wicked the mere raising of a hand against another person. Similarly, since the right to life entailed the right to a livelihood, the rabbis concerned themselves with economic justice, proscribing once-accepted business practices such as cornering a market, misrepresenting a product, and trading on a customer's ignorance. In the same spirit, they pondered a person's rights to honor and reputation. To slander another obviously was forbidden, but they reprehended even putting another to shame, likening the blush of the shamed to the red of bloodshed. Despite the caricature that they were concerned only with legal niceties, their writings show that the rabbis were very sensitive to social interaction. Lying, hatred, infringement on others' liberty—all these were targets of their teachings. The rabbis held that the goods of the earth, which prompt so much human contentiousness, were to be for all people. Thus, after a harvest, the owner should leave his field open for the public to glean; the wealthy are obligated to help the poor; and no bread should ever go to waste. Moreover, the rabbis did not limit their lofty social ideals to the Jewish community. Glossing the injunction of *Leviticus* (19:34) to love the stranger "who sojourns with you . . . as yourself," the Talmudists made little political or social distinction between Jew and non-Jew. Human rights applied to all. The spirit of Talmudic ethics, thus, is both precise and broad. The Talmud goes into extreme detail, but it applies to all humanity. According to the Talmud, the great vices are envy, greed, and pride, for they destroy the social fabric. Anger is also destructive, so the rabbis lay great stress on self-control. On the other hand, self-control should not become gloomy asceticism. Generally speaking, the Talmud views the goods of the earth as being for our enjoyment. We should fear neither the body nor the world. In fact, God, who gives us both the body and the world, obliges us to keep them healthy and fruitful. To spurn bodily or material goods without great reason, then, would be to show ingratitude to God—to withdraw from the order God has chosen to create. Wealth and marriage, for instance, should be viewed as great

through the Messiah. The Messiah would rejuvenate or transform this earthly realm, which was so often a source of suffering. The concept of God's kingdom eventually included a supernatural dimension (heaven), but Judaism rather distinctively has emphasized that personal fulfillment comes through daily life.

The thrust of the Talmud, therefore, is not so much theological as *ethical*. The rabbis were more interested in what one did than in how one spoke or thought. So they balanced considerable theological leeway with detailed expectations of behavior. One could hold any opinion about the subtleties of God's blessings that one should accept with simple thankfulness. For the truest wealth, finally, is to be content with one's lot. The pious Jew tried to raise his sights beyond everyday worries to the Master of the universe, from whom so many good things flowed. The great purpose of religious life was to sanctify this Master's name—to live in such love of God that his praise was always on one's lips.

HALLOWING TIME. Through religious observances, the Talmudists designed the social program for inculcating their ethical ideals. In practice, every day was to be hallowed from its beginning. At rising, the devout Jew would thank God for the night's rest, affirm God's unity, and dedicate the coming hours to God's praise. He was supposed to pray at least three times each day: upon rising, in mid-afternoon, and in the evening (women were exempt, because of their family responsibilities). Ritual washings, as well as the kosher diet, reminded the devout of the cleanliness that dedication to God required. Prayer garments such as the fringed prayer shawl; the phylacteries, or *tefellin* (scriptural texts worn on the head and the arm); and the head covering reinforced this cleanliness. The *mezuzah* (container of scriptural texts urging wholehearted love of God) over the door was a reminder to the entire home to adopt this attitude. Home was to be a place of law-abiding love. When possible, Jews would say their daily prayers together in the synagogue.

The synagogue, of course, was also the site of congregational worship on the Sabbath and on the great feasts that punctuated the year. Primary among such feasts have been Passover, a spring festival that celebrates the Exodus of the Israelites from Egypt; Shavuot, a wheat harvest festival occurring seven weeks after Passover; Booths (Sukkoth), a fall harvest festival whose special feature is the erection of branch or straw booths that commemorate God's care of the Israelites while they were in the wilderness; the New Year; and the Day of Atonement (Yom Kippur). The last is the most somber and solemn of the celebrations: the day on which one fasts and asks forgiveness of sins. It is a time when estranged members of the community should make efforts to reconcile their differences and when all people should rededicate themselves to the holiness that God's covenant demands. There are other holidays through the year, most of

them joyous—like Hanukkah, a feast celebrating liberation by the Maccabees—and collectively they serve the several purposes of a theistic cult: recalling God's great favors (anamnesis), binding the community in common commitments, and expiating offenses and restoring hopes. In the home, celebration of the Sabbath did for the week what the annual feasts did for the year. It gave time a cycle with a peak that had special relevance. From midweek all looked forward to the Sabbath joy, preparing the house and the food for the day that came like God's bride. When the mother lit the candles and the Sabbath drew near, even the poorest Jew could view life as good. Special hospitality was the Sabbath rule; rest and spiritual regeneration were the Sabbath order. Regretful as all were to see the Sabbath end, a glow lingered that strengthened them so they could return to the workaday world.

Explain Judaism using one of the scholarly perspectives we have introduced: Freud, Marx, Otto, Tylor, Frazer, Malinowski, Müller, or another thinker.

EXAMPLE: Explaining Judaism from the perspective of Emile Durkheim, who viewed religion as a system of rituals that served to celebrate and reinforce social cohesion: each element of Jewish religion—doctrine, myth, ritual, and ethics—serves that function.

Jewish *doctrine* is that there is a sacred covenant between the one God and His people. It is easier to see your fellow man as your brother if you both acknowledge the same father: God.

Jewish *myth* involves many stories about their great patriarchs: Abraham, Isaac, and Jacob. The relevance of these stories about the past is that they note common ancestors for the diversity of the twelve tribes.

Jewish *rituals* (e.g., sabbath, Purim, Hanukkah) keep alive those myths by reenacting them in an interpersonal, social context of family (sabbath, Passover) or synagogue (Yom Kippur).

Jewish *ethics* serve two functions. One is to preserve the sacredness of the symbols, rituals, and myths (do not worship idols) and another is to unify the community (helping the poor).

Contribute to this discussion at
http://www.delphi.com/rel101

The principal rites of passage through the life cycle were infant circumcision, through which males entered the covenant community on their eighth day; *bar mitzvah,* to celebrate the coming of age; marriage; and *kaddish* (a funeral prayer requiring ten Jewish males). These rites reinforced the doctrine that life is good (or at least that we should be committed to finding goodness in every stage and challenge of life), that the Torah is life's guidebook, that marriage is a human being's natural estate, and that death is not the final word.

THE MEDIEVAL PERIOD

From the seventh century on, this Talmudic religious program structured the lives of Jews who were mainly under Muslim rule in the Middle East and Spain. As a subjugated people, the Jews tended to look inward for their fulfillment. Muhammad himself took rather kindly to Judaism, because he thought that his own revelation agreed with biblical thought: monotheistic doctrine, daily formal prayers, fasting and almsgiving, the prohibition of swine's flesh. However, things grew more complicated when the Jews refused to convert to Islam, and under both Muhammad and his successors the Jews had to endure some discrimination. Nonetheless, Muslims frequently found Jews useful as translators or businessmen, and Muslim countries were generally tolerant. As long as non-Muslim religious groups posed no threat to security or orthodoxy, they could have a decent, if second-rate, civil status.

During the first centuries of Muslim power, the Jewish community's prestigious center of learning was at the heart of its Diaspora in Baghdad (the former Babylonia). According to Talmudic tradition, the leaders of the Baghdad schools gave *responsa* to points of law and held sway over community religion. They also fixed the pattern of communal worship, which hitherto had been a source of confusion and controversy. During the ninth and tenth centuries, the scholars of the Babylonian schools also standardized the pronunciation for the Hebrew Bible. These scholars (called Masoretes) supplied the vowel points, accents, and other signs necessary to make readable a text that had consisted only of consonants. (Pronunciation, consequently, had been a matter of oral tradition.) The same work went on in Palestine, and

eventually the version of a Palestinian author named Ben Asher won acceptance as the canonical Masoretic text. At the end of the first millennium of the common era, Talmudic scholars emigrated to Europe, North Africa, and Egypt, taking with them the scholarship of the Talmudic school to which they had the closest ties. The Babylonian traditions were more popular, but in countries such as Italy, which had close ties with Palestine, Palestinian influence was great.

The two great Jewish groups in Europe, the **Sephardim** (Spain) and the **Ashkenazim** (eastern European), can be characterized by their subjugation under either Muslim or Christian rule, respectively. The two traditions shared more than they held separately because of the Talmudists, and their different styles in intellectual matters and in piety largely derived from the different cultures in which they evolved.

The Sephardic branch of Jews trace their residence in Spain to the time when the Romans forcefully deported them from Israel in 70 C.E., and they looked for the furthest point in the Empire to which they might be conveniently sent, Spain. The Sephardim established a glorious civilization in the tenth and eleventh centuries, with philosophy, exegesis, poetry, and scientific learning at their peak. Medieval Jewish culture was favored in the southern cities under Muslim rule—Toledo, Cordoba, Sevilla, and Granada—but also did well in Christian areas such as Lisbon and even Avila before the Inquisition. The Sephardim suffered greatly from the Inquisition. When the Catholic monarchs Ferdinand and Isabela completed the reconquest of Spain from the Muslims in 1492, the Jews were given an ultimatum: convert or leave. This expulsion was a trauma so great it led many Jewish cabalists to expect the coming of the Messiah. Many left for Spain's Netherlands colonies. Others emigrated to the Turkish empire, which they hoped would be more benign than the Christian. Even those who converted and remained in Spain were not free from discrimination or persecution. For centuries, the descendants of these converts were accused of practicing Jewish rituals in secret.

PHILOSOPHY. The early medieval period saw a ferment in Talmudic learning. As well, a Jewish philosophical theology arose. Whereas Philo, in the first century of the common era, worked at what could be called philosophical theology, trying to reconcile Hellenistic thought with biblical thought, the medieval thinkers, especially Maimonides, brought philosophy into the Jewish mainstream. Philo's strong point had been reading of scripture on several levels so as to remove the problems that the philosophical mind might have with anthropomorphism). Though he never exerted a decisive influence on his contemporaries, **Maimonides** (1135–1204) did. This physician and scholar from Cordoba combined Aristotelian logic and science. His work was in the form of apologetics, making Judaism a strong contender in the debates that were being conducted by the Western religions on the supposedly common ground of rational analysis. However, Maimonides' work was also constructive, setting Talmudic and traditional learning in the context of a philosophical system. The philosophical services of thinkers such as Maimonides were very useful in internal fights with literalists such as the Karaites, who (despite their fundamentalism about points of biblical law) mocked both biblical anthropomorphism and much of *aggadah* (because it was poetic and symbolic).

The great questions of this period of philosophical debate were the criteria of biblical exegesis, the relation of doctrine to reason, the nature of the human personality and its relation to God, God's existence and attributes, the creation of the world, and providence and theodicy (God's justice). In debating these questions, the philosophers based their work on the Greek view that contemplation (*theoria*) is the most noble human work.

Whereas for the Talmudist study of the Torah was the highest activity, many of the medieval philosophers considered the contemplation of God's eternal forms (through which he had created the world) the highest human activity. Maimonides became the prince of Jewish philosophers largely because he was also learned in the Talmudic tradition and so could reconcile the old with the new. For him philosophical contemplation did not take one away from the Torah, because the proper object of philosophical contemplation was the one Law we find in both scripture and nature.

A key teaching in Maimonides' system was divine incorporeality. God had to be one, which he could

not be if he occupied a body, since matter is a principle of multiplicity. To rationalize the anthropomorphic biblical descriptions of God, where he has bodily emotions if not form, Maimonides allegorized as Philo had done. The dynamic to his system, however, was the conviction that philosophical reason can provide the key to scripture. Maimonides has probably been most influential through the thirteen articles in which he summarized Jewish doctrines, and which even today are listed in the standard prayer book:

1. The existence of God
2. God's unity
3. God's incorporeality
4. God's eternity
5. The obligation to worship God alone
6. Prophecy
7. The superiority of the prophecy of Moses
8. The Torah as God's revelation to Moses
9. The Torah's immutability
10. God's omniscience
11. Reward and punishment
12. The coming of the Messiah
13. The resurrection of the dead

In this summary a philosopher gave the key headings under which reason and biblical revelation could be reconciled.

However, Jewish philosophy before Maimonides expressed a somewhat contrary position. The lyrical writer Judah Halevi (ca. 1086–1145), for instance, insisted that the God of Aristotle is not the God of Abraham and the biblical Fathers. (Halevi's position is reminiscent of the later Christian philosopher Blaise Pascal, and it draws on the same sort of religious experience that made Pascal visualize God as a consuming fire—no Aristotelian "prime mover" but a vortex of personal love.) Halevi did not despise reason, but he insisted that it is less than full religious experience, or love.

MYSTICISM. One of the earliest sources of Judaic mysticism was Ezekiel's vision of the chariot (*merkabah*). In medieval Germany a movement arose among Jews called the Hasidim who upheld a relatively new spiritual ideal. What characterized the truly pious person, this movement argued, was serenity of mind, altruism, and renunciation of worldly things. The renunciation, implying some degree of asceticism, especially ran counter to traditional Judaism, for it seemed to entail turning away from the world. Indeed, Hasidic speech relates to the experience that has always drawn mystics and caused them to neglect the world—the experience of glimpsing the divine being itself, of tasting the biblical "goodness of the Lord." Then the divine love exalts the soul and seems far more precious than anything the world can offer. Hasidism in its medieval Germanic form is not the direct ancestor of the modern eastern European Jewish pietism that goes by this name. Intervening between Hasidism's two phases was a most influential Jewish mysticism, that of the cabala.

Cabala (also known as *cabbala, kabala, kabbalah*) means "tradition," and the cabalists sought to legitimize their movement by tracing it back to secret teachings of the patriarchs and Moses. This Jewish mystical movement started in Spain and flourished during the Middle Ages. The cabalists usually considered themselves followers of the Torah who were developing an esoteric wisdom to complement the esoteric wisdom of the halakic law. In their mystical writings and exercises, the cabalists emphasized the emanations of the divinity into the created world and the symbolic marriage of God with the Torah, which gave religious living a nuptial or erotic symbolism. Such secret or esoteric overtones stamp cabalism as a sort of Jewish **Gnosticism** (secret knowledge). The fullness of knowledge which the cabalists glimpsed in their ecstatic visions ordinary human beings can only conceive symbolically. Hence, cabalists engaged in their own brand of allegorical exegesis of scripture, trying to decode secret symbols about divinity that the Hebrew Bible couched in deceptively simple language.

In the cabalistic perspective, the divine and the human spheres are interdependent. The fallen state of the world (most acutely manifested in the suffering of the Jews, God's chosen people) signals a disruption within the divine essence itself. Human sinfulness, it follows, reflects this divine wounding. On the other hand, human holiness contributes to God's repair, and so every human act takes on cosmic significance. In fact, human life can become a sort of mystery play in which the significant aspect of people's actions is their wounding or repairing of the divine life. When the Spaniards expelled the Jews from the Iberian peninsula at the end of the fifteenth century, the cabalists had the perfect crisis on which to focus their somewhat fevered imaginations.

The paramount book of the cabalistic movement, and the most representative of its symbolism, was the *Zohar,* probably written by Moses de Leon in thirteenth-century Spain. Known as the "Book of Splendor," it consists of imaginative contemplations of the emanations of the divinity through the different layers of creation. From 1500 to 1800, the *Zohar* exerted an influence equal to that of the Bible and the Talmud. The *Zohar* is similar to aggadic materials in that it interprets scriptural texts symbolically and in pietistic fashion rather than in the legal manner of *halakah*. What distinguishes the *Zohar* from traditional *aggadah* is its suffusion with the Gnostic ideas mentioned earlier. For instance, its commentary on the first verse of the Hebrew Scriptures (*Genesis* 1:1) goes immediately to what the divine nature was really like "in the beginning." Within the most hidden recess of the infinite divine essence, a dark flame went forth, issuing the realm of divine attributes, but the mystics saw them as the emanations of God's own being. Such a view makes the world alive with divine essence. It gives human experience eternal implications, because the emanations move through our time, our flesh, our blood. The *Zohar* turns over each word of *Genesis,* searching for hidden clues to the divine plan. It concerns itself with the numerical value of the words' letters (for example, $a = 1$) and correlates clues in *Genesis* with clues from other visionary parts of the Hebrew Bible, such as *Ezekiel,* chapter 1, and *Isaiah,* chapter 6. To align its interpretation with respectable past commentary, it cites traditional rabbis, but the *Zohar's* immediate concern is not the rabbis' interest in ethics but an imaginative contemplation of divinity and the divine plan.

The *Zohar* stimulated many mystics, Hasidim, and even orthodox rabbis to view creation as shot through with sparks of the divine seeking to return to God in redemption. It supported the notion that God is metaphysically married to the Torah and that the splendor of God (Shekina) is a nuptial entity that sets sexual complementarity and love at the center of the heavenly realities.

THE MODERN PERIOD

Thorough exposure to a secularized, technological culture did not come to most of the rural population of the eastern European Jewish *shtetls* (villages), where much of the Ashkenazic Jewish population lived, until the twentieth century. Until that time the eighteenth-century Enlightenment and reform had made little impact, for Talmudic orthodoxy kept the tradition basically unchanged. But the center of eastern European Jewish culture was the restricted urban district known as the *ghetto*. It was in this environment that modern mystical **Hasidism** was developed by Israel Baal Shem-Tov (1700–1760). His movement sought to restore the traditional practices, which they saw as endangered by false messiahs, arid intellectualism, and Talmudic legalism. The key was the pursuit of divine wisdom and joy. The movement quickly caught fire in eastern Europe, and thousands rushed to the Hasidic "courts" where charismatic masters presided.

VILLAGE LIFE. Hasidism remained vigorous in the villages well into the twentieth century. Hasidism set the charismatic holy man rather than the learned rabbi at the center of the community: the *tzaddik* (righteous one). Hasidim revered this holy man for his intimacy with God, his ability to pray evocatively, and his gifts as a storyteller. (As a storyteller he was an updated version of the ancient aggadist.) But the simple ones among them held the *tzaddik* to be a wonder worker.

Hasidism in the *shtetl* commingled with Talmudic tradition, blending legal observance with emotional fervor. Jewish village life hinged on the Sabbath and on three blessings: the Torah, marriage, and good deeds. The Torah meant God's revelation and Law. In practice, it meant the exaltation of learning. *Shtetl* parents hoped that they would have learned sons, well versed in the Law, who would bring glory to the family. Thus, the ideal son was thin and pale, a martyr to his books. From age five or so, he marched off to a long day of study, beginning his education by memorizing a Hebrew that he did not understand and then progressing to subtle Talmudic commentaries. The Torah shaped the economic and family lives of *shtetl* Jews because men tried to free themselves for study, placing the financial burdens on women. The impoverished scholar, revered in the *shul* (synagogue school) but master of a threadbare family, exemplified the choices and value commitments that the Torah inspired. Many men did work in trades (the state usually prevented Jews from owning land and farming), but even they would try to gain dignity by devoting their spare time to learning.

Glory for women came from caring for the home, the children, and often a little shop. So much were those responsibilities part of religion for women that no commandments prescribed for them exact times for prayer, fasting, synagogue attendance, charitable works, or the like. Women's three principal *mitzvoth* (duties) out of the traditional 613 were to remove a portion of the Sabbath bread, to light the Sabbath candles, and to visit the ritual bath (*mikvah*) after menstruation.

In the *shtetl* (village) marriage was the natural human situation and children were its crown. Father and mother were obligated to create a home steeped in Torah and good deeds (fulfillment of the duties and acts of charity). In popular humor, nothing was worse than an old maid, while an unmarried man was pitied as being incomplete. Of course, kosher rules and keen legal observance marked the devout home, which was but a cell of the organic community. That community supported needy individual members with material goods, sympathy in times of trouble, and unanimity in religious ideals. One had to share one's wealth, whether wealth of money or of mind, and the seats of honor in the synagogue went to the learned and the community's financial benefactors.

TRIBULATIONS. The community exacted a steep toll through the pressure it exerted to conform to its ideals and through the gossip and judgment that ever circulated. Nevertheless, most Jews gladly accepted being bound by the common laws and custom, and few could avoid being bound by the equally overt and common suffering. The urban populations in the Russian and Polish ghettos shared an almost paranoid life, with *pogroms* (persecutions) a constant specter, while the rural populations of the rest of eastern Europe never knew when some new discrimination or purge would break out. In both situations, Jews' mainstay was their solidarity in commitment to their traditions. Consequently, we can understand

CASE STUDY: HASIDIC TALES

The Hasidic masters made a deep impression on the Jewish imagination, and some of the tales about them are wonderfully entertaining as well as deeply instructive. For example, there is the story in which Satan was tormented by the good he saw the Baal Shem-Tov doing on earth, so he schemed to overcome the Master. Calling all his servants of darkness together, he disclosed to them a wicked plan. He would station devils on all the roads that led to heaven. Whenever a prayer rose upward, toward heaven's gates, the devils would be able to keep it from getting through. After some days without prayers getting through, Satan would be able to go to God and say, "Look, your people have deserted you. They no longer send you prayers. Even your favorite puppet, Rabbi Israel Baal Shem-Tov, has ceased to pray. Take back his wisdom, then. Take away his people's Torah."

The soldiers of the Evil One listened attentively, and then slunk out to execute the foul scheme. Leaving no bypath unguarded, they lurked silently in wait for any prayer. When a prayer came, they leaped upon it, pummeling and kicking it. They could not kill the prayers, but they flung them sideways into chaos. Thus all of space became filled with wounded prayers, whimpering and moaning, lost from their way. On Sabbaths, the flux of prayers was so great that many got through to heaven's gate, but there a great army of devils saw to it that the prayers were rebuffed. Three weeks passed in this fashion, and Satan thought it time to confront God.

Going before the divine throne, Satan said: "Take away the Torah from the Jews." But God said, "Give them until the Day of Atonement." Satan struck a hard bargain: "Give the command today, but hold back on its execution until the Day of Atonement." So God gave the terrible edict, and the Jews were to lose the Torah. On earth, the archbishop issued a proclamation. In ten days, the bishops were to have all the Hebrew books of learning confiscated. Men were to be sent into the synagogues to seize the Torah, and into all the Jews' homes. Then they were to heap all the He-brew books into a great pile and set fire to them. The bishop of Kamenitz-Podolsky in Russia was the most zealous in obeying, sending his servants into all the Jews' homes. On the Day of Atonement, a great fire would destroy all the books of God's Law.

When the Baal Shem-Tov saw these things happening, he knew Satan was mounting a terrible attack. Yet he did not know how Satan was accomplishing this great evil, nor how to counteract it. Each day the horror mounted as Jews were stripped of the Torah. In home after home, cries of anguish rent the night. Fasting and sleepless, the Baal Shem-Tov struggled on behalf of his people, sending mighty prayers toward heaven day and night. They rose on colossal wings at incredible speed, but the Enemy himself caught them outside heaven's gate and cast them aside. So the heart of Baal Shem-Tov emptied, becoming a great cave of grief. At last the Day of Atonement dawned. Rabbi Israel went into the synagogue to hold the service, and the people saw the fever of his struggle on his face. Hope rose in their hearts. "He will save us today," they said. When the time came to sing the Kol Nidre ("All Vows"), Rabbi Israel's voice poured out the pain of his heart, freezing all who listened.

It was the custom for Rabbi Yacob to read each verse of the lamentations aloud and then for Rabbi Israel to repeat it. But when Rabbi Yacob read out the verse, "Open the Portals of Heaven!" Rabbi Israel did not utter a word. The people first were confused, then waited in growing fear. Once again Rabbi Yacob repeated, "Open the Portals of Heaven!" but still Rabbi Israel did not utter a word.

Then, like a trumpet blast into the monumental silence, Rabbi Israel threw himself upon the ground, beat his head, and roared like a dying lion. For two hours he remained doubled over, his body shaking with the force of his struggle. Those watching in the synagogue dared not approach him. They could only worry and wait. At last, the Baal Shem-Tov raised himself from the ground, his face shining with wonders. "The Portals of Heaven are open," he said, and then he ended the service.

Years afterward, it became known how Rabbi Israel had passed those terrible two hours. He had gone to the Palace of the Eternal, traveling by the road that goes directly to the throne. There he had found hundreds and hundreds of prayers huddled before the gate. Some were wounded, some lay gasping as though they had just ended a terrible struggle, some were emaciated and old, and some were blind from having wandered so long in darkness. "Why are you waiting here?" the Baal Shem-Tov asked them. "Why don't you go in and approach the throne?"

The prayers told Rabbi Israel that only his approach had scattered the dark angels. Before he came, no prayer could pass through the gate. "I will take you in," the Baal Shem-Tov told them.

But just as he started to pass the gate, the Baal Shem-Tov saw the army of evil spirits rush forth to close it. Then Satan himself came forward and hung a great lock, as big as a city, upon the heavenly gate. The Baal Shem-Tov walked all around the lock, looking for a crack through which to enter. It was made of solid iron, however, so there seemed no way he could pass through. Still, Rabbi Israel did not despair. Now, for each of us living on earth, there is an exact duplicate living in heaven. So Rabbi Israel called across the gate to his heavenly counterpart. "What shall I do," he asked, "to bring the prayers before the Name?" Rabbi Israel of heaven told him, "Let us go to the Palace of the Messiah."

They went to the palace, where the Messiah sat waiting for the day when he might go down to earth. As soon as they entered, the Messiah told them, "Be joyous! I will help you," and he gave the Baal Shem-Tov a token. The Baal Shem-Tov took the token back to the heavenly gate. When he brandished the token, the heavenly portals swung open, as wide as the earth is large. So all the prayers entered, going straight to the Throne of the Name. Heaven fell to ecstatic rejoicing, and all the angels sang hymns of praise. But the dark angels fled back to their hellish dungeons, routed and fearful again.

On earth, the bishop of Kamenitz-Podolsky was lighting a great fire. Beside him was a mountain of Hebrew books, which his minions had readied for the flames. He took a tractate of the Talmud and hurled it into the fire. He hurled another and another, until the flames leaped high as the clouds. But then his hand began shaking, and he fell down in a fit. The crowd was seized with terror, and ran out of the central square. The fire soon died down, and most of the books were saved. When the news of this happening spread to other towns, they abandoned their plans to burn the Torahs. Fearing they too would be struck by seizures, the other bishops gave back all the stolen books. That was how the Baal Shem-Tov saved the Torah for the Jews, on the Day of Atonement.

When we reflect on this little story, it reveals volumes about premodern Judaism. The Baal Shem-Tov is the central hero, but there are many other actors in the drama. The evil genius threatening Jewish life is Satan, the angel of power and light who had turned bad. Hating God and everything good, Satan is constantly plotting against God's people. If the Jews had not had saints like Rabbi Israel, there was no telling how their misfortunes might have grown. Bad as life was in the midst of unsympathetic Christians, it would have been much worse without the sainted rabbis.

how threatening were any movements to change those traditions, such as the Reform movement or the Enlightenment must have been. The old ways had been the foundation of Jewish sanity. New conditions, as in Germany and the United States, seemed much less solid than long familiar suffering and endurance.

The bulk of the Jewish population in the late 1700s was in eastern Europe: the Russian empire, Austria, and Prussia. Their life was rather precarious, and attacks by Russians and Ukrainians produced a stream of emigrants to the New World. Yet European Jews contributed to the formation of the notion of the modern secular state, probably because they hoped that it would offer them greater religious freedom. Thus, the Jewish philosopher Baruch **Spinoza** (1632–1672) suggested such a political arrangement, and Moses Mendelssohn (1729–1786), a German man of letters, plumped for a secular state before the French Revolution. Generally, Jews' civil status seemed to prosper in countries or under regimes that were open to the new, liberal ideas of equality. However, when nationalism prevailed, Jews tended to experience more anti-Semitism, since non-Jews then considered them to be outsiders.

DISSOLUTION OF TRADITIONAL JUDAISM. The eighteenth-century European Enlightenment's emphasis on human reason rather than traditional institutional authorities in effect attacked the legal and philosophical underpinnings of traditional Judaism. By extending rights of citizenship to Jews ("Emancipation"), the Gentile thinkers of the Enlightenment in principle took away the basis of the Jewish community—it was no longer a ghetto or a world set apart from the national mainstream, because all citizens were to be equal. By its philosophical turn to individual reason, the Enlightenment attacked the Talmudic assumption that traditional law and its interpretation by the Fathers were the best guides for life. Thus, intellectual Jews who accepted the ideals of the enlightenment tended to abandon Talmudic scholarship (or at least deny that it was the most important learning) and devote themselves to secular learning. This movement spawned the distinguished line of modern Jewish scientists, social thinkers, and humanists, but it meant that the Jewish community lost some of its best talent to secular concerns. It also often meant intellectual warfare between the advocates of the new learning and the defenders of the old.

REFORM. Thus, the traditional legal authority at the heart of rabbinic Judaism crumbled because of both the new secular learning and the greater attractiveness of the charismatic *tzaddik*. In response to this crisis of the tradition came a "Reform" of orthodox conceptions. For the relatively educated, the **Reform** movement meant an effort to accept modern culture and still remain a Jew. In other words, it meant searching for new definitions of Jewishness that would not necessitate alienation from the intellectual and political life of gentile fellow citizens.

Among some of the main personalities of the Reform movement, the emphasis was on rational Jewish ethics and theology (and so applicable to all people). In effect, emphasis shifted from what was distinctive in Judaism, what gave Jews their unique status as God's chosen ones, to what Judaism could offer to all humanity. The stress of Reform was ethical. Reform Jews saw their tradition as offering all peoples a moral sensitivity, a concern for the rights of conscience and social justice, that derived from the prophets and the great rabbis but could serve the dawning future age of equality, political freedom, and mutual respect. Reform Jews tended to be talented people who were either formally or informally excluded from national and university life. As a result, their visions of a new day led them to stress what in their own religious past might abet equal opportunity. Today, most American Jews identify themselves as Reform.

A response to Reform within Judaism was the self-conscious **Orthodox** movement, which insisted that the Torah be the judge of modernity and not vice versa. Positively, however, the Orthodox conceded the possibility that living with Gentiles might be a good, God-intended arrangement. No doubt, the breakup of Christian control over culture that marked the Western shift from medieval to modern times played a strong role in this reevaluation. That is, the Orthodox saw the wisdom in the Reform argument that living among modern Gentiles might free Jews of the prejudice endemic in medieval Christianity by letting Christians see that Jews could be amiable fellow citizens (in its most virulent form, that prejudice branded all Jews as "Christ killers"). However, the most recent strains of Orthodoxy in the United States and Israel seem to favor a return to self-contained rural villages or urban neighborhoods in which Jewish culture may predominate. Although the Orthodox sect is the smallest branch of Judaism in the world, its high birth rates make it the fastest-growing sect of Judaism today.

Conservative Judaism represented an effort to find a centrist position between Reform and Orthodoxy. Its founder was Rabbi Zecharias Frankel (1801–1875), head of a theological seminary in Germany.

JUDAISM IN THE LAST THOUSAND YEARS				
MOVEMENT	WHERE STARTED?	WHERE TODAY?	MAIN THEME	RITUAL
Cabala	Spain	died out	mysticism	study Torah code
Orthodox	Europe	New York and Israel	strict adherence	study Torah rules
Hasidism	Poland	New York and Israel	mysticism and strict adherence	singing
Reform	United States	United States	accommodate to secular world	minimal
Zionist	Europe	Israel	reestablish nation of Israel	resettle Jews in Palestine

Frankel's position was that Judaism should change slowly, remaining true to its traditional character and only allowing slight modifications of traditional practice. In the United States, Solomon Schechter of the Jewish Theological Seminary of America was the central promoter of Conservative Judaism. Its intellectual center is the Jewish Theological Seminary in New York, its rabbinical assembly numbers more than one thousand members, and its league of synagogues (the United Synagogue) numbers more than one thousand congregations. Building on Reform initiatives, the Conservative worship service has introduced family pews, developed a modernized liturgy in the vernacular, and allowed women a fuller role in the congregation's ritual life.

Reconstructionist Judaism, a U.S. Jewish movement founded by Mordecai Kaplan (1881–1983), has taught that past Jewish concern with otherworldly salvation is no longer credible and that consequently Jews should translate their traditional concern for salvation into this-worldly terms: human betterment in health, political rights, education, and the like. Other reconstructionists have kept the same this-worldly emphasis but focused more on Jewish culture than "salvation." Whether this is a specific denomination within Judaism, or more of a secular movement away from Jewish traditional ritual and doctrine, remains to be seen.

ZIONISM. The movement most responsible for the establishment of the modern state of Israel is **Zionism**. Zionism has biblical roots, from the time that Israel gained a land of its own centered on Mount Zion in Jerusalem. During the Exile Jews longed to be back in their promised land, where they alone could sing their native songs joyously. The Diaspora that occurred in the first century C.E. made nostalgia for Zion and the Western Wall that symbolized the Temple ingredient in all Jewish culture. Most of the medieval piety movements anticipated Zionism insofar as their messianism regularly involved the notion of returning to the ancestral land (and to the holiest of cities, Jerusalem). In the eighteenth and nineteenth centuries, Hasidim in Poland sent many people to the holy land, with the result that there were circles of devout Jews in Jerusalem. During the nineteenth century, Jews led by Theodor Herzl (1860–1904) began practical movements to resettle Palestine. The upsurge of nationalism in modern Europe tended to make Jews consider their own national roots, while new movements of social thought, including those led by Marx and Tolstoy, caused many Jews to dream about a new society based on the *kibbutz* (collective).

The greatest impetus to Zionism, however, was the persecutions that convinced European Jews they were in peril on the European continent: pogroms in Russia from 1880 to 1905, Ukrainian massacres

Electronic flashcards and matching games
http://www.quia.com/jg/51429.html

hangman games
http://www.quia.com/hm/18273.html

word jumble games
http://www.quia.com/jw/8467.html

Download multiple choice, true-false, and fill-in drills from
http://www.ureach.com/tlbrink
Click on the public filing cabinet and folder rel7 and download m7.exe, t7.exe, and f7.exe.

from 1917 to 1922, persecutions in Poland between 1922 and 1939, and, above all, the Nazi persecution that began in 1933 and climaxed in the **Holocaust** of perhaps 6 million Jews in Nazi death camps. The aftermath of World War II and the sufferings that Jews had endured in the Holocaust (as the climax of centuries of anti-Semitism in Europe) had made conditions ripe. By 1948, about 650,000 Jews lived within the British Mandate of Palestine, and at the birth of modern Israel many hundreds of thousands more emigrated from Europe and from Arab lands (where, after the 1948 war, conditions were difficult). The main ideologist for the modern Zionist movement was a Viennese named Theodor Herzl. His witness of anti-Semitism during the Dreyfus trial in France at the end of the nineteenth century had convinced him and many other Jews that only by having their own nation could Jews be free of constant persecution.

WORLDVIEW

NATURE

Generally speaking, nature has not been so important in Judaism as peoplehood. In the biblical period nature was quite important, because the earliest "Jews" were shepherds or farmers. The earliest theology appears to have been a veneration of different *els* (gods) related to natural powers, and the constant lament of the prophets and other biblical theologians that the gods of the neighboring peoples (the Canaanites

especially) were seducing the people away from prophetic religion is testimony that the cosmological myth held considerable attraction.

Designated Jewish holidays, the liturgical feasts, though they began as nature festivals, ran through the agricultural year and were expressions of gratitude for harvests. In the Diaspora the sacrificial aspect of early Jewish worship was replaced by the sermonizing and Bible reading of the synagogue. Celebrations still involved food, drink, and dance, but they were probably due more to a social sense, from a desire to affirm a common identity, than from a close connection with mother earth or father sky. (Interestingly, though, in their elaboration of the Torah, the rabbis were remarkably sensitive to animals' welfare. They glossed the biblical injunction not to muzzle the grinding ox, and they demanded that ritual slaughtering be as painless as possible.)

URBAN VALUES. Many of the countries in which Jews lived, as a distinct and often inhibited minority, forbade them ownership of land, while their tradition of study tended to lead them into intellectual occupations and business. The tensions between *shtetl* Jews and Gentiles in eastern Europe, for instance, were due as much to different occupations as to different theologies. The Gentile peasants worked the land and valued rather brutish strength. The *shtetl* Jews did not farm very much, tending rather to engage in small businesses and study. Jews were not to fight, engage in hard labor, drink, or carouse. They were to be disciplined, cultured, and family and community oriented. Because few Jews lived on farms, they had to concentrate on living in densely populated areas. The Gentile peasants needed customers for their goods, middlemen for their trades, craftsmen, and doctors, and Jews tended to fill these roles.

ZIONISM. With Zionism and the return to the holy land, Judaism has brought back to center stage a theme that was prominent in premodern times—the predilection for Israel and Jerusalem as the most religious places, favoring the prosperity of the Jewish denomination. In the centuries of Diaspora, the typical Jew felt something of what the first biblical exiles lamented—the inability to sing and rejoice in a foreign land. That did not afflict the descendants of the actual exiles as intensely, for few of them returned from Babylon when they had the opportunity, but it mixed a certain nature orientation with Jews' desire to have a place of their own. Consequently, Israel became not just a venerable place but also a beautiful, fruitful, arable, desirable land. Thus, the biblical theme of a promised land joined with messianic hopes to link the new age that the Messiah would usher in and the people's return to a place flowing with milk and honey. Zionism drew on these traditional themes, joining them to socialistic (if not utopian) theories of working the land and living together in close cooperation.

Though few American Jews farm, quite a few Israelis live on *kibbutzim* and work the land (and quite a few American Jewish youths join them for a summer or a year). The land, if not nature, is most important to kibbutzniks. Because of Israel's ancient history and Jews' present need to have their own place in the sun, the Israelis now are more agrarian than their recent predecessors were. How that affects their religious consciousness is hard to determine. Many do not consider themselves religious, and they often view their life on the land, even though it brings them close to nature, in sociological rather than naturalistic terms. Frequently, then, they resemble other idealistic groups who form communes and farm in order to augment their freedom (and often to "purify" their lives). On the other hand, those who do form *kibbutzim* out of religious motivations are often fundamentalists trying to regain their biblical heritage. Still, that heritage is not so much harvesting God's earth as living where God made the Jews his special people.

SOCIETY

Few religions are as community minded as Judaism. The Jews were the chosen people—chosen as a group or line rather than as individuals. From tribal beginnings, through kingdom, Diaspora, and ethnic diversification, Jewish religion has always been a group affair. Of course, the Torah is inseparable from this phenomenon, for it is a special law designed expressly for the chosen, covenanted people. It sprang from a group sense that life must flow to "our" God, who led us out of captivity to be his own people. The Torah also specified the theological direction of Jews

by giving election and covenant the forms by which they shaped social life.

Thus, the synagogue has been a popular gathering place, uniting the action of the people. The Christian *ecclesia* ("church") has a similar etymological meaning ("gathering," "being called out"), but the building it names has been almost as much a place for private prayer as for public gathering. Perhaps the relative smallness of the Jewish population has helped it to gain a more worldwide sense of community than Christians have had. Perhaps, as well, the relative mildness of its sectarian divisions has helped to keep Judaism a family affair. In any event, Muslims, despite their democratic worship and pilgrimage, have been less united than Jews have been, and Christians, despite their lofty theology of the Church, have been more individual oriented and divided.

WOMEN'S STATUS. Jews, then, have focused more on culture than on nature. Women have generally been associated with nature, because of menstruation, childbirth, nursing, and—to male eyes—more intuitive, less cerebral behavior. Men have been associated with culture: craft, art, literature, and politics. Though this is a stereotype which does not describe the specific abilities or interests of individuals, many societies have used it, more or less consciously, to characterize sex roles. Therefore, the construct is useful in analyzing how societies view the play of physical nature in human societies.

This gender stereotype is somewhat applicable among Jews. During many periods of Jewish history, women worked or ran the home while the men studied. Women did not read the Torah in the synagogue (usually they could not read Hebrew), did not have many legal obligations (only three *mitzvoth* pertain solely to them), could not be priests or rabbis (until recently), were tabooed during menstruation, and were both indulged and criticized for their "flightiness." Under biblical law, Jewish women were partially considered as property—akin to animals and goods. For instance, the laws concerning adultery and rape were principally intended to protect the rights of the male—the injured husband or father. The principal value of women throughout Jewish history was motherhood. They seldom could have careers and usually had difficulty obtaining the education that would have enabled them to be their hus-

J.T. Carmody

This view of Jerusalem shows the Western Wall ruins of the old temple. The sacred Muslim Mosque, Dome of the Rock, lies directly behind.

bands' best friends. They were the source of the family line and of emotional support, not leaders. In good measure because he enjoyed being the cultural center, the male Jew traditionally prayed thanks to God for not having created him a woman.

JERUSALEM. It is hard for Gentiles to comprehend the dynamics of the current conflict in Palestine, especially the dispute over the holy sites of Jerusalem. From the Jewish perspective, David was the sacred king, the mediator between heaven and earth, the top of the human pyramid, and from his line would spring the Messiah. The city of Jerusalem was the city of David.

When the Jews gained a new homeland in 1948, fulfilling decades of Zionist longings, Jerusalem again became the real center of Jewish geography. All the biblical overtones of the city of David lie inside the old walls. Historically, Jerusalem summons images of kingship, prosperity, a golden age. Sociologically, Jerusalem gives the Jewish people a realized dream, a

place of their own to which, next year, the Messiah just might come and all the blessed might journey. Psychologically, contemporary Jews are apt to overflow with feelings about Jerusalem, some of them quite conflicting. On one hand, there is a desire to support the powers in the new capital that are trying to promote Israel's survival and prosperity. On the other hand, there is the knowledge that the majority of Jews still live outside Israel, often more prosperously than if they lived inside Israel, and that not all the things done in the Knesset (parliament) merit full support. Some policies emanating from the Knesset have made barren land spring back to life. Yet on the West Bank the ecological policies have become so mixed with religious aims that they often seem to be a military weapon aimed against the troublesome Palestinians. It is hard for sensitive Jews to know where to direct their support.

The prophetic emphases on justice, commitment to God, and walking in the ways of the Torah continue to shape daily life in Jerusalem. Down the

CASE STUDY: JEWISH RITUALS

Traditionally, Jewish social life has involved many rituals. To begin with, there was circumcision, the ritual through which males entered the covenant community. In the Jewish perspective, circumcision is not a matter of hygiene. It is a sign of the pledge made between Abraham and God, a sign in the very organ of life. For the rest of his life, the man signed this way stands out from the rest of unsigned humanity. Naked, the Jewish man is clearly a Jew. (At least this was the case before the twentieth century, when the operation became routinely performed on Gentile infants for supposed health reasons.) With or without such health benefits, Jews would continue to circumcise their males on the eighth day after birth, the time when Abraham circumcised Isaac.

The circumcision ritual is called a *bris,* the Hebrew word for covenant. When most children were born at home, the *bris* meant a family feast, with crowds of relatives and friends, learned speeches, and general merrymaking. Each step of the ceremony was something to be stored in the memory for later meditation.

Contemporary ceremonies retain what they can of this tradition, gathering relatives and friends to celebrate the new birth. The *bris* intensifies the ordinary joy parents feel at the gift of a child, by emphasizing that the covenant community is being extended another generation. So the father of the child pronounces a joyous blessing: "Blessed are you, Lord our God, Master of the Universe, who have made us holy with your commands, and have commanded us to bring this boy into the covenant of Abraham our father." Ideally the father would do the circumcision himself, as Abraham did, but the accepted practice has become to employ a *mohel* or ritual circumciser to perform it. The *mohel* may or may not be a medical doctor, but he has been well trained in medical safeguards and antisepsis.

The next rite of passage for the Jewish child is the *bar mitzvah,* or ceremonial accession to adulthood. Recently, American Jews have been quite sensitive about this ceremony. There may be elaborate preparations, incredible eating, and a swirl of family emotions. In the case of American Jews, the *bar mitzvah* seems to have become an occasion to celebrate a relative freedom from discrimination. The religious tradition behind the *bar mitzvah* assumes that a child does not develop the capacity to grasp the concepts of Judaism, nor to fulfill Judaism's disciplines, until the age of thirteen. Before that time, the father is responsible for the child. The *bar mitzvah* marks the child's transition to personal responsibility. Donning the phylacteries that an adult wears when he prays, the boy bar mitzvahed can now receive a call to speak the blessing over a part of the weekly reading of the Torah. In many cases this leads to a renewal of Hebrew studies, so that the ceremony can express a genuine mastery of Judaism's foundations.

With the rise of a Jewish feminist consciousness have come rituals for bringing girls into the covenant and adulthood. Traditionally, women were exempted from most Jewish rituals, that they might be free for family tasks. But as the boys' *bar mitzvah* came to occasion a great party, there were good reasons for girls to want an equal celebration. Thus, there has arisen the *bas* (or *bat*) *mitzvah* ceremony for girls, an improvised way to ritualize girls' graduation from religious-school training and to recognize their new status as adults.

Judaism gives marriage a great deal of attention. Unlike Christian society, Jewish society had no monastic alternative (neither solitary nor communitarian) to marriage and family life. (The Essene community at Qumran, if it was an exception to this rule, was shortlived.) The command to be fruitful and multiply also influenced Jewish attitudes toward marriage. The emotional and social fulfillment of the spouses certainly was much valued, at least in Talmudic times, but a strong focus also remained on procreation. The relatively late development of the notion of personal immortality in Judaism resulted not only from the lack of a clear sense of a spiritual (immaterial) soul, but also to the tendency to think that one continued to exist through one's offspring. In other words, the family line was a sort of concrete immortality. To some extent, this limited the significance of the individual. Therefore, marriage was a treasure of Jewish tradition in part because it prevented the individual from being totally lost in the abyss of death. From this and other benefits attributed to marriage, sexual activity derived a certain dignity, even a certain obligation. Tradition encouraged them to have relations except during the menstrual flow. One of the customs of the Sabbath was that in its leisure spouses should make love. As the cabalists stressed, the Sabbath was the bride of God.

Traditionally, marriages have taken place under a canopy (huppah) supported by four poles, the original purpose of which was to provide the ceremony a sacred space. The day itself usually entailed a fast, and other similarities to the Day of Atonement, in the doctrine that on their wedding day God forgives a couple all their past sins, so that they may begin their life together afresh. Another custom was for the bride and groom to wear white as a symbol of purity. Jewish betrothal occurred by writing a legal document binding on both parties. The rabbi asked the groom if he was prepared to fulfill his obligations as stated in the contract (ketubbah), and the groom answered affirmatively by taking hold of a handkerchief or some other object given him by the rabbi. After the groom signed the contract, the men present surrounded the groom and danced with him over to the bride, who sat regally on a throne. The groom lifted the veil from the bride's face, while the rabbi recited the phrase, "O sister! May you become the mother of thousands of myriads" (Genesis 24:60). The bride and groom then processed to the huppah, the bride circled the groom seven times (entering all seven spheres of her beloved's soul), there were psalms, hymns, a blessing of wine, and then the essential act occurred.

The essential act was the groom putting a ring on the index finger of the bride's right hand and saying, "Behold you are consecrated to me with this ring according to the Law of Moses and Israel." After this the marriage contract was read, seven blessings were recited, and the groom smashed a glass by stamping on it, to conclude the ceremony.

Funeral rites, the last stage on life's way, have involved Jews in a final confession of doctrine. Ideally, the dying person said, "Understand, O Israel, the Lord our God is One. I acknowledge before Thee, my God, God of my fathers, that my recovery and death are in your hand. May it be your will to heal me completely, but if I should die, may my death be an atonement for all sins that I have committed." After death there was a ritual washing of the body, a funeral dominated by the recitation of psalms, a ritualized burial, a meal for the mourners, and then the shivah, a seven-day period of mourning, during which friends were expected to visit and a minyan (quorum of ten) was to gather each day. The mourning period concluded with visiting the synagogue the first Sabbath after the shivah.

streets hurry bearded Hasidic Jews and visiting Americans, devout religionists and Jews nearly completely secularized. The land and the ethnic solidarity have become lodestones to chosen people all over the globe. The Jews of northeastern European origin (Ashkenazim) who have been the main reference point of our story increasingly find that they must accommodate the Jews of Spanish origin (Sephardim) and Middle Eastern Jews. Within a small country, an amazing diversity exists. Fundamentalists (Orthodox) seeking to establish new settlements are committed to fulfill a biblical mandate. Twenty miles away in the Hebrew University, professors teach that such fundamentalism is foolish. Meanwhile, the specter of the Nazi death camps hovers outside Jerusalem at Yad Vashem, the memorial set in the nearby hills. This specter has led many to vow "Never again!"

Infamous gate at Dachau

PROPHECY AND THE CHOSEN PEOPLE. Of the three key biblical figures, Moses predominated, because the Law that came through him has been the backbone of Jewish religious life. As different cultures were assimilated by Judaism, Abraham's lineage became less important than his exemplary commitment to God. Similarly, as political sovereignty became a dim memory, David's kingship became rather metaphorical, propping future hopes more than guiding present living. Moses, however, stayed wholly relevant: he was thought to have authored the code that kept Jews united; he was the mediator of the covenant into which the community circumcised each male. When prophecy had become central to Jewish religion, Moses became the prophet par excellence.

Prophecy, which often distinguishes Western religion from Eastern wisdom religion, is not so much the predictions that appear in today's tabloids as a discernment of what the divine spirit is saying to the people of God. The establishment of Moses as the supreme prophet testifies to the social utility that Jews have expected communication with God to bear. They expected such communication to result in communal renovation, strengthening, and redirection. Prophecy was not a display of individual virtuosity or a matter involving crystal balls. The master of the universe, the Adonai ("My Lord," substituting for Yahweh, which was considered too holy to utter) that all prayers bless, has bound Jews together as his people.

THE LAW. Without abandoning their ideal of the perfect doctrine outlined in Maimonides' thirteen articles, the rabbis generally have focused more on performance than on motivation or thought. One's doctrines about the nature of God (within broad limits) has been less important than keeping the Sabbath and fulfilling one's communal obligations. This attitude encouraged considerable intellectual freedom, including lively debate, tolerance, and theological ambiguity. As well, it prevented the establishment of a clear-cut religious authority and dogma, such as that encountered by Roman Catholics in the magisterium of their councils and popes. The Law, which seemed so specific, had dozens of interpreters. On and on the Talmud grew, because most interpreters had insights worth preserving. One's religious commitment was expressed in action, not in speculation or confession. How one used one's body, money, and time was more important than how one used one's mind or tongue. Such a practical view meant that the community could bind itself through rituals, ethics, and laws without excessive concern about their accompanying doctrines.

THE HOLOCAUST. Last, contemporary Jewish identity has been annealed as a result of the Holocaust. While exodus and entry into the promised land characterized Jews in biblical times, suffering and persecution have characterized Jews since the expulsion from Jerusalem in 70 C.E. Jewish commentators have no consensus on what the recent past and the Holocaust mean, but they do agree that we must not ignore, deny, or explain away the evil of the Holocaust. Thus, Jewish identity, the theme of so many American novels, has yet to be fully resolved.

SELF

After prophets such as Ezekiel and Jeremiah, individual responsibility separated from collective responsibility. Furthermore, both Hellenization and internal legal development set apart individual reason. Jewish thinkers in Alexandria, Egypt two thousand years ago, reflected Platonic, Aristotelian, Epicurean, and Stoic interests in mind and reason. Philo, the luminary of these thinkers, tried to correlate Mosaic teaching with a cosmic law. In the medieval period, Maimonides, Halevi, and others tried to square the Torah with rational demands for a less mythic, more analytic explanation of doctrine. Since the individual soul is the site of reason, such concerns inevitably clarified the personality's partial independence of group thought. That is, it underscored that any particular person might grasp or miss the divine Law.

Moreover, the Torah and the Talmud themselves inculcated something of this sensitivity. As a scriptural religion, Judaism demanded literacy and encouraged learning. But literature and learning are obviously cultural developments deriving from a common human nature that tend to distinguish people according to their talent. Thus, the bright little boy may distinguish himself by the age of ten. Through his unique gifts he may stand out from the crowd and even increase regard for his family. If he develops into a sage, he will join the line of masters whose commentaries on the Law are the classics. So, by stressing personal insight, legal study encouraged individuation.

To a lesser degree, Jewish mysticism and Jewish attitudes toward wealth also encouraged individuation. Mysticism, like study, is a personal inward phenomenon. Despite its debt to tradition and its occurrence within a community of commitment, mysticism is a solitary pursuit involving an "I-Thou" relation. When mysticism flowered in Judaism, it produced revered personalities, such as the Baal Shem-Tov and the Magid of Mezritch. To their disciples, these *tzaddikim* were stunning demonstrations of the ardor that divinity could inspire. Their personalities were special, set apart, distinguished.

Despite the threats that mysticism posed for the traditional rabbinic authority, the mystics were precious for strengthening the common people's commitment. Thus, one could aspire to Hasidic distinction, as one could aspire to rabbinic distinction. Because mystical prowess edified the community, it was a worthy ambition. Analogously, one could aspire to the (lesser) distinction that came with wealth. Judaism is not, comparatively speaking, an ascetic religion. As much as Hinduism, it views wealth or prosperity as a legitimate life goal. For his good fortune and financial talent as well as for his philanthropy, a successful Jew could win recognition. True, with success he was sure to gain a host of petitioners, but their attestation to his generosity somewhat offset the burden they imposed.

This description of the self must be qualified in discussing women. Since their vocation was marriage and practicality, their distinction was basically reflected—that of being a rich man's wife or a scholar's mother. Nevertheless, women had rights to

COMPARISON OF HINDUISM WITH JUDAISM		
COMPARISON	HINDUISM	JUDAISM
Conquering tribe	Aryans	Hebrews
Original economy	herding	herding
Country conquered	India	Israel
Conquest took place	2nd millennium B.C.E.	2nd millennium B.C.E.
Conquered people	Mohenjo-Daro	Canaanites
Economy of those conquered	agriculture, cities	agriculture, cities
Religion of those conquered	mother earth deities	mother earth deities
Scripture recording conquest	*Vedas*	Torah
Individual's place in nation determined by	caste (heredity)	tribe (heredity)
Emerging doctrine about God	monism	monotheism
Dominant persons 1000 B.C.E.	priests	priests
Who were members of	Brahmin caste	Levite tribe
Dietary rules	vegetarian	kosher
Evil behavior	karma	sin
Axial Age figures	mystics	prophets
Axial Age writings	*Upanishads*	prophetic books of Old Testament
Doctrine of afterlife	transmigration	resurrection
Proselytizing	no	no
Heterodox offshoots	Buddhism, Jainism	Christianity
Reaction and commentary	*Bhagavad Gita*	Talmud
Mystical sects	yes (e.g., Vedanta)	yes (e.g., Cabala, Hasidism)
Tools used by mystics	meditation, yoga	Torah number code, singing
Had to live under the rule of	Mogul Muslims, British	Babylonians, Persians, Greeks, Romans, Muslims, Europeans
Gained independence	after World War II	after World War II
Victorious in wars with	Muslim neighbors	Muslim neighbors
Woman leader	Indira Gandhi	Golda Meier

Compare Judaism, point by point, to a nonmonotheistic denomination. So do not pick Christianity, Islam, Akhenaton, or Zoroastrianism. You could select any religion already discussed in this text: Shinto, Jainism, Egyptians, Mesopotamians, Teutons, Celts, Incas, Mayas, Aztecs, Ainus, Inuits, Aborigines, Africans, Melanesians, Polynesians, or Native Americans.

Contribute to this discussion at
http://www.delphi.com/rel101

self-expression, at least regarding nonscriptural matters. The *shtetl* tradition that a woman had no soul did not mean that she had no say. In matters of the home or the shop, she probably had the dominant say. In matters of affection or emotion, she surely did.

MIND-BODY UNITY. Judaism has stressed the unity of mind and body, eschewing a body-soul or matter-spirit duality. Scholars usually contrast biblical Jewish notions of personhood and the then-contemporary Greek notions. This contrast can illumine the tendency of Judaism toward an existential concreteness that most of Western culture has been struggling for centuries to recapture. For instance, Descartes, the father of modern European philosophy, worked hard to reconcile the opposition within the human being between its *res cogitans* (thinking part) and its *res extensa* (material part). In contrast, the "soul" (*nepesh*) of Hebrew biblical thought was a unity of mind and body that could not be divided into thinking and material parts. So the heart rather than the head stood for the center of thought and emotion. Out of the fullness of the heart the mouth would speak. This conviction fought against the Hellenization of Jewish theology, which would have made the mouth speak what reason dictated. It fought against the legalism possible in rabbinic theology, keeping space for aggadic tales whose appeal was more than mental.

THE HUMAN SPIRIT. In prophecy Jewish religion found understandings of God's relationship to the human spirit new to human history. That is, the ecstatic experience of the prophets, who seem to have begun as wandering bands of exultants (*nebi'im*), evolved into something other than ordinary shamanism (which we may take as the typical model of ancient ecstasy). For where shamanism usually kept the world divine and usually confused the relations between imagination and reason in the ecstatic experience (though some shamans were well aware of the divine incomprehensibility), the prophets had experiences that burned below imagination to the base of the spirit. The burning bush, for instance, occasioned the realization that we only know of God what the divine mystery shows in time. Elijah's small, still voice suggested that God comes more through spiritual recollection than through natural storms. Jeremiah, finally, went to the core of the matter: Divine creativity best expresses itself by writing its law upon the human heart. That did not mean that the prophetic, or later the mystical, Jews did not mix myth, symbol, and imagination. The *merkabah* (chariot) imagery dominated even the philosophers' ruminations about God, while the cabalists' bliss was to imagine the divine emanations. Still, the union of the entire *numinous* experience (the entire experience of divinity) with ethical demands refined what it meant to be religious by stressing communion with a transcendent God. Implicit in the prophetic and Talmudic program was the proposition that real religion is doing justice and worshiping purely. Implicit was the twofold commandment of loving God (who is one) and loving one's neighbor (who is another self). This outlook developed a powerful concept of individual conscience: God alone is the mystery that should dominate and constitute the human person in its being or its morality. When Jewish theologians clarified such a monotheism, they dealt a death blow to all idolatry.

ULTIMATE REALITY

The biblical beginnings were deep spiritual experiences: irruptions of divinity that seized and formed the soul (more than they clarified reason). The God who was revealed was lively, personal, and free. Perhaps because the genius of Israelite religion was not reason but spirit, the biblical Jews expressed this God's character as the world's origin and destiny in myths. That is, they expressed the truth of order, of humanity's proper place in and with nature and God, symbolically, from the "dead spot," the bottom of the

CASE STUDY: JEWISH PRAYER

In the Jewish Prayer Book one finds praise for the One God who is King of the Universe: "Praised are you, O Lord our God, King of the Universe." This prayer then itemizes the great things the King of the Universe does. He fixes the cycles of light and darkness. He ordains the order of all creation. He is the source of the light that shines over all the earth. His mercy radiates over all the earth's inhabitants. Because he is so good, he recreates the world day by day. His manifold works reveal his great bounty. Their beauty and order reveal his great wisdom. And what does the devout Jew ask of the King of the Universe? That he continue to love his people. He, the only One exalted from of old, the One praised and glorified since the world began, has been all Jews' shield and protection: He has been the Lord of our strength, the rock of our defense. In his infinite mercy, may he continue to love us. His goodness is for all time, so we may hope for this mercy. Daily he renews the work of creation, so daily he may be our reliance. The Psalmist knew this and sang, "Give thanks to Him who made the great lights, for His loving-kindness is everlasting." O God, make a new light to shine on Zion. Make us worthy to behold its radiance. All praise to you, O Lord, maker of the stars. The One God is also the revealer of the Torah. The Prayer Book expresses this conviction in connection with God's compassion: Out of tender regard for his people's needs, the Lord has taught our Fathers the laws of life. For their sakes, may he continue to teach us. May we, too, learn the divine Laws, trust more and more in the divine guidance. May we observe all the precepts of the divine Law, fulfill all its teachings. If we are to do this, God must enlighten our eyes and open our hearts. He must gather together our scattered thoughts, uniting our whole beings in reverence and love. This reverence and love will keep us from shame, and help us to feel God's aid. If we trust in God's holiness, we will come safely from the corners of the earth to the dignity of our own holy land. It is you, God, who are our deliverance, you who have chosen us from all peoples and tongues. We praise and thank you for having drawn us close to you: "We praise You and thank You in truth. With love do we thankfully proclaim Your unity, and praise You who chose Your people Israel in love."

When the Prayer Book reproduces the Shema, it includes much of the Shema's original biblical gloss. Thus after expressing the call to love God with whole mind, soul, and strength, the Prayer Book reminds the people that the words of the Shema should ever be in their hearts. They should teach these words diligently to their children. They should talk about the Shema at home and abroad, day and night. The words of the Shema ought to be a mark upon the hand, or as frontlets (browbands) between the eyes. They should be inscribed on the doorposts of the home and on every gate. If the people fulfill these injunctions, they will find God favoring. So all Jews should stay mindful of God's words of the Shema, keeping them in their hearts and souls. The words should guide all that the hand works. They should be stamped between the eyes, to guide all that the eye sees, all that the mind conceives. In speaking of God as redeemer, Jewish prayer spotlights his intervention on his people's behalf. God has been the king of each generation, the people's only sovereign guide. He has been the redeemer of each generation, the One to whom all Jews must go in time of need. Creator, he has been a victorious stronghold, a fort no enemy could overrun. Through his redemptive interventions, he has shown that there is no God but he. Though God dwells in the heights of heaven, his decrees reach all of creation. The very ends of the earth stand or fall by God's Laws. Happy is the person who takes these Laws to heart, obeying the commands of God's Torah. Such a person experiences what it really means to have a Lord, a defender and mighty king. The true God is the first and the last. The true people have no king or redeemer but him.

Addressing God directly, the weekly Prayer Book prays: "You, O Lord our God, rescued us from Egypt; You redeemed us from the house of bondage." As though retreating to a favorite haunt of memory, Jewish prayer again and again goes back to the Exodus. God slew the firstborn of the Egyptians, and saved his people's firstborn. He split the waters of the Red Sea, rescuing his followers and drowning the wicked. When the waters engulfed the enemies of Israel, not one of the arrogant remained.

God the redeemer is therefore God the powerful, God the One not to be trifled with. In the Exodus episode, Israel received its greatest lesson in redemption. Ever since, Jews have sung great hymns of thanksgiving to God. Ever since, they have extolled God with psalms of praise. For ever since they have known that the Lord their God is a mighty king, overseeing everything from his high heaven. Great and awesome, he is the source of all blessing, the everliving divinity exalted in majesty. As the *Exodus* episode revealed, the God of Israel humbles the proud and raises the lowly. He frees the captive and redeems the meek. Helping the needy and answering the people's call, he shows himself no respecter of earthly persons, a respecter only of what is right. So let all voices ring out with praise for the supreme God: Ever praised be he! As Moses and the children of Israel sang, "Who is like You, O Lord, among the mighty?" Who is like God in holiness, wonderful deeds, worthiness of praise? There is none like God, because there is only One God. The people God saved in the Exodus sensed this stunning uniqueness. They sang a chorus of praises by the sea. The Lord will reign forever. Rock of Israel, may he ever rise to his people's defense. "Our Redeemer is the Holy One of Israel." Lord of Hosts is our God's name. May the Lord be praised, the Redeemer of Israel.

Such prayer combines a remembrance of God's past deeds with a meditation on God's constant nature. Its regular accent is thankful and praising. God has made everything that exists. He has revealed his will to Israel. And he has saved Israel from its enemies. For these and all his other splendors, he deserves his people's full worship and confidence. Though king, Lord, ruler of heaven, he has deigned to concern himself with his people's needs. Though holy and righteous, he has manifested mercy and steadfast love.

When a person or a group prays in this mood, its words and images fall into an easy rhythm. One image sparks another, one memory brings another memory to mind. Phrases tend to repeat themselves, for the point is not innovation. In their time, God was manifest in nature and was a fellow-warrior, with them against their foes. In their time, good harvests and military victories derived directly from God's hand, while bad harvests and military defeats suggested the people had faltered in their religion.

What has predominated in the Jewish liturgy, however, is the memory of God's saving deeds. In times past God has shown himself the people's redeemer. Reviving their commitment by journeying back to the biblical experiences, generations of Jews have been able to open their spirits to the God who lay ahead of them, in the mystery of the future. God has given his people a way to walk into the future with confidence. Not only has he promised he would reveal himself to Israel through time, he has given his Torah to detail what holy living with him requires.

soul, which revelation seizes. Moreover, having expressed its order mythologically, the Israelite religious genius hardly criticized its symbols, making little effort to interpret them in clearer, if less complete, conceptual terms.

So the God of Moses "is" only what time shows him to be; the God of *Genesis* makes the world "in the beginning" from primal chaos, the status of which is quite unclear; and the God of Isaiah is placed beyond the world by a dazzling cluster of symbols. The fight of the best Jewish theologians has been to preserve the insight, traceable to Moses and the prophets, that God is not one of the visual arts and that the nature of our race cannot be the measure of God. God has to be beyond our measures—visual, emotional, even intellectual. God has to be allowed to be as God presents the divine nature: sovereignly free, though deeply committed to the welfare of human

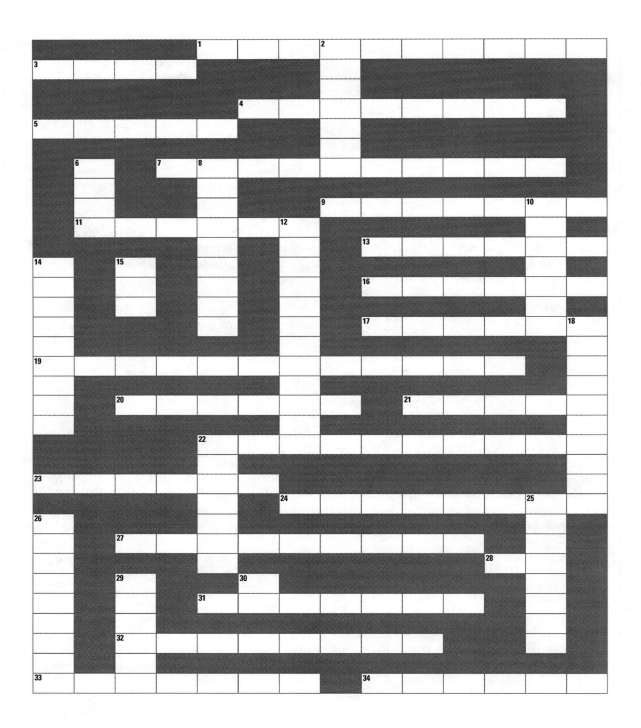

ACROSS

1   Type of commentary in Talmud
3   Children born to a Jewish mother
4   Strict sect of Judaism
5   The Hebrew scriptures; first five books of the Bible
7   Eastern European Jews
9   Contemporary mystical sect of Jews
11   Jewish diet
13   Largest U.S. Jewish sect
16   Language in which the Torah was written
17   Approach of the cabalists
19   The ritual for male infants on the eighth day
20   Contemporary Jewish clergy
21   When Jews were in Babylon in the sixth-century B.C.E.
22   Jewish doctrine about God
23   A Levite who conducted animal sacrifice was a _____.
24   Approach of Moses, Isaiah, Jeremiah, Ezekiel
27   Strict first-century laypeople
28   The Talmud was completed around 500 _____.
31   First-century guerrilla fighters
32   The Roman dispersal of the Jews
33   First-century sect who withdrew to the Dead Sea
34   Book of exegetical commentary

DOWN

2   Non-Jew
6   Kosher diet forbids this meat.
8   Spanish Jews
10   Modern national homeland for Jews
12   Pharisee doctrine of afterlife
14   First-century sect for the wealthy
15   The Torah is a book of _____.
18   The Talmud is a book of exegetical _____.
22   Jewish savior sent by God
25   Contract between God and the Jews
26   Contemporary Jewish house of worship
29   When Moses led the Hebrews out of Egypt
30   The Romans destroyed the temple in 70 _____.

beings. Human beings have to suffer the fact that God is always going to be strictly mysterious: a fullness that human beings can never comprehend, let alone control. The weight of Jewish theological tradition has been that Torah offers guidance for how to live with the God who cannot be visualized, who must always be allowed the divine mysteriousness— guidance that divinity itself had offered as a gracious gift and kindly command. The core of some of the most significant Jewish theology lies in the intimate connection between Torah and the divine mystery— in guidance to honor above all the unimaginable Guide of Jewish existence.

SUMMARY: THE JEWISH CENTER

The center of traditional Judaism is the Torah. That there is a law or guidance, come from God and leading to God, has been Judaism's first conviction and main treasure. With such a guidance, life is relevant, reasonably clear. When such a guidance loses its persuasiveness, as it did for large numbers of Jews in modern times, almost all aspects of life demand rethinking. Then the zeal with which the rabbis studied Torah may shift focus to such new concerns as physical science, social justice, or simply making money. Kept under high pressure for centuries, Jewish intellectual abilities cannot just relax and take a leisurely stroll. In old tracks or new, it has pressed forward to set things clear, gain new knowledge, redress old wrongs. When a Jew marshaled intellectual or moral energy, the old summons suggested that things might subserve a higher plan, society ought to succor its widows and orphans.

RELIGIONS OF ANCIENT CIVILIZATIONS

RELIGIONS OF EARLY CIVILIZATIONS: TWENTY-FIVE KEY DATES	
Date	**Event**
7500 B.C.E.	cereal grain agriculture; domestication of animals
8350–7350 B.C.E.	Jericho (first walled town, 10 acres)
6250–5400 B.C.E.	Catal Huyuk, Turkey (large city, 32 acres)
6000 B.C.E.	rice cultivation in Thailand; pottery and textiles in Catal Huyuk
5000 B.C.E.	irrigation of Mesopotamian alluvial plains; agricultural settlements in Egypt
4000 B.C.E.	bronze casting in Middle East
3500 B.C.E.	invention of the wheel
3100 B.C.E.	pictographic writing in Sumer; unification of Egypt
3000 B.C.E..	spread of copper working
2590 B.C.E.	Great Pyramids at Giza
1750 B.C.E.	Hammurabi has written code of laws
1370 B.C.E.	Akhenaton's "monotheistic" reform
600 B.C.E.	Zoroaster begins prophetic work
550 B.C.E.	Cyrus II founds Persian empire; Zoroastrianism the official religion
525 B.C.E.	Persian conquest of Egypt
521 B.C.E.	Persia extends from the Nile to the Indus
500 B.C.E.	first hieroglyphic writing in Mexico
332–329 B.C.E.	Alexander in Egypt, Persia, India
323 B.C.E.	start of Ptolemaic dynasty in Egypt
312 B.C.E.	start of Seleucid era in Persia
247 B.C.E.	Arsaces I founds the Parthian empire
224 C.E.	foundation of Sasanian dynasty
300 C.E.	rise of Mayan civilization
637 C.E.	Muslims invade Persia
1325–1530 C.E.	Aztec and Inca civilizations

Tribal peoples had technology, and the level of technology (if we can assume that technologies can be ranked) varied greatly from tribe to tribe. All eventually discovered the techniques for the making of fire, and its use in cooking. Most developed the bow and arrow, nets, hooks, and other tools for hunting and fishing as well as the making of houses, clothes, and containers. But in tribal cultures, these advances may take many generations to develop and diffuse from one tribe to another. With the earliest civilizations, the pace of technological innovation increased dramatically, as did the spread of ideas from one society to another.

A great shift in human diet and culture came when some tribes stopped following herds of game and domesticated some of those animals (cattle, sheep, goats, swine, llamas, camels, chickens) for meat, milk, and fiber. Other tribes noticed that the plant they had been gathering would give greater yields if they stayed around and nurtured its growth. Wheat, barley, rice, millet, corn were the cereal grains that permitted farmers to raise enough food to feed their families and have a surplus to trade with others who had dedicated their occupations to making plows or storage bins.

This change in the food supply led to a change in social organization. One of the earliest sociologists studying religion was Emile **Durkheim** who referred to the tribal form of organization as *mechanical*. He chose this term not because hunter-gatherers used machinery, but because members of a society mostly shared the same social function. Each man was a hunter. Each woman was assigned to gather vegetables, sew, cook, take care of the children. There was no real further specialization beyond gender roles (except for the one person who might be assigned the role of shaman). In such a society, it did not matter which man married which woman, much in the same way that in putting standard manufactured nuts and bolts together, you just reach in a bin, grab a nut, reach in another bin, grab a bolt, and you know that they will fit together. With settled agriculture, and especially large cities, came a different form of social organization which Durkheim referred to as *organic*. He chose this term not because city dwellers are closer to the processes of nature, but because their social organization seemed to parallel that of a large organism, with each individual assigned to some specialized function: soldier, miner, smith, potter, weaver, builder, miller.

With agriculture human beings made a great leap in mastery of their environment. Like the domestication of animals, agriculture meant people no longer were at the whim of natural cycles they did not understand. They could stabilize their food supply, lay in better stores for winter, and free some members of their group for artistic work, for developing religious lore, or for planning how to dominate neighboring peoples. The very successes of hunters and gatherers therefore moved these earliest people toward a significantly different way of life (and so toward significantly different religious interests and concepts).

Some of the inventions that spread in the early civilizations may have had roots in tribal cultures: pottery, metal smithing, weaving. But others, like the wheel, would have had little purpose in hunting or herding societies. The wheel is needed only when there are large concentrations of people and large quantities of goods to be moved (e.g., grain, construction materials, copper ore).

Metals deserve special attention. The principal metal was copper and its alloys bronze and brass (discovered about 3500 B.C.E. in the Middle East). They were useful for construction, numerous hand tools, and a simplified method of value exchange—money. More specialized work developed, such as mining, smelting, and casting metal. In turn, this work created more efficient farming implements, which led to the production of surplus food. Surplus food allowed a new class of religious specialists (who were agriculturally unproductive) to arise.

Perhaps the most significant use of metals was as weapons of warfare against other humans. Tribal peoples such as the Melanesians and Teutons had been raiders, invading other tribes to carry off some wealth or trophies of conquest. But as the metal industry grew in importance, it stimulated the exploration and colonization of new territories for raw materials. The early civilizations became military empires designed to protect their flanks and sources of supply against other growing military empires.

From 1900 to 1400 B.C.E., following the Hittite invention of tempering, iron came into widespread use, and the production of bronze and iron further stimulated the human imagination and increased the symbolic content of mother earth. Whereas the earliest iron was a gift from the sky (coming in the form of meteorites), mined iron came from the womb of the earth. Indeed, miners developed regimes of fasting, meditation, and purification since they had to go into the sacred depths and extract a new form of life. Their mythology spoke of elves, fairies, genies, and spirits who inhabited the underground, assisting or witnessing the gestation of mother earth's strangest children, the ores. Metallurgists, like blacksmiths and potters, had to be "Masters of the Fire," which associated them with the shamans, who were masters of inner, magical heat. These metallurgists also took on some of the paradoxical nature of metal itself. Coming from mother earth and being a boon to humanity, metal was sacred. However, being invulnerable and easily made into an instrument of death, metal was also too close to evil for humans to handle comfortably. Thus, the smiths entered the mythology of the gods, fashioning weapons for their heavenly battles and tools for their heavenly enterprises. In India, Tvastr made Indra's weapons for the fight against Vrtra; in Greece, Hephaestus forged the thunderbolt that enabled Zeus to triumph over his enemies.

Perhaps the greatest innovations facilitating the development of civilization would be writing and mathematics. These are less important to a hunting-gathering society, which can rely upon oral traditions to convey information from one generation to another. (The Tasmanians only had three words for numbers: *one, two,* and *plenty;* but that was sufficient to understand how many hunters to bring.) Once there are agricultural surpluses of grain and trade of that grain for cloth and bricks and pots, some means of calculation and permanent records of transactions and contracts are needed. The rich symbolism of pictorial art does not suffice, for what is now required is the precise meaning of concepts that will be interpreted the same way by one person and another, today and tomorrow: weights and measures and laws. To be steady producers of food, human beings also had to calculate the seasons much more precisely. This led to astronomical calculations, astrology, and the worship of planets and stars.

Writing makes the realities of the traditional world mediated, as they previously were not. Spoken language has a holistic quality, conveying its message immediately, in an imperative or at least solicitous way. Written language is more detached and indirect. To the benefit of science, and perhaps the detriment of religion, it tends toward scholarship. For example, once the biblical legends were written down, scholars could dissect them at leisure. In the development of the early civilizations, we glimpse sizable traditions at their very revealing transition from oral to written religion.

These technological changes proceeded alongside changes in the realm of the sacred. Hunters may have understood a sacred solidarity between themselves and the animals they hunted; now there was to be a sacred solidarity between cultivators and plants. Whereas in earliest times blood and bone were the symbolic, most sacred elements of life, in agricultural times the generative elements were seen as masculine sperm and feminine blood. Above all, women dominated agricultural life, and mother earth was the prime focus. Through the millennia before the biology of reproduction became clear, the earth was thought to give birth independently, without need of any male. Because women developed agriculture and controlled it, and because women issued all human life, Mesolithic culture connected women to mother earth. Thus, from this period came the best-known **Great Mothers**, goddesses of fertility. Sexuality be-

came a sacred drive and process, because all nature—the whole cosmos—moved through a religious cycle of conception, gestation, birth, nurturance, growth, decline, and then death (which could be a new conception). Houses, villages, shrines, and burial vaults all reflected the womb architecturally. The earth itself seemed uterine: from it we come, to it we return. Accordingly, very old myths of human creation speak of first ancestors crawling forth from mines or caves, and funerary rituals consign the dead offspring back to the Great Mother. Even during this initial period of agriculture, there was an increased stress on polarities—earth and sky, dirt and rain, yin and yang (the Chinese dual elements).

This focus on the earth in the Mesolithic era continued into Neolithic times, when village life developed into city life, agriculture became more extensive and secure, and arts and crafts such as pottery, weaving, and tool manufacturing were established. Also, in the Neolithic period, cults of fertility and death assumed even greater prominence. From sanctuaries excavated in Anatolia (modern Turkey), we know that around 7000 B.C.E. worship involved skulls and various gifts, such as jewels, weapons, and textiles. The principal divinity was a goddess who manifested in three forms: a young woman, a mother, and a crone (old woman). Figurines represent her giving birth, breasts adorn her cave sites, and drawings portray her among animals, especially bulls and leopards. In many caves the double ax, symbol of the storm god, underscores the fertility theme (stormy rain fecundates mother earth).

Representations of bees and butterflies relate this fertility theme to the burial skulls and gifts, since both bees and butterflies pass through distinct stages in their life cycles. Worshipers likely tried to fit death into such a scheme—to see it as another transformation of the life force, another stage. Subordinate to the goddess was a male god, a boy or youth, who seems to be her child and lover and who has some correlations with the bull.

Roughly ten thousand years ago, settled agriculture became widespread in the river valleys of the Nile, Tigris and Euphrates, Indus, and Huang Ho. The earliest civilizations arose around 4000 B.C.E. (i.e., *before* the *common era* marked in Western culture by the birth of Jesus). The term **civilization** refers to the cities that developed as commercial and ritual

DIMENSION	TRIBAL PEOPLES	EARLY CIVILIZATIONS
Economy built on	gathering, hunting, herding	herding, agriculture, pottery, metals
Durkheimian solidarity	mechanical	organic
Contact with others	raiding	trade, conquest
Religious leader	shaman	priest
Group symbol	totem	patriarch
Ideas preserved by	oral tradition	writing
Control behavior with	taboos	law codes
Deities	primal monotheism animism polytheism	polytheism pantheons henotheism monolatry monotheism
Festivals	rites of passage	calendrical
Sacrifice	animal	animal, grain, human
Creation myths describe	specific origins	instability
Afterlife	contact with ancestors	reward for deeds
Sacred sites	natural hierophanies taboo locations megaliths	pyramids temples
Divination	yes	yes
Exorcism	yes	rare
Mythical figures	tricksters	conquering heros
Puberty rites	yes	rare
Syncretism	after contact with others	after contact with others
Secular society	no	no

centers in the midst of settled agriculture. Unfortunately, the term has conveyed a false sense of superiority, as its opposite, *uncivilized,* is taken to stand for that which is crude, vulgar, unsanitary, or ignorant. Even the adjective *civil* conveys something socially acceptable and well mannered. In this book, all that we want to convey by the term *civilization* is a society based upon city life. When we speak of the "great" civilizations, we are not implying a judgment on their aesthetic accomplishments or moral virtues, but refer to the technological, commercial, governmental, and military abilities that permitted and sustained a large-scale model of human organization.

RELIGIOUS THEMES

Syncretism is the process of blending elements from different religious traditions. One form of syncretism involves incorporating a symbol, myth, ritual, or ethical principle from one tradition into another. One example of this type, suggested in the previous chapter, is the presence of some elements of some Celtic and Teutonic traditions in the Christian holidays of Halloween, Christmas, and Easter. Another example is the spread of the peyote religion among various Native American tribes on the reservation.

Another type of syncretism consists of blending or assimilating different traditions, especially by combining their deities into a structured pantheon. The result usually has been an undigested mixture or rather infertile hybrid. This latter form of syncretism may have been minimal in tribal societies, probably because of the limited forms of contact with other peoples.

Yet another type of syncretism came about as a reaction to (or against) contact with other peoples. During the late nineteenth century, the forced relocation of Native Americans onto the reservations engendered something new: an apocalyptic movement known as the Ghost Dance. During the first half of the twentieth century, the South Pacific saw the growth of the cargo cults in response to airfields and docks constructed by white men.

The rise of civilizations foreordained the syncretism of religions. The heightened contact brought by ever-widening circles of trade was the first stimulus. Later, when civilizations became empires that conquered weaker, surrounding peoples, these contacts between cultures became clashes. As we will see in the remainder of this book, there are different ways that this clash can be resolved. The Hebrews who conquered Canaan and the Aryans who conquered India attempted to destroy the key elements of the religions of the vanquished. Those who later conquered China (e.g., Mongols, Manchurians) and Greece (e.g., Hellenes, Romans) assimilated much of what they found.

Myths also changed their structure, tone, and emphasis under the impact of the early civilizations. In tribal societies, creation myths might explain the origin of the world or the origins of specific things. Frequently these myths would contain totems (animal symbols of a tribe or clan) or tricksters (clever figures often credited with a certain innovation). In the early civilizations, the totem might be replaced by a **patriarch** (e.g., an ancestor such as Abraham for the Hebrews) and the trickster might be replaced by a **culture hero** who brought some cultural innovation or led some primal conquest. The creation myths of early civilizations became extremely important if the society was plagued by instability: these myths served to explain the origin of instability and suggested an approach for its solution.

Doctrines are statements about religious ideas, such as the nature of god (or gods). Both tribal religions and those of the cities could be called polytheistic in that several distinct deities were recognized and worshipped. The animism that characterized so many hunter-gatherers was absent in the early cities. Many of the agricultural societies of the Mediterranean and Middle East had Great Mother goddesses who governed the fertility cycle of plants and domesticated animals.

Conquering peoples (e.g., Aryans, Hellenes, Teutons) tended to have more masculine deities. As they assimilated conquered peoples, they may have kept some of these deities, renaming some to identify with what they had already or placing others in a subservient relation to the gods of the conquerors in a structured relationship known as a **pantheon.** In several (but not most) later civilizations, such polytheism may have led to **henotheism** (worship of some gods over others) or a **monolatry** (worship of one god among many), if not to a complete **monotheism** (only one god exists).

Another twist of doctrine was the elevation of living kings to a divine rank. Many ancient societies saw the monarch as mediating between the people and ultimate reality and concluded that the monarch should be considered a god. Thus the vitality of the king is extremely important, and the moment when the king dies and mediating functions pass to a new ruler is the most dramatic time in the people's existence. Some African tribes approach this doctrine, but its highest form can be found in stable empires such as the Egyptian and Incan, who claimed that their rulers were direct descendents of the sun god.

Rituals changed greatly in the cities. Puberty rites became rare because the transition from boy to adult farmer, builder, weaver or potter is a slow process of apprenticeship. The festivals were now geared more to the seasons of the crops rather than the stages of life, and thus the calendar became even more important. Animal sacrifice was still prevalent in those societies with domesticated animals, but there was an increasing emphasis on other forms of wealth: grain, implements, and even human life.

The sites of rituals were located less and less in natural sites that may have been mentioned in myths as hierophanies (places where something sacred transpired). Now the emphasis was on sites that had been constructed by humans: pyramids and temples more elaborate than the older megaliths had ever been.

One possible impetus in the rise of the city would have been its importance as a ritual center. At first, people may have come to the city to trade and then were told to do some worship and sacrifice while they were there. Later, the temple may have become so important for the society that people traveled to the city to worship, whether or not they had trading to do. In some places, the ritual center may have emerged prior to trade, and the city may have grown around it.

There was also a shift in religious functionaries from the tribal shaman to the priest. The early civilizations had a decreased interest in exorcism. The main duties of priests were to perform sacrifices, rituals, and at least semiofficial interpretations of doctrine and morals. Priests tended to arise alongside writing and to become the custodians of the religious lore that multiplied after writing, but one can find ritualists in oral societies, such as the Druids of the Celts, who fit most of the rest of the priest's profile .

Divination (prediction of future events) was a major theme in many early civilizations, especially those subject to frequent foreign invasions, natural disasters, or problematic weather. The task of predicting the future was handled in certain societies by priests, or it could have had separate, specialized practitioners.

The ethical dimension of religion concerns rules of conduct. This dimension also underwent great changes in the city. Tribal society was composed of a maze of taboos: certain things were wrong because they would involve contact with the profane, disrespect of the sacred, or contact with a powerful sacred (or demonic) force. In the cities, these rules shifted toward the utilitarian dimension of ethics, resulting in the behaviors that kept the city functioning smoothly.

There were rules for the builder, rules for the potter, rules for the soldier, so many rules that they could not all be remembered: they had to be written down in a code of law.

Neither tribal societies nor the early civilizations approximated anything like what we now regard as a secular society. The written laws and tribal taboos were enforced by the religious figures (whether priests or shamans) as well as the rulers (whether tribal chief or emperor). The priests enjoyed so much political power and the "divine" kings required so much priestly recognition that these city-states could be called **theocracies**. Indeed, the power of rulers to tax may have developed out of the power of priests to demand grain for sacrifice.

Afterlife doctrines also shifted in the cities. In tribal societies, the afterlife doctrines and funeral rituals surrounded issues of ancestral contact and veneration. In the cities, the doctrines of afterlife became more closely associated with a future reward for doing one's individual duties in that society.

MESOPOTAMIA

The term **Mesopotamia** means "between the rivers." The two rivers referred to were the Tigris and the Euphrates in the southern part of what is now Iraq. This was the site of several civilizations after 4000 B.C.E.: the Sumerians, the Akkadians, the Chaldeans, the Assyrians, and the Babylonians. The one most important word to remember in the description of this region is *instability*. Agriculture in this area was dependent upon irrigation because the rainfall was uncertain and could lead to drought or flood. Other sources of instability were the constant conflicts between the cities to see who would be the ruling empire. The main features of Mesopotamian religion are a reaction to this chaotic instability: creation myths in which the gods forged an order out of a primal chaos, a written code of laws from King Hammurabi to provide order among human society, and a reliance upon astrology-based divination to find one's personal order in life.

The Sumerians arrived in Mesopotamia as colonizers in prehistoric times and were not related either racially or linguistically to their neighbors to the north, the Akkadians. Sumer was a flat, marshy re-

Many of the ancient religious traditions discussed in this book emphasized the importance of trying to predict the future: the Babylonians used astrology, the Chinese threw objects on the ground, the Africans and Greeks interpreted their dreams. Late-night television advertises many psychic hotlines that claim to be able to predict what will happen.

Do you think that divination can be reconciled with the current doctrines of religions such as Christianity and Judaism?

Contribute to this discussion at
http://www.delphi.com/rel101

gion, and the first settlements consisted of huts built on mud. Flood was a constant, potentially devastating threat. Silt made the land fertile, however, and the Sumerians were able over the millennia to transform the swamp into a garden. They developed *cuneiform* (wedge-shaped) writing approximately two centuries before the Egyptians developed hieroglyphics. By that time they had already built great terraced, multi-storied temple towers (ziggurats) with bricks, and they were using sailboats, wheeled vehicles, animal-drawn plows, and potter's wheels. The country included a dozen small cities, each belonging in principle to its local deity and centered upon his temple. These cities included Eridu (traditionally considered the earliest, dating from about 4000 B.C.E.), Ur, Nippur, and Uruk or Erech. Sumerian kings served as representatives of the gods, enforcing their justice and promoting wealth to be used in their service. Cuneiform writing developed primarily as an instrument for recording contracts and accounts in the affairs of the temples, which controlled up to one-third of the land and owned great wealth.

It was also in Sumer, toward the middle of the twenty-fourth century B.C.E., that the idea of imperial rule was born, when a king named Lugalzaggesi (Zaggesi the Great) conquered a large part of the valley. An inscription that Lugalzaggesi placed on a monument in Nippur tells how Enlil, the supreme god and king of all countries, gave dominion to Lugalzaggesi, who then prayed that his rule might be peaceful and prosperous forever.

Sumerian political power never extended northward into Akkad, but Sumer had enormous cultural influence there. Over the centuries the Akkadians learned writing from the Sumerians and adopted much of their mythology and technology. Despite Lugalzaggesi's prayer for perpetual dominion, he was later defeated in battle and taken captive by an Akkadian, Sargon I, who founded an empire of his own, and also claimed the authority of Enlil. Sargon's rule was shortlived, however, and the Sumerians regained their independence for awhile. But by the time of the lawgiver **Hammurabi** in the eighteenth century B.C.E., the Sumerians were completely absorbed into the civilization that is now known as Babylonian, after its principal city, Babylon (Babilani, or "the gateway of the gods"), which grew to prominence after the demise of Ur.

Although we have some Sumerian fragments, most of the writings now available come from the Babylonian period, so we see Sumerian myths through Babylonian eyes and with Babylonian adaptations. One reason that the evidence is so fragmentary, in addition to its enormous antiquity, is the fact that the cuneiform tablets were not used primarily for the recording of myths, but for business accounts. In many cases the tablets with myths seem to have been the exercise books of schoolboys learning to write by copying out stories. Still, we have enough evidence to provide a fairly clear picture of the religious conceptions not only of the Babylonians, but also of the Sumerians.

The great legacy of Mesopotamia is its creation myths. One of the earliest Sumerian creation myths was the story of Enki and Ninhursag. This takes place in a land pure, clean, and bright, free from death and disease, until the mother goddess, Ninhursag, was impregnated by Enki (variously interpreted as the god of earth or of water). These events took place in primordial time, the time of the ordering of the cosmos. In the myth, Ninhursag and Enki produce a daughter, with whom Enki also mates and who then gives birth to another daughter, with whom Enki also mates. This last birth brings Uttu, Enki's great-granddaughter. Ninhursag warns the girl that Enki lurks in the marsh and lusts for her and that she should not yield herself to him until he offers her the appropriate gifts for a bride. He does so, however, and she gives herself to him joyfully.

At this point it seems (the text is broken) that Ninhursag intervenes, takes Enki's semen, and uses it

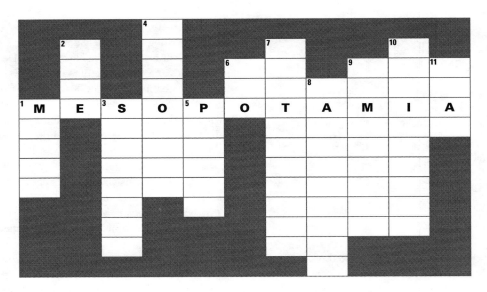

DOWN

1. Mesopotamians had elaborate creation _____.
2. Hammurabi gave a written _____ of laws.
3. The first civilzation in Mesopotamia.
4. Mesopotamians performed divination by using _____.
5. The deities brought order out of _____ chaos.
6. Mesopotamia is the land between _____ rivers.
7. Mesopotamia was plagued by _____.
8. A later Mesopotamian empire
9. The Babylonian king who gave a written code of laws
10. Mesopotamians used astrology to perform _____.
11. Mesopotamia was located near present-day _____.

to bring forth eight plants. Enki, noticing the eight new plants, decides he must "know" them and decide their fate, and therefore he eats them. Ninhursag becomes furious at this usurpation. She curses him and says she will no longer look on him with the eye of life. Enki then languishes and the land becomes dry and dusty. Alarmed, the other gods, with Enlil as their spokesman, intercede through the help of a clever fox to get Ninhursag to restore Enki. She does so by placing her vulva next to the ailing parts of Enki's body and bringing forth eight goddesses, each of whom heals the part with which she is associated. The eight goddesses evidently replace the eight plants that Enki had misappropriated. The poem ends with

the naming of the goddesses and the assignment of their destinies. It is not clear who speaks at that point, Enki or Ninhursag, but since the ending is one of reconciliation and restoration of life, it seems that the naming takes place with Ninhursag's approval. The last line of the surviving text praises Father Enki.

It is not easy to interpret a text that comes to us from a time so distant, in fragments, and possibly with many layers of revision along the way, but the main outline is not too difficult to discern. Clearly the myth depicts the beginning of the ordered world (or "cosmos") as we know it—a world in which nature brings forth living creatures. Before natural life with its cycles of birth, fertility, and death begins, there is

CASE STUDY: *ENUMA ELISH*

Another widespread motif is that of a battle between creative and destructive forces. In the myth of Enki and Ninhursag, this motif takes the form of a personal conflict between mother and father deities. In the famous Enuma Elish myth, it becomes a regular military campaign. Both myths explain the seasonal renewal of nature and also the continuing need for the creative forces in the cosmos actively to counter threats of disorder and returning chaos. (**Cosmos** and **chaos** are Greek terms that have come to be used generally to refer on one hand to the ordered totality of things, including all the levels of being and even the gods, and on the other hand to a state of unformed, unordered being. The term *chaos* originally meant an abyss and comes from the verb "to yawn." *Cosmos* originally referred to the village as compared with its surrounding wilderness. Eventually it came to refer to whatever was harmonious, civilized, beautiful, and constituted an ordered whole.)

The *Enuma Elish* (the title means "When on high" and comes from the first words of the Akkadian text) has come down to us mainly in its Babylonian form, but some fragments of a Sumerian original have also survived. In the Sumerian version everything begins with the union of sky and earth, represented by the first "thing," a cosmic mountain whose base is earth (female) and whose summit is the sky (male). The Babylonian version begins with the precosmic chaos: "When on high the heaven had not been named. Firm ground below had not been called by name. . . . No reed but had been matted, no marsh land had appeared." Neither gods nor humans had yet been created. There was only the primordial pair, Apsu (male, associated with fresh water) and Tiamat (female, the sea), "their waters commingling as a single body." Time and the world begin when they give birth to the first gods (perhaps representing the accumulation of silt where the river water meets the sea). These beget other gods and goddesses who mate in turn to produce the gods of earth (Ea) and sky (Anu) and so on. (Interestingly enough, earth and sky are here both represented by male gods,

evidently because the Babylonians wanted to give honor to the earth god, Ea, progenitor of their own special god, Marduk. They seem to have been more emphatically patriarchal than the Sumerians.)

As the story proceeds, the younger gods annoy their original ancestors through their poor manners and overbearing character. Apsu complains that he can gain no rest by day or by night because of their incessant noise and he proposes to annihilate them. Tiamat, though she too is angry with them, urges restraint, but he ignores her. When the younger gods hear of his plans, they become virtually paralyzed with fear, except for Ea, who casts a spell of sleep on Apsu and then slays him. Afterward Ea builds his home on Apsu's body and begets Marduk. (The image suggests earth, perhaps mud from the river, building up above the level of the water so that habitations may be built and the Babylonians eventually generated.) The poem proceeds with lavish praise of Marduk (the sun), who is said to be the tallest and strongest of the gods. Marduk himself creates the four winds and produces streams, both of which annoy Tiamat. She decides to put an end to all of this nuisance and to avenge Apsu. She takes a new consort, Kingu, and raises an army with which to make war on the younger gods. When they hear of this they are at a loss until they think of asking Marduk to lead them. Ea bids Marduk come to the assembly of the gods. Marduk promises to be their champion but asks in return that he become supreme among them and receive all their authority to "determine the fates." They willingly proclaim him king and confer on him throne, scepter, and royal vestments.

When Tiamat sees Marduk ride into battle against her, she goes wild, taking leave of her senses and shaking to her lowest parts—an image not only of a stormy sea, but of chaos itself. Slaying her, Marduk splits her in two like a shellfish and thrusts one-half upward to make the sky and the other downward to make the sea, setting guards to ensure that her waters will not escape and threaten the world again. He makes the dome of heaven correspond to earth as its heavenly counterpart. Then he executes Kingu and creates human beings from his blood so that the gods will have servants to maintain the earth when they have withdrawn to the heavens. As their final work of creation the gods build Babylon and at its center, as a temple to Marduk, the great ziggurat of Esagila, described as reaching as high as Apsu, as high as the primordial waters were deep.

Notice in this myth that the gods need human beings that they may rest from labor. The gods are not unlimited in power, but constitute only a part of the larger system of things that is the cosmos as a whole. They themselves must struggle to establish creation and keep it in proper order. Also, they do not create the world from nothing but make it from a preexisting reality. The world as we know it comes from the body of the subdued Tiamat, and human beings come from the blood of Kingu. One might say that the gods do not "create" the world in the same sense that the God of the Judeo-Christian-Islamic tradition creates.

The plot of the *Enuma Elish* describes both the creation of the cosmos as a whole and the evolution of the political order of Mesopotamia, as seen from the perspective of Babylonians in the second millennium. The authors are looking back to the origins of an order in which they have preeminence over their neighbors but are themselves under the authority of the gods and divine justice. The movement from a democratic assembly of gods to a centralized monarchic system under the rule of Marduk, god of Babylon, parallels the historical movement from independent city-states in Sumer and Akkad to the Babylonian empire. That the Babylonian emperors interpreted their own authority as subordinate to and representative of an overarching divine order can be seen, for example, in the preamble to the Law Code of Hammurabi (approximately 1750 B.C.E.), which opens with a description of how Anu and Enlil, lords of heaven and earth, committed lordship ("the Enlil functions over all mankind") to Marduk and then called Hammurabi personally to enforce their justice in the land.

The underlying idea in this picture of historical development seems to have been that earthly kingship was conferred from a superhuman source and was an imitation of and participation in the ordering power of a divine original, the order established by the gods of the empire at the beginning of the world. This meant that royal rule was intended to be sacred rule in the service of divine justice. It also meant that human life and its order were connected with the cosmic order and the life of the gods. If human farmers did not cultivate their crops, if reverent worshipers did not offer sacrifices, if justice among human beings was allowed to deteriorate, then the life of the gods would also suffer injury.

This interpretation of the relationship among human beings, the world, and the gods is a good example of *cosmological symbolism:* symbolism in which human life and society are interpreted by analogy with the cosmic order. That was the predominant pattern of symbolism in ancient Mesopotamia, and we will see it again in Egypt. It is not the only possible pattern of symbolic interpretation, but all over the world it seems to have been the first to develop.

Anthropomorphic (human form) *symbolism,* such as that which flourished in classical Greece, likens society and the cosmos to a human existence. Specifically, it depicts reality in terms of the inner order of a wise and virtuous person. Anthropomorphic symbolism usually develops after cosmologically symbolized societies have broken down and disappointed their members so deeply that the members feel the need for an entirely new way of discovering relevance. This sort of disappointment never seems to have afflicted the ancient Mesopotamians, at least not enough to have caused a radically new development in their culture. Most of the myths the Mesopotamians have left us suggest that they found the evil of the universe intelligible in terms of the basic model we have seen: a precarious balance of interdependent forces.

154

Nonetheless, the Mesopotamians did finally wrestle with the problem of a suffering that is genuinely personal and calls the cosmological principle into question. The epic of *Gilgamesh* is their famous meditation on personal suffering. It concerns a famous early king of Uruk in Sumer and probably dates from the late third millennium B.C.E. The most complete surviving text is in Assyrian, but there are fragments of earlier versions in Sumerian and Akkadian.

Gilgamesh was of mingled parentage, divine and human, but he was a mortal all the same, and his mortality is the poem's main theme. At the opening Gilgamesh is a vigorous and effective ruler, in fact too vigorous: his constant demands for labor and military service lead the people of Uruk to appeal to the gods for relief. The goddess Aruru responds by creating another energetic creature, Enkidu, to attract the interest of Gilgamesh. Enkidu is humanity in its most primitive state. He is naked, covered with hair, enormously strong, and lives among animals in the wilderness. Befriending the animals, Enkidu protects them from hunters, who, unable to fight him themselves, appeal to Gilgamesh.

Gilgamesh sends a sacred prostitute, Shamhat, to civilize Enkidu. Shamhat goes to the wilderness to wait for Enkidu by a water hole. When he comes, she attracts his interest by uncovering her body. They enjoy a week of heroic lovemaking, at the end of which Enkidu tries to return to the company of his animals but finds them shying away from him. Shamhat tells him that he no longer belongs among animals but has become wise and godlike. She offers to take him to see the great walls of Uruk and mighty Gilgamesh. Enkidu decides to go with her and to challenge Gilgamesh. He arrives in Uruk at the moment of Gilgamesh's wedding procession and bars Gilgamesh's path to the bride. The two powerful figures hurl themselves at each other and fight like young bulls, shaking the walls of the bride's house. Gilgamesh turns out to be the stronger of the two, but his

generous praise of Enkidu makes them fast friends. Looking for adventure together (Gilgamesh seems to have forgotten all about his bride), they set out to kill a monster named Huwawa. When they return victorious, the goddess Ishtar falls in love with Gilgamesh and proposes to him. He turns her down. Furious, Ishtar appeals to her father, Anu, to unleash the bull of heaven. Anu warns her that this monster will be so destructive that there will be a famine for seven years, but she persuades him to unloose it anyway. However, Enkidu gets behind the bull and twists its tail while Gilgamesh plunges his sword into its neck. Enraged by Ishtar's curses, Enkidu tears off the bull's shank and throws it at the goddess.

This means trouble. The gods hold an assembly and sentence Enkidu to death. Enkidu is horrified and launches into a long lament in which he curses everything that has led to this end: his departure from the animals, his lovemaking with Shamhat, his migration to the city, and even his friendship with Gilgamesh. The sun god Shamash, however, intervenes and persuades him to withdraw his curses and bless his friend before dying. In a dream Enkidu has a vision of Irkalla, the land of the dead. It is a house of dust and darkness, devoid of real life, in which one is no more than a shadow. Far from representing a form of immortality, it is death depicted in the most graphic terms.

After his friend's death Gilgamesh falls into an extreme despondency, not simply because of the loss of his companion, but because death, which had always been a remote abstraction to him, has now become a vivid reality. He realizes that however long and glorious his life may be, death awaits. This thought becomes an obsession, undermining any joy in his own or his city's glory and any consolation from the balance of forces in the cosmos. The thought of his death haunts Gilgamesh day and night. Finally he decides to search for an escape from mortality. He has heard of an ancestor named Utnapishtim who once won eternal life as a gift from the gods and now dwells at the end of the earth. The sun god, Shamash, reproaches him for his lack of moderation, but Gilgamesh is not interested in reasonableness; his heart is set on only one goal: not to die. Eventually he arrives at the shore of the great sea that encircles the earth, where he finds a tavern run by a woman named Siduri. She offers the conventional wisdom, urging him to accept his mortality, enjoy food, drink, and merriment, wear beautiful clothing, bathe in fresh water, rejoice in his children, and give satisfaction to his wife. This, she says, is the task of human beings. Gilgamesh refuses to listen and persuades her to tell him how to find Utnapishtim. She directs him to the boatman, Urshanabi, who takes him to Utnapishtim's island.

The result, however, is bitterly disappointing. Utnapishtim tells Gilgamesh that he did not win immortality through deeds of valor. It happened at a time when the gods had decided to destroy humankind in a great flood. Ea, more foresighted than the other gods, realized that without human beings to maintain the earth the gods would languish for lack of sacrifices. Ea told Utnapishtim to build an ark and save his family and pairs of all animals. (The story is similar in many details to the biblical story of Noah, which, as far as written records indicate, it may predate by perhaps a millennium.) After the flood, the gods realized the fault of their hastiness and were so grateful to Utnapishtim that they conferred eternal life on him. Unfortunately that was something that could happen only once.

Utnapishtim suggests, evidently mockingly, that if Gilgamesh wishes to conquer death, he might begin by trying to conquer sleep. No sooner does Gilgamesh take up the challenge than sleep overcomes him. Utnapishtim would happily let Gilgamesh sleep himself to death, but his wife takes pity on Gilgamesh and persuades Utnapishtim to wake him and let him go home. She also persuades him to tell Gilgamesh about a plant that will perpetually renew his youth. This thorny plant grows in the Apsu, the sweet waters deep under the earth. (In the Mesopotamian cosmology the earth is a great floating island.) Gilgamesh dives for it by tying stones to his feet and sinking to the bottom. When he gets the plant, he is overjoyed, thinking his basic goal achieved. On the way home, however, feeling the heat of the day, he decides to take a swim in a cool pond. He leaves the plant with his clothes and while he is swimming a serpent comes out of its hole and eats the plant. Immediately the snake sloughs off its old skin and is renewed, shiny and young. With that, Gilgamesh completely despairs. Following his despair, however, come resignation and composure. Essentially Gilgamesh accepts the wisdom of Shamash and Siduri that he had rejected earlier. At the end of the poem he takes the boatman around the great walls of Uruk, praising the grandeur of his royal domain.

Myths are told and retold to convey a society's values. Is this poem a lesson in moderation and the acceptance of human limitations, or is it a radical protest against those limitations? There is no easy answer. How far did the challenge to Mesopotamian cosmological assumptions proceed? Did anyone seriously doubt them to the point of considering another perspective? The ending of the poem seems designed to reassert the old doctrines and values. In the perspective of the conclusion, Gilgamesh's obsession becomes a temporary disorder that must be overcome if one is to live in proper harmony with the cosmos and the gods.

no death or disease, but with life comes the problem of evil (theodicy) in its various forms. The form of evil that this story emphasizes is the evil of disorder.

Exactly why Enki's claim to preeminence (that is what his eating of the plants seems to imply) is a source of disorder is not altogether clear. Many ancient myths take the preeminence of the father god for granted, but this one does not. Possibly, therefore, there was an earlier version with a matriarchal emphasis, that is, with the idea that the female principle is preeminent in generation. At any rate, what we see is a struggle between the male and female sources of life to define their relative dignity. When Enki, the male principle, claims eminence that Ninhursag finds excessive, she demonstrates her own importance by withdrawing her life-giving power. The other gods subsequently realize her importance, as does Enki himself, who must ask her to heal each part of his body that is afflicted. At the end an appropriate balance seems to emerge. The masculine principle's usurpation of knowledge and power is represented as a sort of fall that must be purged through suffering and the reestablishment of proper order.

Thus we see a fairly typical mythic pattern in which disorder in creation is repaired by dissolution, and right order is established through a new act of creation (the healing of Enki and the birth of the goddesses who replace the plants). Since this sequence of creation, death, and rebirth is also the pattern of the annual cycle of vegetation, the myth seems to do double duty as both a story of creation and commentary on the cycles of nature.

EGYPT

Modern **Egypt** is a major center of Arab and Muslim culture. Taxi drivers career through Cairo with a *Qur'an* on the dashboard to protect them; common people lay rugs in the train station and kneel at the call to prayer. Yet the treasures of Tutankhamen, the Giza pyramids, and above all the Nile tie modern Cairo to the pre-Islamic Egypt of more than 5,000 years ago. Merely follow the Nile by train to Alexandria and you will see in its delta peasants drawing water with buffalo much as they did in the Old Kingdom.

Egypt described in this chapter is the pre-Arab, pre-Muslim civilization which developed along the Nile River in northeast Africa. The Nile's flow patterns are regular, predictable, and nonthreatening. Egypt had the Sahara desert to the west, mountains to the south, the Mediterranean to the north, and the Red Sea to the east. It was less susceptible to foreign invasion than was Mesopotamia. For the best part of 2,500 years, Egyptian life remained the same. At the Great Pyramids near the Sphinx, the desert seems to have mimicked the Nile's behavior. The endless sand, like the river water, changes with the wind. Actually, though, little changes. Sky, sun, sand, and water—they all endure. Like stable props, they are set on every stage. Egyptian civilization was remarkably *stable,* rigid, static. It lacked the need for divination or myths of primal chaos (so prominent in Mesopotamia). The greatest need was to keep the social order going, and so afterlife came to be emphasized. On the Egyptian stage, pharaohs and peasants enacted a mortality play. Beyond life under the sun, life in the flesh, lay deathlessness. The tomb then was an archway through which everybody passed.

The unification of Upper (southern) and Lower (northern) Egypt occurred about 3100 B.C.E., and with it began the central Egyptian religious dogma—divine kingship. In the prehistoric years before unification, Neolithic culture gradually developed small-town life, characterized by domestic animals, significant crafts (especially pottery), and probably the burial of the dead with hopes of an afterlife. From the beginnings of Egyptian history, local gods had great influence, and throughout the long dynasties they comprised a pantheon (in the form of an assembly of divinities).

Egyptian splendor began vigorously in the period 3100-2200 B.C.E., which historians divide into the Early Dynasties (3100-2700 B.C.E.) and the Old Kingdom (2700-2200 B.C.E.). A famous product of Old Kingdom religion is the Memphite theology, developed to justify the new, unified kingdom centered at Memphis. Central to the justification is that the god of Memphis, Ptah, is the foremost creator god. Ptah originated Atum, the supreme god of the older cosmogony, and the other gods by an idea in his heart and a command on his tongue.

The Middle Kingdom (2050-1800 B.C.E.) was centered at Thebes. It nurtured several trends that brought important changes, although they worked below the surface constancy of Egyptian life. The most important of these trends was a democratization of certain religious rights, as the distance between the pharaoh and the common people narrowed. Also, there was an effort to elevate the more important gods and an increasing inclination to worship gods who were theriomorphic (in the form of animals). The most important religious rights that democratization brought the middle classes were privileges in the afterlife and a chance to participate in ceremonies that had been confined to the king and a few priests. By this time, most middle-class people could afford to have their bodies **mummified** after death.

Sphinx and pyramids

An intermediate period (1800–1570 B.C.E.) dissolved the Middle Kingdom and included a century or so of rule by the Hyksos (Shepherd Kings), who were probably Syrians. The New Kingdom (1570–1165 B.C.E.) began with the famous eighteenth dynasty, which made Egypt a real empire that stretched to the Euphrates. For our limited review of the high points in later Egyptian religious history, the New Kingdom's speculation on the deities is important.

In the nineteenth dynasty under **Akhenaton** (1369–1353 B.C.E.), there was a move to make Aton, previously just the sun disk, the sole deity. Apparently Akhenaton himself bullied through this change (Egypt quickly reverted to polytheism after his death) because of his own spiritual perceptions (which many of his contemporaries considered fanatical and heretical). In a joyful climax, one of Akhenaton's hymns cries out: "The Aton is the creator-god: O sole god, like whom there is no other! Thou didst create the world according to thy desire, while thou wert

alone." Moreover, Aton was not the god of Egypt alone. Akhenaton saw that a real creator god must have established all peoples, whatever their country, speech, culture, or skin. This was truly a remarkable leap toward universalism, especially coming from the leader of a resolutely ethnocentric people, and it was the centerpiece in the so-called Armarna Revolution that gave the New Kingdom a great charge of cultural energy. Whether Akhenaton should be considered one of the first monotheists (claiming the exclusive existence of just one god) or a mere monolatrist (advocating the worship of just one god, but not denying the existence of others) remains a point of scholarly debate, as does the relative role of political and psychological considerations in Akhenaton's actions.

Another high point of New Kingdom theology consisted of the Amon hymns, which probably date from the reign of Ramses II (1290–1224 B.C.E.). They illustrate a return to Amon and the demise of Aton as well as a deep sense that the first creator god must be mysterious. Amon is "far from heaven, he is absent from the underworld, so that no gods know his true form. His image is not displayed in writings. No one bears witness to him. . . . He is too mysterious that his majesty might be disclosed, he is too great that men should ask about him, too powerful that he might be known." Along with the hymns of Akhenaton, these praises of Amon represent the greatest advance in Egyptian theology. Here we see traces of a "negative" theology—a rising of the mind to the true nature of divinity by denying that creatures can represent it adequately.

In the centuries after the New Kingdom, the capital moved to Manis, Bubastis, and Sais—a possible indication of some political turmoil of that era. Persians ruled Egypt from 525 to 405 B.C.E., and the last native dynasties in the fourth century B.C.E. ended with the conquest of Alexander. In the period from Alexander to about 30 B.C.E., the Hellenistic Ptolemies ruled, and the city of Alexandria was the luminary of the eastern Mediterranean. Christian influence rose in the Roman and Byzantine periods (30 B.C.E.–641 C.E.), bequeathing Egypt the Coptic Church. Since 641 C.E., Egyptian culture has been predominantly Muslim.

Except for the brief episode of monotheism under Akhenaton, ancient Egypt was polytheistic. Indeed, the proliferation of Egyptian gods and symbols is overwhelming. The basic hieroglyph for God is a pole with a flag, the emblem flying in front of major temples, which designated purity and the creative life force. Since the Egyptians sensed purity and creativity in many places, they split divinity into many gods. The gods most important in the old cosmogony were four male-female pairs. The males bore the head of a frog, and the females the head of a snake—symbols, apparently, of self-renewal (the frog begins as a tadpole, while the snake sheds its skin). The idea (before the Memphite theology established Ptah as the creator) was that an invisible wind moved over primal waters and used these four pairs of gods to make life.

Throughout Egyptian history, the most important deities were associated with the sun and death (connoting a theme of resurrection). Their names and images varied from cultural center to cultural center, but the most common name for the sun god was Re, symbolized by either the sun's disk or the falcon. Another name was Khepri, represented by a scarab pushing the sun disk; a third name was Atum, whom people at Heliopolis worshiped and represented as the setting sun. In the mythology of Heliopolis, Atum generated himself on the primordial hill of creation (the Pyramids of the Old Kingdom represented this hill). He conquered chaos, took charge of the world, and established maat, the eternal cosmic order. The *Book of the Dead* (17:3–5), from the New Kingdom, says that Re became king of the gods in the earliest times by defeating all his opponents. Maat is his daughter but also his mother, because in his course through the sky, the sun god follows her cosmic order. That course determined Egyptian reality. The west was the land of the dead, and the east was where the daily miracle of the sun's return from the dead occurred. On the walls of royal tombs near Luxor, twelve sections divide the night realm, or underworld, through which the sun god's boat travels. Although the sun god is dead during this time, he still possesses the power of resurrection. Middle night is the realm of Sokaris, who appears in human form with the head of a falcon. His area is a desert through which Re's boat has to be dragged before the sun can reemerge into the light.

It was the deity Osiris, however, around whom developed the funerary cult that made the underworld almost an Egyptian obsession. Nowhere is the myth of his descent to the underworld detailed, but it probably had the following plot. Osiris and Seth were brothers, and the deity Isis was Osiris' sister and wife. Osiris ruled the world as a good regent, but Seth hated him and killed him by guile. He got Osiris into a coffin and sent it down the Nile. Isis recovered Osiris' corpse and uttered a soulful dirge (which inspired litanies used in Osiris' worship). This dirge had a magic power that revived Osiris. Once again Seth moved against Osiris, this time hacking Osiris' body into fourteen pieces and then scattering them. Isis recovered them all and buried each piece properly wherever she found it (this explained the many Osirian sanctuaries). Furthermore, Isis conceived a son Horus by the dead Osiris and brought Horus up in the marshes to hide him from Seth.

When Horus reached manhood, Isis arranged for a trial at which Seth was condemned for murdering Osiris and Horus was recognized as Osiris' heir. Osiris himself remained in the underworld, accepting the roles of lord of the nether realm and judge of the

Egypt had many theriomorphic deities, with part animal bodies.

dead. Osiris seems to represent the growing power of vegetation, which roots in the earth, and he relates to all buildings that are set on the earth, to the moon, and to the dead. Isis represents the throne, the sacred seat of the king. As such, she "makes" the king and is his mother. For instance, on a relief in a temple at Abydos, the pharaoh sits on Isis' lap. Thus, Horus and the pharaoh are correlated. As Horus owed his throne to his mother Isis, so did the pharaoh.

Horus had many appearances, but most frequently he wore the head of a falcon. He was the model son but shows traces of an older sky god. In the Osiris myth, Horus fought Seth and lost an eye, while depriving Seth of his testicles. They reconciled, however, to suggest that life and death are paired. Thoth, originally a moon god, was the agent of their reconciliation. Usually Thoth was represented as a baboon or an ibis. He was also a god of the dead and is thought to have found Horus' lost eye and have re-

turned it to him. This eye became a token of life returned from the dead. All of these myths represent the Egyptian sense of a cosmic order. The term *Maat* described this order. Maat was something like the Law or Logos guiding creation. Personified as a goddess, it had the obligation of constraining or persuading creatures to follow the laws natural to them. The pharaoh mediated Maat to the common people, and the laws of the state sanctioned by the pharaoh spelled out what Maat was to mean in many concrete circumstances. The pharaoh had responsibilities to Maat, but he served as well as a metaphysical link between the order of heaven that Maat expressed and the order of earth that needed ordering. Maat had many competitors in the Egyptian pantheon, probably standing psychologically for the rights of reason in competition with will, desire, fertility, and the other urges of both the conscious and the unconscious mind.

This order was a major reason for the stability of the Egyptian culture. With divinity in their midst, what need the people fear? The greatest threat to social stability, understandably, was the king's death. The care taken for the transition from old pharaoh to new suggests how the office of pharaoh served Egypt as a fence against chaos. Consequently, the most influential mythic cycle was that of Osiris and Isis, which explained where the king (identified with Osiris) had gone at death. Relatedly, the most important ceremonies were the old king's burial and the new king's accession. For a hint of how effective this mythic-ritualistic approach was, consider the pyramids. The common people supplied the immense, brutal labor needed to build the pyramids, because they assured the king's happy afterlife and the state's continuance.

Ancient Egypt had a powerful caste of priests, and at times, despite the dogma of the king's divinity, this caste clashed with the crown. The conflict between Akhenaton and the priests of the old god Amon was a vivid instance of such friction, but conflict was almost always on the verge of breaking out. When Akhenaton moved the capital from Thebes to Amarna, he bruised theological, class, and local sensitivities all at once. The local priesthood, fighting for its own gods and people, consistently defended those sensitivities. As a result, the priesthood was a powerful sociological force.

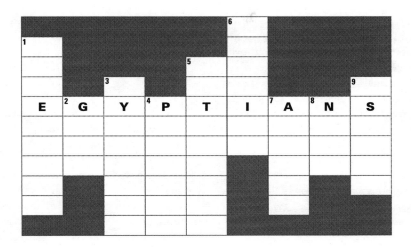

DOWN

1   Monotheist pharaoh of the fourteenth century B.C.E.
2   Egyptians had theriomorphic _____.
3   The _____ may have been used as burial chambers for pharaohs.
4   Egyptian religious leaders
5   Egyptians emphasized this post-death phase.
6   The dead were preserved as _____.
7   Egypt is in northeast _____.
8   Egypt developed along this river.
9   Egyptian god of the underworld who judged the dead.

Women were quite subordinate in Egyptian society but were not without influence and religious importance. The goddesses Hathor, Nut, Neith, Maat, and Isis represented the female aspects of divinity, while the queen had vital roles in the political theology. Hathor, Nut, and Neith were forms of the mother goddess—both sacred representations of fertility and figures of comfort. Maat ruled cosmic justice, while Isis was sister and wife of the god as king. On rare occasions a queen could rule (Hatshepsut, 1486–1468 B.C.E., is the most famous instance), and as the source of the divine king, the queen mother was much more than just another harem wife.

Egyptian proverbs encouraged husbands to treat their wives well so that their property would prosper, but they also pictured women as flirtatious, gossiping and spiteful. Women of the New Kingdom served in the temples and as popular entertainers, but in both cases they risked reputations as prostitutes. In both formal and popular religion, Isis was a focal point for women's own religion, especially in Hellenistic times, after 300 B.C.E. Related to Osiris, she was the ideal wife (and a potent exemplar of grief); related to Horus, she was the ideal mother. Through Isis, then, women in ordinary roles participated in divinity.

Perhaps because of this divinity, legal documents from about 500 B.C.E. suggest that Egyptian women had the right to own property, buy or sell goods, and testify in court. They were taxpayers and could sue; they could inherit from parents or husbands. On the other hand, husbands could dismiss wives at their pleasure (but not vice versa), and concubinage, adultery, and prostitution were widespread. Because many Egyptian women worked the fields or had other important economic roles, their lot was better than that of women in other ancient civilizations (Mesopotamia, for instance). Still, women were not regarded as equal to men.

The Egyptian religious conception of the self relates intimately to the Egyptian concern with death, burial, and the afterlife. The ancient Egyptians loved life, and they looked forward to another, better chapter after death. The remains of many burial sites, well preserved because of the desert sand and dry climate, show that the departed took with them favorite utensils and even favorite servants. The *ba* was that aspect of a person that continued after death, which contrasted with the *ka,* or vital force, the impersonal power animating the living. A third aspect, the *akh,* was the shining, glorious manifestation of the dead in heaven. With these three notions, the Egyptians had a sense of what moves the living and what continues on after death.

The key to a successful afterlife journey was good ethical behavior in this life. As indicated in our outline of his myth, Osiris judged the dead in the underworld. The Pyramid texts of the Old Kingdom, the Coffin texts of the Middle Kingdom, and the *Book of the Dead* from the New Kingdom show a constant concern with judgment, hence a certain awareness of personal responsibility. The *Book of the Dead* contains a famous "negative confession" that illustrates both the posthumous trial Egyptians imagined and some of their principal ethical concerns. The deceased claims before Osiris: "I have not committed evil against men. . . . I have not mistreated cattle. . . . I have not blasphemed a god. . . . I have not done violence to a poor man. . . . I have not made anyone weep. . . . I have not killed. . . . I have not defamed a slave to his superior. . . . I have not had sexual relations with a boy." In all, thirty-six declarations of innocence are made. Then, to complete his show of religious virtuosity, he gives each of the forty-two divine jurors, by name, a specific assurance. For example, "O Embracer-of-Fire, who comes forth from Babylon, I have not stolen. O Eater-of-Entrails, who comes forth from the thirty [judges in the world of the living], I have not practiced usury. O Eater-of-Blood, who comes forth from the execution block, I have not slain the cattle of the god."

We have less knowledge of the rituals in which the average Egyptian may have participated. In most agricultural ceremonies and many regal rituals, the common people could participate. There were probably festivals where grain and animals were sacrificed. Male circumcision and abstinence from pork were practiced, as in some other Middle Eastern traditions.

IRAN

Persia is the name for the ancient area north of Mesopotamia, east of Turkey, south of the Caspian Sea, and west of India and Pakistan. The most recent political regimes of the nation currently occupying that area have preferred the name Iran instead of Persia. That name comes from Aryans, nomadic peoples from the north who invaded and conquered this area during the second millennium B.C.E. We will use the terms *Iran* and *Persia* interchangeably.

Iran has had human habitation for well over ten thousand years. Those first inhabitants were great potters, and archaeologists have found among their relics designs and figurines of a naked goddess, whose mate was likely a god who was her son. This doctrine would be the most direct explanation for the early Iranian customs of marriage between blood relations, descent through the female line, and, in certain tribes (for example, the Guti of Kurdistan), female army commanders. Later archeological remains, dating back to 2000 B.C.E., suggest a people both artistic and hopeful, for impressive pendants, earrings, bracelets, and the like found in gravesites imply a notion of an afterlife.

In the second millennium B.C.E., Indo-Europeans, pressured by population shifts in the neighboring geographic areas, left their homelands in the plains of southern Russia and migrated southeast across Iran. As we shall see in the next chapter, some of them eventually ended up as far south as India. In the west they established the Hittite empire, sacked Babylon, and confronted the Egyptians. From the east, Indo-European tribes called the Mittani conquered northern Mesopotamia and allied themselves with Egypt in about 1450 B.C.E. Linguistic, religious, and social parallels suggest that pre-Zoroastrian Iranian culture, as well as the culture of the peoples who conquered the Indus Valley in India and produced the Vedic culture, derived from the Mittani, Hittite, and other Indo-European **Aryans** (from an Indo-European word meaning "noble"). In particular, the Iranian and Indian Aryans had similar gods and similar social structures.

Recently Iran has been a nation in the throes of choosing its identity and direction. On first view, the principal choices Iran has faced in determining its identity have been Western secularism (almost unavoidable because of Iran's massive petroleum industry) and a form of traditional Islam. In a later chapter we will describe how Islam was brought to Iran and how it developed there.

This chapter will discuss an earlier religion developing in Iran, focusing on a man known as Zarathustra (called **Zoroaster** by the Europeans). He could be described as a priest and prophet. Most historical data indicate that he probably lived in the sixth or seventh century B.C.E., but many modern Zoroastrians claim that he (or his religion) was around several hundred years before then.

The native Iranian religion that Zoroaster challenged was probably controlled by Median priests (the Medes were a later Aryan tribe) from western Iran called Magi. Apparently that religion was an animistic polytheism (devotion to many divine spirits) similar to that of early Aryan India. After Zoroaster's death, the Magi fused their ideas onto his new notions, making Zoroastrianism an amalgam of conflicting gods and practices. Before Zoroaster, Iranian ultimate reality included a number of *ahuras*—good celestial spirits. The most prominent symbols were lucidity (the brightness that glances off the waters or that leaps from fire); the sacred liquor *haoma,* used in the old Aryan rituals; and plain water, symbol of purity and motherliness.

Ancient Iranian society established a pronounced caste system, but most of its ritual practices cut across class distinctions. Some common people were quite interested in magic, but the orthodox leaders feared the occult, treating sorcerers and witches as criminals. Folk remedies and totemic practices (for example, rubbing oneself with the wing of a falcon to ward off an evil spell) flourished, in part because of contact with Mesopotamia. Both divination and astrology were common, and other nations considered the Persian Magi to be specialists in dream interpretation. Occasionally there was trial by fire or molten lead (if the person survived, he or she was deemed innocent).

Zoroaster is estimated to have lived from 628 to 551 B.C.E., but the only direct source for his message is a fragment of the sacred Zoroastrian liturgical text,

the *Avesta.* That portion, called the *Gathas,* along with later Greek and Persian traditions, suggests that Zoroaster's enemies (Magi and men's societies of the old religion) forced him to flee from his homeland into ancient Chorasmia (the area today of western Afghanistan, or Turkmenistan). There, when about forty years old, he found a patron in King Vishtapa and his message began to have social effect.

Zoroaster's doctrine was monotheistic. The one supreme God had the name of Ahura Mazdah, although he was often called the "Wise Lord." This God is the creator of all, having thought it into existence. This God is holy, righteous, immortal, and generous. The great outward symbol of God's "Truth" and power is fire, and the center of the Zoroastrian ritual is the fire altar.

Zoroaster's doctrine was **dualistic** in that he recognized the existence of two powerful and competing forces in the world. The world is divided between "the Truth and the Lie," by which Zoroaster meant God and Satan (who had several different names, including Angra Mainyu, the "destructive spirit").

Zoroaster advocated the doctrine of **free will:** that the creatures of the Wise Lord have the ability to freely choose whether to serve His cause or that of Satan. These creatures include human beings as well as spirit beings (angels). Sometimes the old deities are described as spirit beings who have chosen to serve the evil. Because human beings are free, they are responsible for their own fates. By good deeds they win the eternal reward of possessing Wholeness and Immortality; by evil deeds they merit pain in hell.

Historically, Zoroastrianism may be one of the earliest advocates of **eschatological** doctrine. The conflict between God and Satan was portrayed as apocalyptic (a final battle between these two sides) at which time the dead will be resurrected to fight on one side or the other. Unlike Teutonic eschatology (in which the gods are destined to lose) or Christian-Islamic eschatology (in which God is destined to win), the Zoroastrians say that the outcome hangs in the balance and will depend upon the choices freely made by men and angels.

Zoroaster generates his images of divinity and human destiny apart from nature and toward the inner light of human conscience. Two verses from perhaps the most autobiographical of Zoroaster's hymns suggest the religious experience at the core of his preaching:

> As the holy one I recognized thee, O Wise Lord, When I saw thee at the beginning, at the birth of existence, Appoint a recompense for deed and word: Evil reward to the evil, good to the good, Through thy wisdom, at the last turning-point of creation [43:5].

> As the holy one I recognized thee, O Wise Lord, When he came to me as Good Mind. To his question: "To whom wilt thou address thy worship?" I made reply: "To thy fire! While I offer up my veneration to it, I will think of the Right to the utmost of my power" [43:9].

In Iran in the early sixth century B.C.E., only an exceptional personality could have cut through the welter of Aryan gods, spells, and semimagical practices and discerned a clear religious call to identify God with justice. Similarly, only an exceptional personality could have lingered over abstractions such as Good Mind and the Right and made these terms God's best names. Zoroaster's revelations had a social background and significance. For instance, he championed the farmer over the nomad. Nonetheless, the deeper explanation of Zoroaster's religious power is the interior, spiritual experiences indicated by the *Gathas*. Like Jesus and Muhammad, Zoroaster met a holy, compelling divinity or ultimate reality. His mission was simply to spread this doctrine far and wide. The origins of Zoroastrian history, then, are the visions and insights of a founding genius. Through all its later changes, Zoroastrianism and the world religions that it influenced retained something of the dazzling vision of Zoroaster's Wise Lord.

Zoroaster's basic ethical imperative was to maintain goodness and life by fighting against evil and death. As a result, Zoroastrianism has frowned on fasting, asceticism, and celibacy. Rather, humans have been counseled to foster the powers of generation in nature and humanity alike. One basis for this view was Zoroaster's own stress on the holiness of agriculture, which to him was a cooperation with Ahura Mazdah. The farmer who sows grain, he said, "feeds the religion" of the Wise Lord. Zoroaster himself seems to have disapproved of blood sacrifices, going out of his way to try to protect cattle. Blood sacrifices survived in later Zoroastrianism, though,

the most important being the bull sacrifice. Also important to later Zoroastrians was the preparation and offering of *haoma,* the sacred liquor, which until recently served as a sort of sacrament for the dying. The most important sacrifice and ritual focus, however, has been the fire sacrifice. The flame has to be "pure" (obtained by burning "pure" materials such as sandalwood), and it has to pass to another flame before its fuel becomes embers. The fire sacrifice has overtones of an ancient wonder at the source of light and heat, but its major emphasis has always been to symbolize the blazing purity and potential sensing of the Wise Lord.

Rituals for individuals, including rites of passage at maturity, marriage, and death are important, as are various purifications. Upon entering adulthood, both men and women receive a sacred thread and shirt. The thread is a compound symbol: cosmically it stands for the Milky Way, the thread of the stars through the heavens; mythologically, it recalls Ahura Mazdah's gift of *haoma;* personally, it symbolizes taking up adult responsibilities. The shirt is white, to symbolize purity and the garment that the soul dons after death. Death and bloodshed are prime occasions for purification, because they are prime pollutants. As noted, Zoroastrians have exposed the dead so as not to defile other persons, the earth, fire, or water. In some periods of Zoroastrianism, blood from a cut, an extracted tooth, or even menstrual flow could render a person ritually unclean.

In general, women have played only a small part in the Zoroastrian world. Their part in redemption has been to furnish males to fight against Angra Mainyu. Most of the tradition has held that in the beginning women defected to the Destructive Spirit. Theologically, then, Zoroastrianism has viewed the female nature as unholy.

After the death of Zoroaster, his religion invigorated the Persian empire. The great leaders of the Achaemenid empire who followed Zoroaster were the Persians Cyrus II (599–530 B.C.E.), Cambyses II (530–522 B.C.E.), and Darius I (522–486 B.C.E.). They conquered eastern Iran, the prophet's initial sphere of influence, and we can read in inscriptions that they left something of Zoroastrianism's function as the religious rationale for a new, energetic empire. Following Alexander's victory over Darius III in 331 B.C.E., the Achaemenid dynastic line begun with

Persian reliefs showing emperor Ardechir I receiving his crown from God.

Cyrus II gave way to the Greek Seleucids. Under the Seleucids, for almost a century Hellenistic cultural ideals blended with Persian. Zoroastrian influence probably declined, overshadowed by a Greek-Iranian syncretism. While the practice of pure Zoroastrianism seems to have remained in Fars (the southern province called Persis), the old Iranian goddess Anahita, fused with the Mesopotamian goddess Nanai, complicated the religious picture in other provinces.

Also complicating the picture was the Greek hero Heracles (Hercules), who joined with local gods. Heracles was the patron of the gymnasium, the place of physical exercise, an important feature of Hellenistic culture. Also, he was one of several "savior" gods (gods who made life whole) whose influence grew apace with the disintegration of the previously secure city-state religions. The *Avesta* was probably still evolving at this time, incorporating hymns to the god **Mithra,** who had existed before Zoroaster and later became an important savior god for the Romans. In the *Avesta,* Mithra's main functions are to preserve cattle, sanctify contracts, and render judgment on human actions.

The Greek Seleucids yielded to the Parthians, who entered Iran from the area southwest of the Caspian

Sea. The Parthians dominated Iran, bit by bit, from the first conquest by Arsaces in about 238 B.C.E. until about 226 C.E. While sources are scanty, Zoroastrianism apparently made some gains against syncretism under the Parthians, achieving a privileged status. Nonetheless, in Parthian times the cultures of the different geographic areas varied considerably. Coins, art, and other remains indicate different local preferences for a variety of gods. Ahura Mazdah and Mithra certainly were influential, but the worship of the goddess Anahita was probably the most important. The northern Magis had a custom of exposing the bodies of the dead on mountains or manmade "towers of silence" to be eaten by vultures. This was done because burial would pollute the earth and cremation would pollute the sky. This rite spread as far south as Susa, capital of the old Elamite kingdom. We also know that the Parthians were tolerant of religious minorities, so much so that Jews regarded them as great protectors.

The history of Zoroastrianism under the Parthians remains rather vague. Under the Sasanians (ca. 226–637 C.E.), it is more definite, as is the story of Persian culture generally. The early Sasanian king Papak probably was the director of the shrine to Anahita in Istakhr in Persis (south-central Iran), and his successor Shapur had quite liberal religious policies. That soon changed, however, largely because of the influence of Kartir, a zealous Zoroastrian priest. By the last third of the third century, he had made Zoroastrianism the established Persian denomination. Kartir favored proselytizing, establishing fire temples for worship and instruction, purging Zoroastrian heretics, and attacking all non-Zoroastrian religions. Consequently, he persecuted Jews, Buddhists, Hindus, Christians, and Manichaeans, destroying their centers and proscribing their rituals. From this time, marriage between blood relations became a common Zoroastrian practice, and the Zoroastrian clergy were a political power.

The **Manicheans**—followers of the native Iranian prophet Mani—came to be regarded as the chief heretics. Under Shapur I, Mani had been free to travel and preach, but soon after Shapur's death the Zoroastrians martyred him. Nonetheless, his ideas gained considerable acceptance, both in Iran and throughout the Roman empire. Manicheans stressed a dualism of good and evil, equating good with the spirit and evil with matter. Consequently, they denigrated the body, sex, marriage, women, and food—anything perceived as carnal. As we shall see, Manicheanism had significant effect on Christians, influencing St. Augustine and spawning several medieval heresies. At the end of the fifth century C.E., Persian Manicheans led a socioeconomic movement called Mazdakism (after its leader Mazdak), which preached a sort of communism that included the division of wealth and the sharing of wives and concubines. Many poor people embraced this movement, but Prince Chosroes Anosharvan massacred the Mazdakite leaders about 528 C.E.

In the last decades of Sasanian rule, the Zoroastrian leadership sanctioned a rigid caste system based, somewhat like that of India, on an ideal division of society into priests, warriors, scribes, and commoners. Ritual tended toward a sterile formalism, and a number of speculative or *gnostic* (relating to secret knowledge) tendencies emerged. At the beginning of the Sasanian period, Zurvanism had become the dominant Zoroastrian theology, in good part because of an increasing interest in the problem of evil. Zurvan was Infinite Time. Slowly, he displaced Ahura Mazdah (now called Ohrmazd) as the first principle. Ohrmazd then became identical with Holy Spirit, and Zurvan became his father, as well as the father of Holy Spirit's twin, Destructive Spirit. Thus, Zurvanism begot a dualism: Holy Spirit and Destructive Spirit. However, unlike Mani's dualism, Zurvanism did not make matter evil. For Zurvanite Zoroastrians, nature remained God's good creation.

After the Muslims conquered Persia in the seventh century, the Zoroastrian communities that survived continued to have significant influence. Zoroastrian priests were instrumental in creating a renaissance of religious literature in Pahlavi, the native Persian language in its "middle" period. They kept alive the notion that the prior Sasanian empire had been a fortunate era for the "good religion" that had preceded the Muslims and also for such Zoroastrian doctrines as the coming of the future savior and the approach of an apocalyptic era when judgment would occur. Zoroastrians also fought against the Arabs, Romans, and Turks in their midst, assuring devoted followers that God would soon give them revenge against these interlopers.

DOWN

1 Zoroaster foretold of an _____ end of the world
2 Zoroastrians use this symbol in many rituals.
3 At judgment day, there will be a _____ of the dead.
4 Persia's monotheist prophet of the sixth century B.C.E.
5 Recognizing forces of good and evil
6 Another name for Persia

---

another. In the sixteenth century, they began to exchange texts providing answers to questions that had arisen about ritual and doctrinal matters. The Iranian communities usually felt isolated in the midst of a hostile Muslim environment, but the Indian Parsis flourished and exerted considerable influence on their neighbors, all the more so when British rule gave them special privileges. Bombay (Mumbay) has been the center of India's Parsi community. The result of Parsi contact with the religions of India has been pressure to rethink traditional views about monotheism (Ahura Mazdah) and dualism (Truth and Lie). Indian Zoroastrians (Parsis) have also struggled with internal questions of reforming liturgical rites and doctrine to make them more attractive to modern members. Such matters as the exposure of the dead, questions related to the liturgical calendar for religious celebrations, and interpretations of the scriptures (the *Avesta,* rediscovered in the eighteenth century and thereafter studied with modern philological tools) have all been occasions for debate and division.

When British rule ended in India in 1947, a small group of Parsis (perhaps 5000) were isolated in Pakistan. There was also a small community in Sri Lanka. There may be a quarter million Zoroastrians worldwide, perhaps half of them in India. The Iranian community has been persecuted under the Islamic Republic of the last two decades, and so many have fled to Europe and North America.

However, the actual political revolts that the Zoroastrians attempted tended to be completely crushed. That was dramatically true of an uprising attempted in the city of Shiraz in 979, the result of which was a series of harsh repressions instituted by the Muslim rulers. As a consequence, around the end of the tenth century, Zoroastrians began to leave Iran and head toward India, where their small but successful community became known as the **Parsis.** They left a reduced community in Iran, centered in the regions of Yazd and Kerman. Both these Iranian Zoroastrians and the Parsis have perpetuated the religion begun by Zoroaster, although what one finds practiced nowadays has been deeply transformed by a further millennium of historical changes.

Until the sixteenth century, the Zoroastrian communities in Iran and India had little contact with one

NEW WORLD CIVILIZATIONS

The civilizations of India, China, Greece, and Rome will be discussed in later units. Before we leave this chapter, we will also briefly discuss the civilizations that arose on the continents of North and South America. These civilizations differ in several dimensions from those which arose in the Old World (the continents of Africa, Asia, and Europe). One difference is the dates. Between 4000 and 2000 B.C.E. one could see the stirrings of civilization in Egypt, Mesopotamia, India, and China. In the New World, the civilizations arose in the common era (after the birth of Christ). While the Old World civilizations lasted for thousands of years, those of the Aztecs and Incas were cut short after a few hundred years by the Spanish *conquistadores.* Another difference is that

Mayan pyramids at Chichen-Itzá were ritual centers.

Old World civilizations arose within river valleys: the Nile in Egypt, Tigris and Euphrates in Mesopotamia, Indus in India, Huang Ho in China. New World civilizations arose in less hospitable regions: the rain forest of the Yucatan (for the Mayas) and mountainous inland areas (for the Aztecs and Incas).

The Mayas and the Aztecs will be considered together, although they were separated by time and place. Mayan cities arose first, and were probably largely abandoned by the time the Aztecs began their empire. Although both cultures were centered in present day Mexico, they had little if any geographical overlap: the Mayans in the warm, flat, tropical rain forest of the eastern Yucatan and the Aztecs in the cool central highlands around present-day Mexico City. What unites these two traditions is a similar problem (instability) and a similar system of myths, symbols, rituals, and doctrines for coping with that instability.

If you have been to Cancún, Mexico, you know the Caribbean climate in which the **Mayan** civilization developed. If you arrived by air or cruise ship, you probably noticed how flat and green this area of Mexico is. You might be led to the assumption that the ground is very fertile. But take a handful of it: gravel. The locals have a saying: *La tierra chupa* (literally translated: "The earth sucks"). What they mean is that the frequent rainfall is not sufficient to keep the ground wet and fertile. If you flew in, you probably also noticed some smoke from local forest fires. The Indians learned centuries ago that the ground can only be prepared for corn by the ashes of the burnt rain forest. This fertility allows the harvesting of corn for a few generations, but then the ground becomes exhausted, and the farmers must move on, slashing and burning more rain forest. In a few decades, the rain forest may come back and reclaim the spent farmland.

If you venture out of the prefabricated resort of Cancún and travel a couple of hours south (Tulum) or west (Chichen-Itzá), you will come to some Mayan ruins and maybe see some of the descendents of the Mayas. (Some people in these southern Mexican states, and the mountainous area of Guatemala still converse in their pre-Spanish languages.) Other Mayan ruins lie in remote parts of the Yucatan, overgrown by foliage.

Instability on the Yucatan peninsula was only partially the result of occasional hurricanes and warring tribes (the coastal city of Tulum was walled, but most were not). Instability was also geographical: the farmland, and the cities that grew around it, had to be relocated over and over again.

Much of what we know about the Mayas is pure speculation. Although the Mayas had a pictorial system of writing somewhat similar to Egyptian hieroglyphics, most of their books were destroyed by overzealous Spanish missionaries in the sixteenth century. What we think we know about the Mayas is based upon what has been pieced together from the writings that did survive plus the oral accounts of people several generations removed from the practice of these rituals.

Mayan deities were arranged in a great pantheon with specific functions being assigned to each. Many of the deities were theriomorphic (had animal form or parts). The need for multiple starts is reflected in Mayan creation myths: The theme is of multiple creation. Several worlds were created, and each was destroyed by a different disaster (e.g., a jaguar ate it). The Mayan priesthood was very powerful and developed a calendar based upon precise astronomical observation. The hope was that this calendar would be useful in divination, predicting when the present world would be destroyed (we have less than a dozen years to go!).

The great Mayan symbols for fertility were blood and semen. The Mayan kings would symbolically fertilize the ground to keep the corn crops coming by an annual ritual. A spine from a sea urchin was used to pierce the foreskin and a few drops of blood would fall to the ground. When the corn harvest eventually diminished, a new, more dramatic ritual was substituted. If a few drops of blood from the king was insufficient, perhaps the blood of dozens of commoners would do. The pyramids constructed by the Maya (the world's largest in land area) served as ritual centers for sacrifice).

At first, families regarded it a great honor to have their son or daughter selected for sacrifice. (There was a doctrine of an afterlife, with different levels of

DOWN

1 Mayan deities were animal-formed, or _____.
2 Mayan myths told of multiple _____
3 Mayans frequently had to move their _____.
4 Mayans had a _____ of human blood.
5 Mayan religious leaders

heaven and hell, but it is hard to tell how important this was.) Later, as the number of sacrifices increased, people may have fled the cities. After a few centuries, the Mayan cities were abandoned.

The **Aztecs** began as a tribe somewhere around Utah about a thousand years ago. A shaman had a vision commanding the tribe to migrate southward and to continue the journey until a powerful symbol could be seen: an eagle eating a snake. The journey lasted over two thousand miles until the band arrived at the shores of Texcoco, a stagant lake in a mile-high valley in central Mexico. There they saw the eagle eating the snake. That site is now the Zócalo (central square of Mexico City), and the image of the eagle eating the snake is on every Mexican coin and flag.

The Aztecs did not create the civilization of central Mexico; they merely conquered what had been established by the Toltecs, Olmecs, and other peoples.

(c) Bettmann / CORBIS

Aztecs and other early civilizations turned to human sacrifice in hopes of persuading the gods to show favor.

Aztec ruins are largely confined to Mexico City (some were unearthed in the construction of the subway), but the great pyramids about 40 miles northwest of the city were built for ritual purposes at least a thousand years before the Aztecs arrived.

Central Mexico was also plagued by *instability*. Not only were there frequent and devastating earthquakes and incessant warfare between the tribes, but there was a climatic problem as well. Rainfall in central Mexico stretches from April through October (and then there is a dry spell from October to April).

If the crops are sown early enough, just before it begins to rain, the first harvest should be due around July and a second crop can be sown at that time then harvested around October (if the rains last).

Aztec deities were comparable to those of the Maya: a complex pantheon in which many of the gods of the conquered tribes were renamed or included as subservient to the Aztec gods. Myths of multiple creation reflect the different empires established by previous tribes. The Aztec priesthood was very powerful and used a calendar based upon pre-

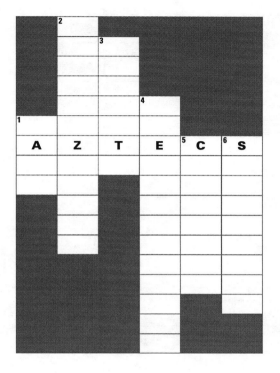

DOWN

1. Aztecs tried to predict the spring _____.
2. Aztecs were not the first _____ in central Mexico.
3. Aztec religious leaders
4. Aztec deities were animal-formed, or _____.
5. Aztecs tried to predict the future with a _____.
6. Aztecs practiced massive human _____.

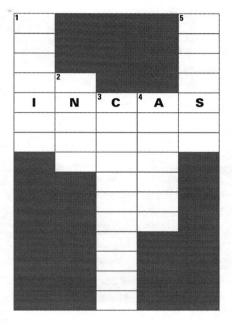

DOWN

1. Incas preserved the dead as _____.
2. Incas lived in these mountains.
3. Inca priests heard _____.
4. Incas lived in South _____.
5. Inca religious leaders

cise astronomical observation. The hope was that this would be useful in divination: predicting when the rains would commence.

Aztec religion also showed an eschatological bent, coming from a myth of a culture hero named Quetzalcoatl. At times he is portrayed as a theriomorphic plumed serpent and at times as a white-faced anthropomorphic god with a beard. The myth foretold that Quetzalcoatl had quarreled with other gods but would return. The Aztec calendar calculated that return to be around 1520 C.E. When Hernán Cortez and his band of a few hundred Spaniards landed on the Gulf Coast near Veracruz, the Aztecs failed to mount a decisive show of force against him, partly out of fear that he might be the returning god.

(Cortez's cannon and horses seemed to be divine instruments.)

The core Aztec ritual was human sacrifice. While the Mayas had been content to sacrifice dozens, the Aztecs required larger and larger numbers until thousands were being killed annually. The thinking went: If they sacrificed a hundred this year and the rains came, better sacrifice at least a hundred next year. If the rains did not come on time, better sacrifice some more next year. The need for victims inspired more military campaigns (the goal was not just land or booty, but people who could be captured and then killed as needed during sacrificial rituals). But military endeavors also required the favor of the gods, so victims had to be sacrificed before a battle to secure

SPECIFIC RELIGIOUS TRADITIONS OF EARLY CIVILIZATIONS					
DIMENSION	EGYPT	MESO-POTAMIA	PERSIA	MAYA AND AZTEC	INCA
Polytheist pantheon	yes	yes	yes	yes	yes
Deity form	therio-morphic	anthropo-morphic	anthropo-morphic	therio-morphic	anthropo-morphic
Mythic culture hero		Gilgamesh		Quetzalcoatl	Viracocha
Divine kingship	yes				yes
Person who changed religion	Akhenaton (pharaoh)	Hammurabi (king)	Zoroaster (prophet)		
What he brought	Monotheism (Aton)	written law code	Monotheism (Ahura Madzah)		
Pyramids	yes	no	no	yes	no
Mummies	yes	no	no	no	yes
Divination	no	yes	yes	yes	no
Environment	stable	unstable		unstable	stable
Creation myths	minor	major	minor	major	minor
Apocalyptic	no	no	yes	yes	no
Priests	yes	yes	yes	yes	yes
Sacrifice	minor grain	minor grain	minor grain animals	major human	minor human
Afterlife	major	minor	major	minor	major

its success so that other victims could be captured (thus creating an endless cycle of sacrifice, war, and sacrifice). Part of Cortez's success was that he easily found allies among the other tribes who would take any opportunity to destroy or weaken the hated Aztecs.

The **Incas** were active about the same time as the Aztecs, but in the Andes region of South America. Their empire stretched from southern Colombia to northern Chile, centering around what is now the nation of Peru. The key to understanding that empire is *stability:* there were no major natural disasters nor armed conflicts. Indeed, most of the Incan extensions had been accomplished by negotiations. Their empire was blessed with relative prosperity based upon potato agriculture and a vast public works system (es-

pecially roads). About a dozen years after Cortez had conquered the Aztecs in Mexico, another small band of *conquistadores* vanquished the Incas, with some of the soldiers boasting that the Indians had no weapons that could defeat an armored Spaniard on horseback.

Inca myths explained the origins of specific things. Potatoes were the result of a primordial murder (similar to the Hainuwele story from Melanesia). Many of the technological innovations of Inca culture were attributed to a mythic culture hero Viracocha, the first Inca emperor and direct descendent of the sun god. The pantheon of active deities was great, incorporating those of many neighboring peoples. There was a powerful caste of priests who performed various rituals at golden temples. Human sacrifice (usually of adolescents) existed, but it was performed on solitary victims.

There was a strict ethical code and the promise of an afterlife. The dead were mummified. The living were told to prepare for the afterlife by purifying themselves and confessing their sins to the priests. (Only the Inca emperor could avoid this ritual and confess directly to the gods without a priest as intermediary.) The priests reacted to confessions by issuing penances, usually in the form of abstaining from sex, alcohol, *chile,* or coca leaves (the source of cocaine).

We are indebted in this section to Professor Eugene Webb of the University of Washington, who furnished us his materials on Mesopotamian religion. Any errors, however, are entirely our responsibility.

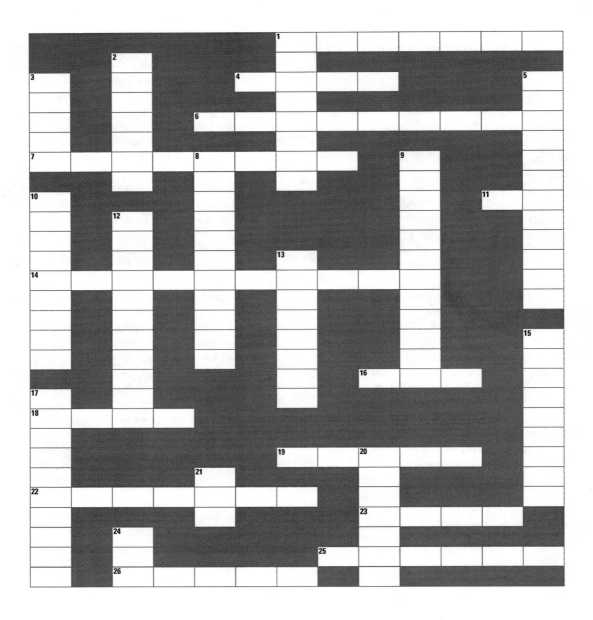

ACROSS

1   Religious leaders of early civilizations
4   South American civilization with priests and mummies
6   Egyptian pharaoh who worshipped one God
7   Mesopotamians had this type of myth.
11 The Aztec and Inca civilizations reached their heights around 1400 _____.
14 Zoroaster warned of a final battle, a great _____.
16 The Egyptian and Mesopotamian civilizations arose around 4000 _____.
18 Zoroaster was from _____.
19 Aztec sacrificial victims
22 Theriomorphic deities take the form of _____.
23 Yucatan religion with myth of multiple creations
25 Zoroaster was from _____.
26 Akhenaton was from _____.

DOWN

1   A structured hierarchy of deities
2   Role of Zoroaster
3   Massive human sacrifices were practiced in this religion.
5   Doctrine of Akhenaton and Zoroaster: only one God
8   Early civilizations gave great power to priests, so they were _____.
9   Early civilizations had many deities, so they were _____.
10 Persian prophet with a dualist apolcalyptic doctrine
12 Religion that emphasized divination and creation myths
13 The Maya and Egyptians had these monuments.
15 Zoroaster saw forces of good and evil; he was _____.
17 Mesopotamians used astrology as a form of _____.
20 Incas and Egyptians turned their dead into _____.
21 Hammurabi gave the first written code of _____.
24 Akhenaton lived in the thirteenth century _____.

Official and Nonofficial Religion

In the United States, the mention of "religion" or "being religious" typically evokes the image of church-oriented religion. When we think of religion, we generally think of Protestantism, Catholicism, and Judaism. When we think of being religious, we tend to locate that religiosity in the social framework of Old First Church, Saint Mary's Church, or Temple Sholom. Church-oriented religion is a prominent and important social form of religion in Western societies, but some other modes do not conform to the "official" model of religion.[1]

How can we interpret the social form of the religious practices and experiences of the following four people, who could be practicing their religion in any number of cities in the United States today?

- Elizabeth thinks a lot about her religion because it is not only an important part of her personal spiritual life, but it is also part of her job: She is a priest in the Episcopalian Church. After years of college and seminary training, Elizabeth is now one of three priests serving a large and active suburban parish. She does a lot of reading and reflection to prepare a sermon each week for the Eucharistic service she performs. Her favorite

---

1. For sources on official religions in the United States, see Castelli and Gremillion, 1987; D'Antonio, 1999; D'Antonio, Davidson, Hoge, and Wallace, 1989; Dillon, 1999; Greeley, 1990; Haddad and Smith, 1994; Heilman, 1995; Hoge, 1999; Hoge, Johnson, and Luidens, 1994; Hunter, 1987b; Lazerwitz et al., 1998; Liebman, 1988; McKinney and Roof, 1990; McNamara, 1992; Meyer, 1999; Roof and McKinney, 1987; Rosenberg, 1989; Seidler and Meyer, 1989.

duties include working with three adult study-prayer groups, serving as parish representative to a local social justice organization, and pastoral counseling, especially with women. How much of this is "work" and how much is her personal religious expression? She would say that there is no boundary between them.

- Rhiannon is also a priest and takes her religion very seriously. Many of the rituals she performs are private, but she tries to perform or participate in important rituals with her Wiccan coven at least once a week. Usually these rituals are done in a member's home, but Rhiannon especially enjoys the ones celebrated outdoors, because many of her deepest spiritual experiences have been in a beautiful natural setting. She is a professional, with a master's degree in Fine Arts; she first learned about Wicca from a coworker at the museum where she works. She has been practicing "the craft" for about eight years now, although she is still a member of a local church. She feels drawn to Wicca because its rituals and community address her sense of herself as a woman better than do her church's teachings and ritual roles for women.

- Rachel has always considered herself Jewish, but was never very observant of Jewish rituals or rules for domestic practices. For the last three years, especially since she got married, however, she has been involved in her religion in a very different way. Now she carefully observes the detailed rules for Jewish practice of the Orthodox branch of Judaism. This represents a myriad of changes in every aspect of her daily life. She keeps a kosher kitchen, restricts her contact with men other than her husband, wears a wig as a public head-covering, and strictly observes the Sabbath, engaging in no work and walking rather than driving if she attends synagogue services.

- Laura is Catholic, but does not attend the parish church to which she "belongs." If she goes to Mass at all, she travels across town to Santa Rosa, where she feels more at home with other Mexican-Americans and a worship service in Spanish. Compared to her mother, Laura thinks she is not very religious, because her mother put hours into preparing special feast-day meals and home devotions, arranging the home altar, saying prayers for the sick, and visiting the old people and helping them in this cold city so far from their homes. Laura does keep a home altar, and she does celebrate important holy days—not just the Anglo ones, but also El Día de los Muertos and the feast days of her two favorite saints—both especially meaningful to people from her part of Mexico. Laura is fluent in Spanish, Portuguese, and English, which are all important in her work for a major airline, but when she prays or meditates before her home altar, her prayers are all in Spanish.

What questions do these vignettes pose for our sociological understanding? How would these portraits be different if they described men, rather than women? What do these differences suggest about the importance of gender roles in official and nonofficial religion today? With this much (and more!) diversity of religions in the United States, how can we research both the religious groups that organize to gather believers and individual religious practice—which sometimes varies dramatically from what official religions preach?

This chapter contrasts official religion and its characteristic expressions of religiosity with "nonofficial" religion and religiosity. Both of these models illustrate the capacity of religion to provide meaning and belonging. A related topic in this chapter is the difficult problem of how to measure or scientifically explore the quality of an individual respondent's religion and religiosity. The Extended Application at the end of this chapter describes the social definitions of women's roles by both official and nonofficial religions and the concurrent shaping of women's religion and religiousness.

THE OFFICIAL MODEL OF RELIGION

The development of a specialized official religion distinguishable from popular or folk religion and other nonofficial religious elements is the result of the historical process of **institutional differentiation.** Earlier religion was relatively diffused throughout all aspects of social life; the practice of religion was relatively unspecialized. Modern religion, by contrast, is characterized by **institutional specialization**: standardization of the worldview in a well-defined doctrine, religious roles performed by specialists, and an organization to control doctrinal and ritual conformity, promulgate group teachings, and promote organizational programs (see Luckmann, 1967:66; see also Bellah, 1964). Interestingly, this same process of differentiation created the possibility of organized irreligion—the institutional expression and consolidation of beliefs and practices of hostility or indifference toward religion. Organized irreligion (e.g., the Secularist, Positivist, and Ethical movements) closely parallels official models of religion (see Campbell, 1971).

Specialized institutions for religion thus become the focus for societal attention to religion. Each institutionally specialized religion typically consolidates its beliefs, values, and practices into a coherent model. These official models typically include a prescribed doctrine, set of ethical standards, cultic expression, and institutional organization.

Doctrine

The official model of a religion is a coherent and consolidated meaning system, articulated by doctrinal experts (e.g., theologians) and typically promulgated only after official approval. Although church doctrine changes over time, a church can state its official model of religion fairly specifically at any one time: "This is what we stand for." Religions vary as to the extent of doctrinal sophistication and the importance of formal, prescribed doctrines. The Roman Catholic Church has a vast, complicated doctrinal system, with some teachings having the weight of dogma (i.e., doctrines to which members are obliged to assent). By contrast, Judaism has no dogma but emphasizes the continual unfolding of religious truths through study of sacred scripture and texts; nevertheless, Judaism has some fairly explicit definitions of its shared meaning system.

Ethics

Official religion also characteristically prescribes a set of norms and regulations consistent with the group's doctrine. These obligations for behavior specify what actions are necessary to be a member in good standing. They include ideals toward which members should strive. Simultaneously, official religion usually uses specialized religious measures for the regulation and control of conduct so that misconduct can be noted and punished. In religions containing normative prescriptions that are complex, the organization sometimes supports specialized religious courts and ethical specialists to interpret the body of regulations. Other religions, whose ethical norms may be just as strong, rely on informal social control measures.

Cultic Expression

Each religion has a set of observances and devotions by which its meaning system is ritually expressed. Official religion tends to encourage standardized cultic expressions such as a liturgy or formal order of worship. Even less central expressions (e.g., devotions) are often standardized. Such standardized forms of expressing religious beliefs and sentiments include the Roman Catholic "Way of the Cross" and the Eastern Orthodox ritual of kissing icons. Some religions emphasize spontaneity in cultic expression; even so, however, the religion encourages certain regularized ways of being spontaneously religious. A minister might pray in his or her own words but choose words appropriate to the King James version of the Bible (e.g., "Almighty God, Thou hast showered us with Thy abundance"). Official religion also typically uses ritual specialists—priests, ministers, cantors, music directors, organists, choirs, and liturgical experts. Thus, official models of religion consolidate and standardize the cultic expression of religion.

Institutional Organization

Official religion typically organizes itself as a specialized association. It develops organizational specialists such as a professional clergy, organizational hierarchies (both lay and clerical), and often a host of auxiliary functionaries (e.g., religious teachers, church librarians, secretaries, program directors, and building service personnel). There are often formal specifications and procedures for membership and jurisdictional boundaries (e.g., parish boundaries). There are programs to be organized—Sunday schools, "outreach" and "mission" programs, fund raising, youth clubs, study groups, and so on.

Especially important in the institutional organization of religious groups is the form of **polity** adopted. *Polity* refers to the arrangements for exercise of legitimate authority in the organization. The three characteristic forms found in most Western religious organizations are episcopal, presbyterian, and congregational polity. *Episcopal* polity refers to an organizational arrangement in which authority is centralized in a hierarchy (i.e., a pyramid of channels of authority). Thus, in the Roman Catholic Church, local parishes are served by priests who are responsible to bishops. The bishops place priests in the local parish, and the congregation has no official authority. Similarly, the bishops are responsible to the pope, using his delegated authority in their dioceses. Other examples of the episcopal form of polity include Eastern Orthodox churches and Episcopalianism; Methodism has a modified form of episcopal polity. *Presbyterian* polity is a form that uses a representative government by both clergy and laity. The local church is run by its clergy and lay-selected representatives. They, in turn, are responsible to a higher authority of elected representatives such as a presbytery, synod, or general assembly (as in Presbyterianism).

The *congregational* form of polity is characterized by high degrees of autonomy of the local congregation, including the power to call or dismiss clergy. This form is characteristic of most Jewish congregations, Baptists, and the United Church. Denominations with congregational polity are less likely to conform with a uniform doctrine and ethical or ritual standards among congregations than are denominations with other kinds of polity.[2] Some observers (see Warner, 1994) suggest that most official religious groups in the United States are converging toward a more congregational mode of polity, regardless of their historical patterns, because structurally religious organizations have become "*voluntary* gathered communities."[3] Similarly, as developed further in Chapter 7, individual congregations in denominations with the congregational form of polity can be highly resistant to external pressures for change, ignoring the urgings of national denomination councils and firing change-oriented clergy. For the same reason, however, congregational and presbyterian forms of polity are more receptive than episcopal polity to the initiatives or needs of local congregations.

---

2. It is therefore not surprising that sociologists trying to research members of these religious organizations have greater problems studying, as aggregates, the adherents of congregational polities such as Southern Baptists, in contrast to hierarchical polities like Mormons (cf. Hadaway, 1989; Cornwall and Cunningham, 1989). Because of the characteristic local autonomy of Southern Baptist polity, it is very difficult for a researcher studying members of many different congregations to identify who is "properly" a Southern Baptist.

3. Interestingly, this change appears to apply not only to Protestant groups but also to Catholic congregations, Pakistani Muslims, Indian Hindus, and Thai Buddhists in the United States, suggesting that it results from a combination of modes of U.S. civic participation and religious groups' location in the voluntary sector of institutional life (Ebaugh and Chafetz, 2000a, 2000b; Warner, 1994). Religious institutions that have been adapted to this characteristically American congregational model of association have become part of the acculturation process for immigrant groups as a place where gender and generational relations are renegotiated (Warner, 1998).

STRUCTURAL SHIFTS
IN OFFICIAL RELIGION

There appear to be some structural changes in how and where official religions operate in modern societies. These developments suggest that, rather than focusing on denominations and other umbrella religious organizations as the unit of analysis, we should try to understand the religious units to which believers are actually committed. If the locus of religious identification has shifted, it is also likely that there are changes in the amount of authority vested in official religious groups by their adherents. Are there, simultaneously, shifts in how much autonomy in belief and practice is exercised by individuals?

Considerable evidence suggests that, at least in the last few decades, people's religious affiliation is not to a denomination or religious organization *per se* (Hadaway, 1993; Hoge et al., 1994). Warner (1994) argues that a growing pattern, at least among Protestants, is for people to identify with a particular local religious organization rather than any denomination with which it is affiliated. When people move to another community, they often switch denominations in order to affiliate with a compatible local congregation. Often, other features of a particular congregation such as ethnic or class makeup are more important bases for affiliation than denomination-defined beliefs and practices. This pattern is corroborated by a Canadian study that found most (60 percent) active laypersons (i.e., regular church participants) believed switching congregations was warranted to be with "people more like yourself" in age, family composition, education, and income. Another feature of compatibility that warranted switching for 46 percent was to be in a congregation with "more people like yourself in terms of ethnic background" (Posterski and Barker, 1993:254–255). If, as some studies suggest (e.g., Bibby, 1993), many congregations serve as homogeneous "clubs" or homogeneous enclaves—albeit with a religious component—their denominational affiliation may be a secondary feature.

This cultural homogeneity as a basis for involvement and commitment at the congregational level may help us understand the schisms that sometimes occur when congregations have internal conflict (see Becker, 1999). One Jewish synagogue, for example, split into two hostile congregations—one redefining itself as liberal Reconstructionist and the other redefining itself as conservative Orthodox. There had been growing disagreements over social and political issues, spurred by a controversial rabbi, but the split came to a head over the issue of women's proper roles in religious practice. The congregation had been able to tolerate considerable internal diversity in religious practice (e.g., offering some worship services mainly in Hebrew and some mainly in English), but the symbolism of the segregation of women was too volatile to be contained and threatened the congregation's core sense of itself (Zuckerman, 1999).

Furthermore, except to religious specialists, the historical distinctions among many denominations have become virtually irrelevant. For example, one active Presbyterian said:

When I was growing up in the fifties and sixties, I don't think there was a dime's worth of difference among Presbyterians, Methodists, or Episcopalians in terms of the way theology impacted on the people. If you get the ministers and priests together, they could have World War III arguing about issues that nobody cares about. But as far as most people are concerned, they're really interchangeable. And I don't think there is any particular value in having a Presbyterian heritage or ethos or way of doing things. The only distinguishing characteristics in the church today deal with our form of government. Anything specifically Calvinistic is gone, and most Presbyterians aren't interested. (quoted in Hoge et al., 1994:120–121)

Thus, asking a respondent's "religious affiliation" may tell a researcher little or nothing about members' actual religious beliefs, practices, commitments, or experiences.

A related development among Protestants is the expansion of "nondenominational" churches. Organized by a dynamic preacher and not constrained by a central denominational organization or belief system, these churches are usually recognizably Protestant, yet often highly idiosyncratic. Even though they are organized as churches (with buildings, Sunday schools, budgets, choirs, clergy, and committees), they are not fully "official religions"—as historically defined. Thus, researchers cannot make any general assumptions of what affiliation with such a church means. Each congregation is independent of external control; some are organized by congregational polity and some are run autocratically by the preacher around whom the congregation gathered. Thus, learning that a respondent belongs to a nondenominational church tells the researcher only that the respondent has a general non–Catholic Christian affiliation and that it is not to any identifiable denomination. For example, one member of a nondenominational "megachurch" (drawing more than 15,000 people each week) said that was precisely what attracted him: "a lack of tradition" (quoted in Niebuhr, 1995). Indeed, some congregations that are affiliated with denominations have dropped the denomination from their name to make the church more appealing to persons who are "put off" by the denomination's historical stance (see Trueheart, 1996; see also Miller, 1998). After Trinity Baptist Church changed its name to Fellowship of Forest Creek, it experienced a growth of new attenders. The minister said, "I'm not ashamed to be a Baptist, but a brand name can be a hindrance" (quoted in Montoya, 1999).

Another factor diminishing the explanatory power of denominational identification is the increasing prominence of special interest groups, voluntary associations organized across denominational lines and focused on specific issues such as abortion legislation, civil rights, or the role of religion in the public schools (Wuthnow, 1988). If deeper loyalty goes to the special interest group, members of a congregation or entire denomination may become profoundly split. Special interest groups have considerable potential for mobilizing religious activism and some sense of group identity, but they are not likely to be a stable locus for religious ritual or experience. Nevertheless, overworked or overcommitted members may feel the need to choose between investing energies and social networks in the religious movement organization or in the local religious congregation..

If some of these hypotheses of structural shifts are accurate, then it becomes far more difficult for sociologists to research and interpret what believing or practicing an official religion means in the actual lives of individual members.

INDIVIDUAL RELIGIOSITY
IN THE OFFICIAL MODEL

Official religion, then, is a set of beliefs and practices prescribed, regulated, and socialized by organized, specifically religious groups. These groups set norms of belief and action for their members, and they establish an official model of what it means to be "one of us." Nevertheless, the actual religion of the individual member may not correspond very closely to the official model. What is the *operative faith* of the individual? What norms, ritual actions, and beliefs hold priority in the individual's life?

The specialized religious institution mediates the official model of religion to the individual member. Thus, for example, being a Presbyterian might be experienced in terms of attending Presbyterian Sunday worship services and Sunday schools in a particular building of one's congregation; receiving communion in the Presbyterian church and being a member of the committee that washes the communion cups; interacting with Presbyterian clergy; singing in the church choir; having a grandfather who is a member of the Session (i.e., elected Board of Elders); having once memorized but now forgotten the Westminster Confession of faith and answers to the catechism; and learning other Presbyterian beliefs and norms in Sunday school and adult discussion groups or from sermons. In other words, the individual member is socialized into the model of his or her church.

For this reason, individual religiosity in official religion can be described in terms of its conformity to the official model. The individual's beliefs are somehow related to church doctrine, and the individual's ethical standards are measured by conformity to the ethical teachings of the official religion. Cultic expressions of the religion are translated in terms of individual observances and devotions. The individual's relationship to the institutional organization is expressed as membership and participation in that organization (see Luckmann, 1967:74).

Thus, it is possible for a sociologist studying an official religion to *operationalize*—to create a working definition of—individual religiosity in terms of the officially defined model. The Roman Catholic Church (especially before Vatican II) used a fairly explicit official model of expected individual religiosity. In his studies of Roman Catholic parishes, Fichter (1951, 1954) was able to operationalize individual religiosity for research purposes, using criteria such as Mass attendance, reception of communion, sending children to parochial schools, participation in parish activities such as Holy Name Society, and interaction with clergy. This approach to operationalizing the concept of religiosity works, to some extent, *only* because the official model of Roman Catholic religion was precise and mediated to individual members.

Nevertheless, we cannot infer that these aspects of official religion explain why the individual member participates in any aspect of it. We cannot infer that those who attend religious services each week do so in precise conformity with what the official model of that religion puts forth as the purpose and meaning of those services. Some attenders may do so. Others may be interested more in sociability, entertainment, or a sense of tradition; some may not even know the "official" version, yet may get a strong subjective sense of meaning and belonging all the same. Thus, although the official model of religion has implications for individual religiosity, there is little indication that all aspects of official religion hold equal importance for each individual believer.

A number of factors bring about this discrepancy between the individual's religion and the official model. One factor is how the individual has been taught and socialized into the official model. Some persons have not learned the official model of their group's religion. The official belief systems of Christian and Jewish groups, for example, generally include a set of moral norms called "the Ten Commandments," but most adults of Christian or Jewish backgrounds cannot name most of those commandments. Many members may not know items of official belief such as catechisms, creeds, and confessions of faith. Furthermore, members vary in how adequately they have internalized the official model. It is one thing to know that one's group holds certain beliefs; it is another to believe them oneself.

The official model is often overlaid with nonofficial religious themes, perhaps drawn from folk religion, mythology, popular culture, or the teacher's own "misinformed" view of the official model. For example, one woman said: "I was in my thirties before I realized that a lot of the stuff I learned about religion in grade school wasn't the official church teaching. I'm sure the church has some theology about sin and grace, but to this day whenever I hear those words I think of what my religion teacher in fifth grade taught us about good angels whispering in our right ears and bad angels urging us in our left ears." Although official religion is characteristically a coherent, consistent body of beliefs and practices, the individual's version of it is not necessarily coherent or consistent. Individuals vary in how much consistency they expect in their own lives, but many people appear to be comfortable with highly incoherent assortments of beliefs and practices (see Bibby, 1983).

Representatives of religious organizations may decry this misinformation or lack of knowledge, but it is an understandable product of socialization. In socialization, the official model is mediated (if taught at all) through other persons who are significant in the child's life: parents, friends, teachers, clergy. The child may be exposed to a relatively incoherent assortment of stories, admonitions, images, threats, and examples.

Individual members may also deviate from the official model of religion in their priorities, often emphasizing aspects of belief and practice that the official model holds as relatively unimportant. Thus, a religious group may emphasize norms against cheating and stealing, whereas an individual member may downplay those norms while emphasizing norms against drinking and gambling. Or a religious group may be divided in its interpretation of "correct" practices and beliefs. Thus what is normal and expected in one "wing" of the group is deviant and negatively sanctioned in another.

Sometimes individual members may disagree with the official beliefs and practices. Of U.S. Roman Catholics, a sizable proportion does not agree with the official church teaching on birth control, abortion, divorce, women clergy, and clerical celibacy. A national study of U.S. Catholics, conducted in 1987, 1993, and 1999, found that there has been a steady increase in the proportion of Catholics who believe the individual should have "final say" on moral issues such as birth control (61 percent in 1999), advocacy of free choice regarding abortion (47 percent), homosexual behavior (48 percent), and extramarital sexual relations (47 percent). The survey also found that most U.S. Catholics felt that a person could be a good Catholic without going to church every Sunday (77 percent), obeying church hierarchy's teachings on birth control (72 percent), or obeying the church's teachings regarding divorce and remarriage (65 percent). Contrary to recent papal or curial pronouncements, a sizable majority approved of the ordination of women and married men, and an even larger majority believed that laity should participate in decision making at the parish level, such as the selection of priests (D'Antonio, 1999; Davidson, 1999; Hoge, 1999; Meyer, 1999; see also Dillon, 1998; Yip, 1997). In the 1950s, when official national organizations of major Protestant denominations made strong statements about Christian responsibility on the issue of racism, many individual members chose to disagree with these teachings (Hadden, 1969). Similar recent disagreement has occurred in Protestant denominations, Roman Catholicism, and Judaism over teachings on homosexuality, women's roles, abortion, war, capital punishment, and divorce.

Adherence to *any* official religious group—church, denomination, or any of the alternative organizational forms described above—is complicated by what some are calling the "new voluntarism" (Roof and McKinney, 1987; see also Ammerman, 1997b). This thesis suggests that, in the modern context, individual believers are and believe they should be free to choose all significant components of their religious belief and practice. Accordingly, denominational affiliation is utterly optional, and selection of a local congregation within that denomination is a matter of personal tastes and "preference" (Marler and Roozen, 1993). Church attendance and ritual participation are viewed as up to the individual.

High proportions (80 percent, according to one Gallup survey) of Americans believe that the individual "should arrive at his or her religious beliefs independent of any church or synagogue" (Gallup Poll and Princeton Religion Research Center, 1988). Many active church members feel free to choose components of their belief system, combining elements of their official religious tradition with other culturally available elements such as New Age spirituality, Asian and Native American religions, popular psychology, and popular religion. One man, a retired educator, said, "I'm a Mennonite hyphen Unitarian Universalist who practices Zen meditation" (quoted in Miller, 1999).

Many others have acquired a greater sense of religious autonomy in response to a growing gap between what official religions' spokespersons teach and the experiences of the laity. One woman (a full-time volunteer worker in a Catholic peace-and-justice center) said, "I think it would be easier to change the color of my eyes or to get a new genetic code than it would be to stop being a Roman Catholic." Later in the interview she added:

> I really set aside exclusive Roman Catholicism. . . . I remained a religious woman and I have never stopped thinking of myself as a religious woman, ever, not for a moment. But I began to weave in understandings of a variety of different religious and . . . spiritual traditions, and . . . ways of behaving in the world—concrete actions. So the traditions that I looked most closely at were Native [American] traditions, the Jewish tradition (and I—because of intermarrying in my family—have a number of men and women who came out of a Jewish faith tradition) and Zen Buddhism and Tibetan Buddhism. (quoted in Spickard and McGuire, 1994)

This sense of religious autonomy, documented among a sizable proportion of Americans (Dillon, 1998; Hammond, 1992; McGuire, 1988; McNamara, 1992; Roof, 1993; Roof and Gesch, 1995) suggests that many official religious organizations have lost much of their authority over their own members. If this voluntarism is characteristic of an emerging pattern of affiliation with official religious groups, then the main distinction among groups (as discussed further in Chapter 5) may be whether they allow voluntaristic commitment or demand totalistic conformity with official group beliefs, norms, and ritual practices.

RESEARCHING OFFICIAL RELIGION
AND RELIGIOSITY

Researching official religion is methodologically easier than researching nonofficial religion because researchers can clearly identify authoritative institutional spokespersons and decision-making bodies. Official religions also typically specify their approved teachings, and ritual practices.[4] Thus, it is possible to compare the Episcopalian position with the Methodist position on some issue (e.g., the ordination of women) or to analyze the liturgy of Lutheran churches or to study the development and effects of a specific institutional change within a religious organization (e.g., a denomination deciding to require candidates for the ministry to obtain a college or postcollege degree preparation for ordination). Using historical data, interviews, archival records,

---

4. Groups vary, however, as to how much authority they vest in the hierarchy and official group agencies and how much autonomy is left to individual congregations and members.

participant observation, and other intensive research methods, many useful research projects have illuminated our understanding of official religions.

It is far more difficult, however, to methodologically tap the religion of individuals. Standard sociological sources, such as census data, opinion surveys, and institutionally generated figures (e.g., membership rolls), can be highly misleading. Survey methods often describe an individual's "religion" by asking respondents their religious affiliation or "preference." A questionnaire may ask the respondent to indicate whether he or she is Protestant, Catholic, Jew, other, or "none." A further refinement of this is specification of the denominational affiliation (e.g., Presbyterian, Southern Baptist, Conservative Jew, Mormon, etc.). These categories then become the basis for broad comparisons of behavior (e.g., college attendance) or attitudes (e.g., approval of desegregation).

Because we need to know more about the values, attitudes, feelings, and experiences that motivate the individual believer, this emphasis on understanding individual religious opinions is worthwhile. The methods and measures used, however, have serious shortcomings that cannot be overcome by minor refinements. One problematic issue is that most of this research has not been interested in the individual's religion *per se* but in generalizations about the "sum" religiosity of larger groups (e.g., denominations or ethnic groups). Thus, the research does not really try to grasp the total picture of each individual's religion and commitment to it; instead, it isolates certain readily measurable aspects of each individual's religion, then lumps these into a composite picture of the larger group.

This methodological approach might be useful *if* members of the larger group (e.g., all Congregationalists, all Nazarenes) were highly homogeneous. That assumption does not hold true for many religious groups, however. Within-group variance among Catholics, Baptists, or Quakers, for example, is often *greater* than between-group variance. So, what does it tell us to find that "on average" persons who identify themselves as Baptist are more likely to believe in "faith" item X than those who identify themselves as Catholics?

Similarly, institutional data tell us little about the actual religion of members. Some churches count the infants of members as full members at baptism; others require an act of commitment in the teen years; yet others admit only adults as members. Some religious organizations enthusiastically encourage attenders to "join"; others neither actively recruit nor readily accept new members. Some religious groups consider a member to be permanently a member unless that person actively quits or is excommunicated; other groups drop inactive members from their rolls; yet others have strict "tests" of membership and expel those who do not live up to their expectations. If religious organizations vary so widely in their definitions of membership, researchers must be very cautious in how they use those figures.

The same is true of official measures of individual religiosity. As official religion sees it, "religiosity" refers to the intensity of commitment to the official belief system as expressed in institutionally identifiable attitudes or behaviors (e.g., receiving communion or agreeing with the group's moral condemnation of certain actions). As with all methodological approaches, this "way of seeing" is also a "way of not seeing" (Burke, 1935:70). A focus on official religiosity highlights certain beliefs, commitments, and practices but simultaneously makes others invisible. For example, most simplistic sociological indices of religiosity include an item about frequency of church attendance. Using such indices, however, we tend to mis-measure Latina Catholic religiosity, which is expressed more in domestic religious expressions (such as devotions at the home altar) than in church attendance.

This methodological set of "blinders" has certain consequences for sociological research. Standard survey approaches are extremely limited in their ability to tap the depth and complexity of each individual's religion and religiosity, because they require respondents to fit their answers into codable (or even precoded) categories determined by official religious conceptions of religious belief and practice. It is entirely possible that such limited categories *never* adequately described individual religiosity. Recent changes in the shape and location of religion in modern—especially religiously plural—societies, however, make survey methodologies even less effective in understanding the quality of individual religiosity. More successful approaches include combinations of ethnographic methodologies, intensive interviews, narrative analysis, and related methods of letting respondents name their own meaningful categories. Whether we are studying religiosity in the official or nonofficial forms of religion, it remains important to leave the definitive categories for individual religiosity open—as part of the research question—rather than assume them to be usable, simply because they are defined as "religious" by historical official religious organizations (see Spickard et al., 2002, for several excellent essays on new ethnographic approaches to the study of religion).

Researchers studying religiosity in the official model recognized that it was a complex feature: No single quality could be used to describe the individual as "religious" or as relatively "more religious" than another individual. Glock (1965) distinguishes five dimensions of religiosity:

1. The **experiential dimension** includes feelings or sensations that are considered to involve communication with "divine essence." It refers, for example, to a feeling that one has been saved or healed, a feeling of deep intimacy with the holy, or a sensation of having received a divine revelation of some sort.

2. The **ritualistic dimension** includes religious practices such as worship, prayer, and participation in certain sacraments.

3. The **ideological dimension** refers to the content and scope of beliefs to which members of a religious group are expected to adhere.

4. The **intellectual dimension** encompasses the individual's knowledgeability about the basic tenets of the group's beliefs and sacred scriptures.

5. The **consequential dimension** includes the effects of religious belief, practice, experience, and knowledge upon the individual's behavior in institutional settings that are not specifically religious (e.g., business, voting, family, and leisure-time activities).

BOX 4.1 Methodological Note: Overreported Church Participation Rates

---

Is there a correlation between attending church and telling the truth? The answer may be "yes," but we cannot rely on social surveys to answer this question, because there is considerable evidence that many respondents do not tell the truth to pollsters. Well-designed social surveys, such as the General Social Survey conducted by National Opinion Research Center at the University of Chicago, have important advantages over other sources of data. They have refined statistical sampling techniques, carefully pretested survey instruments, and such huge sample size that measured variation is statistically significant. Most social scientists and journalists rely on such surveys, at least as starting points for further research or for background national data.

Social surveys have their limitations, however. In recent years, several studies have cast doubt on the accuracy of self-reported church attendance figures reported in several U.S. social surveys.* Since the 1930s, these surveys had regularly asked respondents: "Did you, yourself, happen to attend church or synagogue in the last seven days?" And they regularly reported that, after some decline in the early 1960s, church attendance of Americans was stable—about 40 percent of the populace reported attending that week. These figures were remarkably high compared to Europe, where self-reported church attendance in Britain was about half that in the United States, and figures for France and Scandinavian countries were even lower.

Researchers who used different methodologies challenged the self-report approach. Head counts, time-budget accounts, adult Sunday school attend ance records, and other efforts to produce direct measures of atten-

---

*This description is based upon Marler and Hadaway, 1999; Hadaway et al., 1998; and Walsh, 1998.

These distinctions are useful to remind us that a person can be highly religious in one dimension (e.g., go to church regularly, pray often) and yet not know church teachings (intellectual dimension) or have had any religious experiences. Unfortunately, these dimensions are not all amenable to quantification and measurement through standardizable indices. We need to use different methods to understand, for example, religious experience than we would to study how strongly adherents of official religions agree with their group's ideology.

No research has yet defined these dimensions in terms that are not biased toward the orthodox position of certain historic (i.e., traditional Judeo-Christian) expressions of religiosity. In their study of U.S. church members, Stark and Glock's operational definition of these five dimensions illustrates such a bias (Stark and Glock, 1968:22–80). Thus, a person who assented to a higher proportion of the following beliefs in an index of the ideological dimension was considered more religious than someone who assented to only some:

BOX 4.1 *continued*

dance, all resulted in figures closer to 20 percent—or about half of that reported on telephone surveys. One study used the actual Sunday school rolls in a large evangelical church and compared them with self-reports by telephone interviews of the same church's members; 181 adults said they had attended Sunday school that week, but only 115 actually attended. Frequent attenders may be even more likely than nonattenders to exaggerate their attendance, because they value church attendance more. Their overreporting may not be so much a matter of lying as a matter of somewhat idealized self-representation.

The cumulative results of these studies suggest two conclusions: Americans attend church or synagogue far less frequently than the polls show, and many people misrepresent their behavior when they self-report to survey-takers. People exaggerate or underreport all kinds of behavior (frequency of drunkenness, number of sexual partners,

amount given to charity, etc.), and it is highly likely that other—less observable—behavior, such as prayer and Bible reading, is even more exaggerated in surveys. Surveys will continue to be useful methods for tapping people's expression of their opinions, attitudes, and values, but they will be inadequate for accurately counting other aspects of religion and religiosity—especially those that involve hard-to-verify practices, behaviors, and experiences.

■ Why does this finding of discrepancies in self-reported behavior make it difficult to interpret changes in religious practices over time? What changes might actually be measured?

■ What are some problems with trying to use these measures cross-culturally, comparing the United States with Hungary, France, or Denmark? Why might the rates of overreporting vary from country to country?

---

1. Unqualified certainty in the existence of God
2. Belief in a personal God
3. Belief in miracles as described in the Bible
4. Belief in life after death
5. Belief in the actual existence of the devil
6. Belief in the divinity of Jesus
7. Belief that a child is born into the world already guilty of sin (i.e., original sin)

By these measures, liberal denominations appear less religious than conservative ones, and liberal members of any denomination appear less religious than conservative members. Devout Quakers would, by these measures, probably score very low on religiosity. Subtle cultural and gender biases may also influence these measures. Apparent differences between men's and women's religiosity and between blacks' and whites' religiosity may be, in part, an artifact of how a research instrument operationalizes and measures religiosity (Feltey and Poloma, 1990; Jacobson et al., 1990).

One study asked members from numerous different Christian congregations to rate items according to which they considered most important for living Christian life. The "evangelical" priorities (accounting for 29 percent) corresponded with most indices of "religiosity"; they emphasized prayer, Bible study, witnessing, correct belief (orthodoxy). The single most common approach (51 percent) was what the author called "Golden Rule Christians" who emphasized not ideology, but *practices*—concrete ways of living "right." The third type (about 19 percent) was oriented toward practices such as peace and justice activism. "Golden Rule Christians" would not appear to be so "religious" as evangelicals, by most standard measures, nor would they appear to be as committed to their religious group or congregations as the more sectarian "evangelical" type. Nevertheless, this may be the dominant pattern of (Christian) religiosity today, and it should be recognized as a valid pattern of real religiosity with its own priorities for Christian practice (Ammerman, 1997a).

Recognition of the cultural biases of some ideological items tapped in these "religiosity" scales led Glock and others to formulate parallel measures for emerging religious patterns in the United States. In an ambitious study of nontraditional religious affiliation in a California community, Glock and his coworkers included several non-Christian options such as Eastern mysticism, astrology, Transcendental Meditation, Satanism, and Yoga (Glock and Bellah, 1976; see also Glock and Wuthnow, 1979; Wuthnow, 1976b). This research asked about religious practices other than specifically Christian ones—whether respondents meditated, for example, and what kinds of techniques they used in meditation (e.g., a mantra, drugs, breathing techniques, prayer, etc.). Similarly, a Canadian study tapped several alternative meaning systems beyond the usual official or "visible" religions; researchers identified the "invisible" religious cultural themes as mystical, paranormal, familist, feminist, and positivist (Bibby, 1983). Other researchers have attempted to overcome possible gender biases by eliciting respondents' images of God and by including a measure of perceived closeness to God (see Feltey and Poloma, 1990; Nelsen et al., 1985; Roof and Roof, 1984).

Although such studies greatly expand the range of religious beliefs and practices considered, they are nonetheless limited to discrete, identifiable clusters of beliefs. It may not be possible to devise a research instrument to tap all possible religious beliefs, practices, knowledge, and experiences held by any individual in a culture as diverse as that in the United States. Survey research is predicated on measuring the distribution of opinions, attitudes, or attributes that can be specified in advance (i.e., in wording the questions of the survey). Such a specification is only possible by using the criteria of official religion. A number of features of religion and religiosity in contemporary societies make it problematic to assume that an individual's religion can be adequately described by measuring its correspondence to orthodox official religion (Luckmann, 1973).

Let us now consider some of the ways in which the religion of the individual may differ from official religion.

NONOFFICIAL RELIGION
AND RELIGIOSITY

Alongside or overlaying official religion is another pattern of religious belief—**nonofficial religion.** Nonofficial religion is a set of religious and quasi-religious beliefs and practices that is not accepted, recognized, or controlled by official religious groups. Whereas official religion is relatively organized and coherent, nonofficial religion includes an assortment of unorganized, inconsistent, heterogeneous, and changeable sets of beliefs and customs (Towler and Chamberlain, 1973). Nonofficial religion is sometimes called "common," "folk," or "popular" religion because it is the religion of ordinary people rather than the product of religious specialists in a separate organizational framework.

HISTORICAL PERSPECTIVES:
THE SOCIAL CONSTRUCTION
OF "RELIGION"

Most sociology and historiography has assumed that, at least since the beginnings of Christendom, there has been a radical disjunction between official and popular forms of religion. This disjunction was taken for granted largely because, at the time of the early development of sociology, the official religious organizations had successfully achieved politically legitimated cultural dominance throughout Europe and North America. Social scientists merely accepted official (i.e., Protestant, Catholic, and later, Jewish) groups' definitions of religion's boundaries as "given" (see Trexler, 1984). Failing to question the *social construction* of those boundaries, the social sciences inadvertently supported official religions' definition of their practices and beliefs as "pure" and linked with the "sacred"—that which was to be protected from the "profane" world of everyday life. The residual category, "popular religion," came to be identified as a tainted or impure form of religion, or—worse—as downright pagan.

Thus, the notion of religious **syncretism**—the blending of diverse cultural elements into one religion—came to have a powerfully negative connotation. "Syncretism" was used to imply inauthenticity or contamination, the insidious infiltration of a putatively "pure" religious tradition by meanings, symbols, and ritual practices borrowed from an alien, impure religious tradition. Accordingly, guardians of "pure" Christianity have decried most New World religious expressions such as Umbanda, Santería, and Vodou as syncretism in this negative sense. By contrast, however, recent anthropological thought has debunked the idea of "cultural purity" or "authenticity"—of either the European tradition *or* the alien

Others. Some critics have argued that, in contemporary anthropology, "syncretic processes are considered basic not only to religion and ritual but to 'the predicament of culture' in general" (Shaw and Stewart, 1994:1; for illustrative case studies, see Badone, 1990; Espín, 1994; Glazier, 1996; Shaw and Stewart, 1994; and Stevens-Arroyo and Pérez y Mena, 1995).

Through identifiable historical processes, then, official religion was linked with social and religious elites and nonofficial religion with the uneducated and superstitious "masses" (Brown, 1981; Obelkevich, 1979). The elites promoted "virtuoso" religiosity (conveniently defined in terms of participation in official religious practices) and decried the inferior religiosity of the *hoi polloi*. Religiosity in the official mode was assumed to have "sacred" objectives—holiness, spiritual blessings, and salvation. By contrast, popular religiosity was linked with the profane—for example, giving attention to people's pragmatic, quotidian needs (such as healing, fertility, protection from adverse fortune, obtaining desired material goods, etc.).

In the light of recent scholarship, however, we must reject this assumption for two reasons. First, the sacred/profane dichotomy, upon which the distinction of official, elite religion is based, may produce a misleading conception of religious life. One study of religious beliefs and practices in preindustrial Germany suggests, on the contrary, that the sacred is experienced from within the profane, within the very human context of the historical, cultural, and socially shared situation of believers (Scribner, 1984a:17–18). This generalization finds more recent corroboration in the anthropological analysis of "Los Pastores," a popular religious drama that has been performed in the Mexican barrios of San Antonio, Texas, every Christmas season since 1913. As performed in the backyards and homes, this devotional ritual, with its fulfillment of *promesas* (i.e., pledges of piety in thanks for answered prayers or blessings), meals, and surrounding festivities, creates communal sociability (Flores, 1994). It is precisely because "el Niño Dios" is experienced in the context of the profane—a neighbor's yard, where only last week the neighborhood teenagers were fixing their low-rider cars—that it can speak profoundly to people's lives.

Furthermore, the sacred is experienced in everyday life as it is embedded in human social practices such as calendric rituals, use of space, and meaning-laden postures and gestures (Bourdieu, 1977; Hart, 1992; Muir, 1997; Scribner, 1984a, 1984b). The religious dimensions of people's everyday experience and the so-called profane dimensions often are not merely linked, but interpenetrate (Parker, 1996:242; 1994, 1998).

A second reason sociology of religion should reject the radical disjunction of official and nonofficial religion is that not only the content but indeed *the very definition of religion is a social construction.* The difference between official and nonofficial religion is not an essential quality of religion but is rather the result of a concrete historical process in which certain social groups used their power and authority to privilege certain forms of religious practice over others. The boundary between religion and nonreligion is, thus, a *contested boundary,* and the sociopolitical history of the boundary-setting process itself is more telling than the location of the present dividing lines (McGuire, 2002).

The establishment of an "official" religion by definition excluded—sometimes violently purged—nonofficial "people's" religion. The rhetoric legitimating this hegemonic boundary maintenance spoke of delineating and protecting truth against error, pure practice against the impure or sacrilegious, proper authoritative leadership against nonapproved, and so on. Sociology of religion has already documented the regularity with which these ideas were linked with the class interests of the elites who articulated and enforced them. The process of establishing "official" religion thus generally excluded religious expressions characteristic of the poor, the women, various minorities, indigenous peoples in colonized lands, and other powerless groups.

We seem to assume that once the elites effectively defined nonofficial religion out of existence—as profane—the rest of society gradually became fully incorporated into official religion, albeit with occasional temporary expressions of "heresy" and "superstition," widespread "ignorance" of official teachings, and "laxness" in expected religious practice. Interestingly, for example, some of the earliest ethnographies of New World indigenous peoples[5] were produced to provide the guardians of the official religion (e.g., the Inquisition in Mexico) with a way to distinguish the people's Catholic faith from vestiges of indigenous religiosity (Martin, 1994; see also Curcio-Nagy, 1999). Official religion thus often proceeded hand in glove with colonial domination.

Nonofficial religion did not disappear, however, although its expression may have been hidden in various times and places. Rather, it has existed alongside official religion in a number of fascinating patterns. Latin American popular religion illustrates that, while belonging to the official religion, people can simultaneously engage in nonofficial beliefs and practices that are at least as meaningful or useful to them as are their official religious beliefs and practices. For example, elements of their popular religion address practical needs such as healing, successful harvests, divination, and fertility. This traditional, premodern pattern of religion, although maintained by a very different structural relationship to official religion and to the lay community, is not utterly unlike the pattern of "voluntarism" sociologists describe as characteristic of contemporary U.S. society.

Another reason for studying popular religion is that it often expresses (although sometimes counterproductively) dissent and resistance. For instance, in some popular religious rituals the official order is temporarily inverted or mocked; in some popular religious celebrations, wealth is somewhat redistributed. In some, nonpowerful persons can temporarily refuse to cooperate with the work or other social demands of their bosses, husbands, village rulers, and so on (see Lancaster, 1988:27–54; cf. Benavides, 1994; Comaroff, 1985).

Even in relatively rigid traditional societies, popular religion can express and sometimes activate the concerns of subordinate people. Interestingly, recent historical studies of the interaction between representatives of "official"

---

5. The most famous is Bernardino de Sahagún, *História general de las cosas de Nueva España;* others include Diego de Landa, *Relación de las cosas de Yucatán,* and Hernando Ruiz de Alarcón, *Tratato de las supersticiones.*

religions and whole regions experiencing popular religious beliefs and practices show that the *influence was reciprocal.* Often official religion deliberately accommodated a popular religion, absorbing its beliefs and practices into orthodoxy and orthopraxis (see, e.g., Luria, 1991). Nor were subordinate peoples such as colonized indigenous groups necessarily mere passive recipients; sometimes they were active agents in creating new "shared" meanings in a mestizo (mixed) culture (Carrasco, 1995). Often too, "official" religion was successful at reshaping popular religion, as by inserting observance of approved sacraments into the celebration of a popular pilgrimage.

Along with emphasizing the importance of more study and appreciation of popular religion, however, we must remain critical in our research approaches. One of the most difficult methodological tasks is to avoid romanticizing popular religion. Just because it is a religion "of the people" does not mean popular religion is necessarily any more benign or beneficial than official religion. Some popular religion is intolerant, oppressive, or even violent. For example, both in the Middle Ages in Europe and in the twentieth-century United States, much popular Christian religion promoted anti-Semitism (Lippy, 1994; Vauchez, 1993); popular religion is highly likely to reflect popular prejudices, making it blatantly racist, misogynist, homophobic, or politically chauvinistic. Some popular religion is an obstacle to adherents' educational, occupational, or economic successes; some is antidemocratic and suppressive of certain freedoms, including the free expression of religion itself. Just because popular religion may challenge the status and power arrangements of official religion does not mean that it does not *also* serve to reproduce hierarchical arrangements, such as men's power over women or one tribe's over another.

To the extent that sociology of religion has made paradigmatic the characteristics of such "official" religion, it marginalizes all other forms of religion, all other religious expressions, all other patterns of religiosity. Thus, using this approach, sociologists simply fail to *notice,* much less comprehend, the complex and diverse ways religion is constructed and practiced in people's everyday lives in the modern context.

This is not to imply that popular religion is limited to traditional societies or to marginalized groups. My 1988 study of nonmedical healing groups in a suburban middle-class New Jersey area found many people drawing on a wide range of nonofficial religious beliefs and practices. The Extended Application at the end of Chapter 5 discusses some of these groups and how they may be linked with the location of religion in contemporary societies.

POPULAR RELIGION
IN MODERN SOCIETIES

Since the main distinction between "official" and "popular" religion is whether religious beliefs and practices are under the control of official religious organizations, the United States has a plethora of popular religious expressions. This abundance is partly due to its history of never having allowed an established church—a legally enshrined official church of the nation (although, as shown in Chapter 8, not all religions in the United States have been accepted as legitimate "official" religions). Other historical factors that multiplied unregulated popular religion were the sheer size of the country and the geographical dispersal of the people, especially during frontier expansion.

Many Protestant religious groups have their roots in popular religious expression. The camp meetings and tent revivals of early U.S. Protestantism exemplify the process. Anyone on the frontier who could attract an audience could preach, regardless of training, knowledge, or quality of content (see Lippy, 1994). The official denominations tried to co-opt this religiosity by sending out traveling ministers or by enrolling the local ministers who had attracted followings. They never quite succeeded, though; on the frontier and later in urban revivals, there was almost continual emergence of new religious expressions outside of official control. While perhaps never matching the United States in sheer diversity and numbers of popular religious expressions, Europe has a long history of popular religion, from effervescent religious movements to vestiges of pre-Christian practices, from popular inspirational literature to pilgrimage sites and shrines.

Nonofficial religion is often effective in expressing dissent, precisely because it can draw upon broad cultural resources—including some of the cultural resources of the official religions—and use them in ways unforeseen and uncontrolled by the official religions. For example, slaves who sang spirituals could draw on Judeo-Christian cultural images, such as Moses and the Promised Land, which expressing profound dissent against their oppression. The official religion may promote a practice, such as a pilgrimage or procession, and the nonofficial religion may use the same procession to express dissent or some other meaning, unforeseen by the official religion. The official religion may revere the Bible as a source of sacred scripture, but the nonofficial religion may use the Bible as an object for divination or source of magical powers. People who have been excluded from the official religion may continue to express their religion in unsanctioned ways, the very practice of which is a form of dissent.

A fascinating example of nonofficial religious expression in a modern society is "the Gospel Hour," a two-hour long gospel hymn performance and sing-along in an Atlanta, Georgia, gay bar. Two of the performers, the Gospel Girls, are gay men in drag (wearing sequined gowns, wigs, and makeup), and many of the mostly gay audience participate regularly and enthusiastically in the weekly hymn service. It appears to be an occasion of genuine religious feeling and community for many. One participant said, "my friends and I call it 'coming to services.'" The ritual performance, simultaneously of evangelical Christian gospel hymns and of high drag, serves both to assert an alternative Christian message for gay worshippers and to symbolically erase gender boundaries exaggerated by the dominant society (Gray and Thumma, 1997).

Popular Christianity

Nonofficial religion can draw upon numerous cultural resources in the Christian heritage. In addition to nonofficial preachers, another source of popular versions of Christianity is religious publishing. While much religious publishing is done under the control of official religious bodies (e.g., Sunday school educational materials), the vast majority of religious publications are not edited or reviewed for their "orthodoxy." Unrelated to the official religion of its readers, a large body of inspirational literature promotes religious techniques, values, images, and interpretations. A recent example is the commercially successful spate of books and paraphernalia about angels' presence in people's everyday lives (Kaminer, 1996; Woodward et al., 1993). Also, values and ideological perspectives embodied in popular literature, from *Reader's Digest* to *Gentlemen's Quarterly,* find their way into popular religion (Elzey, 1976, 1988; Moore, 1994).

A parallel and even more popular source of popular religion is inspirational programming on radio and television. Some mass-media preachers gain a sufficient following to build a large-scale organization. Oral Roberts, for example, began as a popular tent revivalist and faith healer and subsequently developed a large, well-financed sectlike organization. Televangelists (i.e., television preachers) exemplify nonofficial religious independence from doctrinal, organizational, and fiscal controls.

There is a complex relationship between religion as promulgated by popular culture and that of official religious groups. On the one hand, studies have found that the "electronic church" (especially television religious shows with popular preachers) is watched almost exclusively by already converted, relatively committed conservative or fundamentalist Christians (Stacey and Shupe, 1982). On the other hand, many organized religious groups (notably including several conservative denominations) have criticized the "electronic church." They question some television evangelists' freedom from outside evaluation and control—especially of their financing and the content of their preaching (Hadden, 1993).

Since televangelists are entrepreneurs, their success hinges on achieving an audience response that can be converted into contributions of money. This necessity is often connected to the beliefs they teach: For example, many entrepreneurial preachers tell their viewers that success, prosperity, and answered prayers come to those who contribute, especially to that particular evangelist's organization (Hadden and Swann, 1981). Thus, while popular evangelists present a version of religion, that version often differs in content and emphasis from orthodox teachings of official religions. Likewise, on the border between popular religion and "official" religion are nondenominational preachers who set up churches as entrepreneurial efforts. The preacher determines the version of religion to be offered and the audience is drawn somewhat like consumers of an entertaining production. This model of congregation and ministry is very different from that of official religious patterns of membership, doctrine, and polity.

Because of its material and pragmatic emphasis, popular religion is particularly open to commercialization. Thus there have long been markets for religious objects, from the time of early Christian purchases of relics (e.g., bones of dead saints) to the contemporary sales of Christian video games, bumper stickers, amusement parks, and jewelry (McDannell, 1995b; see also Moore,

1994). Religious publishing and mass-media evangelism both have clear commercial niches. Official religions also participate in such commercialization (e.g., sales of wedding services and cemetery plots), partly in an effort to control both the religious ideas and the economic resources.

The ideas and practices from popular culture religion are widespread. Artifacts of popular religion bear some resemblance to those of official religion: a wall plaque announcing the presence of angels, a plastic Jesus on the car dashboard, gold-plated crosses on neckchains, bumper stickers proclaiming "My God Is Alive; Sorry About Yours," plaques, posters, and jewelry with messages such as W.W.J.D. (the cryptic reference to "What Would Jesus Do?"). An interesting popular cultural development is the quasi-religious treatment of deceased popular entertainment stars, such as Elvis or Selena, as folk saints to whom petitions can be addressed. For example, pilgrims to Graceland (Elvis's mansion) hold candlelight vigils and ask for Elvis's help with their personal problems (Campo, 1998; Davidson et al., 1990; Nadeau, 1995; Wilson, 1995). Popular religion also includes religious or quasi-religious themes from patriotism or nationalism (explored in detail in Chapter 6). National symbols such as the flag or Statue of Liberty form parts of some individuals' belief systems and are often indistinguishable from elements of official religion.

Magical Beliefs and Practices

Another overlay from common religion onto the official model consists of a variety of magical beliefs and practices. **Magic** refers to rituals performed to influence human or natural events; it is typically based on a conception of suprahuman power that is accessible for human instrumental use. For example, people may say certain words and make a certain mark on the doorways of their houses to protect those within from harm. Often, the emphasis in magical practices is upon technique: The words must be said right and the actions performed correctly in order for the desired effect to be accomplished. For this reason, magic is sometimes viewed as "failed science" (e.g., futile human attempts to deal with disease before the development of "scientific" medical knowledge). Anthropologists since Malinowski (1925/1948), however, have noted that magic—like religion—expresses important meanings in symbolic form. And, like religion, magic relies upon the social group for its shared meanings, including the conception of the external power that magic taps.

Magic has always overlapped religion, but the historical processes (described previously) in late Medieval and Early Modern times involved the Protestant and Catholic churches' concerted effort to purge their religions of magic. Even when the churches reduced or eliminated magical practices from official religion, ordinary people continued to employ magical practices and thinking in their everyday lives. In early New England, Protestant popular religion was full of magical practices for divination, protection of crops and ships, healing and childbirth, and so on (Hall, 1989). Catholic popular religiosity is even more amenable to magical practices, because Catholicism, after its reformation period, continued to encourage use of sacramentals (e.g., blessed water and candles) for domestic use. The Catholic "cult of the saints" also allowed popular religious practices through which believers felt they could tap external, suprahuman powers. While theologians might decry magical beliefs and practices, the actual religion-as-lived by ordinary people often mixes magic into religion with no sense of inconsistency (see, e.g., Orsi, 1997).

One contemporary (generally Protestant) magical practice is stichomancy—the practice of divining or getting a "message" from random opening of the Bible. Similarly, people often participate in religious actions with magical attitudes or conceptions. At the end of a healing service observed in a mainline denomination, the minister offered to bless salt and oil for home prayer for healing. With a rustling of brown paper wrappers, the congregation opened the spouts of salt boxes and lids of cooking oil bottles so the blessing could "get in." This overlay suggests a difficult methodological problem: how to interpret a situation in which members participate in rituals of official religion with attitudes and motives inconsistent with the official model.

The Paranormal and Occult

Other popular religious beliefs and practices concern **paranormal occurrences** (i.e., events outside the usual range of experiences). Belief in paranormal occurrences is fairly widespread. A 1994 *Newsweek* poll reported 13 percent of Americans have sensed the presence of an angel (Kantrowitz, 1994). Various U.S. national surveys have found a sizeable proportion of respondents felt they had experienced being really in touch with someone who had died, reported experiences of déjà vu (i.e., the sense of having already seen a place where they had never been before), and of ESP (extrasensory perception) (General Social Surveys of 1988 and 1998; Gallup and Castelli, 1989). Some persons attribute great significance to paranormal experiences; whole belief systems (e.g., Spiritualism) allocate special meaning to such experiences. Other persons who have had such out-of-the-ordinary experiences recognize them as unusual but place no special interpretation on them.

A study in an English industrial city found comparably high rates of extraordinary religious experiences in a random sample in which very few claimed active membership in an official religious institution. Despite the fact that many of these experiences were described as personally very meaningful, the majority of respondents kept the experiences private or altogether secret for fear of ridicule or being labeled mentally imbalanced (Hay and Morisy, 1985). Thus, some elements of nonofficial religion are "invisible," not so much because of their deviance from official religion, but more because the general culture treats them as inappropriate.

Extrascientific explanations and techniques are also part of common religion. These are ways of interpreting and manipulating the natural and social environment that are not accepted by this culture's official religious or scientific groups. Included are beliefs in astrology, hexing, palmistry, numerology, amulets and charms, water divining, UFOs, divination (by Tarot, pendulum, rod, I Ching, entrails), and witchcraft. We have the mistaken notion that such beliefs and practices are characteristic only of the poorly educated or of recent immigrants from other cultures. Thus, we are not surprised to learn that various Americans seek divination and access to magical powers through Afro-Caribbean religions, such as Santería and Vodou, and Asian religions, such as Taiwanese popular religion.

Numerous studies, however, suggest that extrascientific explanations and beliefs are rather widespread among educated, economically comfortable, native-born Americans. In my own study of nonmedical healing practices among middle-class suburbanites, I found numerous instances of divination (for example, to discover the name of the illness or its imputed causes). Not only adherents of psychic or occult healing approaches, but also adherents of Christian, Eastern, and "New Age" approaches to healing utilized various forms of divination (McGuire, 1988). Another example is the recent interest, among middle- and upper-class Americans not of Chinese cultural background, in Feng Shui, an ancient Chinese approach to divining the most propitious arrangement of a house or other space. Some Americans have completely redesigned their houses, gardens, offices, and Web sites according to the advice of a Feng Shui practitioner.

Similarly, science fiction deals with a number of quasi-religious themes about humanity and its boundaries, which have been embodied in religious groups such as UFO groups that believe they communicate with nonterrestrial beings (see Mörth, 1987). One study found disproportionate numbers of young, highly educated males among those attracted to deviant (or occult) sciences and occult quasi-religious practices (Ben-Yehuda, 1985). It asks, Why this prevalence of nonofficial religion (and nonofficial science) among precisely those social groups most favored in modern technological society?

Another strand of esoteric culture that is a familiar part of common religion is astrology, a set of beliefs and practices predicated upon the idea that impersonal forces in the universe influence social life on earth. Believers try to read and interpret zodiacal signs (e.g., the position of the stars at the time of one's birth) in order to predict outcomes of the influence of those forces. They believe this knowledge helps them choose the best moment for certain actions or the best probable course of action, and to discern when humans bear responsibility or blame for certain outcomes. Under the general category of astrology falls a wide variety of beliefs and practices ranging from highly sophisticated, complex speculations to pop versions such as newspaper horoscope columns (Fischler, 1974).

Astrological beliefs and practices are widespread in modern Western societies. According to a 1990 survey, 25 percent of the U.S. population believes in astrology (Gallup Poll, 1990). Similarly, a Canadian survey found that 34 percent of respondents believe in astrology, and 88 percent consult their horoscopes as least once a month (Bibby, 1993). A study of highly committed adherents found them to be disproportionately well educated, occupationally and economically stable, white, and female compared to the U.S. population (Feher, 1992).

The nature of belief in astrology illustrates the methodological difficulty of studying nonofficial religion. Astrological beliefs are widespread, significant parts of many people's worldviews. Some people hold them in combination with official religious beliefs; for others, they are substitutes for official religion. There is no "church" of astrology. Connections among committed adherents are not commitments to a group but are more like being part of a milieu or "lifestyle enclave" (Feher, 1994). Although there are some individual astrological practitioners, most adherents learn their beliefs and practices through relatively anonymous media—books, newspapers, magazines. Some evidence suggests that, like superstition, commitment to astrology is strongest among traditionally "religious" persons who are not involved in official religion (Wuthnow, 1976a:166).

Beliefs and practices pertaining to paranormal occurrences and extrascientific explanations and techniques are part of what is generally termed the *occult*. **Occultism** is a set of claims that contradict established (i.e., official) scientific or religious knowledge. This focus on the anomalous makes the occult seem strange and mysterious (Truzzi, 1974a:246). The term *occult* refers to the quality of knowledge that is obscured and secret, and thus a source of hidden power. The esoteric and occult have been part of Western societies since their inception. The Enlightenment period of European society marked the beginnings of the attempt to separate scientific ways of knowing from religious and esoteric bases of knowledge, but many wide-ranging innovations began in the "seedbed" of the esoteric. Modern medicine, chemistry, and psychology owe much to the esoteric sciences of earlier times (Tiryakian, 1974:272, 273).

Similarly, secret societies have long been a part of nonofficial religion. Mystery cults, kabbalistic groups, Freemasonry, and Rosicrucianism exemplify their variety. Mystery and awe surround the esoteric knowledge protected by the secret society, and initiation rituals symbolize admission of the member to each level of secret knowledge. The protection of this secrecy promotes the solidarity of the group (Carnes, 1989; Kertzer, 1988; Simmel, 1906; Tiryakian, 1974:266, 267). Seldom is there any clear border between secret societies that are overtly religious and those that are not specifically religious. For example, many groups of the "Women's Spirituality" movement and the "Men's Movement" use secrecy and rituals of initiation (McGuire, 1994). Some explicitly religious movements (e.g., early Mormonism) have similar features because they are organized around a *gnosis* (i.e., special knowledge). Although some of the recent interest in esoteric beliefs and practices may be merely countercultural experimentation or fads, many people take their belief in the occult seriously. Witchcraft exemplifies beliefs and practices followed by adherents with varying degrees of seriousness and involvement. At one end of the spectrum are people for whom paganism is a form of entertainment. Others believe in witchcraft and therefore seek occasional spells for health, protection, and success; they might also ascribe special importance to astrological events such as solstices and eclipses. At the other end of the spectrum are people who are fully involved in the beliefs and practices of witchcraft, belong to a group (i.e., coven), and organize their lives around witchcraft as a counterofficial religion. Their religion structures their sense of time around a ritual calendar; their ritual practices transform ordinary spaces into sacred spaces, and their beliefs and values inform their moral norms about right relationships with others and with the natural environment.

There is a distinction between white and black magic. Wiccans (as many of those practicing modern witchcraft call themselves) hold strong ethical norms about the uses of magical powers for good and not for harm (see Berger, 1999).[6] They often emphasize the continuity of their tradition (sometimes called "the old religion") with the medieval European white witches—"wise women" and men who combined pre-Christian symbolism and lore. It is not uncommon for witches also to belong to church groups of official religion. One interesting contemporary development of witchcraft and neopaganism has been the adoption of some of their symbols and organization for the expression of nonpatriarchal spirituality, thus incorporating Christian and Jewish women in an all-encompassing "goddess" religion (Eller, 2000; Gottschall, 2000; Raphael, 1998). These nonofficial religious beliefs envision feminine features of the divine, and their ritual practices emphasize the empowerment of women (Berger, 1999; Griffin, 1995, 2000; Neitz, 1990, 1994).

While popular, folk, or occult religious beliefs and practices may be defined as "deviant" by arbiters of official religious or scientific knowledge, in everyday life they are in the range of "normal" and plausible to many people (Campbell and McIver, 1987).

INDIVIDUAL RELIGIOSITY
IN THE NONOFFICIAL MODE

One interpretation of nonofficial religion in contemporary societies suggests that modern society is increasingly characterized by a new mode of religiosity in which individuals select components of their meaning systems from a wide assortment of religious representations. But while traditional "orthodox" representations from official religion may be among the components selected, other elements are drawn from popular culture—newspaper advice columns, popular inspirational literature, lyrics of popular music, popular psychology, horoscopes, night-school courses on meditation techniques, and so on (Luckmann, 1967:103–106). This interpretation may somewhat overstate the contrast of this eclectic religiosity with that of earlier times; it is entirely probable that earlier generations held widely varying versions of official religion, melding together combinations of folk beliefs, superstition, pagan customs, and misinformed interpretations of the official model of religion to form individual meaning systems. The sharp contrast between official and nonofficial religion is probably itself a product of relatively recent social processes by

---

6. By contrast, practitioners of black magic use their powers for evil as well as good ends. They believe they have allied themselves with the forces of evil (i.e., Satan), from which they obtain power and direction (Alfred, 1976; Bainbridge, 1978; Moody, 1971, 1974; Truzzi, 1974b).

which society came to define religion as the domain of official religious institutions and by which religious organizations articulated their distinctiveness from popular religion.

The complex threads woven together to comprise the individual's operative religion make it difficult to describe that religion by reference to any single model such as an official religion to which the person may belong. For example, in my own research (McGuire, 1988), one respondent had experienced multiple healings and he devoted two evenings per week to helping others with healing needs; he described himself as "very spiritual" but only "somewhat religious" (a distinction made by many persons whose religiosity was in the nonofficial mode). As part of his spirituality and healing efforts, this person used primarily meditation with visualization (derived not only from Christian sources), as well as yoga, crystals, and reflexology. *And* he was a practicing Methodist, indeed an active clergyman.

This amalgam of beliefs and practices is not at all unusual. Evidence on the distribution of nonofficial religious beliefs and practices shows that many adherents are also adherents of official religion. Only a small portion of nonofficial religion is practiced in lieu of official religion. As suggested in the first part of this chapter, individual religious autonomy and voluntarism may be profoundly affecting official religiosity; those same forces make nonofficial religiosity even more plausible in the modern context. Chapter 5 examines further the organizational effects of these patterns of religiosity.

Merely listing the elements of a person's religion does not adequately describe it. We also need to know which beliefs and practices are central and which are peripheral. How does this complex mixture change over time, and how do some parts recede in relevance? Similarly, we need to know when the individual applies which beliefs and practices. The believer may turn to official religion to help socialize children but seek nonofficial religious help for healing a chronic back problem. We need to understand when and how parts of this eclectic religion generate commitment or community. We need more information about the effective religion of individuals in its complexity and richness.

RESEARCHING NONOFFICIAL RELIGION AND RELIGIOSITY

What does this overview of the varieties of popular religion imply about how we should study religion today? It suggests that official forms of religion—while still of interest—are far less important for understanding the larger religious situation than we had been led to believe. Specifically, we need to give more research attention to those nascent movements (no matter how small) through which religious symbols are being proffered and mobilized, especially in tension with those of religious and other established institutions. For this we need a richer appreciation of the cultural factors in social and political change.

Exactly how is religion employed as a cultural resource? In a structural situation where religion is flexible and relatively autonomous from authoritative control in any institutional sphere, we must focus upon ongoing processes by which believers create, maintain, and change their symbols for making sense of their worlds. These symbol systems are sometimes enduring, sometimes transformed into new meanings, and sometimes completely ephemeral. Nevertheless, given the modern situation of religion, it is the *process*, rather than whether it results in an institutionalized form with a quantifiable membership, that is important for research and analysis.

For study of such flexible and ever-changing processes, we should pay particular attention to rituals, symbols, and other cultural vehicles for world images (whether toward change or preservation) and for shared religious experiences and sense of community. We need greater attention especially to language—such as shared symbolic language, narratives of personal meanings and group experiences, and the structure of discourse and how it develops and changes. Concomitantly, we need less emphasis on quantitative methods such as surveys, opinion research, and formal organizational analysis, because these methodologies presume a relatively fixed, institutional form of religion. They depend upon shorthand identification of people with their institutional location—such as religious affiliation or political party.

We must also drop the assumption that traditional institutional religious symbols, language, rituals, and practices are used for the reasons an institution once intended them. We cannot assume continuity between the functions served by certain religious expressions in another time and place and the meanings of the same expressions today. For instance, we cannot assume that our interpretation of Mass attendance in rural Ireland in the eighteenth century applies, even vestigially, to 1990s Mass attendance of, say, Irish-Americans in Dallas, Texas. Rather than treating traditional meanings as given, we should make them research *questions*. Toward this end, we need to ask people about what is meaningful to them and about what they experience when they participate in official and nonofficial religious practices.

Methodological tools such as ethnography, intensive interviews, participant observation, and ritual analysis are a good start. Anthropological methods are also limited for our task, however, because anthropological research typically has been done among peoples whose beliefs and practices change far more slowly, for whom tradition is more authoritative, and who are relatively isolated from the pluralism that characterizes the modern religious situation. Nevertheless, good ethnography tries to represent the voices and the meanings of the participants themselves. It attempts to derive analytic categories from the culture itself rather than impose ideas, including the researcher's scientific meanings.

We need better methodological tools for studying the richness of religious ritual and experience—whether in the context of official or nonofficial religion. Although it may be one of the most compelling components of many people's religion, it eludes our methodologies based on words and ideas. For

---

BOX 4.2   Historical Perspective: Old-Time Religiosity?

We often imagine that "old-time" religion or religiosity was somehow better than that of our time. For example, Protestants who value Bible-reading admire pictures of Victorian era families gathered around as the grandfather reads aloud from a large family Bible. They presume that, if there had been social scientific surveys in those days, the average person would be categorized as very "religious" by most indices of religiosity (such as church attendance or frequency of reading the Bible). Historians remind us that people's actual practices are more complex.

Family Bibles, marketed aggressively in the latter half of the nineteenth century, represented various meanings—only some of which were religious. They were expensive enough to be listed as part of a person's "estate" in a will, and they were often displayed prominently in a decorous parlor as a symbol of "good taste," as well as of some economic means. They were used as family records (of births and deaths, for example) and as repositories of sentimental poetry, clippings of hair, insurance policies, and dried flowers. One historian observed "Victorian Protestants sought to preserve and make sacred the minutiae of everyday life by physically juxtaposing special memorabilia with the pages of the most sacred object in their household, the family Bible" (McDannell, 1995b:91). Family Bibles were also used for fortune-telling and other religious uses not approved by official religions. Protestant domestic ritual included, not only the reading of the Bible in family worship, but also reverence for the Bible as a sacred object in a place of special attention.

Many family Bibles were bought to show, rather than to read. Indeed, some Victorians believed that, by turning the Bible into a domestic commodity, it could—by its very presence in the home—inspire purified

---

many, religious experience is—almost by definition—ineffable. How, then, can we methodologically tap this critical religious dimension and begin to take it more seriously in our interpretations of people's religion as practiced, as lived?

Our study of religiosity in the nonofficial mode is challenged by the distinction between religiosity and spirituality that many people themselves make. Perhaps we would learn far more about both official and nonofficial religiosity if we included both together in our researches, as complementary and often overlapping resources for individual religious expression. In order to tap both aspects of an individual's religiosity, we need to look with great depth at how people put together all the aspects of their personal religiosity and/or spirituality. Simple catalogs of beliefs and practices may be a start, but they do not adequately tell us how and when the believer draws on one element and not another. One way to focus questions about spirituality is to center on a theme, such as health and illness, childbearing and parenting, dying and loss of a loved one, or other critical experiences for which a respondent could reflect on the whole range of religious responses that was part of each experience. Chapters 3, 4, and 5 report several studies that are promising efforts toward such methodological sophistication.

BOX 4.2 *continued*

sentiments. Church-goers and non-church-goers alike purchased and displayed large, elegant Bibles, so we cannot infer anything about *individual* belief and practice from the rate of sales of this commodity. We know that family Bible-reading was a respected *ideal* among many, but not all, Protestants; it was the theme of posed family photographs, as well as engravings and illustrations of popular tracts. The connection of home Bible-reading with sentimentality and emotionality occurred gradually in the nineteenth century, corresponding to a shift in gender roles and a feminization of Protestant Christianity (McDannell, 1995b). In the depictions of Victorian era Bible-reading, there was a shift from an authoritative male "head of the family"—demonstrating status (and perhaps superior literacy) by reading to the entire household—to a "sweet" and gentle mother reading to her children in an intimate and more individualized relationship.

- Many nineteenth-century Protestants were critical of marketing Bibles as a commodity—as objects to be bought and sold in a marketplace of goods and services. Why does the commodification of religious goods seem sacrilegious to some believers? Why does the commodification of religious services (such as charging a fee for performing a burial or for blessing a new business) seem to diminish their sacred qualities? How is religion commodified differently today?

- Do gender roles and class status (or aspirations to higher class status) affect individual religious practices today, too? What contemporary marketing of religious goods and services is targeted to people wanting progressive gender roles? "Traditional" roles? Is the consumption of such goods nowadays better (or worse) as an indicator of individual religiosity than Victorian consumption patterns?

Expanding our research methods to include nonofficial religion and religiosity makes the research far more complex and requires far greater researcher skill than the seemingly tidy quantitative methods for studying official religion. Nevertheless, both our understanding of official and nonofficial religion and our appreciation of individual religiosity and spirituality will be greatly deepened by the effort.

EXTENDED APPLICATION: WOMEN'S RELIGION AND GENDER ROLES

As we have seen, the individual's religion is a personally meaningful combination of beliefs, values, and practices that is usually related to the worldview of a larger group into which that individual has been socialized.[7] In socialization, the individual typically receives many of these beliefs, values, and practices from representatives of the larger group such as parents and teachers. Much of

---

7. This Extended Application exemplifies concepts in both Chapters 3 and 4.

this received meaning system becomes internalized—that is, made a part of the individual's own way of thinking about self and others. The meaning system received by the individual includes a number of beliefs, images, and norms about that group's definitions of maleness and femaleness. All religions have addressed the theme of human sexuality and gender roles because sexuality is a potent force in human life and because gender is, in most societies, a major factor in social stratification.

This analysis will focus first on how women's religion influences their gender roles and identities, illustrating some of the concepts in Chapter 3 on the individual's religion. A similar application could be drawn for men as males, showing how their gender roles are linked with religion, although this application is not pursued here.

Second, this analysis will illustrate why focusing only on official religion and religiosity is sometimes misleading. As religion became a differentiated institutional sphere, many of women's religious roles and expressions were excluded from official religion and, if continued at all, were kept alive in nonofficial forms such as healing cults, popular religiosity, mediumship, witchcraft, and spiritual midwifery. We need to examine the structural bases for women's status; official religious institutions have historically epitomized the structural and ideological suppression of women. The religious legitimation of their gender role, then, raises some interesting questions about women's religiosity. Do they come to think of themselves as the official model that their religion portrays of them? Impressive historical evidence exists that nonofficial religion is one vehicle for women's assertion of alternative religious roles. A related question is whether official religions are capable of changing to legitimate and express gender equality even if they were to adopt these goals.

Gender Role Definitions

The definitions of maleness and femaleness are culturally established. On the basis of these definitions, a group develops and encourages certain social differences between men and women. The U.S. society expects and encourages little boys to be more active and aggressive than little girls; little girls are expected and encouraged to be more polite, passive, and nurturant. In socialization, males and females are taught their culturally assigned **gender roles**—the social group's expectations of behaviors, attitudes, and motivations "appropriate" to males or females. Historically, religion has been one of the most significant sources of these cultural definitions of gender roles; and religion has been a potent legitimation of these distinctions.

Through socialization, the group's definitions of appropriate women's roles become part of the individual woman's self-definition. She evaluates herself in terms of these definitions: "I am a good girl/daughter/woman/mother/wife." The group's definitions of gender roles are subtly interwoven into the individual's learned "knowledge" about the social world. They are embodied in the language and imagery of the group and thus indirectly shape the members' thought patterns. The culture's use of words such as *bitch, slut, sweetie, doll, housewife,* and *mother* has strong evaluative connotations. These words imply qualities that some people attribute to women and for which there are no obvious male equivalents. Numerous words (e.g., *slut*) exist as negative labels for promiscuous women; there are no equivalent negative terms for promiscuous men. Similarly, a man who is said to "father" a child performs a single biological act; a woman who "mothers" a child provides continuing nurturant care. The language embodies the different standards of the society for men's and women's roles (Lakoff, 1975). In learning the group's language, the individual internalizes these images and symbols. Specifically religious symbols and images also shape the individual's gender role concept.

Although both men and women belong to the same official religions, the individual's religion is not necessarily a small carbon copy of the group's entire official stance. Women's versions of a certain religion are probably very different from men's versions; a woman may focus on those aspects of the group's worldview that speak to her social situation. Thus, an Orthodox Jewish man's personal religion might focus on his public ritual roles (e.g., carrying the Torah and forming part of a minyan, i.e., the ten men necessary for a prayer gathering to be official). He might emphasize the intellectual development, discussion of sacred texts, and careful application of religious law expected of men in the Orthodox community. Women, by contrast, have few ritual duties and none of them are public. Their religion is more likely to be focused on the home: making the Sabbath loaf and lighting Sabbath candles, instructing the very young, and enabling the men of the home to participate in their public religious roles. The very meaning of being Jewish is thus probably very different for the men than for the women. Central religious activities (e.g., attending Sabbath services at the synagogue and family worship around the Sabbath candles) also probably mean something different to each sex.[8]

A woman's religious experience and what she holds religiously most important are qualitatively different from men's religious experience and focus. Women's religion is nevertheless shaped heavily by the larger religious group because it is not a separate religion. The larger group attempts to form the individual's role through its teachings, symbols, rituals, and traditions. Thus, in the example of the Orthodox community, women's religion is strongly influenced by men's ideas of what a properly religious woman should do and be. Men interpret the Law and run the congregation and the religious courts. In most historic (i.e., official) religions, women have had considerably less power than men in establishing social definitions of appropriate gender roles. In the Roman Catholic Church, at least since the time of the early church, men have held all significant positions of authority to set and interpret religious norms, practices, and beliefs. The beliefs, ritual expressions, norms, and organizational

---

8. There is little empirical evidence about exactly how men and women experience religious rituals and events, but some clues appear in Myerhoff, 1978:207–241. Some parallels may also be drawn from studies of how different racial castes, socioeconomic strata, and ethnic groups differently experience similar religious rituals and belief systems.

structure of historical official religions, in short, effectively subordinate women.

The religious legitimation of women's roles is very similar to the religious legitimation of other caste systems. As shown in Chapters 2 and 7, religion is often used to explain why certain social inequalities exist. These explanations justify both the privileges of the upper classes or castes and the relative non-privileges of the lower ones. A **caste system** is a social arrangement in which access to power and socioeconomic benefits are fixed, typically from birth, according to certain ascribed characteristics of the individual. Medieval feudalism exemplifies a caste system, in which individuals born into a given socioeconomic stratum could move up or down relative to others of that stratum but could not aspire to the power and privileges of higher social strata.

Modern societies typically emphasize individual achievements as a basis of socioeconomic status more than traditional societies; however, elements of caste are still important. Race is one ascribed characteristic that still figures into socioeconomic status in most modern societies. Gender is another major basis of caste in modern societies. Women are generally excluded from access to power and socioeconomic status available to men. The expectation that housework is "women's work" exemplifies women's caste status. No matter how great a woman's achievement in art, business, or scholarship, the society still expects her to be the one responsible, by virtue of her gender, for the menial tasks of housecleaning.

Gender-caste status confers necessary, but not sufficient, advantages to men's chances for recognition, power, and prestige. Not all men obtain these privileges in the social system, but maleness is virtually a prerequisite for them. Men's superior caste status does not necessarily make life comfortable and pleasurable for all individual men. Some men also suffer exploitation and discrimination—but not because of their gender. Women's status in most religious groups is circumscribed by gender stratification. Gender is far more important than theological or spiritual qualifications in determining whether an individual can perform certain rituals such as carrying the Torah or consecrating the communion elements.

Religious Legitimation

Religion has historically legitimated gender caste stratification directly (e.g., through religious laws) and indirectly (e.g., by rituals and symbols that reinforce ideas of women's inferiority). We need to remember, though, that there are many complex links between present-day religious beliefs and practices and historical or traditional beliefs and practices. Religions are, in many respects, shaped by their shared memory, their tradition. But there is no direct or deterministic connection between tradition and shared present memory. That is why the same tradition can spawn so many diverse religious groups, each with different ways of living out of their common tradition.

As we examine some of the ways religious groups have historically legitimated women's inferior status, it helps to think of these traditional elements as *cultural resources.* Religious groups "choose" (sometimes consciously, usually not consciously) certain elements of their tradition to remember and apply to people's lives today; other elements of the same tradition become irrelevant or forgotten. Thus, although we can learn about today's religious groups' traditional beliefs and practices, it remains an empirical question for sociology to discover how much of these traditional elements are actually salient in people's lives and religious experience.

Symbolism and Myth Religion contributes to, or legitimates, a caste system in a number of ways. Often religious symbolism embodies a caste-stratification system. It may depict the higher deities as male and the lower deities (or even negative spiritual forces) as female. According to some Hindu tradition, the goddess Kali represents "female illusion," symbolizing in the story of Shiva's entanglement with her the eternal struggle that men must wage against the evils of orientation toward material existence (Hoch-Smith and Spring, 1978:4).

Similar distinctions are embodied in the language of religious ritual. The ritual words of the Catholic Mass had, for centuries, stated that Christ's blood was shed "for all men." After several years of internal pressures, in 1985 the Vatican approved changing the words of the Mass to the gender-neutral term "for all" (see also Wallace, 1988). The language of Orthodox Jewish prayer makes gender-caste distinctions even more explicit. Daily morning prayer includes "Praised are you, O Lord our God, King of the Universe, who has not created me a woman." Conservative Jews have changed this wording to "Praised are you, O Lord our God, King of the Universe, for making me an Israelite"; whereas Reformed Jews do not use this blessing at all (Priesand, 1975:57–60).

Religions vary as to the degree of emphasis they place on a core sacred text (e.g., the Qur'an), but where one is central, the wording of the text can be at the center of many controversies. Some biblical language lends itself to gender-caste distinctions between men and women, although many such distinctions are derived from translations, which embody cultural assumptions of the language of translation overlaid on the distinctions made by the original writers of the many parts of the Bible. Nevertheless, besides the hierarchical, patriarchal language used to legitimate caste distinctions, both the Old and New Testaments include radically antihierarchical images of human relationships with the deity and each other (Ruether, 1989).

Religious groups that have become relatively hierarchical or patriarchal tend to "remember" those biblical images that legitimate their status and power arrangements. For example, Christian worship services and hymns traditionally referred to God by the images of "Lord," "Father," and "King," terms clearly full of masculine and hierarchical—even feudal—imagery. Because the language of worship is linked with social power, potential changes are politically volatile, so much so that the scholars writing the *Inclusive Language Lectionary* (readings for Sunday services) received anonymous death threats (Niebuhr, 1992). Far from being a minor matter of political correctness, language changes aim at reshaping as well as reflecting emerging changes in believers' images of God. Some changes, for example, encourage participants to envision not only powerful males but also women, people of color, infirm or handicapped persons, and powerless people as being "in God's image." Such a reenvisioning has profound theological implications.

Creation stories in male-dominated cultures often assign to women the responsibility for the presence of evil or the troubles of the present world. In these myths, women's presumed characteristics of sexual allure, curiosity, gullibility, and insatiable desires are often blamed for both the problems of humankind and for women's inferior role. The Hebrew myth of Lilith describes that the Lord formed both the first man and the first woman from the ground. The first woman, Lilith, was equal to Adam in all ways, and she refused what he wanted her to do (including his sexual demands). In response to Adam's complaints, the Lord then created Eve from Adam's rib, thus making her inferior and dependent. In one version of the story, Lilith persuaded Eve to eat from the Tree of Knowledge; thus, both the "good" woman through her gullibility and the "bad" woman through her wiliness and willfulness brought about the expulsion of humankind from the Garden of Eden (see Daly, 1978:86; Goldenberg, 1974).

In general, Christianity, Judaism, and (to a lesser extent) Islam and official Buddhism allowed that women were, in principle, equal to men before God, even though they were socially unequal. Thus, unlike other religions of their time, these religions held that women might aspire to salvation or spiritual perfection as much as men. This idea was not only revolutionary but also quite tenuous, however; eight centuries after the founding of Christianity, church authorities continued to express doubts about whether the souls of women were equal to those of men (Weber, 1922/1963:105; see also McLaughlin, 1974).

Moral Norms Religion typically creates or legitimates the **moral norms** that define what is appropriate to male and female gender roles. Thus, each culture has different ideas about appropriate clothing for males and females, and religious norms of modesty often give these concepts a moral connotation. Earlier Christian missionaries in Polynesia and Africa introduced different norms for clothing (especially for women) to the native peoples not merely because they thought Western customs of dress superior but especially because, according to their moral norms, the natives' state of dress or undress was sinful.

Historically, religious moral norms have been very important in defining the appropriate gender behavior of men and women. Many moral norms of religious groups are gender-specific (i.e., separate expectations for women and men). Religion shaped norms pertaining to sexual behavior (e.g., treating women's extramarital sexual activity as a more serious violation than men's). It influenced norms of physical activities, entertainments, drink, and dress (e.g., a "good" woman was expected to be more thoroughly covered, veiled, or screened from view than a "good" man). Religion also legitimated gender distinctions in work roles, home responsibilities, child-care responsibilities, education, marriage responsibilities, political responsibilities, and legal status.

Organization Religious organization is also a framework that supports gender-caste systems. Access to positions of authority and to central ritual and symbolic roles (e.g., the priesthood) is limited or denied to women in most historic religions. Control of ritual and symbolic roles is an important source of social as well as "spiritual" power. Religious organization historically excluded women from economic and decision-making power, except perhaps relative only to other women. Women's lack of power is often symbolized and communicated through their inferior ritual status (see Wallace, 1988, 1997).

Ritual Expression Ritual and symbolic roles (e.g., the role of celebrant of the Mass or reader of the Torah) have become the focus of some women's dissatisfaction with their religion's treatment of women because these roles are important symbols of power and status. Most official religions have allotted women a ritual position in the home. Women light Sabbath candles, lead family rosary, arrange family altars, participate in family Bible readings and mealtime grace, and lead young children in their prayers. Women are typically responsible for arranging the observance of religious holidays in the home, including keeping a kosher kitchen at Passover, preparing feast and fast meals, and arranging candles, Bibles, icons, crêche, or holy water for home devotional use. These ritual activities are seen as consistent with her gender roles as mother and homemaker.

In public rituals, women's traditional roles have been clearly subordinate. Men have traditionally held all important leadership and symbolic roles; women were allowed to be present (under certain circumstances) but silent. Women and children were historically segregated in the congregation, sitting in separate pews or separate parts of the room from men. Sometimes they were further hidden by screens or veils. One explanation is that these arrangements were intended to prevent women's presence from distracting men. Another explanation is that because women are not regarded as real *persons* in the central action, they are merely allowed to observe as unobtrusively as possible. Whatever the historical background, the segregation and veiling of women clearly communicated their inferior status (Borker, 1978). In many religious groups, women were not allowed in certain sacred places (e.g., on the altar platform or behind the screen where central ritual actions occurred). Most religious groups traditionally held that women required special purification after menstruation or childbirth before they could return to participate in group worship or key rituals (e.g., receiving communion).

Religious groups are inherently conservative because they base their beliefs and practices upon the tradition or scripture produced in an earlier era. Thus, Christian groups often justify their exclusion of women from central ritual roles by reference to Saint Paul's views (from the New Testament) of the proper place of women:

I desire then that in every place the men should pray, lifting holy hands without anger or quarreling; also that women should adorn themselves modestly and sensibly in seemly apparel, not with braided hair or gold or pearls or costly attire but by good deeds, as befits women who profess religion. Let a woman learn in silence with all submissiveness. I permit no woman to teach or to have authority over men; she is to keep silent. For Adam was formed first, then Eve; and Adam was not deceived, but the woman was deceived and became a transgressor. (1 Tim. 2:8–15, RSV, 1952)

Similar texts exist in other historic religious traditions. Although the Buddha's approach to women's roles was revolutionary relative to Hindu tradition (e.g., he allowed women to become monks and considered them capable of aspiring to spiritual perfection), he prescribed a greatly inferior role for them in the *samgha* (religious order), where they were forbidden authority and leadership roles. When his favorite disciple Ānanda asked him why women should not be given the same rank and rights as men in public life, the Buddha replied, "Women, Ānanda, are hot-tempered; women, Ānanda, are jealous; women, Ānanda, are envious; women, Ānanda, are stupid" (cited in Schweitzer, 1936:95).[9]

Changing Religious Roles for Women For understanding gender conflict and changing gender roles, a useful distinction is between "women" (i.e., female people) and "Woman"—a "symbolic construct comprised of allegory, metaphor, fantasy, and (at least in male dominated religions) men's psychological projections" (Sered, 1997:2). When women seek to engage in certain religious roles, conflict results from others' (men and women alike) perceiving the core issue as "Woman." This complex symbolic construct raises fears (e.g., of pollution) and images that are remote from the actual meaning of the issue at hand. It is not amenable to rational discourse. Religious opposition to gender equality, thus, can be mobilized as a symbolic opposition to all features of modernity (see Chaves, 1997:128–129).

Acceptance of changes in religious roles for women is greater in groups that do not accept religious traditions as literal truths and divinely ordained. Groups that emphasize orthodoxy to literally interpreted religious traditions are resistant to any kind of change. Thus, Orthodox Judaism, Eastern Orthodoxy, some strains of Roman Catholicism, orthodox Islam, and fundamentalist Protestantism generally oppose changing the ritual and symbolic roles of women. Even the most traditionally oriented religious group, however, represents a *change* from the life idealized by their tradition, because no one still lives in the social context and under the conditions that pertained centuries before, when the remembered events may have occurred.

---

9. No full biographies of Gautama, the historical Buddha, were written until several generations after his lifetime. Early Buddhist scripture suggests that his message was radically egalitarian, but later legends and tales, adopted into the canons of Buddhist schools, portray misogynist attitudes (Gross, 1993).

Other religious groups interpret their traditions or scriptures differently. Thus, some Christian groups believe that Saint Paul's restrictions, as previously quoted, are merely the product of his culture's gender role distinctions rather than part of the central message of the Christian tradition. Similarly, nineteenth-century modernist Muslim interpreters of the Qur'an and Islamic law found much in their tradition that promoted equality for women (Moaddel, 1998). Generally, those religious groups that are least open to change in women's roles are also more conservative toward other social changes as well.

A group's approach to defining women's roles merely reflects its general attitude about the relationship of its tradition to the conditions of modern society. (We will further describe these diverse stances in Chapter 5.) For example, the decades of controversy in many U.S. synagogues over gender-mixed seating (i.e., a whole family sitting together on a pew, in contrast to traditional segregation of women and men) have represented an important symbolic struggle over accommodation to wider U.S. cultural patterns (Sarna, 1986; see also, Zuckerman, 1999). Similar tensions exist in newer immigrant congregations, especially those whose home country's culture had dramatically different roles for women. One study of Lebanese Shi'ite Muslims in the United States found that women were much more likely to be involved in activities at the mosque in the United States than in Lebanon. In the old country, only men participated in daily prayers, Friday services, and other religious gatherings (indeed, many women had never set foot inside the mosque there). In many U.S. congregations, however, women participate in prayers, study, and social functions at the mosque (Walbridge, 1997).

In many religious groups, women are pressing for changes in rituals and symbols in order to reflect their experiences as women and to change the images of women held by the whole group. For example, some Jewish women substitute new, women-affirming blessings for the traditional ones. Others have developed an annual Seder ritual that expresses women's voices in the story of the Exodus (Brozan, 1990). Similarly, in 1990 the Mormon church adapted some of its central ritual, dropping the oath of obedience to their husbands that women previously had taken in place of the men's oath to obey God and the church (Steinfels, 1990).

Thus, the religious heritage of a group does not *determine* its arrangements. Many contemporary religious groups have integrated women more into the central ritual actions; most Protestant and Reformed Jewish congregations allow laywomen the same privileges as laymen. Roman Catholic and Conservative Jewish congregations are more divided in their treatment of laywomen. There is some resistance in Roman Catholic churches to allowing laywomen to serve as lectors, altar servers, and Eucharistic ministers (who distribute communion, especially to homebound and hospitalized parishioners). Similar controversy exists in Conservative Jewish congregations over whether to admit women to central lay ritual roles, such as being called to the Torah (Umansky, 1985).

The issue of the ordination of women is the most controversial because of its great symbolic importance and because the role of the clergy is more powerful than lay roles. The significance of the ordination of women is that it presents an alternative image of women and an alternative definition of gender roles. Thus, the ordination of women has an impact on laypeople as well as clergy.

Women began to press for ordination in the mainline Protestant denominations beginning in the 1880s (about the same time that the Women's Movement began, demanding women's right to vote, own property, etc.). Although some women were ordained in a few denominations in the early part of the twentieth century, only after the 1950s were a substantial number of women granted ordination. The Methodist and Presbyterian churches allowed women clergy beginning in the 1950s, and in the 1970s the Lutheran and Episcopalian churches voted (after considerable controversy and some defections) to ordain women (Hargrove et al., 1985). By the end of the twentieth century, about half of U.S. denominations granted full clergy rights to women. Despite increasing numbers of women in seminaries (from 14.3 percent in 1974 to 31 percent in 1993), women are still greatly underrepresented in the profession. U.S. Census figures for 1990 show that the proportion of women employed in the ministry (roughly 10 percent) was less than half their proportion (between 20 and 25 percent) in medicine or law (cited in Chaves, 1996).

The Catholic Church retains its ban on women clergy, however. In 1976 the Vatican issued a "Declaration on the Question of the Admission of Women to the Ministerial Priesthood," basing continued refusal to ordain women on theological grounds that the sacramental expression of Christ's role in the Eucharist required the "natural resemblance" of Christ to the (male) minister (Sacred Congregation, 1977). Catholic theologians in the United States and elsewhere roundly ridiculed the theological basis of the document (Iadarola, 1985). In 1992, after nine years of work and four controversial drafts, the U.S. bishops failed to agree on a statement on women's roles in the church and remained deeply divided (Steinfels, 1992). In an effort to close further debate on the issue, the Vatican's Congregation for the Doctrine of the Faith announced in 1995 that the church should consider Pope John Paul II's pronouncement forbidding women's ordination to be "infallible" (Steinfels, 1995).

Resistance to women's roles as clergy or ritual leaders is not due merely to the weight of traditional beliefs and practices. Some groups are afraid of harm to the local congregation or denomination that might be caused by internal controversy over the issue (Lehman, 1985). In the Church of England (Episcopalian), the opposition has come from the House of Clergy, rather than the House of Bishops or House of Laity. One study of Church of England clergy found that these attitudes were more strongly correlated with clergymen's notions about women's proper roles in family and society than with any theological or scriptural foundation (Nason-Clark, 1987b). At the same time, studies in the United States and England show lay church members in mainline Protestant and Catholic churches to be generally positive about women in the ministry (Hoge, 1987; Lehman, 1985, 1987; Nason-Clark, 1987a).

Laypersons' opposition to the ordination of women in the Roman Catholic Church has dropped dramatically since Vatican II; indeed, 63 percent of U.S. Catholics surveyed agreed that ordination of women "would be a good thing" (Gallup Poll, 1993).

Nevertheless, the experience of women who have been ordained is far from equality. Women are underemployed, paid lower salaries, and are less likely to be considered for the better positions (such as senior pastor of a large, stable suburban parish). A church may employ a woman as "assistant minister" with special responsibility for youth programs. Although she may occasionally lead worship services, she is not seen as having an important leadership or decision-making role; being in charge of youth activities is consistent with traditional roles of women. Sometimes, male clergy undermine women who "succeed too well," and hiring committees effect a "glass ceiling" barring women from consideration for executive-level ministerial positions (Nesbitt, 1997a; Umansky, 1985; Zikmund et al., 1998).

Women who have had the opportunity to serve in pastoral capacities have often redefined those roles. Their style is generally more relational, less authoritarian, and more democratic, involving the laity in leadership (Nason-Clark, 1987a). Although the Catholic Church does not allow women to be ordained, in many regions nuns and laywomen have taken over many functions of the clergy (due to insufficient numbers of ordained clergy). Similar redefinition of leadership roles appears among these women pastors, who develop collaborative relationships with parishioners rather than hierarchical ones (Wallace, 1991, 1993; see also Lehman, 1993; Lummis, 1994).

Power and Sexuality

Evidence from relatively simple societies suggests that religious distinctions between males and females accompany social distinctions between them, especially in the division of labor. An interplay of power is involved in establishing social inequalities. Religion and human sexuality are both important sources of power, partly because of the mystery, awe, and intensity of the experiences they engender. Those who possess religious power in a social group frequently attempt to control the use of sexual power because they view it as a threat to their power base. Similarly, on the individual level, many religions view the use of sexual power as diminishing or distracting from spiritual or religious power. The regimen of the 3HO movement (Happy-Healthy-Holy—a Western version of Sikh/Hindu religion) severely restricts the frequency of sexual intercourse of members, not because members believe there is anything intrinsically wrong with intercourse but because sexual activity is believed to drain the individual's spiritual energy (Gardner, 1978:120–133; Tobey, 1976).

Men have historically perceived female sexuality—associated with symbolic "Woman" (as described previously)—as a source of dangerous power to be feared, purified, controlled, and occasionally destroyed. General ideas of carnal female sexuality have existed for centuries. Some Western cultural forms of these ideas include images of the enchantress, the evil seductress, the movie queen, and the prostitute. Other cultural images of dangerous female power include the witch, the nagging wife, and the overpowering mother (Hoch-Smith and Spring, 1978:3).

There are several plausible hypotheses for such emphasis on the powers of female sexuality. Douglas (1966) suggests that female sexuality is perceived by males as dangerous and impure because it symbolically represents females' power to counteract the dominance of men. Societies in which there is ambiguity about the legitimate sources of male dominance over females are more likely to develop beliefs in sexual pollution by females than are societies in which women's position is unambiguous. According to Douglas, if formal and informal social power is unambiguous (whether or not a society has established a subordinate position for women), men are less likely to fear sexual pollution. Fear of female sexuality is particularly characteristic of societies in which male dominance over females is a primary feature of social organization. The Pygmies, for example, have a division of labor and power structure in which gender is relatively unimportant and have little concern over sexual pollution.

Douglas (1966) cites the contrasting example of the Lele tribe of Zaire. The men of this tribe use women as something of a currency of power by which they claim and settle disputes. They fight over women and use their dominance over women as a symbol of their status relative to other men. Women of the tribe challenge total male dominance by playing off one man against another and by manipulating men. The men of the Lele have considerable fear of pollution concerning sex and menstrual blood. Women are considered dangerous to male activities, and contact or intercourse with a menstruating woman is believed to be contaminating. Fear of the power of female sexuality is related to the disruptive role that women sometimes play, upsetting the order of a male-dominated system of rewards and privileges in the society. Female sexuality is therefore symbolized as chaotic, disordering, and evil.

Another feared power related to female sexuality is regeneration—the power of life and death. Many cultures observe with awe and some fear the power of female sexuality to create and sustain new life and, by implication, the dangers of female renunciation of this role. For example, the celibate Hindu goddesses are those with feared malevolent powers, whereas goddesses with male consorts are not so dangerous because their power (sákti) can be regenerative and benevolent (Marglin, 1985). The association of female sexuality with fertility, regeneration, and the power of birth makes it both dangerous and potentially fruitful (see Archer, 1990). Thus, religious rituals and social sanctions try to control this source of power.

The theme of sexual pollution is prevalent in historic Western religions as well. The dominant religious images of women in Western societies are built on a dualistic image of female sexuality: The evil side is the temptress/seducer/polluter, and the approved side is the virgin/chaste bride/mother. Religiously approved roles for women are rather narrowly limited to expressions of these images and are defined and legitimated by reference to Scripture, tradition, and such role models as biblical women or and saints (sources of female images in the Christian heritage are explored in

Bynum, 1986; Gold, 1985). In nineteenth-century Catholic piety, Mary was elevated to considerable importance—for example, as a source of miracles and prophetic apparitions. Her power, however, derived from attributes of motherhood and virginity, not fertility or sexuality (which figured into some earlier Mary cults). The promulgation of the controversial dogma of the Immaculate Conception (1854) promoted the new piety for a religious image of Mary as a pure and passive vessel (Pope, 1985). The narrowly defined sexual base of these dominant symbols of femaleness contrasts dramatically with representations of men in ritual and imagery. Whether a man is a virgin matters little in his religious status or participation in ritual. Women are represented as one-dimensional characters in ritual and imagery; their images are based almost exclusively on sexual function (Hoch-Smith and Spring, 1978:2–7).

Women's Religious Identity

Sense of Self-Worth Such imagery serves to reinforce the distinctions of the gender-caste system. On the one hand, it places some value on "good" women's roles. Such symbolism can enhance the individual's sense of self-worth by showing her existence as part or imitative of some larger reality. She may think, "Although my position is lowly, it is part of something bigger"—a larger cosmic picture. The Hindu tradition tells a woman that she may be rewarded in the next life with a higher status if she obediently fulfills the role requirements of a woman in this life. The New Testament quote from Saint Paul presented earlier, outlining women's inferior status, concludes: "Yet woman will be saved through bearing children, if she continues in faith and love and holiness, with modesty" (Tim. 1:15, RSV). Religion often explicitly links spiritual rewards with the fulfilling of gender-caste obligations.

On the other hand, although the religious legitimation of women's roles gives meaning to their subordinate position, it does not necessarily make them happy or give them a positive identity. In Buddhism, as in Western religions, women are used to symbolize to men and women alike the undesirable qualities of human existence, such as suffering and illusory entanglements.

We know very little about the actual impact of these perspectives on women's identities. Such imagery and symbolism surely influence how a woman feels about herself. Does she, by participating in such a religion and culture, come to *perceive* herself as inferior and impure, more prone to sin, and a cause of males' sin and suffering? If participation in such rituals and symbols does not lower a woman's self-image, it must be because she is able to separate herself from them or experience this part of religion in some unofficial way. Do women selectively relate their identities with different aspects of rituals or with different rituals altogether? Do they use gender-linked symbols differently from men?

One study of the writings of religious people during the later Middle Ages— a period rife with misogynistic theological, philosophical, and scientific ideas— found that female and male spiritual leaders used gender images very differently. Male spiritual writers were more likely to view the genders as dichotomous,

---

BOX 4.3   Cross-Cultural Comparison:
Women in the Web of Karma

In the Sinhalese religion in Sri Lanka, for example, both the Buddhist doctrine and the folk religious imagery describe women as vehicles for impermanence and sorrow. The law of karma holds that all actions and thoughts have results in the future, including future rebirths of the individual. The desire for life and the illusions of the world perpetuate rebirths and thus suffering. Suffering refers not only to pain but also to the impermanence, emptiness, and insubstantiality of this existence. Buddha taught that escape from this suffering is possible only by detachment from desire, especially for life in this world.

The Buddhist imagery of women portrays them as particularly caught in this web of rebirth. Because women represent birth, they are themselves a symbol of the force of karma that maintains suffering in the world. They are also seen as the source of men's karma because they are among the things that men most desire. Yet women's desirability (i.e., sex appeal) is as impermanent and illusory as the rest of this world. Thus, women are especially entangled in the web of karma and have greater difficulty detaching themselves (AmaraSingham, 1978).

- The Sinhalese form of Buddhism treats these images of women as "given" in their cultural tradition, whereas American Buddhism has been more successful than American Christianity at sustaining alternative, nontraditional religious images of women's relationship to suffering. How is religious imagery a source of both tradition and change?

- If you were an anthropologist studying women's religious lives* in Sinhalese culture, what features would you examine to understand whether or how these images affect women's actual lives and identities?

---

*See Falk and Gross, 2001, for excellent historical and anthropological studies of women's religious lives.

---

whereas women writers were more likely to use androgenous images, if they addressed gender at all. Men's spiritual ideals focused on conversion and renunciation of the world of wealth and power (for which they invoked gender inversions to symbolize giving up those statuses), whereas women's religiosity emphasized continuity and a relationship to Christ's humanity (and thus physicality). Gender distinctions created genuine restrictions on how women could express their opinions and experiences or achieve heights of spiritual "achievement." For example, both men and women sought renunciation of "the world," but women did not control enough power or wealth to give them up. Thus, women's renunciation was often limited to giving up food or other aspects of daily life over which they did have control. Nevertheless, the religiosity of these outstanding female medieval theologians and mystics was not merely the passive product of the misogynistic ideas of their time. Rather, these women appropriated cultural symbols differently, creating a positive spiritual identity for themselves and their followers (Bynum, 1986).

At the same time, religious traditions have provided women with some positive roles and images (albeit severely limited ones) that bring reward and recognition in their fulfillment. For a woman to aspire to achievements in men's arenas would be deviant and punished by the social group. She may, however, aspire to achievements in women's spheres with no competition from men and be rewarded. These values, too, are internalized. The woman who is successful in fulfilling the mother role comes to perceive herself positively in those terms. She feels good about herself because she has achieved a desired status or has performed valued roles.

In Victorian society, the cultural and religious legitimations of motherhood and women's role in the home achieved a new synthesis. The Victorian ideal of womanhood, as reflected in women's magazines and public statements in the nineteenth century, was one of "piety, purity, submissiveness, and domesticity" (Welter, 1966).[10] The emerging capitalist-industrialist society of the nineteenth century made both the home and religion increasingly marginal to the arenas of power and production. Ideological responses of many religious organizations and revivalists to this privatization struck a responsive chord among middle-class women who were enmeshed in the privatization of the home. An "evangelical domesticity" resulted that emphasized the home and women as the primary vehicles of redemption. The rhetoric of preaching and the themes of gospel hymns of this period portrayed the home as the bastion of tranquillity in a turbulent world. Woman's image was that of the keeper of this refuge who, through her piety and purity, was the foremost vehicle of redemption, in opposition to the aggressiveness and competition of the public sphere (Sizer, 1979; see also McDannell, 1986; Ryan, 1983; Taves, 1986; Welter, 1976). Thus, the religious ideology of evangelical domesticity celebrated the privatization of the home and women's roles, further reinforcing the caste distinctions between men and women. At the same time, it enhanced this narrow role in women's eyes by claiming redemptive significance for it.

Sanctions for Deviance The religious definition of gender roles is supported by religious sanctions (i.e., punishments) for deviance from them. Men as well as women are subject to negative sanctions for failure to fulfill gender role expectations, though conformity to the broader, more powerful male social role is less onerous than complying with the restrictive, less powerful female role. Religion, as we shall see in Chapter 7, is a powerful force for social control. One of the most effective sources of such social control is the individual's own conscience. The person who has been socialized into a certain way of thinking about gender roles feels guilty if he or she fails to fulfill these expectations. One young woman who had learned that "women naturally and instinctively feel great affection for their children" felt guilty

---

10. The instance of Victorian gender roles illustrates the fact that men's roles too are often limiting and burdensome. In this case, men were given the full burden of providing for the family by work away from the "comforts of home." The moral expectations of the husband/father as sole provider for a family are relatively recent in Western history.

that her initial reaction to her newborn child was not a great outpouring of maternal love.

Those who control religious power (especially in official religion) frequently use specifically religious sanctions to enforce gender roles. Recent history provides the examples of a Mormon woman excommunicated for her active support of the Equal Rights Amendment to the Constitution, and Roman Catholic priests and nuns silenced by Vatican officials for challenges to the church's treatment of women (among other issues). In Iran, the political power of fundamentalist Islam has resulted in strong restrictions of women's public roles and appearances, as symbolized by the mandate of returning to the *chador* (i.e., veil).

Historically, the intertwined power of religious organizations with other social institutions gave religion more influence in the control of deviance than in modern society. The persecution of witches in the Middle Ages (and until as recently as the end of the seventeenth century) was focused primarily on women, who were presumed weaker and therefore more vulnerable to the influences of the devil. Authorities typically singled out women who deviated from religiously established norms for females—wise women, healers, midwives. Suspected women (e.g., widows and "spinsters") were disproportionately likely to be relatively independent of men. Witch-hunts such as the massive medieval persecutions were primarily concerned with purification. Women in particular were considered threats to social purity because of cultural assumptions about their sexuality and because anomalous (i.e., independent) women were perceived as dangerous and disruptive. A substantial number of women were put to death or tortured as witches; scholarly estimates suggest that thousands of witches were killed during the Inquisition.[11] There has been no parallel persecution of men *as men,* although men were persecuted as members of other minorities (e.g., Jews).

Alternative Definitions of Women's Status and Roles

Women's Religious Groups One of the most effective social controls of women has been the limitation and prevention of separate, autonomous women's religious groups. Religion has historically had the potential for promoting social change among colonial peoples and subordinated racial and ethnic groups because, in organizing around a religious focus, such groups have often mobilized to press their social and economic concerns. Unlike racial and ethnic minorities, however, women have not generally formed separate religious groups in Western societies. Male-dominated religious organizations

---

11. Recent estimates are that 40,000–50,000 were executed for witchcraft and many thousand more were persecuted. While men made up as many as 25 percent of the victims of European witch-hunts, women were clearly more vulnerable to accusations, trials, and capital punishment (Briggs, 1996). Daly (1978) notes the widespread *religious* legitimation of violence against women. The Indian suttee—cremation of the living wife along with the body of the dead husband—and African clitoral circumcisions are among the rituals she describes as "gynocides." Daly argues that many scholars have glossed over such ritual violence toward women by calling these acts "customs." She doubts that these scholars would have referred to comparable atrocities in the Holocaust as "Nazi customs."

have been understandably threatened by the possible power of autonomous women's groups.

Medieval sisterhoods (including religious orders, lay orders, and numerous unofficial bands of religious women) offered socially approved roles for women who could not or would not fit the primary gender roles of woman as wife and mother. Socially anomalous women (again, typically widows and unmarried women) found in these sisterhoods both security and opportunities for achievement not available to other women in society. Medieval abbesses, for example, were often relatively powerful leaders of large organizations. Church officials, however, kept these groups under relatively tight control (e.g., by regulations restricting sisters' freedom to come and go in "the world"). Like other dissenting, change-oriented groups (e.g., early Franciscans), women's groups that asserted alternative roles were often co-opted and controlled.

Feminism had a specific role in the development of sisterhoods in the Anglican church during the nineteenth century (M. Hill, 1973a). The Victorian image of women, as we have seen, emphasized domesticity. Furthermore, the middle- and upper-class Victorian "lady" was educated to be an ornament in the home; her enforced leisure was evidence of her husband's social status. Women such as Florence Nightingale who asserted any other role for themselves were severely criticized. The Anglican church had dissolved monasteries and convents in its initial break with the Roman church in the sixteenth century, and in the nineteenth century strong voices were raised against reestablishing brotherhoods or sisterhoods in the church. Nevertheless, nascent feminism, combined with a considerable demographic surplus of women, exerted pressures to create acceptable social roles for women who would work in "unladylike" jobs such as nursing, running settlement houses, teaching the poor, and running hospices for derelicts. The creation of acceptable deviant roles for women was perceived as an attack on the Victorian home and women's proper duties. One bishop stated:

> The rules which I have myself laid down as most necessary in my dealing with such communities [the sisterhood] have been the following:—To point out that the first of all duties are those which we owe to our family. Family ties are imposed direct by God. If family duties are overlooked, God's blessing can never be expected on any efforts which we make for His Church. Every community, therefore, of Sisters or Deaconesses ought to consist of persons who have fully satisfied all family obligations. (cited in M. Hill, 1973a:277)

Even among those who approved of the idea of women's religious groups, there was disagreement about the degree of autonomy to allow them. Religious sisterhoods were much more problematic than brotherhoods to church authorities because sisterhoods allowed the possibility of women directing their own work and running their own organizations. The less radical alternative of the office of deaconess (in which women workers would be under the direct supervision of male clergy) was proposed because "women need more support than men" (cited in M. Hill, 1973a:276). Women were gradually allowed into "unladylike" areas of work, partly through the transitional institution of the sisterhood. The potential for feminist protest was, however, somewhat co-opted, especially as women's groups were brought under greater control by authorities and their work was gradually redefined as "women's work." Nursing, for example, was consistent with the serving and nurturant image of women as dependent on (male) doctors for decision making. As women's professions became more respectable, women's religious groups became less important as vehicles for feminist aspirations.

Women's religious groups still remain potentially expressive of women's social and religious interests. Within Roman Catholicism, much of the pressure for the ordination of women comes from the ranks of women's religious orders. Some women's groups have creatively used their greater education and structural independence. While dissenting from the patriarchal stratification of their churches, some women are "defecting in place" (Winter et al., 1994). They are forming their own small group supports for women's spirituality without leaving their churches. They are exploring alternative rituals and religious symbolism that embody their gender and their sexuality (Neitz, 1995).

The main arena for the expression of feminist concerns has become public-sphere organizations. The privatization of religion means that religious achievements are similar to domestic accomplishments: Neither really "counts" as a symbol of achievement in the larger society. Conflicts within religious collectivities over appropriate roles for women primarily result from religion's tendency to continue legitimating traditional roles for women in *both* public and private spheres.

New Religious Movements New religious movements are often a vehicle for the assertion of alternative religious roles for women. Religious movements of nonprivileged classes have typically allotted equality to women, at least in their formative years (Weber, 1922/1963:104–105). Many of the medieval millenarian movements initially allowed women virtual equality. The Protestant Reformation's principle of the "priesthood of all believers" was initially interpreted as opening important roles to both laywomen and laymen. Although their contemporaries were scandalized by the fact, numerous seventeenth- and eighteenth-century religious movements allowed women equal roles in public preaching and prophesying (Garrett, 1987; Mack, 1992; Stuard, 1989).

Many religious movements of the eighteenth century, and later the Great Awakening, granted equality to women. The Shakers believed that their founder, Mother Ann Lee, was the Second Coming of Christ, thus completing the manifestations of Christ (male and female). The Society of Friends (Quakers) was emphatically egalitarian, encouraging women to equal education, leadership, and public-speaking roles. Quaker women such as Susan B. Anthony, Alice Paul, and Lucretia Mott were leaders in the women's suffrage movement; they were also prominent in movements for abolition of slavery, prison reform, fair treatment of Native Americans, and other human rights causes (Bacon, 1986). The late Victorian period was one of nascent feminism, and alternative women's roles were an important part of the beliefs and practices of Pentecostal and Holiness religion, Salvation Army, Seventh Day Adventists, Spiritualism, Christian Science, Theosophy, and New Thought (Baer, 1993; Bednarowski, 1983, 1992; Braude, 1985, 1989; Gilkes, 2001; Robertson, 1970:188, 189; Wessinger, 1993).

New religious movements are more amenable to alternative gender roles because they are based on an alternative source of authority. Traditional ways of doing things are protected by the established religious collectivity, but new religious movements are often based on charismatic authority (see Chapter 7), which is not bound by tradition. The charismatic leader says, in effect, "You have heard it said that . . . , but I say to you. . . ." This new source of authority allows a break from tradition. Weber (1922/1963:104) points out that as the emphasis on charisma fades and the movement becomes established, these movements tend to react against keeping women in roles of authority, typically redefining women's claims to charismatic or other authority as inappropriate or dishonorable behavior. This process is illustrated by changes in the Assemblies of God. In its early years, the Assemblies of God was relatively open to women assuming preaching and pastoral roles because of its emphasis on the "gifts of the Holy Ghost" as a basis for authority and leadership. As the movement became more formalized and bureaucratic and as it came more under the influence of other conservative religious groups' biblical literalism and attitudes toward women, the Assemblies of God greatly restricted women's leadership and decision-making roles. The proportion of women pastors declined from a high in 1915 of 13.5 percent to 1.3 percent in 1983 (Poloma, 1989). Similarly, while always subordinate to male authority, women in the early years of the Mormon church (Latter-Day Saints) had numerous leadership opportunities, but as the movement became established there was greater emphasis on the (male) priesthood line and priesthood authority, thereby greatly increasing the value of men (Cornwall, 1994).

The role of women in developing religious movements is thus a result of alternative sources of authority and power. Many of these movements are understandably appealing to women who are excluded from status and privilege in the dominant religions. Weber (1922/1963:104) accounts for some of the appeal of Christianity and Buddhism by noting that relative to the religious competitors of their times and regions, their subordination of women was less extreme. Similarly, the religious movements of the late Victorian era appealed to women because of their alternate definitions of women's roles.

Several emerging religious movements also focus on gender roles but generally reassert traditional rather than new ones. Thus, the Jesus People, neo-pentecostal movements, evangelicalism, Hare Krishna (Krsna Consciousness), and the Unification Church (of Reverend Moon) define women's roles very conservatively. One study found that many women who "converted" to Orthodox Judaism wanted a traditional religion that offered unambiguous and unchanging gender role expectations and legitimated their desires for a family (Davidman, 1991). Another study describes how a pentecostal women's movement, Women's Aglow, allows women to share experiences of hurt (and sometimes, downright abuse) in a supportive environment, while simultaneously promoting women's submission to men as the authoritative decision makers in all important arenas of life. When these women spoke of their experiences of obtaining god's power, their usage referred to the "power" to live godly lives, not to authority or control (Griffith, 1997a, 1997b; see also Ingersoll, 2003 [forthcoming]). Thus, some newer religious movements may attract women precisely because they reassert traditional, nonmodern gender roles, whereas other religious movements attract other women because they offer totally new ways of thinking about gender and spirituality.

An interesting by-product of the globalization of some Asian religions is that they attract some American and European women by their alternative roles for women. One well-known female Zen (Buddhist) teacher said that she had experienced a deep calling to become a priest, but had been compelled by the sexism of the Church of England (i.e., Episcopalian Church, which at that time, did not allow women's ordination) to turn away from Christianity. To fulfill her spiritual calling, she became a Buddhist monk in a foreign country with a foreign language. Unlike new religious movements from the Hindu or Christian traditions, many Buddhist groups appear to be open to an androgynous leadership style for women (and for men), perhaps because of Buddhism's long tradition of valuing balance between male and female qualities (Puttick, 1997:175–195).

Can official religion create or encompass new or changing roles for women? Sociological analysis suggests the answer is a qualified yes. On the one hand, religious images and symbols are elastic; they can be changed and reinterpreted. On the other hand, traditional images and symbols of women are generally negative and resistant to change. Because much of the power of symbols and ritual is in their reference to tradition, they are essentially conservative. Although religious movements are able to express women's dissent and create new social roles, religious movements have historically returned to traditional, hierarchical, or bureaucratic forms of authority as they become settled—and in so doing have reverted to less innovative and more submissive roles for women. Women's religious groups have the potential of focusing and asserting their social concerns; yet they have been historically controlled and co-opted by (male) authorities of the dominant religion.

Nonofficial Religion While the dominant religious groups have allocated women few if any important ritual roles, women have often found important symbolic roles outside the approved religious structure. Women have been prominent as healers, mediums, and midwives. These roles often paralleled approved religious or medical roles and functions. Just as men have been prominent in official religion as it became a differentiated institution, women have been important in "popular" or nonofficial religion. Nonofficial religion has provided women with a *chance to express their own specific concerns for meaning and belonging*. Midwifery, for example, has traditionally been a highly spiritual role (see Dougherty, 1978).

In nonofficial religion, women have opportunities for leadership and power, as exemplified by the status of women mediums, faith healers, and astrologers (Bednarowski, 1983; Braude, 1985, 1989; Brown, 1991; Haywood, 1983; Puttick, 1997). Nonofficial religion has likewise offered black and Latina women opportunities for ritual leadership and power. For example, Latina women served in nonofficial religious roles as *partera* (midwife), *rezadora* (prayer leader), and *curandera* (healer) in addition to their religious roles in the home (Díaz-Stevens, 1994).

The goddess movement explicitly redefines women's spiritual, social, emotional, and physical roles. The goddess is an image, or symbol, of the divine that is contrary to the image used by patriarchal religions (such as much of the Judeo-Christian heritage). Although much of the amorphous goddess movement is self-consciously outside traditional religious groups, some adherents consider themselves Christians or Jews who are seeking new bases for spirituality in their traditions. Some Wiccans (i.e., practitioners of witchcraft) use the conception of the goddess to balance the gender of the deity as *both* male and female, often combining the idea with a call to a nonhierarchical religion. Others emphasize the goddess as a basis for women's power. One theologian writes:

> The basic notion behind ritual magic and spell-casting is energy as power. Here the Goddess is a center or focus of power and energy: she is the personification of the energy that flows between beings in the natural and human worlds. (Christ, 1987:127)

Some neo-pagan groups take the image of goddess literally, trying to enact older pagan practices dedicated to goddess worship. Others use earlier pagan goddess-imagery more loosely, eclectically weaving old symbols and practices together with new ones to create a new, nonpatriarchal women's spirituality (Neitz, 1990; see also Berger, 1999; Jacobs, 1990).

Although nonofficial religion can be organized as specifically feminist dissent, most nonofficial religion promotes alternative gender roles for women (and men) only indirectly—by providing alternative "world images" (Weber, 1920/1946:280). Women throughout the ages have asserted alternative roles for themselves through religious expression.

Conclusion

Religious groups' treatment of women's roles and women's sexuality is essentially an issue of *power*. If women obtained greater power than they have traditionally had, they could redefine themselves religiously and socially. On the other hand, many religious legitimations and organizations presently work against their obtainment of that power.

This Extended Application, while focusing on women's roles, illustrates more broadly how religion comes to embody and further legitimate caste stratification and power. Our analysis suggests that nonofficial religion sometimes represents one form of counterassertion (albeit often incoherent and fragmented) of power and self-worth by those excluded from power in official religion. If this is true, we need to pay more serious attention to nonofficial religion and its complex relationship with official religion.

SUMMARY

This chapter has contrasted official religion and its characteristic forms of individual religiosity with nonofficial religion and religiosity. Official religion is a set of beliefs and practices that are prescribed, regulated, and socialized by organized, specifically religious groups. Nonofficial religion, by contrast, is a set of religious and quasi-religious beliefs and practices that are not accepted, recognized, or controlled by official religious groups. Official religion is relatively coherent and organized, but nonofficial religion includes an assortment of unorganized, inconsistent, and heterogeneous beliefs and practices.

The official model of religion is clearly identifiable. Its elements—doctrine, cultic expression, ethics, and organization—are mediated by religious institutions. These institutions consolidate and control the religion's definitions of what it stands for. The relative specificity of these official models of religion enables researchers to develop measurable criteria of religiosity. Such measures are, however, bound to the orthodox official models of religion, making them of limited use in understanding religious change and nonofficial religion. Nonofficial religion is more widespread than generally recognized, and it overlaps official religion in both content and adherents.

The Extended Application demonstrates how religion influences women's gender roles and identities. Religious organizational structure, myths, and symbols embody and legitimate subordinate caste status for females—a point of conflict in many religious groups today. As the Extended Application suggests, some aspects of nonofficial religion involve ways by which persons who are unrecognized or even disempowered by official religion have asserted themselves. Thus, nonofficial religion and religiosity are both serious and relevant to our understanding of religion as a whole.

HINDUISM

HINDUISM: TWENTY-FIVE KEY DATES	
Date	**Event**
2750 B.C.E.	growth of civilization in Indus valley
1500 B.C.E.	arrival of Aryans in Indus valley; composition of the *Vedas*
800–400 B.C.E.	*Upanishads*
600–500 B.C.E.	Mahavira and Buddha challenge orthodox Vedic doctrine
500 B.C.E.	Aryans as far south as Sri Lanka
500–200 B.C.E.	epic poetry: *Ramayana, Mahabharata (Bhagavad Gita)*
322 B.C.E.	Chandragupta founds Mauryan Empire
100 B.C.E.–100 C.E.	rise of Bhakti literature
480 C.E.	fall of Gupta empire
680 C.E.	flourishing of Tamil Bhakti movement
788–820 C.E.	Shankara, leading philosopher
800–900 C.E.	rise of Hindu orthodoxy
1017–1137 C.E.	Ramanuja, leading philosopher
1175 C.E.	first Muslim empire in India
1469–1539 C.E.	Nanak, founder of Sikhism
1485–1533 C.E.	Chaitanya, Leader of Krishna Bhakti
1498 C.E.	Vasco de Gama visits India
1526 C.E.	beginning of Mogul Dynasty
1653 C.E.	completion of Taj Mahal
1690 C.E.	British found Calcutta
1818 C.E.	beginning of British rule
1869–1948 C.E.	Mahatma Gandhi
1885 C.E.	founding of Indian National Congress
1947 C.E.	independence from Britain; partition with Pakistan
1971 C.E.	war with Pakistan, followed by founding of Bangladesh

HISTORY

Our sketch of the historical evolution of **Hinduism** unfolds in six chronological phases: the pre-Vedic phase; the Vedic phase; the phase of native challenges to Vedic orthodoxy; the phase when Hindus responded to such challenges (by reforming, renovating, and elaborating the Vedic tradition); the phase when outside, modern Western ideas challenged reformed Hinduism, and the present phase—what we might call recent or contemporary Hinduism. The tendency of Hindu culture not to discard previous ideas and practices so much as to place new ones alongside them means that one can seldom be precise about what was waxing when and what was waning. But one can suggest the "additive" logic of the Hindu religious story by noting the new ideas and movements that slowly enlarged Hinduism into the rich and varied entity one finds today.

PRE-VEDIC INDIA

Before the first invasions of Aryans from the northwest around 2000 B.C.E., an impressive Indian culture already existed. Its beginnings stretch back to the second interglacial period (400,000–200,000 B.C.E.), and its earliest religion, if we conjecture on the basis of ancient peoples living in India today, was shamanist, focusing on the worship of nature—especially on the life force. In 1924, excavations at two sites along the Indus River, called Harrapa and Mohenjo-daro, furnished the first extensive evidence of an advanced ancient Indian culture. This culture, called the Harrapan, stretched over about 500,000 square miles and was distributed in small towns between the two main cities of Harrapa and Mohenjo-daro. Other excavations in what is now Pakistan have disclosed cultures predating the Harrapan, but this Indus Valley culture is the largest source of information about pre-Aryan Indian ways. Carbon dating suggests that the Harrapan culture flourished about 2150–1750 B.C.E., and some evidence suggests that the culture was remarkably stable throughout that period.

Harrapa and Mohenjo-daro seem to have had populations of 30,000 to 40,000. Both were about 1 mile square. That few weapons have been found suggests that their people were not very warlike. Outside each city was a citadel, which was probably used for worship rather than for military defense. There were large granaries in the cities, two-room apartments nearby for the granary workers, and high city walls. Most building was done with kiln-dried bricks, which were standardized by size. Through the city ran an excellent sewage disposal system, with terracotta pipes and manholes through which workmen could enter to clean the pipes. The houses were multistoried dwellings with thick walls and flat roofs.

The entire city plan suggests orderliness: streets were wide and rectilinear, houses had chutes for sliding trash down into collection bins, and apartments had bathrooms and toilets. Larger buildings included a bathhouse 108 by 180 feet, with a tank 20 feet wide by 39 feet long by 8 feet deep. If this tank was used like similar ones outside Hindu temples today, probably its purpose was ritual bathing.

By about 1500 B.C.E., the Harrapan culture was destroyed, after perhaps a millennium and a half of existence. The destructive **Aryan** conquerors were a nomadic people who loved fighting, racing, drinking, and other aspects of the warrior life. They came from the north where they had wandered around the Eurasian steppe with their herds of cattle. (The later

selection of the cow to be a specially revered animal in Hinduism is due to its connection with this ancient Aryan heritage.) Their name means "from the earth" or "noble." All European languages (except Finnish, Hungarian, and Basque) are related to the Aryans' language. The Aryans (or related tribes) pushed through Greece, Italy, Iran, and India during the second millennium B.C.E.

The Aryans moved by horse, ate meat, and hunted with bow and arrow. They knew about iron and fashioned good weapons. Like many other warrior, nomadic peoples (for example, the Celts), they loved storytelling and singing. Indeed, their culture and religion were highly verbal. Their society was male dominated, with a primarily patriarchal family structure, priesthood, and pantheon of deities. Their main deity Indra was exuberant and warlike—a boaster, a thunderbolt thrower, a big drinker, a slayer of dragons. He ruled by seizure rather than inheritance. He had created this world by aggressively seizing the waters of heaven, releasing them, and fashioning the earth. Perhaps Indra was originally a chieftain or culture hero and only later a leading god, but from their earliest time in India, the Aryans undoubtedly looked to him as the source and model of their prowess in war.

These two peoples, the conquerors and the conquered, thus contributed to the beginnings of Hindu culture. If the Harrapan culture was representative, the people who came before the Aryans in the Indus Valley were stable city dwellers who perhaps developed (or took from earlier peoples) important fertility rites. The Aryans were a rough, fighting people who had a much simpler technology than the Harrapans but whose poetry was imaginative. These Aryans became the dominant force militarily and politically, imposing their will and their deities on the subjugated Harrapans (also known as Dravidians or Sramanic people). Inasmuch as the Aryans produced the official scripture of Hinduism, the **Vedas**, Aryan culture always had more official status.

However, Indian culture never lost its native Dravidian features, especially in the less Aryanized south. At most these tendencies were dormant for a while. After the demise of Vedic culture, Dravidian interests in fertility reemerged. The complex devotionalism of later Hinduism is best explained in terms of many non-Aryan factors.

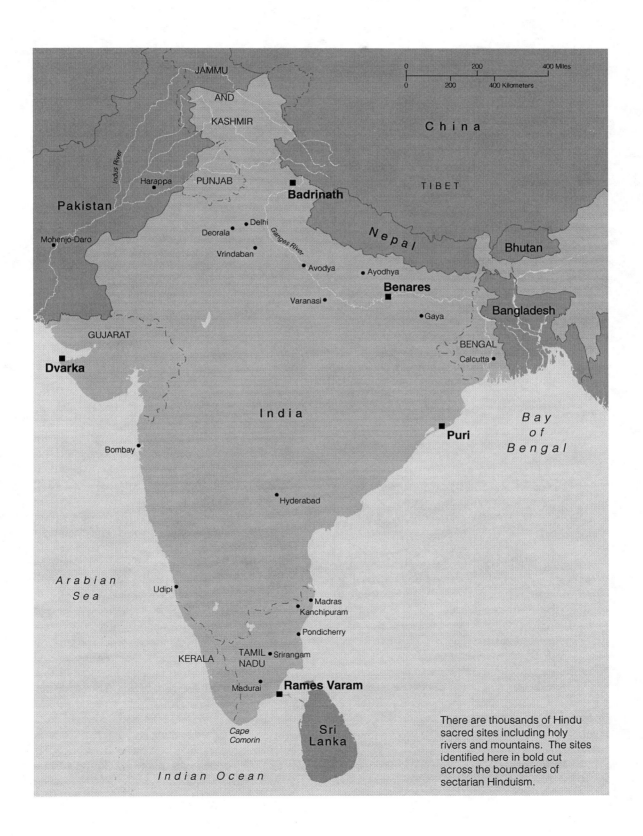

There are thousands of Hindu sacred sites including holy rivers and mountains. The sites identified here in bold cut across the boundaries of sectarian Hinduism.

VEDIC INDIA

By *Vedism* we mean the culture resulting from the mixture of Aryans, Harrapans, and other peoples of the Indus and Ganges valleys. This culture expressed itself in the earliest Indian writings, which are a collection of religious songs, hymns, spells, rituals, and speculations called the *Vedas*. It is convenient to consider them as representing the first stages of Hinduism, for although later India abandoned many of the Vedic gods and practices, the Vedas retained scriptural status throughout the later centuries, weaving themselves deeply into India's fabric.

The word *veda* means "wisdom" (cognates are the English *wit* and the German *wissen*). The Vedic pieces were originally oral. Some of the hymns found in the oldest Vedic literature may have been composed before the Aryans entered India. The hymns honoring the sky and the dawn, for instance, are remarkably like the religious literature of other Indo-Europeans, indicating that they may go back to the time before the Aryans split into their Iranian and Indian branches. Consider, for example, the following lovely verses in praise of Varuna, the deity of moral order:

> He has put intelligence in hearts, fire in the waters, the sun in the sky, and the soma plant on the hills. . . . I will speak of the mysterious deed [*maya*] of Varuna renowned, the Lord immortal, who, standing in the firmament, has measured out the earth, as it were, with a yardstick. (*Rig-Veda* 5:85:2,5)

Although Hindu doctrine has evolved over the past three millennia, the *Vedas* are still regarded as *shruti* (divinely revealed scripture). *Shruti* does not connote that divinities outside the human realm broke through the veil separating heaven and earth in order to impart light from above; as we shall see, Hinduism does not have such a remote view of the divine. Rather, *shruti* implies that the eminent holy person has heard certain things in peak experiences (often induced by the ritual drink *soma*). Therefore, Vedic literature, representing what the rishis (holy men) had heard, was considered the best and holiest presentation of knowledge.

The *Vedas* consist of four separate collections of materials. Together, these four collections are known as the *Samhitas*. *Samhitas* therefore can be a synonym for *Vedas*. The individual collections are called the *Rig-Veda, Sama-Veda, Yajur-Veda,* and *Atharva-Veda*. The *Rig-Veda* is the oldest, largest, and most important. It contains more than a thousand individual units: hymns to the gods, poems, riddles, legends, and the like. They show considerable poetic skill, which argue against their being the spontaneous poetry of freewheeling warriors or rude peasants. More likely, they represent the work of priestly leaders— the careful creation of an educated class concerned with regulating contact with the gods and maintaining its own social status.

Most of the *Rig-Veda*'s hymns have two aspects. First, they praise the god being addressed; second, they ask the god for favors or benefits. For instance, the *Rig-Veda* praises Agni for deeds that show the splendor of his status as the god of fire. (These deeds appear to be not so much mythical allusions to feats the god performed in the beginning as similes drawn from human experience. For example, Agni's flame is like the warrior's battle rush: as the warrior blazes upon the enemy, so the god of fire blazes through the brush or woods.) Then, having admired the god, the hymn singer makes his petition. In *Rig-Veda* 6:6 he asks for wealth: "wealth giving splendor . . . wealth bright and vast with many heroes." The values expressed in the *Rig-Veda* are often utilitarian: a hundred years (longevity), a hundred sons (posterity), and a thousand cattle (prosperity).

Though this ritual exchange is the most usual focus, the *Rig-Veda* has other interests. For instance, it includes petitions for forgiveness of sins (such as having wronged a brother, cheated at games, or abused a stranger) which indicate a developed ethical sense.

Some of the hymns of the *Rig-Veda* show a speculative wondering about the world, a theme developed in later sacred writings. A famous speculative text is 10:129, where the poet muses about the creation of the world. At the beginning there was no air and no sky beyond. It was, in fact, a time before either death or immortal life had begun. Then only the One existed, drawn into being by heat that interacted with the primal waters and the void. However, from desire the One started to think and emit fertile power. Thus, impulse from above and energy from below began to make the beings of the world. But, the hymn asks in conclusion, who knows whether this specula-

MAJOR *VEDAS*	
Rig-Veda	hymns manifesting mythology and prayers
Atharva-Veda	materials concerning magic of special interest to Brahmins
Sama-Veda	mantras chanted at various sacrifices of soma (ritual liquor)
Yajur-Veda	priestly textbook on the Vedic ritual as a whole

tion has intrinsic value? Even the gods were born after the world's beginning, so who can say what happened? Only one who surveys everything from the greatest high heaven knows, if indeed even that being knows.

THE VEDIC GODS. A study of the Vedic gods suggests what the earliest Hindus thought about the deepest forces in their world. The gods are many and complex (tradition said there were 330 million), but of course a few stand out as the most important. Indeed, for many later sages, all the gods were manifestations of a single underlying divinity: "They call it Indra, Mithras, Varuna, Agni, or again the celestial bird Garutman; the one reality the sages call by various names . . ." (*Rig-Veda* 1, 164.46). They are all *devas* (good divinities), as distinguished from *asuras* (evil divinities). (In Iran the terminology is just the reverse, suggesting that the Iranian-Indian split may have been theological.)

The *Vedas* cast most deities in human or animal form. Since the main feature of the *devas* was power, we may consider them functional forces: the warmth of the sun, the energy of the storm, and so on. To express these larger-than-life qualities, later Indian artists often gave the *devas* extra bodily parts. An extra pair of arms, for instance, would indicate prowess in battle; an extra eye would indicate ability to discern events at a distance.

Hermeneutical analysis of the Vedas suggests different generations of the Vedic gods. The oldest group consists of the gods of the sky and the earth that the *Vedas* share with other Indo-European reli-

gious texts. For instance, the Vedic Father Sky (Dyaus Pitar) is related to the Greek Zeus and the Roman Jupiter. Like them, he is the overarching power that fertilizes the receptive earth with rain and rays of sun. The Vedic earth is the Great Mother, the fertile female. These deities are not the most prominent Vedic gods, but they echo in the background as the oldest.

The second oldest group, whose age is confirmed by Iranian parallels, includes Indra, Mithra, Varuna, Agni, and Soma. As noted, Indra was the warrior god of the storm much beloved by the Aryan conquerors. Mithra was the god of the sun. Varuna was the god of cosmic and moral order, and Soma was the god of the exhilarating cultic drink. Known in Iran as *haoma, soma* gave visions so dazzling that it became integral to the sacramental rituals. Agni, finally, was the god of fire, whose importance increased as the sacrifice focused more and more on fire. It is worth noting that most of the deities in this second generation represent earthly and especially heavenly forces. Perhaps the storm, the sun, and the sky were all originally joined in Dyaus Pitar, but later they became separate objects of devotion.

The third generation of gods includes **Brahma** (the creator), **Vishnu** (the preserver), and **Shiva** (the destroyer). This Hindu trinity stands for the complete cycle of generation and regeneration. These deities arose after the Aryans arrived in India and so perhaps indicate Dravidian influences. We will consider them more fully below.

Finally, the fourth generation, which comes to the fore in the philosophical texts called the **Upanishads**, comprises abstract deities such as One God, That One, Who, and the Father of Creation (Eka Deva, Tad Ekam, Ka, and Prajapati). The Upanishadic writers had become dissatisfied with the concrete, world-affirming outlook at the core of the *Rig-Veda* and searched for more mystical approaches.

SACRIFICE. In the early Vedic period, the sacrifice was quite simple. The sacrifice intended to make human beings holy by giving them an operational way to please the gods. It required no elaborate rituals, no temples, no images—only a field of cut grass, some clarified butter for the fire, and soma (poured onto the ground for the gods and drunk by the participants). Later the sacrifice became more elaborate, involving chanting, reenacting the world's creation, and slaying a variety of animals. This elaboration went hand in hand with the increasing importance of the **Brahmin priests.**

One elaborate sacrifice conducted during that era involved a horse, a ceremony that lasted more than a year. In the first step of this complicated ritual, attendants bathed a young white horse, fed it wheat cakes for three days, consecrated it by fire, and then released it and let it wander for a year. Princes and soldiers followed the horse, conquering all territory through which it traveled. After one year, servants brought the horse back to the palace. During the next new moon, the king shaved his head and beard. After an all-night vigil at the sacred fire, the queens went to the horse at dawn, anointed it, and decorated it with pearls. A sacrifice of 609 selected animals, ranging from the elephant to the bee (and sometimes a human), followed.

The sacrifice reached its climax after attendants slaughtered the horse itself and placed a blanket over it. The most important queen then slipped under the blanket to have (simulated?) sexual intercourse with the horse, while the other queens and the priests shouted obscene encouragements. After this, participants ate the horse in a ritual meal. The entire ceremony fits the pattern of ancient celebrations of the new year, which often involved sacrifices and orgies designed to renew the world's fertility. Most of the symbolism centers on the virility of the king, in whose person the people hope to find strength like that of a lusty stallion.

CASTE. When one considers the distinctive organization of traditional Indian society that goes back to the Vedic roots, the word **caste** comes to mind. All human societies tend to stratify by developing social classes: differences in prestige, status, wealth or privilege. In contemporary American culture, it is theoretically possible for an individual to rise or fall in the social order based upon educational or occupational attainments, or changes in income, though about three-quarters of Americans probably end up in the social class of their parents. In classical Indian society, these social classes were fixed at birth, and one was not permitted to change one's caste assignment.

The Sanskrit word for caste was *varna*, the original meaning of which is uncertain but perhaps had connections with color (think of varnish, which em-

THE FOUR CASTES		
Highest	Brahmin	priests
Second	Kshatriya	warriors, nobles
Third	Vaisya	merchants, artisans
Bottom	Sudra	unskilled workers, peasants

phasizes the exterior color of wood). Varna mainly has referred to the division of social ranks and tasks developed by the Aryans and established by them as regulative for the India that they came to dominate. Although this social structure became more pronounced and influential in India than in the other areas (Iran, northern Europe) where Aryan ancestral stock (the proto-Indo-Europeans) prevailed, one finds that ancient Persians, Celts, Greeks, and others shared its general delineation of the main social classes. This delineation was into the three groups of priests, nobles or warriors, and commoners/farmers/merchants. The conquered Harrapan masses formed a fourth, lower caste of workers/servants/peasants. This way, the caste system was a racist attempt to keep Aryans and their descendents at the top of the social pyramid while keeping the conquered peoples out of positions of wealth and privilege.

The function of myth is to tell stories that vindicate the values that we live by today. India thought of *varna* as part of the divinely ordered cosmos—part of the heavenly scheme of things. Thus, the *Rig-Veda* (10:90) speaks of a primal sacrifice of a proto-human being that gave society its four *varnas*. Later, the most influential law code, that attributed to Manu, repeated such Vedic justification, tying the ways Indians had come to think of their principal social classes to the divinely given order of things.

The second Indian word usually covered by the English *caste* is *jati*, which refers to the many particular, familial, clanlike groups that have made Indian society a complex quilt of different groups. Each has a different set of rules governing such issues as acceptable careers, diet, marriage. Most *jatis* require endogamy: that people marry within their own groups. *Jatis* can be considered as subdivisions of *varnas*. Thus, while there might be thousands of differ-

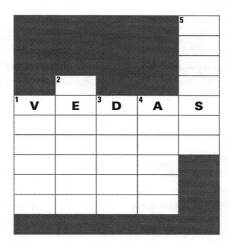

DOWN

1 Vedic god of order
2 Hinduism has millions of these.
3 The *Bhagavad Gita* advocated doing one's caste _____.
4 The invaders of India in the second millennium
5 The Brahmins were _____.

Ganesha

ent brahmin *jatis* separating the priestly caste into various subgroups who could have only limited contact with one another, all such *jatis* held something in common and were more closely connected to one another than to such members of the third social echelon (the farmers/merchants) as barbers, potters, and leather workers.

In practice, the constraints of caste and *jati* have interacted to mean that most Indians have not grown up free to pursue what work and which spouses they might have preferred. The lowest of the lowest caste are assigned to the most unappetizing tasks (e.g., working with animal hides, cleaning public toilets). Modern India has also tried to improve the lot of the untouchables, who lie at the very bottom of the caste system, but they still exist. Thus, even now, only certain groups of people carry garbage, clean homes, work in banks, and so on.

The doctrine of caste may have had an Aryan origin, but it soon came to be buttressed by doctrines of ethics (karma) and afterlife (transmigration) that had not been part of that Aryan tradition. Ideas about reincarnation had been found in some tribal societies and involved the notion that the vital force survives after death and returns to animate a new body, usually in a nearly endless, cyclical way. Each body is merely a temporary housing for the soul. Transmigration of the soul might be human to human, or human to animal.

Karma is an Indian term for the relations among past deeds, present character, and future fate. Karma is the law that governs advancement or regression in this physical world of deaths and rebirths. Karma is the reality that all acts have unavoidable consequences. Karma also explains one's status: A person's present life is shaped by that person's past lives. The only way to escape the round of rebirths, the pain of this *samsara* world, is to advance in one's next life, and this is done by meritorious deeds.

If we put all three together—caste, transmigration, and karma—we get a clever justification for the unjust assignment of social status at birth. The high-caste brahmin could say to the low-caste worker: "It is fair that I was born to the top of the social pyramid and you to the bottom. We are each merely reaping the rewards of our previous lives. If you want a better deal next time around, do the duties of your caste during this life. If you don't, you will be born in lowly animal form next time."

THE *UPANISHADS*. Even during the times of the *Rig-Veda,* people were unhappy with the priests' constant prating. A satire in 7:103, for instance, likens them to frogs croaking over the waters. Intellectuals desired something more satisfying than an understanding of sacrifice that tended to remain on the surface.

As the power of the Brahmin priests increased, the warrior-noble caste grew envious and frustrated. Some of them personally rejected the ritualistic sacrificial formula of spirituality and even their own place in the caste order. Leaving their assigned duties, they went off in the forest and attempted to attain spirituality by means of a more personal (as opposed to formal ritual) notion of sacrifice. The result of this was a series of books known as the *Aranyakas* ("forest books") that took the symbol of the fire's heat (used in the priestly sacrifice) and used it as a personal metaphor for self-discipline.

A related practice was that of **yoga.** It is an Indian term for discipline: to escape pain and gain enlightenment, one had to marshal one's energies and put oneself under discipline. Both Hinduism and Buddhism fostered several different yogas, most of which ideally were in the service of liberation from *samsara.* When we hear the term, we usually think of the physical yogas aimed at improving the body: posture, tone, relaxation, digestion, suppleness, and the like. Those were merely the means; the ends were liberation from the *samsara* world. A discipline focused on the breath might try to unify the matter-spirit composite. The most prestigious yoga was the *jnana* discipline, aimed at gaining an intuitive understanding of reality and so

liberation. The yoga of trance and meditation sought to gain better mental concentration.

These practitioners of yoga and writers of the *Aranyakas* were not priests or prophets, but mystics who hoped that the concentration gained in meditation or yoga would lead to a state known as *samadhi.* This is an Indian term for the highest state of meditation or yoga. *Samadhi* usually is described as an imageless trance, an experience of pure human spirituality. Essentially, it means self-surrender, so that one's life more and more stands free of either worries about the past or troubling anticipations of the future. The yogi who realizes *samadhi* has such control over the body and spirit that the usual constraints of space and time seem broken.

Moksha is the Hindu term for release, liberation, salvation from the bondage of a *samsara* world of suffering in a cycle of death and rebirth. *Moksha* necessarily must be approached "negatively," by way of denying the limitations afflicting daily human experience. So it implies what is not limited, mortal, bound to the cycle of births and deaths, afflicted with desire, deluded, and the rest. Positively, Hindu thinkers have spoken of being, awareness, and bliss. *Moksha* is lasting, self-sufficient, truly real, in contrast to the fragility, passingness, and dubious reality of ordinary existence. It is full of the light of knowing and the joy of loving. As such, it can symbolize a good sufficient to justify the asceticism and toil necessary to escape *samsara.*

Insofar as yoga is trying to defeat *samsara* and lead the person (or the *atman*) to an unconditioned state (*moksha*), *samadhi* is a sort of down payment on *moksha,* much as mystical experience serves many theistic traditions as a down payment on heavenly communion with the deity.

The crowning achievement of this period was a series of books completed from 800 to 300 B.C.E. known as the *Upanishads.* The term means "to sit apart" (in the forest, away from the workaday world). The *Upanishads* reveal the intellectuals' turn to interiority, which furthered this reinventing of the sacrifice (less a matter of slaughter, ritual, and words; and more a matter of soul cleansing and dedication to the divine powers).

The word *Upanishad* connotes the secret teaching that one receives at the feet of a guru (spiritual

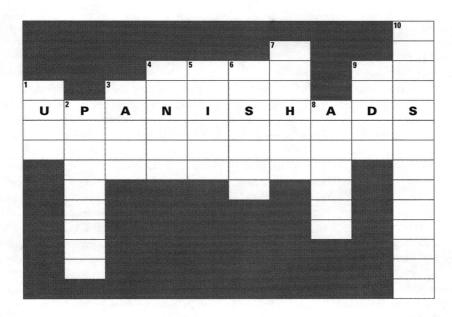

DOWN

1 Spiritual teacher, holy man
2 Doctrine that everything is God
3 Good deeds lead to better rebirth.
4 Doctrine that everything is one reality
5 Doctrine of noninjury to all living creatures
6 Writers of the *Upanishads* were _____.
7 Upanishad name for God
8 One who practices self denial
9 Country where the *Upanishads* were written
10 Doctrine of afterlife

teacher). Out of hundreds of treatises (over the period from 800 to 300 B.C.E.), a few *Upanishads* came to the fore. They show that the intellectuals embraced a variety of styles and ideas and that their movement was poetic as much as philosophical. Whether poetic or philosophical, though, the movement's goal was quite religious: intuitive knowledge of ultimate truths, of the unity behind the many particulars of reality.

The *Upanishads* focus on two terms: **Brahman** and **Atman**. (*Brahman is* the foundation of everything, a pantheistic conception that God is everything and everything is God. Do not confuse this term with the Brahmin caste of priests or with the previously discussed Brahmanist phase of Hinduism.) *Atman* means the vital principle or deepest identity of the individual person—the soul or self. Probing this reality by thought and meditation, the Upanishadic seers moved away from Vedic materiality to spirituality. The internal world, the world of atman and thought, was a world of spirit.

Combining these new concepts of Brahman and Atman, some of the Upanishadic seers found a coincidence—the basic reality within and without, of self and the world, was the same. Atman is Brahman. So in the *Chandogya Upanishad* 6:1:3, the father

Uddalaka teaches his son Shvetaketu that Shvetaketu himself is, most fundamentally, Brahmanic ultimate reality: *Tat tvam asi* ("That thou art"). The soul and the stuff of the world are but two sides of the same single "be-ing" or "is-ness" that constitutes all existing things.

In the *Brihad-aranyaka Upanishad,* one of the most important, an interesting discussion occurs between the thoughtful woman Gargi and the sage Yajnavalkya about the ultimate "warp" of reality (the relevant definition of *warp* is "the basic foundation or material of a structure or entity"). Gargi has pressed the sage to tell her about the weave of reality: "That, O Yajnavalkya, which is above the sky, that which is beneath the earth, that which is between these two, sky and earth, that which people call the past and the present and the future—across what is that woven, warp and woof?" The sage answers that she is asking about space. Sensing that she still has not gained the final goal of her inquiry, Gargi presses one further question: "Across what then, pray, is space woven, warp and woof?" This is the capital question, eliciting from the sage the capital answer: the Imperishable.

To describe the Imperishable, Yajnavalkya launches into a long list of negatives: "It is not coarse, not fine, not short, not long, not glowing, not adhesive, without shadow and without darkness, without air and without space, without stickiness, odorless, tasteless, without eye, without ear, without voice, without wind, without energy, without breath, without mouth . . . without measure, without inside and without outside." Only by denying the limitations implied in each of these attributes can the sage suggest the unique, transcendent character of ultimate reality.

The Imperishable does not consume anything and no one consumes it. It is the commander of the sun and the moon, the earth and the sky, and all other things. Without the knowledge of the imperishable, other religious attainments are of little worth: "Verily, O Gargi, if one performs sacrifices and worship and undergoes austerity in this world for many thousands of years, but without knowing that Imperishable, limited indeed is that [work] of his." For the Imperishable is the unseen Seer, the unthought Thinker, the only One that understands. "Across this Imperishable, O Gargi, is space woven, warp and woof."

The Imperishable, then, is the Upanishadic sage's ultimate wisdom. When pressed for the material cause of things, the "that from which" everything is made, Yajnavalkya can only say "Something that is of itself, something that does not perish."

This is a characteristic answer, one that many sages, West as well as East, have fashioned. Pushing off from the perishable nature of the things of sensory experience, they have conceived of the ultimate foundation of reality as other than sensible things, other indeed than anything within the range of human experience. Reality does not perish, pass away, or suffer change. To uphold the world it must be different from the world. Either in the midst of worldly flux, or apart, it must surpass the "world," the mental construct of the material and spiritual whole that we limited humans fashion.

On the other hand, the ultimate material cause of things must be enough like us, discernible by us, to warrant our giving it negative names and seeking to know it. Were it absolutely other, completely apart from our human realm, we could not even discuss it negatively. It was by pondering this equally primordial fact that the Upanishadic seers came to focus on the human spirit or soul as the best analogue or presence of the Ultimate. This spirit or soul (Atman) seemed the best candidate for the presence of the Ultimate that makes human beings exist. While they live, human beings are imperishable: something keeps them from total change and decay. Thus while they have a given identity they draw upon the Imperishable, depend upon It, and express It. Between It and them must obtain a connection, maybe even an identity. Certainly the most real part of them is the presence of the Imperishable, without which they would actually perish. So perhaps the best way to regard them (ourselves), or anything, is as a form of the Imperishable, one of its myriad extrusions or expressions. If so, one can say that, in the last analysis, only the Imperishable is real or actual or existent. Everything else at best receives a passing reality from the temporary presence to it, presence in it, of the Imperishable. For that reason, Yajnavalkya can rightly call it "that across which even space is woven, warp and woof."

For the Upanishadic thinkers, this realization was liberating because it avoided the multiplicity, externalism, and materialism that had often corroded the

CASE STUDY: THE *ISA UPANISHAD*

The *Isa Upanishad,* one of the shortest, offers a good specimen of the Upanishadic style. Robert Hume, a respected translator of the *Upanishads* into English, divides the Isa into eighteen stanzas.

The strong emotions the stanzas of the *Isa* display remind us that the Upanishadic seers were religious philosophers—people pursuing a vision that would bring them *moksha*. The *Isa*'s passionate quest for a single principle to explain the diversity of the world's many phenomena also reinforces the impression that many of the Upanishadic seers had grown soul-sick from the complexity of the Hindu religion.

The first stanza of the *Isa* announces the monistic theme: Unless we see that the Lord (Isa) envelops all that exists, we misunderstand reality. There must be a stable principle giving rest to all the moving things. Religious people renounce all these moving things and so come to enjoy human life. Such renunciation takes them away from coveting the wealth or possessions of other people, which so frequently is a cause of sadness.

Stanza 2 develops this basis of freedom. It is possible to live in the world, performing the duties of one's station, without being attached to one's deeds. In that case, the deed does not adhere to the personality or weight it down. **Detachment** therefore is the antidote to karma. If one is free from concern about the effects of one's actions, one can work for *moksha*. But, as stanza 3 emphasizes, those who do not detach themselves receive a stern punishment after death. If they have slain the Self (the presence of Brahman within) by desirous, badly motivated deeds, they will go to dark worlds ruled by devils.

Stanza 4 shifts back to a positive viewpoint. The One that does not move, that stands free of the changing things of the world, is swifter than the human mind and senses. Wisdom is placing one's action in this One, reposing one's self in what is so swift it is stable.

Human life therefore faces a paradox, as stanza 5 shows. The principle underlying everything that exists seems both to move and not to move. Insofar as it is the inmost reality of whatever exists, it moves in all things' movement. Insofar as it gives all these things their basis, it is free of their movement, self-possessed rather then dependent on another. So, too, the One can be both far and near, both outside and within any being of the samsaric world.

Stanza 6 suggests a focus to bring this blur into clarity. By looking on all beings as though they reposed in the Self (the world's soul), and looking at the Self as though it were present in all things, the wise person stays close to the Brahman that is the world's ultimate significance.

According to stanza 7, the profit in this focus is the freedom from delusion and sorrow it brings. The person who perceives the unity of reality, seeing the single Self everywhere, achieves a knowledge and joy that the ignorant, mired in the world's multiplicity, never know.

This leads, in stanza 8, to an imaginative flourish. Picturing the world ruler, the human being who has realized full human potential, the Isa unfurls a flag of glowing attributes: wise, intelligent, comprehensive, self-sufficient. By dealing with what is bright, bodiless, pure, and unaffected by evil (by dealing with the Self), this person has reached the summit, come to stand close to eternity.

Stanzas 9 and 10 are quite mystical, probing the nature of religious enlightenment. If those who worship ignorance (who neglect the Self) go into a blind darkness, those who delight in true knowledge go into a greater darkness or mystery, a state beyond the dichotomy between knowledge and non-knowledge.

Stanza 11 adds another dimension: The wise person, holding knowledge and non-knowledge together, passes over death and gains immortality.

The "beyond" or transcendent character of true enlightenment appears even more clearly in stanzas twelve and thirteen. Both non-becoming (changelessness) and becoming (change) can be illusory. The ultimate relevance of Brahman transcends such oppositions. The saving intuition that brings *moksha* takes the perceiver to another realm, where the dichotomies and antagonisms thrown up by ordinary human intelligence do not pertain. According to stanza 14, this saving intuition also conjoins becoming and destruction. If one understands their relation, he can ride destruction across the chasm of death, ride becoming to the far shore of immortality.

The *Isa* concludes prayerfully, in stanza 15 praising the sun as a cover of reality and asking divinity to uncover its face, that we might fulfill our primary human obligation, which is to grasp

reality. (Note that this prayer is answered in the Bhagavad Gita.) Stanza 16 calls divinity the nourisher, the sole seer, the controller of fortunes, the one who is yonder yet the inmost reality of the personality. Stanza 17 prays that while our body ends in ashes, our breath may take us to the immortal wind. This will happen if we remember our purpose, grasp the import of our deeds. The Isa's last prayers, in stanza 18, are addressed to Agni: Lead us to prosperity by a godly path, you who know all the ways. Keep us from the crooked ways of sin, for we want to offer you ample adoration.

ĪŚĀ UPANISHAD

Recognition of the unity underlying
the diversity of the world

1. By the Lord (*īśā*) enveloped must this all be—
Whatever moving thing there is in the moving
world.
With this renounced, thou mayest enjoy.
Covet not the wealth of anyone at all.

Non-attachment of deeds on the person
of a renouncer

2. Even while doing deeds here,
One may desire to live a hundred years.
Thus on thee—not otherwise than this is it—
The deed (*karman*) adheres not on the man.

The forbidding future for slayers of the Self

3. Devilish (*asurya*) are those worlds called,
With blind darkness (*tamas*) covered o'er!
Unto them, on deceasing, go
Whatever folk are slayers of the Self.

The all-surpassing, paradoxical world-being

4. Unmoving, the One (*ekam*) is swifter than the
mind.
The sense-powers (*deva*) reached not It,
speeding on before.
Past others running, This goes standing.
In It Mātariśvan places action.

5. It moves. It moves not.
It is far, and It is near.
It is within all this,
And It is outside of all this.

6. Now, he who on all beings
Looks as just (*eva*) in the Self (*Ātman*),
And on the Self as in all beings—
He does not shrink away from Him.

7. In whom all beings
Have become just (*eva*) the Self of the
discerner—
Then what delusion (*moha*), what sorrow (*śoka*)
is there
Of him who perceives the unity!

Characteristics of the world-ruler

8. He has environed. The bright, the bodiless, the
scatheless,
The sinewless, the pure (*śuddha*), unpierced by
evil (*a-pāpa-viddha*)!
Wise (*kavi*), intelligent (*manīsin*), encompassing
(*paribhū*), self-existent (*svayambhū*),
Appropriately he distributed objects (*artha*)
through the eternal years.

ĪŚĀ UPANISHAD *continued*

Transcending, while involving,
the antithesis of knowing

9. Into blind darkness enter they
That worship ignorance;
Into darkness greater than that, as it were, they
That delight in knowledge.

10. Other, indeed, they say, than knowledge!
Other, they say, than non-knowledge!
—Thus we have heard from the wise (*dhīra*)
—Who to us have explained It.

11. Knowledge and non-knowledge—
He who this pair conjointly (*saha*) knows,
With non-knowledge passing over death,
With knowledge wins the immortal.

The inadequacy of any antithesis of being

12. Into blind darkness enter they
Who worship non-being (*a-sambhūti*);
Into darkness greater than that, as it were, they
Who delight in becoming (*sambhūti*).

13. Other, indeed—they say—than origin
(*sambhava*)!
Other—they say—than non-origin (*a-samb-hava*)!
—Thus have we heard from the wise
Who to us have explained It.

Becoming and destruction a fundamental duality

14. Becoming (*sambhūti*) and destruction
(*vināśa*)—
He who this pair conjointly (*saha*) knows,
With destruction passing over death,
With becoming wins the immortal.

A dying person's prayer

15. With a golden vessel
The Real's face is covered o'er.
That do thou, O Pūshan, uncover
For one whose law is the Real to see.

16. O Nourisher (*pūsan*), the sole Seer (*ekarsi*), O
Controller (*yama*), O Sun (*sūrya*, offspring
of Prajāpati, spread forth thy rays! Gather
thy brilliance (*tejas*)! What is thy fairest
form—that of thee I see. He who is yonder,
yonder Person (*purusa*)—I myself am he!

17. [My] breath (*vāyu*) to the immortal wind
(*an ila*)! This body then ends in ashes! *Om!*
O Purpose (*kratu*), remember! The deed (*krta*)
remember!
O Purpose, remember! The deed remember!

General prayer of petition and adoration

18. O Agni, by a goodly path to prosperity (*rai*)
lead us,
Thou god who knowest all the ways!
Keep far from us crooked-going sin (*enas*)!
Most ample expression of adoration to thee
would we render!

earlier stage of Hinduism. Though sacrifice and the gods continued to have a place in Upanishadic religion, they were quite subordinate to **monism** (the concept that every apparent different separate little thing was merely a manifestation of the same big thing: Brahman).

Upanishadic thinkers felt an urgent need for spiritual liberation (*moksha*), unlike the Vedists. Perhaps the writers of the *Upanishads* worked with experiences they found more dismal, depressing, and afflicting than the first Aryans had. Whereas those vigorous warriors had fought and drunk, living for the moment, these later meditative sages examined the human condition and found it sad. To express their views, they fashioned the doctrines of *samsara* and karma, which did not appear in the early *Vedas*.

Samsara (the doctrine of rebirths or reincarnation) implies that the given world, the world of "common sense" and ordinary experience, is only provisional. It is not ultimately relevant. To take it as ultimate is to delude oneself and thus to trap oneself in a cycle of rebirths. Only when one penetrates Brahman, the truly real, can one escape this cycle. Otherwise, one must constantly travel the scale of animal life (up or down, depending on one's advances or backslidings in wisdom).

THE PERIOD OF NATIVE CHALLENGE

From about 600 B.C.E. to 300 C.E., the Vedic religion, including its Upanishadic refinements, was seriously challenged by some Indians. The *Upanishads* themselves represent a critical reaction to the previous stage of sacrificial rituals, but they are considered to be a movement within Hinduism that charted its later course. The more serious challenges to Hinduism (materialistic, Jain, and Buddhist) first arose in northeastern India, where warrior tribes were more than ready to contest the priests' pretensions to cultural control. By this time (600 B.C.E.), the Aryans had settled in villages and India was a checkerboard of small kingdoms, each of which controlled a group of such villages.

The materialist approach denied the spiritual dimension of reality. These intellectuals, radically opposed to the *Vedas,* strongly attacked the doctrine that there is a reality other than the sensible or material. Ajita, a prominent materialist thinker, said that earth, air, fire, and water are the only elements—the sources of everything in the universe. According to Ajita, the differences among things just reflect different proportions of these elements. Human beings are no exception, and at death they simply dissolve back into these four elements. There is no afterlife, no reincarnation, no soul, and no *Brahman.* During the brief span of their lives, people should live "realistically," enduring pain and pursuing pleasure. Nothing beyond the testimony of the senses is valid knowledge, and what the senses reveal is what is real.

A challenge from a different direction was posed by **Jainism.** This grew from the struggles for enlightenment of its founder Nattaputta Vardhamana, called the Jina (conqueror) or **Mahavira** (great man). He was born to wealth (probably in the warrior caste)

Mahavira with vines growing around his feet to symbolize his asceticism.

but found it unfulfilling, so he launched a life of asceticism. After gaining enlightenment by this self-denial, he successfully preached his method to others. He opposed both the ritualism and the intellectualism of the Vedic tradition. The only significant sacrifice, he said, is that which conquers the self.

The Jina's followers became opponents of all forms of violence and pain inflicted on others. Consequently, they opposed the Vedic sacrifice of animals. Jains became critical of physical matter itself. They did not deny its existence, but developed a **dualistic** view of reality: soul (good) and matter (bad). The Jains viewed karma as a semisolid entity that attached itself to the individual soul through acts in-

DOWN

1. Spiritual exercise for developing mystical experience
2. Acceptance of self-denial, privation
3. Jains accepted no deity as help on the spiritual journey.
4. Jains accepted spirit and matter as reality.
5. Jain diet
6. *Ahimsa* is the doctrine of non _____.
7. Transmigration
8. Ascetic, mystical religion started by Mahavira

---

volving material objects. In memory of the Jina, whom they considered to be a great *tirthankara* ("crosser of the stream of life's sorrows"), Jains rejected eating meat or harming anything thought to have a soul. Since total avoidance of harm was practically impossible, Jains tried to balance any injury that they inflicted or bad karma that they generated by acts of self-denial or benevolence. Mahavira's death was the result of voluntary starvation.

The Jain ethic of noninjury to all life forms is known as **ahimsa**, and has some parallels in the *Upanishads*. The liberated personality would feel no desire to hurt, abuse, manipulate, or otherwise disorder other finite beings and so would be a source of peace in nature as well as society. The preference for a veg-

etarian diet can be found among many Hindu holy men by this time, but the Jains carried *ahimsa* to a greater extreme: forbidding its followers to till the soil, lest a worm be severed by the spade. Jain monks walking through the forest carry a long-handled whisk broom (to symbolically sweep their path of insects) and are supposed to wear a cheesecloth mask to avoid inhaling insects.

The Jain ethic of asceticism also has its roots in Hindu self-discipline carried to an extreme. For the devout Jain, asceticism is more than the avoidance of self-indulgence, but a complete discipline of one's desires, sensual appetites, and spontaneous chatter. This may involve vows of silence, celibacy, poverty, and solitude.

> The notion of salvation in Hinduism and Jainism is that of release from a cycle of life, death, and transmigration. The solution is to meditate until we realize our spiritual identity and escape the hold of karma. This is a very different notion of salvation from that found in Christianity, Judaism or Islam. However, can you find some passage in the Western scriptures that (perhaps if removed from its context) might lend some support to the Hindu / Jain understanding of doctrine, ethics, or ritual?
>
> **Contribute to this discussion at**
> **http://www.delphi.com/rel101**

Jain doctrine is sometimes labeled atheist insofar as it denies the existence of theistic deities who are paths to, or helpers in, our spiritual development. Mahavira challenged his followers to view reality as separate souls striving to cleanse themselves from the stain of karmic matter.

At the time of Mahavira's death, his followers were estimated to have numbered more than half a million. There were more women than men and many more laypeople than monks and nuns. For laypeople and monks alike, however, Jainism developed guiding vows, similar to commandments, which have been a principal reason for the persistence of Jainism in India to the present. The lay vows include commitments not to injure living beings, not to lie or steal, not to be unchaste, not to accumulate large sums of money, not to travel widely or possess more than what one needs, not to think evil of others, and not to pursue evil forms of livelihood. There were also positive vows to meditate and to support the community of ascetic monks.

Today there are about 2 million Jains in India. Prominent centers include Gujarat in the west and Karnatuku in the south. There is also a significant Jain population in Calcutta. In Jain temples one can see pictures of ascetics who represent an ideal of complete detachment, and the Jain doctrine of *ahimsa* (noninjury) has made a permanent impression on Indian culture.

Since we discuss Buddhism at length in the next chapter, we note here only that from a Hindu perspective, Buddhism arose, much like Jainism, as an anti-Vedic protest in the sixth century B.C.E. It was another stimulus to Hindu reform, another flowering of Vedic interest in improving people's ability to cope with an often painful world, another attack on the Vedic sacrifices and their rationale. If by "Hinduism" we mean the full-bodied tradition that evolved in response to the challenges of Jains and Buddhists, then those challenges were crucial to what Hindus later did.

BHAGAVATA. Especially in western India, movements arose that, unlike materialism, Jainism, and Buddhism, brought changes from less radical critics. A collective word for these movements is *Bhagavata* (**devotionalism**), which connotes an emotional attachment to personal gods such as Krishna and Shiva. Devotees (*bhaktas*) continue to claim that such devotion is a way of salvation or self-realization superior to sacrifice or meditation.

In the central Indian city of Mathura, devotion was focused on the god **Krishna**. Local people worshiped him as a personal god and petitioned for gifts. A wealth of legends about Krishna's birth and adventures developed that ultimately made Krishna the most beloved of the Indian deities. In one, demons tried to kill the baby Krishna, but he was stronger than they. When the demoness Putana, who had taken the form of a nurse, tried to offer him a breast covered with poison, Krishna took it and sucked out all her milk and blood. When another demon approached him, Krishna kicked the demon so hard that the demon died. Another cluster of legends describes the child Krishna's pranks (he was always stealing his mother's butter, for which he had a great appetite) and the young man Krishna's affairs with young girls. In later Hindu theology, Krishna is seen as an **avatar**, or manifestation, of Vishnu, whom we discuss shortly.

The premier work of the Bhagavata tradition is a book known as the ***Bhagavad Gita***, in which Krishna is the featured god. (The contrast between the warrior Krishna of the *Gita* and the pranksters of the Bhagavata tradition reminds us that we are dealing with a complex mythological character.) The *Gita* is set in the context of a great battle (the subject of the epic poem the *Mahabharata*), and it deals with the ethical problem of war. The conclusion that Krishna imparts to the reluctant warrior is that it is the caste duty of the warrior to fight. Drawing upon the in-

J. T. Carmody

Hindu Temple

sights of the *Upanishads,* Krishna argues that since individual souls do not die, but are recycled via transmigration, the killer does not really kill.

The *Gita* also concludes that there are many different, but acceptable paths (margas) to salvation: meditation, caste duty, and **personal devotion** to a god. The *bhakti* (devotional love) appears to be the favored path given to (Arjuna) by his guru god (Krishna). In other words, if you cannot dedicate yourself to a life of meditation contemplating the nature of Brahman, just worship lovingly any of the 330,000,000 specific deities that Hinduism offers: it's all the same. The worshiper and the god will be in a reciprocal loving relationship, and through that individual god, the worshiper will reach God (Brahman). This theistic approach has made the *Gita* Hinduism's most influential text.

The devotional cult to Shiva was another reaction against Vedism, and one of its fascinating texts is the *Svetashvatara Upanishad.* For the devotees of Shiva, this text serves much as the *Bhagavad Gita* serves Krishnaites—as a gospel of the personal god's love. It is unique among the *Upanishads* for its theism (focus on a personal god), yet it shares with the monistic *Upanishads* an effort to think logically.

The author begins by asking momentous questions: What is Brahman? What causes us to be born? Then the author rejects impersonal wisdom, materialism, and pure devotion as inadequate answers. His own answer is to interpret Brahman (the ultimate reality) as a kind of god who may become manifest if one meditates upon him. In the *Svetashvatara Upanishad,* the preferred designation for Brahman is Rudra-Shiva. Rudra was probably the Dravidian form of Indra and Shiva a god of fertility. In the post-Dravidian combination of these gods, the accent was on slaying and healing, destroying and creating—Shiva as the lord of the two rhythms of life.

MARGAS (PATHS)		
Dhyana	meditation	experience *samadhi,* unite with Brahman
Jnana	study	study scripture, understand the doctrine
Karma	work	do caste duties; detach action from its rewards
Bhakti	love	devote oneself theistically to a personal god or goddess

According to this *Upanishad,* Shiva is in everything. He has five faces and three eyes, which show his control of all directions and all times (past, present, and future). The devotee of Shiva therefore deals with a divinity as ultimate and powerful as Krishna but whose destructive capacities are more accentuated. Devotion to Krishna (Vishnu) or Shiva, then, satisfies the person who wants religious feeling and a personal god with whom to interact. Probably this sort of person predominated in Hindu history. From the legends about the gods and from the epics (especially the *Mahabharata* and the *Ramayana*), the *bhaktas* found models for religious love and for living as a good child, husband, wife, and so on.

SMRITI. During this period of challenge to Vedic authority, one other development merits attention because it was responsible for a great deal of Hindu religious literature. This movement was commentary on the Vedic literature that was intended to make it more comprehensible, practicable, and contemporary. The authority of this commentary movement is described by the word *smriti* (tradition). *Smriti* has less status than *shruti* and is considered less revelatory, more the product of human reasoning. Where the rishis intuited in mystical vision, the makers of tradition studied and reasoned. On the other hand, *smriti* had great influence in Hindu culture, because any elaboration of the social responsibilities (dharma) of the different castes involved such traditioning.

Smriti provided such diverse literatures as the Dharma Shastras, or law codes (of which the Laws of Manu are the most famous); the writings of the six orthodox schools of philosophy; legendary works such as the *Mahabharata* and the *Ramayana;* the *Puranas* (more legendary materials, often from folk or aboriginal sources); commentaries appended to the *Vedas* (for example, the *Ayur-Veda*—the "Life Veda," devoted to systematic medicine—which tradition added to the *Athavara*); tantric writings on occult and erotic matters; writings (*Agamas*) peculiar to sects such as the Vaishnavites and the Shaivites; and writings on logical or ritualistic forms of thought.

The basic form of the *smriti* was the sutra, an aphorism or short sentence designed to expose the pith of a position. By the end of the third century C.E., the *smriti* tradition had developed some very important and common ways of understanding the Vedic heritage that greatly shaped Hindu social life.

PERSONAL LIFE. From the *smriti* elaboration of Vedic tradition came another influential doctrine, that of the four legitimate life goals. These were pleasure (*kama*), wealth (*artha*), duty (*dharma*), and liberation (*moksha*). Kama was the lowest goal, but it was quite legitimate. *Kama* meant sexual pleasure but also the pleasure of eating, poetry, sport, and so on. Artha was also a legitimate goal, and around it developed learned discussions of ethics, statecraft, manners, etc. Because the person of substance propped society, wealth had a social importance and was thus more significant than pleasure.

Dharma, or duty, was higher than pleasure or wealth. It meant principle, restraint, obligation, law—the responsible acceptance of one's social station and its implications. So in the *Bhagavad Gita,* Krishna appeals to Arjuna's dharma as a warrior: it is his duty to fight, and better one's own duty done poorly than another's done well. *Moksha* meant liberation, freedom, and escape. It was the highest goal of life, because it represented the term of one's existence: self-realization in freedom from karma (the influences of past actions) and ignorance. The concept of *moksha* meant that life is samsaric—precarious and illusory. It also meant that pleasure, wealth, and even duty all could be snares.

As a complement to its exposition of life goals, the *smriti* movement also analyzed the stages in the ideal

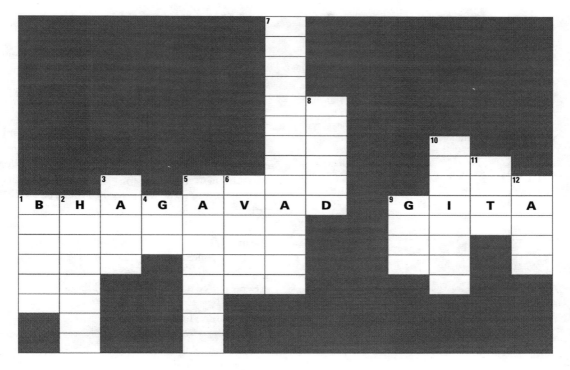

DOWN

1. Hindu term for theistic devotion to a deity
2. Religion that accepts Vedas and caste system
3. What influences rebirth
4. The *Bhagavad Gita* urges theistic devotion to any particular _____.
5. The *Bhagavad Gita* accepts polytheism amid _____.
6. Krishna was an _____ of Vishnu.
7. Doctrine of reincarnation
8. The *Bhagavad Gita* _____ the duty of caste.
9. The *Bhagavad Gita* accepts the existence of many _____.
10. The *bhakti* approach to a god is _____.
11. Krishna told Arjuna to do the _____ of his caste.
12. The *Bhagavad Gita* accepts this Hindu social structure.

unfolding of a life. For the upper classes (excluding the workers), the four stages, or *ashramas,* were student, householder, hermit, and wandering mendicant. In a hundred-year life, each would last about twenty-five years. In studenthood, the young male would apprentice himself to a guru to learn the Vedic tradition and develop his character. Depending on his caste, this would last eight to twelve years and domi-nate the first quarter of his life. Then he would marry, raise children, and carry out social responsibilities. Hindu society honored marriage, and the economic, political, and social responsibilities of the house-holder gave him considerable esteem. (Indeed, the competition posed by Jain asceticism and Buddhist calls for celibacy impelled some Hindu thinkers to reemphasize the dignity of this phase of the life cycle.)

IDEALIZED HINDU STAGES OF (MALE) LIFE		
First	student	study of scripture, meditation with a guru
Second	householder	marriage, caste-defined career, children
Third	retired	retirement, disengagement from material concerns
Fourth	mendicant	renunciation of the material world, live as wandering beggar, devoted to meditation

When the householder saw his children's children, however, *smriti* urged him to retire from active life and start tending his soul. He could still give advice and be helpful in business affairs, but he should increasingly detach himself from the world. Finally, free of worldly concern, seeking only *moksha*, the ideal Hindu would end his life as a poor, wandering ascetic. Thereby, he would be an object lesson in the purpose of human life, a teacher of what mattered most.

In effect, this scheme meant an ideal development (not often realized but still influential) of learning one's tradition, gaining worldly experience, appropriating both tradition and experience by solitary reflection, and finally consummating one's time by uniting with ultimate reality. From conception to burial, numerous ceremonies have paced the Hindu through this cycle. The most important have been adornment with the sacred thread (signaling sufficient maturity to begin studying the *Vedas*), marriage, and funerary rites. Women have fallen outside this scheme. During most of Hindu history, their schooling, such as it was, took place at home, and they were not eligible for *moksha*.

THE PERIOD OF REFORM AND ELABORATION

From about 300 to 1200 C.E., the various movements that criticized or amplified the Vedic heritage resulted in a full reform and elaboration of Hinduism. We can see in the growth of the six orthodox philosophies (described here) and the rise of the major Hindu sects developments that effectively revamped Hinduism.

A convenient distinction in the discussion that follows is that between those who reject the *Vedas* (for example, materialists, Jains, and Buddhists), called heterodox, and those who accepted the *Vedas*, called orthodox.

In other words, if you accept the *Vedas* (and caste) you are still part of the Hindu tradition, but rejecting those components means that you have gone outside of that tradition. Therefore, Jainism and Buddhism are considered different religions, but the *Upanishads* and the *Bhagavad Gita* are considered to be developments within Hinduism.

The orthodox philosophies, or *darshanas,* were conceived as explanations of *shruti* (revelation). There are six such philosophies or schools: Mimamsa, Samkhya, Yoga, Nyaya, Vaisheshika, and Vedanta (the most celebrated darshana).

VEDANTA. Shankara, the greatest of the **Vedanta** thinkers, was a Brahmin who lived about 788–820 C.E. He taught a strict monist doctrine: reality is non-dual and all variety and change should be attributed to illusion. Vedanta may be said to have systematized and deepened the teachings of the monistic *Upanishads,* taking their equation of Brahman and Atman to its logical consequence. Shankara urged celibacy and skipping the two middle stages of the life cycle so that one could pursue liberation wholeheartedly. He tried to systematize the *Upanishads* in terms of "unqualified nondualism" (*advaita*). In other words, he tried to explain the basic Upanishadic concepts of Brahman and Atman with consistency and rigor. To do this, Shankara first established that there are two kinds of knowledge, higher and lower. Lower knowledge is under the limitations of the intellect, while higher knowledge is free of such limitations.

The limitations of the intellect include its reasoning character, its dependence on the senses, and its dependence on the body to act. These limitations are all subjective, since they are limitations of the

CASE STUDY: STORIES FROM THE *MAHABHARATA*

Two stories from the *Mahabharata* illustrate the ambivalent status to which the Brahmins had fallen by the time native Indian developments were challenging and expanding the religious outlook one finds in the *Vedas*.

The first story might be called "The Curse of a Brahmin." It shows the power attributed to Brahmins and also the colorful world of supernatural forces that has long delighted Hindus. Once the great King Parikshit went hunting. Wounding a deer, he chased it deep into an unfamiliar forest. There he came upon a hermitage with an old ascetic priest sitting near some cows. The king approached the Brahmin, told him who he was, and asked him whether he had seen the wounded deer. But the Brahmin gave the king no answer, for he had taken a vow of silence. The king repeated his question, and when he again received no reply, he got very angry. Gazing around, he spied a dead snake, lifted it with the end of his bow, and hung it around the priest's neck to shame him. The Brahmin still did not utter a sound, so the king gave up and returned home empty handed.

The old Brahmin had a son, and when the son's friends heard of the incident, they teased the boy about his father's disgrace. The son asked his friends how his father had come to have a dead snake hung round his neck, and the friends told him the story of King Parikshit's visit. The son reacted angrily, cursing the king: "May Takshaka, the king of the serpents, kill this wretch who placed a dead snake upon the shoulders of my frail old father."

When he returned home, the son told his father how he had cursed the king. The old Brahmin was not pleased. Ascetics, he said, should not behave so impetuously. The son had forgotten that they lived under the protection of King Parikshit, who defended all the priests of his realm. The king had not known of the father's vow, so he should be forgiven much of his anger and bad behavior.

To try to repair the damage of his son's action, the Brahmin promised to send a messenger to warn the king. Both the father and the son knew, though, that the curse of a Brahmin could never be thwarted.

When the old Brahmin's messenger told the king of the curse, Parikshit was saddened by how he had abused the priest. He was also worried about his life, so he took counsel with his ministers about how to protect himself. They advised him to build a high platform, standing on tall posts, so that no one could approach him unobserved, and to remain there for seven days. The king followed this advice and moved his living quarters to the platform.

Toward the end of the seven-day period, the serpent king Takshaka sent several of his servants to King Parikshit disguised as ascetics. Not sensing any danger, King Parikshit allowed the ascetics to mount his platform and accepted their gifts of water, nuts, and fruit. When the ascetics had departed, King Parikshit invited his counselors to enjoy the gifts with him. But just as he was about to bite into a piece of fruit, an ugly black and copper-colored insect crawled out. The king looked at the setting sun, which was ending the seventh day, gathered his courage, and dared Takshaka to assume his real form and fulfill the Brahmin's curse. No sooner had he said this than the insect turned into a huge serpent and coiled itself around the king's neck. Bellowing a tremendous roar, Takshaka killed the king with a single mighty bite.

The story has several morals. First, it teaches the exalted status of priests. Dealing with holy things and marshaling great spiritual power by their ascetic practices, priests can perform marvels that ordinary humans can barely conceive. Therefore ordinary humans, including kings, ought to deal respectfully with priests.

Second, however, a Brahmin's very power imposes on him the responsibility to stay above petty emotions that might lead him to abuse this power. Thus the old father was deeply disturbed by his son's intemperate curse. A Brahmin's power ought to serve the people around him, improving their lives. The many Hindu stories in which priests do not act as ideally as they should suggest that the common people often found their priests wanting.

Third, the story piquantly illustrates the intimacy with nature that popular Hinduism has retained. Even though the *Upanishads* were pressing toward a purely spiritual conception of reality, in which a single Brahmin would relativize the reality of both human beings and snakes, the popular religion that came out of the period of native challenge stayed deeply immersed in the assumption that all things that exist live within physical nature. With this assumption, gods and human beings, serpents and kings, become more alike than unlike one another. This made for a very lively and imaginative "reality," in which curses such as the Brahmin's were plausible enough to teach both priests and commoners a religious lesson.

The second story from the *Mahabharata* might be called "The Well of Life." It offers a dramatic picture of the dangers of samsaric existence (life in this world).

Once there was a Brahmin who wandered into a dark forest filled with wild animals. Indeed, so ferocious were the lions, elephants, and other great beasts of this forest that even Yama, the god of death, would only enter it when absolutely necessary. The Brahmin only came to sense the wicked nature of the dark forest gradually, but then he grew more and more fearful. Panicking, he found himself running in circles, becoming more and more confused.

Finally the Brahmin looked about on every side and saw that the forest was caught in a huge net held by a giant woman with outstretched arms. There were five-headed serpents everywhere, so tall that their heads nearly reached the heavens. Then the Brahmin came to a clearing, with a deep well covered by vines and underbrush. Running frantically from a wild elephant that was pursuing him, he stumbled into the well, fell through the brush, and lodged halfway to the bottom, held upside down by a few vines.

At the bottom of the well was a huge snake. Above him waited the great elephant, which had six faces and twelve feet. To the side, in the vines that held him, were many bees that had built hives and filled them with honey. When the honey dripped toward him, the Brahmin reached out to catch it in his mouth. The more honey he ate, the more he could not satisfy his thirst for it. Meanwhile, black and white rats gnawed at the vines holding him. Though the elephant stood guard above, the serpent stood guard below, the bees buzzed on all sides, and the rats gnawed at his lifeline, the Brahmin continued to grope for more honey.

As many Hindu commentators have made clear, the story is an allegory for the human condition. The forest is the limited sphere of our life, dark and filled with dangers. The woman holding a net over the forest is the process of aging, which allows no human life to escape. The beasts of the forest are the diseases and other forces that can destroy us, while the serpent at the bottom of the well is time, which eventually receives all living things. The six-faced elephant with twelve feet is the year, with its twelve months, while the black and white rats are night and day, the devourers of our life spans. Finally, the honey is the pleasures of life, for which our thirst seems unslakable. The allegory, then, paints human life as tragic. Despite danger on all sides, we persist in pursuing transient pleasures. This is illusion with a vengeance. It is attachment making us oblivious to the great questions of what direction we should be taking and how we ought to be battling death. If we are ever to escape the painful circle of rebirths, which ensures that life after life we will suffer fear and pain, we must realize our self-imposed bondage. Plunging heedlessly into a dangerous life, we are soon fleeing in panic. We have gotten in over our heads, and before long we are upside down in an inescapable pit. Above and below, the many forms of time wait like jailers, ensuring that we stay in terrible danger. Meanwhile, day and night nibble our life span away.

Clearly, the story wants to impress upon its hearers the fearsome nature of unreflective living. If we simply pursue the pleasures of the senses and flee the pains, we will end up in the most trying of circumstances. Only by estimating correctly the lay of the land and refusing to get trapped in life's forests or fall into time's snares can we escape a tragic ending. Only by avoiding the whole battlefield of time can we enter into true freedom.

The Hindu keys to real freedom, therefore, are attention and detachment. We must watch where we are going, and we must stay free of worldly desires. The Brahmin of the story is pathetic because his calling or station especially should have educated him in these virtues. Were he noble in substance rather than just noble in name, he would not have wandered into the forest aimlessly. Simi-larly, he would not have abandoned himself to the sweet honey, forgetting his mortal peril. By meditation, sacrifice, austerities within and austerities without, he would have had hold of his time and been powerful in spirit. Then the beasts would have held no terrors, the well would have gaped to no avail. But, the story implies, few priests or few people of any station are true Brahmins, strong in spirit, so most people find aging a fearsome process.

knower, or subject. The objective limitations to knowledge, due to aspects of the known thing, are space, time, change, and cause-effect relationships. Because of objective limitations, we tend not to see or grasp reality in itself.

Higher knowledge comes by a direct perception that is free of either subjective or objective limitations. In practice, it is the direct vision that the seers who produced the *Vedas* enjoyed *shruti*. Quite likely, therefore, Shankara assumed that the Vedanta philosopher practices a yoga like that of the ancient sages. If so, he assumed that the Vedanta philosopher experiences a removal of the veil between the self and Brahman (with which the self is actually identified).

Shankara then applied this theory of higher and lower knowledge to hermeneutics, the study of textual interpretation. According to Shankara, all passages of the *Upanishads* that treat Brahman as one derive from higher knowledge; all references to Brahman as many or dual derive from lower knowledge. We can paraphrase this by saying that *Brahman in itself* is one and beyond all limitations, while *Brahman for us* (as we perceive it through sensation and reasoning) appears to be multiple—to be both in the world and beyond it, both material cause and prime mover.

With the subtlety of a great philosopher, Shankara wove the two edges of Brahman-in-itself and Brahman-for-us into a seamless whole. With the religious hunger of a mystic, he sought to correlate the within and the without. Shankara's core affirmation in his philosophical construction was that reality within is identical with reality without: Atman is Brahman. In other words, when one realizes through revelation, or higher knowledge, that there is no change, no space-time limitations, no cause-effect qualifications to the real, one then discovers that there is no self. Rather, there is only the Self, the Brahmanic reality that one directly perceives to be the ground of both internal and external being.

From the perspective of lower knowledge, there is, of course, a personal, separate, changing self. In absolute terms, though, there is one indivisible reality that is both subjectivity and objectivity, that is Atman-Brahman. Since we rarely perceive directly, we often live and move in *maya* (illusion). The world of maya is not unreal in the sense that there are no elephants in it to break your foot if you get in the way of a circus parade. The elephants in the world of maya are substantial, their dung is mighty, and their step will crush your foot. But this viewpoint has limited value. From a higher viewpoint, all that is going on is Brahman's illusion: Brahman imagining he is you and Brahman imagining that he is the elephant stepping on your foot.

VAISHNAVISM. In the period of reformation, then, keen speculative minds tried to rehabilitate the Vedic heritage by showing the reasonableness of *shruti*. It is doubtful that they directly converted more than a few intellectuals, but they did impressively demonstrate that orthodox Hinduism, through Vedic revelation, could enable one to make powerful interpretations of reality. The more popular reformations of Vedism were theistic movements that brought the energies of *Bhagavata* (devotionalism) back into the Vedic fold. Such movements centered on Vishnu and Shiva. Although both these movements were targeted at the common person's allegiance and presented quite different versions of divinity, they both advanced Vedic tradition and made a religion that combined some intellectual clout with much emotional enthusiasm. The main determinant of why one clung to one's particular god was a combination of social factors (the religion of one's family, *jati*, geographic area) and personal temperament.

The theistic religion centered on Vishnu (Vaishnavism) got its impetus from the patronage of the Gupta kings in the fourth century C.E. Perhaps the most winning aspect of Vaishnavite doctrine was its notion that the god is concerned about human beings, fights with them against demon enemies, and sends incarnations of himself (avatars) to assist humans in troubled times. In one traditional list there are ten avatars, the most important being Rama (the hero of the epic *Ramayana*), Krishna, Buddha, and Kalki (who is yet to come).

Vishnu himself is associated with water. According to tradition, the Ganges flows from under his feet while he rests on the coils of a great serpent. He is gracious to human beings, sending them many avatars of himself to help them when they are in need. Often he rides the great bird Garuda and is pictured as blue. Like an ancient monarch, he carries a conch shell, a battle discus, a club, and a lotus. Frequently he has four arms, to signify his great power to fight evil, and his consort is the much-beloved Lakshmi.

Vaishnavism promoted itself in several ways. Two of the most effective tied Vishnu to the *bhakti* cult. Between the sixth and the sixteenth centuries, the *Puranas* (legendary accounts of the exploits of gods and heroes) pushed Vishnu to the fore. The *Bhagavata Purana,* perhaps the most influential, was especially successful in popularizing the avatar Krishna. In fact, the tenth book of the *Bhagavata Purana,* which celebrates Krishna's affairs with the girls who tended cows, mixes erotic entertainment with symbolism of the divine-human relationship. As the cow-girls were rapt before Krishna, so could the devotee's spirit swoon before god. When one adds the stories of Krishna's extramarital affairs with Radha, his favorite cow-girl, the religious eros becomes quite intense. The *Puranas* were thus the first vehicle to ele-

vate Vishnu and his prime avatar to the status of *bhakti* (devotional) gods.

Vaishnavite *bhakti* was promoted in southern India during the seventh and eighth centuries. There Tamil-speaking troubadours spread devotion to Vishnu by composing religious songs. However, their wisdom was simply a deep love of Vishnu, a love that broke the bonds of caste and worldly station. The constant theme of the songs was Vishnu's own love and compassion for human beings, which moved him to send his avatars. They were so successful that they practically ousted Buddhism from India, and they were the main reason that Vishnu-Krishna became the most attractive and influential Hindu god.

Vaishnavism also had the good fortune of attracting the religious philosopher Ramanuja, who is now second only to Shankara in prestige. Ramanuja lived in the eleventh century, and his main accomplishment was elaborating the Upanishadic doctrine in a way that made divinity compatible with human love. This way goes by the name *vishishtadvaita*—"nondualism qualified by difference." It opposed the unqualified nondualism of Shankara, whom Ramanuja regarded as his philosophical opponent. For Ramanuja, the Upanishadic formula "This thou art" meant not absolute identity between atman and Brahman but a relationship: the psychological oneness that love produces. The highest way to liberation was therefore loving devotion to the highest lord who represented Brahman. Knowledge and pure action were good paths, but love was better. By substituting Vishnu or Krishna for Brahman or Ishvara, the Vaishnavites made Ramanuja a philosophical defender of their *bhakti.*

SHAIVISM. An alternative to Vaishnavism was Shaivism—devotion to Shiva. Shankara had been a Shaivite, but his intellectualism hardly satisfied the common person's desires for an emotional relationship with divinity. Shiva was the Lord of the Dance of Life and the Destroyer who terminated each era of cosmic time. From the earliest available evidence, Shaivism was a response to this wild god. It was frequently a source of emotional excesses, and its tone always mixed love with more fear and awe than Vaishnavism did.

For an extreme example, one of the earliest Shaivite sects, which the *Mahabharata* calls Pashupati, taught that to end human misery and transcend the material world, one had to engage in such rituals as smearing the body with cremation ashes; eating excrement, carrion, or human flesh; drinking from human skulls; simulating sexual intercourse; and frenzied dancing. Through such bizarre behavior, it wanted to symbolize the reversal of worldly, samsaric values that true religious devotion implied. Less defensibly, members of other sects, such as the eleventh-century Kalamukha (named for the black mark they wore on their foreheads), became notorious as drug addicts, drunkards, and even murderers. Even when Shaivites were thoroughly respectable, their religion was more fiery and zealous in its asceticism than that of the lovestruck but more refined Vaishnavites. Shaivite priests came from all social classes, and Shaivite followers often regarded the lingam as Shiva's main emblem. The lingam symbolized the penis and sexual creativity in general as well as the dedication and intensification of this power through asceticism. There were Shaivite troubadours whose poetry and hymns were a principal factor in Shiva's rise to prominence, especially in southern India.

The Shaivite movement also received royal patronage in southern India from the fifth to the tenth centuries. During those centuries the Shaivites targeted both the Buddhists and the Jains. After winning that campaign, they turned on the Vaishnavites, singing of Shiva's superiority to Vishnu. In their theology they stressed not only the Lord of the Cosmic Dance and the god of fertility and destruction but also the hidden god. (Shiva also had such forms as the householder and the ascetic, representing several stages in the life cycle.) Even the worship of the phallus was enshrouded in mystery by placing it behind a veil. In addition, Shaivites often substituted representations of Nandi, Shiva's bull, or one of his *shaktis* (female consorts) for the god himself. Finally, to stress Shiva's ability to transcend all opposites, his followers often depicted him as androgynous. Since the Shaivite often became identified with the god, Shaivism was more like yoga than was Vaishnavism, in which the worshiper and deity remained two.

The worshiper of Shiva grew conscious that he or she was a sinner through mysterious rituals and Shiva's own symbols of fire and a skull. As a result, there was less equality, less of the lover-beloved rela-

tionship, between the devotee and Shiva than what one found in Vaishnavism. The Shaivite might deprecatingly refer to himself or herself as a dog. That the god would come to such a person was pure grace. Worship, then, was essentially gratitude that the tempestuous god chose to forgive rather than destroy.

SHAKTISM. Even in the Vedas, the male deity was accompanied by a female consort, who represented his energetic force (*shakti*). In developed Hindu speculation, the male principle was cerebral, passive, and detached. The female consorts were the bodily, active, involved, creative side of the divine dimorphism. The *shaktis* needed the control of their male counterparts if they were not to run amok. Many folktales depict the awesome power of a mother goddess or wife of a powerful god on the verge of annihilation.

Shaktism (and later **Tantrism**) focused on secret lore whose prime objective was to liberate the energies of imagination, sex, and the unconscious. Insofar as Shiva's *shaktis* represented the energy of female divinity, they exemplified tantrist powers. The general name of the ancient female divinity is Maha-Devi, whom we discuss later in her form of Kali.

It is hard to know exactly what *shakti* sects had in the way of doctrine or practice, because most of their rites were secret, but one of their main doctrines was that the union of coitus is the best analogy for the relationship between the cosmos and its energy flow. This symbolism seems to have spawned a theory of parallels or dualisms, in which male-female, right-left, and positive-negative pairings all had highly symbolic aspects. Like some of Shaivism, Tantrism downplayed class distinction and violated social conventions to symbolize the reversal of ordinary cultural values implied in religious conversion and realization (of union with divine reality).

One of the many Tantrist rituals for gaining *moksha* was called *chakrapuja* (circle worship). In it men and women (Tantrist groups tended to admit members without regard for gender or caste) used a series of elements (all having Sanskrit names beginning with the letter *m*) that might facilitate union with Shakti: wine, meat, fish, parched rice, and copulation. In right-hand Tantrism, these elements were symbols. Left-hand Tantrism used the actual elements (not hedonistically but with ritual discipline, to participate in *maya*, reality's play). Other Tantrist

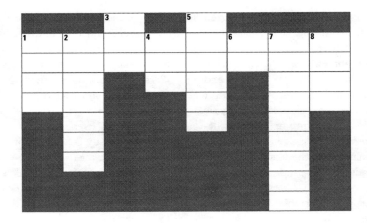

Write each word in a sequential down column:
"Take alcohol and the erotic in spiritual mode."
The second row gives the name of the sect.

practices involved meditation to arouse the *kundalini*—the snake of energy lying dormant at the base of the spine.

Overall, the reformation and elaboration of the Vedic tradition meant expanded roles for some Vedic gods and a shift of popular religion from sacrifice to devotional, theistic worship. The renovators tried to defend and extend their ancient heritage, allowing people to respond to any part of it that they found attractive. In this way they created an eclectic religion tolerant of diversity in religious doctrine and practice.

THE PERIOD OF FOREIGN CHALLENGE

From about 1200 C.E. on, Hinduism increasingly contended with foreign cultures, rulers, and religions. Islam and Christianity both made serious impacts on Indian life, and their presence is felt to this day. Islam, a factor in India from the eighth century on, first affected Indians of the Sind and Punjab regions in the northwestern part of ancient India, where Muslims traded and made military conquests. Invasions in the eleventh century put much of the Indus Valley region under Muslim control, and by 1206 Islam had conquered most of northern India. By 1335, Muslims

controlled the south as well, and their final dynasty, the Mogul, did not end until 1858.

The policies of Muslim leaders toward Hinduism varied. Many were tolerant and allowed the Indians freedom to practice their traditional ways. Others, such as the Mogul zealot Aurangzeb (ruled 1658–1707), attempted to establish a thoroughly Muslim state and so tried to stop drinking, gambling, prostitution, the use of narcotics, and other practices that were prohibited by Islamic doctrine. Aurangzeb destroyed more than 200 Hindu temples in 1679 alone, and he discriminated against Hindus in the collection of taxes, custom duties, and various other ways. The permanent changes that Islam made in Hinduism and that Hinduism made in Indian Islam are hard to determine because the two traditions are intertwined. Islamic architecture and learning influenced Hinduism deeply. On the other hand, Muslim tendencies to regard many Hindu devotional practices (for example, reverencing cows and praying to many deities) idolatrous complicated relations between the religions. Indeed, in modern times tensions have led not only to the partition of India but to much bloodshed.

One definite result of Islam's presence in India was a new religion, **Sikhism**, a blend of Hindu and Muslim traditions. It began as a result of the revelations of the prophet Nanak, a Punjabi born in 1469. Nanak's visions prompted him to sing the praise of a divinity that blended elements of the Muslim Allah and the Hindu trinity of Brahma, Vishnu, and Shiva. This God he called the "True Name." The religious prescriptions for serving the True Name that he set for his followers were rather severe and anticeremonial, steering away from Hindu pilgrimages and devotions and favoring compassion and neighborly good deeds. The Sikhs developed into a small but hardy religious band, and on numerous occasions they proved to be excellent warriors. They number over 6 million in India today, and their golden temple remains in Amritsar in the northwest. Many of the other holy Sikh sites, however, are now in Pakistan because of the 1947 partition.

Christianity has been present in India since the first century C.E., according to stories about the apostle Thomas's adventures there. It is more certain that a bishop of Alexandria sent a delegation to India in 189 C.E. and that an Indian representative attended the Council of Nicaea (325). Only in the sixteenth century, however, did the Christian missionary presence become strong, in the wake of Portuguese (and later Dutch and English) traders. The British East India Company, founded in 1600, increasingly controlled the Indian economy and trade, and after the Sepoy Mutiny in 1857 the company, which had become a sort of government, gave way to direct colonial rule. When India became independent in 1947 after almost a century of British colonial rule, it had some experience with the political ideas and social institutions of the modern West. Christianity therefore usually has had a colonial character. Christianity has not been impressive statistically in terms of the numbers of converts, with less than 3 percent of the population. The impact of Christianity is felt in other ways: hundreds of charitable institutions, especially schools.

MODERN BHAKTI. For Ramananda, a follower of the philosopher Ramanuja, the important thing was to adore God, whom Ramananda called Rama, with fervent devotion. Rama considered all persons equal. In southern India, especially among the people who spoke Tamil, the Lord Vishnu increasingly appeared as a god of pure grace. Self-concern is useless and dis-

tracting, the Tamils told their northern Vaishnavite brethren. Not works but love is redeeming.

In west-central India, from the thirteenth to the seventeenth centuries, a poetic movement called the Maratha renaissance carried the message of *bhakti*. Tikaram (1607–1649), the greatest poet of this movement, stressed God's otherness and the sinfulness of human beings. His god was not the Brahman who was identical with one's innermost self, but a free agent and lover whose goodness in saving sinners was the more impressive because of their distance from him.

In these and other movements, modern Hinduism increasingly focused on *bhakti*, moving away from Vedic orthodoxy. The singers of *bhakti* cared little whether their doctrines squared with the Upanishads or the great commentators. The notions of *shruti* or *smriti*, in fact, meant little to them. They thought that the love they had found undercut traditional views of social classes, sex, and even religions. The god of love was no creator of castes, no despiser of women, no pawn of Hindus against Muslims. With little concern for intellectual or social implications, the singers and seers who dominated modern *bhakti* gave themselves over to ecstatic love.

Perhaps the greatest representative of *bhakti* was Chaitanya, a sixteenth-century Bengali whom his followers worship as an avatar of Krishna. Chaitanya, originally a Brahmin, converted to Vaishnavism and spent his days worshiping Lord Krishna in the great Bengali temple of Puri. Increasingly his devotions became emotional, involving singing, weeping, and dancing. Somewhat typically for modern *bhakti*, Chaitanya repudiated the Vedas and nondualistic Vedanta philosophy as opposing a gracious god. All were welcome in his sect, regardless of caste, and he even sanctioned worship of a black stone, thinking it might help some followers' devotion. He stressed the followers' assimilation with Radha, Krishna's lover, arguing that the soul's relation to God is always female to male.

Yet Chaitanya also stressed the necessity to toil at religious love and opposed those who argued that grace was attained without effort. His followers deified him, seeing his unbounded religious ecstasy as the ideal communion of divinity and humanity. He was the major figure in the devotional surge toward Lord Krishna that produced some remarkable

Bengali love poetry during the sixteenth and seventeenth centuries. His movement has continued in the United States through the work of Swami Prabhupada, founder of the International Society for Krishna Consciousness. The monks in saffron robes on street corners, and his numerous publications, have made **"Hare Krishna"** part of our religious vocabulary.

Partly in opposition to the excesses of *bhakti* and partly because of the influence of Western culture, a group of Bengali intellectuals in the early nineteenth century began to "purify" Hinduism by bringing it up to the standards that they saw in Christianity. The first such effort was the founding of the group Brahmo Samaj by Rammohan Roy in 1828. Roy was a well-educated Brahmin whose contacts with Islam and Christianity led him to think that there should be only one God for all persons, who should inspire social concern and criticism of any abuses, Hindu or Christian. God should, for example, oppose such barbarism as suttee (*sati*), the relatively rare Hindu practice in which a widow climbed on her husband's funeral pyre and burned with him. In 1811, Roy had witnessed the suttee of his sister-in-law, whom relatives kept on the pyre even though she was screaming and struggling to escape. He knew that in Calcutta alone there had been more than 1,500 such immolations between 1815 and 1818. Roy pressured the British to outlaw the practice, and in 1829 a declaration was issued that forbade it (though it did not completely stamp it out). Members of the Brahmo Samaj thought this sort of social concern was essential to pure religion.

Another movement to modernize Hinduism that originated in Bengal in the nineteenth century was the Ramakrishna Mission. Its founder, Ramakrishna, was an uneducated Brahmin who became a mystic devotee of the goddess Kali, whom he worshipped as a divine Mother. After visions of Kali and then of Rama, the epic hero, Ramakrishna progressed through the Tantrist, Vaishnavite, and Vedanta disciplines, having the ecstatic experiences associated with each tradition. He even lived as a Muslim and as a Christian, learning the mystic teachings of those traditions. From such eclectic experience he developed the joyous doctrine that we can find God everywhere: divinity beats in each human heart. Ramakrishna's teachings achieved worldwide publicity through his

disciple Vivekananda, who stressed the theme of worshipping God by serving human beings. The Ramakrishna Mission has sponsored hospitals, schools, and cultural centers, and it keeps an American presence through the Vedanta Society, which has chapters in many American cities.

TAGORE AND GANDHI. In the twentieth century, these currents of domestic and foreign stimuli to religious and social reform inevitably affected the controversies over Indian nationalism and independence. The controversies themselves largely turned on the assets and liabilities of the British and Indian cultures. Not all Indians opposed the British, largely because they did not have a single national tradition themselves. Rather, Indians tended to think of themselves as Bengalis or Gujaratis or Punjabis—natives of their own districts, with their own respective languages and traditions. What the Indian tradition meant, therefore, was far from clear. This fact emerges in the lives of two of the most intriguing modern-day personalities, Rabindranath Tagore and Mohandas Gandhi.

Rabindranath Tagore (1861–1941), modern India's most illustrious writer, won the Nobel Prize for Literature in 1913. His life's work was a search for artistic and educational forms that would instill Indians with a broad humanism. For this reason, he was leery of nationalism, fearing that it would crush individual creativity and blind Indians to values outside their own country. In the West, Tagore found a salutary energy, a concern for the material world, which seemed to him precisely the cure for India's deep cultural ills. However, he despised the Western industrial nations' stress on machinery, power politics, and democracy. In Tagore's renewed Hinduism, India would give and receive—give resources for individual creativity and receive Western energies for using that creativity to improve society.

Mohandas **Gandhi** (1869–1948) was a political genius who made some of Tagore's vision practical. He trained as a lawyer in England and found his calling as an advocate of the masses in South Africa, where he represented "colored" minorities. In India Gandhi drew in part on a Western idealism that he culled from such diverse sources as the New Testament, Tolstoy's writings on Christian so-

Gandhi memorial

J. T. Carmody

cialism, Ruskin's writings on the dignity of work, and Thoreau's writings on civil disobedience. He joined this Western idealism with a shrewd political pragmatism of his own and Indian religious notions, including the *Bhagavad Gita*'s doctrine of karma-yoga (work as a spiritual discipline) and the Jain-Hindu notion of *ahimsa* (noninjury). To oppose the might of Britain, he used the shaming power of nonviolent protests with the message: Indians, like all human beings, deserve the right to control their own destinies.

Gandhi provided an updated doctrine of *ahimsa*: We can strive to minimize our violence and destructiveness by not injuring any fellow creature needlessly. By a vegetarian diet, we can minimize our injury to fellow animals. By such traditions as the protection of the cow, India has long tried to focus nonviolence on a highly visible symbol of animal vitality. Such practices foster self-restraint and compassion, virtues especially needed in modern social affairs. The phenomenon of war, which for Gandhi probably reached its most tragic expression in the

bloody conflicts between Indian Hindus and Muslims that followed upon independence from Britain, depends upon our lack of restraint and compassion. Surely a sagacious society, one that listened to the wisdom of its elders and traditions, would be able to muster the minimal spiritual power needed to keep itself from civil war. That India could not muster such minimal virtue sickened Gandhi's spirit. As a final irony, he ended his life the victim of a Hindu assassin who blamed Gandhi for the civil strife.

CONTEMPORARY HINDUISM: POPULAR RELIGION

As we have already stressed, Hinduism is an umbrella for a great variety of different religious ideas and practices. Of necessity, we have concentrated on the ideas and practices that stand out when one attempts a historical overview. The outstanding ideas, however, tend to be the possession of intellectuals, at least in their reflective form. For the common people, it

COMPARISON OF SECTS FROM INDIA				
DIMENSION	UPANISHADS	JAIN	BHAGAVAD GITA	TANTRISM
Date	800–400 B.C.E.	500 B.C.E.	400 B.C.E.–200 C.E.	1000 C.E.?
Persons		Mahavira	Arjuna (fictional)	
Mysticism	yes	yes	tolerated	using sexual symbolism
Asceticism	yes	yes, extremely	tolerated	rejected
Caste	tolerated	rejected at first	advocated	ignored
Karma	accepted	accepted	accepted	ignored
Transmigration	accepted	accepted	accepted	ignored
Reality	monistic	dualistic	duty of caste	symbolic
Deity	Brahman	atheistic	theistic	paramour

tends to be the many rituals of the Hindu religious year that mediate the sense of unity with the world that religion seeks to inculcate.

Most Hindus have chosen one or more specific deities (out of an estimated 300 million) to worship on a regular basis. Theologically, they all tie back to Brahman. Many are considered avatars of the Big Three: Brahma, Vishnu and Shiva. For example, Brahma (not to be confused with the pantheistic Brahman) is a creator and is sometimes represented by the avatar Ganesha with his blue elephant head.

Most common rituals involve *puja*. This is a Hindu term for ceremonial prayer or worship, especially that which occurs in the home or local temple. The many small offerings, prayers of praise, prayers of petition, sacrifices, vows, and festival celebrations that punctuate the traditional Hindu year suggest that *puja* carried the Hindu spirit along from day to day. What the grand myths and ceremonies did on a great scale, the humble species of *puja* did in the home, for the small group, or for the individual concerned with personal problems. Women were prominent in *puja*, their many devotions to local goddesses, prayers for the health of their families, reverences to Lord Krishna, and the like being a prominent strand in the Hindu tapestry.

The rituals of folk Hinduism vary from geographic area to geographic area, depending on local gods and customs. Among Hindus of the Himalayas, a strong shamanistic influence remains. Many of these people's religious ceremonies involve a shaman's possession (much like the possession of central Indian mediums such as the weaver and carpenter). More often than not, a family calls upon a shaman because of some misfortune. When such things happen, people usually ask a shaman to hold a seance. The shaman may be from any caste, and he tends to make his living by acting as the medium of a particular god. Usually he opens a consultation by singing prayers in honor of his god, to the steady beat of a drum. As he enters into trance, often he becomes impervious to pain, as he demonstrates by touching red hot metal. When the god has taken full possession of the shaman, the god usually uses the shaman's voice to tell the client what is troubling him and what should be done to cure it. The god may also identify thieves or harmful articles that have brought the misfortune. If the clients do not like the god's diagnosis or advice, they simply go to a different shaman.

More often than not, the treatment the god suggests is performing a *puja* (short ceremony) in honor of the being that is causing the trouble. (In the case of a ghost, the *puja* amounts to an exorcism.) Other popular treatments are making pilgrimages or removing harmful objects causing disease. If the case is impossible to cure (for example, a person deranged beyond healing), the god may prescribe an impossible treatment (for example, the sacrifice of a cow; since the cow is sacred to Hindus, sacrificing a cow is unthinkable).

If the suggested cure is performing a *puja,* other religious specialists generally enter the scene. Their job is arranging and executing a ceremony in which the god can enter a human body, ideally that of the victim, dance in it, and make known any further demands. These *puja* specialists usually come from the lower castes, and their basic method of inducing the god's possession of the victim is playing percussion instruments.The ceremony tends to unfold in three parts: the dance, the *puja* or prayer proper, and the offering. Usually the ceremony takes place in the shrine of the god who is concerned. The shrine itself is very simple, generally consisting of one to four iron tridents about 8 inches high. The people place these in a niche in the wall, if the shrine is indoors, or at the base of a large stone, if it is outside, in effect marking off a sacred space. During the ceremonies the shrine is lighted by a small oil lamp, and often a container of rice and small coins hangs near it, as an offering to the god.

The dance, which begins the ceremony, is intended to attract the god (or any other spirit or ancestor who likes to dance in the bodies of humans). The gods are thought to like dancing because it gives them a chance to air their complaints and needs. Dancing most often occurs in the evening, but sometimes it is repeated the following day. As the drummers increase the intensity of the beat and the room fills with onlookers, smoke, and heat, the rhythms become more compelling, until someone, either the victim or an onlooker, starts to jerk, shout, and dance, first slowly but then more wildly. The possessed person is honored with incense and religious gestures and is fed boiled rice, because for the moment he or she is the god. After the god has danced his fill, he usually speaks through the possessed person, telling the cause of his anger (the source of the misfortune) and detailing what it will take to appease him. The victimized person and his or her family then make a short prayer to the god, expressing reverently their desire to comply with his requests, after which they make the offering the god has demanded.

The most frequent offering is a young male goat. The people place the goat before the shrine and throw rice on its back, while the ritual specialist chants mantras. When the goat shakes itself, the onlookers assume the god has accepted their offering. An attendant (usually from a low caste; higher-caste people tend to consider this act defiling) takes the goat outside and beheads it. The attendant then places a foot and the head of the animal before the shrine as an offering to the god, along with such delicacies as bread and sweet rice. The ritual specialist eventually gathers these up as part of his fee, and the family and guests share the rest of the goat.

A third sort of ritual common in contemporary Indian religion deals with a stage of the life cycle, helping a person cope with puberty, marriage, parenthood, or widowhood. Some of these rituals are based upon vows. The vows may last as short a time as a day or as long as the rest of one's life, but whatever their time, they are serious business. As the stories of the *Puranas* emphasize, failure to fulfill a vow can lead to dire consequences.

Consequently, the person who makes a vow usually prepares assiduously to fulfill it by fasting, worshipping gods, taking frequent purificatory baths, abstaining from sexual relations, refraining from drinking water or chewing betel nuts, and not sleeping during daylight hours. From this asceticism, as well as the fulfillment of the vow itself, the vower gains spiritual power. For example, middle-aged women may go on a pilgrimage to a site sacred to Krishna in order to prevent the death of their husbands (trying therefore to protect themselves from the sad fate of the Hindu widow).

CRITIQUE. Modern India is not free of crime or warfare. Despite legal reforms, caste differences endure. To the ancient Aryans, the untouchables were "walking carrion." Gandhi—like other reformers before him—sought to make them part of the holy Hindu system. He called them *Harijans,* children of God. Still, it remains that Hindu caste has been a powerful ingredient in what to the outsider looks like the nearly unrelieved misery of millions of Indian poor. Simply by the accident of their birth, the majority of Indians have been assigned to the bottom levels of the social pyramid. Of course, to the traditional Hindu, birth was nothing accidental. One was born into a priestly caste, or into a caste of workers, in virtue of one's karma from previous lives. While this might provide some consolation—"my fate is what the gods have meted out to me, or what I have earned from previous existences"—it meant that Indian society as a whole could become static. If many people thought that their poverty, or their wealth, was fated, they were less likely to work hard. Certainly, talent and industry could make a difference in any individual life. On the whole, however, the tendency to think of themselves as fenced in by their caste or particular trade sapped the vitality of many Indians. In the worst cases, it also supported discrimination and outright cruelty.

Among all classes, but especially the poor, Indian women have suffered the worst burdens. The poverty, slavery, and general abuse into which untouchable women often have fallen, simply because they had been born into a certain social stratum, call into question all the religions' tendency to justify the status quo as a matter of divine ordinance.

WORLDVIEW

For Hinduism, as all other religious traditions, the relationship between history and worldview is dialectical—that is to say, each influences the other. What Hindus have assumed about the structures of reality (worldview) has developed in the course of their history. Conversely, their worldview has directed many of the choices that have determined the patterns of their existence over time (history).

Perhaps the most significant feature to emerge from Hindu history has been pluralism. Hindus have developed such a wealth of rituals, doctrines, devotions, artworks, social conventions, and other ways of dealing with ultimate reality, one another, and nature that they could not be uniform. More than such religious traditions as the Jewish, the Christian, the Muslim, and the Buddhist, whose basic doctrines have been relatively uncontested, Hindus have admitted variety and debate into the core of their religious

culture. One sees this when examining the impact of such a Hindu notion as that of the four legitimate goals of life. To say that pleasure, wealth, duty, and liberation (salvation) are all legitimate ends for human beings to pursue, and then to allow numerous ways of interpreting each of these ends, has been to ensure that Hinduism would allow a vast range of options in prayer, family life, economic activity, and dealings with the natural environment.

NATURE

For the most part, Hinduism considers nature (the physical cosmos) to be real, knowable, and orderly. The cosmos is a continuum of lives; consequently, human life is seen as an ongoing interaction with the lives of creatures above and below it. Furthermore, most Hindus consider divinity to be more than physical nature and think human self-realization (*moksha*) entails release from the laws of karma. Let us develop these ideas.

The statement that the physical cosmos is real requires some qualification. Through history, the average Hindu, concerned with making a living and caring for a family, has had little doubt that the fields, flocks, and other physical phenomena are real. Also, the hymns of the *Vedas* that revere the sun and the storm express a vivid appreciation of nature. Even many of the philosophers spoke of the world as having being or reality. Only the idealistic thought of the *Upanishads,* as the Vedanta developed and somewhat organized it, called the reality of the physical world into question.

Furthermore, because of the Vedic notion of *rita* (order, duty, or ritual) and the later notion of karma, Hinduism found the natural world quite orderly. *Rita* presided over such phenomena as sunrise, sunset, and the seasons. Karma expressed the Hindu doctrine that all acts in the cosmos result from previous causes or choices and produce inevitable effects. To be sure, there are various religious paths (*margas*) for escaping karmic inevitability, and we discuss those paths here. Nonetheless, *rita* and karma suggest that the world is patterned, regular, and dependable. This does not mean that flood, famine, earthquake, sickness, or war cannot occur, but it does mean that none of these calamities makes the world absurd.

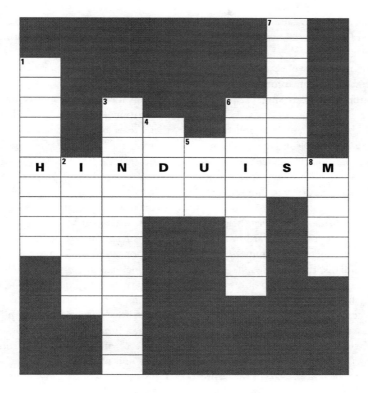

DOWN

1. Doctrine of many deities
2. Aryans' role in 1500 B.C.E.
3. Doctrine of afterlife
4. Most important scripture of Hinduism
5. Do the _____ of one's caste.
6. Spiritual exercise of concentration
7. Doctrine that everything is God
8. Doctrine that everything is one

Karma is connected with the notion of transmigration and rebirth. *Rita* is involved with the vast space-time dimensions in which Hindu cosmology delights. Together these concepts give nature a gigantic expanse that is replete with connections. The connections that most interested the average Hindu linked the myriad living things. Shaivites expressed this interest by venerating the powers of fertility. Ancient rites honoring the Great Mother and other rites stressing Shaktism reveal other Hindu responses to the wonders of life. The symbolism surrounding Shiva and his consorts (such as Kali) explicitly links life with death. At a level above ancient concerns with the vegetative cycle of death and rebirth and the taking of life by life, Hinduism placed the connection between death and life in the context of the universal cycles of creation and destruction.

The Jain notion of *ahimsa*, which many Hindus adopted to varying degrees, implied the connectedness of all lives through its practice of not harming animals. Many Indians refused to eat meat out of the desire not to harm animals. Nonviolence toward the cow, which one might not kill even to help the starving (but which might itself starve), epitomized for many Hindus a necessary reverence for life. Taking karma and transmigration (the passing of the life force from one entity to another) seriously, Hindus thought that life, including their own, was constantly recasting itself into new vegetative and animal forms. Such life was not an evolutionary accident or something that ended at the grave. The inmost life principle continued on, making nature a container of life forces.

Frequently, *maya* and *samsara* carry negative overtones. In fact, the whole thrust toward *moksha* suggests that the natural sphere is of limited value. For more than a few Indians, the natural sphere has been a prison or place of suffering. Yogis of different schools, for instance, have tried to withdraw from materiality to cultivate their mystical experience. Other Hindu mystics have sensed that there was something more ultimate than the ritual sacrifice, the play of natural processes, and even the emotions of the devout worshiper of the *bhakti* god. In this sense *samsara* opposed the freedom suggested by *moksha,* and *moksha* meant exit from what one had known as natural conditions.

However, it is misleading to label Hinduism as world denying or life denying, since India's culture has produced many warriors, merchants, artists, and scientists—a full citizenry who took secular life seriously. Nonetheless, Hindu culture was seldom secular or materialistic in our modern senses, usually stabilizing society by referring to a god or Brahman transcending human space and time. (We may say the same of traditional premodern societies generally.) In addition, Hinduism's reference to metaphysical concepts probably held back its concern with health care, education, and economic prosperity for the masses. When he argued for a secular state and a turn to science rather than religion, India's first premier, Nehru, spoke for many modern educated Indians.

Thus, Hinduism's Aryan beginnings, which were so bursting with love of physical life, and its Dravidian beginnings, which were tantamount to nature and fertility worship, were negated in some periods of history. The most serious blows came from intellectual Hinduism and *bhakti,* which found life good by spiritual exercises and thus were not concerned with social justice or transforming nature for human benefit.

SOCIETY

Hinduism structured society by caste and numerous occupational subclasses. In addition, families traced themselves back through their departed ancestors. Outside the four castes were instances of slavery. The basic structure of the four castes received religious sanction in the *Rig-Veda* 10:90, where the priests, warriors, merchants, and workers emerged from the Great Man's body after he was sacrificed.

The Laws of Manu, expanding the doctrine of casteism, specified the castes' social duties. The Brahmin, for instance, had six required acts: teaching, studying, sacrificing for himself, sacrificing for others, making gifts, and receiving gifts. Brahmins also were to avoid working at agriculture and selling certain foods (such as flesh and salt). Were they to do these things, they would assume the character of people of other castes. In a similar way, Manu set duties and prohibitions for the warriors, merchants, farmers, and workers, giving the entire society a comprehensive dharma. As a result, Hindus considered their dharma to be something given rather than a matter of debate or free choice. Indeed, such caste obligations were the basic cement of the stability of Hindu society.

Nonetheless, various religious inspirations and movements introduced some flexibility. Many of the *bhakti* cults rejected caste distinctions, contending that all people were equal in the god's sight. The possibility of stepping outside the ordinary organization of things to become a full-time ascetic or seeker of liberation loosened the stranglehold of both dharma and caste.

WOMEN'S STATUS. We know little about the earliest Indian women's social status. There is evidence of fertility rites among the pre-Aryans, suggesting a cult of a mother goddess or a matriarchal social structure. In Vedic times women clearly were subordinate to men, but in earlier times they may have held important cultic offices, created canonical hymns, and been scholars, poets, and teachers. In the *Brihad-Aranyaka Upanishad,* the woman Gargi questions the sage Yajnavalkya, indicating that wisdom was not exclusively a male concern. It therefore seems likely that in early India at least, some girls of the upper castes received religious training like the boys'. However, between the first *Vedas* (1500 B.C.E.) and the first codes of law (100 C.E.), women's religious roles steadily declined. A major reason for this was the lowering of the marriage age from fifteen or sixteen years to ten or even five. This both removed the possibility of education (and consequently religious office) and fixed women's roles to wife and mother. In fact, in later Hinduism being a wife was so important that a widow supposedly was prohibited from mentioning any man's name but that of her deceased husband. Even if she had been a child bride or had never consummated her marriage, the widow was not to violate her duty to her deceased husband and remarry. If she did, it was thought she would bring disgrace on herself in the present life and enter the womb of a jackal for her next rebirth.

Thus, the widow was the most forlorn of Hindu women. Without a husband, she was a financial liability to those who supported her. If menstruating, she could be a source of ritual pollution. If barren, she was useless to a society that considered women essentially as child producers. In such a social position, many widows must have concluded that they had little to lose by throwing themselves on their husband's funeral pyre. (Even suttee, though, was not simple. If the widow did not burn herself out of pure conjugal love, her act was without merit.)

Women were sometimes admitted as equals into the *bhakti* and Tantrist sects. However, two circumstances in Tantrism minimized the social liberation that the open admission might have effected. First, the Tantrist sects tended to be esoteric, or secret, which made their public impact minor. Second, the Tantrist interest in tapping *shakti* energies often led to the exploitation of women by men. Thus, the males sometimes tried to gain powers of liberation (*moksha*) by symbolic or actual sexual intercourse, with the result that the females became instruments rather than equal partners. Nevertheless, the Tantrist image of perfection as being androgynous tended to boost the value of femaleness. How much this ideal actually benefited Indian women is difficult to say, but it probably helped some. Nonetheless, women were not generally eligible for *moksha*; the best that a woman could hope for was to be reborn as a man.

There is little evidence that Tantrism eliminated this doctrine, though the *Bhagavad Gita*, 9:32 seems to contradict it.

The overall status of women in Hinduism was that of wards. They were subject, successively, to fathers, husbands, and elder sons. As soon as they approached puberty, their fathers hastened to marry them off, and during their wedded lives they were to honor their husbands without reservation. According to the *Padmapurana*, an influential text, this obligation held even if their husbands were deformed, aged, debauched, lived openly with other women, or showed them no affection. Worse than ward status, however, was the strain of misogyny (hatred of women) running through Hindu culture. The birth of a girl was not an occasion for joy. Hindus attributed it to bad karma in a previous life and frequently announced the event by saying, "Nothing was born." A girl was a financial burden, for unless her parents arranged a dowry there was small chance that she would marry, and the Vedic notion that women were necessary if men were to be complete (which the gods' consorts evidence) lost out to Manu's view that women were as impure as falsehood itself. In fact, Manu counseled "the wise" never to sit with a woman in a lonely place, even if that woman were one's mother, sister, or daughter.

Consequently, Hindu religious texts sometimes imagine a woman as a snake, hell's entrance, death, a prostitute, or an adulteress. In Manu's code, slaying a woman was one of the minor offenses. In the Hindu family, the basic unit of society, woman therefore carried a somewhat negative image; although, of course, some women entered happy households. The high status of the householder did not extend to his wife or female children. India mainly honored women for giving birth and serving their husbands.

MA JNANANANDA. To show the sort of exception that relativizes general statements such as those that we have been making about Hindu women, let us briefly consider a contemporary female guru, Ma Jnanananda of Madras. (*Ma* is a familiar form of "mother".) Jnanananda is a spiritual mother to numerous followers in present-day Madras. She is both a guru and a *sannyasi*. A guru is a religious teacher; a *sannyasi* is one who has taken a formal vow renouncing all worldly life, including family ties and possessions. Such a vow, in effect, means death to one's former life. This renunciation allows full-time pursuit of spiritual goals and fosters spiritual development.

Ma gained her lofty position as a guru because one of the leading Advaita Vedanta figures of contemporary India, Shankaracharya of Kanchipuram, recognized her mystical absorption with Brahman. Jnanananda had done this while living in the world, married and raising five children. That probably accounts for her great ability to relate the teachings of Vedanta to her disciples' daily problems at work or in family life. Photographs of Ma taken before she became a guru show a lovely woman, well dressed and well groomed. The beauty still lingers, but now it seems a reflection of her inner peace. She has traded her fine clothes for a simple sari of ochre cloth, cut her hair short, and painted on her forehead and arms horizontal stripes of a thick paste made from ashes, to symbolize her death to vanity and worldly desires.

In the regime Ma would have a disciple follow, the day begins with some prayer or meditation to the deity of the disciple's choice. After this, the disciple turns to the work of the day, trying to perform duties in such a way that they do not distract the mind from God. The ideal is always to surrender completely to God. When distracting thoughts enter the mind, one should return to God by substituting a prayer or *mantra* (sacred sound). The goal always is "realization" of God, experiential awareness of the divinity in everything. As this realization increases, worldly things lose their allure. Bit by bit, we are skirting the dark forest of fear and desire, moving away from the powers of samsara and time. We can never control all the events of our lives, but we can control our attitude toward them. If we regard what happens to us as intended for our detachment from samsaric things, intended for our attachment to God, all things will become profitable. Such is Ma's teaching.

The final state of realization brings a great love of God. As one's union with divinity increases, one's fulfillment overflows. In this conviction, Ma Jnanananda is a sister to the great mystics of other religious traditions. East and West, they agree that union with God or ultimate reality is the greatest success a human being can attain.

Which theoretical approach would give you the most insight on the history, doctrine, rituals, ethics of Hinduism?

EXAMPLE: *A Marxist perspective.* Marx reduced religion to a method of social control by which the segments of society that possessed power managed to oppress the disenfranchised and maintain power for themselves. In Hinduism, power was possessed by the Aryan invaders of the second millennium B.C.E. The warrior-noble caste used military-political means to maintain power over the disenfranchised majority, and then the priestly Brahmin caste grew out of that and reinforced Aryan control over the social order by introducing karma and reincarnation. Here religion served the Marxist function of "Opiate" in that it distracted people from the plight of their powerlessness, focusing them on preparing for the next life by accepting the injustices of this life, and even justifying the inequities of this life by blaming it on an individual's conduct in previous lives. The result was a remarkably stable socioeconomic order that resisted violent revolution for many centuries.

Select another approach and frame Hinduism within it.

Contribute to this discussion at
http://www.delphi.com/rel101

CONCLUSION. The social rewards of Hindu religion were in the hands of a relative few. By excluding most women, untouchables, and workers, intellectualist Hinduism told well more than half the population that their best hope was rebirth in a better station sometime in the future. (For the most part, only a member of a high caste could reach *moksha*.) However, in the family and the different trades, dharma gave all castes some legitimacy.

SELF

Obviously, the average Hindu did not think about the self in isolation from nature and society. The social caste system and the cosmic *samsara*-transmigration system were the framework of any self examination. Within this framework, however, an individual might set about the task of trying to attain *atmasiddhi*, the perfecting of human nature. This was another way, more concrete perhaps, of posing what *moksha* or the *mahatma* (the "great soul") meant.

In the *Rig-Veda*, *atmasiddhi* was the pious man who recited the hymns and made sacrifices to the gods. Then the changes of Vedic tradition shifted the ideal to the priest who could faultlessly conduct the expanded ritual. The *Upanishads* shifted perfection toward the acquisition of secret knowledge about reality. The *smriti* literature such as the Laws of Manu valued more worldly achievement. There the most excellent man was he who could rule public affairs and lead in community matters. The *Bhagavad Gita* spoke of love as the highest attainment, but it described the realized human personality as being stable in wisdom and having overcome the desires of both the flesh and ambition. Recently Indian saints such as Ramakrishna and Gandhi have stressed, respectively, the mystic loss of self in God and the service of Truth. Clearly, therefore, Hindu tradition allows the self many ideals. Generally speaking, though, full success has implied emotional, intellectual, and spiritual maturity and has honored the social side of human beings, as well as the solitary.

The *Upanishads* jostled the classical life cycle for many. As we have seen, the Upanishadic self was the Atman identified with Brahman. For this revered part of the Hindu tradition, then, the most important aspect of the self was the spiritual core. More than the body, this spiritual core was the key to escaping rebirth. If one was serious about escaping rebirth, why wait for the final stages of the life cycle? Why not cultivate the Atman full time? Some such reasoning surely prompted those who became wanderers long before old age. Whether through study or meditation, they pursued a way that implied that the self's needs or aspirations could outweigh social responsibilities.

In the past thousand years or so, the individual Hindu has therefore had a variety of ways of viewing his or her life journey. The four stages of the life cycle, the Upanishadic or *bhakti* wandering, the household devotions—any of these concepts could give people's lives relevance. Hinduism explicitly recognized that people's needs differed by speaking of four *margas* (paths) that could lead to fulfillment and liberation. Among intellectuals, the way of knowledge was prestigious. In this *marga* one studied the classical texts, the Vedic revelation and commentators'

tradition, pursuing an intuitive insight into reality. Shankara's higher knowledge is one version of this ideal. If one could gain the viewpoint where Brahman was the reality of everything, one had gained the wisdom that would release one from suffering.

But philosophy patently did not attract everyone, and many whom it did attract could not spare the time to study. Therefore, the way of karma (here understood as meaning works or action) better served many people. The *Bhagavad Gita* more than sanctioned this way, which amounted to a discipline of detachment. If one did one's daily affairs peacefully and with equanimity of spirit, then one would not be tied to the world of *samsara*. Doing just the work, without concern for its "fruits" (success or failure), one avoided bad karma (here meaning the law of cause and effect). Gandhi, who was much taken with this teaching of the Gita, used spinning as an example of karma-*marga* or karma-yoga (work discipline). One just let the wheel turn, trying to join one's spirit to its revolutions and paying the quantity of production little heed. When karma-yoga was joined to the notion that one's work was a matter of caste obligation, or dharma, it became another powerful message that the status quo was holy and relevant.

A third marga was meditation (*dhyana*). Contrasted with the way of knowledge, the way of meditation did not directly imply study and did not directly pursue intuitive vision. Rather, it was usually based on the conviction that one can reach the real self by quieting the senses and mental activity to descend without thinking to the personality's depths. In this progression, one approached a state of deep sleep and then went beyond it to nondualism. "Seedless *samadhi*" (pure consciousness) was the highest of the eight branches of yogic progress, but to enter *moksha* one had to leave even it behind. Along the way to *samadhi* one might acquire various paranormal powers (such as clairvoyance or telepathy), but these were of little account. For the many who meditated, the way of *dhyana* usually meant a great sensitivity to body-spirit relationships (through, for example, posture and breath control developed in yoga) and a deepening sense of the oneness of all reality.

Finally, *bhakti* had the status of a *marga*, and, according to the *Bhagavad Gita,* it could be a very effective pathway. Of course, *bhaktas* ran the gamut

CASE STUDY: THE HINDU CHILD

We can get further glimpses into the Hindu sense of the self by considering how Hindus tended to regard their children.

The Hindu child was subjected to religious ceremonies well before birth. For devout Hindus, there were rituals to ensure conception, to procure a male child, and to safeguard the child's time in the womb. Birth itself involved an important ceremony, which ideally took place before the cutting of the umbilical cord, and that included whispering sacred spells in the baby's ear, placing a mixture of butter and honey in its mouth, and giving it a name that its parents were to keep secret until its initiation. Birth made both parents ritually impure for ten days, which meant they were not to take part in the community's ordinary religious rites. Ten days after birth, the child was given a public (as contrasted with the secret) name. Some households also solemnized both an early ear piercing and the first time the parents took the child out of the house and showed it the sun.

There was a pressing motive for parents to have sons, in that at least one son was thought necessary to perform the parents' funeral rites, without which they could not be sure of a safe transit to the other world. Adopted sons were better than nothing, but they were nowhere near so good as natural sons. Girls were of no use whatsoever, because girls could not help their parents in the next world, and at marriage girls passed into the families of their husbands. Although Indian history shows some evidence of female infanticide, this practice seems to have been relatively rare. Despite their lesser desirability, many girls were cared for and petted like sons.

Indian literature suggests that most Hindus had relatively happy, indulged childhoods. In Indian poetry, for example, children are often shown laughing, babbling, and being welcomed onto their parents' laps. On the other hand, poor children were set to work soon after they were able to walk, while wealthier children started their studies as young as four or five. Thus boys usually were set to studying the alphabet by their fifth year. Richer families engaged tutors for their children, and through the Indian Middle Ages (before the Muslim invasions) many village temples had schools attached. The education of girls was considered much less pressing than that of boys, but most upper-class women became literate. Before his initiation, when he was invested with the sacred thread and set to studying the *Vedas,* an upper-class boy usually concentrated on reading and arithmetic.

The initiation of Brahmin boys usually occurred when they were eight. For warriors the ideal age was eleven, and for merchants twelve. The key element in this initiation was hanging a cord of three threads over the boy's right shoulder. The cord was made of nine twisted strands (cotton for Brahmins, hemp for warriors, and wool for merchants). To remove this thread any time during his subsequent life, or to defile it, involved the initiate in great humiliation and ritual impurity. The initiation made the child an Aryan, a member of a noble people, opening the door to his first serious task, that of mastering the sacred Aryan lore. Accordingly, soon after initiation the child was apprenticed to a Brahmin in order to learn the *Vedas.* During this period he was to be celibate, to live a simple life, and to obey his teacher assiduously.

from emotional excess to lofty mysticism. The *Gita* qualified the self-assertiveness that could arise in *bhakti,* however, by making its final revelation not human love of divinity but Krishna's love for humans. On the basis of such revelation, the *bhakta* was responding to divinity as divinity had shown itself to be. In other words, the *bhakta* was realizing human fulfillment by imitating God.

ULTIMATE REALITY

In the early Vedic literature, the gods are principally natural phenomena. It is the wondrous qualities of the storm or fire that elevate Indra and Agni to prominence. By the time that the emphasis on sacrificial ritual dominated, the gods had come under human control. The final stage of Brahmanism was the view that the ritual, if properly performed, inevitably attains its goals—it compels the gods to obey. When we couple this subordinating view of the gods with the notion of *samsara,* the gods become less venerable than human beings. Human beings have the potential to break with *samsara* and to transcend the transmigratory realm through *moksha.* The gods, despite their heavenly estate, are still within the transmigratory realm and cannot escape into *moksha.*

The *Upanishads* moved away from the plurality of gods toward monism. Both the Upanishads and the Vedanta philosophers stated that the knowledge of Brahman or Atman is redemptive. Such knowledge is not simply factual or scientific but has the power to transform one's life—it is light freeing one from existential darkness. Therefore, from the side of the one who experiences Brahman's dominance, we can surely speak of "religious" (ultimately concerned) overtones. Brahman is the basis of everything, if not the creator. It is the supreme value, because nothing is worth more than the ultimate being, which, once seen, sets everything else in light and order.

Attending to Brahman, Hinduism's major concept for ultimate reality, we can note finally that the two aspects of Brahman approximate what monotheistic religions have made of their God. Being beyond the human realm (*nirguna*), Brahman recedes into mystery. This parallels the Christian God's quality of always being ineffable and inconceivable. But because it is within the human realm (*saguna*), Brahman is the basis of nature and culture. In this way it approxi-

mates the Christian conception of the Logos, in whom all creation holds together. Brahman is impersonal, whereas most monotheistic religions conceive their deities on the model of the human personality.

The *bhakti* cults have revered still another form of Hindu divinity. Vaishnavites do not strictly deny the reality of Shiva or Brahma, nor do followers of these other gods deny the reality of Vishnu or Krishna. The mere fact that *bhakti* sects devoted to different gods contend among themselves shows that they take the other gods seriously. But the emotional ardor of the devoted *bhaktas* suggests that they grant their gods the ultimate value of a monotheistic god. The same holds for devotees of goddesses, who may actually outnumber devotees of the male gods.

In Krishna's manifestation to Arjuna in the *Bhagavad Gita,* we can see how this monotheistic value took symbolic form. Krishna becomes the explosive energy of all reality. In the *Gita,* his theophany (manifestation of divinity) is the ultimate revelation of how divinity assumes many masks in space and time. Whatever reality is, Krishna is its dynamic source. Much like the Upanishadic Brahman, he is the one source capable of manifesting itself in many forms. But whereas the atmosphere of Brahman is serene and cool, the *bhakti*-prone Krishna is turbulent and hot. When J. Robert Oppenheimer, one of the developers of the American atom bomb, saw the first nuclear explosion, Krishna's dazzling self-revelation came to his mind: "If the light of a thousand suns should effulge all at once, it would resemble the radiance of that god of overpowering reality" (*Bhagavad Gita,* 11:12).

THE PROBLEM OF EVIL. The problem of evil (**theodicy**) is that so much in human experience seems to be dark and disordered. For many Western observers, Indian philosophy has seemed strangely silent about evil. (Their greater interest was the problem of ignorance—why human beings don't comprehend that only ultimate reality is fully real.) The Hindu doctrine of rebirth shifted the problem of evil away from the Western orientation, in which individuals (like Job in the *Bible*) can accuse God of having dealt with them unjustly, having caused them to suffer through no fault of their own. Rebirth, coupled with the notion of karma, meant that one existed through long cycles of time whose overall justice was beyond human calculation, and that one's fate in a given lifetime was the result of one's actions in a previous existence. Thus there was no unmerited punishment and consequently no "problem" of evil. The gods did not have to justify themselves before innocent sufferers.

One of the early reasons why Hinduism developed an articulate response to the problem of evil was the attacks of the Buddhists, who found evil a soft spot in Hinduism's armor. Thus Buddhist texts satirically ask why the Hindu gods do not set the world straight. If Brahman, for instance, is lord of all things born, why are things so confused and out of joint? Why is there such unhappiness and deception? If we are honest, it seems as though Brahman ordained not dharma (a good working order) but *adharma* (chaos).

Hindu thinkers struggled to meet this challenge. In trying to understand evil, they tended to regard natural disasters, such as earthquakes, and moral wrongs, such as murder, as but two aspects of a single comprehensive phenomenon. In the *Rig-Veda*, probably the moral sense prevails: People are evil-minded, committing adultery or theft. Still, the *Rig-Veda* does not necessarily see such evil as freely chosen. Moral evil or sin may occur without the sinner willing it. Therefore, one finds few prayers of personal repentance in the *Rig-Veda*, though numerous prayers for deliverance from the bad things other people can do.

The *Atharva-Veda* also tends to blend natural and moral evils, and to see moral evil as an intellectual mistake rather than a culpable flaw in character. There are exceptions to these tendencies, such as the Rig-Vedic hymn of repentance to Varuna (5:85), but the overall inclination of the Vedic texts is to regard evil not as something we humans do but as what we do not wish to have done to us.

KALI. One female deity whom scholars have studied thoroughly is Kali, the mistress of death, an important expression of Maha-devi, the ancient great goddess. In her, many of the popular ambivalences about ultimate reality come into focus. Part of the fascination Kali has evoked stems from her dreadful appearance. Usually she is portrayed in black, like a great storm cloud. Her tongue lolls, reminding the viewer that she has a great thirst for blood, and she shows fearsome teeth. Her eyes are sunken, but she smiles, as though enjoying a terrible secret. Round her neck is a garland of snakes, a half-moon rests on her forehead, her hair is matted, and often she licks a corpse. In her hand is apt to be a necklace of skulls. She has a swollen belly, girdled with snakes, and for earrings she has corpses. Her face projects a calm contentment, as if the savage realities of life, its evil and deathly aspects, suit her just fine. (It is interesting that the cult of Kali flourished in areas most profoundly influenced by British colonial rule, as though to express a sense that life had turned horribly oppressive.)

Moreover, certain historic associations have besmirched Kali's name, linking her with some of the most loathsome, degenerate streams in Hindu culture. For example, she has been linked with blood sacrifices, including those of human beings, and she has served as the patron goddess of the Thugs, a vicious band of criminals that flourished from ancient times until the late nineteenth century and devoted themselves to strangling carefully selected victims as a way of honoring the goddess of death. (It is from this group that our English word *thug* has come.) Nonetheless, a careful study of Kali's full history as a major Hindu deity suggests that she has functioned as more than simply a lodestone for the soul's darker passions.

First, Kali does not appear in the earliest Hindu texts, but comes on the scene fairly late. Second, throughout her history it is largely peripheral people, marginal groups that populate her cults. In this her cult reminds one of Shavaism and Tantrism. Third, the geographic areas most devoted to Kali have been Bengal and the Vindhya mountain region of south-central India. Fourth, when Kali became associated with the tantric cults, her appearance changed, for a potential benevolence more clearly emerged. Tantrism's concern with tapping libidinal energies led to the rise of many female deities from the seventh century C.E. on, and by the sixteenth century Kali was intimately connected with the more adventurous "left-hand" tantric sects.

Kali is a personification of the most forbidden thing, death. Therefore, the tantric hero presses on to confront Kali, trying to transform her (death) into a vehicle of salvation. Consequently, the hero is apt to go to Kali's favorite dwelling place, the cremation grounds, meditate on each terrible aspect of her appearance, and try by penetrating her fearsomeness to pass beyond it.

The ordinary Hindu, man or woman, who was not a saint like Ramakrishna, tended to interact with a favorite god or goddess without understanding that this deity was merely the face of a universal divinity or ultimacy. Throughout history, most Hindus have not been literate, so their sense of the gods and goddesses has come from the oral tradition. It was the great cycle of stories about Krishna and Devi, about Rama and Sita, that filled the imagination of the ordinary person and so shaped what he or she said at prayer, thought during the religious festivals, feared in the depths of night or at the bed of a sickly child. This is not to say that the average Hindu had no sense of the unity among the different deities. In all probability, even the humblest peasant accepted that the many different deities were reconciled in the realm of the gods. But for the present age, the trials of this round of the samsaric cycle, it was more helpful to focus on a particular deity than to speculate about a divine unity beyond or underneath all of the divine diversity.

A second feature of popular Hindu religion, the culture of the masses, has been a certain passivity. Ideally, karma moved people to live on the border between acceptance and resignation. Acceptance is something positive: thinking that one's life is in God's hands, thinking that Providence must in the final analysis be benevolent. Resignation is something negative: we can't do much about our situation, in the long run, so we had best detach ourselves from foolish hopes and let happen what will. In their prayers and rituals, Hindus tried to draw from their favorite deities a blend of acceptance and resignation fitting and powerful enough to keep them going. Popular religion certainly had its ecstatic moments, when love of a dazzling deity might move people to transports of delight, but on a daily basis Hindu piety or spirituality tended to be sober.

CONCLUSION. We suspect that Hindus have arranged nature, society, and the self in view of the Agni, Brahman, or Krishna who centered their lives in divine mystery. If Brahman is the ultimate reality, then nature, society, and the self are all versions of *maya*, are all illusion and play. If Agni, the god to whom one directs the fire sacrifice, is the ultimate reality, then nature stands by divine heat, society stands by priestly sacrificers, and the self strives after *tapas* (ascetic heat) or lives by ritual mantras (verbal formulas for controlling the divine forces). Finally, if Shiva is the ultimate reality, then ultimate reality destroys castes, is the arbiter of life and death, and reduces the self to a beggar for grace.

No system of interpretation can truly substitute for the system that the religion itself implicitly uses. In other words, we cannot reduce the religions to their cosmological, sociological, or psychological factors. They must remain essentially what they claim to be: ways emanating from and leading to the divine. For this reason, the concept of ultimate reality in a religion will always be the most crucial concept. God or ultimate reality is by definition the ultimate shaper of a worldview, because divinity determines the placement of the other dimensions and thus the worldview as a whole.

Having had many forms of divinity, Hinduism has had many worldviews. The membership requirements are quite simple: As long as one accepts the divine inspiration of the Vedas and the caste system, one can be called a Hindu.

(c) Joseph Sohm; ChromoSohm / CORBIS

Unlike most Hindu sects, the Hare Krishnas proselytize.

SUMMARY: THE HINDU CENTER

How, overall, does Hinduism seem to configure reality for its adherents? What is the center, or summarizing pattern, that the Hindu "ways" appear to depict? It seems to us that the Hindu center is an alluring sense of unity. From the time of the Vedas, reflective personalities in India sought to put together the many disparate facets and forces of reality. Thus *Rig-Veda* hymns, the *Upanishads,* and the later theistic cults all proposed a mystery, or ultimate reality, or god that stood behind things, promising the devout adherent, or the self-disciplined yogi, a satisfying peace. The peace would come from the order that union with Brahman or Krishna would produce. Thus the individual was not to cling to the passing multiplicity of social, natural, or even personal life. *Samsara* was an enemy trying to keep the individual in a state of disunion, and so of suffering. Illusion was *samsara*'s main ally. If one broke with illusion, ap-

propriated the wisdom of the ancient seers who had fought through to, or been blessed by a vision of, the ultimate unity of all things, one could find being, bliss, and awareness.

Moksha is probably the watchword best symbolizing this typically Hindu cast of mind, yet *moksha* could have several different weightings. For the passionate, those either suffering with special pains or burning for being, bliss, and awareness with a special ardor, *moksha* could be an imperative. There being nothing more important than coming to right order, finding the ultimate relevance of life, the passionate Hindu could pursue *moksha* wholeheartedly, opting out of India's highly structured caste and family life. For personalities either less pressured by suffering or less drawn by the prospects of fulfillment, *moksha* could carry a somewhat comforting and palliative set of overtones. If not in this life, in some future life one could hope to attain *moksha*. With such a good future prospect, the turmoils and troubles of the present life could somewhat slacken.

Theistic Hindus, *bhaktas* devoted to Krishna, Shiva, or one of the goddesses, tended to picture the center in terms of their beloved God. Thus the theophany or revelation that Krisha gives Arjuna in the *Gita* shows Krishna to be the center of all reality, a sort of Brahman, but more personalized, dazzling, and energetic. As the force of life and death, Shiva could have a similarly universal power to organize reality, a similarly profound religious clout. Love for such a god could give the devotee's life ultimate relevance.

Be that as it may (and it may be more descriptive of the recent India than about the India of the pre-

Muslim era), the impression remains that the Hindu center has been as ambivalent in its social effects as most other religious centers have been. By the standards of a radical contemplative wisdom that would penetrate to the core of reality's mystery and a radical social justice that would treat all human beings as equals who deserve fair dealing, the Hindu worldview emerges as more wise than just. So, of course, do most other worldviews, if only because it is usually easier to contemplate the grand source of order, the fair center of a mystery revealing itself as beautiful and healing, than it is to promote other human beings' equal access to the good life that such a mystery suggests.

Electronic flashcards and matching games
http://www.quia.com/jg/51283.html

hangman games
http://www.quia.com/hm/18236.html

word jumble games
http://www.quia.com/jw/8432.html

Download multiple choice, true-false, and fill-in drills from
http://www.ureach.com/tlbrink
Click on the public filing cabinet and folder rel6 and download m6.exe, t6.exe, and f6.exe.

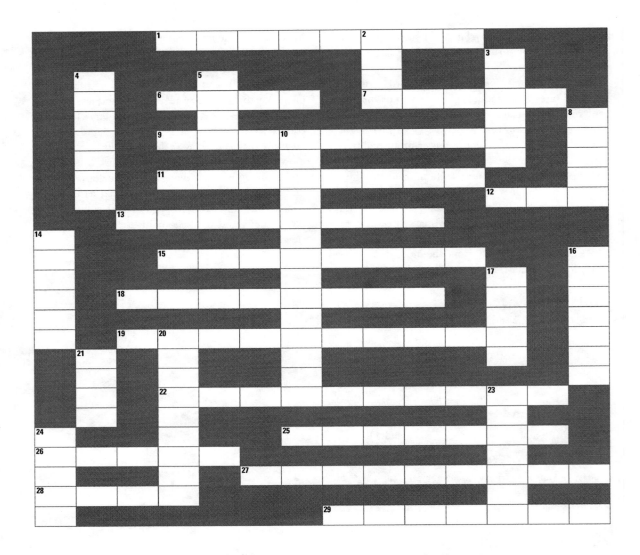

ACROSS

1   The _____ *Gita* is a reaction to Jainism and
    Buddhism.
6   Indian holy man, spiritual teacher
7   People who invaded India in second millennium B.C.E.
9   *Upanishads*, Jainism, Buddhism advocated this
    approach.
11 Ascetic founder of Jainism; lived around 500 B.C.E.
12 The *Upanishads* were written 800–300 _____.
13 The *Upanishads* had this view of reality: all is one
    God.
15 The *Bhagavad Gita* urged this approach to the gods.
18 Heretical sect emphasizing sex and alcohol
19 Self-denial, acceptance of privation, Jain approach
22 Mystical writings of Hinduism
25 Upanishadic term for the one God in everything
26 Place where Hinduism, Jainism, Buddhism arose
27 Upanishadic doctrine of God
28 *Bhagavad Gita* advocates doing the _____ of one's
    caste.
29 The priests belonged to this high caste.

DOWN

2   The *Rig* _____ tells of the Aryan invasion of India.
3   Vishnu the preserver; Shiva the destroyer; _____ the
    Creator
4   Religion founded by Mahavira; ascetic, mystical
5   Krishna told Arjuna to do his _____.
8   Rigid Hindu social class structure
10 Hindu, Buddhist, Jain view of afterlife
14 Preserver deity; Arjuna was his avatar
16 The Brahmin caste was made up of _____.
17 What determines how someone will be reborn
20 Tantrism advocated the use of _____.
21 Physical exercises for spiritual mastery
23 Jain view of reality as spirit and matter
24 Acceptance of *Vedas* and caste makes one a _____.

CHRISTIANITY

CHRISTIANITY: TWENTY-FIVE KEY DATES	
Date	**Event**
ca. 30 C.E.	death of Jesus of Nazareth
ca. 65 C.E.	death of the apostle Paul
ca. 100–165 C.E.	Justin Martyr, leading apologist
ca. 185–254 C.E.	Origen, leading theologian
313 C.E.	Christians freed of legal persecution
325 C.E.	First Council of Nicea
354–430 C.E.	Augustine, leading theologian
451 C.E.	Council of Chalcedon
ca. 480–500 C.E.	Benedict, founder of Western monasticism
ca. 540–604 C.E.	Pope Gregory I, founder of the medieval papacy
787 C.E.	Second Council of Nicea
869–870 C.E.	Intensified disputes between Rome and the Eastern bishops
1054 C.E.	Great Schism between Rome and Constantinople
1096–1099 C.E.	First Crusade to conquer Palestine
1225–1274 C.E.	Thomas Aquinas, leading theologian
1369–1415 C.E.	John Hus, Bohemian reformer
1517 C.E.	Luther's *Ninety-Five Theses*
1509–1564 C.E.	John Calvin, leading theologian
1545–1563 C.E.	Council of Trent
1620 C.E.	Pilgrims sign Mayflower compact
1703–1791 C.E.	John Wesley, founder of Methodism
1869–1870 C.E.	First Vatican Council in Rome
1910 C.E.	beginning of Protestant ecumenical movement
1962–1965 C.E.	Second Vatican Council in Rome

If we gather all its parts, **Christianity** is the largest religion in the world, with about a third of the earth's population expressing at least nominal adherence to a specific Christian denomination. What began as a proselytizing sect within Judaism was carried around the world and mixed with other heritages.

HISTORY

JESUS

Christianity was spread by first-century **apostles** who dedicated their lives to one very singular man, Jesus of Nazareth. It is likely that the word *Jehsus,* a Greek form, derives from the Hebrew *Yeshua,* which means "savior." There is no doubt that Jesus existed, preached, gathered followers, and was executed by the Romans. The historical validity of these facts is attested by such non-Christian authors as Josephus, Tacitus, Suetonius, and Pliny the Younger. Jesus was born about 4 B.C.E. (by current calendars) in Palestine.

BOOKS OF THE NEW TESTAMENT			
BOOK	WHEN	AUTHOR	THEME(S)
James	45 C.E.	James	social justice; need for good works
Galatians	48 C.E.	Paul	need for salvation by grace; against Judaizers
I Thessalonians	52 C.E.	Paul	second coming
II Thessalonians	70 C.E.	Paul?	rebuke idleness while waiting
I Corinthians	54 C.E.	Paul	order within the Church; resurrection; spiritual gifts (tongues; morality)
II Corinthians	55 C.E.	Paul	sex, gossip
Romans	55 C.E.	Paul	need for salvation by grace, not works
Philemon	60 C.E.	Paul	forgiveness and restoration
Colossians	63–90 C.E.	Paul?	against Gnosticism
Ephesians	? C.E.	Paul?	stand against Satan
Philippians	61 C.E.	Paul	rejoice in the exaltation of Christ
I Timothy	62 C.E.	Paul	roles of women, bishops in Church
Titus	62 C.E.	Paul	against Judaizers and Antinomians
I Peter	63 C.E.	Peter	persistence and patience
II Peter	63 C.E.	Peter	against false teachers
II Timothy	63 C.E.	Paul	nature of the Church
Hebrews	60s	?	Jesus fulfills Jewish tradition
Jude	66 C.E.	Jude	against apostates
Mark	60s–70s C.E.	Mark?	Jesus as miracle worker; Son of Man, servant of God; second coming is near
Matthew	60s–70s C.E.	Matthew?	Jesus as King of Jews, Messiah; fulfills Jewish tradition
Luke	60s–80s C.E.	Luke	most comprehensive story of Jesus
Acts	60s–80s C.E.	Luke	chronology of major apostles in the 50s
I John	80s C.E.	John?	against Docetism; sin and Christians
II John	80s C.E.	John?	against false teachers
III John	80s C.E.	John?	encouragement to friends
Revelation	90s C.E.	John?	second coming of Christ
John	90s C.E.	John?	theological view of Christ as God, the Son

NEW TESTAMENT. Beyond that, little can be verified to the satisfaction of objective secular historians. Most of what we know about the life of Jesus is reported in the New Testament. This is a compilation of books including the *Epistles* (letters to early Christians written by the apostles Paul, John, Peter, James, and Jude), the *Acts of the Apostles* (a history written by Luke), and the *Gospels* (the first four books of the New Testament, describing the life of Jesus). While the *Gospels* undoubtedly contain historical facts (such as names of persons and places and descriptions of events) that have not been disputed by any other sources, they also contain other claims that will probably never be verified by sources outside the New Testament. Clearly, the *Gospels* contain some mixture of factual description, myth (in the sense of stories being told because of the values they demonstrate), and interpretation of both myth and fact in order to argue a point of doctrine or explain some ritual developed by the early Christians.

There is a general split of opinion in how the *Gospels* are viewed. In general, more fundamentalist Christian biblical scholars argue that each gospel was written by the man whose name appears at the front (e.g., *Mark* was written by Mark, not a committee). Also, fundamentalists assume that the authors were (except in the case of Luke) eyewitnesses to most of the events they described, especially the crucifixion and the resurrection. The fundamentalists also assume that the *Gospels* were written within a generation of the life of Jesus. The biblical scholars with a more secular orientation assume that the oral recounts of Jesus' life lasted for over a generation before being put in writing (but agree that at least the three synoptic gospels were pretty much in their present form by the end of the first century C.E.). The secular scholars also question if *Mark, Matthew,* and *John* were really written by the individual eyewitnesses of the same name, but could represent composite documents from different sources. The least amount of debate is about Luke, who was a first-century physician turned historian who traveled and may have interviewed eyewitnesses to give a thorough account of the life of Jesus (the gospel of *Luke*) and the movements of the early apostles (*Acts of the Apostles*). One group of secular scholars, the so-called Jesus Seminar, doubts that most of the statements attributed to Jesus (highlighted in some red-letter Bibles) were actually spoken by him at the time; (instead, they were added by the authors to make theological points). Both the more fundamentalist and the more secular scholars tend to dismiss most of the noncanonical writings as written in the next century or written by someone other than the purported author. (The exception seems to be the gospel of *Thomas*, which secular scholars date to about 50 C.E., and that offers some confirmations of many of Jesus' sayings.)

ROLE OF JESUS. We know little about the youth of Jesus except through gospel stories, such as those of his circumcision and his dialogues with religious teachers, and these seem consistent with the assumption that he grew up as a typical Jewish youth of his times. About the year 27 C.E., he started from his native Galilee on a career as an itinerant preacher and healer. (This was not unusual for the time and place, and reflected the frustration of many Jews with Roman rule). When we read the **synoptic gospels** (*Mark, Matthew, Luke*), what is so impressive about Jesus is not the accounts of the healings, but the power of his words: they have the lofty symbolism of a mystic, the tie-in to the past of a teacher, but the new revelatory authority of a prophet (uttered by someone who exorcises and heals like a shaman). Buddha could simply be classified as a mystic, Muhammed a prophet, and Confucius a teacher, but Jesus seems to fill all of these roles. His followers concluded that he had to be more than a man, he must be the Son of God, and the Jewish Messiah.

Apparently Jesus linked his work with that of **John the Baptist,** calling for a spiritual renewal and the expectation of a Messiah. He championed the poor and the socially outcast. He criticized the hypocrisy of the Jewish temple priests, the Sadducees and the Pharisees. The fact that he came from the district of Galilee also seemed to reduce his credentials among the Jerusalem–based Jewish priesthood. To both the Jews and the Romans at the time, that sounded like a call to rebellion against the establishment. His death came by order of the Roman procurator Pontius Pilate on the dubious grounds that he threatened the peace.

Beyond this bare outline, historical and theological interpretations diverge. Indeed, all of the *Gospels* are theological interpretations of Jesus, developed in

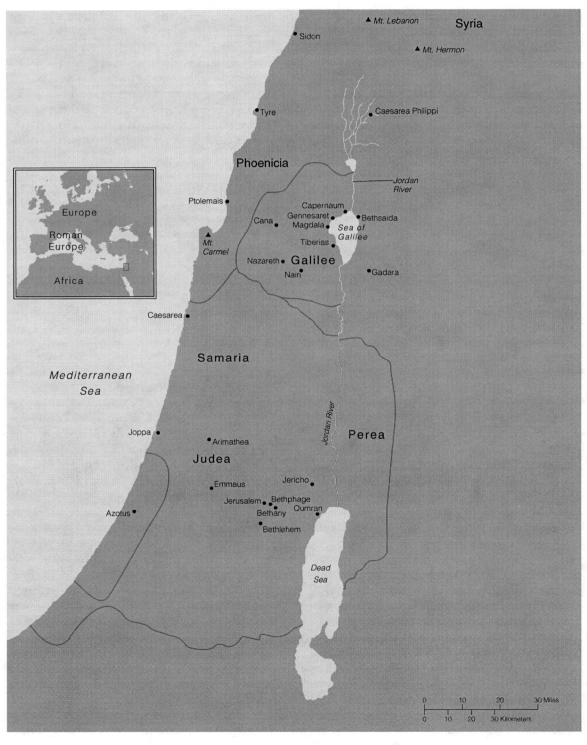

Palestine during the time of Jesus

COMPARISON OF FIRST-CENTURY JEWISH SECTS					
DIMENSION	PHARISEES	SADDUCEES	ESSENES	ZEALOTS	CHRISTIANS
Greek culture	opposed	accepted	withdrew from	opposed	at first ignored, later assimilated
Roman rule	opposed	accepted	withdrew from	rebelled against	persecuted by
Laws of the Torah	strictly followed	loosely followed	other new doctrines	ignored	other new doctrines
Appealed to	poor	wealthy	alienated	robbers	poor
Apocalypse	coming soon	ignored	ignored	start it!	coming soon
Role of Messiah	great	ignored	ignored	ignored	great
Angels	accepted	rejected	ignored	ignored	accepted
Resurrection	accepted	rejected	transmigration	irrelevant	accepted
Heaven and hell	accepted	ignored	ignored	ignored	accepted

Would you describe first-century Christianity as an *ascetic* denomination? Compare the nature and degree of ascetic tendencies in early Christianity to those of Orthodox Jews, Jains, Orphics, or Pythagoreans.

Contribute to this discussion at
http://www.delphi.com/rel101

the light of at least a generation's worth of the Christian community's experience, of controversies with Jews who did not accept Jesus as the Messiah, and of efforts to explain the relevance of Jesus to Gentiles. According to the New Testament and the mainstream doctrine of later centuries, after death Jesus was raised (resurrected) and was disclosed to be "Lord," or the divine Son whose dying and rising brought the world salvation. Another interpretation of Jesus found in the New Testament is that he was the **Messiah**—the anointed king of the age of grace which Judaism had long been anticipating, where grace came to mean not just peace and material plenty but intimacy with God and sharing in divine life. From the titles that the New Testament gives to Jesus, his own

reported claims, and the miracles (healings, raisings from the dead, and so on) that the New Testament attributes to Jesus, we can conclude that the New Testament writers found him most remarkable—so remarkable that he had to be more than human. For them he was the bringer of salvation, God's Word incarnate, the **Christ** (Greek term for God incarnate), the Messiah, and the divine Son.

In the earliest portions of the New Testament, the Pauline *Epistles* (letters), Jesus is a living spiritual reality. The assumption behind Paul's directions for Church life, for instance, is that the "Lord" lives in Christians' midst. After Jesus' death, his followers apparently thought that his movement was finished, but the events of the resurrection convinced them that he had assumed a new form of existence. They stayed together in Jerusalem; at Pentecost (fifty days after Passover, when Jesus had died), they experienced what they called the Holy Spirit, whom they thought Jesus and the Father had sent. The Spirit charged them to go out and preach about Jesus. Thus, the early Christians proclaimed that Jesus' life and death were the definitive act of salvation. The disciples also preached that Jesus was the Messiah. As such, he was

COMPARISON OF MOHISM AND CHRISTIANITY		
DIMENSION	MOHISM	CHRISTIANITY
Who founded?	Mozi	Jesus
Where?	China	Palestine
When?	fourth century B.C.E.	first century C.E.
Who appealed to?	knights	poor
Which commandment?	love	love
Rigid opponents	Confucians	Pharisees
Mystical competition	Taoists	Essenes
Brutal opponents	Legalists	Zealots, Romans
Scripture	fragments in Mencius	New Testament
Fate of founder	unknown	crucified
Fate of movement	died out	grew with proselytizing around Roman empire

in accordance with Jewish tradition and yet responsible for its transformation. From a historical perspective, then, the first Christians appear as sectarian Jews with a new interpretation of messianism. The early Christians thought of themselves as the new Israel because they thought that Jesus had brought, and the old Israel had rejected, the kingdom of God sought by Jewish messianic expectation. This was an apocalyptic position that envisioned a second coming of Jesus, a resurrection of the dead, a final battle with Satan, and a day of judgment.

It took some time for the first interpretations of Jesus to sift out and clarify, and a principal catalyst in that process was **Paul**. From the accounts in *Acts* and his own writings, Paul was a Pharisaic Jew whose conversion on the road to Damascus (*Acts* 9:3–9) was quite dramatic. After his conversion, he tried to show his fellow Jews that Jesus was their Messiah, but their opposition to his preaching, plus his own further reflection on Jesus' life and death, led Paul to think that in Jesus God had opened the covenant to all people—Gentiles as well as Jews. Consequently, Paul made the *gospel* (good news) about Jesus a

transformation of the Torah. Because God had fulfilled in Jesus the intent of the Law, the Law's many detailed prescriptions were passe. Adherence to an external code could not make one righteous (acceptable to God). Only by opening to God's love and healing could one stand before him acceptably. Paul called that opening "faith" by which he understood an absolute personal commitment to Jesus. For him, Jesus was the agent of a shift from the Torah to the gospel, from the old covenant of works to the new covenant of commitment. Jesus the Christ was a new Adam, a new beginning for the human race. Paul began to use the term "body of Christ" to stand for the growing Christian community. All who clung to him became members of his "body." Christ and the Church formed a living entity.

Paul's interpretation of Jesus was the key to early Christianity's developing into a universal religion. Although Paul and the original disciples of Jesus had been Jews, Paul's decision to drop the requirements of the Jewish Law (e.g., circumcision, kosher diet) and extend membership to all (Jew and Gentile) who would base their lives on Jesus, the early Church

CASE STUDY: JESUS' PARABLES

One of the main reasons Jesus has remained fresh for each generation of his followers is that the New Testament authors set down some of Jesus' lively teaching stories, his parables. Puzzling, enigmatic, and vivid, these parables have drawn the attention of preachers and audiences through all the Christian centuries. Today the parables have become a favorite topic of scholarly discussion. We can only hint at the main lines of this discussion, but studying one of Jesus' parables, that of the Great Supper (*Matt.* 22:1–10; *Luke* 14:10–24), will take us a few steps into what New Testament scholars are currently conjecturing about Jesus' own outlook.

As a background to our consideration of the parable of the Wedding Banquet, let us first note the tendency of current New Testament scholars to emphasize the parables' underlying conviction of God's oneness, an absolute mystery. The authors of the parables (Jesus and the writers who set them in their New Testament form) used a paradoxical speech, through which they might hint at God's transcendence—God's overspilling of all human conceptual containers. The parables imply that God cannot be captured in any single set of images. The best way to indicate the divine nature is to juxtapose stories that flash forth now one, now another aspect of what God seems to be like.

Moreover, some of Jesus' parables opposed the assumption of some of his contemporaries that the only way righteous people could experience the rule of God would be through a dramatic, even cosmic, overturning of the prevailing political patterns, so that the sinners presently in charge would be thrown out. Not so, Jesus' preaching suggested. God does not need earthquakes or revolutions. The reign of God is subtler, and more powerful, than any prevailing political or religious conditions. No matter how bad the times, one could always find something of God in them. For Jesus, God was always active, always reaching out to people in need. His gentle speech had a powerful edge; the forgiveness and reconciliation imaged is

demanded for everyone's life. The holiness appropriate to the rule of God belongs to all.

Applied to Jesus' liking for parables, this attitude meant a calm "take it or leave it." A parable was an invitation to enter the world of Jesus' Father, to open oneself to Jesus' view of what God was doing. It was not an oppressive command. The parable of the Banquet suggests that one could meet Jesus and not even realize that this was the most important encounter of one's life. Jesus would not beat his hearers over the head. God would not flash forth lightning or bellow thunder. The Kingdom of God was in people's midst. To find it, they had only to turn around and open themselves to Jesus' good news.

The parable itself tells of a man (or a king) who once gave a great banquet. Deciding to throw this feast, he sent his servants to announce it to those he wanted to invite. The servants told the invitees, "Come, for all is now ready." But the invitees began to make excuses. Not sensing the significance of the invitation, they told the servants such lame tales as "I have bought a field and I must go take a look at it," or "I have bought five yoke of oxen, and I must go examine them," or "I have just gotten married, so I cannot come." (However, *Deuteronomy* 20:5–7 and 24:5 suggest that these may traditionally have been considered legitimate excuses.) In each case, they asked to be excused. The man hosting the banquet got very angry. In Matthew's version, the invitees had treated the man's servants shamefully, even killing them, so the man (who was a king) sent his troops to destroy the murderers and burn their city. In Luke's milder account, the host simply told his servants to go out into the streets and lanes of the city and bring in the most wretched people they could find: the poor, the maimed, the blind, and the lame. When the servants came back to report that they had done this and that there still was room in the banquet hall, the host told them to go out again, this time into the highways and hedges, and make people come in, until the banquet hall was completely full. Those whom he had first invited had shown themselves unworthy of the banquet, but one way or another he would have his house filled.

For Matthew, the story is an occasion to indulge in a bit of allegory. By playing up the theme of the king's punishment of the invitees' bad treatment of the servants, he can allude to the Roman destruction of Jerusalem in 70 C.E., which perhaps he saw as a retribution for the slaying of Jesus. Luke, on the other hand, presents a simpler plot line, and he is more interested in the redoubling of the host's invitation than in any rejection and punishment. Where Matthew makes an irreparable break between the king and the original guests, Luke passes over this relation, allowing the possibility that it might mend. Accenting the good fortune of the new invitees, he stresses that they are an unlikely group, outcasts and strangers. For Luke, the drama lies in the host's seizing the occasion of the original invitees' (the Jews') refusal or inability to come and making it a chance to be generous to another class of people. Thus, when most Jews rejected Jesus' message, God offered the gospel to the Gentiles. In the background of the New Testament's use of the parable is the bitterness between Jews who had accepted Jesus (become Christians) and those who had rejected him. Although they tend to stress the literary structure of the evangelists' different accounts, today's scholars do not neglect the historical or theological dimensions of the parables. For example, they point out that Jewish lore contemporary with Jesus had a story that praised a tax collector for doing one good deed during his (otherwise hateful) life: inviting some poor people to a banquet when the original guests did not come. Similarly, research into the social customs of Jesus' day has revealed a tendency in sophisticated Jewish circles to invite people twice. Important people, at least, did not take seriously a single invitation but had to have their egos stroked a second time. One of the rabbis used a person dressed and ready to go by the time of a second invitation as an example of wisdom, while a person not ready to go by the time of a second invitation, and so excluded from the good time, became an example of foolishness.

Moreover, by choosing the figure of a banquet, both Jesus and the gospel writers inevitably conjured up the messianic time. In the messianic time, when Israel's deliverer had come, Jewish tradition said the people would eat and drink joyously, banqueting together. It may be stretching the original intent of the parable to make it a full symbol of the messianic or heavenly time, as later Christian preachers often have, but the figure itself was bound to suggest inclusion in the occasion of celebrating God's victory or exclusion from it. If one stresses the confrontational side of the invitation and rejection, as Matthew does, one develops a rather harsh, judgmental view of Jesus' messiahship and the invitation to join the Christian community. The understated version of Luke simply hints at what a human situation—a generous host's disappointment that the people he first invited could not come—can reveal about God's ingenuity and goodness. Undaunted, the host finds new outlets for his largess.

Behind Matthew's harsher version probably lie the bitter experiences of the early Christian missionaries, who were confused and hurt that their proclamation of Jesus' good news brought them persecution rather than gratitude. However, this harsh attitude seems to contradict Jesus' own tendencies, which were to keep contact with people, avoid unnecessary ruptures, and find creative alternatives to strategies that had run into dead ends. Behind Jesus' own mission there seems to have lain a rather constant goodwill. If the members of the establishment were not interested in his message, there were always the crowds on society's margins. If the Jews were intractable, there were always the Samaritans and the Gentiles. Jesus may not have worked all this out into an explicit theology of his mission, but it seems latent in his regular style. For all that he seems to have been disappointed by the stupidity and hardness of heart he encountered, he kept speaking provocatively of the Kingdom of God, always hoping he would come upon a few people whom God's Spirit had prepared to accept his words.

In Luke's version of the parable, the social implications of the gospel also are important. It is no accident that the outcasts come into the banquet hall. Luke sees the good news of the Kingdom as especially intended for those people who have little other good news in their lives: the poor, the sick, the despised. At the least, his parable implies, those who have received much from God should share it generously with people less fortunate. The host who insists that his banquet not go to waste should be a role model for Christians.

In recent years, excavations at Nag-Hammadi in Egypt have made available to New Testament scholars Gnostic versions of the gospel (see later) that they can compare with the canonical four *Gospels.* The gospel of *Thomas,* for example, has a version of the parable of the Banquet that is quite spare, more like Luke's than Matthew's account. Interestingly, however, the gospel of *Thomas* makes several of the original invitees excuse themselves for monetary reasons. Thus, one man has some merchants coming the evening of the banquet to pay him money they owe, while another man has bought some property and must go to collect the rent. When the host hears these excuses, he tells his servants to go into the streets and bring back whomever they find. The conclusion of the story is ominous: "The buyers and the merchants shall not come into the places of my Father." Not only does this conclusion make Jesus pass stern judgment on those who reject the invitation, it also castigates business (and by implication all this-worldly affairs) as incompatible with the Kingdom of Heaven.

Overall, the parables remain an absorbing topic for study. Because they stand so close to Jesus' own way of thinking and preaching, they offer some of the best keys to Jesus' intriguing personality. But the parables seldom admit of a clear-cut interpretation, any more than Jesus' other teachings or actions do. They contain so

(c) Dave Bartruff / CORBIS

This is a bishop from a Coptic Church, Egyptian Christians who trace their founding to Mark.

many different levels, possible allusions, and strata of metaphors that one is finally forced to leave off analyzing them and let them make a more synthetic, holistic impact. When one does this, it seems clear that Jesus, like many Eastern gurus, was a man filled with lively speech, because he was a man filled with God's presence, pregnant with God's love.

broke with Judaism irreparably. In the beginning, some followers of Jesus ("Judaizers") had urged keeping the precepts of the Jewish Torah, but they lost out to Paul's vision. The Torah had been the cornerstone of covenantal life. Most Jews, understandably, were not willing to throw the Torah over or enter a new covenant. Unfortunately, Paul and the later gospel writers seem increasingly frustrated with traditional Judaism for not accepting the Christians as the legitimate leaders of Judaism.

The **Gentiles** (non-Jews) who warmed to the gospel lived in a Hellenistic milieu that was ripe for foreign religions offering new concepts of salvation. Just as Judaism was in turmoil, with Zealots, Pharisees, Sadducees, and Essenes all urging different reactions to Roman rule, so, too, were the denominations of the Gentiles. But lacking the Jewish foundation, many of the Gentiles found it difficult to interpret Christian doctrine. Some, such as those in Corinth, fell into an **antinomian** view that since Jesus had died for their sins, they could do whatever they wanted without fear of God's retribution.

A NEW WORLDVIEW. As a result of the gospel and Paul's theology, within a generation of Jesus' death Jewish and Greek thought had combined into a powerful new worldview. From Judaism came the concepts of prophet and messiah. From Hellenism came the notions of savior and god. Jesus was the successor to Moses, the giver of a new Law, Daniel's concept of the Son of Man come to inaugurate the messianic age, the conqueror of death and disorder, and the Logos (Word) of eternal divinity come into time. All past history, from the first parent Adam, had been but a preparation for his coming. All of the future would unfold his implications, climaxing in a final judgment and a fulfillment in heaven.

The new denomination was apocalyptic. The early Christians expected the future to be short: Jesus would soon return in power and glory to consummate his work. As the years went by, the expectation shifted. Jesus had accomplished the essentials of salvation through his death and resurrection. However long it took in God's dispensation for Jesus' salvation to work itself out, there was no doubt of the final success. In the meantime, Christians were to spread the gospel (good news of Jesus).

THE EARLY CENTURIES

The gospel writers (Mark, Matthew, Luke, and John) all interpreted the life of Jesus. Even in the most journalistic portions of the New Testament, they have cast Jesus' sayings and doings in terms of their own theologies. Matthew, for instance, works largely with Jewish notions, trying to show that Jesus is the successor to Moses, the gospel is the successor to the Torah, and so on. The other gospels, as well as the *Epistle to the Hebrews* and the *Book of Revelation,* are similarly theological. John arranges Jesus' public life, giving him a sacramental glow. The second half of John's gospel concentrates on Jesus' "glory": his intimacy with the heavenly Father and his victorious death and resurrection. *Hebrews* tries to show that Jesus fulfilled Jewish types of sacrifice, while *Revelation* is a Christian apocalypse (disclosure) designed to shore up the Christians' commitment against Roman persecution.

By the end of the first century, then, the Church had a variety of theologies. The majority were extensions of Jewish religion in the light of Jesus as the Messiah. The *Apostolic Age* is the period that elaborated what Jesus meant and how the Church was to organize itself. It embraces roughly the period from the death of Jesus (ca. 30 C.E.) to the last decades of the first century. A central concern in both those years and the next centuries was authority. For the early Church, an *apostolos* was a person to whom God had delegated Church authority.

During Jesus' ministry, his twelve intimates were the apostles par excellence, since they had received their commission from Jesus himself. Clearly the Twelve formed a collegial group with Peter as their head, and the Church accepted their authority. However, balancing this apostolic "official" authority was a looser, charismatic leadership expressed through prophecy, teaching, speaking in tongues, and so on. The earliest Church preaching was intended to show that Jesus fulfilled the promises of Jewish scripture. In their teaching, the first apostles relied on oral tradition about Jesus' person and words. The first great problem in the Apostolic Age, as we saw, was the Pauline (pertaining to Paul) problem of opening the Church to the Gentiles.

During the second century, the leadership of the Church passed from those who had seen Jesus them-

Three apostles

selves to those who had received the gospel from eye-witnesses but had not themselves known the Lord. The "Fathers" who led the second-century Church are therefore apostolic in the sense that they had direct contact with the Twelve.

Externally, from the time of Nero (54–68) the Church was ever liable to persecution by the Roman authorities, who worried about secret societies that might sow seeds of revolution. Since the Romans looked on religion as the bond of their realm, they were especially sensitive to groups who did not worship the traditional Roman deities. But Christians continued to expand throughout the Roman empire during the second and third centuries. By 300, they

COMPARISON OF JAINISM WITH GNOSTICISM		
DIMENSION	JAINISM	GNOSTICISM
Time	500 B.C.E.	first and second centuries C.E.
Started in	India	North Africa and Middle East
Spread to	nowhere	Roman empire
Major figures	Mahavira	Mani, Marcion
View of reality	Dualism: spirit and matter	dualism: spirit and matter
View of creator deity	nonexistent	evil
Metaphor	wheel	light
Metaphor adopted by	Buddhism	Christianity
Ethics	asceticism and noninjury	asceticism or antinomianism
Monasticism	encouraged	encouraged
Opposed	Hinduism	Judaism
Rejected scripture	*Vedas*	Old Testament
Rejected doctrine of	caste	incarnation (Docetism)
Verdict of other denominations	declared heretical by Hinduism	declared heretical by Christianity
Core constituency	merchants	
Current status	a few million followers in India	doctrines and symbols recur in new movements

probably constituted the majority population in Asia Minor and Carthage, and they were at least a noticeable fraction of the population along the northern shore of the Mediterranean. Their major political problem, gaining sufferance from the Roman authorities, was not solved until Constantine came to power early in the fourth century.

GNOSTICISM. More potentially destructive than Rome were the heresies known under the general label of **Gnosticism**. This is sometimes covered as another Hellenistic mystery cult, but most of Gnosticism's growth was within Christianity as a competing (later deemed heretical) set of doctrines. Most Gnosticism involved a dualistic mythology: spirit was good, but matter, the negative principle, came from a

Demiurge (something like Satan, a subordinate being whom the spirit Father God begot as Wisdom but who fell from grace). Gnosticism offered a revelation to certain "elect" persons: if they would hate this lower world of material creation (which was under the fallen Demiurge) and commit to the higher spiritual and divine realm, they might return to glory with God. To explain their revelation, the Gnostics taught the myth that each of the elect had a hidden spark from God's eternal world. The sparks fell into matter because of a heavenly war between darkness and light (or, in other versions, because of an accident during the production of the divine emanations). Higher beings would one day dissolve this fallen world, but in the meantime they called to people's hidden sparks by means of saviors, revelations, and rites of baptism.

Gnosticism blended the Hellenistic notion of divine emanation, mystery religion notions about salvation through sacramental rites, and Jewish notions of sin and redemption. It stressed the division between this world and heaven, the evil of matter and the flesh, and the need for asceticism (celibacy and bodily discipline) to gain freedom from matter.

Some Gnostic thinkers, such as Mani, offered a separate denomination which directly competed with Christianity for gentiles open to Middle Eastern religions offering salvation. Mani (216–276) lived in Mesopotamia. At age twenty four, he claimed to be the final revelation, completing the messages started by Zoroaster, Buddha, and Jesus. His system supposed a primeval conflict between light and darkness, and it, too, stressed asceticism. The object of **Manicheanism** was to release the particles of light that Satan had stolen and placed in the human brain. His movement spread to Egypt, north Africa, and even Rome. (During the early years of his adult life, the great Christian thinker Augustine was, for a time, a Manichean.) Mani wound up in Persia, where his Gnostic doctrine had converted the king, who spread it throughout his empire. Unfortunately for Mani, the next king returned to traditional Zoroastrianism and threw Mani into jail, where he died.

The greatest threat from Gnosticism was that it moved within Christianity and tried to shape its doctrine. The ascetic Marcion (85–160 C.E.), who ended up being excommunicated for his preachings, maintained that the Christian gospel is wholly a matter of love rather than a matter of law. On that account, **Marcionism** completely rejected the Old Testament (Jewish scripture), declaring that the God of the Old Testament (who had created the material world) was not the Spirit God, but the Demiurge, Satan.

About the same time, there arose another Gnostic doctrine within Christianity, **Docetism.** It proclaimed that Jesus was the pure Man of Light who brought salvation from the material darkness. It further denied that Jesus could have a material body of flesh. Therefore, his death upon the cross (and his physical resurrection) were merely apparent. Although this doctrine was clearly condemned in the second century, it had great staying power and motivated the Church to issue creedal statements affirming that Jesus did come in the flesh, was crucified, died, and was resurrected.

Forces within Early Christianity

OTHER CHALLENGES. Other threats to Christianity during the early period included Ebionism (an effort to restrict the understanding of Jesus to Jewish categories) and people who claimed revelations setting dates for the second coming of Jesus. This no doubt started in the first century, for Paul and even the later gospels have to caution against setting dates. Perhaps the greatest challenge in this area was that of Montanus in Asia Minor. About the year 160, the aescetic Montanus led a heretical apocalyptic movement based on the primacy of the Holy Spirit. His followers expected the outpouring of the Holy Spirit on the Church. In its own prophecies, **Montanism** saw the beginnings of the bestowal of the Spirit. Montanus set dates for the return of Christ, and many of his followers sold their possessions or decided to stop tilling their fields. When the Church declared Montanism a heresy, it was an important point in its self-definition: Christians were to be an enduring church and not trust a self-appointed prophet who set dates for the imminent return of Christ.

Donatism was an internal challenge dealing with the question of the purity of membership in the Church and clergy that arose in the fourth and fifth centuries, primarily in the north African churches. To understand how this came about, we must understand the gravity of the ongoing persecutions against the Christians. The Roman emperors Decius (249–251) and Diocletian (284–305) made enough **martyrs** to make professing Christian doctrine a serious matter. Christians had to meet secretly in catacombs (caves) or private homes, and their organization had to be informal. Their leaders (bishops and elders)

Which theoretical approach would give you the most insight on the history, doctrine, rituals, ethics of early Christianity? Consider Freud, Marx, Tylor, Malinowski, Otto, Müller, and others.

EXAMPLE: The French sociologist Emile Durkheim viewed religion as a social phenomenon that served to celebrate and reinforce the cohesion of the social group.

Christians in the first century were a small and persecuted band drawn from the ranks of the slaves, workers, and displaced immigrants of the Roman empire. They could not trust the greater Roman society or Jewish authority, only themselves and their savior Jesus.

Luke's history of the apostles (*Acts* 4:32–35) records how they shared material possessions. Although they had come from different lands, they were seen as being of "one blood" (*Acts* 17:26).

Paul's first epistle to the Corinthians (*I Corinthians*) sets out both the ethical rules and the symbolism for the new community. The guiding rule is to avoid offending a brother Christian (8:13). We are not to be concerned with private gain, but with what is best for the community (10:24). Wealth is to be shared (*II Corinthians* 8:13–15).

The powerful symbol Paul uses of the unity of this community comes from the central ritual of the early Church, the Lord's Supper. The bread eaten by all is the Body of Christ. As all partake, they become the Body of Christ; each individual is merely a part (e.g., a toe, an ear) and must serve the whole. Each must appreciate (rather than covet) the diversity of gifts bestowed on other Christians (*I Corinthians* 12).

Contribute to this discussion at http://www.delphi.com/rel101

were indistinguishable from ordinary people, and their teaching had a *disciplina arcani*—a strict code of secrecy. Those who died as martyrs were great heroes, whom heaven would greet with open arms. But many Christians did not have that kind of courage and committed **apostasy** (recanted their commitment to Christ) to avoid torture or death. When the threat of persecution was over, many of these apostates (also known as *lapsi*) felt guilt and asked readmission to the Christian community. Donatus was a local bishop who led a party of rigorists who insisted that such traitors had no place in the Church. He went one step further, declaring that if these lapsed Christians had been readmitted to the priesthood and had administered the sacraments, the holy rites would not be acceptable in God's eyes. Donatism was opposed by many Church thinkers, most conclusively by his fellow north African **Augustine** (354–430) who argued for greater clemency and for Christ's decisive role in the inner effect of the sacraments: the Church is holy even if the people in it are not.

THE CONCILIAR AGE

The Christian church had little power in the secular world until the conversion of the emperor **Constantine** (312), so even when it was not suffering active persecution, it was not very influential. From the time of the Edict of Milan (313), however, Christianity was free to proselytize within the Roman empire.

During the fourth and fifth centuries, a number of meetings (**councils**) of Church leaders were held that formally established the rituals and official doctrine (dogma) that any group in union with the apostolic Church had to adopt. From those meetings came the name for the next period of Christian history. Above all, the meetings, many of which were called by emperors concerned about the unity of the empire, dealt with the central issues of the Christian creed, hammering out the dogmas about God, Jesus, salvation, and the like that became the backbone of Christian theology. Various controversies made Church leaders realize that it was imperative to determine which apostolic sources were genuine expressions of doctrine and which were not. That imperative resulted in the establishment of a Christian scriptural *canon* (list of official books).

Three main factors determined the final canon: whether the writing in question came from an apostle or a close associate of an apostle, whether it was accepted by the Church at large, and whether its contents were consistent with doctrine. As early as 170, leaders in Rome had determined a canon of authoritative books in response to the canon drawn up by the heretic Marcion. Yet for many decades no list was agreed upon by the entire Church because local traditions varied. For instance, the East long hesitated to accept Revelation, while the West was uncertain about Hebrews.

The first great dogmatic (official doctrinal) council occurred at Nicaea by the Black Sea in 325. It produced a consensus that was especially important for clarifying Jesus' divine status as Logos or Son. The Council of Nicaea was called by the emperor Constantine, and without imperial support the Nicene party would not have triumphed. Before Nicaea, most churches had been content to repeat what scripture (Jewish and Christian both) said about God and Jesus. However, Church theologians did not know how to respond to questions that scripture did not address. One such question came from Arius, a priest of Alexandria, in Egypt, who proposed that Jesus, as the Logos of God (the divine Son), was subordinate to the Father. In short, Arianism assumed that if one drew a line between created beings and the uncreated divine substance, the Logos would fall on the side of created beings.

Arius' principal opponent was **Athanasius**, who represented the theologians of Alexandria in Egypt, who descended from Clement of Alexandria (ca. 150–215), one of the first Christian theologians to cast Christian doctrine as a philosophy that might persuade educated Hellenists, and Origen (ca. 185–254), the first great Christian speculator. (Working with Platonic philosophy, Origen had written immensely influential commentaries on scripture and expositions of Christian doctrine.) Athanasius, drawing on this Alexandrian tradition, assaulted Arius' argument. Speaking for what he held to be orthodoxy, he said that the Logos was of the same substance as the Father, possessing the single divine nature. Nicaea agreed with Athanasius, making his position dogma. There were many political machinations, as different political factions chose different theological sides, and Arianism (which was the doctrine of Arius and had nothing to do with the Aryans) thrived among Germanic tribes well into the sixth century. However, the **Nicene Creed**, which codified the position against Arius, was official doctrine.

TRINITARIAN DOCTRINE. The doctrine of the Trinity cannot be found clearly stated in the *Bible*, but most mainline Christian denominations accept it. While most theologians regard the Trinity as a doctrine consistent with scripture, it was not until the

---

Most Christian denominations accept the doctrine of the Trinity, as clarified by the Church councils of the fourth and fifth centuries: that there is one God, taking the form of three persons (Father, Son, and Holy Spirit), co-equal and co-eternal. Take a passage of scripture and interpret it to show how it supports or does not support this doctrine. The scripture can be the *Qur'an,* the Old Testament, the *Book of Mormon, Doctrines and Covenants,* the *Apocrypha,* noncanonical gospels (e.g., *Thomas*), or the canonical New Testament. Identify the translation you are using (especially of the New Testament).

Contribute to this discussion at
http://www.delphi.com/rel101

---

fourth century that Church councils finalized it. Athanasius perceived that the canonical literature gave the Holy Spirit divinity equal to that of the Father and the Son. Therefore, he suggested the word *homoousios* ("of one substance") to include the **Holy Spirit** and so set the lines of what would become, at the Council of Constantinople in 381, the doctrine of the Holy Spirit's divinity. That completed the doctrine of the **Trinity**: one God who was three equal "persons," each of whom fully possessed the single divine nature.

Augustine, bishop of Hippo, in North Africa, was greatly influenced by Plato. It was Augustine who expressed Trinitarian doctrine in terms of a psychological analogy that shaped Western Christian speculation. He proposed that as memory, understanding, and love are all mind, so (but without human imperfections) are Father, Son, and Holy Spirit all divinity. The Father is like an inexhaustible memory (from which all creation comes), the Logos is like the Father's self-awareness, and the Spirit is like their boundless love.

MONASTICISM. Not all early Christian ascetics were Gnostics. The increasing tie between the Church and civil authorities stimulated new religious movements within the Church that opposed the laxness or "accommodation" that worldly success easily begot. The most important reforms generated interest in monasticism and virginity (which overlapped, insofar as monks took vows of celibacy). Communities of celibate, frequently very ascetic monks and nuns grew in this period. Both males and females found a monastic life of dedication to prayer and charitable works a way of maintaining their martyrlike intensity of commitment. Many found that it led them to the North African desert for solitude and asceticism. The great hero of the day, in fact, was the desert father Anthony, who made a great impression on Athanasius. Partly because of the dangers of desert solitude, many monks soon formed communities, and before long these communities admitted women (nuns). In the East, communal (cenobitic) monasticism took form under the guidance of Basil, bishop of Caesarea. In the West, the rule of Benedict predominated. So the dedication that had previously been an informal option (largely in terms of virginity or widowhood) took institutional form. That, too, was an innovation added to New Testament religion, which had no monastic life. The Church's decision that monastic life was truly in keeping with New Testament religion was analogous to the decision to coin new doctrinal concepts. It should not be surprising that the Protestant reformers of the sixteenth century opposed the development of monasticism (as being unbiblical), just as they opposed the development of the Catholic notion of the central authority of the Roman Pope.

CHRISTOLOGY. The councils not only set the pattern of Trinitarian doctrine that dominated the following centuries but also dealt with a host of problems that arose when people started to think about Jesus as the divine Word. Nestorius from Antioch and Cyril from Alexandria squared off in Christological controversy, and Alexandria won. **Nestorianism**, after the teachings of Nestorius, stressed the unity of the Christian God, though he affirmed Christ's two natures (human and divine). Cyril thought that Nestorius' affirmation was not strong enough to safeguard the single personhood of Jesus Christ the God-man, so he pressed for a *hypostatic* (personal) union of the two natures. The Councils of Ephesus (431) and Chalcedon (451) affirmed Cyril's doctrine of one "person" and two "natures." Later Christological development clarified that Jesus had a rational soul, two wills, and two sets of operations, human and divine. This orthodox Christology resulted from trying to systematize the scriptural teaching about God and Jesus. It stressed that only the union of the divine with the human in Jesus could save human beings from sin

and give them divine life. Orthodoxy cast many groups in the shade, branding their positions as heretical, but it also developed the mainline conception of Christ considerably.

CATHOLIC SACRAMENTALISM. The *Gospels* only record two rituals instituted by Jesus. One was a ritual of initiation, baptism, and the other was to be done regularly, the Holy Eucharist (Lord's Supper). Eventually, the Church (which was becoming known as the Holy **Roman Catholic** Apostolic Church) had developed seven **sacraments** (liturgies or rituals), which it understood as being efficacious for channeling God's grace through the Church to its members. The development of these sacraments involved an interesting interplay with the development of doctrines about heaven and purgatory.

The first sacrament was **baptism**. In the *Gospels*, baptism was a rite of initiation into the Christian fold. It was performed in a natural body of water, such as a river, and it was by complete immersion. There is no direct evidence of infants being baptized, although some passages suggest that "whole households were baptized" and we can infer that they might have included children or infants. A doctrine associated with baptism was that it washed away not only original sin, but also any individual sins that the person had committed prior to baptism. Some people petitioned to be rebaptized, because they had fallen into sin again after their conversion, and wished to cleanse themselves of that new stain upon their souls. The Church finally agreed that baptism would be a once-in-a-lifetime, nonrepeatable ritual of initiation.

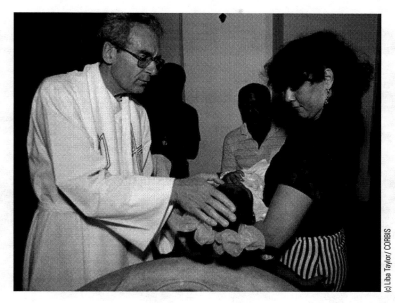

Most Christian denominations use baptism as a ritual of initiation. Here, in Cuba, a Catholic priest baptises an infant by sprinkling. Many Protestant denominations insist on adult baptism by full immersion.

Many people then decided that they would hold off on getting baptized so that it would cover a broader spectrum of life's sins. Deathbed conversions were common into the fourth century.

The Church accordingly made a decision to emphasize baptism as a birth rite, urging that Christian parents get their infants baptized. This entailed a change in the ritual: sprinkling instead of dunking. It also meant that its relevance would not be the initiate's decision to convert to become a Christian; rather, the rite would be more for the parents (and godparents, and the entire local community attending the ceremony), for it would symbolize their commitment to raise the child as a Christian.

This shift opened up several theological issues about the impact of baptism (or its lack) upon an individual in the afterlife. What is the downside if parents do not get the infant baptized? **Pelagianism**, after Pelagius (d. 430), took the humanistic perspective that Adam's sin was an individual fall, not a fall for the entire human race, and therefore, we had no reason to presume that unbaptized infants would go to hell. Augustine challenged Pelagius and reaffirmed Paul's conception of original sin: the entire human race had been stained by the disobedience of Adam, and without the grace of Christ, channeled through the Church, there was no salvation. Medieval theologians, hoping to soften the harshness of this condemnation of the unbaptized, suggested the existence of **limbo**, a place not as bad as hell (for the infant had not been guilty of any personal sins, especially the conscious rejection of Christ) but not as good as the Beatific Vision that was reserved for those in Heaven.

Purgatory, a related concept, tries to answer the question of what happens to adults who, after baptism, commit individual sins. Assuming that these sins are venial (not so serious as to keep one out of heaven), then the soul might have to do a sort of penance in purgatory prior to entering heaven. This is not a place where souls who had rejected Christ while they were on earth will get a second chance to convert, but a place where those Christians who are bound for heaven must serve a little more time in preparation for their eventual destination. Nevertheless, purgatory was not considered that great of a place, and so the motivation was to sin less on earth (or do penance on earth in order to avoid having to spend so much time in purgatory).

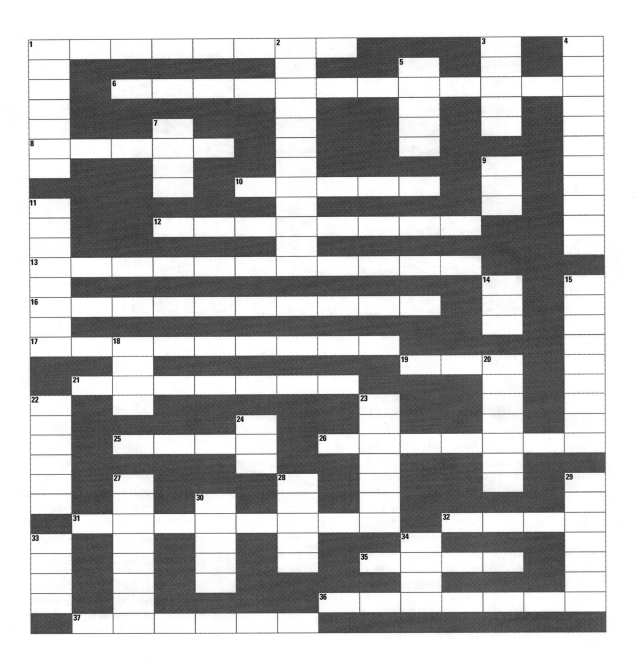

ACROSS

1 Dualists who viewed matter as evil
6 Christianity absorbed Greek and Celtic religion, making it _____.
8 Greek term for "the Word"; Stoic concept
10 Church councils set the _____ of scripture.
12 Priests, monks, and nuns are supposed to be _____.
13 First-century Christianity was _____, expecting the final battle.
16 Augustine was a great fifth-century _____.
17 The Eucharist is known as holy _____.
19 The period before Jesus
21 One God in the form of three persons
25 Author of third gospel and book of *Acts*.
31 Heretical doctrine that Jesus had no physical body
32 Author of *Epistle to the Romans*
35 Author of the book of *Revelation*
36 A Christian not of Jewish origin
37 Docetism was declared to be in _____.

DOWN

1 *Mark, Matthew, Luke,* and *John* are the four _____.
2 Jesus founded this religion.
3 Apostle who became the first pope
4 Doctrines about the end times
5 Catholic doctrine about afterlife
7 The fourth gospel
9 Testament that prophesied a coming Messiah
11 Medieval mystics lived a _____ lifestyle.
14 Testament written by Jesus' followers
15 Fifth-century theologian
18 The earliest gospel
20 A letter written by an apostle
22 Greek title for Jesus
23 Christian ritual of initiation
24 The _____ testament in composed of epistles and gospels.
26 Paul and Peter both had this title.
27 One who renounces a religion and falls away
28 Fifth-century theologian; argued that God was greater than Jesus
29 Part of Palestine Jesus came from
30 The crucified Messiah
33 Author of *Epistles to the Corinthians*
34 Author of the last gospel

While the doctrines of purgatory and limbo were never accepted by any future Christian denomination other than the Catholic, the ritual practice of infant baptism became the norm and has remained so in the Catholic, Eastern Orthodox, Lutheran, Episcopalian, Presbyterian, and Methodist churches. (The return to adult baptism exclusively was advocated by the Baptists, Pentecostals, Mormons, Seventh Day Adventists, Church of Christ, and Jehovah's Witnesses.)

This move toward infant baptism occasioned the need for additional sacraments to take the place of adult baptism. If baptism is not going to be a ritual of personal decision, initiation, for Christians who have come to the age of discretion, then a new sacrament must be developed to fill that void: **confirmation.** This was usually performed by making the sign of the cross with oil on the forehead of the initiate, transforming him or her into a "soldier of Christ."

The main attraction of the deathbed conversion and baptism was that it erased a lifetime of sins. If baptism was to be a birth rite and nonrepeatable, some new sacrament would have to be developed to handle those sins committed after baptism. The earliest form, **confession,** was a public statement of sins to the rest of the Christian community. By the sixth century, a Celtic practice of private confessions of sin directly to a priest became popular, usually associated with the granting of absolution and the assigning of certain penances. (Even serious sins would be forgiven, but the more severe the sin, the greater the time in purgatory to compensate for it.) After Vatican II, the sacrament has been reformulated as the Sacrament of Reconciliation and more public, symbolic options are now available for penitents.

Another attraction of the deathbed baptism was that it helped bring closure to a person's life with a special predeath ritual. After the shift to infant baptism, that was replaced with **last rites** (also known as *extreme unction*). This is a rite of penance (like confession) and anointing with oil (like confirmation). In recent years it has been expanded to the Sacrament for the Sick and can be given to anyone who is ailing or has the risk of death.

The Holy **Eucharist** (Holy Communion, Lord's Supper) has been the principal sacrament in the majority of the Christian traditions. It is practiced weekly (even daily) by the most devout and is based upon the description of the Last Supper that Jesus had with his disciples. The key words recited in the ritual are:

> For in the night in which he was betrayed, he took bread; and when he had given thanks, he brake it, and gave it to his disciples, saying, "Take, eat, this is my Body, which is given for you. Do this in remembrance of me." Likewise, after supper, he took the cup; and when he had given thanks, he gave it to them, saying "Drink ye all of this; for this is my Blood of the New Testament, which is shed for you, and for many, for the remission of sins. Do this, as oft as you shall drink it, in remembrance of me."

Paul's *Epistles* point out that this ritual not only reaffirms the verticle bonds between the Christian and Christ, but the horizontal bonds with his/her community who share the ritual bread and wine.

Marriage also became recognized as a sacramental occasion. The Christian theology of marriage has likened the conjunction of man and woman in matrimony to the union between Christ and the Church, and it has found in the *Genesis* creation account, in which God gave Eve to Adam, a prototype of the nuptial union. A Christian marriage was meant for both the mutual comfort of the spouses and the procreation of children. It had to be entered into freely by both parties, and usually the minister called upon the assembled community not only to witness the parties' vows but also to support them in their marital venture.

Marriage inside the Catholic Church is considered an important sacrament that the individual will not be allowed to repeat again with another spouse (unless the first spouse has died). The current Catholic stand against divorce is seen as the most rigid among Christian churches, but it is quite a bit more complicated than first meets the eye. The Catholics take literally the part about no man being able to put asunder the sacrament of marriage. While the Church recognizes the right of abused spouses to seek legal redress in the form of a divorce granting separation and property settlement, it does not consider such a civil action as freeing the parties to engage in the sacrament of remarriage in the Church. (Indeed, if a divorced Catholic married in a secular or non-Catholic marriage ceremony, the spouses would then be seen as committing adultery). The Catholic Church does have a loophole, nullification or annulment, which says that there must have been something wrong with the first marriage to begin with; therefore we can say that it never really existed, and so a second marriage is really only the first. Unfortunately, this process of a canon law annulment is not well understood, even among Catholics, and tends to be thought of as granted more often to the rich and powerful than to others.

An additional sacrament (and one not undertaken by the laity) is the **ordination** of the Church's ministers. In churches with several ranks of ministers, the bishop has usually presided at the ordination. After satisfying himself that the candidates were qualified, he solicited the approval and support of the community, prayed over the ordinand and then laid hands on the ordinand's head and prayed, "Therefore, Father, through Jesus Christ your Son, give your Holy Spirit to ———; fill him [or her, in churches that ordained women] with grace and power, and make him [or her] a priest in your Church."

Although not an official sacrament, another important ritual was burial rites. These usually focused on the Holy Eucharist for the occasion of death and burial. The Liturgy of the Word featured psalms and scriptural passages concerned with death and the Christian hopes for resurrection, and the person would be buried in consecrated ground with prayers for forgiveness and the life of the blessed in heaven.

Even in the first century, as Christianity moved north and west, the proselytizers often carried with them physical symbols of the religion: perhaps a palm leaf from the Holy Land, or a splinter of wood from the true cross, or a tooth from one of the apostles. These relics were intended to serve as credentials for the missionary, but many times the new Christians venerated these relics as if they possessed magical powers. Later, as the churches became more elaborate, there would be paintings, stained glass windows, and statues representing Jesus or the saints. While these were supposed to be powerful symbols to put the worshipper in a spiritual frame of mind for the worship of Jesus, no doubt some people thought that they were praying to the statue (and thereby committing idolatry).

A related issue is the practice of identifying deceased people as **saints**. Paul used this term broadly to refer to all members of the Christian community. After a generation or two, this title became reserved for exceptional Christians: perhaps the apostles, martyrs, hermits, or exemplary leaders. The Church came to recognize saints as having two functions: their lives could serve as models of piety for the living, and after death they had a role to play in mediating the interaction of heaven and earth. A Christian sometimes prays to a saint in hopes of the saint's serving as an intermediary, someone who will plead the case before God in heaven. The process of selecting saints is a two-step procedure known as beatification and canonization (the maintenance of an official list of saints) and requires action by the Pope.

The greatest of all the saints was **Mary**, mother of Jesus. There is evidence that Christians were praying to her in the earliest Church. The Catholics have introduced some additional doctrines about her: that she was forever a virgin, that when she herself was conceived in her own mother's womb, it was a special immaculate conception so that she would be a vessel free of the taint of original sin, and that after her death she was directly assumed into heaven without having to go through purgatory.

Many Christians from non-Catholic denominations have come to criticize the Catholic leadership for changing the rituals or doctrine from what was reported in the New Testament. Some contemporary fundamentalists might consider the Catholics to be a cult unworthy of the title "Christian." The Catholics respond that all of these extensions of ritual and doctrine were attempts to make the core of Christianity (the worship of Jesus) more relevant to new times and peoples and that it is inappropriate to try to freeze doctrine or ritual to the first century. Furthermore, although the Catholics do respect scripture, they do not consider themselves limited to it (as some fundamentalist Protestants might perceive). The Church sees itself as canonizing the books of the New Testament

The Nelson Atkins Museum of Art, Kansas City, Missouri (Purchase: Nelson Trust) 38-8

Madonna and child

(and later changing that canon over a thousand years later). As one Catholic layman put it, "Jesus did not come to write a book, but to establish a Church." But Catholics can also find scripture to back up the Church's authority to modify doctrine and ritual (e.g., *Matthew* 16:18, which gives Peter as first Pope the keys to the kingdom).

Critique a specific Catholic doctrine, ritual, or ethical stance by citing a scripture from any religion discussed in this book. You might consider:

- Veneration of Mary
- Use of statues
- Purgatory
- Confession
- No remarriage in Church
- Papal authority
- Prohibition of birth control

Contribute to this discussion at
http://www.delphi.com/rel101

Byzantine book cover

The Nelson Atkins Museum of Art, Kansas City, Missouri (Pruchase: Nelson Trust) 66-27

EASTERN ORTHODOX CHURCHES

Orthodoxy has two principal meanings. It may refer to the Eastern **Orthodox Church** that separated from Rome in the **Great Schism** of 1054 or to the "correct doctrine" established by scripture, tradition, and the councils. In this section we address the first concept, describing the growth of Eastern Christianity after the Conciliar Age (most of the great councils took place in the East). The term *Orthodox* was adopted for two reasons: the Orthodox Church thought of itself as keeping the traditional doctrine and rituals alike.

LITURGY. This term means "the work of the people" and refers to public ritual. During the Apostolic Age, the Church had developed a sacramental system in which baptism and the Eucharist ("the Lord's Supper") were especially important. In the early medieval period, when Orthodoxy took form, the liturgy flowered. The result was a full calendar of holy days and a full ritual that involved music, art, incense, iconography, and more. Thus, communal worship became the dramatic center of church life, especially in the Eastern Church.

From the ninth to the fifteenth century, a complicated process of alienation between Byzantine (Eastern) Christianity and Roman Christianity resulted in their separation. Some of the factors in the separation were the fall of the Eastern Roman empire, the failure of the Crusades, the growing antagonism of Islam, the growth of the papacy, the stirrings of what developed into the sixteenth-century Protestant reactions

against the papacy, and the rivalry between Russia and Western Europe. These factors take us to the beginning of modernity in Eastern Christendom, explaining why East and West have remained divided to the present.

RELIGIOUS ISSUES. Thus, the break between Eastern and Western Christianity owed a great deal to political and cultural conflicts. For instance, the patriarch Photius, who presided at the Eastern capital of Constantinople from 858 to 886, drew up a list of what Byzantines considered to be Latin (Western) errors in doctrine. This list reveals how the two portions of Christendom had developed different understandings of orthodoxy. In this list Photius cited irregularities in the observance of Lent (the period of penance before the great feast of Easter when the resurrection of Christ was celebrated), false teaching about the Holy Spirit, and most importantly compulsory celibacy for the clergy (most Eastern priests were married, and now the Pope was trying to make this a requirement).

The most acute point of theological difference between the East and the West was about the Holy Spirit, which came to be known as the *filioque*. According to the Nicene Creed, within the life of the Trinity the Holy Spirit proceeds from the Father. The Western Council of Toledo (589) made an addition to the Nicene Creed: the Holy Spirit proceeds not just from the Father but also from the Son (*filioque* means "and from the Son"). East and West each became attached to its Trinitarian formula, so the *filioque* became a sharp bone of contention. The East claimed that it was heretical; the West claimed it merely articulated a tacit understanding of traditional doctrine that Nicaea had assumed. The practical significance of the difference is not clear, but it probably shows the East's tendency to appreciate the Father's primal mystery—the Father's status as a fathomless source from which everything issues.

In response to Photius, Western theologians composed their own list of complaints about Eastern usage. In their view the Eastern discipline that allowed clerics to marry, that baptized by immersion, that celebrated the Eucharist with leavened bread, and that had different rules for fasting deviated from tradition. The debate even descended to such details as whether bishops should wear rings, whether clergy should wear beards, and whether instrumental music was appropriate at the liturgy. However, the main theological issue continued to be the *filioque,* while the main political issue emerged as the difference in the churches' understanding of authority. The Eastern Church's tradition was a loose federation of bishops, all of whom were considered successors of the apostles. The Eastern Church also stressed the rights of individual churches and ethnic groups. The Western tradition was a "monarchical" leadership by the bishop of Rome. As successor to Peter, he claimed primacy over the other churches.

When the Byzantine empire was about to fall to the Turks, the Eastern and Western factions met for the last time at the Council of Florence (1439). That was long after the mutual anathemas of 1054 (described later), but the East hoped to secure both Church unification and Western help against Islam. On the agenda were only four points (the other disagreements having fallen away as trivial). They were the prerogatives of the bishop of Rome, the *filioque* clause, the doctrine of purgatory (the Roman Catholic teaching that there is an intermediate state between heaven and hell, which the Orthodox condemned as unbiblical), and whether to use leavened or unleavened bread in the Eucharist. In retrospect, theologians have judged the last two items as relatively inconsequential. The first two were interrelated, because the Council of Florence came to focus on the question of whether the Pope had the right to alter an ecumenical creed (that is, add *filioque* to the Nicene Creed). Because of their political problems (the menace of the Turks), the majority of the Greeks (Easterners) accepted the *filioque* and agreed to certain papal prerogatives. The union was confined to paper, though, because back at home Orthodox **synods** refused to ratify the agreements signed by their delegates.

SEPARATION. The pivotal moment in the East-West division was the mutual excommunications of 1054, which were due more to politics (or to snappish personalities) than to theology. Pope Leo IX had sent a Western delegation to Constantinople headed by one Cardinal Humbert. The Normans were menacing Leo and also the emperor Constantine Monomachus, so a major goal was to unite the churches to oppose a common foe. Humbert seems to have been a narrow, contentious type, as was his Eastern counterpart, the patriarch Michael Cerularius. When Pope Leo died in 1054, Cerularius held that Humbert's credentials were void. Humbert responded by laying on the altar of Saint Sophia in Constantinople a letter that excommunicated the patriarch and all his associates. The patriarch then assembled his own council, which excommunicated Humbert in return. The emperor dispatched the cardinal back to Rome with presents, hoping that the next Pope would appoint a new legate who could heal the breach. But the Normans prevented the popes from resuming negotiations, so the mutual excommunications stood until after the Second Vatican Council in the early 1960s.

In the opinion of many contemporary theologians and historians, the division between the Eastern and Western branches of the Church was a tragic accident. (Historians now say much the same of the sixteenth-century Reformation split in Europe.) Political circumstances, differences in traditional ways of celebrating liturgy, and, above all, differences in temperament and cultural backgrounds were more

Here we see priests of the Catholic and Eastern Orthodox Churches. The Episcopalian and Latter Day Saint churches also refer to their leaders as priests.

decisive than hard theological differences. What Orthodox and Catholics (and Protestants and Catholics) held in common was far more significant than what they held apart.

It may be more appropriate to speak of Eastern Orthodox churches (e.g., Greek, Russian) rather than just one Church, because the East has always respected ethnic differences in tradition and local control of church matters (probably because many bishops were under the control of local political leaders, such as the Byzantine emperor, whereas the Pope in Rome often enjoyed much greater power than Western European kings). All the Eastern churches together probably have about 200 million adherents. Most of the priests are married, but most of the bish-

ops are not. The archbishops are sometimes called metropolitans.

In an Orthodox Church, a Catholic will notice fewer statues but more paintings (icons) on the wall. The sign of the cross is made right to left. At the Orthodox liturgy, one feels a Christian *pneumaticism:* The Holy Spirit is dramatically present to effect the sacraments. In the invocation made over the Eucharistic gifts (the *epiclesis*), Orthodoxy stresses the Holy Spirit's role in transforming the bread and wine into Christ's substance. In its baptism and confession of sins, Orthodoxy's accent is sharing God's life—beginning divine life in baptism or repairing it in penance. Overall, Orthodoxy places the mystery of the Christian God to the fore. For the East, God is less a lawgiver or a judge than a spiritual power operating through creation. Creation ought to respond to God's power and beauty, so the Divine Liturgy becomes a song of praise, a hymn to the goodness and love that pour forth from the Father of Lights. Orthodoxy especially venerates Mary, the Mother of God, for her share in the design of grace that raises human beings to participate in the divine immortality.

Both major branches of Eastern Orthodoxy, the Greek and the Russian, have fostered a strong monastic life, and from this strong monastic life has come a steady stream of holy people wise in the ways of the religious spirit, prayer, asceticism, and mysticism. The Orthodox mystical tradition continues, alive and well, in places like Mount Athos in Greece, where monks meditate in the old ways and read the old classics. Like Hasidim lost in the world of Torah, the Orthodox holy men and women are lost in the world of the gospel. For them the gospel words are shining jewels, the gospel scenes are blazing icons. Contemplating those icons, the Orthodox saints have enjoyed wonderful visions of the life of God that fills the holy soul, the mercy of God that courses through the world. Their meditations have made the scriptural scenes contemporary, much the way Jewish prayer has made the Exodus contemporary.

It is shocking to enter the thought-world of the Orthodox monks and nuns, and perhaps equally shocking to realize that a similar thought-world predominated in the Christian West less than 500 years ago. Less than 500 years ago, even theologians studied the *Bible* more for its religious feeling than for its literary structure. Even theologians were more interested in feeling compunction than in knowing its definition. Similarly, the terms of reference are not the historical or literary aspects of the *Bible,* but the spiritual experiences and verities the monastic tradition tells him the *Bible* can promote. What the Holy Spirit did for the apostles, and for all who came after them, the Holy Spirit is poised to do today. After all, Jesus, the eternal Son of God, came from God precisely to give us human beings God's life, which the Holy Spirit wants to nurture in us. God's life, the East always has emphasized, is the perfect community of the Father, Son, and Holy Spirit. It is the Trinity not as the subject of conciliar controversies, or the subject of theologians' dry reflections, but as the spiritual atmosphere in which human beings can live, move, and have their being, if they would open their souls to its power. What the Eastern liturgy has always sung, the Eastern holy people have always stressed: the substantial love of God poured out for the salvation of human beings; humanity's potential elevation to a new, heavenly mode of life.

THE MEDIEVAL PERIOD

In the West, during the third and fourth centuries, most of the Celts converted. During the fifth and sixth centuries, Christian missionaries made considerable inroads among the Germanic tribes. Frequently they would convert tribal leaders from Teutonic religion or Arianist versions of Christianity, and then the entire tribe would convert. From 800 one could speak of the Holy Roman Empire—a tense mixture of political and religious drives for unity. Local bishops found that they could increase their freedom from local secular rulers by increasing their allegiance to the bishop of Rome. The friction between church and state therefore shifted to the interaction between the Pope and the Germanic emperor. A key issue was who should appoint local bishops. The investiture controversy, as it is called, was solved by a compromise in the Concordat of Worms (1122). Secular rulers had to recognize the independence of the local bishop by virtue of his loyalty to the Pope, and the Pope had to consult the emperor and appoint bishops acceptable to him.

During the twelfth century, the **Crusades** to the holy sites in Palestine riveted the Christian imagination, but they tended to increase the alienation between Eastern and Western Christendom. When the Fourth Crusade (1204) conquered Constantinople, set up a Western prince, and tried to Latinize the Eastern church, relations deteriorated to their lowest point. By 1453, after the Councils of Lyon and Florence had done little to heal the wounds of division, and after Easterners had suffered centuries of Western domination, a popular slogan circulated to the effect that Turks would be better rulers than Western Christians.

During the twelfth century, considerable resistance to the established Church power and doctrine arose among some groups, such as the Waldenses, who urged a return to apostolic simplicity and poverty. Groups that owed a debt to the old Gnostic views, such as the French **Cathari** or Albigensians, pushed dualistic views in their war on the flesh and their contempt for the material world.

To meet the challenge of such reformers, the Roman church developed new **orders** of priests and monks, the most important of which were the **Dominicans** and the Franciscans. Dominic (1170–1221) organized his group to preach against the heretics, and one of the devotions it added was the rosary—a string of beads for counting prayers to the Virgin Mary. The **Franciscans** stemmed from the charismatic Francis of Assisi (1181–1226), who dedicated himself to simple living. His angelic love of nature and of the infant Jesus made a deep impression on subsequent generations of Christians. Both Dominicans and Franciscans were innovations on the established (largely Benedictine) model of Western monasticism. Principally, they had more freedom than Benedictines to move out of the cloister. They were mobile and therefore quite effective in responding to different religious trouble spots.

SCHOLASTICISM. The thirteenth century was the high point of medieval intellectual life, and the movement known as **Scholasticism** reached its peak then. The Scholastics systematized the conciliar and patristic (the Fathers') theological doctrines. Augustine (354–430) was their great inspiration, but where Augustine worked with Neoplatonic thought categories (worked out by thinkers such as Plotinus, who developed Plato's ideas), Thomas **Aquinas** (1225–1274), the greatest of the medievals, worked with Aristotelian categories. Between Augustine and Aquinas lived **Anselm** (1033–1109), who said that, on the basis of a firm Christian commitment (rooted in scriptural, conciliar, and patristic doctrines), the theologian ought to learn as much as the divine mysteries allowed. Anselm's definition was a writ of intellectual emancipation. Though they accepted the disciplines of tradition and the Church's teaching office, the medieval theologians seized the right to develop reason and use it to illumine doctrine.

It was Aquinas who gained the greatest following. For Aquinas, philosophy was a universal basis for discussion, regardless of religious allegiance. Jews, Muslims, Christians, and pagans all had reason, and so all could philosophize. Theology, which rested on divine revelation, perfected philosophy, taking it into realms that it could not penetrate on its own (for instance, without revelation philosophy would not know of the Trinity or the Incarnation, the divine Word made flesh). Aquinas developed a powerful system of philosophical theology, but he was by no means the only impressive medieval thinker. His school, Thomism, trusted in reason, had a hopeful view of the world, thoroughly analyzed the Trinity, Christology, grace, and human virtues and vices.

HIERARCHY. The clergy had separated themselves from the laity, and within the clerical order there were numerous ranks: monks, priests, canons, bishops, abbots, archbishops, cardinals, and more. The papacy had a considerable bureaucracy and wielded great secular power. Because the general culture held a Christian worldview, heaven and hell had a vivid reality. Thus, the papal power to bar people from Church membership and so from heaven made people fear the pope greatly. Considerable worldliness entered into the papal use of excommunication, interdict, and the like, because by medieval times the Church had largely laid aside the *parousia* (second coming of Christ) and was concentrating on shaping daily life.

The medieval cathedrals also exhibited hierarchy through their stretching from earth toward heaven. They instruct us about medieval mentality, for towns built them to be a means of indoctrination. One can see this today in the gothic masterpieces of Notre Dame de Chartres and Notre Dame de Paris. The basic architectural thrust is toward heaven, as all commentators point out, yet within the cathedrals are windows and statues that bring God down into daily life. Most cathedrals were built over centuries, and sometimes the townspeople contributed free labor, as if they wanted the cathedral to praise God doubly. Significantly, Chartres and Notre Dame de Paris both bear Mary's name. As the Virgin Mother of God, Queen of Heaven and recourse of weak human beings, Mary was a mainstay of medieval Catholicism.

Around the cathedral walls, in wonderful stained glass, were biblical scenes, pictures of saints, and the like that told even the illiterate what the doctrine meant. With the statues of the Virgin and Jesus, they

(c) Bettmann / CORBIS

Exterior view of elaborate cathedral

lively and alert, giving many psalms a joyous lilt. For solemn moments, such as the celebration of Christ's Passion, chant could express deep sorrow, prefiguring, for instance, the music of Johann Sebastian Bach.

As it developed, the mass increasingly tended to represent Christ's sacrificial death. That did not deny the motif of a common meal, but it shifted emphasis to the consecration of the elements (bread and wine), because in the theologians' interpretation, the separation of the bread and wine stood for the sundering of Jesus' body on the cross. As a prayer (the "sequence") for the feast of Corpus Christi (attributed to Thomas Aquinas) shows, the consecrated host (bread transformed into Jesus' body) came to epitomize God's presence and redemptive action. The consecration was a miracle that the liturgy enacted each day. Paradoxically, the host defied the senses and nourished the soul. Because Jesus' body remained in church, the church was indeed God's house. Indeed, in the host, Jesus made himself available for reverence and prayer. Along with the cult of the Virgin and the cults of the many medieval saints, the cult of the Eucharist gave people at the bottom of the church pyramid another source of comfort.

Thus, the average person went through a harsh medieval life in fear and trembling but with many sources of hope that such a life would lead to heaven. The worldliness of much church life was balanced by the sacramental ceremonies that stressed the primacy of heaven. Rather clearly, the laity knew that they stood between heaven and earth. They were citizens of two worlds, and the best medieval theology and religious art counseled them to live their dual citizenship gracefully. For instance, the cathedral and monastic schools joined piety to learning. The mystery plays and even the *danse macabre* (dance of death) brought home to the common people that death leveled Pope and pauper to strict equality.

THE PERIOD OF REFORM

During the late fourteenth and the fifteenth centuries, the papacy was in great disarray. At one point there were two claimants to the chair of Peter, one in Rome and one in Avignon. In the East the Muslims held Asia Minor and Greece, their most dramatic victory being at Constantinople in 1453. Well into the fifteenth century, southern Spain was under Muslim

gave comfort to the person who slipped into the cathedral's darkness to pray. In its majestic space, one gained a proper perspective on one's problems. At a time when hard work, early death, and many sufferings were the rule, the cathedrals were for many a great support.

Monastic life progressed during the Middle Ages, though new orders such as the Franciscans and Dominicans neither completely replaced the more stable Benedictines nor completely abandoned their regimes. The great work of the monastic community was to celebrate the divine "office": liturgical prayers throughout the day and a communal Mass. By the thirteenth century, the Eucharist involved a rather complex ceremony, with choral music, gorgeous vestments, and precious vessels for the bread and wine. Gregorian chants best represent the music, which was control, while in Italy the spirit of the Renaissance seemed stronger than conciliar attempts to reform the papacy. In addition, there were frictions among local rulers within the Italian, French, and German realms; the middle classes emerged as a result of city life and economic changes; and the pre-Lutheran attacks on Church corruption by the Lollards (followers of John Wycliffe, 1329–1384 in England) and the Hussites (followers of John Hus [1369–1415] in Bohemia) took place.

The spark that set the Protestant **Reformation** blazing was the German, Martin **Luther** (1483–1546), an Augustinian monk whose study and spiritual searches had convinced him that the heart of the gospel was the Pauline justification by "faith" (the doctrine that it is only one's personal commitment to Christ that makes one right with God). Only by reviving this Pauline theme could Christianity regain its pure beginnings. This view claimed that the entire Catholic sacramental system was to be dismissed as a covenant of "works": the mass, the rosary, and so on. Luther was precipitated into action by the prevailing practice of **indulgences** (papal remissions of purgatorial punishment due for sins), which one could obtain for various good deeds, including almsgiving. Behind this practice lay some simple economics. The popes had spent lavishly in their Renaissance enthusiasm for art and culture. Leo X, for instance, was perhaps 125,000 ducats in debt at the time that he endorsed the preaching mission of Johann Tetzel (Luther's great adversary in the debate over indulgences in Germany), the mission included granting an indulgence for a contribution to the building of St. Peter's in Rome. To Luther the whole system—the Pope's extravagance, his pretension to control a treasury of merits generated by the saints, out of which he might draw "credits" to cover sinners' debts, and his focusing his economics on the mass—was blasphemous. On October 31, 1517, tradition says, Luther nailed his *Ninety-five Theses* to the door of the castle church at Wittenberg, which amounted to a formal challenge to the system.

Many Germans who for political or religious reasons had grievances against Rome supported Luther. As his thought expanded, he made scripture the sole arbiter of Christian doctrine and ritual, declared the primacy of individual conscience, upgraded the status of the layperson, and urged the use of the vernacular

(c) James L. Amos/CORBIS

Martin Luther, 16th century German Protestant Reformer

rather than Latin. Luther also stressed the uniqueness of Christ's death on the cross and so taught that the Eucharist principally commemorates the Last Supper, rather than representing Christ's sacrificial death. On the basis of scripture, he judged the doctrine of purgatory unfounded and the practice of monastic life an aberration. Because Luther was a fine preacher, he made these ideas matters for discussion in the marketplace. By translating the *Bible* into marvelous German, he put the central basis for his reform within reach of all literate people (and just about standardized High German in the process). Finally, Luther's departure from monastic life and subsequent marriage led thousands more to leave their monasteries and convents.

THE SPREAD OF REFORMATION. Luther's reform in Germany quickly generated uprisings elsewhere. Not only were many people eager for religious reform, separating themselves from Rome furthered their nationalistic sentiments. In Switzerland, Ulrich Zwingli (among the German speaking) and John Calvin (among the French speaking) led movements with similar themes. In England, Henry VIII and Thomas Cranmer separated their church from Rome. As the Reformation worked out, **Lutheranism** took root in countries with a primarily agrarian economy, such as Germany and Scandinavia, while Calvinism took root in countries with a commercial economy, such as French Switzerland, France, Flanders, and the Netherlands.

John **Calvin** (1509–1564) was a French lawyer who then traveled to Geneva in order to establish a religious community based upon his doctrines. These became known as double **predestination**, and can be summarized in five points, sometimes symbolized by the acronym TULIP. Point one is the *T,* and that stands for the *total* depravity of human nature, and therefore all of humanity is deserving of an afterlife in hell. The second point is the *U,* that God's grace is completely *unmerited* by its human recipients. There is nothing which they could do to earn their own salvation, and, going beyond Luther, Calvin said that humans even lacked the free will to muster their own powers of commitment to turn toward God. Therefore, the salvation accorded any human is completely due to the mercy and sovereignty of God (who has therefore predestined some for salvation). The third point is the *L,* the *limited* atonement of Christ on the cross: he died for the sins of the elect, not for the sins of all. In response to the criticism that this makes God an unfair or capricious dispenser of salvation, Calvin responded that if God were really just, He would consign all humans to hell, the fact that He decides to save some is entirely within his right, and reflects His great mercy. The fourth point is the *I,* which stands for *irresistible* grace: if one is the recipient of God's grace, one will manifest "faith" (and good works) because one has no free will and cannot resist the call of God. The *P* stands for the last point, the *perseverence* of the saints. This is also known as the doctrine of *secure salvation:* if you are saved, you cannot lose your salvation. If someone commits major sins after baptism, that person was obviously not one of the elect to begin with. (Within the Catholic Church, similar ideas about predestination were advanced by a Flemish bishop Cornelius Jansen, 1585–1638.) To

John Calvin, advocate of predestination

(c) Archivo Iconografico, S.A. / CORBIS

CALVIN'S TULIP

- Total depravity of all humankind
- Unmerited grace from God
- Limited atonement: only for the chosen
- Irresistible grace draws the chosen to God
- Perseverance of saints: salvation is secure forever

his credit, Calvin's doctrine opened up a new vista among the Protestants in his Reformed Churches: now one did not have to wonder about salvation and could concentrate on the more arduous task of sanctification, the never-ended task of spiritual perfection via the action of the Holy Spirit.

Critics of Calvinism came from many sectors: Protestants, Catholics, and secular humanists rallied to defend the doctrine of free will. Jacobus Arminius, a Dutch Protestant, argued that although humans were depraved, they had free will, and could always call on God to accept His unlimited atonement. The one downside to **Arminianism** (as his doctrine was

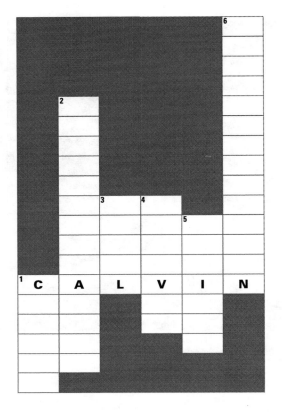

DOWN

1 Calvin said only these few will be saved.
2 Calvin rejected free will in favor of _____.
3 Calvin argued for the _____ depravity of human nature.
4 Calvin said that those who are saved are saved _____.
5 Calvin said that Christ's atonement was _____ to the elect.
6 Calvin's preaching emphasized the need for _____.

Calvin maintained that humans were so evil that they could not, on their own, muster the "faith" necessary to commit themselves to God's grace. So it is God who elects certain persons to receive His grace, and all others will get their just deserts (hell). Therefore, the redemptive act of Christ on the cross was not for all, but only a limited atonement for the elect. If someone has this elect status, then God will not allow that person to fall away. One cannot lose one's salvation. The elect will manifest their status by good deeds: if they don't, then they were not elect in the first place. Calvinist doctrine was accepted by churches such as the Reformed and the Presbyterians.

Arminius opposed Calvin, maintaining that the redemption of the cross was for everyone who freely chooses to accept it. Those who then turn away from God lose their salvation, unless they confess and return to His saving grace. Arminian doctrine was accepted by the Methodists.

Which side of this debate do you accept?

If you accept the Calvinist position, attempt to address a passage of scripture which *appears* to support the position that God has already chosen who will be saved.

If you accept an Arminian position, perform an exegesis of a passage of scripture that *appears* to support the idea that anyone can be saved via an act of free-will acceptance of Jesus.

If you accept neither side, explain your position on free will.

**Contribute to this discussion at
http://www.delphi.com/rel101**

called) is that one can lose one's salvation by backsliding. (Arminius greatly influenced one Anglican priest, John Wesley, 1703–1791, whose movement became known as **Methodism**.) Within the Catholic Church, the major opponents of Jansenism were the Jesuits who defended the doctrine of free will, arguing that God had created man with free will (and that's why Adam fell). Therefore, in order for God's grace to be efficacious, the individual must use his free will to work with Grace (through the sacraments of the Church). The Jesuit position was affirmed by Church councils, and Jansenism was declared heretical.

English **Puritanism** began when the Puritans were inspired by Calvin's desire to honor God by consecrating all of life to his kingship. Consequently, they tried to develop a theocratic state. Calvin's notions of God's sovereignty guided Jonathan Edwards, the first major American theologian, and through Edwards much of the **Great Awakening** (the revivalist movement that Edwards sparked in New England from 1740 to 1743) and subsequent American religious

COMPARISON OF THEOLOGIANS CIRCA 1600				
DIMENSION	CALVIN	ARMINIUS	JANSEN	JESUITS
Where?	Geneva	Holland	Belgium	Spain
Catholic?	no	no	yes	yes
Denominational impact	Presbyterians, Puritans, Pilgrims, Reformed	Methodists, Salvation Army	declared heretical	Catholic
Free will	no	yes	no	yes
Predestination	yes	no	yes	God knows what each one will decide
Human nature	depraved	fallen	depraved	fallen
Salvation open to	a few	all	a few	all
Salvation secured?	forever	can be lost by sin		can be lost by sin
Sinners	never were saved	must return to God		must return to sacraments

life bore a Calvinist imprint. Through the preaching of John Knox, Scotland also became a home to Calvinism, and when they came to America, Scottish immigrants brought their Calvinist tradition (called **Presbyterianism**) to bear on business as well as Church life. Calvin's main work, *Institutes of the Christian Religion,* became the leading text of Reformed (i.e., Calvinist) doctrine, while his efforts to establish a Reformed commonwealth in Geneva provided a model for other communities seeking to live by the gospel.

One recurring theme among reformers has been the desire to get back to original Christianity. That usually involves stripping away some of the accretions that have characterized the Roman Catholic Church over the centuries. For the Eastern Orthodox, it was diminishing the authority of Rome. For Luther, it was indulgences and monasteries and celibacy. **Baptists** strip away all of these and infant baptism. The different forms of Baptists (or **Anabaptists**) that have arisen over the past five hundred years have very little in common doctrinally (there are those who affirm free will and those who affirm predestination), but they agree on the importance of baptism by immersion as a ritual of adult initiation.

From the mid-sixteenth to the mid-seventeenth century, religious wars ravaged much of Europe. In France, they subserved civil frictions. The Edict of Nantes (1598) preserved the status quo: Protestant areas would remain Protestant, Catholic areas (the majority) would remain Catholic. In the Netherlands, the wars had the character of a rebellion against Spain. The northern Netherlands became largely Protestant, while the southern Netherlands remained under Spanish power and so Catholic. Germany was the most furious battlefield. Until the Peace of Munster (1648), there was constant carnage. The upshot in Germany was the famous dictum: each area would follow the religion of its prince.

In England, **Henry VIII** found the Reformation currents useful in his struggle with the papacy to have his marriage to Catherine of Aragon annulled. Henry declared the king supreme in all matters that touched the Church in England, and he eagerly took monastic lands and income to finance his war against France. (This church became known as the **Anglican** "Church of England," or the Episcopalian denomination in the U.S.) From 1553 to 1558, Mary Tudor made England Catholic again, but in 1571, under Henry's daughter Elizabeth I, the English bishops published

Ignatius Loyola, Basque founder of the Jesuit Order of Catholic priests

their *Thirty-Nine Articles of Faith,* which formalized their special blend of Protestantism and Catholicism.

CATHOLIC REFORM. The Catholic response to the Protestant Reformation took place at the Council of Trent (1545–1563). Trent affirmed the reliance of the Church on both scripture and tradition, the effective power of the sacraments, and the possibility of sin after **justification** (denied by some reformers). It also provided for reforms in clerical education and a general housecleaning to remove the laxness and venality that had made the reformers' charges more than credible. Probably the most powerful single agent of the Catholic Reformation was the Society of Jesus (the **Jesuits**), which Pope Paul III approved in 1540. Its founder was **Ignatius of Loyola** (1491–1556), a Basque. Ignatius' companions quickly demonstrated themselves to be the best combination of learning and zealous commitment around. Therefore, they were assigned many of the tasks of teaching and missionizing that were central to Catholic re-

newal. Peter Canisius in Germany, Robert Bellarmine in Italy, and Francisco Suarez in Spain were intellectuals and educators (the first two also became prelates) who had a great deal to do with revitalizing Catholicism in their countries. Jesuit missionaries to Asia such as Francis Xavier, Matteo Ricci, and Roberto di Nobili also had great success. Xavier was a charismatic figure of the first order, able to stir crowds without even knowing their language. Ricci and di Nobili took on the customs of the people with whom they worked (Chinese and Indians) and confronted the vast task of forming indigenous versions of Christianity. Jesuits also ministered underground to Catholics in England (several lost their lives in the effort), and they went to the New World to missionize Canada, the American Southwest, and Latin America.

WORLDVIEW

NATURE

Christianity's Greek and Israelite sources both gave Christianity a realistic orientation toward the natural world. Moreover, the body of Jesus, insofar as Christian doctrine made him the Logos incarnate, was an anchor to realism. Against the Gnostics, who were their foremost adversaries, the early Christian writers insisted on the reality and goodness of matter. If God himself had made the world, and God's own Son had assumed flesh, both the world and human flesh had to be good. Nonetheless, because of the early controversies about the being of God and Christ, the word *physis* (nature) connoted divine and human "whatness" more than it connoted external reality. During the early controversies about free will and sin, Christian speculation finally concluded that the redemption and salvation that Christ had worked were beyond that to which human beings had any right. Thus, they were supernatural gifts that came only by grace. Grace, it followed, was a generosity that God does not owe us. Furthermore, redemption and salvation so transformed human nature that it could share in God's own divine nature (2 *Peter* 1:4). By itself, apart from grace, nature was unredeemed, unsaved, something far from the glory of divinity. These doctrines dominated classical Christian theology (Catholic, Orthodox, and Protestant alike).

As for creation, God stands to the world as its independent, uncaused source, who made it from nothing by his simple free choice. The first mark of the natural world for the traditional Christian, then, has been its subordination to divine creativity. Considerable time passed before the full conceptualization of creation as a Divine making of the world from nothingness developed (from a combination of biblical and philosophical sources), but from the beginning the God of the burning bush was sovereignly free.

In most periods of Christian history, nature was considered mysterious and overpowering, but the *Genesis* story that God gave human beings dominion over nature shaped a doctrine that the physical world existed for humanity's sake. Thus Christianity has taught its followers to husband the physical world and use it. Little in the Christian message proposed that human beings should ravage the world, but equally little proposed integrating human life with nature's ecology or preserving nature's gifts through frugality and reverence. In most periods Christians found nature abundant and generous, so conservation was not a major concern.

Furthermore, the biblical fear of nature gods contributed to a semiconscious Christian effort to make nature undivine. In rural places (among European peasants, for instance), this effort succeeded only partially. Overall, though, it was quite central to the Christian theology of creation. Coming from God, the world was good. But since it came from God by his free choice, springing from nothingness, the world was definitely not divine. Thus, the Christian interest in transforming human nature combined with a continuance of the biblical prophets' objection to the nature gods; thus, the physical world was made a subordinate, even a somewhat ambivalent, concept. Inasmuch as nature and the human body could seem antagonistic to the spiritual destiny of human beings, nature could seem something that human beings had to restrain and control.

SCIENCE. The relative profanity (nonsacredness) that Christians attributed to nature played a rather complex role in the rise of Western science. When the Greek protoscientists, or early natural philosophers, developed a primitive demythologizing of nature, they established the principle that the physical world is open to rational investigation. Thus, it was not blasphemous to pry into nature's secrets, and it could be profitable: Nature yields valuable information to those who pry well.

In Christian hands this demythologizing went several steps further. Pre-Renaissance scholars (many of them monks) worked at what we would call physics or biology, although such work was subordinated to theology. In other words, the basically religious culture preceding the Renaissance determined that theology would be the queen of the sciences. Thus, before the Renaissance, the Catholic Church kept physical science on a rather short leash. The controversy that the new theories of Galileo Galilei (1564–1642) raised shows the Church attitude that still prevailed in the seventeenth century: the doctrine of **geocentric order** had to predominate over the **heliocentric order** supported by the evidence of the senses. Shoring up theological notions (that the earth was the center of the universe was a theological axiom) was more important than allowing intelligence the freedom to investigate nature as it would.

SACRAMENTALISM AND MYSTICISM. Christian sacramentalism has somewhat closed the gap between the place of nature in Christian religion in contrast to pagan religion that was opened by the Western separation of reason from myth. As well, Christian mystics played a large role in the Middle Ages. An example would be figures such as St. Francis who have sensed a divine presence in woods and birds have been rather naturalist in their style. In its worship and sacramental theology, Christian religion often has pressed the scriptural reference that God called creation good. Often, it has applied a mythic and poetic intelligence that made the world mysterious, awesome, and alive. Baptismal water, eucharistic bread and wine, wax, incense, flowers, salt, oil— they have all enriched the liturgy. On the most solemn feast of Easter, the liturgy spoke as though all of creation got into the act, joining in the Exultet—the song of great rejoicing. In the liturgy of Good Friday, which commemorates Christ's death, the tree of the cross (the holy rood) became a new *axis mundi*—a new cosmic pillar linking heaven and earth. Taking over Psalm 150, Christians praised God in his firmament. Taking over other psalms, they made the mountains and the beasts coconspirators to God's praise. All creation, then, was to resound to the

COMPARISON OF BUDDHISM WITH CHRISTIANITY		
DIMENSION	BUDDHISM	CHRISTIANITY
Country of origin	India	Israel
Century of origin	6th century B.C.E.	1st century C.E.
Founder	Gautama	Jesus
His title	the Buddha	the Christ
Social origin of founder	warrior caste	Galilean
Age at beginning of spiritual quest	29	30
Tempted by	Mara	Satan
Duration	40 days	40 days
Reaction to previous scripture	rejected *Vedas*	accepted Old Testament
Accepted local doctrines	karma and transmigration	sin, resurrection, and apocalypticism
Rejected	priestly rituals	priestly rituals, rigid interpretation
Proselytizing?	yes	yes
Followers from all social strata accepted?	yes	yes
Religion went to	East Asia	Roman empire
Canon set	500 years later	300 years later
Decisions about canon and doctrine	Councils of monks	Councils of bishops
Doctrine infected by	Tantrism	Gnosticism
Mysticism preserved by	monastic orders	monastic orders
Mystical doctrine brought in from	Taoism	Platonism
Large vehicle of salvation	Mahayana	Catholicism
Small vehicle of individual salvation	Theravada (Hinayana)	Protestantism
Prophet 1800 years later who demanded a temple	Nichiren	Joseph Smith Jr.

music of the spheres. All creation ought to sing as it labored for redemption. Nature was part of a divine drama, part of a cosmic play of sin and grace. Partly from such liturgical encouragement, Christian mystics have often shown a delight in nature like that of their East Asian counterparts. The accents have been different, since the Christian God is not the impersonal buddha-nature, but they have not been contradictory. For instance, Francis of Assisi felt free to praise God as manifested in nature, and he composed famous canticles to "brother sun" and "sister moon." For the early desert fathers, the wilderness was a place to become sanctified. For many Puritans and early Americans, the wilderness brought to mind Israel's wanderings in the desert—the place where its religion was pure. Thus, a romantic strain of Christian thought has kept nature close to God. Sometimes it has made the city less desirable for religious life than the country. Often it has made solitude close to the elements a privileged place for prayer. As a result, the Christian God has been strong as the seas, everlasting as the hills, lovely as the lilies of the field.

SOCIETY

Central to the Christian notion of how people ought to join together has been the Church. It could oppose the state, standing as the religious collectivity against the secular. It has also been the place where Christian life was supposed to show itself as something mysteriously organic—as the "body" of Christ. In the earliest periods of church history, before Christianity became the official Church of the Roman empire, church leaders led quite unpretentious lives. Meetings of the community tended to be small gatherings in members' homes, and the bishop who led the liturgy might earn his bread as a cobbler or a craftsman. New Testament models suggested that carpentry (the occupation of Jesus) and tentmaking (the occupation of Paul) were more than honorable occupations. The decision to have deacons care for temporal affairs (*Acts* 6:1–6) suggests that Christians quickly established a hierarchy of tasks parallel to the hierarchy of Christian authorities.

POLITY. Christian society has centered on worship through Word and Sacrament. Still, its structural organization was rather fluid at first and varied from place to place. In those early arrangements we can discern elements of all three of the later Church polities: the episcopal, presbyterial (of the elders), and congregational forms of Church government. With time, though, came the monarchical structure of Roman Catholicism, the collegial model of Orthodoxy, and the government by elders that has characterized much of Protestantism. In the West before the Reformation, the structure of the Catholic Church was pyramidal. At the top was the Pope, along the bottom were the laity. In between, in descending order, were cardinals, bishops, and priests. The "religious" (those who had taken vows of poverty, chastity, and obedience, usually in the context of a communal life) were in the middle, though technically most religious groups had both clerical and lay members. Status, naturally and unbiblically enough, was accorded those at the top. Thus, the Council of Trent, reacting against Reformation notions that all Christians are "saints," denounced any diminution of virginity in favor of marriage. As a result, for many Roman Catholics the Church long meant the clergy. That was less true for the Protestants and Orthodox, because their theologies stressed, respectively, the "priesthood" of all Christians (lay and cleric) and the mystical union of all Christians with Christ their head.

WOMEN'S STATUS. In principle, the Christian Church was democratic in that all people, regardless of sex, race, or background, were welcome. Each church member had her or his own gift from God, and each was a unique reflection of God. Thus, there was the Pauline dictum (*Gal.* 3:28) that in Christ there is neither Jew nor Greek, male nor female, slave nor free. In practice, however, women have been second-rate citizens in all branches of Christianity. Neither the Catholic nor the Orthodox churches would ordain women (that remains the case), nor would many Protestant churches. By associating women with Eve, the cause of Adam's fall (1 *Tim.* 2:14), the Church often suggested that they were responsible for human misery and sin. Thus, the fulminations of ascetics (usually celibate males) against women's wiles were a staple of the literature on how to avoid sin.

From the New Testament, men could buttress their supremacy by citing Pauline texts (*Eph.* 5:22–23; 1 *Tim.* 2:11–12) stating that wives were subordinate to their husbands and ought to keep silent in church. From the patristic age they could draw on what we can only call the misogyny of Jerome, Chrysostom, Tertullian, and others who portrayed woman as the gateway to hell. Augustine, perhaps from his personal experience of concubinage, made sexual congress the channel of original sin. Medieval theologians, such as the Dominican authors of the *Malleus Maleficarum* (Hammer of Witches) cited witches as the cause of much psychological imbalance. In the name of preserving the Church, its authorities tortured and killed thousands of witches. Moreover, the Reformation did not relieve women's plight. Luther thought that woman's vocation was to "bear herself out" with children, while John Knox trumpeted against "petticoat" power in the Church. Reformation biblicism, then, meant merely a return to the patriarchy of the scriptures.

With a patriarchal God and an ambivalent role model in Mary the Virgin Mother, Christian women for the most part heard and obeyed, keeping any dissent to themselves. They had some measure of religious self-expression in their convents, and some of them gained leadership roles in the Protestant sects, but from the standpoint of today's egalitarian sentiments, their fate through most periods of Christian history was quite dismal.

CHURCH AND STATE. The Christian view of society outside the Church varied over time. According to the New Testament book of *Revelation,* Roman society was a beast that the coming Messiah had to slay if the earth were to become worthy of God. During the Roman persecutions, which some recent scholarship has downplayed, this view was influential. As a result, earthly life was held cheap compared to heavenly life. When the Church gained security with Constantine, it changed its tune. Eusebius, for instance, virtually ranked Constantine with the twelve apostles. In reaction against this secularization, as we noted, the monastic movement restored the tension between time and eternity. The Western father Tertullian cast doubt on the worth of secular culture, asking what Athens had to do with Jerusalem. However, other patristic figures, such as Clement of Alexandria and Augustine, recognized that Christianity needed an intellectual respectability if it were to prosper, so they started to give their theology an infrastructure of Greek philosophy. By the medieval period, a certain harmony was achieved, as most of the culture was

formed in accordance with Christian ideals (if not practice). There was a balance between reason and revelation, between emperor and pope. In practice, however, the competition between the emperor and the pope was fierce, for each tended to claim ascendancy over the other. Consequently, Church leaders such as Ambrose and Hildebrand, who stood up to kings or even brought them to heel, were accounted great heroes. In the Christian East, however, the emperor had more clearly God given rights.

The Reformation depended in good measure on the political power plays of its day. Through application of the principle that a region would follow the religion of its ruler, a great deal of religious power returned to the local prince. Theologically, Luther tended toward a dualism of powers, religious and secular, while Calvin promoted a theocratic state in which citizens would live under Christian law. Thus, the Reformation did not initially encourage the modern pluralistic state.

SELF

The conceptions of nature and society that we have sketched here suggest the Christian view of the self. The biblical teaching that God placed human beings over nature has meant to Christians that the human person is of much greater value than the plants and animals. Furthermore, as Christian social theory interacted with the secular elaboration of human nature through Western history, the individual acquired greater stature than in Asia. In Asia, as in ancient societies generally, the group predominated over the individual. One was most importantly a member of a tribe and only secondarily a unique person. As an image of God, the individual was more significant under Christianity. Of course, at times both secular and religious authorities crushed individuals ruthlessly. Nonetheless, because they bore the life of Christ, individuals commanded respect. In matters of ethics, for instance, the notion of individual conscience counterbalanced the finespun codes of the canon lawyers and the moral theologians. The sacrament of **penance** epitomized this, for penance was essentially a self-accusation in which the individual, helped by the Church's representative, passed judgment on his or her standing before God.

By standing out from nature and having personal rights, the Christian individual was conscious of being a unique self. Historically, the Church did not lay great emphasis on fulfilling one's unique self by communing with nature, but it did lay great emphasis on fitting into the social body of Christ. In fact, the charity of the community united was to be the primary sign of God's presence. Beyond social fulfillment, however, Christian theology encouraged the self to commune with divinity itself—with the Father, Son, and Holy Spirit. During the biblical period that meant putting on the "mind of Christ." During the Patristic Age it meant that grace was considered a share in divine nature and that religion was a process of divinization. Since the Hellenistic divinity was above all immortal, religion was also a process of immortalization. In medieval speculation, the self's fulfillment was the "beatific vision." By directly perceiving God's essence, our human drives to know and love (Augustine's famous "restless heart") would find a restful bliss. For the Thomists, participation in the divine nature through grace meant sharing in the "missions" of the Son and Holy Spirit. Thus, one's contemplation, knowing, and loving flowed into and out from the dynamic relations that characterized God's own inner life. The Reformation returned to biblical emphases, sending people to study the Word and to work in the world. For Orthodoxy the Divine Liturgy, with special accents on the Holy Spirit and the Mother of God, nourished one throughout life. In many periods, Christians never quite found the balance between life in the world and life that looked to heaven as its true home. Before the Reformation, Christians probably gave greater emphasis to the latter. Since the Reformation and the Enlightenment, they have emphasized social and political commitments in the world.

RELIGIOUS DEVELOPMENT. Stressing communion with God, traditional Christian spiritual masters developed certain models of what happens in the life of the serious religious person. One of the most influential traditions involved the "three ways" that the self would travel. First, one had to walk the *purgative* way, which meant purging oneself of sin and developing virtuous habits. Then one would enter the long way of *illumination,* by which the Christian Word and Sacrament would slowly become one's own. No longer would they be external concepts—in time they would become inner principles of judgment and ac-

tion. Finally, consummating the spiritual life was the *unitive* way, by which the self would unite with God as in a deep friendship or even a marriage. Occasionally such union would produce experiences of rapture, and then one could speak of mysticism strictly so called ("infused contemplation"). Clearly, then, the paradigm of the three ways depended on the notion that final fulfillment was communion with God. The saints who modeled Christian selfhood tended to be wholeheartedly given to communion with God. They also had to manifest charity for their fellows, but the spotlight was on their love of God. Because solitude or monastic withdrawal seemed to foster love of God, by allowing the freedom of deep, leisurely prayer, most saints went outside of family or civic life to lose themselves in devotion. That was the pattern up to the Reformation, and it took Christian selfhood some distance from the New Testament's view that prayer is important but not dominant. Still, as the world became more important, the concept of saintliness expanded to include the service of other human beings. The Church had always honored certain holy married people, certain holy civic leaders, but by late medieval times it had to contend with a more dynamic society.

SIN. Related to the capital question of what the self should most value is the complicated Christian teaching about **original sin** (most developed in Western Christianity—Eastern Christianity has not stressed original sin to the same degree). At its crudest, the teaching said that all people not baptized were in thrall to Satan and on the road to hell. Hell was essentially the deprivation of God (the loss of the beatific vision), but because of a gruesome imagery of fire and brimstone, it was popularly conceived of as a place of physical suffering. The ceremony for infant baptism, then, contained an exorcism of Satan—to save the little one from evil and make it pure for God. (Unbaptized babies who died before reaching the age of responsibility, and so before the possibility of personal sin, went to *limbo,* a state of "natural" happiness without beatific vision. Although limbo was never a matter of fully official Church teaching, it exerted considerable influence.)

A key moment in the development of the doctrine of original sin was Augustine's reading of the Fall as a social act. Adam's sin had alienated all human beings from God, for Adam was the head of the entire race. Augustine took the seeds of this view from Paul (for instance, *Rom.* 5:12–14). It suggested that Christ is the head of a new holy race, but that those not baptized into Christ belong to an old human nature destined for punishment.

The classical Protestant thinkers owed a great deal to Augustine; thus, their reform of theology emphasized original sin. Like Augustine, they interpreted *Genesis* and Paul rather literally, thinking in terms of corporate sinners and saints. The famous double predestination of Calvinism was an attempt to explain human beings' different fates (going to hell or heaven), as members of Adam or members of Christ, without removing the mystery of God's creative vision and providence. Whom God has destined for heaven will surely end up there. Likewise, whom God has set for hell will fall into the flame.

In a fateful development of Calvinistic predestination, the signs of election to heaven became outward decorum and even material prosperity. That meant the double burden of being both poor and damned and the double blessing of being both rich and saved. Eventually more careful *Bible* readers recognized that this correspondence contradicted the Sermon on the Mount, but a lot of Calvinists thoroughly enjoyed storing up plenty in their barns and letting their souls wax fat. How inherently wicked or good the self is was an important question in the Reformation debates between Protestants and Catholics. Protestants, following Luther's stress on justification by "faith" and Calvin's stress on God's sovereignty, tended to emphasize the corruption of human nature through sin. Catholics, partly in reaction to that Protestant position and partly from their own emphasis on the sacraments and the Incarnation, saw an essential goodness in human nature (though they spoke of sin as darkening the mind and weakening the will). Clearly, though, Christianity made the West suspicious of human intuition. Many Christians were indoctrinated that they were virtually bound to be wicked sinners. Often that led them to oscillate between self-punishment and, in compensation, self-indulgence. However, most were taught that through penance one could experience God's mercy—the almost delicious sense of being loved gratuitously. Then the Johannine promise (1 *John* 3:20)—that even when our hearts condemn us God is greater than our hearts—could break out into joyous effect.

The Pauline discussion of sin and grace in terms of "flesh" and "spirit" focused Christian understanding of the self as embodied. That Paul's original language did not intend a matter-spirit dualism was almost forgotten after Christianity took up Greek thought. As a result, extremists tended to deprecate the body, marriage, and the world of human affairs as fleshly pursuits. In response to the Manichean and Albigensian heresies, the Church affirmed the goodness of the body, but the Church's general orientation toward heaven, its introduction of celibacy for holders of high Church offices, and its preference for ascetic saints tended to make the average person regret his or her flesh. For women, this caused considerable suffering, because the male Church teachers often projected their sexual problems onto women. In that case, women became by nature wanton, seductive, and dangerous.

On the other hand, a certain realism about worldly life, in which imperfection if not sin was inevitable, tended to soften this rigorism. Christian moral theologians have usually taught that sins of the flesh are less grievous than sins of the spirit (such as pride, anger, or hatred). And, although at one point Roman Catholic moralists classified all sexual offenses as serious ("mortal" as opposed to "venial" sins), there were usually effective if unauthorized counterforces in the bawdiness of Chaucer and Boccaccio and the frequent concubinage of members of the clergy.

ULTIMATE REALITY

The first Christian conception of God was Jewish. Jesus himself accepted the God of the Fathers—Abraham, Isaac, and Jacob. This God, as we have seen, interacted with human beings and was personal. His guidance of humanity peaked in his liberation of Israel from Egypt and his covenanting with Israel on Mount Sinai. As numerous theologians have pointed out, it was difficult for Jesus to designate himself as divine, because to do so would have confused his identity with that of his "Father." In other words, the God of the Jews was Jesus' Father, his source.

In dealing with the revealed God's inner nature, the concept of the Trinity became paramount. Orthodox catholic (universal) doctrine held that Father-Son-Holy Spirit was attested by the scriptures and defined by the councils. Thus, the God of Christian speculation was perfection, in need of nothing outside himself. He was the Creator and Redeemer, moved only by his own goodness. The Incarnation was the main instance of his outpouring, but glimpses of God abounded everywhere. Subhuman creatures were his "vestiges" (footprints); human beings were his images. Christians were images of his great Image, for they reflected the eternal icon, the Logos-Son. Regarding the Trinity, Christians stood in the Son's position, receiving their likeness to God from the Father and expressing it through Spirit-carried love. The similitude broke down, however, because the divine persons were only relationally distinct (that is, Son and Father differed only as begotten and begetter), while humans remained creatures distinct from God.

BIBLICAL RENEWAL. When Reformation thought returned to biblical conceptions when it found the medieval synthesis too abstract and unhistorical, it revived the notion that "faith" is a living interpersonal relation to God, an ongoing commitment. Between the time of Luther and the nineteenth-century Danish theologian Søren Kierkegaard, such "faith" became paradoxical—a leap. Kierkegaard jumped into the intellectual abyss, proposing that what reason could not fathom divinity could yet do, because it moved by reasons the mind knew not, by reasons of the heart. The Hebrew notion of *hesed* (steadfast, merciful love), which kept God to his freely chosen covenant, encouraged Christians to trust that no situation in their lives was hopeless. If Ezekiel's God could raise dry bones back to fleshly life, Jesus' God could use even suffering and evil to his own inscrutable ends. Was not God's chosen way of salvation, the death of his only begotten Son, the surest sign that no one had ever understood him? As the heavens are above the earth, so were God's ways above the ways of human beings. For that reason, the Reformers wanted only a Pauline formula: God's power and wisdom are Christ crucified.

In contrast to other religions' versions of divinity, Christian theology has stressed the personal, loving character of God that Jesus' flesh disclosed. Jesus was God in human terms. (He was also humanity fulfilled by union with divinity.) As a result, Christianity did not appreciate the impersonal divinity of nature so dear to East Asian and Indian thought. This divinity was implicit in Christian theology, but the personalistic emphasis placed it in the shade.

At its better moments, Christianity was grateful to Judaism, since it had adopted most of Judaism's doctrine of God. As well, it was mindful of the continuing election of Israel that Paul had proclaimed (*Rom.* 9–11). At its worst, Christianity condemned Jews as Christ killers and spoke of their responsibility for Christ's blood. Islam confronted Christianity with claims of a later, perfected revelation and prophecy, and with an adamant insistence on God's unity. For Islam, and for Judaism, the Christian doctrine of the Trinity violated monotheism. Christian claims that God is both one and three seemed to Muslims and Jews incoherent, while Christian allegiance to Jesus clashed with Muslim allegiance to the *Qur'an* and Jewish allegiance to the Torah. Those clashes remain with us yet.

As the center of the Christian worldview, God in Christ dominated Christian conceptions of nature, society, and self. Nature was but God's cloak. It was a lovely gift, but it sprang from nothingness and was wholly under God's control. With each extension of space and time by science, the awe of the sophisticated increased: a more complex nature only magnified their God all the more.

Similarly, God was the norm and goal of Christian society, because his law was the source of all natural law and because eternal life with God in heaven was the goal of all people. God wanted human beings to form a community. Christ showed them the love that could bring that about. Thus, the vocation of the self was to obey the great twofold command: to love God with whole mind, heart, soul, and strength and to love one's neighbor as oneself.

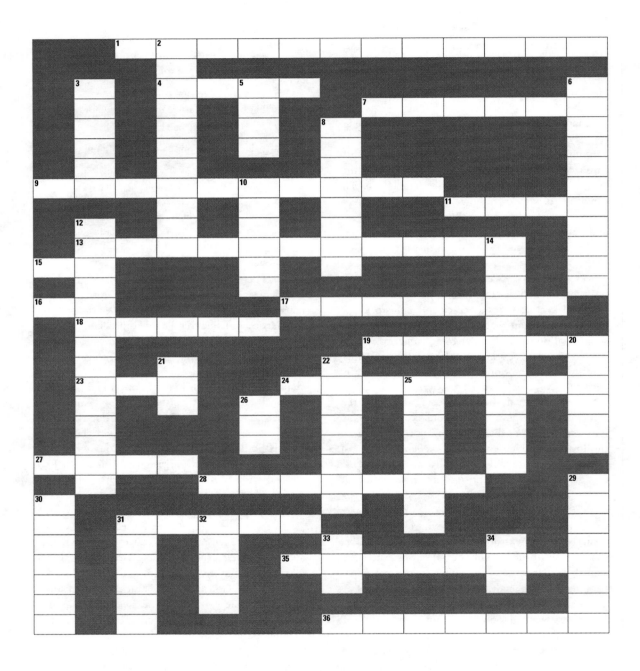

ACROSS

1 Denomination influenced by Calvin
4 Arminius and the Jesuits argued for _____ will.
7 Argued for predestination
9 The _____ Reformation occurred in the sixteenth century.
11 Leader of the Catholic Church
13 The _____ was a period of humanism and great art.
15 The Great Schism occurred in the eleventh century _____.
16 The Renaissance occurred in the fifteenth century _____.
17 Catholics, Calvin, and Luther supported infant _____.
18 Someone canonized after death
19 Founder of the Jesuits, Ignatius _____.
23 Saint Teresa of Avila was a Catholic _____.
24 _____ and Pilgrims brought Calvinism to the United States.
27 A man who lives in a monastery
28 Founder of mystical order; _____ of Assisi
31 Luther argued against salvation by _____.
35 The Church of England
36 Theologian of the thirteenth century; influenced by Aristotle

DOWN

2 The Protestant _____ occurred in the sixteenth century.
3 Martin _____ led the Reformation in Germany.
5 Region of Europe with Orthodox Churches
6 Luther criticized _____ as an abuse of Church power
8 Argued that humans are basically good
10 The East had a _____ with Rome in 1054 C.E.
12 Calvin argued against free will, in favor of _____.
14 The Church of England in the United States.
20 Founder of order of mystics, Francis of _____.
21 The _____ baptists opposed infant baptism.
22 The _____ were the English roundheads influenced by Calvin.
25 _____ Loyola founded the Jesuits.
26 Puritans brought Calvinism to the future nation of the _____.
29 Defended the doctrine of free will against Calvinism
30 A war launched by Catholics against Muslims
31 John _____ was influenced by Arminius; started Methodism.
32 The Holy _____ Catholic Apostolic Church
33 Radical German sect; _____ Baptists of the sixteenth century
34 The period before Jesus

SUMMARY: THE CHRISTIAN CENTER

The Christian center is Jesus, for the God worshipped in the Christian liturgy, served in the Christian ministries, and crucial for the Christian Church is the Father known through the revelations of Jesus. In the New Testament (*John* 14:6) Jesus is the way. For the Christian monk, martyr, or layperson, Jesus has been the strong soldier in combat with Satan, the sacrificial victim dying for human beings' sins, or the good shepherd ever seeking his lost sheep.

The centrality of Jesus the Christ has meant that Christianity is supremely **incarnational**. Its theology, if not always its Church practice, has pivoted around the enfleshment of divinity. Orthodox and Roman Catholic Christians have developed this theology into rich sacramental rites. Protestant Christians have developed it into a profound reverence for the holy scripture.

Religion, Social Cohesion, and Conflict

Religion contributes to both social conflict and cohesion. Some people find it surprising or objectionable that religion should be a force for conflict as well as cohesion. In many respects, however, the aspect of conflict is merely the obverse of social cohesion; some conflict is an integral part of what holds groups together. Religion's importance as an expression of a group's unity also makes it significant as an expression of that group's conflict with another group.

We must keep a neutral conception of conflict and cohesion. A tendency exists in our society to think of conflict, in the abstract, as "bad"; cohesion, in the abstract, seems "good." Yet when we examine some concrete instances of cohesion and conflict, we see that we evaluate the *content,* not the process, as good or bad. Was Moses's confrontation of the pharoah necessarily bad because it was conflict?

In this chapter, we first examine the ways in which religion reflects or contributes to the cohesion of a social group. Particularly problematic is the issue of whether religion contributes to the integration of complex societies such as the United States. Then we analyze the relationship between religion and social conflict, focusing on those aspects of religion and society in general that contribute to or reflect social cleavages. Finally, we apply these understandings to the case of "the troubles" in Northern Ireland, where religion is an important factor in civil strife.

RELIGION AND SOCIAL COHESION

Blest be the tie that binds
Our hearts in Christian love.
The fellowship of kindred minds
Is like to that above.

(Hymn, John Fawcett, 1782)

The theme of social cohesion is central to sociology. What makes society possible? What integrates separate members into a larger whole, the identifiable entity we call "society"? Society is more than an aggregate of people who happen to share a certain time and space. Although made up of individuals, society is not reducible to individual beliefs, values, and behavior. Social norms and traditions existed before the individual and have a force that is external to the individual. In a society with a norm against cannibalism, for example, persons known to violate the norm will be punished regardless of whether they agree with the norm. Another evidence of the external quality of society is the process of socialization, in which the child is confronted with the given expectations, language, and knowledge of that society.

What, then, is the nature of the unity of society that gives it this powerful quality? How is the individual linked to the larger society? How does the society gain the commitment and cooperation of its members? According to integration theories, societal cohesion and stability are ensured by the functioning of institutions (e.g., religion, education, and the family) that represent the larger social reality to the individual and enable the individual to accept personally that definition of reality.

Religion is one important contributing factor in societal integration. Religious symbols can represent the unity of the social group, and religious rituals can enact that unity, allowing the individual to participate symbolically in the larger unity they represent. The Christian ritual of communion is not only a commemoration of a historical event in the life of Jesus but is also a representation of participation in the unity ("communion") of believers. Also, to the extent that a religion imparts important values and norms to its members, it contributes to their consensus on moral issues. Especially significant is religion's ability to motivate believers' commitment and even sacrifice to the group's purposes. By referring to a sphere that transcends everyday life, religion encourages individuals to seek the good of the group rather than their own interests. This consensus and commitment of members is largely a positive effect, but religion also wields powerful negative sanctions for noncooperation. Again, by reference to a transcendent realm, religious sanctions are more potent than earthly punishments.

Integration theories of society stress the equilibrium and harmony of the group. They show the ways that religion helps to maintain equilibrium whenever events threaten it. For example, funeral rituals help a group regain its social balance and morale after the death of a member (Malinowski, 1948:18–24). Religious healing is often a way of reintegrating the deviant member into the group (McGuire, 1988). Changes of social status (e.g., marriage, adulthood, or adoption) are integrated into existing status arrangements through religious symbols and rituals (Van Gennep, 1960). The balance of political and economic power is often ritually expressed and confirmed (Kertzer, 1988). Sometimes religious symbolism and ritual action overcome sources of group cleavages and conflict. In a contemporary Mexican village, the celebration of the fiesta of the Virgin of Guadalupe served to express ethnic cleavages (Maya and *mestizo*) within the community but then to overcome them by affirming the Virgin's protective relationship to all Mexicans (O'Connor, 1989).

Most examples of religion contributing unambiguously to social cohesion are from relatively simple, homogeneous societies. If religion is coextensive with society, its contribution to social cohesion is generally clear. Many societies, however, are not coextensive with a single religion. What is the basis of cohesion in a society such as the United States, in which many competing religions exist and a relatively large number of persons participate in no religious group? What is the function of religion for cohesion where conflicting societies presumably share the same religion (e.g., two warring Christian nations)? How can integration theories explain situations in which a religion arises in a society to conflict with the established ways of that society? Although religion does contribute to social cohesion in complex heterogeneous societies, its role is not very clear-cut. In such societies, the basis of societywide integration is problematic.

Religion as an Expression of Social Cohesion: Durkheim

One approach to social cohesion and religion holds that religion is the *expression* of social forces and social ideals. This perspective emphasizes that *wherever there is social cohesion, it is expressed religiously.* The classical statement of this theoretical approach is Durkheim's, and his insights are sufficiently important to explore in some detail. Throughout Durkheim's works—on the division of labor and on deviance, education, and religion—the theme of social cohesion is central (Bellah, 1973). The relationship of the individual to the larger society was relatively unproblematic for Durkheim because he identified the larger social group as the source of individuation. His theory of religion illustrates this resolution.

Durkheim based his discussion of religion on anthropological evidence about the beliefs and practices of Australian aborigines because he believed that their religion would illustrate the most elementary form. Although some of the material he used has been discounted by later anthropological investigations, Durkheim's general theory of religion is still useful for understanding some aspects of religion, particularly in relatively homogeneous societies. According to Durkheim (1915/1965:22), religion is in its very essence *social*. Religious rites are collective behavior, relating the individual to the larger social group. And religious beliefs are **collective representations**—group-held meanings expressing something important about the group itself. Durkheim may have overstated the social aspect of religion, as Malinowski (1925/1948:65) later pointed out, because subjective and even purely individual religious experiences figure importantly in virtually all religions. The experiences sought by the Christian mystic or a participant in a Sioux initiation rite, for example, are highly individualistic, though their meaning is derived from group-held beliefs and imagery. Furthermore, Malinowski noted, not all times of collective effervescence are religious, nor are all religious gatherings necessarily unifying (see Geertz, 1957). Bringing people together for a periodic religious ritual creates the potential for friction, especially in times of stress or hunger. Nevertheless, Malinowski agreed with Durkheim that religion provides a basis of moral cohesion to the social group.

Durkheim observed that a sense of *force* was central to primitive religions. The totemic principle that represented abstract force to the Australian tribes was comparable with other primitive religions' awe of a force (e.g., *mana, orenda,* and *wakan* in Polynesian and North American tribes). Durkheim emphasized that religious force was not an illusion. Although the symbols for expressing this force are imperfect, the force that people experience is real—it is society. Durkheim described religion as a system of shared meanings by which individuals represent to themselves their society and their relations to that society. Thus, religious meanings are metaphorical representations of the social group, and participation in religious ritual is experience of the transcendent force of society itself (1965:257).

Thus, Durkheim resolved the individual-to-society relationship by presenting individuals as transcending themselves in communion with the greater reality—society itself. But Durkheim added that this force is not entirely outside the individual; it must also become an integral part of the individual's being because society cannot exist except through individual consciousness. By this twofold relationship, religion ensures the commitment of society's members and empowers them to act accordingly. Thus, religious beliefs are idealizations by which society represents itself to its members. Religious rites renew these representations by rekindling the group's consciousness of its unity. At the same time, they strengthen individuals' commitment to the group's expectations and goals (Durkheim, 1965:especially Book 3, Chapter 4).

How do collective representations and collective rituals link the individual to the larger social group? Durkheim's emphasis on language and ritual suggests two ways of understanding this individual-to-society link. First, language and other symbol systems (e.g., religious symbols) depend on shared meanings, and meaning requires a shared reality. By exploring how language and other symbol systems articulate a group's reality, sociologists may come to a better understanding of how people subjectively share that reality (see Fabian, 1974:249–272). Second, studies of ritual can point to how the individual is related to the larger society. Participation in certain religious rituals appears to reduce the sense of boundaries between participants, producing an experience of unity (see Douglas, 1966, 1970; Kertzer, 1988; Spickard, 1991; Turner, 1969, 1974a, 1974b). Both language and ritual articulate the unity of the group and serve to separate that group from others.

Durkheim's emphasis on the significance of ritual for both the individual and the collectivity points to some interesting problems of describing religion in modern society (see Pickering, 1984:442–456). If social cohesion is expressed through tribal collective rituals and meanings, how does it function in a society whose members are from numerous different ethnic backgrounds? Several observers have noted the close link between religion and ethnicity among immigrant peoples. Religious groups provided important resources to newly arrived immigrants, especially during the great waves of immigration in the nineteenth and twentieth centuries. They provided informal networks of association through which the immigrants could obtain jobs, help with housing, and other mutual assistance. They also provided protection from the dominant society, keeping alive the old ways, educating children in "safe" environments where their backgrounds would not be held against them, and providing mutual protection from the hostility of those who did not accept the immigrants. When the historical need for these functions becomes muted or disappears, the ethno-religious community may still be a source of mutual aid, friendship, and a sense of belonging. For these individuals, the ethno-religious group as a set of relationships, not the fact of ethnicity itself, provides a stable source of belonging.

Herberg (1960) analyzed the relationship between religion and ethnic group identity in the 1950s, specifically asking why people in the United States tended to identify themselves in terms of one of three religious "communities": Protestant, Catholic, or Jew. He suggested that as European immigrants had become assimilated into the dominant U.S. culture, ethnic ties superseded localistic ties that had characterized their self-identity and self-location in the old country. According to Herberg, however, those ethnic differences were residual and disappearing. As assimilation proceeded even further, religious identity assumed even greater significance. What matters most about religious identity, however, is not the actual affiliation with a particular religious group, participation in church activities, or even affirmation of the group's belief system but rather it is religion's function as a basis of self-identification and social location. According to Herberg, self-identification in ethnic terms was not altogether satisfactory because it implied incomplete integration into U.S. life. By contrast, *religion* in the United States is an acceptable way for people to differentiate themselves and thus becomes a way for people to define and locate themselves in the larger society. For this reason, people identified themselves with one of the three legitimate religious "communities"—Protestant, Catholic, or Jewish—even though they did not necessarily practice that religion or believe its tenets (Herberg, 1960:6–64).

How applicable will Herberg's thesis be to immigrant groups whose religious traditions are completely foreign to the Judeo-Christian communities? Herberg's analysis was based on earlier waves of European immigrants who fit these three "communities." Indeed, in the period he described, the United States gradually changed from being essentially a Protestant empire to considering itself a Judeo-Christian land. After new immigration laws took effect in 1968, however, both the volume and the sources of new immigrants changed dramatically. By the year 2000, only 15 percent of the foreign-born population of the United States had come from Europe; far more, at least one-fourth, had come from Asia (U.S. Census Bureau, 2000; see also Kivisto, 1993). Nevertheless, the vast majority of new immigrants to the United States are Christian. They include not only those from predominantly Christian countries (e.g., Latin Americans, Filipinos) but also many from countries where Christians are a relatively small minority (e.g., Korea, India, Vietnam) but comprise a disproportionately large number of those migrating to the United States (Yang and Ebaugh, 2000; see also Warner, 2000).

Immigrants whose Christianity was a minority religion in the old country have a very different experience in negotiating their ethno-religious identities in the United States, compared to immigrants whose religion was prevalent or powerful in their native country (see excellent descriptive examples in Ebaugh and Chafetz, 2000a). For example, Vietnamese-American Catholics "fit" an already accepted religious identity in the United States, even though their prior cultural experience of being Catholic was very different from U.S. Catholic culture. By contrast, Vietnamese-American Buddhists must actively negotiate a Buddhist religious identity and work to have it accepted as legitimate in their new community. Several studies suggest that ethnic congregations organize themselves to accomplish this dual feat; both reproducing ethnicity (e.g., by socializing children in their ethnic tradition's language, religion, and customs) *and* adapting to life in their new community (Ebaugh and Chafetz, 2000b). For example, in Houston, Texas, the Vietnamese community has created a temple with many features reminiscent of Vietnam. Unlike in the "old country," however, the temple has become something of a community center, with Vietnamese language classes, frequent social gatherings and meals of Vietnamese food, and networking for jobs and other contacts in the city (Huynh, 2000).

Thus, ethnic group identity appears to be linked with religion for non-Christian new immigrants, even though neither their native religions nor their racial-ethnic identities are as likely as those of earlier European immigrants to be readily accepted as legitimate by the larger society. Those whose religions fit the dominant society's "image" of a religious community (e.g., Hindus, Buddhists) will gain acceptance more readily than marginalized ethno-religious groups (e.g., Cambodian-Americans practicing Hmong folk religion, Cuban-Americans practicing Santería, Jamaican-Americans practicing Rastafari). Like earlier waves of immigrants, the new immigrants face prejudice and discrimination. Even more so than immigrants from Europe, most new immigrants are often victims of outright racism. At the same time, things have changed in the dominant society. Many new immigrant groups benefit from, for example, the extensive civil rights legislation and respect for nongovernmental organizations (NGOs) such as religious organizations that developed since the 1960s. Similarly, new immigrants are not so cut off from the "old country" as previously. Often their social life (including their ethno-religious community) in their new country is closely linked with their home community. One study documented the extent to which Dominican immigrants living in a neighborhood in Boston maintained a "religious life across borders" in close connection with their home community of Miraflores in the Dominican Republic. Such "transnational villagers" managed to accomplish both assimilation and transcultural lifestyles, in the context of increasing globalization (Levitt, 2001).

Herberg's prediction of ethnicity's disappearance as a basis of personal identity in a pluralistic society may have been premature (as the discussion of ethnic self-identity in Chapter 3 suggests). As a basis of group identity, ethno-religious ties are highly salient for many groups in the United States. Creating a sense of solidarity among a fragmented minority has important political implications for groups lacking a voice in their cities, denominations, and nation.

"Latino" group identity, for example, is extremely difficult to forge given the wide range of cultural, geographic, and social-class backgrounds of the more-than-31 million Americans the term was invented to unify (see Cadena, 1995; Nagel, 1994). Catholicism may have initially been a source of group identity for immigrant Latinos, but many Latinos do not find the Catholic Church in the United States to be a strong source of belonging. Some have become Protestant, but many more are marginally involved in Catholic congregations, simply because they do not identify with a Catholicism so foreign to their own cultural experience. Some also feel that the U.S. Catholic Church fails to represent their interests in important political and economic issues as adequately as it represented earlier Irish, German, or Eastern European immigrant minorities (Díaz-Stevens and Stevens-Arroyo, 1998). Some Latino Protestants had changed religious affiliation before coming to the United States. For them, immigration was less disruptive of their identities and social connections if they moved to a locality in the United States that had a congregation of the same Protestant group to which they belonged in the "old country" (Sullivan, 2000a).

Thus, immigrant congregations often serve some of the same functions for new immigrants that local and kinship ties did for the earlier immigrants. They provide temporary living quarters; help in getting a job; guidance in negotiating the intricacies of foreign legal, social service, and educational bureaucracies; and social support and a communication in the immigrants' native tongue and culture. Interestingly, since the Catholicism of the "old country" was often relatively open to popular religious practices, many Latinos combine elements, and even participation in services, of Catholicism and Protestantism. A study of one Mexican-American Catholic congregation observed that some members "are Catholic on Saturday nights and equally Pentecostal, Methodist, or Baptist on Sunday mornings" (Sullivan, 2000b). Thus religion is potentially linked, in sometimes complex ways, with the social cohesion *and* conflict of culturally diverse peoples within a nation.

Moving from primitive religions to world and civil religions, Durkheim (1965:474, 475) asserted that all societies need regular events to reaffirm their shared meanings and central ideas. He saw no basic difference between specifically religious commemorations such as Passover or Christmas and civic rituals such as Independence Day or Thanksgiving. Thus, Durkheim implies that in modern nations (e.g., his own country, France), religious representations and rituals may comprise the civic religion of the national collectivity.

Is it possible for a highly differentiated, heterogeneous society (such as the United States, Canada, and much of Europe) to have a religious expression of its solidarity? Is there a unifying representation of the nation to inform and reflect diverse peoples' sense of "who we are as a nation" and "what kind of nation do we want to be"? What happens when, in the same country, there are conflicting religious representations of the nation? How is religion, then, linked with the nation?

Religious Representations of the Nation

The civil religion thesis is important because it proposes that a religious form exists for the unity of even highly differentiated, heterogeneous societies. **Civil religion** is "any set of beliefs and rituals, related to the past, present, and/or future of a people ('nation') which are understood in some transcendental fashion" (Hammond, 1976:171). Civil religion is the expression of the cohesion of the nation. It transcends denominational, ethnic, and religious boundaries. It includes rituals by which members commemorate significant national events and renew their commitment to the society. Such rituals and representations are religious in that they often represent the nation—the people—as a higher and more valuable reality than mere (i.e., human) social contract and convention. They may also stir religious fervor and sentiments regarding the national collectivity. This concept appears to apply to many features of U.S. religion as it is linked with America as a nation.

American Civil Religion Many civil ceremonies have a marked religious quality. Memorial Day, Fourth of July, presidential inaugurations, all celebrate national values and national unity (Bellah, 1967; Cherry, 1992; Wuthnow, 1994). There are national shrines such as the memorials in Washington, D.C., the Capitol itself, the birthplaces of key presidents, war memorials, and other "special" places to which Americans can make pilgrimages (Campo, 1998). It is not their age or even historical significance but their ability to symbolize the transcendence of the nation as a "people" that inspires awe and reverence. A visitor to Independence Hall said, "Just standing here sends chills down my spine." National shrines are "sacred," in Durkheim's sense of the word.

Similarly, there are sacred objects of the civil religion, especially the flag. Interestingly, the Christian Bible is probably also a sacred object in civil religion, not because of its content but because it signifies an appeal to God as the ultimate arbiter of truth and justice. The extent to which these ceremonies, shrines, and objects are set apart as sacred can be seen in the intensity of outrage at inappropriate behavior or "desecration." Some people were arrested during the 1960s for wearing or displaying a copy of the U.S. flag improperly (e.g., on the seat of their pants), and in the 1990s various legislators introduced bills to criminalize the burning of the U.S. flag in symbolic protests.

Civil religion also has its myths and saints. Lincoln is a historical figure who particularly symbolizes the civil religion. His actions and speeches contributed to the articulation of that religion in a time of crisis, and his life from his humble birth to his martyrdom typifies values of the civil religion. Other "saints" include key presidents (e.g., Washington, Jefferson, Franklin D. Roosevelt, Kennedy), folk heroes (e.g, Davy Crockett, Charles Lindbergh), and military heroes (e.g., MacArthur, Theodore Roosevelt). Similarly, there are stories that exemplify valued traits (e.g., the Horatio Alger rags-to-riches genre) and images (e.g., the frontier). Socially important myths include the American Dream—the land of plenty—unlimited social mobility, economic consumption, and achievement. Although these shrines, saints, and ceremonies are not religious in the same sense as, for example, Greek Orthodox shrines, saints, and ceremonies, they are still set apart as special and not to be profaned. They are an important element of nonofficial religion (as described in Chapter 4) and exist alongside—separate, yet related to—official church religion.

If civil religion is the expression of the integration of a nation, we might expect its especially powerful articulation at the resolution of a conflict. Just as tribal rituals "heal" internal strife and celebrate the unity of the tribe, so too does the rhetoric of inaugural speeches and court pronouncements represent the resolution of conflict and appeal to the overarching integration of the group (Hammond, 1974). The symbolism of civil religion is also very evident when people believe the nation to be threatened by an enemy. During wartime, members' commitments and sacrifices are given special significance. Even one's vegetable garden becomes a symbol of patriotic effort—a "victory garden."

According to Robert Bellah (1967), American civil religion is related to biblical religion, yet is distinctively American. Biblical symbolism has prominent themes (e.g., chosen people, promised land, new Jerusalem, death and rebirth). On the other hand, the civil religion is genuinely American and parallels the biblical religions, not replacing them. Civil religion and Christianity, accordingly, are clearly divided in function: Civil religion is appropriate to actions in the official public sphere, and Christianity and other religions are granted full liberty in the sphere of personal piety and voluntary social action. This division of spheres of relevance is particularly important for countries such as the United States, where religious pluralism is both a valued feature of sociopolitical life and a barrier to achieving a unified perspective for decision making. By having a civil religion for the public sphere and a diversity of particular religions in the private sphere, the social structure has cohesion with the sense of individual freedom of choice. The success of this division is, however, problematic in U.S. society.

What emerges from sociological descriptions of American civil religion is a picture of diverse, even conflicting, values associated with what is central to the people. Bellah's version implies a single, clear-cut, yet ever-developing ideological stance. But is the American civil religion a unified entity? And if not, does it have the capacity to be unifying?

One explanation of diversity in American civil religion is the distinction between "priestly" and "prophetic" versions of civil religion (Marty, 1974; Wuthnow, 1988, 1994). The **priestly version** of American civil religion celebrates the greatness of the nation, its achievements and superiority. The **prophetic version** calls the nation's attention to its offenses against the idealizations for which it stands. Both versions are very much a part of American thought and rhetoric, but they are clearly in conflict. During the 1960s and 1970s, these versions were used to justify opposing stances on U.S. engagement in Vietnam. One set of bumper stickers during that period proclaimed, "America—Love it or leave it!" Another set of bumper stickers retorted, "America—Change it or lose it!" Are these expressions of the same civil religion?

A prophetic version of American civil religion reminds the nation of higher ideals that it must strive to meet. Drawing on this version of civil religion, a group of African-American clergy organized a public challenge to their city's economic development plan, claiming a moral agenda to legitimate their involvement on economic issues. They achieved legitimacy for their dissent by claiming moral "high ground." They accomplished this, not only by reference to their particular religious status and values (e.g., the Catholic Bishops' pastoral letter outlining Catholic values on the economy), but also by reference to civil religious values such as inclusivity and justice drawn from this prophetic version (Williams and Demerath, 1991).

By contrast, the priestly version of American civil religion frequently devolves to nationalistic sentiments and beliefs or to identification of God's will with the aims of "our kind of people." In 1992 President Bush (Sr.) used civil religious imagery to legitimate the U.S. involvement in the war against Iraq in the Persian Gulf. He told a group of Christian radio and television station officials, "I want to thank you for helping America, as Christ ordained, to be a light unto the world" (quoted in Rosenthal, 1992). A priestly version of American civil religion has historically been used to legitimate intolerance, as illustrated by the U.S. history of agitation and discrimination against Asian-Americans since 1850, culminating in the internment of American Japanese during World War II (H. Hill, 1973).

Even the most vulgar forms of American civil religion have considerable appeal and motivating power, exemplified in the prosecutor's speech to the jury at the trial of some American communist labor organizers in 1929:

> Do you believe in the flag of your country, floating in the breeze, kissing the sunlight, singing the song of freedom? Do you believe in North Carolina? Do you believe in good roads, the good roads of North Carolina on which the heaven-bannered hosts could walk as far as San Francisco? . . . Gastonia—into which the union organizers came, fiends incarnate, stripped of their hoofs and horns, bearing guns instead of pitchforks. . . . They came into peaceful, contented Gastonia, with its flowers, birds, and churches . . . sweeping like a cyclone and tornado to sink damnable fangs into the heart and lifeblood of my community. . . . (quoted in Pope, 1942:303–304)

Civil Religion as Legitimating Myth If, in practice, there is no compelling, unifying civil religion in the United States, perhaps we might better conceptualize these religious sentiments and rituals as competing legitimating myths (Hammond, 1994). **Legitimating myths** are stories out of which people live and which they use to justify their values, actions, and identity. Thus, images of America such as being "the Chosen People" or God's vehicle for realizing a millenarian utopia serve both to inform believers' ideas of who they are as a people and to legitimate their nation's collective identity and actions (Moorhead, 1994). Nineteenth-century Populism, for example, drew extensively on civil religious ideas, symbols, meanings, and values to inform and legitimate its ideology, using them as a cultural resource in mobilization of a political movement (Williams and Alexander, 1994). A legitimating myth can be simultaneously a subjectively meaningful source of meaning and belonging and also an ideology. Some of the linkages between religion and ideology, discussed further in Chapter 7, also apply to national legitimating myths.

As legitimating myths, religious representations of the nation are still potentially very powerful. They are cultural resources upon which citizens may draw, both for personal meaning and for mobilizing collective sentiment. Some civil religious themes may recede in usefulness as resources. Some themes may be creatively used and combined in new and unforeseen ways; the application of civil religious themes to the environmental movement is a good example (Albanese, 1992).

If we think of civil religion as a cultural resource available for selective use rather than as a fixed institutional entity, it may help us to make sense of how this *same* civil religion could be a significant source of cultural *conflict* (Wuthnow, 1994). If Americans are in conflict over basic notions of "what it means to be one of us" and "what kind of a people do we want to be," opposing civil religious sentiments are likely to be stirred in debates about abortion, capital punishment, immigration, civil rights, family values, and economic justice, among others. Rather than a taken-for-granted foundation, the social solidarity of modern societies becomes the site of contestation; those engaged in these conflicts actively work to construct and maintain their vision of solidarity (Beckford, 1994).

It may well be that in advanced industrial societies, civil religious elements, like components of individuals' religions, have become somewhat loosened from their institutional coherence, as discussed further in Chapter 8. If this hypothesis is accurate, it suggests that civil religion loses much of its capacity to accomplish solidarity, especially a cohesion that transcends divisions of ethnicity, region, and particular religions. What symbolic power remains may be highly susceptible to political manipulation and commercialization. Many public rituals involve citizens not as voluntarily committed and active participants, but rather as spectators and consumers. Is the quality of civil religious commitment not changed when a Fourth of July celebration is an elaborately staged, professionally orchestrated spectacle, parading U.S. technology, serenaded by a professional band amplified through an elaborate sound system, highlighted by expert lighting technicians and fireworks choreographers, underwritten by corporate contributions, and promoted as a "Kodak moment"? (Wuthnow, 1994).

Why has the religious basis of collective solidarity become an important problematic theme for the social sciences at this time? One reason is the worldwide prominence of religious factors in the splintering of nation-states, such as the former Yugoslavia. Another is the changed location of religion in modern societies (discussed in Chapter 8).

Religion and Nation The priestly form of civil religion is similar to **nationalism**—the ideological expression and building of strong individual identification with the nation, such that national interest becomes preeminent. A useful distinction at this point is between state building and nation building. **State building** refers to developing an authoritative, utilitarian organization for expediently conducting a country's internal and external business. **Nation building** refers to developing a country's sense of solidarity and identity as a people (Eisenstadt and Rokkan, 1973). An example of this analytical distinction is the Quebecois of Canada. Although their primary identification may be regional (i.e., to their province), most Canadians also identify with the Canadian nation, as well as participate in the Canadian state. Many Quebecois, however, do not feel part of the Canadian national identity or solidarity, even though they are subject to the authority of the Canadian state. Their sense of themselves as a people is identified with entirely different symbols, myths, folk heroes, history, and national holidays from that of the rest of the country (Kim, 1993). Indeed, many Quebec residents who voted against separation from the Canadian state did so for economic and political reasons, rather than any sense of national identification with Canada. Existing civil religions in Canada are not nation building.

Many contemporary nation-states came into existence arbitrarily as the result of colonial expansion, division of former colonial territories, or political mergers imposed upon an area by a ruling power. The transformation of these political units (states) into nations is not automatic, and indeed depends upon several cultural factors, including religion (Anderson, 1991).

Civil religion is clearly an element in this process. It can shape a national vision, sacralizing the ideals and "destiny" of a people. It can give national solidarity and identity a religious quality, enabling peoples of diverse tribal, regional, ethnic, and religious groups to come together in a central, unifying cultural experience. Yet, where cultural nationhood is not firmly grounded, where people are divided by religious, ethnic, and linguistic ties, civil religion cannot readily bring people together. Any civil religion arising from tribalistic particularism cannot be a basis of social cohesion for a nation integrating diverse peoples. In the war-torn former Yugoslavia, for example, the legitimating myths supporting Serbian identity as a "people" illustrate this tribalism. They depict Serbian Christians battling Turkish Muslims more than 600 years ago, folk heroes of resistance to Turkish rulers, Serbs displaced by Croats, rural and mountain people resisting urbanization and cosmopolitan attitudes (Kifner, 1994). Such symbols do not have the potential to unite a nation that includes many people of several other ethnic, language, religious, and cultural backgrounds. The problem of tribalistic particularism is discussed further in the second part of this chapter, because such civil religions—as national legitimating myths—are potent sources of social conflict, as exemplified by the situation of Northern Ireland (see Extended Application).

Several factors affect the potency of a religious tie with nationhood. One obvious factor is the degree of religious *homogeneity* in the nation. If a people are already of a single particular religion, that religion can (but does not necessarily) serve as the link with nationhood. Where historically that single religion has been the sole available means of expressing nationality against foreign domination, that religion is especially likely to be expressed as a potent form of civil religion as well (D. Martin, 1978:107; see also Ramet, 1997; Tomka, 1995). This religion–nationalism relationship is exemplified by the situation of Palestine, Cyprus, Poland, and Ireland.

Because religion has considerable potential for legitimating (or delegitimating) the ruling authority of the state, leaders and would-be leaders often try to shape and interpret the religion-to-nationhood linkage in a way that would favor their own power and legitimacy. Sensing the growing influence of oppositional Shi'ite (Muslim) fundamentalist leaders in the 1960s and 1970s, the Mohammad Shah of Iran tried to create a civil religion under the control of the state in order to undermine the traditional religious institutions. He attempted to persuade the people that he was the rightful guardian of the faith. He began to replace religious courts with state-sponsored "Houses of Justice," religious educational institutions with state-controlled ones, and mosques under the control of his religious opponents with state-sponsored ones. The Shah's religious establishment had little effect on the loyalties of most Iranians; indeed, many were incensed, believing that the Shah's civil religion was a perversion of their Islamic tradition (Voll, 1982:292–296). The failure of the ersatz civil religion contributed to the decline of the legitimacy of the monarchy and its eventual overthrow by revolutionary religious fundamentalists.

Often, representatives of particular religions are highly critical of civil religions, especially when the particular religion seeks *hegemony* (i.e., dominant influence) in the state. Some critics decry the dilution or adaptation of the true (particular) faith and its symbols. Others criticize any accommodation with religious perspectives other than their own. In the United States, much of the conflict over prayer in public schools is due to the tension over the state's pluralistic accommodation of non-Christian or nonreligious minorities. Among the most outspoken proponents of prayer in the schools are those who seek a conservative Christian hegemony in the nation. Such tensions over the "proper" religious national vision illustrate that there may actually be conflicting or competing civil religions. The proponents of school prayer have also on occasion tried to yoke elements of the civic faith, such as flag worship, to their political agenda by claiming to be uniquely the "true" patriots.

The development of civil religion in Israel also reflects the influence of particular religious perspectives in trying to shape the image of nationhood. Israel exemplifies a situation in which there are multiple competing national visions with their respective civil religions. Between 1919 and 1945, the Israeli civil religion could be characterized as "Zionist-socialism," uniting around a blend of socialist-worker beliefs and symbols together with an image of the state of Israel as the culmination of Jewish history. "Statism" was the second phase, between 1948 and 1956. It was characterized by an emphasis on the state of Israel itself as a centralized political reality and as a symbol of the collective Jewish people. The statist model, however, did not develop adequate symbols and rituals to be effective. Since 1956 a new civil religion has developed; it focuses more on Judaism and Jewish tradition as a basis for collective Israeli identity and on Israel's connection to worldwide Jewry. Thus, Judaism and Jewishness have become increasingly central to Israeliness. The explicit linkage of the particular religion and national identity has been effectively reasserted (Liebman and Don-Yehiya, 1983). The new emphasis on Jewishness is generally a cultural identification with the language, folkways, and history of the Jewish people. Jews who seriously observe the many prescribed religious practices of Orthodox Judaism account for only about a quarter of the Jewish population of Israel. At the same time, however, even "secular" Jews typically value their Jewish identity and belonging to a Jewish nation; only one-third of those surveyed by the Guttman Institute, in 1991, objected to the extent to which public life and law were controlled by specifically Jewish norms, such as orthodox Jewish regulations regarding marriage, divorce, and family (Liebman, 1997b). Different images of the nation and their relative emphasis on orthodox Judaism have profound influence on the problem of integrating the society, on the treatment of indigenous (Muslim) Palestinians within the country, and on the formulation of a viable diplomatic policy relative to Israel's Arab neighbors (Aran, 1991; Liebman, 1992, 1997a; Lustick, 1988; Sprinzak, 1993).

The comparison of America's and other nations' legitimating myths is useful for an understanding of the religious link between the citizen and nation. It is also related to church–state and religion–power issues, discussed further in Chapter 8.

The civil religion thesis is an important sociological concept. It explains certain aspects of American religiosity that are not related to particular religions. It provides a hypothesis for understanding expressions of national unity in a heterogeneous, highly differentiated society. American civil religion, as described by Bellah and Robertson, is related to the apparent weakness of particular religious institutions in the public sphere. This suggests that the development of a separate civil religion may be related to processes of modernization and secularization, discussed further in Chapter 8.

Finally, the civil religion thesis proposes a basis for the relationship of the individual to the larger modern society. It allows, in theory, the societal needs of cohesion and commitment of members and the individual needs of identity and belonging to be met by the same social processes. To what extent American civil religion really accomplishes this linkage remains unclear. We need to know to what extent people identify their interests and sense of belonging with the nation as a whole. Or, by contrast, to what extent do they locate their interests and community in particular segments of the society that are in conflict with other segments? The relationship of the individual to society is a critical issue in understanding modern societies (Bellah, 1978; Robertson, 1978).

RELIGION AND SOCIAL CONFLICT

Mine eyes have seen the glory of the coming of the Lord.
He hath trampled out the vintage where the Grapes of Wrath
  are stored.
He hath loos'd the fateful lightning of His terrible swift sword.
His truth is marching on.
Glory, Glory, Hallelujah . . .
His truth is marching on.

("Battle Hymn of the Republic," Julia Ward Howe, 1861)

This hymn, which has as its context both particular (Protestant) religions and American civil religion, illustrates the capacity of religion to inspire and reflect social conflict. In this section, we consider factors that make religion a powerful basis or reflection of social cleavages.

Conflict as the Obverse of Cohesion

We must keep in mind that cleavage and conflict are, in many respects, merely the "other side of the coin" of cohesion and consensus. We tend to think of conflict as a breach in sociation, but as Georg Simmel (1906/1955:18) reminds us, conflict is one form of sociation. Simmel emphasized that "a certain amount of discord, inner divergence, and outer controversy, is organically tied up with the very elements that ultimately hold the group together."

Thus, our discussion of religious expression of social cohesion is necessarily related to a consideration of conflict as well. For example, the Doukhobors are a religious sect in Canada and the United States whose values and way of life often conflict greatly with those of the dominant society. Members have often clashed with educational, social welfare, and police authorities; for example, in 1953, Canadian Doukhobors protested educational authorities' toughened stand of public schooling for their children by burning schools and making nude pilgrimages (Woodcock and Avakumonic, 1977). Their strong cohesion as a group sets them off from non-Doukhobors. At the same time, their experience of opposition from the rest of society increases their group's cohesion and commitment. So cohesion at one level of association can produce conflict on another level, and conflict from the outside can contribute to internal cohesion.

Religion has been historically related to conflict at several levels. Perhaps the most obvious has been conflict *between* religious groups, especially when religious boundaries are coextensive with political boundaries. Religion played an important part in the reconquest of Spain by "the Christian monarchs" (end of the fifteenth century). This event was accompanied by powerful "us-against-them" sentiments, resulting both in expulsion of the Moors (i.e., Moslems) and suppression of indigenous Jews. Conflict between religious groups within modern nations tends to be more subtle (e.g., much of the anti-Semitism in America); but when religious boundaries are coextensive with other boundaries (e.g., social class, race, or ethnicity), open conflict can erupt.

Another level of conflict arises *within* a religious group. Conflicts during the early part of the Protestant Reformation exemplify this type, as protesting groups were defined as splinter groups within the Roman Catholic Church. Similarly, many current religious groups came into being as offshoots from larger religious bodies with whom they had some quarrel. The history of U.S. and Canadian Protestantism is the record of many hundreds of such internal conflicts. Today there is considerable conflict within many religious groups, for example, over what should be their group's stand on core moral norms (such as abortion or homosexuality), or whether key scriptures of that faith should be taken as literally true.

Sectarian religious groups also exemplify another level of conflict—between a religious group and the *larger society*. Sometimes the conflict results in reprisals by the larger society, as when courts override family or educational arrangements of the Mormons, Amish, and Doukhobors and jail Quaker and Mennonite conscientious objectors. And sometimes sectarians express conflict only by condemning and withdrawing from the "ways of the world."

Social Sources of Conflict

Social Cleavages Some religious cleavages have their sources in the organization of society. As noted in Chapter 2, religious belonging is one basis of self-identification. A strong sense of belonging (e.g., to a national, religious, kinship, or ethnic group) entails a sense of barrier between members of that group and those outside it. Because religion is one important basis for group identification in society, it is a potential line of cleavage (Coleman, 1956:44, 45). A closer look at religious conflict, however, suggests that the situation is more complex. Often religious boundaries overlap with other lines of cleavage such as social class, race or ethnicity, political or national allegiance, and so on. What appears to be a religious struggle may be also an ethnic or social-class conflict. When religious divisions are coextensive with other lines of cleavage, it is difficult to distinguish the exact role of religion in conflict.

Because religion is often coextensive with other lines of cleavage, it is frequently used as a way of expressing other divisions. A South African could use loyalty to the Dutch Reformed church to express many other loyalties: racial (white, as opposed to black), ethnic (Afrikaner/Dutch, as opposed to English), language (Afrikaans and rabidly anti-English), and political (Afrikaner Nationalist Party) (see Kinghorn, 1997; Moodie, 1978). Similar situations of coextensive identity boundaries have contributed to serious conflict in Lebanon (Labaki, 1988), India (Jaffrelot, 1996; Larson, 1995) , and Northern Ireland (described in further detail in this chapter).

Overlap of cleavage lines also means, however, that religious conflict is often "really" about religion *and* about other seriously divisive issues. In India, for example, state policy regarding education (and by extension economic opportunity) must deal with competing or conflicting demands of groups, defined by coinciding religious-ethnic-language identities (e.g., Aryan Hindus using Sanskrit, North Indian Muslims speaking Urdu, Sinhalese Buddhists using Pali, and Punjabi Sikhs writing Gurumukhi). When these groups conflict over an educational policy, religion is a relevant factor, but it is inextricably intermeshed with ethnic, linguistic, and often economic and regional divisions as well (Oomen, 1989). In such contexts, politico-religious movements (such as Hindu nationalism) mobilize readily unified groups of people whose coinciding identities are linked with shared disprivileged status in a highly stratified society (Basu, 1996; Van der Veer, 1994). Because of this kind of linkage with other important sources of group identity, however, religion has often been a mask or even an overt legitimation for political and economic conflict.

Both the rhetoric and inspiration of religious conflict can cover aspirations for political power or economic gain. Right-wing radio evangelists of the 1930s, Protestant minister Gerald L. K. Smith and Roman Catholic priest Charles E. Coughlin, organized a politico-religious campaign. Virulent anticommunism, anti-Semitism, and nativism were central to their message. Coughlin attracted a radio audience of approximately 10 million weekly listeners, who contributed so much mail and money that he needed 145 clerks. Together Smith and Coughlin organized the Union Party for the 1936 presidential elections. After the defeat of their presidential candidate, Coughlin emphasized anti-Semitism

---

BOX 6.1   Historical Perspective: 1844 Religious Violence in "The City of Brotherly Love"

In 1844, Protestants and Roman Catholics in Philadelphia engaged in armed combat. Protestants were angered that the Catholic bishop had persuaded the school board to excuse Catholic children from Protestant religious instruction, which was then a standard part of the public school curriculum. Mass meetings were held to attack the change, and a Protestant crowd marched into a Catholic neighborhood. Street fighting and general rioting resulted, and Protestant mobs set fire to several houses and Catholic churches. As violence mounted, the governor sent the militia, against which the Protestant mob fought with its own cannon and muskets. Thousands of Catholics fled the city (Shannon, 1963:44).

On the surface, this historical event appears to be a simple case of religious conflict, but the divisions between Roman Catholics and Protestants were also cleavage lines of ethnicity, economic interest, politics, and neighbor-hood. Most Catholics involved were of a despised ethnic group—the Irish, and many were impoverished, recent immigrants.* Protestants were largely part of a rising political stream of anti-immigrant fervor, later culminating in the "Know-Nothing" Party (1854). Economic factors included the competition of immigrants with WASP "natives" for jobs. While the extent of anti-Catholic prejudice at that time should not be understated, it is nevertheless difficult to distinguish elements of religious conflict from other sources of divisiveness.

- What does this historical episode suggest about current debates about religion in the public schools?
- What does it suggest about current debates about the religions of *new* immigrants.

---

*One astute observer entitled his analysis of the social construction (and later diminution) of essentialist ascribed identities for Irish Catholics, *How the Irish Became White* (Ignatiev, 1995).

---

even more, primarily as a symbol of his attack on the country's economic and money system. Although Coughlin received some active church opposition and very little official Roman Catholic support, this right-wing coalition had special appeal to discontented urban Catholics, the elderly, and the rural poor (largely Protestant). The political ambitions of the coalition were served by the anti-Semitic and anti-"subversive" messages proclaimed with religious teachings over the radio (see Bennett, 1969; Ribuffo, 1983). In this example, a religious cleavage between Christians and Jews was exploited to further political ends.

Religion and Nationalism Today religion often feeds nationalism or nationalist aspirations. Occasionally it is captured by them. Ethnic conflict in the former Yugoslavia, for example, is organized more along religious than along other lines. This is not because the Serbs, Croats, and Bosnians are particularly religious people, but because their formal religious allegiances have become the only salient division between them. Serbian identity is historically tied to Eastern Orthodoxy, Croatian identity to Roman Catholicism, and Bosnian identity to Islam. Despite some protestations to the contrary, they share a language, a culture, and a gene pool, but they do not share a national sense of self. Their "ethnicity" is constructed from their communal identity, rather than the other way around (see Asad, 1999; Bauman, 1992; O'Brien, 1993). The Serbs traditionally saw themselves as a vanguard in the historic fight against Islam: the guardians of Europe's eastern gates against the invading Turks. The Croats look west, rather than east—identifying with Rome, not Constantinople. Both continue to look down on Bosnian Muslims as traitors and collaborators—Slavs who converted to Islam during the long Ottoman occupation centuries ago (Ignatieff, 1993).

In this situation religion has become a marker for other social factors that underlie the conflict. Some of these are economic: Poorer provinces resented the advantages given the richer ones when Yugoslavia was united (Botev, 1994). Others are political: Certain politicians found that they could gain power by appealing to nationalist passions (Silber and Little, 1994). But the cultural factors are most important. Serbs, Croatians, and Bosnians imagine themselves each to be "nations," each defined in opposition to the others. Religious differences did not create those nations, but they did mark them off from one another.[1] Once marked, the communities could be mobilized by politicians on all sides.

Religion does not always figure in the creation of such "imagined communities" (Anderson, 1991), but it is a potent resource when it is so used. Sociologists have identified some of the many other factors involved (see Calhoun, 1993; Greenfeld, 1993; Hobsbawm, 1992). Religion is often an important factor in its own right, however: from the nationalism of the French Revolution (Bell, 1995) to the Northern Ireland "troubles" described later in this chapter. Religion can become a "sacred marker" that accentuates and stands for the totality of divisions between people (Hanf, 1994). When conflicting groups treat their religions as cultural *possessions,* the value of which rests not in religious practice itself, but rather in defending the cultural possession against others, religion is particularly likely to serve as such a marker (Tambiah, 1993). Even in modern societies, religion seems to be as salient as ever for dividing people from one another.

The Marxian Perspective Marxian interpretations hold that religious conflict is merely the expression of fundamental economic relationships. Accordingly, the dominant class attempts to impose ideas (including religious ideas) that legitimate its interests. Or it may exploit existing religious divisions among subordinate peoples to prevent them from realizing their true class interests. As we will note in Chapter 7, religion can contribute to legitimation

---

1. Because imagined communities want to believe that their basis for unity is an essential or "pure" quality, they often deny the syncretism (of religion, cultural heritage, language, and genetic makeup) that has inevitably already occurred. For example, Greek nationalism promotes the myth of a racially and culturally direct line back to classical Greek civilization, despite the obvious intervening influences of other cultures (especially those introduced over centuries by the Ottomans). Nationalist rhetoric then claims for Eastern Orthodoxy a pure link with Hellenism, despite its cultural adaptations and syncretic absorption of popular (non-Hellenic) religious practices (Kokosalakis, 1987). These elements—religion, language, cultural tradition, geography, "race"—are woven together to create an imagined community, with obvious political uses (Stewart, 1994).

of the existing social system and also express real conflicts in that system (Turner, 1977).

According to Marxian theory, religious dissent is often an expression of economic dissatisfaction, but its religious nature prevents dissenters from fully realizing their economic-class interests. Religious conflicts have often divided members of the working class when their true interests, according to Marx, would be best served by uniting against the common enemy, the ruling class. In the late nineteenth century, some 100,000 members of the American Protective Association pledged not to vote for, strike with, or hire Catholics if non-Catholics were available (Ribuffo, 1988). Such movements attracted economically threatened working-class persons who might have otherwise benefited from uniting in political and labor movements with Catholics who shared their class interests.

Part of the reason why Marx's predictions of increasing class conflict have not eventuated in many modern societies is that their members are subject to many **cross pressures** other than social-class interest, thus making religion a less volatile source of conflict. Cross pressures refer to the conflicting loyalties that individuals feel when they identify with several different roles and reference groups (Coleman, 1956:46). An example of cross pressures is the conflicting loyalties felt by a black woman who manages the local branch of a bank, lives in an integrated, middle-class suburb with pleasant Jewish and Irish Catholic neighbors, and belongs to a local Baptist church. When an issue arises in which different attachments conflict (e.g., whether tax monies should be used to fund abortions for poor women), she may acutely feel the cross pressures. Her loyalties to poor blacks or to women may urge her to support funding the abortions; her identification with her religion or the privileged classes may press for the opposite stance.

In many societies, this kind of cross pressure is absent or minimal because all major meaningful kinds of personal identification coincide. If the dominant class is of a totally different race, religion, and cultural background from the subordinate class (as in many colonial societies), the potential for social conflict is great because there are few conflicting loyalties within the person. In the United States, lines of cleavage—religious, ethnic, racial, economic, residential, regional, political—are seldom coextensive. Although real status inequalities exist (e.g., whites and Protestants are considerably overrepresented among the political and economic elites), geographical mobility, relative economic mobility, and mass communications have contributed to blurring the lines of cleavage. The existence of these cross pressures within individuals means that the likelihood of concerted conflict along any *one* line of cleavage (e.g., social class or religion) is reduced (Coleman, 1956:47).

Because religious cleavage sometimes masks other cleavages does not mean, however, that there are not real religious interests involved. Protection of religious interests frequently results in conflict. The struggle for *religious liberty*— the freedom to hold and practice the religion of one's choice—has been a recurrent cause of political conflict. Violent suppression of the Huguenots (i.e., French Protestants) resulted in continued conflict from their inception in the early 1500s until 1789. The Huguenots persisted in asserting their right to practice their religion, and the conflict included civil wars, mass emigration, massacres, and torture. To many people today, religious intolerance seems impolite and, at worst, unjust. We find it difficult to understand why religion would be the basis of such strong antagonism.

Conflict over Bases of Authority One of the key reasons why religion can result in such extreme conflict is that it not only reflects lines of cleavage in society, but it can also challenge the bases of legitimacy by which authority is exercised. The French rulers believed (probably accurately) that the Protestant worldview constituted a challenge to the basis of their authority because that authority was justified largely by the Roman Catholic worldview. Religious ideas and interests have historically been significant forces in establishing authority.

Authority, in contrast with power relations, requires that subjects consider it legitimate. **Legitimacy** means the social recognition of an authority's claims to be taken seriously, and it implies negative social sanctions for failure to comply with authoritative commands. Conflict is implicit in authority relationships because they involve dominance and subordination. Yet they are based on more than pure power. Other considerations (e.g., scientific or religious knowledge) may also be sources of legitimacy of authority. There is constant potential for conflict between authorities who base their claims on different sources of legitimacy.

When religion is related to civil disobedience, religion is largely the basis of challenging the civil authority's *source of legitimacy*. In the 1960s, two Catholic priests, Phil Berrigan and his brother Dan Berrigan, together with other Christian peace and justice activists, engaged in a number of nonviolent "direct actions" against America's war in Vietnam. For instance, on one occasion, they broke into the Baltimore Draft Board (Selective Service) offices and poured blood on drawers full of files to protest the involuntary conscription of thousands of (disproportionately inner-city) youth to fight in what protesters considered to be an immoral war. This kind of civil disobedience says, in effect, "Your rules and practices may be right according to your authority, but our actions appeal to a higher basis of authority."

The place of religion in societal authority relationships is complex because religion is both a *basis* of legitimacy and, often, the *content* of authoritative pronouncements. Thus, a spokesperson such as the dalai lama or the pope both pronounces religious messages and bases the claim to speak authoritatively on religious tradition. Religion has historically been an important source of conflict because it offered both a basis for legitimacy of authority and a set of ideas around which conflict centered. The apparent decrease in religion's role as a source of authority in modern society is due partly to its loss of legitimacy— its capacity to compel people to take its claims seriously.

Sources in the Nature of Religion

The nature of religion and religious groups also contributes to social conflict. In many respects, this capacity for promoting conflict is simply the obverse of religion's ability to engender social cohesion. Religion is one way of expressing the unity of the "in-group"—"our people." This in-versus-out dichotomy, however, applies to conflict both outside and within the group.

Conflict with Outsiders: Boundaries This distinction between in-group and out-group implies distancing oneself from outsiders. Just as religious rituals celebrate the identity and unity of the group, they simultaneously maintain the boundary between that group and outsiders. Not only do religious groups protect their external boundaries, but they are also concerned with internal purification—another potential source of conflict (Douglas, 1966, 1970). The we–they dichotomy is both a structural and cognitive framework that includes how people think about themselves and others. This cognitive boundary is based on the fact that "we" have shared central experiences that "they" have not. In-group language embodies these shared experiences and further distinguishes "us" from "them." "Born-again" Christians consider their religious experience an important distinction between themselves and others, and their ways of witnessing to their special experience of being "born again" symbolize this difference.

Religion figures importantly in the socialization of children in most societies and thus becomes part of the "we–they" cognitive framework from an early age. Developing a sense of religious belonging, children come to think of themselves as part of the in-group and share their group's way of perceiving the rest of society. This cognitive framework may also include the perception of others as enemies or inferior to members of one's in-group. The values and attitudes learned in one religious group often vary considerably from those taught to children in another group. Thus, religion's significance in socialization enhances its potential for divisiveness (Coleman, 1956:54, 55; Gorsuch and Aleshire, 1974; Wach, 1944:36).

Conflict with Outsiders: Particularism Certain religious perspectives appear to promote conflict. Particularist worldviews encourage intolerance and prejudice toward the out-group. **Religious particularism** is the viewing of one's own religious group as the only legitimate religion (Glock and Stark, 1966:20). The clash of worldviews in a complex society is resolved in a number of possible stances: "Our way is totally right, theirs is totally wrong"; "Their way is good, our way is better"; "Our ways are both right but appropriate for different people"; "Their way and ours are essentially the same, and apparent differences are only incidental matters." Some religious belief systems include, at their core, tribalistic particularist judgments toward nonbelievers. For example, a study of Canadian racist extremists found that social class and education levels were not closely correlated with involvement in extreme racist activism; rather, the most striking correlation was active membership in certain fundamentalist Christian religions (Barrett, 1987). A U.S. study also found a consistent correlation between fundamentalism and the general tendency to discriminate against others, as well as actual discrimination toward specific targets, such as women, blacks, and homosexuals (McFarland, 1989). Similarly, in Northern Ireland, the foremost religious source of extremist violence is the religious particularism of evangelical Protestants (Brewer, 1998; Bruce, 1994).

Indeed, religious particularism seems to *require* a sense of opposition; one's own religion is seen as triumphant *over* some other. The in-group needs an out-group against which it can compare itself (Glock and Stark, 1966:29; Raab, 1964).[2] Religious worldviews that involve a particularistic stance toward the rest of humankind hold greater likelihood for promoting conflict than less triumphalistic worldviews.

Groups with particularistic worldviews are often able to mobilize the efforts of their members precisely because of this sense of opposition. Particularism enhances militance for one's religious group. The strong element of religious particularism in Islam promoted its early missionary expansion throughout the Middle East, west to North Africa and Spain, east toward India and Southeast Asia, and north toward Eurasia. The fourteenth-century Muslim social historian, Ibn Khaldoun, observed that the genious of Islam was its ability to create a sense of *Al 'Assabiyya* ("group-feeling") among peoples of a wider Arab empire. It made possible transcending the solidarity of nomadic tribes (with their fierce loyalty along lines of kinship) and uniting ethnically and territorially diverse Muslims in a religiously particularist bond: "all of us" (followers of the Prophet) against "all of them" (see Spickard, 2001).

Such particularism, combined with religiously legitimated militance, was also embodied in the *jihad* (i.e., holy war)—a recurrent feature of Islamic conflict. Contemporary conflicts in Afghanistan, Egypt, and Palestine have been viewed as jihads. The idea of missionary expansion is foreign to most non-Western religions because relatively few religions combine the particularism of having "the truth" with the mandate to convert the entire out-group. Interesting parallels with Christianity and Islam, however, are the worldviews of modern totalistic movements such as nazism, communism, and Maoism.

Internal Conflict in the Religious Group: Deviance and Control This same in-group versus out-group dichotomy applies to the relationship of the group toward its own members who are defined as deviant or heretical. Again, conflict is the obverse of cohesion. The way in which a group treats a deviant member involves some form of conflict by which the group exerts its control. **Deviance** is behavior that is contrary to norms of conduct or expectations of a social group. Because it is the group that sets norms and identifies individual instances of deviant behavior, analysis of deviance describes the group as much as the deviant member (Becker, 1963). If a group sets a norm (e.g., against gambling) and labels a member as deviating from this norm, the group is both punishing the gambler-deviant and proclaiming its own identity as a nongambling people.

---

2. For example, some years ago I was talking with a boy of about 12 who had recently been confirmed in his church. Responding to my query about what that ritual meant to him, he said, "It means being willing to fight and even die for Christ." I asked whom he thought he had to fight, and he replied, "I don't know—I guess the Jews." Nascent anti-Semitism perhaps, but probably only a reflection of the boy's sense that his Christianity had to triumph over some other group. The Jews may have been the only non-Christian group of which he had ever heard.

Especially in small, closely knit societies or religious groups, the group's social control over deviant members can be powerful. Mennonites sometimes "shun" deviant members. Family and neighbors refuse any social interaction, sometimes for years, until the deviant repents of a "sin" or recants a "heresy." Because religion is often a source of the social group's norms and values, it is frequently important in the social response to deviance. The actions of the deviant member are seen as not only hurtful to the group but a violation of things that the group holds sacred.

Durkheim (1965:Book 3) emphasized that "piacular rites" (e.g., expiation for wrongdoings and cleansing of impurities) are just as expressive of the group's core unity and force as "positive rites" (e.g., communion). By ritually reincorporating deviant members who repent, both individual and group are strengthened in their solidarity around the norm. Threat of deviance from within is potentially more disruptive than opposition from outsiders because insiders "ought to know better"; outsiders can be dismissed as uninformed and ignorant of the "truth." Insiders must be taken more seriously as "one of us." A fellow member who goes against an important group norm becomes an affront to the essential unity of the entire group.

Deviance may contribute to group solidarity even when the deviant member is not repentant. In uniting against the deviant member, the group is strengthened. Even more than external opposition, internal conflict with the deviant member sharpens the group's sense of its boundaries and norms (see Durkheim, 1938:65–75; Mead, 1918). Collective rejection of the person accused of adultery reminds the entire group how much it should abhor adultery. Sometimes norms may be unclear or changing, and collective treatment of the deviant member may actually articulate the norm. In recent years, for example, numerous community or religious groups have attempted to proscribe or punish homosexual practices. Some have gone so far as to stigmatize AIDS patients due to the association of their disease with homosexuality. One study found that intolerance (e.g., prohibition of children with AIDS from schools) toward AIDS patients is correlated with factors of political conservatism, religious fundamentalism, and lower levels of education and self-esteem (Johnson, 1987). These actions are not merely a reflection of antagonism toward homosexuals; more importantly, they are groups' attempts to assert their norms in a situation where societal norms are unclear or changing. By uniting against what they define as deviance, they are confirming their own norms for themselves.

Religious groups with particularistic worldviews appear especially intolerant of deviance. Their certainty of their own total rightness increases their condemnation of the wrongness they perceive of any other beliefs and practices. Particularistic religious groups give deviant members more reason to fear group sanctions. If you have been socialized in a religion that you believe is uniquely true—the only path to salvation—you are not likely to consider leaving the group. You are likely to try very hard to follow its rules for behavior, accept its punishments for infringement, and hope never to be forced to leave. If you accept the group's claims to be the only true religion, expulsion (i.e., excommunication) is the worst possible punishment. In uniting against the deviant, members of particularistic religious groups gain both a sense of solidarity and a sense of their own moral rightness; they are triumphant over external and internal opposition. The core of righteous members of such groups often develops purist and elitist characteristics, which further promote the likelihood of conflict.

Internal Conflict: Issues of Authority and Heresy Internal strife in religious groups can develop over nonreligious interests too, including socioeconomic issues, leadership and power, and other social cleavages within the group. For example, in the late fourteenth and early fifteenth centuries, the Catholic Church experienced a major schism resulting from a purely political split rather than theological dispute. The same group of cardinals, acting apparently in good faith, elected two rival popes; subsequently, various kings and princes from most regions of Europe sided with one or the other pope to legitimate their own political claims. The subsequent resolution of the schism was due to political rather than any religious rapprochement (see Blasi, 1989).

Nevertheless, conflict over religious ideas and practices frequently centers on the issue of **authority,** which implies control both of the religious organization (however small) and of the articulation of central beliefs and practices. The separation of Eastern ("Orthodox") and Roman Catholicism was fundamentally a conflict over authority. Ostensibly, the schism was over theological issues such as whether Christ was "of the same substance" as God the Father or was "similar" to the Father. Behind these theological issues, however, were deeper sources of conflict: Greek philosophy and polity versus Roman philosophy and law. In particular, the split represented the Eastern patriarchs' dissatisfaction with the consolidation of church power and authority in the hands of the single Western patriarch (i.e., the pope in Rome). The specific theological issues, important as they were to conflicting parties, did not cause the split; the issue of authority in the church was the central source of conflict (Niebuhr, 1929:111–117; "Orthodox Eastern Church," 1943, 16:938–939).

Similarly, the main division between the dominant form of Islam (Sunni) and Shi'ism (the most powerful of the challenging Islamic sects) occurred over the issue of the *imam,* the legitimate successor to the Prophet, Muhammad. According to Shi'ite tradition, there is a line of succession to the imamate from the Prophet through his cousin Ali to their contemporary leaders; the imam is thus the rightful, divinely ordained leader of Muslims (Voll, 1982:7–31).

Other sources of conflict over authority are religious revelations. Because religious experience and ways of knowing are so intensely private, there is always the potential for believers to receive revelations or come to interpretations that differ from official ones. Revelations, prophecies, insights, and new interpretations of scripture and tradition have all been significant sources of intragroup conflict in most major religions.

When members assert a belief or practice that differs in some important way from those authoritatively established, it is often defined as not mere deviance but **heresy.** This kind of dissent implicitly challenges the existing authority structure of the group. It suggests that the entire group should consider a different basis for its core beliefs and practices. The labeling and condemnation of heresy is the official leadership's assertion of its authority in the face of the challenge. The vigor with which labeled heresies have historically been prosecuted illustrates the seriousness of their challenge to established religious authority.

Conflict over authority is exemplified by the Roman Catholic Church's issue of *Americanism,* which Pope Leo XIII condemned as heretical in 1899. *Americanism* generally referred to the idea that religion should be adapted to the individual cultures in which it is practiced. Specifically it meant that the American culture required a different brand of Catholicism than European cultures. The origin of this perspective is attributed to missionaries to the Americans in the mid-1800s. They sought to adapt their missionary appeals to the peculiar characteristics of American culture, especially its democratic and pluralistic organization. Latent in the papal condemnation of Americanism, however, was the assertion of one particular system of church authority (Rome/pope/curia-centered) over another system (national/bishops/collegia-centered). The possibility that any national church authorities might develop separate strains of teaching authority was perceived as a direct challenge to the existing system of centralized authority (Cross, 1958; McAvoy, 1957).

The label of *Americanism* continued to suppress much internal dissent in the American Roman Catholic Church in the first half of the twentieth century. These same issues of authority were central in the deliberations of the First and Second Vatican Councils (1869 and 1962). The politics of the Americanist "crisis" have not been eliminated and continue to recur in clashes between Vatican authorities and some Catholic scholars and clergy (see Kurtz, 1986). The Roman Catholic Church provides clear-cut examples of the definition of heresy because it has developed specific measures for defining and dealing with it. But Protestant history also involves numerous instances of heresy, schism, and clash over authority. While the particularist worldview of many Christian groups promotes this kind of internal conflict, non-Christian religions (e.g., Hinduism, Islam, and Shinto) have also known many schisms and internal divisions.

Internal conflict over heresy is a dynamic process. It can mobilize members of the group for action against the heresy and indirectly promote internal changes, revising its teachings, shifting organizational arrangements, or developing other innovations (e.g., see a case study of the 1953 Boston heresy case [Pepper, 1988]). Or the group can absorb the alternative beliefs and practices, changing in the direction of alternative authority. Even in the suppression of heresy, the group impels adherents of the heresy to form an alternative social movement. The history of Christian sects illustrates this dynamism.

Religion is thus an important factor in social conflict, both within the group and with outsiders. This potential for conflict results both from qualities of religion and religious groups themselves and from the nature of the society as a whole. Nevertheless, the aspect of conflict is basically the obverse of social cohesion; a certain amount of conflict is part of the very structure that holds groups together. And because religion is one important way by which groups express their unity, it is also a significant factor in conflict. This dual relationship is illustrated in the Extended Application section of this chapter: an examination of recent conflict in Northern Ireland.

EXTENDED APPLICATION: THE CONFLICT IN NORTHERN IRELAND

Civil strife in Northern Ireland illustrates religion's capacity to promote both cohesion and conflict. The history of divisions in Northern Ireland is long, complex, and confusing to outsiders. This brief essay focuses on the religious dimension of this struggle, recognizing that other important historical, political, economic, and social factors are also involved. At the writing of this edition, the peace process in Northern Ireland is closer to becoming a political reality than in all the years encompassed by earlier editions of this text. A peace agreement in 1998, ratified by the governments of Northern Ireland, Britain, and Ireland, laid a framework for disarmament of the warring paramilitary units. It provided for a power-sharing Northern Irish governing body to rule the province (since the British took over direct rule some thirty years ago when the nearly exclusively Protestant Northern Ireland Parliament lost legitimacy). Nearly two years later, despite increased outbursts of paramilitary vigilante violence turned against members of their own communities in order to prevent rapprochement, Northern Ireland has moved yet closer to civil society, a just and representative political system, and socioeconomic well-being. Long after the "Troubles" (as the ongoing violence is euphemistically called) are over, however, it will be important for us to understand the causes and the role of religion in promoting conflict and violence, as well as peace and reconciliation.

Religious Conflict?

One often receives the impression from television and newspaper media coverage that the strife in Northern Ireland is purely religious, with two antagonistic camps—Roman Catholic and Protestant—pitted against each other in senseless, deadly violence. Between 1970 and 1998, the sectarian strife claimed between 3,000 and 4,000 lives (or about one in 500 citizens), more than half of whom were civilian noncombatants. Approximately, another 40,000 (or about one in 50) were seriously injured (NISRA, 1998). Neighborhoods and business districts have been bombed or burned, and generations of children have grown to adulthood knowing no other way of life than intermittent warfare in their streets (see McEvoy, 2000).

The image is puzzling to most Americans, who see the antagonists as so similar to each other. Unlike the U.S. national experience with conflict over segregation and discrimination, the opposing sides in Northern Ireland appear to share the same racial stock, language, and social class. These apparent similarities are, however, based on only a casual glance. Participants themselves apply finer distinctions; they are quick to identify someone as "one of us" or "one of them" on the basis of simple items of information—name, address, or school attended.

Nevertheless, the only differences apparent at a superficial level of analysis center around religion. Many Americans find it difficult to believe that religion is so important to anyone as to be worth fighting over. Others note the relative ease with which both Catholic and Protestant Irish immigrants adjusted to the heterogeneous and pluralistic religious scene in America (MacEoin, 1974:1, 2). To participants in the Northern Irish conflict, however, the salience of religion as a genuine source of antagonism is unquestionable. In 1970 a British Broadcasting Corporation (BBC) interviewer asked a Belfast Protestant, "What do you have against the Roman Catholics?"—to which the response was, "Are you daft? Why, their religion of course" (cited in Rose, 1971:247). Americans and other outsiders ask: Is the conflict in Northern Ireland indeed a religious one?

This analysis will suggest that the answer is yes, but with qualifications. The conflict is not over theology or doctrine. It does not center on Protestantism or Catholicism as most adherents of these religions in the United States, Canada, or elsewhere in Europe know them. The conflict in Northern Ireland could perhaps best be understood as the outcome of two mutually exclusive *religious representations of the nation:* one "Protestant" (strongly identified with "Orangeism") and the other "Catholic" (strongly identified with "Republicanism"). Although the concept of civil religion is controversial, it appears useful in explaining the Northern Irish situation of religiously focused political strife.

Conflicting Civil Religions

The role a civil religion takes in a society varies according to the relationship that exists between the particular religions and the civil society. In the United States, civil religious rituals and symbols can represent the cohesion of persons of diverse particular religions (e.g., Episcopalian, Baptist, Catholic, Mormon), in large part because no particular religion has dominance in the state. Separation of church and state makes possible (and, some sociologists would argue, necessary) a civil religion that *transcends* particular religions.

Northern Ireland, by contrast, represents a situation in which religion (Protestant) is not separated from the state. Religion has been a significant consideration in political decision making, in applying social policy, in the actions of police and other officials, in the curriculum of national schools, and in the content of mass media. Relatively few persons in the country doubt that religion should be linked with the state; there is, however, profound dissension over *which* religion should shape the nation.

Both Protestant and Catholic perspectives in Northern Ireland entail visions of nationhood. Whatever their political thrust, both national visions are also intensely religious in both content and style. Each group builds its own version of national identity imbued with religious significance, and each group engenders a strong sense of "us" against "them."

Particular religions (i.e., Roman Catholic and various Protestant groups) contributed to the creation of these opposing visions, but they cannot control them or how opposing factions use them.[3] Thus, religious leaders in both camps who attempt to quell the violence typically have little power over the strong sentiments set into motion in the name of religion. Indeed, church leaders who promote interfaith tolerance and an end to violence have often been ignored or silenced (see Appleby, 2000, for a comparative history of peacemaking and reconciliation).

The opposing civil religions of Northern Ireland illustrate that social cohesion is often the obverse of social conflict. Each group is held together largely by its sense of opposition to the other group. Both groups, especially the Protestants, are thrust into enclaves of tribal togetherness out of fear of the other. Reformation and counter-Reformation symbols and myths that are several hundred years old shape these fears and lock believers into nationalistic ideologies that cannot accommodate full religious pluralism.

The Social Context

Northern Ireland was created in the 1920s after rebellion against Britain, when twenty-six counties of Ireland became a self-governing dominion (eventually recognized as an independent republic). The other six counties, an area of 5,200 square miles in the northeast corner of the island, continued their union with Britain—that is, the United Kingdom. Partition of the island in the 1920s was designed to guarantee Protestant electoral dominance in the North. In the first decades after partition, Protestants were nearly 70 percent of the population (and an even larger proportion of the eligible voters). In the second half of the twentieth century, however, the balance shifted such that now all Protestant denominations combined make up a mere 53 percent majority (Hoge, 1999). The Republic of Ireland, by contrast, is predominantly Catholic, so that on the island as a whole Catholics outnumber Protestants approximately three to one (Prokesch, 1990).

Irish Protestants and Catholics tend to be more fundamentalist and theologically conservative than their counterparts in the United States and England. Both groups have historically been prime examples of *religious particularism,* the belief that one's group has a particular (privileged) connection with the deity and is, thus, the only legitimate religion. The self-righteousness and sense of opposition characteristic of particularistic worldviews make both groups prone to intolerance. Religious polarization in Northern Ireland has produced a social and psychological split in which there are no neutrals; even unbelievers are identified as Protestant or Catholic unbelievers. When bound-

---

3. Further corroboration of the distinction between particular and civil religions in Northern Ireland is found in survey data that show that commitment to particular Protestant religion is only weakly related to "Protestant" political attitudes about the conflict; commitment to Catholic religion is unrelated to "Catholic" political stances (McAllister, 1982).

aries are enshrined by such strident sectarianism, it is difficult for counter-movements to be either nonsectarian or ecumenical. Polarized sectarianism produces a mentality in which neutrality is incomprehensible and ecumenism is anathema.

All aspects of life in Northern Irish cities are divided by these religious poles. There are separate Protestant and Catholic neighborhoods, playgrounds, schools, social clubs, charitable organizations, political parties, youth activities, sports, newspapers, shops, and cultural events. As suggested earlier in this chapter, religion is especially likely to be a source of conflict between groups when it is coextensive with other important sources of identity. In Northern Ireland, religion is something of a "master" identity, with almost all other significant social divisions aligned under it.

Much of the social segregation results from systematic discrimination against Catholics, especially since the 1920s partition. To protect their power and economic advantages, Protestants severely discriminated against Catholics in employment, housing, civil service, public board appointments, electoral districting, and representation. By restricting housing for Catholics to certain neighborhoods and then gerrymandering the boundaries of voting districts, Protestants were able to maintain strong majorities in the councils of communities where they were numerically the minority. Largely due to the polarization and violence of the last thirty years, many communities became more segregated after these policies were ended; by 1991, about half of Northern Ireland residents lived in areas that were more than 90 percent Catholic or 90 percent Protestant (Murray, 1995).

But not all segregation of Catholics was imposed by Protestants. Segregated Catholic schools are supported by the Catholic church hierarchy, partly in order to retain greater control over the socialization of Catholic youths and to protest the (Protestant) religious content of national school instruction (see Brewer, 1998). More recently, the bishops have resisted the spread of integrated schools, arguing that excluding religious education in the schools would lead to secularism (Fulton, 1991). Their emphasis in Northern Ireland has been on achieving equity in building and funding Catholic national schools, while promoting tolerance within segregated schools (Davis, 1994; Murray, 1995; Smith, 1995).

The net effect of such total segregation is that few of the cross pressures that could reduce prejudice and conflict operate in Northern Irish social life. Polarization makes it difficult, if not impossible, to socialize with persons outside one's enclave. "They" are not real persons; "they" are described only by group myths, not by personal contact. Indeed, polarization has produced strong social controls. In-groups punish members who overstep boundaries and are too friendly to the out-group. Members of both enclaves have been beaten, maimed, and even killed for crossing the social boundaries. Sometimes religious sanctions are brought to bear on people who do not stay in their religious enclave. One Catholic bishop refused to confirm children who were not sent to Catholic schools. Some Protestant ministers use their pulpits to denounce fellow Protestants who accept ecumenism.

These current polarizations are the result of a long history, which figures significantly in the myths, symbols, and legends of the two civil religions. This history, however briefly presented here, is critical for understanding contemporary sentiments.

Some Historical Background

Although the history of England's involvement in Ireland may be traced to the twelfth-century Norman conquest, events of the seventeenth century were especially critical in shaping contemporary problems. In the sixteenth and seventeenth centuries, the chief objective of England's Irish policy was to prevent Ireland from becoming a center of English rebels or a stepping-stone for continental enemies. Thus, under the Tudor monarchs, the English began a system of plantations in Ireland, substituting loyal English settlers for potentially disloyal Irish or Old English landholders, predominantly Roman Catholics. The plantation system was particularly important in shaping the religious composition of Northern Ireland (Beckett, 1966:38–63).

Plantation and Insurrection In the seventeenth century, the policy of plantation was extended with vigor and increasingly religious overtones. The most extensive and successful plantation was in the province of Ulster (northern Ireland). Large areas of Ulster were confiscated and given to immigrant English and Scottish landholders. Only about 2,000 British families lived on these Ulster plantations by 1628. Thus, the large-scale removal of native Irish that the government intended did not occur then (Beckett, 1966:64–74; Clarke, 1967). Discontent of the native Irish festered, and in 1641 insurrection broke out, especially throughout the north of Ireland.

The Ulster insurrection had special significance to the English, who were then involved in a civil war between Royalists (largely Catholics and Anglicans) and Parliamentarians (mostly Puritans and Dissenters). Exaggerated tales of the 1641 massacres served as fuel for the English reconquest of Ireland. In 1649 Oliver Cromwell (a Puritan) landed in Ireland with a force of 12,000 soldiers and began a campaign so ruthless that 350 years later he is still identified as perhaps the single most hated symbol of English oppression. Cromwell saw his mission as not only to quell a royalist uprising but also to bring divine revenge for the 1641 massacres. Reporting on his conquest of Drogheda, after which some 2,000 townspeople were put to the sword, Cromwell wrote, "I am persuaded that this is a righteous judgment of God upon those barbarous wretches, who have imbrued their hands in so much innocent blood" (quoted in Beckett, 1966:79, 80).

The settlement following this reconquest solidified English dominance. The settlement forced all "disloyal" landlords to forfeit their lands, and new "loyal" settlers took their places. Catholics were particularly affected by this policy because the English parliament felt that they were, by definition, disloyal to English interests. In 1641 the majority of Irish landlords had been Catholic; after the Cromwellian settlement, the majority were Protestant

(Beckett, 1966:74–81). Catholics lost virtually all political power because representation in parliament was based on landholding.

A subsequent revolution in England further polarized the Irish situation. The English monarch James II (a Catholic) was supplanted by a Dutch (Protestant) ruler, William of Orange (after whom the Orange Order of Northern Ireland is named). Irish Catholics sided with James II, and he brought his army to Ireland, hoping to reconquer England from that base. The Protestant colonists of Ireland had sided with William of Orange, who then brought an expeditionary force to Ireland. James took Dublin and laid seige to Londonderry (i.e., Derry), the main source of Orange resistance, but the city held out for fifteen weeks until reinforcements came. In 1690 the two armies met in a decisive battle at the River Boyne, and James was beaten on July 12. William's victory not only secured his position as king of England but also established Protestant supremacy in Ireland (Beckett, 1966:90–95; Simms, 1967).

These events, which occurred some 350 years ago, are still enshrined in the civil religions of Protestants and Catholics in Northern Ireland. The Catholic civil religion celebrates the heroes of the revolutionary uprising, and the Protestant civil religion commemorates the Orange defenders. In contemporary Derry, an annual (and sometimes violent) Protestant celebration parades the walls of the old city and proclaims to the Catholics living below the walls the seventeenth-century slogan "No Surrender." In Belfast July 12 is a major Protestant holiday with bonfires, parades, speeches, and a mock battle to commemorate William's victory at the Boyne. The defeat is remembered in the Catholic civil religion as merely one of a long string of Protestant and English acts of oppression and injustice (see Thompson, 1967). Thus, the history of "our nation" is remembered differently by the two groups. Events centuries past are the basis for two completely opposed sets of myths, legends, and heroes.

The Deepening Split Events following 1690 further deepened the rift between Protestants and Catholics. Catholics were effectively excluded from parliament, and a number of "penal laws" excluded Catholics (the great population majority of the island) from parliament, army and militia, positions in municipal corporations, all civil service, and the legal profession. Laws of inheritance and land tenure were changed so that it was virtually impossible for Catholic landholders to leave land to a Catholic heir. The laws forbade Catholics from sending their children abroad for education, and Catholics were forced to pay tithes to the (Protestant) Church of Ireland. These laws, in effect for over 100 years, had the desired result of suppressing Catholic political and economic power. The first widespread nationalist movement, arising in the first half of the nineteenth century, focused on the issue of "Catholic emancipation," especially from strictures on political representation and voting. This history laid the basis for the distinctively Roman Catholic character of modern Irish nationalism (Beckett, 1966:96–144).

Meanwhile, Ulster (the northern province) developed the only significant industrial sector in the country, and Ulster business owners feared nationalist separation from Britain—their primary source of markets and supplies. Ulster was also the locus of the only large Protestant enclave, which felt threatened by the prospect of Catholics gaining political power. Some English politicians "played the Orange card," that is, encouraged religious fears and sectarian strife. Lord Randolph Churchill visited Belfast in 1886 to encourage Protestant fears of home rule (i.e., allowing an independent Irish parliament) and left the slogans "Home Rule Is Rome Rule" and "Ulster Will Fight; Ulster Will Be Right." These mottos still resound in contemporary Protestant civil religion in Northern Ireland (Beckett, 1966:146–157).

In the nineteenth century, both Protestant and Catholic national visions grew. Sometimes they were embodied in organizations and movements, but more generally they developed as an attitude or part of a worldview of the respective communities. The development of these nationalisms illustrates the distinction between particular religions (i.e., Roman Catholic, Presbyterian, and Church of Ireland) and Catholic and Protestant civil religions. The Roman Catholic hierarchy frequently opposed the nascent Irish nationalism, even though the movement was heavily Catholic. As the twentieth century approached, church leaders found their interests more closely allied to those of the political establishment. They were particularly unhappy with the socialist strain of the pro-independence labor movement. Thus, while the Catholic hierarchy encouraged a general antagonism toward Protestants, it discouraged the growing Catholic nationalism. Similarly, especially in the North, the Orange Order and related Protestant groups developed their power and beliefs independently of particular Protestant churches, yet with their approval.

The nature of the Irish Revolution (1916–1921) itself laid the grounds for the present conflict. The fighting was primarily between two relatively small, irresponsible armed forces, neither of which was controlled by its government. The British government was unable to exercise control over its special force, the "Black and Tans," and the Irish Republican Army (IRA) was not responsible to the Dail (the newly established Irish independent parliament). Never actually militarily "won," the revolutionary war did prepare both sides for a compromise: the division of the island into a politically independent part and a unionist part (see Beckett, 1966:157–166). In the recent "Troubles," the IRA (Republican nationalist) and Ulster Volunteer Force (Orangeist) are offspring of the irresponsible paramilitary forces of the 1916–1921 strife.

Between Partition and the Civil Rights Movement (ca 1925–1970)
The 1921 treaty that followed the Irish Revolution established partition of the country. Northern Ireland consisted of six counties, which together had a Protestant majority, but the Catholic minority was large and numerically dominant in several localities. These six counties had a parliament in Belfast and remained in "union" with England—thus the political tag "Unionist," retained even today. The other twenty-six counties (overwhelmingly Catholic) were given an independent dominion parliament in Dublin that eventually proclaimed the country a republic. The border was arranged to keep as much economically advantageous area for Northern Ireland as possible while retaining Protestant political dominance. Slogans of Unionists during border disputes

(1922–1925) figure in their contemporary civil religion: "Not an inch" and "What we have we hold" (Brewer, 1998:87–99; McCracken, 1967).

Sectarian strife increased in Northern Ireland after partition. Armed mobs in Belfast viciously attacked Catholic neighborhoods, forcing Catholics to depend on the IRA (i.e., an illegal paramilitary force) to protect them. Often, Protestant fears were deliberately exploited by (Protestant) employers to prevent Protestant and Catholic workers from uniting in labor disputes. In Belfast, unemployment at 30 percent during the 1930s Depression, Catholic and Protestant workers organized a bipartisan demonstration. In response, Orange Order leaders stepped up their appeals to religious sectarianism, suggesting that the dearth of employment was all the more reason to discriminate against Catholics. The grand master of the Belfast Orange Lodge (and subsequent member of the Northern Ireland Senate) said in 1933:

> It is time Protestant employers of Northern Ireland realized that whenever a Roman Catholic is brought into their employment it means one Protestant vote less. It is our duty to pass the word along from this great demonstration, and I suggest the slogan should be: "Protestants, employ Protestants!" (quoted in MacEoin, 1974:66)

The social and political pattern that emerged from increasing sectarianization severely discriminated against the Catholic minority in housing, jobs, law enforcement, and elections. Proportional representation in Northern Ireland's parliament was an early casualty of the Protestant struggle to retain power. Abolition of proportional representation guaranteed that minority parties could not coalesce to counterbalance the Unionist party. The Northern Ireland government also approved a systematic gerrymandering of electoral districts so that Catholic voters were isolated and underrepresented (see McCracken, 1967). As recently as the 1960s and 1970s, gerrymandering resulted in Derry's 20,000 Catholic voters being able to elect only 8 councillors, compared to 12 councillors elected by only 10,000 Protestants. In most large towns, Catholics comprised 61 percent of the population but elected only 9 of the town's 21 councillors; in Dungannon, Armagh, Enniskillen, and other large towns, Catholics were systematically deprived of a fair proportion of power in local government (London Sunday Times Insight Team, 1972:34, 35; MacEoin, 1974:58–59).

Catholics were also discriminated against in housing. This feature was politically significant because until 1969, when the British government forced the Northern Irish government to change its electoral practices, only householders and their wives could vote. Thus, policies that prevented Catholics from becoming householders also kept down their voting strength. City and county councils (which controlled the allocation of much housing, apartments and single-family dwellings alike) gave strong preference to Protestants in existing public housing and drastically reduced the number of new houses built in Catholic neighborhoods. Partly as a result of such political discrimination by the Protestant-controlled city council of predominantly Catholic Derry, over 1,000 single-family housing units were occupied in 1970 by more than one family and sometimes by seven or eight (London Sunday Times Insight Team, 1972:35–37.

Widespread job discrimination was the result of preferential treatment of Protestants in both private and public employment. Belfast's largest employer, the shipyards, had in 1971 only 400 Catholic employees out of 10,000 (London Sunday Times Insight Team, 1972:36). Northern Irish public officials systematically granted more and superior jobs to Protestants. In 1961 Catholics accounted for only 13 of 209 officers in professional and technical grades of Northern Irish civil service, and there was only one Catholic out of 53 people at the top administrative grade of civil service. Catholics were also greatly underrepresented on the twenty-two public boards in charge of such services as housing, tourism, hospitals, and electricity (MacEoin, 1974:67–69).

Despite the extensive discrimination, however, the Protestants generally were not overall much better off economically than Catholics. Because both groups are largely working class, the conflict is not class conflict; Protestants of all classes united against Catholics of all classes (see Rose, 1971; Wells, 1998). The economic discrimination has had direct political implications, however. For decades, there has been higher unemployment among the Catholic working class than among the Protestant working class, forcing workers to emigrate to find jobs (see London Sunday Times Insight Team, 1972:29–31). Protestants also controlled "law and order." Before British intervention in the 1970s, the two main police forces in Northern Ireland were the RUC (Royal Ulster Constabulary) and the B-Specials (Ulster Special Constabulary). The RUC was established at partition and was supposed to be bipartisan. Catholics, however, were never proportionately represented on the force and, at the time of the 1960s Northern Irish Civil Rights movement, were less than 10 percent. The B-Specials was a militia, almost exclusively Protestant. Indeed, the prime minister of Northern Ireland boasted in 1922 that "it is also from the ranks of the Loyal Orange Institution that our splendid B-Specials have come" (quoted in MacEoin, 1974:62). Catholics had a reasonable basis for their suspicions that these police forces used their power against the Catholic community. Besides possessing an arsenal (e.g., armored cars and automatic weapons), both forces were allowed discretionary powers by the Special Powers Act (introduced as a "temporary" measure in 1922 and eventually made permanent). This act, a source of considerable embarrassment to the British government, abridged civil freedoms by allowing any police officer to search, arrest, and imprison suspects without warrant, charge, or trial. In some conflicts, the B-Specials openly joined Protestant mobs against Catholic civilians (see London Sunday Times Insight Team, 1972:132–142).

Grave dissatisfaction with these features of Northern Irish life led to the 1964 formation of the Northern Ireland Civil Rights Association (NICRA), patterned after the American civil rights movement. Its demands were modest. They were (1) "one-man-one-vote" in local elections, (2) removal of gerrymandered boundaries, (3) laws against discrimination by local government and provision of machinery to deal with complaints, (4) allocation of public housing on a (nondiscriminatory) points system, (5) repeal of the Special Powers Act, and (6) disbanding of the B-Specials (London Sunday Times Insight Team, 1972:49). The confrontations that resulted from the generally nonviolent demonstrations of NICRA occurred largely because the Northern Ireland government refused to recognize the legitimacy of the movement's grievances and equated it with Republicanism—the movement for national independence from Britain. Protestant enclaves similarly saw the civil rights demonstrations as "them" organized against "us." The stage was set for a long period of sectarian violence: Protestants versus Catholics and both Protestants and Catholics versus the British.

The Current Troubles After more than three decades of conflict, several of the problems addressed by the Northern Irish civil rights movement continue to be major sources of tension and social problems. One of the most pressing of these issues is inequality of socioeconomic opportunity. Despite nearly comparable attainment of educational qualifications, Catholics (particularly men) continued to be virtually absent from entire sectors of the economy, including better-paid manufacturing jobs, law enforcement, banking, insurance, and big business until the 1990s (Eversley, 1989; Smith and Chambers, 1991). The Northern Irish economy, already disadvantaged relative to England and other parts of Europe further declined in the 1970s and 1980s (Smith and Chambers, 1991). The 1991 census found that, compared with 12.7 percent of Protestant males, 28.4 percent of Catholic males were unemployed. In some Catholic urban ghettos, however, unemployment affected more than two-thirds of all working-age males (Stevenson, 1994). Not until 1990 was a tough equal opportunity act put into effect in Northern Ireland. Ironically, it may have been the secular leveling effect of the European Economic Union, together with a Europe-wide period of economic growth in the 1990s, that rescued Northern Ireland from its history of entrenched unemployment. In Northern Ireland, overall unemployment rates fell from a peak of 17.2 percent in 1986 to 7.2 percent in 1999 (Northern Ireland Executive, 2001).

In the area of housing, major changes have occurred since the early civil rights protests. To eliminate the discrimination in public housing, the British-created Northern Ireland Housing Executive assumed responsibility for building, managing, and allocating public housing (about 40 percent of all new housing is in this public sector). By 1985 most of the worst housing had been replaced, and overcrowding was greatly reduced. At the same time, however, neighborhood segregation had increased. Many previously integrated neighborhoods became all Protestant or all Catholic, as families who were in the minority in each neighborhood left in fear or were actively driven out. Considerable British expenditure in Northern Ireland greatly improved public housing and made it more available to all. There is, however, still a higher proportion of Catholics living in substandard private-sector housing (Melaugh, 1995).

Police actions in the same thirty years have, if anything, generally increased Catholics' sense of injustice. Throughout the 1970s the various police forces in Northern Ireland were expanded, while the proportion of Catholics on the forces remained extremely small (usually less than 5 percent). British "peacekeeping" forces, likewise, used often-lethal violence disproportionately toward Catholics, such as the 1972 massacre of 14 unarmed civil rights demonstrators in Derry (Pringle and Jacobsen, 2001). Simultaneously, the scope of police powers was expanded and civil liberties were curtailed. Police detained several thousand people without ever bringing charges, much less conducting a hearing or trial. Amnesty International investigated conditions in Northern Ireland in 1977 and found evidence of frequent maltreatment of suspects and political prisoners. Police actions were perceived as discriminatory against Catholics. A survey conducted shortly after the Amnesty findings were reported in the media found that some 63 percent of Protestants, but only 20 percent of Catholics, believed that reports of prisoner maltreatment were unsubstantiated (Moxon-Browne, 1983:147). In the 1980s, levels of street violence were lower and police were better disciplined than in the 1960s and 1970s, but the failure to integrate Catholics into their ranks left police forces open to (often well-founded) suspicion of biases and outright partisanship in the administration of justice. The British abolished the B-Specials in 1969, when they took direct control of the province, but it was not until the late 1990s that Northern Ireland began hiring and training a bipartisan police force (see Brewer, 1998; Pringle and Jacobsen, 2001, for details of anti-Catholic violence, 1921–1998).

Public perceptions of the causes of the violence in Northern Ireland are divided. A much larger proportion of Catholics than Protestants view socioeconomic factors such as discrimination, unemployment, inferior housing, and education as significant causes of the "Troubles." Furthermore, actual socioeconomic deprivation is linked with support for the extremists on either "side" (Smith and Chambers, 1991; see also Bell, 1990; Whyte, 1990). Unfortunately, the violence has further polarized communities, such that new building and settlement patterns are generally more segregated than before 1968. Before the Troubles broke out, many small towns and urban neighborhoods were integrated; friendships and marriages between Catholics and Protestants were relatively common. More than thirty years of sectarian violence and widened segregation of two polarized communities has caused greater levels of prejudice, especially among younger generations. One study found that levels of prejudice among those who grew up since the start of the Troubles are as much as 175 percent of the levels among those who grew up in the 1930s and 1940s (Hayes and McAllister, 1999).

This capsule history of strife in Northern Ireland illustrates how two groups, defined by their religions, became so utterly segregated and polarized. The combination of this segregation with the religious particularism of each group makes the situation especially volatile. Systematic political and economic suppression of a large religious minority of natives by a colonial power made the resulting conflict reflect nationalistic as well as religious sentiments. The chief characteristics of the opposing civil religions of Catholics and Protestants illustrate the symbolic link between religion and nation as sources of identity.

Catholic Civil Religion

The national vision identified as Catholic in Northern Ireland is one of a united republic, encompassing all counties of the island. Thus, it is necessary to view the conflict in the context of the religious and political situation of the Republic of Ireland as well. A more militant version of this civil religion draws on the centuries-old Irish revolutionary myth; this version envisions the (Catholic) natives rising up to overthrow the oppressive (Protestant) colonial power. This militant nationalism does not accept the validity of the settlement that partitioned Ireland. A 1968 survey showed that 33 percent of the Catholics in Northern Ireland approved "on balance" the constitution of Northern Ireland, a proportion probably reduced by subsequent polarization. The study concluded that Northern Ireland was a state governed without consent (Rose, 1971:189). A later survey (after various intervening constitutional changes had been tried unsuccessfully) found that about 25 percent of Catholics still favored a United Ireland as the "most workable and acceptable solution" (Moxon-Browne, 1983: 103). Such refusal to accept the Northern Ireland government's right to rule further fed Protestant citizens' notions that Catholics are disloyal or traitorous.[4]

An important factor in the Catholic civil religion of Northern Ireland is its readiness to accept the church–state relations of the Republic of Ireland as normative. Thus, Protestant fears are fed by what they see as the effects of the Catholic Church on political and social policies in the neighboring Republic of Ireland (see Brewer, 1998). Unlike Spain and several other predominantly Catholic countries, Ireland's Catholic Church retained much of its dominance as a public religion and began to make allowances for pluralism and incorporation of minorities only at the end of the twentieth century (see Casanova, 1994, for useful analytical concepts; see also Fulton, 1991).

Although the influence of the Catholic Church in the Republic is indirect, it is still potent (see Fulton, 1991; Morrow, 1995). The Roman Catholic Church includes in its membership some 90 percent of the Republic of Ireland's 3.5 million population. The 1937 constitution of Ireland declared, until it was abridged in 1972, "a special position of the Holy Catholic Apostolic and Roman Church as the guardian of the Faith professed by the great majority of the Citizens" (Article 44, quoted in Whyte, 1980:24–61). The Protestant minority in the Republic is seldom discriminated against; indeed, it is a privileged minority, by all socioeconomic measures. Nevertheless, many Protestants (and Catholics) chafed at the influence of the Catholic Church on legislation and social policy in areas of "private" morality (e.g., divorce, contraception, abortion, and censorship). This indirect power of church hierarchy did not end until public referenda in the 1990s relaxed these laws (Clarity,

---

4. Thus, the 1998 change in the Constitution of the Republic of Ireland, dropping its territorial claim to Northern Ireland, was an important symbol in the trilateral Northern Ireland peace accords.

1994). Thus even though Northern Ireland is politically distinct from the Republic of Ireland, both its Protestant and Catholic nationalisms refer directly to beliefs and practices in the Republic.

The salient imagery and ritual in the Northern Irish Catholic civil religion are symbols of independent Ireland: the flag ("tricolor"), the Irish language, national anthem and ballads of independence, celebration of heroes, and events of revolution. These symbols are often near the surface of interactions with the opposing group. Even nonsectarian events (e.g., civil rights demonstrations) have been the occasion for invoking the symbols of this civil religion; despite organizers' plans, demonstrators sometimes break into singing nationalistic ballads and hymns or unfurl a tricolor flag. These are natural expressions: Catholic militance on behalf of their rights has long been equated with nationalism. Catholic civil religion in Northern Ireland likewise often celebrates, with even more vigor than in the Republic, such heroes and events of Irish revolution as Emmet, Pearse, Connolly, Tone, the Easter Insurrection, the Fenian Rebellion, and Catholic Emancipation.

The Catholic national vision in Northern Ireland is generally more tolerant of Protestants than the Protestant version is of Catholics. This acceptance is largely because Protestants, too, were prominent in the revolutionary heritage of Ireland. Protestants such as Wolfe Tone and Robert Emmet, inspired by the ideals of the French Revolution, led Irish revolts and are celebrated as martyrs in the civil religion of Catholic nationalists.

Protestant Civil Religion

The Protestant civil religion of Northern Ireland is, by contrast, virulently anti-Catholic. Its image of the conflict is a zero-sum contestation, in which any gains experienced by Catholics are viewed as losses by Protestants (Bruce, 1986). Both a 1968 survey and a 1978 comparison found Northern Irish Protestant antipathy to Catholics and Catholicism to be considerably greater than Catholic antipathy toward Protestants and Protestantism (Moxon-Browne, 1983:94–95, 124–136; Rose, 1971:256). The religious form of Protestantism as a civil religion in Northern Ireland is particularly evident in the power and influence of the Orange Order. Orangeism was, until the mid-1970s, essentially the state religion of Northern Ireland. The Unionist Party, which has dominated the government since its inception, has close, overt links with the Orange Order and is almost exclusively Protestant. Lord Craigavon, prime minister of Northern Ireland from 1921 to 1940, proclaimed, "I am an Orangeman first and a politician and a member of this parliament afterwards. . . . All I boast is that we are a Protestant parliament and a Protestant state" (cited in MacEoin, 1974:53). More explicit about the link between the controlling party (i.e., Unionist) and Orangeism is the opinion of Brian Faulkner, prime minister of Northern Ireland before Britain stepped in to rule the province directly in 1972. Faulkner stated:

> There is no alternative to the invincible combination of the Orange Order and the Unionist Party. . . . The Unionist Party relies upon the Orange Order and likewise we in the Order trust the party. That vital

faith must never be jeopardized by either partner. (cited in MacEoin, 1974:243)

The Orange Order, founded in 1795, was especially strong in Northern Ireland in the twentieth century. The grand master of the Belfast Orange Lodge (the largest of the several lodges in the country) described the Order as "basically religious and only coincidentally political, a fellowship of all who embrace the Reformed faith, founded to safeguard the interests of the Protestant people against the aggressions of the church of Rome which historically claims to have power over princes" (cited in MacEoin, 1974:31). The salvation theology of Orangeism requires a sense of opposition: It fights for salvation not only from sin but also from Catholicism.

The Orange Order maintained nearly monolithic control over Protestant opinion in the twentieth century, including in its membership roughly one-third of Protestant men in Northern Ireland. Together with active women's and youth auxiliaries, it involves more than 90 percent of the Protestant community in some localities (MacEoin, 1974:62). The Order includes all social classes, Church of Ireland and Dissenters alike. Indeed, historically it was the main vehicle for establishing Ulster Protestant unity despite significant religious and social-class differences, especially between members of the Church of Ireland and the more fundamentalist Free Presbyterians (Bruce, 1987). Popular support for the Orange Order appears to be waning in recent years, and its active overlap with Protestant paramilitary groups may not be as widespread as earlier in the present conflict (Morrow, 1995; see also Buckley and Kenney, 1995).

The anti-Catholic stance of Orangeism is directly relevant to the Protestant national vision in Northern Ireland; a fundamental premise of that vision is that Catholics must not be allowed power. The Protestant stance is a siege mentality, and militancy is crucial to their religious position (Wells, 1998). When some Catholics attempted to work within the Northern Irish political system in the 1960s, Unionist leaders tried to prevent their participation on grounds of their religion. One of the foremost Unionist leaders stated:

I would draw your attention to the words "civil and religious liberty." The liberty we know is the liberty of the Protestant religion. . . . It is difficult to see how a Roman Catholic, with the vast difference in our religious outlook, could be either acceptable within the Unionist party as a member, or bring himself unconditionally to support its ideals. Furthermore to this, an Orangeman is pledged to resist by all lawful means the Ascendancy of the Church of Rome. (cited by London Sunday Times Insight Team, 1972:37)

According to Northern Irish Protestant civil religion, Catholicism is incompatible with the Protestant conception of democracy, and the Protestant nationalist vision is, by definition, opposed to any Catholic power. One DUP (Democratic Unionist Party, the most extreme Unionist group) member of Assembly, interviewed in 1986, said:

The Christian beliefs held by the vast majority of the DUP clearly influence their political decisions. We believe that Ulster's future is best secured in a society where the gospel message can be preached freely, and that is not under Rome. Where the gospel light in many little towns throughout the Irish Republic has died, it has gone out because of the control of Rome. . . . I'm in politics to preserve this province so that the gospel can be preached freely and the Christian message on any street corner and that cannot be done in a Catholic dominated state. . . . (quoted in MacIver, 1989:367–368)

Protestant group identity is defined mainly by what it is not: Northern Ireland Protestants are adamantly *not* Catholic. Despite the fact that they are a privileged majority, the Protestant enclave experiences itself as "under siege" (Buckley and Kenney, 1995; Darnton, 1995). They are also adamantly *not* Irish. Parallel to the legitimating myths of Catholic nationalist sentiments, Protestant collective representations try to legitimate a separate "Ulster identity." Their legitimating myths include a Protestant reading of history and the claim to be a separate ethnic group. For example, in the 1980s the myth of the Cruthin—supposedly the original inhabitants before the invasion of the Gaelic peoples—was promoted to legitimate the political idea of an Ulster ethnic identity for the Scots-Irish, whose claims on the land would, thus, precede those of the "native" Irish (Davis, 1994). This myth does not appear to be widely held, but it illustrates the extent to which religious and ethnic group identities are very much "imagined communities" (Anderson, 1991). Constructing separate identities in places like Northern Ireland is especially difficult, because the cultural heritage of one group (e.g., Protestant farmers) is largely the same as that of the other group of the same social class and vicinity. Thus, the cultural segregation that has developed has to be actively cultivated, and separate group identities have to be continually carved out and maintained (Buckley and Kenney, 1995).

Nationalism Without Nation Building

The Protestant and Catholic national visions of Northern Ireland appear to fit our model of civil religion, albeit in a different form from that of civil religion in the United States. Both Protestant and Catholic versions are *mutually exclusive images of the nation*. Both entail extensive myths, legends, rituals, and symbols of a long history of growing separation of peoples. Both civil religions entail imagery of the "chosen people." The Protestant version defines themselves as God's chosen people struggling to maintain the truth in a land of paganism and idolatry, whereas the Catholic version describes the Gaelic peoples as the chosen children of God, oppressed by the Protestants. Commenting on this Old Testament imagery, one observer remarked, "One could say that Ireland was inhabited, not really by Protestants and Catholics, but by two sets of imaginary Jews" (O'Brien, 1974:288).

It is proving very difficult for particular religions and religiously motivated parachurch movements to undo the effects of this history and myth. There are many efforts for peacemaking and reconciliation. There may be more peacemakers per capita in Northern Ireland than in any other site of conflict in the world (cited in Appleby, 2000:191), and they do appear to be having some gradual (if uneven) impact. The efforts of nonsectarian political groups, concerned clergy on either side, and various ecumenical peace groups to defuse the religious antagonisms in Northern Ireland are often thwarted because the conflict is less between particular religions than between two civil religions. The differences in belief and practice between the particular religions, Protestant and Catholic, are important but are only a small part of this conflict. The division is essentially over national identity and vision, which are strongly shaped by a long history of experiences and cultural differences between the two groups. So long as people live out of their competing myths, they are incapable of understanding their own agency for change. Their essentialist myths determine who they are: *"The conflict made us who we are. We are defined by our responses to the injustices delivered on us by the enemy. In the stories we tell about the conflict, about our suffering and endurance, we give voice to our deepest sense of meaning and purpose as a people"* (Appleby, 2000:173, italics in original).

As suggested earlier in this chapter, civil religion in many countries has considerable potential for modern nation building, forging unity from diverse peoples of a state and bridging barriers of language, particular religion, tribalism, and regionalism. In the case of Northern Ireland, however, neither civil religion has this potential. Another model of civil religion or of church–state relations would serve the interests of nation building better, but the issue of what nation to build is still a political issue.

SUMMARY

Religion is a source of both social cohesion and social conflict. It contributes to the cohesion of a group and, at the same time, expresses its unity. Durkheim suggests that the moral unity of the group itself is the source of the sense of religious force or power experienced by participants. Thus, religious rituals incorporate members into the group by reminding them of the meanings and obligations of being "one of us." The civil religion thesis is an attempt to understand the expressions of moral unity of modern societies. It suggests that the nation may have a religious expression distinct from the particular religions of the people.

Religion contributes to social conflict because it is one basis of social cleavage. In societies where other loyalties cut across religious ties, religion is less likely to be a focus of serious conflict. Nevertheless, religion's capability for defining the boundaries of "us" against "them" makes it an inherently potential source of conflict. Particularist worldviews especially tend to intolerance and conflict. Religious groups are also subject to internal conflict over issues of deviance and control, authority and heresy.

The aspects of religion that promote both conflict and cohesion are illustrated by the strife in Northern Ireland. While particular Protestant and Roman Catholic religions have historically contributed to the active bigotry and intolerance there, a broader religious division—that between opposing civil religions with national visions, one Catholic and one Protestant—may also exist.

ISLAM

ISLAM: TWENTY-FIVE KEY DATES	
Date	**Event**
570 C.E.	birth of Muhammad
609–610 C.E.	first Qur'anic revelations
622 C.E.	Hejira: flight to Medina
630 C.E.	Muhammad returns to Mecca in conquest
632 C.E.	death of Muhammad
636–640 C.E.	conquest of Damascas, Jerusalem, Egypt, Persia
ca. 650 C.E.	establishment of the canon of the Qur'an
661–750 C.E.	Umayyad Caliphate
680 C.E.	murder of Husain, Shi'ite saint
711 C.E.	Muslims enter into Spain
713 C.E.	Muslims enter Indus Valley
750–1258 C.E.	Abbasid Caliphate
762 C.E.	foundation of Baghdad
909 C.E.	rise of Fatimids in North Africa
956 C.E.	conversion of Seljuk Turks
966 C.E.	foundation of Cairo
1099 C.E.	Christian Crusaders capture Jerusalem
1111 C.E.	death of Al-Ghazali, leading theologian
1258 C.E.	Mongols sack Baghdad
1453 C.E.	Ottoman Turks capture Constantinople
1492 C.E.	end of Muslim presence in Spain
1707 C.E.	decline of Mogul India
1803–1804 C.E.	Wahabism victorious in Mecca and Medina
1924 C.E.	secularization in Turkey
1947–1948 C.E.	creation of Pakistan and Israel

HISTORY

Islam is an Arabic word that means "submission, surrender" (to the will of **Allah**, God). **Muslim** is another Arabic word, this one meaning "one who submits," in other words, a follower of Islam. Muslims understand this God to whom they are submitting to be the same God as He who is described in Genesis, and to whom Jesus prayed.

Islam is one of the best examples of a religion influenced by the place, time, and person who developed it. We will begin our discussion of Islam with Arabs, but not all Arabs are Muslims. Outside Saudi Arabia, there are Arabs who still adhere to various Eastern Orthodox churches (such as Coptic in Egypt, Maronite in Lebanon). Furthermore, most of the world's Muslims are not Arabs, but Indonesians, Bangladeshis, Pakistanis, Afghanis, Turks, Uzbeks, Azerbajanis, Chechens, Bosnians, Albanians, Kosovars, Persians, and Africans. It is estimated that there will soon be more Muslims than Jews in America.

The place and time were the western coast of the **Arabian** peninsula at the beginning of the seventh century of the common era. That land at that time was not the oil-rich nation that we find in modern Saudi Arabia. The main economic activity of this region was trade: shipping across the Red Sea and camel caravans inland. This tribal society was rough and lawless. Some tribes functioned like gangs trying to control the trade. If one group of bandits attacked a caravan and killed some of the drivers, the clan of the victim would resolve to take vengeance against some member of the clan of the (alleged) perpetrators. Clan deities were an important aspect of religious worship.

Arab religion at this time was animistic and polytheistic. Another term sometimes used to describe it was *polydemonistic* since many of the deities or spirits worshiped did not claim divine status. Some of these were good, some evil. The evil spirits or demons had to be warded off with prayers, sacrifices, amulets, and spells. One aspect of polydemonism was a geographical worship of stones, stars, caves, and trees. As the drivers went through various places along the routes, they would have to stop, worship, and pay tribute (not unlike modern toll roads).

The city of Mecca had special status in this regard. It had very many and very important deities honored at a special shrine, a large black stone (possibly a meteorite) set in a shrine known as the Kaaba. This powerful symbol was explained by a myth: that this stone was first consecrated by the father of all Arabs, Ishmael and/or by his father, Abraham. (Recall that Abraham had one child before Sarah gave birth to Isaac. He sired Ishmael through Hagar, the Egyptian handmaiden of Sarah.) A ritual of pilgrimage developed: Arabs who were passing through Mecca should stop at the Kaaba and worship. This ritual became so important that people were convinced they were obligated to come to Mecca to worship, even if they did not have a caravan journey that was passing through Mecca anyway. Some of the local people may have longed for a purer approach to religion, but the Meccan city leaders knew that they had a great attraction to keep business going, and they jealously guarded against any threat to this shrine or the business it generated.

MUHAMMAD

It was into this milieu that **Muhammad** was born in 570 C.E. Little is known of his early life, except that he was born to a widow (his father died during his mother's pregnancy). He was brought up by uncles and he may have lacked much tribal protection. He had to work as a driver on the caravans. Competent and scrupulously honest, he came to the attention of one of the caravan owners, a wealthy widow named Khadijah. She gave him more responsibilities and

when he was twenty five she proposed marriage (she was forty). They had six children, of whom four daughters survived. This marriage was an important factor in his future career, not just economically, for it was his wife's support and encouragement that enabled him to pursue his religious motives.

Around 610, Muhammad began to receive revelations. He often slept in a cave and had visions (perhaps dreams). The revelations are explained by Islamic doctrine as the text of a divine book written by God in heaven, brought by the angel Gabriel, and recited by Muhammad. That book is known as the **Qur'an** (Koran). His first visions, according to the *Qur'an* (53:1–18, 81:15–25) were of someone "terrible in power, very strong." That person hovered near him on the horizon and imparted a revelation. It and subsequent revelations finally convinced Muhammad that God was choosing him to be a messenger, a prophet of God. Muhammad continued to receive revelations for the rest of his life (over twenty years), and those messages, which either he or early disciples wrote down on stones, palm leaves, and leather, form the basis of the Qur'an.

From earliest revelations given to Muhammad, five major themes emerge: God's goodness and power; the need to return to God for judgment; gratitude and worship in response to God's goodness and pending judgment; generosity toward one's fellow human beings; and Muhammad's own vocation to proclaim the message of goodness and judgment.

At first, Muhammad's proclamation met with considerable resistance, principally because it threatened some powerful vested interests. For example, the absoluteness of God threatened the traditional polytheism. However, his message was much more than just a challenge to custom and traditional religion—it was a mortal challenge to the commerce that had grown up around the Kaaba. The livelihoods of the merchants who sold amulets, the soothsayers who sold fortunes, and the semiecstatic poets who lyricized the old gods were all imperiled. Second, Muhammad's call for social justice implied a revolution—if not in contemporary financial arrangements, at least in contemporary attitudes. Third, the message of God's pending judgment was hardly welcome, for no age likes to find itself set before divine justice, hell fire, or the sword of retribution. Last, many Meccans ridiculed Muhammad's notion of the resurrection of the body and apocalyptic images of judgment day.

RISE TO POWER. Initially rejected, Muhammad drew consolation from the fate of prophets who had preceded him. Increasingly, it appears, he learned about Judaism and Christianity from followers of those traditions who either lived in the area or traveled it for trade. The first converts to Muhammad's revelations came from within his own family. When he started to preach publicly, around 613, the leaders of the most powerful clans opposed him vigorously. He thus tended to be most successful among the low-ranking clans and those with young leaders ripe for a new order. Also, those who were considered "weak" (without strong clan protection) found the new prophecy attractive. Muhammad was proposing a religious association based on commitment to Allah that transcended clan allegiances and so might make the weak stronger.

In 619, Muhammad suffered a personal crisis. His wife and uncle, who had been his foremost supporters, both died. Local pressures against him mounted in Mecca. He left, taking a small but loyal band of Meccan followers with him. In 622, he went to Yathrib, to the north, to arbitrate a longstanding dispute between two leading tribes. He settled the dispute with a revelation, and both parties were so impressed that they invited him to remain. The town became Medina, the town of the Prophet.

Muslims call Muhammad's departure or flight from Mecca the **Hejira**, and they view it as the turning point in the history of early Islam. Muhammed became the religious and political leader of Medina. He organized the Meccans who had followed him and the Medina clans into a single group. In Medina he developed a blueprint for a Muslim state.

One problem for Muhammad in Medina was the local Jewish community. Initially, he expected them to recognize him as a modern prophet of the one true God, the God of Abraham, Isaac, and Jacob, the God of the Jews. However, they refused to accept him as a genuine prophet and ridiculed his interpretation of the Hebrew scripture. In the falling out that followed, the Medinans have been accused of driving out the local Jews, or killing them, or selling them into slavery.

After consolidating his power base and building support among the neighboring Bedouin tribes, Mu-

hammad started to challenge his old foes at Mecca. He disrupted their trade in an effort to overturn the city's commercial base, and in 624 his vastly outnumbered troops won a surprising victory at Badr. Finally, after several further skirmishes, Muhammad won a decisive victory at the Battle of the Ditch. Muhammad's greatest triumphs came through diplomacy among the tribes, however. Mecca finally fell in 630 without the stroke of a single sword. In control, Muhammad cleansed the Kaaba of pagan idols. He then consolidated his victory by a final military triumph over resistant Meccans at Hunayn. This settled the matter for most onlookers, and thenceforth the surrounding tribes were in Muhammad's hands.

In the two remaining years of his life, Muhammad further developed the educational program that he had set up in Medina. Muhammad soon became the focus of Arab solidarity throughout the peninsula, and just before his death, he apparently contemplated action against the Byzantine powers in the north, perhaps because Muslim nationalism meant a growing hostility toward the Greeks and their Christian Arab allies. The quick military victories of his successors make most sense on the assumption that they simply executed plans that Muhammad himself had formulated.

PERSONALITY AND RELIGIOUS IMPACT. Although critics have decried Muhammad's violence toward his enemies, he certainly demonstrated an abundant humanity. In addition to his religious sensitivity and his political and military skills, the Prophet apparently manifested a notable sympathy for the weak, a gentleness, a slowness to anger, some shyness in social relations, and a sense of humor. According to the *hadith* (a plural term for traditions about Muhammad), for instance, one day the Prophet's second in command, Abu Bakr, started to beat a pilgrim for letting a camel stray. Muhammad began to smile and then indicated to Abu Bakr the irony that a pilgrim like Abu Bakr (a pilgrim through life) should beat a pilgrim to Mecca.

In glimpses obtained from the *Qur'an* and the earliest levels of the tradition, Muhammad seems to have been an ordinary man whom God singled out to receive revelations. Muhammad's virtue was to accept his commission and keep his commitment until death. The emphasis in the Prophet's own preaching on the sovereignty of God and the divine authority for the Qur'anic message led him to stress his own ordinariness, his liability to error, and the like. For example, at one point he thought that Muslims could compromise with Satan (the "Satanic Verses"), but then he realized that only God could receive Muslim devotion. He made no claim to miraculous power. The central miracle was the *Qur'an* itself—a message of such eloquence that it testified beyond doubt to a divine source.

In keeping with Muhammad's own humility, orthodox Islam has condemned any move to exalt Muhammad above ordinary humanity or to worship him as divine. (There are no statues of Muhammed for Muslims to bow down or pray to.) Nonetheless, popular Muslim religion sometimes seized on hints in the *Qur'an* and made Muhammad superhuman. The most famous of its images is Muhammad's "night journey" (miraculous flight) to Jerusalem, after which he ascended to Paradise, talked with the prophets who had preceded him, and experienced an ineffable vision of God. This story became so popular that it finally entered orthodox doctrine. Later traditions also elaborated on Muhammad's preaching of the coming Last Judgment and tended to think of the Prophet as its shield and intercessor on the Last Day.

QUR'ANIC RELIGION

After Muhammad's death, his followers collected the texts of his revelations and established the orthodox version of the *Qur'an* during the rule of Othman (644–656). However, since this version contained no indication of vowels or diacritical points, variant readings exist and are recognized by most Muslims as of equal authority. Most Muslims insist that the *Qur'an* be recited in Arabic. Muslims consider the *Qur'an* to be written in the purest Arabic. The style of the *Qur'an*, as well as its message, shows that it must have come directly from God.

The present version of the collection of revelations follows the editorial principle that the chapters (*suras*) should be ordered in decreasing length. The result is that the present text tells the reader nothing about the chronology (or theme) of the revelations. While scholars have attempted to distinguish the Meccan utterances from the ones given at Medina, their work is often so refined (distinguishing separate verses within a *sura*) that no one theory of the chronology of the revelations has won universal acceptance. A probable early Meccan passage (96:1–5) emphasizes that Muhammad experienced his call as a command to recite, although what he was to recite only became clear as time passed. *Sura* 53, lines 1–18, richly symbolizes how Muhammad experienced his call. Because of Muhammad's vision of the angel Gabriel, the Muslim theology of revelation granted Gabriel an important role as the mediator in transmitting the *Qur'an*. In *Sura* 81, lines 15–29, are suggestions that Muhammad's early preaching met with rejection and even contempt. Indeed, the Prophet seems to have had to defend himself against the charge of *jinn* (demon) possession. *Suras* 73 and 74 buttress the tradition that Muhammad regularly used to go off to a cave to pray. Wrapped in a mantle against the night cold, he would seek God's comfort. This image has been a model for countless later Sufis and ascetics as they have sought an experiential knowledge of God. Other Qur'anic passages that are considered reflections of Muhammad's early experiences boom forth a praise of God, a sense of God's overwhelming majesty, that suggests Rudolf Otto's classic definition of the holy: the mystery that is both alluring and threatening.

The later passages of the *Qur'an*, those that likely were written in Medina, concern more practical matters. As the head of an established political and religious community, Muhammad had to deal with questions of law and order. Thus, we can find the seeds of later Islamic law on inheritance, women, divorce, warfare. Generally, Muhammad's law and social teaching are advances on the mores of his day. They improved the lot of the downtrodden and humanized both business and war. For instance, Muhammad made widows and orphans the prime beneficiaries of the *zakat* (almsgiving) required of all Muslims. Two points on which outsiders frequently have faulted Muhammad and the *Qur'an* are the doctrines of holy war (*jihad*) and polygamy. Nevertheless, in both cases Muhammad's views were improvements on the pre-Muslim practices and benefited both women and prisoners of war.

THE FIVE PILLARS. On the basis of the *Qur'an*'s prescriptions for Islam, a religion of submission to the will of God, Muslims have elaborated five cardi-

DOWN

1   Muslims engage in this activity during Ramadan.
2   Muslims must _____ that there is but one God.
3   Muslims must pray five times _____.
4   Muslims must give _____ to the poor.
5   Muslims should make a _____ to Mecca.

nal duties known as the Five Pillars of Islam. They are: (1) witnessing (proclaiming the creed), (2) ritual prayer, (3) fasting during the lunar month of Ramadan, (4) almsgiving, and (5) pilgrimage to Mecca. The witness of Islam epitomizes the Muslim's orientation in the universe: There is no God but God, and Muhammad is his Prophet. God is the only fit object of worship, and Muhammad is the last of the prophets—the "seal."

The rigorous monotheism of Islam has both negative and positive aspects. Negatively, in what amounts to an attack on false religion, Islam makes idolatry (associating anything with God) the capital sin. At the onset, then, Muhammad's revelation implied an attack on the prevailing Arab religion. Later it led to a polemic against Christian Trinitarianism and a check on any worldly pride or Mammon that might diminish God's sovereignty.

Positively, Islamic monotheism generated great praise for the "Lord of the Worlds"—the Creator who guided all things, who was the beauty and power by which the world moved. For the later Muslim mystics, the words of the creed swelled with hidden relevance. Like the Jewish cabalists, some Muslim mystics assigned each letter a numerical value and then composed numerological accounts of how the world hung together. Some Muslim mystics pushed the concept of divine sovereignty so far that they denied the existence of anything apart from God. Not only was there no God beside him, there was no being apart from his Being. While the orthodox Muslims found such pantheism blasphemous, the mystics tended to stress the oneness of the Lord's domain. Last, rigorous monotheism implied that Muhammad himself was not divine. His high status was to be the prophetic mouthpiece. (In later devotion, as we have seen, there was a tendency to exalt Muhammad, while later theology often viewed the *Qur'an* as co-eternal with God, much as rabbinic theology saw the Torah as co-eternal with God.)

In this clear statement of monotheism, Muhammad tried to cleanse the Arab psyche of its polytheistic impulses, but he himself accepted the existence of angelic spirits and *jinn*. The *jinn* and angels certainly were not on the same level as God, but they had influence in human life and had to be dealt with. Popular Islamic religion frequently remained quite involved with fighting the *jinn*, retaining longstanding notions about the influence of the evil eye and the need to protect oneself against bad spirits by prayers and regular submission of one's fate to the will of God.

The second pillar of Islam is prayer, which has worked out as an obligation to pray five times daily. Authoritative authors such as Al-Ghazali went to great lengths to specify the postures, words, number of bows, and proper places and times for prayer, but the primary effect of the second pillar on the common people was to pace them through the day in the great Muslim practice of remembrance (*dhikr*). This linked with the Muslim conviction that forgetfulness (rather than intentional sin) was the main reason people disregarded God, fell into idolatry, violated the laws, and so on. Thus the *Qur'an* called for constantly remembering the goodness of God, the promises and favors God had vouchsafed, the teachings of the Prophet, and the like. The call to pray five times a day externalized the importance of *dhikr,* and in general much Islamic spirituality sought to keep the disciple in the presence of the Qur'anic word or attentive to the presence of God to both human beings and the signs of physical nature.

At each call from the minaret (prayer tower), they were to remember the one God whom they served—remember his compassion, his mercy, and his justice. Ideally, by praying fervently at the appointed hours, one might forge a chain that linked together more and more moments of remembrance, so that God progressively came to dominate all one's thought, action, and emotion. Witnessing Muslim prayer is a moving experience. The slow chant of the Qur'anic words becomes haunting, stirring even the non-Arabist. The voice (usually recorded today) is passionate—a lover's near sob, a tremulous witness to God's grandeur.

Fasting in the third pillar. What the prayer times are to the day, the holy month of Ramadan is to the year. **Ramadan** is the month of fasting and (interestingly enough) of celebration that helps give the year its rhythmic turning around God. This lunar based celebration moves around (akin to Easter), but it is not limited to just April. Ramadan may occur when the days are either short and cold or when they are long and hot, which means the severity of the exercise can vary considerably. Through all the daylight hours of Ramadan (from the time that one can distinguish a black thread from a white), no food or drink is to pass the lips. There is as much joy as penitence in this ritual, for there is feasting before dawn and after dusk.

The fast is supposed to discipline both body and mind, reminding all Muslims that their first obligation is to the will of God, and that to fulfill the will of God they need to be masters of their own personal beings. Thereby, the Muslim learns discipline, sacrifice, and the price that divine treasures cost. In contrast to a secular succession of months, in which no time is finally more significant than any other, the Muslim acknowledges the special time of Ramadan, fencing off a portion of time as sacred.

The fourth pillar is pilgrimage. Islam has developed a similar paradigm of the sacred for space by praying toward **Mecca** and by the obligation to make a pilgrimage to Mecca (the Hajj) at least once in one's lifetime. For Muslims, Mecca is the center, the *omphalos* (navel) where the world was born. It is the holy city where Qur'anic revelation was disclosed to the world. Thus, the psychodynamics of the pilgrimage run deep. Without doubt, devout pilgrims understand that they are going to the holiest spot in creation.

On pilgrimage, Muslims dress alike, go through the same traditional actions tying their religion to that of Abraham, their spiritual father, and often experience an exhilarating sense of community. By going through ritual actions associated with Abraham, they dramatize their position that Islam is not an innovation but the religion that preceded Judaism.

The fifth pillar, almsgiving, focuses this sense of community in a practical, economic way. The *zakat* is not a charitable gift but a matter of obligation. How much it should be has varied with local custom (it might be one-fortieth part of one's wealth in some societies, while in others it might be 15 percent of a grain crop, but only 10 percent if irrigation is used). Everywhere it has symbolized the community all Muslims share and the obligations they carry to care for one another. In Muhammad's day clan society had broken down, with considerable suffering for widows, orphans, and others who had no immediate family. The alms in the first place was aimed at helping such unfortunates, but it can also take the form of endowing hospitals, schools, and mosques. The Muslim alms, then, is more than a tiny dole or act of charity—it is an act of social, corporate responsibility. Furthermore, it reminds the advantaged that they are one family with the disadvantaged and that the stern Judge will demand a strict account of what they have done with his gifts.

THE AGE OF CONQUEST

At Muhammad's death in 632, most of Arabia had accepted Islam, though often the allegiance was superficial, as some tribes had been won over more by the political, economic, or military strength of Islam than by a pure attraction to the religious elements. Some tribes took the occasion of the Prophet Muhammed's death to attempt a revolt. General Khalid al-Walid, who served the first caliph (leader), Abu Bakr, crushed them within a year. Thus, when Abu Bakr died in 634, Arabia was united and poised for adventure. The obvious foes were Byzantium and Persia, which threatened Arabian prosperity and were ripe for religious and military conquest. The Muslim armies were amazingly effective. By the end of 636, they controlled both Damascus and Jerusalem. As important in this lightning conquest as their military skill, though, was the unrest of the

CASE STUDY: MARY

Sura 19, entitled "Mary," shows some of the connections between the *Qur'an* and both Judaism and Christianity. The *sura* begins with an interpretation of the story of the birth of John the Baptist (Luke 1:5-80). Zacharias, the father of John the Baptist, approached God and prayed for an heir. He received the answer that he would have a son, to be called John, despite the fact that he and his wife were advanced in years. God instructed John to observe the scriptures with a firm resolve, bestowing on him wisdom, grace, and purity. John grew up to be a righteous man who honored his father and mother and was neither arrogant nor rebellious. So the *Qur'an* blesses the day John was born, and blesses the day of his death.

Then Muhammad receives a command to recount the story of Mary, who left her people and betook herself to a solitary place to the east. God tells Muhammad that he sent to Mary the divine spirit in the semblance of a grown man. Mary saw the spirit and was seized with fear. But the spirit explained that he was a messenger of Mary's Lord, come to give her a holy son. When she asked how this could be, since she was a virgin, the spirit said that nothing was difficult to God and that this miracle was God's will. Thereupon Mary conceived. When her time of delivery came, she lay down by a palm tree, wishing that she had died and passed into oblivion. But a voice from below her cried out that she should not despair. God had provided her a brook to run at her feet, and if she would shake the trunk of the palm tree it would drop ripe dates in her lap.

Mary took her child to her people, who abused her as a harlot. So she pointed to the baby in the cradle, who spoke up and said: "I am the servant of Allah. He has given me the gospel and ordained me a prophet." The child explained that God had commanded him to be steadfast in prayer, to give alms to the poor, to honor his mother, and to be free of vanity and wickedness. God had blessed the day of his birth and would bless the day of his death.

The *sura* then makes a polemical point: This is the "whole truth" about Jesus, the son of Mary, which "they" (probably the Christians) are unwilling to accept. In other words, though Jesus had a marvelous birth, he was in no way the divine Son of God. Only God is Muhammad's Lord, and the Lord of Muslims. Therefore only God is to be served. That is the right path. Any other path is erroneous. Those who cling to the view of Jesus as a member of a divine Trinity (instead of being a mere human prophet, no higher than Muhammed) will experience woe on the day they appear before God, since they are in the grossest error (idolatry).

Next the *sura* takes up the story of Abraham. Abraham was a prophet and a saintly man. He asked his father, "How can you serve a worthless idol, a thing that can neither see nor hear?" Furthermore, he told his father to follow Abraham away from the worship of Satan, who had rebelled against the Lord of Mercy. But Abraham's father only became angry, banishing him from the house and threatening him with stoning. Abraham prayed that the Lord would forgive his father, but he departed, since he could not worship idols. God rewarded Abraham with sons called Isaac and Jacob, prophets of high renown.

The next story in the *sura* on Mary concerns Moses, who was a prophet, an apostle, and a chosen man. God called out to Moses from the right side of a mountain. When Moses came, Allah communed with him in secret and gave him his brother Aaron, also a prophet. Then there was Ishmael, also an apostle, a seer, and a man of his word. Ishmael enjoined prayer and almsgiving on his people, and thereby he pleased the Lord. Last there was Idris (Enoch), another saint and prophet, whom the Lord honored and exalted.

To all these men, God has been gracious. They are the line of prophets, from the descendants of Adam and the people God carried in the ark with Noah. They include Abraham and Israel (Jacob), Moses, David, and Jesus, and they stand out as the line God has guided and chosen. When they received divine revelations, these prophets humbled themselves, falling down on their knees in tears and adoration. In contrast, the generations that succeeded the prophets neglected prayer and succumbed to temptation. Assuredly they shall be lost.

However, those that repent, embrace what Muhammad is preaching, and do what is right will be admitted to Paradise. They shall not be wronged, but shall enter the Garden of Eden, which the Merciful has promised to his servants as their reward. What God has promised, God shall fulfill. In Paradise the just will hear no idle talk, only the voice of peace. Morning and evening they shall receive their sustenance. That is the bliss which the righteous shall inherit. The *sura* then interposes a strange transition: "We do not descend from Heaven save at the bidding of your Lord." Muslim commentators tend to interpret this as the voice of the angel Gabriel, answering Muhammad's complaint that the revelations he was receiving sometimes stopped, making for long intervals of silence. Gabriel reminds Muhammad that revelation like this is solely God's affair. To God alone belongs what is before us and what is behind us, and all that lies between.

Gabriel goes on to comfort Muhammad. His Lord does not forget his servants. God is the ruler of the heavens and the earth and all that is between them. Muhammad's task is simple: Worship him and be loyal in his service. After all, what god compares with God? To whom else can a sane or devout person go?

But all human flesh is weak, so human beings regularly ask, "When I am once dead, shall I be raised to life again" (resurrection)? God's answer is a call to remembrance and patience. Why do human beings forget that God once had to create them from the void?

Unless people put their lives in order, God will call them to account, placing them in the company of the devils, setting them on their knees around the fire of hell. Each sect of dissidents will have its stoutest rebels cast down into hellfire. God alone knows who most deserves to burn. God will deliver those who fear him, but wrongdoers will endure the torments of the fire. God will record every word of vain boasts and determine punishments long and terrible.

Again the *sura* lashes out at Christian doctrine, that God has begotten a son. That is such a monstrous falsehood that the heavens should crack, the earth should break asunder, the mountains should crumble to dust. Those who ascribe to God a son know nothing of the nature of the Merciful. It does not become him to beget a son. His sovereignty is beyond any such thing. For there is none in the heavens or the earth who shall not return to the Lord in utter submission. God keeps strict count of all his creatures. One by one, they shall all approach him on the Resurrection Day. Those he shall cherish are they who have accepted the doctrine Muhammad is preaching and shown charity to their fellows. Concluding, the *sura* has God remind Muhammad that he has revealed the *Qur'an* in Muhammad's own tongue so that Muhammad can proclaim good tidings to the upright and warnings to a contentious nation.

From reading this remarkable bit of the *Qur'an*, one senses the overwhelming sovereignty of Muhammad's God. Not to accept him exclusively is tantamount to blindness or utter corruption of heart. Muhammad finds this way prefigured in the prior prophets of Judaism and Christianity, who deserve high esteem. Jesus, the miraculous child of Mary, the great heroine of commitment to God's plan, was a worthy precursor. But the Christian notion that Jesus was God's son is sheer blasphemy, an effort to diminish the absolute uniqueness and sovereignty of God. The Creator is solely responsible for all that happens in the world. Those who confess this will merit good things in the Garden of Eden. Those who reject it will go to hell, the place of punishing fire and devils.

Courtyard of Cairo mosque

peoples they conquered, who may have seen the Muslims as liberators from Byzantine exploitation. On the eastern frontier, Muslim armies spread into Persian territory, and by 649 all of Persia was in Arab hands.

The quick conquest of Syria released men for further expeditions in the west; by 640 there were conquests in Egypt. Alexandria soon fell, and despite resistance from the Roman emperor Constans, the Arabs established themselves as a marine power operating from the southeastern Mediterranean. By 648, they had conquered Cyprus; by 655, they were in charge of the waters around Greece and Sicily. On land in North Africa, the Muslims conquered the Berber region of Tripoli in 643 and then proceeded to Carthage and to the Nubian regions along the Nile, conquering the Nubian capital city of Dongola. When the Umayyad caliphate established itself in 661, the ventures became even more far reaching. Soon Muslims were as far away as China, India, and

western Europe. By 699, Islam occupied Afghanistan, while various campaigns south of the Caspian and Aral Seas brought Armenia, Iraq, Iran, and eastern India into the Muslim fold by 800.

At the beginning of the ninth century, Arab rule along the southern Mediterranean stretched from Palestine to the Atlantic. Muslims controlled three-quarters of the Iberian Peninsula, and most Mediterranean traffic had to reckon with Muslim sallies. European campaigns had brought Arab soldiers as far north as Orleans, and they strongly influenced the southern portions of the Frankish kingdom. In 732 Muslims had taken Toulouse and then the whole of Aquitaine, moving into Bordeaux and Tours. Charles Martel stopped them at Poitiers, but in 734 they crossed the Rhone and captured Arles, Saint-Remy, and Avignon. Then they fortified Languedoc and recaptured Lyons and Burgundy. In the ninth century, from their positions in southeastern France, they pushed northeast as far as Switzerland. By daring naval raids, they harassed such ports as Marseilles and even Oye on the coast of Brittany.

Toward the end of the ninth century, Islam controlled most of western Switzerland and ruled many of the Alpine passes. In the mid-tenth century Muslims were at Lake Geneva, taking Neuchatel and Saint Gall. Only the attacks of the Huns and the Hungarians from the north and northeast and the deterioration of the Spain-based Umayyad caliphate kept them from ruling all of southern Europe. However, Muslim expansion ended after 1050, when the Normans pushed Islam out of southern France, southern Italy, Corsica, Sardinia, and Sicily.

By 1250, Islam's European presence had weakened considerably. Only southernmost Spain and eastern Anatolia (Turkey) held secure. However, Islam had spread through all of Persia, crossed northern India, and reached the western Chinese border. In East Asia, it had a discernible presence in Sumatra, Borneo, and Java. All of North Africa was securely Muslim, while down the East African coast as far as Madagascar it exerted a strong influence. In many of these regions, of course, substantial portions of the populations remained non-Muslim. For instance, in Egypt many Christians of the Monophysite and Coptic churches remained loyal to their own traditions, as did many Christians in Anatolia and Syria. Nestorian Christians in Iraq north of Baghdad held out, while portions of southern Persia remained Zoroastrian strongholds. In India the majority remained Hindu, especially in the central and southern regions.

MOTIVATIONS. Through this age of conquest and expansion, the basic Muslim strategy revolved around the use of the desert. Just as modern empires, such as the British, made great use of naval power, so the Arabs exploited their experience with the desert, using it for communication, transferring supplies, and retreating safely in time of emergency. In their spread through North Africa, they established main towns at the edge of the desert. In Syria they employed such conquered cities as Damascus to the extent that they lay close to the desert. Through the Umayyad period (to 750), these garrison towns at the edge of the desert were the centers of Arab government. By dominating them and by introducing Arabic as the language of government, the conquerors exerted a disproportionate influence (they usually remained a minority of the total population). The towns served as the chief markets for the agricultural produce of the neighboring areas, and around their markets clusters of artisan quarters developed. By imposing discriminatory taxes on the outlying populations, the Arabs encouraged the citizenry to congregate in the cities, making their control easier.

Religion served as a rallying point for the Arab cause. It stressed the common bond to a single Lord, and it dignified the Arab movement with a sort of manifest destiny. Certainly the generals who dominated the era of conquest were as accomplished in worldly affairs as they were in religion. For Khalid and Amr, two of the most outstanding, the utilitarian values of the Islamic expansion seemed to have been clear.

The Islamic administration of the conquered territories was also quite pragmatic. Rather understandably, the interests served were not those of the conquered subjects but those of the aristocracy that conquest created—the interests of the Arab rulers. Thus, the temper of the Arab military commanders and then of the quasimilitary Arab governors most determined how Islam treated its new peoples. At the beginning of the conquest in Byzantium and Persia, Muslims kept the old administrative structures. In the 640s, though, they shifted to a new format, through which the caliphs could impress their will more directly.

However, at first there was no unified imperial law. The conquerors struck different bargains with different peoples, and some stipulated that local customs or laws remain in force. The Arabs tended to take only the property of the state (and that of the new regime's enemies); other landowners who were willing to recognize the new regime could keep their holdings provided they paid a sizable tax. Nevertheless, there were opportunities for Muslim "speculators," as we might call them, to gain lands outside the garrison center on which they would have to pay only light levies.

At first, the conquered peoples were allowed to retain most of their traditional civil and religious rights. The Muslims grouped most of the conquered non-Muslims together as *Dhimmis*—members of religions that Arab law tolerated. As "peoples of the book," Jews and Christians were *Dhimmis*, with title to special respect. There were nevertheless frictions, especially if Jews or Christians were blatantly derogatory of the Prophet Muhammad and his Book, but usually people were not compelled to convert to Islam. Because Arab rule regularly promised to be more just than Byzantine rule, many Jews and Christians are on record as having welcomed the change. For example, in Palestine the Samaritans actively assisted the invaders. The Arabs were not always sure how to handle such complicity, especially when it developed into a desire to convert to Islam. Islam and Arabism were so synonymous that the first converts had to become Mamali—clients of one of the Arab tribes. In fact, converts seldom gained status equal to born Muslims, especially regarding such material benefits as the booty that warriors received after a conquest.

INTERNAL STRIFE. Despite its enormous outward success in the age of conquest, the Islamic community suffered notable internal divisions. With the exception of Abu Bakr, the first caliphs, known as the rightly guided, all left office by murder. (Despite these assassinations, modern Islam has considered their time the golden age.) Ali, the fourth caliph, was the center of a fierce struggle for control. His main opponent was Muawiya, the head of a unified stronghold in Syria. Muawiya maneuvered to have the legitimacy of Ali's caliphate called into question. As a result, Ali lost support in his own group, and dissidents called Kharijites appeared who had a hand in many later conflicts. A Kharijite killed Ali in 661, and the caliphate passed to the Umayyad dynasty—the followers of Muawiya.

However, Ali's influence did not end with his assassination. In fact, his assassination became part of Islam's deepest division, the one between the **Shia** (party), who were loyal to Ali, and the Sunni (traditionalists). The "party" supporting Ali maintained that the successors to Muhammad ought to come from Muhammad's family—in other words, that Islamic leadership should be hereditary. (As the cousin and son-in-law of Muhammad, Ali was his closest male relative and so his heir.) This conviction was supported by certain verses of the *Qur'an,* in which the Prophet supposedly indicated that Ali would be his successor. The Shia therefore consider the first three caliphs, who preceded Ali, as having been usurpers. After Ali's death, they took up the cause of his sons, Hasan and Husain.

The word that the Shia gave to the power that descended through Muhammad's family line was *imamah* (leadership). Through its history, the Shia has made it a cardinal doctrine that Muhammad's bloodline has an exclusive right to *imamah*. The slaughter of Husain in Iraq in 680 was an especially tragic event, and the Shiites (who have been strongest in Iran) have come to commemorate it as the greatest of their annual festivals. This has developed a religious consciousness dominated by suffering, persecution, and martyrdom. Another distinctively Shiite doctrine has been the expectation for a future prophet (**imam**) to consummate history. Except in Iran, where they are dominant, Shiites have usually been the Islamic minority.

The majority did not follow Ali, but stayed within the **Sunni** (well-trod) path of traditionalism. The Sunnis have considered themselves both more traditional and more moderate than the Shia (or the later Sufis). They have tended to take the generally accepted principles of law and doctrine as the backbone of Muslim culture and to favor religious life that balanced between profession of the uniqueness of God and conviction that God had made the material world good for human beings to develop. Sunnis have predominated in most cultural areas other than Iran. Historically, they supported the view that the successors to Muhammad in leadership of the Muslim community need not be members of the Prophet's bloodline—a position with some foundations in pre-Islamic Arab political custom. During the past quarter century, with strife in Lebanon, Iran, and Iraq, the relations between Shiites and Sunnis have been tense, even combative. Shiites and Sunnis share more doctrines and practices than they hold separately, although the Shiites do have certain distinctive doctrines, such as the expectation of the return of the hidden imam, and certain distinctive festivals, such as the commemoration of the martyrdom of the sons of Ali.

THE GOLDEN CIVILIZATION

The Umayyads had been auxiliaries of the Romans in Syria, so when they established the caliphate in Damascus in 661, they brought an enthusiasm for Hellenistic culture. In particular, they became patrons of the sciences. For example, in 700 they founded an astronomical observatory at Damascus. However, the

Mosque in New Delhi

Umayyads fell to the Abbasids in 749, Umayyad rule continuing only in Spain. The Abbasids set their caliphate in Baghdad and turned to Persian rather than Hellenistic culture, supporting the Persian specialties of medicine and astronomy. Al-Mansur, the second Abbasid caliph, was also devoted to learning, bringing Indian astronomers and doctors to Baghdad and having many Indian scientific treatises translated. Under his successors, translation continued to be a major project, any nation's heritage being fair game. As a result, many Greek treatises (for example, those of Galen and Ptolemy) became available to Muslims. Partly because of Babylonian and Zoroastrian influences, the Baghdad caliphs deemed astronomy especially important. They imported Indian mathematicians to help in astronomical calculations and made Baghdad a center of astronomical learning.

Al-Razi (865–925) collected voluminous lore on medicine from Greek, Indian, and Middle Eastern sources. Indeed, he may even have drawn on Chinese sources, for there is a story that he entertained a Chinese scholar who learned to speak Arabic, and his successors' works include what seems to be the Chinese doctrine of what one could learn from the body's pulses. A Muslim alchemy arose in the ninth century with Jabir ibn-Hayyan, but in Islam alchemy remained somewhat suspect because the authorities linked it with non-Muslim religion. Some radical Sufis became deeply involved in alchemy, but orthodox Sunni had the works of at least one such group, the "Brethren of Purity," declared heretical and burned. The orthodox Muslims had less of a problem with the rational geometry and science of the Greeks.

From 970, the Spanish branch of the Muslim Empire had a distinguished scientific center in Cordoba. Similarly, the religious authorities patronized science, especially medicine and astronomy, at Toledo from the early eleventh century. The Spanish Muslims tended to be critical of Ptolemy and to favor Aristotelian doctrines. **Averroes** (1126–1198), who lived

The Taj Majal, a Muslim building from Mogul India. Muslim art, restrained from making images of God or Muhammed, focused on architecture.

in Cordoba at the same time as the Jewish theologian Maimonides, was a great Aristotelian synthesizer who composed a full philosophical corpus. By conquering the territory between the Muslim East and the kingdom of Sung China, the Mongols expedited trade and the flow of learned information between East and West. Marco Polo (1254–1324) was able to travel to the East because of Mongol rule, which also enabled the Chinese Mar Jaballaha (1244–1317) to come West and become the Nestorian Christian patriarch. When the Mongols conquered China, they left its bureaucratic structure intact. They set up an observatory in Peking and staffed it with Muslims. In the West they conquered the Abbasid capital of Baghdad in 1258, where they continued to support astronomical studies.

Muslim art concentrated on architecture and ornamentation of the mosque rather than painting or sculpture. The preponderance of Muslim art during the golden age was nonpictorial, including rugs,

vases, lamps, and mosques. It reached its peak in the sixteenth and seventeenth centuries, leaving impressive monuments in Ottoman Turkey, Safavid Persia, and Mogul India.

A distinctively Islamic calligraphy developed from the trend to decorate pages from the *Qur'an*. The *Qur'an* itself praises the art of writing (96:4) and speaks of being written on a heavenly tablet (84:2122). The favorite script was Kufic, which originated in the new Islamic town of Kufa near Babylon, and it was the standard scriptural model from about the seventh to eleventh centuries. It is vertical, massive, and angular, while its prime alternate, the Naskhi script, is horizontal, flowing, and rounded. A favorite subject of embellishment has been the *Bismallah*, the prefix to the Qur'anic *suras* ("In the name of God"). Through an extension of calligraphic swirls and loops, Muslims developed an ingenious ability to suggest flowers, birds, lions, and so on. The Sufi interest in numerology also encouraged artistic work.

CASE STUDY: ARCHITECTURE AND POETRY

As we suggested, Islam also influenced architecture. The mosque was a sort of theology in the concrete. Muslim architects tried to embody the conviction that all of life stands subject to God and so that no great distinction should be made between sacred dwellings and profane. The guiding idea in the construction of a mosque was simply to house a space for prayer and prostration. The *hadith* reported that the Prophet led his first companions outside the city, so that they could pray together in an open space. At Medina, the usual place for prayer was the open courtyard of Muhammad's own house. For convenience, the architects tried to construct a churchlike building that had the character of an open space where many Muslims might go through the same rhythmic motions of bowing, kneeling, prostrating, and praying together.

Mosque architecture tended not to differ radically from that of Muslim palaces. Most of the renowned Muslim palaces have crumbled, but the Alhambra, in Granada, Spain, still stands, a glorious tribute to the Muslim golden age. The Alhambra was built between 1230 and 1354 and served as a great citadel for the Moorish kings. It was mutilated after the expulsion of the Muslims in 1492 but extensively restored from 1828 on. Its beauty suggests the Muslim notion of how religion and secular life ought to interpenetrate.

Physically, the Alhambra is located on a hill overlooking the city of Granada. Although it is surrounded by walls and has the look of a fort, only the lowest parts of the enclosure were actually used for military purposes. According to early Islamic tradition, palaces were supposed to be placed as the Alhambra is: close to the city, yet a little bit apart. Thus the Alhambra strikes us as a country villa, yet also like an urban citadel. One gets the same impression from similar palaces in Aleppo (northwest Syria) and Cairo. There, too, the effort was to retain the amenities of a royal palace while fortifying the ruler's residence against possible incursions. Such military considerations led to architectural innovations in the vaulting, gateways, and towers of the urban citadel.

The Alhambra goes beyond a simple fusion of the villa and citadel traditions, however, by breaking its sizable area into a series of separate units. Some of these units are lovely gardens, in the Muslim paradisiac tradition. For example, both Iranian and Indian Muslim palaces frequently sought to prefigure Paradise by developing lovely royal gardens. Of the other units of the Alhambra, the most celebrated is the Court of the Lions. The Court of the Lions has an impressive portico running along several sides, with slim, delicate pillars supporting strong arches. The open space in the center is handsomely tiled, and a small fountain with flowers at the base adds splashes of color. Off the court run complexes of square and rectangular rooms, as though the architect wanted to suggest sumptuousness. This is what one commentator calls the "additive" principle: adding room after room, to imply that the royal resources were limitless. The delicate, filigreed work on some of the wall panelings gives an impression of exquisite lace.

A third feature of the Alhambra, beyond its fortified and multipurpose aspects, is its extraordinary attention to decoration. When one is inside the Alhambra, the most gripping feature is the careful ornamentation of the pillars, walls, ceilings, and floors. If one asks why Muslims lavished such care on the internal aesthetics of their palaces, the Alhambra provides an important clue to the answer. The impressive stalactite domes, and the thin pillars of the Fountain of the Lions, apparently derived from the medieval Muslim understanding of Solomon, the famed biblical king. In the medieval mythology surrounding Solomon, the *jinns* (spirits) made wonderful scenes of beauty for him and his queens. Thus medieval Muslim rulers had a certain stimulus to create scenes of an otherworldly, separate Paradise. Wanting to produce by natural means beauty such as that which Solomon achieved by supernatural power, they came to stress gardens, delicate decorations, and

Built in the seventh century C.E., the Dome of the Rock, Jerusalem, is one of Islam's most splendid shrines. Jerusalem is a city holy to Christians and Muslims as well as Jews.

almost tours de force of engineering (thin pillars holding stupendous domes, for instance).

Less spectacularly, the motivations behind architecture like that of the Alhambra led to the "monumentalization" of many ordinary Muslim buildings. Thus in many urban areas, schools, shops, hostels, hospitals, baths, and even warehouses were built with great facades and intricate decorations. The caravanserais (motels, we might say) of thirteenth-century Anatolia, for example, employed the latest and most sophisticated techniques of construction. A religion that had a large place for "works"—business, pragmatic affairs, military matters—placed great stress on housing its social activities and secular affairs well. Also, in the medieval period Muslims tended to invest in land or buildings rather than trade or industry.

The result was an architecture that little distinguished between the mosque and the secular building. Facades, for instance, seldom gave external viewers a basis for determining what sort of building they were entering. It was the internal decorations of the buildings, or the activity that occurred within them, that gave them their distinction.

From the time of the building of the famous Jerusalem Dome of the Rock in 691, the decoration we stressed in the case of the Alhambra preoccupied Muslim builders. Indeed, increasing the decorative beauty of their buildings seems to have been a prime motivation in the Muslims' development of stucco, in their laying bricks to make bold designs, and in their creation of colored tiles. This concern with ornamentation leads to the question of how Muslim construction and decoration relate, a question historians of Islamic architecture debate with some vigor.

A good case to study is the mosque of Cordoba. In the *mihrab* (niche to designate the direction of Mecca) of the Cordoba mosque the domes contain such unusual features as ribs that appear to support the cupola yet form a static mass with the cupola. The squinches (a characteristic support of domes) that accompany the ribs do not really support anything. In other words, the ribs and squinches are present for decorative, rather than constructive, reasons. The north dome of the great mosque in Isfahan, Persia, built a century after the *mihrab* of the mosque in Cordoba, has an unusual articulation of supports that also seem more decorative than constructive. The supports correspond to every part of the superstructure and give the impression of being a grid or net filled with decorative masonry. Third, the Muslim use of *muqarnas*, three-dimensional shapes used in many different combinations, seems clearly intended for decorative, rather than constructive, purposes. The *muqarnas* draw attention to some principal parts of a building, but they usually have little significance in terms of engineering.

The basic ornamental motif in much other Islamic art is repetition, seemingly endless patterns, whether representational (roses and leaves), semiabstract (vine tendrils and rosettes), or completely abstract (geometric patterns). This motif is known as the *infinite pattern*, and some suggest that it has theological significance. It does not want to rival God by creating anything fixed or permanent. Popular art often violated this pattern, suggesting that it most applied to mosques and official constructions. For instance, a Persian manuscript painting of the sixteenth century portrays Muhammad's ascent to Paradise, complete with winged angels, dishes of fruit, showers of pearls, and rubies.

POETRY. Poetry had always held a place of honor among Arabs, for eloquence had always been considered a trait of a great man, even before the advent of Islam. The ancient poetry was born in the desert, so it was replete with desert images and themes. With expansion and conquest, however, Islam became largely an urban culture, so there was need to reshape its poetry. Meter, rhyme, and new imagery became the chief tools. The result was a very complex style. The thirteenth-century poet Ibn al-Khabbaza fashioned an elegy that epitomized Arab eloquence. The themes that dominate some poetic selections are not especially religious: the beauty of a beloved, trees, battle, and, for humor, the flanks and shanks of an ant.

Still, some of the religious mystics, such as Junaid, Rumi, and the woman Rabia, gained fame for their poetic skills. Most were Sufis—devotees of religious emotion and feeling. Among the religious poets of Islam, the Persians were most eminent. Their themes and images centered on the Sufi goal of self-effacement in the divine immensity. For instance, Rumi often portrayed the soul's sense of abandonment in moments of trial when it could not feel the divine embrace: "Hearken to this Reed forlorn, Breathing ever since 'twas torn from its rushy bed, a strain of impassioned love and pain." In this way, the talented Sufi writers won considerable respect from cultured people. To be able to express their religious vision with eloquence made them seem less eccentric, more representative of traditional Arab cultural ideals.

LAW AND THEOLOGY. Within the inner precincts of Islam, neither science nor art constituted the main cultural development. Rather, the most important flowering of Qur'anic doctrine was the law *Sharia,* (the path, teaching). This concept is similar to the Catholic canon law, or Jewish Torah, or Buddhist dharma. It rose from reflections on the *Qur'an* and the *hadith* that passed on the example and teachings of the Prophet. Generally it tends to connote the orthodox law codes Islam developed, which codified the consensus of the community and the conclusions the Muslim teachers had reached by reasoning from precedents. Traditional Muslims have looked to Sharia for guidance on the path to salvation, although they have admitted notable debate among their teachers over fine points of interpretation. Sharia has been the backbone of traditional Muslim

Meeting of the theologians

oaths, criminal penalties, relations with non-Muslims, partnerships, contracts, the slaughter of animals, use of the land, fines, wills, sports, prohibited drinks, and much more. Some of these topics traditionally got more attention and development than others, in part because the religious courts were more able to detail and enforce laws concerning them: inheritance law, family law, and law concerning pious endowments for good works (schools, hospitals, etc.), for example.

On the whole, Islamic law has most concentrated on what sometimes is called "personal law": marriage, divorce, and inheritance. These areas continued to receive great attention and stay under the influence of religious lawyers even through the twentieth century, somewhat in contrast to the secularization of such other areas as taxation, criminal law, and constitutional law. Interestingly, however, with the rise of fundamentalist influences in many Muslim countries during the last quarter century has come a trend to rethink even these latter, secularized legal areas in terms of older traditions that assumed there was no unreligious, secular dimension in a good Muslim's life.

The early theological discussions dealt with the nature of faith and types of sins (e.g., idolatry). Later debates focused on the unity of God (in the context of discussing the divine attributes) and on the relation of the divine sovereignty to human freedom. While there was a full spectrum of opinions, in Sunni quarters the more moderate positions tended to win favor. Before long, however, Islam effectively curtailed speculation, favoring instead careful efforts to ascertain what legal precedents any practical problem had in the *Qur'an*, the *hadith* of the Prophet, community consensus, or analogous situations. These were the four main sources of religious authority.

The *hadith* were sayings attributed to Muhammad or stories about Muhammad apart from the *Qur'an*. The *hadith* function in Islam as one of the principal sources of authoritative teaching, standing with the *Qur'an*, community consensus, and analogical reasoning. They affirm the paradigmatic role of the Prophet, whose life Muslims have taken as the model or template for Muslim existence. Complicated rules govern how sayings became authenticated and entered the collections of *hadith*. Muslims tend to be confident that what is housed in the several authoritative collections reports what the Prophet said and

culture. As the opening verses of the *Qur'an* suggest, a fundamental concern in Islam is guidance, and Islam went to lawyers, not to scientists, poets, or even mystics, for its most trustworthy guidance.

Traditional Islamic law has thought of itself as derived from God's plan for the proper ordering of human life. Its province has extended to whatever impinged on human beings' passage to Paradise. A term equivalent to *Sharia, fiqh* ("understanding" or "knowledge"), implied that the laws developed by the lawyers expressed what was understood to be behavior that would keep Muslims on the straight path.

The main thrust of the *fiqh* rules is on the "vertical" obligations of the Muslim to God: prayers, pilgrimage, fasting, and the like. Another interest of these treatises bears on what we might call "horizontal" relationships: marriage, divorce, freeing slaves, did, but scholars using the detached techniques of textual criticism find much that seems folkloric and incapable of independent historical verification.

To be sure, Muslims did not view religious law or theology as a human creation. Rather, it was divine guidance, the expression of God's own will. The goal of the teachers was to offer comprehensive guidance for all of life—much as the Jewish rabbis' goal was to apply the Torah to all of life. As they refined their craft, Muslim teachers also distinguished all human actions according to five headings: obligatory, recommended, permitted, disapproved, and forbidden. Thus, one had to confess the unity of God and the Prophethood of Muhammad, one was counseled to avoid divorce, and one was forbidden to eat pork. Since Muslim society was a theocracy, *Sharia* was the code of the land. (While that made for a certain unity and order, it also prepared the way for the Sufi mystic's emphasis on personal devotion as a counterweight to legalism.)

THE PERIOD OF DIVISION

A minor source of division within the Muslim community was the differences in law developed by the various schools. The Hanafite school came to dominate Muslim countries north and east of the Arabian Peninsula. Within Arabia itself, the dominant school was founded by ibn-Hanbal. Northeast Africa was under Shafite and Hanafite lawyers, while Malikite opinions were the most prestigious in northwestern Africa. In Persia the Shia sect had its own law. On the whole, that distribution still holds today.

Given the four recognized legal codes of Sunni, the large Shia minority, and the division of the Islamic empire into eastern and western parts centered at Baghdad and Cordoba, respectively, one can see that religious and political unity was less than perfect. Still, Muslims holding to the Five Pillars and the *Qur'an* had much more in common with one another than they had with any non-Muslim peoples. Thus, legal or creedal differences did not divide Muslim religion severely. In contrast, different devotional styles, such as Sufism, caused considerable conflict.

SUFISM. The **Sufis** were the best known sect of Islamic mystics. The term *Sufi* comes from the Arabic word for wool, which Sufis wore as a gesture of sim-

Sufi mystics use the ritual of the whirling dance.

plicity. In the beginning, the Sufi movement stood for reform and personal piety. In a time when political and military success tempted Islam to worldliness, and the rise of the law brought the dangers of legalism, the Sufis looked to the model of Muhammad at prayer, communing with God. For them the heart of Islam was personal submission to God, personal guidance along the straight path. In later centuries, through its brotherhoods and saints, Sufism set a great deal of the emotional, anti-intellectual, and anti-progressive tone of an Islam that had lost its status as a world power.

Several cultural streams ran together to form the Sufi movement. First was the ascetic current from traditional desert life, which was basic and simple—a daily call for endurance. Out of a keen sense of the religious values in such a harsh life, Abu Dharr al-Ghifari, a companion of the Prophet, chastised the early leaders who wanted to lead a sumptuous court life after their conquests. Second, many of the Sufi ecstatics drew on the Arab love of poetry. Their lyric depictions of the love of God, coupled with the *Qur'an*'s eloquence, drew sensitive people to the side of a living, personal commitment to realize the beauties of Islam. Third, the more speculative Sufis drew on Gnostic ideas that floated in from Egypt and the Fertile Crescent. By the ninth century, Sufi contemplatives (especially the Persian Illuminationists) were utilizing those ideas to analyze the relations between divinity and the world. (The Sufis seem to have found most attractive the emanational ideas—the theories of how the world flowed out of the divine essence—rather than the dualistic theories of good and evil.) This kind of understanding, along with the alchemical interests noted previously, was the beginning of the esoteric and sometimes magical lore for which the orthodox theologians and lawyers held the Sufis suspect. Last, Indian (especially Buddhist) thought apparently influenced the eastern portions of the Muslim realm, and it perhaps was a source of the tendencies toward self-annihilation (loss of personal identity in God) that became important in Sufi mystical doctrine.

Taken at their own word, the Sufis desired to be committed followers of Muhammad and the *Qur'an*. The more honored among them never intended any schismatic or heretical movements. The most famous theologian among them was **Al-Ghazzali** (1058–1111), who withdrew from his prestigious teaching post in Baghdad to pursue the mystic's life.

Like the Jewish Hasidim, the Sufis fashioned stories to carry their messages about the paradoxes of the spiritual life, the need for being focused and wholehearted, the way that God comes in the midst of everyday life. In these stories, the poor man turns out to be rich; the fool turns out to be truly wise. Like their counterparts in other traditions, the Sufis left no doubt that riches and prestige tend to be obstacles to spirituality. Predictably, this challenge to the expectations of society, of the religious authorities, and of the literally minded won the Sufis no love. Perhaps to intensify their opposition, some Sufis became even more provocative, challenging the establishment and suggesting that its religion was little more than dead convention. Along similar lines is a story of a Sufi who meets the devil. The devil is just sitting patiently, so the Sufi asks him why he is not out making mis-

chief. The devil replies, "Since the theoreticians and would-be teachers of the Path have appeared in such numbers, there is nothing left for me to do."

Sufi followers had a *sheikh* (master, similar to a guru in Hinduism) who would help the novice learn meditation. Typically, at the order's local lodge, a small number of professionals resided to teach and lead worship. Most members have been lay adherents who came for instruction when they could and who supported the lodge by contributing money, manual labor, and so on. Each order tended to have its own distinctive ritual, whose purpose was usually to attain ecstatic experience. The ritual was the group's interpretation of the general virtue of *dhikr* (remembrance) that all Muslims seek. For instance, whirling dances characterized many of the Mevlevi **dervish** meetings, while Saadeeyeh Sufis developed a ceremony in which the head of the order rode on horseback over prone devotees.

LATE EMPIRE AND MODERNITY

During the period of empire, at least three general changes occurred in Arabic-speaking society. The first was the transformation of the Islamic Near East from a commercial economy based on money to a feudal economy based on subsistence farming. The second was the replacement in positions of authority of Arabic-speaking peoples by Turks. The Arab tribes retained their independence in the desert regions, where they held out quite well against Turkish rule. In the cities and cultivated valleys (the plains of Iraq, Syria, and Egypt), however, the Arabs became completely subjected, and the glorious language that had been the pride of Islam became the argot of an enslaved population. Psychologically, the Turks grew accustomed to taking the initiative and commanding, and the Arabs grew accustomed to passivity and subjection. The third change was the transfer of the seat of Islam from Iraq to Egypt. Iraq was too remote from Turkey and the Mediterranean to be the base for the eastern wing of Islam, so Egypt—which was on the other principal trade route and which was the most unified area geographically—became the new center.

The Ottoman Turks finally defeated the crumbling Byzantine empire, taking Constantinople in 1453 and renaming it Istanbul. They moved into southeastern

Europe, gaining many converts to Islam among the Albanians and Bosnians. At first many of the subject peoples welcomed the Ottoman takeover from the Mamluks or Byzantines as a return to political order. By the eighteenth century, however, the Ottoman empire was in decay—corrupt, anarchic, and stagnant. The principal religious form of revolt during this period was Sufism. At first Sufism was mainly an escape for oppressed individuals, but with the organization of more brotherhoods, it became a social movement that was especially powerful among the artisan class. The long centuries of stagnation finally ended, however, with increased contact with the West. From the beginning of the sixteenth century, European expansion brought some of the new learning of the Renaissance and the Reformation. The French in particular had considerable influence in the Middle East, and Napoleon's easy conquest of the Ottoman Turks at the end of the eighteenth century was the final blow to Islamic military glory.

THE WAHABIS. Also during the time of Napoleon arose an Islamic reform that was designed to check what it considered to be the infection of Sufism. One of the first leaders in this reform was a stern traditionalist named Muhammad ibn Abd al-Wahab, whose followers came to be known as Wahabis. They called for a return to the doctrines and practices of the early generations, of the ancestors whom they venerated. In law, the Wahabis favored the rigorous interpretations of the Hanbalite school, and they abhorred the veneration of Sufi masters as saints. Thus, they inveighed against supposed holy personages, living or dead, and went out of their way to destroy the shrines that had become places of popular piety or pilgrimage. They further objected that the worship of saints presumed that they were "partners" of God and so was idolatrous. The punishment due such idolatry was death. Some of the more rabid Wahabis went so far as to classify the more lenient lawyers and schools as being guilty of idolatry (and so punishable by death). The Wahabis were based in Arabia, whence they waged war on their dissenting neighbors. They went down to military defeat in their 1818 campaign, but their puritanical reform had much ideological success and spread to other parts of the Islamic world.

An immediate effect of the Wahabi movement was great hostility toward the Sufi brotherhoods. In fact, Muslims interested in renovating orthodoxy singled out the Sufis as their great enemies, although they also attacked the Scholasticism of such theological centers as Al-Azhar in Cairo. One of the leaders of the nineteenth-century reform was the apostle of Pan-Islam, Jamal al-Din al-Afghani, who proposed the political unification of all Muslim countries under the caliphate of the Ottoman sultans. While Pan-Islam has never been realized, it stimulated the widespread search for an effective Muslim response to modernity. In India and Egypt, conservative groups arose that gravitated toward the Wahabi position. Many of the Sufi organizations lost their strength, and those that survived tended to back away from gnosis and return to a more traditional theology.

Even before this conservative threat, however, the Sufis had reformed on their own, sponsoring a number of missions in Africa, India, and Indonesia. For the most part these were peaceful, but occasionally they involved military ventures. In fact, some groups quite consciously took up the Qur'anic tradition of holy war, including the "Indian Wahabis" and the Mahdists in the Sudan. However, even in decline the Sufi brotherhoods kept dear to Islam the notion of bonding together for mutual support.

The organizations that have grown up in recent times, such as the Association for Muslim Youth and the Muslim Brotherhood, seem in good measure an effort to fill the void created by the demise of the Sufi brotherhoods. The new groups differ by operating primarily in pluralistic cultures, where Muslims live in the midst of non-Muslims.

WESTERN INFLUENCE. A characteristic of Islamic modernity was the invasion of Western secular ideas. These ideas came on the heels of modern Western takeovers in the Middle East, at first through the administrations of the Europeans who governed the newly acquired territories and then through the educational systems, which were Westernized. The new classes of native professionals—doctors, lawyers, and journalists—frequently trained abroad or in native schools run by Westerners. One political effect of such training was to raise Muslim feelings of nationalism and to provoke cries for Westernized systems of

CASE STUDY: LESSONS FROM RECENT IRAN

The rest of the Islamic world followed the Iranian upheavals of 1979 with great interest, to say the least, and many interesting commentaries on the relevance of Islam for today have arisen because of the Iranian events. One such commentary appeared in Cairo, at the instigation of the Islamic Student Association of Cairo University. Studying the reflections of this commentary may open a window on the likely future of Islam's blend of religion and politics.

The commentary begins with a quotation from the *Qur'an* (3:26) to the effect that God, the possessor of all sovereignty, gives earthly sovereignty to whomever he wishes. Just as freely, God takes earthly sovereignty away. Only God is powerful over all things. If God wishes to raise someone up, he does. If God wishes to debase someone, he does.

From this theological foundation the commentary moves to the Khomeini revolution in Iran, which was then riveting the whole world. This revolution, says the article, the violence and restraint of which surpassed the calculations and wildest imaginings of most observers, deserves deep study. Muslims must ponder such marvelous happenings, if they are ever to fulfill their Qur'anic destiny (see 3:110) and "assume the reins of world leadership of mankind once again and place the world under the protection of the esteemed Islamic civilization."

Beginning such study, the first lesson the commentary would underscore is the influence of the creed on the Islamic people. The Iranian people, who had appeared completely submissive to death and tyranny, exploded like a volcano, tossing their fears aside. Their spiritual conquest of the steely forces that opposed them recalls the heroes of earliest Muslim times, and it should remind everyone that religious commitment might muster similar power in many situations. Islam is the religion with the power to redress the injustices of all peoples everywhere.

Second, the Iranian revolution reminds us that Islam is a comprehensive religion, legislating for both this world and the next. It provides alike for religion and state affairs, education and morals, worship and holy war. In fact, the Iranian revolution clarifies the errors in modern secularism, which would separate religion from state affairs. Clearly, it shows that secularism is the recourse of idolaters, who want to keep religion out of politics, so that they can plunder the wealth of the common people. The only adequate laws and constitutions are those that derive from the *Sharia* of Islam. When laws and constitutions are manmade, their status is no greater than the idols of the pre-Muslim Arabs. If the pre-Muslim Arabs got hungry, they would eat the Goddess of Pastry. In contrast, the *Sharia* of Islam, which comes from God, is permanent, just, wise, and perfect.

Third, Iranian affairs show that the real leaders of the Muslim people are the sincere, learned men of religion. These men (the *ulama*) have been the guiding lights of all the best modern Muslim liberation movements. The touchstone is justice. For forty years the tyrant shah betrayed his community and brought down on it the most repulsive forms of injustice. God takes his time with the wrongdoer, but when he takes him there is no escaping.

Fourth, shrewd observers will note how the false Iranian leaders had the courage of lions when dealing with their own people but were puppets in the hands of the rulers of the East and the West. Yet the West quickly disowned the shah, abandoning him like a worn-out shoe. To the lesson implied in this, one should add the patent effort of Islam's enemies to exploit the sectarian differences between Shiites and Sunnis and tear the Muslim community apart. As well, the enemies of Islam tried to use the Iranian revolution to instigate local governments to strike out at Islamic movements.

Therefore, rulers in other Islamic locales must realize that their real strength lies in the strength of their people, and that the real strength of their people lies in Islam. Wise leaders are those that place their allegiance in God, his apostle

Muhammad. As the *Qur'an* (5:49) teaches, only those who rule by what God has revealed can expect to be strengthened. Thus, to those who would instigate strife against Islamic movements, one should reply: God suffices for us. The *Qur'an* has said the last word in these matters: "God promised those of you who believe and perform good works that he would make you viceroys on earth as he did with those before and will make it possible for you to follow the religion which pleases you and will change your fear into safety. You will worship me, associating nothing else with me" (24:55).

Several concerns of the Cairo Students' Association merit special comment, because they have been present in the recent resurgence of a passionate Islam in other countries, such as Iran, Afghanistan, and Pakistan. First, some students obviously long for a return to traditional Muslim law. Chafing under what they think is their recent rulers' secularism, the students hope that returning to the principles of the *Qur'an* and traditional Muslim law will speedily redress all current wrongs. In its early stages, the revolution in Iran seemed a great vindication of this viewpoint. Even fervent Muslims were amazed that they were able to bring down so powerful an enemy as the shah. Today, at a greater distance from the events of 1979, and with more experience of what the Ayatollah Khomeini understood the revolution to imply, even zealous students might take pause. The bloody chaos that afflicted the Muslim ranks in Iran after the revolution argues that the *Sharia* is open to markedly diverse and violent interpretations. The long war between Iran and Iraq was a festering sore in the Muslim community.

Second, a great deal of the world does not want to be placed under the protection of Islamic civilization, even when one grants Islamic civilization its great due. Pluralism is a more powerful force than the students seem to realize, and any peaceful assumption of the reins of world leadership will have to handle pluralism quite sympathetically. Any forceful assumption of the reins of world leadership is almost unthinkable, both because Islam is hardly in the position to challenge the West militarily and because military means to power inevitably raise the specter of nuclear war. No nations would profit from a contemporary translation of Islamic "holy war" that led to nuclear confrontations.

Third, students of religion might most profitably focus on the somewhat tacit pleas that run through the Egyptian students' commentary. For example, there is the tacit plea that the rest of the world take seriously and duly honor a proud religious tradition. Islam came on hard times when the West took charge of modernity. Its pride was wounded, and one can trace much of its strong rhetoric, even its hyperbole, to this wounded pride. Now that Islam is on the march again, more than competitive with the Western religions in Africa and other parts of the Third World, it is trying to recoup some of its emotional losses.

Still another plea running through the students' manifesto is for simple justice. Iranians had been suffering injustice. Enough of them had been tortured and abused by the shah to make his regime hated. The popular support for the Khomeini revolution was only explainable on the basis of this hatred. Had the shah's innovations, his programs for modernization and economic development, not been perceived as brutally unjust, as well as destructive of the people's cherished religious heritage, the shah probably would not have become the Iranian Satan. Even when one allows for a considerable emotional excess in the rhetoric of the shah's opponents, and their considerable manipulation by religious leaders quite ambitious for power, the political facts seem clear. The clarion call of the religious revolutionaries was for a restoration of justice. A major attraction in the prospect of restoring a Qur'anic government was the possibility of achieving a much greater justice.

For many secular observers, Khomeini's authoritarianism soon became precisely a demand for idolatrous obedience, precisely the arbitrary rule of a false god.

government. The new ideas challenged the madrasas, or religious schools, too, for it was not immediately apparent that these new ideas could be taught along with traditional theories of revelation and Qur'anic inspiration.

From the nineteenth century on, the economics, politics, education, social habits, and even religion of Muslims were increasingly affected by the upheaval that resulted from the European Renaissance and Enlightenment. Some countries remained largely insulated from Western notions, but they tended to be backward portions of the old empire with little political impact. As we might expect, the cities bore the brunt of the challenge. In theology the outward Muslim reaction was to close ranks. Still, even in the most fiercely traditionalist schools, modern notions—such as the freedom of human beings to shape their own destinies—softened the old propositions about providence and predestination.

Indeed, when it was convenient, theologians incorporated modern science into their argumentation. For instance, some Muslim theologians justified the doctrine that God creates the world continuously by citing atomic theory. The less theologically inclined among the modern educated classes contented themselves by asserting that Islam, as submission to the God as "the Master of Truth," in principle cannot conflict with modern science or with any empirically verified truths.

Controversy over societal matters has been more heated than that over theology because the guidance provided by the traditional legal schools diverged more sharply from Western mores than Muslim theology diverged from Western theology. Slowly Islamic countries have developed civil codes and separated civil courts from religious courts. In the mid-nineteenth century, the Turkish Republic breached the wall of tradition when it abolished the authority of the *Sharia* in civil matters. In other countries the *Sharia* has remained the outer form, but new legislative codes direct the interpretations. The tactic has been to invoke the *Qur'an,* the *hadith,* and the traditions of the schools but to leave the legislators and judges free to choose the authority that is most appropriate. Specifically, the legal reforms have applied primarily to marriage contracts (protecting girls against child marriage), divorce proceedings, and

SCHOOLS OF ISLAM		
SCHOOL	LOCATION	APPROACH
Sunni	Saudi Arabia, Turkey, Bosnia, Albania, Africa, Pakistan, Syria, Palestine, Afghanistan, Indonesia, Bangladesh	consensus interpretation of *Qur'an*
Shia	Iran	living prophet (ayatollah, imam)
Druses	Lebanon	no more converts
Sikh	India	Hinduism and Islam
Sufi	Iran	mysticism
Bahai	Iran	ecumenism
Nation of Islam	United States	racial separation

polygamy—central factors in the traditional family structure.

In considering recent Muslim fundamentalism, one must realize that Islamic secularism never got so advanced as Western secularism. True, fundamentalism attracts a noteworthy number of Christians and Jews, but Christianity and Judaism more clearly differentiate the civic realm, the realm shared with citizens of other religious convictions (or of none), than Islamic culture has done. Conversely, Islam has kept the sacred and the secular more tightly conjoined than Christianity or Judaism has, professing that there is no secular realm—that everything lives by the will and touch of Allah, who is as near as the pulse at one's throat.

WORLDVIEW

NATURE

The key to the Muslim notion of nature is Islam's concept of creation. As much as the biblical religion on which it is built, Islam sees God as the maker of all that is. Several Qur'anic passages establish this doctrine. For instance, *Sura* 10 describes the Lord as "God, who created the heavens and the earth in six days, then sat Himself upon the Throne directing the affair." This is the biblical imagery of creation: Genesis spreading God's work over six days. Moreover, the *Qur'an* finds significance in this creation in that through creation God has given God-fearing people signs of his dominion. By making the sun a radiance and the moon a light, by giving them "stations" so that astronomers can calculate time, and by alternating night and day, God has set over humankind a heaven full of signs. *Sura* 13 repeats this theme, adding earthly phenomena: It is he who stretched out the earth, set firm mountains and rivers, and placed two kinds of every fruit. The abundance of nature testifies to the abundance of nature's source and ought to remind human beings of God's power and provision. Thus, the Creator is not only strong but also admirable in his design of the world and praiseworthy in his concern for human welfare as evidenced by his bounty. In this way the best features of nature become analogies for God in the *Qur'an*. The "Light-Verse" of *Sura* 24 gives one of the most famous of these analogies: God is the light of the heavens and the earth. His light is as a niche where there is a lamp. The lamp is in a glass, the glass is like a glittering star. The lamp is kindled from a Blessed Tree, an olive neither of the East nor of the West, whose oil would shine even if no fire touched it. Light upon light, God guides to the light whom he will.

Religiously, then, nature is replete with evidence from which wise people discern God's creative presence. However, nature is not itself a divinity or a form of God's presence. Unlike East Asian thought, Islamic thought does not mix divinity with the cosmos. Islam separated from the ancient cosmological myth, in that God transcends the world. One may say that the biblical prophets' critique of nature gods combined with Muhammad's negative reaction to the polytheism of his times to correlate transcendence and anti-idolatry. So the signs that nature gives to the God-fearing are not themselves sacraments. They point beyond themselves; the divinity does not come in them. Water, oil, bread, wine—they are not miniature incarnations of divinity. The God of Islam has no incarnation, no personal or material forms by which he becomes present. Creator is Creator, creature is creature, and never the twain shall meet.

Nature never dominated Arab or Muslim culture. The earliest poetry deals more with war and nomadic life than with father sky and mother earth. Pre-Muslim Arabia worshipped natural and agricultural forces, but Qur'anic monotheism attacked them harshly. In religious art, the prohibition on images was not absolute, although religious art tended to avoid representations of natural scenes, let alone representations of God. Still, the prime material for worship, the *Qur'an* itself, contained natural figures and not merely in the context of creation. Thus, it embellished its theme of judgment and recompense with naturalistic imagery. Thus, the *Qur'an* considered nature a factor in the mysteries of judgment, punishment, and reward, as the images of Fire and Garden clearly show. Moreover, mythological elaboration of these themes in popular religion was quite unrestrained. In the popular conception, angels presided over hell, meting out punishments, while heaven became a place for enjoying fruit, wine, and the charming black-eyed virgins.

Islam maintained that justice would be served in the afterlife through reward for the pious and punishment for the non-Muslims. Sex was high on the list of pleasures, so Paradise was rich with sex. Islam depicted sex from the male point of view, with details of "maidens restraining their glances, untouched before them by any man or *jinn*" (55:55). As we shall see below, Islam did not declare the goodness of sex so loudly and clearly for women. In fact, there has often been a double standard concerning sex in Muslim society. Still, the basic fact that Islam does not paint heaven as an ethereal, wholly spiritual realm shows that it blesses human nature.

Muslim spirituality manifests something of the emphasis of keeping human nature under control. By fasting, a Muslim tames the nature closest to the self. By confessing that there is no God but God, a Muslim clears the world of competitors to the Creator and Judge. That means that many devout Muslims' ideal is a bare vista. The Sufis manifested this ideal most fully, for many of them saw life as a pilgrimage to union with a God much more valuable than anything worldly. In less deliberate but still consoling ways, the poor merchant or soldier learned from misfortune how precarious a worldly vista was. Although the physical world was definitely real and on occasion quite good, the human being's role was to observe it closely enough so that it served as a guidepost to heaven. A Muslim can be comfortable in the natural world, then, but only as a visitor. Life in the natural world soon passes, and Judgment depends on higher things, such as one's commitment, one's prayer, and one's generosity in giving alms. The tradition does not teach people that the Judge will ask them how they treated the environment or whether they tore the bosom of mother earth. Those issues are far less important than whether they remembered God and his Prophet.

SOCIETY

The Muslim social unit has been the *Ummah,* the brotherhood and sisterhood of all Muslims. The Prophet was the head of the entire community in his day, but after his death the question of headship of the community became entangled in political and cultural battles. The differences between Shiites and Sunnis have complicated estimates of how the *Ummah* actually subsists in time. But such occasions as the annual pilgrimage to Mecca have allowed Muslims to affirm their solidarity.

The Muslim social ideal has never distinguished between secular and sacred aspects of community life. The Prophet and his successors bore a theocratic power. That is, they had authority in both the religious and the secular spheres, because Islam does not much distinguish the two. Muslims were to bring their disputes to the Prophet or his successors, and they all had a common duty to worship God, to obey God's commands, and to do good and avoid evil. Members were to be to one another as brothers and mutual guardians (*Qur'an* 9:71), respecting life and enjoying its good things.

The Islamic state made a threefold division of humanity: Muslims, covenanters, and enemies. The Muslim peoples who constituted the Dar al-Islam (House of Islam) could not legitimately resort to war against one another. Covenanters were non-Muslims who had made "compacts of peace." Examples would be those Jews and Christians living in Spain and the Zoroastrians of Iran. Muslims had the right to preach to them but not to force them to convert. As long as the covenanters accepted Muslim law in the society, their civil rights and duties were the same as those of Muslims.

Presumably, holy war only resulted when enemies rejected both conversion and covenant. If an enemy responded with hostility, Muslim security necessitated war. Muslims had to fight for brethren in other places who suffered tyranny (*Qur'an* 4:75). For Muslim leaders, the consensus of the community was an important goal, for they wanted a single divine rope to bind the *Ummah* together.

ETHICS. Despite the doctrines of God's sovereignty, Islam considered people to have free will and be morally responsible for their actions. As we noted, the law distinguishes five kinds of action, from the commanded to the forbidden. The *Qur'an* deals with adultery, murder, and theft, prescribing stern punishments for them. Homosexuality is likewise forbidden (though its practice was not absent in Muslim societies which so thoroughly excluded women largely from the daily life of single men).

Muslim dietary rules are comparable to the Jewish kosher restrictions, but they are not as elaborate. Pork is not to be eaten. Meat must be obtained from a butcher skilled in the proper techniques of slaughter. (Today Islamic butchers can be found in European and North American cities with large Muslim populations.)

Two other prohibitions are on alcohol and gambling. These may have had their origin from the need of controlling male behavior on a long caravan (or military campaign). In some Muslim countries (e.g., Saudi Arabia, Afghanistan), alcohol may not be manufactured or consumed. In other Muslim countries, alcohol may be produced and sold to non-Muslims (e.g., Pakistan has a very successful gin distillery started by the British colonialists). Just as not every Catholic is committed enough to avoid committing the sins specified by his denomination, so Muslims sometimes lapse and go into a bar or casino (especially in non-Muslim countries). But God is the most merciful and does forgive.

COMPARISON OF ISLAM, CHRISTIANITY, AND JUDAISM			
DIMENSION	ISLAM	CHRISTIANITY	JUDAISM
Name of followers	Muslims	Christians	Jews
Began	7th century C.E.	1st century C.E.	2nd millennium B.C.E.
Originated in	Middle East	Middle East	Middle East
Founder	Muhammad	Jesus	Abraham
Monotheistic?	yes	yes	yes
Trinity?	no	yes	no
Jesus is	prophet	God, the Son	teacher
Proselytizing?	yes	yes	no
Also spread by	conquest	conquest	diaspora
Adam and Eve?	yes	yes	yes
Old Testament prophets?	yes	yes	yes
Priests	no	some sects	before 70 C.E.
Congregated worship	weekly	weekly	weekly
Place of worship	mosque	church	temple before 70 C.E.; syngagogue
Statues	no	in Roman Catholicism	no
Angels	yes	yes	yes
Resurrection and apocalypse	early Islam	early Christians and some sects	Daniel, Pharisees, some messianic sects
Emphasis on Heaven and hell	major	major in most sects	minor

Racism was an evil targeted by the prophet Muhammad. In the beginning, there was to be no discrimination between Muslims based upon the Arab tribe to which a Muslim belonged. There was never any idea that God was just the God of the Arabs, so this proselytizing religion accepted as converts Turks, Persians, Indians, Slavs, Indonesians and Africans. One story about him was that one of his later wives was an African woman. Another story is that one of his own daughters was given to an African husband.

The *Qur'an* takes slavery for granted, but it commends humane treatment and the freeing of slaves. Only non-Muslim prisoners of war could legally become slaves. Discrimination because of color and race was unlawful, though some racial prejudice mars Islamic history. When the law reached its final stage of development around 1000, its detailed specifications tended to become mechanical. The mystics therefore tried to make ethics spring from a deeper relationship with God. The first virtue they

DIMENSION	ISLAM	CHRISTIANITY	JUDAISM
Salvation	from works	from grace	from works
Scripture	*Qur'an*	*Bible*	Torah
Days of fasting	yes	in some sects	yes
Charity for poor	yes	yes	yes
Ten Commandments as ethical foundation	yes	yes	yes
Polygamy sanctioned	yes, but limited	in some sects	in some periods
Celibacy	never	in some sects	rarely (Essenes)
Male circumcision	puberty	medical option	infant
Pork	prohibited	allowed	prohibited
Alcohol	prohibited	allowed by most sects	allowed
Role of pilgrimage	major	minor	minor
Abraham seen as	ancestor through Ishmael	example of commitment	ancestor through Isaac
Mystics	Sufis	monastics	Cabalists, Hasidim
Had to flee	Hegira from Mecca	persecution from other Christians	Exodus from Egypt, persecution from Christians
Theocratic	when in majority	when in majority	when in majority
Prefer secular society	when in minority	when in minority	when in minority

taught was abstention from everything unlawful or dubious. In other words, one was not to nitpick but to act from the heart and turn away from anything that might displease God. Masters such as Al-Ghazali advocated living every moment in the presence of God. Finally, the general effect of Muslim ethics was to heighten awareness of one's distance from the divine purity and so lead one to beg Allah's mercy and forgiveness.

WOMEN'S STATUS. In the *Qur'an* there is some basis for sexual equality in theory: reward and punishment in the afterlife depend on deeds, not gender. However, Islam has had a gnawing sense that in practice women had too many limitations, such as monthly menstruation, which were bound to interfere with prayer and fasting.

In practice, Muslim law improved the lot of women (over what it had been in Arab lands prior to 600 C.E. Before Islam, women had status little better than that of slaves or livestock. If there was a time of famine, female infanticide would be widely practiced so that the clan did not have to make an investment in a future member who could not drive camels or exact vengeance in the desert. Before Islam, she could be given in marriage or sold as a sex slave before she reached her teens. Islam encouraged formal marriage (but did not ban slavery or concubinage), and (at least in theory) even gave her the right to refuse a marriage proposal. Islamic rules on polygamy limited the number of wives a man could have to four (and having more than one was granted on the condition that he treat them equally, which many theologians have suggested was a back door approach to monogamy). Before Islam, women would not have legal rights to inheritance, but they did under the *Qur'an*. Before Islam, there were few practical hindrances to a man divorcing his wife on a whim. Islamic law still permitted this, but it deterred such a practice by requiring the man to return a portion of the dowry he had received at marriage. Islam also granted women the right to remarry after being widowed, and most importantly, Muslim males the duty to protect pregnant and nursing women.

However, women's rights are not equal to those that the *Qur'an* gives males in either divorce or inheritance. Her value as a witness in court was only half of that of the man. Moreover, the *Qur'an* does not even consider the possibility that women might assume leadership roles in the community, receive an education equal to that of males, teach law or theology, or obtain multiple spouses (as males could). The prime role of a woman in this life was to serve and obey her husband, bearing and caring for his children, and it was in her fulfillment of these duties that her value to Muslim society was judged. Women were portrayed as empty headed and best left illiterate, veiled, and secluded in a harem.

Although on the issues of slavery and women's rights, Muhammad must be viewed as a sincere reformer, making significant improvements by broadening the rights of these classes, the fact that his specific seventh-century reforms have been frozen has created a basis for discrimination in modern times. As contemporary Afghani women hope for the right to work outside the home, and Iranian women struggle for greater opportunities for advancements in education and career, their challenge will be to use the rock of Muhammad's reforms as a steppingstone under their feet rather than a millstone around their necks.

WAR. Muhammad sought to greatly limit the fratricidal strife among Arab tribes. He proclaimed that all Muslims were brothers and abolished the cycle of vengeance for past wrongs. He promulgated the doctrine of **jihad** in order to limit the situations which could justify war. Jihad is frequently misunderstood by non-Muslims (and it does not help matters that there is a terrorist group named "Islamic Jihad" planting bombs against civilian targets). *Jihad* is a Muslim term for holy struggle, warfare in defense, or pursuit, of a good cause. It can connote the whole range of effort necessary to promote Islam in both personal and social life. Moreover, even when it refers to military matters, it need not primarily be offensive. The more ordinary reason for going to war, in the Muslim view of past history, was opposition that would have denied Muslims the chance to practice or spread Islam. Seeing such a denial as opposition to God, the *Qur'an*, and the Prophet, Muslims have felt obliged to fight, as they could feel obliged to fight on behalf of brother and sister Muslims who came under attack. The unity of the Muslim community justified such a sense of social solidarity, Muslims having ties among themselves that relegated their relations with non-Muslims or outsiders to a lower level.

However, most experts on the *Sharia* are clear that the ethics of Islamic warfare protect non-combatants, women and children, the aged, and prisoners of war. Islamic terrorists are condemned by most Islamic theologians, just as terrorist splinter groups of the Irish Republican Army (fighting for the Catholic side in Northern Ireland) have their violence condemned by the Pope.

VARIETY. The different Islamic cultures have all been bonded by the *Qur'an* despite their geographic, linguistic, ethnic, and even theological differences. In India, as noted in a previous chapter, Islamic elements fused with Hindu elements to create **Sikhism** under the inspiration of Guru Nanak (1469–1539). They had a sequence of later gurus who blended Muslim monotheism with Hindu rituals. The men wear turbans and carry symbolic swords. They are prominent in the Punjab district and in India's military. (Most of India remained either Muslim or Hindu, and one of the results of the independence after World War II was a division of the country into a predominantly Hindu republic of India to the south, and the Muslim republics of Pakistan and Bangladesh in the northwest and northeast, respectively).

A thousand years ago, the **Druses** sect was formed by an imam, al-Hakim in Egypt, who had a revelation that only his small group of followers would be saved, and that they were not to accept any additional converts beyond their own descendants. They now number about a quarter million, largely concentrated in an area of southeastern Lebanon.

Islam was also the inspiration behind **Baha'i**, a tolerant, universalist religion that stresses the unity of all traditions and the basic oneness of the human race. It arose in nineteenth-century Persia when a Shiite Muslim, Sayyid Ali Muhammad, declared that he was the twelfth imam—the last messianic leader whom the Shia awaits. Sayyid took the designation Bab ("gate"), and his follower Baha Ullah produced writings that became classic works of Baha'i. Today Baha'i has about 5 million adherents. Its world center is on Mount Carmel in Haifa, Israel, where a lovely garden and shrine are dedicated to the Bab, and there is a beautiful temple just north of Chicago in Wilmette, Illinois. These Baha'i temples are characterized by many entrances, symbolizing the world's different denominations (e.g., Buddhist, Christian, Muslim) all of which are considered acceptable pathways to God.

In Detroit in the 1930s, African-Americans formed a movement called the **Nation of Islam** (also known as the Black Muslims). Although it accepts the *Qu'ran,* and traditional Islamic prohibitions against pork and alcohol, it included doctrines quite different from those of traditional Islam. For example, the movement's mysterious founder, Fard, disappeared and was then heralded as an incarnation of God. The Nation of Islam did not preach racial equality and integration. They had a myth that Satan had created the white man. They advocated a separate homeland in order to secure self-determination. Malcolm X had converted to the movement in prison and became a major spokesman. But after a pilgrimage to Mecca, where he experienced a profound fellowship with blond, blue-eyed Slavic Muslims from

After a pilgrimage to Mecca, Malcolm X found it harder to adhere to the doctrines of the Nation of Islam.

Bosnia, he came to see the racist doctrines of the Nation of Islam as heresy. Malcolm was assassinated in 1965, allegedly by gunmen directed by the Nation of Islam leadership. Although the current head of the movement, Louis Farrakhan, has won widespread praise for his Million Man March, his occasional anti-Semitic remarks have left him a controversial figure. Some of the more famous members of this sect (e.g., boxer Muhammed Ali and basketball star Kareem Abdul-Jabbar) have left it and made full conversions to orthodox Islam.

SELF

The orthodox conception of the self began with the notion of creation. In *Sura 96* the self is described essentially as a small thing that God made from a blood clot or a drop of sperm. The essence of Islam and of being a Muslim was to recognize the creator-creature relation: a sovereign God who is completely the Lord of a very insignificant vassal. The basic scriptural message of Islam is complete submission.

This attitude was no false humility. Rather, it was seen as the acceptance of the human condition. Human beings came from God, and their destiny

CASE STUDY: ISLAMIC RITUALS

Yoruba Muslims of West Africa have ritualized their religion for the life cycle, the religious year, and the ordinary week. By studying these rituals, we may glimpse how Islam has adapted itself to such new geographic areas as West Africa and created a syncretism with tribal aspects of religion.

The life cycle of Yoruba Muslims begins on the day they become members of the worshiping community. This may be the day when, as adults, they formally convert to Islam, or the eighth day after their birth, when they receive their name. The major action in the adult conversion ceremony is an ablution, to symbolize the pure life the convert is entering upon. The candidates take off their clothes and don loincloths. The presiding cleric washes each candidate's right hand three times, the left hand three times, the right leg three times, and the left leg three times. Then three times he washes the elbows, blows each one's nose, and washes the ears. Concluding, he pours water on the head and chest of each candidate, who, having been washed and become clean, is a Muslim.

For the naming ceremony of a newborn child, the presiding cleric receives money in a covered dish. The cleric prays for the child, preaches a solemn sermon (often in Arabic), and then gives the child its name. Some West African Muslims also sacrifice a sheep or cut the infant's hair. (The Yoruba Muslims practice male adolescent circumcision, as well as the drawing of tribal marks on the face or body. Apparently Islam did not introduce these customs to Africa but rather gave them a new interpretation.)

The second major stage on the Yoruba Muslim's way is marriage. The presiding cleric must divine that the proposed match is a good one and pray for the marital partners. Before the wedding, the groom has to pay the bride's family several monies and gifts. In modernized West African Muslim rituals, the presiding cleric asks the groom: "Do you take Miss _____ as your wedded wife? Will you love her, honor her, feed her, clothe her, and lodge her in proper lodging?" Then he quotes the *Qur'an* (4:34), to the effect that one of the signs God has given human beings is creating mates for them, that they may find quiet of mind. Putting love and compassion between these mates, God gives reflective people a sign of his goodness and care. The presiding cleric also asks the bride similar questions, including whether she will love, honor, and obey her husband. He repeats most of the quotation from the *Qur'an* and reminds the bride that "the good women are therefore obedient, guarding the unseen as Allah has guarded." The ceremony concludes with prayers to Allah that he bless this wedding. (Most of the West African Muslim community supports the traditional polygyny.)

Funeral rites complete Islam's ritual impact on the Yoruba life cycle. When a person has died, the neighbors come together and dig a grave. They then wash the corpse, repeating the ablutions of the conversion ceremony. They dress the corpse in a white cap, loincloth, and sewn sheet, and then put it into the grave and cover it with earth. The presiding cleric prays for the deceased person, that God may forgive its sins. The dead person's family is expected to pay the cleric handsomely, with food as well as money. Some modernized sects hold a second ceremony, on the eighth day after the burial, with readings from the *Qur'an*, a sermon, and a eulogy of the deceased.

In addition to these three major ceremonies for the life cycle, Yoruba Islam has an annual cycle of feasting and fasting. The cycle begins with the Muslim New Year, which is a day for hearty eating in most sects and for orgiastic nude bathing and mock battles in a few. The New Year festival recalls Noah, who disembarked from the ark very hungry.

The next festivals in the annual cycle are two celebrations of Muhammad, his birthday and the night of his heavenly journey to Jerusalem and Paradise. The more conservative Yoruba Muslims have made much of the Prophet's birthday, using it as an occasion to display their learning. In their circles children act out scenes from the Prophet's life, and those who teach the Qur'an receive special stipends.

The month of Ramadan is the great time of fasting, but many of the Yoruba elderly fast during the month of Rajab as well. The last Friday of Ramadan is especially important, because then one may ask forgiveness for one's laxities in worship during the past year. Among the modernizing Yoruba Muslims the Ramadan ceremonies include the prayer, "O Allah! whom our obedience does not benefit and our disobedience does not harm, please accept from us what does not benefit you, and forgive us what does not harm you."

The two greatest feasts in the Yoruba Muslim calendar are the Feast of the Breaking of the Fast and the Feast of the Immolation. Each entails two days of public holidays in Nigeria. For the Feast of the Breaking of the Fast, worshipers dress elaborately and bring expensive prayer rugs. The ceremony includes an almsgiving, to solemnize gratitude for a successful conclusion to Ramadan, a visit to the ruler of the Yoruba, and a visit to the graves of the first two imams (religious leaders) of the community. The Feast of the Immolation reminds the Yoruba that their fellow Muslims in Arabia are performing this sacrifice in Mecca, as part of their pilgrimage. The immolation itself usually is the sacrifice of a small goat. After the communal ceremony many individuals also sacrifice goats or rams at the entrances to their own houses.

The last feast of the annual cycle is the Hajj, the pilgrimage to Mecca. Since Nigerian independence, the government has supported the pilgrimage, making the Hajj available to the prosperous farmer, shopkeeper, or local leader. If the individual can make an initial outlay of money, he or she usually will receive supplementary gifts from friends. Once the pilgrims return to their local communities, they enjoy great status, since they have been to the center of the Muslim world. Usually the experience of Islam as a worldwide fellowship greatly broadens the Yoruba pilgrim's horizons. Not all Yoruba Muslims have the opportunity to travel to Mecca, but each year at the time of the Hajj all turn their imaginations to the holy city and picture what is taking place there.

In the weekly religious cycle of Yoruba Muslims, Friday is the crowning day, but Wednesday and Thursday also have special significance. The last Wednesday of each lunar month is esteemed as a day of special blessings. All are encouraged to increase their prayers, that they may protect themselves from the evil every month contains. The darkness of the moon at the end of the month is probably the spark for this attitude.

In folk Islam, Wednesday is considered replete with blessings, as is Thursday. Most Yoruba groups have adopted this folk attitude. Thus, most marriages, celebrations of a student's completion of the Qur'an, and groundbreakings occur on Wednesdays or Thursdays. One of the many functions of the Yoruba cleric is to divine an auspicious date for these celebrations. Conservative Muslims, who tend to be better educated, downplay such divinations, and do not attribute any special significance to particular days of the week.

However, Thursday evening has a special significance, because it is the threshold to Friday, the Muslim Sabbath. Indeed, most Yoruba Muslims offer prayers for the dead on Thursday night. A popular tradition says that on Thursday evening God allows the dead to come back to the world and see what is going on. This ties into a Yoruba tradition of leaving gifts for the deceased. If a dead person does not have gifts left for him, he loses prestige among his peers.

A certain conflict between traditional, pre-Muslim notions about the dead and Muslim ideas confuses many Yoruba Muslims. The traditional pictures show the dead existing in a shadowy heaven, where they need the care of those they have left behind. The Muslim doctrines of judgment and resurrection do not square with these pictures, so the status of the dead is rather murky. Some Yoruba Muslims translate resurrection so that it becomes a state much like the old view, but others accept the more orthodox Muslim notion that resurrection is a wondrous event that will occur in the future.

Friday is the center of the weekly cycle, when all good Muslims are supposed to gather at noon in the main mosque for communal worship. In the large towns the mosques are crowded with male worshipers. (A smaller number of women is allowed to worship, segregated from the males, at the back of the mosque.) The service begins with the call to prayer and then has a sermon in the vernacular. Often this "sermon" turns out to be more like a group session of petitionary prayer. People come up to the prayer leaders and whisper their intentions, which "megaphonists" then repeat in a loud voice, so that God and the community at large can hear them. The sermon sometimes amounts to no more than a few moral exhortations tossed in as editorial comments on the prayers people have offered. The people also con-tribute money. After the sermon comes the heart of the Friday service, the communal ritual prayer. Together the group goes through the actions of the fivefold daily prayer—bowing, kneeling, and touching their foreheads to the ground. Muslim prayer is essentially this doing, this performative act.

Through the life cycle, the annual cycle, and the weekly cycle, the great lesson the Yoruba or any other Muslims are learning is the lesson of prostration. Bowing before God, the Almighty, the Muslim deepens her or his sense that only one power is in charge of the world. To be at peace with God is life's greatest accomplishment; to be at war with God is life's greatest tragedy.

depended on living out the pattern that God had in making them. Thus, they had no basis for self-glorification. Thus, the exclamations of an Al-Hallaj, who claimed identification with God (through mystical union), could only sound blasphemous to the majority, who were immersed in the literal text. Between the divine Lord and the human vassal stretched an impassable gulf. However much genuine love might have drawn the spirit up to God, however much God's intimate mercy might have descended toward human flesh, the essential difference in their states remained.

From other Qur'anic accounts of creation one can gather the impression that, despite their lowliness, human beings have a special status among all creatures. In the stories of Adam's creation (for instance, 2:28, 15:29, 32:8), the angels object to God's making human beings, but God forms this first man from clay and water, gives him a most beautiful form, and breathes his spirit into him. Then he makes the angels bow before Adam, for Adam is the first prophet and viceregent on earth, having in this capacity the right and duty to carry out God's orders. Echoing *Genesis*, *Sura* 2:31 speaks of God's teaching Adam the names of all things, which means giving him power over all things, since to control a being's name was to have power over it. The end God had in mind for such a creature, the recompense that He expected, was ado-ration: "We have created men and *jinn* only for adoration" (51:51). God made the earth subject to human control. Along with the doctrine of God's transcendence, this anthropocentricity in creation helped to deemphasize nature.

The traditional view of human nature conceives of the spiritual faculties having several names. The *nafs* was essentially the animal soul, the source of concupiscence (desire). It had the connotation of belonging to the lower part of the personality—to the flesh that incites evil. (Sometimes, though, it just means "self.") The *ruh* was the spirit, come from God, that animates the human body. Muslims often pictured it as a subtle matter that permeates the human body. Reason (*aql*) was the spiritual faculty by which human beings discern right and wrong. Finally, the mystics spoke of the *qalb*—the heart that is the faculty by which one obtains direct knowledge of God.

For some of the Sufis, the doctrine of creation in God's image was crucial. On occasion, NeoPlatonic or gnostic notions colored this doctrine to mean that the soul wanders in exile. It can return to its home, though, if it appropriates secret teaching or learns certain meditative techniques. From the notion of creation in God's image, the Sufis also developed their concept of the perfect man. Usually they applied it to Muhammad, who contained all the divine attributes and served as a microcosm of divinity.

Which scholarly approach to religion offers the best understanding of the history, doctrine, symbols, rituals, mythology, ethics and/or sectification of Islam? You can use any approach this text has covered: Marx, Freud, James, Malinowski, Durkheim, or another.

EXAMPLE: Rudolf Otto (1869–1937) viewed the core of religion as an emotional experience of the "Holy" or sacred. This is a human experience of our own limitations compared to a wholly other reality, force, or identity.

Muhammad had this kind of profound experience, which he described as his visitation by the angel Gabriel. Those followers who observed the Prophet receiving later revelations said that he would go into a trancelike state.

In the rigidly monotheistic doctrine he developed, Muhammad describes the deity, Allah, as something totally beyond any earthly representation: so no statue of wood or metal could be worshipped, and no human of flesh and blood could claim divine status. The trip to Mecca, in which the pilgrim confronts the presence of Allah behind a veiled stone, is the closest that one may come to this otherly power.

The only Muslims who get beyond this entire otherliness of the deity would be the Sufi mystics, who hope to find Allah within themselves through ascetic lives and dancing rituals, but their goal remains an emotional experience of the divine.

Otto also noted that along with reverence for the deity, religion also generates the opposite emotions (disgust, revulsion) for that which is profane, unclean, or polluted. Much of Muhammad's message is concerned with avoiding things that are unclean (e.g., pork) or tend to pollute our behavior (e.g., alcohol, gambling).

Muslim life is an endless series of purification: daily before each of the five prayer sessions, and also before life's great experience, the pilgrimage.

Contribute to this discussion at
http://www.delphi.com/rel101

Islam did not consider man and woman to be laboring under a "fallen" human nature, for Muslims did not regard the sin of Adam and Eve as being contagious or passed on to their offspring. Thus, Islam did not speak of redemption. The Prophet was a revealer or a medium of revelation; he was not a ransom, a victim, or a suffering servant (as Christians had portrayed Jesus). Instead of sin (in the deep sense of alienation from God by irrational actions), Islam tended to stress human forgetfulness (of God's goodness). Human nature was weak—prone to a kind of religious amnesia.

In the Prophet's own conception of human destiny, men and women have a common responsibility to remember God's goodness and to respond by fulfilling his will. Originally, both men and women were to offer prayer and alms; in later times, however, women's status deteriorated, and they did not have this obligation.

Historically, the major theoretical question concerning the self was the relation of human freedom to divine will. At least in the Meccan sections, the *Qur'an* takes human freedom for granted. Muhammad's call and his preaching make no sense without a capacity to respond. Similarly, the scenes of Judgment Day assume that human beings have been responsible for their actions—that they could have done otherwise than they did. However, later Qur'anic passages emphasize God's omnipotence. As a result, the question arises: Does God lead some people astray—or at least leave them in error? In the Umayyad period a group of strict predestinarians (the Jabriya) stressed God's complete control. Opposing them were the Qasriya, who defended human responsibility. A third group, the Mutazilites, defended both human freedom and God's perfect justice. Still another position, that of Al-Ashari, satisfied many people with the following formula: "God creates in man the will to act and the act, and man acquires the act by performing it." The common people frequently behaved as if life was fated—that it was out of their hands. Among the few monistic mystics, human freedom was lost in the divine nature.

CASE STUDY: MUSLIM SAINTS

When we considered the life cycle rituals, the annual rituals, and the weekly rituals of Yoruba Muslims, we glimpsed Islam's accommodation to the West African religious traditions that predated it. We get another glimpse of such cross-cultural accommodation by studying the different ways the different Muslim ethnic groups have conceived sainthood, the peak achievement of Muslim selfhood. For example, the Indonesian Muslims, who have been greatly influenced by Indian culture, have focused their religious imagination on saints whose style is markedly quieter than the style of the saints Moroccan Muslims have venerated. Since Islam starts to come into focus only when one begins to find the unity underlying such differences, let us attempt a comparative study of the Indonesian and Moroccan Muslim saints.

In Indonesian Muslim lore, Sunan Kalidjaga is the most important of the group of nine "apostles" considered to be the founders of Indonesian Islam. Legend has it that he was born the son of a high royal official of Madjapahit, one of the greatest and last of the Indonesian Hindu-Buddhist kingdoms, which dominated most of Eastern Java during the fourteenth and fifteenth centuries. In the sixteenth century Madjapahit declined, caught between the old Hindu-Buddhist order and the new Muslim order that was emerging. Pressured by this change, Kalidjaga moved to the new harbor state of Djapara, where he met another of the early apostles, Sunan Bonang, and was converted to Islam. Later Kalidjaga so greatly influenced Javanese politics that he is credited with Java's having become solidly Muslim. Symbolically, therefore, Kalidjaga serves as a bridge between the old Indic world of god-kings, ritual priests, and Indian shrines and the new Islamic world of pious sultans, Qur'anic scholars, and austere mosques. Indonesians love to contemplate the story of his conversion, for it recapitulates their good fortune in having gained access to the world of God, and it drives home the conviction that Islam is the best flower of the new phase of their history.

When Kalidjaga arrived in Djapara, he was a ne'er-do-well, accomplished in stealing, drinking, whoring, and gambling. So deep were his vices, he stole all his own mother's money, and when he had dissipated this he set out to steal from the public at large. Eventually he became a highwayman of such renown that people were afraid to go to the Djapara market lest they encounter him and lose all their goods. Into this scene strolled Sunan Bonang, a Muslim (probably an Arab) dressed in gorgeous clothes and expensive jewels, and carrying a cane of solid gold. Naturally he attracted the attention of Kalidjaga, who put a knife to his throat and demanded all his finery. But, to Kalidjaga's amazement, Bonang laughed in his face. Calling Kalidjaga by his name (though he had never met Kalidjaga before), Bonang chided him as though he were a little boy: "Don't always be wanting this thing and that thing. Such material desires are pointless. We live but a moment. It is foolish to be attached to worldly goods. Look: there is a whole tree full of money." Kalidjaga turned and saw a banyan tree transformed to gold and hung with jewels. At a stroke, he realized that material things were nothing compared with Bonang's power. What sort of a man must Bonang be, to be able to turn trees into gold and jewels and yet not care about gold and jewels at all? With this thought, Kalidjaga's life of vice repulsed him, and he begged Bonang to teach him spiritual power. Bonang agreed, but he warned Kalidjaga that such teaching was very difficult. Kalidjaga vowed he would persist until death, but Bonang merely told him, "Wait here, by the side of the river, until I return." Then he took his leave.

Kalidjaga waited by the side of the river for forty years, lost in thought. Great trees grew up around him, floods arose and receded, crowds jostled him back and forth, buildings went up and were torn down. Still he waited, lost in thought. Finally Bonang returned, and he saw that Kalidjaga had indeed been steadfast. So instead of teaching Kalidjaga the doctrines of Islam, Bonang simply told him that he had been a good pupil—

indeed, that he had come to surpass Bonang himself. To demonstrate this, Bonang asked Kalidjaga difficult questions about religious matters, and Kalidjaga answered them all correctly. Then Bonang told him to go forth and spread Islam, which Kalidjaga did with unsurpassed effectiveness.

Because he had reformed his life, and penetrated the implications of his reform, Kalidjaga had become a Muslim. When he walked the meditative way that Indian culture had been impressing on Indonesia for centuries, he came out a Muslim—the new holy man forged in the fires of Indonesia's cultural transformation. So the message that was trumpeted whenever the legend of Java's greatest saint was told was that Islam is the obvious expression of the reformed, converted, highly developed religious personality. If one finds the depths of human authenticity, one eventually realizes that the *Qur'an*, the mosques, and the Muslim scholars are human authenticity's best expressions.

The Moroccan saint Sidi Lahsen Lyusi is quite a contrast to Kalidjaga. Lyusi was born into an obscure tribe of shepherds in the Middle Atlas Mountains of Morocco in 1631. Although he probably was of Berber descent, he claimed to be a *sherif*, or direct descendant of Muhammad. Lyusi died in 1691, so the sixty years of his life coincided with the rise of the Alawite dynasty (which still rules today in Rabat, the capital of Morocco) from the chaos of a preceding sectarian strife. Like Kalidjaga's, therefore, Lyusi's sainthood was intimately tied to a difficult time of transition, when people were looking for models of a new social order. However, where Kalidjaga functioned as a miniature of the new harmony that Indonesia sought, Lyusi directly opposed the power he saw rising in his times. Thus Clifford Geertz, whose description of these two saints we are following, characterizes Lyusi's approach as moralistic, in contrast to the aesthetic approach of Kalidjaga.

The chaos of Lyusi's lifetime is sometimes called the Maraboutic Crisis, and it arose after the collapse of the last of the Berber dynasties, the Merinid. A *marabout* is a holy man, and during the Maraboutic Crisis Morocco splintered into different political groups clustered around different holy men. Lyusi wandered from political group to political group, always restless and on the move. When he arrived in Tamgrut, a desert oasis, he encountered the famous Muslim saint Ahmed ben Nasir. Ben Nasir was sick with smallpox, and so he asked his disciples, one by one, to wash out his loathsome nightshirt. Each disciple refused, repelled by the disgusting garment and afraid for his health. Lyusi, who had just arrived and was not known to ben Nasir, approached the saint and volunteered for the job. He took the shirt to a spring, rinsed it, wrung it out, and then drank the foul water it produced. When he returned to the master his eyes were aflame, not with sickness but with what Moroccans call *baraka*: the supernatural power that makes a *marabout*.

The story summarizes the Moroccan notion of sainthood. The main forces at work in Lyusi's transformation into a man of *baraka* were his extraordinary physical courage, his absolute personal loyalty to his "teacher," his moral intensity, and an almost physical passage of sainthood from teacher to disciple. Thus the Moroccan notion of Muslim sainthood seems more energetic than the Indonesian. Whereas Kalidjaga was transformed by forty years of meditation near a river, Lyusi was transformed by a single act of heroic courage. Thirty years after this event, Lyusi had a momentous confrontation with Sultan Mulay Ismail, the great consolidator of the Alawite dynasty. In 1668, the Alawites had put an end to the Maraboutic Crisis and gained power in Morocco. The confrontation took place in the Sultan's new capital of Meknes, and it reveals the delicate relation between strongman politics and Maraboutism that has dominated Moroccan history. The warrior and the saint have been the two basic forms of heroism in Morocco, and this epic confrontation pitted a great warrior against a greater saint.

When Lyusi arrived in Meknes, Mulay Ismail received him as an honored guest. Indeed, he brought Lyusi to the court and made him his spiritual adviser. The sultan was building a large wall around the city and treating the men working on the wall cruelly. When one of the workmen fell from exhaustion and was sealed into the wall, some of the other workers came to Lyusi secretly to complain. Lyusi said nothing, but that night, when his supper was brought to his chamber, he broke all the dishes. He continued to do this, night after night, until all the dishes in the palace were broken.

Eventually the sultan learned what was happening and ordered Lyusi brought to him. When he asked the saint why he was acting so outrageously, the saint asked in return whether it was better to break pottery of clay or the pottery of God (human beings). Then he proceeded to upbraid the sultan for his cruelty to the workers. The sultan was not moved. Lyusi had abused his hospitality (a high crime in Moroccan culture), so he ordered Lyusi out of the city.

Lyusi left the palace and pitched his tent near the wall that was being built. When the sultan asked why the saint had not obeyed the royal order, Lyusi said that he had left the sultan's city and taken up residence in God's city. At this answer the sultan was so enraged that he charged out on horseback. Interrupting the saint's prayers (another high crime), he again asked why the royal order had been disobeyed. Again he received the answer that Lyusi was now in the city of God. Wild with fury, the sultan advanced to kill the saint. But the saint drew a line on the ground, and when the sultan's horse crossed the line, the horse's legs began to sink into the earth. Terrified, the sultan begged mercy and promised that he would reform. Lyusi said he only wanted a decree acknowledging that he was a *sherif*, entitled to the honors of a direct descendant of the Prophet. The sultan gave him this decree and Lyusi left Meknes (fearing for his life) to preach to the Berbers in the Middle Atlas forests.

After his death a great cult developed at his tomb, and he has since been revered as a most powerful *marabout*. In Lyusi Moroccan Islam has found an ideal embodiment of its moral passion, just as in Kalidjaga Indonesian Islam has found an ideal embodiment of its meditative passion.

Compare Islam, point by point, to a nonmonotheistic denomination. Thus, do not pick Judaism, Christianity, the religion of Akhenaton, or Zoroastrianism. You could choose Buddhism, Confucianism, Shinto, Jainism, Hinduism, or the religions of the ancient Egyptians, Mesopotamians, Teutons, Celts, Incas, Mayas, Aztecs, Ainu, Inuits, Aborigines, Africans, Melanesians, Polynesians, or Native Americans.

Contribute to this discussion at
http://www.delphi.com/rel101

ULTIMATE REALITY

Islam is perhaps the most *theocentric* of the major religions. Before Muhammad, some Arabs had spoken of a high god "Allah" who was above the numerous idols. The divine name itself seems to fuse two words: *al-Ilah* ("the God"). It was an attempt to designate an ultimate divinity, a God who was beyond all demigods. From his visionary experience, Muhammad recognized that God is the only divinity, and that his primary designations are "Creator" and "Judge." As such, God leaves no place for other deities to function in either the world's creation or in the destiny of humankind. Islam polished its theocentricity through controversy with polytheistic Arabs and then with Christians committed to the Incarnation and the Trinity.

The Creator made the world in six days (or in a single moment, according to *Sura* 54:50). Muslims trust that he guides the world wisely and unfailingly. God's knowledge of all creatures is total, and his mercy extends to all who acknowledge him. It is God in whose name every work is being begun and upon whose name will every future action depend. Thus, one has to add *"insha Allah"* ("if God wills") to every sentence that refers to a future act or a new direction of thought. To try to indicate God's fullness, the *Qur'an* encircles him with "most beautiful names." He is the First and the Last, the Inward and the Outward. Above all, he is Merciful and Compassionate. He is the All Holy, the Peace, the Light of Heaven and Earth. Transcendent though he be, he is also as near as the jugular pulse. Wherever one turns, there is his Face (the Qur'anic expression for God's essence).

Angels are also essential objects of Muslim doctrine. According to tradition, God created them from light. The *Qur'an* stresses that they are neither children of God nor female beings. They are intelligent and can become visible. From the *Qur'an,* Muslims know Gabriel as the angel of revelation. Israfil will blow the trumpet at Doomsday, and Azrael is the angel of death. Iblis is the fallen angel. Like Harut and Marut, he is a source of evil. Harut and Marut taught humankind witchcraft, but a beautiful woman seduced them and then imprisoned them in a well in Babylonia. Thus, the sacred space between the creature and the Creator has been abuzz with personages of interest.

Many scholars find the negative portion of the creed ("no God but God") very important, since it unequivocally rejects other peoples' gods. As well, it determined that the greatest sin in the Muslim code would be *shirk*—idolatry or "association" (of other objects of worship with God). The mystics sometimes took this to mean that nothing but God exists—that God alone is real. Among modern Muslims, anti-idolatry on occasion has worked against ideologies such as Marxism, capitalism, and nationalism, which some orthodox Muslims find incompatible with pure monotheism. Insofar as such ideologies gain the ultimate concern of many human beings, they amount to new kinds of idolatry.

After Muhammad's death, debates arose about God's nature. At the beginning, the orthodox clung to the letter and imagery of the received text. That meant accepting descriptions of God that gave him a face, hands, and the like. The Mutazilites, who had contact with Hellenistic rationalism, pointed out the dangers latent in such anthropomorphism: When we think of God in human terms, we think of him as finite. Thus, the Mutazilites clung to the absolute unity of God, accepting as a consequence that God cannot be imagined. In other words, they prized God's difference—the gulf that lies between the Creator and everything created. Indeed, to safeguard God's unity, the Mutazilites even questioned the doctrine of the divine attributes (that God has speech,

sight, and so on). For that reason, the orthodox described the Mutazilites as "those who deny the attributes," a charge of heresy. In these debates, Muslims shared with Jews and Christians the consequences of an exposure to Greek reason. They had to ask whether their descriptions of God could be reconciled with what they could infer from the divine transcendence. For instance, they could infer that a Creator would be independent of the world, unlimited, unimaginable in created terms. From that it followed that any picture of God would be at best a useful fiction that might help some people's understanding. As a further extension of such rationalism, the Mutazilites denied that the *Qur'an* is God's uncreated word. To them that would have made it a co-eternal attribute, something ever existent with God. However, calling the *Qur'an* "created" deeply offended the orthodox, for whom the Arabic text expressed a heavenly prototype. The human *Qur'an* was unalterable (which led the orthodox to resist all attempts to translate it from Arabic), because it derived from eternity. Thus, the Mutazilites and the orthodox clashed in their theologies of revelation.

In contrast, the Sufis tended to forego philosophical speculation, favoring instead a personal experience of the divine. For them the profitable way was not reasoning but intuition. Furthermore, the Sufis opposed Qur'anic fundamentalists by proposing that we should obey God out of love. To the fundamentalists, such a personal relationship seemed novel, for they admitted only a relationship of obedience: the Creator commanded and the creature obeyed.

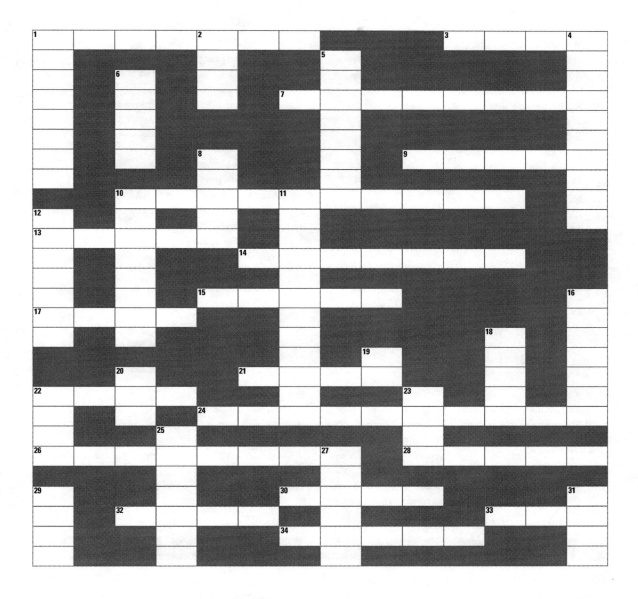

FOLK RELIGION. On the folk level, magical practices mixed with worship. The *Qur'an* gave such practices some foundation by saying that the (bad) angels Harut and Marut taught the Babylonians magic (2:96). Ordinarily, the magician knew formulas that could conjure up the *jinns* or the angels. This has led to an expansion of the ways in which one can imagine the spirits and call them to one's aid. Amulets, reproductions of verses from the *Qur'an,* reproductions of God's names, and so on, are popular expressions of Muslim interest in attaining good luck. Similarly, Muslims continue to dread the "evil eye." To ward off its malignant influence, people constantly intersperse their conversation with "as God wills." As well, they wear amulets or give their children ugly names to keep the evil ones away. Popular religion also retains a considerable interest in astrology and fortune telling. A favorite technique for divining the future is to open the *Qur'an* at random and take the first verse that one's eye falls on as a cipher for what is to come. Other popular methods are reading palms or coffee grounds.

ACROSS

1   Muslims must not drink _____.
3   Muhammed was an _____.
7   Wagering forbidden by Muslim law
9   Muslim doctrine about war
10 Muslims should make a _____ to Mecca.
13 Mulim name for God
14 Followers of Islam
15 Muslim holy book
17 Muslims are supposed to give _____ to the poor.
21 The number of duties for a Muslim is _____.
22 Muslims must not worship an _____.
24 Islam has this doctrine of God.
26 The final Prophet; recited the Qur'an
28 Muhammad received the Qur'an from the _____ Gabriel.
30 Islamic mystic; ritual dancing of whirling dervish
32 Muslims may not eat this meat.
33 Boxer Muhammed _____ converted to Islam.
34 Muslim pilgrimage site

DOWN

1   Muslim theologian
2   Arabic word for pilgrimage
4   Populous Muslim country east of India
5   Muslim theologian, Al- _____
6   Tolerant religion arising in Iran in the ninteenth century
8   Muslims must pray only to _____.
10 Muhammad limited _____ to four wives.
11 What will happen on judgment day
12 Period of fasting
16 Muhammad was not a priest; he was a _____.
18 Major sect of Islam in Arab world
19 Muhammad lived around 600 _____.
20 Islam began around _____ C.E.
22 Iranian living prophet
23 Iranian sect of Islam
25 African-American Muslim, _____ X, advocated equality.
27 Lebanese Muslim group that does not accept converts
29 During Ramadan, Muslims must _____.
31 Synthesis of Islam and Hinduism by Nanak in India

Sacrifice also has a place in Muslim worship of God. Those who can afford it immolate a sheep on the Day of Slaughtering during the annual pilgrimage to Mecca. This sacrifice is in memory of Abraham, who was willing to sacrifice his son Ishmael. People also make votive offerings—cocks, sheep, and so on—at holy places such as the tombs of saints. The animal should be slaughtered ritually, by cutting its jugular vein and its trachea in one stroke; tradition recommends giving it to the poor. Finally, sacrifice is appropriate on almost any important occasion, such as starting construction of a house, celebrating a child's birthday, or expiating an offense.

SUMMARY: THE MUSLIM CENTER

God is certainly the Muslim center, and because the *Qur'an* is the definite expression of God, the *Qur'an* is the central place where the invisible Muslim God has become visible. How, then, does the *Qur'an* portray the Lord of the Worlds, the most ultimate and holy Muslim reality? It portrays him majestically, as a sovereign beyond compare, a power nothing earthly can approach. When God commands, the heavens thunder and the earth quakes. When God consoles, the winds quiet and the soul feels bliss. Were God not compassionate, merciful, life would be utterly terrifying. He is a severe judge, and none can abide the day of his coming. Yet he has sent prophets to warn humanity of his coming, has reset the strict boundaries of his laws. Muhammad is the seal of these prophets, in whom their work has come to complete fulfillment. As there is no God but God, so there is no final prophet but Muhammad.

BUDDHISM

BUDDHISM: TWENTY-FIVE KEY DATES	
Date	**Event**
563–476 B.C.E.	life of Siddhartha Gautama Sakya, the Buddha
519 B.C.E.	Gautama's enlightenment
473 B.C.E.	first Buddhist Congress
363 B.C.E.	second Buddhist Congress
273–236 B.C.E.	reign of Buddhist Emperor Asoka
236 B.C.E.	rise of Mahayana Tradition
160 B.C.E.	*Prajna-paramita* Literature
80 B.C.E.	*Lotus Sutra*
ca. 200 C.E.	Nagarjuna, leading philosopher
220–552 C.E.	Vietnam, China, Korea, Java, Sumatra, Japan missions
430 C.E.	Buddhaghosa, leading philosopher
594 C.E.	Buddhism proclaimed Japanese state religion
749 C.E.	first Buddhist monastery in Tibet
805–806 C.E.	foundation of Tendai and Shingon sects in Japan
845 C.E.	persecution of Chinese Buddhists
1065 C.E.	Hindu invasions of Sri Lanka
1175 C.E.	Honen; Japanese Pure Land Buddhism
1193–1227 C.E.	rise of Japanese Zen sects
1260–1368 C.E.	Tibetan Buddhism influential in China
1360 C.E.	Buddhism becomes state religion in Thailand
1543–1588 C.E.	final conversion of Mongols
1603 C.E.	Tokugawa government dominates Japanese Buddhism
1646–1694 C.E.	Basho, great Japanese Buddhist poet
1868–1871 C.E.	Meiji persecution of Buddhism in Japan
1954–1956 C.E.	sixth Buddhist council in Rangoon, Burma

HISTORY

OVERVIEW

The term **Buddhism** derives from Western scholarly efforts to organize the movements, ideas, and practices that appear to have been spawned by a mystic who founded this religion, a man who bears the title of the Buddha (ca. 563–476 B.C.E.). As well, it covers the diverse acts and thinking of followers of the Buddha, who spread this religion from India throughout Asia and recently have established roots on other continents. Buddhism is the world's first great **proselytizing** religion that became transnational: starting in India and spreading east to the other nations of Asia. Coming from Axial Age India, Buddhism simply shared the assumptions of the Jains and the Upanishads: that earthly existence was a sorrowful cycle perpetuated by rebirths (transmigration) and influenced by the deeds and thoughts of this life (karma) and the need to employ meditation to seek a release. Wherever Buddhism went, it blended with local traditions, modifying the doctrines of karma and transmigration and the practice of meditation, creating a diversity of syncretism.

THE BUDDHA

The man who would later become known as the Buddha was born about 536 B.C.E. outside the town of Kapilavastu in what is now a part of Nepal just below the Himalayan foothills. His people were a warrior tribe called **Sakya** (sometimes spelled *Shakya*) and his clan name was **Gautama**. His given name was **Siddhartha**, so his complete name was Siddhartha Gautama Sakya, and he might be referred to by any of those names (or **Sakyamuni**, as the Japanese termed him) or just the **Buddha**, a term meaning the Enlightened One. Unlike Christianity, which has only one figure who bears the title of Christ (Jesus), Buddhist sects may recognize other Buddhas. Some were mythological figures of the past; others were real people who dedicated their lives to good works and meditation (and therefore earned the title of Buddha) or future Messiahs who would come and end the evil age of a deteriorating society.

The religious climate in which Gautama grew up was quite heated. Some objectors were challenging the dominance of the priestly Brahmin class. As we saw in the chapter on India, there was dissatisfaction with sacrifice burning among intellectuals, while the accounts of the *Mahavira* are evidence of the ascetic movement that also challenged the priestly religion of sacrifice. In secular culture, the sixth century B.C.E. saw a movement from tribal rule toward small-scale monarchy, a growth in urban populations, the beginnings of money-based economies, the beginnings of government bureaucracies, and the rise of a wealthy merchant class. Thus, the Buddha came of age in a time of rapid change, when people were in turmoil over religion and open to new teachings.

Myth heavily embellishes the accounts of Gautama's birth and early life, so it is difficult to describe this period with historical validity. One legend describes his birth as follows: he came out of his mother's side without causing her any pain, stood up, strode seven paces, and announced, "No more births for me!" In other words, the child would conquer the cycle of death and rebirth and would be an Enlightened One.

As Gautama grew, his father surrounded him with pleasures and distractions to keep him in the palace and away from the sights of ordinary life. When Gautama came of age, the father married him to a lovely woman. So Sakyamuni ("sage of the Sakyas") lived in relative contentment until his late twenties. By the time of his own son's birth, however, Gautama (the future Buddha) was restless; he named the child Rahula (fetter). What really precipitated Sakyamuni's religious crisis, though, were experiences he had outside the palace. On several outings he witnessed examples of old age, disease, and death. They shocked him severely, and he became anxiety ridden. How could anyone take life lightly if these were its constant dangers? Meditating on age, disease, and death, the young prince decided to cast away his round of pleasures and solve the riddle of life's ultimate relevance by becoming a wandering beggar concerned only to gain enlightenment.

Renouncing his wife, child, father, and goods, he set off to answer his soul's yearning. (Indian tradition allowed renouncing the world after one had begotten a son.) The teachers to whom Gautama first apprenticed himself when he started wandering in pursuit of enlightenment specialized in meditation and asceticism. Their meditation, it appears, was a yogic pursuit of enlightenment through *samadhi* (trance). From them Gautama learned much about the levels of consciousness but was not fully satisfied. The teachers could not bring him to dispassion, tranquillity, enlightenment, or **nirvana** (a state of liberation beyond *samsara*). In other words, he wanted a mystical experience, a direct perception of how things are, necessitating a complete break with the realm of space, time, and rebirth. He sensed that to defeat age, disease, and death he had to go beyond ordinary humanity and tap the power of something greater.

Gautama spent about seven years on this spiritual quest before he found Enlightenment. First, Sakyamuni turned to asceticism—so much so that he almost starved himself. The texts claim that when he touched his navel, he could feel his backbone. In any event, asceticism did not bring what Sakyamuni sought either.

Because of this, he and his followers have always urged moderation in fasting and bodily disciplines. Theirs, they like to say, is a **Middle Way** between indulgence and severity that strives to keep the body healthy, as a valuable ally should be, and to keep the personality from excessive self-concern. From our perspective of material luxury and comfort, the life of

COMPARISON OF SECTS FROM INDIA					
DIMENSION	*UPANISHADS*	JAINISM	*BHAGAVAD GITA*	TANTRISM	BUDDHISM
Date	800–400 B.C.E.	500 B.C.E.	400 B.C.E.–200 C.E.	1000 C.E.	500 B.C.E.
Persons		Mahavira	Arjuna (fictional)		Gautama
Mysticism	yes	yes	tolerated	Using sexual symbolism	yes
Asceticism	yes	yes, extremely	tolerated	rejected	yes, but limited
Caste	tolerated	rejected at first	advocated	ignored	rejected
Karma	accepted	accepted	accepted	ignored	accepted
Trans-migration	accepted	accepted	accepted	ignored	accepted
Reality	monistic	dualistic	duty of caste	symbolic	
Deity	Brahman	atheistic	theistic	paramour	ignored

a Buddhist monk must seem quite ascetic, but the Buddhists were comparing themselves with much stricter zealous Hindus, who would sleep on a bed of nails, or dedicated Jains, who would sit in meditative postures until their limbs atrophied.

According to the traditional accounts, Gautama's enlightenment (mystical experience) came after he sat under a tree and meditated for forty days. At that point, he became the Buddha (Enlightened One). One symbol used in the mythical account of this experience is that of Mara, the personification of evil or death, who tried to tempt Buddha away from his pursuit. First, he sent a host of demons, but the Buddha's merit and love protected him. Then, with increased fear that this man sitting so determinedly might escape his realm, the evil one invoked his own power. However, when Mara called on his retinue of demons to witness to his power, the Buddha, who was alone, called on mother earth, which quaked in acknowledgment. As a last ploy, Mara commissioned his three daughters (Discontent, Delight, and Desire) to seduce the sage. But they, too, failed, and so Mara withdrew.

ENLIGHTENMENT. The experience of enlightenment can be conceived as the realization of pure ultimate relevance. According to tradition, Buddha had his experience on a night of the full moon. Buddha ascended the four stages of trance (a progressive clarification of consciousness): (1) detachment from sense objects and calming the passions; (2) nonreasoning and "simple" concentration; (3) dispassionate mindfulness and consciousness with bodily bliss; and (4) pure awareness and peace without pain, elation, or depression.

Another traditional way of describing the Buddha's enlightenment is to trace his progress through the night. During the first watch (evening), he acquired knowledge of his previous lives. This is a power that some shamans claim, so it is not Buddha's distinguishing achievement. During the second watch (midnight), he acquired the "divine eye" with which he surveyed the karmic state of all beings—the cycle of dying and rebirth that is their destiny. With this vision he realized that good deeds beget good karma and move one toward freedom from *samsara*, while bad deeds beget bad karma and a deeper entrenchment in *samsara.* This second achievement made Buddha a moralistic philosopher, one who saw the condition of all beings as a function of their ethical or unethical behavior.

During the third watch (late night), the Buddha reached the peak of perception, attaining "the extinction of the outflows" (the stopping of desire for samsaric existence) and grasping the essence of what became the **Four Noble Truths:** (1) All life is suffering; (2) the cause of suffering is desire; (3) stopping desire will stop suffering; and (4) the Eightfold Path (explained below) is the best way to stop desire.

The **Eightfold Path** outlines the lifestyle that Buddha developed for people who accepted his teaching and wanted to pursue nirvana. As such, it is more detailed than a description of what he had directly experienced in enlightenment—something that he probably elaborated later on. The explanation of reality that Buddha developed out of his experience of enlightenment, which became known as the doctrine of *Dependent Co-arising,* also came later. It explains the connections that link all beings. Beings not only depend on one another in what might be called a field of relations, they also arise (come into being) together, thus the "co" in co-arising.

Enlightenment seems to have been the dramatic experience of vividly perceiving that life, which Sakyamuni had found to consist of suffering, had a solution. One could escape the terror of aging, sickness, and death by withdrawing one's concerns for or anxieties about them—by no longer desiring youth, health, or even life itself. By withdrawing in this manner, one could lessen the bad effects of karma, since desire was the means by which karma kept the personality on the wheel of dying and rebirth. Removing desire therefore took away karma's poison. To destroy desire for karmic existence, though, one had to penetrate and remove the illusion of its goodness. That is, one had to remove the ignorance that makes sensual pleasures—financial success, prestige, and so on—seem good. Buddha designed the Eightfold Path and the doctrine of Dependent Co-arising to remove such ignorance and rout desire.

The picture of the Buddha sitting in repose after having gained enlightenment has always been a great consolation to his followers. With the pictures and stories about his kindness as a teacher, his affection for his disciples, his wisdom in instructing kings, and

BUDDHISM BY THE NUMBERS	
3 Jewels	• the Buddha • the Dharma • the Sangha (monastery)
3 Pillars (main concerns)	• wisdom • morality • meditation
3 Marks of All Reality	• painful • fleeting • selfless
4 Noble Truths	• All life is suffering. • The cause of suffering is desire. • We must remove desire to end suffering. • Desire can be removed by the Eightfold Path.
5 Ethical Principals	• Do not kill. • Do not lie. • Do not steal. • Do not have sex outside marriage. • Do not take intoxicants.
8-fold Path	• right views • right intension • right speech • right action • right livelihood • right effort • right mindfulness • right concentration

the like, it has given the Buddha the human qualities most followers of a religious leader seem to need if they are to follow the path with enthusiasm. The general rule seems to be that followers must love the leader if they are to love the path. Admiring the clarity of the leader's teaching and experiencing the benefits of the path are not enough. The leader inevitably becomes the model, the prime evidence, the vindication that the teaching indeed is wholly wise, that the path in fact is fully efficacious. Students did not find his **detachment** something cold and forbidding. They found it just the far side of the **compas-**

sion, the kindness, the charm that made him seem to reach into their very beings and loosen the bonds in which ignorance and fear had kept them tied. These became the central yet polar virtues of Buddha, and the challenge to his followers was to balance the two: to have detachment from the sufferings of the world, yet have enough compassion to stay in the world and minister to those who yet suffer.

THE DHARMA (BUDDHIST DOCTRINE)

Buddhists have seen in Sakyamuni's enlightenment the great act centering their religion. The Buddha is worthy of following because in enlightenment he became shining with knowledge (*bodhi*). What he saw under the *bodhi* tree in the third watch was nothing less than the formula for measuring life and curing its mortal illness. The Four Noble Truths and Dependent Co-arising are two favorite ways of presenting the essential truths of Buddha's knowledge.

DEPENDENT CO-ARISING AND THE EIGHTFOLD PATH. Often Buddhists picture the doctrine of Dependent Co-arising, which provides their basic picture of reality, as a **wheel** with twelve sections or a chain with twelve links (the first and the last are joined to make a circuit). These twelve links explain the round of samsaric existence. They are not an abstract teaching for the edification of the philosophical mind, but an extension of the essentially therapeutic analysis that the Buddha thought could cure people of their basic illness.

The wheel of Dependent Co-arising turns in this way: (1) Aging and dying depend on rebirth; (2) rebirth depends on becoming; (3) becoming depends on the appropriation of certain necessary materials; (4) appropriation depends on desire for such materials; (5) desire depends on feeling; (6) feeling depends on contact with material reality; (7) contact depends on the senses; (8) the senses depend on "name" (the mind) and "form" (the body); (9) name and form depend on consciousness (the spark of sentient life); (10) consciousness shapes itself by *samsara*; (11) the *samsara* causing rebirth depends on ignorance of the Four Noble Truths; and (12) therefore, the basic cause of *samsara* is ignorance.

One can run this series forward and back, but the important concept is that ignorance (of the Four No-

ble Truths) is the cause of painful human existence, and aging and dying are both its final overwhelming effects and the most vivid aspects of *samsara*. Thus, the chain of Dependent Co-arising is a sort of practical analysis of human existence. It is coordinated influences—of how the basic factors shaping reality impact on one another. This chain straddles what we might call the physical and the moral realms, linking desire with death and rebirth but also specifying how desire works through the senses and intellect.

In the Buddha's enlightenment, as he and his followers elaborated it, there is no single cause of the way things are. Rather, all things are continually rotating in this twelve-stage wheel of existence. Each stage of the wheel passes the power of movement along to the next. The only way to step off the wheel, to break the chain, is to gain enlightenment and so detach the stage of ignorance. If we do detach ignorance, we stand free of karma, karmic consciousness, and so on, all the way to aging and rebirth.

The result of enlightenment, then, is no rebirth. **Nirvana** is the state in which the chain of existence does not obtain—in which desire ceases and one escapes karma and *samsara*. A good metaphor for the Buddhist conception of transmigration and nirvana is that a flame (one's life) can be passed from one candle (existence in a body) to another. Nirvana occurs when the flame is blown out. Thus, nirvana begins with enlightenment and becomes definitive with death. By his enlightenment, for instance, the Buddha had broken the chain of Dependent Co-arising; at his death his nirvana freed him from rebirths.

The Eightfold Path (which is the Fourth Noble Truth) details how we may dispel ignorance and gain nirvana by describing a middle way between sensuality and extreme asceticism that consists of (1) right views, (2) right intention, (3) right speech, (4) right action, (5) right livelihood, (6) right effort, (7) right mindfulness, and (8) right concentration. *Right views* means knowledge of the Four Noble Truths. *Right intention* means dispassion, benevolence, and refusal to injure others. *Right speech* means no lying, slander, abuse, or idle talk. *Right action* means not taking life, stealing, or being sexually disordered. *Right livelihood* is an occupation that does not harm living things; thus, butchers, hunters, fishers, and sellers of weapons or liquor are proscribed. *Right effort* avoids the arising of evil thoughts. In *right mindfulness,* awareness is disciplined so that it focuses on an object or idea to know its essential reality. *Right concentration* focuses on a worthy object of meditation.

The first two aspects of the Eightfold Path, right views and right intention, comprise the wisdom portion of the Buddhist program. If we know the Four Noble Truths and orient ourselves toward them with the right spiritual disposition, we are wise and come to religious peace. Tradition groups aspects three, four, and five under morality. To speak, to act, and to make one's living in wise ways amount to an ethics for nirvana, a morality that will liberate one from suffering. Finally, aspects six, seven, and eight entail meditation. By setting consciousness correctly through right effort, mindfulness, and concentration, one can perceive the structures of reality and thus personally vindicate the Buddha's enlightened understanding.

The three divisions of the Eightfold Path compose a single entity, a program in which each of the three parts reinforces the other two. Wisdom sets up the game plan, the basic theory of what the human condition is and how one is to cope with it. Morality applies wisdom to daily life by specifying how one should speak, act, and support oneself. Regular meditation focuses one on the primary points and the reality to which they apply. In meditation the Buddhist personally appropriates the official wisdom, personally examines the ethical life. As a result, meditation builds up the Buddhist's spiritual force, encouraging the peaceful disposition necessary for a person to be nonviolent and kindly.

THE BUDDHA'S PREACHING. Buddha himself apparently debated what to do after achieving enlightenment. On one hand, he had this potent medicine, to dispense as a cure for humanity's greatest suffering. On the other hand, there was dreary evidence that humanity, mired in its attachments, would find his teaching hard to comprehend and accept. Out of compassion (which became the premier Buddhist virtue), the Enlightened One finally agreed to teach. According to tradition, his first sermon occurred in Deer Park near Benares, about five days' walk from where enlightenment took place. He preached first to some former ascetic companions who had rejected him when he turned away from their harsh mortification,

and his calm bearing won them over. What Buddha first preached was the Four Noble Truths, but he apparently prefaced his preaching with a solemn declaration of his authority as an immortal enlightened one. From this preface Buddhists have concluded that one must offer the authority behind the dharma (the teaching) if the dharma is to have its intended effect.

Let us imagine that we are listening to his famous Fire Sermon, preached after the sermon in Deer Park.

O priests, [monks], all things are on fire. The eye is on fire, as are the forms the eye receives, the consciousness the eye raises, the impressions the eye transmits, the sensations—pleasant, unpleasant, or indifferent—that the eye's impressions produce. All that has to do with our seeing is on fire. And in what does this fire consist? It consists in the flame of passion, the burning of hate, the heat of infatuation. Birth, old age, death, sorrow, lamentation, misery, grief, and despair are all expressions of the fire that comes into us through our eyes.

In the same way, the ear is on fire with burning sounds. The nose is on fire with burning odors. The tongue is on fire with flaming tastes. The whole body is on fire with flaming touches. Even worse, the mind is on fire; hot ideas, burning awareness, searing impressions, smoldering sensations. Again I say, the fire of passion, birth, old age, death, sorrow, lamentation, misery, grief, and despair is burning you up.

What, then, should you do? If you are wise, O priests, you will conceive an aversion for the eye and the eye's forms, the eye's consciousness, the eye's impressions, and the eye's sensations, be they pleasant, unpleasant, or indifferent. If you are wise, you will conceive an aversion for the ear and its sounds, the nose and its odors, the tongue and its tastes, the body and the things it touches, the mind and all that passes through it.

If you conceive this aversion, you will divest yourselves of passion. Divesting yourselves of passion, you will become free. Being free, you will become aware of your liberation and know that you have exhausted rebirth. This will prove that you have lived the holy life, fulfilled what it behooved you to do, and made yourselves subject to this world no longer.

When the Buddha finished his sermon, many of the monks' minds became free from attachment and they were delivered of their depravities. This set them on a path toward the heights of meditation where they might defeat the problem of suffering by understanding the illusions on which it feeds.

Can we appreciate the relevance of the Fire Sermon across 2,500 years? We are still possessed of eyes, ears, nose, tongue, and hands eager to touch. We are still the strange animals possessed of minds flowing with ideas, reflex awareness, sensations to drive our days and bedevil our nights. As with the Buddha's contemporaries, unless we have these faculties under control, we are burning with useless passions. Look around you. See how many of your contemporaries rush after money. Others rush after pleasure. A third group hustles to gain power. From dawn to midnight, their brains teem with schemes, images of success, numbers adding up to bigger and bigger bank accounts. Do they not seem feverish? Is there not within them a fire wisdom would have to douse?

The Buddha's preaching won him innumerable converts, men and women alike, many of whom decided to dedicate their lives to following him and his way. A great number entered the sangha (a monastic order) as monks and nuns, assuming a life of celibacy, poverty, and submission to rules of discipline. Other followers decided to practice the dharma while remaining in their lay state, and they frequently gave the Buddha and the Buddhist community land and money. In both cases people became Buddhists by taking "refuge" in the three jewels of the Enlightened One's religion: the Buddha himself, the teaching (dharma), and the community (sangha can mean either the monastic community or the entire community of Buddhists, lay and monastic, past and present). By uttering three times the vow of taking refuge, one became a follower in a strict, official sense.

BUDDHIST CATECHETICS. In time a catechism developed to explain the Buddha's teaching. One of the catechism's most important notions was the "three marks" of reality. The first mark is that all life or reality is painful: the reality of suffering. By this Buddhists do not mean that one never experiences pleasant things or that one has no joy. Rather, they mean that no matter how pleasant or joyous one's life, it is bound to include disappointment, sickness, misunderstanding, and finally death. Since the joyous

things do not last, even they have an aspect of painfulness.

Second, all life is fleeting, or passing. Everything changes—nothing stays the same. Therefore, realistically there is nothing to which we can cling, nothing that we can rely on absolutely. In fact, even our own realities (our "selves") change. On one level, we move through the life cycle from youth to old age. On a more subtle level, our thoughts, our convictions, and our emotions change.

Third, there is no self. For Buddhists, the fleetingness of our own consciousness proves that there is no Atman—no solid soul or self. In this the Buddhists directly opposed Hinduism. All people, it seems, naturally think that they have personal identities. Buddhists claim that personalities consist of nothing solid or permanent. We are but packages of physical and mental stuff that is temporarily bound together in our present proportions.

The tradition calls the component parts of all things, which number five: body, feeling, conception, karmic disposition, and consciousness. Together these *skandhas* make the world and the person of appearances, and they also constitute the basis for clinging to existence and rebirth. To cut through the illusion of a (solid) self—Buddhists do not deny that we have (changing) identities—is therefore the most important blow that one can strike against ignorance. This is done by being open to the flowing character of all life and decisively pursuing nirvana.

The early teachers described the realms of rebirth to which humans were subject and in so doing developed a Buddhist version of the Indian cosmic powers and zones of the afterlife. Essentially, the Buddhist wheel of rebirth focuses on six realms or destinies. Three are lower realms, which are karmic punishment for bad deeds. The other three are higher realms in which good deeds are rewarded. The lowest realm is for punishing the wicked by means befitting their particular crimes. However, these punishments are not eternal; after individuals have paid their karmic debt, they can reenter the human realm by rebirth. Above the lowest realm is the station of the "hungry ghosts," who wander the earth's surface begging for food. The third and least severe realm of the wicked is that of animals. If one is reborn in that realm, one suffers the abuses endured by dumb beasts.

The fortunate destinies reward good karma. The human realm is the first, and in it one can perform meritorious deeds. Only in the human realm can one become a buddha. The two final realms are those of the demigods (Titans) and the gods proper. Both include a variety of beings, all of whom are subject to rebirth. Since even the Buddhist gods are subject to rebirth, their happiness is not at all comparable to the final nirvana. Better to be a human being advancing toward enlightenment than a divinity liable to the pains of another transmigratory cycle. Perhaps for that reason, the Buddhist spirits and divinities, as well as the Buddhist ghosts and demons, seem inferior to the human being. Apparently Buddhism adopted wicked and good spirits from Indian culture without much thought. In subjecting these spirits to the powers of an *arhat* (another term for a buddha, one who achieves nirvana), however, Buddhists minimized their fearsomeness.

Despite its sometimes lurid description of the six realms, the dharma basically stated that each individual is responsible for his or her own destiny. The future is neither accidental, fated, nor determined by the gods. If one has a strong will to achieve salvation, a day of final triumph will surely come. As a result, karma is less an enslavement than an encouragement. If one strives to do good deeds (to live by the dharma in wisdom-morality-meditation), one cannot fail to progress toward freedom. At the least, one will come to life again in more favorable circumstances. Thus, Buddhism ousts the gods and the fates from control over human destiny. This is interesting sociologically, because Buddhism has been most appealing to people who have wanted control over their own lives, such as warriors and merchants. The simpler folk, who might have had to spur themselves to such a sober and confident state of mind, drew encouragement from Buddhist art, which illustrates the delights of heaven and the torments of hell. Many renditions of the wheel of life, for instance, show Mara (Death) devouring the material world and those who cling to it. In the center of the wheel are such symbolic animals as the cock (desire), the snake (hatred), and the pig (delusion), who work to keep the wheel turning.

The dharma, therefore, began as a proclamation of diagnosis and cure. Likening himself to a doctor, the Buddha told his followers not to lose themselves in extraneous questions about where karma or igno-

Original Buddhism was a simple religion:

DOCTRINE: Life is suffering, suffering is caused by desire, desire can only be controlled by a life structured around meditation.

MYTH: The life of the Buddha: a man who meditated, found enlightenment, shared it with others

RITUAL: Meditation

ETHICS: Do not kill, do not steal, do not lie, do not take intoxicants, do not commit sex outside of marriage

Which aspects of Buddhism could you accept?

Which would you reject?

Contribute to this discussion at http://www.delphi.com/rel101

rance comes from. Furthermore, he told them not to concentrate on whether the world is eternal or how to conceive of nirvana. To ponder such issues, said the Buddha, would be like a man severely wounded with an arrow who refuses treatment until he knows the caste and character of the man who shot him. The point is to get the arrow out. Similarly, the point to human existence is to break the wheel of rebirth, to slay the monstrous round of suffering, fleetingness, and emptiness.

For about forty-five years after his enlightenment, the Buddha preached variants on his basic themes: the Four Noble Truths, Dependent Co-arising, and the three marks. His sangha grew, as monks, nuns, and laypeople responded to his simple, clear message. He had to suffer painful threats to the unity of his group, but on the whole he did his work in peace. At his death he had laid the essential foundation of Buddhism—its basic doctrine and way of life. Thus, his death came in the peace of trance. When he asked his followers for the last time whether they had any questions, all stood silent. So he passed into trance and out of this painful realm. According to legend, the earth quaked and the sky thundered in final tribute.

EARLY BUDDHISM

After the Buddha's death his followers gathered to organize the dharma (which for some centuries remained largely oral) in part because he had said it lyze reality by correlating the Buddha's teaching with the experiences of meditation. Therefore, the Buddhist goal in forming a canon of scripture was to establish an authoritative standard by which to measure doctrine and ethics.

However, within a hundred years of the Buddha's death, dissensions split the movement. These were the precursors of the major division of Buddhism into the Theravada and Mahayana schools, which we consider below. The apparent forerunners of the Mahayana schools were the Mahasanghikas, who seem to have considered the monastic rules adaptable, while the Sthaviras (Elders), the precursors of the Theravadins, stressed the importance of the letter of the monastic code. About two hundred years after the Buddha's death, the Pudgalavadins branched off from the Sthaviras. They taught that there is a person or self (neither identical with the *skandhas* nor separate from them) that is the basis of knowledge, transmigration, and entrance into nirvana. These first schisms prefigured later Buddhist history. New schools have constantly arisen as new insights or problems made old views unacceptable. As a result, the sangha has not been a centralized authority and Buddhism has not kept a full unity. Nonetheless, the sangha has given all Buddhists certain essential teachings (almost all sects would agree to what we have expounded of dharma so far). Also, it has fostered a very influential monastic life. The monastic order, which has always been the heart of Buddhism (monks have tended to take precedence over laity as an almost unquestioned law of nature), has been a source of stability in Buddhism.

Head of Buddha from 3rd century C.E., *found in Afghanistan. Some of the largest stone statues of the Buddha in Afghanistan were destroyed in March of 2001 by the Taliban, a group of Muslims who declared that the statues were idols to be smashed.*

should be their leader after him. According to tradition, they held a council of monks to settle both the dharma and the monastic rules. The canon of Buddhist scriptures that we now possess supposedly is the fruit of this council. This is the three baskets of law, the *Tipitaka* (the authoritative collection of materials also known as the *Pali canon* because it was written in the Indian vernacular derived from Sanskrit). It consists of five collections of discourses (*sutras*) that the Buddha supposedly preached. Just one of these collections runs to 1,100 pages in modern printing.

In addition to these sutras and the monastic rules, early Buddhists added to the canon the *Abhidhamma* treatises of the early philosophers, who tried to ana-

MONASTICISM. A major influence on the Buddhist monastic routine has been Buddha's own life. This routine became a model for the monks: rise at daybreak, wash, and then sit in meditation until it was time to go begging for food. Usually devout laity would invite him in, and after eating lightly he would teach them the dharma. Then he would return to his residence, wash, and rest. After this he would preach to the monks and respond to their requests for individual guidance. After another rest he would preach to the laity and then take a cool bath. Originally the monks always wandered except during the rainy season, but later they assumed a more stable setting with quiet lands and a few simple buildings.

The four misdeeds that merited expulsion from the order were fornication, theft, killing, and "falsely claiming spiritual attainments." (This last rule implied that one was not to go around trying to impress people by working miracles or performing divination.) Committing any of thirteen lesser misdeeds led to a group meeting of the sangha and probation. They included sexual offenses (touching a woman, speaking suggestively to a woman, urging a woman to gain merit by submitting to a "man of religion," and serving as a procurer), violating the rules that limited the size and specified the site of a monk's dwelling, falsely accusing other monks of grievous violations of the rule, fomenting discord among the monks, or causing a schism. With appropriate changes, similar rules have governed the nuns' lives. There are hundreds of other things that monks and nuns cannot do, and all of them suggest something about the ideals of the sangha. Prohibitions against lying, slander, stealing another's sleeping space, and "sporting in the water" testify to an ideal of honest and direct speech, mutual consideration, and grave decorum. Similarly, prohibitions against digging in the ground and practicing agriculture reflect the ideals of not taking other creatures lives and of begging one's food. Rules for good posture and table manners indicate that an ideal monk stood erect, kept his eyes downcast, refrained from loud laughter, and not smacked his lips, talked with his mouth full, or thrown food into his mouth. The refined monk also cannot excrete while standing up or excrete onto growing grass or into the water. Finally, he is not supposed to preach the dharma to monks or laypeople who carry parasols, staffs, swords, or other weapons, or wear slippers, sandals, turbans, or other head coverings.

The sangha accepted recruits from all social classes, and many of them were youths. From this circumstance one can understand the concern for the rights of the growing grass and the water. Monks often carried their two principal fears (of taking life or being sexually incontinent) to extremes. Especially regarding matters of sex, the monastic legislation was quite strict.

THE LAITY. From earliest times, Buddhism encouraged its laity to pursue an arduous religious life. Though his or her white robe never merited the honor that a monk's saffron-colored robe received, a layperson who had taken refuge in the Three Jewels and contributed to the sangha's support was an honorable follower. From early times Buddhism has specified morality for the laity in five precepts. The first of these is to refrain from killing living beings. A vegetarian diet was preferred but not always followed. Unintentional killing is not an offense, and agriculturalists have only to minimize their damage to life. The second is to refrain from stealing. The third precept deals with sexual matters. It forbids intercourse with another person's wife, a nun, or a woman betrothed to another man. It also urges restraint with a wife who is pregnant, nursing, or under a religious vow of sexual abstinence. Apparently relations with courtesans were licit. The commentators' explanation of this precept assumes that it is the male's duty to provide control in sexual matters (because females are by nature wanton). The fourth precept imposes restraint from lying, and the fifth precept forbids drinking alcoholic beverages.

This ethical code has been the layperson's chief focus. Occasionally he or she received instruction in meditation or the doctrine of wisdom, and later Mahayana sects considered the laity fully capable of reaching nirvana. (In the beginning only monks were so considered; nuns never had the status of monks, in part because of legends that the Buddha established nunneries only reluctantly.) The principal lay virtues were to be generous in supporting monks and to witness to Buddhist values in the world. The financial support, obviously enough, was a two-edged sword. Monks who put on spiritual airs would annoy the laity who were sweating to support them. On the other hand, monks constantly faced a temptation to tailor their doctrine to please the laity and so boost financial contributions. The best defenses against such abuses were monasteries in which the monks lived very simple, poor lives.

Beyond meditation and the routine of monastic life, early Buddhism did not develop many new ceremonies or rites of passage. The closest was the initiation rite of shaving one's head. Buddhism got its rituals by integrating some of the local celebrations and customs. To this day, most localities do not involve Buddhist priests in birth and wedding ceremonies, but funeral services do. Indian Buddhists commemorated the Buddha's birthday and the day of his en-

CASE STUDY: THERAVADA

The **Theravada** tradition is called "the way of the elders" because it claims ties with pristine early Buddhism. It is sometimes called **Hinayana** (small raft) because it assumes that each individual has to cross the river of suffering by his own efforts: Buddha only provides an example of how to do it. (The followers of this approach prefer to call themselves Theravada, regarding the term *Hinayana* to be one of derision concocted by their opponents.) This approach prevails in Southeast Asia and stresses the importance of meditation for gaining freedom from the illusions of the self. This teaching has experienced a vigorous renaissance in contemporary Myanmar (Burma). By and large, most of the recent Burmese meditation masters have emphasized attaining insight into the true nature of reality, in contrast to meditation masters in other eras or lands who have emphasized attaining a formless yogic trance. Since they claim that insight was the original Buddhist emphasis while trance was the Hindu emphasis, the recent Burmese masters have rather self-consciously

striven to give preference to the Buddhist, rather than the Hindu Brahmanistic, influences that Indian history bequeathed them.

The preferred Burmese focus for observing the human unity is the breath or the body's *tonus* (feeling). By cultivating a regular breathing that integrates the body-mind components and stressing feeling, the Burmese masters have shifted away from the visual emphasis of the yogic tradition. They urge that one try to grow more sensitive to the touch of the breath at the nostrils or the rise and fall of the abdomen. Then, with practice, one can expand this tactile awareness to other dimensions of experience, for example the pleasures or pains one is experiencing. The result should be a heightened attention to what seems most really stimulating, pleasing, or irritating to the body-mind unity at a given moment. Behind the efforts to gain this heightened attention lies the conviction that the three marks, if vividly experienced, will bring one great spiritual progress.

lightenment. However, the *bodhi* tree under which the Buddha came to enlightenment prompted many Buddhists to revere trees. Such trees, along with *stupas* (burial mounds) of holy persons, were popular places of devotion.

Originally, a stupa was simply a mound of earth or stone that served as a shrine to a Buddha or bodhisattua and so became a focus of Buddhist piety. Stupas became more ornate temples as time went on, points of pilgrimage, giving Buddhists access to some of the religious effects pilgrimage regularly produces (entrance into a zone free of ordinary profane concerns, divisions, and sulliedness).

The worship of statues of the Buddha grew popular only under the influence of the Mahayana sect thought after 100 C.E., but earlier veneration of certain symbols of the Buddha (an empty throne, a pair of footprints, a wheel or lotus, or a *bodhi* tree) paved the way. These symbols signified such things as the Buddha's presence in the world, his royal renunciation, and the dharma he preached. The lotus became

an especially popular symbol, since it stood for the growth of pure enlightenment from the mud of worldly life.

MEDITATION. A central aspect of early Buddhist life was meditation, which has remained a primary way to realize the wisdom and inspire the practice that lead to nirvana. Meditation designated mental discipline. For instance, one could meditate by practicing certain devotional exercises that focused attention on one of the three jewels—the Buddha, the dharma, or the sangha. These would be recalled as the three refuges under which one had taken shelter, and the meditator's sense of wonder and gratitude for protection would increase his or her emotional attachment. Thus, such meditative exercises were a sort of *bhakti,* though without sexual overtones.

Indeed, both the saints (*bodhisattvas*) and the Buddha could become objects of loving concentration. However, such devotion was not meditation proper, for this was a discipline of consciousness

Which theoretical approach would give you the most insight on the history, doctrine, rituals, ethics of Hinayana Buddhism?

EXAMPLE: the Freudian perspective. Freud's psychoanalytic approach reduced religion to a social attempt to control unconscious drives of sex and aggression. He also postulated that the human mind could be divided into three components:

ID, which contains those unconscious drives

SUPEREGO, the conscience that attempts to repress those drives

EGO, which is the sense of self, charged with the responsibility of balancing the demands of external reality, as well as balancing the id and superego

From this perspective, Buddhism can be seen as a strategy. The communal life of the sangha (monastic order) serves to strengthen the superego. The first target is the id: both sex and aggression are limited by the rules of the sangha. After these id-based forces are controlled, the Buddhist strategy then targets the ego, using meditative exercises that help the monk transcend any remaining sense of individuality, and tie to external reality. Then only the superego exists, but it has no more opponents, so it may fade away, yielding a tension-free state known as nirvana.

Contribute to this discussion at
http://www.delphi.com/rel101

The monastic lifestyle of **monks and nuns** involves vows of poverty, chastity (celibacy), and obedience. That lifestyle attracted thousands of Buddhist and Christian men and women over the centuries. Do you think that such a lifestyle has any place in the modern world? If not, do you think that any modifications (e.g., a limited commitment of time in the monastery) would be appropriate for today's world?

Contribute to this discussion at
http://www.delphi.com/rel101

---

similar to yoga. As is clear from the story of his own life, Buddha's enlightenment came after he had experienced various methods of "mindfulness" and trance. It is proper, then, to consider Buddhist meditation a species of yoga. From early times the mindfulness of Buddhists has usually been a control of the senses and imagination geared to bringing "one-pointed mental consciousness" to bear on the truths of the dharma. For instance, one fixed on mental processes to become aware of their stream and the *skandhas,* and to focus on the idea that all is fleeting, painful, and selfless. In addition, meditation masters sometimes encouraged monks to bolster their flight from the world by contemplating the contemptibleness of the body and its pleasures.

However, wisdom was more than just attacks on hindrances to freedom and nirvana. In careful meditations, Buddhist adepts tried to replicate the Enlightened One's experience during the night of vision, cultivating first his one-pointedness of mind and then his dispassionate heightening of awareness. Adepts also composed meditations focusing on doctrinal points such as the Four Noble Truths or the three marks in order to see their reality directly. This was similar to the insight practices or the way of knowledge (*jnana-marga*) that Hinduism offered, though of course Buddhist doctrines often differed from Hindu.

MAHAYANA

Maha means large (*maharaja* is a great king; *mahavira* is a great sage), *yana* means boat, so *Mahayana* is the "large raft" (big ferryboat) approach to Buddhism. This theistic approach eventually viewed Buddha as captain of the ferryboat: he is a personal savior and all we have to do is get on his boat. This approach developed about five hundred years after Buddha's death, though there may have been some earlier trends in this area. The role of the laity differed greatly between Theravadins and Mahayanists. Even more, the notion of the Buddha and the range of metaphysics varied considerably. Before its emergence, early Buddhism was fairly uniform in its understanding of Buddha-dharma-sangha and wisdom-morality-meditation. (Theravada has essentially kept early Buddhist doctrine, so the description of Buddhism thus far characterizes Theravada.)

The hallmark of Mahayana was its literature, which placed in the mouth of the Buddha sutras describing a new ideal and a new version of wisdom. Why did Mahayana conceive the need for a greater vehicle? The answer seems to be twofold: the sense that the career of the Buddha showed him to be so full of compassion that one could not limit Buddhist doctrine or practice in any way that confined the outreach of the Enlightened One's mercy, and the sense that people everywhere, indeed all living creatures, needed such compassion—were burning with desire and could only be saved by the wisdom of Gautama. Thus the Mahayanists came to think that the ideal follower of the Buddha, the saint they call a **bodhisattva** (one who had the knowledge and being of a Buddha, who essentially was an Enlightened One, but who decided to remain on this earth a little longer in order to teach others), would so extend compassion that any notion of self-concern would fall away. Somewhat in contrast to the *arhat*, the holy person whose concentration on self-perfection had brought deep wisdom, goodness, and peace, the *bodhisattva* would vow to postpone entrance into nirvana (postpone gaining the fruits of his or her perfection) and stay in the samsaric world to labor for the salvation of all living human beings. In Mahayana, therefore, the self-giving symbolized by Gautama's decision to return to the world and preach the dharma empowered a considerable outreach. Emotionally, horizons expanded to include all beings in need. In terms of missionary impulse, the Mahayanists felt impelled to preach to people everywhere. Culturally, Mahayanists sensed that all aspects of life ideally would be colored and enriched by the Buddha's compassion. As well, they realized that laypeople had to be better appreciated and shown how any state of life, married life and work in the world as much as monastic living, could be a means to enlightenment and a place where one could do good. Finally, the Mahayanists put great effort into developing Buddhist wisdom so that it could accommodate the large heartedness they found in the Buddha's career. Thus their metaphysics came to look for traces of *bodhi*, liberating wisdom, everywhere, and they soon came to question any facile distinction between nirvana and *samsara*.

Historically, Theravada spread to southern India and Southeast Asia, while Mahayana became the "northern" tradition, spreading to Central Asia, China, Korea, and Japan. Today Theravada Buddhism dominates Sri Lanka (Ceylon), Thailand (Siam), Myanmar (Burma), Vietnam and Kampuchea (Cambodia), and Laos. Other Asian countries are dominated by Mahayana Buddhism. Tibet has been dominated by an offshoot of Tantric Buddhism, as we shall see. In focusing on Mahayana doctrine, let us deal first with two innovative teachings of the Mahayana schools, emptiness and mind-only, and then consider the Mahayana views of the Buddha himself.

EMPTINESS. The doctrine of emptiness (*sunyata*) is a hallmark of Mahayana teaching. In fact, the Mahayana sutras known as the *Prajna-paramita* ("wisdom-that-has-gone-beyond") center on this notion. By the end of the Mahayana development, emptiness had in effect become a fourth mark of all reality. Besides being painful, fleeting, and selfless, all reality was empty. Thus, further rumination on the three marks led Mahayana philosophers to consider a fourth mark, emptiness, as the most significant feature of all beings. No reality was a substance, having an "own-being." Obviously, therefore, none could be an *Atman*, be constant, or be fully satisfying.

DIALECTICS. The *Heart Sutra* is an example of this tradition. It employs dialectics (the act of playing both sides of an issue) in analyzing the five *skandhas*: form is emptiness, and this very emptiness is form. Feeling, perception, impulse, and consciousness are all emptiness, and emptiness is feeling, perception, impulse, and consciousness. This identification, the sutra emphasizes, can be seen by anyone "here"—from the viewpoint of the wisdom that has gone beyond. Therefore, reminiscent of Shankara's two levels of knowing Brahman, the *Prajna-paramita* says that there are several ways of looking at ordinary reality. From the lower point of view, feeling, perception, impulse, consciousness, and form are all "something." From the higher viewpoint of enlightenment or perfect wisdom, however, these terms all designate something that is empty, that has no solid core or own-being.

To deal with any dharma as though it were full, therefore, would be to deal with it at least erroneously and possibly desirously—thus, karmically. If, however, we see that nothing is pleasant, stable, or full, then we will deal with all things in detachment, moving through them toward nirvana. So, according to the sutra, a *bodhisattva* sees things without "thought coverings," does not tremble at the emptiness that this attitude reveals, and thereby attains nirvana.

CASE STUDY: THE *DIAMOND SUTRA*

Another good example of the *Prajna-paramita* literature that Mahayana Buddhism developed is the *Diamond Sutra*, which probably originated in India in the fourth century C.E. This sutra begins by setting the stage for a dramatic discourse. Once when the Buddha was dwelling in the garden of a person named Anathapindika, with a group of 1,250 monks, he rose, went on his round of begging, returned, washed his feet, and sat down to meditate. Many monks approached him, bowed at his feet, and seated themselves to await his teaching. One of them, a monk named Subhuti, ventured to ask the Enlightened One how a son or daughter of good family, having set out on the path toward enlightenment, should stand, progress, and control his or her thoughts. The Buddha graciously replied that such a person ought to entertain the thought that although the Enlightened One has led many beings to nirvana, in reality he has led no being to nirvana. How can this be? Because, as any true *bodhisattva* or en-

lightened person understands, the notion of "being" or "self" or "soul" or "person" is actually an illusion. With various subtleties, examples, and further inferences, this is the sutra's main teaching. Thus somewhat later the Buddha repeats the message: *bodhisattvas* are those who do not perceive a self, a being, a soul, or a person. They do not perceive a dharma (individual item of reality), or even a no-dharma. They neither perceive nor nonperceive. Why? Because they have reached a realm beyond the dichotomies that perception usually entails, beyond our ordinary tendency to organize things in terms of beings, persons, or selves.

Such a tendency seizes on individuals and turns aside from the whole. By concentrating on beings, it neglects nirvana. Nirvana is not a thing, nor an entity. Those who think in terms of things or entities cannot enter nirvana. Only those who have gone beyond, to the higher knowledge that is unified, intuitive, and comprehensive, can enter nirvana.

MIND-ONLY. The second major Mahayana school, the Yogacara, which became influential from about 300 C.E. on, proposed another influential teaching on ultimate reality, mind-only. Like the teaching on emptiness, it went beyond early Buddhist teaching, and the Theravadins rejected the sutras that attributed this teaching to the Buddha. The teaching of mind-only held that all realities finally are mental. The Yogacarins wanted a fuller explanation of mental reality, probably because their intuitions grew out of meditational or yogic practices (whence their name).

One of the principal Yogacarin sutras, the Lankavatara, described a tier of consciousness in the individual culminating in a "storehouse" consciousness (*alayavijnana*) that is the base of the individual's deepest awareness, the individual's tie to the cosmic. The storehouse consciousness is itself unconscious and inactive, but it is the repository of the "seeds" that ripen into human deeds and awareness. Furthermore, Yogacarins sometimes called the storehouse

consciousness the Buddha's womb. Thereby, they made the Buddha, or Tathagata (Enlightened One), a metaphysical principle—a foundation of all reality. From the womb of the Buddha issued the purified thoughts and beings of enlightenment. The symbolism is complex (and interestingly feminine, suggesting a Buddhist version of androgyny or primal wholeness). Its main point, though, is clear: The womb of the Buddha (Tathagata-garbha) is present in all living beings, irradiating them with enlightenment. Like the feminine *Prajna-paramita,* then, the ultimate reality of the Yogacarins "mothers" the many individual things (that are themselves empty). It is the great mental storehouse from which they issue, the matrix that holds them all in being. It stimulates their dancing flux.

MAHAYANA DEVOTION. Most major Mahayana schools developed sophisticated theories to correlate the many beings of experience with the simple finality of nirvana. It was not philosophy that brought Mahayana popular influence, though, but its openness to the laity's spiritual needs, its devotional thought. Early Buddhism held monks in great regard, considering them the only true followers of Buddha. They were the teachers, the determiners of doctrine, and the guardians of morality. They were the stewards of tradition who made the sangha a jewel alongside the Buddha and the dharma. Consequently, the laity considered themselves to be working out a better karma, so that in their next lives they might be monks (or, if they were women, so that they might be men). The central lay virtue, as we have seen, was giving financial support to the monasteries, and the sangha seldom admitted laity to the higher occupations of philosophy or meditation.

Mahayana changed this view of the laity. As we have seen, by stressing the Buddha's compassion and his resourcefulness in saving all living creatures, it gradually qualified the Theravadin ideal of the *arhat* (individual saintly monk who worked on his own spiritual perfection) and fashioned a new, more socially oriented ideal, the *bodhisattva.* Mahayana thereby prepared the way for later schools that were in effect Buddhist devotional sects, such as the Pure Land sect. Such sects preached that through graceful compassion, a buddha or *bodhisattva* only required that one devoutly repeat his name and place full trust in him for salvation. In this "degenerate age," the difficult paths of wisdom and meditation were open only to the few. Therefore, the Enlightened One (Buddha) had opened a broader path of devotion, so that laity as well as monks might reach paradise and nirvana. (Or to use the raft analogy: Buddha is the captain of the ferryboat; to get your ticket you just have to accept him as your personal savior.)

Mahayana did not destroy monastic dignity. Rather, it stressed the social side of the ideal. The Mahayanists saw the Theravadin monks as too individualistic. To pursue one's own enlightenment and salvation apart from those of other living beings seemed selfish. Out of great compassion (*mahakaruna*), the full saint would remain in the samsaric world, for eons if need be, content to put off final bliss if that would help save other living beings.

Mahayanists stress six great "perfections" in becoming a *bodhisattva,* and these effectively summarize Mahayana religious living. First is the perfection of giving: giving material things to those in need, but also giving spiritual instructions, one's own body and life, or even one's own karmic merit. In a life of compassionate generosity, everything could be given over to others. Mahayanists understand the five other perfections of morality, patience, vigor, meditation, and wisdom in a similarly broad fashion. Thus, they have applied the traditional triad of wisdom-morality-meditation in more social ways. Giving, patience, and vigor have meant that one became selfless in more than a metaphysical way. For the love of others, for the grand vision of a totally perfected world, the saint may cheerfully donate his goods and talents, suffer abuses, and labor ceaselessly.

Finally, Mahayanists began to contemplate the Buddha's preexistence and the status he had gained as a knowledge being. In this contemplation, his earthly life receded in importance, so much that some Mahayanists began to say that he had only apparently assumed a human body. Then, linking this stress on the Buddha's metaphysical essence with the Indian doctrine of endless *kalpas* of cosmic time and endless stretches of cosmic space, Mahayanists emphasized the many buddhas who had existed before Sakyamuni and the buddhas who presided in other cosmic realms. All became potential objects of adoration and petitionary prayer.

In this way the notion of buddhahood greatly expanded. First it was the quality shared by many cosmic beings of wisdom and realization. Later, in East Asian Mahayana, buddhahood became the metaphysical notion that all beings are in essence enlightenment beings. As we have seen in the *Prajnaparamita* sutra, enlightenment implies grasping how all beings are empty of individual solidity. Enlightenment, therefore, is just realizing one's buddha nature, the knowledge and light that dawn when the grasp of emptiness allows true human nature to show itself. It is the beginning of nirvana, the break with samsara, and the achievement of perfect wisdom all in one.

Buddhahood thus became complex and many-sided. The Buddha came to have three bodies: The dharma body, in which he was the unmanifest aspect of Buddhahood or Enlightenment-being; the human body, in which he appeared on earth; and the glorification body, in which he was manifest to the heavenly beings, with all his marks and signs. Moreover, the distinction between buddhas and great *bodhisattvas* blurred and largely dissolved in the popular mind, giving Buddhist "divinity" a full spectrum of holy beings. Citing the Mahayana understanding of divinity, therefore, is a sure way to refute claims that Buddhism is not a religion. By the fifth or sixth century after the Buddha's death, Mahayana Buddhists were venerating a variety of divine figures. This was especially true in East Asia, where Mahayana devotionalism built on pre-Buddhist traditions (for example, many Japanese *kami* became *bodhisattvas*).

TANTRISM

Tantrism affected (or infected) orthodox Buddhism as well as orthodox Hinduism in the early common era. Buddhist Tantrism in India seems to have originated around the sixth century C.E., flourishing first in the northwest. From the eighth century on it prospered around Bengal, combining with *Prajnaparamita* philosophy and native symbolic practices. It later reached Sri Lanka, Myanmar (Burma), and Indonesia. Often it merged with Shaivism, but in Tibet it combined with native **Bonism**, or shamanist practices, and became the dominant Buddhist sect.

Tantrism had antecedents in both Buddha's teaching and in the surrounding Hindu Brahmanism. Buddha appears to have allowed spells, and the canon contains reputed cures for snakebite and other dangers. *Prajna-paramita* sutras such as the *Heart Sutra* often ended with spells, transferring certain key ideas and words from strictly intellectual notions to mantras. In Brahmanic sacrifices, as we noted, the prayers were understood so literally that they became mantras; if a priest recited a prayer properly, it was sure to accomplish its end.

Buddhist Tantrists took over such sacred sounds as *om*, as well as esoteric yogic systems, such as kundalini, which associated sacred syllables with force centers (*chakras*) in the body. They also used mandalas (magic figures, such as circles and squares) and even stupas (shrines). The Buddhist Tantrists were thus hardly bizarre or innovative, mainly developing ancient Hindu esoteric practices in a new setting.

What novelty the Tantrists did introduce into Buddhism came from their creative use of rites that acted out mandalas and esoteric doctrines about bodily forces. Perhaps under the influence of Yogacara meditation, which induced states of trance, the Tantrists developed rituals in which participants identified with particular deities. If it is true that many meditation schools, such as the Yogacara, employed mandalas for the early states of trance in order to focus consciousness, then the Tantrists probably built on well-established practices. In their theoretical elaboration, however, they retrieved certain ancient cosmological notions.

For instance, they came to see the stupa burial sites as replicas of the cosmos. The railings that separated the stupa precinct from secular ground divided the sacred from the profane. The edge of the moving mandala that the Tantrist troupe would dance or act out had a function similar to that of the railings. Often Tantrism strove to symbolize the entire cosmic plan. Indeed, the Tantrists tried to draw heavenly worlds (*bodhisattva* realms) and gods into their meditations and rituals. A principal metaphysical support of Tantrism was the Madhyamika doctrine of emptiness, which the Tantrists interpreted to mean that all beings are intrinsically pure. Consequently, they used odd elements in their rituals to drive home the doctrines of emptiness, purity, and freedom. For the most part, these ways did not become public, since the Tantrists went to considerable pains to keep their rites and teachings secret. In fact, they developed a cryptic language that they called "twilight speech," in which sexual references were abundant. For instance, they called the male and female organs "thunderbolt" and "lotus," respectively. As with Hindu Tantrism, it is not always possible to tell whether such speech is symbolic or literal. Some defenders of Tantrism claim that it tamed sexual energy in the Indian tradition by subjecting it to symbolization, meditative discipline, and moral restraints. Other critics, however, view Buddhist Tantrism as a corruption of a tradition originally quite intolerant of libidinal practices. For them the Tantrist explanation that, since everything is mind-only, the practice of erotic rites means little is simply a rationalization.

In a typical Tantrist meditation, the meditators would begin with traditional preliminaries such as seeking refuge in the three jewels, cleansing themselves of sins (by confession or bathing), praying to past masters, or drawing a mandala to define the sacred space of the extraordinary reality that their rite was going to involve. Then the meditators would take on the identity of a deity and disperse all appearances of the world into emptiness. Next, using their imaginations, they would picture themselves as the divinities whose identities they were projecting.

So pictured, a man and his consort would sit on the central throne of the mandala space and engage in sexual union. Then they would imagine various buddhas parading into the sacred space of the mandala and assimilate them into their bodies and senses. In that assimilation, their speech would become divine, they could receive offerings as gods, and they could perform any of the deities' functions. So charged with divinity, they would then return to the ordinary world, bringing back to it the great power of a buddha's divine understanding.

The relation of the master (**guru**) and the disciple was central in Tantrism, because the master represented the tradition. (Zen has maintained this stress on the master. The Tantric guru was the authority needed to help the striver receive the original enlightenment disclosed by the Buddha. Texts were too pale and ambiguous.) The Tantric gurus occasionally forced their pupils to engage in quite bizarre and painful practices, to teach them to examine the mirror of their minds, to learn the illusory character of all phenomena, and to stop the cravings and jealousies that clouded their mirror. Pronouncing the death of old judgments and the birth of new ones of enlightenment, the guru might confuse pupils, punish them and push them to break with convention and ordinary vision. When Buddhism had become vegetarian, some Tantric masters urged eating flesh. When Buddhism advocated teetotalism, some urged imbibing intoxicating spirits.

TIBET. Perhaps the best place to examine the Mantric and Tantric tradition full blown is Tibet. Tantrism was welcomed in Tibet and came to dominate in the region between India and China. Our first historical records date from only the seventh century C.E., when Chinese historians started mentioning it. Under King Srongsten Gampo in 632, Tibet borrowed both writing and Buddhism from Kashmir. Toward the end of the eighth century, two notable Indian Buddhist monks came to Tibet and founded a lasting Tibetan sangha. Since that triumph, Tibet has owed more to Indian scholarship and philosophy than to Chinese.

The mandalas, mantras, and chakras (ritual circles within which the gods could be encountered or im-

personated) furthered the Indian academic structures that greatly influenced Tibetan Buddhism. During the Indian Gupta dynasty (320–540 C.E.), great monastic universities became the pillars of Buddhism. The "curricular Buddhism" of these schools encompassed all the arts and sciences. Furthermore, meditation integrated with scholasticism, assuring that the academic efforts to correlate Buddhist doctrine with existing knowledge never divorced themselves from practical religion. The Tibetan adoption of an Indian rather than a Chinese religious style correlated with this union of study and meditation, for the Indian schools favored a gradual penetration of enlightenment in which study could play an important role.

One characteristic of Tibetan Buddhism has therefore been its line of scholars based in monastic universities. They have produced voluminous translations and commentaries for the canonical scriptures, as well as a tradition that learning should inform ritualist life. Learning and ritual, in fact, became the primary foci of the Tibetan monastic life. The king and the common people looked to the monastery for protection through ritual against evil powers, while individual monks utilized both meditation and ritual in their pursuit of enlightenment.

The typical day of a traditional Tibetan monk began with a private ritual contemplation (Tantrist) before dawn for an hour and a half. During the morning, the monk regularly participated in the community's prayers for two hours and then worked in the monastic library. He devoted the afternoon to more work and public ceremony and again meditated in the evening.

Before the Chinese communists occupied and incorporated Tibet into China (and transplanted many ethnic Chinese into Tibet), about a fifth of the adult male population was living in the monasteries. Many monks spent a lifetime in this regime, coming to the monastery at the age of nine or ten and receiving a thorough training in the scriptures, meditation techniques, and ceremonial details. As suggested, the king supported this lifestyle, because ritual could prop his authority. (Pre-Buddhist Tibetan culture thought of the king in ancient sacred terms, as the tie between heaven and earth. Something of this ancient view continued when monks prayed and conducted rituals for the king's good health.) The common people, whose shamanist heritage emphasized many malevolent spirits of sickness and death, saw in the ritual spells and ceremonies a powerful defense. As a result, the monasteries were quite practical institutions for them, too.

One ritual engaged in by both monks and laity in Tibet is the prayer wheel. This is a twelve-sided wheel of stone or bronze. The worshipper spins it rapidly by hand so that the different faces whiz by. Each face has a different prayer stamped upon it. Each time the wheel turns, all dozen prayers are credited to the worshipper. But this can be viewed as more than a relatively high tech approach to send more prayers in less time. The process of spinning focuses the attention and induces a meditative state.

By emphasizing ritual in both public ceremonies and private meditations, Tibetan Buddhism created its own version of the Tantrist doctrine that the imagination, senses, and psychological and bodily powers are all potential sources of energy for enlightenment and wisdom. The Yellow Hat sect of Tantrism is the largest, and the one with the Dalai Lama. They have symbolized the tantric acts. (The Red Hat sect is considered more extreme, with some debased tantrics and some extreme ascetics.) The Tibetan Tantrist cult acted out symbolic situations representing the cosmos, so that the common people could find something comfortingly universal. The worship of the local goddess, for instance, which monasteries and popular festivals promoted, gave the world a motherly and protecting aspect. Monks and laity both prayed personally to Tara for help, while many of Tibet's musical and dancing arts developed through festivals devoted to her.

The success that Buddhism enjoyed in Tibet may also be linked to its ability to capitalize on native shamanist themes and political institutions. The ancient Tibetan *bon* ("he who invokes the gods") was a shaman very like the archetypal Siberian shaman. Beating his drum, whirling in dance, weaving his spells, he fought against the demons of sickness and death. In addition to developing its own Tantrist rituals to cover these interests of the older religion, Tibetan Buddhism also produced a type of wandering "crazy" saint who drew much of the awe and respect that the older shamans had.

The prototype of this ascetic, visionary holy man in Tibet was the much-beloved Milarepa (1040–1123). After a harsh initiation by a cruel guru, he took to the mountain slopes and gained a reputation for working wonders. In his songs he poetically expressed profound insights into both the nature of dharmic reality and the psychology of the ascetic life.

Buddhism capitalized on the demise of kingship in Tibet in the ninth century to establish a theocratic regime with the monastery at its heart. Despite early persecutions during a period of kings' intrigues and assassinations, by the eleventh century the monasteries were strong. Until the communist takeover, in fact, the monasteries and the Dalai Lamas (religious leaders) dominated Tibetan politics (often with much intrigue and sectarian strife). The Mongol emperor Kublai Khan granted Buddhist abbots temporal power over all Tibet, firmly establishing a theocratic rule. By the fourteenth century, however, Tibet was a cauldron of various Buddhist sects vying for power.

Of the sects that developed after the demise of the Chinese Tang dynasty in the ninth century, the most important was the Ge-lug, which shrewdly employed the idea of reincarnation. Consequently, the Mongols both recognized the Dalai Lama as a spiritual leader and considered him a grandson of the Mongol chief. From the sixteenth century onward, the Ge-lug wielded great political clout. The Dalai Lamas, for the most part, have been men of considerable spiritual and political acumen, and their rule has meant a vigorous sangha. The fourteenth, and current, Dalai Lama (b. 1935) was exiled by the Chinese communists, but he is still the spiritual leader of tens of thousands of Tibetan Buddhists, working for the day when Tibetans will again govern their own lives and be free to practice their religion.

One of the implications of the political role of the Tibetan Buddhist leaders, and this emphasis on reincarnation is the practice of identifying small boys as the reincarnation of the Buddha, and therefore the next Dalai Lama. Such a boy would be taken away from his parents and specially trained for his future role. There was a major dispute between Tibetans and the Chinese leadership in the mid-1990s when they had identified different small boys as future leaders of Tibet.

Tibetan Buddhism thus stands out for two things: its Tantrist bent and its especially knotted political history. Few cultures have so absorbed one version of Buddhism as Tibet has absorbed the "thunderbolt vehicle" (Tantrism). Perhaps the most famous Tibetan religious text to reach the West is the *Tibetan Book*

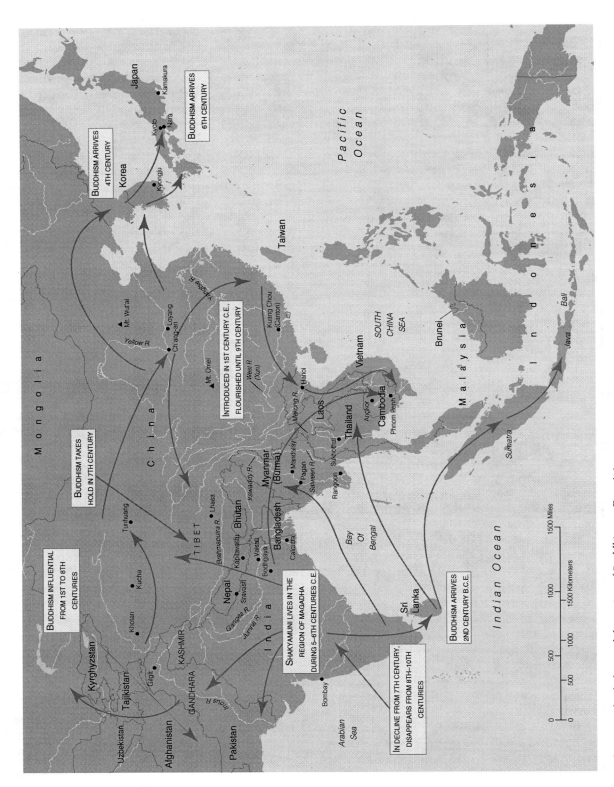

Sakyamuni's birthplace and dispersion of Buddhism to East Asia

SCHOOLS OF BUDDHISM		
SCHOOL	LOCATION	MAJOR THEMES
Theravada (Hinayana)	Myanmar (Burma), Thailand (Siam), Sri Lanka (Ceylon), Kampuchea (Cambodia), Laos, Vietnam	monasticism, meditation, Buddha as guide
Mahayana	China, Korea, Japan	heaven, Buddha as savior
Lamaism	Tibet	Dalai Lama, monasticism, reincarnation, prayer wheels
Tantrism	Tibet	symbolized sex
Zen	China, Japan	monasticism, meditation, mind puzzles
Nichiren	Japan	national shrine, chanting for money

of the Dead, which purportedly describes the experiences of the deceased during the forty-nine days between physical death and entry into a new karmic state. By employing vivid imagery and specifying rituals designed to help the deceased to achieve nirvana, the *Book of the Dead* exemplifies the Tantrist mentality well. It is a journey through the imagination and unconscious that severely challenges most notions of reality, since it maintains that the period right after death is the most opportune time for liberation.

THE DEMISE OF INDIAN BUDDHISM

Buddhism declined in India after the seventh century, only in part because of Tantrist emphases. Invaders such as the White Huns and the Muslims wrecked many Buddhist strongholds, while the revival of Hinduism, especially of Hindu *bhakti* sects of Vishnu and Shiva, undermined Buddhism. Mahayana fought theistic Hinduism quite fiercely, not at all seeing it as equivalent to the Buddhist theology of *bodhisattvas* and buddhas, but Hinduism finally prevailed because of its great ability to incorporate other movements. Indeed, Buddha became one of the Vaishnavite avatars.

By the seventh century the Indian sangha had grown wealthy and held much land—facts that contributed to a decline in religious fervor and to antipathy among the laity. From the time of its first patronage under Asoka (around 260 B.C.E.), Buddhism had enjoyed occasional support from princes and kings, and its ability to preach the dharma, to enjoy favor at court, and to influence culture depended on this support. The Kusana dynasty (ca. 78–320 C.E.), for instance, was a good time for Buddhists, while the Gupta age (320–540 C.E.) revived Hinduism. When the Muslims finally established control in India, Buddhism suffered accordingly. Early missionary activity had exported it to the south and east, however, and Buddhism proved to be hardy on foreign soil. So Hinduism, which has largely been confined to India, became the native tradition that opposed the Muslims.

BUDDHISM IN CHINA

Buddhism may have entered China by the beginning of the first century B.C.E., and possibly earlier. Buddhist missionaries traveled along the trade routes that linked northeastern India and China. Probably the first incursions of Buddhism were not well received by the Chinese. Buddhist monks showed their denial of the body by calling it a "stinking bag of bones" and by shaving their heads. The Chinese revered the body as a gift from the ancestors and wore their hair long to reverence the body. The idea of personal transmigration of souls (which underlay the Buddhist understanding of life's problem and its solution) must have sounded quite foreign to the Chinese.

But the Chinese missionaries were persistent, and by the end of the first century of the common era, a foothold had been established. By 148 C.E., monks such as Anshigao had settled at Luoyang, considerably to the east, and begun translating Buddhist texts.

The first interests of these translators and their audiences appear to have been meditation and philosophy, which suggests that the Chinese first considered Buddhism similar to Taoism. However, as the translating progressed through the Han dynasty (ended 220 C.E.), sutras on morality became popular, too.

From this beginning, Buddhism slowly adapted to Chinese ways. Most of the preachers and translators who worked from the third to the fifth centuries C.E. favored Taoist terminology. This was especially true in the south, where the intelligentsia had created a market for philosophy. By the middle of the fifth century, China had its own sectarian schools, comparable to those that had developed in India. Thus, by that time most of the major Buddhist philosophies and devotional practices had assumed a Chinese style, including the *Abhidhamma* (a system that employed erudite philosophy and psychology in interpreting the scriptures) and the Indian Madhyamika and Yogacara schools. In general, Mahayana attracted the Chinese more than Theraveda, so the native schools that prospered tended to develop Mahayana positions.

The Chinese brought to Buddhism an interest in bridging the gap between the present age and the age of the Buddha by constructing a line of masters along which the dharma had passed intact. The Master was more historical than timeless scriptural texts were, and the authority-minded Chinese were more concerned about history than the Indians had been.

Indeed, conflicts over the sutras were a sore problem for the Chinese, and in trying to reconcile seemingly contradictory positions, they frequently decided to make one scripture totally authoritative. A principal basis for the differences among the burgeoning Chinese Buddhist sects, therefore, lay in which scripture the sect's founder had chosen as most authoritative.

CHAN. The most popular sects were the Chan (later known as **Zen** in Japan), and Jingtu (which were devoted to meditation), and Pure Land (which was more theistic). The Chinese took to meditation from the beginning of their encounter with Buddhism, probably because it was the one aspect of Buddhism with which they could most easily identify (from the Taoist heritage). There are evidences of yogic practices in the Taoist works attributed to Laozi and Zhuangzi, and certainly Taoist imagery of what the sage who knows the "inside" can accomplish had made many Chinese eager to tap interior powers. Chan capitalized on this interest, working out a simple regime and theory that focused on meditation. (*Chan* is the transliteration of the Indian dhyana; the Japanese transliteration is *Zen.*) Its principal text was the *Lankavatara Sutra,* which the Yogacarins also much revered.

Chan (Zen) Buddhism is the most mystical school in all of Mahayana. It urges meditation and other spiritual exercises in order to achieve a Satori experience (similar to the *samadhi* or *moksha* of the *Upanishads.*) The Chan school understands this state to be a pure experience of no-mind action (and Chan found an easy way to conceptualize this in China using Taoist concepts such as *wu-wei*). According to legend, Bodhidharma, an Indian meditation master devoted to the *Lankavatara,* founded Chan in the fifth century C.E. Paintings portray Bodhidharma as a fierce champion of single-mindedness, and he valued neither pious works nor recitations of the sutras. Only insight into one's own nature, which was identical with the dharma-nature of all reality, was of significance; only enlightenment justified the Buddhist life. Tradition credits Bodhidharma with developing the technique of "wall gazing," which was a kind of peaceful meditation—what the Japanese later called "just sitting" (*shikan-taza*).

Probably the most eminent of the Chan patriarchs who succeeded Bodhidharma was the sixth patriarch, Hui-neng. According to the Platform Sutra, which purports to present his teachings, Hui-neng gained his predecessor's mantle of authority by surpassing his rival, Shenxiu, in a demonstration of dharma insight. To express his understanding, Shenxiu had written:

The body is the Bodhi Tree
The mind is like a bright mirror and stand.
At all times wipe it diligently,
Don't let there be any dust.

Hui-neng responded:

Bodhi really has no tree;
The bright mirror also has no stand.
Buddha-nature is forever pure;
Where is there room for dust?

Chinese Buddha

This juxtaposition and evaluation of the two rivals' verse reflects the doctrines of the southern Chan school, which looked to Hui-neng as the authoritative spokesman for its position that enlightenment comes suddenly. Because all Buddha-nature is intrinsically pure, one need only let it manifest itself. The northern school held that enlightenment comes gradually and thus counseled regular meditation. (Hui-neng himself probably would have fought any sharp distinction between meditation and the rest of life: in wisdom all things are one and pure.) The southern school finally took precedence.

One development of Chan was the use of *koan*, mind puzzles, to break the hold of cognitive meaning, thus liberating the individual to perceive ultimate relevance. Perhaps the most famous is "What is the sound of one hand clapping?" Rather than come up with Bart Simpson's quick response of snapping his fingers, the purpose of *koan* is to get the monk to give up trying to find cognitive solutions to life's problems. One rather gross example occurred when one monk asked the master Ummon, "What is the Buddha?" Ummon replied, "A dried shit-stick." (This is a stick used in China instead of toilet paper.) Ummon, asked about the wonderful Buddha-nature that is the true self, makes this shocking and iconoclastic answer. What does he mean? He means that however noble our aspirations, we must remember that we are (in the words of one commentator) "a bag of manure." Nor is it sufficient to give an intellectual assent to this proposition. One who would solve the *koan* must live it, realize it, act it out with his or her body, demonstrate to the master that one has identified with this ugly shit-stick.

PURE LAND. The most popular sect in China was usually Pure Land Buddhism derived from Tanluan (476–542). He sought religious solace from a grave illness, and after trying several systems, he came to the doctrine of Amitabha Buddha and the Pure Land. Amitabha is the Buddha of Light, devotion to whom supposedly assures one a place in the Pure Land (Heaven or Western Paradise). Tanluan stressed commitment to Amitabha and the recitation of Amitabha's name as ways to achieve such salvation. This, he and his successors reasoned, was a doctrine both possible and appropriate in the difficult present age. The Pure Land sect greatly appealed to the laity, and it developed hymns and graphic representations of paradise to focus its imagination. In stressing love or emotional attachment to Amitabha (called *A-mi-to fo* in China), it amounted to a Chinese Buddhist devotionalism. By chanting *"na-mo a-mi-to fo"* ("greetings to A-mi-to fo Buddha"), millions of Chinese found a simple way to fulfill their religious needs and made A-mi-to fo the most popular religious figure of Chinese history.

POPULAR BUDDHISM. Medieval Buddhism also permeated the life of the common people, including the village peasantry, for the government developed a network of official temples that linked the provinces to the capital. On official feast days, ceremonies held throughout the land reminded the people that they shared the same religion. The provinces also used the Buddhist temple grounds for their fairs, thereby making them the centers of the local social, economic, and artistic life. The great feast days were the Buddha's birthday and the Feast of All Souls, when large crowds would gather to honor the Buddhist deities, listen to the sutras, or hear an accomplished preacher expound the dharma.

When local organizations met for vegetarian dinners, clergy and laity had a fine chance to socialize. Fashioning close bonds of mutual interest, these dinners became a great source of fund raising for the monasteries and blessings for the mercantile and personal interests of the laity. The village clergy usually were not well educated, but they tended to know the laity intimately and to provide them considerable solace at such important times as weddings and funerals. Many of the village Buddhist clergy also functioned as healers and mediums, as well as storytellers and magicians.

CHINESE PHILOSOPHY. It was also during its medieval flourishing that Buddhist philosophy became fully Chinese. A hallmark of this domestication was the rendering of the abstractions in which Indians delighted into the concrete images the Chinese preferred. Chan, the school that most stressed meditation, carried the Chinese spirit to the heart of Buddhist spirituality, distrusting abstract words and stressing metaphors, paradoxes, gestures, or direct, person-to-person intuitions. Chan and the other native schools also stressed living close to nature, in the conviction that nature held many of the secrets of enlightenment. This had great appeal for medieval Chinese artists, poets, and philosophers, many of whom would refresh themselves in retreats at Buddhist monasteries.

The concept of nirvana only won acceptance in China after the Buddhists had adapted it to Chinese thought. At the outset, ultimate Buddhist reality seemed wholly contradictory to Chinese concreteness. Thus, Chinese Buddhists accomplished a rather thorough cross-cultural translation. They had predecessors in the Indian Mahayanists, who identified samsara with nirvana, but the Mahayanists were far more abstract than the Chinese. Indeed, Chan probably became the most successful of the sects rooted in Mahayana metaphysics because it most thoroughly domesticated nirvana. Little interested in words or speculations, Chan focused on meditation, by which one might experience nirvana. It also stressed physical work, art, and ritual. Since meditation expresses this commitment to experience via bodily postures that one assumes, one has only to sit squarely in the midst of natural reality and focus on its is-ness. (Not incidentally, one does not close one's eyes. The proper focus is neither a direction within nor a withdrawal to fix on the passing mental stream. In Chan it is a gaze with eyes open toward the end of one's nose.) The objective is to see without reasoning the reality that is right here. Such seeing should not focus on particulars, nor concern itself with colors and forms. Rather, it should appreciate reality's wholeness by not making distinctions.

Through Buddhism, China received a heavy dose of the doctrine of karma. That was most effective in the popular Buddhist sects, among which Pure Land headed the list, but it entered the general religious stream, influencing even those who rarely participated in Buddhist rites. Karma, of course, meant that the self was immersed in a system of rewards and punishments. All its actions, good or bad, had their inevitable effects. Past lives pressed upon the present, and the present was but a prelude to a future life. In popular Buddhism, this doctrine encouraged a sort of bookkeeping. Sometimes quite formally, with ledgers and numbers, Buddhists tried to calculate their karmic situation and plan out a better destiny. More generally, the concept of karma prompted the idea that the self's present existence was a trial that would be evaluated at death. How heavily this sense of trial pressed on the average person is hard to say. Combined with the rather lurid popular pictures of the several hells awaiting the wicked, karma probably sparked its share of nightmares.

The philosophical and meditative Chinese Buddhist sects accepted the traditional doctrine of no-self. So the Chinese thinkers who followed Madhyamika or Yogacara speculation agreed that emptiness or mind-only implied an effort to rout the illusion of a permanent personal identity. To grasp buddha-nature and join the dance of reality, the individual had to annihilate samsaric misconceptions about the substantiality of the self. The Chinese appear to have been more concrete than the Indians in such efforts. That is, where the Indians often reasoned over the self very closely, trying by dialectics to understand the illusion of selfhood, the Chinese tried to get the self to see reality's totality. Such seems to be the intent of pictures that Tiantai and Hua-yen masters drew, as well as the intent of the more radical techniques of Chan. Bodhidharma's "just sitting" and "wall gazing," for example, were exercises designed to make clear that only buddha-nature is real.

GOVERNMENT RELATIONS. The Tang dynasty (618–907) was the golden age of Buddhism in China. A major reason for this growth was the perception of the rulers that Buddhism could help them knit together the northern and southern cultures. Thus the founder of the Sui dynasty presented himself as a universal monarch who was both a pious Buddhist and a generous patron of the sangha. He likened his wars to campaigns to spread the ideals of Buddha, calling his weapons of war incense and flowers offered to the Enlightened One. It is hard to see how this squared with Buddhist nonviolence, but the popularity of Buddhism among the emperor's subjects led him to associate himself with the dharma as much as he could.

On the other hand, both the Sui and the Tang rulers feared the power of the sangha and took steps to limit its influence. Thus they insisted on regulating the admission, education, and ordination of the Buddhist clergy and on licensing the Buddhist temples. As well, the emperors put pressure on the sangha to enforce the monastic rule strictly, for its rules governing monastic life tended to restrict the clergy's economic enterprises. Such imperial efforts to control Buddhism were only partly successful, for many medieval empresses and wealthy merchants saw to it that temple wealth grew. The merchants' support of Buddhism is an interesting example of fitting a religious rationale to economic goals. For the merchants, the Mahayana notion that money gifts should be put to productive use became a justification for widespread commercial enterprise. Since the prevailing economy was, by imperial design, focused on agriculture, the

Mahayana notion in effect buttressed the merchants in their conflict with the state comptrollers.

The government did its best to limit the ways that Buddhist doctrines might become politically subversive, guarding against the revolutionary implications of Mahayana dharma. For example, potential rebels had available to them the Mahayana doctrine that Buddhism would pass through three ages. In the third age, religion would come close to extinction and no government would merit the full allegiance of the Buddhists. A wealthy and powerful sect called the Sanchieh chiao seized on this notion and tried to use it to undermine the imperial authority, but the Tang rulers reacted vigorously and had the sect suppressed. The Mahayana teaching about Maitreya, the future buddha (a sort of messiah), was similarly dangerous. Enough Buddhists expected that the advent of Maitreya was close at hand to present the government a sizable problem. The popular understanding was that when Maitreya came, a new heaven and a new earth would begin. Thus both the Sui and the Tang emperors had to battle rebels moving against them under banners of white (the color associated with Maitreya). Still, the golden age that Buddhism enjoyed in these dynasties flowed from the positive support the emperors gave it. For all their care that Buddhist fervor not become subversive of their own rule, the Sui and Tang leaders made Buddhist ritual an important part of the state ceremony. Thus the accession of a new emperor, the birth of a prince, and the ceremonies in honor of the imperial ancestors all incorporated Buddhist sutras, spells, and prayers. When the emperor ritualized important occasions, the monasteries and temples received handsome donations, which of course increased their patriotic loyalty and pliability.

At the great capital of Changan, Buddhist art dominated a vibrant cultural life. The architecture of the pagodas and temples gracefully blended Indian and native Chinese elements, producing a distinctively Chinese Buddhist appearance. The images and paintings that adorned the temples drew on the full range of sources with which the great Chinese Empire came in contact. With sufficient freedom married to sufficient imperial support, Chinese Buddhist artists enjoyed a period of great prosperity and created a distinctive new style. This sort of syncretism—a core of

Chinese Buddhist inspiration in touch with many other sources of inspiration—extended to literary art. The Tang dynasty was a high point in the history of Chinese poetry, and the moving forces behind this poetry were the two congenial streams of Buddhist and Taoist philosophy.

The state and the sangha therefore had a symbiotic relationship throughout the Sui and the Tang dynasties. Whether pulling in the same direction or wanting to go opposite ways, they were mutually influential. One place where Buddhist views considerably modified traditional Chinese customs was the penal codes. The traditional customs were quite cruel, so the Buddhist ideals of compassion and respect for life served as a mitigating influence. Both the Sui and the Tang rulers granted imperial amnesties from time to time, and when the rulers remitted death sentences they often justified their actions in terms of Buddhist compassion or reverence for life. Specifically, both dynasties took up the custom of forbidding executions (indeed, the killing of any living thing) during the first, fifth, and ninth months of the year, which were times of Buddhist penance and abstinence. The emperors also converted Buddhist notions of the soul to their own ends, using them for the psychological conditioning of the imperial armies. Whereas the traditional Chinese cult of filial piety had weakened martial fervor, teaching that a good son should return his body to the earth intact, out of gratitude to his parents, the Buddhist stress on the soul (or spiritual aspect of the "person") downplayed the importance of the body. The traditional cult had also taught that immortality depended on being buried in the family graveyard, where one's descendants could come to pay tribute. Thus a soldier buried far from home would have no continuing significance. The Sui and Tang dynasties made it a practice to build temples at the scene of foreign battles and endow these temples with perpetual services for the souls of those slain in military service. In this way, they lessened the conflict between a generous service in the army and a generous filial piety.

CHINESE SOCIETY. Medieval Buddhism also increased the charitable helps available in Chinese society. Monks were the first to open dispensaries, free hospitals (supported by the Tang government),

and hostels for travelers. They built bridges, planted shade trees, and generally broadened China's ethical sensitivity. Whereas the native ethic seldom took much charitable interest in affairs outside the clan, Buddhism encouraged an interest in the welfare of all living things. For example, it said that giving alms to poor people outside one's clan was a fine way to improve one's karma. This Buddhist universalism never displaced the formative influence of the Chinese clans, but it did move many Chinese to great magnanimity.

Buddhism downplayed social differences in another way. By teaching that the buddha-nature is present in all reality, it said that equality is more basic than social differentiation. The monastic sangha institutionalized this equality. It would be naive to think that background or wealth played no part in monks' evaluations of one another, but the sangha was governed by a monastic code that underplayed wealth and severely limited monks' possessions.

Furthermore, during many periods in Chinese history, the sangha was genuinely spiritual. That is, its actual raison d'etre was religious growth. In such times, the only "aristocracy" was determined by spiritual insight. For instance, though Hui-neng, who became the sixth Chan patriarch, was born poor (and, according to legend, brought up illiterate), his spiritual gifts mattered far more. Because he was religiously apt, a reading of the Diamond Sutra opened his mind to the Buddha's light. After enlightenment, his peasant origins became insignificant.

The Buddhist sangha also improved the lot of Chinese women. It offered an alternative to early marriage and the strict confinement of the woman's family role. In the sangha a woman did not have full control of her life, but she did often have more peer support and female friendship than she could have in the outside world. In fact, Confucian traditionalists hated Buddhist nuns for their influence on other women, because they demonstrated alternatives to wifely subjection.

One of Taoism's greatest influences on Buddhism shows in Chan's acceptance of individualism. Placing little stock in doctrines or formulas, the Chan master determined enlightenment by the pupil's whole bearing. The flash of an eye, the slash of a sword—a single gesture could indicate an enlightened being.

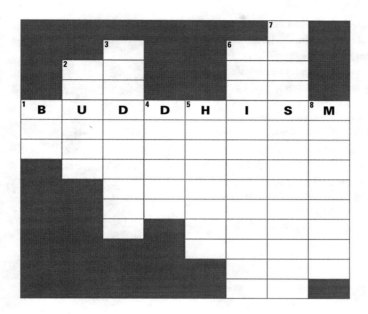

DOWN

1 Buddha lived about 500 _____.
2 Buddhist doctrine: "The Four Noble _____".
3 Who became the Buddha?
4 Hindi and Pali term for doctrine
5 Small-raft school of Buddhism
6 The Buddha's mystical experience of _____
7 Buddha's view of the afterlife
8 Buddha advocated this spiritual approach.

One could even "slay the Buddha"—throw off all traditional guidance—if one had drawn near to the goal. To the unenlightened majority, one's actions and life would be strange. Quite literally, one would be eccentric. But if the Tao or buddha-nature really became the self's treasure, such eccentricity was but the near side of freedom.

BUDDHISM IN JAPAN

Buddhism infiltrated Japan by way of Korea during the second half of the sixth century C.E. It first appealed to members of the royal court with overtones of the prestige of Chinese culture. The Japanese rulers, in the midst of trying to solidify their country, thought of the new religion as a possible means,

along with Confucian ethics, for unifying social life. So, during the seventh century, emperors built shrines and monasteries as part of the state apparatus. In the eighth century, when the capital was at Nara, the Hua-yen school (called Kegon in Japan) established itself and began to exert great influence. The government ideologues expediently equated the emperor with the Hua-yen Buddha Vairocana. Kegon has survived in Japan to the present day and now has about 500 clergy and 125 temples. In general, Buddhism coexisted with Shinto, sometimes in a mutually beneficial syncretism. From Buddhism, Shintoists developed the notion that the *kami* were traces of the original substances of particular buddhas and *bodhisattvas*. As a result, Buddhist deities were enshrined by Shintoists (and *kami* by Buddhists).

TENDAI. The first decades of the Heian era saw the rise of two new schools of Japanese Buddhism, Tendai and Shingon. Dengyo Daishi (767–822), the founder of Tendai, went to China to learn about the latest forms of Buddhist doctrine and practice. Upon returning to Japan, he established a new monastic foundation on Mount Hiei. The school that Dengyo Daishi founded derived from the Chinese Dien-dai sect. Dien-dai taught a quite syncretistic outlook, laying special importance on the *Lotus Sutra*. It was especially interested in joining philosophical speculation to meditation. Dengyo Daishi broadened the syncretistic outlook by adding moral discipline and ritual to the program he wanted his monks to follow. He also gave Tendai a nationalistic aspect, hoping that Buddhist practice would help protect the Japanese nation. The result was a well-rounded school in which just about any traditional Buddhist interest could be pursued. Dengyo Daishi struggled with the government to gain recognition for his group, but after his death his followers got a full go-ahead and could ordain monks. It is difficult to overemphasize the importance of the establishment of Tendai on Mount Hiei, because from its ranks in the Kamakura era (1185–1333) came the leaders of the Pure Land, Zen, and Nichiren sects.

SHINGON. This sect was founded by the monk Kobo Daishi (774–835), who, like Dengyo Daishi, went to China to find fresh inspiration. The term *Shingon* derived from the Chinese term for mantra, and the school that Kobo Daishi established in Japan amounted to a branch of Buddhist tantra. Through elaborate rituals, Shingon expressed deep metaphysical notions thought capable of achieving magical power. Kobo Daishi was a talented writer, so he was able to furnish Japan a full manual on esoteric Buddhism. Through his influence, mantras, mandalas, and *mudras* (ritual gestures) became influential religious vehicles. As well, they made a great impact on Japanese iconography and fine arts.

Both Tendai and Shingon were open to outside influences, so during the Heian period Shinto and Buddhism came into closer contact than previously had been the rule. For instance, there arose numerous *jinguji* (shrine-temples), where Buddhist rituals took place within the precincts of a Shinto shrine. Belatedly, the idea arose that the *kami* were manifes-

Japanese Amida Buddha

tations of the Buddhist *bodhisattvas*. Until the beginning of the Meiji era (1868), when there was an official reform aimed at cleansing Shinto, Tendai, and Shingon fostered such a syncretism between Shinto and Buddhism.

AMIDA. Last, we should note that during the Heian era there arose the conviction that Buddhism was bound to devolve through several ages (on the order of the Indian kalpas), and that the present age was the lowest—a time when religious practice was especially difficult. This eventually laid the foundation for the rise of various savior figures during the Kamakura period—for example, Amida Buddha, the merciful figure who presided in the Western Paradise so eagerly pursued by the Pure Land sects. The Amida, *bodhisattva* of light, became the most influential form of devotional Buddhism. It was popularized by evangelists such as Ippen (1239–1289), who encouraged songs and dances in honor of Amida. By practicing the recitation of "homage to Amida Buddha," followers could gain great merit or even full salvation (entry to the Pure Land). This prescription was simple, practical, and available to all. It did not require deep philosophy or meditation, simply theistic commitment. The laity found Ippen's message very appealing.

Honen (1133–1212) personally suffered persecution for his position and for his success in winning converts. In a letter written to the wife of the ex-regent Tsukinowa, Honen described the essentials that a convert to Pure Land would have to embrace. Sakyamuni came into the world only to reveal Amida's vow to help human beings discover Amida's grace. By prayer even the worst of sinners will come to Amida's mercy, as surely as all mountain water finally comes to the ocean.

NICHIREN. This son of a fisherman named **Nichiren** (1222–1282) came the closest of any Buddhist figure to fulfilling the role of prophet. He agreed with the Pure Land Buddhists that simple devotional forms like the nembutsu were desirable, but he found their stress on Amida unwarranted. For Nichiren the be-all and end-all of Buddhism was the *Lotus Sutra*. He considered this scripture the final teaching of Sakyamuni. Nichiren urged the practice of chanting homage to the *Lotus Sutra*. He also articulated an apocalyptic message: We are in the last days, an evil time. Nichiren demanded the building of a national shrine. Like a stern Israelite prophet of the Old Testament, he warned of disasters to come if the shrine was not built. Legend has it that he predicted the 1257 earthquake, the 1258 typhoon, and the 1259 famine; the Mongol invasion was forestalled only when the government agreed to the building of the shrine, and the divine wind (*kami kazi*) blew the Mongol ships away from Japan.

The strongest contemporary Japanese sect that traces its roots to Nichiren is Nichiren Shoshu with its **Soka Gakkai** ("Value-Creating Society") layman's organization and Komeito (clean government) political party. This movement derives from Makiguchi Tsunesaburo (1871–1944). During World War II, the leaders of Soka Gakkai refused the government's request that all religionists support the military effort, arguing that compliance would compromise the truth of the *Lotus Sutra* (by associating Soka Gakkai with other Buddhist sects and with Shintoists). For this he

Nichiren Shoshu Buddhists (the Japanese Soka Gakkai) claim that vigorous chanting can bring forth blessings of material prosperity. Some Christian denominations cite New Testament and Old Testament passages regarding God's promise of prosperity. Are material wealth and earthly success rewards for a commitment to God (or signs of His favor)? Should we pray to make us rich? Cite scripture to back up your position.

Contribute to this discussion at
http://www.delphi.com/rel101

went to prison. Makiguchi died in prison, but his movement revived after the war through the efforts of Toda Josei, and currently by the leader Daisaku Ikeda. In a time of national confusion, Soka Gakkai's absolutism carried great appeal. According to Soka Gakkai, commitment to the *Lotus Sutra* (and to itself) would dissolve all ambiguities. Many observers have criticized Soka Gakkai as cultlike: Nichiren and contemporary leaders were charismatic and intolerant, and the movement has a vehement missionizing with a "cellular" structure like that of communism, a strict program for daily devotion, pilgrimages to the National Central Temple near Mount Fuji, and an extensive educational program. Under the name Nichiren Shoshu, it has exported itself to the West.

JAPANESE ZEN. Two of the great pioneers who launched Chan on its illustrious career in Kamakura Japan were Eisai (1141–1215) and Dogen (1200–1253). Eisai studied Chan in China and then established himself in Kamakura, the new center of Japanese political power. His teaching won special favor among the hardy war lords who were coming to dominate Japan, and from his time Zen and the samurai (warrior) code had close bonds. For Eisai, mind was greater even than heaven. Buddhism, which concentrated on the mind, had known great success in India and China. Among the different Buddhist schools, the one founded by Bodhidharma especially stressed mastering the mind. From Bodhidharma's missionary ventures in China, Zen had made its way to Korea and Japan. Now it was time for Japan to capitalize on Zen's great potential. By studying Zen, one could find the key to all forms of Buddhism. By practicing Zen, one could bring one's life to fulfillment in enlightenment. To outer appearances, Zen favored discipline over doctrine. Inwardly, however, it brought the highest wisdom, that of enlightenment itself. Eisai was able to convince some of the Hojo regents and Kamakura shoguns of this message and make them patrons of Zen, so he planted Zen solidly in Japan.

If Eisai proved to be a good politician, able to adapt to the new Kamakura times and to benefit from them, Dogen proved to be the sort of rugged, uncompromising character Zen needed to deepen its Japanese roots and gain spiritual independence. After studying at various Japanese Buddhist centers without satisfaction, he met Eisai and resolved to follow in his footsteps and visit China. After some frustration in China, Dogen finally gained enlightenment when he heard a Zen master speak of "dropping both mind and spirit" (in other words, dropping dualism). Returning to Japan, he resisted the official pressures to mingle various forms of Buddhism and would only teach Zen. Nonetheless, within Zen circles Dogen was quite flexible, teaching, for example, that study of the Buddhist scriptures (scholarship) was not incompatible with a person-to-person transmission of the truth (the guru tradition).

Within Zen circles, Dogen also distinguished himself for his worries about the use of *koans*. The Rinzai school of Chan that Eisai had introduced to Japan stressed the use of these enigmatic sayings as a great help to sudden enlightenment. In Dogen's opinion, the Chinese Soto school was more balanced and less self-assertive. He therefore strove to establish Soto in Japan, teaching a Zen that did not concentrate wholly on the mind but rather on the total personality. This led him to a practice of simple meditation (*zazen*) that ideally proceeded without any thought of attaining enlightenment and without any specific problem in mind. Disciplining the body as well as the mind, Dogen aimed at a gradual, lifelong process of realization. The other Japanese Zen approach, Rinzai, has tended to seek sudden enlightenment, urging disciples to strive hard and keep up a firm discipline of work, silence, and obedience.

JAPANESE SOCIETY. Buddhism offered an alternative to the Japanese group orientation. Though the Buddha's own thought was quite social, as manifested by the sangha, his original message stressed the uniqueness of each individual's situation. It is true that each being possessed the buddha-nature (at least according to Mahayana Buddhism, which introduced the Buddha to Japan). This belief, coupled with the doctrine of no-self, led to a conception of the relatedness of reality. Practically, however, the Buddha made the existential personality the religious battleground. Only the individual could remove the poison of karma and rebirth; only the individual could pronounce the Buddhist vows for himself or herself, let alone live them out. However, early Japanese attempts to appropriate Buddhism were sponsored by the state because the state leaders thought they might enlist its magical or ritual power.

CONTEMPORARY BUDDHIST RITUALS

Devout Burmese (Myanmar) Buddhists begin and end the day with devotions performed in front of a small household shrine. This shrine usually consists of a shelf for a vase of fresh flowers and a picture of the Buddha. It is always located on the eastern side of the house (the most auspicious side) and placed above head level (to place the Buddha below head level would be insulting). During the time of devotions, householders light candles and place food offerings before the Buddha. Coming before this shrine, the householders begin by saying: "I beg leave! I beg leave! I beg leave! By act, by word, and by thought, I raise my hands in reverence to the forehead and worship, honor, look at, and humbly pay homage to the three gems—the Buddha, the Law, and the Order—one time, two times, three times, O Lord." Then they would petition to be freed from the four woes (rebirth in hell, as an animal, as a demon, or as a ghost), from the three scourges (war, epidemic, and famine), from the eight kinds of unfortunate birth, from the five kinds of enemy, from the four deficiencies (tyrannical kings, wrong views of life after death, physical deformity, and dull-wittedness), and from the five misfortunes, that they might quickly gain release from their pains. They end the morning prayer by reciting the five precepts, renewing their commitment to abstain from taking life, from stealing, from drinking intoxicants, from lying, and from sexual immorality. Clearly, therefore, the Burmese Buddhists seek to orient each day by honoring the Buddha, begging his protection against misfortune, and rededicating

Thai temple

themselves to the Buddhist ethical code. In the evening many Burmese, especially the elderly, conclude a similar session of homage, petition, and rededication by praying a rosary. The Buddhist rosary consists of 108 beads, one for each of the 108 marks on the feet of the Buddha (which, in turn, represented his 108 reincarnations). While fingering a bead, the devotee usually says either "Painful, selfless, fleeting," or "Buddha, dharma, sangha" three times.

Public ceremonies sometimes have a syncretistic mixture with some of the animistic themes that predates the arrival of Buddhism. Villagers may have a public ceremony every evening after sunset in the village chapel. This is located in the center of the village and consisted of a shed open on three sides. The fourth side encloses an ark containing a statue of the Buddha. Attendance usually is sparse, except in special periods such as the Buddhist Lent, and more sophisticated laity, who think meditation was the central expression of a mature Buddhism, speak disparagingly of the chapel services as magical or superstitious.

Nonetheless, the village service is interesting because it is led by laypeople, rather than monks, and because it uses the Burmese vernacular, rather than Pali, the formal liturgical language. Thus, it is a place where common folk and Burmese youth can experience their religion in a form easy to understand.

The ceremony usually begins with an invocation of the gods, and then an invocation of the Buddha, before whose image fresh cut flowers have been placed. The worshipers ask permission to reverence the Buddha and pray that their worship might bring them to nirvana or the higher abodes (the states near to nirvana). Other prayers follow, asking the Buddha to grant the petitioners strength to fulfill the five precepts and understand the three marks.

The central portion of the village ceremony begins with an offering of flowers, candles, and water—symbols of beauty, reverence, and purification. Following this, the committed laity express their veneration of the Buddha, the teaching, the order, their parents, and their teachers. Next come recitations of parts of the scriptures, a profession of love for all creatures, a recitation of the doctrine of Dependent Co-arising, a recitation of the Buddha's last words, a recitation of the five "heaps" (*skandhas*) of which human individuality is composed, a prayer to the eight planets, and a confession of doctrine.

The ceremony concludes with a water libation that calls the merit of the worshipers to the attention of an ancient earth goddess, the release of the gods who had been called into attendance, and an enthusiastic "sharing of merit" (of the benefit the participants had gained from the service) with the participants' parents and all other beings. Overall, the ceremony reinforces the main points of Buddhist teaching, reminding the participants how to orient their lives and encouraging them to express both their reverence for the Buddha and the main concerns for which they wanted the Buddha's aid.

Since 1970, there has been a successful Buddhist monastery near Mount Shasta in northern California. It has seventeen buildings (a Zendo or meditation hall, a founder's shrine, a shrine to the bodhisattva Kannon, a sewing room, a laundry, a tool shed, a store room, a library, eight residences, and a common room). The monastery was founded by an Englishwoman named Peggy Kennett (Jiyu Kennett-Roshi), who is a guru in the Soto Zen tradition. (Soto and Rinzai are schools that began in China but underwent a further development in Japan.) While maintaining traditional Soto teachings, the Shasta monastery has tried to adapt to American cultural forms. Thus members eat their meals American style at a table rather than Japanese style sitting on the floor, they chant in Gregorian tones rather than Japanese tones, they usually wear Western clerical garb rather than Japanese robes, and they serve English rather than Japanese tea. The central occupation of the monastery is *zazen,* or sitting in meditation. Most members of the monastery spend two to three hours in meditation each day.

During the morning service, the trainees make three bows and offer incense to the celebrant, Kennett-Roshi. The community then intones and recites portions of the Buddhist scriptures. There are three more bows, and then the community processes to the founder's shrine, where they recite more scriptures. During the evening ceremony, in addition to the scripture recitations, there is a reading of the rules for *zazen.* At meals someone recites portions of the scriptures while the food is passed, to help community members increase their sense of gratitude for what they are about to receive. Since the meditation hall is closed on any day of the month having a 4 or a 9 (for reasons not disclosed), six times in most months there is a "closing ceremony." Vespers finish the evening service, and through the day monks say prayers before such activities as shaving their heads and putting on their robes.

The recitation of the Buddhist scriptures potentially has the effect of creating mantras, for when sounds enter consciousnesses that have been purified by discipline and made alert by meditation, they can develop almost mesmerizing cadences. The ritual bows, use of incense, use of flowers, and the like help to engage all the senses and focus all the spiritual faculties, so that the prayer or meditation to be performed can be wholehearted. A major difference between the monastic ritualism of Mount Shasta and the lay ritualism of the Burmese Buddhism we described is the stress the lay ritualism places on petitioning the Buddha for protection against misfortune and help with worldly needs. Part of this difference stems from the greater stress that Theravada lay doctrine places on gaining merit. Whereas the monastic doctrine of Soto Zen stresses the enlightenment, Buddhists live in a thought-world filled with ghosts and gods that constantly make them aware of a need to improve their karmic state. Consequently, Burmese ritual seems more anxious. While the Burmese stress the merit one must attain for a better future, the Soto ritual stresses the grace, harmony, and peace that enlightenment brings. (Of course, Soto ritual is also an effort to inculcate the dispositions that conduce to enlightenment, such as inner silence, gratitude, and a sense of harmony with all of creation.)

WORLDVIEW

Naturally enough, Buddhism has made accommodations for the laity, since they were bound to be the majority of the members of the community. The worldview that we now study has usually come to ordinary laypeople through ceremonies, festivals, traditional stories, and Buddhist culture at large. Music, poetry, views of sickness, views of good fortune—all aspects of a popular religious culture—carry parts of the core religious message. If the core religious message has always been the Four Noble Truths, young people have heard it differently from old people, women have heard it differently from men, the wealthy are bound to stress one side of the message and the poor bound to stress another. That is how popular culture works. It is never straightforward, completely clear, univocal. It is always complex, many layered and many voiced. Thus, you have to imagine the intellectualism that we have stressed working its way out in terms of images and feelings—thoughts and hopes that the average Buddhist seldom brought to clarity or full articulation. The Japanese holy man Shinran (1173–1262) made explicit what many other Buddhist leaders have done implicitly, adapting the dharma to the needs of married people, unlettered people, people who have to work in the world. Shinran went farther than most others, stressing a theistic commitment to the Buddha more than a grasp of the dharma, but whenever it allowed rituals and devotions to multiply, the sangha accommodated the Buddha's Way to the needs of ordinary people.

For example, you have to imagine the typical devout Buddhist family centering its religious life on the little altar in its home. When family members decorate the altar with flowers and fruit and incense, they express concretely their love of the Buddha, their trust that Buddhist tradition would make their lives relevant, their inclination to go to the Buddha and tradition in time of trial. We should not despise religious traditions for being most powerful in time of trial. We ought to accept the fact that, the world over, most human beings only think completely seriously when suffering, death, injustice, evil, and other trials or hardships force them to. Paradoxically, and mercifully, that is how the bad things that happen to good people sometimes turn out to have brought a blessing. The blessing does not remove the badness, but it can become a solid consolation. In the same way, we have to accept the fact that the majority of Easterners, like the majority of Westerners, have gone beyond what a restrained orthodoxy might have preferred and sought human faces in which they might concretize the ultimate reality that they needed to worship. For example, a great many Buddhists have worshiped Gautama, even though some schools of Buddhism have taught that he was only a man who

embodied a universal wisdom. The distinction between venerating a holy man and worshiping a truly ultimate, divine reality escapes many laypeople in many different traditions. The popular treatment of the Virgin Mary in Christianity and of Muhammad in Islam are cases in point. Rather than debating about the propriety of the cult that grew up around Gautama, as around central figures in other religious traditions, we do better to appreciate the human needs that the cult expresses. In the case of the Buddha, the people who have bowed, offered gifts, chanted verses from the scriptures, and in various other ways given flesh to their vow to place their trust in the Buddha (as in the dharma and the sangha) have expressed their need for a center—a holy place of refuge. The Buddha has functioned for most Buddhists as such a place, just as Christ has functioned that way for Christians. The Buddha has meant that reality is not chaotic, suffering is not the final word. More positively, the Buddha has meant that, in the ultimate analysis, human existence is blessedly good and carries a wonderful potential. That is what human beings most need to hear. That is the sort of "place" the human heart most needs to be able to go, if it is not to feel like a motherless child—an orphan in an uncaring, hostile world.

NATURE

Stepping back from the historical view of Buddhism, we find that Buddhist attitudes toward nature do not fit together neatly. From its Indian origins, Buddhism assumed much of Hinduism's cosmological complexity. That meant taking up not only a world that stretched for vast distances and existed for immense eons (kalpas) but also the Aryan materialism and yogic spiritualism that lay behind such a cosmology. However, Buddhism came to contribute its own worldviews. Its numerous "buddha-fields," for instance, are realms with which our earthly space-time system shares the boundless universe. Buddhism has had few equivalents to Vedic materialism, but Buddhism used the doctrine of *samsara* early in its history to justify acceptance of one's worldly situation and working only to improve it (rather than to escape it for nirvana). On the other hand, the ancient Indian yogic practices impressed the Buddha and his followers deeply. Since Gautama had in fact become enlightened through meditation, and since this enlightenment expressed itself in terms of the anti-material Four Noble Truths, Buddhism could never settle comfortably in the given world of the senses and pleasure.

Initially, therefore, Buddhism looked on nature or physical reality as much less than the most real or valuable portion of existence. Only consciousness could claim that title. Certainly the doctrine that all life is suffering reflects a rather negative attitude toward nature, and it indicates that what the eyes see and the ears hear is not the realm of true reality or true fulfillment. Also, to analyze physical reality in terms of three negative marks (pain, fleetingness, and selflessness) further devalues nature. At the least, one is not to desire sensory contacts with the world, because such desire binds one to illusory reality and produces only pain. Thus, Indian Buddhists separated themselves from nature (and society and self).

PHILOSOPHY AND POPULAR BUDDHISM.
Because the great interest of early Buddhist philosophy was an analysis of dharmas (elements of reality) based on probings of consciousness sharpened by intense meditation, the material aspects of the natural realm fell by the way. At best, they were background realities and values. The scholastic Abhidharmists did not deny nature, for they were acutely aware of the senses, but they did deflect religious consciousness away from it. Far more impressive than natural phenomena were the states of consciousness that seemed to go below the gross phenomena to more subtle phenomena. They were the places where the Indian Buddhists preferred to linger. In considering the Buddhist view of nature, we must distinguish between the inclinations of the meditators and scholars, who were interested in nonphysical states of consciousness, and the inclinations of the laity, who saw the world more concretely and less analytically. As we might expect, the laity were more worldly than the monks. When they heard that all life was suffering, they probably thought of their family burdens, their vulnerability to sickness, and the many ways in which nature seemed out of their control. The comforts they received from Buddhist preaching, therefore, lay in the promise that right living would take them a step closer to the kind of existence where their pain would be less and their enjoyment greater.

Thus, it is no surprise that the most popular Buddhist movements were built on the Indian traditions of devotion. Just as popular Hinduism fixed on Vishnu, Krishna, and Shiva, popular Buddhism fixed on Amitabha, Avalokitesvara, and Vairocana. These celestial buddhas or *bodhisattvas* drew the popular religious imagination away from the historical Buddha and the commonplace world of the here and now to the realm of future fulfillment. In that way, popular Buddhism lay in between the deemphasis of the physical realm that the monks and scholars practiced and the simple acceptance of physical life that a worldly or naturalist outlook (such as that of the early *Vedas*) produced.

SAMSARA AND NIRVANA.
We have seen that as the intellectuals and contemplatives worked further with immaterial consciousness and its philosophical consequences, they changed the relationships between samsara and nirvana. In the beginning, Buddhists thought of *samsara* as the imperfect, illusory realm of given, sense-bound existence. Nature, therefore, was part of the realm of bondage. The Buddha himself exemplified this view when he urged his followers to escape the world that was "burning" to achieve nirvana. His original message regularly said that spontaneous experience makes one ill and that health lies in rejecting attachments to spontaneous experience. With time, however, the philosophers, especially the Mahayanists, came to consider the relations between nirvana and samsara more complex. From analyzing the implications of these concepts, the philosophers determined that nirvana is not a thing or a place. The Buddha realized this, for he consistently refused to describe nirvana in detail. But while the Buddha's refusal was practical (such a description would not help solve the existential problems of being in pain), the refusal of the later philosophers, such as Nagarjuna, was largely epistemological and metaphysical. That is, they thought that we cannot think of such a concept as nirvana without reifying it (making it a thing), and that the reality of nirvana must completely transcend the realm of things.

Therefore, nirvana could be the deepest reality of nature. To follow this line of thought is no easy task, so only the elite grasped the philosophy of the *Prajnaparamita*, with its concepts of emptiness and transcendence. That philosophy influenced the devotional life of Mahayana and the ritual life of tantrism, however, because even the simple people could grasp its positive implications as presented by the preachers. These positive implications, which blossomed most fully in the East Asian cultures, amounted to seeing that all reality is related. The other side of saying all dharmas are empty is to say that the buddhanature (or nirvana, or the other ways of expressing the ultimate totality) is present everywhere. Even if one had not entered into nirvana fully, so that no mark of karma remained, one could sense the presence of nirvanic ultimacy as the foundation of nature. For instance, if all things contain the buddhanature, then the natural and social worlds can become glowingly fresh and beautiful, as one realizes their potential.

Tantric Buddhism, finally, shared the doctrine of the nonduality of *samsara* and nirvana that Indian Mahayana developed but differed in its expression of this doctrine through ritualistic imagination. Tibetan practices, for example, played with the world, both loving nature and kicking it away, through sights (mandalas), sounds (mantras), and ceremonies (symbolic intercourse) that engaged the participant both psychologically and physically. All of this, of course, implied using nature as a somewhat sacramental way to gain liberation.

SOCIETY

The Indian society of the Buddha was divided into castes, which were religiously sanctioned as a way of maintaining social order. Moreover, casteism was part of Vedic India's cosmological myth, since according to legend human society's order resulted from the sacrifice of Purusha, the primal human being. In Brahmanism, the priests merited their primary status because they derived from Purusha's mouth.

Buddha, himself a member of the warrior class, brought a message that clashed with this hierarchy. He rejected both Vedas and caste (and therefore his sect would not become just another axial era sect within Hinduism). His dharma taught that beings are to free themselves from painful worldly life. His sangha accepted all persons: both men and women, whether Indians and Nepalese, and from every caste. The Buddhist doctrine and practice refuted the cosmological myth that legitimated casteism. Many warriors and merchants no doubt also found Buddhism a convenient weapon in their struggles with the brahmins for power. So they and others who wanted to change the status quo gave Buddhism a close hearing.

WOMEN'S STATUS. Buddhism offered Indian females considerably more than had been available to them previously. Women were capable of enlightenment and could join the monastic community as nuns. This practice was in stark contrast to the classical Hindu view, which held that women had to be reborn as men to be eligible for *moksha*. By opening religious life to Indian women, Buddhists gave them an option besides marriage and motherhood—a sort of career and chance for independence. No longer did a girl and her family have to concentrate single-mindedly on gathering a dowry and arranging a wedding. Indeed, Buddhists viewed Hindu child marriage darkly, and they thought it more than fitting that women should travel to hear the Buddha preach. In later times, women could preach themselves, but from the beginning they could give time and money to the new cause.

Moreover, by offering an alternative to marriage, Buddhism inevitably gave women more voice in their marriage decisions and then in their conjugal lives. In fact, Buddhism viewed spouses as near equals. The husband was to give the wife respect, courtesy, and authority, while the wife was to give the husband duties well done, hospitality to their parents, watchfulness over his earnings, skill, and industry. One concrete way in which a Buddhist wife shared authority was in choosing their children's careers. For instance, to enter a monastery, a child needed both parents' consent. Married women could inherit and manage property without interference. Buddhism did not require or even expect that widows be recluses, and suttee was abhorrent to a religion that condemned animal sacrifice, murder, and suicide. Finally, Buddhist widows could enter the sangha, where they might find religious companionship, or they could stay in the world, remarry, inherit, and manage their own affairs.

Still, Buddhism never treated women as full equals of men. Though the logic of equal existential pain and equal possession of the buddha-nature could have run to equal political and educational opportunities, it seldom did. Nuns had varying degrees of freedom to run their own affairs in the monasteries, but they were regularly subject to monks. Women never gained regular access to power over males, either in Buddhism's conception of the religious community or in its conception of marriage.

POLITICS. In its relations with secular political powers, Buddhism had varying fortunes. The Buddha seems to have concerned himself little with pleasing public authorities or worrying how his spiritual realm related to the temporal. No doubt his assumption was that if people became enlightened they would relativize social problems and solve them fairly easily. At the time of Asoka, however, the importance of royal patronage became clear. Much of Buddhism's influence outside India began when Asoka dispatched missionaries to foreign lands, and his efforts to instill Buddhist norms of ethics and nonviolence in his government became a model for later ages. As Christians rethought Jesus' dictum about rendering unto Caesar the things that are Caesar's when it found a potentially Christian Caesar in Constantine, so after Asoka Buddhists longed for a union of dharma and kingly authority, thinking that such a union would beget a religious society.

Historically Buddhists tried to gain favor at courts. In Sri Lanka, Burma, Thailand, and the rest of Southeast Asia, this effort often succeeded, and temporal rulers played a large role in Theravada's victory over Mahayana and Hinduism. In China, Buddhism's fortunes depended on whether it fared better or worse than Confucianism in getting the emperor's ear. During the worst periods, it became the object of imperial persecution. The same was true in Japan, where such persecution had much the same rationale: Buddhism was not the native tradition. Overall, however, Buddhism fared well in East Asia. It had to coexist with Confucian and Taoist cultural forces, but it regularly dominated philosophy, funeral rites, and art. Tibet realized the theocratic ideals that Asoka had sparked: throughout most of its history religious leaders doubled as temporal powers. However, the intrigue, murder, and moral laxity that this binding

(c) Craig Lovell / CORBIS

The Dalai Lama, religious leader of Tibet, has been exiled from his country by the Chinese Communist government. Here he is in Santa Cruz, California, on one of his many public speaking engagements.

of the two powers produced during certain periods of Tibetan history suggested rethinking the relation between the religious and the secular powers.

As with Christianity, there is a built-in tension between the Buddhist religious community and any temporal state. The sangha and the church both make claims upon their followers that can bring them into conflict with secular powers. Since these claims are made in the name of dharma or God, they carry an aura of sacredness or of coming from a higher authority. Things that rightly are Caesar's are limited. So long as there is a Christ or a Buddha, a God or a nirvana, Caesar cannot claim everything. One ploy that Caesar can develop, however, is to claim that he, rather than the priests or monks, is the representative of God or dharma. In other words, employing the aspect of the cosmological myth by which the human ruler is the link between heaven and earth, the king can claim a sacredness of his own. Many Christian successors to Constantine claimed this, and in effect many Buddhist rulers after Asoka did also.

Despite its focus on otherworldly matters, then, Buddhism remained knotted in secular-religious controversies. Since it did not clearly establish an authority outside the cosmos (for instance, by coming to a doctrine of creation from nothingness), it was always liable to attack from kingly Buddhists who wanted to make doctrinal dharma serve the state.

THE SANGHA. The sangha alternately raised and dashed hopes that most human beings might live together in harmony and peace. Energetic monasteries, run by learned and holy monks or nuns, were models of what human society could be. Living simply, obeying a common rule and a common authority, such Buddhist professionals acted out a vision of equality and cooperation. When a monastery was in good spiritual fettle, one survived there only if one's motivation was religious. Meditation, hard work, austerity in diet and clothing, long periods of silence, celibacy—these staples of Buddhist monastic life offered little to the worldling. However, monasteries of the devotional sects could be quite different. Often people entered them rather grudgingly and briefly, to learn the minimal ritual and doctrine necessary to function at the inherited family temple. Meditation-centered monasteries also differed from the pampered, court-favored centers of learning, art, and intrigue frequently spawned by East Asian Buddhism. Still, as long as the genuine articles existed, Buddhism was alive and well.

The life of Buddhist laity has always reflected the state of the monastic sangha. When the monasteries were spiritually active, the laity tended to support them generously. In return, the monks usually served the laity spiritually. During these periods, the notion that the layperson's vocational obligation was primarily to support the monks evoked no cynicism. The monastery was embodying the social ideal and so encouraging the whole sangha to think that dharma could be an effective social philosophy. On the other hand, when the monks were lax, the reaction of the laity was ambivalent. The laity enjoyed seeing clay feet under yellow robes, but they missed the examples and teachings that might have dissolved some of their own clay. Ideally, then, the monks and

nuns and the laity have provided mutual supports. A lively interaction between monks and laity could grow from the notion that by giving generously to the monks lay people could draw on the "field of merit" created by monastic holiness. Mahayana and Tantra have acted on this ideal by relating nirvana and samsara in such a way that vocational differences between the laity and the clergy are lessened. Even for these schools, however, the monasteries have symbolized idealistic places of retreat, meditation, study, and ritual devotion.

BUDDHIST AHIMSA. Traditionally, Buddhism laid great stress on the precept of nonkilling, not only because this precept inculcates a respect for all living things, but also because carefully observing it leads to great self-control and promotes peace. For example, if one is to stay away from killing or injuring other creatures, one must control anger, greed, hatred, and the other vices that usually spur our injurious actions and inhibit social justice. Nonetheless, in contemporary countries such as Myanmar (Burma), where many political figures profess to be devout Buddhists, the question of how to apply the precept of nonkilling in public policy has grown quite vexing. Nonviolence probably has been closer to the core of Buddhist tradition than to the core of Christian tradition. Leading Buddhist politicians, such as U Thant, who became head of the United Nations, therefore have had to make some distinctions. Generally they have tried to moderate public policies in the direction of nonkilling but have conceded that a thorough application of *ahimsa* (for example, prohibiting all military action) is not always practical.

Capital punishment is another problem that the precept of nonkilling heightens. Ideally, most Buddhists probably would oppose a law of capital punishment, urging sentences of life imprisonment for capital crimes. Not only would this honor *ahimsa*, it would also offer the criminal an opportunity to repent and be converted to Buddhist convictions. Still, through history to modern times most Buddhist countries have practiced capital punishment. This has caused some analysts to speak of a conflict between the mundane morality of the state and the ideal morality of the Buddhist religion. In their view, the state needs capital punishment to maintain order, so one must reluctantly kill the worst social offenders.

This might seem to relegate Buddhist ideals to complete impracticality, but further reflection has led some ethicians to a more dialectical notion of nonkilling. For these dialecticians, there are circumstances in which not slaying heinous offenders would be a great violence. Those charged with protecting the common good would seriously fail their charge were they to allow murderers to continue operating without fear of capital punishment. So the dialecticians come to the conclusion that committing the lesser evil is doing a species of good. In other words, they justify capital punishment as a necessary evil, a means public officials must employ if they are to honor the precept of noninjury in more general, far-reaching terms. To prevent great injury to the public at large, one must injure some criminal offenders. Once again, it would not be hard to draw parallels to Western debates over capital punishment.

SELF

The practical accent of Buddha's original preaching made the issues related to self paramount. Buddhism has directly addressed individuals, insisting that only the individual can change his or her life. On the other hand, Buddhism has counseled that to escape *samsara* and achieve nirvana, we have to rid ourselves of the notion that we have or are an *Atman*, a soul, or self. This doctrine has prompted some of Buddhism's central meditational practices and philosophical speculation.

Historically, the teaching of "no self" most distinguished the Buddha's way from that of his Hindu predecessors. As we have seen, a staple of Upanishadic wisdom was that the self is part of the great Atman (the interior aspect of Brahman). In yogic meditation, the Hindu tried to realize this ultimate identity, to experience the oneness of everything in Atman. When Buddha turned away from this teaching, calling human identity just a bundle of elements (skandhas) temporarily fused, he laid down a philosophical challenge that Hindu and Buddhist philosophers seldom neglected in later centuries. What motivated this new conception of the human being?

The principal motive, it appears, was Buddha's conviction that the key to human problems is desire. If pain expresses the problem ("All life is painful"), then desire expresses its cause ("The cause of suffer-

ing is desire"). These, we have seen, are the first two Noble Truths. The Third Noble Truth ("The removal of desire leads to the removal of suffering") extends the first two, and when Buddhists pondered its implications, they came to the doctrine of no-self (*anatman*).

The Third Noble truth itself is psychological. For instance, we may analyze the suffering in human relations in terms of desire. Parents desire their children's success and love. When the children choose paths other than what the parents have dreamed, or when the children demand distance in order to grow into their own separate identities, the parents suffer pain. They feel disappointed or rejected, or that their toil and anxiety have gone for naught. Buddhists would tell such parents that their relations with their children have been unwise or impure. Because they have desired success and love, instead of remaining calm and free, they have set karmic bonds that were sure to cause pain. But to cut the karmic bonds, the Third Noble Truth implies, one must get to the root of the desire. At this point one must turn psychology into metaphysics—one must realize that the self from which desires emanate is neither stable, fixed, permanent, nor, ultimately, real. In our distraction and illusion, we gladly accept the fiction that we have stable selves.

In simple terms, the prime reality in our interior lives is flux. At each moment we are different "selves." True, some continuity exists in that we remember past events and project future ones. But this continuity hardly justifies clinging to or relying upon a permanent self. What Buddhists stressed, therefore, was the change and coordination of the components, just as they stressed the interconnectedness and flux of the entire world (through Dependent Co-arising). They developed a view of both the interior realm of consciousness and the exterior realm of nature that became quite relational. Their metaphysics focused on nature's coordinated interdependencies, its continual movement. The self could not be the exception to such a worldview. Humans were too clearly a part of the total natural process to violate the process's fundamental laws. And just as analysis showed all the natural elements to be empty, so, too, analysis showed the self to be empty.

Therefore, Buddhists directly denied what Western philosophers such as Aristotle called a "substance."

To live religiously, in accordance with the facts of consciousness, one had to cast off the naive assumption that the human person is a solid something—one had to slide into the flux. In so doing, one could both remove the basis for desire and open up the possibility for union with the rest of coordinated reality.

This movement toward coordination with the rest of reality became the positive counterweight to the Buddhist negative view of the self. That is, as people advanced in their meditation and understanding, they started to glimpse what Mahayana saw in enlightenment: the realization that all Buddha-nature is nondual. According to the *Prajna-paramita,* ultimately only Buddha-nature existed. All multiplicity or discreteness resulted from a less than ultimate viewpoint. Such a realization, of course, meant the death of the illusion that one was an independent *Atman.*

We have belabored this teaching of no-self because it seems most important to the Buddhist attitude toward the individual. It is also the key to the Buddhist view that nature flows together and that society should strive for ultimate reality by means of enlightenment. Because of no-self, the individual could move toward greater intimacy with nature. There were no barriers of separate identity, no walls making him or her isolated. For those who attained enlightenment through the dharma, this nonseparation of self, nature, and society was a personal experience.

Buddhism regularly counseled the individual to regard the body, the family, society, and even a spouse or a child with detachment. One was to revere and discipline the body according to the Middle Way. Clearly, though, the body was only a temporary station on the way to nirvana or one's next incarnation. Wealth and pleasure were not, as they were for Hinduism, worthy life goals. The family was a necessary unit, biologically and socially, but frequently it was also an impediment to spiritual advancement, as the Buddha's own life showed. Society would ideally be a context for mutual support in realizing enlightenment. Personal bonds, therefore, could not be passionate and karmic, and even a spouse or a child came under this law.

Tantrism seems to qualify the Buddhist view of the self, since it allowed a more intense connection with food, alcohol, sex, and material ritual items. However, according to its own masters, the watchword in Tantrist rituals was still discipline and detachment. To use alcohol or sex licentiously was just a quick way to attachment and bad karma. The point to Tantrist ritual was to master these items and retain the energies that would have flowed out to them.

Even if not carried out, the doctrine of no-self shaped Buddhist culture. Wherever Buddhist religion was vigorous, the doctrine of no-self was influential. In fact, we often can sense its effects in the peace and humor of Buddhist texts. Many texts, of course, are complicated and complex. However, some raise serenity, irony, paradox, and wit to a high religious art. For instance, in one story two monks meet a fetching damsel by a rushing river. One charitably hoists her and carries her across. Later the second monk chastises the first for such sensual contact. The first monk replies, "I let the woman down when we crossed the river. Why are you still carrying her?" The Buddhist ideal was to carry nothing, to have a self utterly free.

ULTIMATE REALITY

Debate has raged over the question of whether Buddhism is a theistic religion. The simple answer is that Theravada has said that it is not, that Buddha has just shown the way; Mahayana has said that it is and encourages us to accept Buddha as savior. Devotional Buddhism certainly has venerated a variety of buddhas and *bodhisattvas,* treating them as other religions treat gods and saints. To be sure, the Buddha himself does not appear to have claimed divinity. Gautama seems to have been a human being who thought that he had found the key to living well. The key was enlightenment, whose expression was the Four Noble Truths. In the enlightenment experience, Gautama encountered ultimate reality. The overtones to this encounter gleaned from the texts are not those of meeting a personal God. Whether that differentiates Gautama's ultimate reality from the God of Western religion is another question, the answer to which depends on careful analysis of peak experiences and conceptions of ultimate reality. The personal character of the Western God is not so simple as many Westerners assume, and the impersonal quality of Gautama's encounter with nirvana is less absolute than many assume.

CASE STUDY: NAGARJUNA

Nagarjuna gained such a lofty reputation in later Buddhism, especially that of Tibet, that he deserves special consideration as an example of the the ideal Buddhist. He probably lived between 150 and 250 C.E., most likely in south India, and his style of argumentation, as well as his analyses of his opponents' positions, suggests that he was trained as a Hindu Brahmin before he converted to the budding movement of Mahayana Buddhism. Although Nagarjuna is known as the most acute of the Mahayana dialecticians, Tibetan tradition also reveres him as a guru who offered his disciples sound ethical advice.

First, Nagarjuna insists that the only way to gain the real relevance of the dharma, the Buddhist sciences, and the holy mantras is directly to experience them. Those who merely analyze the cognitive meaning of words never come to the core. This insistence expresses the conviction of all Buddhist gurus that words can be deceptive. If we allow words a life of their own, detached from the experiences they are trying to describe, words can distract us from reality. To grasp the dharma or the treatises of wisdom, we must both meditate on the realities to which they point and practice the virtues they extol. The same with the holy mantras that the tradition urges us to pray. Unless we experience the states from which they flow, the realities to which the saints have spontaneously directed them, the mantras will be but nonsense sounds.

Nagarjuna then reflects on the sort of knowledge that is intrinsically valuable. We only know what this knowledge is in time of need, when we are hard pressed. Then it is clear that the knowledge contained in books is of little use. Unless we have made an insight our own, it will give us little light or peace. In this, knowledge is parallel to wealth. Time of need shows us that wealth we have borrowed from others is no real wealth. It is nothing on which we can depend, for it can be taken from us at a stroke. Whether it be a matter of knowledge or of wealth, need, pressure, or suffering shows us the stark contrast between what we truly own and what we have merely borrowed. Thus hard times can have a silver lining. If they strengthen our resolve to gain our own wisdom, possess our own (incorruptible) wealth, they can advance us toward fulfillment.

Some people teach with words; others instruct silently. This is reminiscent of the reed-flower, which has no fruit, in contrast to the walnut, which has both fruit and flower. It is also reminiscent of the kataka tree, the fruit of which clears mud from the water. If you only mention the name of the kataka tree, you will not remove the mud. You must make your teaching bear fruit, make it deal with more than words. You must extend it to the realm of action, instructing by silent deeds as well as wordy lectures. Indeed, if you do not apply your knowledge, you are like a blind man with a lamp. Though you have in hand a source of great illumination, you do not shed it on the road, do not light the way for others to travel. Stanza after stanza, Nagarjuna tosses out aphorisms like these. Line after line, his advice is poetic, symbolic, image laden. From deep meditation and reflection, he finds emptiness a font of great illumination. For one who sees, the spiritual life is paradoxical and parabolic. As we come close to enlightenment, the main structures of the holy life stand clear, but these structures (meditation, wisdom, and morality) are capable of endless application. The key is having the experience, grasping the center, knowing emptiness directly. When we realize that reality is a seamless cloth, we can enjoy all its various designs. At that point, Buddhist selfhood will be properly achieved (and empty).

SUMMARY: THE BUDDHIST CENTER

The Buddhist center seems to us to lie in enlightenment. This is the experience that gives the religion its name; this is the experience from which the Middle Way proceeds, to which it conduces. All the philosophical speculation about whether mind exists and about whether there is a big raft or a small one are merely attempts to figure out how to explain or achieve enlightenment.

Nevertheless, as history's first great transcultural religion, it is safe to say that there is more difference in interpreting what all this means within Buddhism than between an Indian Buddhist and an Indian Hindu devoted to the Upanishads.

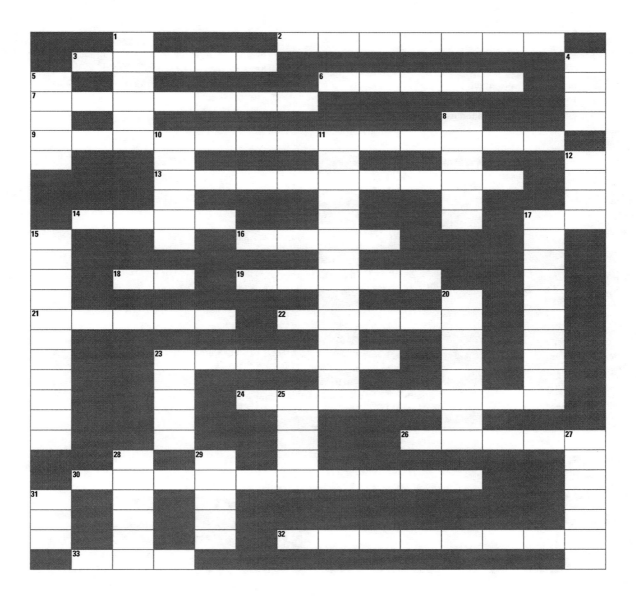

ACROSS

2 Buddha's family name
3 Buddhist symbol of life
6 What influences reincarnation
7 Sect that urged ritual sex
9 Buddhism was _____ and sought converts.
13 Way of the elders; school in southeast Asia
14 Zen mind puzzle
16 The Dalai _____ is the head of Tibetan Buddhism.
18 Number of days Buddha was under the tree meditating
19 Number in the _____ fold path
21 A unit of Buddhist scripture
22 Buddha's clan name
23 Buddha was not a prophet; he was a _____.
24 Small-raft school of Buddhism in Southeast Asia
26 Country of Bushido, Zen, Shinto
30 Buddhism's basic ritual
32 Japanese Buddhist prophet of the thirteenth century
33 Japanese meditative Buddhist sect; uses *koans*

DOWN

1 Japanese indigenous religion
4 Number of "Noble Truths"
5 Buddhist sacred burial site
8 Buddha preached the _____ way between extremes.
10 Buddhist scripture is comprised of _____.
11 Buddhist view of afterlife
12 A male monastic
15 Lifestyle of monks and nuns
17 Buddha's first name
20 The big boat school of Buddhism in Northeast Asia
23 Buddha's followers were _____ and nuns.
25 Country where Buddhism originated
27 The afterlife for a Buddha
28 The cause of suffering is _____.
29 The Dalai Lama represents the Buddhism of _____.
31 Buddha lived about _____ B.C.E.

Electronic flashcards and matching games
http://www.quia.com/jg/51966.html

hangman games
http://www.quia.com/hm/18510.html

word jumble games
http://www.quia.com/jw/8563.html

Download multiple choice, true-false, and fill-in drills from
http://www.ureach.com/tlbrink
Click on the public filing cabinet and folder rel10 and download m10.exe, t10.exe, and f10.exe.

The Impact of Religion on Social Change

The process of social change highlights the relationship between religion and other aspects of the social system, especially the economic and political spheres. This chapter examines some of the key ideas about the interrelationship between religion and social change. Because the issue of religion and social change is so complex, it is useful to separate the ways in which religion supports the status quo and inhibits change from the ways in which it promotes social change. This division is, however, largely analytic: We can speak of aspects of religion that promote or inhibit social change, but in most cases both are occurring simultaneously. We will first examine the ways in which religion supports the status quo and inhibits change, and then examine how religion promotes social change. The concluding analysis poses the questions: Under what conditions does religion have the greatest impact on society, and under what conditions is religion's influence likely to inhibit or promote change? Discussion of these questions is followed by an Extended Application to the case of African-American religion.

FACTORS IN SOCIAL CHANGE

The processes involved in social change are complex. It is difficult to isolate a single aspect such as religion in a chain of events that result in social change. As the example of millenarianism (discussed in Chapter 2) shows, a religious movement that arises in response to social change may itself help to bring about social change.[1] A further complexity is the meaning of religion. Do we mean religious ideas, religious personages, religious movements, or religious organizations? All these aspects of religion need to be considered; yet in any given situation, the relationships are often very complex.

We need to remember that change itself is neither necessarily good nor bad. **Social change** refers to any alteration in the social arrangements of a group or society. Of particular sociological interest is change that results in basic structural rearrangements (e.g., a new basis for social stratification or a change in a group's fundamental mode of decision making). Although the process of change itself is neutral, we often evaluate specific changes and potential changes by culturally established criteria. For example, we might consider the development of modern technology to be good or bad, but the criteria by which we make this judgment are not inherent in the process of change itself.

The effect of religion on a social development is not necessarily intentional. A religious idea or movement may become transformed into something very different from what its originators intended, and the influence of religion is often indirect. The Society of Friends (i.e., Quakers) became one of the foremost reformist sects in Christianity, even though their initial thrust was millenarian and somewhat mystical. As the movement developed, the Quakers' values of hard work and rejection of "worldly" amusements contributed to the wealth of numerous member families. Their other values (e.g., a strong personal conscience on social and political issues) stimulated their active participation in political and social reforms. They were prominent in abolitionism and the underground railroad in the United States, established self-help projects during and after the famine in Ireland, and were active in campaigns for prison and legal reform in England and North America. Thus, the ascetic, inward ideals of the original movement were transformed—first into monetary philanthropy and later into social activism (Baltzell, 1979; Isichei, 1967; Wilson, 1970:178–181). The impetus for its monetary philanthropy was the *unintentional* economic change produced by religious values, and the resulting social activism exemplified an intentional change orientation, or deliberate stance of opposition to the dominant society (Westhues, 1976).

RELIGION SUPPORTS THE STATUS QUO

There is an inherently conservative aspect to religion. Religion can evoke a sense of the sacred precisely because of believers' respect for tradition and continuity. Religious symbols link the believers' present experience with meanings derived from the group's tradition, and religious beliefs that are

---

1. In framing the topic as an interrelationship, we are rejecting theories that treat religion as nothing but an epiphenomenon to other social processes, though we will discuss some of these theories later in this chapter. Any effort to present this complex relationship in the brief space of a chapter necessarily entails great simplification. See the text Web site for sources for further examination of this important theme.

taken-for-granted truths build a strong force against new ways of thinking. Practices handed down through tradition as the god-approved ways are highly resistant to change. Although other aspects of religion promote social change, important elements in religion maintain the status quo.

A central theme in the sociology of religion is the relationship between religious ideas and the nature of the social groups that hold them. Social stratification, in particular, appears closely correlated with religious belief. **Stratification** refers to the differential distribution of prestige and privilege in a society according to criteria such as social class, age, political power, gender, or race. Religion has a different significance to various strata in a society, and different religious ideas will probably appeal to different groups in the society's stratification system. In the United States, Episcopalians and Congregationalists (i.e., United Church of Christ) draw members disproportionately from the upper classes, while Holiness and Pentecostal groups draw relatively large proportions of members from the lower classes (Kosmin and Lachman, 1993). Similarly, religious ideas of a social group often reflect social caste, as illustrated by the discussion of African-American religion later in this chapter.

Interest Theories: Marx and Engels

The connection between stratification and religious ideas has often been explained by interest theories such as Marx and Engels's explanation of religion as ideology. **Ideology** is a system of ideas that explains and legitimates the actions and interests of a specific sector (i.e., class) of society. The classical Marxian approach applies the concept of ideology only to ideas that embody the vested interests of the dominant classes; thus, the term has come to have a negative evaluative connotation. The concept of ideology applies more broadly to religion, however, if it is used neutrally. In this usage, *ideology* also refers to belief systems defending the interests of a socially subordinate group, thus justifying reform or revolution (Geertz, 1964; Lewy, 1974). From this perspective, recent sociology of religion has begun to explore some forms of popular religion as class-based production of religious meanings and practices (Parker, 1998; see also Beezley et al., 1994; Gismondi, 1988; Lancaster, 1988; Maduro, 1982; Nash, 1996; Parker, 1994, 1996).

According to the dominant strain of Marxian analysis, the fundamental basis of social action is **material interests,** referring to considerations that give economic benefits and power to a person or group. Religious and philosophical ideas are seen as mere epiphenomena, after-the-fact explanations that justify or mask real motivations for behavior.[2] Another school of Marxian thought has especially in recent years emphasized the relative autonomy of religion. This school strives to study religious belief systems in themselves, locating them in a larger social-historical context. These theorists retain the insights

---

2. This dominant strain—"dialectical materialism"—is represented by the interpretations of Plekhanov, Bernstein, Kautsky, and later Stalin. Marx himself did not develop a careful, unified theory of religion; the writings of Engels and Kautsky were more fruitful for further development of Marxian theory of religion. For a lucid and critical examination of these early theorists, see McKown, 1975.

of Marx and especially Engels but focus on the complex reciprocal influences between religion and social structure. By treating the relationship as complex, this latter Marxian approach identifies both the passive and active, conservative and revolutionary elements in religion.[3]

Another concept explaining the change-inhibiting aspects of religion is the idea of **alienation,** which is central to the Marxian definition of religion. Marx used this concept to analyze the false consciousness that he believed religion engendered. Marx (1963:122) asserted:

> All these consequences follow from the fact that the worker is related to the *product of his labor* as to an *alien* object. For it is clear on this presupposition that the more the worker expends himself in work the more powerful becomes the world of objects which he creates in face of himself, the poorer he becomes in his inner life, and the less he belongs to himself. It is just the same as in religion. The more of himself man attributes to God the less he has left in himself.

Religion, according to Marx, is the projection of human needs and desires into the realm of the fantastic. Religious alienation is thus the understandable reflection of the false consciousness inherent in this social system. Marx's insight into the change-inhibiting aspects of religious consciousness centers on the sense of domination by an alien force. Religion obscures real sources of conflict of class interests. Only a society that destroys such illusions can establish itself on the "truth of this world."

In this context, Marx stated that religion is the "opium of the people." He considered the distress that people expressed in their religion to be *real* but religion itself as an illusion preventing people from doing anything effective to remedy their condition. Religion, like opium, soothed their distress, but any relief was illusory (Marx, 1963:43, 44). Often religion draws off dissent and zeal that might otherwise promote revolution. Thus, a Marxian reading of the history of the English working class suggests that the development of Methodism precluded revolution by harnessing nineteenth-century workers' dissent and fervor in a religious movement. This thesis was first approvingly suggested in 1906 by British historian Elie Halévy; it was reexplored as a Marxian critique of English class relations by Hobsbawm, 1959, and Thompson, 1968. Parallels have been recently drawn to explain the rise of Pentecostalism in the face of global monopoly capitalism (Csordas, 1992; see also Anderson, 1979).

Although some evidence supports Marx's contention, studies of the correlation between religion and sociopolitical action generally suggest that the relationship is more complex, varied, and unpredictable (see Bastien, 1993; Levine, 1990; Löwy, 1996; C. Smith, 1994). Religion does relieve the tension of economic deprivation by substituting the value of religious achievement for economic achievement, and this substitution may indeed have an opiate effect

---

3. This strain of Marxian thought developed from the interpretations of Gramsci, Lukacs, and the Frankfurt school, among others; see Beckford, 1991; Fulton, 1987; Maduro, 1977; Mansueto, 1988; Mayrl, 1976.

because pressure for change is defused. At the same time, however, religion offers greater self-esteem by informing believers that they are superior, according to these alternative values. Such sense of superiority has transformative power, as exemplified by the zeal of the Puritans (Coleman, 1956:52).

Interest Theories: Weber

Weber, too, noted the extent to which religious ideas served to legitimate existing social arrangements, especially the stratification system. Religion has historically explained and justified why the powerful and privileged should have their power and privilege. The wealthy might justify their privilege as a sign of God's approval of their hard work and moral uprightness. Weber observed that most religions provide theodicies both of privilege and of disprivilege.

Theodicies are religious explanations that provide meaning for problematic experiences—in this case, the discrepancies of stratification. For example, the Hindu doctrine of rebirth simultaneously justifies the privilege of the upper classes and gives meaning and some hope for the conditions of the lower classes. This belief explains that one's present condition is the result of behavior in one's former life. A favored situation (e.g., being born into a high caste) is justified as the result of appropriate behavior in a former incarnation. Prescribed action for both the privileged and disprivileged is therefore to behave appropriately in one's present social situation in order to obtain a more favorable situation in the next life. This theodicy justifies and explains the social status of both privileged and disprivileged and deters the disprivileged from trying to change the existing arrangement—in this life, at least (Weber, 1946:253ff., 1963).

Weber's interpretation of stratification was more complex than that of Marx. Weber distinguished between "class situation" (stratification based on economic factors) and "status situation" (stratification based on factors such as lifestyle, honor, and prestige). Thus, for Weber, the linkage between religion and social arrangements went beyond simple ideological justification for the material interests of a social group; it included ideas that served as a means of **status distinction,** as a focus for group cohesion, and as a basis for controlling economic opportunities (Bendix, 1960:86, 87).

Weber's conceptualization may be useful for understanding the change-promoting and change-inhibiting aspects of the "New Christian Right" in the United States. This movement (and similar movements in America and other societies) is pressing for change, albeit reactionary change. Reactionary movements typically fight the encroachments of "modernity" and urge the cultural return to values and norms of an earlier, more "pure" era. The "New Religious Right," for example, presses for reactionary change in patterns of family life. This goal translates symbolically into crusades against equal rights for women, abortion, sex education in the schools, gay rights, and other nontraditional family lifestyles. A number of studies have shown a strong correlation between religious involvement (e.g., as measured by church attendance) and antifeminist sentiments and activism (see Himmelstein, 1986).

Some observers suggest that the appeal of such movements is based on *status politics*. Accordingly, people whose status (i.e., relative prestige or honor) is threatened by changing cultural norms assert their values politically in order to reestablish the ideological basis of their status (Gannon, 1981; Lipset and Raab, 1981). The differences between supporters and nonsupporters of the "New Christian Right" are less matters of economic class than of cultural lifestyle (Johnson and Tamney, 1984; Shupe and Stacey, 1982; Tamney and Johnson, 1983). One study among U.S. Protestants found that people who were dissatisfied with the amount of social respect given to groups representing traditional values (e.g., people who were involved in churches, people who worked hard and obeyed the law, people like themselves) were especially likely to support the agenda and organization of the Christian right wing (Wald et al., 1989). Another analysis suggested that religion is a major factor in these political stands *both* as a source of traditional images of women and the family *and* as a network from which political traditionalist movements can be mobilized (Himmelstein, 1986). A study of Christian Patriotism, a sometimes-violent, radical right-wing Christian identity movement, found that fundamentalist beliefs powerfully shaped the extremist actions of members through their world images: dualistic conspiratorialism, patriarchal misogyny, inner-worldly asceticism, and dispensationalist millenarianism (Aho, 1990:166–175).

Several researchers have hypothesized that the "New Religious Right" may be a political defense of a set of lifestyle criteria that forms the bases of supporters' social status (Bruce, 1987; Harper and Leicht, 1984; Lorentzen, 1980; Page and Clelland, 1978; Wallis and Bruce, 1986). This political assertiveness may be all the more plausible because of the social and political turmoil of the 1960s and 1970s. Many in the Religious Right interpreted such events as evidence of the failure of modernity and modern values, as well as the vulnerability of the United States as a nation (Simpson, 1983; see also Beyer, 1994). As the previous description of the abortion debate shows (see Chapter 3), lifestyle aspects of status are important. Women whose identity and social status (i.e., relative honor) are bound up in traditional definitions of motherhood and women's proper roles have much to lose when the society shifts to a different set of cultural values (Luker, 1984). Thus, religion may serve to support both socioeconomic class interests and status-group interests. Whether its role is change-promoting or change-inhibiting depends on the social location of the interest group. Furthermore, beyond their purely ideological functions, religious ideas often shape or define the very criteria by which status in a given group is evaluated.

Religious Legitimation

Religious legitimation of the status quo is sometimes the result of direct collusion between the dominant classes and the dominant religious organizations. Religious organizations and their personnel frequently have vested interests, which they protect by alliance with dominant groups in political and economic spheres. At the same time, dominant groups often try to manipulate religion to serve their purposes. Machiavelli recognized the legitimating power of religion and recommended that lawgivers resort to divine authority for their laws. He proposed:

> It is therefore the duty of princes and heads of republics to uphold the foundations of the religion of their countries, for then it is easy to keep their people religious, and consequently well conducted and united. (*Discourses,* Book I, Chapter 12, as quoted in Lewy, 1974)

Through religious legitimation, wars have been justified as "holy wars," obligations have been justified as "sacred duty," and domination has been explained as "divine kingship." The theory of the "divine right" of kings (a Western political theory legitimating monarchies and reaching its apex in the seventeenth century) explained that the monarch's right to rule is God-given and that the monarch's ultimate responsibility for conduct of the state is to God. This theory interpreted the process of monarchical succession and the coronation/anointment of kings as the working-out or expression of that God-given right. By implication, then, a ruler who gained dominance by other means (e.g., by revolution, usurping the throne, or popular choice) was not legitimate in the eyes of God. The monarch had both a civil and sacred role. Divine right made the king priest-mediator of God's will to the state. Belief in the divine right of kings both legitimated the rule of monarchs and suppressed dissent.

In the United States, the constitutionally mandated separation of church and state reduced the direct religious legitimation of political power, but religion has been a significant source of persuasion in political and socioeconomic spheres. Religion has been used to legitimate slavery and racial segregation, industrialization and antiunionism, warfare and international policy—all of which generally served the interests of the dominant sociopolitical groups. The historical processes by which religion was drawn into legitimation of these interests are, however, complex (see sociological studies of specific historical situations such as Yinger's 1946 analysis of church responses to America's participation in World War II; Pope's classic 1942 study of religion's role in quelling a major mill strike; and Hadden's 1969 study of tensions over clergy activism, especially civil rights).

Similarly, religion has been used to legitimate changes favoring a dominant group (e.g., the wealthy or politically powerful). Imperialism and crusades have generally been supported by religious or quasi-religious belief systems. President McKinley explained the decision to wage the expansionist war against Spain by which the United States acquired Cuba and the Philippines as follows:

> I am not ashamed to tell you, gentlemen, that I went down on my knees and prayed Almighty God for light and guidance more than one night. And one night late it came to me this way. . . . There was nothing left for us to do but to take them all and to educate the Filipinos and uplift and civilize and Christianize them and by God's grace do the very best we could by them, as our fellow men for whom Christ also died. (quoted in Ahlstrom, 1972:879)

Religious legitimations and institutional support have also been historically used to promote new economic arrangements such as industrialization. A South Carolina minister, supporting the industrialization of his region, said in 1927:

> To those who can read history it is unthinkable that any one fail to see in it all the hand of God bringing the many thousands from the bondage imposed upon us by social and economic forces which of ourselves we were powerless to control. . . . It is imperative that we think of Southern industry as a spiritual movement and of ourselves as instruments in a Divine plan. Southern industry is the largest single opportunity the world has ever had to build a democracy upon the ethics of Christianity. . . . Southern industry is to measure the power of Protestantism, unmolested. . . . Southern industry was pioneered by men possessing the statesmanship of the prophets of God. . . . I personally believe it was God's way for the development of a forsaken people. (quoted in Pope, 1942:25)

Religious Socialization

Religion legitimates not only the social system but also specific roles and personal qualities appropriate to existing structures. By promoting certain character types (e.g., the "hard-working individualist" or the "fatalistic happy-go-lucky" type) that are appropriate to a socioeconomic system, religion further legitimates that system. In socialization the individual internalizes these roles (as discussed in Chapter 3), which then come to exert an influence often greater than external social controls.

Religious socialization often indirectly supports the socioeconomic status quo by teaching attitudes and values that adapt to that system. For instance, a religion that teaches it is sinful to disobey those in authority indirectly supports those in authority in the existing socioeconomic system. The norms of existing social relations may be inculcated indirectly through religious rituals and socialization.

By observing the moral norms encouraged by a religious group, the individual will come to "fit" better into the existing social arrangement. This effect of religion for suppressing dissent was clearly recognized by a mill official who said: "Belonging to a church, and attending it, makes a man a better worker. It makes him more complacent—no, that's not the word. It makes him more resigned—that's not the word either, but you get the general idea" (quoted in Pope, 1942:30, 31). A restudy of this community found these attitudes still prevalent some thirty years later. Mill managers continue to think that the most valued service of local congregations is developing traits in workers of punctuality, hard work, sobriety, and obedience (Earle et al., 1976:26).

Many sectarian religious groups opposed to "the ways of the world" also teach their members values and behaviors that make them more successful in "the world." Holiness groups, for example, resocialize their members into the values of sobriety, hard work, and forgoing of present pleasures for future rewards (Johnson, 1961). Similarly, Black Muslims internalize a disciplined and

---

**BOX 7.1   Cross-Cultural Comparison:
Reproducing Patriarchy**

In the nineteenth century, the social relationship of the Latin American nobleman-landowner to the peasants who tilled his land was that of the *patron*. The patron granted to the peasant farmers political and economic protection with the use of a portion of land. In exchange, the peasants were honor-bound to serve the landlord and give him their loyalty. This relationship of personal submission was concretized and given moral strength by the religious practice of the "godparent." The nobleman was reciprocally linked to his peasant dependents as godparent to their children at the time of their baptism. Even veneration of the saints in popular religiosity replicated this relationship of dependency relative to the patron. Often villages would think of their community's patron saint as analogous to the human *patron*. The attitudes and values transmitted through the institution of godparent and the popular

emphasis on patron saints indirectly supported the norms of the existing socioeconomic structure (Ribeiro de Oliveira, 1979:314, 315). Long after working-class families had moved to the cities, leaving the semifeudal patronage system of the rural regions, their values (e.g., of special honor toward the ruling class) continued to promote submissiveness.

- Patriarchal relationships (i.e., submission and dependency relative to authority and power) pertain to real kin (e.g., parents), as well as fictive kin (e.g., godparents). How do some religious groups socialize their members into patriarchal relationships in the family, such as between parent and child, husband and wife?
- If religious socialization teaches social relationships that support the socioeconomic status quo, how is change possible?

---

ascetic religious ethic, indirectly producing socioeconomic benefit by enabling them to obtain jobs and run small businesses more readily than other blacks (Lincoln, 1989; Mamiya, 1982; Mamiya and Lincoln, 1988). By legitimating "appropriate" roles and personal norms, religion helps provide motivation for individuals to participate in the existing socioeconomic system (Robertson, 1977).

Social Control

Religion is a potent force for social control. Although social control can be exercised for social change, it is typically change-inhibiting. External forms of religious social control are most evident. Within a religious group, sanctions for deviance from group norms are all the more potent because of their reference to the sacred. The idea of being judged not only by other humans but also by the gods is a powerful deterrent from deviance. Salvation religions such as Christianity exercise control in urging that believers conform to norms in order to ensure their future salvation.

The forms of social control exercised by religious groups include informal sanctions such as ostracizing, shaming, or shunning the offender. Other measures include confession and exclusion or excommunication (Turner, 1977). Some religious groups have highly formal controls such as laws and religious courts. The social control exercised by religious organizations varies according to their power in the society. Societywide religious controls (e.g., the Inquisition and witch-hunts) are less likely in a pluralistic society. Nevertheless, America's modern equivalent of witch-hunts, McCarthyism and related right-wing extremism, was supported largely by members of religious groups that did not (then) favor pluralism—Roman Catholics and fundamentalist Protestants (Lipset, 1963). Even in relatively pluralistic societies such as the United States and Canada, religion forms a significant basis of the laws and formal order, as well as of informal social control.

Another relatively informal aspect of religious social control is the power of group loyalty to ensure conformity. The same loyalty can also be utilized for change-promoting action. When the group supports the status quo, however, religious loyalty ensures that the individual does nothing that would upset the group or work counter to its interests. The greater the accommodation of the religious group to the larger society, the more does members' loyalty to "our kind of people" inhibit change.

Internal religious controls are especially important. A person who is socialized into a religious perspective internalizes religious controls. Although socialization is never "perfect," most people internalize much of the normative content of their upbringing. Socialization has a built-in conservative thrust. When a person does something to have a "good conscience" or refrains from certain behavior to avoid a "guilty conscience," the belief system is exercising its control. Internal social controls are likely to impede change-oriented behavior because the individual feels guilty in breaking away from the learned norms.

RELIGION PROMOTES SOCIAL CHANGE

While certain aspects of religion inhibit social change, other aspects challenge the status quo and encourage change. In some circumstances, religion is a profoundly revolutionary force, holding out a vision of how things might or ought to be. Historically, religion has been one of the most important motivations for change because of its particular effectiveness in uniting people's beliefs with their actions, their ideas with their social lives. Religious movements such as the Great Awakening (i.e., several waves of revivals in the United States beginning in the latter part of the eighteenth century) have had tremendous impact on society, though the outcome may not have been part of the religious goals of the movement itself. These revivals were important sources of the abolitionist movement as well as of later temperance and prohibition movements. They also had an impact on the democratization of the American polity, making way for popular participation in what was largely an oligarchy of economically prosperous citizens (Ahlstrom, 1972:349, 350; Hammond, 1979; Jamison, 1961).

To understand recent developments in modern societies, sociologists have reexamined their classical foundations.[4] Social change issues were central in the works of Marx, Simmel, and especially Weber. These classical theorists have provided explanations for current developments and have inspired contemporary sociologists to new understandings. One product of this new thinking has been a more profound understanding of Weber's analysis of religion and modernization, going considerably beyond the relatively superficial "Protestant ethic" studies of the 1950s. We will discuss this new approach to Weber in more detail later in this chapter.

Religion and Social Dynamics: Beyond Marx

Another product of new perspectives to the classics has been a rethinking of the Marxian approach to religion and social change. A number of neo-Marxian sociologists insist that an appropriately complex empirical approach to the scientific study of religion cannot be substituted for or anticipated by theoretical constructs. Marxian theory is thus used as a perspective from which study can be conducted rather than as a static assumption (Maduro, 1977:366).

This new Marxian approach to religion results in a more complex conclusion than classical Marxian interpretations about the relationship of religion to social change. Starting from some of Engels's later ideas, these sociologists view religion as being relatively autonomous from the economic substructure. These theorists come to a more rich, complex understanding of religion by focusing on its functions as a partially independent variable in social change. In contrast to classical Marxism, neo-Marxian approaches suggest that:

> (1) Religion is not a mere passive effect of the social relations of production; it is an active element of social dynamics, both conditioning and conditioned by social processes. (2) Religion is not always a subordinate element within social processes; it may often play an important part in the birth and consolidation of a particular social structure. (3) Religion is not necessarily a functional, reproductive or conservative factor in society; it often is one of the main (and sometimes the only) available channel to bring about a social revolution. (Maduro, 1977:366)

If religion were not ever autonomous from the dominant economic interests, sociology could not comprehend situations in which religious groups worked for socioeconomic arrangements that were *against* their personal material interests. For example, in the years before World War I, the (pietist) Basel Mission actively opposed and, with the help of their supporters in Germany, effectively blocked the German plantation system in the Cameroons (Africa) on purely

---

4. See especially Beckford, 1989, 1991; Houtart, 1988; Kersevan, 1975; Maduro, 1975, 1982; Mansueto, 1988; O'Toole, 1984; Robertson, 1977, 1979; Thompson, 1986; Turner, 1991.

religious grounds. The Mission's change-promoting activism was despite the fact that its leadership's social-class allegiances were with the officials and investors who shaped Germany's colonial policies (Miller, 1993).

Sociology of religion needs to conceptualize religion as linked with, but not reducible to, economic interests in order to analyze how religion and social change are connected. We have failed to understand religion's role in social change because of an overly institutional conception of religion. When sociologists examine religion as an element of *culture* that can inhibit or promote change, their theoretical interpretations are more complex, nuanced, and useful (see Wood, 1999). The question is no longer "Does religion promote social change?" but rather "In what ways and under what conditions does it promote rather than inhibit change?"

We will consider the change-promoting aspects of religion under three headings: religious ideas, religious leadership, and religious groups. In practice, of course, these frequently overlap (e.g., when a religious leader proclaims a new religious idea to a group of followers).

Religious Ideas and Meanings

Ideas themselves do not directly effect change. Ideas indirectly influence society through people whose interests (i.e., all those things that could benefit them) lie in pursuing those ideas and applying them to social action. Religious ideas therefore effect social action in two ways: They may form the content of what a group of people tries to do; and they may shape people's perception of what their interests are. The movement to abolish slavery in the United States, for example, had important religious impetus. Religious ideas explained the evils of slavery; religious movements created a pool of adherents receptive to abolitionist ideas; and religious interests (e.g., desire for salvation) motivated them to put the ideas into action. For such reasons, it is appropriate for sociologists to examine the emergence of new religious ideas in history.

Religious Breakthrough: Weber By *ideas*, we mean a broad concept of meanings, such as described in Chapter 2, rather than merely the formal ideas of doctrine or theology. Weber used the yet broader notion of **ethic**, referring to the total perspective and values of a religious way of thinking. Weber (1951, 1952, 1958b) examined several world religions for those aspects of their orientations to their god and their social worlds that inhibited or promoted certain socioeconomic changes, especially the process of "modernization." In these studies, Weber examined the social location of religious ideas and innovation in each society. He sought the sources of motivation for individual action, the relationship of the individual to the larger society, and the religious ideas that shaped how individual actors in that society perceived their social world. Weber was especially interested in locating historical points of **breakthrough.** These were periods in the development of a society when circumstances pushed the social group either toward a new way of action or toward reaffirmation of the old way. The movement toward innovation in the social system constituted a breakthrough. Weber noted that religion has been historically prominent in these breakthrough developments.

Like Marx, Weber held that people's vested interests, considered in the context of certain structural conditions, explained their actions. By contrast, he felt that these interests need not be purely economic ones; people could be motivated, for example, to protect their religious standing. Although religious ideas do not determine social action, according to Weber, they are significant in shaping actors' perceptions and interpretations of their material and ideal interests. Weber (1946:280) stated:

> Not ideas, but material and ideal interests, directly govern men's conduct. Yet very frequently the "world images" that have been created by "ideas" have, like switchmen, determined the tracks along which action has been pushed by the dynamic of interest. "From what" and "for what" one wished to be redeemed and, let us not forget, "could be" redeemed, depended upon one's image of the world.

Weber considered religion one of the foremost sources of these ideas that shaped the direction of social action and were "switchmen" in the course of history.

In *The Protestant Ethic and the Spirit of Capitalism* (1958a), Weber analyzed one particularly important breakthrough—the development of the capitalistic mode of socioeconomic organization. He hypothesized a link between the rise of the Protestant worldview and the subsequent emergence of capitalism in Western society. To Weber, capitalism was a significant factor in modernization, a process he viewed with almost prophetic misgivings. The key characteristic of modernization is its *means–end* (i.e., functional) *rationality*. Weber emphasized that capitalism is not mere greed or acquisitiveness but the rational, systematic investment of time and resources toward the expectation of future chances of profit. Furthermore, the expansion of this perspective to a society-wide economic system required socially available roles for performing these tasks: specifically, the role of the entrepreneur (Weber, 1958a:17–27; excellent brief treatments of Weber's thesis include Eisenstadt, 1969, and Robertson, 1977).

Ideas and Individualism: Weber Weber argued that creation of a pool of individuals with the necessary values and characteristics to perform as entrepreneurs was essential to the emergence of capitalism. This development was made possible by a new form of individualism, an unintentional by-product of the main variant of Protestantism at that critical moment in history. Weber reasoned that the social role of the entrepreneur called for someone who valued hard work and considered deferred gratification as almost a virtue in itself. Early Protestantism, especially Lutheranism, contributed to this ethic by its interpretation of work as a vocation. The work of the layperson was thus viewed as a virtue, fulfilling a special call from God.

Capitalism further required persons willing to deny themselves rationally and systematically for the sake of achieving a future goal. The dominant strain of Protestantism (e.g., Calvinism, Puritanism, Pietism, Anabaptism) produced such qualities because of its **inner-worldly asceticism,** encouraging members to be active "in the world"—indeed, to prove their salvation by their socioeconomic actions. At the same time, these forms of Protestantism expected their members to forgo the pleasures "of the world" not to spend their money on luxuries, drink, gambling, or entertainments. The "Protestant ethic" therefore became one of hard work, sobriety, financial care, and deferred gratification. Even though capitalistic gain was far from the goal of these Protestant values, according to Weber, the initial development of capitalism was made possible by the available pool of persons who shared these qualities.

Simultaneously, Protestantism resulted in a powerful new source of motivation for such economic action as capitalism. Protestant beliefs produced a new form of individualism, that is, a new mode of individual-to-society relationship. Under Roman Catholicism, the individual had experienced something of a "blanket" approval. The individual's standing before God and fellow believers was certified by belonging to the church and receiving its sacraments; thus, belonging to the *group* legitimated the individual member. Protestantism, especially its Calvinist varieties, offered no such security. Weber argued that the Protestant ethic made it necessary for individuals to legitimate themselves. This need for self-legitimation, combined with inner-worldly asceticism, produced a strong motivation for the kind of socioeconomic action that capitalism entailed. Weber linked these values and motivations produced by the Protestant ethic with the emergence of capitalism, especially the critical role of the entrepreneur. Once established, however, capitalism no longer needed the Protestant ethic. Mature capitalism, according to Weber, can be self-sustaining.

Numerous scholars since Weber have contested his Protestant ethic hypothesis. Some have argued that the constellation of attitudes and ideas that Weber called the Protestant ethic (if such a mind-set existed) coincided with more important socioeconomic changes such as technological developments, the availability of potential laborers, and the influx of new capital resources (e.g., from colonial holdings). They suggest that these latter factors, among others, were more significant than the Protestant ethic in the development of capitalism. Probably Weber himself would have modified his thesis had he finished his projected sociology of Protestantism before his death. *The Protestant Ethic* was among his earliest writings in the sociology of religion, and his later essays emphasized the change-promoting potential of religious sects as organizations more than the Protestant ethic per se (Berger, 1971; Weber, 1946:302–322).

Religious Imagery Another aspect that contributes to social change is the capacity of religious meanings to serve as symbols for change. Religious symbols frequently present an *image* of future change. They create a vision of what could be and suggest to believers their role in bringing about that change. Change-oriented symbolism is often directed toward the social realm, as exemplified by the ideas of the "heavenly city," the "new Jerusalem," and the "chosen people." Many new religious movements, for example, have articulated visions of the "kingdom of heaven on earth" and of how they ought to proceed to realize that new order (Barker, 1988b).

BOX 7.2 Methodological Note: Historical and Cross-Cultural Comparison

History provides one of the most important sources of sociological data, because all cultural and structural elements of today's societies have a history: At some point in time, they came into existence, and over time they have changed. Sociologists study not only the development and changes in religious beliefs, practices, and collectivities, but also the related changes in the larger society. Max Weber developed a highly sophisticated historical/comparative method for locating and interpreting historical points of breakthrough. He thought that "world images" (such as religious beliefs and inspirations) had their impact in history by changing the direction of people's actions and everyday cultural practices. This box describes (in greatly simplified terms) how the logic of his approach proceeded.

In *The Protestant Ethic and the Spirit of Capitalism,* Weber (1958a) explored key characteristics (or an "ideal type") of the capitalist "spirit" (implying both ways of thinking and motivations that animate action). Having identified several definitive characteristics, Weber first looked at history to see where there were similar characteristics that did *not* lead in the same direction. For example, he noticed that capitalism required delayed gratification and some self-abnegation to invest resources with the uncertain hope of future rewards. He wondered if the asceticism of the Puritans, for example, indirectly (and unintentionally) promoted just such a world image.

But if asceticism were a definitive characteristic, why did other ascetic religious groups *not* develop a capitalist spirit? Weber compared the asceticism of the Puritans with that of Catholic monks; in other volumes, he examined (in great detail) the asceticism of Hindus and other religions, as well. He concluded that what was different was the Puritans' emphasis on individually working out one's salvation by action (including economic action) in *this* world, rather than an other-worldly emphasis exemplified by the other religions. Similarly, he identified rational (means–ends) actions as a feature of the capitalist spirit, so he examined premodern Catholic rational actions (such as the highly disciplined monastic life), as well as Confucianism and other religions that valued rationality. For each comparative analysis, Weber considered why very similar world images led to different historical outcomes.

Historical and cross-cultural comparative methodologies are still important approaches in contemporary sociology. An excellent example is José Casanova's *Public Religions in the Modern World* (1994), which compares the historical trajectories of the public role of religion in several nations, each with different frameworks for linking church and state.

- Why would an understanding of African-American religious expressions today require an understanding of the history of slavery and segregation? What historical and cross-cultural comparisons might enrich our sociological understanding of them?
- If you wanted to understand why, in the United States, Catholics and Quakers are often allies in social justice activism, what historical features of each religious group would you examine? What historical features of U.S. socioeconomic injustices are relevant? Using Weber as a model, what nonactivist religious groups might you use for sociohistorical comparison? What other countries could be compared for "world images" leading to social justice activism?

Religion provides symbols of tradition and continuity, but religious idealization also gives symbols to a group's desire for change. An example of such change-promoting religious imagery is Liberation Theology's sacralization of the community of the poor and identification of this-worldly activism with Christ's struggle to liberate humanity (Lancaster, 1988). For example, in the Nicaraguan *Misa Campesina* (peasants' Mass), the "Kyrie" is sung:

Christ, Christ Jesus
identify yourself with us
Lord, Lord God
identify yourself with us
Christ, Christ Jesus
solidarize yourself
not with the oppressor class
that wrings out and devours
the community
but rather with the oppressed
with my people
thirsting for peace.

(lyrics by Carlos Mejia Godoy, 1981; quoted and translated by Roger N. Lancaster in *Thanks to God and the Revolution* © 1988; reprinted by permission of Columbia University Press)

These symbols enable people to conceptualize their situation and to manipulate change-promoting elements of their social world. Sometimes the specific symbols evoked are not very effective. The future sought by a group may be impossible to realize; but genuine social structural changes are unlikely to occur unless people have new ways of thinking about their social world—a set of symbols that evokes images of change (see Maduro, 1977:366).[5]

Religious symbols are often important as a basis for the legitimacy of a social movement for change. For example, progressive Catholic dissent against a violent and repressive regime during El Salvador's civil war (approximately 1981 to 1992) had considerable cultural legitimacy, due in part to the preexisting respect for the figure of the martyr and the symbolic identification of the martyr's sacrifice with that of Christ (Peterson, 1997; see also Whitfield, 1995).

Religious Leadership

Social change often requires an effective leader who can express desired change, motivate followers to action, and direct their actions into some larger movement for change. Religion has historically been a major source of such leaders largely because religious claims form a potent basis of authority. The prototype of the change-oriented religious leader is the prophet, whose social role is especially significant.[6]

---

5. Maduro's theories utilize the seminal work of Pierre Bourdieu (1977), whose theories of symbolic production are useful to a sociology of religion.

6. This discussion of prophets and charismatic authority follows Weber's theories (1946, 1947:458ff., 1963).

A **prophet** is someone who confronts the powers that be and the established ways of doing things, claiming to be taken seriously on religious authority. There are two types of prophetic roles. One is the **exemplary** prophet, whose challenge to the status quo consists of living a kind of life that exemplifies a dramatically different set of meanings and values. The Buddha is a good example of this kind of prophet, whose very way of life is his message. The other type is the **emissary prophet,** who confronts the established powers as one who is sent by God to proclaim a message. Most of the Old Testament prophets were of this type. The emissary prophet has historically been an important source of change because the message proclaimed offered a new religious idea (i.e., ethic) and a different basis of authority. The prophetic message was often one of judgment and criticism. Whether the message called the people back to a previous way of life or directed them to some new way, it nevertheless called for change.

The role of the prophet is the opposite of the priestly role. A priest is any religious functionary whose role is to administer the established religion—to celebrate the traditional rituals, practices, and beliefs. Most clergy and church officials perform priestly roles. The basis of priestly authority is priests' location in the religious organization as representatives of that establishment, and their actions mediate between its traditions and the people. The prophet, by contrast, challenges the established way of doing things, not only by messages of criticism but also by claiming an authority outside the established authority. Thus, the role of the prophet is essentially a force for change in society.

Weber proposed that **charisma** was the authority basis of leaders such as prophets. *Charisma* refers to "a certain quality of an individual personality by virtue of which he is set apart from ordinary men and treated as endowed with . . . specifically exceptional powers or qualities . . . [which] are not accessible to the ordinary person" (Weber, 1947:358, 359). The authority of the charismatic leader rests on the acceptance of his or her claim by a group of followers and on the followers' sense of duty to carry out the normative pattern or order proclaimed by the leader. Thus, the charismatic leader is a source of both new ideas and new obligations.

The charismatic leader says, in effect, "It is written . . . , but I say unto you. . . ." By word or deed, the charismatic leader challenges the existing normative pattern, conveying to the followers a sense of crisis, then offering a solution to the crisis—a new normative order. Charismatic leaders may arise either outside or within the institutional framework. Charismatic authority is *extraordinary*. It breaks away from everyday bases of authority such as those of officials or hereditary rulers. Thus, in certain periods and social settings, charismatic authority is highly revolutionary.

The authority of the Islamic leader Khomeini in the 1979 revolution against the Shah of Iran illustrates this quality of charisma. Khomeini stood in opposition to the rationalization of Iranian society, the modernization of which had upset large segments of the populace. Counterposing a religious charismatic figure against the political leaders "fit" a traditional Shi'ite model of religious action (Arjomand, 1984, 1988). The combination of Khomeini's personal characteristics and his appeal to Shi'ite Islamic dogma was powerful. Although Khomeini disclaimed his revolutionary function, he was viewed as the leader who, according to prophecy, would deliver the people; the prophecy itself was, in turn, reinterpreted as support for his charismatic authority (Kimmel, 1989).

Pure charismatic authority is, however, unstable. It exists only in *originating* the normative pattern and the group that follows it. By the process of routinization, charismatic authority is transformed into a routine or everyday form of authority based on tradition or official capacity, and the new religious group comes to serve the "interests" of its members. Although this routinization usually compromises the ideals of the original message, it is a necessary process for the translation of the ideal into practice. Routinization frequently dilutes the "pure" ideals and sometimes results in a comparatively static organizational form; however, it is also the process by which charisma comes to have its actual impact on history (see M. Hill, 1973b; Weber, 1963:60, 61).

Cycles of charismatic innovation and routinization into organizational stability have occurred in many religious groups and, indeed, in nonreligious institutions, such as political groups. Charismatic leaders formed many of the Protestant and Catholic Reformation movements. After their movements became established and settled as institutional churches, however, later reformers often arose to decry these institutions' compromises and complacency. The Mormons moved from a highly charismatic form of authority under Joseph Smith and Brigham Young to a stable, routinized form under church officials called "bishops" (many of whom are laymen). Similarly, Black Muslims have undergone several phases of charisma and routinization, each time altering the group's ideology, tactics, and form of organization (Lincoln, 1989; Mamiya, 1982).

The development of mass communications, especially those using image technologies such as television and mass advertising, has added a new and complex dimension to the generation of charisma and the uses of public ritual (Wuthnow, 1994). Mass media possess much more flexible and powerful means to shape the presentation of a leader (or group) to generate the image of exceptional powers or qualities for which the audience might impute charismatic authority. Modern movements may use these mass media to create and sustain a sense of urgency, crisis, or imminent disaster to appeal to a mass constituency (Barkun, 1974).

Not only political figures but also religious leaders can frame their images and their messages for maximum media impact. The television coverage of the journeys of Pope John Paul II resembled a serialized narrative, evoking recurrent themes. In repetitive short news clips, the television viewer "saw" the pope set in images of conquest (e.g., with the keys of the city, honor guards, red carpets, in palatial settings). Other media images included symbolic confrontations with death (e.g., located by cemeteries, concentration

---

BOX 7.3   Historical Perspective: St. Francis as Radical Reformer

The history of the Christian churches is a series of charismatic innovations, routinization of charisma, and stable organization, followed by new appearances of charisma. Saint Francis of Assisi was a charismatic leader, an exemplary prophet whose message was also one of judgment: He urged that Christian life must return to its pristine ideals of poverty, community, and simplicity. The early stages of the Franciscan movement (initiated about 1209 C.E.) were a serious threat to the established church and the sociopolitical order with which the church was intertwined. Early followers eschewed material possessions, in imitation of Jesus, such that they avoided even holding money to purchase food or transportation. Rather, they committed to being mendicant (begging their keep) as they preached their message. They emphasized their equality as "brothers" (i.e., friars), criticizing the stratification, power, and pride of the established church officials. Francis's ideals were utterly radical, relative to the church of his day.

There was little to distinguish the Franciscan movement from other religious "threats" of that period— Albigensians, Waldensians, and various other pietistic movements, each with its own charismatic leaders. Unlike others, however, Francis of Assisi sought the acknowledgment and eventual approval of the pope to establish the Friars Minor and a parallel organization for women. The other religious movements, by contrast, were eradicated, often militarily by the sheer might of the established powers. The Franciscan movement in becoming encapsulated as a lay religious order subject to clerical authority, compromised some of its ideals, and its subsequent routinization made it no longer a serious threat to the church. Nevertheless, the Franciscan ideals had great impact and were periodically raised as a critical standard against the complacency and wealth of the churches.

- Why would living in radical poverty and begging represent a form of religious dissent?
- Why would preaching by laymen and laywomen have been so threatening to the established church of that time?

---

camps, soldiers with machine guns) and triumphal images (e.g., cathartic, expressive images of attentive, cheering people who were waving flags, applauding, and attempting to touch the pope) (Guizzardi, 1989).

Charismatic figures portrayed by the media are thus transformed by the selection process inherent in those media: Images mediate the reality to the audience. Some would-be charismatic figures also deliberately manipulate mass media to enhance their position by creating a sense of awe and power unlikely to be attributed in face-to-face interaction with the leader.

Because it is the *followers* who impute charismatic authority to their leader and who put the charismatic ideal into practice, any analysis of the impact of religion on social change must examine the role of the religious group or community in that change.

The Religious Group

Whether the religious group is a small band following a charismatic leader, a growing religious movement, or a staid and established religious organization, it is a potential force for social change. This potential exists because religion, and especially the religious community, is a source of power, which is a fundamental category in the sociology of religion. The same power can be and usually is, however, used to support the status quo. Religion is not only an experience of power but often also results in the sense of being empowered. Thus, the followers of the charismatic leader may experience a sense of power in their relationship with the leader and with fellow believers that enables them to apply the new order to their social world.

This sense of power, especially when identified with the leadership of a charismatic figure, can give a developing religious movement great dynamism. In 1525, for example, Thomas Muntzer issued this call to battle in the German Peasants' War:

> Do not despair, be not hesitant, and stop truckling to the godless villains. Begin to fight the battle for the Lord! Now is the time! Encourage your brethren not to offend God's testimony because, if they do, they will ruin everything. Everywhere in Germany, France, and neighboring foreign lands there is a great awakening; the Lord wants to start the game, and for the godless the time is up. . . . Even if there were only three of you, you would be able to fight one hundred thousand if you seek honor in God and his name. Therefore, strike, strike, strike! This is the moment. These villains cower like dogs. . . . Have no concern for their misery; they will beg you, they will whine and cry like children. Do not show them any mercy. . . . Strike, strike, while the fire is hot. . . . Have no fear, God is on your side! (quoted in Lewy, 1974:115)

Another potential is the religious group's capacity to unite previously disparate segments of a society. Religious sentiment can bridge barriers of tribe, family, nationality, and race. Enthusiastic religious movements (e.g., Pentecostalism) often experience intense egalitarianism in their early stages. Similarly, in some developing nations, religious groups are sometimes the only forces capable of uniting people steeped in a tradition of tribalism. The followers of Simon Kimbangu in Zaire and Jehovah's Witnesses in Kenya and Zambia exemplify this unifying dynamism. Religion often provides a bridge enabling people of different social-class interests to work together, as illustrated by the early stages of the Solidarity movements in Poland and Catalonia (Johnston and Figa, 1988). The religious community can produce a sense of group consciousness and solidarity that focuses a group's awareness of its needs and interests and strengthens its efforts to achieve its goals (Levine, 1990; Lewy, 1974:217–220).

Another change-related feature of religious groups is that they are microcosms of political participation. Throughout history, members of religious groups often got a "first taste" of political agency through the polity of their religious group, rather than their state. Long before they had the opportunity for democratic participation in their governments, many Presbyterians, Baptists, and Congregationalists, among others, experienced a measure of political agency in their church organization. These experiences may have shaped their eventual image of a good government and prepared them to be more active and effective than people who had no such experience. Similarly, in many countries of Latin America, small Catholic groups called *Communidades Eclesiales de Base* ("base communities") have changed members' expectations for political participation and action toward greater democratization (Cavendish, 1994; Levine and Mainwaring, 1989; see also Brooks, 1999; Bruneau, 1988; Cousineau, 1998; Hewitt, 1990; Krauze, 1999; Levine, 1992; Smith, 1994; Womack, 1999).

Certain forms of religious collectivity typically have greater change-oriented potential. Sectarian collectivities are, by definition, in greater negative tension with society than are denominational or churchly collectivities (see Chapter 5). Sectarian religious groups are particularly likely to mobilize efforts for change because of their characteristic criticism of the larger society and insistence that religion be applied to all spheres of members' lives. Churches and denominations, by contrast, generally have more substantial social bases for action but are less likely to challenge the status quo. As Chapter 5 demonstrates, different kinds of religious collectivities have different potential for change-oriented action. Furthermore, these collectivities experience organizational transformations that reduce or promote their dissent.

FACTORS SHAPING
THE INTERRELATIONSHIP OF RELIGION
AND SOCIAL CHANGE

The earlier parts of this chapter explored those aspects of religion that are change-inhibiting, change-promoting, or both. A more complex question now arises: Under what conditions is religion likely to be either change-inhibiting or change-promoting? The circumstances surrounding a change-oriented effort often determine the degree to which the effort is effective. Thus, we also need to ask: Under what conditions is religion most likely to be an effective source of social change? And what are the social factors that maximize or minimize religion's influence in a society?

Qualities of Beliefs and Practices

Certain qualities of some religions' beliefs and practices make them more likely to effect change than other religions. A sociologist would seek to learn some of these qualities by asking the following questions.

Does the belief system contain a critical standard against which the established social system and existing patterns of interaction can be measured? Those religions that emphasize a critical standard (e.g., a prophetic tradition or a revolutionary myth) pose the potential of internal challenge to the existing social arrangements. The prophetic tradition of the Israelites was a basis for subsequent religious challenges to the established way of doing things (Weber, 1952, 1963). Similarly, nations such as the United States, France, or the Republic of Ireland, where the civil religion embodies a revolutionary myth, have a built-in point of reference for internal criticism (Stauffer, 1974). This prophetic aspect of American civil religion was central to the appeal of the civil rights movement. Kennedy's inaugural address was similarly built on prophetic aspects of American civil symbols.

Ethical standards also provide a basis for internal challenge to existing social arrangements. The social critic can say, in effect, "This is what we say is the right way to act, but look how far our group's actions are from these standards!" Many Americans judged their nation's conduct of the war in Vietnam as immoral. The emphasis of ethical standards within certain religions provides a regular ground for social action and change (Nelson, 1949; Weber, 1963).

Furthermore, the content of norms and ethical standards influences the kinds of resulting social action. Some religious groups emphasize personal or private moral norms such as strictures against smoking, drinking, gambling, premarital and extramarital sexual activities, divorce, homosexuality, abortion, and contraception. Other religious groups put greater emphasis on public morality, focusing on issues such as social justice, poverty, corporate responsibility, ethics of public policy, and war. Both approaches may result in efforts for social change. The temperance movement of the 1920s and the antiabortion movement of recent years both exemplify movements based on personal moral norms; the civil rights movement of the 1960s and the U.S. Central American peace movement of the 1970s and 1980s were efforts to apply moral judgments to the public sphere (Smith, 1996). Religiously motivated social activism is often particularly effective precisely when it is successful in morally de-legitimating its political opponents. For instance, President Reagan's Assistant Secretary of State conceded the effectiveness of religious peace activists, stating "Taking on the churches is really tough. We don't normally think of them as political opponents, so we don't know how to handle them. It has to be a kid-glove kind of thing. They are really formidable" (quoted in Smith, 1996: 380–381).

The existence of such value standards within a group's belief system sometimes provides a basis of legitimacy for leaders who try to move the collectivity to social action. For example, in the 1950s and 1960s, priests ministering to Hispanic farmworkers in California could refer to the Catholic Church's social teachings (e.g., papal encyclicals) regarding social justice and workers' right to organize (Mosqueda, 1986). Despite objections from local clergy and bishops whose congregations (and financial resources) included the grower/employers, these leaders gained legitimacy from the existence of strong standards and ideals taught by their religion at an international level.

How does the belief system define the social situation? Individuals' perceptions of the social situation are shaped largely by how their belief system defines that reality. If a religion informs believers that their misfortune is part of God's plan to test their faith, they are not likely to challenge that misfortune. Believers are unlikely to try changing a situation that the belief system has defined as one that humans are powerless to change. Belief systems that embody this kind of fatalism are not conducive to social activism. Some belief systems promote fatalism as a response to the expected imminent end of the world. One Seventh Day Adventist explained why she did not vote or get involved in Hispanic political efforts in her community: "[T]his world is going to be destroyed anyway. We should be focusing our interest on heavenly things. I fear that if we become too involved in these things, we may overlook important things in life" (quoted in Hernández, 1988).

Similarly, belief systems that are voluntaristic are unlikely to result in concerted efforts for change because they define problems in the social situation as the sum of all the individual shortcomings. Accordingly, social ills can be overcome only by converting all individuals to the right way of life. Certain religious definitions of the situation (e.g., fatalism and voluntarism) are less likely than other religious definitions to result in concerted efforts for structural social change.

How does the belief system define the relationship of the individual to the social world? This question is a generalization of the Weberian theme described earlier in this chapter. Weber pointed out that certain belief systems encourage different kinds of individualism and that this individual-to-society relationship is critical to social action. Weber also distinguished between religions that promote a "this-worldly" as compared with an "other-worldly" outlook. Buddhism's interpretation of the material world and aspirations as illusion discourages this-worldly action. By contrast, many strains of Protestantism emphasize one's "working-out" of salvation in this world and one's "stewardship" (i.e., responsible use) of God-given worldly resources. While "this-worldly" religious perspectives are generally more oriented toward social action, an "other-worldly" focus can serve to withhold legitimacy from the dominant society (Fields, 1985; Goldsmith, 1989). These aspects of the belief system determine the likelihood and direction of action for social change.

The Cognitive Framework of the Culture

Relevant to any discussion of religion's role in social change is the cognitive mode of the culture. What are the main ways that people in a culture think about themselves and their actions? While these qualities of the culture may be related to specific items of religious belief, they are more general. Discovering the cultural aspects that shape the influence of religion on social change would include the following factors.

Is the religious mode of action central to the cognitive framework of the culture? And are other modes of action (e.g., political) foreign to the way people think? Religious modes of action may be the only channel people have for affecting their world; other modes of action may be not only foreign but literally inconceivable. In much of Latin America, most people's worldview is saturated by religion, and religion has the potential to be a viable and vital mode of social action. Economic dissatisfaction and political dissent may be expressed in religious terms and resolved in religious modes of action (Maduro, 1977; Worsley, 1968).

In cultures where the religious mode of action is pervasive, people are unlikely to conceive of other ways of organizing for change. If another mode of action is introduced, people are likely to be highly suspicious because the idea of a group with no religious identity is impossible to them; they cannot conceive of a group for whom religion is irrelevant to mutual activities. The People's Democracy, a radical independent political movement arising in Northern Ireland during the late-1960s strife, was utterly anomalous because in that social context a nonsectarian social group was inconceivable to most persons (Beach, 1977). In the United States, by contrast, nonreligious modes of action are both common and conceivable partly because of the ideological separation of church and state but also because of the high degree of *institutional differentiation* in modern society. Religious institutions are separated from other institutional spheres such as economic and political ones. The difference between these two cultural settings is not only in the social structure but also in the characteristic ways the people think about *themselves and their actions.*

Are religious roles and identification significant modes of individual action in the culture? Does it make sense in the culture for an individual to claim a religious identity or a special religious role? And are religious roles understandable forms of leadership? For Joan of Arc to make religious claims for her leadership made sense to the people of her culture, whereas similar claims in a modern society would probably result in derision or labeling as symptomatic of mental illness. In cultures where religion is important in determining how one thinks of oneself or how others identify one, religion is probably a more significant vehicle for change than in cultures where religious roles are less acceptable.

These aspects of religion suggest that not merely the belief content of religion determines its influence on social change but also the underlying cognitive framework of people in that culture. Sociological analysis of the change-promoting and change-inhibiting characteristics of religion must take into account these cognitive modes, which shape people's ways of thinking about themselves and their world.

The Social Location of Religion

Most sociological analyses of religion's impact on social change have focused on the social location of religion in various societies. They refer to the structural relationship between religion and other parts of society (i.e., where does religion "fit" into the total pattern of how things are done?). Also, the internal structure of religious groups is related to their larger social location. The following criteria suggest some of the structural aspects of religion in relation to society that are relevant for understanding the extent of its impact on social change.

Is religion relatively undifferentiated from other important elements of the society? In most simple societies, religion is diffuse. It permeates all activities, social settings, group norms, and events. Religion, not a separate institution, is undifferentiated even in people's ways of thinking. The person who plants seed with a ritual blessing does not think of the blessing as a separate religious action; it is simply part of the right way to plant seed. One of the definitive characteristics of modernization is differentiation of various spheres of social life. Relatively complex modern societies are characterized by structural (and often spatial) segregation of different parts of social life into identifiable separate institutions.

We can envision societies as falling somewhere on a continuum between these two polar types:

Highly undifferentiated
(religion diffuse)

Highly differentiated
(religion segregated)

In societies where religion is relatively undifferentiated, any change-oriented action is also likely to be religious action. Some of the millenarian movements described in Chapter 2 exemplify religious actions that are also sociopolitical. In relatively undifferentiated societies, religious dissent is often a way of expressing political and economic dissatisfactions. By contrast, although religious action can express other dissatisfactions in relatively differentiated societies such as the United States, members of such societies often think of each institutional sphere as separate and of religious action as irrelevant to the political or economic sphere.

If religion is relatively differentiated from other institutional spheres, do strong ties exist between religious institutions and other structures—especially political and economic ones? The more linkages that exist between religion and other institutional spheres, the more likely that religious movements for change are expressions of dissatisfaction with other spheres as well. Historically, dissatisfaction with political and economic spheres has been prominent, but dissatisfaction with other differentiated institutions is also possible. For example, a number of contemporary religious movements show strong currents of dissatisfaction with the dominant medical system in American society (Freund and McGuire, 1999).

Even in highly differentiated social structures, linkages often exist between institutional spheres. Such linkages range from formal ties (e.g., the state church in England) to highly informal connections (e.g., the "coincidence" of closely overlapping membership between a congregation and other social and political associations in a community). Earlier in this chapter, we saw how religion is often used to legitimate the status quo and serve the interests of the dominant group. Religious organizations themselves often have vested interests such as lands, wealth, and power to protect. These kinds of linkages with political structures and the stratification system are precisely why religion is often used as a vehicle of *dissent against* the political or stratification system.

In societies where religion is closely linked by formal or informal ties with the state, religious movements are especially likely to have political (though not only political) significance. The Protestant Reformation was a highly political movement, but religious ideas were also very important. In the United States, where the official linkages between religion and the state are minimized, there is still a considerable informal religiosity (e.g., congressional prayer breakfasts) and an entire set of beliefs and practices related to civil religion (see Demerath and Williams, 1990). The strong connection between religion and America-love-it-or-leave-it in the 1960s made plausible a specifically religious mode of political reaction. Precisely because the dominant political system was supported by mainstream religiosity, religion was a significant force for political dissent.

Similarly, in situations where religion is closely linked with the stratification system, religious movements are likely to be expressions of socioeconomic dissatisfaction. As the Extended Application in Chapter 6 shows, Catholics were particularly active in the 1960s civil rights movement in Northern Ireland because persistent discrimination against Catholics was embedded in the entire stratification system.

Many theories about the development of religious movements focus on economic or status deprivation (as discussed in Chapter 5). A relationship clearly exists between religious discontent and disprivilege, but it is not so simple or direct as some of these theories imply. The utterly poor and powerless rarely form change-oriented movements because of their fatalism, lack of resources, and the sheer struggle for basic subsistence. At the other end of the socioeconomic ladder, the powerful and privileged rarely form such movements because the established ways of doing things in the society serve their interests well. The broad spectrum of persons between these two poles, however, is difficult to characterize in their likelihood of forming movements for change. Nevertheless, it is possible to generalize that where religion is structurally linked with socioeconomic privilege, religious dissent and movement for change are likely to express dissatisfaction with the existing distribution of privilege and power. Where such dissatisfactions are not adequately handled by the existing religious groups, fertile ground exists for new change-oriented religious movements.

Do other modes effectively compete with religion for the expression of human needs, the development of leadership, and organization of effort toward social changes? In some societies, religious groups may be the most effective vehicle for social change because they are better situated to mobilize change-oriented action. In others, other modes of action such as political or legal action may be better developed and more effective. In some situations, religious organizations and leaders become virtually the only available voices for change due to the co-optation or repression of other avenues. In South Africa, church leaders (except those of the Dutch Reformed churches) protested apartheid from its inception in 1948. By the 1980s, the government had imprisoned, banned, or exiled most secular antiapartheid leaders, so religious leaders (taking considerable risk) became the foremost spokespersons and activist leaders. In 1988 Anglican

Bishop Desmond Tutu (who was awarded the Nobel Peace Prize in 1984), together with twenty-five other church leaders from sixteen denominations, openly defied government bans and called on all Christians to boycott the election for segregated municipal councils. They declared, "By involving themselves in the elections, Christians would be participating in their oppression and the oppression of others" (Thompson, 1990:239). The widespread respect these leaders gained during their protest subsequently made them a more effective voice for reconciliation after apartheid ended and a new government was formed.

Similarly, the Catholic Church became the primary voice for socioeconomic and legal-political changes in Brazil between 1964 and 1985, when a dictatorial military regime had systematically suppressed opposition from political parties and congress, the courts, the press, universities, and labor organizations (Levine, 1990; Smith, 1979). Catholic bishops denounced use of torture and absence of fair trials for political prisoners, published information demonstrating the links between government security forces and private death squads, publicly highlighted the inequitable distribution of wealth, and helped indigenous peoples protect their lands against encroachments by mining and agribusiness developments. Many of the laypeople and clergy involved in these resistance efforts were harassed, arrested, or murdered (Smith, 1979). The bishops openly denounced the military government's economic policies for the poverty they engendered and the injustice of economic development that displaced peasant farmers and indigenous peoples from their lands. The bishops declared "a preferential option for the poor," meaning that, by design, the church was identifying with the masses of poor, trying to represent their needs and interest, and structurally opening itself to their fullest participation in the church and society (Adriance, 1986). After more than a decade of Catholic Church dissent against the oppressive Brazilian military regime, one observer concluded, "The church has become the primary institutional focus of dissidence in the country" (Bruneau, 1982:151).

After 1985, however, the government came under the control of a civilian government and repressive measures were gradually lifted (although serious socioeconomic disparities remain). Other forms of expressing dissent became increasingly legal and viable, and the church has been less vocal on political issues (due partly to constraints from the Vatican and the Conference of Latin American Bishops). At the same time, the Catholic Church lost some of its monolithic status, as Protestant churches gained converts and as Afro-Brazilian movements (already a significant presence) gained recognition. The Brazilian Catholic Church continued to speak out against elitist politics, gross inequalities of wealth and productive resources, serious and widespread poverty, and injustices to peasants and indigenous peoples (Levine and Mainwaring, 1989), but its voice became one among many competing public claims.

What is the social location of religious leaders? The potential of charismatic or traditional religious leaders to effect change largely depends on their social location: ties with a pool of potential followers, links with resources that can be mobilized in a movement, and connections with networks of related movements or leaders. Leaders of any movement require these kinds of ties. Recognizing the importance of these linkages, social organizations threatened by dissent often isolate potential leaders in a social location where they are cut off from the people and resources necessary to establish a change-oriented movement. Church officials, for example, might assign a potential "trouble-maker" to a remote and tiny parish. Although charismatic leaders are less restricted by such official pressures than other leaders, their social location also influences the likelihood of their gaining a sufficient base of support. At same time, when church officials themselves try to promote social change (as exemplified by a case study of Canadian Catholic bishops' social justice programs), their access to both human and material resources make their efforts particularly effective (Hewitt, 1991). Whether or not religious leaders or movements succeed in their efforts for social change depends on their location relative to social resources, organization resources, and a pool of potential followers.

In rural Brazil, "base communities" (*Communidades Eclesiales de Base,* or CEBs) are small Catholic groups that base their social activism on their reflections of the Bible as applied to their social situation. Most of these grassroots organizations were organized and taught this approach by pastoral agents (typically nuns or lay church workers, and sometimes priests), who lived and identified with the people. Their leadership effectiveness was due to their ability to generate local lay leadership and to open new ways of thinking—new images of social relationships in people's ways of thinking about their world. For example, CEBs in rural Brazil encouraged members to consider ways of thinking about land reform in the light of their reading of the Gospel (Adriance, 1994; Cousineau, 1997). A similar leadership role was assumed by a handful of intellectual clerics who identified with the masses of Puerto Rican immigrants to New York (Díaz-Stevens, 1993).

A related aspect of religious leaders' location is their relative autonomy from economic interests of their followers and their opposition: How independent are they? When religious leaders must depend upon powerful interest groups for patronage, they are not likely to challenge the status quo. Oppositional movements require organizational autonomy, not only for control of material resources but especially for control of cultural resources. Local clergy were complicit with local industrialists in putting down textile workers' strikes (studied by Pope, 1942). By contrast, during coal miners' strikes of the same era, religious leaders (some of whom were ministers who came to identify with the workers and some of whom were lay leaders, miner-ministers) helped legitimate miners' struggles for a union (Billings, 1990).

One important factor in the relative influence of religious leaders is the impact of pluralism and institutional differentiation on the salience of religious authority. In a pluralistic religious situation, competing worldviews each have their own spokespersons who can exercise influence that is not necessarily recognized, however, outside their immediate group. A Mormon bishop's pronouncement on a social issue may be printed in national newspapers and read with interest by non-Mormons, but it is not likely to be considered authoritative by persons outside the Mormon fold.

Similarly, institutional differentiation has often led to the idea that religious leaders should speak out only on "spiritual" matters. One survey found that 82 percent of the laity agreed that "clergymen have a responsibility to speak out as the moral conscience of this nation." Nevertheless, 49 percent felt that "clergy should stick to religion and not concern themselves with social, economic, and political questions" (reported in Hadden, 1969:148, 149). This opinion reflects the sense that religious leadership is not relevant to other institutional spheres and that "moral conscience" is generally a matter of private-sphere activities (e.g., marriage and family). Pluralism and institutional differentiation, important features of some modern societies like the United States, considerably diminish the impact of religious leadership and religious movements.

The Internal Structure of Religious Organizations and Movements

In societies where religion is relatively differentiated with distinctive religious organizations, members' access to religious power is an important variable in whether that religious group can be change-promoting. A centralized priestly hierarchy that controls religious "goods" (e.g., salvation) is in a strong position of power to shape the direction and force of that group's efforts. The American Roman Catholic Church was able to racially integrate its congregations and schools long before most Protestant denominations or public schools, because it used an authority that superseded local authorities and opinion (see Campbell and Pettigrew, 1959, for a study of on the tension between local opinion and organizational security in ministers' involvement in civil rights activism).

Centralized religious organizations typically support the societal status quo because they also have vested interests in the economic and political arrangements of that society. In some cases, however, a religious organization identifies with those out of power and privilege (e.g., when it is the religion of a colonial people). A study of turn-of-the-century labor relations in Philadelphia found that interactions between trade unionists and mainstream denominations had considerable *mutual* influence. The popular millennialism of the working-class labor movement and the Social Gospel and ideas of justice of the mainstream Protestants were mutually transformative (Fones-Wolf, 1989).

Access to religious power can be the source of social power, whether for change or stability. Similarly, religions that incorporate a more democratized sense of religious power (e.g., Pentecostalism and other forms of experiential religiosity) have the potential to convert that sense of power to social action. Typically, these groups do not organize themselves for action, however, because other elements of their belief systems do not encourage social action. While the potential for change-oriented action is present in such groups, the loose internal structure of their organizations would lead to a very different form of action than that of a centralized organization.

Another feature of a religious organization that sometimes strengthens its effectiveness in social change is the degree to which a group has larger organizational support outside its immediate situation. Before the fall of the "Iron

Curtain" in Eastern Europe, Roman Catholic clergy in Poland were more able to challenge those in power in the country because theirs was an organization with a supranational base (Mojzes, 1987; see also Chodak, 1987; Chrypinski, 1989). If their religious organization had had only a local base of power and authority, the clergy would have been more vulnerable to suppression or co-optation by the established national political-economic powers (Westhues, 1973).

In some situations, the larger organization tries to foster change in the face of local resistance. In South Africa, the National Council of Churches has been at the forefront of confrontation with the state over the issues of human rights and apartheid (i.e., between 1948 and 1994, the government policy of rigid segregation and stratification of racial groups). The Dutch Reformed Church of South Africa (the denomination of the majority of the dominant white group, the Afrikaners) generally supported apartheid and provided scriptural justification for the policy (Cowell, 1985; Jubber, 1985). When they refused to alter their pro-apartheid stand, two white South African Reformed churches were suspended in 1982 by the international denomination, the World Alliance of Reformed Churches (Barkat, 1983). Finally, in 1986, the Dutch Reformed Church of South Africa rescinded its support of apartheid. While not actively condemning it, as did the international denomination, the church statement did affirm that the "use of apartheid as a socio-political system . . . cannot be accepted on Christian ethical grounds . . ." (quoted in *The New York Times,* October 23, 1986).

The national centralized denomination served a similar role in supporting ministers speaking out against child labor and other working conditions in mills (Pope, 1942:195–198). A study of twenty-eight American religious groups found that the ability of church leaders to carry through controversial policies (such as racial integration) was dependent on the degree of authority given them by a central formal authority. Ministers were in especially weak positions in groups with congregational polity, where their congregations had power to dismiss them without reference to a higher authority (Wood, 1970, 1981). At the same time, however, the larger organization can stifle or suppress local initiatives for change, as illustrated by the tension between the (local) Latin American bishops and the pope at the 1978 Puebla Conference in Mexico, as well as Rome's later pressures to curb Liberation Theology in Latin America.

EXTENDED APPLICATION:
AFRICAN-AMERICAN RELIGIOUS
EXPRESSIONS

As the preceding section suggests, analysis of whether or not religion promotes change in a specific situation must take into account a complex array of variables. Sociologists have analyzed numerous historical developments, such as the spread of evangelical Protestantism in Latin America and the role of religion in worker/union militancy and suppression in the United States. One recurring question is whether U.S. minority religious groups, such as African-American churches, serve to support the status quo or to promote social change for their people. The answer is "yes": Religion both supports the status quo and promotes active social change, often simultaneously. This section examines some developments in the religious experience of African-Americans that illustrate its change-promoting and change-inhibiting aspects.

There is no single entity that is African-American religion; rather, it includes a number of expressions, mostly Christian, that have a common heritage in the experiences of slavery and racism. This common background makes it possible to speak of "African-American religious expressions" even when describing groups with very different belief systems. While the African Methodist Episcopal church is greatly different from the Spiritualist churches and from the Lost Found Nation of Islam (i.e., Black Muslims), all are outgrowths of the historical situation of African-Americans. At the same time, the enormous diversity of African-American religious expressions makes them impossible to summarize in tidy generalizations.

One source of this complexity is that religious groups themselves continually deal with built-in tensions, and they change their resolution to these tensions over time, depending upon the sociohistorical situation. As Chapter 5 and 6 showed, these tensions exist for most Western religions, but minority religions in pluralistic societies experience them differently. The tension between *priestly* and *prophetic* functions pulls each local group between an involvement in the celebration of its own religious life on the one hand and pronouncing God's judgment (including speaking to political and social issues) to the wider community on the other hand. The tension between *other-worldly* and *this-worldly* orientations is another pair of poles simultaneously present in most African-American religious expressions. The tension between *universalism* and *particularism* is present for all Western religions, but it is particularly problematic for ethnoreligious minorities. Another pair of poles is the *communal* and the *privatized;* with other Protestants, most black Christian groups share the pull of privatized religiosity, but African-American popular religious tradition puts a unique and powerful communal "spin" on their Protestantism. Another tension that influences the degree of change-promoting activism is the pull between *charismatic* and *bureaucratic* patterns of authority and organization. Two political options, *resistance* versus *accommodation,* represent another pull experienced by African-Americans and other nondominant groups (Lincoln and Mamiya, 1990:11–15). If we remember that these polar opposites are not one-time, either-or decisions, we can better appreciate how African-American religious groups can be both change-promoting and change-inhibiting.

Afro-Christian Popular Roots

African-American religious expression began under slavery, accounting for a considerable part of its distinctiveness but also of its diversity. The exigencies of slave life, with its omnipresent power relationships and its dialectic of domination and resistance, brought together several religious strands.

Historians disagree about the exact shape of American slave religion, but its general outline is well known. Like all American religions, it had both popular and institutional elements, but the former were stronger. As described in Chapter 4, popular religion is by definition not under official religious control. Thus, it has the potential for expressing a nondominant people's dissent. It is also, however, characteristically loosely organized and fragmented, each local group's beliefs and practices being poorly articulated with those of other adherents. Lacking official clergy or recognized interpreters, it is vulnerable to co-optation or suppression.

Early African-American religions were highly syncretic, with different localities interweaving different elements; some of the recognizable combinations today include mainline, evangelical, and pentecostal/holiness Afro-Christian strands, Creole vodou, Spiritualist, and Afro-Caribbean practices such as Orisha vodou, Santería, and Espiritismo (Baer and Singer, 1992; Chevannes, 1998).[7] Afro-Christian religious expression retained elements of West African oral performance, music and rhythm, and other ritual expression (Pitts, 1993; see also Davis, 1985).[8] The tribal religions of the parts of Africa from which slaves were taken were highly diverse and local, so no single religion could have survived in North America, but African influences were kept in highly syncretized form (Raboteau, 1978). Some recent interpreters have argued that African-American and African-Caribbean religion today is essentially West African (especially Yoruba) religion. They hold that slaves added a thin veneer of Christianity to "trick" the slave overseers. This approach is too simplistic and not based upon the historical evidence of diversity among slaves; tribal religions were themselves diverse, and a considerable number of enslaved Africans in America were practicing Muslims (Joyner, 1994; Turner, 1997). A more balanced interpretation reminds us that: "To underestimate the Africanity of African American Christianity is to rob the slaves of their heritage. But to overestimate the Africanity of African American Christianity is to rob the slaves of their creativity" (Joyner, 1994).

These diverse African tribal religious elements were thoroughly blended with elements of enthusiastic evangelical Christianity spread in the early 1800s by the fervor of the Second Great Awakening—a religious revitalization movement that swept the American countryside from 1770 to 1815. Both blacks and whites were influenced by revivalistic camp meetings, days-long enthusiastic preaching, and a theology that expressed a lively sense of the Holy Spirit. Not all blacks were affected equally, however.

---

7. For sources on Afro-Atlantic and Afro-Caribbean syncretism, see Baer, 1984; Brown, 1991; Chevannes, 1998; Curry, 1997; Desmangles, 1992; Glazier, 1983; Murphy, 1988; Simpson, 1965, 1978; Stevens-Arroyo and Pérez y Mena, 1995.

8. Although the many studies seeking to identify African roots of American religions are a useful corrective to portrayals of slave religion as having abandoned all African influences, they distract us from appreciating the diversity, creativity, and contemporary significance of ongoing syncretism and mutual influence of religious cultures in contact. As Baer and Singer (1992:3) emphasize, "much of the current importance of these African elements derives not from their possible source but in the part they have played and continue to play in the crafting of special mechanisms for social survival, emotional comfort, and transcendent expression under the harshest of physical circumstances."

The conditions of Afro-Christian religious practice varied widely under slavery: Some slaves had extensive opportunities to learn Christian teachings and practices, while others had only fragmented and secondhand knowledge. After a series of slave uprisings, most slave states passed laws forbidding black preaching, forcing slave religious meetings into hiding. Subsequent missions to the slaves (1820s until the Civil War) reached far more people, but also were more compromised by their need to be approved by plantation owners, who typically welcomed Christian teaching if it served to keep the slaves docile and obedient. Nevertheless, by the middle of the nineteenth century, a clearly Christian religion had developed among slaves. It afforded them a chance to gather with each other and exchange social support, to develop their own leadership and social standing, and to express emotionally and spiritually their feelings, despite a social system that treated them as nonpersons. It sometimes also provided opportunities for resistance and escape (Raboteau, 1978).

Particularly significant for our understanding of the change-promoting and change-inhibiting features of African-American religious synthesis is the centrality of its theme of liberation. The Bible, the center of Christian missionary preaching, is replete with stories of liberation, which became central in African-American Christianity. The slaves identified with the suffering Israelites in their bondage. While the Euro-American Protestants thought of their young country as "the New Israel," or even the Promised Land, the African-American experience of it was more like "the New Egypt" of bondage and oppression (Raboteau, 1995). Not only was this theme of liberation preached and sung, for example, in spirituals such as "Go Down, Moses," but it also was embedded in ritual practice, especially the experience of conversion (Dvorak, 1991). What slave Christians "remembered" from biblical stories, hymns, and other Christian practices, thus, was very different from what their southern white Christian counterparts "remembered," even though both practiced a very similar evangelical, intensely emotional, Bible-centered popular Christianity.

Contained within the worldview of slave Christianity were both change-promoting and change-inhibiting themes. Certainly the potential for a prophetic stance is inherent in the themes of liberation and deliverance.[9] The emphasis on communal bonds, of an identity as God's people and commensality (sharing a meal with the Lord and each other), also has potential for promoting solidarity and support—both features of successful movements for change (see Dodson and Gilkes, 1995). On the other hand, the eschatological emphases of the Afro-Christian worldview (e.g., the image of Jesus' future return setting things right) often promoted fatalism rather than activism and typically led to an other-worldly emphasis. But the same symbols have the

---

9. The theme of Moses confronting the pharoah is still prominent in the prophetic stance of African-American churches. When the National Baptist Convention, the nation's largest black religious organization, decided in 1993 to focus on social issues and self-empowerment, the convention chairman told the story of Moses leading his people to the Red Sea, asking God how to get across, and hearing that with the rod in his hand he could part the waters. The chairman concluded: "What we have in our hand is the dollar. What we have in our hand is the vote. We must use what we have in our hand" (quoted in Jones, 1993).

potential to promote change, as the example of millenarianism in Chapter 2 suggests (see Genovese, 1979; Moses, 1993).

Making Their Own Organizations

Independent denominations (e.g., African Methodist Episcopal and National Baptist) are the prominent religious organizations in the African-American community today. Seven historic denominations account for roughly 80 percent of all religiously affiliated African-Americans (Lincoln and Mamiya, 1990:441). The historical split of these groups from their white-dominated parent denominations was neither theological nor caused by dissent over doctrinal or moral purity; it was essentially a split along lines of social caste.

The religious fervor of the Second Great Awakening (1770–1815) was intensely egalitarian. Not only did the belief systems of evangelical groups promote brotherhood, but the shared intense religious experience itself produced a strong sense of equality. In the period after the Revolutionary War, Methodists and other Protestants directly attacked slavery and welcomed African-Americans into their fellowships (Lincoln and Mamiya, 1990; Washington, 1972). In the North and Midwest there were racially mixed congregations of Presbyterians, Methodists, Quakers, Episcopalians, Baptists, and Congregationalists. This form of African-American religious affiliation was, however, typically limited to free persons (indeed, some of them freed because of the antislavery influence of the Second Great Awakening on slaveholders). It was not extended to the masses until slavery was ended (Genovese, 1974; Lincoln and Mamiya, 1990).

From these beginnings grew the major African-American denominations. After the initial egalitarian euphoria waned, African-American Christians found themselves given only limited leadership roles and often segregated participation in their churches, and they challenged these arrangements. When Richard Allen and Absalom Jones protested segregated seating by leading a band of African-American Methodists out of Philadelphia's Saint George's Methodist Episcopal Church in 1787, it was the beginning of separate U.S. African-American denominations. Allen later formed the African Methodist Episcopal Church, a prototype of African-American independent churches (Lincoln and Mamiya, 1990:49–58; Washington, 1972:36–46).

Unlike most other religious splinter groups, these churches did not differ significantly from their parent organizations in their belief systems or patterns of worship. Their dissent was based solely on the treatment of African-American members by predominantly white parent organizations. As a result, their organizations were essentially denominational from the start. They did not exhibit sectarian characteristics such as withdrawal into boundary-maintaining enclaves. These independent denominations were active in abolitionism and the underground railroad, and they organized numerous educational and social service projects to help escaped slaves arriving in northern cities. After the Civil War they were able to extend their leadership and organization to recently freed slaves; indeed, several Methodist and Baptist denominations competed vigorously to establish new congregations in the postwar

South. Also, unlike the popular religious expressions of African-American slaves, denominational expressions promoted the norm of an educated clergy, networks of denominational organization, and regular regional conferences. These organizational features gave them greater coherence and structural supports for new congregations; the denominational organization also curbed idiosyncratic teachings and unorthodox interpretations of the Bible. Thus, while their denominational structure did not itself promote social activism, it increased the effectiveness of those change-promoting efforts mounted by the denominations.

A completely different pattern led to the creation of separate African-American denominational groups in the rural South. Major national denominations, including the Methodists, Baptists, and Presbyterians, had split in the early 1800s, largely over the issue of slavery. The factions of each denomination that were organized separately in the South were segregated, with the all-black congregations in an inferior and subordinate relationship. After Emancipation, the northern denominations successfully intensified their recruitment among southern blacks. In the 1860s and 1870s, partly in response to African-American members' push for greater autonomy and partly due to the white majority's wish to dispense with the black membership, southern denominational organizations spun off their African-American constituents into their own organizations, which eventually became separate denominations (Dvorak, 1991; Lincoln and Mamiya, 1990).

Unlike their northern counterparts, however, these denominations lacked experience with church organization and leadership; their members—most of them only recently slaves—had little education or decision-making experiences and virtually no economic resources. Thus, although they gained nominal local autonomy, it was a very insecure social base. Often they were completely subordinate to local (white) patrons for economic support and vulnerable to the economic injustice, intimidation, and outright violence of the *caste system* that developed after Emancipation. Rural African-American churches became indirectly supportive of the political and socioeconomic status quo, becoming a spiritual escape, a safe emotional outlet, a haven/home. They adopted an almost exclusively other-worldly emphasis: Rewards in the next life would make up for deprivations and abuses in this life. Although nominally denominational, these groups were thrust into sectarian withdrawal by the oppression of the larger society (see Baer and Singer, 1992, for a critical analysis of the economic structures shaping the era).

We must understand African-American denominationalism and sectarianism in the context of the caste system in which they developed. These religious organizations do not, on the surface, appear to fit the standard forms described in Chapter 5, because not even the most "established" African-American denomination is fully integrated into the dominant society. We can understand this apparent discrepancy, however, by realizing the extent to which the *caste system* imposed by the larger society positioned *all* African-American institutions in a situation of somewhat negative tension with the institutions of the larger society.

The caste model suggests that individuals can achieve relatively high status within the African-American community and its own institutions (Dollard, 1949). Black religious organizations are stratified in a way that parallels the social-class bases of white religious organizations. There are relatively prosperous, staid, and genteel African-American denominations and congregations, supporting professional clergy and a wide variety of community programs. Also, there are numerous middle-class and working-class congregations of established African-American denominations. And there are vast numbers of (mainly sectarian) religious groups, such as the storefront churches—appealing primarily to economically marginal persons (Wilmore, 1972:195–197). Some of the sectarian groups are often critical of both the established denominational groups and of the larger society, as are many white sectarian groups, but many groups express this tension by withdrawal into sectarian enclaves. Interestingly, much of this stratification of black churches has a long history, linked with the ghettoization of urban African-Americans in the aftermath of migrations (especially 1910–1920) of rural Southern workers to industrial Northern cities (Gregg, 1993).

The black denominational organizations, however, are also able to be critical of the larger society because of their location in the subordinate caste. Indeed, continuing to the present, the more established denominational congregations are more likely than the sectarian congregations to be involved in the social, political, and economic affairs of their communities. In the 1990s, they also tended to be more socially and politically involved than their white denominational counterparts (Cavendish, 2000; Chaves and Higgins, 1992; Lincoln and Mamiya, 1990; Nelsen and Nelsen, 1975). Nevertheless, neither African-American denominations nor sectarian groups have historically been particularly critical of the dominant society, largely because their adherents have generally accepted the American "way of life"—the dominant cultural values and criteria for success. Although they are conscious of racial grievances and real social inequalities, they have not typically questioned the rest of the established cultural order (Wilmore, 1972:213–214).

In the last decades of the nineteenth century, the churches became the focal point of black community life, but the spiritual message was largely other-worldly and moralistic. We must keep in mind, however, the external social, legal, and economic barriers, which—even more than Afro-Christian belief systems—were responsible for this retreat to quietism.

Quietism, Oppression, and Institution-Building

Despite their increased membership, African-American denominations underwent a dramatic retrenchment from the end of the nineteenth century to the late 1950s. The specific experiences leading to this quietist phase varied from region to region but can be generalized as two major factors: *economic struggle* and *sociopolitical discrimination and repression*. In the South, newly freed blacks struggled to make a livelihood in a shattered economy. The Compromise of 1877 led to the withdrawal of federal troops from the South and abandonment of federal guarantees of African-Americans' civil and political liberties. The last two decades of the nineteenth century were marked by considerable violence toward blacks in the South, and several thousands were victims of lynch mobs (Wilmore, 1972:192). "Jim Crow" statutes created and gave legal force to segregation in every sphere of social life. These local and state laws racially segregated schools, workplaces, building entrances, waiting rooms, drinking fountains, toilets, and seating in public transportation. Statutes enforced the exclusion of African-Americans from theaters, restaurants, parks, and residential areas. Poll taxes and discriminatory "literacy" tests effectively excluded most African-Americans from voting in many southern states. In 1940, only about 2 percent of voting-age blacks in twelve southern states "qualified" to vote (Woodward, 1957). Discrimination in northern regions at the turn of the century was less overt. There was a sizable African-American middle class in many northern communities, but the vast majority were unskilled and suffered considerable discrimination in competing for jobs with waves of European immigrants.

The retrenchment of African-American churches in the face of such massive difficulties is understandable. Individual church leaders (e.g., Bishop Henry Turner) protested the situation, but most congregations retreated into the segregated African-American community where they became the dominant institution, providing alternatives to services and facilities from which their members were otherwise excluded. It was not so much a matter of social activism as of simply meeting their members' needs that inspired black churches to provide recreation and social clubs, social services, insurance, and a "decent" burial.

The massive twentieth-century rural-to-urban migrations of African-Americans created new disruptions. Before World War I, only 28 percent of the black population lived in cities; fifty years later 70 percent were urban dwellers (*Report of the National Commission on Civil Disorders,* 1968). Rural churches were crippled by losses of members and material support. Urban churches were overwhelmed by the needs of the huge influx of rural blacks, many of whom were uneducated, unskilled, and unprepared for the difficulties of the urban ghetto (see Gregg, 1993; Nelsen and Nelsen, 1975:36–47). This period marked the beginning of the greatest increase in sectarian groups, discussed in more detail later in this chapter. The city represented a double threat to many rural immigrants: It represented their first experiences with a general nonreligious worldview and with a social situation where the norms and values of a small, tightly knit community did not hold. One commentator concluded: "With a basically rural orientation, most Black churches retreated into enclaves of moralistic, revivalistic Christianity which tried to fend off the encroaching secular gloom and the social pathology of the ghetto. . . . The socially involved, 'institutional' church was the exception rather than the rule" (Wilmore, 1972:221). From the end of reconstruction to the mid-twentieth century, African-American churches generally retreated from social and political activism.

Nevertheless, the inward turn of African-American denominations in the first half of the twentieth century may have served to build institutions for survival and resistance. In the face of discrimination and segregation, these churches developed schools, savings banks, employment services, day-care facilities, health clinics, and social clubs (see Gilkes, 2001). They were also where members learned participation in decision making and wide-ranging discussion of social issues. African-American women were particularly important in these institution-building efforts, and they were remarkably successful in developing alliances with white churchwomen (Higgenbotham, 1993). While not directly engaging in social activism, such institution-building and grassroots political experience within some churches may have been important platforms on which later activism built.

Religion and the Civil Rights Movement

Several features of African-American religion, especially as practiced in urban denominational congregations, account for much of the success of the 1960s civil rights movement in mobilizing resistance to the widespread segregation, discrimination, and disenfranchisement experienced by American blacks at mid-century.

Internal Organization African-American religious groups have had particular potential for social change because of their special place in their community. Because of the strategies developed during the quietist period, the black churches are very much a symbolic expression of community (see Williams, 1974) and a potentially unifying force, though this potential has seldom been realized. Religious organizations are one area, in the interstices of the larger society, where a minority group can develop its social capital. **Social capital** refers to nonmaterial investments (such as in social networks, values, and bonds of trust) that have potential future "payoffs" in terms of credit, reciprocal obligations, and incentives. Perhaps even more than money, social capital is a valuable resource to further the group's—and not merely individual members'—interests (Harris, 1999:88–89).

Part of the problem of mobilizing black churches is their internal structure; most African-American denominations (especially the Baptists) tend to be highly localized and therefore difficult to organize above the congregational level. Most African-American denominational organizations at the national level were conspicuously absent from 1950s and 1960s civil rights activism. A 1962 split that created a new denomination, the Progressive Baptist Alliance, was not over doctrines or rituals but over the growing activism of progressive members.

In several localities, however, churches of various denominations began to band together to promote change. In 1958, 400 African-American ministers in Philadelphia launched a "selective patronage" campaign (i.e., boycott) against industries that depended heavily on black patronage but discriminated against them in hiring. They used the pulpit for announcing target employers and succeeded in stopping some of the blatant job discrimination. The segregation of churches may have aided this effort, since none of the "opposition" was in the audience (Lincoln, 1974). Similar organizational efforts by local churches were important in the Montgomery bus boycott, sit-ins, and freedom rides (see Fredrickson, 1995). African-American denominations, especially with their broadened national bases, have the potential for promoting nationwide programs for change. Many groups, however, have been involved with the problems of maintaining their organizations, and activism seems threatening to their stability and acceptability.

The Role of the Preacher The example of the "Philadelphia 400" suggests another feature of African-American religion that is effective in promoting change: the role of the preacher. Religious leaders have greater influence in the black community than is characteristic in most white communities. Just as the African-American churches were often the primary institution in the black community, so too the preacher was the community leader (Hamilton, 1972). Although the preeminence of this role is declining in recent years, many African-Americans still look to their preachers for leadership on social and political issues. Studies have shown that blacks are more likely than whites to approve of political activism from their preachers and of using the pulpit to discuss political issues (Harris, 1999; Lincoln and Mamiya, 1990; Nelsen and Nelsen, 1975).

The African-American clergy activists of the 1960s civil rights movement used their influence as religious leaders, and their style of leadership and exhortation was characteristic of the preacher. Clergy such as Martin Luther King, Jr., Leon H. Sullivan, Fred Shuttlesworth, Wyatt Walker, and Ralph Abernathy did not distinguish between their roles as religious leaders and civil activists. It was not just their status as clergy, but indeed their religious experience that was recognized in the African-American community as a basis of authority (Manis, 1991). In the civil rights movement, as in some other 1960s protest movements, dissent itself had a religious quality. It was an integral part of the messianic vision implicit in the theology of the movement (see Moses, 1993). Social movement ideologies can be built upon both priestly and prophetic strands of religious worldviews; the fact that African-American religious groups had a strong preexisting prophetic strand made it possible for such leaders to mobilize a movement for social change (see also Williams and Ward, 2000). The importance of the civil rights movement was not only its specific achievements in gaining voting rights, desegregating educational opportunity, and eliminating discriminatory legislation but also in making African-Americans conscious of their power to effect change.

King's effectiveness resulted, in large part, from his ability to combine a mode of sociopolitical dissent (modeled after Gandhi, another exemplar of religious social action) with the folk religion of his people and the revival technique to which they enthusiastically responded (Franklin, 1994; Wilmore, 1972:24–52). The interweaving of religious with political images and symbols and the utilization of religious modes of expression (e.g., hymns and "shouts") were part of the appeal that enabled religious leaders to mobilize the African-American community for action. King's political speeches were essentially sermons in their structures and imagery:

> We cannot walk alone. . . . We cannot turn back. . . . We cannot be satisfied as long as the Negro is the victim of unspeakable horrors of police brutality. We can never be satisfied as long as our bodies, heavy with the fatigue of travel, cannot gain lodging in the motels of the highways and the hotels of the cities. We cannot be satisfied as long as the Negro in Mississippi cannot vote and a Negro in New York believes that he has nothing for which to vote. We cannot be satisfied as long as the Negro's basic mobility is from a smaller ghetto to a larger one. No, no, we are not satisfied, and we will not be satisfied until "justice rolls down like water and righteousness like a mighty stream." (quoted in Spillers, 1971:24)

The leadership style of the preacher "made sense" in the African-American community, enabling clergy activists to move the people to action.

Conceptions of Religious Action Many African-American religious groups employ a conception of religious action based on spiritual (as well as sociopolitical) efficacy. When a social problem is attributed to spiritual as well as social causes, efficacious religious action to address the problem may be spiritual as well as social. For instance, a socially active African Methodist Episcopal congregation attacked the problems of inner-city drug addiction, not only with programs for youth and a halfway house for recovering addicts, but also by a series of prayer-marches through the area's most notorious housing project. The minister gave the following instructions before the march:

> As we walk through here, everybody stay together and pay attention to what you are doing. There are a lot of spirits over this place, so we are going to have to rebuke those spirits by name. For example, say "Spirit of drug addiction, I rebuke you in the name of Jesus" and then renounce its impact on the lives of the people. (quoted in Nelson, 1997:23)

This conception of religious action holds the prayer to rebuke evil spirits to be equally "real" activism as the building of a halfway house. Interpretations of faith-based social activism that attempt to reduce it to the same terms as secular or self-interested groups' sociopolitical involvements fail to understand this powerful feature.

African-American Religious Diversity

Black urban communities display a fascinating variety of religious groups. In addition to representative churches of African-American denominations, there are many sectarian groups. So far we have considered only the African-American denominations, which are large and growing, but there are many vigorous sectarian and cultic groups in African-American communities. By far the most numerous of these are Pentecostal and Holiness congregations, sometimes referred to as "the Sanctified Church" (Gilkes, 1998b; Sanders, 1996). These religious groups originated at the turn of the century in a series of southern revivals (initially among whites and later among blacks), which also spawned white religious groups such as the Nazarenes and the Assemblies of

God. Both black and white pentecostal groups are characterized by their literal interpretation of New Testament practices, especially manifestations of the Holy Ghost (or Holy Spirit) such as speaking in tongues, divine healing, visions, prophecies, and testimony. Two millenarian sectarian groups, Jehovah's Witnesses and Seventh Day Adventists, are racially integrated, but have attracted a larger African-American following than have most other groups led by whites. Their history of successful missionary proselytization in developing countries has resulted in a high proportion of new immigrants from Latin America, Africa, and the Caribbean. The proportion of Caucasians in the North American Division of the Adventist Church dropped from more than 70 percent in 1980 to about 50 percent in 2000 (see Lawson, 1999).

There are also numerous unaffiliated religious groups in African-American communities. These congregations are frequently very similar to organizationally affiliated congregations but depend solely upon local leadership to establish their beliefs and practices, often based on popular religion. Because of this independence from outside authority, some of these groups are idiosyncratic. Father Divine's Peace Mission (begun about 1932) ministered to several thousand black and white people. Members practiced communalism and extremely strict moral norms. The Mission was active in social welfare (e.g., feeding, clothing, and housing people, opening cooperatives and small business enterprises). It was also politically active, opposing Jim Crow and lynching (see Burnham, 1978; Fauset, 1944). The controversial People's Temple of Jim Jones was a sectarian group that, like Peace Mission, attracted both blacks and whites and had substantial social and political programs (see Hall, 1987).

Some sectarian groups, such as Black Muslims and Black Jews, are not Christian but draw on biblical themes attractive to potential recruits from Christian backgrounds. They are clearly sectarian because of their internal structure and their oppositional stance toward the dominant society *and* its religious organizations. Black Jews, for example, must struggle to be accepted as "real" Jews—in the face of racialized conceptions of Jewishness—*and* as "real" Blacks—confronting the anti-Semitism of many African-Americans (Wolfson, 2000; see also Chireau, 2000; Singer, 2000). One particularly good example of the deliberate appeal to Christian themes is the Shrine of the Black Madonna in Detroit. This group retained much of the faith and practice of traditional African-American denominational churches, but asserted that key biblical figures, especially the Messiah, were black. The leader stated that "the Black Muslims demand too much of a break with the past for African-Americans, most of whom have grown up in a Christian church of some sort. We don't demand a break in faith, or customs" (Cleage, 1967:208).

Afro-Christian religious traditions were, interestingly, utilized by non-Christian African-American leaders. Malcolm X, a spokesperson for Black Muslims, was very much a "prophet" in the black religious style. Since most Black Muslims came from Christian backgrounds, their relationship to their religious leaders was probably styled after Afro-Christian folk religion rather than any Islamic pattern. The message of the Nation of Islam, especially as articulated by Malcolm X, is clearly an example of the revolutionary potential of religious movements. Following Malcolm's lead, the Nation of Islam (renamed the American Muslim Mission in 1980) has become more denominationlike, patterning itself on the Sunni branch of Islam. Although they have become a more staid part of the American religious scene, the Black Muslims are probably one of the most important American religious movements in the twentieth century. In reaction to the main group's move away from an extreme sectarian stance, however, Louis Farrakhan revitalized the messianic and dualistic claims of the movement's founder, W. D. Fard (Baer and Singer, 1992:110–146). Nevertheless, Farrakhan has used traditional Afro-Christian leadership style to maintain his place in the public eye, and he has drawn on themes of self-empowerment that appeal to long-standing self-help traditions nurtured in the black churches.

The religious mosaic of the African-American community includes a number of more cultic expressions, some of which are only superficially religious. As explained in Chapter 5, the cultic stance is more pluralistic and tolerant toward other religious groups than the sectarian stance, but it is nonetheless dissonant from the larger society and lacks the societal acceptance characteristic of denominational groups. Unlike sectarian allegiance, cultic adherence is more segmented; frequently members adhere to several such groups simultaneously. Such groups are diverse, ranging from a faith healer's storefront to a group gathered around a "reader." Some cultic leaders are flamboyant and manipulative, such as Prophet Jones, a healer and fortune-teller whose Detroit church "Universal Triumph, the Dominion of God, Incorporated" is remembered less for its teaching than for the wealth it generated for its leader (Robinson, 1974).

Other cultic groups, however, have fully developed religious worldviews and ritual expression based on more than a century of faith and practice. African-American Spiritual churches and vodou are examples of this cultic pattern of organization (see Chapter 4), as well as the focus on religious power for everyday concerns characteristic of the popular religions that came together in these syncretisms. The Spiritual churches amalgamated elements of (predominantly white) Spiritualism, African-American Protestantism, Roman Catholicism, and vodou or hoodoo. Because, as is typical in cultic religious groups, each congregation is autonomous, individual affiliates also mix elements from New Thought (a turn-of-the-century Metaphysical movement also borrowed by some New Age religious groups), Islam, Judaism, Ethiopianism, and astrology (Baer, 1984; Baer and Singer, 1992).

These religious groups characteristically offer adherents segmented bits of meaning rather than a total package of belief and practice. A believer might seek out a reader's spiritually received advice in a marital problem, go to a healer for rheumatism, send for Reverend Ike's prayer cloth to help get a job, and also go to a local church on Sunday. Although the cultic groups preach a worldview, it is seldom the totalistic worldview like that of the sectarian groups. Adherents may be fervent, but they do not typically belong exclusively to that single religious group. While the cultic groups often provide their members with strong social support networks and a positive identity, their emphasis is totally privatized. Therefore African-American cultic groups rarely challenge the status quo, and they typically lack the stability or influence in the community for any activism. For this reason, the following discussion of change-promoting and change-inhibiting influences focuses primarily upon sectarian religious groups in the African-American community.

The Dynamism of Sectarian Religious Expressions Sectarian congregations are among the most dynamic forces in the African-American community. Their members commit much time, energy, and money to their religious groups. Sectarian groups are able to motivate their members to apply religious norms to everyday life, and many of them enforce strict moral codes. Their creativity in forms of worship and sheer enthusiasm is an important expression of the religious group's sense of community. This dynamism has strong potential for promoting change because conversion to a sectarian worldview can redefine social reality for members. Pentecostals who receive the "gifts" of the Spirit, for example, gain a new way of interpreting themselves and the world around them. The belief systems of sects typically contain a negative judgment of the "ways of the world" and a millenarian vision of a future perfect society. These beliefs are potentially change-promoting; but only rarely, historically, have African-American sectarian groups produced fundamental social change.

Sectarian Quietism The reasons for this general quietism appear to lie in the emphases of their belief systems and the social situations in which they must operate. Many sectarian worldviews are even more other-worldly than those of denominational religious groups. Millenarian sectarian groups, as described in Chapter 2, tend to devote their energies to proselytizing new members rather than trying to change what they believe is a nearly defunct society. The emphasis of many sectarian groups upon divine Providence reduces members' consciousness of human agency. Another emphasis of much sectarian religion that inhibits members from social and political activism is their emphasis on private moral norms and individual responsibility. Many groups are strict about members' behavior. They proscribe the use of tobacco, alcohol, and drugs; insist on hard work, honesty, sexual fidelity, and modesty; and forbid entertainments such as gambling, movies, or dancing. Sometimes religious norms directly discourage activism. One woman said, "In my religion we do not approve of anything except living like it says in the Bible; demonstrations mean calling attention to you and it's sinful" (quoted in Marx, 1967:67). These strict personal moral codes often have the indirect consequence of enabling members to fit more effectively into the dominant society.

One study of black attitudes on civil rights issues found members of sects and cults to have the least militant attitudes. Members of independent African-American denominations (e.g., Methodist and Baptist) were substantially more militant than sect and cult members; but most militant were black members of predominantly white denominations such as Episcopalian, Presbyterian, United Church of Christ, and Roman Catholic (Marx, 1967). African-American sectarian congregations' other-worldliness and emphasis on Providence and private (rather than public) morality make them generally less likely than denominational congregations to be involved in social and political activism.

Some exceptional sectarian groups have been seriously involved in social activism, however. In Chicago, an African-American Pentecostal preacher organized the Woodlawn Organization, a neighborhood association that operated successful tenants' rights and consumer protection programs (Brazier, 1969). A recent reexamination of civil rights era opinion surveys of African-Americans suggests that religion may have also been indirectly related to individual activist involvement and movement mobilization even among members of traditionally quietest churches. By promoting a sense of self-worth and personal empowerment and efficacy, some black churches encouraged their members to use religious resources in their activism. For example, one civil rights organizer in Mississippi said, "We stood up. Me and God stood up" (quoted in Harris, 1999:69). There is also some indication that a younger generation of Pentecostal and Holiness preachers is more involved in social activism. For example, one activist black Pentecostal preacher in a northern city said, "Basically I tell [my congregation] that we don't just read the Bible, we *live* it. . . . Injustice is a sin, right? It's *sinful*. So we gotta fight against it" (quoted in McRoberts, 1999:62).

The social location of a religious group may be an important factor in the extent to which it emphasizes activism. Direct social and political action may be a luxury that the absolutely poor have neither the material nor personal resources to consider. Many African-American sects have emphasized comforting and taking care of their members. One early Pentecostal leader said, "The members of my church are troubled and need something to make them happy. My preaching is not about sad things, but always about being saved. The singing in my church has 'swing' to it, because I want my people to swing out of themselves all the mis'ry and troubles that is heavy on their hearts" (quoted in Washington, 1972:67).

These groups provide a small, close-knit community of mutual care and concern, often in the center of an otherwise harsh and anonymous urban environment (see Kostelaros, 1995). African-American sects may have withdrawn from action in society both from opposition to the "ways of the world" and as a response to the threatening atmosphere of their social situation. A small, close-knit group of fellow believers serves as protection against the influences of "the world," but it also narrows members' lives to a "safe" enclave. These aspects of the social situation surrounding black sects and cults, as much as the content of their belief systems, help to explain their general nonactivist orientation.

The Changing Effectiveness of African-American Religious Social Activism

This Extended Application has examined the factors contributing to change-promoting or change-inhibiting qualities of African-American religious expression. We have considered aspects of the belief systems, the cultural framework, the social and historical situation, and the internal structure of the various kinds of religious groups that bear upon their orientation toward social and political change. These aspects suggest that African-American religious groups are highly appropriate vehicles for change-oriented actions, though they have not always been used to promote change. In particular, within the cognitive framework of many (perhaps most) African-Americans, it "makes sense" to pursue goals through religious groups and under religious leadership. Indeed, until recently religious organizations may have been the only viable indigenous vehicle for African-American social action.

The same line of analysis, however, suggests that African-American religion may have a considerably diminished role in future social change because of at least four factors: increased member complacency, alienated youth, a changing U.S. social structure, and religious privatization. Many religious leaders themselves name *members' complacency* as the most obvious factor (Wilmore, 1972:195–197). There is a growing economic disparity between middle-class and lower-class African-Americans. If these two communities become disconnected from one another, analysts worry that those who are relatively well-off socioeconomically may be less likely to utilize their increased resources for dramatic change (Lincoln and Mamiya, 1990; the nature of social-class and racial ties among African-Americans is controversial; see Wilson, 1980).

Yet there is considerable evidence that many middle-class black churches are far less complacent than their white counterparts, even though social problems are arguably more overwhelming than before the civil rights movement: crumbling inner cities, crack and AIDS epidemics, massive unemployment and underemployment, and vanishing social security "nets" (for health care, child care, food, housing, old-age income, etc.) for all Americans (see Billingsley, 1999; Wilson, 1987). In 1986 the total revenue of all U.S. religious congregations was $49.6 billion, of which $1 billion was spent on assistance for the poor; by 1991, despite the fact that their revenue had slipped to $48.4 billion, the churches increased their aid to the poor to $7 billion. Overall, the black churches spent proportionately more of their revenues. For example, Progressive Community church, an inner-city African-American congregation in Chicago, spent about half of its total budget on programs for the poor: an all-purpose community center offering hot meals, day care, youth programs, clothing aid, referrals for emergency housing, job counseling, and more (*New York Times,* 1995). In the face of such massive societal problems, minority communities simply do not have the resources or the social structural leverage to make meaningful changes (Gilkes, 1995).

A second and related factor is *alienated youth*. Few of the urban youth most affected by this serious social decline are involved in religious groups. While both Christian and non-Christian African-American leaders have appealed for renewal of black families and good male models and mentoring for youth, many young people have little respect for religion of any kind. Younger Americans are generally less likely to be involved in religious groups than older persons, but in northern cities, younger blacks with lower educational levels have particularly low rates of religious involvement (Nelsen and Kanagy, 1993; see also Gilkes, 1995).

Many religious groups have made strong appeals to involve black men, such as the 1995 "Million Man March" in Washington, D.C. Bethel African Methodist Episcopal Church in Baltimore, one of the nation's oldest denominational churches, for example, has developed active all-male church organizations, including men's Bible study groups, a large male choir, and programs and rituals for young men to take Christian manhood more seriously (Mamiya, 1994). Although such programs have been successful in increasing the proportion of men in middle-class and working-class religious groups, whether they can attract alienated youth of the inner city remains to be seen. Unfortunately, this "emergent militant black manhood" may undermine the significant roles and autonomous infrastructures of women in African-American religious organizations (Gilkes, 1998a, 2001).

A third factor is the *changing structure of U.S. society.* The very successes of the civil rights movement meant that nonreligious modes of action (e.g., political and legal) became increasingly accessible to African-Americans. As people master these modes, religious modes of social action will have less importance and will stand to lose even more significance as people come to think in terms of alternatives. Increasingly, nonreligious modes of action are accessible and "make sense" to African-Americans.

The fourth factor in the diminished role of black religion in promoting change is that the *general forces of religious privatization* appear to be making inroads into the African-American community, much as they have among whites in the last several decades. The forced segregation of that community had protected the religious worldview of its members, even as immigrant Italian, Irish, and Jewish communities protected their religious worldview in the first half of the twentieth century. "Making it," however, means participating in a public sphere—the worlds of work, politics, education, and law—in which religion is treated as largely irrelevant. Although people can also enjoy the private sphere (e.g., community, family, religion, leisure, etc.), the meanings and values of the private sphere are increasingly voluntary and not compelling in the public sphere. The "new voluntarism" (described in Chapter 4) applies to much African-American religiosity; especially in urban and suburban contexts, religion is private and voluntary (Nelsen and Kanagy, 1993). Unlike earlier periods of quietism, however, this voluntarism is structural. In many respects, in the modern world no religion has sufficient structural power to undo the preeminence of public-sphere institutions, especially the economic and political ones, that both create the conditions under which people suffer and control the terms of discourse about the direction of society.

SUMMARY

Certain qualities of religion tend to support the existing socioeconomic arrangements; at the same time, however, religion also promotes social change and has considerable potential for change-promoting action in certain social situations. Interest theories explain that religion frequently supports the vested interests of the dominant social classes, legitimating their dominance, socializing believers to comply with it, and utilizing religious social controls for deviance from it. Religious elements can be potent forces for social change; religious groups, leadership, ideas, and images can promote change-oriented action.

Because the relationship between religion and social change is complex, we have focused on the conditions under which religion is likely to be change-inhibiting or change-promoting. Social structural aspects of religion are important variables that influence the impact of religion on social change in any given situation. The social location of religion, the relationship of religious institutions to other institutions in society, and the internal structure of religious organizations are all criteria in determining whether religion is change-promoting or change-inhibiting and its degree of effectiveness in social action.

These factors that shape the interrelationship of religion and social change are illustrated by the African-American religious expressions, which both promote and inhibit social change. At critical historical moments, the unique qualities of African-American religious groups made religious leadership and organization plausible forces for human rights and socioeconomic change.

Religion in
the Modern World

MEREDITH B. MCGUIRE
JAMES V. SPICKARD

Major changes have occurred in the social location and significance of religion in Western societies over the last several centuries. Indeed, it appears that no developed or developing country (including non–Western ones) has remained untouched by these processes. The situation of religion in the modern world is different than it used to be; the linkages of religion with societal and individual life have changed. Any examination of the nature of religious change must be grounded in an understanding of other major changes in the structure of society—or indeed, the world.

Classical sociologists (such as Weber, Marx, and Durkheim) paid particular attention to religion and religious changes in an attempt to *explain the emergence of the modern world*. They, and many other social theorists since then, felt that modern society differs absolutely from what came before it (Luckmann, 1967:16, 17). Not only has the pace of social change increased in the century since these classical social theorists wrote about religion, but also the scope of change has broadened widely. We can now speak of a *globalized* modern social situation. There is considerable evidence that the modern world is qualitatively different from the past. At the same time, this extensive qualitative difference may merely signal that we are in a period of transition—not yet fully in the social reality of the next historical era.

When we think about rapid social change, especially with regard to religion, we must avoid romantic notions about the "good old days." Our image of traditional "old-time religion" is often historically very limited (e.g., referring to a period of the heyday of church religiosity that, in the United States, encompassed only several decades ending in the mid-twentieth century). We conveniently forget that throughout much of America's relatively short history the majority of Americans were apparently unchurched, highly susceptible to an uncontrolled assortment of nonofficial religious teachings, superstitious, or ignorant of church doctrines and practices. Much of what we identify as "traditional" religious morality, such as norms regarding gender roles, abortion, incest, and abstinence from undesirable substances, dates primarily from Victorian times, with the domestication of religion in the face of early industrialization.

Nor were the "good old days" necessarily all that "good." Yes, the quaint little church on the village green back then had the potential to be a place of neighborly warmth and cohesion, where everyone knew everyone else, and where religious belief, practices, and shared values were more fully supported in everyday life by all in the community. That same firm sense of tradition and community, however, also gravely restricted individual freedom: Choices of marriage partners, occupations, leisure-time activities, and political options were all controlled, sometimes subtly and often overtly. The societies that so firmly supported traditional religion were generally authoritarian, patriarchal, highly stratified, and nondemocratic. Indeed, the very discovery of the individual, with emotional needs and human rights and prerogatives of choice, is a peculiarly modern feature of a society, as discussed later in this chapter. So, in trying to understand the location of religion in modern society, let us strive for a more neutral appreciation of social changes: Some qualities we may value have been lost or transformed; other valuable features have been gained.

Each chapter of this book has described some of the changes that have occurred in the nature of religion, religious belief and practice, religious movements and organizations, and individual religiosity. Religion is still a valuable focus for sociological understanding, however, and for some of the same reasons the classical sociologists focused on it: religion's place in the linkage of the individual to society, its role in providing meaning and belonging, its function as legitimation for authority and stratification, its dual roles in public life and private religious expression and experience, and so on. Thus, sociology of religion helps us understand *society itself,* not merely the religious aspects of it.

This chapter first examines four of the narratives that sociologists of religion have used to interpret the place of religion today and to project its future. Each of these narratives gives a very different picture of religion, with different implications for religion's location and future roles. Subsequently, we look briefly at two critical issues for which sociology of religion gives us a way of understanding society itself: how individuals are connected with their larger society (i.e., Durkheim's twin themes of individuation and social cohesion), and the connection of religion, authority, power, and order in the modern world.

FOUR NARRATIVES
IN THE SOCIOLOGY OF RELIGION

If we ask, "What is happening to religion today?" and "What will religion be like in the years to come?" we get several different stories. Some sociologists see religion in decline and tell us about its loss of influence in daily affairs. Other sociologists see denominations shrinking but independent congregations growing; they tell us about religious reorganization. Still others see religion as increasingly a matter of personal choice; others think that personal choice has always been present, and focus their story on the shape of the markets for religious "goods" in which personal choices are made. Each scholarly view puts forth its supporting evidence, but puts that evidence into a *narrative* that tells us where we are now and what we can expect in times to come.

We use the words *story* and *narrative* deliberately here (instead of *paradigm, theory,* or any other scientific-sounding word), because scholars, like others, are led by their imaginations. Not that they ignore data; far from it. Isolated data do not make sense all by themselves, however; they make sense only when embedded in a story that gives them meaning. The membership declines of American mainline Protestant denominations, for example, can be interpreted as a result of growing secularization, as a shift in the relative strength of denominations and congregations, as a sign of growing religious individualism, or as the result of these denominations' failure to deliver a religious product that appeals to American consumers. Data alone do not tell us which of these interpretations is the "correct" story.

Four main narratives currently dominate the sociology of religion: each answers differently our questions about religion's present and about its future. Thematized below as secularization, reorganization, individualization, and supply-side market analysis, these narratives paint fundamentally different pictures of religion's place in the modern world.

Secularization

The story of **secularization** has a long tradition in sociology, although it is invoked less frequently in recent years. Auguste Comte (1798–1857), who coined the word *sociology*, claimed that society had moved from the "theological" through the "metaphysical" to the "scientific" stage—the last typified by the triumph of reason over dogma and the withering away of religious thinking. Max Weber (1864–1920) portrayed modern life as a "disenchanted" world. The ideals that had motivated the early Protestant reformers had lost their religious content, yet lived on as an "iron cage" of rational self-repression that compelled modern folks to work hard at their professions without hope of transcendent reward.

The idea that "religion is not what it once was" has some empirical support. There is the aforementioned decline in American mainline Protestant church membership, stretching back to the 1950s (Roof and McKinney,

1987). Despite the rise (and recent decline) of the Christian Right (Fowler et al., 1999:137–154) American religious organizations have nowhere near the social influence that they had two centuries ago, neither in public life nor over their own members. Young American evangelicals increasingly disagree with their churches' moral stances, though not on all matters (Hunter, 1987b:59). The majority of Jews no longer attend synagogue (Davidman, 2002), and Roman Catholic church attendance has fallen by one-fourth since 1965 (Greeley, 1990). In sum, there is considerable evidence that religion is a smaller part of American life, both public and private, than it once was.

Europe has seen an even steeper religious decline. In Britain, membership dropped from 30 percent to 14 percent of the adult population between 1900 and 1990 (Bruce, 1999:213). Sunday attendance in the Nordic countries now amounts to something less than 2 percent of the adult population (Bruce, 1999:217). Even the opponents of the secularization story recognize that Europe's Catholic bishops have less political power than before, and that public life is no "longer suffused with religious symbols, rhetoric, or ritual" (Stark and Finke, 2000:60). As Steve Bruce (1999:7–8) recently framed that story:

> The road from religion embodied in the great European cathedrals to religion as personal preference and individual choice is a road from more to less religion. From the Middle Ages to the end of the twentieth century, religion in Europe (and its offshoot settler societies) has declined in power, prestige, and popularity.

This is the narrative underlying the secularization view. Once nearly universally **established**—that is, supported by and identified with the state—contemporary religions are now largely voluntary organizations, a declining part even of private life. Sweden's recent disestablishment of Lutheranism (i.e., no longer recognizing it as the "state church") is merely part of a trend.

Facts such as these give the secularization story its *prima facia* plausibility. Looked at closely, however, the picture is not so simple. The secularization narrative is not a unified story of religious decline, but comes in several interconnected versions.

The first of these versions emphasizes **institutional differentiation:** the fragmentation of social life, as specialized roles and institutions are created to handle specific tasks or functions that were formerly joined (Dobbelaere, 1981, 1999). According to this version, churches used to be much more central to social life than they are now, because there were once fewer organizations among which to divide the labor. Today, the Poor Box has been replaced by the Welfare Office, the pastoral counselor by the psychologist, the religious order's hospice by the hospital corporation. Yes, we still have Poor Boxes, pastoral counselors, and medical religious orders, but they treat a far smaller proportion of the population than they once did. Their professions have been secularized, although the remaining religious practitioners have not.

Particularly important is religious institutions' loss of control over the definition of deviance and the loss of the ability to control it (Wilson, 1976:42).

During the Middle Ages, religious institutions defined and prosecuted deviant behavior, exercising social control both through informal measures (e.g., confession or community ostracism) and formal measures (e.g., church courts). In most modern societies, however, religious institutions have no such direct control. Courts are more independent, and law is the province of specialists. Medical institutions have similarly acquired much power over social control, defining deviance as "sick" and calling medical social control measures "therapy" (Conrad and Schneider, 1980). The net effect of this differentiation is that separate institutional specialists *compete* for areas of control that previously were mainly church prerogatives. Although religious institutions still proclaim their definitions of deviance, their influence is seriously limited in most modern societies.

A second approach emphasizes **societalization.** Bryan Wilson (1982:154) describes this process as the way in which "life is increasingly enmeshed and organized, not locally but societally (that society being most evidently, but not uniquely, the nation state)." Almost everywhere in the modern world, small-scale communities have lost power to large-scale organizations: huge corporations, mass media and marketing, political bureaucracies, and the like. Religion, tied up with the life of the local community, has suffered that community's erosion. Local churches have to compete not just with other religious organizations, but with television, sports, national politics, and other forms of mass entertainment. To the degree that these other forces become stronger, religion becomes relatively weaker. Religion may still be important for some individuals, but it is no longer at the center of community life.

A third strand emphasizes **privatization:** the increasing relegation of religion to the private sphere. Most Americans see religion as a private matter; indeed, they object to churches playing a political role. Accordingly, religion can influence individual morality, but it should avoid trying to direct public policy.[1] Though clergy still attend national festivals and bless public events, their presence is more decorative than central. Instead, religion is supposed to shape individual morality and private life, becoming, along with the family, "a buffer zone in which individuals receive support that helps them absorb the stresses and strains brought on by their public activities in other institutional spheres" (Pankhurst and Houseknecht, 2000:24). Though not an absolute decline, this is certainly a retreat from the very public role that religions played in past eras. Ole Riis (1989) describes a similar process in Scandinavia, where religious organizations have even less public importance than in the United States, but a privatized "Protestant Humanism" still plays a significant role in legitimating the liberal status quo.

Institutional differentiation, societalization, and privatization are large-scale developments, acting at what sociologists call "the macro level" (Lechner,

---

1. The General Social Survey in 1991 (the most recently the question was asked) found half of its American respondents opposed to clergy trying to influence the government, and nearly two-thirds opposed to clergy trying to influence voters.

1991a). But secularization may occur at the level of the individual, according to some scholars who argue that **decline in individual religious belief** is just as important as these macro-level changes. Peter Berger (1967:107–108) put this point eloquently:

> The process of secularization has a subjective side as well. As there is a secularization of society and culture, so there is a secularization of consciousness. Put simply, this means that the modern West has produced an increasing number of individuals who look upon the world and their own lives without the benefit of religious interpretations.

According to the secularization narrative, one chief cause of this decline in religious belief is **pluralism:** the fact that the modern world brings together many people with many different views, and that modern societies expect them to behave civilly toward each other with toleration for their differences. The story goes like this: In premodern times, people were surrounded by people of like faith and, thus, not likely to question their own group's beliefs. The religion of the Other (if it existed nearby) was unthinkable, in part because each group's lives could be lived utterly apart. But nowadays people of diverse cultures and religious persuasions live in the same communities. They are aware of the fact that their neighbors and coworkers do not share their beliefs and practices. This may lead them to wonder whether their own views are right or whether any religion is right. The "growing pluralism" version of the secularization narrative tells us that religions are threatened by the presence of multiple views of the world. It suggests that, where worldviews coexist and compete as plausible alternatives to each other, the credibility of all is undermined. The pluralistic situation relativizes the competing worldviews and deprives them of their taken-for-granted status (Berger, 1967:151).[2]

According to the secularization narrative, another posited cause of decline is growing **rationalization.** Modern societies value rational thinking—rational science, rational business organization, and rational law. The paradigmatic instance of this "threat" to religion's place in the world is the supposed conflict between religious and scientific explanations of the world. Whether or not religion and science are at odds is immaterial; people have long believed that they are, and have acted on those beliefs. Thus, in 1999, the Kansas State Board of Education banned the teaching of evolution in the public schools, to protect Christian children from having their faith undermined by their science teachers. Though recently reversed, this policy was a typically sectarian attempt to protect religious belief by forbidding competing ways of thinking. As the massive negative publicity accorded the incident shows, it is increasingly difficult for religious groups to limit what their members hear.

Rationalization affects economic action as well. An increasingly educated workforce has learned to apply systematic rational thinking to many tasks and goals. Corporate planning, for instance, usually involves rational accounting

---

2. Daniel Olson (1999) has provided new empirical support for this view.

and market analyses, not divination. Governments that wish to increase a nation's prosperity consult economists, not prayer leaders. While religion may still create personal meaning, the story goes, rational thinking creates material results; and an increasingly large part of social life values those results as a priority.

There is a bit of a red herring in all this, of course, for governments and businesses have always been results-oriented, as have been—by the way—religious organizations. But most secularization narratives have at least implied the withdrawal of personal religiosity from public life in favor of rational decision making, as well as the decline of personal religiosity in general. The fact that many scientists are themselves religious does not undercut this trend, as their religiosity is private; religious belief may give their lives meaning, but rationality governs their scientific work.

As this brief overview shows, there are many secularization narratives. One does not have to accept them all to recognize the changed place of religion in modern life. While most scholars grant that macro-level social changes give religion a different social role than it once had, there is considerably less agreement about whether religion is "declining" (and, if so, how). In evaluating the claims of the secularization story, some unresolved issues stand out. First, we have the question of whether religious decline is limited to Europe, and so whether the secularization narrative is yet one more attempt to generalize European experience to the rest of the world (Martin, 1996; Swatos and Christiano, 1999).

Second, we have the question of whether religious belief is declining at all, or whether—instead—people are becoming not less religious, but differently religious. The rise of New Age religion, for example, can be read as evidence against the secularization hypothesis: new religious beliefs and practices are simply replacing old ones. Some observers, however, see New Age beliefs and practices as a kind of self-worship (Heelas, 1996); is this evidence for, or against, religious decline? Third, individuals may not be less religious, but other aspects of religion in society may be declining. Mark Chaves (1994:750), for example, argues that secularization should be defined not as "declining religion but as the declining scope of religious authority." Secularization narratives have raised important questions about the legitimation of authority in modern societies, some of which we discuss later in this chapter.

Religious Reorganization

While the secularization story got much of its plausibility from Europe's steep religious decline, sociology of religion's second narrative arose from the American religious context. The United States has long been a religious nation, but one focused on local congregations, not on a single large institutional church. Recently, sociologists have noticed the shifting religious balance between local congregations and the denominations to which many of them belong. They tell a tale of religious **reorganization** that well describes the American scene.

R. Stephen Warner (1993, 1997) points out that Europe was traditionally a region of villages, each dominated by a single church, the focal point both of religious life and of religious rebellion. The United States, in contrast, has long had a plurality of churches, none of which could long dominate local, much less national affairs. Moreover, American churches were typically organized as local congregations: communities of believers whose religious and personal lives were entangled to a much greater degree than was the case in the European homeland. Except for the earliest colonial years, there was no state church, so religion was voluntary. Americans joined and left churches for the myriad personal reasons that people have for doing anything. And for the most part, their choices depended on a local congregation's ability to meet their religious needs (Finke and Stark, 1992). The same is true today: Americans join religious groups, not so much on the basis of a denominational "brand" loyalty as on a sense of connection with a local congregation. They look to that congregation as a community to which they can contribute and in which they can flourish (Warner, 1994). Finding "the right" community is less a matter of matching the group's theology to individual beliefs, than it is a matter of finding a congregation whose social patterns one finds congenial. Indeed, one study found community attachment to be more important than shared beliefs in maintaining church support and participation (Roof, 1978).

There is no denying the membership declines of the major Protestant denominations, one of the verified trends of the last forty years (Roof and McKinney, 1987). Hidden beneath that trend, however, is the rise of independent congregations, small and large, which attract increasing numbers of adherents (Miller, 1998). From congregations made up of a few families to megachurches with membership into the thousands, these groups typically do not affiliate with the established denominations. Instead, they welcome all comers, play down theological distinctiveness, and focus on providing a warm community.

This community takes many forms, as recent congregational ethnographies show (e.g., Ammerman, 1987; Davidman, 1991; Davie, 1995b; Neitz, 1987; Tweed, 1997; Warner, 1988). Like all religious groups, these congregations find ways to help people make sense of their lives and make them feel a part of the social community, as described in Chapter 2. What is new about the current situation is precisely the decline of *supra*congregational religious structures. It seems no longer so important that a congregation affiliate with a denomination, whether it be Lutheran, Methodist, Presbyterian, or Baptist. For example, some Baptist congregations have recently dropped "Baptist" from their names, wishing to de-emphasize their ties to a denomination widely seen to have sectarian tendencies (Montoya, 1999). Catholic congregations are, of course, a bit different, as they do not so readily disaffiliate from their mother church. But even the Catholic hierarchy plays communitarian themes, recognizing that it cannot compel religious obedience from above.

The story of religious reorganization tells us about this decline of supracongregational religious structures and about the importance that religiously involved people place on their local ties. Rather than a tale of religious weakening, this narrative claims a growing importance for local religiosity in the American landscape.

As noted in Chapters 3 and 6, congregation-level religious groups have provided a very important site for the integration of new immigrants into American life. Several recent studies of immigrant churches have documented the importance of religious communities in giving new immigrants both a connection with their former countries and a toehold in the new (Ebaugh and Chafetz, 2000a; Levitt, 2000; Warner and Wittner, 1998). The opening of Chapter 1 describes such congregations in San Antonio, providing a cultural and spiritual "home" for new immigrants from Lebanon, Egypt, Russia, Mexico, India, China, and so on. There are also ethnic congregations for the older immigrant groups, for example, those from Greece, Poland, and Bohemia (Czech).

If the reorganization narrative is right, such cases are not just properties of immigrant religion, but of American religion in general. (This narrative does not try to predict anything but the *American* religious future.) Unlike the old model of Roman Catholicism as "the immigrant church," helping European Catholic immigrants adjust to American society (Alvarez, 1979; Dolan, 1983), the reorganization model emphasizes not so much adjustment but *continued localism*. That is, it does not tell us that religion is important to these immigrants only while they are adjusting to American life, predicting that this function will later fade away. Instead, it tells us that religion has become a source of community for immigrants, as it has continued to be for everyone else! People may not need to be connected to denominations and other big religious groupings any more, but they still want a rich congregational life—perhaps more than ever. This is a story of religious restructuring, not decline.

Why, however, might religious localism be so important today? The secularization narrative looks at macro-level social trends to predict religion's future; what might the reorganization narrative see? So far, no group of scholars has worked this out in detail, but here is one possible account of what is going on.[3]

Among the social changes of the last century has been the growth of large-scale social and economic institutions, which have greater and greater influence in individuals' lives. Variously termed the "mass society" (Vidich and Bensman, 1968), "globalization" (Robertson, 1992), and "late modernity" (Giddens, 1991), this social order greatly expands the reach of governments, big industries, and commercial enterprises and restricts individuals' sense of control over their own fates. One result is a retreat to family and friends as a source of support and identity: a return to localism as a haven in a difficult world. The religious congregation stands alongside the family in offering personal support and close social ties (Wuthnow, 1994)—as a locus of *religious emotion*, to use Danièle Hervieu-Léger's concept (Champion and Hervieu-Léger, 1990). The growth of a mass society makes such personal connections all the more important; religion, in its local manifestation, becomes increasingly socially important.

---

3. Various social theorists have made points similar to the following, though not from a "reorganization narrative" point of view. See Peter Beyer's (1994) work on religion and globalization, which does not limit itself to any of the four narratives proposed here.

Specifically, the reorganization narrative might see the local congregation as better able to meet people's need for community than the previously influential denominations. Local congregations give people a sense of belonging without mirroring the institutional world that dominates their work lives. Broader than family, but emotionally safer than the political/economic sphere, local religion fills an important personal gap for many people.

This sociological explanation of religious reorganization, speculative though it is, supports some of the versions of the secularization narrative, while opposing others. It can easily accommodate the issues of institutional differentiation and privatization, as these social processes underlie mass social development. Unlike Wilson (1982), however, it does not conclude that societalization leads to religion's decline; on the contrary, the local becomes more important, not less, as large-scale institutions grow. And this explanation does not suppose that the growth of mass society undercuts religious belief, in part because it does not view belief as central to congregational religious life. Religious *belonging* is much more important to understanding current trends.

Religious Individualization

A third narrative also involves religious restructuring, but not from one organizational level to another; it involves a fundamental shift in the locus of religion from institutions to individuals. We call this the story of religious **individualization,** although we could just as easily use the term **autonomization.** Both concepts refer to the degree to which individuals pick and choose among various religious options, crafting a custom-made religious life, rather than choosing a package formulated by religious institutions.

The story goes like this. In the past, religions centered around church life. People's membership in one or another church pretty much predicted their beliefs and actions, in part because they had been socialized into their church's institutional package of beliefs and practices. One could expect a Catholic to believe in the Trinity, to attend Mass, to venerate the saints, and to eat fish on Fridays; one could expect a conservative Baptist to read the Bible daily, to pray in a specific manner, to believe in personal salvation, and to avoid dancing and drink. As described in Chapter 4, there was presumably a good match between the prescribed "official" religion and individuals' religious expressions.

That was the past. Now, however, says this narrative, religious diversity has grown, not just between churches but *within* them. Where once most individuals accepted what their leaders told them, today they demand the right to decide for themselves: their core beliefs as well as the details. And they do not feel compelled to switch religious communities when their religious views change. Official and unofficial religiosity are thus out of synch, with the latter growing in importance. Nor are all self-described religious people churchgoers. The 1994 General Social Survey reported that 10 percent of Americans who never attend church describe themselves as strongly religious, and another 54 percent see themselves as somewhat religious. In short, this narrative, too, describes a religious revolution: neither one of religious decline nor of religious reorganization, but one in which individuals are freer than ever before to shape their own religious lives.

A good deal of evidence from the U.S. and Europe supports this story. Religious individuals today do not generally believe everything that their leaders say they should; indeed, members of many churches display a diversity of religious beliefs and practices that formerly would have been defined as heresies. Numerous studies, as detailed in Chapter 4, have documented widespread religious eclecticism (Davie, 1995a, 1995b; McGuire, 1998; Roof, 1999; Spickard, 1996). Even Catholics, with their historic identification with a common tradition, insist on autonomy in how their faith is practiced in the modern world (Dillon, 1998, 1999; McNamara, 1992; Spickard and McGuire, 1994).

The religious individualism narrative sees these developments as examples of the growing *autonomy* of religious believers. Individual religion no longer mirrors an institutionally defined package of beliefs and practices. Rather, individuals construct their faiths out of many disparate elements, not limited to one tradition. Indeed, Danièle Hervieu-Léger (1999:196ff.) shows how individuals no longer feel the need to conform themselves to the established churches, but instead practice "religion *à la carte*"—a *bricolage* in which institutionally validated beliefs are less and less important in individual lives. Nancy Ammerman (1997b) suggests that this effort to craft a spiritually meaningful life may be part of the postmodern condition: a central aspect of the shape of individuality in our era.[4] In sum, there is as much evidence supporting this narrative as there is for either of the other two discussed so far.[5]

Such interpretations of religious voluntarism often build on Thomas Luckmann's (1967, 1990) description of religious privatization and individual autonomy. Luckmann argues that these processes do not point to the disappearance of religion but to a shift toward individualized religion, rather than "visible" religious institutions, as the most important unit of analysis. Thus, narratives of religious individualization and autonomy address a larger sociological question about the relationship between the individual and society in the context of "late" or "high" modernity. (We discuss some of these interpretations later in this chapter.) Luckmann (1967:99) suggests that religion's voluntary quality contributes to a sense of autonomy in the private sphere, perhaps making up for the individual's lack of autonomy in institutions of the public sphere:

---

4. Ammerman suggests that this individualism is nowhere near so socially corrosive as social critics like Robert Bellah (Bellah et al., 1985) and Robert Putnam (1995) claim. In her view, religious voluntarism nurtures civic virtue rather than undercutting it; people make lives together in religious congregations, where they learn the social skills they need to build communities elsewhere.

5. Besides the evidence mentioned so far, there are also the results of Hammond's (1992) survey of religious adherents in Ohio, Massachusetts, South Carolina, and California. Hamberg (1992) and Riis (1994) found similar patterns in Scandinavia, as did Hervieu Léger (1986) in France.

Once religion is defined as a "private affair" the individual may choose from the assortment of "ultimate" meanings as he sees fit—guided only by the preferences that are determined by his social biography. An important consequence of this situation is that the individual constructs not only his personal identity but also his individual system of "ultimate" significance. (used by permission)

This self-selected construction is, according to Luckmann, the contemporary social form of religion. While church-oriented religion continues to be one of the elements that some people choose for their constructions, other themes from the private sphere (e.g., autonomy, self-expression, self-realization, familism, sexuality, adjustment, and fulfillment) are also available in a supermarket of "ultimate" meanings (Luckmann, 1990, 1967:100–114). This process not only explains the rise of new religious movements and New Age religions, but the acceptance of New Age beliefs by mainstream church members. The religious individualization narrative tells us that these developments are not so much reactions to the collapse of religious worldviews (as in some secularization narratives), as they are evidence of a shift in the *locus* of religious meaning. Where once religious institutions were dominant, now individuals are. This, the story goes, is a fundamental change.

There are, however, at least two problems with this story, insofar as it is presented as a general picture of religious change. First, its picture of the past is inaccurate: it is not likely true that people once simply accepted the views of their church leaders as their own. McGuire (2000) notes that before the reformations of the sixteenth and seventeenth centuries, European Christian individual belief and practice was markedly eclectic. Individuals had a vast array of daily religious practices to choose or reject, saints to venerate or ignore, festivals to celebrate or avoid. Both elite and common versions of popular religiosity focused on ritual *practice,* rather than orthodox *belief,* and—as long as they adhered to core required practices, such as Baptism and Holy Week obligations—individuals had considerable choice as to which other ritual practices they employed in their personal and domestic religious expression (Muir, 1997; Scribner, 1984a, 1984b).

The Protestant and Catholic Reformations, however, both strove to "reform" the Church by purifying it of unorthodoxies. They labeled many popular beliefs and practices "not religious," and attempted to purge them from their adherents' lives. There is not, in this view, a general shift from religious authority to religious individualism; there is, instead, a historically specific growth of religious authoritarianism and institutional control that has been reversed in recent decades. Individuals may be no less religious now than in times past, just as individuals may have been as religious—but differently religious—in the Middle Ages as in the early modern period after the reformations' establishment of boundaries and control. Perhaps the balance has merely shifted from religious eclecticism and cultic tolerance to religious centralism and narrow, controlled boundaries, and then back again.

The second problem has to do with the ethnocentrism of the individualization narrative. Regardless of whether religious life was once more controlled by religious authorities in Europe and the Americas, it was not so ruled throughout much of the rest of the world. Spickard (1998b, 2000) has argued that religions in places like China, India, and the Muslim empires were never as directed from the top as was Western Christianity. Chinese religion, for example, has never been church religion. Instead, it has traditionally consisted of an agglomeration of household cults, memorial shrines, and ethical teachings that provided great scope for individual religious *bricolage* while stabilizing the social order. In this sense, modern Western religious individualism potentially looks a great deal more like traditional Chinese religion than it looks like the West's own past.

Despite these problems, the religious individualization narrative captures something of what is happening to religion in the modern world. If its description of the past is suspect, its description of the present deserves attention. Like the secularization and reorganization narratives, it describes a piece of what is happening and focuses on facts that other stories miss. None of these three stories, however, fully answers our two core questions: "What is happening to religion today?" and "What will religion be like in the years to come?"

The Supply Side of Religious Markets

A fourth religious narrative claims to answer these questions fully, with a "general theory" of how religion works in *all* times and places. It begins with the idea that churches do not exist in social isolation; instead, they compete for "customers" in religious "markets." Those markets may consist of hundreds of competing "firms"—small churches each trying to attract members. Or they may consist of one or a few large churches or religious organizations that hold a religious monopoly. Postulating that the "demand" for religious "goods" is nearly always constant, the **supply-side story** claims that the dynamics of religious life are merely a special case of the dynamics of all market behavior. If one knows something about the characteristics of religious "firms" and the applicable religious market structure, one can predict any specific religious future.

The most prominent historical application of this method is Finke and Stark's (1992) analysis of the rise and fall of several Protestant denominations over the last 200 years. Unlike Europe, with its state-supported monopoly churches, the United States has long had a relatively free market for religion. Those churches that can attract members prosper; those churches that cannot do so decline. Finke and Stark chart the growth and relative decline of Congregationalists, Methodists, Baptists, and various sectarians—the market share of each rising as it exploits promising market niches, and falling as it liberalizes its theology and accommodates to the world. This version of the supply-side story is relatively simple: It claims that "Successful" (i.e., growing) churches are other-worldly and conservative; churches decline as they move "up-market" by appealing to the liberal elite rather than to the conservative masses. It says that religious monopolies reduce religious participation, as clergy do not depend for their livelihood on "selling" their "product."

Religious competition increases total religious activity, though particular "firms" may lose members. According to this story, the secularization narrative is simply wrong in its portrayal of contemporary religious decline.

What, then, does this narrative recommend to religious leaders who wish their churches to remain strong? First, deregulate the religious marketplace; and second, emphasize the supernatural! The end of religious monopolies, we are told, will increase the total number of church members and attenders, as a higher proportion of the population finds churches that cater to their specific needs. Not everyone wants a metaphysical religion, but some people do; they will stay away from church unless a deregulated market gives them access to their kind of worship. The same is true for biblical literalists, mystics, Wiccans, and the ritualistic: a religious free market increases the total supply of religious "goods," increasing the trade in religion overall. Yet, most people, according to Finke and Stark, want an "old-time religion" that promises salvation and sure answers. Their creative analysis of Protestant church membership trends claims to show a cross-cultural preference for supernaturalistic religions that offer a vision of a "life beyond." Historical data provide some support for this conclusion, as does the growth of contemporary evangelical, fundamentalist, and pentecostal denominations (including the various charismatic renewals). The membership declines of American mainline Protestantism fit this pattern well (Kelley, 1972; Roof and McKinney, 1987).

This narrative, thus, has the same kind of *prima facia* plausibility that we saw with the other narratives. Like the secularization narrative, it also has several interlocking parts that are sometimes hard to separate in its advocates' work. The first and most widely accepted part of this story is its emphasis on religious **markets.** It seems clear that churches do operate in market-like conditions, and that the secularization, reorganization, and individualization narratives have not spent much time analyzing them. To the extent that churches see a growing membership as a sign of success, market structure makes a difference: It is very hard to increase the size of a small church under a religious monopoly. And free religious markets make it much easier for people to start and join churches than do restricted markets. Yet, the supply-side emphasis on formal membership and attendance as the criteria of religious success biases the measurements, such that some groups will appear to be more vital no matter what the market structure (Carroll, 1996:227–228). And, conversely, these criteria result in other religions seeming to disappear from the religious scene when they are perhaps just as vital as the groups that supply-side definitions notice. The claim that free markets increase the total amount of religion may be an artifact of such measurement, a possibility that the advocates of the supply-side view have neglected to explore.

One interesting feature of this narrative is its emphasis on the **supply** of religious goods rather than the *demand* for them. Our previous three narratives claimed that recent changes in social life altered the demand for religion, either by lowering it (secularization), changing its desired institutional location (reorganization), or changing its locus (individualization). A narrative that reminds us that religious suppliers are also important is thus a welcome balance. Yet, this is not an either-or situation: In theory, both supply and demand can vary in amount and type, though the extent that each (or either) does so in a particular time and place ought to be an empirical issue.

Some advocates of the supply-side narrative, however, go further. Laurence Iannaccone argues that "the ultimate preferences (or 'needs') that individuals use to assess costs and benefits tend not to vary much from person to person or time to time" (Iannaccone, 1997:26; see also Iannaccone and Finke, 1993). Although this formulation does not make religious demand absolutely constant, it minimizes the importance of any variations. It especially obscures changes in the type of religion that people find valuable—the very changes in life-orientation and worldview that the other narratives chart (Demerath, 1995; Riis, 1994). There is no reason that a new emphasis on the suppliers of religious "goods" has to deny changes in religious demand, but the advocates of the supply-side narrative have often made it do so.

Two of this narrative's other elements are even more controversial. One, based on **exchange theory,** seeks to "examine elementary principles about what humans are like and how their aspirations exceed their opportunities," and charts these principles' application to religious matters. The result is a vast set of propositions, beginning with claims about why people seek the supernatural and then describing the results of their doing so. Boiled down, this story says that people use religion to seek other-worldly rewards: Religious rewards are used as "compensators" for the trials of life (in these authors' earlier versions of the story, Stark and Bainbridge, 1985). Or (according to the authors' most recent version) people use religion as a tool to get what they cannot otherwise have (Stark and Finke, 2000:83).

Unfortunately, the notion of "compensators" or "tools" is a bit hard to test empirically, as its advocates can easily redefine the results to fit their narrative. Indeed, there are scholarly reports of rather vital religious groups that do not believe in the supernatural at all (Buckser, 1995).[6] These data throw at least some doubt on the central role that supernatural belief is supposed to play in the supply-side definition of religion—and also throw doubt on the notion that other-worldly "compensators" or "tools" are as central to religious life as the advocates of the supply-side narrative claim.

The other controversial element derives from **rational-choice theory:** the idea that individuals rationally maximize their gains in their everyday actions, including religious ones.[7] Supply-side advocates argue that this idea connects market behavior with individual religious action (Finke and Iannaccone, 1993; Stark and Finke, 1993; Stark and Iannaccone, 1993).

---

6. Whether one counts these cases depends, of course, on the definition of "religion" one employs, as was discussed in Chapter 1. At the beginning of the twenty-first century, sociologists of religion are seriously rethinking the very definition of "religion" (see Greil and Bromley, 2002).

7. Abell (1996) notes that rational-choice theory in mainstream sociology is considerably more complex than the classic economic model that is used by most sociologists of religion. Our present discussion is limited to the theory's recent use by sociologists of religion, not its use in general.

Economists have argued for decades that markets work the way they do because of the millions of decisions made daily by consumers and producers, each rationally calculating profit and loss. The version of the supply-side narrative that emphasizes individual rational religious choice imports this model, arguing that its success at predicting market-level behavior tells us how religious consumers act. Specifically, this approach lets us throw out old notions about religious irrationality. Religious people are not loony or deluded; they use the same reasoning processes as everyone else to gain the benefits they seek. The supply-side narrative thus claims that the European philosophical bias against religion—which variously degraded it as "false consciousness" (Marx), "neurosis" (Freud), or "masochism" (Nietzsche)—need not rule (Finke and Stark, 1992:250).

It is important to note that the notion of "rational" used by rational-choice theorists is not the same as the previously mentioned notion of "rationalization." The secularization narrative saw "rationalization" as the growing use of means-ends thinking in both public and private life. According to that narrative, religious and moral values are increasingly deemed irrelevant, especially in the public sphere. Rational-choice theorists, on the other hand, claim that people have *always* chosen to maximize their gains, in all places and eras. For them, religion is like any other good that either succeeds or fails in the marketplace.

One novel application of this rational-choice idea is the claim that conservative churches are strong precisely because they ask so much of their members (Iannaccone, 1994). Though one would think that having a religion that requires several-days-a-week attendance, large financial contributions, and considerable ideological commitment would drive people to seek an easier alternative, rational-choice theory says that this is not the case. True, strict churches "cost" a lot to join and membership in them costs a lot to maintain, but their "rewards" do not have to be shared with the tepidly faithful. Strict churches have no "free riders" to eat up the benefits of membership without contributing their share. Thus, religiously committed sectarians get a rather large reward for their participation, compared to the religiously committed who belong to more liberal groups. If one is so inclined, it thus "pays" to join a church that is hard to get into, where the ratio of one's benefits to one's costs is much higher.

The emphasis on religious rationality may be a needed corrective, though not for recent sociology of religion, which has rarely treated religious people as irrational. Yet, there is some question about whether the rational-choice portion of the supply-side story is actually talking about real, empirical people's choices, or whether it is merely modeling the *results* of those choices. Arguing for the latter interpretation, Spickard (1998a) notes that the assumptions on which its proponents say that a rational-choice theory must rest are either demonstrably false or are so vague as to be nearly useless. Though any person's behavior can be modeled as means–ends rationality, that person's *actual motivations* may take distinctly different forms. Thus, it is one thing to describe a person's decision to join a church *as if* the person were trying to maximize his or her benefits; it is something different to claim that the person's *actual* thoughts in joining measured his or her potential gains against potential losses. It is impossible to demonstrate that people actually think this way (and few people would admit to doing so). Empirical motivations are much more complex than the rational-choice approach allows.

Further, the assumption of stable religious preferences, which justifies the emphasis on changing religious *supply* rather than changing religious *demand,* can be shown not to refer to *individual* religious preferences, which demonstrably change, but at best to religious *populations:* aggregations of individuals whose pattern of religious preferences are somewhat predictable. But this shift negates the rational-choice attempt to connect the market model of religion to individual religious acts. In short, Spickard shows that the rational-choice component of the supply-side narrative cannot tell us anything about religious individuals, as it claims, although it can provide an interesting model of the behavior of religious populations in the aggregate. Individual religious behavior remains unexplained in supply-side terms.

One last problem: The supply-side narrative distorts history at least as much as do the other three approaches. Religious vitality in late medieval/early modern Europe, for example, is not simply measurable by church membership and attendance—the primary yardstick the supply-siders use to measure vitality today (Gorski, 2000). Still, the supply-side narrative provides a trenchant critique of the secularization narrative, against which it has largely defined itself (Stark, 1999). Rather than seeing religions in decline, it sees them flourishing or declining based on market conditions and the religious "product" that they offer on that market. Nostalgia for the supposed "good old days" when religion was strong is ludicrous, says this narrative, because the same factors were at work then as now. Just redesign your religion so that it will be more popular, and church members will flow through your doors.

Beyond Narratives

We have, then, four stories about what is happening to religion today and about what will happen to it in the future. Much current work in the sociology of religion revolves around one or another of these stories: either supporting, critiquing, or testing them for their applicability to contemporary life. All four stories are plausible, based on accumulated evidence; each highlights different aspects of religious life. Few scholars are wedded to any single story, though most scholars prefer one or two over the others. Yet, there are enough conflicts between them that simply splitting the difference between them does not create a coherent picture of religion's present and future.

There remains one proto-narrative, less formed than our others because it described social processes in general rather than a story about religion in specific. This is the "story" of globalization, which we discuss later in this chapter. Although several sociologists of religion are working in this area (Beyer, 1994; Robertson 1992; Simpson 1996), they have as yet produced no single narrative of religion's future. Is this a bad thing? We think not. If each of our four stories about religion's future sensitizes us to various aspects of religious life, we need not rush a fifth story to a premature conclusion.

INTERPRETING MODERN SOCIETIES

Examining these narratives has shown some of the different ways sociologists interpret religion—past, present, and future; but a more important question is how these interpretations can help us to understand the larger society. These broader questions motivate some of the most exciting current studies in the sociology of religion. If the location or role of religion has changed, *so what?* Sociologists have focused on two critical issues: (1) What is the nature of the individual and the individual's connection to the larger social "group" (e.g., family, community, nation, humankind)? (2) How is religion now involved in the legitimation of authority (e.g., legal, political, personal, moral)?

Some of the narratives we have discussed address these issues directly. The secularization and individualization narratives particularly speak to the issues of the individual-to-society connection. Because their conceptions of religion are more limited, the reorganization and the market narratives address this connection only indirectly, and as relatively unproblematic. Similarly, the secularization narrative raises the legitimacy and authority issue, while the reorganization and individualization narratives address the issue less fully but with promising insights. The market model does not concern itself with legitimacy at all. But we do not need to accept any of these narratives to recognize the importance of these two social issues, as well as appreciating the role religion plays in each.

The Individual-to-Society Connection

How does a social group of individual members hold together? How is the individual's self-identity linked with the group identity—as tribe, ethnic group, community, or nation? How does the individual come to think of him- or herself apart from the life of that group? These are core questions asked by sociologists, at least since Durkheim. Like him, sociologists have usually found religion to be part of their answer. Several features of modern societies make these questions—and religion as a partial answer—compelling still.

We have already mentioned **privatization,** the process by which certain differentiated institutional spheres (e.g., religion, family, leisure, the arts) are segregated from the dominant institutions of the public sphere (e.g., economic, political, legal) and relegated to the private sphere. This segregation means that the norms and values of these private spheres are treated as irrelevant to the operations of public-sphere institutions (Berger, 1967:133). It also typically implies that the functions of providing meaning and belonging are relegated to private-sphere institutions.

Religion's recent history demonstrates this trend. Not only are all but a few late modern societies religiously plural, but most allow no single faith to rule public life. The individual's religion (or irreligion) is largely a matter of personal choice. One's identity as a Catholic, Buddhist, Wiccan, or Baptist helps define one, both to oneself and others. The privatization hypothesis holds that everything that contributes to making, maintaining, or changing personal identity is located in the private sphere.

On the one hand, such privatization promotes some of the personal freedoms many enjoy in modern societies. One freedom is the extent to which one's reference groups (i.e., those whose opinion of one "counts" in shaping one's behavior) are not imposed by kin or neighborhood but are more freely chosen. Rational-choice models of behavior may be correct in emphasizing that humans choose rationally, but they fail to appreciate that for *most* people, historically, choice did not reside with the individual but with some collectivity (e.g., family, tribe, congregation) in which the affected individual may have had little voice, much less autonomy. Thus, the choice to marry off a daughter to affirm economic ties with another family and the decision to sell a son into indentured servitude to support the larger family unit both represent highly rational choices, but are clearly *not* the choice of the individual daughter or son.

Our sense that the individual *ought* to have the right to choose for him- or herself is very recent, even in the history of Europe and North America. For example, in the United States, it was only in the twentieth century that the vestiges of slavery and women's historic lack of self-determination were stricken from the laws. The fact that such choices are matters of intense debate in human rights discourse worldwide shows that our "modern" notions of the individual are *contested* and hardly universal. The very idea that individuals could freely choose their religious groups is a thus peculiarly modern (and Western) idea. Jean-Paul Willaime (1998) notes that this "ultra-modernity" frees individuals from religious institutions while simultaneously reducing those institutions' role in society at large. This increases the range of individual choice—both between religions and whether to participate in religious life at all.

On the other hand, religious privatization causes two types of problems. First, the processes of differentiation make it harder for society to mobilize the commitment and efforts of its members whose identities are located in the private sphere. Values from one separate sphere do not readily motivate behavior in another. Why should one vote in an election, serve in the army, or work hard on the job? In societies with relatively little institutional differentiation, behavior in work, politics, and social or military service is often motivated by values from other spheres—family, community, religion, and tradition. In contemporary society, the main motivating force in public spheres appears to be the promise of certain levels of consumption, that is, a material standard of living (Fenn, 1974:148).

Second, privatization apparently results in problems of meaning and integration for many individuals. As noted in Chapter 2, individuals seem to require **plausibility structures** to maintain their religious faith—indeed, to maintain *any* faith in the context of a pluralistic world. Churches provide such structures, as do families and other communities of belief and collective memory (Hervieu-Léger, 1999). But where the distance between public and private is large, some people have difficulty constructing a stable identity. This problem may be reflected in the relatively widespread quest in Western societies for holistic worldviews, as expressed by many alternative health movements, agrarian communes, and contemporary religious movements. Holistic perspectives such as these express a desire for integrating all aspects of life, gaining a sense of wholeness in social, physical, psychic, and spiritual life. The question comes down to one of personal integration: How does one understand oneself if the community of memory, the tradition, has become voluntary and uncertain? Some people thrive in this situation, but others suffer. Some of the more unusual manifestations of contemporary religion may be partly a response to such need.

The issue of **autonomy** is another problem in linking individual to society in the late modern context. Thomas Luckmann (1967) notes that contemporary religion supports personal autonomy, but it also redefines individual autonomy to mean *not* the ability to control one's own actions and commitments. Instead, autonomy has come to mean the absence of external restraints and traditional limitations in the *private* search for identity. Autonomy in one's public life, on the other hand, is increasingly limited because the institutions of the public sphere (such as corporations and states) have growing and *real* power over the individual. Performance of one's roles in these public spheres must conform to institutional requirements, making them a realm of little or no freedom for many (Luckmann, 1967:109–115).

Luckmann (1967:115–117) observes this discrepancy between the *subjective* autonomy of the individual in modern society and the *objective* autonomy of the major institutions of the public sphere. He wonders if the removal of value considerations other than means–ends rationality (e.g., the value of cost-effectiveness) from public institutions has not contributed to the dehumanization of the social order. The irony, then, would be that privatized religiosity, by sacralizing the increasing subjectivity of the individual, supports such dehumanization. By withdrawing into privatized religious expressions, this new mode of religiosity fails to confront the depersonalized roles of the public sphere. If this is true, modern forms of religion do not have to legitimate society directly— they support it indirectly by motivating retreat into the private sphere.

Late modern societies also experience the impact of **individuation.** This is the process by which the individual and his or her concerns come to be seen as distinct from the social group and its concerns.

Robert Bellah (1964) argues that historic religions (especially Judaism and Christianity) "discovered" the self; early modern versions of these religions enabled a greater acceptance of the self; and modern religions represent an even greater emphasis on the autonomy and responsibility of the self. Accordingly, modern religion is characterized by an image of the dynamic multidimensional self, able (within limits) to continually change both self and the world. The mode of action implied by this image is one of continual choice, with no firm, predetermined answers. The social implications of modern religion include the image of culture and personality as perpetually revisable. Bellah notes, however, that whether the freedom allowed by this perspective will be realized at the *social* rather than purely individual level remains to be seen (Bellah, 1964:374).

Roland Robertson's synthesis of themes from Weber, Durkheim, and Simmel similarly emphasizes the twin processes of *individuation* (especially the quest for individual autonomy) and *societalism* (i.e., the growth in societal power over individual members). He suggests that the individuation process has proceeded so far that large-scale institutions of the public sphere cannot easily resist it. Some emerging religious movements of recent years may prompt a new mode of relationship between the individual and society (Robertson, 1977:305, 1978:180, 1979; see also Dreitzel, 1981; McGuire, 1988, 1996). Indeed, the very privatized form of modern religiosity may make it more effective than traditional religiosity as a bridge between autonomous individual actors on the one hand and societal institutions and humankind on the other (Riis, 1989, 1993).

In this vein, James Beckford (1989, 1996) contends that religion is no longer a source of prefabricated identities, but functions as a cultural resource out of which individuals must forge a sense of who they are. Through a process of religious *bricolage,* they construct a personal religious identity out of the bits and pieces of various religious traditions. Hervieu-Léger (1990:S22) comments that, in this sense, religious phenomena are "vehicles of an alternative rationality which is as much in harmony as in contrast with modernity." Rather than weaknesses, features of privatized religion are, thus, particularly effective strengths in modern society. For example, the purely voluntary associative basis of religious networks makes them more flexible supports for the mobile modern individual. Similarly, the contemporary religious emphasis on personal experience and the individual's "right to subjectivity" are well suited to personal motivation and decision making in a societal situation where values and ends are not institutionally "given."

Yet, this role for religion raises the problem noted before: If values and ends are open to contestation (and individual choice), what happens to religious values and norms and other nonmaterial goals? Not only does this contestation cause dissonance on the individual level, but it also reflects societal conflict between an increase of corporate control in the public sphere and the relegation of individual autonomy to the private. The modern economic situation is characterized by the increasing power and scope of **corporate actors** in conflict with the power and rights of individuals. The corporate actor is one who fills a role in an institution; the role, rather than the individual, is part of the corporate world (Fenn, 1978:66), and the corporate role is functionally rational in the institutional arena. In contemporary society, there is no necessary integration of the meaning of institutional roles into the subjective meaning system of the individual actor.

This increasing anonymity of functionally specialized roles makes the individual replaceable, and it also makes the corporate actor less morally responsible for individual actions (Fenn, 1978:81, 82). In countless war-crimes tribunals, the world heard this refrain: "It's not my fault; I was only following orders." Corporate executives, likewise, deny their personal responsibility for perpetrating sweatshop and child labor, environmental degradation, and urban decay by claiming, "It's not my responsibility; my job is only to implement company policy." This is technically true, precisely because corporate rationality denies the importance of anything but the "bottom line" (i.e. corporate profit). The other side of religious privatization, increasing individual religious autonomy and increased religious individuation, is thus the withdrawal of all but economic values from the public sphere. "Doing good" is increasingly a matter of choice, not compulsion, in both the public and the private world (Luckmann, 1967:96, 97).

Authority and Legitimacy

Changes in religion's roles in individuals' lives also let us think more clearly about changes in social **legitimacy.** *Legitimacy,* as discussed in Chapter 6, refers to the *bases of authority* of individuals, groups, or institutions by which they can expect their pronouncements to be taken seriously (Fenn, 1978:xiii). Legitimacy is not an inherent quality of individuals, groups, or institutions, but is based on the *acceptance* of their claims by others. If an individual proclaims "it is absolutely imperative for Americans to reduce their consumption of gas and oil by 15 percent," on what basis does this person claim to be taken seriously? Such a statement by the president of the United States would be based on a different source of legitimacy than the same statement by a spokesperson for the Union of Concerned Scientists, the editor of the *Houston Chronicle,* the National Council of Churches, or, for that matter, a Los Angeles taxi driver.

Religion legitimates authority indirectly in traditional societies by its pervasive interrelationship with all aspects of society. Myth and ritual support the seriousness of all spheres of life. The chief, priest, or matriarch can speak with authority because their roles correspond to or reflect the authority of divine beings. Historic religions legitimate authority more directly, as shown in Chapter 7. Such historic religions as Christianity, Islam, and Judaism have similarly given authority to pronouncements on education, science, economic policy, law, family life, sport, art, and music. Whether directly or indirectly invoked, the images and symbols of the sacred are a source of legitimacy (Fenn, 1978:xiii). The *taken-for-granted quality* of religion as a source of legitimacy characterizes all of these earlier societal situations.

Because legitimacy and authority are the underpinnings of government and law, shifts in the nature of authority and the sources of legitimacy have profound implications for how modern societies can operate. The location of religion in contemporary societies reflects societal changes in the *bases* of legitimacy. Sociologists of religion, thus, are probing the serious implications for the larger society of religion's changed location and roles.

Conflicting Sources of Authority The process of institutional differentiation has resulted in a rise of competition and conflict among the various sources of legitimate authority in modern society. As Bellah (1964) suggests, early differentiation of religious from political institutions meant that religious institutions could come into conflict with political institutions. The potential to legitimate implies the corollary ability to *delegitimate* power, whether in the context of government, courts, workplace, or family (see Luckmann, 1987; Riis, 1998b). Historically, the churches could authoritatively evaluate whether the state was engaged in a "just" war and could authoritatively criticize business practices they judged as "usurious" (i.e., charging unfair interest rates on loans). In contemporary society, by contrast, religious institutions must actively compete with other sources of legitimacy. Personal, social, and political authority are now more uncertain.

This competition for legitimacy can be seen in a number of issues in recent years. As examples in Chapter 7 show, civil disobedience over civil rights, abortion, sanctuary for political refugees, and the U.S. involvement in wars in Vietnam and Central America was often based on a different *source of authority* than that of the prevailing legal or political ones. Civil disobedience often claimed religion or higher human values as the basis for conflict with civil authorities.

Often court events involve a clash of several different sources of legitimacy. In one court case, for instance, a young person had been comatose for months and "as good as dead" in the commonsense view. Eventually her parents sought the court's permission to terminate the "extraordinary" measures that were keeping her body alive. The court case was complicated, and no single authority held uncontested legitimacy. Medical experts gave their opinions on the medical definitions of death. Legal experts raised issues of the legal rights and guardianship of comatose patients. Theological experts offered briefs on the borderlines of life and death, and the girl's father made a thoughtful personal statement about the parents' request. What is relevant sociologically is that medical, legal, religious, and parental figures vied in court to have their statements taken seriously (Fenn, 1982; Willen, 1983). In late modern, rapidly changing societies, authority is contested, not "given." Religion is often in the fray—sometimes as a *contestant,* sometimes as the supporting *basis* of a person's (or group's or government's) authority, sometimes as the *content* over which various authorities vie.

Pluralism, particularly, undercuts univocal notions of legitimacy. This feature is an especially important characteristic of the American, Canadian, and Australian religious scenes, given their histories of religious diversity and church–state relationships, together with waves of immigration and (belated) acknowledgment of native religions. It is also increasingly characteristic of much of Europe, where patterns of immigration, changing church–state relationships, and regional economic integration have dramatically affected the legitimacy of authorities of all kinds. Even outside the West, the considerable cultural diversity of several southeast Asian countries, for example, makes pluralistic tolerance an appropriate basis for civil society—*if* it can be achieved—as an alternative to ethno-religious strife and supremacy.

Historic official religions were characteristically monolithic: They established the worldview of their society and had a monopoly over the ultimate legitimation of individual and collective life. Where alternative views coexisted

---

BOX 8.1 Historical Perspective: Differentiation and Legitimacy of Medical Authority

Western medicine is a good example of a source of authority that now competes with religious and other sources of authority. First, medicine was differentiated from other institutions, including religion. Long before there was any distinctive occupation of medicine, healing was the function of mothers and other nurses, herbalists, folk healers, religious persons, midwives, diviners, and so on. Characteristics of the institutional differentiation of medicine include the development of a distinctive body of knowledge, a corps of specialists with control over this body of knowledge and its application, and public acknowledgment (or legitimacy) of the authority of medical specialists (Freidson 1970).

The specialized occupation of "doctor" did not develop until the Middle Ages, when healing was highly supernaturalized. Christian church authorities attempted to control healing, because the power to heal was believed to come from spiritual sources—evil or good. The Lateran Council of 1215 (which represented the apex of church power in the Middle Ages) forbade physicians from undertaking medical treatment without calling in ecclesiastical advice. Healing that took place outside clerical jurisdiction was suspected of having been aided by the devil. The two main groups of healers that were thus suspect were Jewish doctors and "witches" (typically women). Jewish and Moorish physicians had kept their ancient medical lore alive throughout the Middle Ages, while the dominant European medical knowledge was a stagnant and less effective form of

late Greek medicine. Therefore, Jewish physicians were sought by the wealthy, to the disgust of Christian clergy who proclaimed, for example, that "it were better to die with Christ than to be cured by a Jew doctor aided by the devil" (cited in Szasz, 1970:88).

The masses, however, were served by an assortment of folk healers such as village women who used herbs, potions, magic, charms, and elements of pre-Christian religions to cure disease and ward off evil influences (see Ehrenreich and English, 1973). These healers were a special target of the Inquisition in several countries. A papal bull (i.e., official writ), the *Malleus Mallificarum* (1486), became a manual for witch-hunts, singling out women healers as especially dangerous, because:

All witchcraft comes from carnal lust, which in women is insatiable. . . . Wherefore for the sake of fulfilling their lusts they consort with devils. . . it is sufficiently clear that there are more women than men found infected with the heresy of witchcraft. . . . And blessed be the Highest Who has so far preserved the male sex from so great a crime. (Sprenger and Kramer, [1486] 1948)

The specialized occupation of doctor developed largely through the establishment of university medical schools, the creation of medical guilds, and the later state regulation of credentials for physicians. This political process legitimated the increasing monopoly of physicians

---

with the dominant one, they were absorbed and co-opted or effectively suppressed and segregated. Examples of absorption include the incorporation of early monasticism into church–controlled monastic orders and the development of sects within Hinduism. The alternative worldviews of medieval Jews among

BOX 8.1 *continued*

against the claims of other healers. Nevertheless, the formally recognized physicians were unable to command a monopoly over healing services, largely because the state of their craft did not inspire public confidence until recent times.

In the United States, that professional legitimation did not occur until well into the twentieth century (Freidson, 1970; Starr, 1982). By mid-century, however, physicians' monopoly of legitimacy was so great that pastoral counselors and religious healers risked legal prosecution if their efforts to help someone could be construed as "practicing medicine without a license"(Anthony and Robbins, 1995). Jehovah's Witnesses believe that blood transfusions are forbidden by Scripture, but the courts have generally upheld the medical authorization of transfusions, even for unwilling recipients (*United States v. George*). Religious believers who used prayer or other religious practices to address their children's health needs could be prosecuted for endangering their children by failing to seek "legitimate help"—that is, medical intervention (Beck and Hendon, 1990; Richardson and Dewitt, 1992).

Thus, medical authority supersedes parental authority even when medical ability to prevent death is doubtful (precedent cases cited in Burkholder, 1974:41; see Wilson, 1990, for parallel British cases). A number of court decisions have upheld medical judgments to perform cesarean sections even over the strenuous religious objections of patients and their families, and despite the fact that subsequent medical developments showed that most of the operations were not medically necessary (Irwin and Jordan, 1987).

■ What criteria could a court apply to determine if a religious healer's or minister's practices to help a person get well should be allowed, even if contrary to medical advice, under the "free practice" clause of the Constitution?

■ Imagine you are the judge to whom a hospital has applied for an emergency ruling to override a woman's refusal to consent to undergo cesarian section (a serious surgical procedure to deliver an unborn child).

• The hospital's physicians argue that tests show the fetus has some probability of being "distressed" and, without immediate intervention, might become stillborn or handicapped. They admit they do not know for certain that the fetus is in danger, but assert that even a small chance is not worth the risk of failing to intervene medically.

• The parents argue that their god watches over them and their unborn baby and that their deeply held faith tells them not to intervene medically, because god's will and providence will determine the outcome of the natural birth process. To them, allowing the cesarian is an affront to god and a sign of lack of faith.

• Would you give greater weight to the physicians' authority or the parents'? On what basis?

Christians, as well as Zoroastrians (i.e., Parsees) among Hindus, were little threat to the monopolies of these dominant worldviews because the minority religions were effectively suppressed and segregated (Berger, 1967:134, 135).

In the contemporary pluralistic situation, however, the various authorities in society, in the state, in the world, compete for legitimacy. No single view has such uncontested legitimacy that a person expressing it authoritatively can be *certain* of being taken seriously (Berger, 1967:151). Thus, religious perspectives are not only competing with each other, but they are also competing with other groups that base their claims to authority on such other foundations as science, medicine, professional expertise, and so on.

More than simply describing the predicament of religion in the contemporary world, these features—differentiation and pluralism—raise important questions about the larger societal (indeed, world) social order. The problem of legitimacy at the societal level involves the society's very basis for authoritative decision making and its grounds of moral unity or integration. Such problems highlight the issues of church–state tensions and the nature of civil religions and religious nationalisms.

Pluralism and Legitimacy in the United States Both pluralism and the religious bases of legitimate authority have a complex history in the United States. In colonial America, the principles of pluralism and religious tolerance were gradually established, but colonial society was far from pluralistic in the modern sense. It was narrowly Protestant and adamantly Christian, even though less than 10 percent of the populace actually belonged to churches (see Wood, 1988). Colonial Massachusetts, for example, was virulently anti-Catholic, with stringent laws against "popish" ideas and practices. Quakers and Baptists were also suppressed, sometimes violently. Only Pennsylvania, Rhode Island, and—for a period—Maryland and New York had some legal support for religious tolerance, but even there religious minorities were not treated equally before the law. Many of the colonies denied Catholics, Jews, and minority Protestant groups such rights as voting, holding public office, and conducting religious services in public (Ribuffo, 1988). Later, the Constitutional Convention of 1787 prohibited any religious test for public office, which dramatically reshaped church–state relations in the new republic. This change ultimately eliminated preferential treatment not only for *any one religion* but also of *religion over nonreligion* (Wood, 1988).

The principle of religious liberty, together with the growing multiplicity of religious views, pressed the government and especially the courts to resolve conflicts. The courts needed moral answers to resolve legal questions, yet the increasing ethno-religious diversity of the country made it impossible for the courts to resort to the language and legitimacy of orthodox Protestantism. In 1879 the Supreme Court considered whether polygamy (in this case, plural marriage) would be legally permitted if it were part of a religious group's (i.e., Mormons') practices (*Reynolds v. United States*). The court decided against making "religious" exceptions to "the law of the land" (Hammond, 1974:129–130).

The further the beliefs and practices of a religious minority were from those of the Protestant dominant culture, the more likely that group was to have legitimation difficulties before the courts (Mazur, 1999). Indeed, as of the year 2000, "no Jew, no Muslim, and no Native American has ever won a free exercise case before the Supreme Court, despite numerous efforts" (Witte, 2000:234–235). Historically, the religious minorities most affected have been Native Americans, Mormons, and Jehovah's Witnesses, but new immigrants have introduced new religious minorities and new challenges to the Protestant assumptions embedded in U.S. legal authority.

Similar conflicts arose in the twentieth century over whether to allow exemptions on religious grounds from national ceremonies (e.g., saluting the flag) and military service, release time from public schools for religious instruction, prayer in public schools, taking prohibited drugs for religious purposes, and so on (Witte, 2000; see also Demerath and Williams, 1987; Hammond, 1987). It would be a mistake to see these conflicts as "merely" church–state issues. The very *process* of their resolution reflects the pressure of an increasingly pluralistic situation in which *no* single religious worldview is granted legitimacy. Note the change between the language of cases in 1892 and 1965:

Church of the Holy Trinity v. United States, 143 U.S. 226, 1892:

Mr. Justice Brewer wrote that events in our national life "affirm and reaffirm that this is a religious nation." Deciding that a statute prohibiting importing aliens for labor was not intended to prevent a church from hiring a foreign Christian minister, the Court quoted with approval two earlier judicial opinions stating that "we are a Christian people, and the morality of the country is deeply ingrafted upon Christianity" and "the Christian religion is a part of the common law of Pennsylvania."

United States v. Seeger, 380 U.S. 163, 1965:

In a conscientious objection case, the Court determined that "belief in relation to a Supreme Being" (thus exemption from military service) shall be determined by "whether a given belief that is sincere and meaningful occupies a place in the life of its possessor parallel to that filled by the orthodox belief in God of one who clearly qualifies for the exemption." Exemption is not limited to monotheistic beliefs. Mr. Justice Clark noted the prevalence of a "vast panoply of beliefs," thus Seeger's beliefs qualified as "religious" and he was exempted. (cited in Hammond, 1974:130, 131)

More than just religion is at stake here. Philip Hammond (1974) suggested the pluralistic situation creates problems of defining order, because no monolithic worldview exists to authoritatively define it. The society still needs order, however, so legal institutions are called on to establish and interpret it. The result is a constellation of legal institutions with a "decided religio-moral character" (Hammond, 1974:129). According to this interpretation, the courts are trying to articulate a basis for moral unity where no such foundation is given by specifically religious institutions. What some people decry as "secularity" is not the result of lost belief followed by immoral behavior. Instead, society has lost its overall sense of moral community and consensus (literally "thinking and feeling together"). Without agreement on the way to live together, claims of moral authority make no sense (MacIntyre, 1967:54).

This problem affects *societal* decision making. How is it possible for human values to determine public policy in a pluralistic society? Is the role of religion in political decision making reduced to that of one more interest group vying with opposing interest groups? Or is it even possible for a pluralistic society to agree on human values at a societal level? The obvious examples of religious groups asserting themselves on a national level have typically been issues of legislating what might be called "private morality"—homosexuality, abortion, pornography, divorce, gambling, or drinking. Less publicized but still important have been the efforts to apply religious values to decision making on "public morality"—civil rights, the Vietnam War, arms proliferation, and the environment.

The difficulties of reaching a consensus on social values in a pluralistic society can be illustrated by the issues involved in developing a national energy policy for the United States. The energy situation could be viewed as merely the conflict of competing interests: producers versus consumers, producers versus environmental protection groups, voters versus major campaign contributors, Californian-based corporate interests versus Texas-based corporate interests, the United States versus other nations, and so on. Policy decisions could reflect a juggling of these interests according to relative power, influence, technological expertise, financial muscle, or political pressure. Nevertheless, important human values have also been raised by religious people and institutions. These issues include the fair distribution of scarce resources, a concern for the "have-nots," human health and safety, our society's responsibility to future generations, and our country's responsibility in international relations. None of these interests or values specifies the exact outcome of any policy decision, but they are hotly contested in pulpit and pew, as well as in public life. In the end, those factors which the powers-that-be accept as relevant in the decision-making process *do* make a difference. Is consensus on values necessary or even possible? And if so, does the society consider human values relevant or important to decisions in the public sphere?

Richard Fenn (1972:27) argues that having unstable sources of legitimacy produces two seemingly disparate social responses: *the development of minority and idiosyncratic definitions of the situation, together with increasingly secularized political authority.* On the one hand is pressure to desacralize the political authority—for example, removing any ideological notions of what is "good" from decision making and replacing them with functionally rational criteria such as due process and technical procedures (see also Hammond, 1974). On the other hand, individuals and groups develop their own particular (i.e., "idiosyncratic") views and symbols for which they claim the same seriousness as recognized religions. Individual and group claims to social authority multiply as the uncertainty of boundaries becomes evident (see Fenn, 1978:55).

Court cases present some interesting examples of the ambiguities at this stage. The religious use of peyote (a hallucinogen) by some Native Americans has had a long tradition. The Native American church, instituted in 1918, ties together themes from Native American religions and incorporates peyotism in its ritual. In 1962 a group of Navajos using peyote in their religious ceremony was arrested and convicted under a California law prohibiting possession of peyote. The California Supreme Court overturned the conviction (*People v. Woody*), however, granting Native Americans immunity under the First Amendment of the Constitution, which guarantees free exercise of religion. Despite the promulgation of federal policies to protect Native American religious freedom (see Michaelson, 1987), few court battles have upheld those freedoms. In 1990 the U.S. Supreme Court overturned a lower court's decision and refused to grant religious exemption from Oregon's laws against possession or use of peyote (*Oregon Employment Division v. Smith*).[8]

The courts were even more pressed on the religious freedom issue when individuals and groups in the larger culture began to use hallucinogens for religious purposes. A number of "psychedelic churches" (e.g., the Church of the Awakening and the League of Spiritual Discovery, both founded in the mid-1960s) have tried to establish their constitutional immunity for the religious use of drugs (mainly marijuana, peyote, and mescaline). The best-known case on this issue was in the mid-1960s, when Dr. Timothy Leary was convicted and sentenced to thirty years in jail and $40,000 in fines for illegal possession of marijuana. Dr. Leary, a researcher of psychedelic drugs, claimed that marijuana use was an integral part of his religious practice. On appeal, the court upheld the conviction, commenting that Leary's religious use of marijuana was occasional, private, and personal. The court declared a "compelling state interest" in drug prohibition:

> It would be difficult to imagine the harm which would result if the criminal statutes against marijuana were nullified as to those who claim the right to possess and traffic in this drug for religious purposes. For all practical purposes the anti-marijuana laws would be meaningless, and enforcement impossible. . . . We will not, therefore, subscribe to the dangerous doctrine that the free exercise of religion accords an unlimited freedom to violate the laws of the land relative to marijuana. (*Leary v. United States*, 383 F.2d 841, 1967)

This kind of conflict illustrates the lack of moral unity and problems of legitimacy in modern societies such as the United States. Similar cases involving idiosyncratic perspectives include conflict over whether military or prison worship opportunities should be provided equally for minority religions such as Wiccans and Black Muslims, whether Transcendental Meditation (TM) should be allowed in the schools, whether faith healers or Scientologists could be banned as fraudulent, and whether to allow movements with strong political overtones (e.g., Christian Patriots) the prerogatives of religious organizations

---

8. The *Smith* case represented a repoliticization of the legal issues, though, in that the Court was clearly reflecting the "statist" shift that characterized the presidencies of Reagan and Bush, who had appointed most of that Court. This shift was away from tolerance of marginal religions toward greater state control of all aspects of private life. However, a coalition of religious groups, including most mainstream denominations, pressured Congress to restore the earlier criteria for legitimate "free exercise." The 1993 Religious Freedom Restoration Act, passed overwhelmingly by both chambers of Congress, reaffirmed protection for minority religions in the United States (see Richardson, 1995a; Smith and Snake, 1996; Williams, 1995), although the future enforcement of such legislated protection is uncertain.

(see Alley, 1988; Burkholder, 1974; Mazur, 1999; Pfeffer, 1974, 1987; Richardson, 1995a, 1995b; Robbins, 1981, 1985; Witte, 2000).

Legitimation problems are disturbing because they undermine the ability of society to maintain belief in a symbolic whole that transcends the separate identities and conflicting interests of society's component parts (Fenn, 1978:8). Pluralism and institutional differentiation make it impossible to achieve a new firm source of societal integration and legitimacy. At the same time, however, they increase the likelihood that people will need and seek some ideological symbolic whole.

Rationalization and the Legitimacy of Authority. *Rationalization* is the process by which certain areas of social life are organized according to the criteria of *means–ends* (or "functional") *rationality*. This linkage was a central thread in the works of Weber (1947, 1958a), who viewed a special form of rationality as the foremost feature of modern society.[9] According to Weber, modern Western society is characterized by a "rationalized" economy and a concomitant special "mentality." A **rational economy** is functionally organized, with decisions based on the reasoned weighing of utilities and costs. The rational mentality involves openness toward new ways of doing things (in contrast with traditionalism) and readiness to adapt to functionally specialized roles and universalistic criteria of performance. Although these forms of rationality originated in the economic order, they have extended into political organization and legal order—the modern state. Weber argued that religious motives and legitimations played a central role in bringing about this form of organization and mentality. He traced, for example, the religious sources of universalistic ethics (i.e., the norm of treating all people according to the same generalized standards) and the development of religious drive for rational mastery over the world. Despite its religious origins, this rationality became divorced from its historical source and acquired an impetus of its own (Weber, 1947, 1958a).

Weber (1958a) closed his early essay on the Protestant ethic with an almost prophetic evaluation of possible outcomes from the process of rationalization. He observed that the rationally organized order of modern society presents itself to the individual as an overwhelming force. *All* people engaged in the extensive system of market relationships are bound by the norms of functional rationality, whether they agree with them or not. This constraint is exemplified by how very difficult it is to establish alternative economic arrangements, as countercultural communes have discovered. The ultra-rational conditions of the modern economic order have become an *"iron cage" of instrumentality,* which in Weber's opinion is far from desirable:

> No one knows who will live in this cage in the future, or whether at the end of this tremendous development entirely new prophets will arise, or

---

9. Note, however, that Weber used the concept of rationality in several ways, giving rise to some ambiguities in his theories; see Luckmann, 1977:16, 17. Note also, that Weber was describing *social* changes, not all aspects of individuals' lives and actions. This is one of the differences between his concept of "rationalization" and the uses of the concept of "rational" in rational-choice theory, described earlier.

there will be a great rebirth of old ideas and ideals, or, if neither, mechanized petrification, embellished with a sort of convulsive self-importance. For the last stage of this cultural development, it might well be truly said: "Specialists without spirit, sensualists without heart"; this nullity imagines that it has attained a level of civilization never before achieved. (Weber 1958a:182)

Weber's analysis suggests that the differentiation process alone does not account for important changes in contemporary society. Rationalization specifies the direction of differentiation: Differentiation proceeds according to the criteria of means–ends rationality. Businesses can (and many do) specialize tasks according to nonrational criteria. Nevertheless, the main thrust of organization in business (and increasingly in other spheres such as schools, government, churches, and other voluntary organizations) is to extend the criteria of functional rationality: effectiveness, efficiency, cost–benefit analysis, and specialization of tasks. While differentiation alone produced separate norms appropriate to each institutional domain, rationalization of public-sphere institutions means that nonfunctional values (e.g., kindness, honesty, beauty, meaningfulness) are generally irrelevant to action within these institutions. The ethical regulation of an impersonal rational organization is thus impossible (Weber, 1958a:331).

If modern society is indeed moving in the direction of increasing functional rationality, this process implies problems at two levels: the location of individual meaning and belonging, and a conflict between corporate control and values versus personal autonomy and values. Personal meaning is not only relegated to the private sphere but is also undermined by the dominant rationality of other spheres. Rationalized medical practice, for example, does not deal with the "meaning" of childbirth. It is more functional to treat the woman's and child's bodies as objects to be manipulated. Personal meaning, satisfaction, and emotions in giving birth are not overtly denied by the medical process, but they are subordinated to "rational" criteria of efficiency and medical management. The individual seeking to apply meaning to personal experiences is in a weak situation relative to the powerful institutions for which individual meaning is irrelevant.

This issue of loss of meaning appeared earlier in this chapter under the guise of "secularization"; here we see it in more complex form. This very fact tells us that the sociology of religion is more than just the study of churches, church membership, and religious belief. Instead, it takes us to the core of social processes that shape late modernity.

RELIGION, POWER, AND ORDER
IN THE MODERN WORLD

World events in recent years have highlighted the extent to which religion is an appropriate focus for the study of the continuing tensions between tradition and modernity. The resurgence of fundamentalist Islam in Mideastern politics, the political effects of both Christian liberationist movements and evangelicalism in Latin America, and the intensification of church–state issues in the United States and Britain exemplify the relationship of religion to political and economic life in modern and modernizing societies.

The first part of this chapter described four prominent sociological narratives of social change as they apply to the situation of religion and the future of religions. We also suggested that a fifth story is emerging to interpret religion's role in the modern world, one based on the analysis of globalization. There is no doubt that one must look beyond the borders of any given society for the full impact of social changes. One interpreter of the modern situation, Roland Robertson, describes **globalization** as the "compression of the world and the intensification of consciousness of the world as a whole" (1992:8). It is the ongoing and complex process by which "the world as a whole" comes to be experienced as a "single place" (1991a:283). Globalization does not mean harmonious integration, nor that the world is becoming a better place.

The *fact* of globalization can be illustrated by the 1995 incident in which a prestigious transnational university press withdrew its contract to publish a book in response to death threats toward that press's staff in an Asian country. Euro-American academics were outraged at the abrogation of one of the most cherished modern norms, freedom of expression of ideas. The militant religious group issuing the threat was, likewise, participating in the global "single place." Its violent activism was meant to enforce its will, not merely in its own country but in all countries—regardless of their particular laws and norms defining "objectionable" material. This is globalization: the situation in which we are all connected with each other (i.e., structural integration), even if we lack agreement on virtually everything (i.e., cultural integration).

In the modern world, globalized compression results from systems of communication and technologies that create an immediacy impossible to imagine even three decades ago. In writing this chapter, we were able to carry on extended conversations with several European and South American colleagues by electronic "mail" in order to be sure that we had their most current writing. Images on television, over the Internet, and in print media bring to people around the world a consciousness of the larger world. Many groups that resist westernization find that the allure of modern media technologies makes isolation of their people from global influences very difficult. Urban Iranians, for example, can use their satellite dishes to receive European and North American television programming, undercutting religious authorities' efforts to limit their exposure to a "decadent" outside world.

Modern compression is, particularly, a result of the globalization of economic activity. Whereas in the not-too-distant past most economic activity was local or regional, increasingly the scope of economic interdependence has broadened—to whole societies, whole continents, and ultimately the entire world. The scope of a global economic situation is difficult to imagine. It means that decisions made in distant places by unknown powerful people affect most aspects of one's own everyday economic situation.

In traditional societies, most economic relationships were within the community, and transactions were handled face-to-face: Producing, buying, and selling of all needed goods and services took place in the immediate community. Modern Western societies in the twentieth century became accustomed to a larger scope; societal economies are now taken for granted. In 1975, when a company opened a new factory in Texas and closed its older plants elsewhere, its employees in New Hampshire may have been frustrated and angry about losing their jobs, but they could at least envision some of the societal economic factors influencing their plight. It takes a considerable leap of knowledge and sociological imagination, however, for displaced U.S. workers in the twenty-first century to understand increasingly *global* factors in their economic fate, such as: when rising global interest rates limit their company's access to capital, or when management lays off productive workers in order to keep stock prices high, or when the company closes its U.S. operations to avoid costly pollution controls by locating across the border in Mexico. Other experiences of global economic interdependence facing Americans, like all citizens of highly developed nations, include: the impact of World Trade Organization (WTO) policies and trade agreements, NAFTA (the North American Free Trade Agreement) and the parallel European Economic Union, international commodity cartels (oil, coffee, cocoa, etc.), trade embargoes, massive World Bank and U.S. government worldwide lending and borrowing, and vast transnational corporations with assets greater than the entire gross national product of many countries.

People of developing countries of the Third World have a different experience of this global interdependence. Their economies were initially developed as colonies of First-World nations, and the colonial legacy often makes economic, social, and political independence extremely difficult. Furthermore, developing countries are often totally dependent on the international economic powers for markets, development loans, and imported technology. Often these countries have only a few export products (typically natural resources such as minerals) and cannot even set their own prices for the sale of these in the international economy. "Development" in these contexts frequently means only that the Third-World country allows transnational corporations to build factories, extract natural resources, affect the environment, and pay reduced taxes in return for the employment of a number of that country's unskilled or semiskilled workers. The fragility and one-sidedness of this kind of "development" are linked to total dependence on a vast world economy in which the developing countries have little or no leverage.

Compression of political systems is also inevitable in the modern world. While retaining somewhat separate national cultures, the states of Europe are thrust together to work out complex political and legal issues, partly due to their economic union, but more generally due to their need for concerted action and international interdependence. The articulation and expansion of international law is, thus, closely linked with globalization (Lechner, 1991b).

Furthermore, the fact of supranational economic structures makes necessary political and judicial institutions on the same scale. As noted in the second part of this chapter, modern national polities lack the moral consensus they need if they are to wrestle with their problems; this is even more true of emerging international polities. In Europe, there are new supranational political and judicial institutions that are grappling with such issues as pluralism in a complex transnational economic system (Richardson, 1995b)[10] for some of the church–state issues in a pan-European context). Religious issues are paramount for these decisions—the meaning of life, the moral legitimacy of the social order, and so on. In Europe, as in the United States, religion has a renewed role in the legitimation and critique (and, thus, potential delegitimation) of various systems of power and systems of community (Riis, 1998b). Religion is relevant to these developments precisely because many of the changes in the modern world (described earlier in this chapter) explain the difficulty—and importance—of dealing with issues of moral order, legitimacy, and the basis of human rights in an increasingly globalized social system.

Although the fact of globalized economic and political involvement makes supranational moral discourse *necessary,* it is extremely difficult for supranational institutions to establish norms or criteria for judgment that constituent members would accept as legitimate. The problem is acute because different religious and philosophical traditions have radically different conceptions of the individual, the nature of freedom, and the nature of rights. In some religious/cultural traditions, for example, rights adhere to a group unit such as a family, rather than to individuals as in European and American conceptions of rights. By contrast, in Euro-American thought, law, nature, and religion are separated; the individual is considered to be a legal entity separate from the collectivity, conceptualized as an autonomous person and as a citizen (Lechner, 1991b). There may be grounds on which a supranational, multicultural moral consensus can be established, but at present we do not have one—a fact with grave social and religious consequences (Spickard, 1994).

Robertson argues that globalization evokes religious and political responses largely because it is profoundly relativizing (Robertson, 1991a, 1992). Globalization results in a disjunction of time and space that produces an ongoing negotiation and reconstruction of what constitutes "authenticity." Whereas formerly people relied on orienting polarities that framed identity and difference (such as home and away, local and global, "us" and "them"), globalization now relativizes those distinctions (Beyer, 1998a). Historically religions have had "homes"; for example, Christianity's home was Europe, Hinduism had India as home, Islam's home was the Middle East, and Buddhism's was East and Southeast Asia. Religions have been linked to their own sense of time and place by their constructed histories, languages of sacred texts and worship, and other chosen cultural components. Globalization creates the possibility—indeed, the necessity—of defining "authentic" religion in terms that transcend those location-based and ethnic boundaries. For example, in New York City, it is possible to be a "real" Muslim from an African-American background and worship together with other "real" Muslims who have emigrated from the

---

10. The treatment of religious minorities is becoming something of a global "human rights" legal test-case (see Richardson and Introvigne, 2001, and the entire *Nova Religio,* 2001, symposium on "New Religions in Their Political, Legal, and Religious Contexts Around the World").

Middle East. Such globalized notions of authentic religious identity raise problematic issues about authority (e.g., who has the authority to define what is accepted as "authentic"?) and legitimation. These issues bring with them problems of power.

The nature of the linkage between religion and politics depends partly on the nature of the religious belief systems and political systems involved. Chapters 6 and 7 suggest some of the factors shaping the relative activism and influence of a religion in sociopolitical spheres. The connection between religion and politics varies widely from one society to another.

Religion, Power, and Legitimacy Issues in Europe

The history of European religious diversity is very different from that of the United States, and each country has a different resulting way of framing religion's role vis-à-vis the state, its laws, its political institutions, and its treatment of religious minorities (see Casanova, 1994). We must remember that the diversity among Christians that prompted U.S. constitutional protections had a long prior history in Europe. Even today the results of realignments between political institutions and religious institutions that occurred throughout Europe many centuries ago continue to shape the *contested* borderlines as to what is properly the realm of secular authority and what is properly the realm of religious authorities and institutions. Thus, the Western notion of a clear-cut division between sacred and secular realms is the result of a long historical process; the outcome was the product of power and contests over the legitimacy of authority. The Reformation wars expressed both (proto-)national loyalties and religious aims (Riis, 1998b). We should not underestimate the extent to which many of those boundaries were established by raw power and domination.

The early modern development of European national cultures was firmly linked with people's religious identities. Such linkage is exemplified by the linkage of Lutheran identity with Swedish identity, Catholic identity with Irish identity, and Anglican identity with English identity. Even when (in recent decades) thus-formed nation-states have eliminated the designation of a "state" or "established" church, the deeply embedded assumptions based on their national religions have often remained in law, public policy (such as use of tax revenues), institutional arrangements (such as in the schools), and understanding of the nature of "secular" authority. For example, in England, research suggests that the prevailing religion is a generalized Anglican "believing without belonging": a religion of the no-longer churched but the still faithful (Davie, 1994). Such religion still has immense public impact, for example, creating form and space for the public grieving of the death of Princess Diana (Davie, 2000b). Thus, as Europe developed, both religious identities and national identities were sociopolitically constructed and linked, sometimes in national churches (as in Britain) and sometimes in civil religions (as in France).

By the end of the twentieth century, however, globalization had challenged the neat polarities upon which religious and national identities were constructed. Britain experienced several waves of immigration from its former colonies in South Asia and Africa; because of that colonial heritage, these people may consider themselves to be properly British, even though they are relatively newcomers to English soil. British policy has been to treat the immigrants as cultural minorities; for example, schools may teach about religious holidays as a way of encouraging children to understand and respect the different practices of classmates. British Muslims, however, have been politically restive, challenging the modern tendency to relegate religion to the private sphere (Modood, 2000). Church–state tensions are, thus, inextricably intertwined with the problematic issue of legitimating authority in the context of profound difference—a situation greatly exacerbated by increasingly global ties.

Church–State Tensions in the United States

As the degree of interdependence at the global level increases, church–state tensions at the societal level are likely to increase. This is because church–state issues are the locus of societal struggles to articulate a national identity and moral character, both of which globalization makes more problematic (Robertson, 1981:193; 1989:19). There are two particular areas of church–state tension in the United States. One is legal conflicts over what may be properly called "religion," and the other involves political conflicts over the religious stance of the American people and its proper role in public life.

Religious Boundaries and the Law Two historical mandates shape the church–state relationships in the United States: (1) a firm constitutional prohibition against the state establishing any religion as *the* religion of the land (later this was further articulated as a "wall of separation" between church and state) and (2) constitutional protection for free practice of religion (i.e., "religious liberty"). These two central norms have been the focus for various church–state tensions throughout the history of the United States (see Alley, 1988; Jelen and Wilcox, 1995; Witte, 2000).

Two societal factors made church–state relations more problematic, especially after World War II. One major change was the increased number, socioeconomic status, and influence of American Catholics; this was the first important challenge to taken-for-granted Protestant assumptions in the nation's concept of "religion." Subsequent proliferation of diverse new religious movements (both inside and outside of Christian traditions) and of new immigrant religious groups (including non-Western religions) has confronted the state with an even more varied array of beliefs and practices claimed as "religious."

The second major change is the nature of the Supreme Court itself, which has been more willing to hear church–state cases in recent decades (Demerath and Williams, 1987). Furthermore, in attempts to reassert influence in the public sphere, numerous religious groups and religious social movements have turned to litigation and legislation, for example, over issues of public education, abortion rights, homosexual rights, and religious communication (Pfeffer, 1992; Williams, 2000). The depth of U.S. pluralism makes it unlikely that either new laws or court decisions will satisfy these groups' wish for a decisive break with state neutrality on religion (Hammond, 1987; see Hunter, 1987a, 1991). Such politicization of religion reflects changes in the nature of the modern state (discussed later) and has parallels in other countries (such as Egypt and Israel) where orthodox religions, confronting the pluralism of the modern world, are attempting to reassert control through the law.

As shown earlier in this chapter, numerous precedent-setting cases have arisen over whether a given practice (e.g., polygamy, taking of hallucinogenic drugs, exemption from military service, or refusal of blood transfusion) should be allowed under the protection of the principle of religious freedom. A key criterion in such decisions was whether the practice was part of what could be considered a valid religion. Should the courts protect immigrant religious practices that offend nonminority sensibilities or laws? Should the courts allow the animal sacrifices of Santería, the Rastafari ritual smoking of ganja (marijuana), or the male and female ritual "circumcisions" practiced by some Muslim peoples? If the courts ban these religious practices, on what grounds do they do so?

To enforce the principle of religious liberty, therefore, the courts must define religion. In the twentieth century, in several cases regarding conscientious objection (to war), the Supreme Court adopted very broad definitions. Subsequently, however, various courts were faced with cases requiring decisions as to whether deviant religious movements (such as the Unification Church or Children of God) were indeed "religion" and thus deserved protection of their religious liberty (see Beckford, 1993; Bohn and Gutman, 1989; Pfeffer, 1987; Richardson, 1995a; Robbins, 1987; Robbins and Beckford, 1993; Wald, 1997; Witte, 2000).

Further complications arise as to which aspects of a religious group's actions deserve protection. Most modern religious organizations are extensively involved in activities that are not purely spiritual—running hospitals and schools; investing in real estate and stocks; operating TV, radio, and film studios; offering life insurance; and so on. Many court cases have had to delineate which aspects of religious organization deserve protection under the "free practice" clause. For example, should religious groups be exempt from laws governing fair wages and hiring practices, corporal punishment of children, or fraudulent advertising?

Church–state tensions have been exacerbated by the steady increase of government regulation of a wide range of activities affecting religious groups. In recent years, religious groups have been subject to many new tax laws, labor regulations, immigration investigations, and licensing and accreditation regulations for institutions and personnel. The increasing internal power of the centralized state has made the boundary between church and state yet more problematic.

In 1985 the U.S. government charged eleven clergy and laypersons with violation of federal immigration statutes; the defendants made no secret of their intent to assist Central American refugees to enter the country illegally and to provide them with "sanctuary." The Sanctuary Movement held strong religious motivations for their aid to refugees who were fleeing political oppression in countries like El Salvador and Guatemala. The movement argued that the U.S. government was breaking its own immigration law, which requires asylum to victims of political oppression in other countries (see Cunningham, 1998; Smith, 1996). Whether the activities of the Sanctuary Movement could be defined as "religious practices" became a key issue in the court case (*United States v. Aguilar*) because the government's primary evidence was based on testimony from paid infiltrators. Is the free practice of religion compromised by government infiltration? Spokespersons for the government argued that the "bugged" gatherings were not really church services and prayer meetings because they included discussion of nonspiritual issues; the Sanctuary workers argued that these were very much religious gatherings and that their religion was not limited to a purely spiritual realm (Wogaman, 1988).[11]

Religion and Politics In the context of increased power of the centralized state, conflicts over what is properly "religion" (and thus rightfully handled by religious groups) are also conflicts over what is properly "the state" (and thus rightfully under the aegis of the government). The push of the state to expand the boundaries of its influence has brought a political response from numerous religious groups of varying theological and political persuasions. Public issues such as sex education in the schools, "gay rights," or "the right to die" have become arenas for political battles in which various religious groups assert their diverse moral judgments and argue that the state is not the proper agency for deciding the matter. Religion-oriented political activism (both conservative and progressive) is one response to the state's expansion of the scope of its control (see Robbins, 1993; Williams, 2000). Direct political power is not the only impact of modern religion, however. Religion often has significant power through its cultural influence, by which it exercises symbolic roles such as shaping the terms of political discourse (Demerath and Williams, 1990). Nevertheless, in a pluralistic society such as the United States, even pervasive cultural influence cannot be monolithic as in premodern societies.

More important than the specific legislative and regulatory influences of the modern government apparatus, however, is the sense that the modern state (in all its forms and agencies) is increasingly deciding the very purpose and direction of the society (Robertson, 1981:194). Citizens perceive the state as having greater power and influence over their lives and everyday well-being.

---

11. The court decided to allow use of the tapes obtained by government infiltrators, but ironically the government lawyers subsequently decided not to use the tapes because they were so full of church members' testimony of their moral convictions and descriptions of atrocities from which refugees sought sanctuary that the prosecution feared the tapes would actually help the defense. Subsequently, the Presbyterian Church (U.S.A.), the American Lutheran Church, and four local congregations in Arizona filed suit over damages wrought by government infiltration of churches; the suit was supported by several other religious bodies, including the National Council of Churches.

Concern over the growing power of the government appears to be linked with the political mobilization of churchgoers in the United States. One study concluded that active churchgoers were likely to become politically involved if their attitudes toward certain issues (e.g., defense, abortion, welfare services, affirmative action) were combined with the feeling that the government was generally becoming too powerful (Wuthnow, 1988:318).

Internal attention to church–state tensions, civil religion, and nationalism reflects concerns about national identity, especially in a world context. If we ask, "Who are we, as a nation?" all answers to this question have profound religio-moral implications. Are we, as a nation, the kind of people who protect the "little guy," support ruthless dictators, retaliate against terrorists, invade countries that disagree with us, stand up for our values? And, if so, what are the values that our nation collectively holds dear enough to fight for? Internally, should ours be the kind of nation whose laws permit drinking, birth control, child abuse, divorce, gambling, abortion, same-sex marriages, pornography, or possession of handguns? What values should we apply in deciding priorities for spending our national monies? Are we the kind of people who care most about health care, education, nuclear arms, space exploration, scientific research, decent housing, highways, or the environment? These are all value-laden issues, and thus of religious concern, but rarely are the specific moral and civil religious implications of such judgments made explicit in political discussions.

Power and Order in the Global Context

The twin themes of power and order have been virtually ignored in much of the study of the sociology of religion. These aspects may, however, be among the most important for understanding the linkage of religion to other spheres of life at all levels: individual, societal, and global (McGuire, 1983). Power has a range of meanings, all of which can be applied to religion in the modern world; in understanding religion, the most important advantage of an emphasis on the concept of power is that it highlights the *intentional* production of foreseen events (Beckford, 1983). Such a focus avoids overly reductionistic interpretations and recognizes the extent to which religious action often involves the deliberate assertion of power.[12]

In the global context, the concepts of power and order highlight the underlying problem of *legitimation*. Legitimation involves the justification of power and its uses in terms other than the simple fact of holding power. Legitimation must therefore point to values, beliefs, and ideologies; the exercise of legitimate power cannot be merely a matter of technical procedures or

---

12. This use of the concept of power thus differs from the more reductionistic, materialistic interpretation of the global situation given by "world systems" theorists; furthermore, "world systems" approaches treat separate nation-states as the relevant units in an international rather than global order. For a critical appraisal of this approach, see Beyer, 1994; see also Robertson, 1985, 1991b.

**BOX 8.2   Cross-Cultural Comparison:
The "Headscarf Affair" in France**

In 1989 two Muslim schoolgirls were expelled from their secondary school in France for wearing a *hijab* (Muslim veil). The issue was hotly debated in Parliament over several years, and many more girls who insisted on wearing the *hijab* were expelled from other schools around the country. This controversy was not over school dress codes and discipline, nor was it about race relations and prejudice toward a minority (Muslims are the second most numerous religious group in France, after Catholics). Rather, at the heart of the controversy in France was the viability of that nation's particular form of church–state relationship, which dates back at least to the Revolution. Particular religion (such as Islam or even Catholicism) in the schools represents a threat to civil religion because the French schools, even more so than the American, were designed to be the cradle of citizenship and civil religious collective sentiment.

The 1789 *Déclaration des Droits de l'Homme et du Citoyen,* a foundational document comparable to the U.S. Bill of Rights in the Constitution, states, "No citizen shall be disturbed because of his views, if they are religious views, as long as their expression does not disturb the public order established by law." Individual freedom of religion (including freedom not to accept *any* religion) is guaranteed, but the republican principle of *laïcité*— requiring the State and its agencies (including the state education system) to be religiously neutral—is no longer needed to prevent intrusion by the Catholic Church (Willaime, 1998).

The French education system historically has emphasized civic and moral education, essentially promoting civil religious ideals and practices in place of particular religious practices and moral norms. The religion-free, uniform education system has been identified with reproducing French identity. Thus, the wearing of

---

rationalized operations of due process, but it always functions in the context of symbols held meaningful by those who accept the exercise of power as legitimate (Kokosalakis, 1985). One good example of the interface of religion and political life at the global level is the widespread attention to issues of human rights, justice, and abuses of power. Thus, problems of moral order and the wish for transnational or transcultural norms are evident. Religious groups are uniquely poised to question the legitimacy of regimes whose continued power rests on gross violations of norms of human rights.

Similarly, religious groups speak to the issue of relative poverty and wealth among the nations. Robertson (1987) suggests that the world economy suffers *de*legitimation precisely as the strong national state gains legitimation because it becomes more difficult to justify the existence of enormous economic inequalities among the nations. Because it refers to values and sources of authority that transcend the economic situation, religion is one of the foremost vehicles for both expressing dissatisfaction with the global economic situation and proffering alternatives.

BOX 8.2 *continued*

the *hijab* was extremely upsetting to those who saw it as a breach of the principle of religious neutrality in the schools (MacNeill, 2000). If children were to be socialized into French civic ideals and identity, they had to be protected from religions claiming primacy over that civil religion, promoting ideals and identity *other* than the French. For example, some saw the Muslim requirement of headwear for women as an affront to the national ideal of equality. Others saw it as a form of fundamentalism, which (even in its Christian version) undermines certain civil religious ideals.

Another—albeit less common—interpretation of *laïcité,* however, emphasizes respect of cultural and religious diversities (Molokotos Liederman, 2000; Willaime, 1998). This approach may be especially apt in a multicultural France, with now more than 4 million Muslims (more than half of whom are citizens), mainly recent immigrants from former French colonies in North Africa.

Nevertheless, it does not resolve the problem of how to socialize children of a culturally heterogeneous country into French identity and norms of citizenship. School uniforms and regulations, school pageants and celebrations of civic holidays, and other normative practices are equally important as the content of school books and lessons in teaching children what it means to be one of "us." That is why they are so hotly contested, as the latest skirmish on the boundaries of church and state.

- The "headscarf" issue was motivated by concerns other than prejudice alone, but what evidence would you look for to determine whether the controversy may also have involved prejudice toward Muslims (or toward North African–French)?
- What constitutional principles exist in the United States that (sometimes) produce different outcomes in similar cases?

To understand the role of religion in the modern world, it is therefore useful to look beyond the scope of societal changes to global changes. The foremost problematic issue appears to be legitimation of the global order. Related religion–politics tensions are also promoted by global interdependence; thus, this global perspective provides another window for understanding intrasocietal religious developments, such as church–state legal conflicts, nationalisms, the New Right, and liberation theologies.

THE SOCIOLOGY OF RELIGION IN THE MODERN WORLD

Weber closed his work on the Protestant ethic with an almost prophetic statement, wondering if society were heading toward the ultimate nullity of a totally rationalized, disenchanted world. In this chapter, we explored this and related theses about the future of religion. Following Weber and Durkheim, we have used our examination of religion to provide a picture of the world at the beginning of the twenty-first century and the individual's place in it.

Events of recent years make the sociology of religion a particularly useful approach to understanding this relationship between individual and society. In the second half of the twentieth century, just as some observers were predicting that religion was declining and would virtually disappear, new religious movements and new patterns of spirituality arose among the very sectors of society that were supposed to be most secularized. New forms of religiosity highlight a number of questions about the future of religion: Do they presage new modes of individual-to-society relationship? Do they highlight individual autonomy, or are they new forms of authoritarianism? Do they represent religion's potential for bringing about socioeconomic change, or are they so privatized that they exemplify the disempowerment of individuals in modern society? These questions remain to be addressed by further sociological research.

Similarly, the issue of religion's role in modern societal coherence is critical. Studies of civil religions, nationalism, ethnic congregations, political messianism, and church–state relations in modern and modernizing societies will be useful to our understanding of this issue. We need to know more about fundamental processes such as legitimacy and authority in the context of modern societies and global economic interdependence. Contemporary sociology of religion has the potential to contribute to our understanding of these important topics.

Although these themes suggest that our focus must be broader than the narrow, institutionally specific sociology of religion, much is yet to be learned from the study of church-oriented religion. Religious organizations continue to be important in the lives of many individuals; their membership, organization, and basis of social support make religious institutions perhaps the most important kind of voluntary association in the United States, and their direct and indirect influences in society are still worth studying. Besides official religion and religiosity, however, sociologists also need to study nonofficial religion and religiosity. We have been too quick to accept the official model of religions in our research. More important, the sociology of religious institutions needs to ask larger questions. Rather than focus on religious organizations (e.g., parishes or denominations) as ends in themselves, we must ask: Of what larger phenomenon is this an example? The model of religious collectivities presented in Chapter 5 illustrates such a broader perspective. Thus, the concepts of church and sect can be seen as broad developmental models of any group in particular kinds of tension with its social environment.

Sociology has strived for an unbiased or objective approach to social reality. But sociologists of religion, while guided by this ideal, sometimes find themselves uncomfortable with its implications. Specifically, we cannot assume the superiority or necessity of religious worldviews; at the same time, however, we wonder about the direction society would take if it were utterly nonreligious. Without higher sources of authority for appeal, is legitimacy in modern society to be based on raw power and domination? What becomes of human freedom in the face of powerful public-sphere institutions, especially those of modern scope such as huge transnational corporations, which are effectively free of societal normative constraints? There is no necessary religious "solution" to these issues, but the sociology of religion is uniquely poised to raise them.

SUMMARY

The social location and role of religion (including nonchurch religion) in contemporary society suggest that important social changes have occurred. These changes have apparently resulted in qualitatively different patterns of relationships and meanings. Religion, as well as other institutions, has been profoundly affected by larger changes in society. Although religion appears adaptable and vital in its numerous social forms, these larger changes raise some important questions about the continued ability of religion—and other institutions of the private sphere—to influence other important aspects of society. Particularly apparent is that major changes in the relationship of the individual to society have occurred, and any examination of the nature of religious change must be linked with an understanding of other major changes in the structure of society.

We have examined four main narratives (or stories) that many sociologists of religion use to make sense of these complex developments. Some have told stories of secularization and religious decline; others have framed historical changes as reorganization and change in focus of religious commitment. Some have used narratives of growing individualization and autonomy, while others have depicted religious developments as the result of market decisions. Each of these stories frames the definition, history, and significance of religion differently. And each poses different implications for the importance of certain aspects of religion and their probable future. Each narrative proffers useful insights, but no single one is adequate for interpreting religion's role in the many facets of societal (indeed, global) changes. Nor do any adequately explain the implications of these massive changes for the individual-to-society nexus.

Understanding the role of religion in modern societies requires looking beyond the level of individual or society. The interface of religion with power and order in the subsocietal, societal, and international arenas constitutes one very important item on the sociological research agenda. Due to increasing transnational economic interdependence, a global context is a necessary perspective for understanding religion and modernity. Recent history suggests that religion is one of the foremost forces speaking to issues of legitimation of power and moral order at the global level.

Are All Religions True?

Introduction

Suppose there were only one religion in the world. Let's call it the religion of Bliss. Suppose further that most people were Blissians. They participated in its rituals and conducted their lives, for the most part, according to its teachings. There were some dissenters, some anti-Blissians, but very few.

One consequence of this imaginary situation would probably be that the teachings of Bliss would seem true. There would be no real alternatives, no other religions teaching different doctrines or disputing the truth of Bliss. No one would have to worry about what attitude to take toward rival religions. It would not be necessary. Blissians would have a monopoly on religious truth.

We do not live in such a world. Instead we live in a world with diverse religious traditions that have been and are in conflict. We cannot avoid contact with people of other faiths, and the very existence of such religious pluralism calls into question the truth of each. In the diverse religious world in which we live, we must develop some view about how our religion, if we profess one, relates to the others.

One possibility is to claim that only members of our religion will be saved because only our religion teaches the true path to salvation. Truth belongs to us exclusively. Another possibility is to claim that, although other religions teach some truth and although adherents to other religions can be saved, *our* religion teaches the *full* truth. It is the fulfillment of what the others have only dimly glimpsed. This sort of inclusivism seems more charitable than the exclusive attitude, but it is not so charitable as a third possibility often called pluralism. According to pluralism, all religions are valid paths to salvation.

If we adopt a pluralistic attitude, we need some sort of explanation of why the teachings of all these valid religions appear so different and often seem to conflict. One possibility is to argue that the differences are real but that they involve trivial matters. On important issues there is basic agreement. Another possibility is to argue that the differences are not real but merely apparent. On the surface the different religions seem to contradict each other, but when properly understood, they do not. Or one might admit real differences even on important matters but claim this does not affect the salvific value of each of the great traditions.

In addition to the attitudes of exclusivism, inclusivism, and pluralism, one might argue that today religions interpenetrate one another. Religions no longer exist isolated from one another, but in mutual relationship. What others believe and do helps me better understand my own religion.

We live, as it were, in a religious supermarket with competing brand names and products. Suppose we are shopping. How do we decide what to buy? Do we judge all the other religions by the standards of our own religion? Do we judge the other religions by their own standards? Do we develop some neutral set of rational criteria that enable us to judge impartially and fairly the truth claims of each?

Perhaps this whole business of judging the truth of other religions is misguided. Perhaps it simply cannot be done, or even if it could, it would miss the point. Perhaps we should concentrate on cooperation among the various religions on important moral and social issues, such as helping the poor and stopping violence and war.

Maybe the question "Are all religions true?" is misleading. It is certainly ambiguous. Does it mean that the teachings of the various religions are true? Does it mean that the rituals and rites practiced by the various religions are effective? Does it mean that the social organizations of the various religions are conducive to building community? If we restrict its meaning to the teachings alone, does the question mean that before a religion is true, all (every single one) of its teachings (however trivial) must be true? Further, the question seems to presuppose that there is some sort of religious truth that humans are capable of discovering. Perhaps there is no such thing as objective, absolute truth. What we call "truth" is nothing more than human constructions and conventions that reflect cultural values and biases. Perhaps truth is localized and relative to particular historical periods. After all, many different religions and societies have managed to flourish and survive on this planet while responding to the problems of human existence in very different ways. Perhaps what works for each is the only truth there is.

11.1 Four Attitudes

Consider the following cases:

CASE 1. I believe my religion teaches what is true. If what it teaches is true, then opposing views must be false. Hence there is no salvation for anyone apart from my religion.

CASE 2. I believe my religion teaches what is true. Other religions also teach things that agree with my religion, so other religions must contain some truth as well. However, only my religion teaches the full truth that the others only partially realize. Nevertheless, adherents to other religions may attain salvation insofar as they follow implicitly the path explicitly taught in my religion.

CASE 3. I believe my religion teaches what is true. I also believe other religions teach what is true. Therefore, the different religions must be different paths leading to the same goal, just as there are different paths up a mountain leading to the same summit. Each is right; they just constitute different ways of getting to the same end.

CASE 4. I believe all religions are seeking understanding. This search is enriched in a process of interpenetration, integration, and mutual appreciation. No human is a island and it is the same with religion. We come to understand ourselves, by understanding others.

Raimundo Panikkar was born in 1918 in Spain. He lived in India for many years and became a citizen of India. There he became intimately acquainted with the Indian religious traditions, although he eventually became a Roman Catholic priest and a professor of religious studies at the University of California in Santa Barbara. Because of his multicultural background and interests, he has been deeply involved in interreligious dialogues for a number of years, seeking to promote mutual understanding among the world's religions. His experience has taught him that people often enter such dialogues with four distinct attitudes. In the following selection, he characterizes these attitudes.

The first attitude he calls exclusivism; case 1 above reflects that viewpoint. Only my religion provides salvation and truth. Case 2 illustrates the second attitude, which Panikkar labels inclusivism. This attitude is clearly more tolerant and generous than the first, but it still singles out one religion-(mine) as the best or highest among all the rest. The third attitude, illustrated by case 3 and labeled parallelism by Panikkar (it is also frequently called pluralism), is more tolerant. It neither restricts truth and salvation to one religion nor insists that one religion is better than all the rest. Case 4 reflects an attitude Pannikkar calls interpenetration. We approach other religions with the conviction that the more we know about and understand other religions, the more our own is enriched.

There are problems with each of these views, and Panikkar describes some of them. There are also other possible views that he does not discuss. For example, imagine a case 5 that maintains that none of the religions is a bearer of truth or salvation. This is a skeptical attitude and is distinct from the other four. However different the other four are, they all ascribe some value to religion. The skeptical attitude may also find some value (such as social utility) in religion, but it finds neither truth nor a means of salvation.

Reading Questions

1. What is exclusivism, and what are its difficulties?
2. What is inclusivism, and what are its difficulties?
3. What is parallelism, and what are its difficulties?
4. What is interpenetration, and what are its difficulties?
5. Does any of these four views reflect your own attitude? Which? Why?

Four Attitudes*

RAIMUNDO PANIKKAR

THE CHAPTERS THAT FOLLOW do not elaborate a theory of the religious encounter. They are part of that very encounter. And it is out of this praxis that I would like to propose the following *attitudes* and *models* for the proper rhetoric in the meeting of religious traditions.

I do not elaborate now on the value of these attitudes or the merits of these models. This would require studying the function and nature of the metaphor as well as developing a theory of the religious encounter. I only describe some attitudes and models, although I will probably betray my sympathies in the form of critical considerations. The dialogue needs an adequate rhetoric—in the classical sense of the word.

1. Four Attitudes

A. EXCLUSIVISM

A believing member of a religion in one way or another considers his religion to be true. Now, the claim to truth has a certain built-in claim to exclusivity. If a given statement is true, its contradictory cannot also be true. And if a certain human tradition claims to offer a universal context for truth, anything contrary to that "universal truth" will have to be declared false.

If, for instance, Islam embodies the true religion, a "non-Islamic truth" cannot exist in the field of religion. Any long standing religious tradition, of course, will have developed the necessary distinctions so as not to appear too blunt. It will say, for instance, that there are degrees of truth and that any "religious truth," if it is really true, "is" already a Muslim one, although the people concerned may not be conscious of it. It

will further distinguish an objective order of truth from a subjective one so that a person can be "in good faith" and yet be in objective error, which as such will not be imputed against that person, etc.

This attitude has a certain element of heroism in it. You consecrate your life and dedicate your entire existence to something which is really worthy of being called a human cause, to something that claims to be not just a partial and imperfect truth, but a universal and even absolute truth. To be sure, an absolute God or Value has to be the final guarantee for such an attitude, so that you do not follow it because of personal whims or because you have uncritically raised your point of view to an absolute value. It is God's rights you defend when asserting your religion as "absolute religion." This does not imply an outright condemnation of the beliefs of all other human beings who have not received the "grace" of your calling. You may consider this call a burden and a duty (to carry vicariously the responsibility for the whole world) more than as a privilege and a gift. Who are we to put conditions on the Almighty?

On the other hand, this attitude presents its difficulties. First, it carries with it the obvious danger of intolerance, hybris and contempt for others. "We belong to the club of truth." It further bears the intrinsic weakness of assuming an almost purely logical conception of truth and the uncritical attitude of an epistemological naiveté. Truth is many-faceted and even if you assume that God speaks an exclusive language, everything depends on your understanding of it so that you may never really know whether your interpretation is the *only* right one. To recur to a superhuman instance in the discussion among two religious beliefs does

*A shorter verision was first published in *The Intrareligious Dialogue* by R. Panikkar. Copyright © 1978 by Raimundo Panikkar. New York: Paulist Press. This longer version was published by Asian Trading Corporation in 1984. Reprinted by permission.

not solve any question, for it is often the case that God "speaks" also to others, and both partners relying on God's authority will always need the human mediation, so that ultimately God's authority depends on Man's interpretation (of the divine revelation).

As a matter of fact, although there are many *de facto* remnants of an exclusivistic attitude today, it is hardly defended *de jure*. To use the Christian *skandalon,* for instance, to defend Christianity would amount to the very betrayal of that saying about the "stumbling block." It would be the height of hypocrisy to condemn others and justify oneself using the scandal of God's revelation as a rationale for defending one's own attitude: divine revelation ceases to be a scandal for you (for you seem to accept it without scandal)—and you hurl it at others.

B. INCLUSIVISM

In the present world context one can hardly fail to discover positive and true values—even of the highest order—outside of one's own tradition. Traditional religions have to face this challenge. "Splendid isolation" is no longer possible. The most plausible condition for the claim to truth of one's own tradition is to affirm at the same time that it includes at different levels all that there is of truth wherever it exists. The inclusivistic attitude will tend to reinterpret things in such a way as to make them not only palatable but also assimilable. Whenever facing a plain contradiction, for instance, it will make the necessary distinctions between different planes so as to be able to overcome that contradiction. It will tend to become a universalism of an existential or formal nature rather than of essential content. A doctrinal truth can hardly claim universality if it insists too much on specific contents because the grasping of the contents always implies a particular "*forma mentis.*" An attitude of tolerant admission of different planes will, on the contrary, have it easier. An umbrella pattern or a formal structure can easily embrace different thought-systems.

If Vedanta, for example, is really the end and acme of all the Vedas, these latter understood as the representation of all types of ultimate revelation, it can seemingly affirm that all sincere human affirmations have a place in its scheme because they represent different stages in the development of human consciousness and have a value in the particular context in which they are said. Nothing is rejected and all is fitted into its proper place.

This attitude has a certain quality of magnanimity and grandeur in it. You can follow your own path and do not need to condemn the other. You can even enter into communion with all other ways of life and, if you happen to have the real experience of inclusivity, you may be at peace not only with yourself, but with all other human and divine ways as well. You can be concrete in your allegiances and universal in your outlook.

On the other hand, this attitude also entails some difficulties. First, it also presents the danger of hybris, since it is only you who have the privilege of an all-embracing vision and tolerant attitude, you who allot to the others the place they must take in the universe. You are tolerant in your own eyes, but not in the eyes of those whose challenge your right to be on top. Furthermore it has the intrinsic difficulties of an almost alogical conception of truth and a built-in inner contradiction when the attitude is spelt out in theory and praxis.

If this attitude allows for a variegated expression of "religious truth" so as to be able to include the most disparate systems of thought, it is bound to make of truth a purely relative. Truth here cannot have an independent intellectual content, for it is one thing for the parsi and another for the Vaiṣṇava, one thing for the atheist and another for the theist. So, it is also another thing for you—unless you jump outside the model because it is you who have the clue, you who find a place for all the different world views. But then your belief, conception, ideology, intuition or whatever name we may call it, becomes a supersystem the moment that you formulate it: you seem to understand the lower viewpoints and put them in their right places. You cannot avoid claiming for yourself a superior knowledge even if you deny that your conviction is another viewpoint. If you "say," furthermore, that your position is only the ineffable fruit of a mystical insight, the moment that you put it into practice nothing prevents another from discovering and formulating the implicit assumptions of that attitude. Ultimately you claim to have a fuller truth in comparison with all the others who have only partial and relative truths.

As a matter of fact, although there are still many tendencies in several religious traditions that consider themselves all-inclusive, there are today only very few theoretical and philosophical formulations of a purely inclusivistic attitude. The claim of pluralism today is too strong to be so easily bypassed.

C. PARALLELISM

If your religion appears far from being perfect and yet it represents for you a symbol of the right path and a similar conviction seems to be the case for others, if you cannot dismiss the religious claim of the other nor assimilate it completely into your tradition, a plausible alternative is to assume that all are different creeds which, in spite of meanderings and crossings, actually run parallel to meet only in the ultimate, in the *eschaton*, at the very end of the human pilgrimage. Religions would then be parallel paths and our most urgent duty would be not to interfere with others, not to convert them or even to borrow from them, but to deepen our own respective traditions so that we may meet at the end, and in the depths of our own traditions. Be a better Christian, a better Marxist, a better Hindu and you will find unexpected riches and also points of contact with other people's ways.

This attitude presents very positive advantages. It is tolerant, it respects the others and does not judge them. It avoids muddy syncretisms and eclecticisms that concoct a religion according to our private tastes; it keeps the boundaries clear and spurs constant reform of one's own ways.

On the other hand, it too is not free of difficulties. First of all, it seems to go against the historical experience that the different religious

and human traditions of the world have usually emerged from mutual interferences, influences and fertilizations. It too hastily assumes, furthermore, that every human tradition has in itself all the elements for further growth and development; in a word, it assumes the self-sufficiency of every tradition and seems to deny the need or convenience of mutual learning, or the need to walk outside the walls of one particular human tradition—as if in every one of them the entire human experience were crystallized or condensed. It flatters every one of us to hear that we possess *in nuce* all we need for a full human and religious maturity, but it splits the family of Man into watertight compartments, making any kind of conversion a real betrayal of one's own being. It allows growth, but not mutation. Even if we run parallel to each other, are there not *sangams, prayāgs,* affluents, inundations, natural and artificial dams, and above all, does not one and the same water flow "heavenwards" in the veins of the human being? Mere parallelism eschews the real issues.

Notwithstanding, this attitude presents on the other hand more prospects for an initial working hypothesis today. It carries a note of hope and patience at the same time; hope that we will meet at the end and patience that meanwhile we have to bear our differences. Yet when facing concrete problems of interferences, mutual influences and even dialogue one cannot just wait until this *kalpa* comes to an end or the *eschaton* appears. All crossings are dangerous, but there is no new life without *maithuna*.

D. INTERPENETRATION

The more we come to know the religions of the world, the more we are sensitive to the religiousness of our neighbour, all the more we begin to surmise that in every one of us the other is somehow implied, and vice-versa, that the other is not so independent from us and is somehow touched by our own beliefs. We begin to realize that our neighbour's religion does not only challenge and may even enrich our own, but that ultimately, the very differences which separate us are somewhat potentially within the own world of my religious convictions. We begin to accept that the other religion may complement mine and we may even entertain the idea that in some particular cases it may well supplement some of my beliefs provided that my religiousness remains an undivided whole. More and more we have the case of Marxists accepting Christian ideas, Christians subscribing to Hindu tenets, Muslims absorbing Buddhist views, etc. and all the way remaining Marxists, Christians and Muslims. But there is still more than this. It looks as if we were today all intertwined and that without these particular religious links my own religion would be incomprehensible for me and even impossible. Religions are ununderstandable without a certain background of "religion". Our own religiousness is seen within the framework of our neighbor's. Religions do not exist in isolation, but over against each other. There would be no Hindu consciousness were not for the fact of having to distinguish it from Muslims and Christians, for example. In a word, the relation between religions is neither of the type of exclusivism (only mine), or inclusivism (the mine embraces all the others), or parallelism (we are running independently towards the same goal), but one at a *sui generis perichoresis* or *circumincessio*, i.e. of a mutual interpretation without the loss of the proper peculiarities of each religiousness.

The obvious positive aspect of this attitude is the tolerance, broadmindedness and mutual confidence that it inspires. No religion is totally foreign to my own; within our own religion we may encounter the religion of the other; we all need one another; in some way we are saying not just the same but mutually complementing and correcting things. And even when religions struggle for supplementation, they do it within a mutually acknowledged religious frame.

On the other hand, this attitude is also not free from dangers. First of all, one has to ask if this is not a little wishful thinking. Are we so sure of this interpenetration? Do "Karma" and "Providence" interpenetrate or exclude each other? On what grounds can we establish it? Is this attitude not already a modification of the selfunderstanding of the traditions themselves? This could be answered by justifying the role of creative hermeneutics. Each interpretation is a new creation. But can we say that such hermeneutics really exist in all the minutiae of the world religions? Or is it not a kind of new religiousness which makes a selective use of the main tenets of the traditions while neglecting the others? There may be a religious universe but is it sufficiently broad as to allow for insuperable incompatibilities?

But again this attitude may offer perspectives which the others lack. It may put us on a way which is open to all and which nobody should feel reluctant to enter. It can contribute to the spiritual growth of the partners: even interpreting other beliefs as exaggeration or distortions of our own we touch a more fundamental frame of reference, and without losing our identity, we weaken our assertive ego. It can contribute to a mutual enrichment within a synthesis. The values of the other tradition are not merely juxtaposed to those of our tradition but truly assimilated and integrated to our beliefs and in our own being. It is an open process. . . .

11.2 Conflicting Truth Claims

Consider the following statements:

1. Ultimate reality is personal.
2. Ultimate reality is impersonal.
3. After we die we will be reincarnated.
4. After we die we will not be reincarnated but will go to heaven or hell.
5. The Bible is the final revelation of God's will.

6. The Qur'an is the final revelation of God's will.
7. We need to be redeemed from sin.
8. We need to find release from suffering.
9. We need to find liberation from ignorance.

All of these are claims made by different religions. Could all of these statements be true? Clearly they could all be false, but it seems unlikely that they could all be true, because some appear to contradict others. If I claim the Bible is the final revelation of God's will and you claim that it is not, one of us must be wrong, or so it would seem.

John Hick, author of the next selection, recently retired from Claremont Graduate School after a long and distinguished career teaching philosophy of religion in both England and the United States. One of his primary concerns has been to develop a theory of religion that would harmonize the conflicting claims of the different world religions. He has proposed a pluralistic hypothesis to account for religious differences. Behind all the personal gods and impersonal absolutes proposed by religious thinkers stands *the Real in itself*. This Real is experienced in different ways in different traditions. If this hypothesis is correct, then how do we account for the differing and often contradictory claims that different religions make? Can all religions somehow be reflecting the same reality when they speak of it in such different and conflicting ways?

Reading Questions

1. What is the skeptical argument that arises from the conflicting truth claims of the various religions?
2. How does the proposal to treat each religion as a distinct form of life with its own language game avoid the problem of conflicting truth claims?
3. What is the difference between "doctrinal disagreements" and "basic religious disagreements"?
4. What is "illicit reification," and how does it affect the concept of religion?
5. What are three areas of differences among religions, what is an example of each, and how does Hick propose that they be overcome?
6. What is Hick's hypothesis about the unity underlying religions?
7. What is the Kantian distinction between noumenal and phenomenal, and how does Hick use this to show how the *personae* and *impersonae* might be related?
8. Do you find Hick's hypothesis plausible? Why or why not?

Conflicting Truth Claims*

JOHN HICK

Many Faiths, All Claiming to Be True

Until comparatively recently each of the different religions of the world had developed in substantial ignorance of the others. There have been, it is true, great movements of expansion which have brought two faiths into contact: above all, the expansion of Buddhism during the last three centuries B.C. and the early centuries of the Christian era, carrying its message throughout India and Southeast Asia and into China, Tibet, and Japan, and then, the resurgence of the Hindu religion at the expense of Buddhism, with the result that today Buddhism is rarely to be found on the Indian subcontinent; next, the first Christian expansion into the Roman Empire; then the expansion of Islam in the seventh and eighth centuries C.E. into the Middle East, Europe, and later India; and finally, the second expansion of Christianity in the missionary movement of the nineteenth century. These interactions, however, were for the most part conflicts rather than dialogues; they did not engender any deep or sympathetic understanding of one faith by the adherents of another. It is only during the last hundred years or so that the scholarly study of world religions has made possible an accurate appreciation of the faiths of other people and so has brought home to an increasing number of us the problem of the conflicting truth claims made by different religious traditions. This issue now emerges as a major topic demanding a prominent place on the agenda of the philosopher of religion.

The problem can be posed very concretely in this way. If I had been born in India, I would probably be a Hindu; if in Egypt, probably a Muslim; if in Sri Lanka, probably a Buddhist; but I was born in England and am, predictably, a Christian. These different religions seem to say different and incompatible things about the nature of ultimate reality, about the modes of divine activity, and about the nature and destiny of the human race. Is the divine nature personal or nonpersonal? Does deity become incarnate in the world? Are human beings reborn again and again on earth? Is the empirical self the real self, destined for eternal life in fellowship with God, or is it only a temporary and illusory manifestation of an eternal higher self? Is the Bible, or the Qur'an, or the Bhagavad Gita the Word of God? If what Christianity says in answer to such questions is true, must not what Hinduism says be to a large extent false? If what Buddhism says is true, must not what Islam says be largely false?

The skeptical thrust of these questions goes very deep; for it is a short step from the thought that the different religions cannot all be true, although they each claim to be, to the thought that in all probability none of them is true. Thus Hume laid down the principle "that, in matters of religion, whatever is different is contrary; and that it is impossible the religions of ancient Rome, of Turkey, of Siam, and of China should, all of them, be established on any solid foundation." Accordingly, regarding miracles as evidence for the truth of a particular faith, "Every miracle, therefore, pretended to have been wrought in any of these religions (and all of them abound in miracles), as its direct scope is to establish the particular religion to which it is attributed; so has it the same force, though more indirectly, to overthrow every other system." By the same reasoning, any ground for believing a particular religion to be true must operate as a ground for believing every other religion to be false; accordingly, for any particular

*From *The Philosophy of Religion*, 3d ed. by John Hick. © 1983. Reprinted by permission. Prentice-Hall, Inc., Upper Saddle River, NJ. Footnotes deleted.

religion there will always be far more reason for believing it to be false than for believing it to be true. This is the skeptical argument that arises from the conflicting truth claims of the various world faiths.

W. A. Christian's Analysis

In his book *Meaning and Truth in Religion*, W. A. Christian begins with the idea of a "proposal for belief." Belief is here distinguished from knowledge; if I look at my watch and tell you the time, or if I look out of the window and report that it is raining, I am giving information, not making a belief proposal in Christian's sense. The context in which proposals for belief are made is that of common interest in a question to which neither party knows the answer, and in relation to which there is accordingly scope for theories that would provide an answer. Such a theory, offered for positive acceptance, is a proposal for belief. The following are examples of well-known religious belief-proposals:

Jesus is the Messiah.
Atman is Brahman.
Allah is merciful.
All the Buddhas are one.

These examples are drawn respectively from Christianity, Hinduism, Islam, and Buddhism. It is clear that these belief-proposals are all different; but are they incompatible? Do they, as put forward by these different faiths, conflict with one another?

Consider first what looks like a very direct religious disagreement. Christians say that (A) "Jesus is the Messiah," whereas Jews say that Jesus is not the Messiah and the Messiah is still to come. But William Christian points out that when we take account of what each party means by the term "Messiah" it turns out that they are not directly contradicting one another after all. For "Jews mean by 'the Messiah' a nondivine being who will restore Israel as an earthly community and usher in the consummation of history. Christians mean a promised savior of mankind from sin. Two different Messiah concepts are being ex-

pressed; hence two different propositions are being asserted." Thus the Jew's denial that Jesus is the Messiah does not contradict the Christian's assertion that Jesus *is* the Messiah.

This could suggest the following view: the concepts used in the belief-proposals of a particular religion are peculiar to that religion. Christians use the concept of the Messiah (= divine savior); Jews, the concept of Messiah (= human agent of God's purposes); Buddhists, the concept of Nirvana; Hindus, the concept of Brahman; and Muslims, for example, the concept of the Sharia. Each of these ideas, as it occurs within these religions, gains its meaning from its use within the context of that religion and is thus peculiar to it and has meaning only as part of its discourse. Hence there cannot be a case of two religions employing the same concept and saying contradictory things about it. The Christian, for example, does not say that Allah is not merciful, for Allah is not a Christian concept and Christian discourse does not include any statements about Allah. Or again, the Muslim does not say that Atman is not Brahman, for the question does not arise within the circle of Islamic discourse.

This position could be developed along lines for which some have found inspiration in the later writings of Wittgenstein. Each religion, one might say, is a "form of life" with its own "language-game." Christian language—employing such distinctively Christian concepts as Incarnation, Son of God, and Trinity—derives its meaning from the part that it plays in the Christian life. The criteria of what it is appropriate to say, and thus of what is to be accepted as true, are peculiar to this realm of discourse. These rules of the Christian language-game treat the Bible and Christian tradition as important sources of knowledge. But nothing that is said in the context of Christian faith can either agree or disagree with anything that is said within the context of another religion. The Christian and, say, the Buddhist, are different people, belonging to different religious communities and traditions and speaking different religious languages, each of which has meaning within the context of a different religious form of life; accordingly there is no question of their making rival belief-proposals. Such a theory has the great attraction that it avoids entirely the otherwise vexing problems of the apparently conflicting truth claims made by different religions.

However, William Christian goes on to show that any such solution would be only apparent. Returning to our original example, it is true that Jews and Christians mean different things by "the Messiah" and thus that when the one says that Jesus is not the Messiah and the other that he *is,* they are not directly contradicting each other. However, we can go beyond these two Messiah concepts. We can speak of "the one whom God promised to send to redeem Israel," it being left open whether this is a human or a divine being. We then have the belief-proposal (B), "Jesus is the one whom God promised to send to redeem Israel," this being a proposal that the Christian accepts and the Jew rejects. At this point there is a real disagreement between them about the truth concerning Jesus, a disagreement that was only temporarily masked by noting the different concepts of Messiah that were in use. Indeed, if there were no such genuine and substantial disagreement, it would be difficult to account for the original splitting off of Christianity from Judaism and for the religious polemics that followed. The persisting disagreement does not have to involve any hostility or bitterness; it does not have to prevent Christians and Jews from rejoicing in all that they have in common; and it is compatible with close friendship and cooperation between them. But it is also clear that they do in fact hold different and incompatible beliefs about the nature and significance of Jesus—as also about a large number of other related matters.

Thus, whereas (A) "Jesus is the Messiah" has different meanings for Christian and Jew, when we go behind this formula to (B) "Jesus is the one whom God promised to send to redeem Israel," we find that at this point there is direct Jewish-Christian disagreement. Furthermore, W. A. Christian points out that this process can be carried further to uncover differences between Christian and Jew on the one hand and, say, Sto-

ics on the other. For it is a presupposition of (B) that (C) "The being who rules the world acts in history," for that being is said to "promise," to "send," and to "redeem Israel." However, a Stoic would deny that the Divine does any of these things or indeed acts in history in any way. He thinks of the Divine quite differently, so that the question, "Has God acted in history in such-and-such a manner?" can never arise: since the world-ruler does not act in history at all, there is no scope for debate as to whether or not the world-ruler has acted by sending Jesus.

This process of formulating presuppositions that become the loci of religious disagreement can go yet further. The Jew, the Christian, and the Stoic all hold that there is a Being who rules the world: according to Jew and Christian, that Ruler acts in history, whereas according to the Stoic, not. But there are other faiths that would deny the presupposition that (D) "The source of all being rules the world." The Neoplatonist, for example, denies this, as does the Buddhist and the Hindu of the Advaita-Vedānta school . . . .

William Christian further points out that besides religious disagreements of this kind, in which different predicates are affirmed of the same subject (he calls these "doctrinal disagreements"), there are others in which different subjects are assigned to the same predicate; these latter he calls "basic religious disagreements." For example, the theist says that "God is the ground of being," but the pantheist says that "Nature is the ground of being." Other basic religious predicates attributed to different subjects in different religions are "the supreme goal of Life" (this is the Beatific Vision in Christianity, Nirvana in Buddhism); "that on which we unconditionally depend" (Allah in Islam, the God and Father of our Lord Jesus Christ in Christianity); "more important than anything else" (knowledge of one's true nature in Hinduism, worship of Jahweh in Judaism); "ultimate" (the Absolute, or Brahman, in Hinduism; Truth in humanism); "holy" (God in the theistic faiths, man in humanism). William Christian offers a complex and interesting theory of the relation between basic religious proposals and doctrinal proposals, but we are concerned at the moment only with his demonstration of how disagreements between religions may be located by one's uncovering the presuppositions of statements that might at first seem to have meaning only in the context of a particular religion, and thus not to be candidates for either agreement or disagreement on the part of other religions. We have seen that there are real disagreements concerning religious belief-proposals; that is to say, there are many belief-proposals that are accepted by the adherents of one religion but rejected by those of another.

So far, then, the problem posed at the beginning of this chapter has refused to be banished. There is, however, another approach to it which deserves to be considered.

Critique of the Concept of "A Religion"

In his important book *The Meaning and End of Religion,* Wilfred Cantwell Smith challenges the familiar concept of "a religion," upon which much of the traditional problem of conflicting religious truth claims rests. He emphasizes that what we call a religion—an empirical entity that can be traced historically and mapped geographically—is a human phenomenon. Christianity, Hinduism, Judaism, Buddhism, Islam, and so on are human creations whose history is part of the wider history of human culture. Cantwell Smith traces the development of the concept of a religion as a clear and bounded historical phenomenon and shows that the notion, far from being universal and self-evident, is a distinctively Western invention which has been exported to the rest of the world. "It is," he says, summarizing the outcome of his detailed historical argument, "a surprisingly modern aberration for anyone to think that Christianity is true or that Islam is—since the Enlightenment, basically, when Europe began to postulate religions as intellectualistic systems, patterns of doctrine, so that they could for the first time be labeled 'Christianity' and 'Buddhism,' and could be called true or false." The names by which we know the various "religions" today were in fact (with the exception of

"Islam") invented in the eighteenth century, and before they were imposed by the influence of the West upon the peoples of the world no one had thought of himself or herself as belonging to one of a set of competing systems of belief concerning which it is possible to ask, "Which of these systems is the true one?" This notion of religions as mutually exclusive entities with their own characteristics and histories—although it now tends to operate as a habitual category of our thinking—may well be an example of the illicit reification, the turning of good adjectives into bad substantives, to which the western mind is prone and against which contemporary philosophy has warned us. In this case a powerful but distorting conceptuality has helped to create phenomena answering to it, namely the religions of the world seeing themselves and each other as rival ideological communities.

Perhaps, however, instead of thinking of religion as existing in mutually exclusive systems, we should see the religious life of mankind as a dynamic continuum within which certain major disturbances have from time to time set up new fields of force, of greater or lesser power, displaying complex relationships of attraction and repulsion, absorption, resistance, and reinforcement. These major disturbances are the great creative religious moments of human history from which the distinguishable religious traditions have stemmed. Theologically, such moments are seen as intersections of divine grace, divine initiative, divine truth, with human faith, human response, human enlightenment. They have made their impact upon the stream of human life so as to affect the development of cultures; and what we call Christianity, Islam, Hinduism, Buddhism, are among the resulting historical-cultural phenomena. It is clear, for example, that Christianity has developed through a complex interaction between religious and non-religious factors. Christian ideas have been formed within the intellectual framework provided by Greek philosophy; the Christian church was molded as an institution by the Roman Empire and its system of laws: the Catholic mind reflects something of the Latin Mediterranean temperament, whereas the Protestant mind reflects something of the northern Germanic temperament, and so on. It is not hard to appreciate the connections between historical Christianity and the continuing life of humanity in the western hemisphere, and of course the same is true, in their own ways, of all the other religions of the world.

This means that it is not appropriate to speak of a religion as being true or false, any more than it is to speak of a civilization as being true or false. For the religions, in the sense of distinguishable religiocultural streams within human history, are expressions of the diversities of human types and temperaments and thought forms. The same differences between the eastern and western mentality that are revealed in characteristically different conceptual and linguistic, social, political, and artistic forms presumably also underlie the contrasts between eastern and western religion.

In *The Meaning and End of Religion* Cantwell Smith examines the development from the original religious event or idea—whether it be the insight of the Buddha, the life of Christ, or the career of Mohammed—to a religion in the sense of a vast living organism with its own credal backbone and its institutional skin. He shows in each case that this development stands in a questionable relationship to that original event or idea. Religions as institutions, with the theological doctrines and the codes of behavior that form their boundaries, did not come about because the religious reality required this, but because such a development was historically inevitable in the days of undeveloped communication between the different cultural groups. Now that the world has become a communicational unity, we are moving into a new situation in which it becomes both possible and appropriate for religious thinking to transcend these cultural-historical boundaries. But what form might such new thinking take, and how would it affect the problem of conflicting truth claims?

Toward a Possible Solution

To see the historical inevitability of the plurality of religions in the past and its noninevitability in the future, we must note the broad course that

has been taken by the religious life of mankind. The human being has been described as a naturally religious animal, displaying an innate tendency to experience the environment as religiously as well as naturally significant and to feel required to live in it as such. This tendency is universally expressed in the cultures of primitive people, with their belief in sacred objects, endowed with *mana,* and in a multitude of spirits needing to be carefully propitiated. The divine reality is here crudely apprehended as a plurality of quasi-animal forces. The next stage seems to have come with the coalescence of tribes into larger groups. The tribal gods were then ranked in hierarchies (some being lost by amalgamation in the process) dominated, in the Middle East, by great national gods such as the Sumerian Ishtar, Amon of Thebes, Jahweh of Israel, Marduk of Babylon, the Greek Zeus, and in India by the Vedic high gods such as Dyaus (the sky god), Varuna (god of heaven), and Agni (the fire god). The world of such national and nature gods, often martial and cruel and sometimes requiring human sacrifices, reflected the state of humanity's awareness of the divine at the dawn of documentary history, some three thousand years ago.

So far, the whole development can be described as the growth of natural religion. That is to say, primitive spirit worship expressing man's fears of the unknown forces of nature, and later the worship of regional deities—depicting either aspects of nature (sun, sky, etc.) or the collective personality of a nation—represent the extent of humanity's religious life prior to any special intrusions of divine revelation or illumination.

But sometime after 1000 B.C. a golden age of religious creativity, named by Jaspers the Axial Period, dawned. This consisted of a series of revelatory experiences occurring in different parts of the world that deepened and purified people's conceptions of the divine, and that religious faith can only attribute to the pressure of the divine reality upon the human spirit. To quote A. C. Bouquet, "It is a commonplace with specialists in the history of religion that somewhere within the region of 800 B.C. there passed over the populations of this planet a stirring of the mind, which, while it left large tracts of humanity comparatively uninfluenced, produced in a number of different spots on the earth's surface prophetic individuals who created a series of new starting points for human living and thinking." At the threshold of this period some of the great Hebrew prophets appeared (Elijah in the ninth century; Amos, Hosea, and the first Isaiah in the eighth century; and then Jeremiah in the seventh), declaring that they had heard the word of the Lord claiming their obedience and demanding a new level of righteousness and justice in the life of Israel. During the next five centuries, between about 800 and 300 B.C., the prophet Zoroaster appeared in Persia; Greece produced Pythagoras, and then Socrates and Plato, and Aristotle; in China there was Confucius, and the author or authors of the Taoist scriptures; and in India this creative period saw the formation of the Upanishads and the lives of Gotama the Buddha, and Mahavira, founder of the Jain religion, and around the end of this period, the writing of the *Bhagavad Gita*. Even Christianity, beginning later, and then Islam, both have their roots in the Hebrew religion of the Axial Age, and can hardly be understood except in relation to it.

It is important to observe the situation within which all these revelatory moments occurred. Communication between the different groups of humanity was then so limited that for all practical purposes human beings inhabited a series of different worlds. For the most part people living in China, in India, in Arabia, in Persia, were unaware of the others' existence. There was thus, inevitably, a multiplicity of local religions that were also local civilizations. Accordingly the great creative moments of revelation and illumination occurred separately within the different cultures and influenced their development, giving them the coherence and confidence to expand into larger units, thus producing the vast religiocultural entities that we now call the world religions. So it is that until recently the different streams of religious experience and belief have flowed through different cultures, each forming and being formed by its own separate environment. There has, of course, been contact between different religions at certain points in history, and an influence—sometimes an important influence—of one upon another; nevertheless, the broad picture is one of religions developing separately within their different historical and cultural settings.

In addition to noting these historical circumstances, we need to make use of the important distinction between, on the one hand, human encounters with the divine reality in the various forms of religious experience, and on the other hand, theological theories or doctrines that men and women have developed to conceptualize the meaning of these encounters. These two components of religion, although distinguishable, are not separable. It is as hard to say which came first, as in the celebrated case of the hen and the egg; they continually react upon one another in a joint process of development, experience providing the ground of our beliefs, but these in turn influencing the forms taken by our experience. The different religions are different streams of religious experience, each having started at a different point within human history and each having formed its own conceptual self-consciousness within a different cultural milieu.

In the light of this it is possible to consider the hypothesis that the great religions are all, at their experiential roots, in contact with the same ultimate divine reality but that their differing experiences of that reality, interacting over the centuries with the differing thought forms of differing cultures, have led to increasing differentiation and contrasting elaboration—so that Hinduism, for example, is a very different phenomenon from Christianity, and very different ways of experiencing and conceiving the divine occur within them. However, now that in the "one world" of today the religious traditions are consciously interacting with each other in mutual observation and dialogue, it is possible that their future developments may move on gradually converging courses. During the next centuries each group will presumably continue to change, and it may be that they will grow closer together, so that one day such names as "Christianity," "Buddhism," "Islam," and "Hinduism" will no longer adequately describe the then current configurations of man's religious experience and belief. I am not thinking here of the extinction of human religiousness in a universal secularization. That is of course a possible future, and indeed many think it the most likely future to come about. But if the human creature is an indelibly religious animal he or she will always, even amidst secularization, experience a sense of the transcendent by which to be both troubled and uplifted. The future I am envisaging is accordingly one in which the presently existing religions will constitute the past history of different emphases and variations, which will then appear more like, for example, the different denominations of Christianity in North America or Europe today than like radically exclusive totalities.

If the nature of religion, and the history of religion, is indeed such that a development of this kind begins to take place in the remaining decades of the present century and during the succeeding twenty-first century, what would this imply concerning the problem of the conflicting truth claims of the different religions in their present forms?

We may distinguish three aspects of this question: differences in modes of experiencing the divine reality; differences of philosophical and theological theory concerning that reality or concerning the implications of religious experience; and differences in the key or revelatory experiences that unify a stream of religious experience and thought.

The most prominent and important example of the first kind of difference is probably that between the experience of the divine as personal and as nonpersonal. In Judaism, Christianity, Islam, and the important strand of Hinduism which is focused by the *Bhagavad Gita,* the Ultimate is apprehended as personal goodness, will, and purpose under the different names of Jahweh, God, Allah, Krishna, Shira. Whereas in Hinduism as interpreted by the Advaita Vedānta school, and in Theravada Buddhism, ultimate reality is apprehended as nonpersonal. Mahayana Buddhism, on the other hand, is a more complex tradition, including, for example, both nontheis-

tic Zen and quasi-theistic Pure Land Buddhism. There is, perhaps, in principle no difficulty in holding that these personal and nonpersonal experiences of the Ultimate can be understood as complementary rather than as incompatible. For if, as every profound form of religion has affirmed, the Ultimate reality is infinite and therefore exceeds the scope of our finite human categories, that reality may be both personal Lord and nonpersonal Ground of being. At any rate, there is a program for thought in the exploration of what Aurobindo called "the logic of the infinite" and the question of the extent to which predicates that are incompatible when attributed to a finite reality may no longer be incompatible when referred to infinite reality.

The second type of difference is in philosophical and theological theory or doctrine. Such differences, and indeed conflicts, are not merely apparent, but they are part of the still developing history of human thought; it may be that in time they will be transcended, for they belong to the historical, culturally conditioned aspect of religion, which is subject to change. When one considers, for example, the immense changes that have come about within Christian thought during the last hundred years, in response to the development of modern biblical scholarship and the modern physical and biological sciences, one can set no limit to the further developments that may take place in the future. A book of contemporary Christian theology (post-Darwin, post-Einstein, post-Freud), using modern biblical source criticism and taking for granted a considerable demythologization of the New Testament world view, would have been quite unrecognizable as Christian theology two centuries ago. Comparable responses to modern science are yet to occur in many of the other religions of the world, but they must inevitably come, sooner or later. When all the main religious traditions have been through their own encounter with modern science, they will probably have undergone as considerable an internal development as has Christianity. Besides, there will be an increasing influence of each faith upon every other as they meet and interact more and more freely within the "one world" of today.

In the light of all this, the future that I have speculatively projected does not seem impossible.

However, it is the third kind of difference that constitutes the largest difficulty in the way of religious agreement. Each religion has its holy founder or scripture, or both, in which the divine reality has been revealed—the Vedas, the Torah, the Buddha, Christ and the Bible, the Qur'an. Wherever the Holy is revealed, it claims an absolute response of faith and worship, which thus seems incompatible with a like response to any other claimed disclosure of the Holy. Within Christianity, for example, this absoluteness and exclusiveness of response has been strongly developed in the doctrine that Christ was uniquely divine, the only Son of God, of one substance with the Father, the only mediator between God and man. But this traditional doctrine, formed in an age of substantial ignorance of the wider religious life of mankind, gives rise today to an acute tension. On the one hand, Christianity traditionally teaches that God is the Creator and Lord of all mankind and seeks mankind's final good and salvation; and on the other hand that only by responding in faith to God in Christ can we be saved. This means that infinite love has ordained that human beings can be saved only in a way that in fact excludes the large majority of them; for the greater part of all the human beings who have been born have lived either before Christ or outside the borders of Christendom. In an attempt to meet this glaring paradox, Christian theology has developed a doctrine according to which those outside the circle of Christian faith may nevertheless be saved. For example, the Second Vatican Council of the Roman Catholic Church, 1963–1965, declared that "Those who through no fault of theirs are still ignorant of the Gospel of Christ and of his Church yet sincerely seek God and, with the help of divine grace, strive to do his will as known to them through the voice of their conscience, those men can attain to eternal salvation." This represents a real movement in response to a real problem; nevertheless it is only an epicycle of theory, complicating the existing dogmatic system rather than going to the heart of the problem. The epicycle is designed to cover theists ("those who sincerely seek God") who have had no contact with the Christian gospel. But what of the nontheistic Buddhists and nontheistic Hindus? And what of those Muslims, Jews, Buddhists, Hindus, Jains, Parsees, etc., both theists and nontheists, who have heard the Christian gospel but have preferred to adhere to the faith of their fathers?

Thus it seems that if the tension at the heart of the traditional Christian attitude to non-Christian faiths is to be resolved, Christian thinkers must give even more radical thought to the problem than they have as yet done. It is, however, not within the scope of this book to suggest a plan for the reconstruction of Christian or other religious doctrines.

A Philosophical Framework for Religious Pluralism

Among the great religious traditions, and particularly within their more mystical strands, a distinction is widely recognized between the Real or Ultimate or Divine *an sich* (in him/her/its-self) and the Real as conceptualized and experienced by human beings. The widespread assumption is that the Ultimate Reality is infinite and as such exceeds the grasp of human thought and language, so that the describable and experienceable objects of worship and contemplation are not the Ultimate in its limitless reality but the Ultimate in its relationship to finite perceivers. One form of this distinction is that between *nirguna* Brahman, Brahman without attributes, beyond the scope of human thought, and *saguna* Brahman, Brahman with attributes, encountered within human experience as Ishvara, the personal creator and governor of the universe. In the west the Christian mystic Meister Eckhart drew a parallel distinction between the Godhead (*Deitas*) and God (*Deus*). The Taoist scripture, the *Tao Te Ching*, begins by affirming that "The Tao that can be expressed is not the eternal Tao." The Jewish Kabbalist mystics distinguished between En Soph, the absolute divine reality beyond all human description, and the God of the Bible; and among the Muslim Sufis, Al Haqq, the Real, seems to be a similar concept to En Soph, as the abyss of Godhead underlying the self-revealing Allah. More recently Paul Tillich has spoken of "the God above the God of theism." A. N. Whitehead, and the process theologians who follow him, distinguish between the primordial and consequent natures of God; and Gordon Kaufman has recently distinguished between the "real God" and the "available God." These all seem to be somewhat similar (though not identical) distinctions. If we suppose that the Real is one but that our human perceptions of the Real are plural and various, we have a basis for the hypothesis, suggested tentatively in the previous section, that the different streams of religious experience represent diverse awarenesses of the same limitless transcendent reality, which is perceived in characteristically different ways by different human mentalities, forming and formed by different cultural histories.

Immanuel Kant has provided (without intending to do so) a philosophical framework within which such a hypothesis can be developed. He distinguished between the world as it is *an sich,* which he called the noumenal world, and the world as it appears to human consciousness, which he called the phenomenal world. His writings can be interpreted in various ways, but according to one interpretation the phenomenal world *is* the noumenal world as humanly experienced. The innumerable diverse sensory clues are brought together in human consciousness, according to Kant, by means of a system of relational concepts or categories (such as "thing" and "cause") in terms of which we are aware of our environment. Thus our environment as we perceive it is a joint product of the world itself and the selecting, interpreting, and unifying activity of the perceiver. Kant was concerned mainly with the psychological contribution to our awareness of the world, but the basic principle can also be seen at work on the physiological level. Our sensory equipment is capable of responding to only a minute proportion of the full range of sound and electromagnetic waves— light, radio, infrared, ultraviolet, X, and gamma— which are impinging upon us all the time. Consequently, the world as we experience it represents a particular selection—a distinctively human selection—from the immense complexity and richness of the world as it is *an sich.* We experience at a certain macro/micro level. What we experience and use as the solid, enduring table would be, to a micro-observer, a swirling universe of discharging energy, consisting of electrons, neutrons, and quarks in continuous rapid activity. We perceive the world as it appears to beings with our particular physical and psychological equipment. Indeed, the way the world *appears* to us is the way the world *is for us* as we inhabit and interact with it. As Thomas Aquinas said long ago, "The thing known is in the knower according to the mode of the knower."

Is it possible to adopt the broad Kantian distinction between the world as it is in itself and the world as it appears to us with our particular cognitive machinery, and apply it to the relation between the Ultimate Reality and our different human awarenesses of that Reality? If so, we shall think in terms of a single divine noumenon and perhaps many diverse divine phenomena. We may form the hypothesis that the Real *an sich* is experienced by human beings in terms of one of two basic religious concepts. One is the concept of God, or of the Real experienced as personal, which presides over the theistic forms of religion. The other is the concept of the Absolute, or of the Real experienced as nonpersonal, which presides over the various nontheistic forms of religion. Each of these basic concepts is, however, made more concrete (in Kantian terminology, schematized) as a range of particular images of God or particular concepts of the Absolute. These images of God are formed within the different religious histories. Thus the Jahweh of the Hebrew Scriptures exists in interaction with the Jewish people. He is a part of their history and they are a part of his; he cannot be abstracted from this particular concrete historical nexus. On the other hand, Krishna is a quite different divine figure, existing in relation to a different faith-community, with its own different and distinctive religious ethos. Given the basic hypothesis of the reality of the Divine, we may say that Jahweh and Krishna (and likewise, Shiva, and Allah, and the

Father of Jesus Christ) are different *personae* in terms of which the divine Reality is experienced and thought within different streams of religious life. These different *personae* are thus partly projections of the divine Reality into human consciousness, and partly projections of the human consciousness itself as it has been formed by particular historical cultures. From the human end they are our different images of God; from the divine end they are God's *personae* in relation to the different human histories of faith.

A similar account will have to be given of the forms of nonpersonal Absolute, or *impersonae*, experienced within the different strands of non-theistic religion—Brahman, Nirvana, Sunyata, the Dharma, the Dharmakaya, the Tao. Here, according to our hypothesis, the same limitless ultimate Reality is being experienced and thought through different forms of the concept of the Real as non-personal.

It is characteristic of the more mystical forms of awareness of the Real that they seem to be direct, and not mediated—or therefore distorted—by the perceptual machinery of the human mind. However, our hypothesis will have to hold that even the apparently direct and unmediated awareness of the Real in the Hindu *moksha*, in the Buddhist *satori*,

and in the unitive mysticism of the West, is still the conscious experience of a human subject and as such is influenced by the interpretative set of the cognizing mind. All human beings have been influenced by the culture of which they are a part and have received, or have developed in their appropriation of it, certain deep interpretative tendencies which help to form their experience and are thus continually confirmed within it. We see evidence of such deep "sets" at work when we observe that mystics formed by Hindu, Buddhist, Christian, Muslim, and Jewish religious cultures report distinctively different forms of experience. Thus, far from it being the case that they all undergo an identical experience but report it in different religious languages, it seems more probable that they undergo characteristically different unitive experiences (even though with important common features), the differences being due to the conceptual frameworks and meditational disciplines supplied by the religious traditions in which they participate.

Thus it is a possible, and indeed an attractive, hypothesis—as an alternative to total skepticism—that the great religious traditions of the world represent different human perceptions of and response to the same infinite divine Reality.

11.3 Religious Pluralism and Advaita Vedanta

For centuries many religions could live isolated, for the most part, from others. When they did come in contact, their relationship tended to be characterized by warfare and conflict rather than by harmony and tolerance. Today that isolation is no longer possible. Telecommunications, modern travel, and immigration have resulted in ever greater contact. Will this cause greater religious conflict than in the past? Or will the religions learn ways to get along?

Centuries ago, in India, different religions could not live in isolation. There was constant contact, and ways of dealing with others had to be worked out. Long before modern philosophers began to wrestle with the issue of conflicting religious truth claims, Indian philosophers grappled with the same problem.

In the next selection, Arvind Sharma, Birks Professor of Comparative Religion at McGill University, compares Hick's views on conflicting truth claims with the views worked out in Advaita Vedanta (see Reading 2.2). Sharma finds both similarities and differences, but the similarities are striking enough for Sharma to conclude that there are "very strong family resemblances" between Hick's hypothesis and the Advaita Vedanta view.

Some might question whether such comparisons are really possible. The language, culture, tradition and philosophical assumptions of an ancient Indian philosophy, such as Advaita Vedanta, are so very different from the modern situation and the framework in which Hick is operating that comparing their views may be like comparing apples and watches. In other words, the incommensurability between the two is so great that there may be no sure way of translating claims that Hick makes about *the Real in itself* and claims that Shankara makes about Brahman. The fact that both assert that ultimate reality is beyond our ordinary experience further complicates matters.

Reading Questions

1. How does the parable of the blind man and the elephant illustrate a point different from Hume's contention that in religious matters, "whatever is different is contrary"?
2. What are the key points of the Advaitic view of Reality?
3. What is the Advaitin response to the Christian's analysis of religious disagreements, and why do doctrinal disagreements within Vedanta *not* lead to intolerance?
4. How does the Advaitin respond to Smith's analysis of religions as cumulative traditions?
5. How does Advaita Vedanta respond to the three differences among religions identified by Hick?
6. What five points does Sharma make in comparing Hick's philosophical framework with Advaita Vedanta?
7. Do religions give different names to the same ultimate reality? What do you think and why?

Religious Pluralism and Advaita Vedanta*

ARVIND SHARMA

Introduction

It is sometimes claimed that whereas in the past great movements of religious expansion such as those of Buddhism, Christianity and Islam did involve contact among followers of different religions, such contact for the most part represented "conflicts rather than dialogues." It is only during the past few centuries that such contact has stimulated inquiry into the actual beliefs and practices of various religions in a less combative atmosphere and has "brought home to an increasing number of us the problem of the conflicting truth claims made by different religious traditions."

Although this may be true globally, it seems that India had to face the issue of religious

*From Arvind Sharma, *The Philosophy of Religions and Advaita Vedanta: A Comparative Study in Religions and Reason.* University Park: The Pennsylvania State University Press, 1995, pp. 211–224. Copyright
© 1995 The Pennsylvania State University. Reproduced by permission of the publisher. Footnotes deleted.

pluralism—and that of the conflicting truth claims inherent in such a situation—at least as far back as the sixth century B.C.E. This may or may not be what Heinrich Zimmer had in mind when he wrote: "We of the Occident are about to arrive at a crossroads that was reached by the thinkers of India some seven hundred years before Christ," but conflicting truth claims were certainly an element in the situation Indian thinkers had to reckon with at the time. This point is well illustrated by the following parable:

Buddha, the Blessed One, gives of the blind men and the elephant to illustrate that partial knowledge always breeds bigotry and fanaticism. Once a group of disciples entered the city of Śrāvasti to beg alms. They found there a number of sectarians holding disputations with one another and maintaining "This is the truth, that is not the truth. That is not truth, this is the truth." After listening to these conflicting views, the brethren came back to the Exalted One and described to him what they had seen and heard at Śrāvasti.

Then said the Exalted One:

"These sectarians, brethren, are blind and unseeing. They know not the real, they know not the unreal; they know not the truth, they know not the untruth. In such a state of ignorance do they dispute and quarrel as they describe. Now in former times, brethren, there was a Rājā (king) in this same Śrāvasti. Then, brethren, the Rājā called to a certain man, saying: 'Come thou, good fellow! Go, gather together all the blind men that are in Śrāvasti!'

"'Very good, Your Majesty,' replied that man, and in obedience to the Rājā, gathered together all the blind men, took them with him to the Rājā, and said: 'Your Majesty, all the blind men of Śrāvasti are now assembled.'

"'Then, my good man, show the blind men an elephant.'

"'Very good, Your Majesty,' said the man and did as he was told, saying: 'O ye blind men, such as this is an elephant.'

"And to one he presented the head of the elephant, to another, the ear, to another a tusk, the trunk, the foot, back, tail and tuft of the tail, saying to each one that was the elephant.

"Now, brethren, that man, having presented the elephant to the blind men, came to the Rājā and said: 'Your Majesty, the elephant has been presented to the blind men. Do what is your will.'

"Thereupon, brethren, the Rājā went up to the blind men and said to each: 'Have you studied the elephant?'

"'Yes, Your Majesty.'

"'Then tell me your conclusions about him.'

"Thereupon those who had been presented with the head answered 'Your Majesty, an elephant is just like a pot.' And those who had only observed the ear replied: 'An elephant is just like a winnowing basket.' Those who had been presented with the tusk said it was a ploughshare. Those who knew only the trunk said it was a plough. 'The body,' said they, 'is a granary; the foot, a pillar; the back, a mortar; the tail, a pestle; the tuft of the tail, just a besom.'

"Then they began to quarrel, shouting, 'Yes, it is!' 'No, it isn't!' 'An elephant is not that!' 'Yes it is like that!' and so on, till they came to fisticuffs about the matter.

"Then, brethren, that Rājā was delighted with the scene.

"Just so are these sectarians who are wanderers, blind, unseeing, knowing not the truth, but each maintaining it is thus and thus."

The parable is significant in that it follows a direction opposite to the one taken by the Western philosophy of religion, which has evolved on the principle laid down by Hume "that, in matters of religion, whatever is different is contrary." The parable here illustrates that whatever is contrary is not necessarily contradictory. John H. Hick elaborates Hume's point made in relation to miracles—that while it constitutes the proof of one religion it must constitute the disproof of another—thus: "By the same reasoning, any ground for believing a particular religion to be true must operate as a ground for believing every other religion to be false; accordingly, for any particular religion there will always be far more reason for believing it to be false than for believing it to be true."

Advaita Vedānta takes a different view on this point because it emphasizes experience rather than belief. "To say that God exists means that spiritual experience is attainable." Because it is attainable in different forms, each attainment confirms rather than contradicts attainment or expression of it. It is Hume's assumption that different attainments represent different and contradictory beliefs but "Hindu thinkers warn against rationalistic self-sufficiency" in these matters which takes the form of dogma and maintain that different attainments represent different apprehensions of the one Reality, which is infinite, so that "toleration is the homage which the finite mind pays to the inexhaustibility of the Infinite." This is recognized by Śaṅkara, who contended with other schools of thought but also proclaimed the insufficiency of any one school of thought in relation to the divine.

The key points to be noted here in the Advaitic vision of Reality are as follows: (1) The Absolute is beyond human words and may be brought within the limits of comprehension in many diverse but not necessarily mutually negating ways. (2) This Absolute or the Real is one, which explains the "attitude of acceptance of other cults." In this context the following line of the ṚgVeda (1.164.46) is often invoked: "The Real is one, the learned call it by various names, Agni, Yama, Mātariśvan." (3) The Real is known through experience, and the experience of a modern Hindu mystic such as Rāmakṛṣṇa (1836–86) confirms the view that various religions represent different approaches to the same Reality. Thus the Advaitin position tends to be very different from that of Hume, as is obvious from the statement of S. Radhakrishnan on this very point.

It is sometimes urged that the descriptions of God conflict with one another. It only shows that our notions are not true. To say that our ideas of God are not true is not to deny the reality of God to which our ideas refer. Refined definitions of God as moral personality, and holy love may contradict cruder ones which look upon him as a primitive despot, a sort of sultan in the sky, but they all intend the same reality. If personal equation does not vitiate the claim to objectivity in sense perception and scientific inquiry, there is no reason to assume that it does so in religious experience.

W. A. Christian's Analysis

W. A. Christian analyzes religious disagreements among world religions as consisting of basically two kinds: (1) "doctrinal disagreements," in which "different predicates are affirmed of the same subject"—for example, Jesus was "the One whom God promised to send to redeem Israel," a statement about which Jews and Christians substantially differ, as over the statement that "Jesus is the Messiah," over which they may be seen to only nominally differ on account of different conceptions of the Messiah, and (2) "basic religious disagreements," in which "different subjects are assigned to the same predicate," as when the *ultimate* is regarded as God in Christianity, Brahman in Hinduism, and Tao in Taoism.

The Advaitin response to Christian's analysis is basically consistent with its position described earlier: that whether it is a case of affirming different predicates of the same subject or of assigning different subjects to the same predicate, the language-barrier in relation to Brahman is never overcome.

Within this broad limitation, however, in Advaita Vedānta "doctrinal disagreements" play a more important role than "basic religious disagreements." Advaita has little difficulty with different predicates being assigned to the same subject. Thus Śaṅkara quotes the following text in his Aitareya-Upaniṣad Bhāṣya: "Some speak of it as Agni, some as Manu, Prajāpati, Indra, others as Prāna, yet others as the eternal Brahman."

But the situation is different in the case of doctrinal disagreements. Just as one can speak of the Messiah in the context of Judaism and Christianity, one can speak of Brahman in the context of the Vedantic tradition. Advaita accords primacy to *nirguṇa* Brahman, but some other schools of Vedānta accord primacy to *saguṇa* Brahman. In fact, "The main issue that was debated by the Vedantins who came after Śaṅkara was whether *Brahman* is *nirguṇa* or *saguṇa*." Troy Wilson Organ graphically illustrates the difference involved in the two approaches: water is water, no doubt, but it is quite different when experienced as H_2O or as a cold splash on one's face.

This doctrinal disagreement within Vedānta, however, has characterized it from the earliest times to the present, and has continued through the centuries *without compromising tolerance* within it in any marked degree. This is because the issue arises at the level of the ultimate. No school of Vedānta rejects the validity of either the *saguṇa* or *nirguṇa* formulation: the issue is of relative priority rather than absolute truth. Indeed, Gauḍapāda, a famous predecessor of Śaṅkara, says that Advaita Vedānta "is pleasing to all, has no dispute with anyone, and is not hostile to anyone."

W. C. Smith's Analysis

Just as W. A. Christian probed the nature of belief in the context of conflicting truth claims, W. C. Smith probes the nature of religion itself. He concludes that it represents the Western habit of "turning good adjectives into bad substantives" through "illicit reification," which manifested itself after the Enlightenment in the form of raising the question about the truth or falsity of a religion as an intellectual system. Religions should really be viewed as cumulative traditions. As he puts it, "It is not appropriate to speak of a religion as being true or false, any more than it is to speak of a civilization as being true or false."

It seems that Smith is arguing against a religion being related to theories of truth on the one hand and advocating a Wittgensteinian "culture-game" theory on the other. Both of these are questionable from an Advaitin point of view. The correspondence theory is hard to verify in relation to religions, but even if it is accepted that the various religions represent distinct "truth-systems" in accordance with the coherence theory, so to speak, and are "relative," even then what is true of one may not be true of another. It is true that Smith blunts this last point by arguing that religions are to be viewed as culture-systems rather than truth-systems. However, the followers of the religions regard them as making truth claims, and from that point of view the problem persists.

The "culture-game" theory on the model of the "language-game" does have the merit of avoiding the truth-falsehood issue but opens up the Santayanan point that "religions are not true or false but better or worse." Here again Smith would not like to force the issue—but the Advaitin would—of whether the issue is veridical or functional. If the question of whether religion is true or false is *not* asked, then the question of whether it is good (useful) or bad (useless) needs to be asked. A modern Advaitin, S. Radhakrishnan, for instance, states: "Let us frankly recognize that the efficiency of a religion is to be judged by the development of religious qualities such as quiet confidence, inner calm, gentleness of the spirit, love of neighbour, mercy to all creation, destruction of tyrannous desires, and the aspiration for spiritual freedom, and there are no trustworthy statistics to tell us that these qualities are found more in efficient nations."

The point here is not that these virtues cannot be quantitatively measured but rather that they form the qualitative propaedeutic for the study of Advaita according to Śaṅkara.

John H. Hick's Analysis

John H. Hick distinguishes among three kinds of differences among the religions of the world: (1) differences in modes of experiencing the divine Reality, especially as personal or impersonal; (2) philosophical and theological differences; and (3) differences in the "key or revelatory experiences that unify a stream of religious experience and thought." Hick seems to think that differences in the first two categories are not hard to overcome. He writes, for instance, that the personal and impersonal modes of encountering reality could be "understood as complementary rather than as incompatible." Similarly, in the philosophical and theological realms the various religions may converge in the future as they face the challenges of critical scholarship, science, and globalization together and overcome or moderate their historical specificities. It is the differences of the third kind which Hick sees as constituting "the largest difficulty in the way of religious agreement. Each religion has its holy founder or scripture, or both, in which the divine Reality has been revealed—the Vedas, the Torah, the Buddha, Christ and the Bible, the Qur'an. Wherever the Holy is revealed, it claims an absolute response of faith and worship, which thus seems incompatible with a like response to any other claimed disclosure of the Holy."

Advaita Vedānta seems to confirm Hick's view on the first point—that the personal and impersonal approaches to the divine may be viewed as complementary. It also seems to confirm his second point—that modernity will reduce religious differences. In this matter Advaita Vedānta may well have anticipated modern developments. We may now examine the third kind of difference, which according to Hick may prove to be a major obstacle in resolving conflicting truth claims. The issue here turns on the founder and scripture of the tradition.

Advaita Vedānta dispenses with the issue of the founder in accepting the Vedas as *apauruṣeya;* that is, as possessing neither a human nor divine author. But what about its claim that only the Vedas can supply humanity with saving knowledge?

Some scholars, K. Satchidananda Murty among them, have argued very strongly that salvation must be mediated through the Vedas in the context of Advaita Vedānta. This does seem to be the general position, despite problems, but it is not entirely clear whether this is a substantial or a nominal position and even whether the position within Advaita Vedānta might not be more charitable than it has been made out to be.

In this context Brahmasūtra 1.1.4 is significant, as it declares that the Upaniṣads, are to be interpreted *tat tu samanvayāt* (on the principle of harmony). The well-known modern thinker, S. Radhakrishnan has suggested that "today the *samanvaya* or harmonization has to be extended to the living faiths of mankind"—and, one might add, to the *scriptures* of all the living faiths of mankind. Such an approach might have the effect of rendering the third difficulty identified by Hick more tractable.

A Philosophical Framework for Religious Pluralism in John H. Hick and Advaita Vedānta: A Comparison

John H. Hick then goes on to propose a philosophical framework for religious pluralism, the basic principle of which is that we can "think in terms of a single divine noumenon and perhaps many diverse divine phenomena." In elaborating this position Hick makes several remarks that are quite significant from the point of view of Advaita Vedānta: (1) Hick identifies the "similar (though not identical) distinctions" found within the major religious traditions between the Real as such and the Real as experienced by human beings.

In the west the Christian mystic Meister Eckhart drew a parallel distinction between the Godhead (*Deitas*) and God (*Deus*). The Taoist scripture, the *Tao Te Ching*, begins by affirming that "the Tao that can be expressed is not the eternal Tao." The Jewish Kabbalist mystics distinguished between En Soph, the absolute divine reality beyond all human description, and the God of the Bible; and among the Muslim Sufis, Al Haqq, the Real, seems to be a similar concept to En Soph, as the abyss of Godhead underlying the self-revealing Allah. More recently Paul Tillich has spoken of "the God above the God of theism." A. N. Whitehead, and the process theologians who follow him, distinguish between the primordial and consequent natures of God; and Gordon Kaufman has recently distinguished between the "real God" and the "available God."

Hick draws on Immanuel Kant's concept of "the world as it is *an sich,* which he called the noumenal world, and the world as it appears to human consciousness, which he calls the phenomenal world." Taking his cue from this, Hick forms "the hypothesis that the Real *an sich* is experienced by human beings in terms of one of the two basic religious concepts" ("the Real as such and the Real as experienced by human beings"), which when experienced are "made more concrete (in Kantian terminology, schematized) as a range of particular images of God or particular concepts of the Absolute." Thus, on the one hand, are the *different* images of God as found in the various theistic religions explained and on the other the different forms of nontheistic religions which refer to the Absolute—"Brahman, Nirvana, Sunyata, the Dharma, the Dharmakaya, the Tao."

Hick further maintains that although it is sometimes claimed of the absolutistic experience that it is unmediated, unlike the theistic, by the human mind, "our hypothesis will have to hold that even the apparently direct and unmediated awareness of the Real in the Hindu *moksha,* in the Buddhist *satori,* and in the unitive mysticism of the West, is still the conscious experience of the human agent and as such is influenced by the interpretative set of the cognizing mind." Ultimately, Hick concludes that "it is a possible, and indeed an attractive hypothesis—as an alternative to total skepticism—that the great religious traditions of the world represent different human perceptions of and response to the same infinite divine Reality."

The reader will recognize that this position is very similar to the one developed by modern Advaitin thinkers. However, the difference between the position advocated by John H. Hick and the position of the Advaitin on these points needs to be clarified.

1. The reader will notice, and Hick specifically mentions, the similarity of the distinctions between Godhead and God, and so on, to the distinction drawn between *nirguṇa* and *saguṇa* Brahman in Advaita. Here the point to be kept in mind from the Advaitic point of view is that "God as immanent (*saguṇa*) and God as transcendent Reality (*nirguṇa*) are not two any more than the man on the stage and the man outside the stage are two." This is an allusion to Śaṅkara's analogy of the actor—a shepherd who appears on the stage in the *role* of a king is not two people, a shepherd and a king. In other words, Advaita would insist, the *nirguṇa* and *saguṇa* refer to two aspects of the *same* Reality.

2. Immanuel Kant's concept of *Ding an sich* must be used with some caution in the context of Advaita. This becomes clear from certain observations made by M. Hiriyanna while concluding a discussion of *nirguṇa* Brahman:

> Here naturally arises the question whether such an entity is not a sheer abstraction. Śaṁkara recognizes the force of this objection. It is, indeed, the very objection he seems to have raised against a certain other monistic view (*sattādvaita*) of Upanishadic teaching which was in vogue in his time, viz. that Brahman is universal Being. Śaṁkara's monism differs from it in that it views the ultimate reality not as objective, but as identical *at bottom* with the individual self (*ātmādvaita*). This altered conception secures the maximum certainty to the reality of Brahman, for nothing can possibly carry greater certitude with it than one's belief in the existence of oneself. "A man," it has been said, "may doubt of many things, of anything *else;* but he can never doubt of his own being," for that very act of doubting would affirm its existence. It is thus eventually through something in ourselves that, according to Śaṁkara, we are able to judge of reality and unreality. Such a view does not mean that the self is known to us completely. Far from it. But, at the same time, it does not remain wholly unknown, being our own self—a fact which distinguishes the advaitic ultimate from not only the universal Being referred to above, *but also (to mention a Western parallel) the thing-in-itself of Kant.*

In Advaita, the thing-in-itself is knowable in a metempirical way, as the *ātman,* though there is considerable controversy surrounding the issue of how it is known. In this debate the role of the *mind* is one of the points at issue. According to one school, for instance, *direct* knowledge of the ultimate Reality, Brahman, is possible because as "Brahman, which is to be known, is not different from the knower (the subject) immediate knowledge is possible." Another view is that "though the knowledge of Brahman derived from scripture is not itself immediate, Brahman is immediate; and Brahman is immediately experienced by mind only."

Although the latter position is closer to Hick's, neither position would agree with his statement that the experience is "*influenced* by the interpretative set of the cognizing mind," as the dispute between them is over the mechanics of Realization alone. What is crucial to note here is the possibility of "immediate knowledge not involving sense-perception. The empirical self, for instance, is immediately known, but it cannot be said to be *presented* to any sense. Hence the word pratyakṣa, which literally means 'presented to a sense,' is here replaced by the wider term aparokṣa or 'not mediate.'" It is also important to note, in a broader context, the pervasive significance of the Ātman = Brahman identity in Advaita.

However, although the *experience* as such is not influenced by the cognizing mind—because, in the technical jargon of Advaita, the internal organ (*antaḥkaraṇa*) is merged with nescience (*avidyā*), *of which it is a product,* before the latter is sublated, leading to Brahman-*experience*—our *knowledge* of it may be influenced by the internal organ "for no knowledge, whether mediate or immediate, is possible in the absence of the internal organ," although the self, *ātman,* is ontologically prior to the "false identity of the self and the not-self," which presupposes *avidyā* or ignorance."

3. The previous discussion clarifies the view whether, from the point of view of Advaita, one can agree with Hick that "even the apparently direct and unmediated awareness of the Real . . . is still the conscious experience of the human subject and as such is influenced by the interpretative set of the cognizing mind." The Advaitic position would seem to suggest that the awareness of the Real is unmediated and direct, but when it becomes recognized *as* the conscious experience of the subject it is influenced by the mind-set. On the analogy of sleep it may be pointed out that our personality has nothing to do with the *state* of deep sleep; "None of the features of sleep . . . is 'known' at the time, for no knowledge, whether mediate or immediate, is possible in the absence of the internal organ. But they are nevertheless realized then as shown by the fact of their being recalled afterwards." At the stage of recall the internal organ is again active and the mind-set now comes into play.

4. The Advaitin philosophical framework, nevertheless, for religious pluralism, is very similar to Hick's and shares its attractive features. It is, however, capable of an extension that is possible while one is functioning from within an Advaitic framework but perhaps not possible if one is operating within the framework suggested by Hick. Nor is it entirely clear whether the new position represents any advance or possesses any advantage over that advocated by John H. Hick. It, however, needs to be taken into account as it does actually appear in the history of Advaita Vedānta. It is rooted in the Advaitic position that in the final analysis only one ultimate reality exists, which is called *Brahman* or *ātman*. But if there is really only one reality, are we left with any other position to even contend with? Thus a modern exponent of Advaita Vedānta can affirm that

> Advaita is *non-dual-ism*. Reality, according to its insight, is non-dual, not-two. Advaita does not profess to formulate conceptually what Reality is. It is not, therefore, a system of thought, an *ism*. It is not a school among schools of philosophy. It does not reject any view of Reality; it only seeks to transcend all views, since these are by their very nature restricted, limited, and circumscribed. The pluralisms, theistic or otherwise, imagine that they are opposed to Advaita. But Advaita is not opposed to any of the partial views of Reality.

Such an affirmation is in keeping with the tradition of Advaita Vedānta, for an early exponent of it, Gauḍapāda (seventh century C.E.) declared: "The dualists (i.e. pluralists) are conclusively firm in regard to the status of their respective opinions. They are in conflict with one another. But, Advaita is in no conflict with them. Advaita, verily, is the supreme truth; dvaita is a variant thereof. For the dualists, there is duality either way (i.e. both in the Absolute and in the phenomenal manifold). With that (duality) this (non-duality) is not in conflict."

Such a view has the merit of being nonconflictual, but at the cost of dismissing the other party out of hand. This is apparent in a remark Śaṅkara makes in his commentary on the verses of Gauḍapāda quoted above. Śaṅkara writes: "As one who is mounted on a spirited elephant does not drive it against a lunatic who stands on the ground and shouts, 'Drive your elephant against me who also am seated on an elephant,' because he (the former) has no notion of opposition, even so (is the case with the non-dualist). Thus, in truth, the knower of *Brahman* is the very self of the dualists. For this reason, our view is not in conflict with theirs."

In point of fact, however, Śaṅkara did engage other schools in debate and dialogue. Perhaps if it is realized that Śaṅkara is talking here from a metempirical point of view, whereas all discourse is carried on within the empirical realm, the contradiction is converted into a paradox.

5. The founder and the scriptures loom large as an issue in Hick's agenda, but Advaita Vedānta deals in the eternal rather than the historical. It could be argued that it apotheosizes the Veda; however, the Veda also belongs to the realm of *mithyā;* moreover, some say that the Vedas are endless, which creates room for the acceptance of other scriptures. Finally, experience takes precedence over the Vedas, on which their own claim to validity really rests. Thus what John H. Hick identifies as the main obstacles to the accommo-

dation of conflicting truth claims turn out to be less problematical in the case of Advaita Vedānta.

Conclusion

Despite these divergences there is little doubt that there exists a very strong family resemblance in the philosophical frameworks offered by John H. Hick and Advaita Vedānta for resolving conflicting truth claims. This becomes quite clear from such Advaitic statements as the following found in the Yogavāsiṣtha (III.1.12; III.5, 6, 7; V.8.19):

> Many names have been given to the Absolute by the learned for practical purposes such as Law, Self, Truth.
>
> It is called Person by the Sāṁkhya thinkers, Brahman by the Vedāntins, pure and simple consciousness by the Vijñānavādins, Śūnya by the Nihilists, the Illuminator by the worshippers of the Sun. It is also called the Speaker, the Thinker, the Enjoyer of actions and the Doer of them.
>
> Śiva for the worshippers of Śiva, and Time for those who believe in Time alone.

11.4 The Transcendent Unity of Religions

Many people have distinguished the esoteric (hidden, secret, inner, spiritual) aspect of religions from the exoteric (public, historical, institutional) aspect. Some have come to believe that the esoteric side of religions expresses and embodies a *philosophia perennis*—an ancient wisdom about a divine Reality that constitutes an absolute unity transcendent to the empirical reality we know. This Perennial Philosophy, some claim, can be found in rudimentary and fragmentary forms in the myths of pre-literate peoples and in more fully developed forms in all of the major world religions.

Frithjof Schuon, born in Basel, Switzerland, in 1907 and author of the next selection, became interested in the *philosophia perennis* at an early age and has devoted a lifetime to its study. He studied Sufism in Algeria and Morocco and was strongly influenced by the Algerian Sufi Ahmad Al-Allawi. He became convinced that there exists a universal, ancient, and sacred wisdom that has shaped and informed all of the diverse religious traditions. He became particularly attracted to the Islamic Sufi tradition because of its mystical spirituality and its claim that in Allah is revealed the transcendent unity of all reality. If there is such a unity, then it must constitute the transcendent unity of religions.

On the exoteric level, religions are diverse. They make what appear to be contradictory claims. They regard certain religious founders and prophets as unique givers of truth and salvation. The exoteric, however, is finite, relative, particular, and perspectival. The esoteric has to do with what is infinite, absolute, universal, and integral. The true unity of religions is in the esoteric dimension. Those who understand the esoteric (those who know the ancient *philosophia perennis*) see that the conflicts and differences among the diverse traditions are really superficial. Beneath the surface lies a wondrous unity that mystics of all ages and all faiths proclaim—or so Schuon argues.

Many question whether there is such a thing as a *philosophia perennis* (a term first coined by the German philosopher Leibniz, 1646–1716). Still others wonder whether it can be at the core of all religions. In part, the arguments are historical. What sort of evidence do we have, and what does it prove? In part the arguments are philosophical. Can one simply ignore what appears to be genuine religious diversity and disagreement by reinterpreting it as an exoteric expression of a hidden unity and truth?

Although Schuon does believe there is agreement among diverse traditions about the ideas of the Perennial Philosophy, he also believes that the true unity of religions must be ultimately located at a deeper level—the level of the divine unity itself. Here is found the transcendent unity not only of religions but of all reality. Ultimately, all diversity and plurality are but accidental variations on a unitary divine theme.

You might wonder whether Schuon somewhat arbitrarily elevates one particular philosophical notion of the divine to the status of highest truth and relegates the rest to a lesser, exoteric status. Read and see what you think.

Reading Questions

1. What does philosophy ignore, according to Schuon?
2. What, according to Schuon, is the difference between a dogmatic affirmation and a speculative formulation?
3. Do you agree with Schuon's assertion that "if God were on the side of one religious form only," then its persuasive force would be such that "no man of good faith would be able to resist it"? Why or why not?
4. How does Schuon support his claim that anyone who tries to prove the truth of one religion to the exclusion of others cannot provide such a proof?
5. If, as Schuon asserts, "pure and absolute Truth can only be found beyond all its possible expressions," then it would seem that we can never state this *Truth*. If we cannot, then how do we know that what Schuon claims about "absolute Truth" is true?

The Transcendent Unity of Religions*

FRITHJOF SCHUON

THE TRUE AND COMPLETE understanding of an idea goes far beyond the first apprehension of the idea by the intelligence, although more often than not this apprehension is taken for understanding itself. While it is true that the immediate evidence conveyed to us by any particular idea is, on its own level, a real understanding, there can be no question of its embracing the whole extent of the idea, since it is primarily the sign of an aptitude to understand that idea in its completeness. Any truth can in fact be understood at different levels and according to different conceptual dimensions, that is to say, according to an indefinite number of modalities that correspond to all the possible aspects, likewise indefinite in number, of the truth in question. This way of regarding ideas accordingly leads to the question of spiritual realization, the doctrinal expressions of which clearly illustrate the dimensional indefinitude of theoretical conceptions.

Philosophy, considered from the standpoint of its limitations—and it is the limitations of philosophy that confer upon it its specific character—is based on the systematic ignoring of what has been stated above. In other words, philosophy ignores what would be its own negation; moreover, it concerns itself solely with mental schemes that, with its claim to universality, it likes to regard as absolute, although from the point of view of spiritual realization these schemes are merely so many virtual or potential and unused objects, insofar at least as they refer to true ideas; when, however, this is not the case, as practically always occurs in modern philosophy, these schemes are reduced to the condition of mere devices that are unusable from a speculative point of view and are therefore without any real value. As for true ideas, those, that is to say, that more or less im-plicitly suggest aspects of the total Truth, and hence this Truth itself, they become by that very fact intellectual keys and indeed have no other function; this is something that metaphysical thought alone is capable of grasping. So far as philosophical or ordinary theological thought is concerned, there is, on the contrary, an ignorance affecting not only the nature of the ideas that are believed to be completely understood, but also and above all the scope of theory as such; theoretical understanding is in fact transitory and limited by definition, though its limits can only be more or less approximately defined.

The purely "theoristic" understanding of an idea, which we have so termed because of the limitative tendency that paralyzes it, may justly be characterized by the word "dogmatism"; religious dogma in fact, at least to the extent to which it is supposed to exclude other conceptual forms, though certainly not in itself, represents an idea considered in conformity with a theoristic tendency, and this exclusive way of looking at ideas has even become characteristic of the religious point of view as such. A religious dogma ceases, however, to be limited in this way once it is understood in the light of its inherent truth, which is of a universal order, and this is the case in all esoterism. On the other hand, the ideas formulated in esoterism and in metaphysical doctrines generally may in their turn be understood according to the dogmatic or theoristic tendency, and the case is then analogous to that of the religious dogmatism of which we have just spoken. In this connection, we must again point out that a religious dogma is not a dogma in itself but solely by the fact of being considered as such and through a sort of confusion of the idea with the form in which it is clothed; on the other hand, the outward dogmatization of universal truths is perfectly justified in view of the fact that these truths or ideas, in having to provide the foundation of a religion, must be capable of being assimilated in some degree by all men. Dogmatism as such does not consist in the mere enunciation of an idea, that is to say, in the fact of giving form to a spiritual intuition, but rather in an interpretation that, instead of rejoining the formless and total Truth after taking as its starting point one of the forms of that Truth, results in a sort of paralysis of this form by denying its intellectual potentialities and by attributing to it an absoluteness that only the formless and total Truth itself can possess.

Dogmatism reveals itself not only by its inability to conceive the inward or implicit illimitability of the symbol, the universality that resolves all outward oppositions, but also by its inability to recognize, when faced with two apparently contradictory truths, the inward connection that they implicitly affirm, a connection that makes of them complementary aspects of one and the same truth. One might illustrate this in the following manner: whoever participates in universal Knowledge will regard two apparently contradictory truths as he would two points situated on one and the same circumference that links them together by its continuity and so reduces them to unity; in the measure in which these points are distant from, and thus opposed to one another, there will be contradiction, and this contradiction will reach its maximum when the two points are situated at the extremities of a diameter of the circle; but this extreme opposition or contradiction only appears as a result of isolating the points under consideration from the circle and ignoring the existence of the latter. One may conclude from this that a dogmatic affirmation, that is to say, an affirmation that is inseparable from its form and admits no other, is comparable to a point, which by definition, as it were, contradicts all other possible points; a speculative formulation, on the other hand, is comparable to an element of a circle, the very form of which indicates its logical and ontological continuity and therefore the whole circle or, by analogical trans-

position, the whole Truth; this comparison will, perhaps, suggest in the clearest possible way the difference that separates a dogmatic affirmation from a speculative formulation.

The outward and intentional contradictoriness of speculative formulations may show itself, it goes without saying, not only in a single, logically paradoxical formula such as the Vedic *Aham Brahmasmi* ("I am Brahma")—the Vedantic definition of the yogi—or the *Ana 'l-Ḥaqq* ("I am the Truth") of Al-Ḥallāj, or Christ's words concerning His Divinity, but also, and for even stronger reasons, as between different formulations each of which may be logically homogeneous in itself. Examples of the latter may be found in all sacred Scriptures, notably in the Koran: we need only recall the apparent contradiction between the affirmations regarding predestination and those regarding free will, affirmations that are contradictory only in the sense that they express opposite aspects of a single reality. However, apart from these paradoxical formulations—whether they are so in themselves or in relation to one another—there also remain certain theories that, although expressing the strictest orthodoxy, are nevertheless in outward contradiction one with another, this being due to the diversity of their respective points of view, which are not chosen arbitrarily and artificially but are established spontaneously by virtue of a genuine intellectual originality.

To return to what was said above about the understanding of ideas, a theoretical notion may be compared to the view of an object. Just as this view does not reveal all possible aspects, or in other words, the integral nature of the object, the perfect knowledge of which would be nothing less than identity with it, so a theoretical notion does not itself correspond to the integral truth, of which it necessarily suggests only one aspect, essential or otherwise.[1] In the example just given, error corresponds to an inadequate view of the object whereas a dogmatic conception is comparable to the exclusive view of one aspect of the object, a view that supposes the immobility of the seeing subject. As for a speculative and therefore intellectually unlimited conception, this may be compared to the sum of all possible views of the object in question, views that presuppose in the subject a power of displacement or an ability to alter his viewpoint, hence a certain mode of identity with the dimensions of space, which themselves effectually reveal the integral nature of the object, at least with respect to its form, which is all that is in question in the example given. Movement in space is in fact an active participation in the possibilities of space, whereas static extension in space, the form of our bodies, for example, is a passive participation in these same possibilities. This may be transposed without difficulty to a higher plane and one may then speak of an "intellectual space," namely, the cognitive all-possibility that is fundamentally the same as the Divine Omniscience, and consequently of "intellectual dimensions" that are the internal modalities of this Omniscience; Knowledge through the Intellect is none other than the perfect participation of the subject in these modalities, and in the physical world this participation is effectively represented by movement. When speaking, therefore, of the understanding of ideas, we may distinguish between a dogmatic understanding, comparable to the view of an object from a single viewpoint, and an integral or speculative understanding, comparable to the indefinite series of possible views of the object, views that are realized through indefinitely multiple changes of point of view. Just as, when the eye changes its position, the different views of an object are connected by a perfect continuity, which represents, so to speak, the determining reality of the object, so the different aspects of a truth, however contradictory they may appear and notwithstanding their indefinite multiplicity, describe the integral Truth that surpasses and determines them. We would again refer here to an illustration we have already used; a dogmatic affirmation corresponds to a point that, as such, contradicts by definition every other point, whereas a speculative formulation is always conceived as an element of a circle that by its very form indicates principally its own continuity, and hence the entire circle and the Truth in its entirety.

It follows from the above that in speculative doctrines it is the point of view on the one hand and the aspect on the other hand that determine the form of the affirmation, whereas in dogmatism the affirmation is confused with a determinate point of view and aspect, thus excluding all others. . . .

Exoteric doctrine as such, considered, that is to say, apart from the "spiritual influence" that is capable of acting on souls independently of it, by no means possesses absolute certitude. Theological knowledge cannot by itself shut out the temptations of doubt, even in the case of great mystics; as for the influences of Grace that may intervene in such cases, they are not consubstantial with the intelligence, so that their permanence does not depend on the being who benefits from them. Exoteric ideology being limited to a relative point of view, that of individual salvation—an interested point of view that even influences the conception of Divinity in a restrictive sense—possesses no means of proof or doctrinal credentials proportionate to its own exigencies. Every exoteric doctrine is in fact characterized by a disproportion between its dogmatic demands and its dialectical guarantees: for its demands are absolute as deriving from the Divine Will and therefore also from Divine Knowledge, whereas its guarantees are relative, because they are independent of this Will and based, not on Divine Knowledge, but on a human point of view, that of reason and sentiment. For instance, Brahmins are invited to abandon completely a religion that has lasted for several thousands of years, one that has provided the spiritual support of innumerable generations and has produced flowers of wisdom and holiness down to our times. The arguments that are produced to justify this extraordinary demand are in no wise logically conclusive, nor do they bear any proportion to the magnitude of the demand; the reasons that the Brahmins have for remaining faithful to their spiritual patrimony are therefore infinitely stronger than the reasons by which it is sought to persuade them to cease being what they are. The disproportion, from the Hindu point of view, between the immense reality of the Brahmanic tradition and the insufficiency of the Christian counterarguments is such as to prove quite sufficiently that had God wished to submit the world to one religion only, the arguments put forward on behalf of this religion would not be so feeble, nor those of certain so-called "infidels" so powerful; in other words, if God were on the side of one religious form only, the persuasive power of this form would be such that no man of good faith would be able to resist it. Moreover, the application of the term "infidel" to civilizations that are, with one exception, very much older than Christianity and that have every spiritual and historic right to ignore the latter, provides a further demonstration, by the very illogicality of its naive pretensions, of the perverted nature of the Christian claims with regard to other orthodox traditional forms.

An absolute requirement to believe in one particular religion and not in another cannot in fact be justified save by eminently relative means, as, for example, by attempted philosophico-theological, historical, or sentimental proofs; in reality, however, no proofs exist in support of such claims to the unique and exclusive truth, and any attempt so made can only concern the individual dispositions of men, which, being ultimately reducible to a question of credulity, are as relative as can be. Every exoteric perspective claims, by definition, to be the only true and legitimate one. This is because the exoteric point of view, being concerned only with an individual interest, namely, salvation, has no advantage to gain from knowledge of the truth of other religious forms. Being uninterested as to its own deepest truth, it is even less interested in the truth of other religions, or rather it denies this truth, since the idea of a plurality of religious forms might be prejudicial to the exclusive pursuit of individual salvation. This clearly shows up the relativity of form as such, though the latter is nonetheless an absolute necessity for the salvation of the individual. It might be asked, however, why the guarantees, that is to say, the proofs of veracity or credibility, which religious polemists do their utmost to produce, do not derive spontaneously from the Divine Will, as is the case with religious demands. Obviously such a question has no

meaning unless it relates to truths, for one cannot prove errors; the arguments of religious controversy are, however, in no way related to the intrinsic and positive domain of faith; an idea that has only an extrinsic and negative significance and that, fundamentally, is merely the result of an induction—such, for example, as the idea of the exclusive truth and legitimacy of a particular religion or, which comes to the same thing, of the falsity and illegitimacy of all other possible religions—an idea such as this evidently cannot be the object of proof, whether this proof be divine or, for still stronger reasons, human. So far as genuine dogmas are concerned—that is to say, dogmas that are not derived by induction but are of a strictly intrinsic character—if God has not given theoretical proofs of their truth it is, in the first place, because such proofs are inconceivable and nonexistent on the exoteric plane, and to demand them as unbelievers do would be a pure and simple contradiction; secondly, as we shall see later, if such proofs do in fact exist, it is on quite a different plane, and the Divine Revelation most certainly implies them, without any omission. Moreover, to return to the exoteric plane where alone this question is relevant, the Revelation in its essential aspect is sufficiently intelligible to enable it to serve as a vehicle for the action of Grace, and Grace is the only sufficient and fully valid reason for adhering to a religion. However, since this action of Grace only concerns those who do not in fact possess its equivalent under some other revealed form, the dogmas remain without persuasive power—we may say without proofs—for those who do possess this equivalent. Such people are therefore "unconvertible"—leaving aside certain cases of conversion due to the suggestive force of a collective psychism, in which case Grace intervenes only *a posteriori*, for the spiritual influence can have no hold over them, just as one light cannot illuminate another. This is in conformity with the Divine Will, which has distributed the one Truth under different forms or, to express it in another way, between different humanities, each one of which is symbolically the only one. It may be added that if the extrinsic relativity of exoterism is in conformity with the Divine Will, which affirms itself in this way according to the very nature of things, it goes without saying that this relativity cannot be done away with by any human will.

Thus, having shown that no rigorous proof exists to support an exoteric claim to the exclusive possession of the truth, must we not now go further and admit that even the orthodoxy of a religious form cannot be proved? Such a conclusion would be highly artificial and, in any case, completely erroneous, since there is implicit in every religious form an absolute proof of its truth and so of its orthodoxy; what cannot be proved, for want of absolute proof, is not intrinsic truth, hence the traditional legitimacy, of a form of the universal Revelation, but solely the hypothetical fact that any particular form is the only true and legitimate one, and if this cannot be proved it is for the simple reason that it is untrue.

There are, therefore, irrefutable proofs of the truth of a religion; but these proofs, which are of a purely spiritual order, while being the only possible proofs in support of a revealed truth, entail at the same time a denial of the pretensions to exclusiveness of the form. In other words, he who sets out to prove the truth of one religion either has no proofs, since such proofs do not exist, or else he has the proofs that affirm all religious truth without exception, whatever the form in which it may have clothed itself.

The exoteric claim to the exclusive possession of a unique truth, or of Truth without epithet, is therefore an error purely and simply; in reality, every expressed truth necessarily assumes a form, that of its expression, and it is metaphysically impossible that any form should possess a unique value to the exclusion of other forms; for a form, by definition, cannot be unique and exclusive, that is to say, it cannot be the only possible expression of what it expresses. Form implies specification or distinction, and the specific is only conceivable as a modality of a "species," that is to say, of a category that includes a combination of analogous modalities. Again, that which is limited excludes by definition whatever is not comprised within its own limits and must

compensate for this exclusion by a reaffirmation or repetition of itself outside its own boundaries, which amounts to saying that the existence of other limited things is rigorously implied in the very definition of the limited. To claim that a limitation, for example, a form considered as such, is unique and incomparable of its kind, and that it excludes the existence of other analogous modalities, is to attribute to it the unicity of Existence itself; now, no one can contest the fact that a form is always a limitation or that a religion is of necessity always a form—not, that goes without saying, by virtue of its internal Truth, which is of a universal and supraformal order, but because of its mode of expression, which, as such, cannot but be formal and therefore specific and limited. It can never be said too often that a form is always a modality of a category of formal, and therefore distinctive or multiple, manifestation, and is consequently but one modality among others that are equally possible, their supraformal cause alone being unique. We will also repeat—for this is metaphysically of great importance—that a form, by the very fact that it is limited, necessarily leaves something outside itself, namely, that which its limits exclude; and this something, if it belongs to the same order, is necessarily analogous to the form under consideration, since the distinction between forms must needs be compensated by an indistinction or relative identity that prevents them from being absolutely distinct from each other, for that would entail the absurd idea of a plurality of unicities or Existences, each form representing a sort of divinity without any relationship to other forms.

As we have just seen, the exoteric claim to the exclusive possession of the truth comes up against the axiomatic objection that there is no such thing in existence as a unique fact, for the simple reason that it is strictly impossible that such a fact should exist, unicity alone being unique and no fact being unicity; it is this that is ignored by the ideology of the "believers," which is fundamentally nothing but an intentional and interested confusion between the formal and the universal. The ideas that are affirmed in one religious form (as, for example, the idea of the Word or of the Divine Unity) cannot fail to be affirmed, in one way or another, in all other religious forms; similarly the means of grace or of spiritual realization at the disposal of one priestly order cannot but possess their equivalent elsewhere; and indeed, the more important and indispensable any particular means of grace may be, the more certain is it that it will be found in all the orthodox forms in a mode appropriate to the environment in question.

The foregoing can be summed up in the following formula: pure and absolute Truth can only be found beyond all its possible expressions; these expressions, as such, cannot claim the attributes of this Truth; their relative remoteness from it is expressed by their differentiation and multiplicity, by which they are strictly limited.

NOTE

1. In a treatise directed against rationalist philosophy, Al-Ghazzālī speaks of certain blind men who, not having even a theoretical knowledge of an elephant, came across this animal one day and started to feel the different parts of its body; as a result each man represented the animal to himself according to the part that he touched: for the first, who touched a foot, the elephant resembled a column, whereas for the second, who touched one of the tusks, it resembled a stake, and so on. By this parable Al-Ghazzālī seeks to show the error involved in trying to enclose the universal within a fragmentary notion of it, or within isolated and exclusive aspects or points of view. Shri Ramakrishna also uses this parable to demonstrate the inadequacy of dogmatic exclusiveness in its negative aspect. The same idea could, however, be expressed by means of an even more adequate example: faced with any object, some might say that it "is" a certain shape, while others might say that it "is" such and such a material; others again might maintain that it "is" such and such a number or such and such a weight, and so forth.

11.5 Whose Objectivity? Which Neutrality?

What criteria should we use in sorting out the conflicting truth claims among the various religions? Do we have a set of principles and procedures for going about deciding who is right and who is wrong? If we lack such principles, why? Is it impossible to decide such conflicts? Or maybe it is possible, but we just have not figured out how to do it yet.

Can we appeal to religious experience in order to settle conflicts? When it comes to questions of truth, how should we interpret such experiences? Should we appeal to historical facts? Does proving that Jesus lived (or the Buddha or Muhammad) prove anything about the truth of their messages?

Perhaps we should use a pragmatic criterion. Does faith x help people live better lives? How do we determine that? If it does, how does this bear on its truth? It may help me get through some really depressing moments to believe that angels are watching over me and keeping me from harm, but does that prove angels exist?

The list of questions and suggestions could go on and on. When it comes to settling disputed claims to truth among the world's religions, there are many more questions than answers. There are, however, several different options, and a careful exploration of each might give us some guidance. One of the biggest problems is the issue of objectivity. Is it really possible to be objective when judging different religions?

Gavin D'Costa, professor of religion at the University of Bristol, explores some of the options in the next selection. He is quite skeptical of claims to neutrality. Objectivity is illusive, he thinks, when it comes to deciding religious truth. Should we give up and stop trying? D'Costa thinks not. Can he convince you?

Reading Questions

1. What four options are available for judging the truth claims of religions?
2. What two axioms does D'Costa hope to establish?
3. According to D'Costa, what is wrong with Netland's two definitions and eight principles?
4. What is Ward's argument, and what is wrong with it?
5. What does D'Costa conclude about the impasse regarding conflicting truth claims?
6. Do you think D'Costa's conclusion is correct? Why or why not?

Whose Objectivity? Which Neutrality?*

GAVIN D'COSTA

I

There is an impasse in the discussion as to how to judge a religion other than one's own. On the one hand judging another religion by the criteria and standards of one's own tradition has become a highly problematic exercise. The metaphor used by some critics for such an approach is that of jingoistic flag-waving. Criticisms of this strategy are numerous and interdisciplinary in their nature. For instance, it is argued that such an enterprise is part and parcel of the political–economic imperialism of western (Christian) history. Such geo-political–religious imperialism is intolerable in a post-colonial age. Sociologically, anthropologically, and philosophically it has been argued that disparate traditions are quite simply incommensurable, each operating with their own rules and grammar. Hence, to judge one religion against another is like judging the goodness of an apple against a vacuum cleaner. The degree of incommensurability varies, so that at the lower end of the scale, the appropriate analogy is that of judging the goodness of apples against or-

anges. Such criticisms involve a range of disputed questions such as the possibility of successful translation of one language into another alien and different language, the epistemological logocentricism of western philosophical thought, and so on. I should state before proceeding that despite such criticisms I am a supporter of a nuanced form of this first strategy. I shall return to this point in due course.

If, on the one hand, judging another religion by one's own is deemed problematic, the alternative has proven equally so. Here it is maintained that it is inappropriate to use criteria from one's own religion to judge another religion. One may judge another religion by that religion's criteria alone or one should desist from such a task altogether as it is conceptually impossible. However, critics point out that if one judges another religion purely by its own criteria then the whole problem of conflicting truth claims is bypassed which was in fact the reason for trying to find criteria for judgement. Judging religions by their own criteria may be helpful in some contexts, but it takes us no further in trying to arbitrate

*From "Whose Objectivity? Which Neutrality? The Doomed Quest for a Neutral Vantage Point from Which to Judge Religions" by Gavin D'Costa. *Religious Studies 29*. Copyright © 1993 Cambridge University Press, 79–95. Reprinted by permission. Footnotes deleted.

between two rival religious claims. Critics also point out that total incommensurability is self defeating and such relativism is finally conceptually indefensible. Such relativism effectively ghettoises religions by emasculating any public relevance they may claim. In response, relativising the relativisers means that those who stipulate against religions making judgements on other religions commit the very error they are opposed to by carrying out judgements on all religions.

Stalemate? There are two other options. One would be to question the necessity of such a task and re-centre attention on more pressing issues such as poverty and hunger, political exploitation of women and minorities, child abuse, and the global destruction of parent earth (an inverse form of child abuse). This could be labelled the liberationist/pragmatic strategy that moves the focus away from conflicting doctrines and truth claims and tries to focus on common social and environmental problems. While the agenda is unquestionably urgent, such a pragmatic strategy does not really circumvent the problem. Questions of "justice" and "virtue" are involved in addressing such social and moral problems, and inevitably critiques of a tradition other than one's own, as well as one's own, will be required in trying to eradicate "child abuse" or "exploitation" of women. Hence, such a strategy meets the same difficulty, for most religions circumscribe their world and thereby define the activities that can and should go on within those boundaries. Religions are not just doctrinal entities, but traditions which fuse and hold together doctrine, practice, liturgy, ritual and so on. Philosophically, such an emphasis on morality as the uncontroversial bridge to avoid the impasse described above stems from an impoverished form of Enlightenment natural ethics which assumes incontestable universal moral norms that would be adhered to by all sensible persons. It should also be said that such a pragmatic approach is sometimes suggested by those who are frankly indifferent to religions and essentially wish to impose a humanistic agenda homogeneously upon all religions.

So what of the fourth option which could deliver us from this impasse? This strategy is subtle and interesting and in limited respects a variant on the above. It is also deceptively straightforward. It is the path of neutrality. Find neutral, commonly acceptable criteria which could not sensibly be rejected by any thinking adherent of any religious tradition. Apply these criteria and one will find a way through the impasse and provide a basis for judging true from false religions. Utopian? Just such a strategy has been suggested by two philosophers of religion: Keith Ward and Harold Netland in *A Vision to Pursue* and *Dissonant Voices* respectively. Ward and Netland could not, of course, refer to each other's work, but one might expect from both of them a consensus on criteria, or at least an agreement in principle with each other's criteria. It would be less fair to expect agreement on the outcome of the application of their criteria for this of course would be quite a complicated task. However, when we turn to their two books we find something surprising, although perhaps quite predictable. Not only are their criteria very different, but Ward suggests all religions would achieve worthwhile scores and thereby supports a form of pluralism (p. 191f), while Netland on the other hand suggests that Christianity alone "satisfies the requirements of all the . . . criteria" (p. 193) and hence, alone amongst the traditions, is true. Such an outcome should alert us to the inherent problem in such allegedly neutral strategies. What I wish to do is critically examine each of their proposals to show that such strategies are futile. In so doing, I will be implicitly arguing for a version of the first position outlined above.

I also hope to show the truth of two axioms. The first is that *in relation to the increased specificity of an alleged neutral proposal its neutrality diminishes*. The second is that *in relation to the decreased specificity of an alleged neutral proposal its usefulness diminishes*. The underlying logic of these two axioms is that whatever criteria are specified they are always and necessarily tradition specific. To give them the status of tradition-transcending robs them of the specificity that ensures their critical cutting edge. And the degree to which they have a critical cutting edge, the more they are rendered tradition specific so they cannot be deemed neutral and capable of acceptance by *all* sensible persons. The implication of this claim would be that by definition any claim to break the impasse by means of the neutrality route is doomed to failure because it is illusory.

II

Harold Netland's proposals are advanced in an interesting defence of Christian "exclusivism" (there is no salvation outside faith in Christ). I do not wish to discuss Netland's book here but am only concerned with his allegedly universally acceptable and binding proposals for determining the truth or falsity of competing religious worldviews. Netland's proposals come after a convincing and robust criticism against relativist strategies (mainly Hick and Knitter—but he would probably add Ward to his list) and less convincing criticisms of fideist strategies. He is dissatisfied with both for their inability to settle questions of truth. He notes that his proposals are not exhaustive and in need of further explication (p. 183), but what he offers is sufficient for discussion. He advances eight principles (P), which are dependent on two prior definitions (D) of religion. I quote from his summary (pp. 192–3):

> D1: p is a defining belief of R if and only if being an active participant in good standing within the religious community of R entails acceptance of p.
>
> D2: A religion R is true if and only if all of its defining beliefs are true; if any of its defining beliefs are false, then R is false.
>
> P1: If a defining belief p of a religion R is self-contradictory then p is false.
>
> P2: If two or more defining beliefs of R are mutually contradictory at least one of them must be false.
>
> P3: If a defining belief p of R is self-defeating it cannot reasonably be accepted as true.
>
> P4: If the defining beliefs of R are not coherent in the sense of providing a unified perspective of the world, then R cannot plausibly be regarded as true.
>
> P5: Any religious worldview which is unable to account for fundamental phenomena associated with a religious orientation or which cannot provide adequate answers to central questions in religion should not be accepted as true.
>
> P6: If a defining belief p of R contradicts well-established conclusions in other domains, and if R cannot justify doing so, then p should be rejected as probably false.
>
> P7: If a defining belief p of R depends upon a belief in another domain (e.g. history) which there is good reason to reject as false, then there is good reason to reject p as probably false.
>
> P8: If one or more defining beliefs of R are incompatible with widely accepted and well-established moral values and principles; or if R includes among its essential practices or rites activities which are incompatible with basic moral values and practices, then there is good reason for rejecting R as false.
>
> P9: If the defining beliefs of R entail the denial of the objectivity of basic moral values and principles; or if they entail the denial of the objective distinction between right and wrong, good and evil, then there is good reason for rejecting R as false.
>
> P10: If R is unable to provide adequate answers to basic questions about the phenomenon of moral awareness this provides good reason for rejecting R as false.

Before turning to the proposals, it should be noted that it seems odd for an evangelical Christian like Netland, who insists that faith in Christ is required for salvation, to propose such a scheme. It would appear that his exclusivist claim should in fact be that salvation is only granted to those who accept his ten principles and two definitions, for he writes that "I should state that the reason I believe one is *justified* in accepting the Christian faith as *true* is because it is the only worldview that satisfies the requirements of all the above criteria" (p. 193, my emphases)—not apparently, because of who Jesus was and who his community proclaimed him to be. The truth of revelation is subject to the truth of the ten principles and two definitions! But let us turn to his proposals.

Netland acknowledges that regarding his definition D1 (p is a defining belief of R if and only if being an active participant in good standing within the religious community of R entails acceptance of p) there is a difficulty in that religions heatedly debate what beliefs precisely constitute "defining beliefs," but he does not think this problematic in terms of the overall logic of his proposals. However, it may be argued that it is for the following reasons. Firstly, precisely because within any one religion there is considerable debate as to what its defining beliefs may be, it is spurious to suggest a cohesive and unified referent to the term "religion." In this respect there are many Christianities and many Buddhisms, both now and in times past, so that in principle the application of the evaluating criteria would have to be applied to *every possible* manifestation of *every possible* religious tradition before Netland's claim that "the [*sic*] Christian faith . . . is the only worldview that satisfied the requirements of all the above criteria" (p. 93) could be seen to be true. While he prefaces this claim that "although this cannot be argued here" I would maintain that while such a task is in principle possible, in practice it would be virtually impossible. It would require *a posteriori* studies using Netland's principles which to my knowledge has not even been started, let alone suggesting that it could be achieved by a single person in a single lifetime. Hence, while this does not jeopardize Netland's overall aim in principle, it suggests a misplaced confidence in his claiming Christianity to be the winner, on such terms, of the judging competition.

Furthermore, while Netland tends to reify religion into a single unified substance, the interesting philosophical and theological factor is precisely the phenomena of change and transformation within religious tradition. William Christian has shown very clearly that besides holding defining beliefs, religious persons also have the mechanisms by which they control, establish and discern defining beliefs and may in one period change what counts as a defining belief for very good theological or philosophical reasons, without thereby changing or denying the "same" religious adherence. The point about this was that even within a unified denomination we can see that there are mechanisms by which it can demote "defining beliefs" to the status of peripheral beliefs without necessary self-contradiction.

Hence, D2 could be rendered tautologous in stipulating that "A religion R is true if and only if all of its defining beliefs are true; if any of its defining beliefs are false, then R is false." Historically, short of changing religion, in times of credibility crisis regarding a defining belief, religious thinkers would tend to relegate that belief in status, rather than hold it as a defining belief with self-consciousness of its error. Again, this does not bear immediately on the question of neutral criteria, but suggests the difficulty with embarking on any evaluating exercise outside of a tradition-specific starting-point.

Finally, what if the defining beliefs of a religion were avowedly fideistic or relativist and such were their subsequent definitions of "truth"? In practice, relativism seems to be quite a recent phenomenon amongst liberal western educated members of religions, but fideism has a distinguished pedigree within different traditions. Fideistic predestination, for example, is evident in Madhava's theology and in Augustine's later thought. This raises the difficulty of the very definition of religion being non-neutral and acceptable to all, for Netland has concealed in his proposal an unstated D3: that is, "Truth is propositional and realist and religions can only define themselves in this way." Hence, what masquerades as an apparently *neutral definition* of religion is in fact a *prescriptive evaluation* of what constitutes genuine true religion, before we even get to the principles which are supposed to perform precisely the task of discerning genuine true religion. This is hardly a promising start.

Let us now turn to the principles that Netland offers and for the moment grant that the project of defining religion is trouble-free. Netland's first and second principles, which rely on notions of identity, non-contradiction and excluded middle, are a promising start for literate, speculative, self-reflective traditions. (I'm not sure the Azande would subscribe to entering this scheme so that they could be evaluated.) I think that here Netland genuinely isolates tradition-transcending principles which would be acceptable to many literate, speculative, self-reflecting persons in different religions. But without looking at the way in which such principles are applied and used from within a specific tradition, they do not really help in settling disputes over truth, except in discerning muddles. Take two examples. If we apply P1 and P2 (if a defining belief p of a religion R is self-contradictory then p is false; and if two or more defining beliefs of R are mutually contradictory at least one of them must be false) to a Zen koan, "listen to the sound of one hand clapping," a koan which is essential as a means to realizing satori, Netland would rule Zen out because such a statement is meaningless in his terms. But Zen Buddhists accept such rules of logic only to show that satori transcends logical conceptuality and definition. A Mādhyamika Buddhist such as Nāgārjuna, who also accepts such rules of logic only to show why no logical system can be held, would also be disqualified by Netland. In fact, Netland may also end up dismissing certain scientists for claiming that light is both a wave and not a wave, or an Einstein for suggesting that the speed at which we observe an object travelling would be both the same and different, depending on our observational position.

The problem here is that these principles do not help in the task of evaluation. One must observe the ways in which they are used within different communities, where such principles may be accepted but are subordinated to more fundamental truths of revelation by which they are regulated. So that while conversation between Netland, Nāgārjuna and Einstein could be possible in accepting the validity of the principle of identity, non-contradiction and excluded middle, the way in which they would each utilize and understand logic would be quite different, yet internally consistent and defensible. Netland is partly aware of this for he notes that some would say that the notions of nirvāna, satori and the Trinity are all contradictory and adds "whether any of these doctrines is indeed self-contradictory is of course a separate and complex question" (p. 184). But is it a separate question? I think Netland here moves too quickly, for whether they are indeed self-contradictory is established by the way that a specific tradition regards and utilizes these principles. Isolating the principles

outside of a particular context does not really get us very far. Recall my axioms: in relation to the increased specificity of an alleged neutral proposal its neutrality diminishes and secondly, in relation to the decreased specificity of an alleged neutral proposal its usefulness diminishes. The latter might be applied to P1 and P2 without claiming that they are entirely without merit, although one must acknowledge their limited provenance, namely literate, speculative, self-reflecting persons within religions and their limited provenance, namely subordination to truths of revelation or meditative experience.

Of P3 (if a defining belief p of R is self-defeating it cannot reasonably be accepted as true) it may be observed that it amounts to no more than P1, for "self-defeating" is by Netland's own definition tantamount to self-contradiction. He writes of self-defeating statements that they "cannot be true because they provide the grounds for their own refutation" (p. 184) and the example he gives, that of thorough-going relativism being self-refuting, is obviously an example of self-contradiction. P4 (if the defining beliefs of R are not coherent in the sense of providing a unified perspective on the world, then R cannot plausibly be regarded as true) amounts to coherence *within* a religious system and as with P1 and P2 Netland does, I believe, isolate a tradition-transcending criterion which would be acceptable to most literate, speculative, self-reflecting persons within different religions. As he notes himself, "coherence of a worldview in and of itself is not sufficient to guarantee truth of a worldview, but lack of coherence does provide good reason for its rejection" (p. 186). It should also be noted that the notions of coherence may vary as we will see below in relation to the notion of "adequacy."

P5 seems to amount to a tautologous criterion for judgement, for it dismisses a religion which is "unable to account for fundamental phenomena associated with religious orientation" and one "which cannot provide adequate answers to central questions in religion." The reason for suggesting tautology here is that "fundamental phenomena" are not something self-evident to any neutral on-looker who can then judge between different explanations of these same phenomena and then choose the best. Rather, religious world views actually define and select what they perceive to be fundamental phenomena and their very power lies in the answers they give to the type of question they perceive. Take for example the central way in which the question of God is not seen as necessary for enlightenment by the Buddha and does not need to feature in the notion of dukkha, its cause and the means to remove it. The "fundamental phenomena" here are radically and differently constructed from those perceived by a Richard Swinburne who in suffering sees the problem of evil because of a belief in a loving God, and must then "answer" this problem by defending a good and loving God. While Buddhists and Christians share the same physical world it would pre-judge a whole range of questions to suggest they interpret/experience and experience/interpret the world in a common way, implying common fundamental phenomena or even a sense of what counts as an "adequate" answer to very different questions. Adequacy, for example, is intrinsically a theological and philosophical notion highly dependent on the tradition within which the term is used. For instance, certain Christian critics of free-will theodicies (adequate answers to the question of evil in the face of a loving God, a non-question for a Buddhist) will find the free-will defence entirely inadequate on the grounds that the attempted justification of suffering is un-Christian. Such a position is advanced by Kenneth Surin. Now defenders of the free-will argument like Swinburne can argue endlessly, but such critics as Surin will *a priori* refuse their overall vision for they have, one might say, incommensurable criteria of adequacy. Critics may try and show why such defences are internally problematic, as does Surin, but ultimately they have different senses of "adequacy," such that Swinburne will be satisfied with a rationally plausible answer while Surin requires that the answer, if "adequate," must satisfy the child being burnt to death in the ovens of Auschwitz. Again, Netland is aware of such problems for he writes that "there is not always agreement concerning just what phenomena fall

within the reference range of a religious world-view and what constitutes a satisfactory answer to the basic questions of religion. This fact, however, does not call into question the legitimacy of the criterion itself but simply indicates the difficulty of applying it to particular religious worldviews" (p. 187). But this final sentence avoids the problem, as I have tried to show, for this criterion does not actually mean anything without the specification that Netland seems to think is an entirely separate question. Netland further perpetuates the kind of essentialism about "religion," the "world" and "common questions" in a manner that is quite ahistorical in assuming such cohesive, reified and unitary entities.

P6 to P10 begin to bear features of "thick" description where tradition specific characteristics are much more obvious and unmask the alleged neutrality of the proposals. P6 and P7 use "well-established conclusions in other domains," such as science, history and archaeology, upon which to judge the claims of religion, either in the case of direct contradiction (P6) or dependency (P7). The difference between P6 and P7 could be a difference of degree rather than of kind. But that is not relevant, for more importantly Netland situates his criteria very clearly in a specific tradition. Netland's neutrality is that of the enlightened western secularist where there is a distinct separation between theological "science" and the historical, scientific and archaeological sciences, each one given sovereign reign within its own field and ever increasingly the latter group given sovereign reign over religious territory. But such presuppositions are very tradition specific. Admittedly with the internationalization of western secular culture many societies and religions are going through some similar fragmentationary processes, although it must be noted, they react very differently. For example, in some Islamic thought there is no autonomy granted to secular sciences in the way presupposed by Netland such that religious truth is determined and controlled by secular truths. The same could be said for some forms of Chinese and early Indian thought where "scientific theories" were actually part of religious worldviews, for example in the evolutionary framework of Sāmkhya-Yoga where Netland's distinction between science and religion would not make sense, let alone be applicable. And one can also find resurgent within some forms of Christianity a strong resistance to such fragmentation coming from both conservative evangelicals, who oppose scientific theories of evolution and from radical post-modernists, who oppose scientific notions of history. Here again, I am not suggesting that Netland's criterion is entirely unhelpful, but that without tradition-specific specification it is unuseable, and insofar as it can be used, betrays its neutrality.

P8 and P9 are perhaps the most blatantly non-neutral and given my first axiom that in relation to the increased specificity of an alleged neutral proposals its neutrality diminishes, it is not surprising that these principles are the ones which might take us on some distance in actually carrying out a process of judgement. P8 states: "If one or more defining beliefs of R are incompatible with widely accepted and well-established moral values and principles; or if R includes among its essential practices or rites activities which are incompatible with basic moral values and practices, then there is good reason for rejecting R as false." This unashamedly privileges western secular tastes and sensibilities in deeming religions true in accordance with their conformity to current notions of good taste and decency. Netland seems unaware of the huge and questionable set of assumptions implicit in this criterion. Firstly, he is guilty of the now consistent danger of "essentialism"; assuming some homogeneous coherence and consensus on moral values, principles and practices. But this begs the question as to which society will Netland turn to find this alleged consensus: the Azande, the Aztec, the Crusader Christians of the middle ages, Tibetan Buddhism before the entry of the Chinese, present-day Saudi Arabia, present-day England, present-day Chicago, or where? And when he has chosen that society, which group's morality is he to take as normative, and what about the plurality of moral values, principles and practices that he will inevitably find? Strangely, Netland seems to ignore such intractable difficulties, but rather cites ex-

amples of this allegedly neutral common morality: "Thus, a religious world view which includes child sacrifice or cannibalism as an essential rite or adopts as a basic tenet the inherent superiority of whites over blacks should, for this reason, be rejected as probably false" (p. 190). These are a curious set of examples, because in present day Chicago and England it would seem that public morality as a whole accepts as a basic moral value the right to choose what the Roman Catholic Church views as "child sacrifice": abortion. And in certain parts of Protestant Northern Ireland, there are still leaflets circulated where the communion rite of the Catholic mass is seen as cannibalism and "God's vicar on Earth" as "Satan's representative."

The point I am making is this. There are no sets of basic moral values which are neutral and acceptable to all people, and as soon as one tries to specify some their historical and tradition-specific nature becomes evident. Prohibition on suicide in one tradition amounts to martyrdom in another, avoiding meat only on a Friday in one tradition amounts to a six-day species-genocide in the eyes of another. My view does not in itself exclude the possibility of overlap, family resemblances, and so on. However, I would question the possibility that there is a homogeneous neutral publicly acceptable morality. Furthermore, if such an entity were found there seems to be no good reason to advance such a criterion as deciding the truth or falsity of a religion. For nearly all religious traditions the logic operates in the reverse direction. For example, in some forms of Judaism, Islam and Christianity, good and bad are defined from the basis of revelation and certain streams of privileged tradition stemming from that revelation, and this has then often been the basis for criticising the societies in which Jews, Christians and Muslims then find themselves. Netland's P8 suggests a reverse logic which is difficult to defend historically.

P9 has especially interesting results for its specifies that "if the defining beliefs of R entail the denial of the objectivity of basic moral values and principles; or if they entail the denial of the objective distinction between right and wrong, good and evil, then there is good reason for rejecting R as false." Here, more than almost anywhere else, the tradition-specific nature of Netland's proposals becomes evident. He gives no grounds for assuming that it is universally acceptable that such a realist view of ethics is the case, or why it is uncontroversial that there is an objective distinction between right/wrong, good/evil. This obvious weakness would allow those groups who do not agree with these assumptions to question (quite rightly given Netland's project) whether such proposals are objective neutral criteria for evaluating religions. One can imagine an Advaitin specifying that any religion that viewed the distinction between evil/good as an objective one could not be true because it undermines the absolute undifferentiated nature of Brahman, which is of course beyond the provisional duality of good and evil. Netland would no doubt reply that this was rather loading the dice. But oddly, he does the same with a curious air of innocence. Hence, he concludes that a

> strong case can be made for the view that Advaita Vedanta Hinduism and Zen Buddhism—insofar as they make a fundamental ontological distinction between levels of reality and truth and maintain that the highest Reality and Truth is absolutely undifferentiated unity, allowing no distinctions whatever—are incompatible with moral objectivity. It is hard to see how Advaita Vedanta or Zen can accommodate an objective distinction between good and evil, right and wrong (p. 190).

and hence they are probably false religions. It is also clear that such a proposal would be far from acceptable to most Advaitins or Zen Buddhists. Needless to say, the battlefield over the question is entirely misconstrued by Netland. He wins, so to speak, on very loaded and pre-judged terms which settle the question of religious truth before it has actually been discussed properly. This hardly overcomes the impasse regarding questions of conflicting truth claims, but rather propounds an answer of neutral criteria which we have seen to be far from neutral.

Little need be said about P10 (if R is unable to provide adequate answers to basic questions about the phenomenon of moral awareness, this provides good reason for rejecting R as false.) As with my criticisms of P5, it must be urged that the notion of "adequacy" is far from clear and involves strong theological and philosophical judgements as to what it constitutes. And as with my criticisms of P5, it must also be asked whether there is any agreed phenomenon of "moral awareness" or whether Netland simply once again creates essences out of a complex multiform phenomenon. Zen Buddhists clearly think that they do provide "adequate answers" and that the "inadequate" answers are given by theists (who are dualists) like Netland and their notions of adequacy are not derived from classical logic, but from the basic experience of satori, which conceptually defies the norms of classical logic.

If Netland's attempt to frame neutral criteria by which to judge religions is deeply problematic, as I hope to have shown, will Ward's fare any better? The logic of my criticisms suggests that the answer must be "no" for the two axioms have so far proven true: in relation to the increased specificity of an alleged neutral proposal its neutrality diminishes and that in relation to the decreased specificity of an alleged neutral proposal its usefulness diminishes.

III

Keith Ward's proposals are advanced in the context of his vision of Christianity in the twenty first century. He follows in the tradition of John Hick's pluralism, adopting a unitarian Christology and wishing to forge peaceful and harmonious relations between religions by means of overcoming exclusivist Christologies. As with Netland's book, I am concerned solely to assess his proposed neutral criteria by which to judge religions. Ward suggests that there are "certain common features of being human" (p. 178) such that it will be possible to specify "the criteria of excellence which are appropriate to human beings and the nature of the goal which is proper to humanity as such" (p. 179). Hence Ward wishes to establish that there "is a set of fundamental values which are given by the very nature of human being itself, and which are not merely conventional or matters of arbitrary and wholly subjective preference" (p. 179). Once more, we see a curious logic whereby religions will be told what constitutes their truthfulness in terms of some foundational Archimedes point outside of all religious traditions. This Archimedian point is that of a Kantian form of natural theology.

Ward, like Netland, criticises relativist and fideist positions and sees the way out of the impasse regarding conflicting truth claims in the provision of universal criteria. These are established by conditions for the possibility of reflectively using the concept of "value." This allegedly avoids the difficulties of dealing with the very different types of values held, but probes deeper, into the transcendental arguments from the notion of value. Ward notes analogies here with Kant's transcendental arguments for the possibility of scientific and mathematical knowledge. But this analogy should alert us to two possible dangers. Firstly, that in specifying general conditions for being able to hold values nothing specific is said about the content of values and their possible conflicts, which is ultimately the issue at stake. The point is not that every one has and is able to make truth claims, but rather that the truth claims themselves, if taken seriously, often conflict. Second, Kant operates within a very specific tradition and the history of philosophy since testifies to the controversy as to whether he had attained for pure and practical reason the transcending role he claimed for it. There are strong philosophical counter-traditions questioning the entire Kantian project which is germane for indicating the problem of any alleged neutral starting point.

What is Ward's argument? I hope I convey it correctly for at times in his text the different steps and stages are not always clear. Firstly, he argues that the notion of "value" presupposes preference and choice, and that value, if it is worthy of being sought, must be an intrinsically worthwhile

state of consciousness. Secondly, he argues that "happiness" is a basic value which admittedly "does not show what sort of conscious state happiness is" (p. 182), and that such happiness can be found in different ways, although one must qualify it by stating that it "is always wrong to cause sorrow or suffering, in the absence of further justifying factors" (p. 182). Thirdly, to seek to make choices to attain happiness, a further basic value is presupposed: that of knowledge. Hence, with qualifications, it can be said that it "is an unequivocally good thing to have the capacity to know what can be chosen and how best to achieve it" (p. 184). Knowledge is not simply a grasp of the facts, but a "deep sensitivity to and appreciation of beauty and order and a compassionate empathy with the sufferings of all creatures" and involves "an understanding of the nature of things and the explanation for their existence, so far as this is available" (p. 184). Fourthly, choice, happiness, and knowledge presuppose freedom to make such choices. Ward summarises his argument thus: "if I value anything at all, I have a good reason to value the realization of intrinsically satisfying conscious states, the capacity of knowing which states are actual and possible, of reasoning about how to obtain them, and of being free to realize them. These basic values are presupposed by the analysis of value in terms of rational preference" (p. 186). In order to render this as a universally applicable truth, Ward adds a fifth value, which he calls "justice; which simply reminds us that whatever is a basic value for us is one for anyone like us in the relevant aspects" (p. 186), meaning that if pursuing the attainment of values is good for x, and all factors being equal for y, then justice requires that it is good for y similarly to pursue the attainment of values.

In keeping with the Kantian transcendental nature of the argument, it should be noted that all Ward has provided (if his argument is correct) are certain formal, rather than material, elements constitutive of human beings as value seeking. Realizing intrinsically satisfying conscious states, knowing about such states, being able to know how to obtain them and being free to do so, are all formal properties of moral agents, specifying nothing whatsoever about the contents of the moral vision they hold. But Ward goes on to say that in so much as these conditions hold, one can claim to have arrived at an "autonomous," "objective" and "absolute" "standard or test for the acceptability of values. Any values which frustrate or destroy any of the set of basic values are less acceptable than values which, in a particular context, can be seen as encouraging the realization of the set of basic values" (p. 187). But can material choices actually effect the formal conditions required for making choices? Is Ward guilty of a category confusion? I think that he is guilty because what he calls "the set of basic values" are not actually material choices available, but the conditions for making any material choices. If it is otherwise, then these cannot be transcendental conditions for value-seeking that Ward claims them to be. Precisely because the "basic set of values" are conditions for choice-making and value-seeking they cannot specify the material contents of choice-making and value-seeking. Hence, they can hardly apply as criteria for granting truthfulness to material choices, but only as stating the necessary conditions for material choices.

In fact it should be noted that even the way in which Ward has specified the transcendental conditions of value seeking human beings is not neutral. For instance, he presupposes some very tradition specific notions of rationality and knowledge. Rationality is defined as "the capacity to discern the true nature of things and the deepest patterns of intelligibility in the world" (p. 184), a definition which smacks of traditional theistic natural theology. What of the Nāgārjunas of this world, who far from noting that the nature of things constitutes deep patterns of intelligibility in the world, note rather that nothing within this world is properly intelligible and therefore nothing within this world is properly satisfying? The same could be said for Śankara's Advaita Vedānta, for on the ultimate level of truth the world is actually unintelligible (anirvicanya) and has no proper status (māyā). A similar criticism could be advanced regarding Ward's definition of knowledge which requires an "appreciation of beauty and order," an aspect of deep illusion according to most Buddhists. And similarly, for Ward's concession that while happiness can admittedly be found in different ways, he would qualify it by saying it "is always wrong to cause sorrow or suffering, in the absence of further justifying factors" (p. 102). But the notions of "sorrow" and "suffering" are in danger of being essentialised (à la Netland), for surely such terms are actually defined and have their meaning within tradition-specific contexts, not in a general and universal sense as implied by Ward? Suffering and sorrow, for a Buddhist, constitute the marks of dukkha and are part of the nature of empirical existence, whereas within certain forms of Christianity they are not essential to empirical existence and exist as a result of sin. Hence, at one level to be freed of the illusion of God as an essential being is to be freed from suffering and sorrow (within Buddhism), while entirely the opposite could be the case with Christianity. The list of differing constructions and construals given to this term could be multiplied and the point I am making is simple. I wish to stress that there is no neutral language and concepts and hence, even within Ward's formal definition, there is no neutrality. But let us for the moment grant Ward's argument a potential coherence to see how he further slips from stating common *formal* requirements to equating these with common *material* goals, compounding his category mistake.

Having rejected any seeking of values that destroys those absolute values which presuppose the conditions for seeking value, Ward goes on to distinguish between being *merely* human (being capable of pursuing these values) and being *fully* human (realising these values as fully as possible) (p. 188). So where does religion enter the picture? Ward's answer is that the religions all share a common "structure" which consists "in a maximal instantiation of the five basic values" (p. 189). But at this level of generality Ward's criteria do not really take us very far in resolving any conflicts concerning "maximal instantiation," for herein lies the problem of conflicting truth claims, and he seems to partially recognize this when he adds "and one can see how different faiths interpret such a maximal case in different ways" (p. 189). This amounts to saying that all religions have in common is a desire to achieve a way of life in which adherents are fulfilled and of course this is not saying very much regarding the evaluation of what counts as fulfilling or not. How, for instance, is martyrdom discerned as authentic or inauthentic in the cases of St Peter, the Jonestown disciples, and the followers of Hizballah (the Party of God)? All persons in the above cases may fully believe that they are achieving a "maximal instantiation" of pursuing that which is most valuable. It is at this point that Ward most clearly jumps the tracks and introduces a concealed assumption that actually negates the thrust of his argument from neutrality.

He begins to argue that while different faiths may interpret maximal cases in different ways, the differences "are subtle differences of interpretation" (p. 189) and have a commonality of content; that is "a turning-away from selfishness by relating individuals to a supreme objective value which is their ultimate goal" (p. 188). Or again, he says "there is agreement on the need to move from self towards a supreme objective value and an agreement on the sort of value this will be which forms a deeper structure underlying particular differences of interpretation" (p. 190). But this is surely a classical case of a category mistake; the confusion of the categories of form and content. Ward simply jumps from assuming a common structure (a movement towards a supreme objective value) to conflating that structure with content, and therefore a common goal. Hence, rather than attempting a solution to the problem, Ward dissolves it by not taking conflicting claims seriously. It is worth quoting at length the following passage which demonstrates this:

> It might be better to see the different faiths, not as in radical opposition but as having a range of agreed values, but varying ways of interpreting them in the light of a developing understanding of the world. There is an important sense in which differing faiths are engaged in a common pursuit of supreme value, though they conceive this in diverse ways. The theist will seek to transcend self by achieving a conscious relationship to God which enables her to share and reflect the supreme perfections of God. She seeks to make her will one with the divine will. The Buddhist seeks to transcend selfish desire, to make her nature one with the Buddha nature. The Vedantin seeks to realize her self as one with the Self of all, unlimited being, consciousness and bliss. Is there so much difference here? Are the deep agreements not more important that the countless unsettlable disputes which litter the libraries of professional dogmatists? (p. 190).

Presuming "professional dogmatists" is a term of abuse, I must plead guilty to being such a character, for it seems to me that the reverse of what Ward observes is the case. There seems to be very deep disagreements of content, even if there is a commonality of structure within different religions. For example (if one can generalize for the moment) the Christian's entire morality and pursuit of supreme value is based on difference and participation, difference from God but finally participation in his love, charity and goodness. Difference, distinction and participation are all upheld as ontological categories by means of the doctrine of the Trinity. The Advaitin on the other hand is entirely orientated towards unity without difference and oneness without duality: the "experience" of anubhava in which Brahman is realized as the sole existent, one without a second. Not only is the goal different, but so is the entire basis of morality and what counts as the ultimate truth for the Christian and Advaitin. And Rāmānuja and Madhva, as Vedāntins, certainly felt that the errors of Śankara were serious enough to condemn his teachings, to criticise his false understanding of Brahman and thereby the basis of Śankara's ethics. Without even drawing the Buddhist in at this point, and the differences between different schools of Buddhism are considerable, the "countless unsettlable disputes" are far from insignificant. It seems that the deep structure actually testifies to something very different from what Ward sees. Despite various commonalities in formal structure, and perhaps commonalities in values at varying levels of theory and practice, at a fundamental level there are substantial ontological differences that cannot be dissolved. This it should be recalled is the purpose of the exercise: to adjudicate between such differences. But Ward's strategy is to relegate such differences to "subtle differences of interpretation" and one suddenly realizes that the transcendental argument for the condition of value-seeking, has dropped entirely out of sight. And this is not insignificant.

Ward's allegedly neutral path of adjudication is, it seems to me, independent of the conclusions which he draws for two basic reasons. The first is that he commits a category mistake in applying his argument. From a similarity of formal structure, he assumes a common goal. Secondly, the criteria are not in fact neutral for Ward has already decided earlier in the book (and has begun to do so in his earlier work: *Images of Eternity,* 1987) that religions present "iconic" visions, where "iconic" plays a similar function to John Hick's category of "myth"; that is, something is "revealed" but it cannot be held to be an absolute truth and it must always be open to correction and transformation. Hence, disputes between the ultimate nature of reality can always be relegated to complementary perspectives and not finally taken seriously at all. It is curious that those wishing better relationships between religions and who are anxious to dispose of exclusivist claims, end up inadvertently not respecting the integrity of the different traditions and the seriousness and absoluteness of their claims and thereby erect a new exclusivism.

IV

I have endeavoured to achieve certain limited goals. Firstly, I have tried to show that the impasse in the problem of conflicting truth claims cannot be met by means of advancing neutral criteria for adjudicating between religions. As has been demonstrated by my examination of Ward and Netland, it can be argued that in relation to the increased specificity of an alleged neutral proposal its neutrality diminishes and secondly, in relation to the decreased specificity of an alleged neutral proposal its usefulness diminishes. In Netland's case we saw that his criteria were either so underspecified as to be incapable of the task, or so overspecified to be obvious form of tradition-specific (at least theistic) criteria that they could not count as performing the task they were set up to perform. In Ward's case we saw that his criteria were far from neutral and when they actually achieve results in application, they only did so by changing their nature through a category mistake.

Where does this leave us in the impasse regarding conflicting truth claims? Slightly better off I think, in avoiding certain options. In arguing implicitly that one cannot start from other than a tradition-specific starting point I hope to have shown the necessity for pursuing the question along the avenues set out in the first of the options outlined at the beginning of the paper. However, it remains to be shown how one can profitably counter the various objections to such an approach and to argue that this is in fact the only credible way in which to judge religions other than one's own.

11.6 A Problem for Radical Pluralism

If I hold that my religion has an exclusive monopoly on the truth and that all others are wrong, I assume there is such a thing as religious truth. If I hold that my religion is inclusive of the truth found in all religions insofar as it articulates such truth in its fullest extent, I assume there is such a thing as religious truth. If I think that all religions are true and that all present a plurality of valid paths to salvation, I assume that there is religious truth. If I go even further and adopt a more radical position, arguing that every religion ought to learn from and include within its own traditions the truth discovered in the other traditions, I assume that there is religious truth.

What if there is no such thing as THE TRUTH? What if all religions construct diverse human responses to the pressures of life, making sense of human experience as best they can given their historical and social locations? There may be no absolute and objective Truth, but only localized, constructed, cultural methods for coping with the problems of human existence. Perhaps we should not assume there is religious truth but only that there are varied responses to the issues and problems of being human.

Purusottama Bilimoria, who teaches religion and philosophy at Deakin University in Australia and is the author of the next selection, raises the question of whether the assumption of truth behind the various responses to religious plurality is appropriate. He suggests a "critical pluralism" that recognizes that there is no such thing as THE TRUTH in any absolute sense. Rather, he acknowledges various traditions struggling to construct meaning as best they can in a world that is often hostile.

If religious truth is a humanly constructed idea, if it is an artifact of human existence, then a type of hopeless relativism appears to engulf us. What is true for you is false for me, and what is true for me is false for you. Where does this leave us? If my religion teaches that human sacrifices must be made in order to ensure that the sun will come back and give us life, should you say, "Well, that's true for you, but in my religion it is false"? Should you then go on to say, "Nevertheless, go ahead, sacrifice those people. After all, truth is a humanly constructed notion, localized in time and place and unique to various experiences and traditions"?

Reading Questions

1. What is a more radical form of pluralism according to Bilimoria?
2. What is the implicit assumption of radical pluralism?
3. Why is the "ontotheological-metaphysical" presupposition questionable?
4. How does deconstructive a/theology reconceive God?
5. What is the post-onto/theocentric challenge?
6. If a new kind of critical pluralism is built around the idea that all conceptions of truth are equally constructed human artifacts and that there is no TRUTH in any absolute sense, then how could that critical pluralism escape being just another constructed truth like exclusivism, inclusivism, pluralism, and radical pluralism?

A Problem for Radical Pluralism*

PURUSOTTAMA BILIMORIA

Preamble

An aspect of Max Charlesworth's practical philosophy has engaged the following set of problems: If a culture X takes its episteme, theological (or, secular) framework and set of values to be paradigmatic or in some ways privileged, then what does this mean for the different religious worldviews, values and ideals of other cultures, and of the sub-cultures within it? How is it possible in a pluralistic society where people have very differing ethical views to reach any kind of community consensus on significant moral issues? What if they also have altogether differing views about the foundations of ethics or morality and the nature of the ethical enterprise, and about the precise relationship of ethics to law? Further, the ethical views of certain minority communities are based on or derived from *religious* foundations which may be radically different from, sometimes in conflict with, those of the majority society (whether quasi-religious or secular). What then are the implications for any due process in legal discourse about the claims of one group over another—e.g. Australian Aboriginal claim to their "sacred" land iconically linked with the Ancestor Spirits as against British Australian law?

Max Charlesworth's discursive handling of the questions and issues that arise in this confrontation have helped inspire wide-ranging discussions and even reviews of customary practices and opinions. But this matter is best left for more detailed treatment at another occasion. I want merely to pose a question for one facet of these problems, for the problem precipitated by pluralism, albeit religious/theological pluralism . . . .

I. Religious Pluralism

The contemporary Swiss-German theologian Hans Küng has suggested that the "boundary between the true and false today, even as Christians see it, no longer runs simply between Christianity and other religions, but at least in part *within* each of the religions."

The conventional discourse on religious pluralism has hitherto been framed in terms of the encounter of Christianity with "other" or "non-Christian" religions and the kind of response Christians might or might not make to people of non-Christian persuasion in all their diversity and complexity. The positions and attitudes adopted within the pluralist ("dialogue-ic") paradigm have ranged from forms of "exclusivism" (that all religions have some worth, but Christianity offers the only valid path, *extra ecclesiam nulla salus*), "inclusivism" (that other religions have great spiritual depth and revelations, but are not sufficiently salvific), and "pluralism" (that the truth-content of faith can have a variety of articulations each of which is legitimate), with shades in between. Ernest Troeltsch, William Hocking and Paul Tillich first suggested the idea of pluralism, although with differing interpretations and implications of the claim to finality or normativity for Christians. The consensus in more recent times seems to gravitate towards *pluralism* in one or the other of its interpretations. The more popular understanding of religious pluralism, as articulated by W. C. Smith, John Hick, Paul Knitter, D'Costa among others, maintains that "other religions are equally salvific paths to God, and Christianity's claim that it is the only path (exclusivism), or the fulfilment of other paths (inclusivism) should

*From "A Problem for Radical (onto-theos) Pluralism" by Purusottama Bilimoria, *Sophia* 30 (1991):21–33. Reprinted by permission. Footnotes deleted.

be rejected for good theological and phenomenological grounds."

In other words, the traditional universalism and absolutism attached to the Christian position is bracketed and the independent validity of other religions—even in their "otherness" or *alterity*—is now recognised. Much thought has been given as to how the differences between religions, the great diversity of beliefs, practices, rites and symbolisms, might be reconciled or a *rapprochement* brought about among them. And there has been much optimism about learning from other religions and the mutual enrichment or upliftment that can be experienced anew in "dialogues and conversations" with people whose religious instincts appear not to have been scorched by centuries of internal theological disputes, doubts and argumentations, and by the rapid shifts that the modern (beginning with Western) societies have made towards secularism, scientism and technocratic utopianism.

A corollary of this mitigated position is a more radical form of pluralism which argues that the established and dogmatic traditions should turn over to and enmesh (integrate) themselves as much as practicable with the currency of other, possibly less dogmatic, ("world" and "primal") traditions with radically different (maybe more ancient) historical roots and wealth of outlook on nature, on the human condition, on the cosmos, on liberation, and so on. While during the colonial-imperial phase the distant and marginalised traditions were infiltrated, expropriated and recast to look more like the dominant tradition (e.g. Christianity in Hindu-Muslim India, typified in R. Panikkar's earlier The Hidden Christ of India), the trend now is to reverse the process and appropriate the "other" traditions into one's own tradition in the intra-religious context. (Which, of course, echoes a process already operative in the intra-traditions context, e.g. bhakti or devotionalism appropriated into the mainstream ritualistic Brahmanism that led to the emergence of Hinduism vis-à-vis Buddhism and Jainism.) Pluralism becomes a means of preserving the old in the guise of the new or other.

This task, it is urged, is a matter of some urgency now that there is widespread recognition of the historical contingency of every cultural artifact—as surely religion is one—as well as our growing awareness of the unavoidable "prejudices" and the questionable assumption undergirding the privileged or paradigmatic access to the "Ultimate" claimed in each religion. Together the religions may be able to heal the scars left by the clashes of disparate cultures, and inject some sanity, hope and insightful wisdom towards preventing nature and humankind from the threat of human-engendered destruction, if not also work toward the betterment of human beings as indeed the goal of each religion appears, in principle at least, to be absolutely committed to.

Thus, Christianity could be Judaised, Judaism Hinduised, Hinduism Islamised, Islam Buddhised, Buddhism Koori-ised, and so on. Imagine the prospect that Australia presents for such a "crucible of a radical spirituality," situated as it is in the Pacific-Asia region with an indigenous (aboriginal) tradition that goes back some 50,000 years, and is now a home for a plethora of ethnic and culturally diverse groups that have brought their own faith-traditions to its shores! This would seem to be the challenge of what goes under the rubric of "radical pluralism," which, while it acknowledges the historical relativity of each religion, nevertheless accedes to the intrinsic intentionality or drift towards the essential truth, the *telos,* as well as submitting to the fundamental integrity, insights, virtues and spirituality of each tradition. Even if the form of relativism it implicitly admits to is merely "provisional," there appears to prefigure here an assumption that truth might just be plural; or, more likely, that truth is one but that it conceals itself behind a kaleidoscopic facade.

There are versions of radical pluralism that, pushed to further degrees of ambivalence, attempt to ride over the limitations imposed by the excluded middle, contrary to Parmenides' intuition; thus in calling for the non-exclusion of other truths from one's own, we have a simultaneity of "One and Many." But there is a more serious suggestion that supervenes on the distinction that some want to draw between truth in science, in religion, in ethics, in human disciplines, in personal orientations, and so on. And this turns on a revision of the classical (Aristotelian) notion of truth (culminating in science as its key model). Thus, it follows that, if religions are plural, truth must also be plural.

II. *Plurality of Truth*

The question of how one might legitimate the claim to a variety of truth qua truth aside, there is another problem which the pluralist paradigm seems least self-conscious of. As the post-modern critics are at pains to point out, radical pluralism continues to trade on the implicit assumption that there is such a thing as religious truth, or that there is an "ultimate something" that answers to the description of truth in each religion. In short, the assumption is that there is some one *ultimate* being or reality, the universal spirit as the absolute (*logos, onto-theos*), which transcendentally sediments as the core intentionality of all religions. The ultra-radical pluralist might say that because the ultimate reality is ineffable and language presents a barrier to this hidden reality, the best we can do is to pursue the different names of the absolute (as we would if we were looking for the "ultimate ice cream" or playing different "language-games"). The pluralist approach, then, in conceding to different paradigms of the ultimate reality, unequivocally affirms that there is an absolute of which each religious truth is an attempted articulation. The term "God" names the "ultimate reality" in Western religious traditions; the terms "Brahman" in Hinduism, and "*nirvāna/śūnyatā* (emptiness)" in conjunction with "*Dharma/dharmakāya*" and "refuge in Buddha" in Buddhism, have analogous function to that of the term "God."

In other words, religious truths are, if not simply a variety of reflecting articulations of the ultimate truth, modes of representations of the one true Ultimate (*ens realissimum*). It is only that we are not yet able to decide as to which of these is the final manifestation or decisive articulation, or as to which captures best the distinctive mark of the Ultimate: the truth of truths (the "highest truth" *à la* neo-Vedānta discourse). Perhaps history in its *n*th fulfilment, or another (or the deferred) revelation, or a prophet, or avatāra, or total submission, etc., will in due course disclose it to us.

III. *The Questionable Presupposition*

It is the very ontotheological-metaphysical presupposition just sketched, whether it is based on the identity of God and being (intuited through reason as in philosophical theology and argued in philosophy of religion) or based on revelation and faith as in the discourse of theology, or on the scriptural evocation of Brahman, and so on, that has now become suspect. Reason itself (more persistently since Kant) has come in the firing line as being an insufficient tool to explain and defend the claims supposedly derived from sources more transcendental to it. Theoretical reason knows only this world of "appearance," and not the whatever-in-itself. For Kant, the postulate of God, just as the ideas of the "world" and "self," is a matter of reasonable trust (and not quite a matter of faith), intended to guide and govern our wisdom and tenets. Thus if reason is not universal in all matters—or not universal at all—there can be no truth, still less religious truth, that can lay claim to being universal.

Thus it seems that while the earlier form of absolutism that underpinned the exclusive (and to an extent, inclusive) truth—claim of one religion over the others (i.e. in respect of being in possession of the truth, regardless of its content—and this applies, *pari pasu,* to strong forms of Judaism, Hinduism, Islam, and Buddhism) is rejected, the absolutism *in* the truth-content (i.e. the meta-*écrit* in respect of the ontology of God, Brahman, Allah, Buddha-nature, the Dreaming, etc.) is not really set aside or bracketed sufficiently. For, to reject the latter kind of absolutism would be to risk undermining the very doctrinal formations and foundations of religious discourse altogether. But it is precisely this *foundationalism* that has for so long stood its own ground within religion, and returned to in the thinking of great philosophers like Plato,

Śankara, Hegel, Schleiermacher, Rahner, *et al.,* which now has come under the hermeneutics of suspicion.

This critique is not simply a rehearse of the attack of positivists and sundry philosophers, although it takes notice of it, but has come about in part as a result of the problems raised regarding the formation and function of God as an onto-theological concept in the history of Western thought, by Nietzsche, Heidegger, Kierkegaard, Barth with other German theologians, later Wittgenstein and French deconstructionists. The metaphysical presupposition or prejudgment implicitly determining much of religious thought anywhere in respect of the ever constant presence, the *sacra arché* and spiritual telos or its inspirations to a transcendentalised utopia, is increasingly thrown into the open as a possible source of all that has gone wrong in the current historical situation. Thus the facticity and particularity of Western thought in respect of its presupposition and faith in the historical uniqueness of its development has been brought home by Heidegger, Gadamer and Derrida among others, who have in their own inimitable ways tried to address the "crisis" (and *décadence*) now upon the very foundations of (modern) European culture, thought, ethics, and religion. The illusion of the apparent universality and necessity of the metaphysical flight has apparently been dispelled by reaching back to the ground of metaphysics and the specific thinking, or the unthought, on which it has been based. Metaphysics is looked upon as a "*supplément*" (addition and substitution) for naive discourse "about things." The thought of Being or "truth" is tantamount to an "intrusion within language's closure upon itself." Grammatology (the science of writing) shakes this complacency, and reveals the inconsistencies in the codes and signifiers which served to maintain the constancy of the logos, the absolute *arché* or *telos* that never was.

IV. Deconstruction in Theology

Similar critical reflections have occurred and are perhaps continuing in Eastern traditions as well, which in the particular case of Buddhism may be traced back to Nāgārjuna's (2nd cent BCE) dialectical critique of Brahmanic metaphysics and orthopraxy, continued in Vijñānāvada's ambivalence over the Absolute of Vedānta, and more recently in Nishitani's work on *No-thingness* (combining Buddhist and Heideggerian insights for a critique of "Eastern modernity").

In the Anglo-American world there have been echoes of this problematic in the so-called "Death of God" theology (with Robinson's *Honest to God* assault) and in the deconstructionist twist it (has) received in the hands of Thomas Altizer Jr., Carl Raschke, Robert Scharlemann, and Mark C. Taylor. Even though, it may be pointed out, that while in deconstructive a/theology the project of revealing the "absence" and "NOTHNESS" of the theistic image of deity is meticulously completed, there is implicit in its discourse a "leap" (transgression) beyond the text (the "Word," which writing both forgets and wrenches from its *unconscious*) to the projected (often interiorised into the equally abnegated self) return of the "noncentred whole," the "Wholly Other." It is in the *otherness,* the *Alterity,* of God which theism had forgotten and which lay buried beneath the metaphysical speculations, that the "traces" can be retrieved. This "absent" God is discernible only in the "space" marked by the *uncertainty* of its *différance* (read as Hegel's subversion of absolute idealism in the notion of absolute negativity). The play on "*difference*" harkens back via Derrida to Heidegger's uncovering of the "ontological difference," that is, the difference between being and entities, as well as to his larger task of the "destruction" (*Destruktion*) of the history of ontology. A "spacing" is then made possible which does not tolerate an identity (total self-presence) that closes in upon itself. While the entitative notion of God as the transtemporal or metaphysical entity ("being as Being") is arrested (and dismembered), along with all the conventional signifiers attuned to this traditional conception, God is re-conceived (re-constituted) as the being that is not God or, better still, when God is not being God. It is in its *totaliter aliter,* without remainder, as the "negated presence" rather than absolute nihilism, that truth arises as the "ghost" that continues to dance on the tomb of the dead (Crucified) God: "a self-consciousness which itself becomes absolute by passing through the death of God."

Bonhoeffer (already in conversation with followers of Mahatma Gandhi who had raised doubts about the historicity of Jesus) is particularly important in this regard for being perhaps the earliest of such "deconstructionists" to have issued the challenge to Christianity to rethink its traditional self-understanding. As he wrote from his prison cell: "Religious people speak of God when human perception is (often just from laziness) at an end, or human resources fail: it is really always the *Deux ex machina* they call to their aid, either for the so-called solving of insoluble problems or as support in human failure—always, that is to say, helping out human weakness or on the borders of human existence. Of necessity, that can only go on until men can, by their own strength, push those borders a little further, so that God becomes superfluous as a *Deus ex machina*." Of course, while in one sense Bonhoeffer was, as the saying goes, pulling the rug from under the feet of the Church, in another sense he was preparing Christianity for a radically different conception of the "ultimate" in his rejection of the metaphysical and theological notion of deity, and in his concern with the secular world. This challenge is still being worked out for its fuller implications in Christian theology (particularly with Barthian thesis of the historical reality of revelation that cuts across theism and atheism, believers and unbelievers alike); and it has had a tremendous impact on "third world" theology as well (especially on liberation theology). But in other ways, the discourse has not moved much beyond the acceptance of Christ as the incarnation of truth [or the erased term] in history.

There is a further difficulty with deconstructive a/theology. While it does make considerable overtures towards, particularly Buddhist tradition (most evident in Altizer's recent writings with unmistakeable Buddhistic signifiers), the concepts from varying traditions are treated as "remains, what is left over, to be used or discarded at the whim of the theologian," without giving full regard to their context, or to the damning indictment their further *reductio* might entail for what a/theology would not withstand, viz. its own self-destruction. Thus "Buddhist nothingness," "śunya," the "utter self-emptying and emptiness of . . ." abound in the rhetorical fits of a/theology. Once emptied, however, the "space" is quickly filled up again—not on account of the spectre of relativism, but in the anxiety of stark nihilism, the *abyss* that might swallow everything/being and itself too. But why does a/theology evade this ultimate consequence of its own deconstituting endeavour? If a/theology is to be true to the dual *aporias* of pluralism and radical deconstruction, must it not countenance the possibility of its own structural subversion, capitulation? Indeed, there is already some disquiet among deconstructive theologians as they criticise each other's *excesses,* quasi-transcendentalisms, false inversions (e.g. of the *Geist in the structure and language of the Unconscious*), and misappropriation of the role of interpretation in the deconstructive enterprise.

V. The Post-onto/theocentric Challenge

In the light of the foregoing analysis, the challenge staring us in the face in the late hour of the 20th century may be formulated thus: We might well be content and adapt ourselves to living in a pluralist milieu wherein each one accepts and tolerates the respective "faith-path" chosen by adherents of other religions, but can we accept that there is therefore a plurality of "absolutes"? That alongside God, there is in the deepest (or "highest") reality, also Allah, Brahman, the Dreaming, Buddha-nature (or the converse)? That these are not simply different manifestations of the same "One and Only One," or "Not-Two, nor-Many," "Not Another" (*non aliud*) being or truth, but are Ultimates in their own right? Or, we might be forced to ask, where does radical pluralism draw the line before the legitimacy it accords to each religion transgresses the boundary of the truth-claim with respect to the "Ultimate" in each religion? The question is not about the different ways in which the Ultimate is conceived (e.g. as the absolute in identity, in relativity, in *identity-in-difference*, in non-difference, in utter *difference*, or its "*altar-ity*," and so on), but it is about the presupposition that beyond the indefinite dissemination of the signs there is a referent (a signified), some constant, whether in its "pleroma" (infinite, "fullness") or its "emptiness" ("non-beingness," "nothingness"), that answers to the description? (Even if that absolutising is intransitive, i.e. without subject or predicate.)

And what response can a sanguine religious pluralism make to those (within religion and outside religion, say, in philosophy and science) who reject the idea or possibility of any "absolute" altogether as a hopelessly futile metaphysical project in whose traps religions fell and have remained entangled? This critique, then, disqualifies any and all claims to universal truth in or across religions: all religious truth is henceforth considered to be local, partial, and constructed. Here all truth stands de-absolutised. So the differences in myth and doctrine across religions are not differences in truth-claims nor are they "alternative maps, in different projections, of the universe . . ." but are simply different ways of making sense of the existential facticity of life and different ways of dealing with this non-transcendental or relative subjectivity in the day to day activities and concerns of people. (While Hick appears to be saying something close to this, for him the *soteriological* significance, and its afterlife verification, nonetheless leads us away from the relative to some unarticulated notion of the absolute, once again.)

Again, it is insisted, the differing orientations are not simply variations on the same invariant objective truth, but categorically distinct historical experiences which resist reduction to a unitary symbolic process, or revelation, or way of knowing. It resists reduction to even anything like a common denominator of the rather safe and pervasively non-cognitive "numinous" that Otto sought on the cognitive model provided by Kant's epistemology, much less to the spiritual unity or its *telos* in transcendental subjectivity as pursued by theologians inspired by the Cartesian-Husserlian project in phenomenology.

Hence to rescue religion and maintain genuine plurality of spiritual life-worlds, some argue, one ought seriously to consider rejecting belief in the Absolute (of any kind or form) altogether, and any claim to the universal and normative for all and sundry. For it is this belief, fundamental to most if not all religions, rather than the confrontations of differences in conceptions of the absolute and the practices and histories of the religious traditions amidst us, that gives rise to intolerance, competition, self-righteousness, dogmatism, barbarism and such adverse conducts as the other history of religions has made amply evident.

Indeed, it would be argued in such a critique that overall what is more important to emphasise is the fact of the differences *qua difference* in the cluster of social-historical phenomena, and irreducibly so. And that there need be assumed nothing in particular, or of a general kind, of which these are differences; that is to say, at no point in the inquiry should one presume to have arrived at an understanding of some common "Archimedean centre" ("the centre of the centre"), from which the lines of differentiation have, as it were, shot out. This predilection towards finding the core central myth, the universal arche(type), the projected confirmation in eschatology/soteriology/orthopraxy, and such other epithets ("name of the names") that express this universalist proclivity across the differences in the religious orientations (described to us profusely by anthropologists and religious dialogists) ought to be indefinitely deferred, suspended, or even erased. Nor need this be a cause for celebration, but possibly a sombre lamentation that such a goal is, in the final analysis, unattainable.

The Jainas in India pre-empted this move by suggesting that it is neither possible *nor necessary* to have an absolute view on anything, still less on matters of "ultimate concern," such as whether there is or is not an absolute. (Pyrrho perhaps imbibed "imperturbability" and "*epoche*" in matters ultimate from the Jainas when he accompanied Alexander to India.) Genuine tolerance and "conversation," the Jainas preached, is only possible when "one-sidedness" (*ekānta*) in thinking is clearly set aside. (Jaina philosophy, it may be noted in passing, provided a seven-term dialectic which allowed the possibility of holding, that from varying points of view: "x is," "x is not," "x both is and is not," "x is inexpressible," "x is both not and inexpressible," "x is, is not, and is also inexpressible.")

The challenge in the "post-modern" human condition targets at the underfoot of radical pluralism in suggesting that there is neither one "absolute" or "decisive" truth-content (logos, presence) in religion (contrary to the exclusivist presupposition), nor a plurality of expressions or articulations inscripting the same deep truth-content (contrary to the inclusivists assumption). Indeed, it argues that all conceptions of truth are equally constructed artifacts, which have thus to be contextualised and understood in the horizons of the disparate and possibly unique experiences, tradition and aspirations of each cultural group.

If the arguments on which this challenge is pivoted go through, then what kind of *pluralism* is possible, without risking ambiguity, equivocation, deep uncertainty and *angst* that characterise radical pluralism? Is "critical pluralism" that can countenance and come to terms, albeit creatively rather than destructively, with the kinds of problems and questions raised, a real possibility? Might this be the direction or turn we could more fruitfully take in our reflections at this juncture of the history of reflections on religion and particularly on the confrontations of vastly different traditions, denominations and sub-cultures within and between the religions of the world? . . .

Suggestions for Further Reading

Adler, Mortimer J. *Truth in Religion: The Plurality of Religions and the Unity of Truth*. London: Collier Macmillan, 1990.

Anderson, Sir James Norman Dalrymple. *Christianity and World Religions: The Challenge of Pluralism*. Downers Grove, IL: Inter-Varsity Press, 1984.

Bilimoria, Purushottama, ed. "Tradition and Pluralism." *Sophia: A Journal for Philosophical Theology and Cross-Cultural Philosophy of Religion* 34 (March–April):1995.

Chatterjee, Margaret. "Reflections on Religious Pluralism in the Indian Context." In *Culture and Modernity: East–West Philosophic Perspectives*, edited by Eliot Deutsch. Honolulu: University of Hawaii Press, 1991.

Christian, William. *Oppositions of Religious Doctrines*. New York: Herder and Herder, 1972.

Cobb, John. *Beyond Dialogue*. Philadelphia: Fortress Press, 1982.

Connolly, William E. *The Bias of Pluralism*. New York: Atherton Press, 1969.

Coward, Harold G. *Pluralism: Challenge to World Religions*. Maryknoll, NY: Orbis Books, 1985.

———. *Religious Pluralism and the World Religions*. Madras, India: Radhakrishnan Institute, University of Madras, 1983.

———, ed. *Modern Indian Responses to Religious Pluralism*. Albany: State University of New York Press, 1987.

Copleston, Frederick Charles. *Religion and the One: Philosophies East and West*. New York: Crossroad, 1982.

Das, Bhagavan. *The Essential Unity of All Religions*. Wheaton, IL: The Theosophical Society, 1939.

D'Costa, Gavin. *Theology and Religious Pluralism: The Challenge of Other Religions*. New York: Basil Blackwell, 1986.

———, ed. *Christian Uniqueness Reconsidered: The Myth of a Pluralistic Theology of Religions*. Maryknoll, NY: Orbis Books, 1990.

Dean, Thomas. *Religious Pluralism and Truth: Essays on Cross-Cultural Philosophy of Religion.* Albany: State University of New York Press, 1995.

Donovan, Peter. "The Intolerance of Religious Pluralism." *Religious Studies* 26 (June 1993):217–229.

Hick, John, ed. "Religious Pluralism." *Faith and Philosophy* 4 (October 1988).

———. *God and the Universe of Faiths.* London: Macmillan, 1973.

———. *God Has Many Names.* Philadelphia: Westminster Press, 1980.

———. *Problems of Religious Pluralism.* New York: St. Martin's Press, 1985.

———. *Truth and Dialogue in World Religions.* Philadelphia: Westminster Press, 1974.

———. *An Interpretation of Religion: Human Responses to the Transcendent.* New Haven: Yale University Press, 1989.

Huxley, Aldous. *The Perennial Philosophy.* New York: Harper & Row, 1945.

Knitter, Paul F. *No Other Name? A Critical Survey of Christian Attitudes Toward the World Religions.* Maryknoll, NY: Orbis Books, 1985.

Kraemer, H. *The Christian Message in a Non-Christian World.* London: Edinburgh House Press, 1938.

———. *Why Christianity of All Religions?* London: Lutterworth Press, 1962.

Lipner, Julius. "Truth-Claims and Inter-religious Dialogue." *Religious Studies* 12 (1976): 217–230.

Nasr, Seyyed Hossein. *Knowledge and the Sacred.* Albany, NY: State University of New York Press, 1989.

Newman, Jay. *Foundations of Religious Tolerance.* Toronto: University of Toronto Press, 1982.

Radhakrishnan, S. *Eastern Religions and Western Thought.* 2d edition. London: Oxford University Press, 1940.

Rouner, Leroy S., ed. *Religious Pluralism.* Notre Dame, IN: University of Notre Dame Press, 1984.

Senor, Thomas D., ed. "Part II Religious Pluralism" (articles by Plantinga, van Inwagen, Runzo, and Mavordes defending exclusivism or critiquing pluralism) in *The Rationality of Belief and the Plurality of Faith: Essays in Honor of William P. Alston.* Ithaca, NY: Cornell University Press, 1995.

Smart, Ninian. *A Dialogue of Religions.* SCM Press, 1960.

Smith, Huston. *The Forgotten Truth; The Primordial Tradition.* New York: Harper & Row, 1976.

Smith, William Cantwell. *Religious Diversity.* Edited by Willard G. Oxtoby. New York: Harper & Row, 1976.

———. *Towards a World Theology.* Philadelphia: Westminster Press, 1981.

Stetson, Brad. *Pluralism and Particularity in Religious Belief.* Westport, CT: Praeger, 1994.

Tillich, Paul. *Christianity and the Encounter of the World Religions.* New York: Columbia University Press, 1963.

Ward, Keith. "Truth and the Diversity of Religions." *Religious Studies* 26 (March 1990):1–18.

———. *Religion and Revelation.* Oxford, England: Clarendon Press, 1994.

Yandell, Keith. "Religious Experience and Rational Appraisal." *Religious Studies* 8 (June 1974).

Yearley, Lee H. *New Religious Virtues and the Study of Religion.* Phoenix, AZ: Arizona State University Press, 1994.

The Individual's Religion

Sociology of religion emphasizes religious groups and social expressions of religion. The individual members of religious groups are, however, social actors—that is, persons with motives and meanings of their own. Although the individual actor's attitudes, conceptions, and behavior may be strongly influenced by social groups, there is no neat or deterministic correlation between what the group believes and what the individual member personally holds central. To understand religious behavior, we must know how religion shapes and is expressed by the *individual* actor.

Chapter 2 suggested how religion provides *meaning,* in the context of *belonging* to a religious group. This chapter examines the processes by which the individual adopts and becomes committed to a religious worldview and community. We might think of a religious group as a *community of memory,* in which past, present, and future members are linked in a chain of collective memory (or tradition, in the broadest sense of the word). In rituals and other religious practices, the group reminds itself of important events, relationships, and meanings that are central to the religious group's very reason for existence. The re-creation and transmission of this dynamic collective memory is a central feature of religion, but—as this chapter and Chapter 8 suggest—conditions in modern social life make sustaining a community of memory very difficult (Hervieu-Léger, 1998, 2000). First, we will explore the social forces shaping and maintaining the individual's worldview as it develops and changes over the life cycle. Second, we will analyze the process of conversion by which an individual may dramatically change that worldview. Finally, we will examine the

process of commitment, by which old and new believers alike commit themselves to the group of fellow believers.

SHAPING THE INDIVIDUAL'S RELIGION

The meaning-providing and belonging features of religion, described in
Chapter 2, are important to shaping the individual's religion. Through *social*
interaction the individual learns religious meanings and experiences a sense of
personal and group identity. The individual subjectively experiences religion in
social contexts, influenced by socially shaped, learned meanings.

Meaning, Belonging, and Identity

These learned meanings are conveyed by specific people. The child does not
(indeed cannot) internalize the group's meaning system without having a sense
of belonging to the group in which that meaning system is grounded.
Typically, in societies with relatively homogeneous meaning systems, belonging to the group means coming to take its worldview for granted.

In societies with competing worldviews, socialization into one's own group
includes some awareness of the existence and differences of other groups
around one's own. The child's identity typically includes an important sense of
belonging to a specific religion, ethnic group, or nation, as well as a feeling of
contrast with others not of that religion, ethnic group, or nation.

Religion is often an important part of how an entire *group* thinks of itself:
what it means to be "one of us." For example, the religious identity of "Italian-
American Catholic" includes religion and other political and cultural meanings
pertaining to belonging to a particular community. The connection of religion
and group identity is explored in more depth in Chapter 6. Another link of
religion and identity includes all the ways that religion informs the individual's
self-identity.

Self-identity refers to each person's biographical arrangement of meanings and interpretations that form a somewhat coherent sense of "who am I?"
Often the question "Who am I?" is answered in terms of "This is where I
belong." Thus, a woman might describe herself as "a mother, a wife, a Catholic,
a Polish-American, a member of the town volunteer ambulance squad, in the
church choir, and vice president of the PTA." These roles represent not merely
formal memberships but—more important—social locations of her identity.
Religion pervades all such social roles in relatively undifferentiated societies. In
modern, highly differentiated societies, however, religion is only one source of
the individual's sense of belonging and identity.

Self-identity is profoundly *social,* because it is constructed through ongoing
interactions with others. Although those others—especially important persons
like parents, spouse, close friends—are powerful influences on the individual's
developing self-identity, their influence is never deterministic. Nor is identity
fixed. It is continually changing as the individual takes on new roles, interacts
with new people, and grows older. Even in very rigid, traditional societies, for

example, a woman's self-identity as a new mother is very different from her later self-identity as an old woman.

The construction of self-identity in modern societies may, however, be qualitatively different from that in traditional societies. In modern societies, the individual's social situation is not rigidly determined by *ascribed* (socially fixed) statuses and roles. Thus, self-identity tends to be malleable, selectively constructed, and changing (cf. Giddens, 1991:53–55). In late modernity, individual self-identity is more eclectic, more like *bricolage*—an edifice constructed from a wide range of culturally available options (Beckford, 1989; Luckmann, 1967).

Components of the individual's self-identity, including religion, family identification, ethnic identity, aesthetics, and even gender, appear to be more open to reflexive *choice* in the modern world. Religion thus becomes an optional resource for the ongoing project of constructing personal identity. If this thesis about modern self-identity is accurate, it means we need to think of such social processes as childhood socialization, conversion, and commitment as more tentative and changeable ongoing projects.

Like all identity projects, the individual's religion develops and changes over the life course. A person is not born with a set of religious beliefs and practices; religion is developed and nurtured (or ignored) in the socialization of the child. Although many have reached an identifiable religious perspective or commitment by young adulthood, this is not the end of their religious development. The individual's religion continues to develop and change, perhaps less dramatically, throughout the rest of life. Indeed, the very meaning of "being religious" changes in different periods of life, and the place of religion in the individual's life also changes. In keeping with this dynamic perspective on religious development, this section follows the life cycle of an individual believer in a contemporary Western society. It focuses (as does religious practice itself) on certain critical periods: early childhood, adolescence, marriage and procreation, and old age and dying. One intermediate period, for which there are no special religious rituals or events, is included: middle age.

One of the difficulties in describing an adequately complex picture of religious development in modern societies is that much of the research in this area has focused on narrowly defined church-oriented religion. Not only does much modern religious life take place outside religious organizations, but also religious affiliation is not a very satisfactory indicator of each individual's actual religion. (See Chapter 4 for related methodological issues.) The following description, then, suggests a line of reasoning that future studies might pursue in exploring the relationship between religion and family, community, identity, life cycle, and human development.

Childhood, Family, and Community

Childhood Early childhood is a critical period in the development of the individual's religion. The child begins to learn what it means to be "one of us" (our society, our ethnic group, our religion, our family, our tribe, etc.). Specifically, in socialization, the individual internalizes the social group's moral norms and basic values. Socialization also accounts for the development of the individual's attitudes and values, such as attitudes about authority or the value of acquiring material possessions. These attitudes and values are closely linked with religious belief, and they vary according to the type of religiosity that individuals acquire through socialization into their group.

In relatively simple societies, there is no distinction between socialization into the larger group and religious socialization. Becoming religious—however defined in that society—is simply part of gradually becoming an adult, responsible member of society. Religious roles in simple societies are not differentiated from other roles such as mother, healer, or chieftain. Similarly, the child's religious roles simply involve the child's participation in ongoing social activities. The child might assist the father in his work and observe the father praying over his tools. Or a child might learn, in helping the grandmother, that one should bless the hearth and fire each morning upon rekindling the fire. He or she might learn the central myths of the tribe from sitting beside a storyteller after a meal. The pervasiveness of religion in simple societies enables the religious socialization of children to occur informally and continuously. Complex societies, by contrast, place more emphasis on intellectual learning and formal religious knowledge. The society's differentiation of religious knowledge from other relevant formal knowledge complicates the child's acquisition of religious knowledge.

Learning the content of the meaning system of one's group is, however, not sufficient. Children need to internalize this meaning system, to make it their own. A computer could teach a child an entire catechism, but that knowledge of itself would probably have very little significance in the child's life. Internalization of the group's meaning system occurs through interaction of the child with specific other members of the group who mediate the group's way of thinking and doing to the child. In early socialization, the child's family is the foremost influence.

The Family The first, perhaps most enduring source of the individual's sense of belonging is the family. The very young child is not *in* society but is a part of the family, only indirectly participating in society. Later full participation in society is typically organized according to values, motivations, and attitudes acquired in childhood. One study of religious socialization reminds us that "the most memorable aspects of growing up religious occur within families, especially through the daily routines and sacred objects, the holidays, and the intimate relationships of which families are composed" (Wuthnow, 1999:69).

Rituals and symbols allocate identity even in early childhood. One of the most significant and widespread rituals is naming the child. The choice of given names, the affirmation of kinship networks (e.g., naming the child after a grandparent), and the bestowing of the family name (or refusal to bestow it) are highly symbolic acts. Many groups have special ritual occasions for giving a new family member this initial identity. Other occasions of childhood (e.g., birthday celebrations) also affirm the child's identity. The status of the child is relatively clear in most societies. Thus, major rituals and symbols of identity are often used to make important transitions (such as the identity change from child to adult). The family home is also a religious site—the location of sacred space and objects, the place where religious practices occur. For example, a Mexican-American home is likely to have a home altar, where the mother arranges candles and religious objects, photos of loved ones, and other reminders for family and individual prayer or devotions. As Chapter 4 reminds us, overemphasis on official religion and public religious services has diminished our awareness of domestic religious ritual and symbolism. Yet, especially for women and children, the family and home are central religious sites.

Many parents may try to reproduce a religious worldview for their children. For some, their children's religious training is a major consideration in adults' decisions to reestablish their church attendance (Gallup and Castelli, 1989:144; Roozen et al., 1990). One study (Wilson and Sandomirsky, 1991) found that marriage and parenthood were the strongest predictors of whether women who were previously religiously unaffiliated would join and become active in a religious group. The authors suggest that, for women at least, the decision to affiliate with a church or synagogue is an interdependent one, aimed at a collective good for the whole family. A related phenomenon, however, is that once the family "nest" is nearly empty, parents of the current middle-aged generation (sometimes called "baby boomers") are less likely to participate in their religious group than parents of younger children (Roozen, 1993). Indeed, it appears that the "return" to organized religion that the media touted in the 1990s was just a temporary involvement, done for the "sake of the children" (Roof, 1999:232–234).

Family involvement in official religious activities and religious education for children declined substantially in the latter half of the twentieth century. In 1952 only 6 percent of adults in the United States had received no religious training as a child; this figure had risen to 18 percent in 1988 (Gallup and Castelli, 1989:66–68). Religious socialization is far more complex than merely ensuring that children attend Sunday school or Hebrew school or catechism classes. Although other agents of socialization, throughout the entire life course, contribute to a person's religious involvement, early religious socialization appears to be the strongest influence (Sherkat, 1998). Informal religious socialization is also formative, however. One study found that family roles themselves—actual or fantastic—were an important factor in shaping children's images of God. Children identified God with parental (or grandparental) roles and qualities: big, authoritative, nurturing, understanding, forgiving, controlling, wise, angry, and so on (Heller, 1986; see also Wuthnow, 1999). Regardless of race, socioeconomic status, or religious affiliation, children in another study (Dickie et al., 1997) perceived God as like their parents in terms of nurturance and power. There were differences according to gender, however; girls' God-images were more strongly linked to their parents' style of discipline and parental attributes of authority and power than boys' perceptions of God.

The family is more than an agent of religious socialization. It is often, indeed, a primary religious group, a fundamental unit of the institution of religion. The trite adage "the family that prays together stays together" is probably reversed in its reasoning. It is entirely likely that any cohesive family expresses, rather than originates, its unity in rituals and symbols that, in most cultures, are also fundamentally religious. At the same time, religion has historically legitimated the family, established rituals to celebrate family unity, and provided norms and social controls to protect the institution of the family. The scope of the family unit in modern society is greatly narrowed from the extended family and large kinship networks of earlier periods. Like other bonds, modern commitments to family may be shorter-term commitments (Rubin, 1996), weakening families as sources of ongoing identity formation.

The Community Another major source of identity is based on the individual's sense of belonging to a distinctive group—tribe, nation, ethnic group. The U.S. and Canadian history of immigration makes ethnicity an important factor in many people's experience. In the second half of the twentieth century, much of Europe also experienced considerable immigration from parts of the world where religions were dramatically different from Europe's. In a culturally plural society, a close-knit ethnic community may be an important plausibility structure supporting the group's religious worldview (Berger, 1967:46). Ethnicity may be an important basis for a person's choices of neighborhood, friends, job, marriage partner, leisure-time activities, and organizational memberships. For another person, ethnicity may be irrelevant to such choices.

The process by which the child is socialized into the family and ethno-religious group is gradual. It begins with the child's simple experiencing of group membership as a taken-for-granted part of life. Later the child may learn terms for identification with the group (i.e., "I'm a Catholic," "My people are Korean"). In a multicultural context, these group identities are often linked with a sense of "us" compared with multiple Others ("them"). The child's sense of "us" is not necessarily oppositional; just as they learn to distinguish family from nonfamily, children also learn how to distinguish other ethnic or religious groups from the groups with which they are identified. One anthropological study in an ethnically homogeneous south Asian neighborhood of London found that religion, far more than ethnicity, was an important feature of children's self-identities. Hindu, Muslim, and Sikh children studied and played together amicably, even though in their parents' homelands these religious groups have historically been in conflict. The children (7–10) experienced elements of each others' religion, as well as the dominant Christian culture, in part because the school encouraged plays and celebrations to learn about each others' cultures. The study found that the children had fairly accurate ideas of core differences among the religions and a strong sense of belonging to their own. Even as they crossed boundaries to participate in each other's religious traditions, they kept a clear sense of the distinction. For example, Hindu, Sikh, and Muslim children often exchanged cards or gifts at Christmas. One Muslim girl explained that Christmas gifts were okay, because "Jesus is our prophet . . . BUT we do not believe he is the son of God" (quoted in Larson, 2000).

The communities of family, neighborhood, friendship, and ethno-religious group provide an initial sense of belonging and a foundation for identity. Subsequent communities provide a base of support for maintaining that identity or for changing it (as our later discussion of conversion will show). They are also the social bases for the continued plausibility of the group's entire meaning system (Berger, 1967:45–47). Thus, the meaning-providing and belonging aspects of religion are directly connected.

Social changes and developments such as *pluralism* (i.e., the coexistence of competing worldviews) seem to have undermined some of the cohesiveness and effectiveness of these communities. As children emerge from the taken-for-granted small communities of family and neighbors, they will probably encounter a bewildering variety of other groups with other belief systems and ways of life. Some individuals remain immersed in the initial network that supported the plausibility of early beliefs and identity; others detach themselves from these bonds and seek elsewhere a social base for their beliefs and sense of who they are. The very existence of this element of *choice* in identity and belief system characterizes only certain kinds of society. The possibility of detaching oneself from the taken-for-granted beliefs and social groups into which one has been socialized provides greater freedom—and simultaneously makes both belief and identity problematic (Berger, 1967:137, 151).

There is considerable evidence that both ethnicity and religion may have become less salient as sources of identity for many Americans. For white Americans at least, ethnic identity, like religious identity, has become essentially voluntary (Hammond, 2000). Since race is still largely an ascribed characteristic in the United States, despite the increasing proportion of the population that is of mixed racial and ethnic backgrounds, nonwhites experience more limited options for their ethnic self-identities (Waters, 1996). Nevertheless, they also construct ethnic self-identities creatively and eclectically by choosing *which* cultural elements to make personally meaningful (see Conzen et al., 1990; Sollors, 1989). For example, one individual might choose to make participation in an ethnic congregation a central expression of self-identity, while another might emphasize ethnic dances and festivals.

In a pluralistic context, it does not even matter whether the chosen ethnic identity is accurately part of the individual's ancestry. For example, one African-American woman who was an enthusiastic member of a Brazilian dance troupe in Chicago explained that she had no reason to believe that her ancestors came from Brazil or the parts of Africa from which Brazilian blacks may have come. Nonetheless, Brazilian music and dance were now the most valued part of her current identity as a black person in the United States. In modern, pluralistic societies, individuals are relatively freed of structurally given identities, relatively freed to pick and choose culturally available elements to construct a picture of who they are (see Conzen et al., 1990; Sollors, 1989). Ethnic and religious elements of self-identity thus function as *culturally plausible myths*—stories out of which one lives.

This connection between the ethnic and religious elements of self-identity helps us understand the special role of ethnic congregations in the lives of new immigrants. A study of two Hindu communities in California found that they were substantially modifying Hindu practice to adapt to the U.S. religious climate, for example, by organizing the equivalents of Sunday school and worship groups—which do not typically exist in India. Through participation in ethnic congregations of Americanized Hinduism, new immigrants could both reaffirm their ethno-religious heritage and come to "fit in" in a way that is culturally recognizable by Americans (Kurien, 1998). Similarly, many American Muslim mosques serve as the place where marriage ceremonies take place and where community celebrations involving feasting and dancing are held; this is in marked contrast to Middle Eastern Muslim practice which treats such uses of the mosque as highly inappropriate (Haddad and Smith, 1996).

Many immigrant religions emphasize religious practices in the home. Both ethnicity and religion are celebrated, simultaneously, at home shrines and altars, domestic rituals (such as lighting candles and incense), prayers and blessings, and special holiday meals. A study of immigrant congregations in Houston found that such domestic religious practices were important in reproducing ethnicity for young and old alike (Ebaugh and Chafetz, 2000a: 385–401). They are important (often, more important than what happens at the public religious services) for the socialization of children into their ethno-religious tradition. They confirm central religious roles for women in the transmission of both ethnic and religious practices. And they produce patterns of sociability in the home and community that support ethno-religious identities. This study also found, however, that ethno-religious identities were more conflicted for subsequent generations. One youth explained:

> Hinduism is an important part of life; it sort of defines me. It shows myself and others where I come from. But it is different for me than it would be for my parents because they are used to more traditional ways. I believe that my being both Indian and American causes me to regard religion in a different way from them. But it is important because it is part of my culture and I'll never deny it. (quoted in Ebaugh and Chafetz, 2000a: 439)

Problems of Family and Community in Contemporary Society Many processes in contemporary society have seriously weakened the ability of family, community, and religion to offer the individual a stable source of belonging and identity. Neighborhood communities are decreasingly characterized by face-to-face intimacy and personal, affective bonds. Furthermore, family, neighborhood, and religion alike have been undermined by **privatization**— the process by which certain institutional spheres become removed from effective roles in the public sphere (especially in the arena of economic production and power). Chapter 8 will examine the impact of privatization on religion in greater detail, but it is important here to note the link between privatization of the family and religion.

The power of religion to legitimate other institutions such as the family has been undermined. There is little support for the family from public institutions. What support exists is largely due to the family's significance as an economic unit of consumption and to the family's symbolic importance (e.g., in the rhetoric of politicians). These processes, together with the pluralism of society, have weakened the norms governing family interaction. At the same time, however, greater demands are made on the family. The weaknesses of the neighborhood and community in providing support for members' identities result in greater pressure on the family to be a complete repository of identity (Brittan, 1977:58, 59).

Economic and demographic changes have made the type of family idealized in the 1950s (i.e., two or three children living with both biological parents, the mother not working outside the home) only a small minority of U.S. families today (Marler, 1995). Single-parent families, blended families, adoptive families, homosexual families, commuter families (where one spouse works in a distant city and commutes "home" on weekends), and dual-career families are also prevalent patterns for family life. In recent decades, perhaps the biggest single stress on the family's ability to meet its members' needs has been workplace and related economic changes. Compared to the 1950s, parents have had to spend greatly increased proportions of their time on the job in order to provide for their families (Hewlett, 1991; Schor, 1992).

As the individual's control over life in the public sphere diminishes—and as the institutions of the public sphere become less and less concerned with providing meaning for their participants—the individual seeks more fulfillment, security, control, and meaning in the private sphere (Berger, 1967; Luckmann, 1967:106–114). Privatization thrusts the search for personal identity out of the public sphere. The nature of work and division of labor in modern societies make it difficult for people to derive their primary sense of identity from their work role. Yet the family cannot sustain the burden of providing all personal identity for its members.

The local community (as a social unit, not just a political or geographical one) has also been undermined. Religion has traditionally been inextricably intertwined with community; the boundaries of one were frequently coextensive with the boundaries of the other. Social and geographical mobility, however, along with the influx and incorporation of waves of immigrants, has changed the patterns of community in U.S. society. Local communities are increasingly voluntaristic, segmented, and irrelevant to institutions of the public sphere. The voluntary nature of community has the advantage of freeing individuals to choose their community of identification, but it also reduces their power relative to institutions of the public sphere and their ability to provide stable sources of identity for members. The process of privatization is not inexorable, but its impact on family and community is already evident.

Alternative Modes of Family and Community One historical alternative to the dominant mode of family and community has been the ethno-religious group that withdraws from the society in order to preserve its distinctiveness. Examples of this kind of community include the Jewish Hassidim, the Amish, Doukhobors, and Hutterites. The Hassidim are particularly interesting because their withdrawal is not to a rural refuge; instead, they have organized their life within urban areas to sustain their religious identity.

The Hassidim are an ultraorthodox group of Jews, mostly first- and second-generation immigrants who fled persecution in central and eastern Europe (see Belcove-Shalin, 1995; Kephart and Zellner, 1991; Poll, 1969; Shaffir, 1974). There are proportionately few U.S. and Canadian converts to

---

**BOX 3.1 Cross-Cultural Comparison:
An Ethno-Religious Community**

Italian-Americans who immigrated to New York City between the 1880s and 1920s developed a close-knit community in East Harlem around their parish church, Church of Our Lady of Mount Carmel. Their language, family patterns, and other aspects of rural Italian culture were embedded in and expressed by their religious practices, such as the annual nine-day *festa* of the parish's patron saint (Orsi, 1985). Following centuries-old traditions from their old country, they celebrated their parish's patron saint's feast day with a major procession in the streets, devotions and Masses in the church, followed by eating, drinking, dancing and merriment. With greater prosperity, the Italian residents became dispersed in the suburbs, often no longer living in ethnically homogeneous neighborhoods. And their old neighborhood became predominantly Puerto Rican, later intermingled with Mexicans, Dominicans, and West Africans. The Italian-Americans still sponsor and produce the *festa* in East Harlem, but the events have become multiethnic.

Interestingly, Haitian pilgrims from other parts of the city (and, often, from distant cities) predominate numerically in the celebration, because Our Lady of Mount Carmel is identified with sites of religious power in Haiti—including popular religious sites of Creole folk Catholicism and Vodou (McAlister, 1998; see also Brown, 1991).

- Is it possible to separate ethnicity from religion as a basis of community? As a basis of self-identity?
- Do congregations of religious groups serve different functions for new immigrants than for members whose families have been living in the society for several generations?
- If a community of memory coheres around a tradition, such as that of turn-of-the-(twentieth)-century rural Italian Catholic culture transposed to New York City, does the religious community of another Catholic culture, such as that of rural Haiti, practice the *same* religion?

Hassidism, although the largest branch (Lubavitcher) proselytizes successfully among less orthodox Jews (Davidman, 1991; Davidman and Stocks, 1995; Kaufman, 1995; Shaffir, 1978). An estimated 200,000 Hassidim live in the United States, and large Hassidic communities also exist in Canada. The Hassidic community is carefully organized to enable members to follow the 613 rules regulating everyday life for orthodox Jews. Members must live close enough to the synagogue to be able to walk there for services on the Sabbath. Food that passes the highest levels of kosher regulations must be available. Outside the home, men and women are segregated at all times, partly because of religious rules designed to protect men from defilement by contact with a menstruating woman. Thus, the men of the community arrange their work so that they have no interaction with women (e.g., by working in the neighborhood or in an all–male trade). The men further arrange their work time to be free for frequent daytime religious services.

The Hassidic community has its own system of law and its own shops, trades, and schools. The rebbe (i.e., spiritual master) is the final authority in both spiritual and secular matters. Indeed, there is no distinction between spiritual and secular issues; religion pervades all spheres of life. The socialization of children into the group's approved way of life is relatively unproblematic because of the group's success in limiting outside influences. Children attend religious schools, are heavily occupied with their studies and (in adolescence) with their own religious duties, and are seldom exposed to outside media such as television or movies. The community enclave makes the Hassidic way of life a taken-for-granted reality to the child. Personal identity and a sense of belonging are similarly unproblematic. Roles and norms for appropriate behavior are fixed, with roles available to males varying considerably from those for females. Boys clearly learn their roles as men, and girls learn clear-cut expectations of women; both are rewarded by the close-knit community for meeting these role expectations.

A related kind of local community, the **intentional community,** is one in which members choose to live together communally. This arrangement turns the voluntary nature of its commitment into a virtue. Religious communalism has a long tradition in Western society; monastic communalism dates back to the sixth century C.E. A wide variety of groups dissatisfied with the values and structures of contemporary society have adopted a communitarian form of organization. Intentional communities are potential alternatives to the modes of both family and community life of the larger society. The intentional community allows the group to alter all aspects of social interaction—work, leisure, marriage, family, decision making, education, and so on. Thus, a group can integrate the spheres of work and religion for its members because, in the separate community, these spheres need not be segregated as they are for most members of society. The intentional community also provides a potentially stronger base of personal identity and a stronger sense of belonging than the privatized family and community can. Communitarian groups often resemble traditional communities with their close-knit, affective interpersonal relationships; they differ, however, in being essentially voluntary. Members cannot take their belonging for granted, although certain practices of the group may make it difficult for the member to consider leaving. The group's continual point of reference is the dominant society from which its way of life departs.

Twentieth-century commune movements in the United States, Canada, and parts of Europe illustrate some of these themes. Communes such as Twin Oaks, The Farm, and Ananda organized themselves as alternatives to the dominant mode of personal, family, and community life. Many intentional communities are outgrowths of specifically religious movements; twentieth-century examples include the Jesus People, Hare Krishnas (Krsna Consciousness), Unification Church, Catholic Pentecostalism (later called Catholic Charismatic Renewal), and the Bruderhof (Society of Brothers). Most Catholic Charismatic prayer groups, for example, consist of persons who live in typical middle-class neighborhoods and maintain ordinary middle-class family styles. Their prayer group attempts to provide additional sources of community support, bolstering families and individual members in their distinctive beliefs and practices. This movement also spawned a number of "covenant communities"—intensive groups whose living arrangements, finances, child care, and other family functions are communally shared. Such communities enable members to have a much stronger base of social support for their way of life than would be otherwise possible. Privatization robs communitarian groups of their impact. Establishing a communitarian enclave, no matter how dissident, is a somewhat expanded way of "doing your own thing" in the private sphere of family, religion, and community.

Adolescence

Whereas childhood is a period of initial socialization into a group's way of life and meaning system, the transition to adulthood is a critical transformation in most cultures. Childhood is important in establishing identity and group belonging in a general way, but the transition to adulthood means passage to a new identity involving responsibility, knowledge, ritual and symbolic roles, and acceptance into adult circles. The dramatic quality of this transition is ritually expressed in many cultures by rites of passage for adolescents.

Rites of passage are rituals that accompany a change of place, state, social position, and age. One interpretation suggests that rites of passage enable societies to effect an orderly, meaningful transition for individuals and groups who move from one socially recognized stable state (e.g., childhood) into another (e.g., adulthood). The stable statuses have clearly defined rights, obligations, and roles. The transition between them, however, is dangerous because rights, obligations, and roles are temporarily ambiguous and disordered. Both the social group and the individual member are thus served by these rituals that express, yet circumscribe, the ambiguity and disorder of this period.

These rites consist of three phases: separation, marginality, and aggregation. In the separation phase, ritual actions symbolize detachment of the individual from the previous stable state; the individual metaphorically dies to the old self. The phase of marginality symbolizes the ambiguity of the transition. It represents a structureless realm in which previously taken-for-granted roles and relationships are brought into question. The phase of aggregation unites the individual with others in the new status group. It includes the transmission of knowledge needed by the individual in the new role together with the symbolic features of the new role (e.g., clothing representing the new self). Rites of initiation in simple societies illustrate these processes (Van Gennep, 1960; see also Eliade, 1958; Turner, 1974a, 1974b, 1979).

Contemporary religious groups have rituals that are remnants of earlier rites of passage; baptism, for example, has many features of initiation rites. Confirmation among Christians and bar or bat mitzvahs among Jews also represent the transition from childhood to adulthood in the religious group. These rituals are, however, relatively weak in effecting such transition in modern society. One study noted that, ironically, decline in adolescent religious observance and adherence to traditional beliefs of their religion generally began soon after confirmation, bar or bat mitzvah, or other rituals for adolescents—for most, the last obligatory religious training (Ozorak, 1989). Contemporary rituals of transition are ineffective partly because religious groups allow ritual adulthood to members whom they do not consider really adult. A 13-year-old boy who had recently become a full member of the Presbyterian church (having attended communicants' classes, made a profession of faith, and participated in his first communion service) wrote to the elders (governing board) of the church suggesting changes in church activities. His letter was received with mirth: "Isn't that cute that he thinks he's old enough now to be telling us what to do?" A stronger example of the ambiguity of adult status is the use of forcible "deprogramming," in which parents of legally adult "children" refuse to accept their offsprings' choice of religious identities.

Another more serious basis of this weakness is the quality of adolescence in this society. There is no clear-cut event that confirms adult status. Puberty marks the end of biological childhood, but social adulthood is many years away. The economic structure requires years of preparation for adulthood. A 20-year-old student who is not fully self-sufficient and independent of parental and school control is no longer a child but is not socially recognized as fully adult. Demarcation events such as leaving home, a first self-supporting job, and marriage are recognized as the beginning of adulthood for some individuals but not for others.

Rather than the *medium* by which transition to adulthood is structured, religion in this society often ends up as the *content* over which adolescent rebellion is staged. Adolescence is often a time of identity crisis because the ambiguity is not culturally resolved. The assertion of one's identity (separate from the child's identity, which is defined by family and community values) sometimes takes the form of religious rebellion. The young person tries to assert an adult self by denying those aspects of life perceived as symbolic of the childhood self and tie to parents or family. An obvious example of this rebellion is the youth who joins a religious group that appears diametrically opposed to his or her childhood religion. A very different pattern—the young person who becomes hyperreligious in the childhood religion—is another way of expressing rejection of the family's "low level" of religiosity and their "hypocrisy." A holier-than-thou stance is comparable to changing religions as a way of asserting an independent identity and rejecting parental values (Greeley, 1979). These seemingly dissimilar adolescent strategies may account for a number of contemporary religious expressions: the attraction of youth to countercultural religious movements, their seemingly fanatical adherence to both old and emerging religious groups, and the agonizing struggles between parents and youth over a newly asserted religious identity.

Most research has focused on how successfully specific religious denominations have been able to retain the affiliation, attendance, and participation of succeeding generations of youth members (see Dudley, 1999; Hyde, 1990; Wilson and Sherkat, 1994). They shed some light on the problem of transmission of religious identity in the context of highly voluntaristic and pluralistic societies. For a deeper understanding of the problems of sustaining any community of memory, we need more qualitative studies of the social interactions that incorporate adolescents into such communities.

Marriage, Sexuality, and Procreation

Marriage marks a status passage and the beginning of a new family of procreation. Especially for women in most cultures, marriage is the entry to full adulthood. A wealth of ritual and symbolism accompanies and defines this status passage. Religion often directly promotes the ideal of marriage by setting the norms for marriage and establishing the appropriate behavior of members before, during, and after the marriage ceremony. In societies where several religious or ethno-religious groups coexist, religious groups also delimit the pool of acceptable spouses; members are not supposed to marry "outside the fold."

Images evoked in the marriage rituals of historic religions symbolize this status passage. For instance, the practice of the father "giving away" the bride symbolized the traditional transition of the woman from her father's possession to her husband's. Some religious groups have attempted to change this symbolism to fit the realities of contemporary family life—for example, by having both parents escort the bride to the groom or by allowing the bride to present herself. Nevertheless, the symbolism represents a fundamental transition of status for both bride and groom. Other symbols (e.g., wedding bands, ceremonial binding of hands, exchange of ceremonial crowns) represent the unity of the new social group—husband and wife.

Although historically religion has been closely linked with family life and the regulation of marriage and sexual behavior, its impact in contemporary family life appears to be more indirect and perhaps weakened. Unfortunately, the data available are narrowly limited to the impact of religion on marriage in four particular areas of social control: *endogamy* (i.e., marrying within one's ethno-religious group), *sexual norms* (e.g., restrictions of premarital, extramarital, homosexual, or "deviant" sexual activities), *divorce,* and *reproduction.* Furthermore, these data describe only relatively recent attitudes and behavior. We have no comparable information about the impact of religion on family life in, say, 1830 or 1600. These data are also generally based on a narrow consideration of the term *religion*; correlations usually refer only to "religious affiliation."

In the twentieth century, U.S. Catholics, Jews, and Protestants all experienced steady increases in the rate of exogamous marriage (McCutcheon, 1988). Religious exogamy (i.e., marrying outside one's group) is the most frequently given reason for switching denominations, as one spouse changes to the religious affiliation of the other (Demerath and Yang, 1998). Data from a national survey showed that religious exogamy is related to marital dissolution; marriages in which one spouse adopted the religion of the other, however, achieved a higher rate of stability than marriages that were homogamous (i.e., both partners of the same religion) from the beginning (Lehrer and Chiswick, 1993).

Although all Jewish and Christian groups emphasize the ideal of permanent marriage, divorce rates and attitudes toward divorce have been changing.

In the second half of the twentieth century, the rate of marital disruption of U.S. Protestants, Catholics, and Jews rose steadily, as did the proportion of members who approved of divorce (and remarriage of divorced persons). Although the official teachings of the Roman Catholic Church are strongly against divorce and remarriage, only about 15 percent of Roman Catholics disapprove of divorce (see Goodstein and Morin, 1995).

One study observed that religion's influence on marital commitment is often indirect. For example, it shapes the degree of emphasis on caring for one another and the couple's definition of gender roles, which subsequently have an impact on the marriage relationship and partners' commitment to that relationship (Scanzoni and Arnett, 1987). Another study found, however, that the wife's religious beliefs concerning "marital commitment and non-marital sex are more important to the stability of the marriage than the husband's beliefs" (Call and Heaton, 1997: 391).

Family life—a broader category than marriage alone—is also linked with religion. A study of black families found that religious involvement and commitment to religious upbringing of children was strongly linked with positive subjective assessments of family life (Ellison, 1997). Subjective assessments of "satisfaction," however, are ambiguous variables; does religion produce an objectively happier marriage and family life, or does it teach the person to define and interpret whatever exists as "happy"? (Ellison, 1991).

Interestingly, most U.S. religious groups appear to be far more concerned about regulating families' procreative sexuality than with domestic violence. They seem more upset about out-of-wedlock childbirth than about child beating, more outspoken against divorce than against spousal rape, and more cognizant of the national abortion rate than of the existence of incest in their own families. We must remember that religion is not always a source of marital happiness and well-being. It is sometimes linked with causing or at least condoning serious family and marriage problems, such as spousal or child abuse (Nason-Clark, 1995, 1997). Some studies show that father-daughter incest often occurs in morally rigid religious families (Imbens and Jorker, 1992), where daughters are expected to be totally submissive to parental authority. Similarly, some religious groups encourage parents and other adults to physically abuse children, if necessary, to break their will and force submission to "God's will" (Capps, 1992; Ellison et al., 1996; Greven, 1991). While religious participation may mitigate against (self-reported) spousal abuse generally, men whose religious views are much more conservative than their wives' are especially likely to engage in wife-battering and other domestic violence (Ellison et al., 1999). Overall, it appears that religions emphasizing obedience in hierarchical relationships (e.g., father/husband exercising dominance over his children and wife) are more likely to condone, if not encourage, domestic abuse and violence.

Social science's emphasis on a limited range of religion's social control functions in marriage is imbalanced. It would be useful to know how religion (defined more broadly than religious affiliation) influences the extent to which people perceive themselves as *having choices* in life (e.g., the choice not to stay married). How does religion influence the individual's general orientation toward life (e.g., fatalism or hopefulness) and toward others (e.g., are others perceived as basically good or bad)? What impact, if any, does religion have on the individual's sense of self-worth and independence; does the individual's religion contribute to the sense of self outside the marriage or family? These broader influences of religion are probably more critical for our understanding of marriage and divorce than are formal moral norms of specific religious organizations.

Similarly, it would be fruitful to explore what kinds of marriages result from different kinds of religious orientations. For example, are the religious orientations and perspectives of the spouses important in determining the power relationships between them? Their ideals of married love? The degree of interpersonal communication in their marriage? The allocation of tasks, resources, decision making, and rewards in the marriage and family? Probably religion is one important factor in shaping the quality of marriage relationships, but the precise nature of its influence has yet to be documented.

A related correlation is the influence of religion on gender roles. Various religious perspectives lead to different images of maleness and femaleness. Gender roles are extremely important in marriage, as in other institutional settings. What a man expects of himself and what others expect of him as a man directly influence the kind of activities and relationships in which he engages. If it is considered unmanly to care for babies, a man is likely to avoid situations in which he would do (or be seen doing) this. Religious beliefs, myths, images, and symbols have been important forces in shaping gender roles, as illustrated in the Extended Application section of Chapter 4.

Similarly, a broader approach to the influence of religion on childbearing, childbirth, and family life is needed. Numerous studies have correlated religious affiliation and fertility, but they have focused too much on the differences between religious organizations' norms for control over the reproductive behavior of members. Far more interesting would be information about how religion shapes the attitudes of men and women toward children. How is the meaning of having children different for men than for women, for older couples than for younger ones, for Italians than for Germans, for Jews than for Baptists, and so on? What exactly is the impact of the individual's religion on his or her attitude toward children—especially one's own children? Also, what is religion's impact on attitudes toward reproductive events *per se?* How does religion shape the individual's ideas of and feelings about menstruation, intercourse, pregnancy, and childbirth? How does religion influence the person's experience of these events?

One important step in this direction is a study of women's activism on the abortion debate. Female "pro-life" activists and female "pro-choice" activists were found to operate from totally different worldviews, which entailed radically different meanings of motherhood, family, women's roles, children, and the importance of the individual. Although religious affiliations informed these opposing worldviews, another explanatory factor was the difference in the two groups' socioeconomic situations. Pro-choice activists tended to have experience and educational credentials to pursue careers and higher-paid jobs; ability to control their reproductive functions was crucial in being able to achieve their career goals. By contrast, pro-life activists had chosen life patterns generally outside of the paid workforce (and most were ill-prepared to succeed in that sphere); for them, childbearing and childrearing were central parts of their sense of purpose and self-esteem. Indeed, because of their values about children and motherhood, these women were typically opposed to the use of "artificial" birth control, even though its use would obviate the need for many abortions. From their respective worldviews, both groups of women had made life commitments that limited their ability to change their minds and life directions (Luker, 1984:158–215). Some of the fervor of the abortion debate is fueled by the stakes that persons on both sides have invested in their worldviews.

Finally, the narrow focus of research on attitudes toward sexual norms has failed to tap the broader issue of sexuality itself. All religions have attempted to interpret sexual themes or experiences. Religious symbolism frequently deals directly with themes of sexuality. Important parallels exist between spiritual and sexual ecstasy; sexual images are linked with religious images in the writings of famous Christian mystics (Bynum, 1991; Milhaven, 1993). Unfortunately, our society's understanding of sexuality is far too narrow—far too focused on artificially dichotomous ideas of properly masculine or feminine sexuality, conceived merely in genital and/or erotic terms (Giddens, 1992; Marcuse, 1966). This narrow approach produces the mistaken notion that the main sociological issue about sexuality is how to interpret homosexuality.[1] This limitation prevents us from appreciating other possible expressions of human sexuality, such as nursing a baby. It also tends to view the choice of celibacy as aberrant asexuality, rather than a valid alternative pattern of sexuality (see Cline, 1993).

Religion's link with human sexuality is understandable because both are direct, personal experiences of *power,* which evokes a sense of chaos and need for control, pollution and need for purification, danger and need for protection (Douglas, 1966). Religion, with its capacity to give meaning and order, offers control, purification, and protection from the chaotic power of sexuality. The establishment of moral norms to regulate sexual behavior is only one aspect of this control. Other important aspects include religious interpretation of sexual experiences and events (e.g., interpreting marital intercourse as imitative of the marriage of the gods). Religion also provides rituals and symbols to deal with some of the more potent and awesome aspects of sexuality. Many religions have a ritual of purification for women after childbirth (e.g., the "churching" of women in some Christian groups). Indeed, the human body and its functions are potent symbols. Corporality (the quality of being a body) is a common metaphor for social and religious cohesion (see Turner, 1980, 1991). Religion also offers ways of channeling sexual energies into spiritual

---

1. Note how many sociology texts, if they treat the topic of "sexuality" at all, discuss it only in terms of homosexuality, sexual identity, or the social control of sexual deviance.

energies. Many religious groups believe that sexual activity reduces one's spiritual energies; thus, norms of abstinence from sexual intercourse are based not on notions of right and wrong but on the idea of heightening one's spiritual powers. These reflections about the interrelationship of religion and sexuality suggest some of the directions that further study could take.

Middle Age

Significantly, there are no rites of passage to middle age. In earlier times, fewer people lived in relatively good health much beyond the time their children became adults. Now, however, with increased longevity and smaller families, a gap of twenty or more years between the time children leave home and parents reach retirement age is not uncommon.

Middle age is often a period of "identity crisis" for both men and women. Many women discover that they have invested their sense of purpose in their families, but their status as "mother" means little in middle age. The correspondence of this social loss with the time of biological change (i.e., menopause) can be doubly traumatic if women consider their reproductive capacity a basic part of their sense of self and personal worth. Interestingly, religious involvement appears to decline somewhat in middle age, once children's socialization and family involvement in organized religious activities is past. But, for many women, *spirituality* (a more personal interior quest) may increase in middle age. The kinds of attitudinal openness to change, personal growth, and creativity developed through their spirituality are predictive of a sense of well-being in later life (Dillon and Wink, 2000).

Although the existence of a male biological equivalent to menopause is debated, the social transitions of men in middle age are often as pronounced as those of women. A man may have invested much energy and time in his career and, in middle age, begin to realize that his career goals are unlikely to be achieved. Or he may come to doubt the goals and values that had motivated him in earlier years of his career. Precisely at the stage when his children are becoming more independent of their parents, he may begin to want a closer relationship with them. The structure of family and work in this society makes middle age a problematic time: One's chances of achieving socially desirable goals in family and job are considered past or severely reduced, but one is not yet free to quit striving for those goals.

In Western societies, chronological age is a key criterion by which social roles are linked. It becomes an evaluative criterion when the individual or social group measures the age-appropriateness of the person's achievements and activities. Statements such as "He is too young to be married" or "She is too old to be working full time" exemplify the social basis of these definitions of age-appropriateness. The person may be physically capable of full-time work or marriage and childbearing, but the society has established its criteria of the appropriate ages for these roles (Kearl, 1980; see also Berger et al., 1973:73).

Age is also a key criterion in comparing oneself with others. As age progresses, however, opportunities for comparing favorably with others of one's cohort decrease. By middle age, many people sense that their number of remaining years and resources for competition severely limit their likelihood of "getting ahead." Middle age brings the peak of socioeconomic mobility; for many individuals, it may mark the beginning of the downward mobility characteristic of old age. Retirement marks the worker's entry into "old age"— again, a socially defined threshold of age-appropriate behavior. Generally, middle age is not a valued life period in our culture, the dominant values of which emphasize youthfulness: youthful standards of beauty, energy, bodily functioning, and carefree lifestyle. Contemporary religious groups do little to smooth this status passage with ritual or symbolism.

Old Age

Popular imagery holds that religion is more important in the lives of old people. Studies of religion and aging have found that, as people age, generally they do not dramatically change their religious involvement. While health problems may cause them to reduce public participation in religious services, there appears to be no reduction in private forms of religious involvement (for a review of the literature, see Idler, 1994).

Problems of meaning and belonging may be particularly acute for older persons. Difficulties of financial and physical limitations may compound the broader problem of the society's general devaluation of old age. While coping with their own diminished vitality, elderly persons must often cope with the difficulties of their spouse's and friends' chronic illness, disability, and death. Some 35 percent of the persons giving care to the elderly are themselves older than 65 (cited in *The New York Times,* May 13, 1989). The extra burdens of caregiving and the very real losses, not only through death but also of everyday abilities, such as driving a car or playing a beloved musical instrument, pose serious psychological, social, and spiritual problems for many elderly persons.

One longitudinal study (Idler and Kasl, 1992) found that public religious involvement of the elderly has significant protective effects against disability, as well as helping believers cope with or avoid depression. Furthermore, persons who belonged to Christian or Jewish groups were less likely to die in the month before their respective religious holidays than the nonaffiliated. The authors concluded that religious involvement has a strong positive effect on health and, while some of this effect can be explained by social factors (such as religious norms for healthy behaviors like avoiding smoking), other aspects of religion (such as ritual experience and meaning) also play a role.

Another study (Futterman et al., 1999) used psychological measures to distinguish whether or not elderly respondents' use of religion was as a spiritual "quest." Researchers found that, for many older persons, deep belief and religious commitment go hand in hand with doubt and an active search for meaning. Such a quest-orientation appears to promote adaptation and coping in old age. For instance, one elderly woman (78), an active participant in the same church for more than thirty years, said that she began to wonder about an afterlife after her husband's death:

First place, I don't think there's any hell or purgatory. And I thought that . . . I don't think that heaven's a place. I don't think it's up there, I

BOX 3.2 Methodological Note: Operationalizing Religiosity

In old age, do people become more religious than in their youth? Do women have different patterns of religiosity and religious commitment than men? Does a high level of religiosity in adolescence predict continued religiosity in middle age? In order to address interesting questions such as these, sociologists and social psychologists must first find a good way to operationalize "religiosity"; that is, they need concrete and uniformly applicable ways to measure or rate the core quality to which "religiosity" refers. One of the many problems of operationalizing "religiosity" is that researchers rely on survey questionnaires and interviews, so they can tap only respondents' opinions, attitudes, values, and self-reported behaviors (Chapter 4 discusses some other methodological problems). Some studies also ask such questions as: "How religious a person do you consider yourself to be?" or "How important is religion in your life?" Such methodologies, unfortunately, fail to tap people's *actual* religious practices. Also, depending upon whether religiosity is viewed as socially desirable, some respondents are likely to understate their religiosity or overestimate it. What is measured is respondents' sense of what they *ought* to say, not what is their *actual* practice.

One innovative study* tried to get around this problem by rating participants based upon their responses to open-ended questions in interviews that *had already been conducted* as part of a much larger, longitudinal study. The study was about many aspects of participants' lives, so respondents' attention was not focused on religion and there was no special value (except the wider cultural norms of the time) to emphasizing religiosity in their responses to these broad questions. Participants were studied intensively in childhood and adolescence, and then interviewed at length in adulthood (four times—in their 30s, 40s, mid-50s and early 60s, and late 60s and early 70s). Interviewed participants also responded to various written questionnaires and self-reports. Some of the open-ended questions asked specifically about religious beliefs and practices; others asked about any interests and activities, often eliciting spontaneous mention of religious or spiritual practices and attitudes.

The researchers first agreed on what criteria they would consider evidence of each level of their scale of religiosity (and a separate scale for rating spirituality). Questionnaires had asked about frequency of church attendance, but most beliefs, values, and practices were elicited indirectly, in response to open-ended questions. Thus, the researchers decided that the rating scales should reflect mainly presence or absence (not intensity or frequency) of each criterion. Next, two trained coders rated (on a scale of 1–5) hundreds of interview segments, "blind" to any information identifying the respondent or the year in

---

don't think it's . . . I don't know. But I felt that he had a place to go after he died. But I wasn't sure. I wanted to be sure . . . I just felt it couldn't be a house or anything. [she laughs with embarrassment] Maybe a spirit world . . . After my husband died, I didn't change my mind so much as I just started thinking about it more. I just don't know now. (quoted in Futterman et al., 1999: 165)

BOX 3.2 *continued*

---

which the interview was conducted. The researchers compared the coders' ratings for each respondent to verify they were applying the same criteria. Then they compared their measures of religiosity for respondents in the older adulthood interviews with participants' self-reported answers on a standardized "religiosity" index. High levels of correlation assured them that their measures were internally consistent and tapping much of the same phenomenon that the best available pencil-and-paper measures had measured.

Operationalizing "spirituality" was more difficult, because there were no existing measures with which to compare their ratings. The researchers did succeed in establishing criteria for the coders that were internally consistent, yet these produced *very* different ratings for each respondent than did the religiosity measures. In the life course of one individual, for example, high religiosity and low spirituality ratings at age 30 might change to medium-low religiosity and high spirituality by age 55. Having operationalized and rated "religiosity" and "spirituality," the researchers could then correlate these measures with other variables, such as age and gender, and with other measures, such as respondents' scores on various (already administered) attitude and personality scales. They found, among other things, that "highly religious individuals tended to be other-oriented, involved in creative activities, low in narcissism, and exhibited authoritarian characteristics.

Individuals high in spirituality tended to be involved in communal activities, generative, creative, and interested in personal growth. They tended to be non-authoritarian" (pp. 28–29).

- Why are respondents more likely to understand the same thing by a questionnaire's wording when they are asked "how religious" they are but less likely to understand the same thing by the question "how spiritual"?

- This study's sample was largely of fully Protestant background (70 percent), with nearly all the rest of the respondents coming from fully Catholic or mixed parentage. If the study were to be applicable to non-Christian religious minorities, as well as to Christians, how would the researchers have to change the criteria to tap the "religiosity" of, say, Hindus or Muslims?

- Suppose you had access to a remarkable source of personal reflections (such as the journals and letters of all the inhabitants of a Midwestern town during the Great Depression and World War II). What categories of beliefs, attitudes, values, and practices would you look for in that trove in order to give a good depiction of the role of religion in people's lives and over the course of growing older?

---

*This description is based upon an early report from the research of Michele Dillon and Paul Wink (2000), presented at the annual meeting of the Society for the Scientific Study of Religion.

Popular notions sometimes suggest that the greater religiosity of old age is something of a last-chance "cramming for the final exam." Although there may be some validity to this conception, the religiosity of the elderly is probably more of a reflection of their social situation. Old people may emphasize spiritual and human relationship values in their lives because the society has relegated them to the private sphere—out of the world of work. Our society places great value on one's work role (especially for men, but increasingly also for women) throughout the individual's adult life, and old age brings the often abrupt end of that role. Retirement effectively means, for many people, leaving the public sphere. Thus, the elderly person must find all bases of identity and self-worth in the private sphere—family, leisure-time activities, religion, neighborhood. Perhaps because they have been characteristically confined to the private sphere, women often adjust better than men to old age. They have already developed more social roles in the private sphere, and society has not expected them to invest themselves in their employment roles (if any) as heavily as men (Myerhoff, 1978).

By contrast, some societies provide recognizable spiritual roles for elderly persons to assume. In India, elderly persons can assume valued spiritual roles (especially if they are economically comfortable enough to "retire" from economically productive roles). Hindu men who have raised and supported their children to adulthood are allowed to retire in honor to a life of contemplation and spiritual exercises. Upper-class, married Hindu women are allowed a similar freedom after menopause to perform *habisha*—rituals to protect their husbands and develop their own spirituality. Women's freedom is temporary, however, ending when they become widows and must observe the social and ritual prohibitions for that status (Freeman, 1980).

Elderly women in other cultures often have spiritual roles as healers and midwives—positions of culturally recognized spiritual power; elderly men may be diviners, healers, or seers. Urban Western cultures, characteristically, do not provide such roles. Individuals may be recognized and honored for their "holiness" or "goodness" within their own immediate religious group, but such roles are *privatized*. The honor an elderly woman may receive at her Wednesday-night prayer meeting does not carry over to her treatment by the Social Security bureaucracy, hospital clinic, or other tenants in her apartment building.

One of the critical problems of meaning in middle and old age is modern society's sense of time. Primitive religions integrate all human action into cosmic time; the events of one's life can be interpreted as part of a larger cosmic drama. The individual's passage through the life cycle repeats and imitates the deities' birth, adolescence, marriage, childbirth, parenting, work, play, fighting, aging, and death. In this religious perspective, time has sacred significance. It collapses past and future into an eternal present.

Historic religions such as Christianity and Islam also give sacred significance to time. The past is full of the deities' self-revelation to humans; the present is important in the working out of the deities' will for humans; the future will bring the full realization of that will and celebration of a glorious reward. In this perspective, time promises immortality. Old age has sacred meaning, both as a fulfillment of divine will and as a threshold to higher levels of spiritual rewards. Modern society, by contrast, encourages a profane image of time. Time "passes," and its passage signifies decay or entropy. Time is a resource to be used but contains no special meaning; when the resource is depleted, life ends. In this context, old age has no special significance with reference to past accomplishments (e.g., social rewards for living a good life) or to future rewards (e.g., heaven, nirvana). Old age means merely the end of full life opportunities (Kearl, 1980).

The U.S. society values economic roles especially highly. The individual's occupational role shapes the society's evaluation of that person and his or her own identity. Consumer roles are equally important. Social status is based partly on evaluations of the individual's ability to maintain a certain standard of consumption (e.g., quality of house, car, neighborhood, clothing). Elderly persons are often deprived of valued statuses in both kinds of economic roles; they are retired from their work roles, and, simultaneously, their fixed incomes leave them unable to maintain valued standards of consumption.

The legitimation offered for this loss of valued statuses is the idea of "retirement." Retirement is supposed to be an economic and moral vindication for growing old. It is described as a time for individualism (e.g., the freedom to move away to a retirement resort, play golf, lounge around, putter in the garden, and escape social obligations). The concept of retirement implies that the individual has earned this escape by having fulfilled life's social obligations. This individualism (if, indeed, the retired person can afford such luxuries in retirement) does epitomize what younger members consider to be freedom and a desirable reward. It cannot, however, provide meaning to life and death, a sense of belonging or self-worth, for the retired person (Kearl, 1980).

This life is made even more problematic in its ending. Often biological death follows the individual's social death by many years; the individual may become physically, financially, or mentally unable to sustain interactions that the society considers "alive." Yet the person is kept biologically alive, often by extreme measures of medical intervention. It becomes difficult to die "on time" (Kearl, 1993). The medical supervisors of death not only treat it as meaningless but also often segregate dying persons from family, neighbors, or friends who could support their personal meaning system. Religion has traditionally given meaning and dignity to old age and dying. Attempts to retain these values are not supported, however, by the structure of modern society. Old age and dying are generally perceived as times to fear.

CONVERSION

The capabilities of religion for providing the individual with a sense of both meaning and belonging are especially evident in the process of conversion. **Conversion** means a transformation of one's *self* concurrent with a transformation of one's basic *meaning system*.[2] It changes the sense of who one is and how one belongs in the social situation. Conversion transforms the way the

---

2. Throughout this discussion we will emphasize the broad concept of *meaning system* more than the specific term *religion*. This usage is helpful because the processes described here apply to other comprehensive meaning systems as well as to specifically religious ones. The processes of conversion and commitment can apply not only to religious changes but also to psychotherapeutic and political transformation.

individual perceives the rest of society and his or her personal place in it, altering one's view of the world.

This definition of conversion distinguishes simple changes in institutional affiliation from more fundamental alterations in the individual's meaning system. An Episcopalian who marries a Roman Catholic may join the Catholic church to accommodate the spouse's wishes. Such a change of affiliation is not necessarily a conversion. Similarly, a Presbyterian who moves to a new town and, finding no local church of that denomination, joins a Congregational church has probably not—strictly speaking—converted. Such denomination switching is relatively common in the United States. Some 40 percent of the U.S. populace have switched denominations at least once (Roof and McKinney, 1987:165), but when they do, they are highly likely to stay in the same "larger denominational family" (Hadaway and Marler, 1993:102). These findings are corroborated by Canadian studies, which suggest that people switch along lines of "comfort zones" in the worship services of religious groups other than one's own (Bibby, 1999). Thus, when other factors (such as marriage, friendship, geographical and socioeconomic mobility) cause people to consider changing religious affiliation, they are highly unlikely to change their religion dramatically. Such changes are not conversions but simply changes of affiliation from one organization to another.

Conceptualizing Conversion

There is considerable diversity among conversions. One distinction is the degree of personal transformation that takes place. How different are the new meaning system and self from the former ones?

The extreme case is a *radical transformation of self* and meaning system such as when a highly committed Conservative Jew converts to a fundamentalist Christian worldview. Not only are such extreme conversions relatively uncommon, but they rarely occur as dramatically as popular imagery implies. The processes by which such radical transformations occur are actually similar in kind, though usually not in degree, to less extreme conversions (see Berger and Luckmann, 1966:157–163). These processes are described in greater detail in the next section.

Less extreme cases include conversions in which the new meaning system and self represent a *consolidation of previous identities.* Some young men who became *ba'ale teshuvah*—members of strict Orthodox Jewish *yeshivot* (i.e., commune-schools)—had come from non-Orthodox Jewish homes but rejected their Jewish way of life and had then tried various alternative worldviews. Becoming newly Orthodox eventually enabled these members to consolidate elements of both their former identities into a new, "superior" self (Glanz and Harrison, 1977; see also Danzger, 1989).

Another less extreme type of conversion is essentially a *reaffirmation* of elements of one's previous identity. Many "born-again experiences" fit this model. It is difficult to specify how much change such conversions really entail. Often they involve no change in one's religious affiliation, yet exhibit real changes in the individual's personal religious behavior and sense of identity. This type of conversion does not necessarily entail a total rejection of the previous meaning system.

Some identity-consolidating conversion experiences involve little or no change in meaning system and sense of self. Many religious groups expect young members to make a personal faith decision and to undergo a conversion experience as they approach adulthood. Such groups provide opportunities such as youth revivals in which the necessary conversion experience is more likely to occur. These experiences, although very real and meaningful to participants, are better understood, not as conversions, but rather as rituals of reaffirmation of the person's existing identity and meaning system (Wimberley et al., 1975). Reaffirmation experiences are part of a process of commitment in which the individual's self-concept as a religious person becomes more central (see, for example, Staples and Mauss, 1987).

Conversion in the Context of Modern Societies Modern societies are characterized by the expectation that more areas of life are matters of *individual* decisions. In modern societies, individuals believe they are free to make such significant *choices* as marriage partner, occupation, place of residence, and religion. They also typically have more real options for choice than do persons in traditional societies. At the same time, however, many people are genuinely ambivalent about such individual freedom and try to constrain these choices by other means. While parents may no longer arrange marriages, they still try to limit their children's range of choice of partners by, for example, sending them to small colleges attracting the desired ethnic, religious, and social class groups of students. Similarly, although in principle modern societies hold that religion is a matter of individual choice, few people would agree that all religions are valid "acceptable" options.

Ironically, unlike in traditional societies, religions in modern contexts must actively work at generating members' individual choices and commitments. In modern societies the religious training of youth, for instance, is aimed largely at keeping them in "the faith" as adults when they face many other options. By contrast, in highly traditional societies, young people's belonging to the group's religion in the future is taken so for granted that youth need only to learn how to perform their own roles in that group. In the modern context, some religious groups consciously orchestrate social occasions at which the "correct" individual choices will be made, yet be experienced as freely and fully chosen.

Social scientists are particularly fascinated with conversion and commitment, because these processes highlight important features of the relationship between the individual and society in the changing contexts of modern life. **Individuation** is the process by which cultural and social structural arrangements come to consider each individual as a separate entity—in relation to group entities such as the family, tribe, religious group, or political and judicial institutions. Modern societies are characterized by a much higher degree of individuation than traditional societies, but modern societies differ culturally in how they think about the individual and about individual choices and rights. For example, Protestant Christians have traditionally emphasized individual repentance and salvation, whereas Eastern Orthodox Christians have emphasized being saved in a community united by ritual practices. A social scientist would ask how these two groups adapt their understandings of the individual-to-society relationship in the context of largely urbanized modern social and economic conditions.

Because of this cultural diversity, however, we must be cautious not to confuse our own cultural "rhetorics" for the essential or definitive features of conversion. For example, Euro-American cultures assume that religious belief and practice are (or ought to be) matters of voluntary *individual* choice, but many other cultures view decisions about religious affiliation and practice to pertain to the entire family, so if the head of the family changes religion, the entire family changes. Similarly, most U.S. religious groups believe that conversion entails accepting a new set of religious ideas or beliefs; other cultures downplay religious beliefs and emphasize changed ritual practices. One anthropologist (Rosaldo, 1989) recounts his failure to comprehend the conversion of a tribesman of the Ilongot (of the highland Philippines) to evangelical Christianity. Christian beliefs—including beliefs about death or heaven—were unimportant to this man who was suffering greatly the death of seven children in a short span; what mattered was that the new religion offered religious *practices* that enabled him to cope with his grief and rage. In the traditional Ilongot way of life, the grief and rage experienced in bereavement had been ceremonially dealt with by head-hunting. After Marcos's declaration of martial law in 1972, the government forbade and severely punished head-hunting, so tribesmen had no way of dealing with these intense emotional experiences. In this example, the man's abandonment of the Ilongot way of life probably preceded his embrace of a Christian way of life, but Christian *beliefs per se* appear not to have been a significant feature of his conversion.

Conversion Accounts and Rhetorics The main difficulty in distinguishing the degree of change that occurs in any given conversion is that the individual who converts *reinterprets past experiences* in relationship to the new meaning system. Therefore, it becomes difficult to determine what amount of the convert's description of the changes experienced represents the objective process of conversion and how much expresses the convert's subjective reinterpretation of those events. The convert constructs the story of conversion, drawing on a socially available set of plausible explanations, or *rhetoric*.

Several rhetorics are available to converts to use to "explain" their conversion (Burke, 1953). Rhetorics of choice emphasize how much the change resulted from a personal, often agonizing decision. Our society places much value on individual decision, so these rhetorics are prominent in explanations of conversion. In cultures where personal decision is less valued or even discouraged, rhetorics of choice are not emphasized; indeed, often converts do not even experience "making a personal decision" (Tippett, 1973). Rhetorics of change emphasize the dramatic nature of personal change in the conversion. Converts may compare the evil or unhappiness of their previous way of life with how wonderful their new way is. Rhetorics of continuity focus on the extent to which one's new meaning system and self are the logical extension of earlier beliefs and experiences. The convert might remember important past experiences as tentative steps toward the newfound truth.

Religious groups themselves often encourage the application of one type of rhetoric over another. Thus, the Catholic Charismatic Renewal encourages new members to interpret their "born-again" experiences as continuous with their former way of life, whereas many Pentecostal sects encourage new members to interpret their similar "born-again" experiences as a dramatic change and repudiation of their former way of life. Because the main source of information about conversion is the converts themselves—and because their explanations of events surrounding their conversions are reinterpretations consistent with their new meaning systems—evaluating evidence about conversions is difficult. Sociological theories of conversion must not mistake these interpretations and rhetorics that express them for the objective events of the conversion (Beckford, 1978a; Machalek and Snow, 1993).

Explaining Conversion

A theoretical understanding of how conversion occurs is nevertheless worthwhile because it reveals much about the connection between the individual's meaning system, social relationships, and very identity. Because conversion consists in a change of the individual's meaning system and self, it has social, psychological, and ideational components. The social component consists of the interaction between the recruit and other circles of associates (e.g., parents, friends, coworkers). The psychological component refers to emotional and affective aspects of conversion as well as to changes in values and attitudes. The ideational component includes the actual ideas the convert embraces or rejects during the process. These ideas are rarely very philosophical or theological; they are simply a set of beliefs that both justify the new meaning system and negate the former one.

Factors in Conversion An adequate theory of conversion must take all the aspects mentioned into account without overemphasizing any single component. Some theories give too much weight to social factors by creating the image of a passive person being pushed and pulled by various social forces. Although very real social pressures are exerted on the potential convert, the person who converts is not a passive object of these pressures. Conversion entails an interaction during which the recruit constructs or negotiates a new personal identity (Beckford, 1978a; Kilbourne and Richardson, 1989; Straus, 1979). Furthermore, only some of those exposed to such social pressures do decide to convert (Barker, 1983).

Some theories of conversion overemphasize ideational components of the process. These theories are consistent with the ideological claims of the religious groups themselves. Religious groups like to believe that the truth value of their beliefs alone is sufficient to compel a person to convert. The content of the belief system *is* a factor in conversion. Some beliefs are more appealing than others to people in certain circumstances; indeed, the potential convert will likely be recruited to a group whose perspective is consistent with that person's previous outlook, even though the specific content of the group's beliefs may be unfamiliar (Greil, 1977). Also, we must acknowledge people's religious reasons for their religious behavior and not try to reduce every motive to some psychological function.

Nevertheless, ideas alone do not persuade a person to convert. Even in the scientific community where objective facts and the truth value of interpretations are supposed to be paramount, there is considerable resistance to change from an established interpretive paradigm to a new one—even when the old paradigm is inconsistent with the "facts" (Festinger, 1957; Kuhn, 1970). How much more are religious believers, with their emphasis on supraempirical reality, likely to resist changing their ideas? Thus, although the ideational component is important in the appeal of a new belief system, it is not sufficient to bring about conversion.

Other theories place too great an emphasis on psychological factors in conversion, explaining the change entirely in terms of the individual's personality, biography, and personal problems. Psychologistic explanations are attractive because they mesh with many of our individualistic cultural values. Nevertheless, they are too one-sided, leaving out social situational factors and other important components. Also, some of these theories tend to assume that conversion to unusual religious groups entails "sick" behavior. Yet adherents' behavior is quite understandable and rational within their alternate meaning systems. If one believes that astrological forces influence human events, it is perfectly rational to act in accordance with those forces. Likewise, if one believes that the world is coming to an end in the very near future, it is not irrational or "sick" to give up one's possessions or career plans.

"Brainwashing"　One particularly misleading psychologistic model of conversion is the "brainwashing" metaphor. This model is based on studies during the 1950s of the processes by which certain U.S. military personnel in the Orient were pressed to convert to Chinese communism. The popular image applied to this process was "brainwashing," conveying the idea that the convert's mind was cleansed of prior beliefs, values, and commitment, then filled with a new belief system. Psychological studies of this process identified several factors contributing to conversion without cooperation of the converts (Lifton, 1963; Sargant, 1957). Various social scientists have subsequently generalized the interpretations of this drastic type of political conversion to other forms of conversion. Some accurate parallels do exist between forcible "brainwashing" and conversion, but these characteristics apply to all forms of resocialization. Thus, the training of soldiers for combat and the rehabilitation of juvenile delinquents also involve these processes. To say that conversion is a form of resocialization does not mean that it is therefore an extreme, involuntary form of resocialization.

The key problem with the "brainwashing" metaphor is its ideological use and potential application for abuses of civil liberties. Nonconverts often feel threatened by the conversion of someone close to them. The convert has rejected their own dearly held views and norms and has indirectly threatened the nonconverts' own meaning system. When people cannot understand why an individual would *want* to convert to an unfamiliar religious perspective, they find "brainwashing" an attractive explanation. This metaphor implies that the converting individual did not change voluntarily. The metaphor also allows people to negate the ideational component of the convert's new meaning system. A convert's parents can feel, "He doesn't believe those ideas because they are meaningful to him but because his mind has been manipulated." In its extreme form, the "brainwashing" metaphor has been recently used to justify the denial of converts' religious liberty on the ground that they do not know their own minds (Anthony and Robbins, 1992, 1995; Richardson, 1991, 1993c).

An interesting parallel with the current anticult charge of "brainwashing" is the nineteenth-century anti-Mason movement. Freemasonry is now a legitimate, middle-class form of fraternal organization, but it was severely attacked in the nineteenth-century United States as subversive to democracy. Other now respectable groups that were attacked (often violently) were Roman Catholics and Mormons. The key themes of the movements against Masonry, Roman Catholicism, and Mormonism emphasized that, unlike conventional denominations that claimed only partial loyalty of their members, these groups allegedly dominated their members' lives, demanded unlimited allegiance, and conducted some activities in secrecy (Holt, 1973; Vaughn, 1983).

This parallel suggests that the "brainwashing" controversy is an ideological issue at another level (see Robbins and Anthony, 1979). The society defines as "deviant" one who is *too* committed to religion, especially authoritarian religion. The resocialization processes themselves are less of an issue than the legitimacy of the group's religion itself. To illustrate this discrepancy, two researchers compared conversion and commitment processes of the Unification Church of Sun Myung Moon and similar late-twentieth-century sects with the nineteenth- and early-twentieth-century practices of the now socially acceptable Tnevnoc "cult." The Tnevnoc practices were essentially comparable and seem bizarre until we discover that the authors were actually referring to life in the convent—which, spelled backward, is Tnevnoc (Bromley and Shupe, 1979). The chief difference between many modern "cults" and groups such as Roman Catholicism, Freemasonry, and Mormonism is that the latter groups have now achieved social legitimacy.[3]

Keeping these cautions in mind, we can examine some of the factors in conversion. By emphasizing conversion as a *process* rather than an event, we take into account the fact that the convert has both a history and a future. Although an individual may experience conversion as a discrete event, numerous other experiences lead up to and follow that event that are also parts of the

---

3. To reduce the impression that conversion and commitment processes characterize only "weird" religions, I have drawn examples from both traditional and "new" religions.

conversion. The following description examines the sequence of events in the process of conversion; but let us remember that no single step in the sequence is itself sufficient to "cause" conversion (Beckford, 1978a; Heirich, 1977; Machalek and Snow, 1993; Richardson, 1985).

Predisposition to Conversion

Several personal and situational factors can predispose people to conversion by making them aware of the extent to which their prior meaning system seems inadequate to explain or give meaning to experiences and events. By contrast, if individuals can satisfactorily "handle" experiences and events within the framework of their meaning system, they have no desire to seek alternative meanings for their lives. Sometimes the individual who acutely feels the need for a new set of meanings becomes a *seeker*—that is, a person who actively looks for a satisfactory alternative belief system. A seeker often tries many different alternative beliefs and practices (Balch and Taylor, 1977). One American (a business analyst) convert to Soka Gakkai, a recent Japanese form of Buddhism, described her previous path:

> I practiced Christianity [in] the Reorganized Church of Jesus Christ of Latter-day Saints [Mormons], which taught [that there was] no salvation outside the Church, yet there were some good people outside. My church was very rigid (drinking rules and such). In 1971, Transcendental Meditation—I was looking for balance, for a daily rhythm. It helped me feel good—computer work is very stressful. It was more powerful than praying to God. I did Transcendental Meditation for a year. I also met Gurdjieff teaching in 1974, and was part of the Gurdjieff Society from 1974 to 1977. I was against organized religion—protocol, ceremony. A lady I met in the Gurdjieff group was starting chanting. She said "Try it!" When she chanted I felt sick—I was against trying it. However, I felt the strength. I was searching, but blocked. (quoted in Wilson and Dobbelaere, 1994:82)

Often, however, the individual experiences the desire for a more satisfactory meaning system as a vague tension, a malaise.

Many converts describe a crisis that they felt was a turning point in their lives. It is very difficult to evaluate the extent to which such crises actually precipitate the individual's conversion. Some crises may disrupt a person's life so completely that the individual has difficulty integrating them into the previously held meaning system. Natural disasters, war, and personal tragedy are particularly acute challenges. Serious illness or unemployment may be experienced as turning points. Social events such as an economic depression or anxiety over social conditions (e.g., crime or erosion of morals) may predispose people to conversion. Nevertheless, such crises do not *cause* religious conversion. Religious conversion is one among several possible resolutions of tensions and problems created by the crisis. Thus, serious illness might predispose one person to convert to a new meaning system; another person with a similar illness might find great meaning and comfort in his or her existing meaning system and have that belief confirmed by the crisis experience. Diverse other responses are possible, including alcoholism, political conversion, psychotherapy, suicide, and so on. Individuals converted to religious meaning systems are typically people whom previous socialization has predisposed to a religious perspective (see Greil, 1977; Lofland, 1966, 1977).

Determining to what extent the convert's description of a crisis experience is the result of after-the-fact interpretation of events is also difficult. Some religious groups encourage their members to witness about their conversion experience by telling the group how they came to "see the light." Whether the events thus described were really critical when they occurred is therefore difficult to reconstruct. Often the new group itself promotes the recruit's experience of a crisis. Many groups raise the recruit's anxiety over social and personal problems. Jehovah's Witnesses, for example, often approach strangers with a message about common worries—war, inflation, crime. By "mediating" anomie, the group encourages the individual to convert. The group encourages an experiential crisis of meaning by emphasizing order-threatening conditions and magnifying the potential convert's feelings of dissatisfaction, fear, and anxiety, which the person may have previously felt only vaguely (Beckford, 1975b:174).

Initial Interaction

Most recruits are drawn to the group by friends or relatives. Besides introducing the newcomer to the group and its beliefs, these preexisting networks of friendship account for the plausibility of the beliefs and the attractiveness of belonging. Thus, a person might be impressed by a roommate's happiness in a religious group and be curious enough to "check it out." The fact that a person whom one knows and likes belongs to the group attests to the normalcy or desirability of the group's way of life (Gerlach and Hine, 1970; Lofland, 1966). Even groups such as the Nichiren Shoshu (a Japanese movement brought to the United States in 1960), which conspicuously proselytize in public and anonymous settings, typically recruit most of their members through preexisting networks of friends and relatives (Snow et al., 1980).

Through interaction with members of the group, the recruit is gradually resocialized into that group's way of life. This resocialization consists of the individual's reshaping of identity and worldview to become consistent with those considered appropriate by the group. Several social processes enable the individual to make this transformation. Group support is particularly important. The recruit enjoys warm, affective relationships with the new group. Members of the Unification Church, for example, shower the potential member with attention and affection. These bonds affirm the new self and meaning system. As the recruit gradually withdraws from competing social relationships, the new group's opinions become increasingly important (Berger, 1967:50–51). Intensive interaction and close affective bonds with group members are central to the conversion process because they link the individual's new identity with the organization's perspective and goals (Greil and Rudy, 1984).

At the same time, the recruit also weakens or severs those relationships that support the old self. Former attachments compete with new commitments, symbolize a worldview that the recruit wishes to reject, and are based on an identity that the recruit wishes to change. Imagine, for example, that through two good friends you are introduced to a group of U.S. Sufis (Sufism is a mystical sect within Islam). Suppose that you learned enough about the group that you decided you would like to join them. How would your non-Sufi friends and relatives react? Your roommate might say, "Oh, come off that mysticism kick. I liked you better when you were a drinking buddy." Imagine your parents' reaction when you announce at supper that weekend, "Guess what, Mom and Dad, I've decided to join this fantastic bunch of Sufis, and I'm going out to the West Coast to live in a commune with some of them!" Most converts find their former set of friends less than supportive of their newfound truth and new self. Relationships with the new group therefore become even more important to counteract opposition from others.

During this resocialization, recruits learn to redefine their social world. Relationships once valued become devalued, and patterns of behavior once undesirable become desirable. New believers may redefine their families to exclude the biological family and to include the new family of fellow believers. A Shaker hymn thus celebrates the severance of old family ties:

Of all the relations that ever I see
My old fleshly kindred are furthest from me
So bad and so ugly, so hateful they feel
To see them and hate them increases my zeal . . .
My gospel relations are dearer to me
Than all the flesh kindred that ever I see . . .
(quoted in Kanter, 1972:90)

This process results in a whole new way of experiencing the world and oneself. The individual comes to "see" the world with an entirely different perspective; indeed, the new believer may say, "I once was blind, but now I see." This phrase is not merely metaphorical because the new perspective actually causes the individual to *perceive* the world differently. That which was marginal to consciousness becomes central, and that which once was focal becomes peripheral. Every worldview entails the selective perception and interpretation of events and objects according to its meaning system. Conversion means adopting new criteria for selecting (Jones, 1978; Snow and Machalek, 1983).

Recruits also redefine their own biographies. They remember episodes that appear consistent with the newfound perspective and interpret them as "part of what led me to the truth." Events are reinterpreted in terms of new beliefs and values. Remembering how proud she was to have achieved scholastic honors in school, one young woman said, "What a fool I was back then to have put so much store on worldly achievements."

The actual interaction between the recruit and the group is especially important in bringing about this transformation of worldviews. The most obvious action of religious groups is **proselytizing** potential converts. *Proselytizing* means that an individual or group actively tries to persuade non-believers to become believers. Some religious groups (e.g., Jehovah's Witnesses) do much proselytizing among nonbelievers; others (e.g., Conservative Jews) do virtually none. Although proselytizing activities are relatively conspicuous to outsiders, they are important primarily as a commitment mechanism for already converted members (Beckford, 1975b; Festinger et al., 1956; Shaffir, 1978). One study of a growing Pentecostal denomination found that members with extensive religious experience (e.g., speaking in tongues, divine healing) were especially vigorous evangelizers of potential recruits (Poloma and Pendleton, 1989). Thus, a mutually reinforcing relationship developed between members' involvement in the group and their attempts to share their religious faith and experience.

Mutual witnessing within existing friendships appears to be especially effective in bringing about the recruit's conversion to a new meaning system. Thus, the newcomer may mention an apparent coincidence that had recently happened, and a group member may respond, "That was no coincidence. That was God trying to show concern for you so that you will change your life." Or a member might say, "I used to be just like you. I had my doubts and didn't know what to believe, but now it all fits together. Now I can see what I was missing." Through these informal interactions, the recruit may gradually "try on" the interpretations suggested by members and apply their meaning systems to personal experiences. Thus, the new recruit comes to share their distinctive worldview.

Symbolizing the Conversion

The part of the conversion process typically identified as "the conversion" is essentially some form of *symbolizing* the transformation that has already been occurring. The convert affirms the new identity by some symbolic means considered appropriate in that group. In many Christian groups, baptism is meaningful as a symbol of conversion. Other ritual expressions of the new self include speaking in tongues (i.e., *glossolalia*) and witnessing. Some groups have very formal means for symbolizing transformation; others have more informal symbols that are not obvious to the nonbeliever (Gerlach and Hine, 1970; Lebra, 1972).

Although conversion is a gradual process, many recruits who have decided to convert adopt some of the symbols of conversion rather dramatically. Part of the resocialization itself is learning to act, look, and talk like other members of the group. Indeed, groups such as the Unification Church may focus on teaching recruits to display signs of commitment to the neglect of socializing them to actual commitment (Long and Hadden, 1983:9). The imitation of signs of commitment—which might be called "doing being converted"—

may be one part of the resocialization process. It is, however, often mistaken by observers as evidence that a dramatic conversion has been accomplished.

Some groups may encourage the new member to seek a conversion experience. This special emotional and spiritual event thus symbolizes the person's full conversion. Such experiences, however, are only part of the larger conversion process but are valued ways of symbolizing the transformation in some groups. Often these conversion experiences are brought about in carefully orchestrated settings. In a revival meeting, the timing of the altar call is synchronized with music and spoken message to proclaim, in essence, "Now is the appropriate time to have that special experience you came for" (W. Johnson, 1971; Walker and Atherton, 1971).

Another symbolic expression of the new self is changing one's name. Nuns traditionally changed their names upon taking their vows. The new name both symbolized the person's new identity and helped confirm that identity every time she was addressed. Some groups also encourage converts to confess the wrongness of their previous way of life. Among the Society of Brothers (Bruderhof), such a confession event symbolizes the conversion and demonstrates how new members' views of themselves have been transformed (see Zablocki, 1971:239–285). In the confession, converts affirm their new selves by derogating the behavior of their old selves. These symbols of conversion illustrate the complexity of the larger process of resocialization (see Goffman, 1961, especially his comparison of the "mortification of self" in several different institutional settings).

COMMITMENT

The process of conversion does not end when the recruit formally joins the group and symbolically affirms the conversion. Rather, the conversion process is continued in the **commitment** process, by which the individual increasingly identifies with the group, its meaning system, and its goals. Groups that have highly effective recruitment strategies may not be able to keep and effectively deploy their members if their commitment processes are not also effective (Long and Hadden, 1983). Popular imagery somehow envisions the converted recruit as permanently changed. The turnover of members in contemporary religious movements belies this notion. A British study found that, in the tightly organized Unification Church, the majority of converts leave the group of their own free will within two years (Barker, 1983). Similarly, a Canadian study of numerous new religious and parareligious movements found that, while participation rates were relatively high, the proportion of adherents staying in these movements was extremely low (Bird and Reimer, 1982).

Commitment is a problem not only for contemporary movements. George Whitefield, an eighteenth-century Calvinist preacher, observed that his efforts were not as successful as those of John Wesley, the principal founder of Methodism. The key difference was that, although both preachers achieved many converts, Wesley insisted that the localities where he preached should establish "classes" to ensure the commitment of new converts (Snow and Machalek, 1983). Relative commitment of members is no indicator of the truth or "deviance" of a religious group. Maintaining commitment to *any* group is always problematic, and it is especially difficult in a modern, pluralistic, mobile, individualistic society.

Commitment means the willingness of members to contribute in maintaining the group because the group provides what they want and need. *Commitment* therefore implies a reciprocal relationship. The group achieves its goals by fulfilling the needs of its members, and the members satisfy their desires by helping to maintain the group. Persons who are totally committed to a group have fully invested themselves in it and fully identify with it. Commitment is the link between the individual and the larger social group. A person cannot be coerced into commitment but decides to identify with the interests of the group because of personal values, material interests, or affective ties (Kanter, 1972:65–70).

Conversion is a resolution of the individual's problems with former meaning systems and former self, but conversion alone is not sufficient to resolve new problems. The group's commitment processes help prevent the individual's doubts and new problems from undermining the conversion. The final result of the entire conversion process is not merely creating new members but creating members who will invest themselves in what the group is believing and doing. The same process also ensures the commitment of all members, new and old, to the group's values and objectives. *Commitment processes build plausibility structures for the group's worldview and way of life.*

The level of commitment that a group expects varies. Most major denominations in the United States do not expect intense commitment from their members or for that commitment to influence all aspects of their lives. At the opposite extreme, religious groups such as many fundamentalist and Pentecostal churches, as well as most communal groups ranging from Hassidic Jews to Trappist monks, expect members to demonstrate intense religious commitment in all spheres of daily life. Commitment mechanisms in dissenting or deviant groups are especially important because of their difficulty in maintaining their worldview in face of opposition both from established religious groups and the larger society. All social groups, however, need some commitment from their members in order to maintain the group and achieve their goals (see Gerlach and Hine, 1970). And all social groups (including nonreligious groups such as the army) utilize commitment measures similar to those used by religious groups.

The processes by which the group fosters commitment are similar to processes of conversion. Both processes urge members to *withdraw* from competing allegiances and alternate ways of life, and both processes encourage members to *involve* themselves more deeply in the life of the group, its values and goals. These commitment mechanisms are used to some degree by all social groups. Groups desiring more intense or total commitment of members, however, are likely to use more extreme commitment processes. Groups gain greater commitment of members by asking them to sacrifice something for the group, but the degree of required sacrifice varies widely. Most religious bodies ask their members to give up some of their money and time for the group's goals and projects; and some groups expect their members to tithe a specific, substantial percentage of their income. Still other groups ask members to give up all belongings to the group and to live communally.

Withdrawal from Competing Allegiances

Any degree of sacrifice enhances the individual's commitment because giving up something makes the goal seem more valuable. Sacrifice gives observable evidence to the group that the member is committed, and it "weeds out" members who are not sufficiently committed. Religious groups further encourage sacrifice by signifying it as a consecration, so the act of sacrifice gains sacred status. Some groups ask members to sacrifice time and energy (e.g., devoting a certain number of hours each week to proselytizing new members). Some groups expect members to abstain regularly or periodically from certain foods or from alcohol, tobacco, drugs, or sexual relationships. Several Christian groups encourage or require their members to fast during Lent. Either for all members or for an elite core group, many religious groups place special value on celibacy. Other groups may expect members to do without "worldly" pursuits (e.g., dancing, going to movies, wearing makeup or stylish clothing). Such sacrifices are demanded by most contemporary religious groups, especially marginal ones. Celibacy, for example, figures in the commitment process of such diverse groups as Roman Catholic clergy, some neo-Pentecostals, the Divine Light Mission, and the Unification Church. Vegetarianism and abstinence from smoking, drinking, and drugs are commonly required sacrifices (see Kanter, 1972, for examples from nineteenth-century communal groups; for contemporary examples, see Gardner, 1978).

Some sacrifices may also be interpreted as forms of **mortification,** the process of stripping the individual of vestiges of the "old self." Groups seeking to resocialize their members into a new identity consistent with the group's beliefs and values often encourage mortification. Members are asked to let go of those areas of life that compete with the new, desired self. They may have to wear prescribed dress and hairstyle, do without makeup or jewelry, and give up certain prized possessions. They are asked to sacrifice not because these things are wrong in themselves but because using them supports the "old self." Other forms of mortification include public confession, giving up control over one's time and personal space, and relinquishing personal choice in a wide range of matters (Goffman, 1961; see also Chidester, 1988; Zablocki, 1971). Some groups use rituals in which participating members must violate taboos pertaining to their former way of life. Thus, ritually consuming some formerly forbidden food or engaging in formerly taboo sexual practices, for example, serve as group commitment mechanisms (Palmer and Bird, 1992).

The group sometimes promotes further withdrawal of members from their former way of life by asking them to renounce competing relationships. Many sectarian groups discourage members from interacting with the "outside

---

BOX 3.3   Historical Perspective: Mortification of Self in a Protestant Communitarian Sect

As the tour guide, dressed in clothing of the style the Sisters wore, took us from monastic cell to cell, I tried to imagine what it was like to live and work and pray in the Cloister at Ephrata. This communitarian settlement in Pennsylvania was founded in 1732 by Pietist immigrants from Germany. Every aspect of their schedule, buildings, and interactions was designed to mortify the self in order to shed all their worldly ways in order to fully practice their Christian faith. Each tiny cell had a small window, a wooden bench for a bed, and a block of wood for a pillow. The Sisters and Brothers arose each day while it was still dark, dressed in their plain work clothes, and made their way to the chapel for the first of several daily periods of prayer. They read only what was approved, and they had minimal interaction with the nonbeliever neighbors. They

spent the day hard at work in the fields, barns, kitchens, and laundries of the community. Their food was simple, vegetarian fare, grown and cooked in their own community. Members of the Cloister were celibate, but a few "Outside" coreligionists lived with their wives and children in cottages nearby (Longnecker, 1994).

Reaching the end of the tour, one of the women in our entourage exclaimed admiringly: "You don't see that kind of Christian commitment nowadays!"

- If we did see it, would the media label it a "cult," and would social service workers try to wrest the children away?
- Why is extreme asceticism deviant in our society?
- Why does our society distrust extreme religious commitment?

---

world" and may adopt special social arrangements to insulate members from outside influences. Groups such as some Mennonites, Jesus communes, the early Hare Krishna movement, and centuries of Christian monks geographically separate themselves from the rest of society. Other groups insulate their members by operating their own schools, places of work, and social clubs. For instance, numerous conservative evangelical groups have instituted home schooling or separate sectarian schools (see Peshkin, 1986; Rose, 1988; Wagner, 1990). The group may also exercise control over the communication media to which members are exposed or may limit interaction with outsiders.

More important than physical withdrawal from "the world" is the creation of psychic **boundaries** between the group and the outside. By use of these boundaries, members come to think of the group as "we" and the rest of society as "they." Furthermore, members perceive their in-group as good or superior and the outside as evil or degraded. Thus, the individual member's withdrawal from competing activities is motivated not only by controls that the group exercises but especially by the wish to identify with the in-group and to avoid the negative influences of the outside. Even groups that have not withdrawn fully from the larger society often create these kinds of psychical boundaries, for example, by urging members to join parallel religious organizations rather than secular organizations. Thus, groups like Christian Veterinarian's Fellowship or Fellowship of Christian Athletes provide some of the prestige and business networks of professional associations, while protecting members from secular society (Elzey, 1988).

Withdrawal from competing relationships often entails changes in the member's relationships with parents, spouse, and close friends. Typically, the individual identifies with outside relationships less and less, while simultaneously drawing closer to fellow group members. Many religious groups try to exert some control over the member's choice of a marriage partner. Marriage to someone who does not support (or who even opposes) one's worldview can undermine the believer's meaning system.

The group frequently tries to guide or control even its members' relationships within the group. Close relationships among a small part of the group may detract from commitment to the group as a whole. The attachment of a married couple to each other or of parents to their children can compete with their involvement in the larger group. Groups that seek intense commitment from their members often have special structural arrangements to reduce this competition. The Oneida commune of the nineteenth century had a form of "open marriage" that diminished the pairing off of couples. The Unification Church treated their entire movement as the "united family," based on Reverend Moon's teachings that the family was essential to the salvation of the nation and world. The Church chose marriage partners and scheduled mass weddings, promoting the sense that members' commitment was primarily to the united family rather than the spouse or immediate family (Christiano, 2000).

These processes all promote commitment to the group by encouraging individual members to withdraw themselves from those aspects of their former life that prevent them from being fully a "new self." The degree to which any given religious group asks its members to withdraw from nongroup loyalties depends largely on the type of group. The more marginal, sectlike groups typically expect high levels of attachment. Their commitment processes are therefore more intense and extreme than those of ordinary denominations.

Attachment

At the same time that groups encourage members to withdraw from other allegiances, they also urge members to become more and more involved in the group itself, drawing them into greater oneness with the group. This sense of unity is clearly related to the concept of belonging, discussed in Chapter 2. The provision of a sense of belonging may be as important, if not more important, than the specific beliefs of sectarian groups in maintaining high levels of member commitment (Ammerman, 1987; McGaw, 1980).

Activities that draw the members into the fellowship and consciousness of the larger group promote both the cohesion of the group and the commitment of individual members. These commitment mechanisms make belonging to the group an emotionally satisfying experience. Commitment mechanisms for attachment are also likely to differ according to the intensity of the commitment desired by the group. Groups that expect intense commitment of members use stronger measures to promote attachment to the group.

The "we feeling" of group consciousness is promoted by homogeneity of membership. The more alike members feel, the easier it is for the group to gain a sense of unity. Established religious bodies typically achieve member homogeneity by self-selection. Individuals choose to join a church or synagogue with membership characteristics comparable to their own social status, racial, ethnic, or language group, and educational and religious background. Sectlike groups, by contrast, have more selective memberships, screening out or discouraging unacceptable members. Sectlike groups put greater emphasis on resocializing new members, thereby *creating* more homogeneity (Kanter, 1972:93, 94).

Group unity is also enhanced by the sharing of work and possessions. The extreme form of such sharing is full communal living, in which all possessions are held in common and all work is performed together. At the opposite pole are nominal forms of sharing, such as gathering Thanksgiving baskets for the needy or a painting party to decorate Sunday school rooms. Even these minimally demanding kinds of sharing promote a sense of unity in the group. Much sharing in religious groups consists of people taking care of each other. Group members may aid the family of a hospitalized member by caring for the children, preparing meals, and comforting the worried spouse. This kind of sharing promotes the commitment not only of the family receiving care but also especially of those giving the care.

Regular group gatherings also bring about greater commitment of members, and such gatherings need not be for overtly religious purposes. A church supper helps increase members' feeling of belonging to the group. For example, ethnographies of African-American churches note the centrality of preparing church suppers and of eating food together as an expression of group solidarity and sharing (Goldsmith, 1989; Williams, 1974). Communal groups meet very frequently, sometimes each day. Other sectlike groups also urge their members to meet often. Some groups hold prayer meetings three nights a week in addition to Sunday services and church socials.

Not all religious groups, however, identify commitment to the congregation as critical. Some groups emphasize both family-level religiosity and supracongregational commitment as very important. Religious gatherings of the family (e.g., the family saying the prayers of the rosary together or praying special Sabbath blessings, *Shabbat b'rachot*) serve similar functions of commitment but not necessarily to the congregation.

The content of group gatherings can also promote the commitment of individual members. **Ritual** is one particularly important aspect of a group gathering. By ritual, the group symbolizes meanings significant *to itself.* Ritual gives symbolic form to group unity, and participating individuals symbolically affirm their commitment. Ritual both reflects and acts on the group's meaning system. Too often we tend to think of ritual as being empty and a matter of "going through the motions." Even going through the motions can promote a sense of unity, but in many groups the content of ritual is highly meaningful and especially successful in creating a sense of oneness. Rituals important in many religious groups include communion and other ritual meals, healing services, symbols of deference, embraces, special prayer postures, hymns, and rituals of purification.

Mutual **witnessing** continues to be as important in the commitment process as in the initial socialization or conversion of the believer. Through witnessing, members show themselves and others how their daily lives can be interpreted in terms of the group's meaning system. This kind of public witnessing is prominent in evangelical and charismatic Christian prayer meetings and in the *satsang* of some imported neo-Hindu movements. Witnessing transforms all events, thoughts, and experiences into significant events, meaningful thoughts, and special religious experiences. Witnessing explicitly devalues everyday and nonbelievers' interpretations of events and replaces them with approved religious interpretations. Witnessing can be relatively public or can occur in the setting of a small fellowship group or family. The public proselytizing of Jehovah's Witnesses, Mormons, and Hare Krishnas is different from the relatively private witnessing of the evangelical Women's Aglow movement or the Catholic Charismatic movement. Religious groups that consider themselves in opposition to the rest of "the world" are more likely to emphasize witnessing as a commitment mechanism (on witnessing in religious groups, see Ammerman, 1987; Kroll-Smith, 1980; McGuire, 1982; Shaffir, 1978). Mutual witnessing is an important commitment mechanism in nonreligious groups, as well. For instance, it has functions in Alcoholics Anonymous and other "twelve-step" groups: Overeaters Anonymous and Christian diet groups (e.g., Jesus is the Weigh); psychotherapeutic groups; and quasi-religious corporations such as Amway (see Bromley, 1998c; Griffith, 1999; Jones, 1975; Lester, 1999; Rice, 1994; Rudy and Greil, 1987, 1989).

Commitment to a group can be strengthened if the group convinces the member that the group itself is extraordinary. Groups (such as those described in Chapter 2) that expect the imminent end of the world typically portray themselves as the elect who will be saved. Their elaboration of millenarian catastrophic prophecies often intensifies group members' commitment (Wessinger, 2000a). Other groups represent their rituals and practices as necessary for salvation in the next life. Many of these groups teach that fallen-away members will be even worse off than people who never knew the "right" way.

Group practices that promote a sense of awe further emphasize the significance of the group itself. These practices make the actions of the group appear more than mundane; mystery, magic, and miracles surround the group actions. When the leaders "receive directions" from God, as among Mormons and Pentecostals, the directions seem far more awesome than if members had voted on them. Social and symbolic distance also promotes a sense of awe. Thus, medieval churches used physical barriers (e.g., rood screens) and space to separate the body of the congregation from the central ritual performance. Even today many religious groups have certain sacred spaces in their places of worship where ordinary members cannot routinely go. These practices may not have been deliberately created to generate commitment, but the production of a sense of awe does result in enhancing members' commitment.

DISENGAGEMENT

Although many members continue or increase their commitment to their religious group, others become less committed or drop out of the group. In many respects, the process of **disengagement** is the reverse of conversion. Like conversion, disengagement typically entails a transformation of self and basic meaning system. When a religious meaning system and identity have been especially central in a believer's life, the process of altering self and meaning system may be a wrenching transformation.

Both conversion and disengagement are forms of "status passage" in which the individual leaves one role and enters another (Glazer and Strauss, 1971). Persons in modern, mobile societies may go through many role-exit experiences, such as moving out of one's parents' home, divorcing a spouse, being discharged from the armed services or hospital or prison, moving away from a community, changing jobs, retiring, or quitting a social club. Some of these roles are more central to the individual's identity, and thus role exit may be more complex and emotion-laden than for other secondary roles. If the religious group has been the primary source of all other parts of the member's identity and social life, leaving can be particularly socially and emotionally wrenching. One Israeli who left the ultra-Orthodox *haredi* (Jewish) community said:

> You feel an emptiness, a very deep emptiness, and there's also confusion.
> You have nobody to talk to, nobody who really understands what you're
> going through. The loneliness can be overpowering. You're cut off. The
> close friends you've had since childhood, you never see again (quoted in
> Shaffir, 1995)

The exit process itself depends not only upon the individual's identity, roles, and social relationships, but also upon the group or organization's response. If a person leaves after a long struggle to change a group from the inside, and the group's stance toward that person has been one of hostility or even intimidation, then the process of disaffiliation itself is fraught with considerable emotion and social tensions. Interestingly, the position of the religious group itself, relative to the larger society, has considerable influence on the exit process for individual members (see Bromley, 1998a). For example, the high moral status of the Catholic Church enabled it to control the role exit of priests and nuns, treating their quitting the priesthood or religious order as defection or as personal failure. By contrast, a group such as Hare Krishna, which was already under considerable pressure from an organized anticult movement, had little control to prevent its former members from taking new roles, with considerable social (and economic) support as active apostates.

Although these organizational factors help us understand religious role exit, they apply also to other forms of defection and role exit, such as the whistle-blower in business or political organizations.

Stages of Disaffiliation

Like the commitment process, the disengagement process involves the pushes and pulls of various social influences. Individuals must weigh what they are accomplishing by being members against opportunities to reach those (or other) goals elsewhere. Typically, members reach the decision to leave the group only gradually, but just as members' retrospective accounts of their conversions are transformed to fit their new beliefs and image of self, so too are ex-members' accounts of the events and decisions that led up to leaving the group transformed. Four stages characteristic of role exit include (1) first doubts, (2) seeking and weighing role alternatives, (3) a turning point, and (4) establishing an ex-role identity (Ebaugh, 1988).

Disengagement is often the result of a breakdown or diminished effectiveness of the plausibility structure (described in Chapter 2) that supports the religious group's beliefs and practices. One study found that this breakdown of plausibility resulted from such factors as reduced isolation from the outside world, competing commitments (such as intimate dyadic relationships within the group or family links outside the group), lack of movement success, and apparent discrepancies between leaders' words and actions (Wright, 1987). Particularly if the social-emotional climate of a religious group was important in a recruit's initial conversion or commitment, those interpersonal experiences that fail to fulfill the believer's affective needs can be disconfirming (see Jacobs, 1989).

Just as social networks initially brought members into the group and sustained their commitment to its worldview, so too competing social networks make disengagement plausible and attractive. One study (Aho, 1994) of persons who voluntarily left hate groups (such as the KKK or the Aryan Nations Church) found that voluntary exit was promoted by social pushes (e.g., harassment by colleagues) and social pulls (e.g., falling in love with a nonbeliever). One elaborated ex-role identity is that of the vocal apostate. In contrast to people who simply take leave of their religious group, apostates are defectors who subsequently aid the opposition, making public claims against the group. Becoming an apostate is like a new conversion, in which the former religious identity is construed as "lost" and the new one as "found" (Wright, 1997).

Just as conversion involves coming to take a new member role for granted as part of the recruits' identity, so too the "first doubts" stage of role exit typically involves experiences that call that taken-for-granted reality into question. Often the doubts are not about the group's beliefs; for example, many nuns who eventually left the convent were not doubting their Christian faith but rather their role commitments as nuns (Ebaugh, 1988). Like the conversion experience, disengagement often entails a turning point, which is remembered more vividly in retrospect than many other parts of the gradual change. Just as the researcher must be careful when interpreting retrospective conversion stories, so too must tales of disaffiliation be treated with caution (Richardson et al., 1986).

The believer might respond to first doubts in a number of ways, such as seeking advice from other believers, trying to relieve doubts, reaffirming belief and allegiance to the group, or reconsidering commitment. Furthermore, persons who are disengaging from a group typically try to identify and weigh their alternatives to the member role. Whatever the outcome, neither conversion nor disaffiliation is a passive, mindless process.

Coerced and Voluntary Exit

The inadequacies of the "brainwashing" explanation of conversion become particularly acute in interpreting disengagement. If, as the "brainwashing" thesis holds, converts are coercively persuaded to belong to a religious group, then once converted and held in the group they would be unable to exercise the will to change beliefs and leave the group. This interpretation became the justification for the practice of forcible "deprogramming," by which believers were kidnapped, held against their wills, and subjected to a barrage of tactics designed to turn them against their former religious group and to convert them to an alternative perspective.

Sociological studies of disengagement from religious groups show, however, that the brainwashing/deprogramming conceptualization is a grossly inaccurate portrayal of these processes. Using this model, sensationalistic media have conveyed the impression that converts are trapped, indeed "lost" indefinitely. In fact, much conversion (especially to demanding religious groups) is temporary (Wright and Ebaugh, 1993), and most persons exiting religious groups—even intensely demanding ones such as Unification Church, Hare Krishna, and Children of God/Family of Love—do so voluntarily (Wright, 1991). For example, even socially "acceptable" conversions to well-established religious movements (like a Billy Graham crusade) are often very tenuous and short-lived (W. Johnson, 1971).

The Unification Church is one of the religious movements frequently accused of brainwashing its recruits; however, a sociological study found that most recruits' involvement was temporary. During the movement's growth period in the 1970s, of some 1,000 recruits who were interested enough to attend a residential workshop, only 8 percent joined and remained as full-time members for more than one week. And of those few who did join, only about 5 percent remained full-time members for a year. Those recruits most likely to have joined with enthusiasm and later disengaged were those who had converted with idealistic expectations that the movement would make the world a better place, whereas those who continued in the movement were more likely to have joined for personal spiritual goals. The study concluded that it was "perfectly plausible" for the action-oriented idealists to decide to disaffiliate from the Unification Church when it appeared not to live up to its promise as an agent of social change (Barker, 1988a). Those converts who stayed in groups expecting high levels of commitment were hardly passive; they influenced and sometimes changed the group, even while the group influenced them (Richardson, 1993b). Mounting evidence from studies of the many "new religious movements" of the last three decades indicates that new members of unconventional religious movements are hardly the malleable, passive, gullible dupes portrayed in the media. Rather, recruits to religious groups are both open to the spiritual alternatives and yet relatively resistant to conversions that entail high levels of commitment and drastic changes in identity (see Bromley, 1998b, for a recent summary of arguments questioning the brainwashing thesis).

Role exit from intensely committed religious groups in which much of each member's identity is invested can be extremely difficult. Similarly, disaffiliation in the context of a small, close-knit village is likely to be more difficult than in a large urban area. Most religious groups in modern societies get far less commitment and investment from their members. Religious disaffiliation from a casual or peripheral religious role is simple and needs no social support.

Collective Forms of Disengagement

Doubts and unsatisfied needs may propel a member to leave a religious group, but individual disaffiliation is not the only response. One possible response to doubts and disillusionment is internal reform of the religious group. For example, during one of my own research projects, members of a large meditation group gradually realized that their guru was using his esteem and influence in sexual advances to several women members. Because the disappointed members still very much believed in their group's spiritual practices and ideals, instead of leaving the group they began discussing how to change the group. They decided to send the guru back to India and continue without him.

A related response is when a group of dissatisfied members collectively defect over movement politics, often staging their departure to make a strong statement to the leadership of the movement organization. For example, a group of former ISKCON (Hare Krishna) members formed the "Conch Club" to collectively defect from the national organization, which they rejected as unworthy of their commitment, due to its direction after the death of its founding guru. They continued to retain their beliefs and identity as Krishna devotees, locating themselves within the larger movement but rejecting the organization of that movement (Rochford, 1989). Similarly, many former residents of Rajneeshpuram, the Oregon commune of disciples of Bhagwan Shree Rajneesh, had generally positive retrospective accounts of membership in the movement and living at the commune. Because the commune and movement organization were disbanded by the guru, they had not left as defectors, and many retained friends in the movement, so role exit was less drastic (Latkin et al., 1994).

Another historically important form of disengagement is for dissatisfied members to break off from the religious group and form a separate group. Rarely do schismatic groups consider themselves to be *leaving* their faith;

rather, they view their exit from the group as keeping the true faith. Often, they view their new ideology as more pure and their new practices as more faithful than those of the parent group. For example, the Cooperative Baptist Fellowship is an alliance of former Southern Baptist Convention (SBC) churches and individuals, formed in 1991 in response to the growing control of the more fundamentalist faction over the denomination's seminaries, publishing, and management. The Fellowship holds that the SBC had violated core principles of their Free Church heritage and congregational polity. Ironically, that same Free Church tradition makes it virtually impossible for the SBC to excommunicate the Fellowship members (see Hadaway, 1989), so the dissenters do not need to form a new denomination.

Similarly, the founding members of many of today's mainstream religious organizations had to cope with the decision and social agonies of disaffiliation. Virtually all of the Christian denominations formed in the Early Modern era were created in dissent and disaffiliation. Such collective forms of disaffiliation are also occasions of some role transition and perhaps personal anguish, but they are rarely so wrenching as individual role exit because members have the mutual support and idealism of a group making the exit together.

SUMMARY

This analysis of the processes of religious socialization, conversion, and commitment illustrates the interrelationship of religious meaning and religious belonging. The individual's meaning system is socially acquired and supported through early socialization and interaction with other believers throughout life. If the individual changes meaning systems, it is through social interaction. And the processes that promote commitment to the meaning system and the group supporting it are fundamentally social processes.

Social factors are important in shaping the individual's religion, and examination of critical periods in the individual's life cycle suggests some of these factors. Early socialization in the context of the family, neighborhood, and ethno-religious community is particularly important in establishing not only the basic beliefs and values but also the connection between the individual's belief system and very identity. Rites of passage to new statuses are often filled with religious significance. Passage to adulthood and marriage illustrates some of the ways in which religion can shape critical moments as the individual takes on a new social identity. The society's secularized conception of time may be an important cause of some of these problems. Evidence about the nature of the interrelationship between the individual's religion and social factors is, however, generally limited either to nonmodern examples or to studies of narrowly defined, church-oriented religion. Thus, this chapter has suggested some of the directions that further research into the individual's religion might take.

Conversion is essentially a form of resocialization similar to nonreligious resocialization. Through interaction with believers, the recruit comes to share their worldview and takes on a new self consistent with that meaning system. Mere transfers of organizational affiliation are not real conversions of world-view and identity. The process of conversion funnels recruits from a general predisposition to conversion, through interaction with group members, to growing identification with the group and its belief system. The conversion process is generally gradual, although it may appear sudden and dramatic because of the way it is symbolized by some individuals or groups.

Commitment mechanisms promote the loyalty and attachment of all members, new converts and old members alike. Groups such as most denominations, which expect only partial commitment of members, typically use less extreme commitment mechanisms than do sectarian groups, which expect members' total commitment and immersion in the life of the group. The process of commitment involves simultaneously the individual's withdrawal from competing allegiances (e.g., by sacrifice) and greater attachment to the group (e.g., by frequent interaction with fellow members). Through these commitment processes, the group builds a firm plausibility structure for its meaning system. Like conversion, disengagement from religious commitment entails a transformation of self and worldview supported by a changed plausibility structure.